ISBN 978-1-5284-5608-1
PIBN 10945005

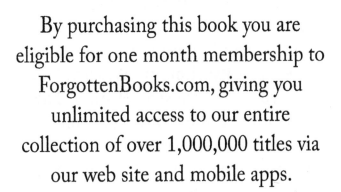

English
Français
Deutsche
Italiano
Español
Português

www.forgottenbooks.com

Mythology Photography **Fiction**
Fishing Christianity **Art** Cooking
Essays Buddhism Freemasonry
Medicine **Biology** Music **Ancient
Egypt** Evolution Carpentry Physics
Dance Geology **Mathematics** Fitness
Shakespeare **Folklore** Yoga Marketing
Confidence Immortality Biographies
Poetry **Psychology** Witchcraft
Electronics Chemistry History **Law**
Accounting **Philosophy** Anthropology
Alchemy Drama Quantum Mechanics
Atheism Sexual Health **Ancient History**
Entrepreneurship Languages Sport
Paleontology Needlework Islam
Metaphysics Investment Archaeology
Parenting Statistics Criminology
Motivational

OFFICIAL REGISTER O
HARVARD UNIVERSIT

VOLUME IX   APRIL 2, 1912   NUMBER

REPORTS OF THE
PRESIDENT AND THE TREASUI
OF HARVARD COLLEGE

1910—11

PUBLISHED BY THE UNIVERSITY
CAMBRIDGE, MASS.

REPORTS OF THE
ESIDENT AND THE TREASI
OF HARVARD COLLEGE

1910—11

CAMBRIDGE
PUBLISHED BY THE UNIVERSITY
1912

CONTENTS

TREASURER'S STATEMENT

274438

PRESIDENT'S REPORT FOR 1910–11

To THE BOARD OF OVERSEERS: —

The President of the University has the honor to submit the following report for the academic year 1910–11: —

At the close of this academic year Dr. Thomas Dwight died, having borne a prolonged illness with conspicuous courage. With the exception of a single year he had been on the instructing staff of the Medical School continuously since 1872, and since 1883 as Parkman Professor of Anatomy. Following Dr. Oliver Wendell Holmes, who had held this position for thirty-five years, he held it for twenty-eight, and during that time he rendered great service to the School as instructor and investigator. The University has also lost by death Dr. Walter Remsen Brinckerhoff, who had recently been appointed Assistant Professor of Pathology after a devoted mission as Director of the Leper Colony at Molokai; Mr. Thomas Hall, who kept up his teaching in spite of growing blindness; and Dr. Ray Madding McConnell, who had been doing excellent work as Instructor in Social Ethics. It has lost by retirement Professor Silas Marcus Macvane, who began as Instructor in Political Economy in 1875, became Instructor in History in 1878, Assistant Professor of the same subject in 1883, Professor in 1886, and finally, in 1887, McLean Professor of Ancient and Modern History; Dr. John Templeton Bowen, who to the regret of his colleagues in the Medical School was constrained by his health to resign his professorship of Dermatology; and Frederick Caesar de Sumichrast, who retired from his associate professorship of French after teaching thirty-four years.

Some of the recent changes in the regulations of the College that went into operation for the first time during the past academic year, have begun to show their effects. The one with which a student is brought earliest into contact is the new requirement for admission. The reasons for a change in this matter were set

5

forth in the last annual report; but since those reasons were based
not so much on dissatisfaction with the old examinations in the
cases of those boys who were prepared for them, as on the barrier
they erected against boys from good schools over the country
which do not direct their chief attention to preparation for these
examinations, the new requirement has been set up only as an
alternative to the old one. The two stand, and probably will
long stand, side by side. Nevertheless, the new requirement
differs essentially from the other in character and in aim.
The old examinations are designed to test all the secondary school
work done, and can be taken a few at a time, an examination
being passed on each piece of work when completed. The system
is one of checking off studies and accumulating credits. The
new requirement is an attempt to measure, not the quantity of
work done, but the intellectual state of the boy; a certificate being
accepted for the quantity of his school work, and examinations
being held on sample subjects to test the quality of his scholarship. The regulations in full will be found in an appendix to this
report (p. 25), but the main outlines of the system may be briefly
pointed out. To be admitted to examination the boy must present
a statement from his school of the studies he has pursued, and these
must be the content of a good secondary school course devoted
mainly to academic subjects. Four subjects must then be offered
for examination, and must be offered at the same time. One of
them must be English; another must be Latin or Greek, if the
student is to be a candidate for the degree of Bachelor of Arts, but
may be a modern language in the case of a candidate for the degree
of Bachelor of Science; the third must be Mathematics, or Physics
or Chemistry (the reason for the option being the difficulty that
some intelligent boys find in doing themselves justice in an examination in Mathematics); and the fourth may be any subject
of an academic character, not already offered, that the boy may
select. As these are sample examinations covering subjects which
are of primary importance or in which the candidate feels most
confidence, they must be passed well. But it must be borne in
mind that the object is to discover whether the boy is fit for
college work, not to measure his proficiency in particular studies.

Information about the new requirement was sent out freely;
yet the plan was new, untried, and formulated only a few

months before the June examinations, and under such conditions the number and geographical distribution of the applicants was highly encouraging. Of these there were in all, in June and September, 185, of whom 46 were discarded by reason of defective school records, — for the most part because they had pursued no subject consecutively. The remaining 139 were allowed to take the examinations; and of these 83 were admitted and 56, or 40.2 per cent, were rejected; while of the boys who presented themselves for final examination under the old plan 17.1 per cent were rejected, and 8.1 per cent of the June candidates did not reappear to complete their examinations in September. It had been supposed by some people not connected with the University that the new plan would be virtually a form of admission by certificate, in which examination would play a subordinate part, and hence would mean a letting down of the bars; but the result of the first experiment has dispelled that impression. In fact, four of the candidates who failed under the new system in June tried the old one with success in September; while only one succeeded in a second assault upon the new examinations. The masters of the regular preparatory schools seem now inclined to offer only their best pupils under the new plan. A boy, indeed, whose capacity to enter is doubtful would be wise in trying the old plan, for he has thus a larger chance of being admitted, although with conditions; whereas a boy who is sure to get in will do better to adopt the new plan and come in without conditions, which are always a handicap in college.

One of the chief objects of the new plan, as already observed, was to open the road to Harvard College to the pupils from good schools, and more particularly from good public schools, throughout the nation. In this respect, also, the figures are gratifying. Of the students entering under the old plan in June and September, 1911, 72 per cent were prepared in Massachusetts, 85 per cent in schools in New England, only 8.5 per cent in schools in the other Atlantic states, and only 4.5 per cent in schools west of the Alleghanies. Whereas of those admitted at the same time under the new plan only 41 per cent came from schools in Massachusetts, 47 per cent from schools in New England, while over 31 per cent came from schools in the other Atlantic states, and 21 per cent from those west of the Alleghanies; there being represented twelve states from whose schools no boy was admitted under the old plan.

The comparison of public with private or endowed schools (including therein private tutors) is not less striking. Under the old plan the public schools sent 46 per cent of the candidates admitted. Under the new plan they sent 84 per cent. With such conditions in regard to the situation and character of the schools from which they come, it might be supposed that the greater part of the boys admitted under the new plan would offer a modern language in place of Latin. But although the boys who do so form a larger proportion under the new plan than under the old one, they are still a small minority. They were 6.5 per cent under the old plan and 20.5 per cent under the new.

As yet the new plan has not been in operation long enough to forecast its final effects. That it is perfect no one would assert, but that on the first trial it gives evidence of fulfilling the objects for which it was designed can hardly be denied. The difficulty in its application comes in the preparation of examination papers that will test the quality of scholarship acquired rather than the quantity of ground covered. The art of examining demands experience, and adjustment to a change of aim requires time, but continued improvement will certainly come with practice. That the new plan brings within reach of Harvard College boys from schools which had hitherto not sent them seems certain, and it is not less clear that this result has been attained without lowering the standard of admission. Whether in scholarly qualities the students entering by the new method will be better or not so good as those admitted under the old plan remains to be seen; but that they are far from indolent, or handicapped at the outset, is proved by the fact that not a single one of the eighty-three was put on probation for low marks at the examinations in November, 1911.

Another change which has gone into effect during the past year is the new regulation for the choice of electives in college. This was first applied to the class that entered in September, 1910. Its members were called upon in the spring of their Freshman year to outline a plan for the remainder of their college course in accordance with the rule requiring both concentration and distribution of studies. In particular they were required to designate their subject of concentration and to select three, at least, of the courses to be taken in the following year. This they did after consultation with a member of the Faculty or an instructor, each of these advisers having under his charge, as a rule, only four members of the class. To ensure that the choices complied with the rules, or to prepare requests that an exception be allowed by the Committee on the Choice of Electives, the plans were all submitted to Professor Charles P. Parker, the Secretary of the Committee, to whom the success in administering the system has been mainly due.

The rules have worked with little friction, because they appear to supply for most men a good basis for planning a college course of study; and the cases of failure to submit valid plans were generally the result of a misunderstanding of some kind. The requests also for exceptional treatment were not numerous and almost always fell into one of two classes: first, those of men who desired to concentrate in an eminently proper subject, — such as Biology, — which is not included in a single existing department or regular field for a degree with distinction. These were of course allowed. Second, those of men who wanted to avoid any real concentration by taking almost exclusively elementary studies in many fields. These were clear violations of the essential principle of the rules and were refused. More numerous were the requests in the autumn to change single courses selected in the spring for the coming year. Such requests are natural at the outset of a new system, and they were generally granted, unless the obvious motive was to take easy courses.

It may be interesting to note the number of men concentrating their work in the different departments; for while the result is no surprise to persons familiar with the choice of electives by students in recent years, it displays their preferences in an unusually vivid way. The following table, taken from Professor Parker's article in the *Harvard Graduates' Magazine*, shows for each department, or field of distinction, in one column the number of men who have selected it as the object of concentration, and in a second column the number of men who, while concentrating elsewhere, have announced their intention of taking two

or more courses therein. This second column includes only a
part of the men who will ultimately take two or more courses in
a department outside of their main field, because they are by no
means obliged to choose all their electives at so early a stage in
their college career; yet it may serve as an indication of the
trend of student thought.

CHOICE OF SUBJECTS BY CLASS OF 1914

Department	Concentration (4 or more courses)	Distribution (2 or 3 courses)
Romance Languages	45	41
English	42	22
The Classics	12	4
Germanic Languages	9	30
Comparative Literature	3	2
History and Literature	9	..
Fine Arts	12	2
Music	9	10
Architecture	6	..
Inadequately expressed as "modern languages" or "Group 1"	9	
Total, Group 1	156	
Engineering	55	4
Chemistry	38	13
Biology	14	..
Geology	5	3
Physics	4	2
Too vaguely expressed as "Group 2" or "Natural Sciences"	2	..
Anthropology	1	1
Total, Group 2	119	
Economics	133	39
History	41	6
Government	25	9
Too vaguely expressed as "History and Political Science," or more vaguely	33	
Total, Group 3	232	
Mathematics	9	34
Philosophy	3	84
Total, Group 4	12	

Percentages of Concentration

Language, Literature, Fine Arts, Music	30%
Natural Sciences	23%
History, Economics, Government	45%
Philosophy and Mathematics	2%

It will be observed that much the largest number of choices are in the group of History and Economics, nearly one-half of the students selecting this group; and that of the single departments by far the most popular is Economics, which attracts more than a quarter of all the men in the class. This is in accord with the tendency of public thought at the present day. The next largest group is that of Language and Literature, the choices being chiefly, and in about equal number, in English and the Romance Languages. The group of the Natural Sciences is the third in size, but of the men concentrating in this field nearly one-half are really beginning in college to study their profession of Engineering; and, except for Chemistry, no other subject attracts a considerable number of students. The men who concentrate in the fourth group are few, and in fact the neglect of both Classics and Mathematics as the principal fields of a college education is as marked as it is deplorable; the former subject appealing to only a little more than two per cent and the latter to an even smaller proportion of the members of the class. It may be noted, however, that as a secondary study Mathematics has a much larger following, and this is even more the case with Philosophy, which has far the largest number in the second column, — a number larger indeed than any figure in the first column except for the case of Economics. The figures in the second column are decidedly significant; although it must be borne in mind that even the two columns taken together fail to express either the total number of students or the amount of instruction given in the different subjects; for almost every man takes in some department a single course, which this table does not show, and often before graduation will take more. It will be interesting to examine hereafter the choice of courses when the class has completed its college work; and it will be instructive to collate the courses chosen with the careers that the men embrace, for it will throw light on their motives for the choice. The selection of college studies by undergraduates may not always be judicious, but in most cases the choice of the main field, at least, is serious. As Professor Parker says, " No wise body of teachers can afford to disregard the states of mind in which young men approach instruction. Wherever we wish to lead them we must begin where they are."

A third change which went into effect during the year is that of requiring every student before he is registered as a Junior to be able to read ordinary French or German. It has been applied for the first time to the Class of 1914, and in view of the fact that each student had already been required to pass an entrance examination, or take a college course, in both languages, the results are striking. The members of the class have had four opportunities to present themselves for the oral examination — in October, 1910, and in February, June, and October, 1911. Among the five hundred and nineteen students who entered the Freshman class in 1910, three hundred and ninety-nine attempts have been made to pass the French examination, and about half as many to pass the German.[1] In each case almost precisely one-half have failed, so that out of the five hundred and nineteen who entered college in September, 1910, only two hundred and one had shown an ability to read either French or German by Christmas of the next year.

Such a result is the best proof that an examination of this kind was needed. It shows how insufficient is the entrance examination, or the requirement of a college course, to secure an ordinary reading knowledge of a language; yet it is clear that at the present day almost no subject can be properly pursued, to the extent to which it must be pursued in college by any student who concentrates his six courses therein, without a fair reading knowledge of at least one modern language. Many of the students who fail in the oral examination have nevertheless reached the point where with a little serious effort, a little persistent practice by themselves, they could read with reasonable accuracy and fluency; and when experience of the new examinations has impressed the need of attaining that proficiency, they will no doubt profit more by the existing instruction. In the meanwhile it is proposed

[1] The figures are given in this way because some men have tried more than once.

to offer special summer courses, which will not count for a degree, but will be devoted to preparation for the oral examinations by practice in reading the language.

The efforts of the students, encouraged in every possible way by the College authorities, to promote solidarity among themselves, to prevent the student body from being divided into exclusive groups, to make the College, in the common use of the term, more democratic, have had a notable growth. One of the most palpable signs of this, initiated by the students, is the practice on the part of the Seniors of getting together for their final year in the College Yard. This was mentioned in the report of last year, and it has been continued to an even larger extent, the Seniors filling substantially all the rooms in Hollis, Stoughton, Holworthy, and Thayer. For this purpose the steam heat and new plumbing were extended to the south entry of Thayer, and during the summer just passed Holworthy has been wholly refitted with new plumbing; so that all the dormitories at the north end of the Yard are now provided with shower baths, and all except a part of Holworthy with steam heat.

· Another means of bringing students together is found in the dining halls. The habit that has grown up among them of late years of taking their meals sporadically in different places without constant companions is unfortunate. Men would not be social creatures if they were not gregarious at meals. Moreover, it is doubtful whether proper food would be provided at a moderate price for so great a number of students if dining halls were not maintained by the University, and this cannot be done unless the students come in large numbers. But the problem is not altogether simple, for the students tend to weary of the monotony of a big dining hall as the months go by; and it is therefore satisfactory to find that both Memorial and Randall Halls were fairly well filled during the year and that both earned more than their running expenses. At Memorial the average membership was 681, and 447,513 meals were served; while at Randall, where the payments are not made by the week, and hence there is no registration, 433,829 meals were served. Memorial earned the interest on its debt for improvements and equipment and a small balance toward the sinking fund; Randall substantially the

whole of its interest and sinking fund. In order to be able to
improve the supply of food without increasing the price of board,
the Corporation has determined to remit all charges upon Memorial Hall for interest and sinking fund above the sum of four
thousand dollars a year.

In Appleton Chapel, the Sunday morning service, which began
in January, 1910, has been continued throughout the past year
with gratifying results. The average attendance of students increased from 146 in 1908–09, and 151 in 1909–10, to 244 in 1910–11.
Perhaps even more significant is the growth of their minimum
attendance from 40 in 1908–09, and 50 in 1909–10, to 104 in 1910–
11, while the churches in the neighborhood report that the presence of students at their services has not materially diminished.
The attendance at the Chapel of persons other than students
has changed very little, but it is composed in far larger part of
members of the Faculty and their families. In short, the Chapel
is becoming what it ought to be, a real university chapel, and
this fact impresses anyone who attends the services.

For the graduate and professional schools the year has been
one of progress. The reports of the various Deans explain the
condition of these schools, and it is necessary here to allude only
to the changes made during the year, or to matters where comment may be of general interest. Attention is called to the
report of the Dean of the Graduate School of Arts and Sciences,
and especially to his statement of the benefits that might flow
from research fellowships which would enable and induce a few
young men of rare original power to devote some of their most
creative years to work that may bear fruit in enlarging the bounds
of knowledge, instead of consuming most of their energy in teaching when others with different gifts could do that as well, or
better, than they. Such fellowships might be in part honorary,
and should all be highly honorable, for the time has come in
America when creative scholarship should attract ambitious
youth as strongly as other kinds of activity. That the desire
to advance human knowledge should be so largely confined among
college graduates to men who must use it as a means of support
is not wholly creditable to our universities. Of John Harvard

Fellowships without stipend awarded to scholars of high grade there were last year three among the travelling fellows, but not a single one among the resident students in the Graduate School of Arts and Sciences. Almost every career in life must be pursued mainly by persons who obtain their livelihood thereby, but above all else knowledge of the mysteries of nature and of man ought to attract a few men solely by its charm and its boundless possibilities.

The Graduate School of Applied Science has had notable additions during the year. The Department of Architecture has been strengthened by the coming of M. Eugène Joseph Armand Duquesne as Professor of Design; and a new Department of Sanitary Engineering has been created by the appointment of Professor George Chandler Whipple, who will take up his work in the course of this year. The new department touches on one side the instruction in Engineering in this School, and on the other the Department of Preventive Medicine in the Medical School. The number of students may not be large at the outset, but the instruction will supply a rapidly growing need in the community.

In the Law School the fourth-year course, leading to the degree of *Scientiae Iuridicae Doctor*, was opened during the year, with a small number of students. There was neither expectation nor desire that they should be numerous, for the additional year is not designed for men who intend to devote themselves to practising the art of the profession. The regular three years' course serves that purpose, and experience has proved its excellence in attaining its object; but the province of a law school extends also to the production of jurists who will advance legal thought, and the fourth year is established with that view. Men of this kind will always be few, and quality, not numbers, is the criterion of the value of the course.

In the Medical School the changes during the year have been noteworthy. Here also an additional year of work leading to a new degree went into effect. Eight students were registered in the graduate course in Preventive Medicine, of whom two completed the work and received the new degree of Doctor of Public Health.

The greatest need of the School has been a closer connection with the hospitals of the city, and marked progress in this direction has been made. The construction of the Peter Bent Brigham Hospital, adjoining the Medical School, was begun during the past summer and the building is expected to be finished and ready for patients in the autumn of 1912. By an understanding with the Hospital its chief physician and surgeon are nominated to the Trustees by the Corporation of Harvard University, and the subordinate medical officers are to be nominated by these chiefs. Similar arrangements have been made with the Children's Hospital, the Infant Asylum, and the Infants' Hospital, and the same practice has been followed in the Free Hospital for Women and the Infants' Department of the Boston Dispensary, while the Collis P. Huntington Memorial Hospital for Cancer is intimately associated with the School. It cannot be repeated too often that the object of these agreements is not to subordinate the hospital to the Medical School, but to promote the interest both of the School and of the patients through a joint appointment by the two institutions. This will make it possible to secure the best medical talent by combining a chair in the School and a clinic in the hospital.

During the year the Faculty discussed a radical change in the process of examination leading to the degree of Doctor of Medicine. Hitherto the degree has been conferred upon the completion of a fixed number of courses, those in the first three years being required and those of the fourth year elective; and, since the intensive method is pursued, the student, in the earlier part of his course at least, devoted his whole energies for a certain length of time to a single subject, passed an examination upon it, and bade it farewell. Complaint was made that the system was inelastic, lacking in stimulation; and that the student might graduate without retaining sufficient knowledge, without coördinating it, and without inducement to review it. In the spring of 1910, a committee was appointed to consider means of lessening the rigidity of the medical curriculum. Members of the committee examined carefully the system prevailing in Ameri can medical schools of granting the degree upon an accumulation of credits in separate courses, required or elective, and the European system of holding general examinations, first upon the general scientific or laboratory subjects, and later upon the clinical branches. The committee was convinced that the latter plan afforded a better test of medical preparation, gave to the student more latitude in his work, and directed his attention more to acquiring a thorough command of medical science. It reported, therefore, in favor of two general examinations, partly practical, partly oral, and partly written, designed to measure the student's comprehension, judgment and skill, rather than to test his detailed information; the first examination to cover the laboratory subjects taught in the first year and a half, the second to cover the clinical subjects studied later, the examination in special courses to be retained only for the purpose of certifying that the student has completed the courses required and can be allowed to present himself for the general examination.

The essential principles in the report of the committee were adopted provisionally by the Faculty on March 4, and another committee, composed mainly of different members, was appointed to consider a practical method of giving effect to the plan. The second committee modified the plan in some respects and carried it into far greater detail. It was then discussed both by the Faculty Council and the Faculty, and finally adopted in October, 1911. In its complete form it will be found in an appendix to this report (p. 26).

General examinations of this character involve a marked departure from the prevalent American system of counting points and accumulating credits by examinations passed in separate courses. It will be observed that they are based upon the same principle as the new plan for entrance and the oral examinations in reading French and German already introduced in the College; and their possible application is by no means limited to the Medical School. Examinations are in all cases defective instruments. In a primitive golden age, if a college consisted of a log with the president on one end and the student on the other, examinations might perhaps be dispensed with altogether, but in an institution of any size they are a necessity, and where they exist their character and scope will inevitably determine in large measure the attitude of the student toward his studies. If he obtains his degree by passing examinations in separate courses, each course will be to a great extent an end in itself; whereas if he must look forward to a general examination in the future, the course becomes a means to an end, a part of a larger whole. The difference is even more marked where the courses are elective than where they are required, because in scoring points toward graduation the indolent student is tempted to select courses which require little work, and is attracted therefore to those which cover ground already in part traversed; whereas, if he is preparing for a general examination, he is drawn to choose those which will give him the knowledge he will require. The value of any general examination must depend upon the skill with which it is administered; and that skill can be attained thoroughly only by experience. The art of conducting examinations is not less difficult and worthy of cultivation than the art of passing them; and in the Medical School the organization of committees for the purpose seems to promise good results. Among other things it makes abundant provision for a matter vital to a general examination upon a subject, as distinguished from an examination upon a course; to wit, that the majority of the examiners in any subject shall not be the persons who have given the student his instruction therein. In order, indeed, to avoid a narrow and technical aim, the rules go so far as to require that on each examining board for the oral examinations on a laboratory subject, there shall be a representative of the clinical subjects, and *vice versa*. No doubt time will be needed to perfect the system, but well administered it can hardly fail to promote a thorough mastery of the essentials in a medical education.

The adoption of the principle of a general examination upon subjects, instead of scoring credits in particular courses, is also under consideration in the Divinity School, both for the ordinary degree of Bachelor of Divinity and for an advanced degree of Master of Divinity. The students in that School are not numerous, and their number is far less important than that the School should maintain for its degree a standard which shall be universally recognized as both high and rigorously enforced.

The Divinity School has been strengthened during the year by the accession of Professor James Richard Jewett to a chair of Arabic; and its equipment has been enriched by the joint Andover-Harvard Library built by Andover Theological Seminary. To this the theological books of both schools have been transferred. As the great collections of books at Harvard and in other libraries in this neighborhood become larger, the difficulty and the importance of avoiding needless duplication, and of making the collections readily accessible to all persons who can profit by them, increase year by year, and give scope for the energy and tact of the Director of the University Library.

The organization of the extension work of the University under a Dean and Administrative Board, the coöperation therein, save for the Summer School, of the other institutions of higher learning in and about Boston, and the establishment of a special degree for students in these courses, were described in the last annual report. For the work done during the past year the reader is referred to the report of the Dean, but a few words may be said here about the general policy involved. The development of the great state universities in the West, and their success in meeting the needs of the communities by which they are maintained, have thrown a new light upon the functions of a seat of learning. Too sharp a distinction is sometimes drawn between the endowed universities and those supported by the state. The fact that the former are neither directed by the public authorities, nor maintained by public funds, does not relieve them from the duty of serving the public. They are public institutions, the crown of the educational system, and although their first duty is to give the highest education possible to all men, rich and poor, who are capable of profiting by it, they can, and should, give aid to those who seek instruction but are unable to abandon their occupations to enter the regular curricula. This need not involve any lowering of the standard, for what the people should desire is not degrees cheaply obtained, but the best of instruction and a means of measuring their progress by the regular college standards strictly maintained. Harvard has had an unfortunate reputation of being a rich man's college, and undeservedly, for a very large percentage of the students are obliged to earn money to pay their way, or to seek scholarships or aid from loan funds. It has had the reputation also of being exclusive, of holding aloof from the mass of men. This impression we must seek to remove until every man in the community in which we stand feels that he has a potential stake in the University, is proud of it, and takes an interest in its welfare.

The University has no funds directly applicable to extension work. The Summer School is now self-supporting, but the public courses in term time must be carried on at a loss. The Boston Chamber of Commerce has given some help, while the Lowell Institute, of which the writer happens to be the trustee, defrays the greater part of the expenses not covered by students' fees. The founder directed that a part of his lectures should be popular and others "more erudite and particular." In fact, he seems to have had in mind what we now call university extension, but he did not realize how difficult it would be in this country to give effect to his project save by a close connection with a college. This portion of his design is now carried out by means of a coöperation with institutions of college rank in this neighborhood, partly through the extension work organized under the joint committee described in the last annual report, and partly in other ways. Unfortunately, perhaps, John Lowell, Jr., limited the fee in his courses to the price of two bushels of wheat per term, but if this limits the resources of the extension teaching, it provides the public with instruction of high grade at a very low cost to the student.

Under the arrangement for an exchange of professors with Germany we had the benefit during the first half-year of Professor Max Friedländer of Berlin, whose courses and public lectures on music will be long remembered. At the request of the Prussian Government, Professor Hugo Münsterberg was sent in return to Berlin.

For a number of years Mr. James Hazen Hyde maintained at his own expense an exchange with France whereby an American professor lectured at the French universities for half a year, and a Frenchman delivered a course of public lectures at Harvard. Last year President John H. Finley, of the College of the City of New York, was sent to France, and Professor Emile Boutroux, the eminent head of the *Fondation Thiers*, lectured here. The interchange has been highly profitable, but it was felt that it would be better still if we could obtain a French professor who would give regular instruction in the University for a half-year. The French government accepted the proposal cordially, and an agreement was made for a biennial exchange of professors. Such an exchange will be of great value in bringing our students into close contact with the rich scholarship of contemporary France.

An affiliation has been made also with a number of the best colleges in the West, and it has been made on their initiative. They are academic descendants of the old New England colleges, and do not attempt to maintain professional or graduate departments, but have a firm faith in the merits of a four-year college education. They find themselves pressed by the competition of the western state universities, which have far larger resources, and offer the attractions of the so-called "combined degree" whereby one or two years of study in the professional school of the university is treated as equivalent to college work, and is credited toward the degree of Bachelor of Arts as well as toward the professional degree. By that process a student obtains both degrees in a shorter period than if he completed his college work before entering upon the study of his profession. This is not the place to discuss the merits and defects of such a telescoping of curricula. It is a distinct advance over admission to the professional schools without any college work; but, on the other hand, the education it furnishes is unquestionably less than that of a full college course followed by a full professional course. No doubt it will appeal strongly to the greater part of American young men; but there are many others who prefer to obtain the more complete education. Nevertheless, it places these western colleges at a disadvantage, because the man who takes their full course must spend a year or two longer before he can practice his profession; and they turned their thoughts to Harvard as almost the only university which does not permit the taking of a combined degree. The colleges included at present are Knox in Illinois, Beloit in Wisconsin, Grinnell in Iowa, and Colorado College. Harvard is annually to send one of its professors for a half-year, who will spend a month at each of the colleges, giving regular instruction to the students; and each college may send to Cambridge for half a year one of its instructors, who will give a third of his time to teaching in the University, and spend the rest of it in study or research. The colleges are to provide the maintenance and travelling expenses of the visiting professor, and Harvard is to pay each of her visitors the salary of an assistant in a course. The direct advantages of the affiliation are only a part of its object; the indirect benefits are greater still, for the alliance enlarges the influence and usefulness of both institutions.

The friends of the University have as usual been generous, the total amount received in gifts and legacies during the fiscal year ending July 1, 1911, having been $1,745,438.72. Among the largest separate sums received are: from the estate of Gordon McKay, an additional payment of $382,377.86; from the estate of Alexander Agassiz, $201,507.50, partly for the cost of the publications of the Museum of Comparative Zoölogy, and partly for its general expenses; $141,000 for the construction and maintenance of the Collis P. Huntington Memorial Hospital from subscriptions received through Dr. J. Collins Warren; $100,000 from the Class of 1886 for its Twenty-fifth Anniversary Fund; $100,000 from Mr. Adolphus Busch, to be added to his gift for the construction and maintenance of the Germanic Museum; $92,568.75 to be added to the Anonymous Fund; from the estate of Mrs. Mary Hemenway, $45,000, for the Mary Hemenway Fund for Archaeology in the Peabody Museum; from the estate of John Harvey Treat, $40,797.11, for the purchase of books for the Library.

Most of these gifts are restricted to special objects, and in spite of generosity we are in want. By rigid economy, severely felt in some cases, the deficit for the University, College and Library was reduced from $50,100.88 to $28,532.84. Economy must be practiced until our resources increase, although several departments are undermanned and should be enlarged if we are to do the work the public properly expects. In many directions we need funds for buildings or endowment.

For the Freshman Dormitories over eleven hundred thousand dollars, including the Smith bequest, has been subscribed, and seven hundred thousand more is required for the buildings and furniture.

The Library is in a deplorable physical condition. We have a magnificent collection of books. It is the greatest treasure of the University. Much has been done to make it more useful. The classification has been carried forward. The catalogue has been improved, arrears in cataloguing are being made up and cards of standard size are being introduced. But this precious collection is housed in an old building which is not fireproof. For want of space some seventy thousand volumes are stored in the basements of other buildings; more are constantly moved out to make room for accessions; there are no proper places for professors and students to work; and, in brief, if we are not shortly to lose much of the usefulness of this great scholars' library, we must have a large addition to the structure. An excellent plan for a new building has been made by a number of architects employed by the Committee of the Overseers. To build it will cost over two million dollars, and to maintain it the income of a million more. If this sum cannot be raised, at least enough must be secured to begin at once a substantial portion of the work.

The foundations of the research laboratory for physical chemistry have been laid, and it is a pleasure to think that this productive branch of investigation is placed on a satisfactory basis. But it does not relieve the general condition of chemical instruction, for which Boylston Hall is wholly inadequate. The importance of Chemistry to natural science, to health and to industry, has increased rapidly, and its development in the future is measureless; yet we are almost entirely limited to a single building constructed more than half a century ago. If Harvard is not to fall hopelessly behind the times in this branch of science, we need laboratories, which, with the fund for maintenance, will cost a million dollars.

The School of Business Administration was projected with contributions of twenty-five thousand dollars a year for five years; and, since that period comes to an end in 1913, adequate provision must be made for an endowment of the School. It has proved its value and deserves to be put on a permanent foundation.

In order to enable the Medical School to call eminent clinical professors from other parts of the country — which it must do in order to maintain itself as a national institution of the first rank — it needs funds to pay them adequate salaries. More pressing still is the condition of the Dental School. The new building

is admirable, and the number of students has increased largely.
The operating rooms provide a dental hospital in which great
numbers of patients are treated, and the importance of this work
to public health is being more and more recognized. The building has been erected by the efforts of the staff, and in order to
place the School where it stands, the clinical instructors have
for years foregone their salaries altogether; but it is neither
just nor possible that this should continue longer, and to resume
the payment of salaries an endowment of at least five hundred
thousand dollars is required.

These are only the most obvious and pressing needs of the
University. There are others only less urgent. If they appear
large, it is because the usefulness of the University in its existing
fields of work is great. With improvements in equipment, the
expense of all effective instruction has increased, and this is
multiplied by the growing cost of everything. It is no mere
spirit of rivalry with others, but a desire to serve the country in
the best way that compels a statement of our lack of resources.

The following reports by the Deans, the Directors of Laboratories, and the heads of other branches of work are respectfully
referred to the Overseers.

A. LAWRENCE LOWELL, President.

CAMBRIDGE, January 25, 1912.

APPENDIX TO PRESIDENT'S REPORT

I

REQUIREMENTS FOR ADMISSION TO HARVARD COLLEGE WITHOUT COMPLETE EXAMINATION

A. EVIDENCE OF THE COMPLETION OF AN APPROVED SECONDARY SCHOOL COURSE

1. Tabulated Statement

A candidate shall present to the Committee appointed to administer this plan evidence as to his secondary school work in the form of an official detailed statement showing: —

(a) The subjects studied by him and the ground covered.

(b) The amount of time devoted to each.

(c) The quality of his work in each subject.

2. Approved School Course

An "approved secondary school course" must

(a) extend over four years,

(b) concern itself chiefly with languages, science, mathematics, and history.

No one of these four subjects may be omitted.

At least two studies of a school programme must be carried to the stage required by the present advanced examinations of Harvard College, or by the equivalent examinations of the College Entrance Examination Board.

B. EXAMINATION IN FOUR SUBJECTS

1. Subjects

A candidate who presents evidence that he has satisfactorily completed an "approved secondary school course" shall offer himself for examination in the four subjects named below. A satisfactory record in these examinations shall admit to Harvard College without conditions.

(a) English.

(b) Latin, or, for candidates for the degree of S.B., French or German.

(c) Mathematics, or Science (Physics or Chemistry).

(d) Any subject, not already selected under (b) or (c), from the following list: —

Greek	History	Chemistry
French	Mathematics	Physics
German		

2. The Examination Papers

(*a*) The preparation presupposed by the examination papers in the several subjects shall not be less than is ordinarily required for the present elementary examinations. The papers shall contain a sufficient number of alternative questions, and shall be so framed as to permit variety in the methods of school instruction. They shall also include advanced questions, thus permitting each student to reveal the full amount and the quality of his attainment. In any subject offered for examination which the candidate has pursued to an advanced grade he must present evidence of that grade of attainment. The papers shall not, however, presuppose a greater length of preparation than is ordinarily required for the present Harvard examinations.

(*b*) Time of examinations.
The four examinations must be taken at one time, in either June or September.

(*c*) Judging the examination books.
A copy of the candidate's school record shall be given to the readers of the examinations. In judging the books the examiner shall submit a full statement of his opinion of each book. In addition, at the option of the examiner, a grade may be given.

3. A Satisfactory Record

A " satisfactory record " shall not be construed to require that a candidate attain distinction in all four subjects, but shall mean that in the judgment of the Committee on Admission the candidate's examination record as a whole, when viewed as the basis for a general estimate of his quality, is such as to make his admission to college advisable.

II

EXAMINATIONS IN THE MEDICAL SCHOOL

The Committee appointed to devise a plan for general examinations in the Medical School submits the following report which was adopted without change: —

There shall be a Committee on Examinations, appointed from the Faculty by the President, which shall have full charge of all examinations in M.D. courses in the School.

There shall be two kinds of examinations, general and practical.

A. General Examinations

Two general examinations shall be required of the candidate for the M.D. degree: the first, after the end of the second year; the second, after the completion of the fourth year of medical study.

I. *The First General Examination*

  (a) Time of Examination.

      The student may choose either June or September for his first general examination.

  (b) Requirements for Admission to Examination.

      No student shall be admitted to this examination until he has completed all courses included in this examination, and has passed examinations in the practical work thereof.

  (c) Subjects of Examination.

      The subjects comprised in the first general examination shall be anatomy, histology and embryology, physiology, biological chemistry, pathology, and bacteriology; but this examination shall assume and require an elementary knowledge of physics, inorganic and organic chemistry, and biology.

II. *The Second General Examination*

  (a) Time of Examination.

      The student may choose either June or January for his second general examination.

  (b) Requirements for Admission to Examination.

      No student shall be admitted to this examination until he has passed satisfactorily the first general examination, has completed four years of medical study in four different calendar years, including at least one year of resident study at the Harvard Medical School, has completed all courses included in this examination, and has passed examinations in the practical work thereof.

  (c) Subjects of Examination.

      The subjects comprised in the second general examination shall be preventive medicine and hygiene, materia medica and therapeutics, medicine, surgery, pediatrics, obstetrics, gynaecology, dermatology, syphilis, neurology, psychiatry, ophthalmology, otology, and laryngology.

III. *The Character of the General Examinations*

      The general examinations shall be partly written and partly oral.

  (a) The Written Examination.

      The written part of each general examination shall consist of questions selected and arranged by the Committee on Examinations from lists of questions submitted by the departments concerned. The written test shall be divided into two or more parts of three hours each, and shall be given on successive days of the general examination. The examination books shall be read and graded as the Committee on Examinations shall determine, and the grade shall count as forty per cent of the final mark.

(b) The Oral Examination.

The oral part of each general examination shall be conducted by examining boards, of five members each, appointed from the teaching staff by the Committee on Examinations. Each board shall have not less than two professors. On each board for the first general examination there shall be one representative of clinical subjects, and at least one representative of each of the following groups: normal structure (anatomy, histology, and embryology), normal function (physiology and biological chemistry), abnormal structure and function (pathology, comparative pathology, and bacteriology). On each board for the second general examination there shall be one representative of the laboratory subjects, and at least one representative of each of the following groups: medicine, surgery. No single department shall have more than one representative on a single board. Any board may request the Committee on Examinations to appoint other members of the teaching staff to aid in conducting the examination.

The oral part of a general examination shall not be held on the same days with the written examination. The oral part of the second general examination shall include the electives taken in the fourth year. The board shall determine by conference and vote the grade of the student, and it shall count as twenty per cent of the final mark.

IV. *Repetition of General Examinations*

No student who has failed to pass a general examination shall be permitted to repeat the examination within the calendar year in which he failed. Any student who fails three times in a general examination shall be debarred from further attempts.

B. PRACTICAL EXAMINATIONS

The practical examinations shall be conducted by the several departments in conference with the Committee on Examinations, and the departments shall give no other examinations which shall count for the degree. These examinations shall be planned to measure the student's practical knowledge and skill, and to this end the second examination shall include a thorough test of the student's capacity in diagnosis and treatment under conditions of actual practice. Every student may choose whether he will take the practical examinations at the end of each course or near the time of the next general examination. In order to be admitted to a general examination the student must have passed all the practical examinations in the subjects of that examination.

Forty per cent of the average percentage grade of each student in the practical examinations shall count in the final mark of each of the general examinations. In estimating the average percentage grade the marks in the practical examinations in medicine and surgery shall each be multiplied by three, in obstetrics and pediatrics each by two, and in the other departments by one.[1] In departments giving only lectures and demonstrations an oral, instead of a practical, examination shall be held, and the marks counted as if secured in the practical test.

C. ADMISSION TO ADVANCED STANDING

The preceding rules governing general examinations shall be applied to students seeking to enter the Harvard Medical School with advanced standing, as follows: —

Both general examinations including the practical examinations shall be required of every student admitted to the Harvard Medical School, and these examinations, including practical examinations, shall be given under the supervision of the Committee on Examinations as provided above. The requirements for admission to each general examination shall be the same for those entering for advanced standing as for those regularly enrolled in the Harvard Medical School from the beginning of the first year of medical study, except that courses pursued at other recognized medical schools in character and quality equivalent to similar courses in this School will be accepted in place of these courses in this School when satisfactory evidence of having pursued such courses is presented to the Dean. No student shall be admitted to the third year work until he has passed the first general examination, and no student shall be admitted to the second general examination who has not spent at least one year in resident study at the Harvard Medical School.

A graduate of another medical school of recognized standing may obtain the degree of M.D. at this University after a year's study in the undergraduate course, by fulfilling all the requirements for admission to the first and second general examinations, by passing these examinations, by fulfilling all requirements of laboratory and practical work required in the full undergraduate course, and by fulfilling all requirements for admission.

---

[1] This is in accord with the system at present in vogue in making up the students' general average, by which a subject with a three-hour or a two-hour examination counts proportionately more than one with a one-hour examination.

REPORTS OF DEPARTMENTS

THE FACULTY OF ARTS AND SCIENCES

To the President of the University: —

Sir, — I have the honor of presenting a report on the work of the Faculty of Arts and Sciences for the academic year 1910–11.

Besides the President, the Faculty contained eighty-five Professors, two Associate Professors, sixty Assistant Professors, one Lecturer, eighteen Instructors, the Acting Dean of Harvard College, and the Recorder, — in all, a hundred and sixty-nine members.

Instruction in 1910–11

With the following list of courses of instruction that were actually given under the authority of the Faculty, I print a statement of the number and the classification of the students in each course. The figures are those officially returned to the Recorder by the several instructors at the close of the academic year, and take no account of persons who, regularly or irregularly, attended the exercises and did the work of a course without being officially recognized as members of it. The abbreviations are those ordinarily used in such lists: *Se.*, Senior; *Ju.*, Junior; *So.*, Sophomore; *Fr.*, Freshman; *Sp.*, Special Student; *uC.*, Unclassified; *Gr.*, Graduate School of Arts and Sciences; *G.S.*, Graduate School of Applied Science; *G.B.*, Graduate School of Business Administration; *R.*, Radcliffe; *Di.*, Divinity; *And.*, Andover; *Me.*, Medical School; *Ext.*, Department of University Extension; *Instr.*, Instructor.

COURSES OF INSTRUCTION GIVEN IN 1910–11
Semitic Languages and History

For Undergraduates and Graduates : —

1¹. Professor Lyon and Dr. Davey. — Hebrew. Selections from the prose narratives of the Old Testament. 1 Se., 1 Ju., 2 So., 2 Fr., 2 Di. Total 8.

2². Professor Lyon and Dr. Davey. — Hebrew (second course). Syntax. Extensive reading in the Old Testament.

2 So., 2 Fr., 1 uC., 1 Di. Total 6.

4. Professor Lyon. — History of Israel, political and social, till the capture of Jerusalem by the Romans. 3 Se., 6 Ju., 6 So., 5 Di. Total 20.

5. Professor G. F. MOORE. — History of Jewish Literature from the Earliest Times to 200 A.D.   2 Ju., 1 Sp., 4 Di., 4 And.   Total 11.

A6. Professor ARNOLD. — Religion of Israel. History of the religious ideas and institutions of Israel from the earliest times to the Maccabaean age.
2 Di., 9 And.   Total 11.

12 hf. Professor LYON. — History of Babylonia and Assyria.
3 Ju., 1 Di.   Total 4.

Primarily for Graduates: —

‡10. Professor LYON. — Assyrian.   1 Ju.   Total 1.

‡13. Dr. DAVEY. — Arabic. Brünnow's Chrestomathy.   1 Gr., 1 Ju.   Total 2.

18. Dr. DAVEY. — Classical Aramaic (Syriac). Selections from the Peshitto; Syriac prose of the classical period.   1 Se., 1 Di.   Total 2.

COURSES OF RESEARCH

‡20a. Professor LYON. — Assyrian: Unpublished inscriptions.   1 Di.   Total 1.

20b hf. Professor G. F. MOORE. — Old Testament: Methods of Historical Investigation, with special reference to the Old Testament.
1 Gr.   Total 1.

Egyptology

For Undergraduates and Graduates: —

3 hf. Asst. Professor REISNER. — History of Egypt.
1 Gr., 14 Se., 20 Ju., 15 So., 2 Fr., 1 Me.   Total 53.

4 hf. Asst. Professor REISNER. — History of Egyptian Art.
1 Gr., 19 Se., 19 Ju., 22 So., 5 Fr., 1 uC., 1 Di.   Total 68.

Indic Philology

For Undergraduates and Graduates: —

1a hf. Professor LANMAN. — Elementary Sanskrit.   1 Se.   Total 1.

1b hf. Professor LANMAN. — Elementary Sanskrit (continued). Hertel's Pancha-tantra.   1 Se.   Total 1.

The Classics

Primarily for Undergraduates: —

GREEK

G. Asst. Professor C. N. JACKSON. — Course for Beginners.
4 Gr., 1 Ju., 3 So., 15 Fr., 3 Sp., 1 uC., 1 And.   Total 28.

A. Dr. K. K. SMITH. — Greek Literature. Homer, Odyssey; Euripides and Aristophanes.   1 Se., 3 So., 6 Fr., 2 uC.   Total 12.

B. Professor GULICK, Asst. Professor C. N. JACKSON, and Dr. POST. — Greek Literature. Plato; Lysias; Elegiac, Iambic, and Lyric Poets; Euripides.
4 So., 27 Fr.   Total 31.

E hf. Dr. WEBB. — Greek Prose Composition (first course).
1 Gr., 1 Ju., 5 So., 1 Fr.   Total 8.

1a 'hf. Mr. Fobes. — Greek Literature. The Period of Athenian Supremacy. Herodotus; Aeschylus; Plutarch. 1 Ju., 3 So., 4 Fr., 1 uC. Total 9.

1b 2hf. Dr. Post. — Greek Literature. The Period of Athenian Supremacy. Thucydides; Aristophanes; Sophocles.
1 Se., 3 So., 3 Fr., 1 uC. Total 8.

2. Professor Clifford H. Moore and Associate Professor C. P. Parker. — Greek Literature. Aristophanes; Thucydides; Aeschylus; Sophocles.
1 Gr., 10 So. Total 11.

3 hf. Asst. Professor C. N. Jackson. — Greek Prose Composition (second course). 1 Gr., 1 Ju., 4 So. Total 6.

LATIN

A. Mr. Miller. — Cicero (selected speeches). Virgil.
1 Ju., 1 So., 7 Fr., 1 Sp., 1 uC. Total 11.

B. Associate Professor C. P. Parker, Professor E. K. Rand, Drs. Webb and K. K. Smith, and Messrs. Fobes and Miller. — Latin Literature. Livy; Horace; Terence. 2 Ju., 7 So., 83 Fr., 1 Sp. Total 93.

E hf. Dr. K. K. Smith. — Latin Composition (first course). Translation of English Narrative. 1 Ju., 5 So., 1 Fr. Total 7.

1. Professors Clifford H. Moore and E. K. Rand. — Latin Literature. Tacitus; Catullus; Horace. 1 Se., 2 Ju., 14 So., 2 uC. Total 19.

2a 'hf. Mr. Fobes. — Latin Literature. General View of Latin Poetry.
1 Se., 1 Ju., 1 So., 1 Fr. Total 4.

2b 2hf. Dr. Webb. — Introduction to Latin Prose Literature. Tacitus.
1 Ju., 2 So., 1 Fr., 1 uC. Total 5.

3 hf. Mr. Fobes. — Latin Composition (second course).
1 Gr., 2 Ju., 5 So., 2 uC. Total 10.

For Undergraduates and Graduates: —

GREEK

6. Professor Weir Smyth and Dr. Post. — Greek Literature. Demosthenes; Aeschines; Aeschylus; Sophocles; Aristophanes.
1 Gr., 2 Se., 6 Ju., 1 So., 1 And. Total 11.

7 hf. Professor Gulick. — Greek Prose Composition (third course).
4 Gr., 4 Se., 2 Ju. Total 10.

9. Professor Ropes. — Introduction to the Study of the New Testament. Origin and History of the New Testament Writings; The Teachings of Jesus Christ and of the New Testament Authors.
7 Di., 4 And. Total 11.

8. Professor Goodwin and Associate Professor C. P. Parker. — Plato; Aristotle. Survey of Greek Philosophy from Thales to Aristotle.
3 Gr., 9 Se., 3 Ju. Total 15.

10. Professor GULICK. — The Life of the Ancient Athenians, described and illustrated by the aid of the Literature and of the Monuments.

1 Gr., 24 Se., 30 Ju., 18 So., 3 Fr., 3 Sp.   Total 74.

12. Professor WEIR SMYTH. — History of Classical Greek Literature.

7 Gr., 3 Se., 3 Ju., 2 So., 1 uC.   Total 16.

LATIN

6. Professor HOWARD. — Latin Literature. Suetonius; Pliny; Juvenal; Martial.   2 Gr., 3 Se., 4 Ju., 2 So.   Total 11.

7 *hf*. Associate Professor C. P. PARKER. — Latin Composition (third course).

5 Gr., 6 Se., 3 Ju.   Total 14.

8. Professors CLIFFORD H. MOORE and E. K. RAND. — Latin Literature. Cicero; Lucretius; Plautus.   6 Gr., 7 Se., 3 Ju.   Total 16.

15. Professor E. K. RAND and Dr. WEBB. — The Works of Virgil, with studies of his Sources and of his Literary Influence.

2 Gr., 2 Se., 1 Ext.   Total 5.

Primarily for Graduates : —

CLASSICAL PHILOLOGY

25 *hf*. Professor E. K. RAND. — Introduction to the Interpretation and Criticism of Classical Authors. History of Classical Studies.   6 Gr.   Total 6.

53 *hf*. Professor GULICK. — Introduction to the Critical Study of Homer.

1 Gr., 1 Sp.   Total 2.

66 *hf*. Dr. POST. — Greek Culture in the Sixth Century B. C.

3 Gr., 1 Ju.   Total 4.

27 *hf*. Professor GULICK. — Greek Political Theory. Aristotle (Politics).

1 Gr., 1 Ju., 1 uC.   Total 3.

36 *hf*. Professor E. K. RAND. — Cicero and Humanism.   3 Gr.   Total 3.

64 *hf*. Associate Professor C. P. PARKER. — The Philosophy of Motion. Heraclitus, Protagoras, Democritus.   2 Gr.   Total 2.

26 *hf*. Professor WEIR SMYTH. — Theocritus, Bion, and Moschus. Greek Pastoral Poetry.   2 Gr.   Total 2.

68 *hf*. Asst. Professor C. N. JACKSON. — Lucian and his Times.

4 Gr., 1 uC., 1 Di.   Total 6.

‡60. Professor ROPES. — The Gospels of Matthew, Mark, and Luke.

4 Di., 1 And.   Total 5.

52 *hf*. Professor CLIFFORD H. MOORE. — The Comedies of Plautus.

4 Gr., 1 Se.   Total 5.

67 *hf*. Mr. FOBES. — Catullus and the Elegiac Poets.

3 Gr., 1 Se., 1 Ju.   Total 5.

46. Professor HOWARD. — The Second Punic War. Livy (Books XXI–XXX).

5 Gr.   Total 5.

21 *hf*. Dr. K. K. SMITH. — Introduction to Greek Epigraphy.   6 Gr.   Total 6.

22 ²*hf*. Professor CLIFFORD H. MOORE. — Latin Grammar (Sounds and Inflections). 8 Gr. Total 8.

32 ¹*hf*. Professor CLIFFORD H. MOORE. — The Religion and Worship of the Romans. 8 Gr. Total 8.

CLASSICAL ARCHAEOLOGY

For Undergraduates and Graduates : —

1a ¹*hf*. Asst. Professor CHASE. — Greek Archaeology.
8 Gr., 9 Se., 2 Ju., 1 So., 1 Fr. Total 16.

1b ²*hf*. Asst. Professor CHASE. — Etruscan and Roman Archaeology.
2 Gr., 2 Se., 6 Ju., 1 So., 2 Fr., 1 Sp. Total 14.

Primarily for Graduates : —

5 ²*hf*. Asst. Professor CHASE. — Greek Numismatics. 1 Ju. Total 1.

20. THE SEMINARY OF CLASSICAL PHILOLOGY.

Professors WEIR SMYTH and HOWARD, Directors for 1910-11. — Training in philological criticism and research. Text-criticism and interpretation of Greek and Latin authors: for 1910-11, Aeschylus and Suetonius.
6 Gr. Total 6.

English

ENGLISH COMPOSITION

Primarily for Undergraduates : —

A. Professor BRIGGS and Asst. Professor GREENOUGH, Mr. HERSEY, Drs. BIRNBAUM, LONG, CROSS, and LEACH, and Messrs. M. McLEOD, FRENCH, HUNT, SHIPHERD, and C. A. MOORE. — Rhetoric and English Composition. 1 Gr., 1 G.S., 1 Se., 7 Ju., 8 So., 468 Fr., 6 Sp., 10 uC. Total 502.
Of this number, 49 (1 Ju., 43 Fr., 2 Sp., 3 uC.) were relieved of the prescription of English at the end of the first half-year; 22 Fr. took the second half-year's work as an elective half-course.

28a *hf*. Mr. T. HALL, assisted by Mr. COUES. — English Composition. Practice in writing in connection with English 28. 6 Fr., 2 uC. Total 8.

D¹˜²*hf*. Dr. WEBSTER, assisted by Dr. CROSS and MESSRS. HUBBARD and HUNT. — English Composition.
1 G.S., 5 Se., 8 Ju., 54 So., 53 Fr., 1 Sp., 8 uC. Total 130.

31. Mr. HAGEDORN. — English Composition.
1 Gr., 1 Se., 1 Ju., 11 So., 7 Fr., 3 Sp., 1 uC. Total 25.

22. Dr. MAYNADIER, assisted by Mr. COUES. — English Composition.
11 Se., 32 Ju., 15 So., 9 Fr., 3 Sp., 6 uC. Total 76.

18. Mr. STONE. — The Forms of Public Address.
12 Se., 28 Ju., 6 So., 1 Fr., 1 Sp., 2 uC. Total 50.

30 ¹*hf*. Mr. STONE. — Debating. 9 Se., 3 Ju., 1 So., 1 Fr., 1 Sp. Total 15.

For Undergraduates and Graduates : —

12. Asst. Professor COPELAND. — English Composition.
1 Gr., 7 Se., 8 Ju., 7 So., 1 Fr. Total 24.

57 *hf.* Professor PERRY. — English Composition.

11 Gr., 1 G.S., 2 Se., 1 Ju., 2 Fr., 2 Sp.   Total 19.

Primarily for Graduates : —

5. Professor BRIGGS. — English Composition (advanced course).

12 Gr., 7 Se., 7 Ju., 1 So., 1 Fr., 2 uC., 1 Di.   Total 31.

47. Professor BAKER. — English Composition. The Technique of the Drama.

12 Gr., 1 Ju., 1 Sp.   Total 14.

ENGLISH LANGUAGE AND LITERATURE

Primarily for Undergraduates : —

28 *hf.* Professors BRIGGS, BLISS PERRY, KITTREDGE, BAKER, and NEILSON, and Mr. T. HALL. — History and Development of English Literature in outline.
1 Gr., 63 Fr., 2 Sp., 2 uC.   Total 68.

41. Professor WENDELL, and Mr. W. R. CASTLE, assisted by Messrs. WITH-INGTON and HUNT. — History of English Literature from the Elizabethan times to the present.
12 Se., 27 Ju., 44 So., 10 Fr., 1 Sp., 4 uC.   Total 98.

37 *²hf.* Dr. MAYNADIER. — The Story of King Arthur.
11 Se., 13 Ju., 26 So., 16 Fr., 2 uC.   Total 68.

For Undergraduates and Graduates : —

8a *¹hf.* Dr. WEBSTER. — Anglo-Saxon.
19 Gr., 5 Se., 3 Ju., 1 So., 1 Fr., 1 uC.   Total 30.

1. Professors KITTREDGE and F. N. ROBINSON. — Chaucer.
20 Gr., 5 Se., 2 Ju., 1 So.   Total 28.

2. Professor KITTREDGE. — Shakspere.
28 Gr., 19 Se., 28 Ju., 31 So., 2 Fr., 2 Sp., 4 uC.   Total 114.

11a *¹hf.* Professor NEILSON. — Bacon.
9 Gr., 5 Se., 14 Ju., 6 So., 1 Sp.   Total 35.

11b *²hf.* Professor NEILSON. — Milton.
7 Gr., 7 Se., 15 Ju., 11 So., 5 Fr., 4 uC.   Total 49.

61 *²hf.* Asst. Professor GREENOUGH. — Eighteenth Century Periodicals, particularly the Tatler, Spectator, Rambler, and Adventurer.
7 Gr., 2 Se., 4 Ju., 7 So., 2 Fr., 1 Sp.   Total 23.

53 *²hf.* Asst. Professor COPELAND, assisted by Mr. SHEAHAN. — Scott.
2 Gr., 34 Se., 25 Ju., 27 So., 10 Fr., 3 Sp., 1 uC.   Total 102.

55 *²hf.* Professor BLISS PERRY. — Tennyson.
22 Gr., 41 Se., 66 Ju., 39 So., 3 Sp., 8 uC.   Total 179.

48 *²hf.* Professor BRIGGS. — Browning.
16 Gr., 4 Se., 6 Ju., 6 So., 1 Fr.   Total 33.

Primarily for Graduates : —

19 *²hf.* Professor F. N. ROBINSON. — Historical English Grammar.
16 Gr., 1 Sp.   Total 17.

3b²hf. Professor KITTREDGE. — Anglo-Saxon. Béowulf.
22 Gr., 1 Se.   Total 23.

4. Professors NEILSON and F. N. ROBINSON. — Early English. English Literature from 1200 to 1450. Mätzner's Altenglische Sprachproben.
24 Gr.   Total 24.

40²hf. Professor NEILSON. — Scottish Literature from Barbour to Lindesay.
12 Gr.   Total 12.

Comp. Lit. 26¹hf. Professor KITTREDGE. — The Early English Metrical Romances. (See Comparative Literature.)   2 Gr.   Total 2.

14. Professor BAKER. — The Drama in England from the Miracle Plays to the Closing of the Theatres.   42 Gr., 4 Se., 10 Ju., 2 So., 5 Sp.   Total 63.

62¹hf. Asst. Professor GREENOUGH. — The Character, with some Consideration of Related Forms.   8 Gr., 2 Se.   Total 10.

49¹hf. Professor NEILSON. — Shakspere. Study of Special Topics.
13 Gr., 1 Ju.   Total 14.

50²hf. Dr. BERNBAUM. — Dryden and the Transition from the Seventeenth to the Eighteenth Century.   18 Gr., 1 Se.   Total 19.

54¹hf. Professor BLISS PERRY. — Carlyle.
15 Gr., 11 Se., 14 Ju., 4 So., 1 uC.   Total 45.

29¹hf. Dr. MAYNADIER. — The English Novel.
6 Gr., 2 Se., 5 Ju., 2 So., 1 Fr., 2 Sp.   Total 18.

COURSES OF SPECIAL STUDY

20. The instructors in English held themselves ready to assist and advise competent Graduate Students who might propose plans of special study in the language or literature of the periods or in the topics mentioned below. Such plans, however, must in each case have met the approval of the Department.   2 Gr.   Total 2.

a. Professor F. N. ROBINSON. — Anglo-Saxon.   3 Gr.   Total 3.

c. Professor NEILSON. — Modern English Literature.   6 Gr.   Total 6.

d. Professor BAKER. — The English Drama: its history, and its relation to Continental Drama.   5 Gr.   Total 5.

Public Speaking

Primarily for Undergraduates: —

1. Mr. BUNKER. — Voice Training.
2 Gr., 1 G.B., 3 Se., 3 Ju., 3 So., 22 Fr., 1 Sp., 2 uC.   Total 42.

2 hf. Asst. Professor WINTER, and Messrs. WILLARD and BUNKER. — Masterpieces of Public Discourse.
2 Se., 4 Ju., 8 So., 8 Fr., 1 uC.   Total 23.

3hf. Asst. Professor WINTER, and Messrs. PERRET and R. H. SMITH. — Platform Speaking.
2 Gr., 2 G.B., 22 Se., 32 Ju., 24 So., 7 Fr., 3 Sp.   Total 92.

4 hf. Asst. Professor WINTER and Mr. PERRET. — Dramatic Interpretation.
3 Se., 1 Ju., 1 So., 2 Sp.   Total 7.

5. Asst. Professor WINTER, and Messrs. WILLARD, PERRET, and BUNKER. —
Advanced Training in Platform Speaking and in Dramatic Interpretation.
1 Gr., 6 Se., 1 Law.   Total 8.

Germanic Languages and Literatures

GERMAN

Primarily for Undergraduates : —

A. Drs. WEBER, EISERHARDT, and PETTENGILL, and Messrs. IBERSHOFF, HER-
RICK, A. E. RAND, and SIEVERS. — Elementary Course.
8 Gr., 4 Se., 11 Ju., 18 So., 161 Fr., 8 Sp., 14 uC., 1 Di.   Total 215.

B. Asst. Professor W. G. HOWARD. — Elementary Course (counting as two
courses).   2 Gr., 4 So., 18 Fr., 1 Sp., 8 uC.   Total 28.

C. Dr. PETTENGILL and Mr. HERRICK. — German Prose and Poetry.
1 Se., 1 So., 26 Fr., 1 Sp., 1 uC.   Total 80.

1a. Drs. LIEDER and PETTENGILL. — German Prose and Poetry.
1 Se., 6 Ju., 27 So., 16 Fr.   Total 50.

1b. Dr. LIEDER. — German Prose.   Subjects in History and Biography.
1 Se., 4 Ju., 22 So., 11 Fr., 1 Sp.   Total 89.

1c. Dr. LIEDER. — German Scientific Prose.   Subjects in Natural Science.
2 Gr., 2 Se., 5 Ju., 15 So., 16 Fr., 2 uC.   Total 42.

Fhf. Mr. HERRICK. — Practice in speaking and writing German (first course).
2 Se., 1 Ju., 5 So., 5 Fr., 1 uC.   Total 14.

Hhf. Dr. EISERHARDT. — Practice in speaking and writing German (second
course).   1 Se., 2 Ju., 1 So.   Total 4.

2a. Professor VON JAGEMANN and Dr. EISERHARDT. — Introduction to German
Literature of the Eighteenth and Nineteenth Centuries. Lessing, Goethe,
and Schiller. German Ballads and Lyrics.
5 Se., 7 Ju., 17 So., 17 Fr., 1 uC.   Total 47.

2b. Professor H. S. WHITE and Dr. LIEDER. — Introduction to German Literature of the Eighteenth and Nineteenth Centuries. Lessing, Goethe, and
Schiller. German Ballads and Lyrics.
1 Se., 8 Ju., 23 So., 44 Fr., 1 uC.   Total 77.

2c. Dr. WEBER. — German Prose.   Subjects in German History.   Freytag;
Heyck; Kugler; Biedermann; Tombo.
1 Gr., 1 G.B., 3 Ju., 5 So., 7 Fr., 1 uC.   Total 18.

3. Dr. WEBER. — Schiller and his Time.   Der Dreissigjährige Krieg; Wallenstein; Maria Stuart; Die Jungfrau von Orleans; Die Braut von
Messina; Gedichte.   3 Se., 5 Ju., 14 So., 2 Fr.   Total 24.

4. Professor WALZ. — Goethe and his Time.   Works of the Storm and Stress
Period; Autobiographical Works; Poems; Egmont; Iphigenie; Tasso;
Faust.   4 Se., 12 Ju., 17 So., 9 Fr., 1 Sp., 1 uC.   Total 44.

25 1 hf. Professor FRANCKE, assisted by Mr. T. K. BROWN, Jr. — History of
German Literature in outline.
29 Se., 25 Ju., 15 So., 6 Fr., 2 uC.   Total 77.

For Undergraduates and Graduates : —

6 hf. Dr. WEBER. — German Grammar and practice in writing German (advanced course).   4 Gr., 1 So. Total 5.

1 hf. Mr. GROSSMANN. — German Correspondence.
                                   1 Gr., 1 Se., 2 So., 1 Fr., 1 uC. Total 6.

7 *¹hf.* Professor FRANCKE, assisted by Mr. GROSSMANN. — History of German Culture from the French Revolution to the end of the Wars of Liberation.
                                   14 Gr., 2 Se., 3 Ju., 1 So. Total 20.

Comp. Lit. 8 *²hf.* Professor FRANCKE. — Goethe's Faust; with a study of kindred dramas in European Literature. (See Comparative Literature.)
                      8 Gr., 1 G.B., 1 Se., 4 Ju., 5 So., 3 Fr., 1 Sp. Total 23.

Comp. Lit. 10 *²hf.* Professor WALZ. — The Influence of English Literature upon German Literature in the Eighteenth Century. (See Comparative Literature.)   7 Gr., 1 Se., 7 Ju., 1 So., 2 Fr. Total 18.

26a *¹hf.* Asst. Professor W. G. HOWARD. — German Literature in the first half of the Nineteenth Century. Kleist; Uhland; Heine.
                                   9 Gr., 2 Se., 7 Ju., 5 So., 1 Sp. Total 24.

26b *²hf.* Asst. Professor W. G. HOWARD. — German Literature in the second half of the Nineteenth Century. The Development of the Novel and the Drama.   9 Gr., 1 Se., 4 Ju., 2 So., 1 Sp. Total 17.

32. Professor H. S. WHITE. — Bismarck's Life and Writings. — Selections from Bismarck's speeches, state papers, and private correspondence; with some study of the development of Germany as illustrated in Bismarck's utterances.   2 Se., 6 Ju., 5 So., 2 Fr. Total 15.

8. Professor WALZ. — German Literature in the Twelfth and Thirteenth Centuries. Nibelungenlied; Kudrun; Hartmann; Wolfram; Walther von der Vogelweide. Translation into modern German.
                                   8 Gr., 1 Se., 2 Ju., 1 Sp. Total 12.

Primarily for Graduates : —

‡Comp. Lit. 34 *²hf.* Asst. Professor W. G. HOWARD. — The Dramatic Works of Grillparzer considered in their relations to European Literature.
                                                         8 Gr. Total 8.

28. Professor H. S. WHITE. — Goethe's Italienische Reise. Readings and translation, with some examination of the original letters and diaries upon which the narrative is based, and with illustrations of the course of Goethe's travels and art studies.   4 Gr., 1 Se., 1 Ju. Total 6.

‡12a *¹hf.* Professor VON JAGEMANN. — Gothic. Introduction to the Study of Germanic Philology. General Introduction; Phonology.
                                   22 Gr., 1 Se., 1 Sp., 4 R. Total 28.

‡15 *²hf.* Professor WALZ. — Old High German.   11 Gr., 1 Sp., 5 R. Total 17.

21. Professor VON JAGEMANN. — History of the German Language.
                                   8 Gr., 1 Se., 1 Ju., 3 R. Total 13.

SEMINARY COURSES

‡20a ¹hf. Professor FRANCKE. — Lessing's Laokoon.

3 Gr., 1 Sp., 4 R.   Total 8.

‡20b ²hf. Professor FRANCKE. — Schiller's Philosophical Poems.

2 Gr., 1 R.   Total 3.

20c ²hf. Professor VON JAGEMANN. — Hartmann von Aue.

2 Gr., 1 Se., 1 R.   Total 4.

20d ¹hf. Professor WALZ. — Bürger and the Poets of the Hainbund.

5 Gr., 1 Instr., 4 R.   Total 10.

SCANDINAVIAN

Primarily for Graduates :

2. Dr. LEACH. — Icelandic (Old Norse). The Sagas, the Younger Edda, and
   the Elder Edda.   2 Gr., 1 Se. Total 3.

Romance Languages and Literatures

FRENCH

Primarily for Undergraduates : —

A. Dr. WHITTEM, Drs. HAWKINS, MACKENZIE, and WILKINS, and Mr. LINCOLN.
— Elementary Course. French prose and composition.
18 Gr., 1 G.S., 1 Se., 6 Ju., 9 So., 64 Fr., 8 Sp., 18 uC., 3 Di.   Total 118.

1b. Asst. Professor BABBITT, Dr. HAWKINS, MACKENZIE, and WILKINS, and
Mr. LINCOLN. — French Prose, historical and general. Translation from
French into English.

1 Se., 10 Ju., 21 So., 39 Fr., 2 Sp., 2 uC.   Total 75.

1a. Associate Professor DE SUMICHRAST and Mr. BRUN. — Reading, translation, grammar, and composition.

5 Ju., 19 So., 14 Fr., 2 Sp., 3 uC.   Total 43.

2c. Asst. Professor POTTER, Drs. HAWKINS and WHITTEM, and Messrs. LIN-
COLN and WESTON. — French Prose and Poetry. Corneille; Racine;
Molière; Victor Hugo; Alfred de Musset; Balzac; Mérimée; Flaubert;
Daudet; Loti; Zola. Composition.

5 Se., 8 Ju., 25 So., 58 Fr., 1 Sp., 3 uC.   Total 100.

2a. Asst. Professor WRIGHT, Dr. HAWKINS, and Messrs. BRUN, ALLARD, and
WESTON. — French Prose and Poetry. Corneille; Racine; Molière;
Victor Hugo; George Sand; Alfred de Musset; Rostand. Composition.

1 Se., 5 Ju., 24 So., 105 Fr.   Total 135.

3. Mr. ALLARD. — French Composition (elementary course).

7 Se., 3 Ju., 4 So., 10 Fr., 1 uC.   Total 25.

4 ¹hf. Mr. BRUN. — French Composition (intermediate course).

1 Gr., 5 Se., 5 Ju., 6 So., 7 Fr., 1 uC.   Total 25.

5 ²hf. Mr. BRUN. — French Composition (advanced course).

1 Gr., 1 Se., 5 Ju., 5 So., 6 Fr.   Total 18.

For Undergraduates and Graduates : —

6c. Professor GRANDGENT. — General View of French Literature.
>1 Gr., 2 Se., 2 Ju., 11 So., 2 Fr., 1 Sp. Total 19.

6. Associate Professor DE SUMICHRAST. — General View of French Literature.
>1 Gr., 5 Se., 10 Ju., 20 So., 9 Fr., 1 uC. Total 46.

7. Associate Professor DE SUMICHRAST. — French Literature in the Eighteenth
Century.   5 Gr., 8 Se., 13 Ju., 1 uC. Total 27.

9. Asst. Professor WRIGHT. — French Literature in the Seventeenth Century.
>2 Gr., 3 Ju. Total 5.

10. Asst. Professor WRIGHT. — French Literature in the Sixteenth Century.
>3 Gr., 2 Ju. Total 5.

16. Mr. ALLARD. — The French Drama in the Nineteenth Century.
>4 Gr., 1 So., 1 Fr., 1 uC. Total 7.

18 *hf.* Mr. ALLARD. — French Correspondence.
>1 Se., 2 Ju., 3 Fr., 1 Law. Total 7.

Primarily for Graduates : —

14. Professors SHELDON and FORD. — French Literature in the Fourteenth and
Fifteenth Centuries.   5 Gr., 2 R. Total 7.

19 *hf.* Professor FORD. — Historical French Syntax.   6 Gr. Total 6.

22 *hf.* Asst. Professor WRIGHT. — Studies in the French Drama of the Seventeenth Century. Corneille; Racine; Molière.   .   7 Gr. Total 7.

ITALIAN

Primarily for Undergraduates : —

1. Dr. WILKINS and Mr. WESTON. — Elementary Course.
>1 Gr., 1 Se., 10 Ju., 12 So., 10 Fr., 2 Sp., 2 uC. Total 38.

For Undergraduates and Graduates : —

5. Dr. WILKINS. — Modern Italian Literature. Prose and Poetry of the
Eighteenth and Nineteenth Centuries. 1 Gr., 3 Se., 2 Ju., 1 So. Total 7.

2. Professor FORD and Mr. WESTON. — Italian Literature of the Fifteenth and
Sixteenth Centuries. Torquato Tasso; Ariosto; Machiavelli; Benvenuto
Cellini.   5 Gr., 3 Se., 1 So. Total 9.

10. Professor GRANDGENT. — The Works of Dante, particularly the Vita Nuova
and the Divine Comedy.   10 Gr., 5 Se., 1 Jr., 2 Fr., 1 uC. Total 19.

SPANISH

Primarily for Undergraduates : —

1. Asst. Professor POTTER, Drs. WHITTEM and MACKENZIE, and Messrs. LIN-
COLN and RIVERA. — Spanish Grammar, reading, and composition.
Modern Spanish Novels and Plays.
>2 Gr., 2 Se., 12 Ju., 42 So., 40 Fr., 7 uC. Total 105.

17 *hf.* Dr. HURTADO. — Spanish Composition.
>2 Gr., 5 Se., 7 Ju., 4 So., 1 Sp. Total 19.

For Undergraduates and Graduates: —

18 *hf.* Dr. HURTADO. — Spanish Correspondence.   1 Gr., 1 Ju., 1 Sp. Total 3.

4 *hf.* Professor FORD. — A General View of Spanish Literature.
                              5 Gr., 4 Se., 4 Ju., 2 So., 1 Fr. Total 16.

2. Professor FORD and Dr. WHITTEM. — Spanish Literature of the Sixteenth
  and Seventeenth Centuries.   Cervantes; Lope de Vega; Calderón.
                              6 Gr., 4 Se., 2 Ju., 4 So., 1 Sp. Total 17.

Primarily for Graduates: —

‡3. Professor FORD. — Early Spanish. The Poem of the Cid. Spanish Literature to the Fifteenth Century.   12 Gr., 1 Sp., 1 R. Total 14.

ROMANCE PHILOLOGY

Primarily for Graduates: —

3. Professor SHELDON. — Old French. Phonology and inflections. The oldest
  texts. La Chanson de Roland; Chrétien de Troyes; Aucassin et Nico-
  lette.   17 Gr., 1 Se. Total 18.

4. Professor GRANDGENT. — Provençal. Language and literature, with selections from the poetry of the troubadours.   6 Gr., 1 R. Total 7.

Celtic

Primarily for Graduates: —

1 *hf.* Professor F. N. ROBINSON. — Old Irish. General Introduction to Celtic
  Philology.   1 Gr. Total 1.

2 *hf.* Professor F. N. ROBINSON. — Middle Irish. Windisch's Irische Texte.
  The history of Irish Literature.   2 Gr. Total 2.

THE CELTIC CONFERENCE

Fortnightly conferences were held in Celtic subjects for reading and for the
presentation of the results of investigation. In 1910–11 the meetings were
chiefly devoted to the study of Ossianic texts in Irish and Scottish Gaelic.

Slavic Languages

For Undergraduates and Graduates: —

1a. Asst. Professor WIENER. — Russian.   2 Ju., 1 So., 2 Instr. Total 5.

4 *hf.* Asst. Professor WIENER. — Introduction to the History of Russian Literature.   1 Gr., 5 Se., 6 Ju., 6 So., 2 Sp. Total 20.

5 *hf.* Asst. Professor WIENER. — Tolstoy and his time.
                              1 Gr., 9 Se., 5 Ju., 1 So., 2 Fr., 2 Sp. Total 20.

Primarily for Graduates: —

3b *hf.* Asst. Professor WIENER. — General Survey of Slavic Philology.
                                                      1 Gr. Total 1.

Comparative Literature

Primarily for Undergraduates: —

1 *hf.* Professor WENDELL, assisted by Dr. LEACH and Mr. HAGEDORN. —
  European Literature. General Survey.
                        12 Se., 24 Ju., 41 So., 17 Fr., 1 Sp., 7 uC. Total 102.

For Undergraduates and Graduates : —

7. Asst. Professor POTTER. — Tendencies of European Literature in the Renaissance. 3 Se., 3 Ju., 1 So., 2 Fr. Total 9.

10 ²*hf*. Professor WALZ. — The Influence of English Literature upon German Literature in the Eighteenth Century.

7 Gr., 1 Se., 7 Ju., 1 So., 2 Fr. Total 18.

11. Asst. Professor BABBITT. — The Romantic Movement in the Nineteenth Century. 11 Gr., 11 Se., 8 Ju., 8 So., 1 Sp., 1 uC. Total 40.

12 ¹*hf*. Professor BLISS PERRY and Dr. T. P. CROSS. — Types of Fiction in the Eighteenth and Nineteenth Centuries.

22 Gr., 57 Se., 49 Ju., 33 So., 8 Fr., 6 Sp., 7 uC. Total 182.

8 ²*hf*. Professor FRANCKE. — Goethe's Faust; with a study of kindred dramas in European Literature.

8 Gr., 1 G.B., 1 Se., 4 Ju., 5 So., 3 Fr., 1 Sp. Total 23.

Primarily for Graduates : —

16*b* ²*hf*. Asst. Professor POTTER. — The History of Pastoral Literature. The Pastoral in modern European Literature.

2 So., 2 Fr., 1 Sp., 1 uC. Total 6.

19 ¹*hf*. Professor BAKER. — The Forms of the Drama.

26 Gr., 3 Se., 1 Ju., 1 So., 4 Sp., 1 uC. Total 36.

22. Asst. Professor BABBITT. — Literary Criticism since the Sixteenth Century.

12 Gr., 1 Se. Total 13.

24 ²*hf*. Professor BLISS PERRY. — Political Satire in Europe since the Renaissance. 12 Gr., 4 Se., 1 Ju., 1 So., 2 Sp., 1 uC. Total 21.

26 ¹*hf*. Professor KITTREDGE. — The Early English Metrical Romances.

2 Gr. Total 2.

‡34 ²*hf*. Asst. Professor W. G. HOWARD. — The Dramatic Works of Grillparzer, considered in their Relations to European Literature. 8 Gr. Total 8.

35 ²*hf*. Dr. WEBSTER. — Life in the Middle Ages, as illustrated by Contemporary Literature. 5 Gr. Total 5.

COURSES OF SPECIAL STUDY

20. Professor KITTREDGE. — Opportunities were afforded to competent students, under the guidance of instructors, for original investigations in special topics, such as were not covered by regular courses in the Department.

1 Gr. Total 1.

20*c*. Professor WEIR SMYTH. — The Relations of Greek Literature to European Literature in other Tongues. 1 Gr. Total 1.

20*h*. Professor FORD. — The Relations of Spanish Literature to European Literature in other Tongues. 3 Gr., 1 Se. Total 4.

Comparative Philology

Primarily for Graduates : —

2*a hf*. Professor GRANDGENT. — General Introduction to Linguistic Science. Phonetics. The Pronunciation of English, French, German, and Latin.

7 Gr., 3 R. Total 10.

History and Government

INTRODUCTORY

Primarily for Undergraduates : —

History 1. Professor HASKINS and Dr. GRAY, assisted by Messrs. VARRELL, HARING, OLSEN, and PACKARD. — Mediaeval History (introductory course). 2 Ju., 32 So., 228 Fr., 2 Sp., 9 uC. Total 273.

History 2. Modern European History.
2a *¹hf*. Asst. Professor MERRIMAN, assisted by Mr. PERKINS. — History of Western Europe from the close of the Middle Ages to 1715.
7 Se., 25 Ju., 77 So., 13 Fr., 2 Sp. Total 124.

2b *²hf*. Professor MACVANE, assisted by Mr. PERKINS. — History of Europe from 1715 to the present day.
8 Se., 17 Ju., 61 So., 6 Fr., 2 Sp. Total 89.

Government 1. Asst. Professor MUNRO, assisted by Messrs. DAVIS, GREGG, STEPHENSON, S. C. McLEOD, and CLEARY. — Constitutional Government.
3 Ju., 91 So., 250 Fr., 6 Sp., 18 uC. Total 368.

I. ANCIENT AND ORIENTAL HISTORY

For Undergraduates and Graduates : —

History 4. Asst. Professor FERGUSON. — History of Greece to the Roman Conquest. 4 Gr., 2 Se., 5 Ju., 3 So., 1 Fr., 1 uC. Total 16.

Primarily for Graduates : —

History 35. Asst. Professor FERGUSON. — Roman Constitutional History.
7 Gr., 1 Sp. Total 8.

Course of Research

History 20i. Asst. Professor FERGUSON. — Research in Greek and Roman History. 1 Gr. Total 1.

II. MEDIAEVAL HISTORY

For Undergraduates and Graduates : —

History 8 *²hf*. Dr. GRAY. — History of France to the accession of the Valois kings. 2 Gr., 2 Ju., 2 So., 1 Fr. Total 7.

Primarily for Graduates : —

History 25 *hf*. Professor HASKINS. — Historical Bibliography and Criticism.
7 Gr., 1 Di. Total 8.

‡History 21 *¹hf*. Professor HASKINS. — Introduction to the Sources of Mediaeval History. 2 Gr. Total 2.

History 26¹. Professor EMERTON. — History of Christian Thought, considered in its relation to the prevailing philosophy of each period, from the earliest time to the Eighteenth Century. 3 Di., 1 Ju. Total 4.

History 45 *²hf*. Professor HASKINS. — Diplomatics. 5 Gr. Total 5.

Courses of Research

History 20a ¹*hf.* Professor EMERTON. — Readings from the Literature of the Reformation Period.   1 Gr. Total 1.

History 20c. Professor HASKINS. — Mediaeval Institutions.   2 Gr. Total 2.

III. MODERN EUROPEAN HISTORY

For Undergraduates and Graduates: —

History 7a ¹*hf.* Professor EMERTON. — The Era of the Reformation in Europe. First part: from the rise of Italian Humanism to the close of the Council of Basel (1350–1448). 5 Gr., 5 Se., 5 Ju., 2 So., 1 Fr., 1 Di. Total 19.

History 12a ¹*hf.* Professor MACVANE. — English History from the Revolution of 1688 to the Reform of Parliament.
                5 Gr., 25 Se., 18 Ju., 19 So., 6 Fr., 1 Sp., 1 uC. Total 75.

History 12b ²*hf.* Professor MACVANE. — English History since the Reform of Parliament. 3 Gr., 25 Se., 22 Ju., 20 So., 8 Fr., 2 Sp., 1 uC. Total 81.

History 14. Asst. Professor JOHNSTON. — The French Revolution and Napoleon I.
                10 Gr., 22 Se., 19 Ju., 6 So., 3 Fr., 1 uC. Total 61.

History 27 ²*hf.* Asst. Professor JOHNSTON. — The Historical Literature of France and England since the Close of the Eighteenth Century.
                1 Gr., 2 Se., 2 Ju. Total 5.

History 16. Asst. Professor MERRIMAN. — History of Spain and the Spanish-American Colonies.   10 Gr., 3 Se., 2 Ju. Total 15.

History 15. Dr. LORD. — History of Russia.   3 Gr., 1 Ju., 1 Fr. Total 5.

History 18 ¹*hf.* Professor COOLIDGE. — History of the Far East in the Nineteenth Century.   3 Gr., 7 Se., 8 Ju., 8 So., 2 Fr., 1 Sp. Total 24.

History 30 ²*hf.* Professor COOLIDGE. — The Colonial Expansion of Europe in the Nineteenth Century and the Growth of the British Empire.
                2 Gr., 14 Se., 14 Ju., 6 So., 3 Fr., 2 Sp., 1 uC. Total 42.

History 34 ¹*hf.* Asst. Professor JOHNSTON. — The Political Geography of Europe.
                2 Se., 2 Ju. Total 4.

History 24a ¹*hf.* Professor E. C. MOORE. — The History of the Christian Church in Europe within the last three centuries.
                14 Se., 27 Ju., 9 So., 3 Fr., 2 Sp., 1 Di., 2 And. Total 58.

History 24b ²*hf.* Professor E. C. MOORE. — The Expansion of Christendom in the Nineteenth Century.
                12 Se., 35 Ju., 23 So., 7 Fr., 2 Sp., 3 Di., 1 And. Total 83.

Courses of Research

History 20d. Professor COOLIDGE and Asst. Professor JOHNSTON. — History of Continental Europe and of Asia in the Eighteenth and Nineteenth Centuries.   1 Gr. Total 1.

History 20f ¹*hf.* Asst. Professor MERRIMAN. — English Institutions in the Tudor and Stuart Periods.   3 Gr. Total 3.

History 20g. Professor COOLIDGE and Asst. Professor MERRIMAN. — History of Continental Europe in the Sixteenth Century.   2 Gr. Total 2.

‡History 20j. Professor MACVANE. — Recent English History.   1 R. Total 1.

IV. AMERICAN HISTORY

For Undergraduates and Graduates : —

History 10a ¹hf. Professor CHANNING. — American History to 1760.
10 Gr., 8 Se., 5 Ju., 15 So., 5 Fr., 4 uC. **Total 42.**

History 10b ²hf. Professor CHANNING. —American History (1760–1789).
10 Gr., 2 Se., 6 Ju., 11 So., 4 Fr., 2 uC. **Total 35.**

History 48a ¹hf. Professor CHANNING. — Selected Readings in American History. Lecky's " England in the Eighteenth Century."
1 Gr., 4 Se., 3 Ju. Total 8.

History 48b ²hf. Professor CHANNING. — Selected Readings in American History. Rhodes's "United States."   1 Gr., 4 Se., 3 Ju. Total 8.

History 17. Professor TURNER. — The History of the West.
16 Gr., 16 Se., 18 Ju., 13 So., 1 Fr., 1 uC. Total 65.

History 13. Professor A. B. HART, assisted by Mr. MORISON. — Constitutional and Political History of the United States (1789–1907).
5 Gr., 27 Se., 45 Ju., 39 So., 9 Fr., 2 Sp., 3 uC. Total 130.

Primarily for Graduates : —

History 28a ¹hf. Professor CHANNING. — Selected Topics in the Historical Development of American Institutions. The Constitutional History of the Revolutionary Period, 1774–1783.   8 Gr., 1 Se. Total 9.

History 28b ²hf. Professor CHANNING. — Selected Topics in the Historical Development of American Institutions. The Economic History of the Critical Period, 1783–1787.   7 Gr., 1 Se. Total 8.

History 44. Professor TURNER. —Selected Topics in Van Buren's Administration.   9 Gr. Total 9.

History 46 hf. Mr. W. C. FORD. — Manuscript Materials of American History.
4 Gr., 1 R. Total 5.

Courses of Research

History 20e. Professor CHANNING. — American History.
3 Gr., 2 Se., 1 Ju. Total 6.

History 20k. Professor TURNER. — American History.   2 Gr. Total 2.

V. ECONOMIC HISTORY

For Undergraduates and Graduates : —

Economics 6a ¹hf. Professor GAY, assisted by Mr. KLEIN. — European Industry and Commerce in the Nineteenth Century. (See Economics.)
12 Gr., 1 G.B., 10 Se., 22 Ju., 12 So., 2 Fr., 1 Sp., 1 uC. Total 61.

Economics 6b ²hf. Professor GAY, assisted by Mr. KLEIN. — Economic and Financial History of the United States. (See Economics.)

18 Gr., 1 G.S., 1 G.B., 19 Se., 52 Ju., 22 So., 7 Fr., 1 Sp., 3 uC. Total 119.

Economics 11. Professor GAY. — Modern Economic History of Europe. (See Economics.) 6 Gr., 2 Se., 1 Ju. Total 9.

VI. CHURCH HISTORY

History 5, 6, 7a, 24a, 24b, 26, and 20a are courses in Church History. In addition to these, the following courses in Andover Theological Seminary (offered Primarily for Graduates) were open to students in Harvard University: —

History A1. Professor PLATNER. — History of the Church in Outline.

1 Ju., 3 Di., 8 And. Total 12.

History A3. Professor PLATNER. — Christian Institutions, historically and comparatively considered. 2 Gr., 4 Di., 3 And. Total 9.

History A4 ¹hf. Professor PLATNER. — History of the Church in England.

1 Di., 1 And. Total 2.

History A5 ²hf. Professor PLATNER. — History of the Church in America.

1 uC., 1 Di., 1 And. Total 3.

VII. HISTORY OF RELIGIONS

Primarily for Graduates: —

History of Religions 10 ¹hf. Professor PLATNER. — The Elements of Christianity.

5 Se., 7 Ju., 7 So., 1 Fr., 1 Sp., 1 uC. Total 22.

For Undergraduates and Graduates: —

History of Religions 2. Professor G. F. MOORE. — History of Religions in Outline. — *First half-year:* The Religions of China and Japan, Egypt, Babylonia and Assyria, and the Western Semites (including Judaism and Mohammedanism). *Second half-year:* The Religions of India, Persia, the Greeks, Romans, Germans, and Celts; Christianity.

1 Gr., 4 Se., 3 Ju., 5 So., 2 Sp., 19 Di., 3 And. Total 37.

History of Religions 4 ²hf. Professor G. F. MOORE. — Judaism, from 198 B.C. to modern times. 1 Ju., 1 So., 1 Sp., 6 Di. Total 9.

History of Religions 5 ¹hf. Professor G. F. MOORE. — Islam. Life of Mohammed; the Koran; the Moslem conquests; Mohammedan law and theology. 1 Gr., 2 Ju., 5 Di., 2 And. Total 10.

VIII. MODERN GOVERNMENT

For Undergraduates and Graduates: —

Government 3. Dr. HOLCOMBE. — The History and Organization of Parties.

2 Gr., 18 Se., 23 Ju., 13 So., 7 Fr., 1 Sp., 1 uC. Total 60.

Government 10. Mr. YEOMANS. — The Government of England.

2 Gr., 4 Se., 3 Ju., 7 So., 2 Fr. Total 18.

Government 17. Asst. Professor MUNRO, assisted by Mr. HULL. — Municipal Government. 1 Gr., 2 Se., 30 Ju., 23 So., 5 Fr., 1 Sp., 3 uC. Total 65.

Government 24 *hf.* Professor HATTON (Western Reserve University). — Municipal Reform in the United States.

6 Gr., 12 Se., 24 Ju., 26 So., 4 Fr., 1 Sp., 8 uC.   Total 76.

Government 32 *hf.* (formerly Economics 24 *hf.*). Dr. HOLCOMBE. — Municipal Ownership and Control in Europe and Australia.

2 Gr., 8 Se., 6 Ju., 11 So., 1 Fr., 1 Sp., 1 uC.   Total 25.

Primarily for Graduates: —

Government 7. Asst. Professor MUNRO and Professor HATTON (Western Reserve University). — Problems of Municipal Administration in Europe and America.   5 Gr., 8 Se.   Total 13.

‡Government 12. Professor A. B. HART. — The American Political System, national, state, and municipal.

22 Gr., 7 Se., 4 Ju., 1 uC., 1 Law, 6 R.   Total 41.

Courses of Research

Government 20e. Professor A. B. HART. — American Institutions.

3 Gr., 1 Se.   Total 4.

IX. LAW AND POLITICAL THEORY

For Undergraduates and Graduates: —

Government 6. Mr. YEOMANS. — History of Political Theories.

9 Gr., 2 Se., 3 Ju., 2 Di.   Total 16.

Government 25 *hf.* Mr. JOSEPH WARREN. — Elements of Jurisprudence.

2 Gr., 15 Se., 10 Ju., 3 So., 2 Fr., 1 Sp., 1 uC.   Total 34.

Primarily for Graduates: —

Government 19. Professor STIMSON. — American Constitutional Law: A study of constitutional principles and limitations throughout the United States.

7 Gr., 6 Se., 6 Ju., 1 Sp., 1 Di., 2 Law.   Total 23.

X. INTERNATIONAL LAW AND DIPLOMACY

For Undergraduates and Graduates: —

Government 4. Professor G. G. WILSON. — Elements of International Law.

8 Gr., 18 Se., 20 Ju., 3 So., 1 Fr., 1 Sp., 2 uC.   Total 53.

Primarily for Graduates: —

Government 15. Professor G. G. WILSON. — International Law as administered by the Courts and as observed in International Negotiations.

7 Gr., 3 Se., 1 Ju., 2 Sp.   Total 13.

Course of Research

Government 20c. Professor G. G. WILSON. — International Law.

2 Gr., 1 Se.   Total 3.

Economics

Primarily for Undergraduates: —

1. Professor TAUSSIG, assisted by Drs. HUSE, E. E. DAY, and FOERSTER, and Mr. BALCOM. — Principles of Economics.

4 Gr., 1 G.S., 14 Se., 96 Ju., 272 So., 99 Fr., 15 Sp., 30 uC.   Total 531.

7 ^2hf. Dr. Huse, assisted by Messrs. Eldred and Hess. — Public Finance considered with special reference to the Theory and Methods of Taxation.

1 G.S., 30 Se., 63 Ju., 69 So., 18 Fr., 2 Sp., 9 uC. Total 192.

I. Economic Theory and Method

For Undergraduates and Graduates : —

2. Professor Taussig. — Economic Theory.

16 Gr., 1 G.B., 15 Se., 5 Ju., 2 So., 1 Sp., 1 uC., 1 Law. Total 42.

4. Professor Young (Leland Stanford Jr. University). — Statistics. Theory, method, and practice.   5 Gr., 8 Se., 9 Ju., 1 So., 2 Fr., 1 uC. Total 26.

14a ^1hf. Professor Carver. — The Distribution of Wealth.

5 Gr., 1 G.S., 28 Se., 36 Ju., 9 So., 2 Fr., 3 uC., 2 Di. Total 86.

14b ^2hf. Professor Carver. — Methods of Social Reform. Socialism, Communism, the Single Tax, etc.

5 Gr., 1 G.B., 20 Se., 32 Ju., 7 So., 1 Fr., 3 uC., 4 Di. Total 73.

Primarily for Graduates : —

‡15. Professor Bullock. — History and Literature of Economics to the year 1848.   6 Gr.   Total 6.

II. Economic History

For Undergraduates and Graduates : —

6a ^1hf. Professor Gay, assisted by Mr. Klein. — European Industry and Commerce in the Nineteenth Century.

12 Gr., 1 G.B., 10 Se., 22 Ju., 12 So., 2 Fr., 1 Sp., 1 uC. Total 61.

6b ^2hf. Professor Gay, assisted by Mr. Klein. — Economic and Financial History of the United States.

13 Gr., 1 G.S., 1 G.B., 19 Se., 52 Ju., 22 So., 7 Fr., 1 Sp., 3 uC. Total 119.

11. Professor Gay. — Modern Economic History of Europe.

6 Gr., 2 Se., 1 Ju. Total 9.

III. Applied Economics

For Undergraduates and Graduates : —

5 ^1hf. Professor Ripley, assisted by Mr. Whitnack. — Economics of Transportation.   4 Gr., 48 Se., 65 Ju., 18 So., 5 Fr., 2 uC. Total 142.

8a ^1hf. Dr. Huse. — Money. A general survey of currency legislation, experience, and theory in recent times.

2 Gr., 30 Se., 50 Ju., 18 So., 2 Fr., 5 Sp., 1 uC. Total 108.

8b ^2hf. Dr. E. E. Day. — Banking and Foreign Exchange.

1 Gr., 26 Se., 55 Ju., 27 So., 5 Fr., 5 Sp., 4 uC. Total 123.

9a ^1hf. Professor Ripley, assisted by Mr. Whitnack. — Problems of Labor.

6 Gr., 17 Se., 29 Ju., 8 So., 1 Fr., 1 uC., 2 Di. Total 64.

12 ^1hf. Dr. E. E. Day. — Commercial Crises and Cycles of Trade.

1 G.B., 40 Se., 43 Ju., 10 So., 2 Fr., 2 Sp., 1 uC. Total 99.

16. Professor Bullock. — Public Finance (advanced course).

5 Gr., 1 Se., 1 Ju. Total 7.

17 ²hf. Dr. Huse. — Municipal Finance.

> 3 Gr., 11 Se., 5 Ju., 1 So., 1 Sp.   Total 21.

23 ²hf. Professor Carver. — Economics of Agriculture, with special reference to American conditions.

> 5 Gr., 1 G.S., 21 Se., 24 Ju., 10 So., 5 Fr., 1 Sp., 6 uC.   Total 73.

28 ²hf. Professor Young (Leland Stanford Jr. University). — Insurance and Speculation.

> 3 Gr., 1 G.B., 27 Se., 35 Ju., 12 So., 1 Fr., 2 Sp., 3 uC.   Total 84.

Primarily for Graduates : —

30 ¹hf. Professor Ripley. — Problems in Railroad and Corporation Finance.

> 2 Gr., 9 Se.   Total 11.

IV. Courses Preparing for a Business Career

For Undergraduates and Graduates : —

18. Asst. Professor Cole, assisted by Messrs. Johnson and Platt. — Principles of Accounting.

> 3 Gr., 6 G.S., 26 G.B., 118 Se., 59 Ju., 2 So., 5 Fr., 2 Sp., 2 Law.
>
> Total 223.

21 ¹hf. Professor Wyman, assisted by Mr. R. M. Johnson. — Principles of Law governing Industrial Relations.

> 4 Gr., 1 G.S., 1 G.B., 108 Se., 47 Ju., 3 So., 3 Fr., 2 Sp.   Total 164.

V. Sociology

For Undergraduates and Graduates : —

3. Professor Carver, assisted by Mr. Bristol. — Principles of Sociology. Theories of Social Progress.

> 8 Gr., 9 Se., 27 Ju., 3 So., 2 Fr., 3 Sp., 6 uC., 3 Di.   Total 61.

(See Social Ethics)

Social Ethics 1 ²hf. Professor Peabody, Dr. McConnell, Dr. Ford, and Dr. Foerster. — The Ethics of Modern Industrialism.

> 2 Gr., 27 Se., 29 Ju., 27 So., 7 Fr., 4 Sp., 3 uC., 4 Di., 1 And.   Total 104.

Social Ethics 2 ²hf. Dr. Brackett. — Practical Problems of Social Service : Public Aid, Charity, and Neighborhood Work.

> 7 Gr., 3 Se., 3 Ju., 2 Di.   Total 15.

Social Ethics 4 ¹hf. Dr. Brackett, Dr. McConnell, Dr. Ford, and Dr. Foerster. — Selected Topics in Social Ethics.

> 5 Gr., 3 Se., 2 Ju., 4 So.   Total 14.

Social Ethics 5 ¹hf. Dr. McConnell. — The Moral Responsibilities of the Modern State.   2 Gr., 3 Se., 1 Ju., 2 So., 2 Di.   Total 10.

Social Ethics 6 ²hf. Dr. Foerster. — Social Amelioration in Europe.

> 4 Gr., 4 Se., 6 Ju., 3 So., 2 Sp., 1 Di.   Total 20.

Social Ethics 7 ¹hf. Dr. Ford. — Rural Social Development.

> 4 Gr., 3 Se., 1 Ju., 2 So., 1 Sp., 2 Di.   Total 13.

‡Social Ethics 20a ²hf. Professor Peabody. — Seminary of Social Ethics. Religion and the Social Question.   3 Gr., 1 So.   Total 4.

‡Social Ethics 20b²hf. Professor PEABODY. — Special Researches in Social Ethics. 2 Gr., 1 R. Total 3.

Social Ethics 20c. Dr. BRACKETT. — The School for Social Workers.
5 Gr., 1 Ju., 1 Ext. Total 7.

VI. COURSES OF RESEARCH

Primarily for Graduates : —

‡20b. Professor CARVER. — The Laws of Production and Valuation.
1 Gr., 1 R. Total 2.

20d. Professor TAUSSIG. — The Economic History of the United States, with special reference to Tariff Legislation. 1 Gr., 1 Se. Total 2.

20g. Asst. Professor SPRAGUE. — Banking. 2 Gr., 1 Se. Total 3.

THE SEMINARY IN ECONOMICS

Meetings were held by instructors and advanced students for the presentation of the results of investigation.

Business

I. ACCOUNTING

Economics 18. Asst. Professor COLE. — Principles of Accounting. (See Economics.)
3 Gr., 6 G.S., 26 G.B., 118 Se., 59 Ju., 2 So., 5 Fr., 2 Sp., 2 Law.
Total 223.

Business 1. Asst. Professor COLE. — Accounting Practice. 15 G.B. Total 15.

Business 2. Asst. Professor COLE. — Accounting Problems. 3 G.B. Total 3.

II. COMMERCIAL LAW

Business 5. Asst. Professor SCHAUB. — Commercial Contracts.
23 G.B. Total 23.

Business 6. Asst. Professor SCHAUB. — Law of Business Associations.
1 Gr., 6 G.B. Total 7.

Business 7 ¹hf. Asst. Professor SCHAUB. — Law of Banking Operations.
2 G.B. Total 2.

III. ECONOMIC RESOURCES

Business 10. Mr. CHERINGTON. — Economic Resources of the United States.
1 Gr., 25 G.B. Total 26.

Business 11. Mr. CHERINGTON. — Commercial Organization and Methods.
19 G.B., 1 uC. Total 20.

Business 14 ²hf. Mr. DOWNS, Mr. CHERINGTON, and the following lecturers: Messrs. HERBERT BARBER, JOHN BIRKINBINE, C. L. CHANDLER, T. A. EDDY, W. C. FARABEE, H. N. FISHER, H. G. GRANGER, H. R. A. GRIESER, ALBERT HALE, A. S. HARDY, W. G. REED, Consul-General RICHLING, L. S. ROWE, W. H. SCHOFF, Professor J. RUSSELL SMITH, and W. H. STEVENS. — Economic Resources and Commercial Organization of Central and South America. 2 G.B., 1 uC., 1 Law. Total 4.

Business 16. Mr. CHERINGTON. — Economic Resources of the United States (advanced course). 1 G.B. Total 1.

IV. INDUSTRIAL ORGANIZATION

Business 17 ¹hf. Professor GAY and Mr. GUNN, and the following lecturers:
Messrs. M. W. ALEXANDER, C. G. L. BARTH, CHARLES DAY, W. B.
DICKSON, HARRINGTON EMERSON, J. O. FAGAN, W. C. FISH, H. L.
GANTT, C. B. GOING, H. F. J. PORTER, RUSSELL ROBB, W. F. RUSSELL,
GERSHOM SMITH, J. E. STERRETT, and F. W. TAYLOR. — Industrial Or-
ganization.   1 G.S., 35 G.B., 1 uC.   Total 37.

Business 18. Mr. GUNN and the following lecturers: Mr. F. M. FEIKER and Mr.
S. E. THOMPSON. — Industrial Organization (advanced course).
                                                          8 G.B.   Total 8.

Business 20c ²hf. Messrs. H. L. BAKER, A. E. BARTER, H. L. BULLEN, J. C.
DANA, A. W. ELSON, E. B. HACKETT, W. C. HUEBNER, H. L. JOHNSON,
C. C. LANE, A. D. LITTLE, C. E. MASON, J. H. McFARLAND, A. F. MAC-
KAY, H. M. PLIMPTON, W. S. TIMMIS, J. A. ULLMAN, and D. B. UPDIKE.
— An Introduction to the Technique of Printing.   9 G.B.   Total 9.

V. BANKING AND FINANCE

Business 21. Asst. Professor SPRAGUE. — Banking.   12 G.B.   Total 12.

Business 22. Asst. Professor SPRAGUE. — Banking (advanced course).
                                                          2 G.B.   Total 2.

Business 24 ²hf. Mr. J. F. MOORS. — Investments.   29 G.B.   Total 29.

Business 25 ²hf. Asst. Professor SPRAGUE and the following lecturers: Messrs.
GROSVENOR CALKINS, Hon. W. H. CORBIN, W. J. CURTIS, A. L. DICKIN-
SON, R. F. HERRICK, J. F. HILL, Judge C. M. HOUGH, T. W. LAMONT,
G. O. MAY, H. L. STIMSON, and G. W. WICKERSHAM. — Corporation
Finance.   1 Gr., 14 G.B.   Total 15.

VI. TRANSPORTATION

Business 28. Asst. Professor CUNNINGHAM. — Railroad Operation.
                                                  1 G.S., 7 G.B.   Total 8.

Business 29. Mr. RICH. — The Railroad and the Shipper: The Theory and
Practice of Rate Making, with special reference to the Interstate Commerce Act.   8 G.B., 1 Law.   Total 9.

Business 30 ²hf. Mr. HOBBS. — Railroad Accounting.   8 G.B.   Total 8.

Business 32. Asst. Professor CUNNINGHAM. — Railroad Operation (advanced
course).   1 G.B., 1 Law.   Total 2.

VII. INSURANCE

Business 35a ¹hf. Mr. MEDLICOTT. — Fire Insurance.
                                          1 Gr., 3 G.B., 1 Law.   Total 5.

Business 35b ²hf. Mr. DOW. — Life Insurance.   5 G.B.   Total 5.

Philosophy

Primarily for Undergraduates: —

A-E. INTRODUCTION TO PHILOSOPHY

A ¹hf. Professor PALMER. — History of Ancient Philosophy.
            1 G.S., 33 Ju., 85 So., 79 Fr., 3 Sp., 12 uC., 1 Di.   Total 214.

B $^2hf.$ Professor SANTAYANA. — History of Modern Philosophy.
1 G.S., 20 Ju., 54 So., 52 Fr., 1 Sp., 16 uC. Total 144.

C $^1hf.$ Professor ROYCE. — Logic.
1 Se., 10 Ju., 10 So., 20 Fr., 4 Sp., 7 uC. Total 52.

D $^1hf.$ Asst. Professor R. B. PERRY. — General Problems of Philosophy.
1 Gr., 1 G.B., 17 Ju., 16 So., 15 Fr., 2 Sp., 3 uC. Total 55.

E $^2hf.$ Asst. Professor HOLT. — Psychology.
39 Ju., 47 So., 81 Fr., 4 Sp., 8 uC. Total 179.

For Undergraduates and Graduates : —

2 $^2hf.$ Dr. LANGFELD. — Advanced Psychology.
11 Gr., 5 Se., 7 Ju., 2 So., 1 Sp., 2 uC., 1 And. Total 29.

14 $^1hf.$ Asst. Professor HOLT, assisted by Dr. LANGFELD. — Experimental
Psychology. 8 Gr., 4 Se., 4 Ju., 2 So., 2 Fr., 1 And. Total 21.

13b $^1hf.$ Asst. Professor YERKES. — Comparative Psychology. Mental Development in the Individual. 10 Gr., 9 Se., 6 Ju., 2 So., 2 uC. Total 29.

6 $^2hf.$ Asst. Professor YERKES. — Educational Psychology.
12 Gr., 7 Se., 2 Ju., 1 So., 1 Fr., 2 Sp. Total 25.

21a $^2hf.$ Asst. Professor YERKES. — Animal Psychology. A study of forms of
activity and consciousness in the animal kingdom.
2 Gr., 1 Se., 1 Ju., 1 Fr. Total 5.

3 $^1hf.$ Asst. Professor R. B. PERRY.— Philosophy of Nature, with especial reference to Man's Place in Nature. Conceptions of nature in the light of
moral and religious interests.
2 Gr., 4 Se., 10 Ju., 14 So., 5 Fr., 1 Sp., 2 uC., 1 Di. Total 39.

4. Professor PALMER. — Ethics. The Theory of Morals, considered constructively. 6 Gr., 6 Se., 8 Ju., 5 So., 1 Fr., 2 Sp., 9 Di. Total 37.

9. Professor ROYCE. — Metaphysics. The Fundamental Problems of Theoretical Philosophy. The Concepts of Truth and Reality. Realism, Modern
Pragmatism, and Idealism, in their Relations.
18 Gr., 5 Se., 2 Ju., 1 Sp., 10 Di. Total 36.

24 $^1hf.$ Asst. Professor R. B. PERRY. — Present Philosophical Tendencies. A
brief survey of contemporary Materialism, Idealism, Pragmatism, and
Realism. 12 Gr., 13 Se., 2 Ju., 3 So., 1 Fr., 1 uC., 1 Di. Total 33.

16 $^1hf.$ Professor FENN. — Theism. 1 Gr., 5 Di., 1 And. Total 7.

19. Professor E. C. MOORE. — Philosophy of Religion.
1 Gr., 1 So., 16 Di. Total 18.

15. Professor ROYCE. — Advanced Logic. Modern doctrines regarding the
thinking process and regarding the principles of the Exact Sciences.
Outlines of a Theory of Knowledge. The Relations of Deduction and
Induction. 5 Gr., 3 Se., 1 Ju., 2 So., 1 uC. Total 12.

18. Asst. Professor WOODS. — Philosophical Systems of India, with special
reference to Vedanta, Sankhya, and Yoga. 3 Gr., 1 Se., 2 So. Total 6.

12. Professor SANTAYANA. — Greek Philosophy, with special reference to Plato.
7 Gr., 6 Se., 8 Ju., 4 So., 1 Sp., 5 Di. Total 31.

7b²hf. Asst. Professor R. B. Perry. — History of Ethics. Utilitarianism. Bentham, Mill, Spencer, Sidgwick.

3 Gr., 4 Se., 6 Ju., 3 So., 3 Fr., 2 uC., 2 Di.   Total 23.

11a ¹hf. Asst. Professor Woods. — Descartes, Spinoza, and Leibnitz.

3 Gr., 1 Se., 2 Ju., 1 Di.   Total 7.

11b²hf. Asst. Professor Woods. — English Philosophy from Locke to Hume.

3 Gr., 1 Se., 2 Ju., 3 So., 1 Fr., 1 Di.   Total 11.

8 ¹hf. Professor Royce. — The Kantian Philosophy.   8 Gr., 2 Di.   Total 10.

10 ¹hf. Professor Santayana. — Philosophy of Art.

9 Gr., 10 Se., 15 Ju., 7 So., 1 Fr., 3 Sp., 3 uC.   Total 48.

Primarily for Graduates : —

COURSES OF SPECIAL STUDY

‡20a. Asst. Professor Holt and Asst. Professor Yerkes. — Psychological Laboratory. Experimental investigations in Human and Animal Psychology by advanced students.   6 Gr., 1 Se.   Total 7.

‡20b. Asst. Professor Holt. — Seminary in Psychology. Recent Developments in Experimental Psychology.   8 Gr.   Total 8.

‡20c. Professor Royce. — Seminary in Logic. A Comparative Study of those Concepts of Human Thought which have to do with the Relations of Cause and Effect.   7 Gr., 1 Ju.   Total 8.

‡20d. Professor Palmer. — Seminary in Ethics. The Systematization of Ethics.

7 Gr., 2 Di., 1 R.   Total 10.

‡20e hf. Asst. Professor R. B. Perry. — Seminary in the Theory of Knowledge. Consciousness.   15 Gr., 1 Se., 1 Di.   Total 17.

20f hf. Professor Royce. — Seminary in the History of Philosophy. Hegel's Dialectical Method.   4 Gr., 1 Di., 1 R.   Total 6.

20i²hf. Professor E. C. Moore. — Seminary in Theology. Modern Theology, especially as influenced by Ritschl: a survey of constructive work in Theology during the last twenty years in Germany, England, and America.

1 Sp., 2 Di., 1 R.   Total 4.

Social Ethics

For Undergraduates and Graduates : —

1 ²hf. Professor Peabody, Dr. McConnell, Dr. Ford, and Dr. Foerster. — The Ethics of Modern Industrialism.

2 Gr., 27 Se., 29 Ju., 27 So., 7 Fr., 4 Sp., 3 uC., 4 Di., 1 And.   Total 104.

2 ²hf. Dr. Brackett. — Practical Problems of Social Service: Public Aid, Charity, and Neighborhood Work.   7 Gr., 3 Se., 3 Ju., 2 Di.   Total 15.

4 ¹hf. Selected Topics in Social Ethics.

Dr. Brackett. — The State and Charity.

Dr. McConnell. — The Ethical Relations of the State to Industrial Affairs.

Dr. Ford. — The Ethical Aspects of Industrial Coöperation.

Dr. Foerster. — The Ethics of Immigration.

5 Gr., 3 Se., 2 Ju., 4 So.   Total 14.

5 ¹*hf.* Dr. McConnell. — The Moral Responsibilities of the Modern State.
2 Gr., 8 Se., 1 Ju., 2 So., 2 Di. Total 10.

6 ²*hf.* Dr. Forster. — Social Amelioration in Europe.
4 Gr., 4 Se., 6 Ju., 8 So., 2 Sp., 1 Di. Total 20.

7 ¹*hf.* Dr. Ford. — Rural Social Development.
4 Gr., 8 Se., 1 Ju., 2 So., 1 Sp., 2 Di. Total 18.

Primarily for Graduates : —

COURSES OF RESEARCH

‡20a ²*hf.* Professor Peabody. — Seminary of Social Ethics. Religion and the Social Question. 8 Gr., 1 So. Total 4.

‡20b ²*hf.* Professor Peabody. — Special Researches in Social Ethics.
2 Gr., 1 R. Total 8.

20c. Dr. Brackett. — The School for Social Workers.
5 Gr., 1 Ju., 1 Ext. Total 7.

Education

For Undergraduates and Graduates : —

1a ²*hf.* Professor Cubberley (Leland Stanford Jr. University). — The History of Education in Europe since the Reformation.
7 Gr., 6 Se., 6 Ju., 7 So., 4 Fr., 3 Sp., 3 uC. Total 36.

2a ¹*hf.* Professor Hanus. — Introduction to the Study of Education. Discussion of Educational Principles.
8 Gr., 39 Se., 31 Ju., 29 So., 12 Fr., 6 Sp., 3 uC. Total 128.

2b ²*hf.* Professor Hanus. — School Administration as a Branch of Municipal Affairs. Contemporary Tendencies and Problems.
4 Gr., 10 Se., 9 Ju., 2 So., 4 Fr., 2 Sp., 2 uC. Total 33.

6a ¹*hf.* Asst. Professor Holmes. — Educational Theory in the Early Nineteenth Century. Froebel. 3 Gr., 3 Se., 1 Ju., 1 So., 2 Sp. Total 10.

6b ²*hf.* Asst. Professor Holmes. — Educational Theory in the Early Nineteenth Century. Pestalozzi, Herbart, and their Followers. The Influence of Pestalozzi, Froebel, and Herbart on the Development of Modern Schools.
7 Gr., 4 Se., 4 Ju., 3 So., 2 Sp. Total 20.

Primarily for Graduates : —

‡8a. Professor Hanus. — Organization and Management of State and City Schools and School Systems. Rural School Systems. Duties and Opportunities of Superintendents and Principals.
8 Gr., 8 Se., 1 uC., 1 R. Total 13.

‡8b. Professor Hanus and Asst. Professor Holmes. — Secondary Education : Public High Schools, Endowed and Private Schools.
10 Gr., 7 Se., 1 Ju., 6 R. Total 24.

8c. Asst. Professor Holmes. — Elementary Education. Programmes of study, equipment, methods. 5 Gr., 7 Se., 1 Sp., 1 uC. Total 14.

SEMINARY COURSES

‡20a. Professor Hanus. — Seminary. Contemporary Problems in Education.
12 Gr., 1 Se., 3 R. Total 16.

20c *hf. Professor CUBBERLEY (Leland Stanford Jr. University). — Seminary. The Evolution and Present Status of Education in Certain Selected States.
3 Gr., 2 Se. Total 5.

The Fine Arts

Primarily for Undergraduates : —

1. Asst. Professor POPE and Mr. MOWER, assisted by Mr. R. E. JONES. — Principles of Drawing and Painting, with elementary practice.
2 G.S., 1 Se., 6 Ju., 11 So., 37 Fr., 1 Sp., 3 uC. Total 61.

For Undergraduates and Graduates : —

2a. Asst. Professor POPE and Mr. MOWER. — Freehand Drawing (formerly Architecture 8a).
6 G.S., 2 Se., 8 Ju., 8 So., 1 Fr., 2 Sp., 1 uC. Total 28.

2b. Mr. MOWER. — Freehand Drawing (advanced course).
4 G.S., 8 Se., 4 Ju., 2 Sp. Total 18.

3. Asst. Professor CHASE, assisted by Mr. FROST. — History of Ancient Art. Architecture, Sculpture, and Painting in Egypt, Assyria, and Greece, with some account of the lesser arts.
13 Se., 27 Ju., 12 So., 6 Fr., 1 Sp., 1 uC. Total 60.

4a. Mr. FITZPATRICK, assisted by Mr. BORDEN. — The Fine Arts of the Middle Ages and the Renaissance.   1 Gr., 4 Se., 18 Ju., 3 So. Total 26.

4c *hf. Mr. FITZPATRICK. — History of Renaissance Sculpture.
1 Se., 2 Ju. Total 3.

5 *hf. Mr. W. C. LANE. — The History of the Printed Book.
1 G.B., 2 Se., 1 Sp. Total 4.

8a *hf. (formerly Architecture 7a). Asst. Professor POPE and Mr. E. O. PARKER. — The Theory of Pure Design.
1 Se., 5 Ju., 3 So., 1 Fr., 1 uC. Total 11.

8b *hf. (formerly Architecture 7b). Dr. Ross and Mr. E. O. PARKER. — On Drawing and Painting: Theory and Practice.
4 Ju., 3 So., 3 Fr., 2 uC. Total 12.

9. Dr. POST. — The Art and Culture of Italy in the Middle Ages and the Renaissance.   1 Gr., 5 Se., 6 Ju., 4 So., 1 Fr., 3 Sp., 4 uC. Total 24.

Primarily for Graduates : —

COURSE OF SPECIAL STUDY

‡20a. Mr. FITZPATRICK. — History and Principles of Engraving. Investigation of technical processes. Consultation of authorities; examination of prints.
1 Se., 2 R. Total 3.

20b *hf. Mr. E. W. FORBES. — Florentine Painting.   1 Gr., 1 Se. Total 2.

20c *hf. (formerly Architecture 20b). Dr. Ross. — Advanced Practice in Drawing and Painting.
1 Gr., 2 Se., 1 Ju. Total 4.

Architecture

For Undergraduates and Graduates: —

1a. Professor H. L. WARREN and Mr. FROST. — Technical and Historical Development of the Ancient Styles, with especial reference to Classic Architecture. 7 G.S., 5 Ju., 10 So., 2 Sp., 1 uC. Total 25.

1b. Professor H. L. WARREN and Mr. FROST. — Technical and Historical Development of the Mediæval Styles of Architecture.
9 G.S., 7 Se., 7 Ju., 3 So., 1 Fr., 3 Sp. Total 30.

2a. Mr. FROST and occasional criticism by Mr. E. T. PUTNAM. — Elementary Architectural Drawing. Elements of Architectural Form. The Orders.
3 Ju., 2 So., 1 uC. Total 6.

2b. Mr. E. T. PUTNAM, assisted by Mr. FROST. — Descriptive Geometry, Shades and Shadows, and Perspective.
1 G.S., 2 Se., 2 Ju., 5 So., 1 Fr., 1 uC. Total 12.

3b. Mr. H. B. WARREN and Mr. MURPHY. — Freehand Drawing (second course). Drawing from the Life. 10 G.S., 1 Se., 2 Ju., 1 Sp. Total 14.

Primarily for Graduates: —

3c. Mr. H. B. WARREN and Mr. MURPHY. — Freehand Drawing (third course). Architectural Subjects and from the Life. 1 Se., 1 Fr., 1 Sp. Total 3.

3d. Mr. H. B. WARREN and Mr. MURPHY. — Freehand Drawing (fourth course). Architectural Subjects and from the Life. 1 Gr., 3 G.S. Total 4.

4a. Mr. E. T. PUTNAM, with lectures by Professor H. L. WARREN. — Elementary Architectural Design. 3 G.S., 3 Se., 1 Ju. Total 7.

4b. Professor H. L. WARREN. — Architectural Design (second course).
10 G.S., 2 Se., 1 Fr., 3 Sp. Total 16.

4c. Professor DESFRADELLE (Mass. Institute of Technology), assisted by Mr. FROST. One Problem under the direction of Mr. R. A. CRAM. — Architectural Design (advanced course). 3 G.S. Total 3.

5a. Asst. Professor KILLAM. — Construction of Buildings: Materials and Methods. 4 G.S., 2 Ju., 1 So. Total 7.

5d²hf. Asst. Professor KILLAM. — Resistance of Materials. Elementary Structural Design. 1 G.S., 2 Ju., 1 Sp., 1 uC. Total 5.

COURSES OF SPECIAL STUDY

20a. Professor H. L. WARREN. — History of Architecture.
1 Gr., 2 G.S. Total 3.

20c. Asst. Professor KILLAM. — Advanced Practice in Construction of Buildings.
1 G.S. Total 1.

Landscape Architecture

For Undergraduates and Graduates: —

1. Asst. Professor PRAY. — Principles of Landscape Architecture.
2 G.S., 15 Se., 25 Ju., 15 So., 10 Fr., 4 Sp., 2 uC. Total 73.

Primarily for Graduates : —

2. Mr. H. V. HUBBARD, with occasional instruction by Asst. Professor PRAY. — Practice in Design (first course). 5 G.S., 1 Sp. Total 6.

3. Asst. Professor PRAY and Mr. H. V. HUBBARD, with occasional instruction by Professor OLMSTED. — Practice in Design (second course). Park and city planning. 6 G.S. Total 6.

4. Mr. H. V. HUBBARD. — Principles of Construction (first course). 6 G.S. Total 6.

5. Mr. H. V. HUBBARD, with occasional instruction by Asst. Professor PRAY. — Principles of Construction (second course). 6 G.S., 1 Sp. Total 7.

6. Mr. WATSON. — Elements of Horticulture. 4 G.S., 1 Ju. Total 5.

7. Mr. WATSON. — Plants in Relation to Planting Design. 3 G.S., 1 Ju., 1 Sp. Total 5.

8. Mr. WATSON. — Planting Design (first course). 4 G.S., 1 Sp. Total 5.

9 Mr. WATSON. — Planting Design (second course). Advanced work following the methods of Course 8. 6 G.S. Total 6.

10. Asst. Professor PRAY, with occasional conferences with Professor OLMSTED. — Principles of City Planning, illustrated by a critical study of examples. 11 G.S., 1 Sp. Total 12.

11. Mr. H. V. HUBBARD, with occasional instruction by Asst. Professor PRAY. — Elementary Drafting, with special reference to forms used in Landscape Design. 4 G.S., 1 Ju. Total 5.

20. Asst. Professor PRAY. — Competent students were directed in special work in design following Landscape Architecture 3, or in research on some special topic. 1 Gr., 1 Se. Total 2.

Music

For Undergraduates and Graduates : —

1. Asst. Professor HEILMAN, assisted by Dr. DAVISON. — Harmony, the Grammar of Music. 2 Gr., 4 Se., 3 Ju., 9 So., 30 Fr., 1 uC. Total 49.

2. Asst. Professor HEILMAN. — Counterpoint. 2 Se., 2 Ju., 1 So., 3 Fr. Total 8.

2a *hf.* Asst. Professor SPALDING. — Vocal Composition; part-writing, strict and free, together with analysis of choral works of the great composers. 1 Gr., 1 So., 1 Fr. Total 3.

3. Asst. Professor SPALDING. — History of Music from the time of Palestrina to the present day. 1 Gr., 8 Se., 18 Ju., 21 So., 10 Fr., 1 Sp., 2 uC. Total 56.

9 *¹hf.* Professor MAX FRIEDLÄNDER. — The Life and Works of Beethoven, with musical illustrations. 2 Gr., 1 G.B., 1 So. Total 4.

10 *¹hf.* Professor MAX FRIEDLÄNDER. — Romanticism in Music, from von Weber and Chopin to Berlioz and Schumann, with musical illustrations. 2 Gr., 1 G.B., 1 So. Total 4.

4. Asst. Professors SPALDING and HEILMAN. — The Appreciation of Music; analytical study of masterpieces from the point of view of the listener. 2 Gr., 6 Se., 14 Ju., 12 So., 5 Fr., 1 Sp., 2 uC. Total 42.

8 ¹ʰf. Professor Max Friedländer. — General History of Music of the Eighteenth Century, from Scarlatti to Haydn and Mozart.

1 Se., 6 Ju., 2 So., 1 Sp.　Total 10.

4a hf. Asst. Professor Heilman. — Brahms, Tchaikovsky, and Franck: an analytical and appreciative study of their works, with reference to style, structure, and content.　　1 Gr., 1 Se., 3 Ju., 3 So.　Total 8.

4b hf. Mr. Hill. — D'Indy, Fauré, Debussy: a critical study of their respective contributions to modern music.　2 Se., 2 Ju., 3 So., 1 Sp.　Total 8.

Primarily for Graduates: —

¡6. Mr. Hill. — Instrumentation.　　1 Gr., 4 Ju., 1 So., 1 Sp.　Total 7.

20 ¹ʰf. Professor Max Friedländer. — Studies in General Musical Knowledge, for advanced students. Interpretation of selected standard works of musical literature.　　1 Ju., 1 Sp., 1 uC., 1 R.　Total 4.

Mathematics

Primarily for Undergraduates: —

F. Asst. Professors Whittemore and Coolidge. — Trigonometry and Plane Analytic Geometry.　　5 Ju., 13 So., 73 Fr., 1 Sp., 3 uC.　Total 95.

A ¹ʰf. Mr. Fullerton. — Logarithms; Plane and Spherical Trigonometry.

2 Se., 5 Ju., 5 So., 30 Fr.　Total 42.

C. Professor Byerly. — Plane and Solid Analytic Geometry (extended course).
1 Gr., 1 G.S., 4 Ju., 7 So., 38 Fr., 1 Sp., 4 uC.　Total 56.

D ²ʰf. Mr. Fullerton. — Algebra.　2 Se., 2 Ju., 8 So., 25 Fr., 1 Sp.　Total 38.

E ¹ʰf. Mr. Fullerton. — Solid Geometry.

4 Se., 3 Ju., 3 So., 17 Fr., 1 Sp.　Total 28.

H ²ʰf. Asst. Professors Huntington, Coolidge, and H. N. Davis. — A Brief Survey of Mathematics for the General Student.

3 Ju., 11 So., 16 Fr., 1 uC.　Total 31.

2. Professor Bôcher. — Differential and Integral Calculus (first course).
1 Gr., 1 G.S., 3 Se., 18 Ju., 42 So., 6 Fr., 1 Sp., 6 uC.　Total 78.

4. Asst. Professor H. N. Davis. — The Elements of Mechanics.

6 Gr., 1 G.S., 1 Se., 3 Ju., 4 So., 2 uC.　Total 22.

For Undergraduates and Graduates: —

3. Asst. Professor Coolidge. — Introduction to Modern Geometry and Modern Algebra.　　6 Gr., 2 Se., 4 Ju., 4 So., 1 uC.　Total 17.

1 ¹ʰf. Dr. Dohmen. — The History of Mathematics.

1 Gr., 4 Se., 2 Ju., 1 So.　Total 8.

5. Professor Osgood. — Differential and Integral Calculus (second course).
7 Gr., 11 Ju., 1 So., 1 Fr., 2 Sp., 2 uC.　Total 24.

12 ¹ʰf. Professor Osgood. — Infinite Series and Products.

13 Gr., 2 Se.　Total 15.

14b ²ʰf. Professor Osgood. — Algebra. Galois's Theory of Equations.
8 Gr., 2 Se., 1 R.　Total 11.

9. Professor Byerly. — Dynamics of a Rigid Body.

5 Gr., 4 Se., 1 Sp.　Total 10.

Primarily for Graduates : —

‡13. Asst. Professor WHITTEMORE. — The Theory of Functions (introductory course). 7 Gr., 2 Se. Total 9.

‡16a ¹hf. Asst. Professor WHITTEMORE. — The Calculus of Variations.
4 Gr. Total 4.

‡16b ²hf. Asst. Professor WHITTEMORE. — The Equations of Mechanics.
1 Gr., 1 Se., 1 R. Total 3.

‡28 ¹hf. Asst. Professor COOLIDGE. — Projective Geometry.
2 Gr., 2 Se., 1 Sp., 1 R. Total 6.

‡29 ²hf. Asst. Professor COOLIDGE. — Non-Euclidean Geometry.
2 Gr., 2 Se., 1 Sp. Total 5.

‡10. Professors BYERLY and B. O. PEIRCE. — Trigonometric Series. Introduction to Spherical Harmonics. The Potential Function. 3 Gr. Total 3.

‡17. Professor OSGOOD. — The Theory of Functions (advanced course). The Algebraic Functions and their Integrals. The Logarithmic Potential.
4 Gr. Total 4.

‡19. Professor BÔCHER. — Ordinary Linear Differential Equations. 5 Gr. Total 5.

33 ¹hf. Associate Professor E. B. WILSON (Mass. Institute of Technology). —
Statistical Methods in Theoretical Physics. 3 Gr. Total 3.

‡SEMINARY IN THE THEORY OF FUNCTIONS

Professor OSGOOD and Asst. Professor WHITTEMORE. 5 Gr., 2 Se Total 7.

COURSES OF RESEARCH

‡20e. Professor BÔCHER. — Fourier's Series and Analogous Developments.
2 Gr. Total 2.

‡20f. Asst. Professor COOLIDGE. — Topics in Higher Geometry 1 Gr. Total 1.

Astronomy

Primarily for Undergraduates : —

1. Professor WILLSON and Dr. DUNCAN. — Descriptive Astronomy
1 G.S., 10 Se., 11 Ju., 22 So , 3 Fr , 3 Sp., 4 uC Total 54.

2 ¹hf. Professor WILLSON. — Practical Astronomy. Application of Astronomy to Navigation and Exploration.
1 Gr., 2 G.S., 5 Se., 5 Ju.. 1 So , 2 Sp. Total 16.

E ¹hf. Dr. DUNCAN. — Astronomy for Engineers. A modification of the first half-year of Astronomy 1, in which special attention was given to the methods of determining the meridian, finding the variation of the compass, time and latitude by theodolite. etc.
5 Se., 9 Ju., 4 So , 2 Fr. Total 20

For Undergraduates and Graduates : —

3. Professor WILLSON. — Practical Astronomy. Portable and fixed instruments. Time and longitude by transit; latitude by zenith telescope; meridian circle. 2 Gr., 2 Se.. 2 Ju , 1 Sp. Total 7.

4a $^1hf.$ Dr. DUNCAN. — The Determination of Orbits. Olbers' method for the parabolic orbits; Gauss' method for elliptic orbits. 1 Se. Total 1.

4b $^2hf.$ Dr. DUNCAN. — The Determination of Orbits. Leuschner's method for orbits of any eccentricity; orbits of visual and spectroscopic binary stars. 2 Se. Total 2.

Primarily for Graduates: —

5. Professor WILLSON. — Practical Astronomy. Instruments of the fixed observatory. Meridian circle; almucantar; equatorial instrument; absolute determinations. 1 Se. Total 1.

Physics

Primarily for Undergraduates: —

B. Professor HALL, Asst. Professor G. W. PIERCE, and Mr. CHAFFEE. — Elementary Physics. 5 Ju., 11 So., 28 Fr., 3 Sp., 1 uC. Total 48.

C. Professor SABINE, Asst. Professors G. W. PIERCE, LYMAN, H. W. MORSE, and H. N. DAVIS, Dr. BRIDGMAN, and Mr. HAYES. — Experimental Physics. Mechanics, Sound, Light, Magnetism, and Electricity.
4 Gr., 3 Se., 15 Ju., 37 So., 60 Fr., 6 Sp., 8 uC. Total 133.

1. Professor HALL and Mr. R. D. DAVIS. — General Descriptive Physics.
4 Se., 3 Ju., 7 So., 10 Fr., 2 uC. Total 26.

11 $^1hf.$ Asst. Professor H. W. MORSE. — The Theory of Primary and Secondary Batteries. 4 Se., 2 Ju., 1 So. Total 7.

For Undergraduates and Graduates: —

2 $hf.$ Professor SABINE and Asst. Professor LYMAN. — Light.
3 Gr., 2 Se. Total 5.

3. Professor B. O. PEIRCE, assisted by Mr. R. H. KENT. — Electrostatics, Electrokinematics, and parts of Electromagnetism.
1 G.S., 3 Se., 12 Ju., 4 So., 1 Sp. Total 21.

12 $^1hf.$ Asst. Professor LYMAN. — Electric Conduction in Gases and Radioactivity, with special reference to Modern Theories of the Constitution of Matter.
1 Gr., 2 G.S., 2 Se., 7 Ju., 1 So., 1 Se. Total 14.

17 $^2hf.$ Asst. Professor G. W. PIERCE. — Electric Waves and their Application to Wireless Telegraphy.
3 G.S., 1 Se., 6 Ju., 3 So., 1 Sp., 1 uC. Total 15.

4. Asst. Professors G. W. PIERCE and LYMAN. — Magnetism, Electromagnetism, and Electrodynamics. 3 Gr., 5 G.S., 2 Se., 2 Ju., 1 Se. Total 13.

5. Professor SABINE. — Light. 4 Gr., 2 Se. Total 6.

6a $^1hf.$ Professor HALL. — Elements of Thermodynamics.
1 Gr., 1 Se., 2 Ju., 1 Fr. Total 5.

6b $^2hf.$ Professor HALL. — Modern Developments and Applications of Thermodynamics. 1 Gr., 1 Se., 2 Ju. Total 4.

14 $^2hf.$ Asst. Professor H. W. MORSE. — The Theory of Photography.
1 Se., 3 Ju., 2 So. Total 6.

15 $^1hf.$ Asst. Professor G. W. PIERCE. — Radiation. 3 Gr., 1 Se. Total 4.

Primarily for Graduates : —

:7 ·*hf.* Professor HALL. The Kinetic Theory of Gases.   4 Gr.   Total 4.

:9 Professor B. O. PEIRCE. — The Mathematical Theory of Electricity and Magnetism.   9 Gr., 1 Sp.   Total 10.

COURSES OF RESEARCH

20d. Professor SABINE. — Light and Heat.   8 Gr.   Total 8.

20*e* Asst. Professor G. W. PIERCE. — Radiation and Electromagnetic Waves.
                                    1 Gr., 1 G.S.   Total 2.

20*f.* Asst. Professor H. W. MORSE. — Molecular Physics.   1 Gr.   Total 1.

20*g.* Asst. Professor LYMAN. — Light of Short Wave-Lengths   1 Gr.   Total 1.

20*h.* Asst. Professor H. N. DAVIS. — Heat.   2 Gr.   Total 2.

Chemistry

Primarily for Undergraduates : —

1. Dr. LATHAM CLARKE, Messrs. KELLEY and FISKE, assisted by Messrs. HOOVER, BOLTON, W. N. JONES, and PATCH. — Descriptive Inorganic Chemistry.   1 Gr., 6 Se., 19 Ju., 50 So., 172 Fr., 5 Sp., 9 uC.   Total 262.

2 *¹hf.* Mr. KELLEY, assisted by Mr. M. W. Cox. — Organic Chemistry (elementary course).
                2 G.S., 8 Se., 25 Ju., 49 So., 12 Fr., 2 Sp., 8 uC.   Total 106.

3. Dr. G. S. FORBES, assisted by Mr. COOMBS and Messrs WOODWARD, CONROY, and BREHAUT. — Qualitative Analysis.
                3 G.S., 4 Se., 21 Ju., 34 So., 3 Fr., 1 Sp., 3 uC.   Total 69.

For Undergraduates and Graduates : —

4. Asst. Professor BAXTER, assisted by Mr. VOTER — Quantitative Analysis, gravimetric and volumetric.
                4 Gr., 2 Se., 14 Ju., 14 So., 2 Fr , 3 uC   Total 39.

8 *²hf.* Professor RICHARDS and Dr. G. S. FORBES, assisted by Mr. BARRY. — Elementary Theoretical and Physical Chemistry, including the Historical Development of Chemical Theory.
                2 Gr., 1 G.S., 3 Se., 17 Ju., 28 So., 3 Fr., 8 uC   Total 62.

11. Dr. LATHAM CLARKE. — Industrial Chemistry.
                10 Gr., 6 Se., 12 Ju., 3 So , 1 uC.   Total 32.

9 *¹hf.* Asst. Professor BAXTER, assisted by Dr. C. J. MOORE. — Advanced Quantitative Analysis.   6 Gr., 4 Se , 2 Ju., 1 So , 1 uC.   Total 14.

10 *²hf.* Asst Professor BAXTER, assisted by Dr. C. J. MOORE. — Gas Analysis.
                6 Gr., 4 Se., 3 Ju., 1 uC.   Total 14.

5. Associate Professor F. J. MOORE (Mass. Institute of Technology), assisted by Mr. ESSELEN. — The Carbon Compounds.
                6 Gr., 5 Se., 14 Ju., 5 So., 1 Sp , 3 uC   Total 34.

15 *²hf.* Asst. Professor HENDERSON. — General Biological Chemistry.
                5 Gr., 8 Se , 10 Ju , 9 So., 3 uC   Total 35

Primarily for Graduates : —

6. Professor RICHARDS and Dr. G. S. FORBES, assisted by Mr. SHIPLEY. — Physical Chemistry.   8 Gr., 5 Se. Total 13.

12 *¹hf.* Asst. Professor BAXTER. — Photochemistry, including the use of Optical Instruments in Chemistry.   4 Gr., 1 Se. Total 5.

7 *²hf.* Dr. G. S. FORBES. — Electrochemistry.   3 Gr., 1 G.S., 2 Se. Total 6.

13 *²hf.* Dr. G. S. FORBES. — Experimental Electrochemistry.
    1 Gr., 1 Se. Total 2.

14 *¹hf.* Dr. G. S. FORBES. — Advanced Physical Chemistry.   4 Gr. Total 4.

16 *¹hf.* Mr. KELLEY. — The General Reactions of Organic Chemistry.
    8 Gr., 3 Se., 1 Ju. Total 12.

17 *²hf.* Mr. KELLEY. — Special Topics in Advanced Organic Chemistry.
    6 Gr., 2 Se., 3 Ju., 1 So. Total 12.

COURSES OF RESEARCH

20a. Professor RICHARDS. — Inorganic Chemistry, including Determination of Atomic Weights.   2 Gr. Total 2.

20c. Dr. LATHAM CLARKE. — Organic Chemistry.   8 Gr. Total 8.

20d. Professor RICHARDS. — Physical Chemistry, including Electrochemistry.
    4 Gr. Total 4.

20f. Asst. Professor BAXTER. — Inorganic Chemistry, including Determination of Atomic Weights.   4 Gr. Total 4.

Engineering

Primarily for Undergraduates : —

1e. Mr. GAYLORD, and Messrs. DONAHUE and FORT. — Trigonometry, Algebra, and Analytic Geometry.
    1 G.S., 1 Se., 3 Ju., 2 So., 36 Fr., 1 Sp., 2 uC. Total 46.

1d *²hf.* Mr. GAYLORD. — Analytic Geometry.
    5 So., 9 Fr., 1 Sp., 1 uC Total 16.

1c. Asst. Professor HUNTINGTON, and Messrs. MOULTON and D. L. WEBSTER. — Differential and Integral Calculus.
    2 G.S., 1 Se., 11 Ju., 25 So., 3 Fr., 2 Sp., 2 uC. Total 46.

3a. Asst. Professors KENNEDY and A. E. NORTON, and Messrs. NINDE and THOROGOOD. — Mechanical Drawing.
    1 Gr., 2 G.S., 5 Se., 13 Ju., 21 So., 24 Fr., 1 Sp., 4 uC. Total 71.

3b *¹hf.* Asst. Professor A. E. NORTON and Mr. THOROGOOD. — Descriptive Geometry.   2 G.S., 6 Se., 20 Ju., 22 So., 4 Fr., 1 Sp. Total 55.

3d *²hf.* Asst. Professor A. E. NORTON, and Messrs. NINDE and THOROGOOD. — Mechanism. Study of Gearing and Mechanical Movements.
    2 G.S., 6 Se., 16 Ju., 16 So., 2 Fr., 2 Sp. Total 44.

10a. Mr. MARKHAM. — Chipping, Filing, and Fitting.
    2 Se., 6 Ju., 9 So., 1 Fr., 1 uC., 7 S.S. Total 26.

10b. Mr. MARKHAM. — Blacksmithing.
2 Se., 6 Ju., 10 So., 1 Fr., 8 S.S.   Total 27.

10c. Mr. MARKHAM. — Pattern-making and Foundry Practice.
1 Se., 6 Ju., 7 So., 1 Fr., 6 S.S.   Total 21.

10e. Mr. MARKHAM. — Machine Shop Practice.
1 Se., 5 Ju., 7 So., 1 Fr., 1 uC., 11 S.S.   Total 26.

5b ^1hf. Professor L. J. JOHNSON and Mr. NICHOLS. — Elementary Statics. Graphic and Algebraic Methods.
9 G.S., 4 Se., 27 Ju., 21 So., 6 Fr., 4 Sp., 2 uC.   Total 73.
At Harvard Engineering Camp.   Mr. H. U. RANSOM.
1 G.S., 4 Ju., 4 So., 1 Fr., 1 Sp., 1 uC., 1 S.S.   Total 13.

5c ^2hf. Asst. Professor HUNTINGTON and Mr. D. L. WEBSTER. — Elementary Kinematics and Kinetics.
4 G.S., 8 Se., 17 Ju., 15 So., 1 Fr., 2 Sp., 2 uC.   Total 44.
At Harvard Engineering Camp.   Mr. H. U. RANSOM.
1 Ju., 2 So., 1 Sp., 1 uC.   Total 5.

For Undergraduates and Graduates : —

4a. Asst. Professor HUGHES, assisted by Mr. C. F. EBERLY (Topographer, U. S. Geological Survey), Mr. MORRISON, and other assistants. — Plane and Topographical Surveying.
2 G.S., 2 Se., 23 Ju., 28 So., 37 Fr., 2 uC., 1 Sp., 1 Me., 6 S.S.   Total 102.

4chf. Asst. Professor HUGHES, assisted by Mr. C. F. EBERLY. — Geodetic Surveying.   1 Ju., 1 So., 1 Sp., 2 S.S.   Total 5.

4d. Asst. Professor HUGHES, assisted by Mr. H. U. RANSOM and other assistants. — Railroad Engineering (first course).
1 G.S., 2 Se., 12 Ju., 15 So., 17 Fr., 1 uC., 4 S.S.   Total 52.

5a ^1hf. Asst. Professor HUNTINGTON and Mr. D. L. WEBSTER. — Kinetics (second course).   5 G.S., 10 Se., 15 Ju., 1 So.   Total 31.

5c ^2hf. Professor HOLLIS and Mr. BEARD. — Elementary Resistance of Materials.
5 G.S., 12 Se., 24 Ju., 2 So., 1 Fr., 2 Sp., 1 uC.   Total 47.

6a ^1hf. Asst. Professor HUGHES and Mr. PAIGE. — Elementary Hydraulics.
8 G.S., 12 Se., 15 Ju., 1 So., 1 Sp.   Total 37.

11a ^2hf. Professor HOLLIS, and Messrs. MARKHAM and BEARD. — Steam Machinery (introductory course).
3 G.S., 13 Se., 37 Ju., 27 So., 6 Fr., 2 Sp.   Total 88.

12b ^1hf. Professor MARKS and Mr. WOLFARD. — Elements of Thermodynamics. Theory of Heat Engines.   10 G.S., 9 Se., 26 Ju., 1 So., 1 Sp.   Total 47.

13a. Professor MARKS, assisted by Messrs. WOLFARD and DODDS. — Engineering Laboratory. A course in experimental methods.
8 G.S., 2 G.B., 12 Se., 11 Ju., 2 So., 1 Sp., 1 uC.   Total 37.

14a. Asst. Professor KENNEDY and Mr. NINDE. — Machine Design (introductory course).   1 Gr., 2 G.S., 5 Se., 8 Ju., 1 Sc.   Total 17.

16a. Professor KENNELLY, and Messrs. CRANE, J. W. DAVIS, and HEALEY. — Generation, Transmission, and Utilization of Electrical Energy (elementary course).   9 G.S., 1 G.B., 10 Se., 6 Ju., 1 So., 2 Sp., 1 uC.   Total 30.

Primarily for Graduates : —

4e². Asst. Professor HUGHES and Mr. PAIGE. — Road Engineering.
5 G.S., 2 Se. Total 7.

4f¹. Asst. Professor HUGHES and Mr. PAIGE. — Railroad Engineering (second course). Problems in railroad construction, economics, and maintenance.
5 G.S., 5 Se. Total 10.

5f. Professor L. J. JOHNSON and Mr. NICHOLS. — Mechanics of Structures.
1 Gr., 5 G.S., 3 Se. Total 9.

5g¹. Professor HOLLIS. — Mechanics of Machinery and Boilers.
2 G.S., 2 Se., 1 Ju. Total 5.

6c². Asst. Professor HUGHES and Mr. PAIGE. — Hydraulics (third course). Water Supply and Sewage Disposal.
8 G.S., 3 Se. Total 11.

6d¹. Asst. Professor HUGHES, and Messrs. SAFFORD and PAIGE. — Hydraulics (second course). Stream Flow; Measurements of Flow; Water Power.
8 G.S., 3 Se. Total 11.

7b. Professor SWAIN, Asst. Professor KILLAM, and Mr. NICHOLS. — Theory and Design of Structures of Wood, Stone, and Metal. 5 G.S., 3 Se. Total 8.

8a¹. Asst. Professor KILLAM. — Foundations, Masonry, and Fireproofing.
1 Gr., 4 G.S., 4 Se. Total 9.

12a². Professor MARKS and Mr. WOLFARD. — Efficiency and Economics of Heat Engines.
5 G.S., 3 Se. Total 8.

13b². Professor MARKS, assisted by Messrs. WOLFARD and DODDS. — Mechanical Engineering Laboratory.
2 G.S., 1 Se. Total 3.

14b¹. Professor HOLLIS, assisted by Mr. ORDWAY. — Machine Design (second course).
2 G.S., 1 Se. Total 3.

16b. Professor CLIFFORD. — Elements of Electrical Engineering (second course).
4 G.S. Total 4.

16j¹. Professor ADAMS and Mr. DOGGETT. — Direct Currents and Direct-Current Machinery.
6 G.S., 7 Se., 1 uC., 1 Sc. Total 15.

16k¹. Mr. CRANE and Mr. DOGGETT. — Direct-Current Machinery.
7 G.S., 7 Se., 1 uC., 1 Sc. Total 16.

16l². Professor CLIFFORD and Mr. J. W. DAVIS. — Alternating Currents.
5 G.S., 5 Se., 1 uC., 1 Sc., 1 Law. Total 13.

16m². Mr. CRANE and Mr. J. W. DAVIS. — Alternating-Current Laboratory.
5 G.S., 5 Se., 1 uC., 1 Sc. Total 12.

16n¹. Professor CLIFFORD and Mr. J. W. DAVIS. — Alternating-Current Machinery.
6 G.S., 1 Sp., 1 uC. Total 8.

16o¹. Professor ADAMS and Mr. DOGGETT. — Alternating-Current Machinery.
5 G.S. Total 5.

16p¹. Professor KENNELLY. — Electric Transmission and Distribution of Power.
2 Gr., 4 G.S., 1 Sp. Total 7.

17b². Professor KENNELLY. — Telegraphy and Telephony.
2 Gr., 1 G.S., 3 Se., 1 uC., 1 Sc. Total 8.

17c². Professor KENNELLY and Mr. HEALEY. — Illumination and Photometry.
1 G.S., 2 Se., 1 Sc.   Total 4.

17d. Professor ADAMS and Mr. DOGGETT. — Dynamo Design.   3 G.S.   Total 3.

18a². Professor HOLLIS, assisted by Mr. ORDWAY. — Power Station Design.
5 G.S., 1 Se.   Total 6.

21². Professors SWAIN, HOLLIS, and KENNELLY. — Conference on Engineering
Subjects.   8 G.S., 1 Se., 1 Sp., 1 Sc.   Total 11.

22². Professor WYMAN. — Contracts and Specifications.   General Principles of
Common Law governing Construction Contracts.
14 G.S., 8 Se., 1 Ju., 1 So., 1 uC., 1 Sc.   Total 26.

COURSES IN SPECIAL FIELDS

20a. Professor ADAMS. — Electrical Engineering Research.   1 G.S.   Total 1.

20b. Professor CLIFFORD. — Electrical Engineering Research.   6 G.S.   Total 6.

20c. Professor KENNELLY. — Electrical Engineering Research.   2 G.S.   Total 2.

20e. Professor SWAIN. — Structures of Wood, Masonry, and Metal.
5 G.S.   Total 5.

20m. Asst. Professor HUGHES. — Stream Flow and Water Power.
1 G.S.   Total 1.

Forestry

*None of the Courses in Forestry can be counted towards the degree of
A.B. or S.B.*

3a. Asst. Professor JACK. — Forest Botany. Systematic Study of Local Species
in Autumn Characters.   11 G.S.   Total 11.

1a. Asst. Professor FISHER. — Silviculture. Silvical Studies. Forest Description and Treatment.   11 G.S.   Total 11.

2. Asst. Professor CARTER. — Forest Measurements.   11 G.S.   Total 11.

1c. Asst. Professor JACK. — Silviculture. Forest Planting and Nursery Work.
9 G.S.   Total 9.

7b. Asst. Professors FISHER and CARTER. — Forest Management. Construction of a Complete Working Plan.   7 G.S.   Total 7.

7c. Asst. Professors FISHER and CARTER. — Forest Management. Logging
Operations in the Harvard Forest.   8 G.S.   Total 8.

3b. Asst. Professor JACK. — Forest Botany. American Species.
7 G.S.   Total 7.

1b. Asst. Professor FISHER. — Silviculture. Forest Regions and Forest Influences.   9 G.S.   Total 9.

4. Asst. Professor JACK. — Forest Protection. Diseases of Trees. Forest
Fires.   7 G.S.   Total 7.

7a. Asst. Professors FISHER and CARTER. — Forest Management. Theory of
Forest Regulation and Valuation.   8 G.S.   Total 8.

9. Mr. BAILEY. — Forest Products.   12 G.S.   Total 12.

6a. Mr. CARY. — Lumbering. General Logging and Forest Engineering.
8 G.S.   Total 8.

6b. Asst. Professor CARTER. — Forest Surveying and Timber Estimating.
8 G.S.   Total 8.

Botany

Primarily for Undergraduates: —

1 ²*hf.* Asst. Professor Osterhout, assisted by Mr. Tupper and other assistants. — Botany (introductory course).
2 Gr., 1 G.S., 7 Se., 12 Ju., 18 So., 76 Fr., 2 Sp., 7 uC. Total 125.

2 ¹*hf.* Professor Thaxter, assisted by Mr. Colley. — Morphology of Plants.
1 Gr., 3 G.S., 9 Ju., 9 So., 1 Fr., 1 Sp. Total 24.

For Undergraduates and Graduates: —

3 ¹*hf.* Professor Jeffrey, assisted by Mr. Hemenway. — General Morphology, Histology, and Cytology of Vascular Plants.
4 Gr., 1 G.S., 3 Se., 5 Ju., 1 So., 1 uC. Total 15.

6 ²*hf.* Professor Thaxter, assisted by Mr. Colley. — The Bacteria, Mycetozoa, and Higher Fungi.
2 Gr., 1 G.S., 2 Se., 2 Ju., 3 So., 1 Fr., 1 uC. Total 12.

7. Asst. Professor Fernald, assisted by Mr. Darlington. — Classification and Distribution of Flowering Plants, with special reference to the Flora of New England and the Maritime Provinces.
4 Gr., 1 Se., 3 Ju., 3 So. Total 11.

8 ¹*hf.* Professor Jeffrey and Mr. Bailey, assisted by Mr. Blades. — Structure of Woods: microscopic features. 1 Gr., 10 G.S. Total 11.

10 ²*hf.* Professor Jeffrey, assisted by Mr. Hemenway. — Special Morphology of the Higher Vascular Plants, the Conifers, Gnetales and Angiosperms.
3 Gr., 2 G.S., 1 Se., 3 Ju., 1 So. Total 10.

11 ²*hf.* Professor W. E. Castle and Asst. Professor East.—Variation, Heredity, and the Principles of Animal and Plant Breeding. (See Zoölogy 11 ²*hf.*)
3 G.S., 3 Se., 2 Ju., 3 So. Total 11.

13. Asst. Professor Osterhout and an assistant. — Plant Physiology.
3 Gr., 2 G.S. Total 5.

Primarily for Graduates: —

12 ²*hf.* Asst. Professor East. — Variation and Heredity. 3 G.S. Total 3.

Courses of Research

20*a.* Professor Jeffrey. — Structure and Development of Vascular Plants.
4 Gr. Total 4.

20*b.* Professors Farlow and Thaxter. — Structure and Development of Cryptogams. 5 Gr. Total 5.

20*d.* Asst. Professor Fernald. — Researches in Geographic Botany.
2 Gr., 1 G.S. Total 3.

20*e.* Asst. Professor Osterhout. — Researches in Plant Physiology.
2 Gr., 1 G.S. Total 3.

20*f.* Asst. Professor East. — Variation, Heredity, and the Principles of Plant Breeding. 1 Gr., 3 G.S. Total 4.

Zoölogy

Primarily for Undergraduates : —

1 ¹*hf.* Professor G. H. PARKER, Mr. E. C. DAY, and other assistants. — Zoölogy (elementary course).

3 Gr., 11 Se., 8 Ju., 28 So., 69 Fr., 5 Sp., 6 uC.   Total 130.

2 ²*hf.* Professor W. E. CASTLE and Mr. DETLEFSEN. — Morphology of Animals.

1 Gr., 7 Ju., 7 So., 7 Fr., 1 uC.   Total 23.

For Undergraduates and Graduates : —

3. Asst. Professor H. W. RAND and Mr. LAURENS. — Comparative Anatomy of Vertebrates.   3 Gr., 3 Se., 5 Ju., 3 So., 1 Fr.   Total 15.

4 ¹*hf.* Asst. Professor H. W. RAND and Mr. BOYDEN. — Microscopical Anatomy.

1 Gr., 1 Se., 1 Ju., 1 So., 1 Fr.   Total 5.

5a ²*hf.* Professor MARK, Asst. Professor H. W. RAND, and Mr. KORNHAUSER. — Embryology of Vertebrates.   Early Stages of Development.

1 Se., 1 Ju., 1 So.   Total 3.

11 ²*hf.* Professor W. E. CASTLE and Asst. Professor EAST. — Variation, Heredity, and the Principles of Animal and Plant Breeding.

3 G.S., 3 Se., 2 Ju., 3 So.   Total 11.

12 ¹*hf.* Professor MARK and Mr. KORNHAUSER. — Cytology, with special reference to Heredity.   3 Gr.   Total 3.

Primarily for Graduates : —

7a ²*hf.* Professor WHEELER and Mr. BRUES. — Morphology and Classification of Insects.   4 Gr., 2 G.S., 1 Se., 2 Ju., 1 Fr.   Total 10.

7b ²*hf.* Professor WHEELER and Mr. BRUES. — Habits and Distribution of Insects.   2 Gr., 2 G.S., 1 Se., 2 Ju., 1 Fr.   Total 8.

7c ²*hf.* Mr. BRUES. — Practical Entomology.   2 G.S., 2 Se.   Total 4.

‡14b ¹*hf.* Professor G. H. PARKER. — The Structure and Functions of Central Nervous Organs.   7 Gr., 3 G.S., 2 Ju.   Total 12.

17 ¹*hf.* Asst. Professor H. W. RAND. — Experimental Morphology.   The Form-determining Factors in Development and Growth. 2 Gr., 1 G.S.   Total 3.

COURSES OF RESEARCH

20a. Professor MARK. — Embryology.   1 Gr.   Total 1.

20b. Professor MARK. — Cytology, with special reference to Heredity.

2 Gr.   Total 2.

20c. Professor G. H. PARKER. —The Structural and Functional Basis of Animal Reactions.   5 Gr.   Total 5.

20e. Asst. Professor H. W. RAND. — Developmental and Growth Processes. Comparative Anatomy of Vertebrates.   1 Gr.   Total 1.

20g. Asst. Professor H. W. RAND. —Experimental Morphology. 1 Gr. Total 1.

20d. Professor W. E. CASTLE. — Variation, Heredity, and the Principles of Animal Breeding.   3 G.S.   Total 3.

20f. Professor WHEELER. — Economic Entomology.   4 G.S.   Total 4.

Geology

GEOLOGY AND GEOGRAPHY

GENERAL GEOLOGY

Primarily for Undergraduates : —

4 ¹*hf.* Asst. Professor WOODWORTH, assisted by Messrs. LAWRENCE and WIG-
GLESWORTH. — Introduction to Geology. Dynamical and Structural
Geology.
1 Gr., 6 G.S., 16 Se., 32 Ju., 28 So., 22 Fr., 1 Sp., 2 uC.   Total 108.

5 ²*hf.* Asst. Professor WOODWORTH, assisted by Mr. LAHEE. — Introduction to
Historical Geology.   1 Se., 10 Ju., 9 So., 9 Fr.   Total 29.

For Undergraduates and Graduates : —

8 ¹*hf.* Asst. Professor WOODWORTH, assisted by Mr. SEDGWICK SMITH. —
Advanced General Geology. 2 Gr., 7 G.S., 6 Se., 3 Ju., 2 uC.   Total 20.

16 ²*hf.* Asst. Professor WOODWORTH. — Glacial Geology.
1 Gr., 1 G.S., 1 Ju., 1 uC.   Total 4.

12 (formerly 22). Mr. LAHEE. — Geological Field Work in the Vicinity of
Boston.   1 Gr., 2 G.S., 2 Se.   Total 5.

Primarily for Graduates : —

20c. Professors DAVIS, WOLFF, and H. L. SMITH, and Asst. Professor WOOD-
WORTH. — Geological Investigation in the Field and Laboratory.
1 Gr.   Total 1.

ECONOMIC GEOLOGY

For Undergraduates and Graduates : —

18 ²*hf.* Professor WOLFF, and Asst. Professors WOODWORTH and PALACHE,
and an assistant. — Economic Geology of the Non-Metalliferous Substances.   1 Gr., 2 G.S., 1 Se., 2 Ju., 1 Fr., 1 Sp., 1 uC.   Total 9.

GEOGRAPHY

Primarily for Undergraduates : —

A ¹*hf.* Asst. Professor D. W. JOHNSON and Mr. REED. — Physical Geography
(introductory course).
2 Gr., 1 G.S., 3 Se., 2 Ju., 10 So., 23 Fr., 1 Sp., 2 uC.   Total 44.

For Undergraduates and Graduates : —

6 ²*hf.* Asst. Professor D. W. JOHNSON. — Physiography of the United States.
1 Gr., 3 Se., 2 Ju., 3 So., 2 Fr., 1 uC.   Total 12.

10 ²*hf.* Asst. Professor D. W. JOHNSON. — Geomorphology.
1 Gr., 1 Ju., 1 So., 1 uC.   Total 4.

Primarily for Graduates : —

20a. Professor DAVIS and Asst. Professor D. W. JOHNSON. — Physiography
(research course).   6 Gr., 1 R.   Total 7.

METEOROLOGY AND CLIMATOLOGY

Primarily for Undergraduates : —

B ^{3}hf. Professor WARD, assisted by Mr. REED. — Meteorology (elementary course).   1 Gr., 2 G.S., 4 Se., 6 Ju., 14 So., 33 Fr., 4 uC.   Total 64.

For Undergraduates and Graduates : —

1 ^{1}hf. Professor WARD. — Climatology of North America.

2 Se., 3 Ju.   Total 5.

19 ^{1}hf. Professor WARD. — General Climatology.   1 Se., 2 Ju.. 1 uC.   Total 4.

Primarily for Graduates : —

20e. Professor WARD. — Climatology (research course)   1 Gr.   Total 1.

Mineralogy and Petrography

Primarily for Undergraduates : —

2. Asst. Professor PALACHE, assisted by Mr. R. E. SOMERS. — Mineralogy (including Crystallography, Physical and Chemical Mineralogy, and Descriptive Mineralogy).

1 Gr., 3 G.S., 2 Se., 10 Ju.. 4 So., 1 Fr.   Total 21.

For Undergraduates and Graduates : —

12. Professor WOLFF, assisted by Mr. ROBERT HARVIE. — Petrography.

2 Gr., 8 G.S., 4 Se.. 1 Fr.   Total 15.

Primarily for Graduates : —

14 ^{2}hf. Professor WOLFF. — Advanced Petrography.

1 Gr.. 8 G.S , 1 Se., 1 Sp.   Total 11.

Mining and Metallurgy

Primarily for Undergraduates : —

A ^{1}hf. Professor PETERS and Mr. WEEKS. — Introduction to Mining and Metallurgy.   43 Ju., 48 So., 55 Fr.. 2 Sp , 4 uC.   Total 152.

B ^{2}hf. Professors SAUVEUR and PETERS, assisted by Messrs BOYLSTON and FREEMAN. — General Metallurgy.

5 G.S , 1 Se., 6 Ju., 7 So , 5 Fr.   Total 24.

1 ^{2}hf. Professor H. L. SMYTH and Asst. Professor RAYMER, assisted by Mr. WEEKS. — Elements of Mining.   Prospecting and Exploring. Breaking Ground; Hydraulic and Open-pit Mining: Stamp-milling and Ore-concentration.   4 G.S., 5 Se., 13 Ju., 6 So., 6 Fr.. 1 uC.   Total 35.

2. Professor H. L. SMYTH, Asst. Professor GRATON, and Mr. WEEKS — Ore-deposits.   Origin and occurrence.

1 Gr , 6 G.S , 1 Se.. 5 Ju , 1 uC.   Total 14

3 ^{1}hf. Asst. Professor RAYMER, assisted by Mr. FREEMAN — Fire Assaying.

4 G.S., 3 Se., 3 Ju , 2 So , 1 Fr.   Total 13.

4 ^{2}hf. Asst. Professor C. H. WHITE, assisted by Mr. KINGSBURY — Metallurgical Chemistry.   The Analysis of Ores   2 G.S . 3 Ju.. 1 Fr   Total 6.

For Undergraduates and Graduates : —

7^{1}. Mr. WEEKS. — Metal and Coal Mining; Exploitation

4 G.S . 5 Se   Total 9.

8 *hf.* Asst. Professor RAYMER. — Mining Plant.   5 G.S., 4 Se.   Total 9.

10. Mr. WEEKS. — Mining.   The study of mining operations.
    2 G.S., 4 Ju., 1 So.   Total 7.

11 *hf.* Professor SAUVEUR, assisted by Mr. BOYLSTON. — Metallurgy of Iron and
    Steel.   8 G.S., 3 Se., 7 Ju., 3 So., 1 Fr., 1 Sp., 1 uC.   Total 24.

12 *hf.* Professor SAUVEUR, assisted by Mr. BOYLSTON. — Metallography.
    1 Sp.   Total 1.

14 *hf.* Professor PETERS, assisted by Messrs. WEEKS and KINGSBURY. — Metal-
    lurgy of Copper, Lead, Zinc, and the Minor Metals, and of the Precious
    Metals in connection with Copper and Lead.   8 G.S., 1 uC.   Total 9.

15 *hf.* Professor PETERS. — Metallurgy of Zinc, Nickel, Tin, Mercury, and the
    Minor Metals.   1 G.S., 1 Se., 1 Ju., 1 uC.   Total 4.

17². Asst. Professor RAYMER. — Ore-dressing, Concentration, and Milling.
    4 G.S., 4 Se.   Total 8.

19. Asst. Professor C. H. WHITE. — Metallurgical Chemistry (advanced course).
    1 Ju., 1 Sp., 1 uC.   Total 3.

Primarily for Graduates : —

21¹. Asst. Professor C. H. WHITE. — Leaching Processes for Gold and Silver
    Ores.   9 G.S.   Total 9.

22 *hf.* Professor PETERS. — Advanced Course in the Metallurgy of Copper,
    Lead, and the Minor Metals.   2 G.S.   Total 2.

24². Professor H. L. SMYTH. — Mine Examination and Reports.
    9 G.S.   Total 9.

26¹. Asst. Professor RAYMER. — Mine Surveying.   9 G.S.   Total 9

28 *hf.* Mr. LAHEE. — Geological Surveying.   3 G.S., 4 Se.   Total 7.

30². THE INSTRUCTORS IN THE DIVISION. — Mining and Metallurgical Projects
    and Design.   9 G.S.   Total 9.

COURSES OF RESEARCH

20a. Professor SAUVEUR, assisted by Mr. BOYLSTON — Metallurgy and the
    Physics of Metals.   1 G S.   Total 1

20b. Asst. Professor GRATON. — Problems in ore-deposits.
    1 Gr., 7 G.S., 1 Se., 1 Sp.   Total 10

20c. Professor PETERS. — Problems in Metallurgy.   1 G.S.   Total 1.

Anthropology

Primarily for Undergraduates : —

1. Drs. FARABEE and TOZZER, assisted by Dr. HOWE. — General Anthropology
    1 Gr., 1 G.S., 11 Se., 15 Ju., 35 So., 6 Fr., 3 Sp., 3 uC.   Total 75

For Undergraduates and Graduates : —

5. Asst. Professor DIXON. — American Archaeology and Ethnography.
    2 Gr., 2 Se., 4 Ju., 1 Fr., 2 Sp.   Total 11.

4 *hf.* Dr. FARABEE. — Prehistoric European Archaeology and European Eth-
    nography.   1 Se., 1 Sp.   Total 2.

7 *hf.* Asst. Professor DIXON. — Ethnography of Oceania.   1 Se.   Total 1.

Primarily for Graduates : —

2 ¹*hf.* Dr. FARABEE. — Somatology.   2 Gr., 1 Se., 1 Ju., 1 Sp.   Total 5.

9 ¹*hf.* Dr. TOZZER. — Archaeology and Hieroglyphic Systems of Central America.   3 Gr., 1 Se., 1 Ju., 1 Sp.   Total 6.

10 ²*hf.* Dr. TOZZER. — Archaeology and Ethnography of Mexico.
3 Gr., 1 Se., 1 Ju., 1 Sp.   Total 6.

COURSES OF RESEARCH

‡20*a.* Asst. Professor DIXON. — American Archaeology and Ethnology.
1 Gr.   Total 1.

‡20*b.* Dr. FARABEE. — Advanced Somatology.   2 Gr.   Total 2.

‡20*c.* Asst. Professor DIXON. — Studies in American Languages. 1 Gr.   Total 1.

20*e.* Dr. TOZZER. — Central American and Mexican Hieroglyphic and Picture Writing.   1 Gr., 1 Sp.   Total 2

Physiology

1. Asst. Professor DARLING, and Drs. PROVANDIE, BACON, HAPGOOD, and GOODRIDGE. — Elementary Anatomy and Physiology. Personal Hygiene. Emergencies.   18 Se., 40 Ju., 50 So., 63 Fr., 4 Sp., 5 uC.   Total 180.

In accordance with the vote of the President and Fellows whereby the Faculty may under certain conditions authorize a Doctor of Philosophy or a Doctor of Science to give instruction gratuitously or for such fees as he may himself collect, Günther Jacoby, Ph.D., was authorized to give in the first half-year a course of lectures on Schopenhauer; and Karl Schmidt, Ph.D., in the second half-year, a course of lectures on "The Logical Structure of Mathematical and Inductive Systems."

The Faculty has adopted the custom of inviting those visiting professors who conduct Harvard courses to be guests at its meetings.

With the Freshman Class that entered College in 1910 the new scheme requiring of every student a certain amount of work in each of four elective groups and work of a reasonably advanced character in one of the four, was put into effect. With it came the use of the whole Faculty and of many instructors outside of the Faculty as advisers. It is too early to judge the degree of success in the new scheme. Many persons doubtless believe that Group I contains too much and Group IV too little; scarcely any two persons would agree about all the details in the plan, and some of these details must be worked out further or they will prove confusing: but, with every deduction, the plan, in theory sound, is in practice full of promise. Incidentally it tends to familiarize College teachers with the Elective Pamphlet, with the rules of the College Office, and with the work of their colleagues, giving "concentration" along with "distribution" to their dealings with the students. The Elective Pamphlet, by vote of the Faculty, has been rearranged in accordance with the four-group system.

When the undergraduate part of the Lawrence Scientific School was merged in Harvard College, no specific arrangement was made for the degree of S.B. with Distinction. In November, 1911, the Faculty voted "That the degree with distinction be open to candidates for the degree of S.B."

In April Professor C. P. Parker, Secretary of the Committee on the Choice of Electives, presented the following report, and moved that it be approved by the Faculty and sent to all Chairmen of Divisions, Departments, and Committees administering Degrees with Distinction: —

The Committee reports that there is need of more general agreement as to the quality of work required for the Degree with Distinction. The degree does not indicate knowledge of a professional character, but ought to be within reach of an undergraduate of good ability as part of his general education. The Degree with Distinction carrying a *cum laude* should, in the opinion of the Committee, indicate that the candidate has shown by his marks and other tests that he is of *B* quality. The higher grades of distinction should indicate a certain amount of brilliancy, and not merely diligence in study. A *magna cum laude* should indicate that a man is, in the opinion of the Committee in charge, of *A* quality. The Faculty has already voted (November 15, 1910,) that for the degree of A.B. *summa cum laude* a candidate should show marked ability not only in his special field, but also in studies outside his field of distinction. (The recommendation for the degree of A.B. *summa cum laude* must, however, come from the Division in which he specializes.) The Committee on the Choice of Electives believes that there should be a general agreement of the Faculty on some such standard as the foregoing.

The motion was carried.

The most important act of the Faculty in the whole academic year — and its most important act in many years — concerned admission to Harvard College. At the first meeting in the autumn the Faculty received a communication from the Board of Overseers: —

Voted, to transmit to the Faculty of Arts and Sciences the Report of the Committee on the Relation of the University to Secondary Schools, presented to the Board of Overseers on June 29, 1910, with the request that they consider the same.

REPORT OF THE COMMITTEE ON THE RELATION OF THE UNIVERSITY TO SECONDARY SCHOOLS

To THE BOARD OF OVERSEERS OF HARVARD COLLEGE: —

The Committee on the Relation of the University to Secondary Schools desire to call the attention of the Board of Overseers to the fact that the College draws very few students from public high schools beyond those of Eastern Massachusetts. The Committee also desire to express their belief that changes now being made in the curricula of public high schools throughout the country for the purpose of satisfying community needs will result in decreasing yet more the connection between those schools and Harvard College.

In view, therefore, of the present relations between the College and public high schools, the Committee respectfully suggest that the Board of Overseers request the Faculty of Arts and Sciences to consider the present requirements for admission with a view to determining whether changes may not be made in those requirements which will bring the College into closer relations with public high schools throughout the country.

The Committee desire to express their conviction that it is of the highest importance that the College should be more accessible to graduates of public high schools in all parts of the country, and that the requirements for admission should be so defined as to promote relations between such schools and the College which will enable good students in the one to pass freely into the other.

ROBERT GRANT,
LOUIS A. FROTHINGHAM,
GEORGE WIGGLESWORTH,
JOHN G. HART,
WILLIAM B. MUNRO,
JOSEPH WARREN,
ALFRED ERNEST STEARNS,
WILLIAM ORR,
GEORGE P. HITCHCOCK.

Harvard requirements for admission have had wide influence and, for the most part, good influence; but that they have warped the curricula of some schools is scarcely questioned, and that they have cut off from the College many of the ablest and best pupils in strong high schools, especially in those of the West, is not questioned at all. The trouble has been, not in the height of their standard, which was helpful, but rather in the eccentricity of their standard, which made it impossible for a boy outside of Harvard preparatory schools to meet the requirements without special instruction or without self-preparation in subjects no better than those of the school curriculum as tests of power. The comparatively small cost of living at state universities, admission by certificate, local pride, and marked improvement in local opportunity have sent to the state universities boys whose presence in Harvard College would be highly advantageous both to the College · and to themselves. Even slight acquaintance with the situation shows the mistake under which Harvard College has been laboring. No high school can adapt its curriculum to the requirements of any one university, unless it be a state university. No boy from a distance can be expected before he knows any college to pick out that college far away whose requirements for admission offer most obstacles, unless the obstacles are of a stimulating kind. Convince a boy that the hardest thing is the best thing, and he will do it. Thus there have always been boys whom no persuasion could keep away from the Harvard admission examinations; but most boys have acquired no conviction on this subject strong enough to resist surrounding influence. Though no friend of Harvard College wishes to make admission easy, every friend who has known the situation in the last few years has longed for some change whereby the ablest and the best-trained boys in any good high school shall not find that their way to Harvard College is blocked by an eccentricity of requirement which throws some doubt on the wisdom of the University as a whole.

The communication from the Overseers was referred to a committee of the Faculty composed of Professor Baker (Chairman), Professor E. H. Hall, Professor von Jagemann, Professor G. H. Parker, Professor C. H. Moore, Professor Ropes, Professor Munro, Mr. J. G. Hart, and Mr. W. R. Castle, Jr. This committee brought forward the new scheme of admission, expounded on page 25, and secured its adoption.

Too much credit cannot be given to this committee of the Faculty. No committee within my recollection has had harder steering, and few have steered so well.

The new scheme meets certain great needs — simplicity, avoidance of waste, and such natural connection with strong schools as shall enable a boy of vigorous mind to come to Harvard normally. It is thus a long step in the economic administration of all that relates school to college. Incidentally it indicates a policy for want of which the Faculty has long worked at a disadvantage. As the Faculty has grown larger and more unwieldy, it has proved quite unable to settle details with wise efficiency; yet it has often adhered to its old feeling of responsibility for details, and has clouded its debates on general policy with every conceivable small side issue. In the new scheme

of admission it has enunciated the general principle of entrusting
to a committee of experts — or of men who must soon become
experts — every administrative detail. By adopting a scheme
firm in big things and flexible in little ones, it has shown its desire ·
to rid itself of detailed formalism and to maintain the only policy
by which a Faculty of its size can live.

L. B. R. BRIGGS, *Dean.*

THE COLLEGE

To THE PRESIDENT OF THE UNIVERSITY: —

SIR, — As Acting Dean of Harvard College for the academic year 1910–11 I have the honor of submitting to you a report on Harvard College, along the lines established by Dean Hurlbut in his several annual reports.

The number of students in the College at the time the lists were compiled for the Catalogue of 1910–11 was two thousand two hundred and seventeen, divided as follows: —

Seniors	382
Juniors	482
Sophomores	516
Freshmen	671
Total number of Undergraduates	2,051
Special Students	75
Unclassified Students	91
Total	2,217

Compared with the figures at the corresponding time of the preceding year these show a loss of forty-eight: —

	Gain	Loss
Seniors	15	
Juniors		23
Sophomores	17	
Freshmen	7	
Special Students		51
Unclassified Students		13
	39	87
Net gain		48

During the year the following students died: —

Arthur Louis Max Dejonge, '14, . . . February 15, 1911.
Sherman Pratt Parsons, Unclassified, . . . May 13, 1911.
Arthur Elwin Smith, '11· . . . . June 27, 1911.

Four hundred and fourteen candidates — sixteen in February and three hundred and ninety-eight in June — received the degree of Bachelor of Arts in course. Of these, two hundred and eighty-eight were registered as Seniors. The registration of the others is shown in the following table: —

On leave of absence all the year 22
On leave of absence first half-year 1
On leave of absence second half-year 10
Graduate Students in Arts and Sciences 9
Graduate Students in Applied Science 7
Registered in the Law School 16
Registered in the Medical School 5
Registered in the Business School 9
Registered in the Junior Class 16
Registered in the Sophomore Class 1
Registered in the Freshman Class 2
Registered as a Special Student 1
                                                        ——
                                                        99
To be designated " as of 1912 " in the *Quinquennial* . . . 27
                                                        ———
                                                        126

Forty-one candidates received the degree of Bachelor of Science. Their registration is indicated in the next table: —

Senior Class 29
Junior Class 4
Freshman Class 2
                                                        ——
                                                        35
Graduate School of Applied Science 1
                                                        ——
                                                        36
On leave of absence all the year 4
On leave of absence second half-year 1
                                                        ——
                                                        41

The next two tables show the losses and gains in the three lower classes between November, 1910, and the latter part of October, 1911: —

	November, 1910	Loss	Gain	November, 1911
Class of 1912 . .	(Juniors) 482	180	70	(Seniors) 372
Class of 1913 . .	(Sophomores) 516	99	118	(Juniors) 535
Class of 1914 . .	(Freshmen) 671	228	56	(Sophomores) 499
		507	244	

Net loss in the three classes between Nov., 1910, and Nov., 1911, 263
(31 less than in 1910).

	Class of 1912	Class of 1913	Class of 1914	Total for three classes
LOSSES				
Left College before the end of the year . .	15	15	36	66
Left College at the end of the year	126	21	26	173
Were "dropped" and left College	19	11	22	52
Entered a lower class	17	24	102	143
Entered a higher class	3	28	42	73
Total loss	180	99	228	507
GAINS				
From higher classes	8	17	24	49
From lower classes	33	37	. .	70
Newly admitted	29	64	32	125
Total gain	70	118	56	244
Net loss	110	. .	172	263
Net gain	. .	19	. .	. .

The next table shows the losses and gains in the number of Special Students since December, 1910: —

*In attendance, December, 1910 75
Left College before the end of the year 10
Left College at the end of the year 31
Entered a College class 10
   Total loss 51
Reëntered College in 1911 as Special Students . . . 24
Newly admitted 20
   Total 44
   Net loss 31

The Freshman Class in 1911–12 numbers seven hundred and forty, a gain of sixty-nine over 1910–11. The number admitted by examination is ninety-three more than that in 1910: —

Admitted by examination in 1911 593
Admitted by examination before 1911 25
Admitted from another college 6
†Admitted from a higher class 115
Admitted from the Special Students 1
   Total 740

* Catalogue figures of 1910–11.
† Dropped from 1914: by low record, 15; by admission conditions, 64; by both record and conditions, 23. Readmitted Freshmen: formerly in 1911, 1; formerly in 1912, 0; formerly in 1913, 4; formerly in 1914, 3. Total 115.

The Assistant Dean makes the following statement in regard to the Class of 1914: " During the year 1910–11 one hundred and four Freshmen were at one time or another on probation. Of these seventy-four came from private schools and thirty from public schools. Fourteen of those on probation were dropped out of College at the end of the year because they failed to win their promotion. In addition to these fourteen, five had their connection severed because they failed either to pass three courses or to get at least one grade of *C*. Eighteen who were not on probation were dropped for having failed to pass three courses with at least two satisfactory grades. On the whole, this record is distinctly better than it was during the preceding year."

In June, 1911, admission examinations under the new plan were held for the first time. As previously set forth, this plan does not take the place of the old plan; it provides another method of admission for good scholars.

To be admitted to Harvard College, a candidate

(1) Must present evidence of an approved school course satisfactorily completed; and

(2) Must show in four examinations, as explained below, that his scholarship is of a satisfactory quality.

School Record

A candidate must present to the Committee on Admission evidence of his secondary school work in the form of an official detailed statement showing

(a) The subjects studied by him and the ground covered.

(b) The amount of time devoted to each.

(c) The quality of his work in each subject.

To be approved, this statement must show

(a) That the candidate's secondary school course has extended over four years.

(b) That his course has been concerned chiefly with languages, science, mathematics, and history, no one of which has been omitted.

(c) That two of the studies of his school programme have been pursued beyond their elementary stages, i. e., to the stage required by the present advanced examinations of Harvard College or the equivalent examinations of the College Entrance Examination Board.

•

THE EXAMINATIONS

If the official detailed statement presented by the candidate shows that he has satisfactorily completed an approved secondary school course, he may present himself for examinations in four subjects as follows: —

(a) English.

(b) Latin, or, for candidates for the degree of S.B., French or German.

(c) Mathematics, or Physics, or Chemistry.

(d) Any subject (not already selected under (b) or (c)) from the following list: —

Greek	History	Physics
French	Mathematics	Chemistry
German		

These four examinations must be taken at one time, either in June or in September.

The following figures in regard to the candidates for admission under the new plan may be of interest.

Candidates whose high school records were not approved	46
Candidates rejected	57
Candidates admitted	83
Total	186

In June and September, 1911, 83 boys were admitted to the Class of 1915 under the new plan. Their preparatory schools were as follows: —

ALABAMA:
Marion, Marion Institute 1
COLORADO:
Colorado Springs High School . 1
CONNECTICUT:
Lakeville, The Hotchkiss School 3
DISTRICT OF COLUMBIA:
Washington, Central High School 1
Washington, Western High School 2
GEORGIA:
Augusta, Academy of Richmond
County 1
ILLINOIS:
Chicago, University High School 1
La Grange, Lyons Township High
School 1
KENTUCKY:
Louisville, Male High School . . 1
MAINE:
Skowhegan, High School 1
South Berwick, Berwick Academy 1
MASSACHUSETTS:
Belmont, High School 1
Boston, English High School . . 6
Boston, High School of Com-
merce 3

MASSACHUSETTS:
Boston, Latin School 3
Cambridge, High and Latin School 1
Concord, High School 1
Danvers, Holten High School . 1
Fall River, High School 1
Fitchburg, High School 1
Hingham, High School 1
Hyde Park, High School 1
Lawrence, High School 2
Lowell, High School 1
Malden, High School 1
Mount Hermon, Mount Hermon
School 1
New Bedford, High School . . . 1
Newburyport, High School . . . 1
Quincy, High School 1
Rockland, High School 1
Roxbury, High School 1
Springfield, Central High School 1
Stoneham, High School 1
Waltham, High School 1
Weymouth, High School 1
MICHIGAN:
Detroit, Central High School . . 1

MINNESOTA:
Winona, High School 1
MISSOURI:
Cape Girardeau, State Normal
School 1
Kansas City, Westport High School 1
NEBRASKA:
Harvard, High School 1
NEW JERSEY:
Hammonton, High School . . . 1
Montclair, High School 3
Newark, Barringer High School 1
NEW YORK:
Baldwin, High School 1
Brooklyn, Boys' High School. . 2
Buffalo, Central High School . . 1
Buffalo, Masten Park High School 1
Buffalo, Nichols School 1
Elmira, Elmira Free Academy . 1
Fulton, High School 1
Hudson Falls, High School . . . 1
New York, Ethical Culture School 1

NEW YORK:
New York, Horace Mann High
School 1
Rochester, West High School. . 1
OHIO:
Cincinnati, Franklin School . . 1
Cleveland, Central High School 1
Cleveland, University School . . 1
PENNSYLVANIA:
Allegheny, High School 1
Bradford, High School. 1
Philadelphia, Central High School 1
Pittsburgh, High School 1
VERMONT:
Brattleboro, High School . . . 1
VIRGINIA:
Roanoke, High School 1
WASHINGTON:
Seattle, Broadway High School . 2
Tacoma, High School 1
WISCONSIN:
Milwaukee, West Division High
School 1

E. H. WELLS, *Acting Dean*

ATHLETIC SPORTS

Sir, — As Chairman of the Committee on the Regulation of Athletic Sports I have the honor of making a report for the academic year 1910–11.

Assistant Dean Castle took the place of Dean Hurlbut, who was on leave of absence throughout the academic year. Otherwise the graduate membership of the Committee was unchanged. The undergraduate members were Roger W. Cutler, 1911, Herbert Jaques, 1911, and Heyliger de Windt, 1912. Paul Withington, 1909, served as Assistant Graduate Treasurer throughout the academic year. He has exceptional knowledge of athletic sports and of present athletic conditions in the University. He has, also, the confidence of both officers and students. The Advisory Committee on Baseball was formed to give our players the benefit of the best Harvard tradition and the best Harvard knowledge. Dr. E. H. Nichols, 1886, was Chairman; Barrett Wendell, Jr., 1901, and Dr. Channing Frothingham, Jr., 1902, were appointed with him; and to these were added, *ex-officio*, Mr. Garcelon and Captain C. B. McLaughlin. On the recommendation of this Advisory Committee, Dr. Frank J. Sexton was engaged as coach for two years.

The Committee on the Regulation of Athletic Sports, though unable to bind future committees, expressed a willingness to coöperate with the Trustees of the Harvard Union in an addition to the Harvard Union Building. On February 21st it voted: —

That it is the sentiment of this Committee that after the balance due for the completion of the Stadium has been paid in full, this Committee is willing to appropriate, each year, a sum not exceeding $2500 towards the repayment of the cost of a building to be built by the Union, and to be available for general athletic purposes, and now planned to be used by the Varsity Club; such payment in no event to exceed one-third of the amount at the disposal of the Committee for general athletic purposes in any one calendar year; such payments to continue until the sum of $25,000 has been so appropriated by this Committee. This action to be submitted to the Corporation, and if disapproved by them, to be void, and to be further subject to agreement with the Trustees of the Union as to the description and nature of the building to be built and the limitation of its purposes.

The addition to the Union will be built as a memorial to Francis Hardon Burr, 1909, and will be paid for, in great part, by money given for that purpose.

The class in general athletics for beginners was successfully conducted by Mr. Garcelon and Mr. Withington. It can no longer be called an experiment; it is a great opportunity for those who need to strengthen their bodies and to ventilate their minds.

In April the Committee authorized an expense of $1,000, for tennis courts near the Medical School, since the use of the courts on the Soldier's Field and Jarvis Field by medical students is impracticable.

In the four major sports Harvard University teams won a reasonable share of victories. The football score of 0 to 0 against Yale was almost universally regarded as a defeat for Harvard, since Harvard was believed to have a stronger team than Yale and the strongest team in many years. The record of the track team was sad: Harvard not only lost to Dartmouth and Yale, but was distressingly weak at the intercollegiate games, qualifying only six men and winning only six points and not a single first place. The crews have sustained the reputation of Harvard crews in the last few years. The baseball team, with mediocre material and experimental pitchers, played and won its first Yale game at New Haven and won again at Cambridge, rendering a third game unnecessary. The players were drilled and disciplined with strictness and intelligence; the men who directed them were masters of the game to whom an earnest player could not but respond.

The fundamental question whether baseball is a fit game for college students cannot be answered until those in charge of the game make clear what is and what is not baseball. A recent writer for the *American Magazine*, Mr. Hugh S. Fullerton, has taken the bull by the horns: "'Sportsmanship,'" he says, "is a relative quantity"; and later, "Almost anything is ethical and proper in baseball that will win games except maiming or injuring opponents, playing for a personal record rather than for the team, and 'laying down.'"

Again Mr. Fullerton says, —

"Fixing" the grounds so as to give the home team the advantage and handicap the visiting players is the commonest form of trickery, yet in professional ball it is not considered wrong, any more than a commander of a defensive army would consider it wrong to prepare breastworks to meet an enemy. . . . There probably is not a major or minor league grounds in the country on which the home players have not the advantage, and visiting teams are forced to be on the alert from the moment they enter a field to discover, if possible, what they are up against.

Still again, —

If a manager has a staff of tall, overhand pitchers the pitcher's box is a mound, sometimes more than a foot high, to add to the angle the ball must take from the overhand pitcher's hand to the plate. If the team has a pitching force of short, underhand or side-arm pitchers, the slab is level with the rest of the diamond, or lower.

One of the best examples of " doping " grounds to favor the resident team was the Baltimore grounds, during the epoch of McGraw, Keeler, Kelley, Jennings, and Robinson, — all great baseball generals. The team was composed of fast men, several of them left-handed batters and good bunters. The players were extremely fast going to first base and they ran the bases well after reaching that vantage point. From the stands the grounds looked much like all other grounds — but they did not look that way to the players. The base lines and portions of the infield had been filled in with a concretelike substance, which, when dampened and tamped down hard, was as fast and springy almost as gutta percha. The first base was quite two feet lower than the home plate, second base still lower, third base just a little higher than second, and the runners needed alpine stocks to come home from third. The pitcher's slab was elevated or depressed to suit the style of the pitcher, center and left fields were level, while right field, where the clever and speedy little Keeler played, was at such a sharp down grade that when Keeler played " deep " the batter scarcely could see him. The field was kept rough and the weeds and grass grew high. The visiting right fielder was all at sea as to which way a batted ball would roll, or how to reach it, while Keeler knew the angles perfectly and sprinted along rabbit tracks known only to himself. The " Orioles' " favorite method of attack, especially against slow teams, was bunting toward first base, the team being one of the pioneers in using the bunting attack as a method of demoralizing the defensive infield. The bunting was varied by " chopping "; that is, hitting the ball on top, to make it bound high. The hardness and springiness of the grounds made the chopped balls bound to enormous height, and the fast sprinters beat out scores of chopped balls while the helpless infielders were waiting for the ball to come down. Not satisfied with all these advantages, they banked up the base lines until they resembled billiard cushions, in order to keep bunted balls from rolling foul.

I quote at this length to give Mr. Fullerton's article a chance and to show with some fulness my reason for believing that base-ball, — which I regard as almost or quite the best game in existence, — is on trial as a game for gentlemen. One of the " great baseball generals " named in the last passage I have quoted used to coach a Harvard team; something very like one of the plays illustrated by a diagram " showing how the pitcher, pretending to back up the first baseman on a throw from the shortstop, interferes with the base-runner by passing in front of him, impeding his progress," was used in a Harvard team a year or two ago, till means were taken for stopping it. Mr. Fullerton asserts that "every year baseball advances in real sportsmanship," and he derives comfort from the fact that an excited, partisan crowd indignantly repudiated the throwing of a bottle and some other object at a visiting catcher when he was waiting for a foul ball to drop. Nevertheless he says, "Baseball indeed has the strangest code of ethics of any game played by men."

If it is baseball to bank up a portion of the field in a fashion scarcely noticeable to visitors, and to practise bunting into sloping places carefully prepared for one's private use, — if this, of which at least one important University has been accused, and of which, according to Mr. Fullerton, any professional team may be guilty, is baseball, baseball is no game for a decent man. Granted that no two persons will draw precisely the same line between honorable strategy and a low trick, there remains a fundamental difference between sport and sharp practice that even a child can understand. If students are wax in the hands of unprincipled coaches, if generosity to a rival is ignorance of the game, if, in short, the game is not the game but an intricate collection of such devices as would ostracize a man in anything else, college baseball should be stopped at once and for ever. If it is the duty of patriotic students to make all the noise they can while the visiting pitcher is facing their representatives, if it is the duty of the catcher to "steady" the pitcher by remarks that (incidentally) unsteady the batsman, if baseball must, as the *Yale Alumni Weekly* puts it, "degenerate into vocal competitions on the part of the players, or into efforts to rattle the opposing pitchers on the part of the grandstands," the sooner we have done with the game the better.

Yet the facts are these: Here is a fascinating game with every legitimate opportunity for a quick body and a quick mind. Not a single act to which an intelligent observer can object belongs to baseball. Baseball, properly played, baseball brilliantly played, may be not merely a great game, but a school of health, self-control, and honor. Unhappily it is like the man (in the small boy's version) who "went down to Jericho and fell among thieves, and the thieves sprang up and choked him."

Students are often charged with wasting opportunities for study; they may with equal justice be charged with wasting opportunities for sound athletic sport, for wide and generous courtesy, for turning rivals into friends, or rather for recognizing rivals as friends. It is good to see signs of improvement; to know, for example, that on the night of a Yale football game at Cambridge some of our dormitories are full of Yale guests: but it is not good to see and hear what we still see and hear at athletic contests, or to know that at many a conference about dates of games the successful college representative is he who can get the upper hand of the others. Those of us who have faith in the radical soundness of American youth believe that, however slowly, a better day will come, — a day when in the arrangements for a game and in the game itself, every man thought fit to represent a college will give full measure of all accessory advantages to the college that is not his own.

L. B. R. BRIGGS.

THE GRADUATE SCHOOL OF ARTS AND SCIENCES

To THE PRESIDENT OF THE UNIVERSITY: —

SIR, — As Dean of the Graduate School of Arts and Sciences, I have the honor to submit a report on the School for the academic year 1910–11.

The following tables present in summary form information concerning the number and distribution of the students, recommendations for degrees, and the assignment of fellowships and scholarships.

Table I shows that the number of students registered in the School was four hundred and eighty-four, an increase of thirty-two over the preceding year. Of this number four hundred and fifty-eight were resident, and twenty-six non-resident, all of whom were travelling fellows. Of the resident students four hundred and sixteen were in attendance during the whole year, of whom three hundred and eleven were doing full work. Of the remaining forty-two resident students twenty entered the School after November 1 and twenty-two withdrew before the end of the year.

TABLE I. — NUMBER AND CLASSIFICATION OF STUDENTS

	1908–09	1909–10	1910–11
I. Resident Students doing full work in the School for the whole academic year	290	279	311
Resident students not doing full work or not working for the whole year as Resident Students	123	156	147
	—413	—435	—458
Non-Resident Students holding fellowships	15	15	26
Non-Resident Students not holding fellowships	1	2	0
	— 16	— 17	— 26
II. Students whose studies lay chiefly in			
Semitic Languages and History	0	0	2
Ancient Languages (Classics and Indic Philology)	28	26	22
Modern Languages (including Comparative Literature)	127	117	164
History and Political Science	85	77	93
Philosophy	50	59	52
Education	12	23	16
Fine Arts (including Architecture)	6	2	5
Music	3	3	4
Mathematics	23	30	22
Physics	18	14	15
Chemistry	34	26	34
Engineering	1	2	0
Biology	18	29	30
Geology	9	9	12
Mining and Metallurgy	1	0	0
Anthropology	5	9	5
Medical Sciences	4	5	3
Unclassed Students	5	21	5
	—429	—452	—484
III. First-year Students	245	254	257
Second-year Students	104	110	136
Third-year Students	52	53	53
Fourth-year Students	18	24	24
Students in fifth year or later	10	11	14
	—429	—452	—484
IV. A.B.'s and S.B.'s of Harvard University and of no other institution	120	122	150
A.B.'s and S.B.'s (and holders of similar degrees) of other institutions and also of Harvard University	5	6	9
Students not holding the Harvard degree of A.B. or S.B.	304	324	325
	—429	—452	—484
V. Students holding the Harvard degree of A.M., S.M., Ph.D., or S.D.	95	106	120
Students holding the Harvard degree of A.B. or S.B., but not of A.M., S.M., Ph.D., or S.D.	87	86	111
Students holding no Harvard degree in Arts, Philosophy, or Science	247	260	253
	—429	—452	—484

In Table II similar facts concerning residence and amount of work are set forth for a period of twenty years. Tables III and IV show the percentage of students in their first and following years and the percentage of students without Harvard degrees.

TABLE II. — NUMBER OF STUDENTS: 1891–1911

	1891-92	1892-93	1893-94	1894-95	1895-96	1896-97	1897-98	1898-99	1899-1900	1900-01	1901-02	1902-03	1903-04	1904-05	1905-06	1906-07	1907-08	1908-09	1909-10	1910-11
Resident Students doing full work in the School for the whole academic year	108	127	162	161	175	194	171	218	227	226	218	216	289	273	280	281	287	290	279	311
Resident Students not doing full work or not working for the whole year as Resident Students	70	73	86	94	105	96	107	103	99	113	86	94	123	105	133	105	119	123	156	147
Whole number of Resident Students	187	200	248	265	280	290	278	321	326	339	304	310	412	378	393	386	406	413	435	458
Non-Resident Fellows	9	9	10	12	13	14	15	12	13	14	11	15	14	15	16	21	17	15	15	26
Other Non-Resident Students	4	7	1	5	6	2	:	3	2	:	:	:	1	2	:	:	1	1	2	:
Whole number of Non-Resident Students	13	16	11	17	19	16	15	15	15	14	11	15	15	17	16	21	18	16	17	26
Whole number of students	200	216	259	272	299	306	293	336	341	353	315	325	427	395	409	407	424	429	452	484
Percentage of Resident Students doing full work for whole academic year	58	64	65	63	63	67	62	68	70	67	72	70	70	72	66	73	71	70	64	68

TABLE III. — PERCENTAGE OF STUDENTS IN THEIR FIRST AND
FOLLOWING YEARS: 1898–1911

	1898-99.	1899-1900.	1900-01.	1901-02.	1902-03.	1903-04.	1904-05.	1905-06.	1906-07.	1907-08.	1908-09.	1909-10.	1910-11.
	%	%	%	%	%	%	%	%	%	%	%	%	%
First-year Students.	55	53	54	50	54	61	60	53	56	57	57	56	53
Second-year Students	21	25	23	26	26	21	24	26	21	23	24	25	28
Third-year Students	13	11	15	12	11	12	11	13	14	12	12	11	11
Fourth-year Students and Students of longer residence	11	11	8	12	9	6	5	8	9	8	7	8	8

TABLE IV. — PERCENTAGE OF STUDENTS WITHOUT HARVARD
DEGREES: 1898–1911

	1898-99.	1899-1900.	1900-01.	1901-02.	1902-03.	1903-04.	1904-05.	1905-06.	1906-07.	1907-08.	1908-09.	1909-10.	1910-11.
	%	%	%	%	%	%	%	%	%	%	%	%	%
Percentage of Students holding no Harvard degree	41	44	44	40	46	46	52	52	55	58	58	58	52
Percentage of Students holding no Harvard first degree in Arts or Sciences	55	61	62	56	62	59	65	64	67	71	71	71	67

Tables V, VI, and VII indicate that the School continues to maintain its national character in the geographical distribution of its students and of the institutions from which they come to Harvard.

TABLE V. — COLLEGES AND UNIVERSITIES REPRESENTED BY FOUR OR MORE GRADUATES IN THE SCHOOL: 1906–07, 1907–08, 1908–09, 1909–10, 1910–11

1906–07.

College	No.
Harvard	185
Dartmouth	10
Boston Univ.	8
Toronto	8
Amherst	7
Columbia	7
Yale	7
Michigan	6
Vanderbilt	6
Bowdoin	5
California	5
Cornell Univ.	5
Haverford	5
Indiana	5
Kansas	5
Missouri	5
Queen's	5
Rochester	5
Arcadia	4
Brown	4
Chicago	4
Ohio Wesleyan	4
Princeton	4
Toronto	4
Vanderbilt	4
State Univ. of Iowa	4

1907–08.

College	No.
Harvard	182
Amherst	10
Michigan	8
Brown	8
Dartmouth	8
Rochester	7
Williams	7
Bowdoin	6
Brown	6
California	6
Texas	6
Yale	6
Columbia	5
Indiana	5
Ohio Wesleyan	5
Chicago	5
George Washington	5
Leland Stanford Jr.	5
Mass. Inst. of Tech.	5
Missouri	4
Mt. Allison	4
Princeton	4
Toronto	4
Vanderbilt	4
Washington	4

1908–09.

College	No.
Harvard	182
Columbia	11
Amherst	9
Brown	9
Dartmouth	9
Bowdoin	8
Michigan	7
Princeton	7
Haverford	6
Mass. Inst. of Tech.	6
Northwestern	6
Williams	6
Boston University	5
Chicago	5
Missouri	5
Mt. Allison	5
Texas	5
Toronto	4
West Virginia	4
Yale	4
Acadia	4
Allegheny	4
California	4
Kansas	4
Oberlin	4
Ohio Northern	4
Ohio State	4
Southern California	4
Tufts	4
Wesleyan (Conn.)	4

1909–10.

College	No.
Harvard	199
Amherst	14
Dartmouth	10
Chicago	8
Haverford	8
Princeton	8
Williams	7
Bowdoin	7
Kansas	7
Missouri	7
Syracuse	6
Yale	6
Brown	6
Indiana	6
Mass. Inst. of Tech.	6
Michigan	6
Northwestern	6
Texas	5
California	5
Columbia	5
Ohio State	5
Tufts	5
Charleston	4
Georgia	4
Mount Allison	4
Oberlin	4
Ohio Wesleyan	4
Western Reserve	4

1910–11.

College	No.
Harvard	218
Dartmouth	11
Bowdoin	9
Amherst	8
Chicago	8
Northwestern (Ill.)	8
Boston Univ.	8
Brown	7
Yale	7
Indiana	7
Syracuse	6
North Carolina	6
Toronto	6
Missouri	6
Williams	6
Central (Ky.)	6
Columbia	5
Cornell	5
Monmouth	5
Wisconsin	5
Mt. Allison	5
Mass. Inst. of Tech.	5
Tufts	5
Kansas	4
Allegheny	4
Dalhouse	4
Leland Stanford Jr.	4
Ohio State	4
Ohio Wesleyan	4
Trinity (Conn.)	4
California	4
McGill	4

Total Membership.	1906–07	1907–08	1908–09	1909–10	1910–11
	407	424	429	452	484

TABLE VI. — STUDENTS FROM HARVARD AND TWENTY-FIVE OTHER COLLEGES: 1895-96 — 1910-11

	1895-96	1896-97	1897-98	1898-99	1899-1900	1900-01	1901-02	1902-03	1903-04	1904-05	1905-06	1906-07	1907-08	1908-09	1909-10	1910-11	Total
Harvard	178	174	178	196	191	197	189	174	232	192	197	185	182	182	199	218	3064
Amherst	7	7	5	5	7	10	8	10	14	8	8	7	10	9	14	8	137
Brown	6	5	7	8	5	11	8	11	12	7	12	4	8	9	6	7	126
Dartmouth	3	6	6	2	3	6	5	7	12	9	6	10	8	9	10	11	113
Bowdoin	7	4	3	6	4	9	8	7	7	5	3	5	6	8	7	9	98
Yale	4	2	4	10	4	7	4	6	9	7	8	7	6	5	7	7	97
Michigan	2	4	3	4	7	7	2	7	10	5	10	6	9	7	6	3	92
California	6	7	6	8	8	7	7	6	4	3	3	5	6	4	5	4	89
Ohio Wesleyan	2	1	4	2	2	3	5	5	8	14	12	4	5	3	4	4	78
Haverford	2	2	3	5	5	4	4	5	7	5	5	5	3	6	8	8	77
Kansas	8	8	8	5	4	5	2	3	3	2	3	5	3	4	7	5	75
Williams	2	2	-	2	4	6	3	4	7	7	7	3	7	6	8	6	74
Toronto	1	1	5	6	5	6	6	3	4	5	3	8	4	5	2	6	70
Boston Univ.	2	1	2	3	4	6	1	1	5	5	7	8	6	5	3	7	66
Wesleyan (Conn.)	8	8	5	3	5	5	3	3	4	2	3	3	3	4	2	2	63
Tufts	4	5	2	6	5	5	4	6	6	3	1	2	-	4	5	5	63
Indiana	2	6	4	5	4	2	3	3	2	3	4	5	5	3	6	6	63
Columbia	3	2	3	1	-	1	1	6	5	1	4	7	5	11	5	5	60
Northwestern	1	2	5	6	6	5	1	6	2	2	1	1	2	6	6	8	60
Leland Stanford Jr.	2	4	4	7	6	2	3	6	4	5	3	3	4	1	1	4	59
Chicago	-	1	3	2	2	3	3	7	1	3	4	4	4	5	8	8	58
Oberlin	2	7	5	3	6	9	4	1	-	1	3	3	3	4	4	-	55
Princeton	1	3	5	1	2	3	4	3	2	-	3	4	4	7	8	3	53
Texas	2	2	2	1	3	3	3	5	5	3	1	2	6	5	6	3	52
Dalhousie	3	2	2	3	4	4	5	2	2	2	4	2	3	3	3	4	48
Mass. Inst. of Tech.	4	3	4	3	3	2	1	1	1	1	2	2	4	6	6	5	48
Total Membership	299	306	293	336	341	353	315	325	427	393	409	407	424	429	452	484	

TABLE VII. — BIRTHPLACES OF GRADUATE STUDENTS: 1908-11

	1908-09	1909-10	1910-11
Students born in the New England States	129	132	148
Students born in other Northern States east of the Mississippi River	166	160	158
Students born in Southern States east of the Mississippi River	17	37	42
Students born in States west of the Mississippi River	58	61	65
Students born in the Dominion of Canada	27	27	32
Students born in other foreign countries	32	35	39
Total number of students	429	432	484
Percentage of students born in New England	30	29	30
Percentage of students born elsewhere	70	71	70

Tables VIII and IX set forth the number of candidates recommended for higher degrees and their distribution throughout the various Divisions and Departments.

TABLE V. — COLLEGES AND UNIVERSITIES REPRESENTED BY FOUR OR MORE GRADUATES IN THE SCHOOL : 1906–07, 1907–08, 1908–09, 1909–10, 1910–11

1906–07	1907–08	1908–09	1909–10	1910–11
Harvard 185	Harvard 182	Harvard 182	Harvard 199	Harvard 218
Dartmouth 10	Amherst 10	Columbia 11	Amherst 14	Dartmouth 11
Boston Univ. 8	Michigan 9	Amherst 9	Dartmouth 10	Bowdoin 9
Toronto 8	Brown 8	Brown 9	Chicago 8	Amherst 8
Amherst 8	Dartmouth 8	Dartmouth 9	Haverford 8	Haverford 8
Columbia 7	Rochester 8	Bowdoin 8	Princeton 8	Chicago 8
Yale 7	Williams 7	Michigan 7	Williams 7	Northwestern (Ill.) 8
Michigan 6	Bowdoin 7	Princeton 7	Bowdoin 7	Boston Univ. 7
Vanderbilt 6	Brown 6	Haverford 6	Kansas 7	Brown 7
Bowdoin 6	California 6	Mass. Inst. of Tech. 6	Missouri 7	Yale 7
California 6	Yale 6	Northwestern 6	Syracuse 7	Indiana 6
Cornell Univ. 5	Columbia 6	Williams 6	Yale 6	Syracuse 6
Haverford 5	Indiana 5	Boston University 6	Brown 6	North Carolina 6
Indiana 5	Ohio Wesleyan 5	Chicago 5	Indiana 6	Toronto 6
Kansas 5	Chicago 5	Missouri 5	Mass. Inst. of Tech. 6	Missouri 6
Missouri 5	Queen's 5	Mt. Allison 5	Michigan 6	Williams 6
Queen's 5	George Washington 5	Texas 4	Northwestern 6	Central (Ky.) 6
Rochester 5	Leland Stanford Jr. 5	Toronto 4	Texas 5	Columbia 5
Acadia 4	Mass. Inst. of Tech. 5	West Virginia 4	California 5	Cornell 5
Brown 4	Missouri 4	Yale 4	Columbia 5	Monmouth 5
Chicago 4	Mt. Allison 4	Acadia 4	Ohio State 5	Wisconsin 5
Ohio Wesleyan 4	Princeton 4	Allegheny 4	Tufts 5	Mt. Allison 5
Princeton 4	Toronto 4	California 4	Charleston 5	Mass. Inst. of Tech. 5
Vanderbilt 4	Vanderbilt 4	Kansas 4	Georgia 4	Tufts 5
State Univ. of Iowa 4	Washington 4	Oberlin 4	Mount Allison 4	Kansas 5
		Ohio Northern 4	Oberlin 4	Allegheny 4
		Ohio State 4	Ohio Wesleyan 4	Dalhousie 4
		Southern California 4	Western Reserve 4	Leland Stanford Jr. 4
		Tufts 4		Ohio State 4
		Wesleyan (Conn.) 4		Ohio Wesleyan 4
				Trinity (Conn.) 4
				California 4
				McGill 4
Total Membership, 407	424	429	452	484

TABLE VI. — STUDENTS FROM HARVARD AND TWENTY-FIVE OTHER COLLEGES : 1895-96 — 1910-11

	1895-96	1896-97	1897-98	1898-99	1899-1900	1900-01	1901-02	1902-03	1903-04	1904-05	1905-06	1906-07	1907-08	1908-09	1909-10	1910-11	Total
Harvard	178	174	178	196	191	197	189	174	232	192	197	185	182	182	199	218	3064
Amherst	7	7	5	5	7	10	8	10	14	8	8	7	10	9	14	8	137
Brown	6	5	7	8	5	11	8	11	12	7	12	4	8	9	6	7	126
Dartmouth	3	6	6	2	3	6	5	7	12	9	6	10	8	9	10	11	113
Bowdoin	7	4	3	6	4	9	8	7	7	5	3	5	6	8	7	9	98
Yale	4	2	4	10	4	7	4	6	9	7	8	7	6	5	7	7	97
Michigan	2	4	3	4	7	7	2	7	10	5	10	6	9	7	6	3	92
California	6	7	6	8	8	7	7	6	4	3	3	5	6	4	5	4	89
Ohio Wesleyan	2	1	4	2	2	3	5	5	8	14	12	4	5	3	4	4	78
Haverford	2	2	3	5	5	4	4	5	7	5	5	5	3	6	8	8	77
Kansas	8	8	8	5	4	5	2	3	3	2	3	5	3	4	7	5	75
Williams	2	2	–	2	4	6	3	4	7	7	7	3	7	6	8	6	74
Toronto	1	1	5	6	5	6	6	3	4	5	3	8	4	5	2	6	70
Boston Univ.	2	1	2	3	4	6	1	1	5	5	7	8	6	5	3	7	66
Wesleyan (Conn.)	8	8	5	3	5	5	3	3	4	2	3	3	3	4	2	2	63
Tufts	4	5	2	6	5	5	4	6	6	3	1	2	–	4	5	5	63
Indiana	2	6	4	5	4	2	3	3	2	3	4	5	5	3	6	6	63
Columbia	3	2	3	1	–	1	1	6	5	1	4	7	5	11	5	5	60
Northwestern	1	2	5	6	6	5	1	6	2	2	1	1	2	6	6	8	60
Leland Stanford Jr.	2	4	4	7	6	2	3	6	4	5	3	3	4	1	1	4	59
Chicago	–	1	3	2	2	3	3	7	1	3	4	4	4	5	8	8	58
Oberlin	2	7	5	3	6	9	4	1	–	1	3	3	3	4	4	–	55
Princeton	1	3	5	1	2	3	4	3	2	–	3	4	4	7	8	3	53
Texas	2	2	2	1	3	3	3	5	5	3	1	2	6	5	6	3	52
Dalhousie	3	2	2	3	4	4	5	2	2	2	4	2	3	3	3	4	48
Mass. Inst. of Tech.	4	3	4	3	3	2	1	1	1	1	2	2	4	6	6	5	48
Total Membership	299	306	293	336	341	353	315	325	427	393	409	407	424	429	452	484	

TABLE VII. — BIRTHPLACES OF GRADUATE STUDENTS : 1908-11

	1908–09	1909–10	1910–11
Students born in the New England States	129	132	148
Students born in other Northern States east of the Mississippi River	166	160	158
Students born in Southern States east of the Mississippi River	17	37	42
Students born in States west of the Mississippi River	58	61	65
Students born in the Dominion of Canada	27	27	32
Students born in other foreign countries	32	35	39
Total number of students	429	452	484
Percentage of students born in New England	30	29	30
Percentage of students born elsewhere	70	71	70

Tables VIII and IX set forth the number of candidates recommended for higher degrees and their distribution throughout the various Divisions and Departments.

TABLE VIII. — RECOMMENDATIONS FOR DEGREES IN 1909–11

	1909	1910	1911
I. Graduate students recommended for A.M.	109	130	150
Graduate students recommended for S.M.	3	4	—
Graduate students recommended for Ph.D.	38	34	40
	—150	—168	—190
II. Professional students recommended for A.M. on special courses of study	5	13	14
Professional students recommended for Ph.D. on special courses of study	– 5	3 16	1 15
Total number recommended for A.M., S.M., and Ph.D.	155	184	205
III. Harvard Bachelors of Arts or Science, not previously graduated elsewhere	38	50	51
Harvard Bachelors of Arts or Science, previously graduated elsewhere	2	1	4
Students not Harvard Bachelors of Arts or Science	115	133	150
	—155	—184	—205

TABLE IX. — DIVISIONS AND DEPARTMENTS IN WHICH RECOMMENDATIONS FOR THE HIGHER DEGREES WERE MADE IN 1911

Division	Department	Degrees A.M.	Degrees Ph.D.
Ancient Languages		5	2
Modern Languages			
	English	41	6
	Germanic Languages and Literatures	10	–
	French, and other Romance Languages and Literatures	9	1
	Comparative Literature	–	1
	In more than one Department	1	–
	Total in Modern Languages	— 61	— 8
History, Government, and Economics			
	History and Government	23	
	Economics	9	–
	Total in History, Government, and Economics	— 32	— 4
Philosophy		12	6
Education		7	–
The Fine Arts		1	–
Music		–	1
Mathematics		9	1
Physics		4	2
Chemistry		8	8
Biology			
	Botany	1	2
	Zoölogy	3	3
	Total in Biology	— 4	— 5
Geology		1	2
Anthropology		2	–
Medical Sciences		–	1
Undivisional		4	–
Professional Students:			
	Divinity School	13	1
	Medical School	1	—
	Total	164	41

The degree of Doctor of Philosophy was conferred upon the forty-one men named below.

WILLIAM EWART MAURICE AITKEN, A.B. (*Univ. of Toronto*) 1908, A.M. (*ibid.*) 1909.
> *Subject*, Philology. *Special Field*, Semitic Philology. *Thesis*, "Beelzebul, Baalzebub: A Contribution to the Study of Hebrew Proper Names and of Jewish Demonology." J. H. Thayer Fellow, American School for Oriental Study and Research at Jerusalem.

THOMAS BARBOUR, A.B. 1906, A.M. 1908.
> *Subject*, Biology. *Special Field*, Zoölogy. *Thesis*, "A Contribution to the Zoögeography of the East Indian Islands." Member of the Faculty, Peabody Museum of American Archaeology and Ethnology, and Curator of Oceanica, Harvard University Library.

FREDERICK BARRY, A.B. 1897, A.M. 1909.
> *Subject*, Chemistry. *Special Field*, Physical Chemistry. *Thesis*, I. "The Molecular Refractions of Hydrochloric Acid and of Stannic and Stannous Chlorides." II. "The Heats of Combustion of Homologous Hydrocarbons." Assistant in Chemistry and in the History of Science, Harvard University.

HAROLD EUGENE BIGELOW, A.B. (*Mount Allison Univ.*) 1903, A.B. (*Harvard Univ.*) 1907, A.M. (*ibid.*) 1908.
> *Subject*, Chemistry. *Special Field*, Organic Chemistry. *Thesis*, I. "Some Derivatives of Bromtriioddinitrobensol and Related Compounds." II. "The Heat of Solution of Barium." Professor of Chemistry, Mount Allison University.

WALTER RAY BLOOR, A.M. (*Queen's Univ.*) 1902, A.M. (*Harvard University*) 1908.
> *Subject*, Medical Sciences. *Special Field*, Biochemistry. *Thesis*, "The Carbohydrate Esters of the Higher Fatty Acids." Associate in Biological Chemistry, Medical School of Washington University.

SOLON JUSTUS BUCK, A.B. (*Univ. of Wisconsin*) 1904, A.M. (*ibid.*) 1905.
> *Subject*, History. *Special Field*, American History. *Thesis*, "The Granger Movement." Research Associate in History, University of Illinois.

PAUL WHITTIER CARLETON, A.B. 1906, A.M. 1907.
> *Subject*, Chemistry. *Special Field*, Organic Chemistry. *Thesis*, "Some Derivatives of Certain Quinones and Aromatic Diketones." Instructor in Chemistry, University of Wisconsin.

EMORY LEON CHAFFEE, S.B. (*Mass. Institute of Technology*) 1907, A.M. (*Harvard Univ.*) 1908.
> *Subject*, Physics. *Special Field*, Electricity. *Thesis*, "A New Method of Impact Excitation of Undamped Electric Oscillations and their Analysis by Means of Braun Tube Oscillographs." Instructor and Bayard Cutting Fellow for Research in Physics, Harvard University.

STANLEY PERKINS CHASE, A.B. (*Bowdoin Coll.*) 1905, A.M. (*Harvard Univ.*) 1906.
> *Subject*, Philology. *Special Field*, English Philology. *Thesis*, "William Hazlitt as a Critic." Instructor in English, Union College.

PHILIP GREELEY CLAPP, A.B. 1909 (1908), A.M. 1909.
> *Subject*, Music. *Special Field*, Composition. *Thesis*, "Modern Tendencies in Musical Form." Teaching Fellow in Music, Harvard University.

FLETCHER BARKER COFFIN, A.B. 1895, A.M. 1896, LL.B. 1898.
> *Subject*, Chemistry. *Special Field*, Inorganic Chemistry. *Thesis*, "A Revision of the Atomic Weights of Cobalt and Arsenic." Professor of Chemistry, Lake Forest College.

HARRY TODD COSTELLO, A.B. (*Earlham Coll.*) 1908, A.M. (*Harvard Univ.*) 1910.
> *Subject*, Philosophy. *Special Field*, Logic. *Thesis*, "The Fundamental Characteristics of Organisation, especially as Illustrated by those Organisations through which the Results of Science are Applied in the Arts and Industries." Frederick Sheldon Fellow, continuing his studies at Paris.

HARVEY WARREN COX, PH.B. (*Nebraska Wesleyan Univ.*) 1902, A.M. (*Univ. of Nebraska*) 1906, A.M. (*Harvard Univ.*) 1910.

Subject, Philosophy. *Special Field*, Epistemology and Psychology. *Thesis*, "The Rise of the Motor Theory of Consciousness." Professor of Philosophy, University of Florida.

EDWARD CARROLL DAY, A.B. (*Hamilton Coll.*) 1907, A.M. (*Harvard Univ.*) 1908.

Subject, Biology. *Special Field*, Zoölogy. *Thesis*, "The Effect of Colored Lights on Pigment Migration in the Eye of the Crayfish." Parker Fellow, continuing his studies at Bonn, Germany.

WILLIAM GEORGE DODD, A.B. (*Bethany Coll., W. Va.*) 1893, A.M. (*Harvard Univ.*) 1908.

Subject, Philology. *Special Field*, English Philology. *Thesis*, "The Treatment of Love by Chaucer and Gower." Professor of English, Florida State College for Women.

ROBERT FISKE GRIGGS, S.B. (*Ohio State Univ.*) 1903, A.M. (*Univ. of Minnesota*) 1906.

Subject, Biology. *Special Field*, Botany. *Thesis*, "The Development and Cytology of Rhodochytrium." Assistant Professor of Botany, Ohio State University.

HARVEY CORNELIUS HAYES, A.B. 1907, A.M. 1908.

Subject, Physics. *Special Field*, Magnetism. *Thesis*, "An Investigation of the Errors in Cooling Curves and Methods for Avoiding these Errors; also a New Form of Crucible." Assistant and Fellow for Research in Physics, Harvard University.

VIRGIL LAURENS JONES, A.B. (*Univ. of North Carolina*) 1899, A.M. (*Carson and Newman Coll.*) 1901, A.M. (*Harvard Univ.*) 1910.

Subject, Philology. *Special Field*, English Philology. *Thesis*, "English Satire, 1650–1700." Associate Professor of English, University of Arkansas.

GEORGE LESLIE KELLEY, S.B. 1907.

Subject, Chemistry. *Special Field*, Organic Chemistry. *Thesis*, I. "The Constitution and Reactions of certain Halogenated Orthobenzoquinopyrocatechin Hemiethers." II. "The Transition Temperature of Sodium Chromate." Instructor in Chemistry, Harvard University.

RALPH HAYWARD KENISTON, A.B. 1904, A.M. 1910.

Subject, Philology. *Special Field*, Romance Philology. *Thesis*, "Garcilaso de la Vega: A Critical Edition of his Works, together with a Life of the Poet." Assistant Librarian, Hispanic Society of America, New York.

FREDERICK HENRY LAHEE, A.B. 1907, A.M. 1908.

Subject, Geology. *Special Field*, General Geology. *Thesis*, "A Study of Metamorphism in the Carboniferous Formation of the Narragansett Basin." Instructor in Geology, Harvard University.

DANIEL WOLFORD LARUE, A.B. (*Dickinson Coll.*) 1904, A.M. (*ibid.*) 1905, A.M. (*Harvard Univ.*) 1907.

Subject, Philosophy. *Special Field*, Epistemology. *Thesis*, "Type Studies in the Methods of Escape from Subjectivism." Teacher of Psychology and Pedagogy, State Normal School, E. Stroudsburg, Pa.

HENRY LAURENS, A.B. (*Coll. of Charleston*) 1907, A.M. (*ibid.*) 1908.

Subject, Biology. *Special Field*, Zoölogy. *Thesis*, "The Reactions of Amphibians to Monochromatic Lights of Equal Intensity." John Thornton Kirkland Fellow, continuing his studies at Bonn, Germany.

HENRY WHEATLAND LITCHFIELD, A.B. 1907.

Subject, Philology. *Special Field*, Classical Philology. *Thesis*, "Quibus Virtutum Vitiorumque Moralium Exemplis ex suorum Annalibus sumptis Scriptores Latini Antiqui usi sint quaeritur." Instructor in Greek and Latin, Harvard University.

JACOB LOEWENBERG, A.B. 1908, A.M. 1909.

Subject, Philosophy. *Special Field*, History of Philosophy. *Thesis*, "The Genesis of Hegel's Dialectical Method." Assistant in Philosophy, Harvard University.

CHARLES HOWARD MCILWAIN, A.B. (*Princeton Univ.*) 1894, A.M. (*ibid.*) 1898, A.M. (*Harvard Univ.*) 1903.

Subject, History. *Special Field*, English History. *Thesis*, "The High Court of Parliament and its Supremacy." Assistant Professor of History, Harvard University.

HERBERT EUGENE MERWIN, S.B. 1908 (1907).
Subject, Geology. *Special Field*, Mineralogy and Petrography. *Thesis*, "Mineralogical and Petrographical Researches, with special Reference to the Stability Ranges of the Alkali Feldspars." Assistant Petrologist, Geophysical Laboratory, Carnegie Institution of Washington.

SAMUEL MOORE, A.B. (*Princeton Univ.*) 1899, A.M. (*ibid.*) 1908.
Subject, Philology. *Special Field*, English Philology. *Thesis*, "Chapters in the History of Literary Patronage from Chaucer to Caxton." Lecturer in English Philology, Bryn Mawr College.

WILLIAM JAMES MUSGROVE, A.B. (*Univ. of California*) 1905, A.M. (*Harvard Univ.*) 1906.
Subject, Philosophy. *Special Field*, Philosophy of Mind. *Thesis*, "Animal Psychology and the Concept of a Mind." Instructor in Philosophy, University of Washington.

WILLIAM LEONARD PUGH, A.B. (*Parsons Coll.*) 1897, A.M. (*ibid.*) 1901, A.M. (*Northwestern Univ., Ill.*) 1908.
Subject, Philology. *Special Field*, English Philology. *Thesis*, "The Strong Verb in Chaucer." Assistant Professor of English, Wofford College, Spartanburg, S. C.

EMILE RAYMOND RIEGEL, S.B. 1908, S.M. 1910.
Subject, Chemistry. *Special Field*, Inorganic Chemistry. *Thesis*, I. "The Quantitative Determination of Antimony by the Gutzeit Method." II. "The Action of Sulphur Trioxide on Carbon Tetrachloride and Silicon Tetrachloride." Chemist, with the Cochrane Chemical Co., West Works, Everett, Mass.

DWIGHT NELSON ROBINSON, A.B. 1908, A.M. 1909.
Subject, Philology. *Special Field*, Classical Philology. *Thesis*, "Quibus Temporibus Religiones ab Oriente ortae et Romae et in Provinciis Romanis floruerint desierintque quaeritur." Instructor in Latin and Greek, Yale University.

WILLIAM OSCAR SCROGGS, S.B. (*Alabama Polytechnic Institute*) 1899, S.M. (*ibid.*) 1900, A.M. (*Harvard Univ.*) 1905.
Subject, History. *Special Field*, American History. *Thesis*, "The Financial History of Alabama, 1819–1860." Associate Professor of History and Economics, Louisiana State University.

CLARENCE LIVINGSTON SPEYERS, PH.B. (*Columbia Univ.*) 1884.
Subject, Chemistry. *Special Field*, Physical Chemistry. *Thesis*, "The Compressibilities and Surface Tensions of Water and Six Hydrocarbons." Professor of Thermodynamics, University of Pittsburgh.

ALBAN STEWART, A.B. (*Univ. of Kansas*) 1896, A.M. (*ibid.*) 1897.
Subject, Biology. *Special Field*, Botany. *Thesis*, "A Botanical Survey of the Galapagos Islands." Instructor in Botany, University of Wisconsin.

THORBERGUR THORVALDSON, A.B. (*Univ. of Manitoba*) 1906, A.M. (*Harvard Univ.*) 1909.
Subject, Chemistry. *Special Field*, Inorganic and Physical Chemistry. *Thesis*, I. "A Revision of the Atomic Weight of Iron." II. "Methods for the Adiabatic Determination of Heats of Solution of Metals in Acids." Edward William Hooper Fellow, continuing his studies at Dresden.

MASON WHITING TYLER, A.B. (*Amherst Coll.*) 1906, A.M. (*Harvard Univ.*) 1908.
Subject, History. *Special Field*, English History. *Thesis*, "Anglo-French Relations under James II." Instructor in History, Simmons College.

SAMUEL EVERETT URNER, PH.B. (*Baker Univ.*) 1906.
Subject, Mathematics. *Special Field*, Analysis. *Thesis*, "Certain Singularities of Point-Transformations in Space of Three Dimensions." Assistant Professor of Mathematics, Miami University.

FRANCIS COX WALKER, A.B. (*Univ. of New Brunswick*) 1892, A.B. (*Harvard Univ.*) 1894, A.M. (*ibid.*) 1902.
Subject, Philology. *Special Field*, English Philology. *Thesis*, "Syntax of the Infinitive in Shakspere." Instructor in English, Washington University.

SHOGORO WASHIO, PH.B. (*Drake Univ.*) 1909, A.M. (*Harvard Univ.*) 1910.
  Subject, Philosophy. *Special Field*, Epistemology and Metaphysics. *Thesis*, "A Criticism of the Realism of G. E. Moore and B. Russell." Continuing his studies at Berlin.

CHARLES EDWARD WHITMORE, A.B. 1907.
  Subject, Philology. *Special Field*, Comparative Literature. *Thesis*, "The Supernatural in Tragedy." Instructor in English, Harvard University.

Forty fellowships were assigned for the year 1910–11, including three John Harvard Fellowships without stipend. There were fourteen resident and twenty-six non-resident appointments. A list of the incumbents follows. After the name of each fellow is given the name of his fellowship, the subject that he studied, and his present occupation. The place of study of the non-resident fellows is also indicated.

TRAVELLING FELLOWS

ROBERT PIERPONT BLAKE, John Harvard Fellow. Ancient History. Berlin.
  Reappointed. Continuing his studies at St. Petersburg.

OSCAR JAMES CAMPBELL, Frederick Sheldon Fellow. Comparative Literature. Paris.
  Instructor in English, University of Wisconsin.

PHILIP GREELEY CLAPP, Frederick Sheldon Fellow. Music. Stuttgart.
  Teaching Fellow in Music.

EDGAR DAVIDSON CONGDON, Frederick Sheldon Fellow. Zoölogy. Vienna.
  Instructor in Anatomy, Cornell University Medical College.

MELVIN THOMAS COPELAND, Frederick Sheldon Fellow. Economics. London.
  Instructor in Economics, New York University.

SUMNER WEBSTER CUSHING, Frederick Sheldon Fellow. Geology. India.
  Instructor in Geography, State Normal School, Salem.

HENRY WADSWORTH LONGFELLOW DANA, Fellow of the Ministry of Public Instruction of the French Republic. Comparative Literature. Paris.
  Frederick Sheldon Fellow, at Paris.

LLOYD DIXON, John Harvard Fellow. Mathematics. Oxford.
  Continuing his studies at Oxford.

ARTHUR JOHNSON EAMES, Frederick Sheldon Fellow. Botany. Australasia.
  Austin Teaching Fellow in Botany. Fourth-year Graduate Student.

ARTHUR LEON EATON, Rogers Fellow. Romance Languages. Madrid and Paris.
  Instructor in French, Indiana University.

GEORGE HAROLD EDGELL, John Harvard Fellow. Fine Arts. Rome.
  Reappointed. Fellow of the American School of Classical Studies at Rome.

GRIFFITH CONRAD EVANS, Frederick Sheldon Fellow. Mathematics. Rome.
  Reappointed. Continuing his studies at Rome.

DONALD FISHER, Henry Bromfield Rogers Memorial Fellow. Philosophy. Gras.
  James Walker Fellow, at Berlin.

EDWIN WILLIAM FRIEND, Rogers Fellow. Classics. Berlin.
  Instructor in Latin, Princeton University.

NORMAN SCOTT BRIEN GRAS, John Thornton Kirkland Fellow. Economic History. London.
Frederick Sheldon Fellow, at London.

PERCY HAZEN HOUSTON, Parker Fellow. English. London.
Continuing his studies in Europe.

DUNHAM JACKSON, Edward William Hooper Fellow. Mathematics. Göttingen and Bonn.
Instructor in Mathematics.

JOHN AVERY LOMAX, Frederick Sheldon Fellow. American Ballads.
Reappointed. Assistant Professor of English, University of Texas.

WILLIAM EDWARD LUNT, Frederick Sheldon Fellow. History. London.
Thomas Brackett Reed Professor of History and Political Science, Bowdoin College.

ROBERT GRANT MARTIN, Frederick Sheldon Fellow. English. London.
Instructor in English, Northwestern University.

RAYMOND EDWIN MERWIN, Fellow in Central American Archaeology. Anthropology. Belize.
Continuing his studies in Central America.

OLIN HARRIS MOORE, Parker Fellow. Romance Languages. Paris.
Instructor in French, English High School, Boston.

SERGIUS MORGULIS, Parker Fellow. Zoölogy. Vienna.
Frederick Sheldon Fellow, at Berlin.

HENRY MAURICE SHEFFER, Frederick Sheldon Fellow. Philosophy. Cambridge, England.
Instructor in Philosophy, University of Washington.

EDMUND WARE SINNOTT, Frederick Sheldon Fellow. Botany. Australasia.
Austin Teaching Fellow in Botany. Fourth-year Graduate Student.

LANGDON WARNER, Frederick Sheldon Fellow. Oriental Art. Japan.
Assistant Curator of the Department of Chinese and Japanese Art, Boston Museum of Fine Arts.

RESIDENT FELLOWS

CHARLTON ANDREWS, MacDowell Fellow. Dramatic Composition.
Head of Department of English, State Normal School, Valley City, No. Dak.

FREDERICK LANSDOWNE CANDEE, South End House Fellow. Social Problems.
Director, South Bay Union, Boston.

PAUL WHITTIER CARLETON, Edward Austin Fellow. Chemistry.
Instructor in Chemistry, University of Wisconsin.

HARRY TODD COSTELLO, James Walker Fellow. Philosophy.
Frederick Sheldon Fellow, at Paris.

ALFRED OTTO GROSS, Edward Austin Fellow. Zoölogy.
Assistant in Zoölogy. Third-year Graduate Student.

RALPH EMERSON HEILMAN, Robert Treat Paine Fellow. Social Science.
Reappointed.

THOMAS COOKE McCRACKEN, South End House Fellow in Social Education. Social Education.
Reappointed.

SAMUEL MOORE, Christopher M. Weld Scholar.   English.
Lecturer in English Philology, Bryn Mawr College.

JAMES HAMILTON PICKEN, Francis Parkman Fellow.   Philosophy.
Christopher M. Weld Scholar, at Berlin.

ROBERT JACKSON RAY, Henry Lee Memorial Fellow.   Economics.
Professor of Economics, Keiogijuku University, Japan.

CHARLES MANFRED THOMPSON, Ozias Goodwin Memorial Fellow.   History
and Government.
Assistant in History, University of Illinois.

THORBERGUR THORVALDSON, Edward Austin Fellow.   Chemistry.
Edward William Hooper Fellow, at Dresden.

HENRY ASA VAN LANDINGHAM, Willard Scholar.   English.
Associate Professor of English, Richmond College, Va.

CHARLES EDWARD WHITMORE, Edward Austin Fellow.   Comparative Literature.
Instructor in English.

TABLE X. — FELLOWSHIPS AND SCHOLARSHIPS (1909–12)

1. *Applications and Appointments*

	1909–10	1910–11	1911–12
Spring applicants for reappointment or promotion	73	59	73
Spring applicants for a first appointment	272	300	285
Later applicants	37	39	40
	—382	—398	—398
Appointed to fellowships	24	24	47
Appointed to scholarships	86	91	88
Appointed instructors, teaching fellows, or assistants	23	32	33
	—133	—147	—168
Deduct for repetitions	5	1	3
	—128	—146	—165
Entered or continued in the Graduate School of Arts and Sciences without receiving any of the above-named appointments	47	68	72
Entered undergraduate classes of Harvard College	2	2	0
Entered other Departments of the University	6	8	5
	— 55	— 78	— 77
Applicants who were at the University in the year following their applications	183	224	242
Applicants not at the University in that year	199	174	156
	—382	—398	—398

2. *Classification of Applicants and Appointees*

	1909–10		1910–11		1911–12	
	Applicants	Appointees	Applicants	Appointees	Applicants	Appointees
Students of Philology	134	41	161	44	121	38
Students of History, Political Science, Philosophy, or Education	132	34	131	40	168	55
Students of Mathematics, Physics, or Chemistry	68	21	67	20	66	27
Students of Natural History	37	12	32	10	36	14
Students of other branches, or unclassified . .	11	2	7	1	7	1
	382	110	398	115	398	135
Students in Graduate School of Arts and Sciences	131	51	131	53	129	51
Students in Harvard College	23	5	22	4	18	5
Students in other Departments of the University	2	–	5	–	2	–
Former students in some Department of the University	34	8	33	8	37	9
Persons never previously members of the University	192	46	207	50	212	70
	382	110	398	115	398	135
Harvard Bachelors of Arts or Science, not previously graduated elsewhere	40	18	37	18	41	17
Harvard Bachelors of Arts or Science previously graduated elsewhere	2	–	6	3	3	1
Graduates of other institutions, not Harvard Bachelors of Arts or Science	269	73	298	70	303	93
Undergraduates of Harvard College or Lawrence Scientific School, not already graduated elsewhere	23	5	21	4	18	4
Undergraduates of other institutions and other non-graduates	48	14	36	20	33	20
	382	110	398	115	398	135

The members of the Administrative Board for 1910–11 were Professors W. M. Davis, Mark, G. F. Moore, B. O. Peirce, H. W. Smyth, Kittredge, Turner, Walz, Baxter, R. B. Perry, and the Dean. Ten meetings were held during the year. The opening meeting of the Graduate School of Arts and Sciences and of the Graduate Schools of Applied Science and Business Administration was held in the Faculty Room on the evening of Friday, October 7, 1910. The chief address was by Professor George Foot Moore, who discussed certain recent tendencies in college and university instruction. President Lowell and Mr. H. N. Hillebrand, President of the Graduate Club, spoke briefly.

Probably the most troublesome administrative question connected with the Graduate School of Arts and Sciences is that of admission to the School and to candidacy for a degree, a difficulty arising from the wide differences in the requirements for bachelor's degrees in American colleges. Some institutions confer the degree of A.B. for the studies of the secondary school; others publish standards of admission and graduation which they do not enforce; others do work which is good as far as it goes but does not constitute the full equivalent of a standard college course. Consequently some applicants cannot be permitted to register as graduate students, while others can with propriety be admitted to graduate standing but cannot be allowed to become candidates for a degree without a longer period of residence than is regularly required. Moreover, all graduates of the same college ought not to be treated alike; special consideration should be given to those who bring distinguished records, and there should always be an opportunity for revising the conditions of candidacy in the cases of students whose work at Harvard shows unusual excellence. A just decision in each individual case demands an amount of local knowledge and accumulated experience such as the authorities of no single graduate school can ever hope to possess. Fortunately the problem is one that concerns all American graduate schools, and an excellent beginning has been made in the direction of coöperative effort. In connection with the meeting of the Association of American Universities at Charlottesville in October, 1910, there was held a conference of deans and similar officers of the graduate schools of the institutions there represented, at which the question of admission was specially considered. Provision was made for the exchange of information between different universities, and the United States Bureau of Education was asked to assist in collecting and classifying facts bearing upon the standing of the bachelor's degrees of American colleges. This task was entrusted to the Bureau's Specialist in Higher Education, Dr. Kendric C. Babcock (Ph.D. Harvard '96), who made a careful examination of the records of the various graduate schools and of such bodies as the Carnegie Foundation and the General Education Board, and has recently issued a preliminary " Classification of Universities and Colleges with reference to Bachelor's Degrees." This list, the first attempt to reduce to some sort of order the chaos of American college degrees, is necessarily tentative, but it has already rendered valuable service to the authorities of graduate schools and in revised and enlarged form will serve as the principal supplement and corrective to the results which have been gained in our own experience. It should also be found useful in other departments of Harvard University, for under the system of organization which requires collegiate graduation for admission to the professional schools, the evaluation of college degrees becomes a necessity for these schools likewise. Diversities of practice in this respect have been a source of embarrassment to particular schools and to the University as a whole, and the establishment of a substantially uniform university standard is much to be desired.

One of the notable deficiencies in the students who enter the Graduate School is the inability on the part of a majority of them to make ready use of French and German books in their studies. Men come to us each year who have studied but one of these languages, and in making good this defect of preparation they are obliged to spend time which ought to be given to higher work. Harvard University requires an elementary knowledge of both French and German on the part of candidates for the degree of Master of Arts, yet so inadequate are the standards of the American baccalaureate as regards acquaintance with modern languages, that even this minimum is more than the general practice of American universities demands for the master's degree. Nevertheless, since a reading knowledge of one of these languages will after 1913 be demanded of all candidates for the A.B. and S.B. in Harvard College, it would seem necessary that Harvard should add a similar requirement for the degree of A.M., if the master's degree is to maintain its standing with reference to the A.B. In the case of candidates for the degree of Doctor of Philosophy a reading knowledge of German and French is regularly enforced, but often at the expense of valuable time on the part of those whose preparatory and collegiate education has been deficient in such training. This is one of the most obvious points at which graduate studies could be helped by increased efficiency in the American college.

It is the source of satisfaction to note the progress of the higher work of the school, as seen in the increasing number of students who remain more than one year (compare Table III) and in the growing resort to the more advanced and special courses. From certain points of view these courses of special training and research may be considered the most important which the University offers, for they are the nurseries of productive scholarship.

In them the contact between professor and student is most constant and most intimate, and through them the investigators of the future are trained and the productive capacity of the professor multiplied by the researches of his students. Such courses can never be large, else their purpose is defeated, and they are inevitably costly of the professor's time and the university's money; but the cost must be paid, and paid generously, if the university is to continue and develop as a centre of the highest scholarship. There are departments in which the provision of advanced courses is plainly inadequate, whether measured by the intrinsic importance of the subject or by the demands of actual and prospective students, and increased resources for maintaining and extending advanced instruction constitute the most pressing need of the Graduate School of Arts and Sciences. A gift of one million dollars could be immediately and advantageously used for such purposes; the eight professorships which it would support need not be confined exclusively to graduate instruction, but they should be devoted primarily to filling the most serious gaps in our advanced teaching. The endowment of particular professorships of this type would, of course, be a contribution to the same end.

A further means of stimulating productive scholarship would be furnished by the creation of a group of research fellowships for men of proved capacity for original investigation. The needs of those whose studies can only be continued elsewhere are now met by the Frederick Sheldon fund and other travelling fellowships, but for a great variety of investigations the libraries and laboratories of Cambridge offer opportunities of which our best students need to avail themselves for a longer period than is now generally possible. Each year men who have made a brilliant beginning in research are obliged to enter immediately upon instructorships which offer neither the leisure nor the facilities for advanced study and may ultimately cripple or destroy their impulse to productive work. The first few years after leaving the university are the critical period in the life of the potential investigator, and the opportunity of one or two years of comparative freedom would often turn the scale. Moreover, a group of picked and trained scholars of this sort, enjoying the income of a paid fellowship or the equivalent distinction of a John Harvard appointment, would by their presence and influence in Cambridge give stimulus and encouragement to the most ambitious men in the Graduate School. Such Fellows would ordinarily, though not necessarily, have taken the doctor's degree; they might well give a small amount of time to teaching, but their primary occupation should be research. It is to be hoped · that such foundations may be encouraged by the excellent example of the Bayard Cutting Fellowship for Research in Physics, established in 1911 with an income of $575. The conditions of tenure prescribe that "this Fellowship, to be considered as a reward for men of the very highest intellectual attainments, is to be conferred upon a successful investigator, in order that he may remain in the University in the pursuit of his special research. This Fellowship shall carry with it the rank and privileges of an instructor, and may be conferred on the holders of other University appointments."

The productive work of the Graduate School of Arts and Sciences would also be greatly assisted by a publication fund which would ensure the publication of such important books and monographs, both of professors and of advanced students, as yield no commercial return and cannot find a place in the existing series of university publications. The best form which such a fund could take would be the liberal endowment of a University Press for the whole University.

CHARLES H. HASKINS, *Dean.*

THE GRADUATE SCHOOL OF APPLIED SCIENCE

To the President of the University: —

Sir, — I beg to submit the following report in regard to the Graduate School of Applied Science for the academic year 1910–11.

There was during the year one student enrolled in the Lawrence Scientific School whose graduation in June closed the process of reorganization of the Scientific School.

The enrolment by subject in the Graduate School of Applied Science at the time of the issue of the Annual Catalogue was as follows: —

	1909	1910
Civil Engineering	14	17
Mechanical Engineering	7	3
Electrical Engineering	17	15
Mining and Metallurgy	18	26
Architecture	5	20
Landscape Architecture	9	13
Forestry	12	19
Applied Chemistry	0	1
Applied Physics	1	0
Applied Biology	4	9
	87	123

Subsequent to the issue of the Catalogue there were ten additional enrolments distributed as follows: —

Civil Engineering	1
Architecture	2
Landscape Architecture	2
Applied Chemistry	1
Applied Biology	4
	10

The total enrolment in the School therefore, during the academic year 1910–11, was one hundred and thirty-three.

COLLEGES AND UNIVERSITIES REPRESENTED BY GRADUATES IN THE
GRADUATE SCHOOL OF APPLIED SCIENCE

Amherst College	1	New Hampshire College	1
Bowdoin College	1	Ohio State University	1
Brown University	1	Oxford University (England)	1
Carleton College	1	Park College	1
Colorado College	1	Princeton University	1
Colorado Agricultural College	1	St. Mary's College	1
Columbia University	1	South Dakota State College of	
Cornell University	1	Agriculture and Mechanic Arts	1
Dartmouth College	5	South Eastern Agricultural Col-	
Hamilton College	1	lege (Wye, England)	1
Hamline University	1	Swarthmore College	1
Hampden-Sidney College	1	Trinity College (Conn.)	1
Harvard University	69	Tufts College	1
Heriot-Watt College (Edin-		University of California	1
burgh, Scotland)	1	University of Idaho	1
Hobart College	1	University of Maine	1
Indiana University	1	University of Nebraska	1
Iowa Agricultural College	1	Washington and Jefferson Col-	
Japanese Naval College	1	lege	1
Lake Forest College	1	West Virginia University	1
Massachusetts Agricultural Col-		Williams College	2
lege	2	Yale University	3
Massachusetts Institute of			
Technology	3		

As shown by the above table, the total number of colleges and universities represented by graduates in the Graduate School of Applied Science was forty, as compared with thirty-one of the preceding year.

In the Division of Engineering the most notable event of the year was the appointment as Gordon McKay Professor of Sanitary Engineering of Mr. George C. Whipple, of the firm of Hazen and Whipple in New York. Mr. J. W. M. Bunker and Mr. Melville C. Whipple were appointed Instructors in Sanitary Engineering, as assistants to Professor Whipple for the organization and development of the department. During the latter part of the year extensive changes and installations were carried out in the organization of the laboratory courses in the subject. A strong argument for the early organization of this subject in the University was the opportunity for coöperating with the Department of Preventive Medicine and Hygiene under Professor Rosenau in the Medical School. Through the combined departments the University is undertaking one of the most modern of scientific developments in a unique manner.

The principal addition to the laboratory equipment of the Division of Engineering during the year was in the subject of electrical engineering on which the Division had agreed to concentrate its immediate efforts. With the exception of certain large equipments, such as that for high tension work, this department is rapidly becoming admirably equipped. Provision cannot be made for work in high tension phenomena without some large pieces of apparatus, of which the most expensive is a high voltage transformer, and without a small building especially adapted to the work.

The Engineering Camp has for several years been one of the best managed institutions for undergraduate instruction. All who have been connected with the Camp, whether as students or as junior instructors, and all who have visited the Camp agree that the character of the work done by the students has been of a high order and the discipline excellent. Great credit is due Professor Hughes for these admirable results. In the past the Camp has been on an independent budget and self supporting. The Camp is of so much importance to the higher work in engineering that it may well be made dependent on the same resources as the other work in the Division of Engineering and share in the support from the McKay bequest. In view of the diminished count allowed the summer courses in engineering toward the Bachelor's degree there will be without question a diminution in the number of students in the next and ensuing years. In view of this certain prospect in the diminution of attendance and therefore in the receipts of the summer courses, and in view of their importance not merely in their present form but in an even more enriched form, it is desirable that these courses and the maintenance of the Camp should be placed on the budget of the Scientific School.

In addition to the installation of the laboratories in sanitary engineering and the rearrangement of rooms which this rendered necessary, other changes have been made in Pierce Building. Space has been made for an office and lecture rooms for the Division of Forestry during its winter term. In the library a space has been reserved for the books of the Division of Forestry. This has been accomplished at a considerable sacrifice on the part of the Division of Engineering. Other changes made in the arrangement of the library, providing for a separation of the stacks from the reading room, have rendered possible greater care and oversight of the books and their use.

The Division of Mining and Metallurgy, with an unusually strong staff, still remains in need of better physical equipment. It is cramped in its quarters. In many fields it is cramped in its laboratory resources. Its library is ill housed and is lacking in books and periodicals. The lack in periodicals is especially deplorable in view of the fact that the instruction in the Division is in so large a measure conducted by reference to current literature, a form of instruction on the whole characteristic of the School and consistent with the best traditions of the University. There is also great need for the equipment of a course in electrical and magnetic ore separators, and in the application of electrical and magnetic methods to mining and metallurgical processes in general.

The year under review was one of great change and reorganization in the Department of Architecture. It is especially noteworthy for the acceptance of a Professorship in Architectural Design by Professor Eugène J. A. Duquesne, and the acceptance of an Assistant Professorship in Architectural Design by Mr. John S. Humphreys. Professor Duquesne began his work in April, Professor Humphreys at the close of the academic year. Professor Duquesne came from the École des Beaux Arts, and it was his atelier above all others to which American students, going to Paris for further study in architecture, resorted. Professor Humphreys came from the firm of Carrère and Hastings in New York. Great credit for this reorganization and the present perfect condition of the Department, both in its large lines and in its details, is due Professor Warren.

There were no changes in the staff of the Department of Landscape Architecture, but the Department continued the improvement of its equipment, now one of the best in the country. The recognition of the Department by the practising profession is perhaps best indicated by the fact that it has been chosen as a place for deposit of all of the plans submitted for membership in the American Society of Landscape Architects. The Department continued its bibliography of landscape architecture and city planning, a production of value to the profession.

Through the active assistance of the Visiting Committee of the Board of Overseers the Division of Forestry was enabled to make a strong addition to its teaching staff and to undertake important extensions in its programme of studies. During the year Mr. Austin Cary returned to the service of the Department as Lecturer in Lumbering and Forest Engineering, and Mr. E. E. Carter, Assistant Forester in the United States Forest Service, accepted an appointment as Assistant Professor of Forestry to fill the vacancy left by the resignation of Mr. MacKaye. The physical equipment was still further perfected and great improvement rendered in the buildings, grounds, and farm outfit.

The Division of Forestry again suffered during the winter from its inadequate accommodations in Cambridge, its library and its lecture room being in a cramped and ill lighted and ill heated building. During the year, however, arrangements were made with the Division of Engineering, looking toward the housing of the Division of Forestry for the ensuing year in Pierce Hall.

The Bussey Institution, representing the work of the School in Applied Biology, grew in its physical equipment and in the number of students and the interest which its work produced. The prime work of the Bussey Institution being advanced instruction and research, its activity could be adequately represented only by a list of its important contributions.

The best land of the Bussey Institution was transferred many years ago to the Arnold Arboretum. Of that which remains comparatively little is of such location and quality as to be of service. The low land which lies between South Street and the railway track, across the street from the main buildings of the Bussey Institution, is fertile and because of its protected location of great value to the Bussey Institution and above all things should be retained against all inroads. It is about the only land now left which is of value. That which lies between the railway tracks is so exposed to depredations, so stripped of its surface soil in enriching the land of the Arnold Arboretum, or else so low in level as to be of comparatively small value either to the Bussey Institution with its old form or with its new purpose. As it lies within the city limits and at the end of the elevated railway as well as near an important station of the New York, New Haven, and Hartford Railway, there are many reasons why it should be added to the developed and taxed property of the city. Could permission be obtained from the General Court for the disposal of this angle of land, the resulting increase in endowment would enable the Bussey Institution to develop as an even more vigorous and more complete institution of biological research.

During the year the School of Applied Science was placed on independent financial resources and thus under the necessity of operating under the limitations of a well defined budget. In this process the Corporation voted that the resources of the School from other than the McKay Endowment should be annually less by an amount equal to one quarter of the increase from the McKay bequest until the income of the School from other resources than the McKay bequest should be equal to that at the time of the death of Mr. Gordon McKay.

WALLACE C. SABINE, *Dean.*

THE GRADUATE SCHOOL OF BUSINESS ADMINISTRATION

To THE PRESIDENT OF THE UNIVERSITY: —

SIR, — I have the honor of presenting my report upon the Graduate School of Business Administration for the academic year 1910–11.

The number of students registered is shown in the following comparative table, counting as "regular" students college graduates taking full work in the School: —

	Number of Students		
	1908–09	1909–10	1910–11
Regular students:			
First-year	33	42	43
Second-year		8	10
	33	50	53
Special students:			
(a) College graduates taking partial work	25	15	15
(b) Not holding college degrees	22	26	26
	47	41	41
Totals	80	91	94

GRADUATES OF COLLEGES

Amherst College	1	Peking University	1
Brown University	1	Princeton University	1
Clark College	1	Trinity College (Conn.)	1
College of the City of New York	1	Tufts College	3
Cornell University	1	Université de Rennes (France)	1
Dartmouth College	3	University of Arkansas	1
Guilford College (N.C.)	1	University of North Carolina	1
Harvard University	43	University of Southern California	1
Mass. Institute of Technology	1	University of Wisconsin	1
Monmouth College	1	Yale University	1
Otterbein University	1		
Ouachita College (Ark.)	1		68

(22 colleges represented, as compared with 14 in 1908–09 and 19 in 1909–10.)

Geographical distribution of students: —

STATES:

		STATES:	
Alabama	1	New York	9
Arkansas	2	North Carolina	2
Connecticut	1	Ohio	4
Georgia	1	Pennsylvania	2
Illinois	3	Rhode Island	1
Indiana	1	Vermont	1
Maine	1	Virginia	1
Maryland	1	Wisconsin	1
Massachusetts	54		
Michigan	1	FOREIGN COUNTRIES:	
Minnesota	2	China	3.
New Jersey	1	France	1.

(20 states and 2 foreign countries, as compared with 12 states and 2 foreign countries in 1908–09 and 16 states and 5 foreign countries in 1909–10.)

Average ages of students (taking age in years and months on dates of registration in each academic year): —

	1908–09	1909–10	1910–11
First-year men	23.22 years	22.95 years	23.26 years
Second-year "	—	24.75 "	24.67 "
Special students	31.65 "	32.06 "	31.68 "
with degree	30.11 "	27.89 "	27.63 "
without "	32.66 "	34.47 "	34.01 "

The degree of Master in Business Administration was conferred in June, 1911, upon eight men, John Frederic Spence receiving this degree " *with distinction*." The names of the graduates and the subjects of the graduation theses are as follows: —

Edgar Stratton Chappelear, A.B. (*Dartmouth Coll.*) 1909.
Thesis subject: " Capitalization of Industrial Corporations."
Ting-chi Chu, A.B. 1909.
Thesis subject: " Currency Reform in China."
Carroll Dunham, 3d, A.B. 1910.
Thesis subject: " Bank Stocks as an Investment."
Bryant Burwell Glenny, Jr., A.B. (*Yale Univ.*) 1909.
Thesis subject: " Paying Workmen in Industrial Plants."
Herman Goepper, A.B. 1909.
Thesis subject: " The Statistical Use of some Accounting Records in Telephone Operation."
Laurence Edward Poland, A.B. 1909.
Thesis subject: " The Application of Scientific Management in a Small Factory."
John Frederic Spence, A.B. 1910.
Thesis subject: " The Relation of the Packers to the Leather Trade."
Clarence Birch Stoner, A.B. (*Otterbein Univ.*) 1896.
Thesis subject: " Y. M. C. A. Accounts."

The two prizes of one hundred dollars and fifty dollars, offered annually by Mr. George Oliver May of New York, for the two best graduating theses, were awarded to Mr. Herman Goepper and Mr. C. B. Stoner.

Because of lack of satisfactory candidates, only three of the five University Scholarships for the year 1910–11 were awarded, as follows: —

> John David Plant, A.B. (*Cornell Univ.*) 1910.
> Frank Starr Spring, A.B. 1910.
> Clarence Birch Stoner, A.B. (*Otterbein Univ.*) 1896.

The following changes in courses were made from 1909–10: Business 7 (Law of Banking Operations) was shortened to a half course; Business 11¹ (Commercial Organization and Methods) was lengthened to a whole course; Business 12² (Economic Resources and Commercial Policy of the Chief European States) was omitted. The Department of Public Business was transferred to the new Department of Government. A course entitled An Introduction to the Technique of Printing was given for the first time, with Mr. C. C. Lane, Publication Agent, in charge. The Business School supported during this year Fine Arts 5 ¹hf. (The History of the Printed Book), given by Mr. W. C. Lane, Librarian, under the Department of Fine Arts.

The new course in printing was given by outside lecturers, chosen in coöperation with the Advisory Committee on Printing, and the conduct of this course, even during its first year, has been unusually satisfactory. We can no longer regard as experimental the coöperative lecture courses in which business men assist as specialists. When properly organized, they have proved successful. Moreover, the opportunity of meeting and questioning men of large experience in affairs is valuable to and highly appreciated by the students of the School. This feature of the School's instruction should be continued, although for various reasons changes will undoubtedly be made from time to time in the amount of such outside assistance in any particular course. This method of instruction may be extended with advantage to some courses in which it has not hitherto been applied, whereas in other courses the number of lecturers will be diminished owing to changes in circumstances. During the past year, for instance, Professor Sprague has taken upon himself an increasing part of the instruction in the course on Corporation Finance.

The outside lecturers in these courses were as follows during 1910–11: —

BUSINESS 14²: ECONOMIC RESOURCES AND COMMERCIAL ORGANIZATION OF CENTRAL AND SOUTH AMERICA

Herbert Barber of New York: "Shipping Business between the United States and the River Plate."

Dudley Bartlett of Philadelphia: "Cuba."

John Birkinbine of Philadelphia: "Industrial and Trade Conditions of Mexico."

Charles Lyon Chandler, American Consular Assistant at Buenos Aires: "The Trade of the Argentine"; "Industrial Development of the Argentine," and "Foreign Investments in the Development of the Argentine."

Dr. W. C. Farabee: "The Rubber Industry."

Colonel Horace N. Fisher of Brookline: "Resources and Trade of Chili."

Henry G. Granger of New York: "Colombia."

H. R. A. Grieser of New York: "The West Indies and United States Interests, with especial attention to Haiti and Santo Domingo."

Dr. Albert Hale of Washington, D. C.: "Trade Possibilities and Methods in Central America, Colombia, and Venezuela."

A. S. Hardy of New York: "Nicaragua."

Hon. George A. Loud of Washington, D. C.: "Panama Canal."

W. G. Reed: "Geographical Factors in South American Commerce."

J. Richling, Consul General from Uruguay: "Uruguay."

Professor L. S. Rowe of the University of Pennsylvania: "Attitude of the Latin-American Nations toward the United States."

Wilfred H. Schoff of Philadelphia: "Peru"; "Bolivia," and "Ecuador."

Professor J. Russell Smith of the University of Pennsylvania: "Relation of the Panama Canal to American Shipping" and "The Panama Canal with Relation to the West Coast of South America."

W. H. Stevens of New York: "Banking, Currency, and Foreign Exchange."

BUSINESS 17¹: INDUSTRIAL ORGANIZATION

M. W. Alexander of Lynn: "Training of Men," and "Training of Men for Industrial Efficiency."

Carl G. Barth of Philadelphia: "Routing."

M. L. Cooke of Philadelphia: "Training and Development of Workers."

Charles Day of Philadelphia: "Routing."

Harrington Emerson of New York: "Securing Efficiency in a Railroad Organization."

J. O. Fagan of Boston: "The Limitations on Management by Trade Organizations and by other Factors" and "The Limitations on Workmen's Efficiency by Trade Organizations."

W. C. Fish of Lynn: "Decentralized Management."

H. L. Gantt of New York: "The Compensation of Workmen; paying for Time versus paying for Results," and "Training of Workmen in Habits of Industry and Coöperation."

C. B. Going of New York: "The Relation of Industrial Engineering to Industrial Organization."

H. F. J. Porter of New York: "Industrial Betterment; developing the Efficiency of the Human Element in a Working Organisation."

Russell Robb of Boston: "Organization."

W. F. Russell of Harrisburg, Pa.: "Cost Accounting in Manufacturing Establishments."

Gershom Smith of Washington, D. C.: "Mechanical Aids in Accounting and Statistical Departments" and "The Distribution of Indirect Costs by the Machine-hour Method."

J. E. Sterrett of Philadelphia: "The Relation of the Accountant to Economical and Efficient Management."

F. W. Taylor of Philadelphia: "Task Management and its Nature"; "Task System and Workingmen," and "Planning Department; general Principles."

BUSINESS 18: INDUSTRIAL ORGANIZATION (advanced course)

Frederick M. Feiker of Chicago: conduct of field work in course for six weeks, ending March 22, 1911.

Sanford E. Thompson of Newton Highlands: special instruction in time study in course for eight weeks, ending May 26, 1911.

BUSINESS 20c^2: AN INTRODUCTION TO THE TECHNIQUE OF PRINTING

H. L. Baker of New York: "Printing Machinery."

A. E. Barter of Norwood, Mass.: "Binding."

Henry L. Bullen of Jersey City: "Commercial Printing."

J. C. Dana of Newark, N. J.: "Introductory Lecture."

A. W. Elson of Boston: "Reproducing Processes."

E. B. Hackett of New Haven, Conn.: "Copy."

H. L. Johnson of Boston: "The Principal Printing Offices of the World."

C. C. Lane of Cambridge: "Distribution."

A. D. Little of Boston: "Physical Qualities of Paper."

J. H. McFarland of Harrisburg, Pa.: "Printing Office Management."

A. F. MacKay of Philadelphia: "Machine Composition."

C. E. Mason of Boston: "Paper Making."

H. M. Plimpton of Norwood, Mass.: "Binding."

W. S. Timmis of New York: "Printing Office Equipment and Routing."

J. A. Ullman of New York: "Printing Ink."

D. B. Updike of Boston: "Type and Composition."

BUSINESS 25^2: CORPORATION FINANCE

Grosvenor Calkins of Boston: "Incorporation Organisation and Power of Corporations."

Hon. William H. Corbin of Hartford, Conn.: "Taxation."

W. J. Curtis of New York: "Local Public Service Corporations."

A. Lowes Dickinson of New York: "Determination of Profits."

J. F. Hill of Boston: "Issue of Securities."

Judge C. M. Hough of New York: "Bankruptcy."

T. W. Lamont of New York: "Underwriting."

G. O. May of New York: "Disposition of Surplus."

H. L. Stimson of New York: "Federal Control of Corporations."

F. W. Whitridge of New York: "State Control of Corporations."

The lectures on subjects of general business interest, given under the auspices of the School and open to the students of the University, were as follows: —

Henry White Cannon, Chairman of the Board of Directors, Chase National Bank, New York: "The National Banking System."

Henry E. Hess of New York: "The Proper Assessment of Fire Insurance Rates in Great Cities."

Hon. Seth Low of New York: "New Business Problems."

F. I. Kent, Vice-President of the Bankers' Trust Company, New York: "Foreign Exchange."

Julius Kruttschnitt, Director of Maintenance and Operation, Union Pacific System, Chicago, Ill.: "The Operating Efficiency of our Railroads."

Hon. Franklin MacVeagh of Washington, D. C.: "The Life of the Business Man."

There were special lecturers in the following courses: —

ECONOMICS 18

Professor H. R. Hatfield of the University of California: "History of Accounting," on May 10, 1911.

BUSINESS 1

Professor H. R. Hatfield of the University of California: "Comparison of English, French, and German Methods of Accounting with our Own," on May 12, 1911.

BUSINESS 10

Professor J. Russell Smith of the University of Pennsylvania: "Organisation of Ocean Shipping," on March 17 and 20, 1911.

BUSINESS 11

J. R. Simpson of Boston: "Retail Merchandising," on March 8 and 10, 1911.
H. N. McKinney of Philadelphia: "Advertising," on March 20, 1911.

BUSINESS 24

Samuel H. Ordway of New York: "Defects and Proposed Reforms of the New York Stock Exchange," on April 6, 1911.

A considerable addition was made during the year to the list of firms which have agreed to allow their plants to be inspected and studied by students of the School. The following firms should be added to the list given in last year's report: —

American Rubber Co., East Cambridge.
American Steel and Wire Co., Worcester.
American Watch Tool Co., Waltham.
Atwood and McManus, Chelsea.
Beggs and Cobb, Winchester.
Boott Mills, Lowell.

Boston Bookbinding Co., Cambridge.
Boston Bridge Works, East Cambridge.
Boston Rubber Shoe Co., Malden.
William S. Butler Co., Boston.
M. W. Carr and Co., West Somerville.
Edwin Clapp and Sons, East Weymouth.
Commonwealth Shoe and Leather Co., Whitman.
Commonwealth Trust Co., Boston.
Converse Rubber Shoe Co., Malden.
John H. Cross Co., Cambridge.
Lewis A. Crossett, North Abington.
A. H. Davenport Co., East Cambridge.
P. Derby and Co., Gardner.
Doten-Dunton Desk Co., Cambridge.
W. L. Douglas Shoe Co., Brockton.
George H. Ellis Printing Co., Boston.
Faunce and Spinney, Lynn.
Farley Harvey Co., Boston.
Gilchrist Co., Boston.
Griffin Wheel Co., Chelsea.
P. J. Harney Shoe Co., Lynn.
Hornblower and Weeks, Boston.
Houghton Mifflin Co., Boston.
Ivers and Pond Piano Co., Boston.
Kidder, Peabody Co., Boston.
Kitson Machine Shop, Lowell.
Lawrence and Co., Boston.
A. C. Lawrence, Boston.
Maverick Mills, East Boston.
W. H. McElwain Co., Boston.
Mead-Morrison Manufacturing Co., Cambridge.
National Shawmut Bank, Boston.
New England Confectionery Co., Boston.
New England Maple Syrup Co., Cambridge.
Old Boston National Bank, Boston.
Poland Laundry Machinery Co., Roxbury.
Rickard Gregory Shoe Co., Lynn.
Reed and Prince, Worcester.
Saco-Pettee Co., Newton Upper Falls.
A. Shuman and Co., Boston.
Simplex Electrical Co., Cambridge.
B. F. Sturtevant Co., Hyde Park.
Talbot Mills, North Billerica.
Tileston and Hollingsworth Co., Hyde Park.
Watertown Arsenal, Watertown.
Walker-Stetson Co., Boston.
Wellington-Sears Co., Boston.
R. H. White Co., Boston.
Whittenton Manufacturing Co., Taunton.
Women's Educational and Industrial Union, Boston.

The coöperation of business firms in taking students for summer employment is again to be noted. For special reasons only six of the ten students returning for the second year's work were employed during the summer, a smaller proportion than in previous years. The reports from employers continue to be remarkably favorable.

The Reading Room in Lawrence Hall, referred to in last year's report, has been in use during the year and has become an indispensable part of the School's equipment. In this Reading Room are placed reference books for use in connection with each of the courses in the School, together with a large number of corporation reports and other similar material. There are now approximately twelve hundred and fifty volumes and nine hundred and sixty pamphlets in this Reading Room. A few additions were made during the year to the list of confidential business documents for the Business Archives, a collection to which attention should be drawn and which will doubtless increase with the growth of the School and the interest and confidence shown in it by business firms.

In close proximity to the Reading Room in Lawrence Hall there has been assigned, with President Lowell's consent, a room for the use of the Business School Club, a student organization which commenced its activity in the second year of the School's existence. The Club has furnished this room as a place for Club meetings and purposes of study.

Mr. A. F. Crowley, Superintendent of the Reading Room, made during the year a visit to libraries in Philadelphia, New York, and Washington, which specialize in collecting books and other material in relation to business, in order to study their methods and resources.

A study tour was made by Mr. P. T. Cherington, Instructor in Economic Resources, during the summer of 1910, to Panama, Costa Rica, and Guatemala. During the latter part of this same summer Mr. Cherington made a short trip to Pittsburgh, Cleveland, Cincinnati, Louisville, Washington, Philadelphia, and New York, to get material on the trade in certain products of those cities.

During this last academic year Mr. Selden O. Martin, appointed Instructor in the School, on leave of absence, has been making an extended tour in South America, in preparation for his course on Economic Resources and Commercial Organization of Central and South America, to be given in 1911–12, during the second half-year.

Such study tours by instructors and others connected with the School are a part of the general policy of furtherance of research which is at once the opportunity and the duty of a graduate school such as ours. The study tours are undertaken primarily to provide further equipment for the direct work of instruction, since in many of the subjects which must be offered in the School the necessary knowledge can be obtained only as a result of careful and prolonged personal inquiry. While benefiting the School, such studies have, however, the advantage of being of service to the community or to the industries investigated. Such, for example, has been the work done under Professor Cole's direction by the advanced students in Business 2, where practice in auditing was given at the Women's Educational and Industrial Union, an educational and charitable organization in Boston that conducts many enterprises and has many kinds of receipts and expenditures. The members of the class worked also with the instructor in devising a system of accounting for a group of local hospitals.

In this connection mention should also be made of an enterprise inaugurated during the year which promises to give notable results. Through the initiative and generosity of Mr. A. W. Shaw of Chicago, Editor of *System*, a fund was established to be known as the Shaw Fund for Business Research. It was determined after a series of conferences to commence with a study of retail conditions in the boot and shoe industry, and preparations were made to send two investigators into the field for the summer of 1911.

There has been promised the School annually by Mr. Joseph E. Sterrett, of the firm of Price, Waterhouse and Company, one hundred dollars which the Administrative Board has voted to be used to buy additional books on accounting, such purchases to have a bookplate indicating the fund from which they were made.

Of significance for the future of the School was the investigation and report of the sub-committee, appointed by our Visiting Committee. This sub-committee inspected the methods and the programme of instruction of the School. Some of its members visited classes, and expressions of opinion in regard to the work of the School were obtained from a large majority of former students and from some of their present employers. On the basis of this evidence the Visiting Committee reported favorably upon the scope of instruction and the quality of the work done in the School, and the report to the Board of Overseers states that the Committee is convinced of the wisdom and expediency not only of continuing the work of the School but of continuing it upon a broader and more permanent financial basis. Some increased expenditure would be necessary to carry such plans into effect, but even to continue the present work of the School on the most economical plan will require an income of at least $30,000 a year, in addition to the estimated receipts from students. It should be noted, however, that with this minimum income, no provision would be made for a building or for additional new courses or for the appointment of additional instructors. It is hoped that steps will be taken soon to provide, preferably by endowment, for the needs of the School.

EDWIN F. GAY, *Dean*.

THE DIVINITY SCHOOL

To the President of the University: —

Sir, — As Dean of the Divinity School I have the honor to present the following report for the year 1910–11.

With the exception of Professors Peabody and Emerton who were absent during the first and second half-year respectively, all the members of the Faculty were in residence and gave their courses as announced. On account of illness, Professor Coe was unable to give the course on Religious Education (Homiletics 10^{1}hf) provided by the generosity of Mr. Sears, but Asst. Professor H. W. Holmes, who was to have been his assistant, gallantly undertook at very short notice to conduct the course and carried it through successfully and profitably. Thanks to the continued kindness of Mr. Sears the arrangement made with Professor Coe last year has been renewed and his course is included in the offering for the present year.

Experience seems to demonstrate that students will not ordinarily attend lectures or courses of lectures, however good, which do not count towards a degree. Therefore it has seemed inexpedient to provide such lectures. Last year, however, the Reverend Rodney F. Johonnot, LL.B., S.T.D., gave two lectures on "The Legal Relations of a Minister to his Parish," which were well attended and highly appreciated.

By vote of the Faculty no session of the Summer School of Theology was held in 1911. This does not necessarily mean that the School has been permanently abandoned, but in the circumstances it seemed best to omit it for at least one year. Through the King's Chapel Lectures under the auspices of the Lowell Institute, the Sunday afternoon preaching services in King's Chapel by members of the Faculty, and especially through the *Harvard Theological Review*, the Divinity School is now rendering far wider public service than was the case ten years ago, and the need of the Summer School has become correspondingly less. Moreover, the annual deficit, constituting a drain upon the resources of the regular School, makes it doubtful whether we ought to curtail the opportunities of students preparing for the ministry in order to continue the Summer School attended for the most part by ministers in active service. No final decision, however, has been reached with regard to the continuance of the Summer School.

During the past year 55 students were enrolled in the regular School, of whom 3 left at the end of the first half-year and 3 entered at the beginning of the second half-year. The distribution was as follows: —

Resident Graduates	13
Senior Class	6
Middle Class	5
Junior Class	4
Special Students	11
Andover Students	16
	—
Total	55

Thirty-six colleges were represented as follows: —

Alabama Polytechnic Institute	1	Marietta College	1
Amherst College	5	University of Michigan	1
Berea College	1	Missouri Wesleyan College	1
Boston University	1	Nebraska Wesleyan University	1
Bowdoin College	1	University of North Carolina	1
Brown University	3	Northwestern University	2
Carson and Newman College	1	Ohio Northern University	1
Central College	1	Olivet College	1
University of Chicago	1	Syracuse University	3
Colgate University	1	Tarkio College	1
Columbia University	1	University of Toronto	3
University of Denver	1	Tufts College	1
Drake University	3	Vanderbilt University	1
Drury College	1	Wesleyan University	1
Earlham College	1	Western Reserve University	1
Harvard University	10	Yale University	1
Kansas Normal College	1		—
University of Kansas	1		58
Kentucky School of Medicine	1	Counted more than once	7
Leland Stanford Jr. University	1		—
			51

Fourteen theological seminaries were represented by graduates as follows: —

Bangor Theological Seminary	1
Boston University	5
Chicago Theological Seminary	2
Doshisha Theological Seminary, Japan	1
Drake University	2
Drew Theological Seminary	1
Garrett Biblical Institute	1
Harvard University	2
Meadville Theological School	1
Pacific Theological Seminary	1
Tohoku Gakuin, Japan	1
Union Theological Seminary	1
Theological School of Van, Turkey	1
Victoria University	1
	21
Counted more than once	2
	19

The interchange of instruction between the Faculty of the School and the Faculty of Arts and Sciences indicates the extent of the contribution made by the Divinity School to the general work of the University. This interchange between the two Faculties in 1910–11 was as follows: —

Divinity students electing courses offered primarily by the Faculty of Arts and Sciences: —

Semitic	1 election.
Egyptology	1 "
Greek	1 "
Classical Philology	1
English	1
German	1 "
French	3 elections.
History	1 election.
Government	4 elections.
Economics	11 "
Philosophy	39 "
Social Ethics	9
	73

Non-Divinity students electing courses offered primarily by the Divinity School: —

Old Testament	32 elections.
Church History	158 "
History of Religions	19 "
Theology	5
Ethics	106
	—
	320

The interchange of instruction between the Harvard Divinity School and Andover Theological Seminary was as follows: —

Harvard Divinity students electing courses offered primarily by Andover Theological Seminary: —

Old Testament	2 elections.
New Testament	8 "
Church History	10 "
Theology	5
Homiletics	15
	—
	40

Andover students electing courses offered primarily by the Divinity School: —

Old Testament	4 elections.
New Testament	6 "
Church History	3 "
History of Religions	5 "
Theology	1 election.
Ethics	3 elections.
Homiletics	7 "
	—
	29

Six members of the School received the degree of S.T.B. (one *cum laude*), eleven the degree of A.M., and one the degree of Ph.D. The degree of A.M. was also conferred, in February, upon one person for work done in the Divinity School in the year 1908–09.

The following is a list of the Courses of Instruction given in the School in the year 1910–11. With each course is a statement of the number of students electing it from the Divinity School, Andover Theological Seminary, the Graduate School of Arts and Sciences, Harvard College, and Radcliffe College. In such Andover courses as were taken only by Andover students, no record of attendance is given. A list of the lectures delivered in the Lowell Institute course in King's Chapel is appended to the list of regular courses.

COURSES OF INSTRUCTION

OLD TESTAMENT

1¹. Dr. DAVEY.—Hebrew.—Morphology. Selections from the prose narratives of the Old Testament. *First half-year.* 2 Div., 6 Col.

2². Professor LYON.—Hebrew (second course).—Syntax. Extensive reading in the Old Testament. *Second half-year.* 1 Div., 5 Col.

18. Dr. DAVEY. — Classical Aramaic (Syriac). — Brockelmann's Syrische Grammatik; selections from the Peshitto; Syriac prose of the classical period. 1 Div., 1 Col.

4. Professor LYON. — History of Israel, political and social, till the capture of Jerusalem by the Romans. 5 Div., 15 Col.

5. Professor G. F. MOORE. — History of Jewish Literature from the earliest times to 200 A.D. 4 Div., 4 And., 3 Col.

A6. Professor ARNOLD. — Religion of Israel. — History of the religious ideas and institutions of Israel from the earliest times to the Maccabean age. 2 Div., 9 And.

10. Professor LYON. — Assyrian. 1 Col.

20. Professor LYON, Professor G. F. MOORE.— Research courses. 1 Div., 1 Gr.

NEW TESTAMENT

2. Professor ROPES. — Introduction to the Study of the New Testament. *First half-year:* The origin and early history of the New Testament writings. *Second half-year:* The teaching of Jesus Christ, and the theological and ethical ideas of the New Testament writers.
7 Div., 4 And.

3. Professor ROPES. — The Gospels of Matthew, Mark, and Luke.
4 Div., 1 And.

A7 ¹hf. Professor RYDER.— The Acts of the Apostles. *Half-course (first half-year).* 3 Div., 1 And.

A8²hf. Professor RYDER. — The Epistle to the Romans. *Half-course (second half-year).* 2 Div.

15 ¹hf. Professor FENN. — The Theological Method of Jesus and Paul. *Half-course (first half-year).* 6 Div., 1 And.

A16 ¹hf. Professor HINCKS.— New Testament Religion. *Half-course (first half-year).*

A19²hf. Professor RYDER. — The Epistle to the Hebrews. *Half-course (second half-year).* 3 Div., 1 And.

CHURCH HISTORY

A1. Professor PLATNER. — History of the Church in Outline.
3 Div., 9 And., 1 Col.

3a ¹hf. Professor EMERTON. — The Era of the Reformation in Europe. First part: from the rise of Italian Humanism to the Council of Basel (1350–1448). *Half-course (first half-year).* 1 Div., 5 Gr., 13 Col.

4a ¹hf. Professor E. C. MOORE. — The History of the Christian Church in Europe within the last three Centuries. *Half-course (first half-year).*
1 Div., 2 And., 55 Col.

4b ²hf. Professor E. C. MOORE. — The Expansion of Christendom in the Nineteenth Century. *Half-course (second half-year).*

3 Div., 1 And., 79 Col.

A3. Professor PLATNER. — Christian Institutions. — An historical and comparative study of the organisation and government, the forms of worship, and the doctrinal standards of the main branches of the Christian Church. 5 Div., 3 And., 2 Gr.

A4 ¹hf. Professor PLATNER. — History of the Church in England. *Half-course (first half-year).* 1 Div., 1 And.

A5 ²hf. Professor PLATNER. — History of the Church in America. *Half-course (second half-year).* 1 Div., 1 And., 1 Col.

5¹. Professor EMERTON. — History of Christian Thought, considered in its relation to the prevailing philosophy of each period from the earliest time to the Eighteenth Century. *First half-year.* 3 Div., 1 Col.

6 ¹hf. Professor EMERTON. — Practice in the Study and Use of Materials for Church History. *Half-course (first half-year).* 1 Gr.

HISTORY OF RELIGIONS

2. Professor G. F. MOORE. — History of Religions in Outline.

18 Div., 3 And., 1 Gr., 14 Col.

4 ²hf. Professor G. F. MOORE. — History of Judaism. *Half-course (second half-year).* 4 Div., 3 Col.

5 ¹hf. Professor G. F. MOORE. — Islam. — The Life of Mohammed; the Koran; the Moslem conquests; Mohammedan law and theology. *Half-course (first half-year).* 5 Div., 2 And., 1 Col.

THEOLOGY

1 ¹hf. Professor FENN. — Theism. *Half-course (first half-year).* 5 Div., 1 Gr.

A1 ²hf. Professor EVANS. — The Philosophic Basis of the Christian Religion. *Half-course (second half-year).* 1 Div., 3 And.

2¹. Professor FENN. — Outlines of Systematic Theology. *Second half-year.* 6 Div.

A ²hf. Professor EVANS. — Systematic Theology. The Distinctive Truths of Christianity. *Half-course (second half-year).* 4 Div., 8 And.

3 ¹hf. Professor FENN. — New England Theology. *Half-course (first half-year).* 4 Div.

7. Professor E. C. MOORE. — Philosophy of Religion.

15 Div., 1 And., 1 Gr., 1 Col.

20a ²hf. Professor E. C. MOORE. — Modern Theology, especially as influenced by Ritschl: a survey of constructive work in Theology during the last twenty years in Germany, England, and America. Lectures, reading, and reports. *Half-course (second half-year).* 2 Div., 1 Col., 1 Rad.

ETHICS

1 ^{1}hf. Professor Peabody, Dr. McConnell, Dr. Ford, and Dr. Foerster. Social Ethics. — The Ethics of Modern Industrialism. Lectures, special researches, and prescribed reading. *Half-course (second half-year).* 3 Div., 2 Gr., 97 Col.

20a ^{2}hf. Professor Peabody. — Seminary of Social Ethics. — *Subject for the year:* Christian Ethics and Modern Life. *Half-course (second half-year).* 4 Div., 3 And., 3 Gr., 1 Col.

20b ^{2}hf. Professor Peabody. — The instructor directs special researches of competent students in Social Ethics. *Half-course (second half-year).* 2 Gr., 1 Rad.

HOMILETICS AND PASTORAL CARE

A1a ^{1}hf. Professor Fitch. — The Philosophy of Preaching: An Introduction to the Historic Ideals and Present Possibilities of the Ministry. *Half-course (first half-year).* 5 Div., 10 And.

A1b ^{2}hf. Professor Fitch. — The Technique of the Preacher: the minister as maker of sermons, leader of worship, administrator, and pastor. *Half-course (second half-year).* 5 Div., 7 And.

2. Professors Peabody, E. C. Moore, Fenn, and Fitch. — Preaching. 8 Div., 2 And.

A2 ^{1}hf. Professor Fitch. — The Homiletic Teaching of the Old Testament. *Half-course (first half-year).* 2 Div.

A3 ^{1}hf. Professor Fitch. — Christian Preaching and Christian Doctrine. *Half-course (second half-year).* 3 Div.

10 ^{2}hf. Asst. Professor Holmes. — Principles and Methods of Religious Education. *Half-course (second half-year).* 6 Div., 5 And.

PUBLIC SPEAKING

1. Asst. Professor Winter and Mr. Bunker. — Training in Voice and Speech. Preparatory to Course 2. *Once a week.* (Not counted for a degree.) 4 Div.

2 hf. Asst. Professor Winter and Mr. Bunker. — Sermon Delivery, Scripture Reading, Oral Discussion. *Half-course.* 9 Div.

KING'S CHAPEL LECTURES

The Eastern Church

Professor J. W. Platner. — Three lectures: The Historic Development of Greek Christianity; The Patriarchate of Constantinople; The National Church of Armenia.

Professor G. F. Moore. — Two lectures: The Nestorians and Theological Education; The Nestorians and Missionary Activity.

Professor E. C. Moore. — Two lectures: The Patriarchate of Moscow; Reforms in the Russian Church.

Professor Leo Wiener. — One lecture: The Russian Church and the Russian People.

Professor W. W. Fenn. — One lecture: The Theology of the Eastern Church.

The following is a report of the Divinity Library for the year from July 1, 1910, through June 30, 1911. There were added to the Library 467 volumes and 79 pamphlets by purchase, 169 volumes and 209 pamphlets by gift. July 1, 1911, there were in the Library 38,794 volumes and 11,074 pamphlets. During the year 793 titles were catalogued in the author catalogue and 28 titles in the subject catalogue. There were borrowed from the stack for home use 872 volumes, from the stack for hall use 544 volumes, from the reserved books for overnight use 605 volumes.

W. W. FENN, *Dean.*

THE LAW SCHOOL

To the President of the University: —

Sir, — I have the honor to present my report upon the Law School for the academic year 1910–11.

The first table below shows the growth of the School from year to year since 1870 in the number of students, the number and percentages of college graduates, and the number of colleges represented by their graduates. A feature of this growth which will gratify the friends of the School is the steady increase in the number of graduates of other colleges than Harvard, and in the number of colleges represented. The fact that all parts of the country are so well represented in the student body cannot fail to be of much benefit both to the students and to the institution.

The second table gives the courses of study and instruction during the year, the text-books used, the number of weekly exercises in each course, and the number of students who offered themselves for examination in each course at the end of the year.

During the twelve months from August 1, 1910, to August 1, 1911, 6,260 volumes and 586 pamphlets were added to the library. On August 1, 1911, the library contained about 126,860 volumes and about 13,976 pamphlets. The increase of purchase over the previous year was due in part to the fact that purchases were delayed on account of Mr. Ames's death which would otherwise have been made during the year 1909–10.

One of the most important additions to the library during the year was the collection of *Bar Association Proceedings* belonging to Francis Rawle, Esq., of Philadelphia. This remarkable collection contained many volumes which it is practically impossible to find at the present time. The School has been trying for a long time to fill the gaps in its collection, but up to last year more than one hundred volumes were still lacking. By this purchase we have obtained substantially all these rare volumes, and we shall have no difficulty in disposing of the duplicates to good advantage. The library now contains what is believed to be the only complete collection of *Bar Association ·Proceedings* in existence. These volumes contain valuable matter, the importance of which is likely to increase in the future.

Year	Whole No. of Students	Total of College Graduates	Harvard Graduates	Graduates of other Colleges	Non-Graduates	Per cent of College Graduates	No. of Colleges represented
1870–71	165	77	27	50	88	47	27
1871–72	138	70	34	36	68	51	25
1872–73	117	66	34	32	51	56	25
1873–74	141	86	49	37	55	61	25
1874–75	144	82	63	19	62	57	18
1875–76	173	93	60	33	80	54	25
1876–77	199	116	74	42	83	58	30
1877–78	196	121	80	41	75	62	30
1878–79	169	109	71	38	60	64	24
1879–80	177	118	90	28	59	66	20
1880–81	161	112	82	30	49	70	19
1881–82	161	99	66	33	62	61	22
1882–83	138	93	58	35	45	67	32
1883–84	150	105	75	30	45	70	25
1884–85	156	122	85	37	34	78	31
1885–86	158	122	83	39	36	77	29
1886–87	188	143	88	55	45	76	34
1887–88	225	158	102	56	67	70	32
1888–89	225	158	105	53	67	70	32
1889–90	262	189	122	67	73	72	41
1890–91	285	200	135	65	85	70	33
1891–92	370	257	140	117	113	69	48
1892–93	405	266	132	134	139	66	54
1893–94	367	279	129	150	88	76	56
1894–95	418	310	139	171	108	75	74
1895–96	475	380	171	209	95	80	82
1896–97	490	408	186	222	82	88	82
1897–98	551	490	229	261	61	89	77
1898–99	564	503	212	291	61	89	78
1899–00	613	557	236	321	56	91	67
1900–01	655	605	252	353	50	92	88
1901–02	633	584	247	337	49	92	92
1902–03	644	600	241	359	44	93	94
1903–04	743	695	272	423	48	94	111
1904–05	766	711	286	425	55	93	114
1905–06	727	716	295	421	11	98	118
1906–07	705	696	260	436	9	99	126
1907–08	719	712	276	436	7	99	122
1908–09	690	680	256	424	10	99	121
1909–10	765	759	257	502	6	99	˙127
1910–11	790	778	240	538	12	98	135
1911–12*	808	795	215†	580	18‡	98	145

Other important additions to the library were collections of very rare early Acts of Massachusetts, New Hampshire, and Ohio; a large collection of early English Colonial Laws; an almost complete set of the Pennsylvania District Ordinances;

* Up to October 30, 1911.

† 21 Harvard Seniors who have completed the full College course, but have not received their diplomas, are reckoned as graduates. Prior to 1905–06 Harvard Seniors were not reckoned as graduates but as non-graduates.

‡ Eight of the thirteen non-graduates are graduates of law schools.

Instructors	Studies and Text-books	Exercises per week	Number of students examined
	First Year		
Prof. Wambaugh and Mr. Joseph Warren	Agency. Wambaugh's Cases on Agency	2	324
Asst. Prof. Scott	Civil Procedure at Common Law. Ames's Cases on Pleading (2d ed.)	2	309
Prof. Williston	Contracts. Williston's Cases on Contracts	3	305
Prof. Wyman; Prof. Beale and Asst.	Criminal Law and Procedure. Beale's Cases on Criminal Law (2d ed.)	2	302
Prof. Scott; Prof. Warren	Property. Gray's Cases on Property, vols. 1, 2 (2d ed.)	2	322
Prof. Thayer	Torts. Cases on Torts: Ames, vol. 1 (3d ed.), Smith, vol. 2 (2d ed.)	2	317
	Second Year		
Prof. Brannan	Bills of Exchange and Promissory Notes. Ames's Cases on Bills and Notes and Brannan's Negotiable Instruments Law	2	90
Prof. Thayer	Evidence. Thayer's Cases on Evidence (2d ed.)	2	266
Prof. Pound	Jurisdiction and Procedure in Equity. Ames's Cases in Equity Jurisdiction, vol. 1	2	267
Prof. Gray and Mr. Gray	Property. Gray's Cases on Property, vols. 3, 4 (2d ed.)	2	269
Prof. Williston	Sales of Personal Property. Williston's Cases on Sales	2	256
Mr. Dutch	Admiralty. Ames's Cases on Admiralty	1	7
Prof. Williston	Bankruptcy. Williston's Cases on Bankruptcy	1	41
Prof. Beale	Carriers. Beale's Cases on Carriers (2d ed.)	1	198
Prof. Wambaugh	Insurance. Wambaugh's Cases on Insurance	1	63
Prof. Brannan	Damages. Beale's Cases on Damages (2d ed.)	1	14
Mr. Joseph Warren	Persons. Smith's Cases on Persons	1	19
Prof. Wyman	Public Service Companies. Wyman's Cases on Public Service Companies	1	189
Prof. Pound	Quasi-Contracts. Scott's Cases on Quasi-Contracts (2d ed.)	1	19

Third Year

Professor	Course		
Prof. Beale	Conflict of Laws. Beale's Cases on the Conflict of Laws	2	168
Prof. Wambaugh	Constitutional Law. Thayer's Cases on Constitutional Law	3	102
Prof. Warren	Corporations. Warren's Cases on Private Corporations	2	191
Prof. Brannan	Partnership. Ames's Cases on Partnership	2	22
Prof. Gray	Property. Gray's Cases on Property, vols. 5, 6 (2d ed.)	2	59
Prof. Wyman	Suretyship and Mortgage. Ames's Cases on Suretyship. Wyman's Cases on Mortgage (revised ed.)	2	106
Asst. Prof. Scott	Trusts. Ames's Cases on Trusts (2d ed.)	2	170
Prof. Brannan	Bills of Exchange and Promissory Notes. Ames's Cases on Bills and Notes and Brannan's Negotiable Instruments Law	2	18
Prof. Thayer	E . . . Thayer's Cases on Evidence	2	5
Prof. Pound	Jurisdiction and Procedure in Equity. Ames's Cases in Equity Jurisdiction, vol. 1	2	1
Prof. Gray and Mr. Gray	Property II. Gray's Cases on Property, vols. 3, 4 (2d ed.)	2	6
Prof. Williston	Sales of Personal Property. Williston's Cases on Sales	2	5
Mr. Dutch	Admiralty. Ames's Cases on Admiralty	1	2
Prof. Williston	Bankruptcy. Williston's Cases on Bankruptcy	1	62
Prof. Beale	Carriers. Beale's Cases on Carriers	1	10
Prof. Brannan	Damages. Beale's Cases on Damages	1	23
Prof. Pound	Equity III. Ames's Cases in Equity Jurisdiction, vol. 2	1	113
Prof. Wambaugh	Insurance. Wambaugh's Cases on Insurance	1	32
Prof. Beale	Municipal Corporations. Smith's Cases on Municipal Corporations	1	32
Prof. Wyman	Public Service Companies. Wyman's Cases on Public Service Companies	1	9
Mr. Joseph Warren	Persons. Smith's Cases on Persons	1	15
Prof. Pound	Quasi-Contracts. Scott's Cases on Quasi-Contracts	1	7

Fourth Year

Professor	Course		
Prof. Wyman	Administrative Law. Goodnow's Cases on Administrative Law and Cases on Officers	1	1
Prof. Beale	History of the Common Law. No text-book	1	1
Prof. Wambaugh	International Law. Scott's Cases on International Law	1	2
Prof. Beale	Jurisprudence. No text-book	1	3
Prof. Pound	Roman Law. No text-book	2	1

15 volumes of early Constitutional Convention Proceedings; Pynson's Nova Statuta of 1496–97; an edition of the tract entitled "Diversity of Courts," printed by Pynson in 1526; a first edition of Fitzherbert's Book of Justices; and a collection in 477 volumes of the Reports of the Supreme Court and the Courts of Appeal of the Argentine Republic.

The collection of portraits of judges and lawyers has been increased during the year by 7 engravings, 6 photographs, 1 photogravure, and 1 lithograph. Four colored prints of buildings were also added.

It was voted by the Faculty that beginning with the year 1911–12, every candidate for the degree of Bachelor of Laws will be required to take twelve hours a week in the second year, instead of ten hours a week as heretofore. It was also voted that hereafter students in the second year shall not be allowed to remain in the School unless they obtain an average on the work of that year at least five per cent higher than the usual passing mark. This is additional to the existing requirement that no student may remain in the School who has more than two conditions standing against him, and carries further the policy of making a high standard of capacity and diligence a condition of remaining in the School. The wisdom of this policy has been confirmed by experience.

As will be seen by the table, the courses in Criminal Law and in Civil Procedure have each been extended to cover two hours a week.

During the year an additional scholarship with an income of $250 has been established through the generosity of anonymous friends of the School. The purpose of this scholarship is to encourage research in problems of law reform, and it is to be awarded to a student of the fourth-year class who, in the opinion of the Faculty, gives promise of ability to do effective work in the investigation of such problems. The holder will be required to write a dissertation embodying the results of his study. This scholarship has already been awarded to a graduate of the Class of 1911.

With the approval of the Corporation the Faculty voted to offer two prizes of $200 and $100 respectively to the winners of a competition between law clubs in the second-year class. These prizes were offered from the income of the gift of $10,000 made by Mrs. James Barr Ames in fulfilment of a wish expressed by Mr. Ames, and mentioned in last year's report. This use of the income from Mr. Ames's generous gift was deemed appropriate in view of the great interest which he always felt in the law clubs. The competition should result in substantial benefit to the work of the law clubs, both of the first and second year. It will hereafter be open only to second-year clubs, the members of which have attended faithfully and systematically to their law club work during their first year.

The Board of Advisers appointed, as explained in the last report, from the third-year class, has the task of regulating the competition, and of supervising the work of the first-year law clubs in order to see that it is kept up to the required standard of excellence. Last year's experience gave good reason for believing that the advisers can help the first-year men greatly both in their law club work and in other ways. The duties of the board have been extended this year, and the membership has been increased to eight.

EZRA RIPLEY THAYER, Dean.

THE FACULTY OF MEDICINE.

To the President of the University: —

Sir, — As Dean of the Faculty of Medicine, I have the honor to present my report for the academic year 1910–11.

In recent years there has been a steady increase in the number of physicians taking courses in the Medical School. Such of these courses as are offered in the summer months, constituting a Summer School of Medicine, were reorganized in 1908–09 with a Director in charge, and this form of organization has been a success. During the present year, the Faculty voted to organize graduate courses into a definite subdivision of the Faculty of Medicine, with a Dean, and an administrative board in charge, and this form of organization will be put into effect during the next year. It is believed that many improvements in the courses will result from this change, and that an important part of the work of a Medical School, namely, furnishing to physicians the opportunity of improving their equipment for work, will be developed more systematically.

Last year announcement was made of courses leading to the degree of Doctor of Public Health. During this year, eight students registered in these courses, and to two the degree was awarded in June. This new degree appears to have aroused much interest, and the character of preparation and work determined upon as the requirement for this degree very generally has been commended.

The report of the first year of Dr. Dexter's work as Director of Scholarships indicates that this form of administration of student aid has been a success. Many conferences were held by Dr. Dexter with students seeking aid, and, in addition to those receiving scholarships, twenty-six men were helped with $2,225, very largely in the form of loans. Sums of money, large or small, can, I am confident, be used wisely through Dr. Dexter to aid deserving students.

Last year's report made mention of a close affiliation between the Peter Bent Brigham Hospital and the Harvard Medical School. During the current year, similar affiliations were made with other hospitals, so that in addition to the Peter Bent Brigham Hospital, the Children's Hospital, the Infants' Hospital, the Infants' Asylum, the Children's Department of the Boston Dispensary, and the Free Hospital for Women are now organized with the continuous service plan, the Chief-of-Staff in each case appointed on nomination from the Medical School. This insures to the Medical School ample clinical facilities to which men desired to fill positions in the Medical School may be called, with no limitations as to their place of residence. Now the same freedom of choice in clinical teachers is possible that has long existed in the case of laboratory teachers. Such hospitals constitute a very considerable addition to the plant available to the Harvard Medical School for teaching and investigation, and give the opportunity for the development of the clinical branches on a scale commensurate with that of the laboratory branches, provided the necessary endowment is procured. Enlarged opportunities call for increased funds. It is believed that new and large sums of money can be wisely expended in connection with these developments, and must be forthcoming if the Harvard Medical School is to develop symmetrically and broadly. Friends of the School have provided a splendid group of buildings and means of maintenance for the laboratory departments, which we believe is being used well. Similar generosity is now asked for the clinical departments.

Construction began during the year on the Peter Bent Brigham, the Infants', and the Collis P. Huntington Memorial Hospitals, all on land immediately adjacent to the Medical School buildings. Of these the Collis P. Huntington Memorial Hospital is for the investigation of cancer under the auspices of the Cancer Commission of Harvard University. Funds for its erection were secured through the enthusiastic efforts of Dr. J. Collins Warren, who already in many ways has rendered inestimable service to the Medical School.

Assistant Professor Wolbach spent a portion of the year on the West Coast of Africa in company with Dr. J. L. Todd of McGill University, the two making up an expedition under the auspices of the Liverpool School of Tropical Medicine. They studied sleeping sickness, and other protozoan diseases, collecting much material for subsequent investigation and instruction. Such an expedition is a new activity for the Medical School.

Through the generosity of Dr. F. C. Shattuck, the Henry P. Walcott Fellowship in Clinical Medicine has been established, paying a stipend of $1000, to enable some recent graduate to conduct clinical investigation. In its purpose, in its name, and from its donor, this Fellowship is most welcome.

During the year the Rebecca A. Greene bequest of $25,000 for general Medical School purposes became available. Such unrestricted gifts are particularly useful to the School. There have been also many gifts for immediate use for various special purposes, aggregating in all $27,239.90. These gifts make possible much investigation that could not be undertaken otherwise.

No great changes have been made during the year 1910–11 in methods of instruction. The death of three of the officers of the Medical School, Dr. Thomas Dwight, Parkman Professor of Anatomy; Dr. Walter R. Brinckerhoff, Assistant Professor of Pathology, and Dr. Emma W. Mooers, Custodian of the Neuropathological Collection, have brought changes in the School that will be long felt.

In February and June 101 men were recommended to the President and Fellows for degrees: —

Medical School	For the degree of M.D. (February)		8
	" " " *cum laude* (February)		1
	" " " (June)		61
	" " " *cum laude* (June) .		17
	" " Dr.P.H. (June)		2
			89
Dental School	For the degree of D.M.D. (February) . . .		0
	" " " (June)		10
	" " " *cum laude* (June)		2
			12
	Total		101

HENRY A. CHRISTIAN, *Dean.*

THE MEDICAL SCHOOL

Sir, — As Dean of the Medical School I have the honor of presenting my report for the academic year 1910–11.

The Administrative Board was constituted as follows: Drs. H. A. Christian, C. M. Green, F. B. Harrington, G. G. Sears, F. B. Mallory, J. L. Morse, W. B. Cannon, John Warren, and E. E. Southard.

The Faculty Council was composed of the following: Drs. H. A. Christian, W. T. Councilman, G. G. Sears, Myles Standish, W. B: Cannon, John Warren (Secretary), J. B. Blake, and the President of the University.

Buildings and Grounds. — Numerous minor changes have been made in the various buildings. On the roof of Building E a commodious animal house has been erected for the use of the Department of Surgery. In the rear of Building B, two lawn tennis courts have been built by the Athletic Association of the University.

Anatomy. — The Department of Anatomy has suffered a great loss in the death of Professor Dwight. Dr. Dwight had been connected with the Medical School since 1872 as a teacher of Anatomy, and for twenty-eight years had served as Parkman Professor of Anatomy, having succeeded Dr. Oliver Wendell Holmes in 1883. Dr. Dwight had done very much to develop the teaching and research work in the Department, and had made most valuable additions to its collections and to the Anatomical part of the Museum of the School. As a teacher and investigator he will be a great loss to the Department and to the Medical School. In 1910–11 Professor Dwight gave all the regular lectures of the first-year course. In spite of the fact that his physical condition was such as to cause most men to give up work, his abilities as a lecturer were never seen to better advantage. He also added to his former communications on variations in the bones, and among other contributions reported a case of a secondary cuboid bone in both feet, which is practically unique. He continued to take an active share in the administration of his Department until the end.

Dr. Warren has published studies on the paraphysis and pineal region in reptilia, and Dr. Z. B. Adams on the relations of the articular process of the vertebrae in the production of congenital scoliosis.

The first-year course in Anatomy has been rearranged so that dental and medical students will receive separate instruction, and the work for each has been modified in a way to improve this instruction.

Physiology. — Instruction has been improved by total separation of medical and dental students. This change has permitted trying the experiment of giving to adequately trained medical students the alternatives of routine laboratory work, and special research. In consequence, nine students of medicine were engaged in investigation during the course. Of these Messrs. A. T. Shohl and W. S. Wright finished with Professor Cannon an investigation on emotional glycosuria; J. C. Aub and C. A. L. Binger secured interesting results in observations on the effect of nicotine on the secretion of the adrenal glands; Mr. A. L. Washburn obtained important evidence as to the nature of hunger.

The Staff of the Department has been carrying on researches while not engaged in teaching as follows: Mr. E. L. Porter on irritability of the central nervous system; Dr. J. B. Ayer on the effects of intrathoracic and atmospheric pressure on cardiac activity; Assistant Professor Martin on the standardization of electrical stimulation and the application of these methods to physiological problems; Dr. Alexander Forbes on the dynamics of inhibition and stimulation in spinal reflexes; Professor Cannon on the mechanical factors of digestion, and with Dr. D. de la Paz on the influence of emotional states on adrenal secretion, and with Dr. R. G. Hoskins on the effects of asphyxia, hyperpnoea, and sensory stimulation on the activity of the adrenal glands.

During the year the laboratory was also used by Dr. Hoskins (Professor of Physiology at Starling-Ohio Medical College), in a critical investigation of biological methods of testing for epinephrin, and by Drs. F. T. Murphy and Beth Vincent in a study of the cause of death in intestinal obstruction.

Comparative Physiology. — The following investigations were conducted during the year: Dr. Russell Richardson, an instrument for measuring the blood flow through perfused organs; Drs. W. M. Boothby and A. Ehrenfried, the technique used in the transplantation of organs, and an improved apparatus for anaesthesia; Miss A. H. Turner (Associate Professor of Zoölogy at Mt. Holyoke College), the electrical properties of muscle, and, with Professor Porter, the nervous control of respiration. Professor Porter worked out improvements in certain physiological apparatus, and confirmed by a new method his discovery of the vasoconstrictor nerves of the heart.

Bacteriology. — The particularly notable event was the taking up of his duties by Assistant Professor Wolbach in the autumn of 1910, and his departure on the expedition of the Liverpool School of Tropical Medicine to the Gambia, holding the added position of Sheldon Travelling Fellow. During the year Assistant Professor Wolbach has published papers on swamp fever in horses (with J. L. Todd), cell inclusions in granulomatous lesions, trachoma (with S. H. McKee) and colophonium in certain staining reactions. A considerable part of the work on several of these papers was done in this laboratory. The results of the expedition to the Gambia are being worked out, and the first report on the diagnosis and distribution of human trypanosomiasis in the Gambia has been published. Subsequent reports will deal with parasitic protozoa found in animals, a malarial index of the Gambia, chronic ulcers, and filtration experiments with trypanosomes. Collateral work of Dr. Wolbach's part of the expedition was the collecting of flies for Professor Thaxter, and a considerable number of insects and small animals for the Museum of Comparative Zoölogy in Cambridge, so that the benefits of the expedition extend beyond the Medical School.

The work of the Department has gone on as usual, with a fair degree of success.

Pathology. — During the past year the laboratory has suffered a great loss in the death of Assistant Professor Brinckerhoff. Dr. Brinckerhoff, after serving as an assistant here in Pathology, took charge of the United States Government Station for the Investigation of Leprosy at Molokai, where he remained for four years, until his appointment as Assistant Professor of Pathology at Harvard. He was an able and indefatigable investigator and an unusual teacher, combining rare skill in the orderly presentation of knowledge with the faculty of stimulating enthusiasm in the student. The place made vacant by the death of Dr. Brinckerhoff has been filled by the appointment of Dr. Howard T. Karsner, formerly a teacher in the University of Pennsylvania. Assistant Professor Karsner's work in the Department will be principally in experimental pathology. Dr. Richards resigned his position as Instructor in Pathology to accept a position in Clinical Medicine in the newly organized Department of Medicine in the University of Minnesota.

The laboratory continues to render a valuable service to physicians and to hospitals without a pathological department in making post-mortem examinations and in examining material. During the past year there have been 191 post-mortem examinations, and 980 specimens have been examined and reported upon. The cost of conducting this work is to some extent met by charges, and the material so obtained is of great service in teaching.

The pathological laboratories of the Massachusetts General Hospital and the Boston City Hospital render a valuable service, being used chiefly in teaching students in elective and graduate courses.

Comparative Pathology. — At the beginning of the year the Department lost the services of Dr. E. L. Walker, who accepted a position with the Philippine Government, for which he was to continue his researches in medical zoölogy. Dr. Walker was an indefatigable worker here, and the author of a number of papers.

During the year seven publications appeared from the Department, and several others were nearly ready for the press. Mr. J. H. Brown, assisted by a grant from the Rockefeller Institute for Medical Research, studied a number of cultures of anaerobic bacteria. A considerable amount of work was done, with the aid of a fund generously contributed by several persons, upon the possible relation of infantile paralysis to household pets and other domestic animals. In this work Mr. Carlon Ten Broeck gave very material assistance.

Preventive Medicine and Hygiene. — The degree of Doctor of Public Health was awarded to Dr. Edward B. Beasley, who presented a thesis entitled " An Investigation on the Permeability of Slow Sand Filters to Bacillus Typhosus," and to Dr. Arthur I. Kendall, with a thesis upon " Certain Fundamental Principles Relating to the Activity of Bacteria in the Intestinal Tract: Their Relation to Therapeutics." Dr. F. M. Allen, Charles Follen Folsom Teaching Fellow, continued his study of metabolism in relation to infection; Drs. W. P. Lucas and H. L. Amoss investigated the vaccine treatment in the prevention of dysentery; Dr. A. I. Kendall continued his studies upon intestinal bacteria, and published a number of papers. In some of the publications Dr. Kendall has been associated with Drs. C. A. Herter, A. W. Walker, R. M. Smith, T. M. Rotch, A. A. Day, and M. R. Edwards.

Professor Rosenau served on a Commission appointed by Governor Draper to study the milk question and report the draft of a bill to the Legislature. He also completed a study of organic matter in the expired breath, prepared a section on Tropical Diseases with Dr. J. F. Anderson in a Handbook of Practical Treatment, and with Drs. Amoss and Sheppard conducted experimental investigations on anterior poliomyelitis. Dr. E. H. Schorer, Fellow in Preventive Medicine and Hygiene, is studying milk in its relation to public health, under the auspices of the Milk and Baby Hygiene Association, and in connection with this is investigating various problems of scientific and practical interest.

One of the rooms in the Department has been set aside for a Board of Officers from the United States Navy, who will investigate certain hygienic problems connected with submarine boats.

In numerous ways members of the Department have again taken an active interest in philanthropic and public health movements which have a bearing upon preventive medicine, and have coöperated in the work of several of the public health organizations of the community.

Pharmacology. — Dr. Louis Nelson studied the chemistry of recin; Drs. Emerson and Nelson, the action of caffein and its salts; Dr. D. H. Williams, chaparro amargoso; Dr. L. M. Freedman, the galvanic reaction of nystagmus; and Dr. Hartwell completed his studies on the artificial circulation in the extirpated liver.

Theory and Practice of Physic. — The investigations mentioned in last year's report as being made by Professor Christian and Drs. R. M. Smith, Walker, Talbot, Pratt, Spooner, and C. Frothingham, Jr., were continued, and in large part have been completed and published.

Clinical Medicine. — In February, Dr. James Marsh Jackson, after many years of fruitful service, resigned, and Dr. G. Cheever Shattuck was appointed as Assistant in his place. Dr. C. H. Lawrence, Jr., served through the greater part of the year as Henry P. Walcott Fellow, and the results of his investigations are soon to be published. Only minor changes were made in the general scheme of student instruction. Publications by the members of the Department were numerous, as already listed in the *Gazette.*

Pediatrics. — A notable increase in the teaching service and in the amount of valuable clinical material has been made during the year. Drs. Fritz B. Talbot and Richard M. Smith, Fellows, conduct instruction for fourth-year men and graduates at the Massachusetts General Hospital, where the Department of Children has been placed under the direction of Dr. Talbot, assisted by Dr. Smith. Dr. Bowditch has been given charge of the Massachusetts Infants' Asylum, and about thirty beds have thus been rendered available for teaching throughout the year. In like manner Dr. Lucas has been appointed to a continuous service in the Children's Department of the Boston Dispensary, which not only renders available for teaching purposes a clinic amounting to about 11,000 children in the year, but will also later add to the teaching service about thirty hospital beds.

Publications from members of the Department have been reported in the *Gazette*. Among these are papers by Professor Rotch, Assistant Professor Morse, and Drs. Ladd, Dunn, Bowditch, Lucas, Talbot, Smith, and Place.

Surgery. — The Department has to report with regret the resignation of Dr. F. T. Murphy, who resigned his position as Assistant in Surgery to become Professor of Surgery in Washington University, St. Louis.

The course in genito-urinary surgery previously given in eight lectures at the Medical School, in October and November, was rearranged, and the instruction was given in sixteen clinical lectures at the Boston City Hospital from February to June, by Dr. Paul Thorndike, and the section work was given by Dr. Hugh Cabot at the Massachusetts General Hospital.

The Laboratory of Surgical Research was in continuous use during the year under the immediate charge of Dr. John Homans. Papers based on work done in the laboratory have been published by Drs. Homans, Vincent, Osgood and Lucas, and Quinby, and have been recorded in the *University Gazette*. The facilities of the laboratory have been greatly augmented by the construction of an animal house on the roof of Building E, well equipped for the care of animals. Rooms previously used for this purpose are utilized for other uses.

The Animal Farm noted in the previous report is in operation, and has materially helped not alone the work of the Surgical Department, but the other departments in the Medical School, by facilitating the securing and taking care of animals.

During the year fifty-one papers on surgical subjects were published by the members of the Department of Surgery, and were noted in the *Gazette*.

Obstetrics and Gynaecology. — Instruction in these allied subjects has continued essentially the same as in the preceding year. In clinical teaching the Harvard Medical School is richly provided for. In Obstetrics, the Boston Lying-in Hospital affords an ample clinic, and each student receives a large amount of clinical instruction. Each group of students has the entire time of a graduate house-officer in the observation and supervision of his work, in addition to the instruction of the visiting staff in pathological cases. In the class receiving the degree in June, 1911, the average number of obstetrical cases attended under supervision and instruction was twenty-two, more than three times the number required for the degree, and this was in addition to numerous cases observed in the work of the Hospital. To still further increase the clinical instruction, the Department has received the generous offer of the Harvard Medical School Alumni Association to provide a salary for an Alumni Assistant, a graduate who will devote the greater part of his time to individual clinical instruction.

In Gynaecology the School has an ample clinic at the Boston Dispensary, the Free Hospital for Women, and the Boston City Hospital. During the year arrangements have been consummated by which the Free Hospital for Women has become closely affiliated with the Harvard Medical School, and Dr. William P. Graves, the Surgeon-in-Chief, has been made a Professor in Gynaecology.

Warren Anatomical Museum. — The chief addition to the Museum was the splendid gift by the late Dr. Charles G. Weld of the Tello collection of ancient trephined Peruvian skulls, numbering about 500 specimens. Another valuable gift was from Dr. Henry O. Feiss of Cleveland, Ohio, of working models showing the mechanism of scoliosis and deformities of the pelvis. The Curator has added about 200 specimens, chiefly of new growths removed in the Surgical Service of the Massachusetts General Hospital. The work of re-carding the specimens has progressed satisfactorily, and adds greatly to the appearance of the shelves.

During the year the Museum lost a devoted friend by the death of Professor Dwight, who gave much of his time to the part devoted to Anatomy, and the collection of variations of bones, especially of the vertebrae, will be a lasting monument to his patience and zeal.

Proctor Fund for the Study of Chronic Diseases. — During the year appropriations were made from this Fund as follows: to Dr. J. H. Pratt for the continuation of his work on the study of pancreatic disease; to Dr. W. P. Lucas for experimental work on the coagulation of the blood; to Dr. F. T. Lord for the continuation of his work on actinomycosis; to Dr. R. M. Smith for experimental studies on diseases of the heart and kidney; to Dr. R. B. Osgood for the continuation of experimental investigations in poliomyelitis; and to Dr. F. M. Allen for experimental studies of diabetes. $1000 yearly for four years was appropriated from the accrued income for the care of patients with cancer in the new Huntington Memorial Hospital, which has been erected on the grounds of the Harvard Medical School. It was thought that the use of the Fund for the investigation of cancer was among the purposes for which the Fund was given. In view of the important aid which the Proctor Fund has given to the study of chronic diseases, it is the desire of the Trustees of the Huntington Memorial Hospital to name one of the beds in this Hospital the Proctor Bed.

The Proctor Fund has been of increasing usefulness. The requests for assistance from the Fund have multiplied. Up to the present time it has been used chiefly to further laboratory and experimental investigation of chronic conditions. Its usefulness in the future will be greatly increased by the erection in close relation to the School of the group of hospitals of which the Huntington Memorial Hospital will be the first to be opened.

The Cancer Commission of Harvard University. — Research has been carried on under the direction of Dr. E. E. Tyzzer, who has been studying the nature of immunity reactions to tumors. He has also discovered a group of minute animal parasites, which, though having no direct bearing on the tumor problem, are of biological importance. They represent a new genus, and two distinct species of this genus have been discovered and described.

Dr. E. H. Risley has completed investigations on the serum treatment of cancer, on the diagnostic value of the haemolytic test for cancer, and on the Gilman-Coca vaccine treatment of cancer. His work has been carried on under the direction of the Cancer Commission at the Massachusetts General Hospital, where cordial coöperation in his work has been given by the administrative officers, the Trustees, and the Staff of the Hospital.

The building of the Collis P. Huntington Memorial Hospital, which now nears completion, marks a new era in the activities of this Commission. Primarily designed for the investigation of cancer as it occurs in the human being, it should provide the most approved treatment for a limited number of selected cases which are to remain under constant observation, so as to afford opportunity for a complete study of each case. The Hospital also furnishes facilities for an out-patient clinic. The more important functions of this Hospital will be to provide for the clinical investigation of cancer, improvement in the care of cancer patients, and facilities for the early diagnosis of the disease. Dr. Thomas Ordway, formerly Director of the Bender Hygienic Laboratory at Albany, New York, will serve as Physician-in-Charge of the Hospital.

Clinic in the Harvard Medical School. — During the year the Clinic has had 4,086 visits from patients for treatment. Of these, 1,511 were visits for the first time, or new patients. The development of the Clinic has been satisfactory. It has been in operation now for one and two-thirds years, gradually increasing in usefulness during this period.

Statistics. — The statistics of the School will be found in the following tables: —

FINAL EXAMINATIONS

	1907				1908				1909				1910				1911			
	Passed	Failed	Total	% Failed	Passed	Failed	Total	% Failed	Passed	Failed	Total	% Failed	Passed	Failed	Total	% Failed	Passed	Failed	Total	% Failed
First Class:																				
Comparative Anatomy	72	10	82	12	79	7	86	8	51	3	54	5	54	3	57	6	59	8	67	12
Biological Chemistry	63	11	74	15	64	15	79	19	47	17	64	26	58	5	63	9	48	11	59	18
Anatomy	62	13	75	17	65	16	81	20	54	9	63	14	62	2	64	3	61	6	67	10
Physiology	77	11	88	12	77	16	93	17	56	13	69	18	54	12	66	22	66	6	72	8
Second Class:																				
Pathological Anatomy	61	4	65	6	66	13	79	16	84	12	96	12	50	3	53	6	56	3	59	5
Bacteriology	54	15	69	22	62	22	84	26	81	12	93	12	53	2	55	4	59	4	63	6
Hygiene	51	17	68	25	73	5	78	6	87	3	90	3	48	3	51	6	58	0	58	0
Third Class:																				
Theory and Practice	65	1	66	1	60	6	66	9	60	7	67	10	95	3	98	3	53	2	55	4
Surgery	64	1	65	1	62	3	65	5	68	1	69	1	90	0	90	0	50	0	50	0
Obstetrics	60	7	67	10	58	9	67	13	69	16	85	19	84	9	93	10	51	2	53	4
Pediatrics	69	0	69	0	67	0	67	0	75	0	75	0	89	3	92	3	51	2	53	4
Dermatology	65	3	68	4	61	8	69	12	70	7	77	9	93	2	95	2	53	2	55	4
Gynaecology	65	0	65	0	57	10	67	15	72	5	77	6	75	19	94	20	54	2	56	4
Neurology	62	5	67	7	66	4	70	6	74	2	76	3	87	6	93	7	55	2	57	4
Therapeutics	59	16	75	21	59	13	72	18	68	14	82	17	84	10	94	12	31	4	35	11
Clinical Medicine	62	7	69	10	63	7	70	10	73	7	80	9	89	3	92	3	56	0	56	0
Clinical Surgery	63	0	63	0	61	0	61	0	73	0	73	0	90	0	90	0	54	0	54	0
Syphilis	66	0	66	0	64	0	66	0	78	0	78	0	87	4	91	5	52	2	54	4
Ophthalmology	71	2	73	3	59	7	67	10	69	11	80	14	91	2	93	2	49	2	51	4
Otology	65	1	66	1	64	3	68	5	73	1	74	1	92	1	93	1	53	0	53	0
Laryngology	64	2	66	3	66	2	68	3	73	0	73	0	90	2	92	2	53	0	53	0
Psychiatry	66	0	66	0	65	3	68	4	73	2	75	2	91	0	91	0	53	0	58	0

Fourth Class. — Electives: [*]

	1	2	3	4	5	6	7	8	9
Anatomy	40	49	49	38	34	30	31	88	88
Comparative Anatomy	.	.	.	8	8	4	4	8	8
Embryology	.	8	8	.	.	0	0	0	0
Physiology	1	10	10	2	9	8	8	8	8
Comparative Physiology	.	2	2	0	0	0	0	1	1
Biochemistry	2	5	5	1	1	2	2	2	2
Bacteriology	6	.	.	1	1	1	1	4	4
Pathology	.	14	14	30	30	32	32	42	42
Comparative Pathology	.	2	2	3	3	1	1	5	5
Protozoölogy	2	.	.	.	.	2	2	0	0
Neuropathology	6	.	.	1	1	4	4	3	3
Preventive Medicine and Hygiene	.	1	1	0	0	3	3	19	19
Pharmacology	66	.	.	.	.	9	9	5	5
Medicine	28	83	84	49	50	111	111	110	110
Theory and Practice	65	45	45	46	46	59	59	68	63
Pediatrics	6	70	70	47	47	72	72	93	98
Clinical Surgical Pathology	.	2	2	0	.	1	1	3	3
Roentgen Ray	66	.	.	58	59	1	1	4	4
Surgery	.	102	102	58	59	94	94	95	95
Genito-Urinary Surgery	17	6	6	3	3	1	1	0	0
Orthopedics	2	19	19	21	21	17	17	23	23
Surgical Pathology	59	2	2	0	0	1	1	0	0
Obstetrics	20	58	58	51	51	58	58	72	72
Gynecology	8	25	25	24	24	24	24	40	40
Dermatology and Syphilis	19	3	3	8	8	1	1	17	17
Neurology and Psychiatry	1	28	28	11	11	22	22	14	14
Ophthalmology	1	9	9	1	1	3	3	5	5
Otology	8	7	7	2	2	2	2	7	7
Laryngology	.	16	16	11	11	13	18	21	21

* In the table of electives, not the total number of students taking electives are enumerated, but the number of courses elected. Each course represents the work of one student for a period of one month. Eight electives constitute the work of the fourth year, but a student may take more than one month's work in a single subject. This system of fourth-year work went into effect in 1906.

GENERAL STATISTICS OF THE SCHOOL

Candidates for the Degree of Doctor of Medicine

New matriculants	80

The number of students in attendance : —

Fourth Class	88
Third Class	46
Second Class	54
First Class	76
Special Students	7
Total	271
Applicants for Degree of M.D. (February)	9
Applicants for Degree of M.D. (June)	81
	90
Rejected	3
Graduated	87

Of the 87 students who received the degree of Doctor of Medicine, 18 received the degree *cum laude*.

Candidates for the Degree of Doctor of Public Health

The number of students in attendance	8
Applicants for Degree of Dr.P.H. (June)	3
Rejected	1
Graduated	2

	SUMMER COURSES					GRADUATE COURSES				
	1907	1908	1909	1910	1911	1906–07	1907–08	1908–09	1909–10	1910–11
Courses taken	281½	178	291	299	510	93½	125	128	151	184
Students . .	194	136	210	197	267	68	81	111	111	153
Receipts . .	$8501.50	$4886.50	$8729.50	$8622	$13370	$2141	$2932.50	$3187	$3605.77	$4085

Students in courses of the regular medical curriculum . . .	271
Students in Graduate Medical courses	153
Students in Summer Medical courses	267
Students in Doctor of Public Health courses	8
Total students, October 1, 1910, to October 1, 1911, . .	699

HENRY A. CHRISTIAN, *Dean.*

THE DENTAL SCHOOL

To the President of the University: —

Sir, — As Dean of the Dental School I herewith hand you my report for the academic year 1910–11.

The enrolment of students was as follows: —

Graduate students	3
Third-year students	17
Second-year students	39
First-year students	57
	116

In the fall of 1909 our registered students numbered 88. This number was an increase of 24 students over our last registration in the old building on North Grove Street. Our registration for the session of 1910–11 numbered 116, an increase of 28 students over that of the previous year, and a total gain of 52 students since moving into our new building. This showing is a healthy indication of our new environment.

Instruction was given as follows: —

Anatomy. — Professor T. Dwight, Asst. Professor Warren, Demonstrator Cheever, Instructors Mosher and Shepard, Assistants Flagg, Hartwell, Green, Boothby, Ehrenfried, Whittemore, Smith, Fellow Adams. 424 hours.

Comparative Anatomy. — Professor Minot, Asst. Professor Lewis, Demonstrator Bremer, Instructors Williams, Shepard, Johnson, Teaching Fellow Danforth, Austin Teaching Fellow Heuser. 252 hours.

Physiology. — Professor Cannon, Instructors Martin and Forbes, Fellow Ayer, Austin Teaching Fellow Porter. 348 hours.

Physiological and Dental Chemistry. — Lecturer H. Carlton Smith, Assistant C. F. MacDonald, Jr. (Chemistry). 302 hours.

Bacteriology. — Professor H. C. Ernst, Asst. Professor Wolbach, Instructor Frothingham, Assistants Page, Perry, Worthington, Everett, and Tobey, Austin Teaching Fellow Floyd. 160 hours.

Materia Medica and Therapeutics. — Professor E. C. Briggs, Instructor Cooper. 38 hours.

Dental Pathology. — Professor C. A. Brackett. 32 hours.

Neurology. — Instructor Taylor. 4 hours.

Crown and Bridge Work. — Professor Cooke, Instructors Eldred and Hovestadt. 128 hours.

Orthodontia. — Professor E. H. Smith, Asst. Professor Baker, Instructor Howe. 128 hours.

Orthodontia, Juniors. — Asst. Professor BAKER. 10 hours.

Prosthetic Dentistry, Juniors. — Asst. Professor CROSS. 32 hours.

Prosthetic Dentistry, Laboratory, Seniors.— Asst. Professor CROSS, Instructors
  HAYDEN, HALEY, L. A. ROGERS, CLARK, LANGLEY, Demonstrator KAZAN-
  JIAN. 496 hours.

Prosthetic Dentistry, Laboratory, Juniors. — Asst. Professor CROSS, Instructors
  DORT, EAMES, FURBISH, PETERS, and BECKFORD, Assistant STRANGMAN,
  Demonstrator KAZANJIAN. 544 hours.

Anatomical Articulation, Mechanical Treatment of Fractured Jaws, Cleft Palates,
  and other Deformities. — Asst. Professor CROSS. 21 hours.

Extracting and Anaesthesia. — Professor POTTER, Instructors FARRINGTON,
  SQUAREBRIGS, STONE, MIDGLEY, GILPATRIC, and NORWOOD. 477 hours.

Porcelain Inlays and Carving Teeth. — Instructors HADLEY and MOFFATT.
  142 hours.

Roentgenology. — Assistant CUMMINGS. 208 hours.

Surgery, Surgical Pathology, and Oral Surgery. — Professor MONKS, 12 lectures
  and demonstrations; Professor MONKS, Instructor MINER, Assistant TAFT,
  clinics, 160 hours. Instructor BLAKE, 9 clinics at City Hospital.

Syphilis. — Instructor C. MORTON SMITH. 6 lectures and clinics.

Oral Hygiene. — Lecturer GEORGE H. WRIGHT. 15 lectures and clinics at Nose
  and Throat Department, Massachusetts General Hospital.

Operative Dentistry, Seniors. — Professor POTTER. 32 hours.

Operative Dentistry, Juniors. — Lecturer DILL. 32 hours.

Operative Dentistry, Infirmary, Seniors. — Professor SMITH, Instructors LOVE-
  LAND, JEWELL, EDDY, BLAISDELL, FURFEY, PAUL, STANLEY, ELLIOTT, and
  COOPER. 624 hours.

Operative Dentistry, Infirmary, Juniors. — Lecturer DILL, Instructors LITTIG,
  WHITEHILL, PIKE, STEVENS, WHITCHURCH, COOPER, WYMAN, SPINNEY,
  CHUTE, LEAVITT, F. T. TAYLOR, Assistants O. S. SMITH and ESTES.

The work of the School is outlined in the following tables: —

OPERATIVE DEPARTMENT

No. of treatments of teeth and gums	1,888
" " " pyorrhoea alveolaris	120
" sets of teeth cleaned	1,211
" fillings — gold	936
" " gutta percha	371
" " cement	1,365
" " amalgam	1,740
" " amalgam and cement	1,140
" " silicate	260
" patients	3,199
" operations	9,868

PROSTHETIC DEPARTMENT
Service to Patients

No. of sets of artificial teeth 176
" " " " repaired 102
" partial sets of artificial teeth 136

Practice Work

No. of specimen plates 254

ORTHODONTIA
Service to Patients

No. of patients treated for irregularities of the teeth 36
" appliances 99
" models of regulating cases 68

Practice Work

No. of appliances for irregularities of the teeth 126
" models for regulating cases 42

CROWN AND BRIDGE WORK
Service to Patients

No. of crowns and caps 92
" crowns repaired 22
" pieces of bridge work 54
" " " repaired 24

Practice Work

No. of crowns and caps 201
" bridges 114
" carved teeth models 14

INLAY WORK
Service to Patients

No. of porcelain inlays and tips 36
" gold inlays 58

Practice Work

No. of porcelain inlays 80
" gold inlays 80

FRACTURED JAWS
Service to Patients

No. of cases 29
" appliances 29

Practice Work

No. of appliances 44

ARTIFICIAL PALATES

SERVICE TO PATIENTS

No. of cleft palates   2
  "   "   palate appliances   4

SURGICAL DEPARTMENT

No. of patients   570
  " cases of stomatitis   4
  "   "   non-erupted teeth   6
  "   "   syphilis   4
  "   "   alveolar abscess   26
  "   "   impacted lower third molars   12
  "   "   tri-facial neuralgia   1
  "   "   necrosis   6
  "   "   fibroma   4
  "   "   cysts   3
  "   "   alveola sinus   6
  "   "   chronic osteitis   1
  "   "   imbedded roots with abscess   2
  "   "   imbedded root involving antrum   1
  "   "   amputation of root   5
  "   "   maxillary sinusitis   7
  "   "   cervical adenitis   2
  "   "   mucus cyst of lip   1
  "   "   acute pyorrhea   2
  "   "   ranula   1
  "   "   replantation   1
  "   "   stricture of Stenson's duct   1
  "   "   tubercular abscess   1
  "   "   neuroma   2
  "   "   sarcoma   2
  "   "   carcinoma   1
  "   "   fractured jaws   4
  " radiographs   208

SUMMARY

No. of operations in Prosthetic Department   801
  "   "   Operative Department   9,067
  "   "   Surgical Department   3,406
                                       ————
                                      13,274

An evening course was conducted from October 25 until March 14, open to graduates and practitioners of repute. The following subjects were offered: —

Porcelain Inlays. JOHN Q. BRYAM, D.D.S., Indiana Dental College, Indianapolis, Ind.

The Muscles of Facial Expression. GEORGE H. MONKS, M.D., Harvard Medical and Dental Schools.

Anatomical Articulation, Correctable Impression, Cleft Palate and Fractured Jaws. HAROLD DEW. CROSS, D.M.D.

Crown and Bridge. JULIUS F. HOVESTADT, D.M.D.

Relation of Mastication to the Work of the Digestive Glands. WALTER B. CANNON, M.D., Harvard Medical School.

Diseases of the Heart. FRANCIS W. PALFREY, M.D., Harvard Medical School.

Inlay Technique. HENRY W. GILLETT, M.D., New York, N.Y.

Syphilis. C. MORTON SMITH, M.D., Harvard Medical and Dental Schools.

Sterilization. WILLIAM H. POTTER, D.M.D.

Roentgen Rays. EARLE C. CUMMINGS, D.M.D.

Orthodontia. CALVIN S. CASE, D.D.S., M.D., Chicago College of Dental Surgery, Chicago.

Interstitial Gingivitis. EDWARD C. BRIGGS, D.M.D., M.D.

Oral Surgery. LEROY M. S. MINER, D.M.D., M.D.

Nitrous Oxide and Oxygen. CHARLES K. TETER, D.D.S., Cleveland, O.

Laryngology. HARRIS P. MOSHER, M.D., Harvard Medical School.

Oral and Nasal Hygiene. GEORGE H. WRIGHT, D.M.D., Harvard Medical and Dental Schools.

Actinomycosis. FREDERICK T. LORD, M.D., Harvard Medical School.

Orthodontia. ALFRED P. ROGERS, D.D.S.

Trigeminal Neuralgia. EDWARD W. TAYLOR, M.D., Harvard Medical and Dental Schools.

Orthodontia. LAWRENCE W. BAKER, D.M.D., and HORACE L. HOWE, D.M.D.

Removable Bridge Work. RALPH B. RITZ, D.D.S., New York, N.Y.

A summer course in Prosthesis was conducted by Assistant Professor Harold DeW. Cross which was attended by eleven students.

Preliminary steps were taken during the year to rearrange the courses of the first year which are given in the Medical School by teachers from the Medical staff. After much discussion on the part of the Administrative Boards of the Medical and Dental Schools a committee of five was appointed by the President to take into consideration the merits of the proposed changes made by the Medical men. The Committee was made up as follows: Dean Smith (chairman), Drs. Potter, Minot, Warren, and Folin. The result of the deliberation of the Committee led to a rearrangement of the courses so that the Dental students, who are now increasing in numbers, will be able to have the necessary laboratories to themselves under special teachers.

The following arrangement was adopted: —

Physiological and Dental Chemistry, Histology and Embryology, including the dissection of the animal, during the first half-year; Anatomy, including the dissection of the human, and Physiology, during the second half-year.

This plan, of course, is a radical innovation in the method of teaching these fundamental branches of medicine, but is looked upon with favor by many who feel that the Dental student having had little or no biological work in his preliminary training will be better prepared to benefit by the courses in Anatomy and Physiology by being first trained in Histology and Embryology, which includes the dissection of the animal.

The Dean was appointed as delegate to the meeting of the Dental Faculties Association of American Universities, held in Iowa City in March. The meeting was attended by the Deans of the Dental Departments of the University of California, State University of Iowa, University of Michigan, University of Minnesota, University of Pennsylvania, and Harvard University.

One of the important results of this meeting was the agreement entered into by the members of the Association to adopt the Harvard standard of entrance requirements, namely, a four years' high school training which must include Physics and Chemistry which were formerly taught during the first year of the Dental course.

The Deans of the schools were most hospitably entertained by President MacLean of the University of Iowa, and by the Faculty of the University.

Dr. Robert T. Moffatt, a graduate of our School in the Class of 1895, has placed $500 at the disposal of the Administrative Board, $100 to be given each year for five years to a needy student or students, preferably seniors or juniors, who, in the opinion of the Board, are most worthy. A vote of thanks was extended to Dr. Moffatt for his generous gift.

The Chemistry Department, under the charge of Mr. H. Carlton Smith, has continued the investigation of oxydizing enzymes, and the study of saliva in its relation to disease. This work is new and has been carried on in connection with cases from the Boston Dispensary.

Dr. George H. Wright read a paper before the National Dental Association in Cleveland, Ohio, on "A New Instrument for Comparative Measurements demonstrating Changes in Nasal Fossae when Readjusting the Maxillary Arch." He lectured before the physicians of the Brookline Medical Society on the "Teeth and Their Relation to Functional Disturbances." He has also been making a study of malformations of the orbit coincident with maxillary irregularities.

Professor William H. Potter delivered seven lectures on Oral Hygiene in New England, and one before the Institute of Stomatology, New York. August 7, he spoke upon the "Condition of Oral Hygiene in the United States" before the International Commission for Dental Hygiene, in London, England.

The Library has been enriched by the bequest of the late Dr. Luther D. Shepard of his dental library, and by the gift of valuable books by Dr. George H. Monks.

In recognition of the very great interest taken by the late Dr. Dwight M. Clapp in the development of the X Ray in connection with dentistry, and for his valuable service to the School as teacher and member of the Administrative Board, the Board voted to give his name to the X Ray department.

At the request of the International Hygiene Committee the School sent an exhibit to the Hygiene Exhibit in Dresden, Germany, which was open from May until October, the essential features of which were: —

1. Photographic reproductions of experimental work done by Assistant Professor BAKER upon animals, showing changes in the bony development of the head due to a loss of teeth.

2. Salivary analysis exhibit (methods and apparatus).

3. Formalin-gelatin mounts of carious teeth.

4. Papers (printed) upon school dental examinations, relation of erupting teeth and enlarged tonsils.

In March, 1911, Dr. Miner read a paper before the American Academy of Dental Science on "Clinical Studies from Cases in Oral Surgery." This paper was the result of studies of cases from the surgical clinic of the Harvard Dental School, the dental clinic of the Massachusetts General Hospital, and from his private practice.

Dr. Miner has spent much time during the year in the study of certain tumors of the alveolar process generally known as epulis. He has also made investigations in the Bacteriology of Pyorrhoea, and in the vaccine treatment of the cure of this disease. He has further investigated into the pathological conditions and treatment of ununited fractures of the jaw. The result of his findings will soon be published.

The Committee on the raising of funds for the school did a great deal of work during the past winter and succeeded in obtaining a few thousand dollars for the Endowment Fund. The task of raising a suitable endowment for the School is a difficult one. The efforts of the Committee, however, will be continued with the hope that the School will soon be placed on a good financial basis and thereby be better able to carry on its work of education and charity.

EUGENE H. SMITH, *Dean*.

THE LIBRARY

Sir, — As Director of the University Library and Chairman of the Council of the College Library, I beg to submit my report covering the year from July 1, 1910, to June 30, 1911.

The past year has not been an eventful one for the College Library. Owing to the shortening of the previous fiscal term a heavy charge on unpaid bills was carried over into the next, considerably reducing our immediate resources for the purchase of books. The Council accordingly saw itself obliged to cut off all unexpended appropriations except those from restricted funds. This has borne hard on several departments. Fortunately the situation was helped out by generous gifts from several quarters, so that the total amount spent was almost exactly that of the average for the last five years. We have also come into possession of an unusual number of new funds from gifts or bequests, which will serve as a much needed compensation for the loss of revenue due to the transfer of a portion of the Pierce fund from book buying to administrative purposes. The most notable gift of books that we have received has been the Joan of Arc collection of the late Francis C. Lowell, which we shall be able to continue and increase, thanks to the fund established in his memory. It should be remembered that all our collections, with the exception of a very few specially provided for, can be enriched only through the liberality of friends of Harvard. The ordinary resources of the Library suffice at best to meet somewhat inadequately the needs of the various departments for the current scholarly and scientific literature on their subjects. Yet it is the special collections that constitute the strength and glory of a great library, and we must never lose a chance of adding to those we possess, no matter how inadequate may be our present accommodation for them.

In my report of last year I pointed out four administrative tasks which the Library must attend to without delay, — namely, the catching up of our back work in cataloguing, the making of new classifications, reforms in the subject catalogue, and the change from our small size catalogue cards to standard ones.

I am glad to be able to report progress in all of these directions, though in some of them the work has been that of preparation rather than of actual advance. We have at least ceased to add to our back work by putting certain cards into the official catalogue only, where they are useless to the public. Henceforth our accessions will be recorded as promptly as possible in the public catalogues; we have begun to make up arrears and expect to proceed much faster with this in the future. Secondly, we have classified on the shelves some thirty-five thousand volumes, previously unarranged or in a defective arrangement. Thirdly, we have made improvements in our subject catalogue and shall continue to do so from year to year, but without attempting any fundamental changes which, desirable or not, would be impossible under our present financial conditions. At the same time we have carefully considered, modified, and, I believe, much improved our rules as to subject cataloguing. Finally, since January 31, 1911, we have made out only cards of standard size, although for a while this necessitated a special catalogue case to hold them. In connection with this whole change many preparations had to be made, especially with regard to the installation last summer of new catalogue cases with 2,424 trays into which had to be placed about one million and a half cards. For instance, the mere preliminary boring of holes in the cards took nearly three months.

There is nothing now for me to add on the subject of our supreme need, a new building. Each year we waste more and more money, and we are put to and put others to more and more inconvenience by storing fresh thousands of volumes in some stray cellar and by continually shifting thousands in Gore Hall in order to obtain a little more space where most needed. It is now getting common to see in our book stacks volumes lying on tables or on the floors of the passageways for weeks at a time owing to the fact that it means hours and sometimes days of work in book moving before the necessary room can be created in a given spot. A preliminary committee of architects has prepared an extremely interesting tentative ground plan for a new building. This has been accepted by the Overseers, but until the necessary funds are forthcoming it represents only one more pious wish. In the meanwhile the danger of a fire like that which recently destroyed the State Library of New York is a fact we can do nothing to meet, and we dread even to think of. The consequences of such a catastrophe to the whole future of the University need no pointing out.

The Departmental Libraries are at least better housed and their growth continues to be satisfactory. The library of the Divinity School is being moved over to the new building of the Andover Theological Seminary, to be gradually merged with the collection there. A new wing is to be added to the Gray Herbarium which will give it needed additional space for its valuable possessions. At the present time, the special reference libraries, being merely parts of the College one, though not located in Gore Hall, make their purchases through the central ordering department, but the departmental libraries, with the exception of the Gray Herbarium, buy and catalogue their own new books. Although this is probably not the most economical system, and leads to duplication, it is necessary as we are situated. Many of the departmental libraries are growing faster relatively than is the College Library, which is now totally incapable of handling their work for them, and they prefer to do it for themselves even at greater cost. The existing arrangement has distinct advantages. It is more flexible and may accomplish more, as the departmental libraries have their own specially trained staffs, besides which their professors take a keen personal interest in their growth and give them invaluable aid. The vote of the Corporation of January 30, 1911, requiring these libraries in future to send to Gore Hall cards for their acquisitions, will in time build up there a central catalogue indicating the resources of all parts of the Harvard University Library. Unfortunately it will be many years before we can hope to make up deficiencies due to our having been unable to keep a complete record in the past.

The question of the desirability of transferring books from the custody of one of our libraries to that of another is of growing importance. At first sight it would seem that as officially " the University Library consists of all the collections of books in the possession of the University," those in any portion of it should be placed where they will be most useful. This could be insisted upon if all of them had been paid for from a common fund. In point of fact, however, the departmental libraries (and even most of the special reference ones) have their own budgets and resources and not unnaturally regard their volumes as their personal property. But even admitting this claim, we may wonder whether the different parts of the University Library might not do more to help one another than they sometimes have. Should they not, for instance, ordinarily be willing to present their duplicates to one another rather than sell them to outsiders ?

Should they not also consent to hand over to each other books which, though not duplicates, are not likely to be needed by them and may be useful elsewhere, reserving to themselves in each case the right of decision. As the College Library is a general collection, there has been an increasing demand on it from the departmental and the special libraries, and thousands of volumes have been transferred to them. The decision is often difficult to make in individual instances, and is complicated by the fact that few of the other libraries are willing to be or can be as liberal in lending out their books as Gore Hall; therefore a transfer of books to them means putting greater restrictions on the use of those books. Nevertheless, I believe that this process should continue and that a number of works now in Gore Hall could wisely be sent elsewhere, but if this is true it is equally true that in certain other cases, even if so far they have not been numerous, books from the departmental libraries should be turned over to the central one, or to each other. It matters little that such exchanges will be unequal, that for instance usually Gore Hall, as in the past, will give more than it will receive. A broad liberal policy in these matters is the only wise one. The component parts of the Library of Harvard University should not assume an attitude of bargaining with one another but should be glad to be as generous as possible without injustice to themselves. Their combined resources and their utmost mutual aid will be none too great in view of the competition that the Harvard Library, like the rest of Harvard University, is meeting in other institutions of this country.

ARCHIBALD CARY COOLIDGE.

APPENDIX TO THE LIBRARY REPORT

I

ACCESSIONS

The accessions to the libraries of the University for the year, and the present extent of each are shown in the following table: —

ACCESSIONS	Volumes added	Present extent in	
		Volumes	Pamphlets
College Library : —			
Gore Hall Collections	23,231	564,088	392,896
Thirty-two Special Reference Libraries . . .	4,349	61,456	. .
Law School	6,260	126,051	14,256
Divinity School	636	38,794	11,074
Medical School	1,552	17,780	36,000
Dental School	46	1,675	12,000
Bussey Institution	68	3,818	11,000
Museum of Zoölogy	1,095	47,952	44,369
Peabody Museum.	277	4,172	4,003
Astronomical Observatory	297	13,508	30,000
Gray Herbarium	657	12,784	10,017
Arnold Arboretum	2,222	24,747	6,659
Total	40,690		
Deduct, transfers between Gore Hall and Department Libraries	305		
Totals	40,385	916,275	571,774
Andover Theological Seminary	. .	64,000	37,000
Total number of volumes and pamphlets . .		1,589,049	. .

The additions to the Gore Hall collection alone for the last five years have been as follows: —

ADDITIONS TO GORE HALL	1906–07	1907–08	1908–09	1909–10 11 mo.	1910–11
Volumes by purchase or exchange .	7,520	8,765	9,759	8,577	9,939
Do. by binding serials	1,478	1,699	1,841	1,924	2,382
Do. by binding pamphlets . . .	852	1,099	1,122	974	1,315
Do. by gift	4,852	7,153	17,939	9,141	9,547
Total volumes added	14,702	18,716	30,661	20,616	23,183
Maps in sheets	512	699	1,181	525	555
Pamphlets by purchase or exchange	1,899	2,010	1,820	3,051	2,044
Do. by gift	14,128	14,872	19,611	17,348	21,848
Total gifts (vols. and pams.) . . .	18,980	22,025	37,450	26,489	31,395

INCOME AND EXPENDITURE FOR BOOKS

The following table shows the income of the book-funds, receipts from other sources for the purchase of books, and expenditures for books during the last six years: —

INCOME AND EXPENDITURE	1905–06	1906–07	1907–08	1908–09	1909–10 11 mos.	1910–11
From book funds, —						
Balance from previous year .	$4,781	*$5,140	$5,726	$5,723	$5,029	$2,163
Income of the year	19,063	†20,259	19,773	20,917	19,111	21,426
Total available	23,844	25,399	25,499	26,640	24,140	23,589
Spent for books	19,324	19,673	19,776	21,611	21,977	19,332
Balance to next year	4,520	5,726	5,723	5,029	2,163	4,257
Special gifts, sales, etc. —						
Balance from previous year .	2,814	4,279	3,802	3,321	4,860	‡4,241
Received during the year . .	9,484	10,115	5,351	7,246	11,948	11,521
Total available	12,298	14,394	9,153	10,567	16,808	15,762
Spent for books	8,019	10,592	5,832	5,707	8,567	11,425
Balance to next year	4,279	3,802	3,321	4,860	8,241	4,337
Total spent for books, —						
College Library	$27,343	$30,265	$25,608	$27,318	$30,544	$30,757
Dep't and Spec. Ref. Libraries (orders through Coll. Lib.)	9,357	7,642	5,914	7,436	8,339	9,239
Total	$36,700	$37,907	$31,522	$34,754	$38,883	$39,996

* Includes $620 accumulated income of the Boott Fund, not previously reported.
† Includes a special appropriation of $1000.
‡ The balance of last year is diminished by the transfer of $4,000 to the Coolidge-Hay Fund.

SPECIAL REFERENCE LIBRARIES

The present extent of these libraries is as follows: —

SPECIAL REFERENCE LIBRARIES	Perma-nent	On Deposit	Totals
1. Chemical Lab. *Boylston Hall*	3,088	1,230	4,318
2. Physical Lab. *Jefferson Phys. Lab.*	689	19	708
3. Botanical Lab. *University Museum*	1,279	120	1,399
4. Geological Lab. Do.	236	. .	236
5. Mineralogical Lab. Do.	873	212	1,085
6. Phys. Geography Lab. Do.	251	180	431
7. Zoölogical Lab. Do.	401	. .	401
8. Plant Physiology Laboratory. *Botanic Garden* .	133	. .	133
9 Astronomical Lab.	71	. .	71
10. Statistical Lab. *Dane Hall*	247	. .	247
11. Physiological Lab. *Lawrence Hall*	64	. .	64
12. Classics. *Harvard Hall 3*	4,777	148	4,925
13. History. *Harvard Hall R. R.*	5,869	39	5,908
14. Economics. Do.	1,661	34	1,695
15. Social Ethics. *Emerson Hall.*	3,300	. .	3,300
16. Philosophy (Robbins Library and Psychol. Lab.). *Emerson Hall*	4,071	44	4,115
17. Child Memorial (English). *Warren House* . . .	5,256	90	5,346
18. Lowell Memorial (Romance). Do. . . .	1,632	6	1,638
19. German. Do. . . .	1,558	. .	1,558
20. French. Do. . . .	2,614	. .	2,614
21. Sanskrit. Do. . . .	1,027	31	1,058
22. Semitic. *Semitic Museum*	1,844	24	1,868
23. Mathematics. *Sever 22*	965	69	1,034
24. Mining and Metallurgy. *Rotch Laboratory* . . .	400	71	471
25. Engineering. *Pierce Hall*	7,508	197	7,705
26. Music. *Holden Chapel*	1,048	. .	1,048
27. Education. *Lawrence Hall*	6,433	. .	6,433
28. Business. Do.	212	1,247	1,459
29. Fine Arts (incl. Gray and Randall Coll.). *Fogg Museum*	1,179	13	1,192
30. Architecture. *Robinson Hall*	2,084	16	2,100
31. Preachers' Library. *Wadsworth House*	186	. .	186
32. Phillips Brooks House Library	500	. .	500
Totals	61,456	3,790	65,246

SHELF DEPARTMENT

During the year the following groups were permanently classified: —

Church History	12,485	volumes
Forestry	497	"
General Geography	2,129	"
Heraldry	120	"
International Law	1,585	
British History	18,158	"
Total	34,924	

II

FROM THE REPORT OF THE LIBRARIAN

The diminution in the Library's income for the purchase of books, caused by the small balance carried forward from the previous year and by the application of the entire income of the Pierce Fund to administrative expenses, was fortunately made up by the receipt of an unusually large number of gifts and by the establishment of several new funds (aggregating over $75,000) the income from which will henceforth be continually available for the increase of the Library in special fields.

The new funds received are the following: —

Coolidge and Hay Fund, $4,500. From Professor A. C. Coolidge and Mr. Clarence Leonard Hay, '08, for the purchase of books relating to South America. This fund insures the regular increase of our South American collection, of which the chief foundation was the library of Luis Montt, of Santiago de Chile, received two years ago as a gift from Messrs. Coolidge and Hay.

Cutting Fund, $12,500. A legacy from W. Bayard Cutting, Jr., 1900, a constant and generous friend of the Library, the income to be used for the purchase of books on modern European history and the history of the countries of North Africa, preference being given to books on the history of France, Switzerland, or Italy, and to the history of Morocco, Algiers, or Egypt. In addition to the income of this book-fund, one-half of the income of the Bayard Cutting Fellowship Fund of $25,000, in any year when the Fellowship is not awarded, is to be used for the purchase of books of permanent value, preferably in French or Italian literature.

Gross Fund, $1,590. Established in memory of the late Charles Gross, Professor of History, by his friends and pupils, the income to be used for the purchase of books on English history and institutions.

Lodge-Stickney Fund, $3,125. Established as a memorial of George Cabot Lodge and Joseph Trumbull Stickney, the income to be used to purchase rare and choice works of English and French Poetry.

Francis Cabot Lowell Fund, $10,000. Given by Mrs. Lowell in memory of her husband, Judge Lowell, a member of the Corporation, the income to be used to supplement his collection of works on Joan of Arc (bequeathed by him to the College Library) by the purchase of books of historical value on countries and periods more or less closely related thereto.

Treat Fund, $41,000. Legacy of John Harvey Treat, of the Class of 1862, being the residue of his estate. By the terms of Mr. Treat's will, the income is " to be used for the benefit of the Library for the purchase of books relating to the Church of England and other churches in communion with her, the Roman and Greek Churches, and the Episcopal Church in the United States of America, especially as regards ritual matters of the same general character as the collection presented [by Mr. Treat] in 1888; also books relating to Christian archaeology. If the funds are more than sufficient for the purpose designated, they may be used for other departments at the discretion of the Librarian." Mr. Treat's previous gifts for the same purpose have been chronicled in almost every one of the Librarian's reports for many years. These have been mainly devoted to the building up of a collection of works on the Roman Catacombs, in which subject Mr. Treat was especially interested.

Twentieth Massachusetts Regiment Fund, $600, to accumulate until it amounts to $1,000. In December, 1910, the University received from Col. Charles L. Peirson, S.B. '53, of Boston, the sum of $861.50, representing the balance of the fund raised for a memorial to the Twentieth Massachusetts Regiment of Volunteer Infantry, which served throughout the War of 1861-65. The bulk of the original fund was used in placing one of the St. Gaudens lions on the stairway of the Boston Public Library and in establishing in that library a fund of $5,000 for the purchase of books of a military or patriotic character. The income of the College Library fund, when it has reached its designated limit, is to be used for buying books of a similar character, those on the American Civil War having preference. The balance of the gift may be spent from time to time in a similar way as needed.

Welsh Fund, $3,000. Established as a memorial of Julian Palmer Welsh, of Philadelphia, of the Class of 1897, and given by a number of his friends. The income is to be spent in buying books in English and American literature. An engraved bookplate, by Mr. Bruce Rogers, has been provided.

The establishment of the Craig Prize in Dramatic Composition will provide a regular income for the purchase of books on the history of the English stage so long as the prize is awarded, since one-half of the prize of $250 is to be given to the College Library for this purpose.

An annual gift of $1,000, in memory of Charles Elliott Perkins, of the Class of 1904, is for books on the history of the Western states. The donor remains anonymous. With these successive gifts, it may be expected that an extremely valuable collection of Western history will be built up.

Other gifts received in continuation of former ones, which have been some annual and some occasional, are as follows: From Mrs. R. L. Adlercron, of London, formerly Miss Hester Bancroft, $600 for books on Japan; from Thomas Barbour, '06, of Brookline, $35 for books on Oceania; from Harold J. Coolidge, '92, of Boston, $50 for books on China; from the Dante Society of Cambridge, $50 for books on Dante; from Ellis L. Dresel, '87, of Boston, $50 for books on German drama; from Professor G. L. Kittredge, '82, of Cambridge, $100 for books on the history of witchcraft; from John S. Lawrence, '01, of Boston, $10 for books on the biography of successful men (received after the close of the financial year); from James Loeb, '88, of New York, $100 for labor periodicals; from Edwin S. Mullins, '93, of Hyannisport, $50 for folklore; from Walter W. Naumburg, '89, of New York, $200 for books on Shakespeare; from William Phillips, '00, of the American Embassy in London, $100 for books on London (received just after the close of the financial year); from Horace B. Stanton, '00, of Boston, $25 for books on Molière.

Mr. Alexander Cochrane, of Boston, has supplemented his gift of some years ago by another gift of $1,000, of which $750 is for English Literature and $250 for Scotch History and Literature.

Professor A. C. Coolidge's gifts for books have amounted to $2,137, and have been devoted principally to works on German and French History, on Morocco, and on the Ottoman Empire.

Other welcome gifts have been received as follows: From Harold W. Bell, '07, of Cambridge, $137 for a set of the " Numismatic Chronicle"; from James F. Curtis, '99, of Boston, $50 for books on the Western states; from Mr. William B. Cutting, of New York, to fulfil the expressed intentions of his son, $150 for books on Napoleon, Florence, and Switzerland; from James L. Derby, '08, of New York, $25 for books on the Philippines; from Henry Stephens, 3d, '05, formerly of Waters, Michigan, now living in Zalaegerszeg, Hungary, $550 for the purchase of the extremely rare set of the " Codex diplomaticus Hungariae " (40 volumes); from Horace E. Ware, '67, of Boston, $100 for books on Comparative Philology.

Gifts for the purchase of books in English Literature have been received from Robert Bacon, '80, of New York, $100; Henry W. Cunningham, '82, of Boston, $100; E. P. Merritt, '82, of Boston, $100; James A. Stillman, '96, of New York, $100; George Wigglesworth, '74, of Boston, $100; Lucius Wilmerding, '01, of New York, $150. To these sums the Department of English added $132 and an anonymous giver $53. Much of this money would have been spent at the Hoe sale if the prices given had not been exorbitant. A large part of these gifts has been actually applied with great advantage to the purchase of original issues of English poetry of the seventeenth and eighteenth centuries, in folio form, offered for sale by Pickering and Chatto in London.

Unrestricted gifts for the purchase of books were received from William Endicott, Jr., '87, $1,500; Godfrey Morse, '70, of Boston, $50; and Evan Randolph, '03, of Philadelphia, $100.

An anonymous gift of $500 for the purchase of books on Fine Arts, and another anonymous gift of $25 for the purchase of books on Oceanic Linguistics, were likewise received. All these gifts, the number and variety of which is unusual, made it possible to maintain the normal increase of the Library in most departments and to add particularly valuable collections in certain fields.

The total number of volumes received by gift, as distinguished from those bought with money given, was about the same as usual, in spite of the fact that no very large collections were received from any individual donor. The most notable gift of the year was the bequest from Judge Francis C. Lowell of his books relating to Joan of Arc and French

History of the fifteenth century, a collection which has particular value because of the discriminating care with which it was formed. It numbers over five hundred volumes and pamphlets, but sixty-five of the volumes are made up by binding many pamphlets together. The memorial fund given by Mrs. Lowell insures the constant addition to the collection of whatever may be had that is valuable.

From the Spanish Government we received 382 volumes of the " Actas " of the Castillian Cortes, 1559–1598, and of the Spanish Cortes from 1809 to date.

From the French Government came 157 volumes of the " Annales du Sénat," in continuance of previous gifts of the same set.

The governments of Prussia, Austria, and of many of the Prussian provinces have continued to send us their current official publications, making a collection of great historical and statistical value.

The books received in July, 1910, from the estates of Professor J. B. Greenough and of Professor Charles Gross were mentioned in last year's report. The family of Professor F. J. Child have added about sixty volumes and a number of pamphlets to their former gifts from Professor Child's library. From the library of Professor A. S. Hill, we have received thirty volumes; and from that of Professor C. L. Smith, 678 volumes, 49 pamphlets, and 40 serials. From the Estate of Robert Treat Paine we received 63 volumes. Mr. Samuel S. Shaw, '53, of Boston, has sent us from time to time a number of interesting letters and papers from his father's correspondence, illustrating undergraduate life many years ago. Dr. Osler, of Oxford University, had the kindness to send us photographs of early Commencement Theses and Quaestiones which he had found in the Hunterian Museum in Glasgow. The Commencement Theses are for the years 1643, 1646, 1647, 1653, and 1678. Those for 1643, 1647, and 1678 had been known hitherto only from copies preserved in the collections of the Massachusetts Historical Society; the others are probably unique, and all of them were lacking in the Harvard collection.

From the Netherland Bible Society have been received nearly a hundred volumes of translations of the Bible and its parts into African and East Indian languages.

One of the interesting purchases of the year was a collection of pamphlet and broadside material relating to the French Revolution and the Commune. This has been supplemented by a gift from an anonymous donor of ninety-seven broadside proclamations relating to the French Revolution.

Mr. Daniel B. Fearing, of Newport, has continued to send, for the Morgan collection of Persius, rare and valuable editions of that poet hitherto wanting in the Morgan collection.

Such are a few of the interesting or valuable gifts received in the course of the year. Any detailed enumeration of them is impossible within the limits of this report, but the thanks of the College are transmitted to each donor as his gift is received, and at this time only a general expression of gratitude is possible.

APPLETON CHAPEL
AND PHILLIPS BROOKS HOUSE

To the President of the University: —

Sir, — I alluded in my last report to the change of hour of the Sunday service at Appleton Chapel, which had taken place after the Christmas recess in the previous year, 1909–10. I was able to report as to the effect of that change for the period only from January to June, 1910. On twenty-four Sundays during that period the average attendance had been 339, the average number of students being 168. The Chapel Committee appointed by the Phillips Brooks House have furnished the following table for the report of the Association, of which I avail myself:

	1908–09	1909–10[1]	1910–11
Student attendance, average	146	151	244
Student attendance, maximum	450	459	700
Student attendance, minimum	40	50	104
Student attendance, number of Sundays below 100	16	9	0
Student attendance, number of Sundays 200 or over	9	8	20
Student attendance, percentage of total attendance	34 2	47.6	47.5
Total attendance, average	426	317	513

It had been the judgment of the Board of Preachers that the first effect of the change of hour might easily be a falling off in the total number of those in attendance, since the proportion of residents of Cambridge availing themselves of the Chapel services would certainly be diminished. The figures above given show the justice of that judgment, though the averages for the second half-year are better than for the first. But the year just closed shows the increase which was hoped. That increase is entirely in the number of students and of members of the Faculty and their families. Representatives of the churches in the immediate vicinity of the University assure the Board of Preachers that the resort of students to these churches has not been seriously diminished. At the same time the Chapel service has been given the central place in the life of the University which is fitting. Obviously, also, a need in the life of certain members of the Faculty and of their families is being filled. Up to a certain point an illustration is being given of the possibility of an interdenomina-

tional church. At the request of many who have made the
Chapel their church home it has been arranged that the Sunday
services shall be continued during the periods of recess, excepting,
of course, the long summer vacation. In limited degree the
request has been made on behalf of certain families that permanent
sittings be assigned to them. It has been easy to accede to this
request. On the other hand, it should be said that there are many
who prefer to ask for no restriction of this sort.

The average number of students and instructors in attendance
upon the daily service of morning prayers during the year 1910–
11 was, for two hundred and ten services, exactly 100. The
corresponding figure the previous year was 90.

If it is permissible to speak of the greatest need of the Chapel
at this moment, that is certainly the need of a new organ.

The Phillips Brooks House Association and its constituent
societies reported June 1, 1911, membership as follows: —

Phillips Brooks House Association (direct)	40
Harvard University Christian Association	220
St. Paul's Society	200
St. Paul's Catholic Club	150
Graduate Schools' Christian Association	50
Law School Society	20
Harvard Divinity Club	55
	735

of whom 300 are reckoned as paying members.

The Social Service Committee reported men at work under
its direct appointment and supervision as follows: —

Teaching (Sunday School work not included)	147
Boys' Clubs	123
Home Libraries	11
Miscellaneous (reading to the blind, tutoring, juvenile court work, friendly visiting, etc.)	11
	292

This service was rendered in thirty institutions.

The Committee having Charge of Bible Study reported men
engaged in Bible Study or in the consideration of religious problems as follows: —

Classes	Number	Sessions	Enrolment	Average Attendance
Normal (for leaders)	3	5	19	15
Led by Professors	7	8	201	104
Led by Students	15	7	99	78
	25	20	319	197

These figures are taken from the report of Mr. Joseph S. Davis, '08, the retiring Secretary, to whom much of the success of the work at the House in the past two years is due.

The Secretary for this year is Mr. Arthur Beane, who was associated with Mr. Davis last year as Social Service Secretary and who is now giving full time to the work of the Phillips Brooks House. The Social Service secretaryship is now held by Mr. Eliot Dunlap Smith, '12. A pamphlet on "Social Service," published by Mr. Smith in September, 1911, with the report of Mr. Davis above referred to, gives information in detail as to the voluntary undertakings, religious and philanthropic, which have their centre at the Brooks House. The magnitude and variety of that work must surely win the attention and gain the sympathy and coöperation of the friends of the University.

Besides the University Teas and the College Teas, the regular meetings of the Society of Harvard Dames have been held at the Phillips Brooks House. This Society is designed to bring together the women connected with the families of students in the various departments of the University temporarily resident in Cambridge. The meetings of several learned societies have been held at the House in the course of the year and the House is always placed at the disposal of women in attendance at the Summer School.

EDWARD CALDWELL MOORE.

THE GRAY HERBARIUM

To THE PRESIDENT OF THE UNIVERSITY: —

SIR, — During the academic year 1910–11 the regularly employed staff of the Gray Herbarium has consisted of the Curator (Asa Gray Professor of Systematic Botany), an Assistant Professor of Botany, a collector, a librarian, an assistant engaged partly in bibliographical work and partly in the distribution of specimens, and an assistant employed chiefly in the mounting of specimens. The following persons have also been employed during portions of the year as supplementary aids: Miss H. E. Day, in bibliographical indexing; Messrs. C. A. Weatherby and A. W. Cheever, in determinative work as well as in the sorting and distribution of specimens; Miss June Adkinson, in sorting and labelling; and Mr. Joseph Kittredge, Jr., as assistant in field work.

By the death of Cyrus Guernsey Pringle, May 25, 1911, the Herbarium lost a skilled and discriminating collector. For nearly thirty years he had been connected with the establishment, — a position at first depending upon informal agreements with Dr. Gray and Dr. Watson, but in later years confirmed by Corporation appointment. During this period he made annual journeys of exploration to the wilder portions of the Southwestern and Pacific States and especially to Mexico. Combining in a highly exceptional manner the close observation and exact methods of the scientist with the energy and courage of a tireless and intrepid explorer, he attained well-merited distinction in his profession and leaves a long and enviable record of valuable discoveries and arduous work well done.

The more noteworthy collections of plants received during the past year have been as follows: I. *By gift, in exchange, or for identification:* from the United States National Museum, 1,831 plants, chiefly from the western and northwestern United States; from the New York Botanical Garden, 250 plants of Utah and 439 plants of Cuba and Jamaica; from the Arnold Arboretum, 322 herbaceous plants from Korea and Manchuria; from Mr. W. C. Lane, his private herbarium, consisting of 541 plants, chiefly from New England; from the Geological Survey Department of Canada, through Messrs. John and James M.

Macoun, 115 plants, chiefly from the Hudson Bay region; from Miss Grace Gilbert, formerly of Cambridge, her private herbarium, consisting of 1135 mounted plants; from Mr. E. B. Bartram, 321 plants, mostly from Pennsylvania and the pine barrens of New Jersey; from the United States Department of Agriculture, 77 plants of Turkestan; from Mr. C. C. Deam, 65 plants of Guatemala, and from Mr. W. S. Cooper, 153 plants of Isle Royale. II. *Acquired by purchase:* from Mr. L. A. Goodding, 577 plants of Arizona; from Mr. T. S. Brandegee, 489 plants of southern central Mexico, collected by Mr. C. A. Purpus, many of them species of special rarity and interest; from Mr. W. H. Blanchard, 153 critically identified specimens of the difficult genus *Rubus;* from Mr. J. E. Dinsmore, 100 plants of Palestine; from Mr. C. R. Orcutt, 786 plants of Mexico; from Mr. J. C. Blumer, 252 plants of Arizona; from Mr. Max Koch, 242 plants of Australia; from the late Dr. Edward Palmer, 452 plants of northeastern Mexico, a noteworthy collection, the last to be made by this veteran explorer of long and distinguished record; from Dr. Ezra Brainerd, 181 specimens of North American violets, selected and prepared with special care to illustrate critical studies in this difficult group; from Miss Alice Eastwood, 170 plants of Colorado; from Mrs. C. F. Wheeler, 3,636 specimens chiefly of the genus *Carex* from the herbarium of the late C. F. Wheeler of the Department of Agriculture; from Mr. Karl Fiebrig, 845 plants of Paraguay and 301 plants of Bolivia; from Professor A. A. Heller, 320 plants of Utah, Nevada, Montana, and Oregon; from Mr. B. F. Bush, 281 plants of Missouri; from dealers: Fiori's *Flora Italica Exsiccata,* centuries 13–14; Baenitz's *Herbarium Americanum,* issues 17–22; also 250 plants of Brazil collected by E. M. Reineck and 152 plants of New Caledonia collected by R. Schlechter. III. *Collected by members of the staff:* 7,570 plants of Newfoundland and Labrador, secured by Professor Fernald and assistants.

The entire number of specimens received from all sources has been 20,552. The number of sheets of mounted specimens added to the organized portion of the Gray Herbarium has been 16,457, the largest recorded annual addition, bringing the whole number of sheets in the herbarium to 467,581. To the laboratory collection, used in instruction, there have been added 536 sheets of illustrative material.

To the library of the Gray Herbarium there have been added 657 volumes and 449 pamphlets. On June 30th, 1911, the library contained 12,786 volumes and 10,015 pamphlets. There have been four issues of the Card-index of New Genera and Species of American Plants, together including 9,209 cards and bringing the total number of cards in the index to 92,705.

During the summer of 1910, Professor Fernald, accompanied by Professor Karl M. Wiegand of Wellesley College (who gave gratuitously his effective and valued coöperation), made a very successful exploring expedition to western Newfoundland and the portions of Quebec and Labrador adjacent to the Straits of Belle Isle. They were aided by Mr. Joseph Kittredge, Jr., and accompanied by Mr. Alfred V. Kidder from the Peabody Museum of Harvard University. The territory traversed had for the most part never been explored by trained botanists and yielded a large number of highly interesting plants giving new and important data regarding the relations of vegetation to the underlying rock-strata and furnishing much of the information which has since been published by Professor Fernald in evidence of a postglacial land connection between Newfoundland and the North American Continent. More than 7500 specimens of plants were collected, which greatly amplify botanical knowledge of the regions visited.

During the year notable progress has been made toward a safe housing and adequate equipment for the Herbarium. The Gray residence has been removed in accordance with an agreement mentioned in the preceding report, and the Herbarium is thereby relieved of a considerable fire-menace. A quantity of further steel equipment has been installed, chiefly in the Kidder Wing, including 32 new herbarium cases with a joint capacity of some 80,000 sheets. Finally, two patrons have with great generosity subscribed the sums needed to effect important changes in the building. One of these gifts, amounting to $25,000, from a donor who wishes to be anonymous, is to be used to rebuild, extend, and refurnish the library. The other gift was from Mr. George Robert White of Boston, for many years a member of the Visiting Committee, and will be devoted to the rebuilding, enlargement, and complete re-equipment of the laboratories lying between the main portion of the Herbarium and the Conservatories. For these purposes Mr. White has contributed the generous sum of $31,500, it being estimated that the construction will cost $21,500 and the extensive steel furnishings $10,000. This important portion of the building will hereafter be known as the George Robert White Laboratories of Systematic Botany.

It would be difficult to overstate the advantages which will accrue to the Herbarium from these gifts. The old library, small, imperfectly lighted, and by no means safe from fire, was quite inadequate for the proper shelving of the books of reference, which were in consequence so closely crowded, often in double series upon the shelves, as to be difficult of access and especially subject to injury, confusion, and loss. On the other hand, the new library wing will give every facility for convenient shelving of the books, as well as methodical provision for the extensive card-catalogues, indices, maps, stored publications, filed manuscripts, etc., in all these respects greatly facilitating reference, economizing the time of the staff, and above all giving the safety merited by collections of such value. The second story of this wing will be divided into private offices and rooms for special collections.

The old laboratories, maintained by the College, were antiquated in construction and had fallen into some disrepair. They were also so full of inflammable wooden fittings and furnishings as to constitute a real danger. The George Robert White Laboratories, which will replace them and which are to be administered as a part of the Herbarium building, will possess as perfect safety as can be secured by the scrupulous exclusion of inflammable materials. They will, moreover, have complete modern equipment, greatly facilitating the work both of the instructors and students. The ample space in the second story will give the Herbarium for the first time in its history proper facilities for the safe storage of valuable collections awaiting identification or distribution. Such stored collections are especially difficult to guard from destructive influences, such as predatory insects, dust, dampness, etc., all of which, it is believed, will be thoroughly eliminated by the air-tight metal cases to be provided through Mr. White's liberality. There will also be an instrument room, a private office, and finally a large, well-lighted, and completely furnished room where the New England Botanical Club is to be permitted to keep its valuable local herbarium, a collection which, duly installed in such convenient and readily accessible quarters, will render the building in even higher degree a working center for students of the New England flora, both professional and amateur.

Plans for the new construction were matured during the spring of 1911, by Mr. W. L. Mowll, the architect of the Kidder Wing, and the rebuilding both of the library and laboratories is now in progress.

To complete the extensive programme of reconstruction and enlargement, begun about three years ago when the Kidder Wing was planned, it remains only to rebuild the central, original section of the Herbarium, an undertaking which appears to be free from structural difficulty. Some changes are also contemplated in the arrangement and grading of adjacent portions of the Botanic Garden. These will give an appropriate setting for the building when finished, and it is confidently believed that it will possess character and dignity as well as great convenience and safety.

Among the gifts received by the Gray Herbarium during the year have been a copy of Hoola van Nooten's elaborately illustrated folio publication upon the flowers and fruits of Java, a work of value, contributed to the library by Mrs. William G. Weld of the Visiting Committee; also a bust of the late Alphonse de Candolle, a distinguished botanist of Geneva. The latter was given to the Herbarium by his son, Mr. Casimir de Candolle, in recognition of the long and intimate friendship which existed between his father and Dr. Gray.

The Visiting Committee again issued its annual circular in the interests of the Herbarium, and in prompt and generous response gifts for present use, aggregating $1800, were received from no less than 133 subscribers, whose names and contributions are stated in the report of the Treasurer. These gifts, used chiefly to further botanical exploration and permit an increased output of scientific publication, are of great service to the establishment.

During the year twenty papers have been published by the Gray Herbarium. As their titles have been fully recorded in the *University Gazette*, they need not be repeated here.

B. L. ROBINSON, *Curator.*

THE BOTANIC GARDEN

To the President of the University: —

Sir, — I have the honor as Director to submit my second annual report on the progress and condition of the Botanic Garden.

The range of greenhouses which faced the main garden was taken down early in the year and later replaced by buildings of metal construction. In the report for 1909–10 the reasons for this extensive change were given in detail. The new range simply replaces the old one, but by altering the position of a few partitions and by a rearrangement of the walks it proved possible to increase the area devoted to plants, to secure better light and to establish a more efficient conservatory. The central part of the old range, which was originally designed for a palm house, has not been wholly satisfactory. In recent years the palms had outgrown their quarters and had rendered the conditions under them unfavorable for other plants which were, through necessity, overcrowded in adjoining houses. It was decided to abandon the plan of making a special exhibition of palms, in inadequate quarters, with the hope that sometime in the future a spacious and suitable palm house might be erected. It was further decided to convert the space occupied by the old palm house into a stove house for the excellent representation of foliage plants cultivated at the garden, and by exchanging the tallest palms and retaining young plants of the same species as duplicates, to enrich the general collection.

Early in the year the greenhouses were painted inside and out and all necessary repairs in the north range were made at a very slight expense. One of the chief causes for repairs is the quality of the steel used in the construction of the modern greenhouse bench. These benches rust out very quickly and are costly to replace. As an experiment the centre benches in the new stove house were constructed of reinforced concrete. Aside from their permanency, assured by the use of cement and metal, these benches have this advantage: they soak up water, dry out slowly and tend to keep the air favorably charged with moisture. In the future it may be well to substitute concrete benches for our metal ones and so eliminate the constantly recurring expenses of painting and replacement.

At present the two large ranges of greenhouses are in good condition, are modern throughout, and should be free from the necessity for repairs for several years.

Through exchange and by gifts, the collections were enriched from time to time. A most valuable gift came to us from Dr. N. L. Britton, Director of the New York Botanical Garden, who sent several rare forms or varieties of *Paphiopedilum insigne*. From J. H. Maiden, Director of the Botanic Gardens, Sydney, 44 packets of seeds were received. From Mexico a number of orchids were sent to the Director by Mr. C. R. Orcutt for identification. From Australia and New Zealand many seeds were sent by Messrs. Eames and Sinnott, graduates of the University, who were conducting botanical studies abroad. From the Philippines several interesting plants came to us from Mr. C. M. Weber, collector for the Ames Botanical Laboratory. Messrs. R. & J. Farquhar & Co. generously presented a large collection of bulbs which were used for the display of early spring flowers and for laboratory work. For a number of years Messrs. R. & J. Farquhar & Co. have continued to send, as a gift, bulbs and seeds, and through their kindness it is possible to make a much better floral display than we should otherwise attempt with our restricted income.

As a matter of record the report of Mr. Robert Cameron, the Head Gardener, is here included: —

The summer of 1910 was dry and severe on vegetation, but with the adequate supply of city water we were able to carry most of our plants successfully through the prolonged drought.

The trees and shrubs in the garden were thoroughly sprayed with " Disperene " at the end of May and we had no difficulty whatever with insects of any kind during the summer or fall months.

The principal work in the fall was taking down the old range of greenhouses and grading the ground for the new one.

All the plants in the greenhouses had to be stored in the upper houses through the winter. On completion of the new greenhouses they were rearranged and now look more healthy and vigorous than ever before.

During the winter there were no heavy snow storms, consequently for the greater part of the time the ground was free from snow. Such conditions are not the best for herbaceous species, and the frequent thawing and freezing injured some of these; the losses, however, were not heavy.

The hot weather came so early in the spring that our bulbous plants in the borders and beds failed to grow or flower as well as in previous years.

Shortly after Mrs. Gray's death it was decided that the Garden House, generally known as the Asa Gray House, would be, in its original location, a constant source of danger in case of fire to the valuable collections of botanical specimens preserved in the Gray Herbarium. Consequently the sale of the house and its removal were deemed advisable. In 1810 the house was built, in 1910 it was moved. After having been intimately associated with the history of American botany for a century it is fortunate that the house is to remain near the Garden, almost opposite the Gray Herbarium, on the westerly side of Garden Street.

In 1910–11 the garden was extensively used for instruction and research. During the year the physiological laboratory and the adjoining greenhouse were in continuous use by Professor Osterhout. Some of the results of his researches regarding the permeability of protoplasm have already been published (*Science*, N. S., vol. xxxiv, No. 867, pp. 187–189) and the material for future publications is at hand. In connection with his experiments Professor Osterhout has had installed an elaborate equipment for the supply of water, at different temperatures, to his cultures of aquatic plants. He reports that gratifying results are being obtained.

After the mid-year examination period the students in Botany 13 conducted work at the Garden. For this work additional space was furnished in the section adjoining the greenhouse of the physiological laboratory. (Cf. Report for 1909–10, p. 191.) Under Professor Osterhout's supervision experiments with water cultures were conducted. These proved successful, although at first rendered futile by the depredations of mice.

Mr. Bradley M. Davis continued his interesting investigations on the genus Oenothera. For this work additional space was furnished near Raymond Street. In the experimental plot on the upper terrace an extensive culture of hybrids between *Oenothera biennis* and *O. grandiflora* was grown and in addition several races or strains of the species which were crossed during the season. These furnished important material for the paper, "Some Hybrids of *Oenothera biennis* and *O. grandiflora* that resemble *O. Lamarckiana*" (*American Naturalist*, vol. xlv, p. 193). This paper presented a working hypothesis that *Oenothera Lamarckiana* arose as a hybrid between forms of these species and that its peculiar habit of giving rise to mutants, as described by De Vriese, is explicable as the behavior of a hybrid which is splitting off strongly marked variants.

In the late winter and spring of 1911 about one third of the space in the north range of hot-houses was devoted to a series of Davis' Oenothera cultures started for investigations in the summer of 1911.

Although a large part of the space available for experimental work was given over to Dr. Davis for his researches, and the services of the gardeners were furnished freely for the potting and transplanting of the numerous seedlings necessary in his work, the results promised seemed of sufficient value to warrant the Director in giving every aid at his command.

During the year Mr. B. M. Watson conducted his class in horticulture at the Garden, using the potting shed of the north range as a lecture room and the greenhouses for the cultivation of demonstratory plants.

In connection with the State Forester's Office, the propagation and distribution of the fungus-disease of the brown-tail moth larvae was continued this season under the supervision of Mr. R. H. Colley, Austin Teaching Fellow in Cryptogamic Botany, and about two hundred square feet of space in the central bed of House 14 were devoted to this purpose. The disease was successfully carried through the winter and propagated in the spring, and during the month of May a large area, including Ayer, Massachusetts, and the towns in its vicinity, was planted; several thousand bags of infected caterpillars being furnished from the disease boxes in the greenhouse for this purpose. In addition to these plantings, between one and two hundred mailing cases containing infected larvae were sent to private individuals who had applied to the Forester's Office for the material. The results of these plantings were satisfactory; although the epidemics produced were inhibited to a considerable extent by cold and dry weather, these unfavorable conditions continuing throughout the period of planting. After the completion of the spring plantings, the fungus was propagated at the Garden during the summer, and caterpillars from ten bushels of cold storage nests were reared for use in the fall plantings. The latter were continued from August 20th to September 12th, between one and two hundred thousand larvae being infected and distributed among fifty towns in eastern Massachusetts. The weather during this period was unusually favorable for the purpose in view, and the results were very gratifying; epidemics being started in every instance, which are likely to be effective in producing early natural infections next season.

The fungus disease of the gypsy moth larvae, brought from Japan in 1909 by Dr. Clinton, was again started from resting spores wintered out of doors, and a general infection in the breeding boxes was obtained by June 18th. It was not found possible, however, to make more than three plantings from this material; since, after this date, the wilt disease destroyed the larvae in the breeding and infection boxes with such rapidity that all trace of the fungus was lost early in July, and no more material was available for further plantings. No results, moreover, were observed to follow the three plantings mentioned; a general mortality from wilt being present in all of the localities where they were made. The experiences of last season were thus repeated, as far as this disease is concerned, and it seems probable that in view of the great difficulty which appears to be associated with its propagation, and its decidedly less contagious character, that results comparable to those obtained from the use of the brown-tail fungus are not to be hoped for in the future, even if the disease proves not to have been wholly lost.

As in former years material was furnished to the classes in botany, and plants required for special studies were cultivated in the greenhouses. The research courses, conducted under Professor Jeffrey's supervision in the Botanical Laboratories at the University Museum, were constantly supplied with specimens. Several papers which have been published or are about to be published from these laboratories have been wholly or in part based on plants furnished by the Botanic Garden. Taken in the aggregate the amount of material required for purposes of instruction and research is large, and in its production much space is used and a great deal of labor expended. As far as possible and to a reasonable extent specimens for botanical study are freely furnished when called for, to the schools of Cambridge.

The labels out of doors are rapidly becoming illegible through the action of the weather and must very soon be entirely replaced by new ones. Through the summer Mr. H. T. Darlington was employed in an attempt to discover by experiment some simple and reasonably permanent, yet inexpensive, form of label. A smaller label than that formerly in use, made of metal, was selected for experimental work and a method of printing from type was adopted. Hand-printed labels are costly and to look well must be printed by one skilled in lettering. Mr. Darlington's experiments with different paints, different types, and different metals were very instructive, and after the samples prepared by him have been thoroughly tested in the open air for a year an effort will be made to replace the majority of the labels. In connection with his work Mr. Darlington prepared a detailed report which is in the files of the Garden.

A botanic garden in which the plants are wrongly named is a discredit to those who maintain it and wholly at variance with the spirit of accuracy which should characterize a scientific establishment, yet the ease with which labels are misplaced both by the workmen, and by visitors who remove a label to read it and then return it to the wrong place, and the likelihood of a single vigorous species taking possession of a whole bed where several weaker species have struggled for existence are sources of error against which it is difficult to contend. Many years have passed since any serious attempt has been made to correct the errors which have arisen through erroneous replacements of labels, mistaken judgment in naming plants, or by changes in nomenclature sanctioned by botanists. Consequently one of the most pressing scientific needs at the Garden at the present time is a thorough revision of the labels which will discover and eliminate errors and bring the nomenclature of the collections into accord with modern usage. In order to accomplish this the services of a competent systematic botanist should be secured whose entire time for at least one year could be devoted to the verification of names and the identification of doubtfully determined species.

Although the Curator of the Herbarium is ready at all times to render assistance in naming the plants in the garden submitted to him for identification, the extent of the work now to be done calls for special effort.

As in former years plants, and flowers when available, have been freely furnished for decorative purposes at college entertainments.

Monthly reports received from Mr. R. M. Grey, superintendent of the Harvard Experiment Station near Cienfuegos in Cuba, contain a detailed account of the operations for the year and indicate clearly that the economic flora of the island may be greatly enriched by the introduction of plants from tropical and subtropical countries.

Requests for material or information have been received from time to time from the United States Department of Agriculture, and these have been granted whenever possible. Several kinds of sugar cane for cultivation in Greenville, Texas, were forwarded in October, 1910. Tobacco seed for experimental work in connection with the Granville Tobacco Wilt were supplied in November. By special request a report on *Ceratonia Siliqua* L. (the carob tree) was prepared by Mr. Grey. In return for such services the Station receives from the Department of Agriculture desirable material which is of value in determining the adaptability of certain economic plants to the climate of Cuba.

The production of sugar cane from seed continues to be one of the special undertakings at the Station. This work is generally successful, notwithstanding the fact that for several years it has been hampered by unusual droughts. Some of the seedlings secured have given promising economic results, and real progress has been made.

In October, 1910, the violent storms which devastated plantations in western Cuba did not reach Cienfuegos but strong winds were felt which shook the fruit from orange and grape-fruit trees and did slight damage to the larger plants grown at the Station. On June 3, 1911, a violent whirlwind advanced directly on the Station accompanied by heavy rain. The full force of the storm lasted for forty-five minutes and in that length of time caused serious and in some cases irreparable damage. All of the large buildings, the greenhouse and windmill, were either destroyed or badly damaged. The plantations were covered deep with broken branches and other debris distributed by the winds, for the removal of which two days were necessary.

OAKES AMES, *Director.*

THE BOTANICAL MUSEUM

To the President of the University: —

Sir, — I have the honor of presenting the following report on the condition of the Botanical Museum.

The changes which have been made in one of our exhibition rooms by substituting plate-glass shelves for the thick wooden ones have resulted, as we had hoped, in giving to the cases much more light as well as somewhat more space. The heavy cost appears to be fully justified.

The steady growth of the Museum in illustrative material has been wholly due to the generosity of two anonymous friends of the University, who have borne the expense of collecting, preparing, and labelling the new acquisitions. To one of these friends we are also greatly indebted for numerous new books on the subject of economic or industrial botany. The rapid development of the subject, of late years, demands the replacement of many of the older works by more exhaustive treatises and especially by recent monographs.

A large part of our newly acquired material has been placed in insect-proof containers of an improved pattern, and installed in suitable cases in one of our store-rooms. Over fifteen hundred objects have been installed and authentically labelled for reference and consultation. These specimens have attracted so much attention from visitors, on the few days when the private rooms have been opened to the public, that steps are to be taken for adequately lighting the cases for exhibition purposes. The expense of introducing electric lights into these rooms is to be met by a friend of the University.

Our authentically named specimens of " raw " industrial plant products, such as fibres, gums, resins, tanning-barks and leaves, and the like, are more and more studied by visiting manufacturers, for accurate identification. Since it has become known that the Curator stands ready to assist in this work of identification, his gratuitous services have been largely sought and freely given.

The well-arranged material is now available for continuing the instruction in economic botany which was interrupted when Mr. Oakes Ames declined reappointment as Instructor. Mr. Ames was an inspiring teacher, conversant with many practical aspects of plant-improvement and plant uses, and he was, moreover, familiar with the material now available in our Museum for illustration and research. The loss of his services is much to be regretted.

Owing to the admirable collections exhibited in the Museum of the Arnold Arboretum, we do not feel justified in devoting more than a very small amount of our space to the illustrations of woods and forest products. But with that reservation, it is designed to have within reach in our rooms an exhaustive collection of the plant products which are in most common use or which are promising for future development. Only those specimens will be placed on our shelves for exhibition purposes which best illustrate morphology, ecology, and economic botany. The rest of the material will be stored in convenient containers for ready consultation.

A part of our morphological material consists of the large collection of fossil plants, entrusted to the Museum by the late Alexander Agassiz, and rearranged by Dr. Robert T. Jackson. This valuable collection is now accessible to palaeontological students of sufficient training, on application to Dr. Jackson.

A large and important invoice of Mr. Blaschka's glass models of plants is looked for this summer. Until it arrives no further change in the arrangement of the models will be made in any of the rooms. During the year a short sketch of the Blaschkas and their work for the Museum was published for free distribution to the crowds of visitors, and the edition was speedily exhausted. Another and enlarged edition may be prepared after the next invoice of models arrives.

The Curator would respectfully call attention to the imperative need of soon securing for the Museum an Assistant Curator who can familiarize himself with the details of its administration. During the many years in which the Museum has been growing, there have been no less than six excellent assistants whose services have been perfectly satisfactory, and who would have made good curators, but all of them have been taken away from the service of the Museum by the much larger salary offered elsewhere. The retention of a suitable Assistant Curator is therefore largely a matter of remuneration. At present we have absolutely no invested funds from which to draw for the support of such an officer, all of our expenses being met solely by gifts for present use.

GEORGE LINCOLN GOODALE,
Honorary Curator.

THE ARNOLD ARBORETUM

Sir, — I have the honor to submit the following report on the progress and condition of the Arnold Arboretum during the year ending June 30, 1911.

Beyond extending the existing groups of trees and shrubs with new species and varieties little planting has been accomplished since the appearance of my last report. An interesting new plantation will, however, be found on the southern slope of Bussey Hill just below the Overlook. Here in a bed 650 feet long and 15 feet wide have been planted in groups with several individuals of a species many of the plants raised from the seeds collected by Wilson during his first Arboretum expedition to China. The position is an exposed one and has been selected that the hardiness of these plants may be well tested.

After an absence of a year Mr. Wilson returned to the Arboretum in April from his second expedition to China. In spite of a serious accident in September, 1910, which nearly cost him his life, he succeeded in securing the seeds of all the cone-bearing trees from the mountains near the Tibetan frontier. To obtain information about these trees and to introduce them into cultivation were the principal objects of this journey; and the Arboretum is fortunate in having been able to distribute in this country and in Europe the seeds of these important trees which, with few exceptions, are new to science, and may be expected to play an important part in economic and ornamental planting.

The results of this second journey are the seeds of 462 species of trees and shrubs, a number of plants, including many willows and poplars, now first introduced, a large collection of lily bulbs and of terrestrial Cypripediums, 2,500 sheets of herbarium specimens, and 374 photographs of trees and forest scenery.

Good results have been obtained from Mr. Purdom's second season in China, passed among the little known mountains of southern Shensi. He returned to Peking at Christmas and, having forwarded his collections of seeds and herbarium specimens, started west again for Kansu, where he arrived in May.

At the end of 1911, his contract with the Arboretum ends and he will return to England.

During the year, 9,280 sheets have been inserted in the herbarium. This is the largest addition that has been made to it in any year since the herbarium was established.

The library now contains 24,747 bound volumes and 6,659 unbound pamphlets, 2,222 volumes and 423 pamphlets having been added during the year. The classified arrangement of the books on the shelves has been finished.

The interchange of plants and seeds with other horticultural and botanical establishments has been continued during the year. 10,222 plants, including grafts and cuttings, and 2,256 packets of seeds have been distributed as follows: To the United States, 8,854 plants and 561 packets of seeds; to Great Britain, 1,082 plants and 1,261 packets of seeds; to the continent of Europe, 286 plants and 366 packets of seeds; to Japan, 33 packets of seeds; to New Zealand, 28 packets of seeds; to Hawaii, 7 packets of seeds. There have been received 5,736 plants and 1,949 packets of seeds; of these 4,886 plants and 105 packets of seeds came from the United States; from Great Britain, 742 plants and 26 packets of seeds; from the continent of Europe, 108 plants and 175 packets of seeds; from Japan, 54 packets of seeds; from China, 1,589 packets of seeds (Purdom, 304; Wilson, 1,285).

During the year instruction in dendrology has been given at the Arboretum by Assistant Professor Jack to students in forestry and to a class of thirty-three special students, principally teachers.

The printing of the Bradley Bibliography has proceeded steadily through the year. The first volume will be issued during the summer and the printing of the second volume is well advanced. Work on the catalogue of the library and of the living collections has been continued.

To facilitate the study of the living collections an illustrated Guide to the Arboretum, with a map showing the position of all roads, walks, and groups of trees, has been published. During the spring twelve weekly *Bulletins of Popular Information* were distributed without charge to persons interested in the Arboretum and in the cultivation of plants. The object of these *Bulletins* is to give, from time to time, in popular language, authentic information about the plants in bloom or otherwise worthy of special visits. The demand for these *Bulletins*, not only from persons living near Boston but from all parts of the country, seems to justify the cost of publication. To the Guide-book and to these *Bulletins* is probably due the large increase in the number of interested visitors to the Arboretum during the spring and summer of this year.

I take this opportunity to express again my thanks to the Trustees of the Massachusetts Society for Promoting Agriculture for their annual grant to increase the knowledge of trees, and to the members of the Visiting Committee who have been active and successful in enlarging the income of the Arboretum.

C. S. SARGENT, *Director.*

THE CHEMICAL LABORATORY

To THE PRESIDENT OF THE UNIVERSITY: —

SIR, — In the absence of the Director, the Chemical Laboratory was in charge of Assistant Professor Baxter during the year 1910–11.

The number of students taking both laboratory and lecture courses showed a substantial increase over that of the previous year, and the number of research students was also slightly larger. The last named class of students must necessarily be somewhat limited as long as two causes continue to operate, viz., the demands upon individual instructors, owing to the smallness of the teaching force, and the restricted laboratory quarters. To the latter cause must also be assigned our inability to offer new courses, from which suggestions for research are always gained.

Twenty-six men were engaged in original investigations, under the direction of the various members of the Division, upon the following subjects: Surface tension, compressibility, boiling point, and heat of combustion of certain organic compounds; heat of neutralization of acids and bases; new methods for determining heat of solution of metals; transition temperatures of chromate and carbonate of sodium; preparation of barium and determination of its heat of solution and amalgamation; applications of the method of floating for the determination of the specific gravity of liquids, with reference to several analytical and thermometrical problems; investigation of salts fused at high temperature, with reference to residual moisture.

Atomic weights of phosphorus by analysis of the tribromide; of arsenic by titration of arsenious acid against iodic acid; of iron by the reduction of ferric oxide; vapor pressure of iodine; changes in volume during solution of certain salts in water; dissociation of phosphorus oxychloride.

Action of sulphur trioxide on silicon tetrachloride; preparation and properties of pyrosulphuryl chloride and chlorsulphonic acid.

Alkali-insoluble phenols; preparation of new octanes and nonanes; oxidation products of iodanil; derivatives and reactions of certain benzhydrols; action of ethyl and propyl magnesium bromides on anthraquinone, and other reactions of ethyl magnesium bromide.

Preparation of formaldehyde; investigation of certain perfumes; production of ethylene by cracking gas oil.

Twenty-three papers were published, chiefly on investigations conducted during 1909–10, and their titles may be found in the *University Gazette*. The grants of money from the Carnegie Institution of Washington, to Professor Richards of $2500 and to Assistant Professor Baxter of $1000, which have done so much for research in this laboratory, were continued during the past year.

The plans for the Wolcott Gibbs Research Laboratory, for which something over $105,000 has been raised, are completed, and ground will be broken in the autumn of 1911. The building, of which Mr. A. W. Longfellow of Boston is the architect, will be situated on Divinity Avenue, south of the Peabody Museum, and is planned as one of the group of buildings which the Division of Chemistry earnestly hopes will be erected in a few years. The Gibbs Laboratory provides only for research, chiefly in inorganic and physical chemistry. Upon its occupation, which will be at the beginning of the year 1912–13, a few more rooms will be available in Boylston Hall for the purposes of research, or for small laboratory courses, but the acquisition of this building affects very slightly the situation which has so long confronted us, — that of " an old building, badly overcrowded, very ill-ventilated and quite inadequate for its purposes," as stated by you in your report for 1909–10.

During the past year was formed the Association of Harvard Chemists, of which certain of the Visiting Committee on the Chemical Laboratory constituted the nucleus. An enthusiastic meeting of the Association was held in Boston, April 10, 1911, at which steps were taken toward an organized effort to obtain money for the proposed new buildings, a sketch of which appeared in the *Harvard Bulletin* of February 8, 1911. Committees were appointed to solicit subscriptions in New York, Boston, Cleveland, and Milwaukee.

CHARLES R. SANGER, *Director*.

THE JEFFERSON PHYSICAL LABORATORY

To the President of the University: —

Sir, — In the past, it has been the policy of the instructors in the Division of Physics, in planning their own work and in guiding students engaged in research, to pursue exhaustively a single subject rather than to change the topic frequently. The following list of researches pursued in the Laboratory during the year illustrates the application of this principle: Professor Hall, Thermal Properties of Iron; Professor B. O. Peirce, Researches in Magnetism; Professor Sabine, Problems in Acoustics. During the progress of this work, tests of the acoustic properties of various materials used in the interior finish of buildings have been made. The work has been done with the coöperation of the Johns-Manville and Guastavino Companies of Boston and part of the expense has been paid by them. Professor G. W. Pierce, Wireless Telephony; Professor Morse, Storage Cells; Professor Lyman, Spectrum Analysis in the Schumann Region; and, in connection with Mr. Bovie of the Department of Botany, Experiments on the Effect of Light on Living Organisms; Professor Davis, Problems in Thermodynamics; Dr. Bridgman, Properties of Matter under Extremely High Pressure; Dr. Chaffee, The Wireless Telephone and the Velocity of Cathode Rays; Dr. Hayes, The Study of Alloys.

The titles of researches of students working in the Laboratory are as follows: Mr. Evans, Electric Conductivity of Crystals; Mr. Royster, The Joule-Thomson Effect in Thermometric Gases; Mr. Sawtelle, The Nature of the Spark Discharge; Mr. Swan, The Minimum Audible Intensity of Sound; Mr. Trueblood, The Joule-Thomson Effect in Steam; Mr. Uyeda, Electrically Coupled Circuits; Mr. Webster, The Absorption of Light.

The Laboratory is not closed during the summer and the Division of Physics has always welcomed investigators from other universities during this season. This year, Dr. Tolman of the University of Cincinnati and Mr. Smith of the University of Kansas have carried on research work during July, August, and September.

The Cutting Fellowship for Research was awarded for the first time in June; the recipient was Dr. Chaffee. The Fellowship for Research, formerly held by Dr. Bridgman, was given to Dr. Hayes. It is to be regretted that the fund for this latter Fellowship will be exhausted at the end of this year.

The building during term time was in its usual crowded condition as far as undergraduate students were concerned. The new rooms made vacant by the removal of the boilers will give some relief to the crowding among the advanced students in future.

The fire risk in the Laboratory increases from year to year. The Director believes that this risk may be greatly reduced by a sprinkling system; he therefore earnestly recommends that such a system be installed without delay.

This Division is justly proud of the amount of original work which this Laboratory turns out, but work of this kind involves very great expense. If the activity of the Laboratory is to continue unimpaired, the Endowment Fund must be increased.

The volume of Contributions for 1910 contains papers by the colleagues and former students of Professor Trowbridge as well as by men working in the Laboratory. It bears the following dedication: —

TO JOHN TROWBRIDGE

who projected a great physical laboratory for Harvard University and found the means to build and equip it, who by his foresight, invention, and care has kept this laboratory among the foremost in opportunities for scientific achievement, and by his magnanimity has made it a place proverbial for good feeling, this volume is gratefully and affectionately dedicated by those who have profited by his labors and enjoyed his friendship.

THEODORE LYMAN, *Director.*

PSYCHOLOGICAL LABORATORY

To the President of the University: —

Sir, — The Psychological Laboratory, which during my absence in Berlin was under the control of Professor E. B. Holt, was carrying on research during the year in a variety of directions, some of the investigations being continuations of work in previous years. The following pieces of research which led to definite results may be mentioned. A. S. Ford studied "Time Reversals in Suspended Perception." D. I. Patch tried to approach the problem of suggestion in some new lines. R. E. McCormick analysed experimentally "The Time Curve of the Inhibitory Effect Produced by Sensations." Probably the most important research in human psychology carried out by a graduate student was the work of J. H. Picken called "The Transition States between Various Tasks of Thought and their Relation to Feeling." In the realm of animal psychology H. W. Huntley studied "The Psychogenesis of the Rabbit."

The instructors and assistants in the laboratory were engaged in the following researches: Professor Holt continued his studies in dizziness, devoting himself last year to the localization of auditory sensations in dizziness. Professor Yerkes studied "Inheritance in the Rat." Dr. Langfeld continued his work on "Suppression and Association of Ideas," and Dr. Kallen experimented with "The Psychology of the Comic."

The experimental training course of Professor Holt and Dr. Langfeld transcended the limits of our technical capacity. We consider twenty men as the normal limit for the course. The apparatus of the laboratory was supplemented by some valuable instruments, especially in the field of vision and space perception. To be sure, Professor Holt again felt strongly the rather chronic difficulty of the laboratory, namely, that its means do not allow such buying of new instruments as would be necessary if the laboratory were really to be modernized constantly. It may appear as if a yearly budget of about fifteen hundred dollars, of which twelve hundred dollars come from the Robinson Fund and three hundred from appropriation and fees, ought to be sufficient for keeping the laboratory not only in running order, but in a state of steady improvement. Yet it must be considered that this budget of the Psychological Laboratory is burdened to an unusual degree with expenses which do not enrich its lasting equipment. Firstly, the laboratory has to pay for all the psychological books for the library on the second floor of Emerson Hall, the periodicals as well as the monographs. The Emerson Hall library at present subscribes to thirty-six scientific magazines which have been classed as belonging to psychology. Some of them, of course, are physiological or psychiatric or pedagogical or partly philosophical. But as they are kept in the interest of the psychologists, they are charged to the account of the laboratory. Some of them might perhaps be eliminated, but it seems unwise to stop the subscription to magazines which the library owns from the first volume, as the whole value of such magazines lies in the unbroken sets. On the other hand, we believe that the periodicals are the most important part of such a library, inasmuch as the student working on research may be able to secure single books anywhere, but would have great difficulty in finding the older volumes of the magazines. These magazines now cost the laboratory two hundred dollars every year. If the collection of books, which is very small indeed, in the field of psychology is to be adjusted to the needs of the seminaries and courses, it seems that at least a hundred dollars must be spent for them every year. Thus there is an expense account of three hundred dollars which does not really touch the laboratory at all.

A second expense of only indirect interest for the laboratory work is the money which we spend for buying a hundred and fifty reprints of every publication which comes from this laboratory. As we lack the funds to print new volumes of the *Harvard Psychological Studies*, volumes which proved to be very expensive and which naturally had a very small sale, last year we went over to a less expensive policy. We publish the papers at various places in the magazines or as supplement monographs of archives, and buy a hundred and fifty reprints of them in order to collect them in volumes, which will be sent out free of charge under the old title, *Harvard Psychological Studies*. A large number of these volumes will be again put at the disposal of the Gore Hall library and be used, as previously, as material of exchange in the interest of the whole University. The expenses for these reprints are also considerable after all, and reduce the available funds of the laboratory by about a hundred to two hundred dollars more. Moreover, the laboratory finds a most serious difficulty in the fact that it cannot well do its work without a high class mechanic in its workshop, and yet that the volume of work needed by the laboratory is hardly in proportion to the wages which a mechanic of high quality has a right to expect. We have to pay eighty dollars a month, if we are to have that type of mechanic who alone can be really useful to us, although we feel that the amount of work which is demanded by the character of our investigations hardly justifies such a luxurious appointment, as he may have plenty to do in one week and very little in another. Some psychological laboratories try to overcome this difficulty by using the free time of the mechanic for the manufacture of instruments which they sell, but so far we have not believed in the desirability of this method for the Harvard Laboratory. The small amount of money which remains after all these deductions is necessarily spent in the first place for the material, the chemicals, metals and wood, tools and supplies, which are needed from day to day. The animals, too, which are used for the psychological experiments need their regular food. In short, if all this is to be spent, hardly anything can remain to satisfy the highly important desire to buy instruments invented in other laboratories. There is no doubt that our establishment still has many glaring defects in its equipment.

HUGO MÜNSTERBERG.

THE OBSERVATORY

To the President of the University: —

Sir, — The success of a really great institution depends on its adoption and maintenance of a permanent policy. Thus, the Greenwich Observatory has attained its position by observation of the Moon and planets continuously, during more than two centuries. In like manner, for nearly a century, the Pulkowa Observatory has been the highest authority on the absolute positions of the stars. By thirty years of continuous labor, and the expenditure of more than a million dollars, the Harvard Observatory has created a field of work which is not occupied elsewhere, in photometry, photography, and spectroscopy. It is estimated that the equivalent of the entire time of one assistant is now required to furnish replies to the requests for facts which are received here from the observatories of Europe and America. These requests, each year increasing in number, generally relate to the spectrum or brightness of certain stars, and the material for reply exists only at this Observatory. It is obviously desirable that the organization required to supply this demand should be placed on a permanent basis. While no one would suggest that a plan should be continued when more useful work could be found, yet it is the first principle of good business management to provide for a demand as long as it exists. To change an established system in accordance with the wishes of any individual would be as foolish as for the trustees of a great library to convert it into an art museum because they wished to appoint a man having an extensive knowledge of art. In a large institution, the officers must be adapted to the place; in a small one, the plan of work may be changed to accord with the officers.

The excess of the expenses of the Observatory over its income has continued. Accordingly, the photographic work at the Arequipa Station has been diminished, and expenses reduced in other ways. This has not been allowed to interfere with the publication of the Annals, which has made better progress than ever before. The amount accomplished has been limited by the demands of the University on the Publication Office, otherwise, still better progress would have been made. For several years, copy has been supplied more rapidly than it could be printed.

Fortunately, an accumulation of the income of the Quincy Fund has permitted several volumes to be issued, without drawing on the general funds of the Observatory.

The Observatory has suffered a severe loss by the death, on May 21, 1911, of Williamina Paton Fleming, Curator of Astronomical Photographs. She was an Honorary Member of the Royal Astronomical Society, an Honorary Fellow of Wellesley College, and last winter received the gold medal of the Mexican Society of Sciences. Mrs. Fleming's record as a discoverer of new stars, of stars of the fifth type, and of other objects having peculiar spectra, was unequalled. Her gifts as an administrative officer, especially in the preparation of the Annals, although seriously interfering with her scientific work, were of the greatest value to the Observatory.

OBSERVATORY INSTRUMENTS

East Equatorial. — The observations with the 15-inch East Equatorial have been made by Professor O. C. Wendell and have been of the same general character as in previous years. Over eight thousand photometric comparisons have been made, mainly with the polarizing photometer with achromatic prisms. A part of the measurements relate to stars of the Algol type, others to stars whose variability is small, or doubtful, this instrument permitting slight changes to be detected with certainty. More than a thousand settings have been made on Nova Lacertae, and its comparison stars. 184 photometric measures have been made on 12 nights of the nucleus of Brooks' Comet 1911c.

With a second photometer, adapted to the measure of adjacent objects, nearly four thousand settings have been made on double stars. Thirteen eclipses of Jupiter's satellites have been observed photometrically, making 910 in all. 384 settings have been made on δ Orionis, suspected of variability. The occultations of several stars during the Lunar Eclipse of November 16, 1910, were also observed.

Meridian Circle. — The principal work of the Meridian Circle is now substantially completed and published, with the exception of the proper motion of the 8,337 stars contained in the zone $-9°\,50'$ to $-14°\,10'$. The reduction of previous catalogues to 1900.0, for comparison with the results of the present work, has been provisionally completed, and the comparison itself is so far advanced that the study of the systematic differences between the catalogues has been begun, in preparation for the examination of those stars in which such motions are known, or suspected, to exist. The instrument is now used only for time determinations, and should be reconstructed throughout before it is used for any large investigation.

HENRY DRAPER MEMORIAL

The number of photographs taken with the 11-inch Draper Telescope is 147, making 18,330 in all; with the 8-inch Draper Telescope, 449, making the total number 37,302. The entire number of photographs of the stars taken at Cambridge during the year is 3,796. The Draper Memorial Photographs continue to contribute liberally to our lists of stars having peculiar spectra. Mainly from the study of these photographs, Mrs. Fleming found two new stars, eight variables, two stars having the hydrogen lines bright, one star of the fifth type, and one gaseous nebula. Miss Cannon has found two new stars, ten variables, and two stars in which the hydrogen lines are bright. Miss Mackie has found five variables, Miss Leland and Miss Breslin, one each. The discovery of four novae in a single year is without precedent.

Plans are being made for a Revised Draper Catalogue, covering all parts of the sky, and including about fifty thousand stars of the eighth magnitude, and brighter. The classification of the spectra will be undertaken by Miss Cannon, but the time required to complete the work will depend on the force available for the laborious work of identifying with certainty every spectrum measured.

Various investigations have been carried on by Mr. King, including the determination of the photographic magnitude of the Sun and planets, comparison of the light of the Pole-star with two standard electric lights, kindly furnished by the Bureau of Standards at Washington, variability of the Pole-star and a Orionis, photographs of stars through yellow and blue screens.

BOYDEN DEPARTMENT

As Mr. Hinkley will leave Arequipa shortly, Mr. Leon Campbell was sent there to take his place, and took charge of the Station on June 1, 1911. He will divide his time between the photographic work and observations of the southern variable stars. The number of photographs taken with the 13-inch Boyden Telescope is 125, making 12,959 in all. 751 photographs were taken with the 8-inch Bache Telescope, making 42,735 in all.

The total number of stellar photographs taken at the Station during the year was 2,042. 642 estimates of variable stars have been made. The weather has continued to be extremely cloudy.

Bruce Photographic Telescope

The number of photographs taken with the 24-inch Bruce Telescope was 205, making a total of 10,509. 35 photographic charts having exposures of two hours were made of the selected areas of Kapteyn. 100 charts having exposures of one hour and 61 special plates were also made.

Blue Hill Meteorological Observatory

The Observatory is directed and supported by Professor A. Lawrence Rotch. Mr. S. P. Fergusson, assistant and mechanician of the Observatory for twenty-four years, resigned to become professor of meteorology at the University of Nevada. The usual observations and records were maintained at the Observatory and its two lower stations. The exploration of the air was continued by means of kites and pilot-balloons. Kites carrying meteorographs were flown on twelve of the days fixed by the International Committee for Scientific Aeronautics, and reached a mean height of 6,825 feet above sea level, which is slightly lower than the average for the two previous years. The maximum altitude was 10,900 feet. The air currents alone were observed with pilot-balloons on five international days, when the wind was insufficient to lift the kites, up to a mean height of 15,650 feet, and a maximum of 27,400 feet.

During the last summer a bulletin was posted daily at the Observatory gate containing the weather forecast, the morning observations, and their departure from normals, which was read by thousands of visitors. Data useful for aerial navigation, collected above Blue Hill, St. Louis, and the Atlantic Ocean, have been published in a series of charts entitled " Charts of the Atmosphere for the Use of Aeronauts and Aviators."

Miscellaneous

Variable Stars. — The continuity of the observation of the northern variable stars of long period is likely to be seriously affected by the absence of Mr. Campbell, in Arequipa. This will, however, enable us to secure observations of the southern stars, many of which have been observed but little. The number of observations of variable stars communicated to us by other astronomers this year has been unusually large. 1,111 observations have been received from the observers at Amherst College Observatory; 748, from Mr. M. W. Jacobs, Jr., of Harrisburg, Pa.; 544, from Mr. W. T. Olcott, of Norwich, Conn.; 59, by Mr. J. H. Eadie, of Bayonne, N. J.; 56, by Mr. S. C. Hunter, of New Rochelle, N.Y.; and during the last month, 14, by Mr. W. P. Hoge, of Pasadena, Cal. All those sending their observations here the first of each month, are recognized in the publications in *Popular Astronomy* which shows the progress of the work. To increase this material, Circular 166 was issued, pointing out the importance of continuous observations of these stars, which is almost the only way in which an observer with a small telescope can obtain results of real scientific value; also, that it is extremely important that these stars should be followed with large telescopes, when too faint for observation with less powerful instruments. All charts and other material needed for the work were promised to those who could make use of them. The replies have been most gratifying. The Editor of *Popular Astronomy* proposed the formation of a Section of observers, and Mr. W. T. Olcott undertook the laborious work of correspondence and detailed supervision. It seems probable that the amount of valuable material thus collected will be greatly increased.

Observatory of the Rev. J. H. Metcalf. — 55 photographs have been taken by Mr. Metcalf and his assistant with the 12-inch and 6-inch doublets, with an average exposure of 70 minutes. The total number of photographs to December 27, 1910, is 1,153. Owing to Mr. Metcalf's removal from Taunton to Winchester, the telescopes were not used for several months. They have now been remounted in Winchester, and are in working order.

The 16-inch Metcalf Doublet has been in regular use in Cambridge. 686 photographs have been taken, making the total number 1,297. It is now used to supplement, for the northern stars, the work of the Bruce Telescope in Arequipa. A large number of the Kapteyn Selected Areas and Harvard Standard Regions have been photographed. Unfortunately, the illumination of the sky at night by the lights of Boston and Cambridge prevents the use of very long exposures.

An investigation of the greatest importance has been undertaken with this instrument in determining the position of the Moon by photography. 106 plates have been taken, and a discussion of 11 of them by Professor Russell of Princeton shows that the position of the Moon can be determined in this way with an accuracy slightly greater than that of the best observations with meridian circles.

Additional Investigations. — Besides the work described in other portions of this report, many other investigations are in progress. Miss Leavitt has derived final values of the photographic magnitudes of the sequence of stars near the North Pole. As these magnitudes were derived by several independent methods it is probable that they represent a true scale. Measures of the photographic magnitudes of 48 sequences distributed throughout the sky have been continued by Miss Leland. A systematic search for variable stars in all parts of the sky, mainly by Miss Cannon and Miss Leavitt, is now two-thirds completed. Reduction of the precise positions of sixteen thousand faint stars published in H.A. 1, 2, and 6, by Miss Harwood, is nearly completed and copy for the printer has been prepared for the first five hours.

Library. — The Library of the Observatory has been increased by 288 volumes and 1,675 pamphlets, making the total number 13,530 volumes and 31,272 pamphlets. It is scattered through the various rooms of the Observatory, and continues in constant danger of destruction by fire.

Telegraphic Announcements. — Forty-seven telegraphic announcements have been made, mainly relating to the discovery and observation of comets. They are sent to all who wish for them, free of expense beyond that charged in each case by the telegraphic company. The introduction of the Night Letter system permits messages to be sent in ordinary language, instead of in cipher, without increased expense, and generally without serious delay. A change in the rules of the telegraph company has doubled the cost of the cipher messages on land lines. Subscribers are given the option of either service.

Cablegrams intended for this Observatory should be addressed "Observatory, Boston," and all telegrams, "Harvard College Observatory, Cambridge, Mass." All correspondence should be addressed to the Director.

Forty-two neostyle bulletins have been issued, making the total number 467. They form a very quick and convenient method of keeping astronomers informed of current work. Many interesting facts are communicated to us and thus distributed to our subscribers without charge.

Publications. — Good progress has been made in the publication of the Annals, and it is expected that still better results, as regards the completion of volumes, will be made during the coming year. **56**, No. **5**; **59**, Nos. **6**, **7**, and **8**; **64**, No. **7**; **65**; **66**; **68**, Part **2**; **71**, No. **1**, have been distributed. Of the unfinished volumes, **47**, Part **2**, Photographic Magnitudes of 107 Variable Stars of Long Period, is nearly completed, and will be sent to the printer in a few weeks. **56**, No. **6**, Stars having Peculiar Spectra, is about two-thirds in type. **59**, No. **9**, Tests of Photographic Plates, 1902 to 1910, is in the hands of the printer. **61**, Part **3**, A Statistical Investigation of Cometary Orbits, is in type. **62**, Part **2**, Ledgers of Stars in the Zone $-9° 50'$ to $-14° 10'$, is printed and at the binders. **63**, Part **1**, Observations of 328 Variable Stars of Long Period, is nearly all in type. **67**, Catalogue of 8,337 Stars in the Zone $-9° 50'$ to $-14° 10'$, was sent to Germany to be printed, more than a year ago. Proof of the first few pages has recently been sent to us. **71**, No. **2**, Spectra and Photographic Magnitudes of Stars in Standard Regions, is ready for distribution. **72**, No. **1**, Position of the Moon determined Photographically, is in type. **72**, No. **2**, 1655 New Nebulae, is in the hands of the printer. A few pages of **73**, Part **1**, Blue Hill Meteorological Observations, 1909, are in type.

The set of the Annals, from **1** to **60**, is therefore completed and distributed, with the exception of portions of **47**, **56**, and **59**. **65**, **66**, **68**, **70**, and portions of **61**, **62**, **64**, **69**, and **71** are also distributed. **74** is the first volume which is not partly in type. It is hoped that **1** to **70** will be completed this year with the exception of Part **2** of **63**, and **69**. A description of the contents of the Annals is also in type.

Four Circulars have been issued, whose numbers, titles, and dates are as follows: —

163. *181325.* Nova Sagittarii, No. 3. H.V. 3306. January 19, 1911.
164. Nova Sagittarii, No. 4. Five New Variable Stars. March 18, 1911.
165. Three New Variable Stars in Harvard Map, No. 22. April 10, 1911.
166. Coöperation in Observing Variable Stars. June 29, 1911.

Various other publications by officers of the Observatory are described in the *Harvard University Gazette*, each month.

EDWARD C. PICKERING, *Director.*

MUSEUM OF COMPARATIVE ZOÖLOGY

To the President of the University: —

Sir, — Twenty courses in Zoölogy were given during the academic year 1910–11 by Professors Mark, Parker, Wheeler, Castle, Rand, East, and Mr. Brues to two hundred and fifty-four students in Harvard University.

Messrs. E. A. Boyden, E. C. Day, John Detlefsen, S. I. Kornhauser, Henry Laurens, C. C. Little, W. R. B. Robertson and R. A. Spaeth served as Assistants in these courses.

The Virginia Barret Gibbs Scholarship was held by Mr. R. A. Spaeth, and the income of the Humboldt Fund aided three students, two while at work at the Bermuda Biological Station for Research and one engaged in research at Woods Hole.

Five courses in Zoölogy were taken by thirty-five students of Radcliffe College. This instruction was given by Professors Mark and Rand and Mr. D. W. Davis. Messrs. Boyden, Kornhauser, and Spaeth were the Assistants for the Radcliffe instruction.

During the academic year 1909–10 the number of students and of courses was: —

Harvard, seventeen courses, two hundred . and ninety-seven students; *Radcliffe*, four courses, twenty-four students.

In the Department of Geology and Geography the instruction by the regular staff was given by Professors Davis, Ward, Woodworth, Johnson, and Dr. Lahee, assisted by Messrs. S. C. Lawrence, W. G. Reed, Jr., R. E. Sawyer, Sedgwick Smith, and Edward Wigglesworth. Dr. Lahee also assisted Professor Woodworth in one course.

By the courtesy of the Massachusetts Institute of Technology five students of Harvard University were admitted to courses in Palaeontology given by Professor H. W. Shimer at the Institute.

Seventeen courses were taken by three hundred and fifteen students in Harvard University and six courses were taken by twenty-one students in Radcliffe College.

In 1909–10 the number of courses and of students was: — *Harvard*, eighteen courses, two hundred and fifty-five students; *Radcliffe*, six courses, twenty-one students.

The income of the Josiah Dwight Whitney Scholarship Fund aided two students in geological and geographical work in Montana, Washington, and British Columbia.

A marble tablet inscribed: —

In memory
of
Alexander Agassiz
1835–1910
Omnia quae hic vides monumentum

has been set in the wall of the Entrance Hall (Oxford Street) of the Museum. The tablet is the gift of Mr. Agassiz's sons, George Russell Agassiz, Maximilian Agassiz, and Rodolphe Louis Agassiz.

The Corporation has installed automatic sprinklers in the boiler rooms, preparators' rooms, work shops, and photographic rooms in the basement. The windows of a few rooms between the Museum halls and the Zoölogical laboratories have been refitted with resistant glass, and a very large proportion of the windows throughout the whole Museum have been furnished with metal weather strips. Tested to a limited extent a few years ago this appliance gave most satisfactory results, and its introduction throughout the Museum and especially in the basement during the past winter showed at once that both for cleanliness and as an economizer of fuel it will be of great and permanent usefulness. Following the policy of recent years the renovation of the work rooms and of the exhibition cases has been continued; three rooms have been renovated this year and new exhibition cases have been built for the systematic collection of mammals and for the North American faunal collections. For the research collections new cases have been built for the ornithological, herpetological, and entomological departments.

To Dr. Thomas Barbour and Mr. Louis A. Shaw the Museum's thanks are due for financial aid which has been used for improvements in the work rooms and for their better equipment.

Mr. John E. Thayer continues a most generous contributor to the collections of the Museum. His gifts to the ornithological department in many cases have anticipated its needs and have made it a most effective study collection of the birds of the world.

Through Mr. Thayer's liberality the Museum also possesses the valuable series of letters and drawings of Alexander Wilson and John J. Audubon, formerly the property of the late Joseph M. Wade. The Wilsoniana contains seventy of Wilson's original drawings of birds, a sketch of his school house, and one of the "Sorrel Horse Inn." These drawings vary as to completeness; some are but rough outlines, while others are finished in all details and are superior both in perspective and in delicacy to the engraved plates by Alexander Lawson in the "American Ornithology." There are sixteen autograph letters of Wilson ranging in date from 1803 to 1810, two autograph poems, and his book of receipts for the engraving and coloring of the plates of his "American Ornithology."

The Auduboniana included in Mr. Thayer's gift consists of five original drawings by John J. Audubon and seventy-three of his autograph letters written chiefly to Dr. John Bachman. There are a few letters of Mrs. Audubon, one letter of her son, John W. Audubon, and sixty letters of another son, Victor G. Audubon.

Letters of John Bachman, J. G. Bell, T. M. Brewer, Richard Harlan, Edward Harris, Robert Jameson, George Ord, J. K. Townsend, and many others, are included in Mr. Thayer's gift.

Some of these letters, together with extracts from the ledgers and day-books kept by John J. Audubon and his sons during the publication of their works on the birds and mammals of North America, will be published at some future date.

The Museum is also the fortunate possessor, through the kindness of Mrs. Anna Davis Hallowell, of an Alexander Wilson memento of very great interest. This is a vertical sun-dial made by Wilson himself during the closing years of the eighteenth century. The dial is a simple slab of fine white marble, about thirteen inches square, with

1800

Alex   Wilfon

cut in; the gnomon is of iron. Mrs. Hallowell writes me that this sun-dial was given to her by her " father, Edward H. Davis of Philadelphia some time about 1870. He bought it from an old woman who had a garden on the Old York Road, near Milestown Pa., who had inherited it from her parents, and knowing my father's knowledge of birds and gardening, offered it to him. In like manner he gave it to me, and as our old house at South Yarmouth had the same date, (1800) I have kept it in our garden, until my brother, Professor Wm. M. Davis, suggested that it would be safer with you. I therefore desire to present the dial to the Museum of Comparative Zoölogy."

From Dr. John C. Phillips the Museum has received large and valuable series of birds and mammals; among the latter especial mention should be made of a remarkably fine skull with horns attached of a male of the typical southern race of the White

Rhinoceros (*Rhinoceros simus*). This race is now practically extinct, and though Dr. Phillips's specimen lacks data, it, without doubt, came from Zululand. The front horn is massive and measures thirty-one and one-half inches; it is typical in form with recurving tip, while the hind horn is quite small, only ten inches in length, and has a short compressed smooth tip. This skull has been placed on exhibition on the wall of the Divinity Avenue Entrance Hall.

Dr. Phillips, in addition to his valuable gifts to the collections, has most generously supplied the means by which an additional Preparator has been added to the Museum staff. Since August, 1910, Mr. Walter R. Zappey has been engaged almost continuously upon the research collections of birds and mammals, where his skill and industry are rapidly improving specimens received in the rough. He has also, in addition to several small mammals prepared for the exhibition rooms, mounted for the North American room a pair of Nelson's Sheep, *Ovis nelsoni*, collected by Dr. Phillips in Lower California.

Dr. Thomas Barbour has worked on the collections of amphibians and reptiles throughout the year; his generous expenditure of time and money has greatly enhanced the value and extent of these collections. He has also presented many valuable specimens to the collections of other departments of the Museum, especially the ornithological and entomological departments.

For a handsome male Javan Peacock, *Pavo muticus*, acknowledgment is due Mr. William Barbour. This specimen, mounted by Mr. Zappey, is shown in the Indo-Asiatic room.

The thanks of the Museum are tendered the New York Zoological Society which has given, as in former years, a considerable number of reptiles; most of these have made, through Mr. Nelson's skill, admirable exhibition mounts. It was a satisfaction to the Museum to be able to offer this Society, as a slight return for similar favors in past years, a living Haytian Solenodon which had been in the Museum since 8 December, 1908; unfortunately, however, it survived in New York but a few months, and its skeleton, prepared by Mr. Nelson, is on exhibition in the systematic collection of mammals.

For a collection of shells of great scientific value, the Museum is indebted to Mrs. F. Woodward Earl (Marie Binney Earl). Dr. Amos Binney, Mrs. Earl's grandfather, was the author of a work on the terrestrial mollusks of. the United States which remains to-day unexcelled. The manual, " The Terrestrial Air-breathing

Mollusks of the United States and the Adjacent Territories of North America," by her father, William Greene Binney, was published as volumes four and five of the Bulletin of this Museum. These volumes, with the several supplements issued later, maintain the reputation of Amos Binney.

Mrs. Earl's gift, the William Greene Binney collection, consists of nearly nine hundred lots of pulmonate gasteropods with the types and typical material illustrative of W. G. Binney's studies; though lacking large numbers of specimens of any form, its well-selected series show in admirable detail the variation and distribution of the species represented.

During his studies of Palaeozoic Echini, Dr. R. T. Jackson amassed a large series of specimens of recent forms. These he has most generously presented to the Museum, and, though the Museum's series of recent Echini is an especially large and complete one, Dr. Jackson's donation contains many that are most desirable additions, including all the Mesozoic and recent forms figured in his monograph of the Echini (*Memoirs Boston Society of Natural History*, vol. 7). There are also a large number that can be used advantageously for exchanges.

In the early years of this Museum its stores were enriched by large and valuable collections gotten together by zealous missionaries in many parts of the globe. One of the notable instances of this work was that of the Rev. M. M. Carleton. Mr. Carleton's collections, received during the early seventies, were made almost entirely about Amballa and Koolloo, India, and their value is increasingly recognized each year.

It is especially gratifying to record a similar service this year. To the Rev. George Schwarb the Museum is much indebted for many and most desirable additions to its series of reptiles and amphibians. Collected in western equatorial Africa, Mr. Schwarb's specimens add a number of species previously unrepresented in the Museum collections, and they are, moreover, in excellent condition for study.

In the name of the late Francis A. Pierce, Mrs. Pierce has most kindly given the Museum a collection of skulls and horns of ungulates, some of which have been mounted by Mr. Nelson and are shown on the wall of the Divinity Avenue Entrance Hall.

The Museum is indebted to Mr. L. J. de G. de Milhau for another instalment of Icelandic birds. These as well as previous sendings have been prepared by Rowland Ward and are presented as the joint gift of Mr. de Milhau and the late Mr. J. W. Hastings.

The Museum is also indebted to Miss H. E. Hooker, and to Messrs. E. N. Fischer, Henry Hales, and William McNeil for specimens for its collection of domestic fowls; to Col. John Caswell, for a skin and skeleton of the rare African Nandi Maned Rat, *Lophiomys testudo;* to Mr. R. A. Spaeth, for a series of copepods; to Professor W. M. Wheeler, for some desirable arachnids and myriopods from the western United States, and to the American Museum of Natural History, for the skin and skeleton of the West Indian Seal, *Monachus tropicalis.* Professor J. B. Woodworth and Mr. R. W. Sayles have presented fossils of value, and acknowledgment is also due Mr. W. T. Davis and the Honorable Mason Mitchell for specimens sent to the Museum.

Thanks to the kind interest of Mr. J. H. Emerton and Miss E. B. Bryant the collection of Araneida is in excellent condition; by their work and their gifts the value of the collection is greatly enhanced.

The Museum is indebted to Professor S. F. Clarke for the identification of a series of hydroids loaned him for study several years ago. Professor A. E. Verrill has studied at the Museum such of the alcyonarian corals as relate to his report on the species collected by the U. S. Coast Survey Steamer "Blake." For this report ninety-eight plates have been delivered and the text and remaining plates are well advanced.

The ornithological collections have profited greatly by the zealous work of Mr. Bangs. The addition of a large case for the research collection of skins has enabled him to arrange the passerine families, Fringillidae to Streperidae inclusive, in the order of Sharpe's Hand-list; this work necessitated the reidentification of many skins and also took considerable time for labelling and cataloguing. In addition to the above, Mr. Bangs has kept the ordinary current work of the ornithological department well in hand.

Mr. Robert W. Sayles who has had charge of the exhibition collections in the Geological Section of the Museum since December, 1906, is rapidly making the rooms devoted to these collections instructive to students and attractive to the general visitor. Attention may be called to a model illustrative of earthquake action and to one of a Japanese earthquake-proof house, that have been installed this year.

Dr. G. M. Allen has continued his work on the collection of mammals; he has finished the revision of the Muridae, Spalacidae, and Geomyidae and also the alcoholic specimens of monotremes, marsupials, and primates.   Dr. Allen spent five weeks in Grenada collecting in the interests of the Museum and, as in previous years, he has devoted a portion of his time to research.   One of the results, Mammals of the West Indies, was issued as Bulletin M. C. Z., vol. 54, no. 6, pp. 175–263; another, an account of the species of Proechidna, is practically complete.

Mr. W. F. Clapp was employed for a few months on the Molluscan collections.   Under Dr. Faxon's direction and with the voluntary aid of Mrs. N. A. Clapp, a large amount of routine work was accomplished.   Mr. Clapp also collected for the Museum large series of shells in New England and in Florida.   The Museum is very much indebted to Mrs. Clapp for her earnest work throughout the year.

Mr. Nelson's work has, as usual, been varied in scope: it includes the remounting and repair of a considerable number of skeletons of reptiles, birds, and mammals, a work long needed and one which has improved the appearance of the exhibition cases.   He has made and mounted some skeletons not previously shown in the exhibition series, has continued his successful work of mounting reptiles for exhibition, and has also mounted a series of finches for the West Indian faunal collection.   As in previous years his handiwork, both photographic and mechanical, is serviceable throughout the Museum.

The Museum is again under obligations to Messrs. Faxon, Brewster, Woodworth, Bangs, Bigelow, and Sayles for their interest in their respective departments.

To the exhibition collections have been added a number of fishes mounted by Mr. S. F. Denton.   Mr. Denton has also mounted several specimens of Salmon, *Salmo salar*, which Dr. John Collins Warren was good enough to send from Quebec for this purpose.   A few North American mammals obtained through the kind coöperation of Mr. H. E. Redmund have been mounted by Mr. Nelson, and an especially handsome specimen of the European Bison, *Bos bonasus*, purchased of Rowland Ward, fills a place too long vacant in the systematic collection.   The Museum has also obtained by purchase a skin with skeleton of Père David's Milou Deer, *Elaphurus davidianus*, a very rare species found only in northern China and closely related to North American forms.

For its research collections the Museum has acquired some selachians of unusual interest; fragments of fossil fishes from the

Lower Old Red Sandstone of Scotland; fossil vertebrates from the Cretaceous of western Kansas; and additional series of Rotifera.

Drs. Clark and Bigelow collected for two weeks in August, 1910, at Grand Manan, and the same length of time was spent at the same place in July, 1911, by Dr. Clark. Though the results of the dredging and of the surface collecting were rather meagre, some interesting forms were obtained by shore work. Dr. Clark also made quite an advance toward a satisfactory preparation of starfishes. During the past summer Dr. Bigelow devised and tested satisfactorily a closing net for horizontal towing. This work was carried on in Massachusetts Bay and in the Gulf of Maine, and for the opportunity to undertake it as well as the expedition to Grand Manan in 1910, acknowledgment is due Mr. Joseph S. Bigelow, Jr., who most kindly placed his yacht at the disposal of Drs. Bigelow and Clark.

Dr. G. M. Allen and Mr. C. T. Brues collected, during their stay of five weeks in Grenada, B. W. I., many desirable mammals, birds, and reptiles, together with some invertebrates of exceptional interest. The generosity of Dr. Thomas Barbour enabled Messrs. Allen and Brues to undertake this work for the Museum.

The Library contains 48,019 volumes, and 44,442 pamphlets; the accessions for the year are 1,095 volumes, and 1,075 pamphlets.

An Audubon plate of peculiar interest, a gift of Mr. John E. Thayer, has been hung in the Library; it represents *three* Clapper Rails in place of *two* shown in Audubon's published works; both the arrangement of the birds and the background differ from the Havell plate. The plate given by Mr. Thayer was printed by Childs and Inman, Philadelphia, and is dated 1832; the date of the Havell plate is 1834.

There have been placed in the Library two noteworthy records of Mr. Agassiz: one, the original manuscript from which the abstract of his first scientific paper on the mechanism of the flight of Lepidoptera (*Proc. Boston Society of Natural History*, February, 1859) was made, and the other, a case with a number of beautiful drawings on wood, the work of Mr. Agassiz during the early years of the Museum; these figures were drawn for a text-book of zoölogy, proposed, but never carried to completion, by his father. The manuscript is the property of Mrs. George R. Agassiz and has been kindly loaned by her.

The publications for the year include one volume and four numbers of the Memoirs, eight numbers of the Bulletin and the

Annual Report, a total of 975 (681 quarto, 294 octavo) pages and 138 (110 quarto, 28 octavo) plates.

The volume and two numbers of the Memoirs contain reports on the scientific results of expeditions carried on under Mr. Agassiz's direction. Mr. Springer's Memoir is a continuation of his studies of fossil crinoids, some of which have been published in earlier volumes of the Memoirs. The other Memoir and six numbers of the Bulletin represent work of the Museum staff or reports on collections of the Museum; one number of the Bulletin is a Contribution from the Zoölogical Laboratory and one number contains Sir John Murray's address on Mr. Agassiz's life and scientific work.

To assist in the publication of Contributions from the Zoölogical and Geological Laboratories the Corporation has continued the usual appropriation of $350.

For the publication of the Reports on the expeditions of the "Blake" and "Albatross," and for some other Memoirs in which he was interested, Mr. Agassiz made provision by his will. Of the "Blake" reports that of Dr. Hartlaub on the Comatulae is in type and will be published during the coming year. Mention has been made of the progress of Professor Verrill's work on the alcyonarians and it is hoped that this also will be issued before the close of the Museum year 1911–12. With these extensive reports published there is, with the exception of the Crustacea now in the hands of Professor Bouvier, but little "Blake" material still unworked. For the three expeditions of the "Albatross," those of 1891, 1899–1900, and 1904–05, the reports of Dr. Hansen on the schizopods, Dr. Bigelow on the siphonophores, and that of Messrs. Kendall and Radcliffe on the shore fishes of the expedition of 1904–05, will be issued during the year. Mr. Garman's monograph of the plagiostomes will also be published at an early date. Several other reports on the collections of the "Albatross" are in a forward state of preparation.

SAMUEL HENSHAW.

THE ZOÖLOGICAL LABORATORY

To THE PRESIDENT OF THE UNIVERSITY:—

SIR,— Aside from the changes due to the regular alternation of certain courses, the courses of instruction in Zoölogy during 1910–11 were substantially the same as in 1909–10, with one exception,— the addition of Zoölogy 7d, Forest Entomology. Merely formal changes were: the substitution of "Practical Entomology" for "Common Economic Insects and Methods of Controlling Them" as a description of Zoölogy 7c, and the designation by new numbers of two of the fields of research previously offered: "20b, Cytology, with Special Reference to Heredity," and "20g, Experimental Morphology."

As usual, the following tables show the number of students in each of the several classes who attended each of the courses in Zoölogy. The first table exhibits the facts for Harvard University, the second for Radcliffe College.

TABLE I

Courses 1910–11	Graduate A. & S.	Ap. Sci.	Senior	Junior	Soph.	Fresh.	Special	Uncl.	Total
Zoölogy 1	3	. . .	10	8	30	68	4	6	129
" 2	1	. . .	. . .	7	8	7	. . .	1	24
" 3	3	. . .	3	5	3	1	. . .	. . .	15
" 4	1	. . .	1	1	1	1	. . .	. . .	5
" 5a	. . .	. . .	1	1	1	. . .	. . .	. . .	3
" 7a	4	2	1	2	. . .	1	. . .	. . .	10
" 7b	2	2	1	2	. . .	1	. . .	. . .	8
" 7c	. . .	2	2	. . .	. . .	. . .	. . .	. . .	4
" 7d	. . .	9	. . .	. . .	. . .	. . .	. . .	. . .	9
" 11	. . .	2	3	2	3	. . .	. . .	. . .	10
" 12	3	. . .	. . .	. . .	. . .	. . .	. . .	. . .	3
" 14b	7	3	. . .	2	. . .	. . .	. . .	. . .	12
" 17	2	1	. . .	. . .	. . .	. . .	. . .	. . .	3
" 20a	2	. . .	. . .	. . .	. . .	. . .	. . .	. . .	2
" 20b	3	. . .	. . .	. . .	. . .	. . .	. . .	. . .	3
" 20c	5	. . .	. . .	. . .	. . .	. . .	. . .	. . .	5
" 20d	2	1	. . .	. . .	. . .	. . .	. . .	. . .	3
" 20e	1	. . .	1	. . .	. . .	. . .	. . .	. . .	2
" 20f	. . .	3	. . .	. . .	. . .	. . .	. . .	. . .	3
" 20g	1	. . .	. . .	. . .	. . .	. . .	. . .	. . .	1
Sums ..	40	25	23	30	46	79	4	7	254

TABLE II

Courses 1910-11	Gr.	Senior	Junior	Soph.	Fresh.	Special	Total
Zoölogy 1	. . .	3	8	2	8	3	24
" 2	. . .	1	3	. . .	1	1	6
" 3	1	. . .	1	1	. . .	. . .	3
4	1	. . .	. . .	. . .	. . .	. . .	1
" 5a	1	. . .	. . .	. . .	. . .	. . .	1
Sums	3	4	12	3	9	4	35

Nineteen students (fourteen registered in the Graduate School of Arts and Sciences, four in the Graduate School of Applied Science, and one Senior) carried on researches, five each under Professors Mark and Parker, and three each under Professors Wheeler, Castle, and Rand.

Of these, four met the requirements for, and received in June, the doctor's degree, three — Messrs. Barbour, Day, and Laurens — receiving the degree Ph.D., and one — Mr. Titus — the degree S.D. The thesis of Thomas Barbour was entitled "*A Contribution to the Zoögeography of the East Indian Islands*"; that of Edward C. Day, "*The Effect of Colored Light on Pigment Migration in the Eye of the Crayfish*"; that of Henry Laurens, "*The Reactions of Amphibians to Monochromatic Lights of Equal Intensity*," and that of Edward G. Titus, "*Monograph of the Genera Phytonomus and Hypera.*" Mr. Samuel C. Palmer completed the requirements for the degree of Ph.D., but too late for recommendation in June. His thesis is entitled "*The Numerical Relations of the Histological Elements in the Vertebrate Retina.*" The thesis of Mr. J. W. Chapman, on "*Insects Injurious to the Trees in the College Yard*," was accepted and will be published soon. Satisfactory work was accomplished by the other research students.

Two students received aid from the income of the Humboldt Fund to the amount of $138.57 while working at the Bermuda Biological Station, and one while working at Woods Hole received from the same source $58.00.

The Bermuda Biological Station was opened June 26, and closed August 5. Of the four persons enrolled, three were connected with Harvard University. Three numbers of the Contributions from the Station have been published during the year.

During the April recess Professor Mark delivered a lecture at Colgate University on "Some Vestigial Organs in Man."

Professor Parker spent much time during the year in perfecting an appliance for the production of spectral light of measured intensity. He also wrote for "Folia Neurobiologica" reviews of the American papers on the physiology of the nervous system.

Professor Wheeler's assistant, Mr. W. Reiff, devoted one half his time to a continuation of the study of the wilt disease of the gypsy moth, in coöperation with the State Forester, the other half being given to work on the Bussey collection of insects.

During November and December Professor Castle delivered a course of eight lectures at the Lowell Institute in Boston on "Heredity in Relation to Evolution and Animal Breeding." The lectures are to be published. In February, 1911, he delivered a lecture on "The Nature of Unit Characters," before the Harvey Society of New York, and in July, 1911, at the University of Chicago, two lectures, on "The Methods of Evolution" and on "Heredity and Sex." These three lectures are also to be published. Professor Castle has had in his research work the coöperation of Research Fellow Dr. J. C. Phillips.

Mr. Brues has devoted some time to the preparation of a poster for the Women's Municipal League illustrating the activities of the housefly.

The Zoölogical Club held twenty-three meetings; twenty original papers and seven reviews were presented. The average attendance was between fourteen and fifteen.

During the period covered by this report 41 zoölogical papers have been published. As their titles have been recorded in the *University Gazette*, and in the annual report of the Curator of the Museum of Comparative Zoölogy, they need not be repeated here.

EDWARD L. MARK, *Director*.

MINERALOGICAL MUSEUM AND LABORATORIES OF MINERALOGY AND PETROGRAPHY

To the President of the University: —

Sir, — The public Mineralogical Collections have been increased by about one hundred specimens, received in larger part as gifts from a dozen different donors. The most valuable and important single acquisition comprised a dozen blocks of the translucent green Smithsonite (zinc carbonate) from Kelly, New Mexico, weighing in all 600 pounds, which, after some of the larger surfaces had been cleaned and polished, was placed on exhibition; this was the gift of Mr. Robert W. Bull, '96, at the suggestion of Mr. A. F. Holden, '88, who keeps the interests of our Museum constantly in mind. Other important specimens include a large group of Colorado vivanite, a large white topaz from Texas, and pyrargyrite from Mexico. In a trip made by the instructors and students of the Department to Franklin Furnace and Paterson, New Jersey, a number of fine specimens were obtained from these well-known localities.

The Curator has spent some time in a study of the serpentines of Newfane, Vermont. The usual courses of instruction were given in the laboratories and the teaching plant maintained at its present high standard and even improved.

JOHN E. WOLFF, *Curator*.

THE PEABODY MUSEUM OF AMERICAN ARCHAE-
OLOGY AND ETHNOLOGY

To the President of the University: —

Sir, — It is my sad duty to begin my annual report by recording the loss of two of our distinguished and honored associates. Judge Francis Cabot Lowell died on March 6, 1911. Mr. Lowell was elected Trustee and Treasurer of the Board of Trustees at a meeting held on June 22, 1885. From that time Mr. Lowell was an interested and active member of the board, and, according to our records, he never missed a meeting for thirteen years. When in 1896 the Trustees decided that it would be for the best interests of the Museum to make over their trust to Harvard University, Mr. Lowell took an active part in attending to the legal matters pertaining to the transfer of the trust. On the accomplishment of this transfer, January 1, 1897, Mr. Lowell became a member of the Faculty of the Museum, of which the other members were President Eliot, Stephen Salisbury, Charles P. Bowditch, and the Peabody Professor. After Mr. Lowell's appointment as United States District Judge, and later, in 1905, as Circuit Judge, his arduous duties prevented him from attending the meetings regularly, but he came when he could. The last time we had him with us was at the annual meeting in 1908, but his interest in the Museum continued, and he was often consulted by other members of the Faculty on important matters relating to its welfare.

Another member of the former Board of Trustees, Dr. Samuel Hubbard Scudder, died on May 17, 1911, after a lingering illness of several years. Mr. Scudder became a member of the Board of Trustees in 1880, succeeding Mr. T. T. Bouvé as President of the Boston Society of Natural History. In 1897 he resigned that office, but remained a Trustee by election on the resignation of Colonel Lyman owing to ill health. Mr. Scudder continued a member of the Board of Trustees until it ceased to exist by the transfer of the Trust to the University in 1897. During the time that Mr. Scudder held this office several important matters came before the Board of Trustees for settlement, and the records show that he was appointed on special committees in which he

took an active part. As a distinguished and broad-minded
naturalist, brought up in the school of Agassiz, he fully appreciated the objects of the Museum, and was one with whom the
Curator could confer on all scientific and administrative matters
with the surety of receiving valuable advice and cordial support.

By the establishment of the new assistantship provided for by
the Mary Hemenway Fund for Archaeology, much has been
accomplished in connection with the cataloguing and arranging
of portions of the archaeological collections that have long been
in storage. This important work can now be continued until
many thousands of specimens, still in storage, are catalogued,
numbered, and made available for research.

Thanks to the interest of Mr. Augustus Hemenway, who has
provided for the repairs and painting of the exhibition halls and
for the repainting of the interior of the cases, Mr. Willoughby
has been able to rearrange the collections in several halls, and to
place on exhibition some recent accessions and a few collections
that have been in storage. During this rearrangement Mr.
Willoughby has prepared many general and special labels which
have been printed. With the assistance of Mr. Guernsey he has
been able to catalogue and care for the accessions during the
year.

As a protection in case of accident we are now having copies
made of the fifteen early volumes of the manuscript catalogue
of the specimens in the Museum. Beginning with the sixteenth
volume, the catalogue has been made in duplicate. These duplicate volumes will eventually be kept in the contemplated fireproof vault.

Assistant Professor Dixon, Librarian of the Museum, reports
that 277 volumes and 547 pamphlets have been added during
the year, and our anthropological library now contains 4,172
volumes and 4,003 pamphlets. A new iron book stack and a new
case of drawers for the standard catalogue cards have been added
during the year.

From funds furnished by the Committee on Central American
Research the Museum has published and issued under one cover
Memoirs, Vol. V, Nos. 1 and 2, 135 pages, 47 text figures, 2 maps,
and 30 plates, 1911. No. 1 is the final report by Mr. Teobert
Maler, who was for several years employed by the Museum to
explore various prehistoric sites in Central America. This report
is on the Ruins of Tikal in Guatemala and contains heliotype
reproductions of thirty of Mr. Maler's unexcelled photographs of

the temples and buildings of the prehistoric city, as well as plans
and drawings of many of the ruined structures.   No. 2 is a preliminary report on Tikal by Dr. A. M. Tozzer, who was in charge
of the Museum Expedition of 1909–10.   It contains a large map,
with cross sections of the city, and plans of numerous buildings,
not given in Mr. Maler's report.   The two complementary reports
thus give as full an account of the ruins of Tikal as is possible
at this time.

The Committee also provided for the expedition of 1910–11,
under the charge of Mr. R. E. Merwin, Central American Fellow.
This expedition made an exploration of Holmul, a ruined city
discovered by the expedition of 1909–10, and visited several
sites in the District of Peten.

Another publication of special importance is that of the Archaeology of the Delaware Valley by Mr. Ernest Volk, — Papers,
Vol. V, 258 pages, 26 text illustrations, 125 plates, 1911.   This
is Mr. Volk's report on twenty-two years of research under my
direction in the Delaware Valley.   In this volume are given the
facts as discovered and presented by Mr. Volk, relating to the
long controverted subject of Glacial Man in America.   The
evidence is given showing that man was contemporaneous, during
the closing period of the glacial age, with the deposition of the
Trenton gravel and the yellow drift in the valley.   For the publication of this volume we are indebted to the interest and generosity of Dr. Charles Peabody.

In addition to the above, the Museum has received the following gifts of money for various purposes during the year: —

Mr. John Stetson, his annual gift of $100 and an additional gift of $100 for the purchase of books	$200.00
Professor H. W. Haynes, his annual gift for the library . .	55.00
Dr. John C. Phillips, cost of typewriter for the library . .	86.00
A Friend, for binding books in the library	100.00
Mrs. N. E. Baylies, annual gift for Museum incidentals .	25.00
Miss Mary L. Ware, for a salary	480.00
Mr. Augustus Hemenway, toward repairs in exhibition halls	244.83
Dr. Charles Peabody, toward exploration in the Delaware Valley	200.00
A Friend, annual gift for explorations	100.00
Mr. Clarence B. Moore, annual gift for explorations . . .	500.00
A Friend, for salary of temporary assistant	100.00
A Friend, for the purchase of a collection	500.00
A Friend, for the purchase of a collection	5500.00
	$8090.83

The income of the Huntington Frothingham Wolcott Fund was used for the purchase of collections from British Guiana, Africa, Pacific Islands, and North America, thus adding many valuable specimens to the Museum.

The income of the Henry C. Warren Fund for Exploration was used for explorations in the Delaware Valley, in Ohio, in Iowa, and in New Brunswick. We were thus able to carry on the exploration of several archaeological sites, which is in accordance with Mr. Warren's expressed wish previous to specifying the bequest in his will.

A portion of the income of the Mary Hemenway Fund is applied to the Hemenway Assistant in Archaeology. The balance of this income can be appropriated for archaeological explorations, for obtaining archaeological collections, or for work on such collections.

The accessions to the Museum by gift, purchase, and exploration have been of unusual number and importance during the year, but only those received as gifts from friends are here mentioned: —

By a bequest we have received, from the estate of the late Dana Estes of Brookline, a large collection of prehistoric objects in pottery, bronze, iron, and bone. The collection was formed during the exploration, under Mr. Estes' supervision, in 1884 and 1885, of a series of tombs near Belluno, Italy. It contains many personal ornaments, weapons, implements, and vessels of bronze, and is particularly rich in fibulae of several forms. Mr. Charles P. Bowditch has presented the Museum with the complete paraphernalia for a Javanese shadow play, also a collection of cloth illustrating the methods of printing and dyeing textiles by wax painting among the Javanese, a collection of pottery and baskets from Java, baskets from Borneo, Luzon, and Ceylon, charms from Japan, and photographs of stone carvings and ruined buildings in India. Mr. Lewis H. Farlow has given an unusually fine collection of baskets, implements, utensils, clothing, personal ornaments, and ceremonial objects, from the Shasta, Karok, Yurok, Cayuse, Wasco, Clatsop, Skokomish, Yuki, Hupa, Sac and Fox, and Blackfoot Indians. Many of these specimens are of great scientific value and cannot be duplicated. Mr. Oric Bates collected and presented to the Museum 109 crania from a cemetery of plundered rock-cut tombs at Siwa, the ancient Ammonium in the Libyan Desert, northern Africa. The date of these tombs is approximately 400 B.C. to 100 B.C. The burials may in some cases be intrusive and as late as Roman times. They are all, however, pre-Islamic. From Professor Arlo Bates we have received two crania from the shell-heaps at North Haven, Maine: one of these shows a perforated palate and is the only instance we have of a " hair-lip " among the crania of North American Indians; from Mr. Clarence L. Hay, stone carvings, pottery, and shell objects from Mexico, and a Quechua loom from Cuzco, Peru; from Professor T. A. Jaggar, Jr., several Aleutian baskets and basket material, wallets, mats, and sea-otter darts, also photographs of the native people of the Aleutian Islands, collected by him in 1907; from Dr. William McM. Woodworth, a large collection of ethnological specimens from the Northwest coast and the Pueblo region, also from northern Africa and the Pacific Islands; from Mr. Edward Thompson, a nearly complete costume of a Mixteco Indian woman, and yucca fibre carrying bags from the same people; from Miss Grace Nicholson, a model of a tule rush canoe of the Pomo Indians of California, and 106 photographs of the various northern California Indians visited by her the past summer; from Professor J. B. Woodworth, quarry material from chert beds at the head of Spring Cañon, near Virginia City, Montana; from Dr. John C. Phillips, a painting of a buffalo hunt on deer skin by a Sioux Indian, also an Eskimo child's suit from Greenland; from Mr. A. V. Kidder, metate and axe from the ruins at Rito de los Frigoles, New Mexico, two old Navajo blankets, two very old birchbark buckets from a rock-shelter at Grand Sable, a stone maul from Isle Royal, Michigan, a grooved axe from New Mexico, and a bowl from Santa Clara, New Mexico; from Mr. Louis Cabot, through Dr. Bigelow, a soapstone pot from Iredell Co., North Carolina; from Mr. Henry E. Cornell, a Chukchi mat of skin with applied figures; from Miss Mary Brooks of Gloucester, a cranium with a metopic suture, from a cave in Tarmatambo, Peru; from Dr. Charles G. Weld, a Peruvian mummy, gourd cups, small stone effigies, and textile fabrics, from Peruvian graves; from Mr. Alanson Skinner, copper spear point from Menominee reservation, Wisconsin; from the estate of Dr. Weld, through Dr. Thomas Barbour, 31 large photographs of natives of New Zealand, New Guinea, and New Hebrides; from Mr. Harrison W. Smith, bow and six arrows from Ceram Island, Molucca group; from Mr. Clarence B. Moore, pottery from mounds in the Mississippi valley; from Mrs. W. H. Wightman, a stone hammer from northern Ireland; from Mr.

H. J. Winn, 32 Addis gallery photographs of Indians; from the Duke of Loubat, four bronze medals.

Assistant Professor Dixon was given leave of absence for the last half of the year in order to prepare the report on the Indian Tribes of the United States for the Census Bureau.

Dr. Charles Peabody, Assistant in European Archaeology, was in Europe during several months. He represented the Museum at the Congrès Préhistorique de France, and visited several archaeological sites, where he secured a number of specimens for the Museum.

Mr. A. V. Kidder, Austin Teaching Fellow, was in New Mexico during the winter continuing his study of the ancient pottery from the Pueblos.

It will be recalled that, in 1897, Miss Phoebe Ferris bequeathed to the Museum the land occupied by an Indian cemetery. This is the site where, with the assistance of Dr. C. L. Metz, I began to explore in 1881. Since that time parties from the Museum have from time to time been engaged in its exploration, and it has been a training place in field work for a number of the graduate students in the Department. During the present season this exploration has been completed by Mr. Bruce W. Merwin. The large amount of material obtained during all these years is being studied by Mr. R. E. Merwin who has taken a prominent part in the explorations. The land which belongs to the Museum can now be made into a public park for the city of Madisonville, Ohio, under such conditions as the University may determine in accordance with Miss Ferris' bequest.

Miss Alice C. Fletcher, the holder of the Thaw Fellowship, has completed her report on the Omaha tribe. This embodies the results of her long continued research on the history, life, ceremonies, customs and arts of the Omahas. By an agreement with the Museum this important volume is issued in the series of reports of the Bureau of Ethnology.

The close association of the teachers in the Division of Anthropology with the Museum, of which they are officers, keeps the instruction in anthropology closely connected with the work of the Museum as established on the foundation of the Division under the Faculty of Arts and Sciences. The Museum and its library are thus essential to the Division.

In May last, the Association of American Museums held one day's session of the Boston Meeting in Cambridge. The Museum was visited by the officers of many museums in this country and our methods were studied by those interested in museum technique.

The Visiting Committee appointed by the Board of Overseers held a meeting in the Museum, on January 12, for the purpose of discussing the possibility of completing the south wing of the University Museum in order to give to the anthropological section the much needed additional room and extended facilities. After a consideration of the plans, which had been prepared under my direction, for closing the gap between our present building and the southwestern corner of the Oxford Street façade, the Committee discussed the form of a report to the Board of Overseers. It was decided that such a report should present the scope, importance, and value of the Museum in its various lines of activity with a statement of its financial condition, and should be accompanied by an appeal to the Overseers on the part of the Committee for the completion of the building at an estimated cost of $125,000. This report was prepared and signed by the twelve members of the Committee, all of whom are graduates of the University. It was presented by the Chairman, Mr. Markham, at the meeting of the Overseers on April 12, 1911.

F. W. PUTNAM,
Honorary Curator of the Museum.

THE SEMITIC MUSEUM

To the President of the University: —

Sir, — The year 1910–11 has seen several changes in the personnel of the Semitic Department. Professor George F. Moore has withdrawn, in order to devote his teaching entirely to the Department of the History of Religions. Dr. William R. P. Davey has accepted an appointment in Syracuse University. Professor James Richard Jewett, who graduated at Harvard in 1884, has come to us as Professor of Arabic, after long service in Brown, Minnesota, and Chicago Universities.

The Semitic Museum has been enriched during the year by the addition of several hundred specimens. Among these are a collection of eleven Babylonian-Assyrian stone cylinder seals, and a collection of eight hundred and twenty cuneiform tablets from Babylonia. Most of the tablets date from the early Babylonian period, and relate to matters of business, religion, and private and social transactions. We have also received from Jerusalem specimens of eighty-six varieties of the trees and shrubs of Palestine. These are the first instalment of a collection which F. Vester and Co. of Jerusalem have been engaged for several years in gathering for our Museum. Each variety is represented by two specimens, one giving a cross section, and one a longitudinal cut showing the grain of the wood. These specimens of wood have been placed on exhibition in one of the table cases of the Palestinian room.

In the previous report the expectation was held out that a full account of the work of excavation done at Samaria in 1908–10 might be published during the year 1911. It is now clear that this expectation cannot be realized, because the explorers have had other engagements which made heavy demands on their time. It is hoped that the publication of the report may not be long delayed. Its appearance is eagerly awaited by scholars, and ought to arouse such general interest as shall provide the means for a resumption of the work of excavation. The Israelite palaces and the Hebrew writings found at Samaria are unique, and justify the hope of still greater surprises for the explorer.

The amount of publication of a Semitic nature now provided for suggests that the time has come for the projection of a series of occasional volumes, to be issued by the Semitic Department. In such a series the account of the work at Samaria naturally belongs, as does also a volume which has been prepared by Dr. Mary I. Hussey on the early Babylonian tablets belonging to the Museum. The means to publish these two works have been provided by the generosity of Mr. Jacob H. Schiff, Chairman of the Committee to visit the Semitic Department. Before coming to us Professor Jewett was engaged in preliminary arrangements looking to the publication of a series of Arabic volumes. These also might form part of the Harvard Semitic series. The cuneiform tablets, Babylonian-Assyrian seals, pottery from Palestine, and Arabic and Syriac manuscripts would furnish material for additional volumes.

DAVID G. LYON, *Curator*.

THE FOGG ART MUSEUM

To the President of the University: —

Sir, — I have the honor to present the following report on the Fogg Art Museum for the year 1910–11.

The Fogg Museum has received by gift the following additions to its permanent collections of works of art: two water color drawings by John Ruskin — Convent and Alpine Pass, and Pass of Faido — presented by friends and pupils of Professor Charles H. Moore, the first Director of the Fogg Museum, in recognition of his devoted service to the Museum and to the University; from the French government, eight pieces of Sèvres porcelain, which were presented to Harvard University and placed in the Fogg Museum; a Japanese painting by an early Ukiyoye master, a Japanese book of songs, fourteen Japanese prints, some Italian bobbin lace, and seventeen ancient gems, from Mr. Owen Bryant, '04; Chinese porcelains, consisting of three tall jars, two tall beaker-shaped vases, and three large bottles, from Mrs. W. Wheeler Smith of New York; and from Mr. James Loeb, '88, thirty-six plaster casts of Arretine moulds and fragments to replace some of the original pieces which, together with his collection of vases and bronzes, Mr. Loeb removed to his home in Munich.

A Venetian painting representing the Holy Family, attributed to Bonifazio, was bought from the income of the Randall fund with the help of gifts from Dr. Denman W. Ross, '75, and Mr. Charles C. Walker, '92.

To the print collection an unusually large number of additions have been made. The Museum Collection has acquired by gift from Mr. Paul J. Sachs, '00, Rembrandt's Great Jewish Bride, the Shepherdess Knitting by Millet, sixty-one etchings by Jacquemart, and fifty-one etchings by Herman A. Webster; from an anonymous giver, the Furnace Nocturne, an etching by Whistler; from Mr. Francis Bullard, '86, a third state of the Clyde from Turner's Liber Studiorum, and Lupton's copy of the Mill near the Grand Chartreuse, from the same series; and from Mr. James C. Smillie, thirteen etchings by his father, James D. Smillie. The Nocturne, a lithotint by Whistler, was purchased from the income of the Gray fund.

The Museum has added 541 photographs and 507 slides to its collections. To its library 61 volumes have been added, of which 24 were gifts. The most notable purchases were the L'Oeuvre gravé de Rembrandt by Rovinski, and the first two volumes of Max Lehrs' Geschichte und kritischer Katalog des deutschen, niederlandischen und französischen Kupferstichs im XV. Jahrhundert. Both these books are scarce and valuable, and important for the student. Their purchase was made possible by the fact that there was at this time an accumulated income in the Searle fund, from which our books are purchased. The remaining acquisitions include 18 gallery catalogues, and 11 volumes for students' use.

The Fogg Museum has received as an indefinite loan a painting of S. Fabian, Pope, attributed to Antoniazzo Romano, and a small pinnacle from an altarpiece with S. Agnes and the lamb, attributed to Ambrogio Lorenzetti, one of the important early Sienese masters; as a temporary loan, a tondo attributed to Raffaellino del Garbo, and a Madonna adoring the Child, from Mr. Harold W. Pearsall. Several of the Italian paintings mentioned in the last report, which were lent by Mr. and Mrs. C. B. Perkins and the Misses Norton, remained in the Museum through this year also. The Misses Norton lent, in addition, a water color drawing of Scott's house in Edinburgh, by J. M. W. Turner. Mr. Owen Bryant, '04, lent five Japanese prints; Mr. Richard Norton, '92, two moulds from Tripoli; and Mr. Edward W. Forbes, '95, two water color drawings of Greek marbles in Athens, by Mr. Joseph Lindon Smith, and a Spanish Gothic chest of the fifteenth century.

The principal special exhibition of the year was of works of Degas, this being the first exhibition of his paintings ever held in Boston. Mr. Alfred Atmore Pope of Farmington, Conn., lent three remarkable paintings; Mr. Harris Whittemore of Naugatuck, Conn., one of Degas' most important and beautiful works; Messrs. Durand-Ruel of New York, two oils and a pastel; Mr. Frank Gair Macomber of Boston, an oil and a pastel; and the Museum of Fine Arts, Boston, an oil, two pastels, and also reproductions of drawings and photographs of paintings and pastels by Degas, which were shown in the print room. This exhibition attracted a total of 2,551 visitors during the ten days it was held, the attendance ranging from 64 on the first day to 533 on the last. It was the most popular special exhibition the Fogg Museum has had. A catalogue of the exhibition, with an introduction by Professor Arthur Pope, was prepared for free distribution.

The Degas exhibition was followed by one of facsimile photographs in color of early Flemish paintings, which were loaned by the College Library for the purpose.

The Rembrandt exhibition in the print room was replaced by an exhibition of modern etchings, including, besides prints already belonging to the Museum, some of those by Jacquemart and Webster given by Mr. Sachs, and works of Meryon, Whistler, Haden, Lalanne, Lepère, Palmer, Bone, Zorn, and others, lent by Mr. Bullard.

During the year the Fogg Collection, with the exception of the paintings, was catalogued. 761 engravings were catalogued and lists were made of the plates represented in the collection by series of states, and of those of which there are duplicate states in the Museum.

Engravings and photographs were mounted for other departments of the University and for a few outsiders. For this work the Fogg Museum received $38.97. The receipts from the sales of photographs, post-cards, and catalogues have amounted to $22.70.

In the photograph department 507 slides and 1,532 photographs were catalogued, and in addition, about 450 photographs, mainly of Italian painting, were recatalogued with changed attributions. The table adjoined shows the growth and record of the photograph and slide collections for a succession of years: —

	1905–6	1906–7	1907–8	1908–9	1909–10	1910–11
Photos received during year	2,076	670	1,926	525	859	541
Photos catalogued during year	1,250	1,276	1,481	683	2,535	1,532
Photos remaining uncatalogued	2,262	2,932	3,551	3,372	1,696	647
Total number accessions	35,144	36,420	37,901	38,595	41,129	42,661
Total number in Museum	37,406	39,352	41,452	41,967	42,825	43,308
Slides catalogued		67	84	98	52	472	507
Total number in Museum	3,570	3,654	3,752	3,804	4,276	4,783

About a year and a half ago, a standard size of photograph mount, 14x18 inches, was adopted, that previously used having been 13¾x21¼ inches. The task of cutting down the mounts of approximately 40,000 photographs from 21¼ to 18 inches in height was then begun. This involved also the rewriting of catalogue numbers on each mount. The work was nearly completed on the first of September, to the general satisfaction of users of the photographs.

Photographs were lent 133 times, and slides 220 times, chiefly to members and departments of the University and to Radcliffe College.

The number of registered visits for the study of photographs was 972; of these 925 were by members of the University and 47 by outsiders.

The total number of visits made to the print room for purposes of study was 287. Of these 195 were by members of the University and Radcliffe College.

Since the Fogg Museum was built in 1895 the conditions have changed. It contains now a valuable and growing collection of original paintings, which cannot be displayed properly in the present gallery. Better lighting of the gallery is needed, and additional space for exhibition. Members of the Fine Arts Department are anxious to have a room in the Fogg Museum where the drawing classes may be conducted. The Fogg lecture room is too large and the little lecture room too small for most of the Fine Arts courses which are given in them. The members of the Fine Arts Department are now engaged in planning how best the needs of the Museum and the Department may be filled by certain changes in the present building and the addition of a wing. It is expected that the plans will mature soon, and it is greatly to be desired that means of procuring the necessary money for these changes will be found. Moreover, additional funds are needed for the purchase of works of art. Those applicable to that purpose are so small that it is very difficult for the Museum to grow as fast as it ought to grow, although opportunities to buy important works of art frequently come.

EDWARD W. FORBES, *Director*.

THE GERMANIC MUSEUM

To the President of the University: —

Sir, — The academic year 1910–11 marks a decided advance in the Germanic Museum cause and has raised new hopes for the future.

The most important event of the year was the decision reached in regard to the architect of the new building. It was Mr. Busch's desire that the new building should be a characteristic specimen of German architecture and that it should therefore be designed by a leading architect in Germany. Through the kind intercession of Geheimrat Schmidt, of the Prussian Ministry of Education, who has done so much to facilitate the interchange of professors between Harvard and Berlin, we succeeded in obtaining the services of Professor German Bestelmeyer of Dresden, one of the foremost architects of contemporary Germany, whose recently completed Central Hall of the new University buildings at Munich is an undoubted work of genius and justly enjoys a more than national reputation.

Professor Bestelmeyer, entering upon his task with earnest enthusiasm and rare insight, has produced a plan remarkably consistent and simple and at the same time strikingly original. The Corporation at once accepted it and have authorized him to proceed with elaborating the working plans and specifications. In this Professor Bestelmeyer will be assisted by our own Professor H. Langford Warren, who all along has taken a keen interest in the Germanic Museum and to whose intelligent and expert advice we owe much. In the absence of Professor Bestelmeyer, the supervision of the construction of the building itself is to be committed to Professor Warren's firm (Warren & Smith).

The site generously accorded to us by the Corporation is the corner lot between Frisbie Place, Kirkland Street, and Divinity Avenue, opposite Randall Hall. It is one of the finest sites in all Cambridge, and affords the architect ample scope for monumental and pleasing effects, — an opportunity of which Professor Bestelmeyer has skilfully availed himself.

The whole building embraces an oblong rectangular space of about 130 feet on Kirkland Street and about 200 feet on Divinity

Avenue and Frisbie Place. But the Museum proper consists of two wings of unequal length, placed at right angles to each other, the longer one facing Divinity Avenue, the shorter one stretching from Divinity Avenue to Frisbie Place, parallel with Kirkland Street, but set back from it some 100 feet. The space between the two wings is conceived of as an ornamental court, with shrubs, statuary, and water-basins, connected with the Museum itself by cloister-like arcades running along Kirkland Street and Frisbie Place. A massive tower rising at the point of junction of the two main wings holds the various parts of the design firmly together. It is an interesting illustration of the catholicity of Harvard taste, that at the same time that modern French architecture has come to be so happily represented at Cambridge in the person of Professor Duquesne, there should arise here a German building thoroughly characteristic of the best in modern German art, full of originality and power and at the same time harmonious, measured, and restrained.

The exact date when ground will be broken for the new building has not yet been settled. Meanwhile, it is gratifying to note that gifts both of money and of objects for the rounding out of our collection continue to come to us.

Mr. Otto H. Kahn of New York has given the sum of $1,000 for the purchase of reproductions of German sculptures, preferably to be used toward the acquisition of a bronze copy of Rietschel's Goethe-Schiller monument at Weimar.

His Highness, Johann Albrecht, Duke of Mecklenburg and Prince-Regent of Brunswick, has signified his intention of giving a bronze copy of the Brunswick Lion, the bronze monument erected in 1166 by Duke Henry the Lion of Saxony in front of Brunswick Castle as a symbol of his territorial sovereignty. This interesting specimen of German Romanesque metal work will be placed in the court in front of the new Museum building and will add much to the mediaeval effect of the south façade.

Professor Hugo Lederer of Berlin has given a cast of his colossal statue of " The Fighter," recently exhibited at the Paris Salon. This remarkable work of one of the foremost sculptors of contemporary Germany has provisionally been placed in our present building and forms a welcome counterpart to " The Fencer " by the same master, already in our possession.

The Provincial Government of Rhenish Prussia has notified the Curator that it is preparing for the Museum a collection of casts of monumental and architectural sculpture of the Rhineland from the Romanesque period to the Renaissance.   This collection will embrace among other objects a Romanesque portal of Trèves Cathedral, the main portal of the Church of our Lady at Andernach, reliefs from the Tympanon of the Church of our Lady at Trèves, choir-stalls from St. Gereon at Cologne, the Visitation group from Xanten, and a number of monumental tombs from various Rhenish churches.

Finally, the Society of Arts and Crafts of the Rhineland and Westphalia announces that it is preparing a similar gift representing the development of the industrial arts in western Germany in the Middle Ages and the Renaissance. Both collections together will contain about twenty large and some forty smaller objects.

These two collections are being prepared under the supervision of Professor Paul Clemen of Bonn University, German Visiting Professor at Harvard in 1907–08, at whose suggestion both gifts were made. They are therefore a direct outcome of the interchange of professors between Germany and Harvard University, which in its turn had its first inception from the Museum propaganda.

KUNO FRANCKE, *Curator*.

PUBLICATION OFFICE

To the President of the University: —

Sir, — I have the honor to submit my report for the academic year 1910–11.

During this year the Publication Office has been particularly busy.

In the printing department more than 1700 pieces of work were handled, including the Annual Catalogue, the President's Report, and the University Directory, and representing a business of more than $56,000. During the year a new press has been installed and an addition made to our monotype equipment. Every foot of available space in University Hall is now in use, but the office is still unable to do more than a portion of the printing which the various needs of the University require.

In addition to its work as a distributing centre for the official publications of the University the Publication Office has had charge of the mailing of the *Harvard Theological Review* and the *Quarterly Journal of Economics*, and the publishing of several books and periodicals.

The following publications were issued during the year: —

A Guide to Reading in Social Ethics.
Harvard University Directory, 1910.
Banking Reform in the United States. By O. M. W. Sprague.
Applied Ethics. By Theodore Roosevelt.
Railway Rate Theories of the Interstate Commerce Commission. By M. B. Hammond of Ohio State University.
A Laboratory Course in Physiology. By W. B. Cannon.
Harvard Theological Review. Vol. 4.
Harvard Studies in Classical Philology. Vol. 22.
Quarterly Journal of Economics. Vol. 25.
Annals of Mathematics. Vol. 12.
Annals of the Astronomical Observatory. Vol. 56, Pt. 5; Vol. 59, Pts. 6 and 7; Vol. 64, Pt. 7; Vol. 65; Vol. 66; Vol. 68, Pt. 2.

The following books are in press: —

Manual for Northern Woodsmen. By Austin Cary. Third edition.
The British Postoffice. By J. C. Hemmeon of McGill University.

The demand for these publications has been encouraging, the University Directory in particular having had a very wide sale. The receipts up to date on the latter book amount to more than

$12,500, and several hundred copies have been sold and not yet paid for. Leaving out of consideration the receipts on the Directory account, the total sales of publications for the year amounted to more than $11,000.

I should like again to call your attention to the need of more adequate publication facilities. Works of high scholarship are being prepared by members of the University, and because of our lack of publication funds and our inadequate equipment many of these books are never issued or are sent to other presses. The loss to scholarship as well as to the prestige of the University is real. To quote from the *Harvard Alumni Bulletin:* " Only last year an historical treatise of great importance, written by a Harvard master of arts, now a member of the Faculty of Arts and Sciences, was given to the press of a sister institution for publication." And although the University has the largest Sanskrit publication fund of any institution in this country, it has no facilities for printing a Sanskrit book.

Volumes that are commercially profitable can usually find a publisher, but the test of a book's merit is not always its salability, and if the University's reputation for productive scholarship is to be maintained a subsidized institution is needed for the publication of books that can never pay in dollars and cents.

That this is becoming generally recognized is evidenced by the recent establishment of presses at several American universities. No one of these is comparable with the presses at Oxford or at Cambridge, England, and in that fact, it seems to me, lies the opportunity for this University. There is a very definite need in this country for a learned press where large fonts of type of Arabic, Hebrew, Sanskrit, Russian, and other tongues might be found, where compositors skilled in setting foreign languages and mathematical formulae might be gathered, and where work of scholarly accuracy might be executed. The first press of adequate scope to be established in the United States will draw to it, from all parts of the country, learned work which is now sent abroad, and Harvard University has still the chance to establish such an institution. The opportunity is not one that can be postponed, however, for the need is so well recognized and the advantages to be derived are so considerable that within the next few years some university is sure to take advantage of the situation.

C. CHESTER LANE,
Publication Agent.

UNIVERSITY EXTENSION

Sir, — The following report covers the work of University Extension for the academic year 1910–11, including the Summer School of Arts and Sciences for 1911.

I. The Summer School of Arts and Sciences

The general courses of the Summer School were given by twenty-eight officers of the Faculty of Arts and Sciences, including one lecturer, eight assistant professors, fifteen instructors, three assistants, one Austin Teaching Fellow, together with four professors and one assistant professor from other institutions, and four gentlemen not at present holding any academic position. Eight persons were employed as assistants in these courses. In addition, two Harvard professors offered research courses for which no student applied. As usual, besides the general courses, the Physical Education courses were given by the Director of the Hemenway Gymnasium with a large staff of lecturers, instructors, and assistants, and the courses in Surveying and Mechanics were given at the Engineering Camp.

Certain courses given in previous years, but taken by a very small number of students, were omitted in 1911. The most noteworthy addition to the list was the course on Vocational Guidance, given by Mr. Meyer Bloomfield, '01, Director of the Vocation Bureau of Boston, and taken by forty-two students. This course, which the School owed to the generosity of Mr. Bloomfield and the Executive Board of the Vocation Bureau, is the first attempt to give systematic instruction at a university in this newly-developed and useful field of the teacher's work. It is hoped that the course, which attracted attention throughout the country, can be again offered in an enlarged form in the coming summer.

The School also had the advantage of a course of six lectures on the " Massachusetts Idea of Vocational Education," arranged by the State Board of Education of the Commonwealth, and given by the Commissioner of Education and by other officers of the Board and of industrial and agricultural schools in Massachusetts. It is hoped that this may be the beginning of permanent close coöperation between the Summer School and public educational authorities in furthering the interest of teachers.

The number of persons in attendance at the School was as follows: —

	1909	1910	1911
Total number of students	933	873	787
" " " men	438	476	400
" " " women	495	397	387
Percentage of men	47%	54.5%	51%

This body of students was made up as follows: —

	1909	1910	1911
Students at Engineering Camp [1]	12	31	19
Harvard students of preceding academic year: [2]			
Members of graduate and professional schools	17	19	10
Undergraduates in good standing	46	61	43
Undergraduates with deficient record	42	57	35
Radcliffe students of preceding academic year	7	11	6
Students in physical education courses	160	170	186
Students from outside in general courses	653	528	492
	937	877	791
Names counted twice	4	4	4
	933	873	787

As the above figures show, the diminution in numbers was due largely to the falling off of Harvard students. This was partly occasioned by the rule, made this year for the first time, that students who have failed in college work will be admitted, for the purpose of making up failure, to three courses only, — Trigonometry, German, and French. These courses were especially planned to be of a disciplinary character, and the rule was strictly enforced, with a result entirely satisfactory.

The composition of the group entitled " Students from outside in general courses " was as follows: —

[1] Not including Engineering Camp students who were at the time members of Harvard University.

[2] Not including Harvard students in shopwork courses.

	1909	1910	1911
Teachers and school officers:			
Professors and college instructors.	52	40	40
Normal school teachers	16	14	5
High school teachers	121	98	94
Grade school teachers	63	100	75
Endowed and private school teachers	64	54	52
Other teachers	86	34	38
Superintendents, supervisors, and principals	59	55	50
	—	—	—
Total, teachers and school officers	461	395	354

Men	163	162	135
Women	298	233	219
Percentage of men . .	35%	40%	38%

	1909	1910	1911
Students from other colleges	48	39	27
Students from preparatory schools	2	7	5
Other students	47	21	11
Other occupation than teaching	33	34	45
Occupation not given	62	32	50
	—	—	—
	192	133	138
	461	395	354
	—	—	—

Total, students from outside taking General Courses	653	528	492
Men	261	243	209
Women	392	285	283
Percentage of men . .	40%	46%	42.5%

In this body of students from outside there were:—

	1909	1910	1911
Holders of A.B. or S.B. or some equivalent degree	173	148	170
Holders of a higher degree	71	57	48
Members of the Summer School in one of preceding five years	146	99	136

The geographical distribution of this same group was as follows:—

	1909	1910	1911
New England States	327	257	261
Middle States	157	124	94
South Atlantic States	57	26	36
South Central States	19	26	26
North Central States	66	72	52
Western States	6	5	5
Foreign countries	21	18	18
	—	—	—
	653	528	492

The Harvard Summer School not only aims to maintain an exacting standard of work, but its methods are peculiar in two respects. First, under the arrangement of our instruction a student, in order to get any "credit" at all, must complete the full equivalent of one half-course. In consequence, he has as a rule no time to pursue seriously more than one subject in the six weeks. The majority of teachers who undertake summer study prefer to take more than one subject, hearing several lectures a day but giving less time to private study in each course. Moreover, if they are working for a degree, they are also eager to secure the greater amount of "credit" usually to be secured under that plan. The second peculiarity of Harvard is that the University does not grant the degree of A.M. on the ground of summer study alone. Hence the numerous college graduates who wish to earn that degree by studying for a series of summer vacations do not find at Harvard what they want, unless, in exceptional cases, they choose to take a Harvard course in preparation for a degree from another university.

It is thus manifest that the number of persons whose needs are met by the Harvard Summer School is limited. Nevertheless, in both these policies the Harvard position is sound, and the service to the country rendered by the University in maintaining the distinctive character of our summer work and of our Master's degree far outweighs the repute which greater size would bring us. There is no reason to doubt that much greater numbers could be secured by a different policy in these two respects, but no one who has observed how even some intelligent and very earnest school teachers gain here a new conception of what study is, will wish to make a radical change in our methods of teaching, while the high standard of our Master's degree is its prime attraction.

It seems likely that by great care and economy the Summer School can be maintained on this basis without serious annual expense to the University. The quality of the students is excellent, and the testimony of both students and instructors leaves no doubt that the work of our six-week courses is the full equivalent of a half-course in term time.

In any case, the chief constituency of the Summer School must be sought among teachers and other mature persons, and among students who either (as in the case of prospective medical students taking chemistry) require certain special subjects for professional purposes or else have definite aims of general culture. The use of the Summer School by undergraduates making up failures, and by undergraduates merely wishing to score summer credit in order to shorten their college course, was not a part of the original purpose of the School, and is a purely incidental and somewhat dangerous function of its present activity.

The courses in Physical Education at the Hemenway Gymnasium have been conducted by Dr. Dudley A. Sargent since 1887, and are intended to train directors of gymnasiums and of physical education in colleges and schools. The number of students taking them has grown in a remarkable way, and the proportion of men among the students has also shown a gratifying increase in recent years.

Year	Students	Percent. of Men	Year	Students	Percent. of Men
1887	57	32	1900	119	29
1888	45	38	1901	111	32
1889	59	37	1902	130	31
1890	83	30	1903	165	26
1891	95	36	1904	134	25
1892	111	33	1905	150	24
1893	56	39	1906	127	28
1894	77	40	1907	125	32
1895	90	39	1908	158	39
1896	104	37	1909	160	37.5
1897	124	26	1910	170	39
1898	84	19	1911	186	45
1899	72	39			

The deficit on the Summer School account for the fiscal year 1910–11 (being a part of the deficit made by the Summer School of 1910) amounted to $4,213.27, and was charged to the College Account.

The account of the General Courses of the Summer School for 1911 (of which the expenses necessarily fell in two fiscal years) shows, as given below, a deficit of about $500.00, which was met from the surplus earned by the courses in Physical Education.

GENERAL COURSES

Income

	1910	1911
Registration fees	$1,614.00	$2,232.00
Tuition fees (not including Phys. Educ.)	15,196.67	13,805.00
Auditors' fees	850.00	930.00
Stated contribution from Phys. Educ.	250.00	250.00
Gifts for special objects	—	320.00
	$17,910.67	$17,537.00
Deficit	5,467.20	494.14
	$23,377.87	$18,031.14

Expenses

Salaries and grants for instruction	$16,584.00	$12,080.00
Public exercises and hospitality	1,016.21	761.76
General expenses	344.55	414.21
Expenses for Shopwork courses	176.00	528.00
Administration and office expenses	2,197.02	2,159.03
Advertising and circulars	1,989.93	1,103.21
Postage	289.19	231.02
Tution fees remitted	100.00	135.00
University Charge:		
Bursar's Office	180.57	382.00
Publication Office	285.93	236.91
Annual Catalogue	214.47	—
	$23,377.87	$18,031.14

PHYSICAL EDUCATION COURSES

Fees for tuition	$6,250.00	$6,900.00
Salaries and expenses	5,804.65	5,130.48
Surplus	$445.35	$1,769.52

II. COMMISSION ON EXTENSION COURSES

The Commission on Extension Courses consists of representatives of the following institutions: —

Harvard University	Boston University
Tufts College	Museum of Fine Arts
Mass. Institute of Technology	Wellesley College
Boston College	Simmons College

Since the general administrative services for the courses of the Commission were provided by Harvard, it is proper here to make record of the work of the Commission for 1910–11. The following table exhibits the courses, the number of students in each, and the number of certificates granted to students who completed the courses. The number of certificates earned was about 46 per cent of the whole enrolment.

	Enrolment	Certificates
English Literature and Composition (Professors Copeland and Greenough and Mr. Hersey of Harvard)	258	64
Experimental Electricity (Professor Derr of Institute of Technology)	27	11
Elementary Economics (Professor Metcalf of Tufts) . . .	116	64
Psychology (Professor Yerkes of Harvard)	20	7
Advanced English Composition (Professor Sharp of Boston University)	82	27
History of English Literature (Professor Black of Boston University)	80	46
German Literature (Professor Perrin of Boston University) .	18	10
Elementary French (Professor Geddes of Boston Univ.) .	23	8
French Literature (Professor Colin of Wellesley)	13	5
Physics (Professor Kent of Boston University)	12	9
Ancient Art and Civilization (Dr. Fairbanks of Museum of Fine Arts).	29	13
Roman, Byzantine, and Gothic Art (Professor Sumner of Institute of Technology)	21	9
Dynamical and Structural Geology (Professor Barton of Teachers' School of Science)	23	15
Mineralogy (Professor Barton of Teachers' School of Science)	23	14
Physical Geography (Professor Johnson of Harvard) . . .	74	69
Physiological Botany (Professor Osterhout of Harvard) . .	44	24
	863	395

The students in these courses are not members of, nor even directly affiliated to, Harvard University, but the courses authorized by the Commission, having been approved by the Harvard Administrative Board for University Extension, were accepted by the Faculty of Arts and Sciences (on recommendation of the Faculty's committee on instruction) to be counted toward the degree of Associate in Arts. Each course counts as a full-course, a two-thirds course, a half-course, or a quarter-course, according to the amount of work required. All the courses given by the Commission in 1910–11 were also accepted for the degree of A.A. by the Faculties of Tufts College and Wellesley College.

The Boston School Committee has accepted the degree of A.A. from Harvard, Radcliffe, Tufts, and Wellesley as the equivalent of the A.B. in establishing the qualifications of teachers, so that the courses of the Commission are now fully available for the purposes of Boston school-teachers. A large number of teachers have availed themselves of this opportunity by taking these courses. This is probably one reason why but a small number of Boston teachers take courses in the Harvard Summer School.

The experience of the first year of the Commission's work
gives confidence that the general plan which has been followed is
suited to the end in view, and that the lines laid down can be
pursued in the further development of University Extension in
Boston.

The financial statement of the Commission's courses is as
follows: —

Expenses

Salaries		$12,224.50
Lecture-room expenses		604.41
Advertising		117.60
Printing		423.94
Postage		188.35
Office and clerical expense		197.24
Teachers' School of Sciences		
Expenses for equipment and administration	$1,042.21	
Less gifts and minor income	197.47	844.74
		$14,600.78

Income

Fees	$5,169.50
Lowell Institute	8,027.53
Chamber of Commerce subscription	1,403.75
	$14,600.78

For 1911–12 about the same number of courses have been
provided, and the number of students is about twenty-five per
cent greater than in 1910–11. More than one fifth of the persons
taking courses this year were in last year's courses also. The
valuable Courses for Teachers maintained by Boston University
and the courses of the Commission supplement each other, and a
full and gratifying coöperation is maintained between the two
groups.

III. Extension Students in Regular Courses

In 1910–11 five persons were registered as Extension Students of the University. Of these two were members of the School for Social Workers, and one was a student in the Episcopal Theological School.

In 1911–12 eleven persons are registered as Extension Students, of whom one is a member of the School for Social Workers, one each a student in the Episcopal Theological School, the New England Conservatory of Music, and Andover Theological Seminary. This class of Extension Students is understood to include non-graduates whose main occupation is not that of a Harvard student, but who wish to work in Harvard courses. They would formerly have been classed as Special Students in Harvard College; as Extension Students they are not members of Harvard College. The distinction has proved decidedly convenient, and makes it easier to render Harvard instruction available for a varied group of highly deserving non-graduate students who wish to take courses under the Faculty of Arts and Sciences.

JAMES HARDY ROPES, *Dean.*

RADCLIFFE COLLEGE

To the President of the University:—

Sir, — I have the honor to submit the report of Radcliffe College for the academic year 1910–11.

The number of students in actual attendance during the year was 500, as against 485 during the preceding year.

Graduate Students	71
Seniors	62
Juniors	74
Sophomores	61
Freshmen	106
Special Students	117
Unclassified Students	9
Total	500

At Commencement in June, 1911, sixty-seven students, four of whom had completed their residence in an earlier year, received the degree of Bachelor of Arts. Three students who had not been registered as Seniors received the degree, and two students who had been so registered failed to receive it. Three of the sixty-seven received the degree *magna cum laude*; twenty-six received it *cum laude*.

Seventeen candidates received the degree of Master of Arts. Six of the seventeen had taken their first degree at Radcliffe; the others represented the following colleges: Mount Holyoke College (two); Wellesley College (two); Hollins College, Leland Stanford Jr. University, McGill University, Middlebury College, Newcomb College, Smith College, Vassar College (one each). Eight received the degree in English, four in History and Political Science, two in German, two in Philosophy, and one in Chemistry

Three hundred and forty-three candidates presented themselves for admission. Twenty-one were candidates for admission as special students. Forty-six candidates took part of the examinations or worked off admission conditions. One hundred and sixty candidates took the preliminary examinations, and one hundred and sixteen the final examinations. Sixteen candidates who took wholly or in part the examinations of the College Entrance Examination Board are included in the foregoing classification; of these students two were admitted to the Freshman class. The new plan for admission adopted by Harvard College in 1911 was tried by twenty-four admission candidates in June and September. Of these sixteen candidates passed successfully.

The results of the final examinations are given in the following table: —

	Admitted	Admitted clear	Rejected
June	65	38	13
September	29	5	5
	94	43	18
Total rejected	18		
Candidates in June who did not reappear in September . . .	4		
	116		

The entering class of 1911–12 numbers ninety-three, who were admitted, eighty-three by examination in 1911, eight in 1910, and one in 1909, and one by the Committee on Admission from Other Colleges in 1911.

Seventy-one graduate students registered during the year 1910–11, forty-six of whom were from colleges other than Radcliffe. Twenty-nine students were admitted to thirteen whole courses, and twenty-nine students to fourteen half-courses, of the " Courses primarily for Graduates in Harvard University open to competent students of Radcliffe College."

The Caroline I. Wilby Prize was awarded to Ruth Holden, 1911, for a thesis entitled " Reduction and Reversion in the North American Salicales." The Captain Jonathan Fay Diploma and Scholarship were also awarded to Ruth Holden, 1911. The Fellowship of the Woman's Education Association of Boston was awarded for 1911–12 to Maud Elizabeth Temple, A.B. (Bryn Mawr) 1904, A.M. (*ibid.*) 1905, Radcliffe graduate student, 1909–10. The Craig Prize in Dramatic Composition was awarded in 1911 to Florence Agnes Lincoln, a special student in Radcliffe College. The Doctor's thesis written by Edith Nason Buckingham, A.B. 1902, Ph.D. 1910, " Division of Labor among Ants," was published as Radcliffe Monograph number 16.

The members of the Academic Board for 1910–11 were Professor Byerly (Chairman), and Professors E. L. Mark, S. M. Macvane, H. S. White, E. H. Hall, H. W. Smyth, A. A. Howard, G. L. Kittredge, C. H. Grandgent.

Mrs. Josiah Parsons Cooke, an Associate of Radcliffe College, died May 19, 1911. She was one of the earliest supporters of Radcliffe. Her long, faithful, and generous service to the College will never be forgotten. There have been three elections of new members to the Council during the year 1910–11: Mr. Frederick Perry Fish, an Associate since 1904, was elected for a term of seven years from 1909, to fill the vacancy caused by the resignation of Professor Ezra Ripley Thayer; Miss Anna Florena Wellington, of the Class of 1904, was elected for a term of seven years from 1908, to fill the vacancy in an elective office caused by the resignation of the first Dean and the appointment of the second; Professor Fred Norris Robinson was elected for a term of seven years from 1905, to fill the vacancy caused by the resignation from the Council of Professor William Watson Goodwin. Professor Goodwin's distinction as a scholar and teacher, and his large experience in the academic life of Harvard have made his services to the College both as instructor and as administrator of inestimable value. His continuance on the Board of Associates ensures for the College his uninterrupted interest in its welfare. Mrs. Frances Parkman was reëlected member of the Council for seven years from 1911. Miss Harriet Dean Buckingham, of the class of 1895, was elected Secretary of the College in December, 1910. Miss Grace E. Machado resigned her position as Mistress of Grace Hopkinson Eliot Hall at the end of the year 1910–11. Miss Machado displayed marked capacity for executive work, and the power to create in the students a spirit of democracy and of loyalty to the College, in the opening years of the Hall. Miss Machado's position has been filled by Miss Elinor Mead Buckingham, of the Class of 1892.

In the beginning of the past academic year the Council definitely undertook to secure the money for a third hall of residence to be named Sarah Whitman Hall, in memory of Mrs. Henry Whitman. This hall seemed to them an imperative need, because further increase in the number of students from a distance was impracticable until more halls could be provided. At the beginning of the summer of 1911, although only a little less than half the required $75,000 had been subscribed, it was decided to start the building in the hope that further contributions would be made later, and with the understanding that such part of the fund as was not secured by subscriptions should be made up from the general funds, and repaid gradually from the income of the hall. Sarah Whitman Hall is to stand in Walker Street, facing the Radcliffe field. The architects are Messrs. Kilham and Hopkins.

The resources of the College have been strengthened during the year by a few important gifts of money. The Cambridge Latin School Club gave in May, 1911, $2,500, which it had secured by long-continued effort, — one-half the sum necessary to endow a scholarship. A member of the Class of 1911 gave $1,000 toward the fund for instruction. Toward this same fund for instruction, in which the Alumnae are seriously interested, the Class of 1896 made its fifteenth anniversary gift of $400, and the Class of 1901 its decennial gift of $1,000. The bequest of Mrs. Martha T. Fiske Collord, two hundred shares of the capital stock of the Standard Oil Company, was received October 19, 1910. By the terms of Mrs. Collord's will this bequest may be held as a trust fund to be known as the Fiske Fund, and the income may be applied to the general uses of the College until such time, if ever, as the College wishes to use the fund for the erection of a building, to be known as the Fiske Building. The Council determined to use the income of the fund for the salaries for instruction, and accordingly increased the salaries of full professors and of assistant professors in 1911–12, and thereafter, $100 for each course. The will of Mrs. Rebecca A. Greene of Dartmouth provided that the College should receive, on the death of her husband, $\frac{100}{100}$ of her residuary estate. Since Mr. Greene's death in April, 1911, $175,000 has been paid to the College on account of this bequest. The Council hopes to keep intact the greater part of these two bequests to enable Radcliffe " to pay for a reasonable share of the time of such eminent Harvard professors as are willing to teach women." The President has already expressed the belief that " the time will come when Radcliffe teaching is in no sense extra work," and that " the coming of such a time will benefit both Radcliffe College and Harvard College."

During the year the College came into possession of the house and 20,269 square feet of land at 61 Garden Street, adjoining the Radcliffe halls of residence, bequeathed by Mr. J. Rayner Edmands. It was found necessary to use the Edmands House in 1911–12 in order to give rooms to seven of the twenty-six students who could not be accommodated in the halls. The Greenleaf House, on the estate which was given to the College in 1905, by the generosity of two hundred friends of the College, has been restored to its original use as a dwelling house, and is now occupied by the Dean. The College purchased in 1911 two additional pieces of property in the square bounded by Garden and Brattle Streets, Mason Street, and Appian Way, — the property at 77 Brattle Street, and that at 15 Appian Way, — thus enlarging the holdings of the College by 14,570 square feet.

Several bequests to the College, which have not yet been received, were announced during the year: Miss Alice M. Curtis left $25,000 to found the Marion H. Curtis Scholarship or Scholarships; Mrs. Lydia Augusta Barnard, of Milton, $30,000 to found the Anna Parsons Scholarships, $75,000 for the erection of a dormitory to be known as James and Augusta Barnard Hall, the net income therefrom to be used for scholarships to be known as the James and Augusta Barnard Scholarships, and $10,000 for the same scholarships, subject to certain life interests; Mr. Francis B. Greene, of Dartmouth, provided that after the payment of certain gifts, and after the lapse of annuities and a trust fund, the College should receive the rest of his property, one-half for its general fund, one-half to found the Rebecca A. Greene Scholarships; Mrs. Josiah P. Cooke left $5,000 to found the Josiah Parsons Cooke Scholarship, and $5,000 subject to certain life interests. These scholarships will contribute toward the best welfare of the College by bringing desirable students who would not otherwise be able to obtain a college education. To do the work which lies before Radcliffe is expensive in teachers, in books, and in laboratory facilities. The sum total of three of the bequests mentioned before is $150,000, but it is probable that no considerable part of this money will be available for two years at least. Even if we take into account all these bequests, the rate at which the endowment is increasing to-day is not sufficient to ensure an exceptionally strong institution to-morrow. Radcliffe should obtain during the next few years a position of preëminently commanding importance.

Everyone realizes that great issues are under discussion in the education of women to-day. American parents are constantly demanding better education for their daughters, and there is a rapid increase in the number who are looking toward college. Radcliffe gives promise of large usefulness in the education of girls, not only from Massachusetts but from the South and West. No act of Harvard College was ever more generous or more timely than the recognition by the President and Fellows of " their ultimate responsibility for Radcliffe College " in the series of votes by which they constituted themselves a Board of Visitors of Radcliffe, and made it a duty of the Harvard President to countersign the Radcliffe diplomas as equivalent to Harvard diplomas. This vital relation between Harvard and Radcliffe has ensured to the women's college a plan that works well, and is fundamentally sound. Radcliffe has remained true to its original and single purpose, to open to women instruction by Harvard teachers of the same grade as that given in the University. Notwithstanding the fact that a student's achievement is largely determined for her by her gifts and her circumstances, much may be added to her natural attainments if she is privileged to draw on Harvard's long-treasured store of knowledge and learning. Radcliffe tolerates no artificial distinctions; it is intellectually thorough; it honors the student who works. It now sends out every year one hundred young women, holders of its degrees. In all it counts 1,176 alumnae, 156 who hold from Radcliffe the degree of Master of Arts only, and 13 who hold the degree of Doctor of Philosophy. They are loyal in spirit and ready to show their loyalty by sending their pupils and their sons and daughters to Harvard and Radcliffe. Moreover, these women are uniting with thousands of graduates of other colleges in serious public and educational interests. Like Harvard, Radcliffe encourages its students to study not only the history and literature of the past, but the great industrial and scientific problems of the present.

MARY COES, *Dean.*

APPENDIX

REPORT OF THE MEDICAL ADVISER

To THE PRESIDENT OF THE UNIVERSITY: —

SIR, — I have the honor to present in tabular form a report of the work of the Medical Adviser and of the Stillman Infirmary for the academic year 1910–11.

The five hundred and eighty-one patients cared for at the Stillman Infirmary are included in Tables I and II. It is gratifying to note that of these five hundred and eighty-one patients, there was no death, and only eight were discharged unrelieved. Of these eight, one, Paul Mariett, is still suffering from an incurable disease.

The number of cases of appendicitis was markedly less than for the preceding year, and only ten operations were required, as compared with nineteen for 1909–10.

I have knowledge of only three deaths among the student body at large: —

    A. L. M. Dejonge, February 15, pneumonia.
    S. P. Parsons, May 13, drowned.
    A. E. Smith, June 27, prussic acid poisoning.

It is interesting to note the increasing preference of the students for the wards over private rooms at the Infirmary. The relation of room to ward patients for the nine years since the Infirmary was opened is as follows: —

	1902–03	1903–04	1904–05	1905–06	1906–07	1907–08	1908–09	1909–10	1910–11
Room ...	89	117	113	91	99	83	93	102	94
Ward....	134	173	264	341	368	458	366	473	487

I think these figures show how the beautiful wards presented by Mr. Stillman with the Infirmary have gone far toward removing the common prejudice to hospital wards as the students have become more familiar with their attractiveness and comfort. A large per cent of room patients are not cared for in the ward simply because the nature of their illness requires either isolation or complete quiet.

        MARSHALL H. BAILEY, *Medical Adviser.*

TABLE I

ILLNESS REPORT, 1910–11

Diseases	Sept.	Oct.	Nov.	Dec.	Jan.	Feb.	Mar.	Apr.	May	June	Total
Appendicitis	1	3	1	4	8	4	7	1	4	..	33
Asthma	..	1	2	1	1	..	..	..	..	..	5
Bronchitis	..	6	2	1	12	6	4	1	3	..	35
Chicken-pox	..	..	2	..	1	1	1	..	..	..	5
Colds — unclassified	..	22	50	42	62	39	50	41	16	3	325
Coryza	..	5	3	4	8	1	4	3	2	..	30
Diarrhoea	..	8	1	..	2	1	3	1	4	..	20
Diphtheria	..	..	1	1	2	..	..	..	..	..	4
Ear, of the	..	5	..	2	8	7	1	1	1	1	26
Eye, of the	..	6	13	8	14	13	30	36	36	5	161
General Debility	..	4	7	6	14	17	11	20	12	1	92
Headache	..	..	1	1	2	..	..	1	3	..	8
Heart, of the	..	..	1	..	..	..	..	..	..	..	1
Indigestion	..	5	10	6	8	12	17	8	7	..	73
Insomnia	..	..	4	2	1	2	..	..	1	1	11
Jaundice	..	4	5	2	2	6	2	..	3	..	24
La Grippe	..	7	12	11	91	64	46	14	2	..	246
Laryngitis	..	1	1	1	5	2	1	..	..	..	11
Malaria	..	2	3	..	..	..	1	2	1	..	9
Measles	..	..	1	1	2	2	8	7	3	2	26
" German	..	..	..	..	1	1	20	19	10	1	52
Miscellaneous	3	33	45	38	37	22	35	25	30	3	271
Mumps	..	..	..	..	..	..	..	1	..	2	3
Neuralgia	..	..	2	..	1	1	3	1	..	1	9
Pertussis	..	..	..	..	..	1	..	1	..	..	2
Pharyngitis	..	5	1	6	2	1	5	1	9	..	30
Pleuritis	..	..	2	..	1	..	..	..	1	1	5
Pneumonia	..	1	..	1	3	..	..	3	..	..	8
Rheumatism	..	3	3	2	3	3	6	2	1	2	25
Scarlet Fever	..	1	..	..	2	..	..	2	2	..	7
Skin, of the	..	..	3	2	2	4	2	3	1	1	18
Surgical	..	36	32	37	25	15	25	22	26	8	226
Teeth, of the	..	3	5	3	4	1	3	1	1	..	21
Tonsillitis	1	6	12	18	33	27	23	16	49	3	188
Totals	5	167	225	200	357	252	308	233	228	35	2010
Visits	..	93	113	115	226	153	163	112	215	100	1290
Office consultations, medical	12	244	288	229	427	246	331	264	318	98	2457
Office consultations, surgical	7	97	101	120	125	93	129	80	99	47	898
Total number of consultations	19	434	502	464	778	492	623	456	632	245	4645

Cases not seen by the Medical Adviser 765

TABLE II

ILLNESS REPORT AS RELATED TO THE DIFFERENT SCHOOLS

Diseases	College						Instructors	Law	Graduate	Totals
	1	2	8	4	Sp.	Un.				
Appendicitis	7	6	5	7	..	2	..	2	4	33
Asthma	1	4	..	..	..	..	..	..	..	5
Bronchitis	11	9	5	4	..	..	..	4	2	35
Chicken-pox	..	1	1	..	..	..	..	2	1	5
Colds, unclassified	117	88	66	32	3	4	1	6	8	325
Coryza	11	8	6	2	..	..	..	3	..	30
Diarrhoea	9	3	2	2	..	1	1	1	1	20
Diphtheria	1	1	1	..	..	..	..	1	..	4
Ear, of the	11	5	2	1	..	..	..	5	2	26
Eye, of the	49	47	42	18	..	3	..	1	1	161
General Debility	22	19	16	9	4	7	..	2	13	92
Headache	3	3	..	2	..	..	..	..	..	8
Heart, of the	..	1	..	..	..	..	..	..	..	1
Indigestion	27	17	13	9	..	1	1	2	3	73
Insomnia	1	2	4	2	1	..	..	1	..	11
Jaundice	5	9	2	2	..	..	..	3	3	24
La Grippe	82	51	38	33	1	3	..	23	15	246
Laryngitis	4	3	..	3	..	1	..	..	..	11
Malaria	..	2	2	2	..	..	..	1	2	9
Measles	7	4	3	3	..	..	..	4	5	26
" German	16	13	6	9	..	..	..	2	6	52
Miscellaneous	78	56	47	31	5	6	1	26	21	271
Mumps	1	..	1	..	..	..	..	..	1	3
Neuralgia	4	1	4	..	..	..	..	..	..	9
Pertussis	1	..	1	..	..	..	..	..	..	2
Pharyngitis	10	5	8	5	..	..	..	2	..	30
Pleuritis	1	1	1	..	..	..	..	1	1	5
Pneumonia	5	1	..	..	..	..	..	..	2	8
Rheumatism	7	5	4	5	1	..	..	1	2	25
Scarlet Fever	2	..	1	2	..	..	..	1	1	7
Skin, of the	6	5	5	..	..	..	1	..	1	18
Surgical	60	50	46	30	1	7	2	20	10	226
Teeth, of the	5	8	4	3	..	..	1	..	..	21
Tonsillitis	63	42	32	14	..	2	..	18	17	188
Totals	627	470	368	230	16	37	8	132	122	2010
No. of Students	671	516	482	382	75	91	..	802	..	
% of "Sign-offs"	93	91	76	60	21	41	..	16	..	
No. of Students at Infirmary	121	80	98	71	6	11	7	98	86	
% of "Sign-offs"	18	16	20	19	8	12	..	12	..	

TABLE III

STILLMAN INFIRMARY

LIST OF CASES, 1910–11

Abscess — miscellaneous	6	La Grippe	133
" peritonsillar	7	Laryngitis	3
Anemia — pernicious	1	Malaria	3
Appendicitis	18	Measles	18
Bronchitis	14	" German	37
Burns	5	Melancholia	1
Chicken-pox	4	Miscellaneous Medical	36
Colds — unclassified	43	Miscellaneous Surgical	47
Concussion — cerebral	2	Mumps	5
Debility	6	Otitis Media	12
Diphtheria	3	Pharyngitis	7
Dislocation — of elbow	1	Pleuritis	5
Enchondroma	1	Pneumonia	7
Fracture — of fibula	1	Rheumatism	7
" " tibia	1	Scarlet Fever	5
" " ulna	1	Sprains	7
Hernia	4	Synovitis — of knee	5
Herpes Zoster	4	Tonsillitis	60
Indigestion	8	Tonsillectomy	3
Infected knee and general sepis	1	Wounds	5
Infections — localized	19	No diagnosis	11
Insomnia	7		
Jaundice	7	Total	581

Room patients	94
Ward patients	487
Total	581

Discharged — well	406
" relieved	167
" not relieved	8
Total	581

Total number of hospital days	3,883
Daily average	14.22
Total number of operations	46
Operations for Appendicitis	10

REPORT OF THE APPOINTMENT OFFICE

To the President of the University: —

Sir, — The following Report, rendered by the Appointment Office, describes the work of that Office in 1910–11. The work consists of the recommendation of Harvard men (A) to fill *academic* positions in universities, colleges, schools, or institutions of research; (B) to fill positions *not academic*, including institutional, technical, or business positions. These recommendations may be made by the Chairmen or other representatives of the Divisions and Departments of the Faculty of Arts and Sciences, by the Deans of the Professional Schools,[1] by the representatives of the Faculty in coöperation with the Office of the General Secretary of The Harvard Alumni Association, or by that Office independently.

It may be well to call attention to some of the facts which the following tables show. In the number of academic appointments those in Universities and Colleges lead with 122; then follow in order Private Schools, 40; Public Schools, 13; and Technical Schools, 10. According to the classification by subject English leads with 50; then follow History, 15; Philosophy, 13; Mathematics, 12. In the table of appointments other than academic an attempt has been made this year to classify more carefully than before the nature of the appointments made. Numerically, General Manufacturing leads with 42, 13 of which are in Manufacturing proper; Public Service Corporations follow with 14; Construction and Consulting Engineering, 12; Banking and Brokerage, 7.

In the table of the general summary it is noticeable that 97 out of 200 academic appointments are in the North Atlantic Section of the United States. Out of the 112 appointments not academic 89 are in that same section. In the preparation of these figures men employed by a corporation have been regarded as working wherever the central house of that corporation may be, though they may have been delegated to other parts of the country. In 1910, out of 165 academic appointments 92 were in the North Atlantic States, and out of 74 appointments not academic 62 were in the same section.

In 1910 the average salary reported for academic positions was $1,297; in 1911, $1,310; the average salary reported for a position not academic was in 1910, $991; in 1911, $888. In the case of academic appointments in both years these averages are made somewhat higher by the fact that in several instances the salaries were unusually large. The disparity between the average salary for teaching and for business positions may be accounted for by the fact that the business positions were in many cases appointments where the training was a large part of the return, whereas the salaries of the teaching positions begin higher and look for less future financial advancement.

---

[1] No official reports have been made by the Deans of the Professional Schools.

(A) ACADEMIC

I. Registration of Teachers

(a) Available[1] 684
(b) Unavailable[2] 1496

Total 2180

II. Calls for Teachers

(a) Direct from universities, colleges, and schools 544
(b) Indirect:
From institutions requesting endorsement of candidates, or from candidates requesting endorsement of candidacy . 124
From teachers' agencies 209

Total 877

III. Appointments

(a) Teaching and Administrative

	Number of Positions	Number of Salaries Reported	Aggregate Salaries Reported
1. Universities or Colleges			
Regular Teachers			
Direct	92		
Indirect	24		
Substitute Teachers			
Direct	6	122	113	$146,381
2. Technical Schools			
Direct		10	9	8,330
3. Normal Schools			
Direct	2		
Indirect	2		3	4,100
4. Industrial Schools			
Direct		2	2	3,200
5. Public High Schools			
Direct		13	13	17,035
6. Private or Endowed Schools			
Direct	33		
Indirect	7	40	39	52,375
Total...............		191	179	$231,421

[1] File containing candidates active at any time.
[2] File containing candidates available only for advancement, or for other reasons unavailable.

Classification according to Subjects and Departments: —

1. Subjects

	Number of Positions
Greek	3
Latin	2
Greek and Latin	3
Greek and Mathematics	1
Greek, Latin, and Elementary Mathematics	1
Latin, German, and Spanish	1
Latin and General Elementary Subjects	1
English	50
English and French	1
English, French, German, and History	1
English and History	1
English and Mathematics	1
English, Mathematics, and Latin	1
Journalism	1
Public Speaking	1
German	5
German and English	1
German and Latin	1
German, Latin, and Spanish	1
Romance Languages	2
French	5
French and Elementary Subjects	1
French and German	8
French, German, and Spanish	1
French and Latin	1
French and Spanish	1
Spanish	1
History	15
History and Political Science	1
History, Mathematics, Physics, and Physiography	1
Economics	5
Economics and History	1
Philosophy	13
Philosophy and Education	1
Social Ethics	1
Education	2
Music	1
Mathematics	12
Mathematics, Physics, and Botany	1
Engineering	2
Physics	2
Chemistry	9
Chemistry and Geography	1
Economic Geography	1
Forestry	2
Biology	7
General Science	1
General Elementary Subjects	4
Physical Training	1
Carried forward	— 181

Brought forward...............		181

2. Administration

Dean	1	
Directors	2	
Head-master	1	
Principals	2	
Assistant Principal	1	
Supervising Principal	1	
Superintendents	2	
		10

Total		191

(b) Scientific Research

	Number of Positions	Number of Salaries Reported	Aggregate Salaries Reported
1. Anthropology	1		
2. Astronomy	2		
3. Biology			
Economic Entomology ... 1			
Genetics 2			
Horticulture 1			
Plant Pathology 1	5		
4. Chemistry	1		
Total	9		$6,800

(B) NOT ACADEMIC
I. Registration

(a) Engineers (Association of Harvard Engineers)		30
(b) Business Men (Harvard Alumni Association)		
Available	515	
Not available	1212	1727
		1757

II
Calls upon The Harvard Alumni Association   229

III. Appointments

	Number of Positions secured through		Number of Salaries Reported	Aggregate Salaries Reported
	Faculty	Harvard Alumni Association		
(a) Government Service				
1. Consular	1			
2. Customs		1		
3. Diplomatic		1		
4. Forest	2			
5. Interior				
6. Tariff	1	9	3	$4,900
Carried forward.......		9	3	$4,900

Brought forward			9	3	$4,900
(b) Institutions not Academic					
1. Association (Secretary)					
2. Church (Minister)	1				
3. Hospital (Medical Assistant)	1				
4. Library (Secretary)		2			
5. Research (Treasurer)	▲		6	5	5,900
(c) Business					
1. Accounting and Auditing ...		2	2	2	2,800
2. Banking and Brokerage	1	7	8	8	2,710
3. Engineering (Construction and Consulting) ...	11	1	12	5	4,200
4. Insurance and Real Estate ..		2	2	2	1,870
5. Journalism					
Advertising		2			
Reporting		1	3	3	3,904
6. Manufacturing					
Shop and Manufacturing proper	13				
Sales	1	6			
Management (Efficiency)..	2	6			
Technical					
Chemistry	6	3			
Engineering	4	1	42	35	29,216
7. Mercantile					
Wholesale and Brokerage .	1	4			
Management		2	7	7	3,444
8. Plantation Management ...		1			
9. Publishing		2	2	2	1,820
10. Public Service Corporations					
Railroad					
Engineering	8	2			
Telephone					
Administration	1	▲			
Engineering	2		14	9	11,812
11. Secretaryships (Private)		4	4	4	4,416
Total....................			112	85	$76,902

(C) GEOGRAPHICAL DISTRIBUTION

	Universities Colleges	Technical Schools	Normal Schools	Public Schools	Private Schools	Industrial Schools	Scientific Research	Not Academic	Totals for States	Totals for Divisions
NORTH ATLANTIC DIVISION:										186
Maine	4	..	1	..	..	..	..	1	5	
New Hampshire	4	1	1	1	3	..	..	1	11	..
Vermont	2	..	..	..	..	..	..	..	2	..
Massachusetts	7	2	1	5	16	2	1	52	86	..
Rhode Island	4	..	1	..	1	..	..	..	6	..
Connecticut	2	..	..	1	1	..	1	2	7	..
New York	8	1	..	1	2	..	3	24	39	..
New Jersey	2	..	..	..	5	..	..	3	10	..
Delaware	1	..	..	..	..	..	..	2	3	..
Pennsylvania	10	1	..	1	1	..	..	4	17	..
SOUTH ATLANTIC DIVISION:										24
Maryland	..	..	..	1	2	..	..	..	3	..
District of Columbia	1	..	..	..	..	..	2	7	10	..
Virginia	2	..	..	1	..	..	..	..	3	..
West Virginia	1	..	..	..	..	..	..	..	1	..
North Carolina	2	..	..	..	..	..	..	..	2	..
South Carolina	2	..	..	..	..	..	..	..	2	..
Georgia	..	1	..	..	1	..	..	..	2	..
Florida	1	..	..	..	..	..	..	..	1	..
SOUTH CENTRAL DIVISION:										23
Kentucky	2	..	..	1	..	..	..	..	3	..
Tennessee	1	..	..	..	..	..	..	..	1	..
Arkansas	4	..	..	..	..	..	..	..	4	..
Oklahoma	..	..	1	..	..	..	..	..	1	..
Texas	1	1	..	..	..	..	..	..	2	..
Missouri	6	..	..	1	4	..	..	..	11	..
Kansas	1	..	..	..	..	..	..	..	1	..
NORTH CENTRAL DIVISION:										42
Ohio	4	..	..	..	2	..	..	..	4	..
Illinois	5	..	..	..	2	..	..	10	17	..
Michigan	1	1	..	..	..	..	..	1	3	..
Wisconsin	13	..	..	..	..	..	..	..	13	..
Minnesota	2	..	..	..	..	..	..	..	2	..
North Dakota	1	1	..	..	..	..	..	..	2	..
South Dakota	1	..	..	..	..	..	..	..	1	..
WESTERN:										21
Colorado	3	..	..	..	..	..	..	1	4	..
Utah	1	..	..	..	..	..	..	..	1	..
Washington	6	..	..	..	..	..	..	..	6	..
Oregon	4	..	..	..	..	..	..	..	4	..
California	4	..	..	..	2	..	..	..	6	..
CUBA	..	..	..	..	..	..	..	1	1	1
HAWAII	..	..	..	..	..	..	1	..	1	1
ARGENTINE REPUBLIC	..	..	..	..	..	..	1	..	1	1
CANADA	8	1	..	..	..	..	..	1	10	10
ENGLAND	..	..	..	..	..	..	..	1	1	1
INDIA	..	..	..	..	..	..	..	1	1	1
JAPAN	1	..	..	..	..	..	..	..	1	1
Total Positions	122	10	4	13	40	2	9	112	312	312

(D) SUMMARY OF APPOINTMENTS

Geographical Distribution	Academic 1911	Not Academic 1911	Academic 1910	Not Academic 1910
North Atlantic....................	97	89	92	62
South Atlantic	17	7	12	4
South Central	23		4	
North Central	31	11	40	5
Western	20	1	11	1
Dependencies	3	1		
Foreign Countries	9	3	6	2
	200	112	165	74
Total		312		239
Aggregate Salaries	$229,821	$76,992	$210,209	$68,388.40

L. B. R. BRIGGS, *Dean,*
Faculty of Arts and Sciences.

E. H. WELLS, *General Secretary,*
The Harvard Alumni Association.

REPORT OF THE SECRETARY FOR STUDENT EMPLOYMENT [1]

An easy method of indicating recent achievements and present needs of the Office for Student Employment is given in the following summary:

	1909–10	1910–11
Men registered for term-time work	560	599
Men who secured term-time work	436	272
Men registered for summer work	584	638
Men who secured summer work	204	138
Total registration for term-time and summer work, allowing for men registered for both	956[2]	1021[2]

An increase of 65 men registered and a decrease of 230 employed.

The division of the registration among the different Departments of the University is as follows: —

College	619	Dental	8
Medical	38	Scientific	18
Law	128	Extension	2
Graduate	124	Special	23
Business	13	Unclassified	30
Divinity	9	Assistants	9
		Total	1,021

	1909–10	1910–11
Amount earned by 436 men through the aid of the office during term-time	$45,699.32	
Amount earned by 278 men through the aid of the office, the departments of the University, and The Alumni Association during term-time		$63,263.29
Amount earned by 204 men through the aid of the office during the summer of 1910	20,062.40	
Amount earned by 157 men through the aid of the office, the departments of the University, and The Alumni Association during the summer of 1911		23,568.64
Total amounts	$65,761.72	$86,831.93
[3]Total amount reported earned independently by men registered with the office during term-time		31,823.55
Total amount reported earned during the year		$118,655.48

[1] On July 1, 1911, Roger Alden Derby, '05, resigned as Secretary for Employment, and Edward Eyre Hunt, '10, was appointed his successor. The statistics in the following report, therefore, are based on the figures of Mr. Derby's year.

[2] 1909–10, 188 duplicate registrations; 1910–11, 216 duplicate registrations.

[3] To 571 inquiries 231 replies were received, and these replies reported 25,580¾ working hours.

It appears from the foregoing summary that there has been a distinct tendency to concentrate the work in the hands of a very few, and to give it, therefore, to the best fitted or to the most needy. Frequently, of course, the most needy are the best fitted; but the terms are not synonymous. Whatever the cause, there is danger to the service in this concentration. Too small a proportion of the men registered are given even a preliminary trial. They lose interest or else they are obliged to look for employment elsewhere. It is now commonly understood among the students that unless a man really needs work, he should not register with the office. The man who would like to work and the man who must work are thus differentiated even before registration, and after registration the more needy man receives preference over the less needy. In other words, there is and always has been an inevitable tendency to give to the service of the Employment Office a semi-philanthropic cast. Employment very often, like stipend-bearing scholarships or aids, has been awarded on a basis of need.

It is not because less attention should be paid to the wants of the needy but because wider scope should be offered to the talents of the able that this comment is made. Remedy for much of the difficulty lies in an extension of the opportunities for employment, and the first steps should be (1) an adequate study of the seasonable demand for part-time employment in Boston and Cambridge, and (2) an insistent policy of judicious publicity directed at those who have such employment in hand. An endowment seems the prerequisite for such a programme. The Students' Employment Office is to help men to help themselves; and its purpose will be clearer when all the men registered can be given a thorough test, and when the community at large can feel that in employing Harvard men it secures competent, punctual, business-like service guaranteed by the University.

That it is necessary for the office to instruct students in habits of business accuracy and promptness is evidenced by the fact that in answer to 571 letters of inquiry sent to men registered during term-time, in an attempt to compile statistics of the total sum of money earned independent of the efforts of the Employment Office on behalf of such men, but 231 replies were received. Such a lackadaisical attitude toward the Office is obviously harmful to the service which it tries to render.

In an effort to minimise the handicap of distance from the Cambridge office under which men labor in the Medical and Dental Schools, the Secretary for Student Employment keeps an office hour once a week in the Administration Building, Longwood Avenue, Boston.

The following table shows the number of temporary positions filled — 1,942 in all — through the aid of the Office, the Departments of the University and The Alumni Association: —

Agent	15	Literary work	
Attendant	4	Critic	1
Boatman	3	Editor	1
Camp Councillor, tutor	11	Newspaper correspondent	1
Canvasser, solicitor	48	Meter Reader	6
Cashier	2	Model	3
Cataloguer	8	Monitor	111
Chauffeur	2	Musician	16
Choreman	53	Night School Teacher	7
Clerk, unclassified	192	Office Boy	1
Clerk, office	10	Outing Class Teacher	1
Club employee	2	Photographer	2
Coach	2	Playground Director	2
Companion	16	Proctor (examination)	110
Computer	2	Proof-reader	2
Detective	4	Reader	6
Draftsman	9	Room for Services	9
Electrician	1	Salesman	17
Errandman	52	Scene Shifter, Chair Mover	11
Expressman	7	Secretary	4
Farm Hand	2	Settlement Worker	3
Forester	7	Statistician	2
Gate Keeper, Guard, Usher	72	Stenographer	32
General Man on Estate	2	Substitute for Schools	5
Geologist	1	Supernumerary	4
Guide	169	Supervisor of Study	19
Hotel Employee	5	Supervisor and Tutor	8
Interpreter	1	Surveyor	3
Legal work	2	Ticket Taker	436
Library work		Translator	13
Attendant	3	Tutor and Companion	[1]52
Classifier	2	Tutor (special subjects)	110
Messenger	1	Typewriter	105
		Waiter	128
		Watchman	1

1,942

[1] Six of these are tutoring positions for one year.

Term-Time Employment

September 30, 1910 — June 27, 1911

Positions	No. of positions	Hours	Amount	Number of men employed	Average number of hours worked per man	Average amount earned per man
Agent [2]	6	..	$318.65	6	..	$53.10
Attendant	4	..	442.00	4	..	110.50
Canvasser, Solicitor	48	..	383.33	42	..	9.12
Cashier	2	..	561.50	2	..	280.75
Cataloguer	6	386	140.50	6	64⅓	23.41
Chauffeur	2	..	690.00	2	..	345.00
Choreman	38	1,093	287.97	25	43¾	11.52
Clerk	155	4,212½	1,435.94 [1]	32	131⅝	44.87
Coach	2	..	41.00	2	..	20.50
Companion	7	..	1,593.25 [1]	7	..	227.61
Computer	2	..	.. [1]	2	..	..
Detective	4	27	27.00	4	6¾	6.75
Draftsman [2]	8	411 [1]	371.20	4	102¾	92.80
Electrician	1	4	1.25	1	4	1.25
Errandman	49	125	35.99	38	3¼	.95
Expressman	7	380	58.95	7	54¼	8.42
Gate Keeper	48	503	215.25	46	10⅞	4.68
General Man	1	..	800.00	1	..	800.00
Guide	162	283½	202.90	30	9½	6.76
Hotel Employee	3	..	619.50	3	..	206.50
Interpreter	1	..	20.00	1	..	20.00
Legal Work	2	123	123.00	2	61½	61.50
Library Work [2]	4	..	499.50	5	..	99.90
Literary Work	3	..	495.00	3	..	165.00
Meter Reader	6	..	272.86	6	..	45.48
Model	3	84	47.00	4	21	11.75
Monitor	111	..	639.20	110	..	5.81
Musician	16	..	310.50 [1]	12	..	25.88
Night School Teacher	3	..	354.00	3	..	118.00
Outing Class Teacher	1	..	52.00	1	..	52.00
Photographer	2	5	3.00 [1]	2	2½	1.50
Proctor	109	2,744½	2,727.04	106	25⅞	25.73
Proof-reader	2	9½	2.37	2	4¾	1.19
Reader	6	235	100.85	4	58¾	25.21
Room for Services	6	..	616.50 [1]	5	..	123.30
Salesman [2]	16	..	341.92	16	..	21.37
Scene Shifter, Chair Mover	11	3 [1]	30.66	7	½	4.38
Secretary [2]	3	..	1,450.00 [1]	3	..	483.33
Settlement Worker	3	254	219.00	4	63½	54.75
Statistician	2	182 [1]	100.00	1	182	100.00
Stenographer	27	..	412.34	14	..	29.45
Substitute for Schools	5	..	660.00	4	..	165.00
Supervisor [1]	19	..	2,042.00 [1]	17	..	120.11
Supervisor and Tutor	7	..	6,178.00	4	..	1544.50
Surveyor [2]	1	..	330.00	1	..	330.00
Ticket Taker	399	..	700.00	396	..	1.77
Translator	9	60½	137.50	10	6	13.75
Tutor	93	2,020 [1]	3,647.95 [1]	78	25⅞	46.77
Tutor and Companion [2]	18	..	20,545.00	12	..	1712.09
Typewriter	104	..	606.77	23	..	26.38
Waiter	128	44,988½ [1]	11,373.15 [1]	128	351½	88.85
	1,675	58,132¾	$63,263.29			

[1] Statistics compiled upon number of men who reported only. Thirty-five men have not reported.

[2] Six positions filled by the Departments of the University or The Alumni Association.

SUMMER EMPLOYMENT
June 28, 1911 — September 28, 1911

Positions	No. of positions	Hours	Amount	Number of men employed	Average number of hours worked per man	Average amount earned per man
Agent [2]	9	..	$447.00	7	..	$63.86
Boatman	3	..	313.00 [1]	3	..	104.33
Camp Councillor, Tutor	11	..	2,163.50	11	..	196.68
Cataloguer	2	65	18.80	2	32½	9.40
Choreman	15	174	49.39	12	14½	4.12
Clerk	37	759½ [1]	222.91	28	27	7.96
Club Employee	2	..	545.00	2	..	272.50
Companion	9	..	2,856.35 [1]	9	..	317.37
Draftsman [2]	1	..	10.50	1	..	10.50
Errandman	3	18	4.74	3	6	1.58
Farm Hand	2	..	459.00	2	..	229.50
Forester [2]	7	..	.. [1]	7	..	..
Gate Keeper	24	..	236.00	24	..	9.83
General man on estate	1	..	210.00	1	..	210.00
Geologist	1	3	5.00	1	3	5.00
Guide	7	963	803.45	7	140½	114.78
Hotel Employee	2	..	722.00 [1]	2	..	361.00
Library Work	2	820	174.40	2	410	87.20
Night School Teacher	4	..	14.00	4	..	3.50
Office Boy	1	117	15.00	1	117	15.00
Office Clerk [2]	10	..	1,185.60 [1]	10	..	118.56
Playground Director	2	..	370.00	2	..	185.00
Proctor	1	3	3.00	1	3	3.00
Room for Services	3	..	15.50	2	..	7.75
Salesman [2]	1	..	50.00	1	..	50.00
Secretary	1	..	.. [1]	1	..	..
Stenographer	5	..	211.50	5	..	42.30
Supernumerary	4	..	28.00	4	..	7.00
Supervisor and Tutor	1	..	225.00	1	..	225.00
Surveyor [2]	2	..	.. [1]	2	..	..
Ticket Taker	37	..	928.00	37	..	25.08
Translator	4	41	37.00	4	10½	9.25
Tutor	17	694½	1,553.50 [1]	11	63	141.22
Tutor and Companion	34	..	9,535.50 [1]	34	..	264.28
Typewriter Teacher	1	12	12.00	1	12	12.00
Watchman	1	..	144.00	1	..	144.00
	267	3,690½	$23,568.64			

[1] Statistics compiled upon number of men who reported only. Seventeen men have not reported.

[2] Nineteen positions filled by the Departments of the University or The Alumni Association.

EDWARD EYRE HUNT,
Secretary for Student Employment.

ORDINARY DEGREES CONFERRED, 1907–11

	1907	1908	1909	1910	1911
Bachelors of Arts	448	379	421	452	414
Bachelors of Arts out of course . . . . ·.	63	60	73	52	62
Bachelors of Science	79	50	60	57	44
Bachelors of Science out of course	17	10	13	12	25
Bachelors of Divinity	7	12	12	6	6
Bachelors of Divinity out of course	0	0	0	0	0
Bachelors of Laws	183	159	163	182	168
Bachelors of Laws out of course	23	13	14	11	13
Bachelors of Agricultural Science	6	7	5	1	0
Bachelors of Agricultural Science out of course	2	0	0	1	0
Doctors of Public Health	0	0	0	0	2
Doctors of Medicine	70	69	55	73	85
Doctors of Medicine out of course	0	2	3	0	2
Doctors of Dental Medicine	24	18	10	24	12
Doctors of Dental Medicine out of course . . .	0	0	5	0	0
Masters of Arts	124	116	112	142	163
Masters of Arts out of course	8	8	7	0	0
Masters of Science	2	4	3	4	0
Masters of Science out of course	0	0	0	0	0
Doctors of Philosophy	33	43	38	37	41
Doctors of Science	1	0	0	0	1
Metallurgical Engineers	0	0	0	0	1
Mining Engineers	1	3	5	3	8
Masters in Civil Engineering	2	1	2	1	5
Masters in Mechanical Engineering	0	3	0	4	1
Masters in Electrical Engineering	0	1	3	4	8
Masters in Electrical Engineering out of course	0	0	0	1	0
Masters in Architecture	2	1	2	2	0
Masters in Landscape Architecture	1	1	0	1	4
Masters in Forestry	2	4	5	3	5
Masters in Forestry out of course	0	0	0	0	1
Masters of Science in Chemistry	0	0	0	0	1
Masters of Science in Botany	0	0	0	0	3
Masters of Science in Zoölogy	0	0	0	0	1
Masters in Business Administration	0	0	0	8	8
Totals	1098	964	1011	1081	1084
Commencement Certificates	0	1	1	1	1

INDEX

TREASURER'S STATEMENT

TREASURER'S STATEMENT

CONTENTS

TREASURER'S STATEMENT FOR 1910–11

To the Board of Overseers of Harvard College: —

The Treasurer submits the annual statement of the financial affairs of the University, for the year ending June 30, 1911.

The net income of the general investments for this period was divided at the rate of 4.85 per cent among the Funds to which these investments belong.

From the income of all bonds bought at a premium for general investments $9,058.01 was credited to the various accounts concerned, and for special investments $655.12, as the fair yearly repayment to make good the premiums at the maturity of the bonds.

CHARLES F. ADAMS, 2d, *Treasurer*.

Boston, November, 1911.

BALANCE SHEET
June 30, 1911

ASSETS

CASH IN BANKS:
Bursar, ...	$73,841.59	
Treasurer — General, ...	182,522.33	
Treasurer — Special — Schedule 1, ...	7,062.04	$263,425.96

ACCOUNTS RECEIVABLE:
Term Bills of January, 1911, ...	$168.42	
Term Bills of June, 1911, ...	122,512.95	
Sundry accounts of Bursar's office, ...	7,453.46	
Interest accrued, ...	3,383.49	133,518.32

INVENTORY — Stores, ... 10,076.13

INSURANCE UNEXPIRED, ... 23,644.41

INVESTMENTS:
Securities — Special — Schedule 1, ...	$2,630,045.84	
Securities — General — Schedule 2, ...	17,362,797.59	
Land and Buildings — Special — Schedule 1,	1,518,035.86	
Land and Buildings — General — Schedule 3,	2,965,986.14	24,476,865.43

$24,907,530.25

BALANCE SHEET

June 30, 1911

LIABILITIES

ACCOUNTS PAYABLE:

Salaries and Aids, ...	$159,001.26	
Deposits and Advance Payments, ...	27,251.97	$186,253.23

CAPITAL:

Gains and Losses for General Investments, ...			589,020.28
Income on General Investments Unapportioned, ...			5,649.94
Funds and Gifts, July 1, 1910, ...	$22,766,854.54		
General Suspense, July 1, 1910, ...	107,613.90		
	$22,659,240.64		
Gifts for Capital — Exhibit D, $1,283,138.02			
Gains and losses in valuation of Special Investments, . .	10,532.86		
Unexpended balances of new gifts for buildings, ...	194,307.83		
	$1,487,978.71		
Expenditures charged to General Suspense, ...	94,326.69	1,393,652.02	
		$24,052,892.66	
General Surplus — Exhibit B, ...		73,714.14	
Funds and Gifts — June 30, 1911, Schedule 4, ...	$24,323,194.54		
General Suspense, Credit Balances, June 30, 1911, Schedule 5, ...	154,158.81		
	$24,477,353.35		
Less General Suspense, Debit Balances, June 30, 1911, Schedule 6, ...	350,746.55	$24,126,606.80	24,126,606.80
			$24,907,530.25

CONSOLIDATED STATEMENT OF INCOME AND EXPENDITURE

For the year ended June 30, 1911

INCOME

RESTRICTED INCOME:

From SPECIAL INVESTMENTS,

Interest and Dividends — Schedule 1, ...	$123,214.32		
Rents of Land and Buildings, . . $137,016.57			
Less Operating Expenses, . . . 55,774.55	81,242.02		
Net income — Schedule 1, ...		$204,456.34	

From GENERAL INVESTMENTS,

Interest and Dividends on

Securities — Schedule 2, . . . $735,738.99			
Bank Balances, ... 4,385.56			
Advances to Departments and			
Miscellaneous, ... 17,317.31	$757,441.86		
Rents of Land and Buildings, . . $296,275.75			
Less Operating Expenses, . . . 113,659.69			
Net Income — Schedule 3, ...	182,616.06		
Total Income General Investments, ...	$940,057.92		
Less balance remaining after apportion-			
ment to the Funds and Gifts, ...	5,486.30		
Net Income General Investments appor-			
tioned, ...		934,571.62	
Gifts for Immediate Use — Exhibit E, ...	$462,300.70		
Less Unexpended balances of new gifts for			
buildings, added to Funds and Gifts —			
Exhibit A, ...	194,307.83	267,992.87	
Miscellaneous income, ...		58,478.52	

GENERAL INCOME:

Tuition Fees, ...	$651,200.84	
Laboratory Fees, ...	33,970.85	
Other Fees, ...	68,393.16	
Gross Rents of College Dormitories, etc.	86,661.72	
Miscellaneous income, ...	115,010.10	955,236.67
		$2,420,736.02

CONSOLIDATED STATEMENT OF INCOME AND EXPENDITURE

For the year ended June 30, 1911

EXPENDITURE

From Restricted Income for:

Administrative Purposes,	$3,804.80	
Educational Purposes,	460,809.27	
Other Activities,	442,612.51	
Aids.	168,908.65	$1,076,135.23

From General Income for:

Administrative Purposes,	$99,317.68	
Educational Purposes,	907,075.83	
Other Activities,	83,172.12	
Aids,	15,230.00	1,104,795.63
Repairs and equipment of College dormitories,	$11,307.10	
Caretaking and operating expenses of College dormitories,	30,471.09	41,778.19
Repairs and equipment of land and buildings for general purposes,	$29,251.67	
Caretaking and operating expenses of land and buildings for general purposes,	95,061.16	124,312.83
		$2,347,021.88
General Surplus to Exhibit A		73,714.14

$2,420,736.02

	INCOME		
	Restricted	General	Total
University (Sch. 7), ...	$77,788.73	$19,757.60	$97,546.33
College, including Graduate School of Arts and Sciences, (Sch. 8), . .	461,645.55	565,305.07	1,026,950.62
Library (Sch. 9), ...	66,630.24	224.62	66,854.86
Graduate School of Applied Science (Sch. 11), ...	147,091.54	100,496.52	247,588.06
Graduate School of Business Administration (Sch. 12), ...	31,714.37	8,832.00	40,546.37
Divinity School (Sch. 13), ...	32,906.74	9,524.38	42,431.12
Law School (Sch. 14), ...	40,821.92	119,694.02	160,515.94
Medical School (Sch. 15), ...	196,326.45	83,588.82	279,915.27
Dental School (Sch. 16), ...	4,487.27	22,672.77	27,160.04
Bussey Institution (Sch. 17), ...	14,067.73	. . . . . .	14,067.73
Arnold Arboretum (Sch. 18), ...	53,684.50	. . . . . .	53,684.50
Botanic Garden (Sch. 19), ...	16,002.09	. . . . . .	16,002.09
Botanical Museum (Sch. 20), ...	3,050.00	. . . . . .	3,050.00
Gray Herbarium (Sch. 21), ...	19,031.04	. . . . . .	19,031.04
Observatory (Sch. 22), ...	52,227.84	. . . . . .	52,227.84
Museum of Comp. Zoölogy (Sch. 23),	41,948.81	. . . . . .	41,948.81
Peabody Museum of American Archaeology and Ethnology (Sch. 24), . .	21,860.36	. . . . . .	21,860.36
Semitic Museum (Sch. 25), ...	1,886.38	. . . . . .	1,886.38
Germanic Museum (Sch. 26), ...	5,297.69	. . . . . .	5,297.69
William Hayes Fogg Art Museum (Sch. 27), ...	5,921.35	. . . . . .	5,921.35
Appleton Chapel (Sch. 28), ...	9,783.34	. . . . . .	9,783.34
Phillips Brooks House (Sch. 29), . .	1,664.32	. . . . . .	1,664.32
Hemenway Gymnasium (Sch. 30), . .	. . . . . .	1,853.50	1,853.50
Stillman Infirmary (Sch. 31), ...	3,984.31	19,100.78	23,085.09
Funds and Gifts for Special Purposes (Sch. 32), . . $354,171.20			
Less Unexpended balances of new gifts for buildings, 194,307.83	159,863.37	. . . . . .	159,863.37
Less Deficits of the following departments included in the above expenditure of other departments and deducted to show the total net expenditure :			
Appleton Chapel (Sch.28), $552.67			
Hemenway Gym.(Sch.30), 10,843.70			
	$1,469,685.94	$951,050.08	$2,420,736.02

10

BY DEPARTMENTS

June 30, 1911

EXPENDITURE	GENERAL		Disposition of General Deficit or Surplus FUNDS AND GIFTS		GENERAL SUSPENSE	
	Deficit	Surplus	Debit	Credit	Debit	Credit
$47,078.18	......	$50,468.15	......	$50,468.15	......	......
1,024,016.57	......	2,984.05	$26,624.96	28,909.00	$5,716.83	$6,366.84
98,659.99	$31,805.18	......	36,325.64	3,954.22	207.22	773.51
215,429.73	......	32,158.33	......	23,295.06	2,662.39	11,525.66
37,770.87	......	2,775.50	285.90	......	250.00	3,311.40
38,429.12	......	4,002.00	......	2,688.05	......	1,318.95
147,468.09	......	13,052.85	......	3,625.93	......	9,426.92
273,049.02	......	6,866.25	......	16,765.87	9,899.81	.19
35,410.98	8,250.94	......	......	1,091.00	9,341.94	......
21,125.04	7,057.31	......	......	......	7,057.31	......
49,564.16	......	4,120.34	......	4,120.34	......	......
14,850.67	......	1,151.42	......	30.62	......	1,120.80
1,434.29	......	1,615.71	......	......	......	1,615.71
20,032.44	1,001.40	......	......	......	1,001.40	......
56,300.94	4,073.10	......	6,116.41	2,605.88	562.57	......
48,276.17	6,327.36	......	7,002.58	337.31	......	337.91
16,266.81	......	5,593.55	......	2,246.60	160.00	3,506.95
21,505.97	19,619.59	......	20,546.39	926.80	......	......
1,095.95	......	4,201.74	......	3,484.32	......	717.42
6,847.11	925.76	......	586.07	......	339.69	......
10,518.10	182.09	......	......	......	182.09	......
1,561.78	......	102.54	225.27	327.81	......	......
12,697.20	......	......	......	......	......	......
23,051.79	......	33.30	......	374.80	341.50	......
135,982.28	......	23,881.09	......	23,234.90	3,930.40	4,576.59
$2,358,418.25						
11,396.37						
$2,347,021.88	$79,242.68	$152,956.82	$97,713.22	$168,481.66	$41,653.15	$44,598.85
	79,242.68		97,713.22			41,653.15
		$73,714.14		$70,768.44		$2,945.70

11

GIFTS FOR CAPITAL
June 30, 1911

ESTABLISHING NEW FUNDS OR INCREASING OLD ONES

From the estate of Alexander Agassiz, $50,000 in cash, and real estate valued at $50,000, " the income of which is to be devoted to the general uses of the Museum of Comparative Zoölogy."

From the estate of Alexander Agassiz, $101,507.50, " the income of which is to be used in defraying the expenses of publication in the Memoirs of the Museum of Comparative Zoölogy or in the Bulletin of the Museum, of sundry publications now preparing, a list of which I have left in the hands of the Curator of the Museum." The President and Fellows are authorized to pay $500 of the income yearly to a properly qualified person who shall superintend and edit such publication, but no allowance is to be made for salaries from this fund: " the income of this fund shall be wholly expended for the expenses necessary for the illustrations and their production, and the preparation of the text." If the income is in any year insufficient, the principal may be used.

If, after the publications are completed, any part of the original $100,000 remains, the inc me shall be called the Publication Fund of the Museum of Comparative Zoölogy and be used for expenses connected with the publication of the Memoirs, or of its Bulletins.

From an anonymous giver, $18,456.25 and securities valued at $74,112.50, to be added to the Anonymous Fund, without restriction beyond the payment of a certain annuity.

For addition to the principal of the Fund for the Professorship of Hygiene, $10,000, from the anonymous founder of this Fund.

For the Arnold Arboretum Fund, from

B. F. Keith	$110
Massachusetts Society for Promoting Agriculture . . .	500
	$610

From Mr. and Mrs. Bayard Thayer $2,500 each, for the general uses of the Arnold Arboretum. This $5,000 is to be credited for the present to the Arnold Arboretum Construction Fund, with the idea that it will eventually become part of a special Thayer Endowment Fund.

From the estate of Walter Farnsworth Baker, $29,410.79 and real estate valued at $46,000, further payments on account of his unrestricted bequest of one third of the residue of his estate "to the Corporation of Harvard University to be used for any purpose to help my beloved Alma Mater."

From the estate of Mrs. Caroline M. Barnard, $6,000, "to be used and applied for scholarships known as 'The Warren H. Cudworth Scholarships,' desiring that preference should be given as far as possible to students from East Boston, Lowell and Everett, in Massachusetts, in aid of whom I have heretofore contributed."

From the estate of Mrs. Caroline M. Barnard, $6,000, on account of her bequest of the balance of the estate as follows: "The balance, if any, remaining after these payments I give and devise to the several Institutions, Corporations and Societies named as Beneficiaries in this my said will, to be shared by them pro rata: that is to say, in the proportion which the respective bequests hereinbefore given to each, bear to the total amount of all the bequests to said beneficiaries."

For the purpose of building and endowing a Hospital for Incurable Cases of Cancer under the management of The Cancer Commission of Harvard University, $101,000, received through Dr. J. Collins Warren, from sundry subscribers.

From members of the Class of 1844, $207.09, to be added to the "Fund of the Class of 1844."

From William Gibbs Peckham, $2,000, to be added to the "Class of 1867 Scholarship."

From members of the Class of 1881, $1,270, to be added to the "Twenty-fifth Anniversary Fund of the Class of 1881."

From members of the Class of 1882, $9,868.59, to be added to the Fund of the Class of 1882, established on the twenty-fifth anniversary of their graduation.

From members of the Class of 1883, $7,104.41, to be added to the " Class of 1883 Fund," established on the twenty-fifth anniversary of their graduation.

From members of the Class of 1884, $1,050, to be added to the " Class of 1884 Fund," established on the twenty-fifth anniversary of their graduation.

From members of the Class of 1885, $3,208.98, to be added to the " Twenty-fifth Anniversary Fund of the Class of 1885."

From members of the Class of 1886, $100,000, to establish the " Twenty-fifth Anniversary Fund of the Class of 1886."

From Archibald Cary Coolidge and Clarence Leonard Hay, $500, to be added to " The Archibald Cary Coolidge and Clarence Leonard Hay Fund," the income to be used for the purchase of books relating to South America, for the College Library, with the right to withdraw the whole or such part of the principal as may be necessary for the purchase of any library or collection of books on South America.

From the estate of John Clarence Cutter, $244.26 and securities valued at $1,078, on account of Mr. Cutter's residuary bequest, one-half the income thereof to be expended to pay a certain annuity and one-half to maintain an annual course of lectures to be called the " Cutter Lectures on Preventive Medicine."

In memory of Bayard Cutting, of New York, of the Class of 1900, $25,000, to endow a fellowship " to be known as the ' Bayard Cutting Fellowship.' The money is to be invested by the Corporation, and the annual income paid, according to the standing rules of the Corporation, to the incumbent appointed by the President and Fellows, on the nomination of the department in which the student in question is working, or with which he is affiliated as a teacher or other officer.

" It is the desire of the participants in this memorial that the Bayard Cutting Fellowship should be reserved exclusively for men of the highest intellectual attainments and of the greatest promise as productive scholars. It is never to be given to the best among any number of applicants, unless the best man is one of first rate and well-rounded excellence.

"With this general provision, the Fellowship is open, in the first place, to students of history, preference being given to students of modern European history, diplomatic history, international law, or colonial government. If no student of history, of the quality indicated above, is available in any given year, then the Fellowship is open to students of European literature, preference being given to students of French or Italian literature. If in any given year no student of the quality desired is available in either of the above-mentioned subjects, then the Fellowship is to be open to students in economics, preference being given to students of the history of economics. If in any given year no properly qualified candidate is available, then one-half the income of the fund for that year shall be paid into the principal, and the other half be assigned to the College Library for the purchase of books of permanent value, preferably in French and Italian literature.

"This Fellowship may be assigned to the same man for two or more successive years, if such an assignment is in the best interests of scholarship. This Fellowship is not limited to resident students, but may be held by non-resident students who may pursue their studies either in foreign parts or in any other university in the United States. Travelling or non-resident incumbents of the Fellowship must, however, have spent at least one year in Cambridge, either as a resident student, or as an officer of instruction or government. The Fellowship may be held, however, by resident students during their first year of residence."

From the estate of W. Bayard Cutting, Jr., $25,000, " to be used for such appropriate objects and purposes of said Corporation as shall be designated and appointed in writing by Edgar Huidekoper Wells, of Boston, Massachusetts, or, in case of his death before me, then by Theodore Lyman, of Brookline, Massachusetts." According to Mr. Wells's written request, one-half of the income is to be expended on books for the College Library and the other half to maintain the Bayard Cutting Fellowship for Research in Physics.

From William F. Drea, $10 additional, towards the Class of 1909 Dental Endowment Fund.

For an endowment for the benefit of the Harvard Dental School, to be used for education, research, or the general expenses of the Infirmary, from

Anonymous	$10
Mrs. Arthur W. Blake	200
Shepherd Brooks	1,000
T. Jefferson Coolidge, Jr.	250
Miss Sarah H. Gaston	25
Mrs. Ernestine M. Kettle	100
William H. Potter	50
James M. Prendergast	100
Wallace F. Robinson	500
Henry O. Underwood	1,000
	$3,235

From sixteen anonymous givers, $482 additional, to be added to the Harvard Dental Alumni Endowment Fund.

From the estate of Mrs. Francis B. Greene, $25,000 for the use of the Medical School.

From friends and former pupils of the late Professor Charles Gross, $1,576.06, to form a library fund in his memory, the interest to be used for the purchase of books on English History, especially in those branches of the subject in which Professor Gross's studies lay, from

C. M. Andrews.
Roswell P. Angier.
James F. Baldwin.
Joseph Henry Beale.
Justin De Witt Bowersock.
Hiram Bingham.
William Garrott Brown.
Edward Channing.
Charles Motley Clark.
Gilman Collamore.
Archibald Cary Coolidge.
George Cunningham.
H. W. C. Davis.
William C. Dennis.
David A. Ellis.
Sidney B. Fay.
Carl R. Fish.
H. A. L. Fisher.
Kuno Francke.
Edwin F. Gay.
Elliott H. Goodwin.

Howard L. Gray.
Henry Gross.
Marks Gross.
Emanuel M. Grossman.
Ernst T. Gundlach.
Albert Bushnell Hart.
Charles H. Haskins.
Louis C. Hatch.
Harold D. Hazeltine.
Charles R. Henderson.
L. J. Henderson.
William Hudson.
Gaillard T. Lapsley.
Henry B. Learned.
Walter Lichtenstein.
Felix Lieberman.
Robert H. Lord.
A. Lawrence Lowell.
Charles H. McIlwain.
Selden O. Martin.
Roger B. Merriman.

Percy Muloch.
William B. Munro.
Nellie Neilson.
Watson Nicholson.
John Noble, Jr.
Percy V. Norwood.
Robert E. Olds.
Wilfred A. Openhym.
Stephen W. Phillips.
George W. Prothero.
Miss Bertha H. Putnam.
Conyers Read.
N. Thayer Robb.
Arthur B. Schaffner.
William H. Schofield.
Henry L. Shattuck.
Walter J. Shepard.
Adelbert Smith.

St. John Smith.
W. H. Smith.
James Tait.
Frank W. Taussig.
Theodore C. Tebbetts.
Frederick L. Thomson.
T. F. Tout.
Crawford H. Toy.
Eliot Tuckerman.
Paul Vinogradoff.
Frederick S. Weis.
R. G. Wellington.
Edgar H. Wells.
George P. Winship.
James E. Winston.
Arthur Mayer Wolfson.
J. H. Wylie.

From the estate of Charles L. Hancock, $8,641.40, the balance of his residuary bequest, to be added to the Charles L. Hancock Fund.

From the estate of William P. Harding, $5,000, to establish "The Selwyn L. Harding Scholarship of the Class of 1886," " the annual income of said fund in an amount not exceeding $350 to any one beneficiary thereof, to be paid to such needy, worthy, and industrious student as shall have been connected with the University's undergraduate department for one year at least." High grade marks are not a requisite, but " my wish is rather that the benefits shall go to that class of young men who have striven to do the best work that they were capable of."

From the Harvard Edda Club, $250, the first payment towards a scholarship fund, the income to be used for Scandinavian students.

From the estate of Mrs. Mary Hemenway, $45,000, for the benefit of the Peabody Museum of American Archaeology " to be known as 'The Mary Hemenway Fund for Archaeology,' the income only thereof to be applied in accordance from time to time with the wishes of the Faculty of the Peabody Museum, to the benefit of its archaeological department for the prosecution of original research or purchase of exhibits or the salaries of teachers, including assistants."

From the estate of Mrs. Mary Upham Johnson, $2,000, " to found a scholarship in the Medical Department of the University, to be called the ' William Otis Johnson Scholarship,' in memory of my husband, the late William Otis Johnson, M.D., of the Class of 1845."

Through Harold C. Ernst, $3,000, " to be used as the nucleus for establishing a fellowship in the Medical School under the following conditions:

" The fund is to be known as the John R. Kissinger Fund, and is intended to commemorate the action of the private in the United States Army of that name who volunteered for the first yellow fever inoculation, suffered an attack of the disease, and refused compensation for his act.

" The fund is to be allowed to accumulate until it reaches the minimum sum of $20,000. The income of this fund is then to be used to found a fellowship to pay the salary of an individual who shall engage in the investigation of the causation of infectious diseases, preferably, but not necessarily, in the direction of tropical medicine. If at any time it seems advisable, the income may be used to pay the expenses of similar investigations instead of paying the salary of an individual. The income is to be administered upon the recommendation of the Professor of Bacteriology in the Medical School." The income may be made subject to a certain annuity.

From the estate of Solomon Lincoln, of the Class of 1857, of Boston, Mass., $10,000, " for the general use of the Department of Romance Languages and Literature in the University."

For a memorial to the late George Cabot Lodge and Joseph Trumbull Stickney, of the Class of 1895, $3,102.40, " to establish a fund the income of which shall be used by the Harvard College Library to purchase rare and choice works of English and French poetry, in which shall be put a book-plate with their names," from

Brooks Adams.	Mrs. L. R. Cheney.
Mrs. John W. Ames.	Archibald Cary Coolidge.
William Sturgis Bigelow.	William C. Endicott.
George E. Barton.	Mrs. William C. Eustis.
Walter v. R. Berry.	Mrs. James T. Fields.
Mrs. Donald Cameron.	Miss L. Frelinghuysen.

Mr. and Mrs. Augustus P. Gardner.
William Amory Gardner.
Mrs. Walter Gay.
Miss Harriet Guild.
George A. James, 2d.
Lady Johnstone.
Mrs. Sergeant Kendall.
Charles R. Lanman.
Mr. and Mrs. Henry Cabot Lodge.
Mrs. E. M. McClellan.
Mrs. L. M. L. Mathewson.
Miss Marjorie Nott.
Mrs. R. Burnside Potter.
Spring Rice.
Mrs. Douglas Robinson.
Mrs. Theodore Roosevelt.
George Santayana.
Frederick Cheever Shattuck.
Mrs. Albert Stickney.
Mrs. Edward Wharton.

From Mrs. Francis Cabot Lowell, $10,000, the income of the fund to be used to supplement, by the purchase of books of historical value more or less closely related to the subject, the collection of works on Joan of Arc, given by Francis Cabot Lowell, of the Class of 1876, of Boston, Mass.

From the estate of Gordon McKay, $179,408.28 and securities valued at $202,969.58, to be added to the Gordon McKay Endowment Fund.

To establish the " George Herbert Palmer Fund," " for the foundation at Harvard of a prize or scholarship in Ethics to be named for Professor Palmer," $1,301.44. " The precise manner in which the income from this fund is to be employed will be designated later by the undersigned or their successors appointed by them

> C. M. Bakewell
> Reginald C. Robbins
> Ralph Barton Perry
> W. R. Warren."

From the estate of Trenor L. Park, of the Class of 1883, of New York City, $21,914.79, being his bequest of $25,000 plus interest at six per cent., less $1,250, the inheritance tax of New York and $131.04, the interest thereon, less $5,000, which by vote of the Corporation has been credited to the " Class of 1883 Fund."

From the estate of Henry L. Pierce, $100, to be added to the Henry L. Pierce Residuary Bequest.

From Miss Emily Dutton Proctor, $10,000, " to be used towards the maintenance of the new Cancer Hospital which The Cancer Commission of Harvard University is building on the grounds of the Harvard Medical School and for the care of patients therein to its normal capacity." Principal or income, or both, may be used at the discretion of the Corporation.

From the estate of Freeborn F. Raymond, 2d, of Newton, $5,000, "for the establishment of the Thomas William Clarke Scholarship."

From the estate of Amey Richmond Sheldon (Mrs. Frederick Sheldon), of Newport, R. I., $4,339.83, additional, for the Frederick Sheldon Fund, "the income thereof to be applied in the discretion of and under rules to be prescribed by the President and Fellows aforesaid to the further education of students of promise and standing in the University by providing them with facilities for further education by travel after graduation, or by establishing travelling scholarships."

From Norman G. Reoch, $100, to be added to the Joseph Warren Smith, Jr., Memorial Fund, the income of which is to be used for general purposes of the Harvard Dental School.

From members of the Class of 1877, $254.09 additional, to be added to the Edward Henry Strobel Memorial Fund.

For the Teachers' Endowment Fund, $8,062.25 additional, from previous contributors.

From the estate of John Harvey Treat, $14,491.94, and securities valued at $26,305.17, on account of his residuary bequest, "the income whereof to be used for the bene it of the Library for the purchase of books relating to the Church of England and other Churches in Communion with her, the Roman and Greek Churches, and the Episcopal Church in the United States of America especially as regards ritual matters."

To establish a fund to be known as the Fund of the Twentieth Massachusetts Regiment of Volunteer Infantry, for the purchase of books on Military History, preference being given to books dealing with the War of the Rebellion, 1861–1865, from

Mrs. Guy Norman	$100
Through Charles L. Peirson	500
	$600

From the estate of Ira D. Van Duzee, $4,905.42, being his bequest to Harvard College "in trust to use the income to aid in the support and education of one worthy student, the fund to be known and recognized as the Ira D. Van Duzee Scholarship."

From Frederick Cheever Shattuck, $8,000 additional, the final payment on account of his offer of $25,000 to establish "The Henry P. Walcott Fellowship in Clinical Medicine."

In memory of Julian Palmer Welsh, $650 additional, for the memorial fund established in 1910, which is to accumulate until it amounts to $3,000. "The income of the fund is then to be spent in buying for the Harvard College Library books in English and American literature, two subjects in which Mr. Welsh was much interested. The income of this fund is, however, to be charged on demand with the expense (not to exceed $100) of designing and engraving a book-plate."

From the estate of Jerome Wheelock, of Worcester, Mass., $10, the eighth payment of that amount for establishing the Jerome Wheelock Fund of $100,000.

From the estate of Miss Florence E. Wilder, $2,000, being her bequest for a prize to be known as "The Elizabeth Wilder Prize," the income to be given annually to freshmen needing financial aid who pass the highest examination in German at the mid-year examination.

From the estate of Charles J. Wister, $800, "the income to be awarded each year to the student who passes his examination with the highest combined average in mathematics and music, the same to be designated 'The Wister Prize' and be awarded in money or a medal at the option of the recipient."

The total amount of these gifts for capital account is $1,283,138.02, as shown in Exhibit A.

GIFTS FOR IMMEDIATE USE
June 30, 1911

From Edwin H. Abbot, $400, in accordance with the terms of his letter of gift, to be added to the income of the Teachers' Endowment Fund.

From John S. Ames, $350 additional, for the purchase of apparatus for certain courses in Botany.

Through Thomas Dwight, $500 additional, for anatomical research.

From anonymous donors, $545, towards the work of The Cancer Commission of Harvard University.

From an anonymous giver, $100, towards defraying the travelling expenses of members of the Faculty of Arts and Sciences.

From an anonymous giver, securities valued at $25,000, for an additional building to the Harvard Union in memory of Francis Hardon Burr.

From an unknown donor, $500, " for extra musical expenses."

From an anonymous friend of the University, $500, to pay tuition fees of three members of the Class of 1915.

From anonymous friends of the University, $250, to be awarded to a student of the fourth-year class of the Law School who, in the opinion of the Faculty, gives promise of ability to do effective work in the investigation of problems of law reform. The student will be required to write a dissertation embodying the results of his study.

From an anonymous giver, $600 additional, for a Fellowship in the Graduate School of Arts and Sciences, for the study of Central American Archaeology and Ethnology.

From an anonymous giver, $150, towards defraying the expenses in 1910–11 of a certain student in the Graduate School of Arts and Sciences.

From an anonymous giver, $150, to be utilised as a loan fund for fourth-year students or recent graduates of the Medical School to help defray expenses incident to their hospital service.

From an anonymous giver, $300, to pay for eight lectures on " The Principle of Relativity " in physics, given in the spring of 1911 in Cambridge by Professor Gilbert N. Lewis, of the Massachusetts Institute of Technology.

From an anonymous giver, $350, for the Ricardo Prize Scholarship for 1911–12.

From an anonymous giver, $10,000, for the rebuilding and extension, as well as the furnishing of the Library of the Gray Herbarium.

From an anonymous giver, $1,000, " to Harvard University," upon certain defined conditions.

From an anonymous giver, $300, " to increase a salary in the Medical School."

From an anonymous friend of the University, $400, to be added to a certain fellowship.

From an anonymous giver, $2,000, to meet certain expenses at the College Library.

From an anonymous giver, $250, for the salary of a secretary for The Cancer Commission of Harvard University.

From an anonymous giver, $200, to secure a certain salary under The Cancer Commission of Harvard University.

From an anonymous giver, $50, to be used as the income of Scholarship Funds is used.

From an anonymous giver, $3,500, " for immediate use by the Department of Social Ethics."

To increase the income of the Arnold Arboretum for the year 1910–11, from

Mrs. George R. Agassis	$1,000	Amount brought forward	$2,200
Thomas Allen	100	Miss Mary S. Ames	200
Frederick L. Ames	1,000	Oliver Ames	100
John S. Ames	100	Charles W. Amory	100
Amount carried forward	$2,200	Amount brought forward	$2,600

FOR THE ARNOLD ARBORETUM (continued)

Amount brought forward	$2,600
Mrs. Charles W. Amory	100
Lars Anderson	100
Mrs. Lars Anderson	100
Anonymous	400
Anonymous	100
Anonymous	100
Miss Ellen S. Bacon	100
Walter C. Baylies	100
E. Pierson Beebe	100
George N. Black	100
Mrs. Arthur W. Blake	100
Francis Blake	100
Peter B. Bradley	100
Robert S. Bradley	100
Mrs. Edward D. Brandegee	100
Mrs. John L. Bremer	100
Miss Helen O. Brice	50
Peter C. Brooks	100
Shepherd Brooks	100
E. S. C.	100
Mrs. Louis Cabot	100
Alexander Cochrane	100
Mr. and Mrs. James M. Codman	100
Miss Alice S. Coffin	100
Charles A. Coffin	100
T. Jefferson Coolidge	100
F. G. Crane	100
W. Murray Crane	100
Zenas Crane	100
Miss Sarah H. Crocker	50
Mrs. Charles P. Curtis	100
Mrs. Charles H. Dalton	100
Mr. and Mrs. Ernest B. Dane	500
Mrs. Arthur E. Davis	100
Frank A. Day	100
Philip Dexter	100
Mrs. George A. Draper	100
Miss Hannah M. Edwards	100
Mrs. George R. Emmerton	50
William Endicott, Jr.	100
Arthur F. Estabrook	100
Mrs. Robert D. Evans	1,000
In the name of Mr. L. Carteret Fenno	100
Desmond Fitzgerald	100
Miss Cornelia A. French	100
Amount carried forward	**$8,550**

Amount brought forward	$8,550
Mr. and Mrs. Henry C. Frick	1,000
George A. Gardner	200
John L. Gardner	100
William A. Gaston	100
R. H. I. Goddard	100
Mrs. Henry S. Grew	100
Charles Hayden	100
Mr. and Mrs. Augustus Hemenway	200
Henry Hornblower	100
Henry S. Howe	100
Henry S. Hunnewell	100
Mrs. Henry S. Hunnewell	100
Walter Hunnewell	100
Eben D. Jordan	100
George G. Kennedy	100
Nathaniel T. Kidder	100
Mrs. David P. Kimball	100
Horatio A. Lamb	100
Gardiner M. Lane	100
George B. Leighton	200
John M. Longyear	100
Percival Lowell	100
Arthur T. Lyman	100
Mrs. Theodore Lyman	100
Thomas L. Manson	100
Mrs. Charles E. Mason	100
Miss Ellen F. Mason	25
Miss Fanny P. Mason	100
George von L. Meyer	100
George H. Mifflin	100
Thomas Minns	100
J. Pierpont Morgan	100
Mrs. J. Pierpont Morgan, Jr.	100
John T. Morris	100
Mrs. John T. Morse, Jr.	100
Frederick S. Moseley	100
John Parkinson	100
Frank E. Peabody	100
George A. Peabody	100
Charles L. Peirson	100
John C. Phillips	50
Mrs. John C. Phillips	100
Dudley L. Pickman	100
Mrs. Dudley L. Pickman	100
Wallace L. Pierce	100
Amount carried forward	**$14,125**

FOR THE ARNOLD ARBORETUM (*continued*)

Amount brought forward	$14,125	Amount brought forward	$17,825
David Pingree	500	Miss Evelyn Thayer	100
Laban Pratt	100	Mrs. E. V. R. Thayer	100
William A. Read	100	John E. Thayer	100
Mrs. Jacob C. Rogers	100	Mrs. John E. Thayer	100
Mrs. Robert S. Russell	100	John E. Thayer, Jr.	100
Mrs. John L. Saltonstall	500	Nathaniel Thayer	100
Richard M. Saltonstall	100	Mrs. Nathaniel Thayer	100
Charles S. Sargent	100	Nathaniel Thayer, 2d	100
Mrs. Charles S. Sargent	100	Miss S. B. Thayer	100
Winthrop Sargent	100	Miss Susan Thayer	100
Mrs. Winthrop Sargent	100	Samuel Thorn	50
Henry F. Sears	100	William A. Wadsworth	100
Mrs. J. Montgomery Sears	100	Edwin S. Webster	100
Mrs. Knyvet W. Sears	100	Mrs. Edwin S. Webster	100
Mrs. G. Howland Shaw	100	Frank G. Webster	100
Mrs. Robert G. Shaw	100	Mrs. Frank G. Webster	100
C. R. Simpkins	100	Laurence J. Webster	100
John T. Spaulding / William S. Spaulding	100	Mrs. Laurence J. Webster	100
		Charles G. Weld	100
Charles A. Stone	100	C. Minot Weld	100
Mrs. Charles A. Stone	100	Stephen M. Weld	100
Galen L. Stone	200	Mrs. Stephen M. Weld	100
Nathaniel H. Stone	100	Mrs. William G. Weld	100
Charles E. Stratton	100	Mrs. Henry C. Weston	100
Charles W. Taylor	100	William P. Wharton	50
Bayard Thayer	100	George R. White	100
Mrs. Bayard Thayer	100	William Whitman	100
Miss Constance Thayer	100	John D. Williams	100
Duncan F. Thayer	100	Robert Winsor	100
Amount carried forward	$17,825		$20,625

From Mrs. George M. Nowell, $150, towards furnishing a room in the new greenhouses at the Botanic Garden.

For present use at the Botanic Garden, from

Anonymous	$250
Ernest B. Dane	1,500
Arthur F. Estabrook	1,000
	$2,750

Towards the new greenhouses at the Botanic Garden, from

John S. Ames	$1,000
Miss Mary S. Ames	1,000
Mrs. Oliver Ames	1,112
Edwin F. Atkins	1,000
Ernest B. Dane	1,000
	$5,112

For present use at the Botanical Museum, from

Anonymous $50
Anonymous 1,500
Anonymous 1,500
$3,050

For the botanical exploration of Western China, begun in 1906 by Ernest Henry Wilson, on behalf of the Arnold Arboretum, from

Sundry subscriptions from persons in England, through F. R. S. Balfour $3,394.92
James Veitch and Sons 1,473.85
$4,868.77

From W. Graham Bowdoin, Jr., $250, for the "W. Graham Bowdoin, Jr. Scholarship" for 1910–11.

From Miss Abby A. Bradley, $600 additional, to be added to the income of the William L. Bradley Fund for the Arnold Arboretum.

From Heman Merrick Burr, $90, "for the benefit of the University."

From Adolphus Busch, $100,000 additional, for the Germanic Museum.

Towards meeting the third year's expenses of the Graduate School of Business Administration, in accordance with the pledges which made the undertaking possible, from

Oliver Ames $500
George F. Baker, Jr. 100
Walter C. Baylies 500
Charles S. Bird 500
J. A. Lowell Blake 500
Edward D. Brandegee . . . 100
Allston Burr 100
Benjamin P. Cheney 1,000
Charles A. Coffin 200
" E " 1,000
Estate of Robert D. Evans . 1,000
Charles S. Fairchild 500
William A. Gaston 100
General Education Board . . 14,750
Robert Goelet 250
Robert Walton Goelet . . . 250

Amount carried forward . $21,350

Amount brought forward $21,350
Henry S. Howe 100
A. Lawrence Lowell 1,000
George S. Mandell 500
J. Pierpont Morgan, Jr. . . 1,000
Nathaniel C. Nash 100
Bradley W. Palmer 100
George L. Peabody 200
James H. Proctor 100
Estate of William B. Rice . . 500
Horace S. Sears 200
Herbert N. Straus ⎫
Jesse I. Straus ⎬ 500
Percy S. Straus ⎭
Members of the Class of 1879 1,000

$26,650

For the general purposes of the Graduate School of Business Administration, from

H. W. Cannon	$50
William J. Curtis	100
A. Lowes Dickinson	100
George L. Duval	100
Franklin MacVeagh	50
Charles E. Mason	100
Frederick W. Taylor	150
	$650

From Warren Delano Robbins, $100, to be applied to expenses of work in South America, in connection with the Graduate School of Business Administration.

From Daniel Waldo Field, $500, towards the equipment of the reading-room of the Graduate School of Business Administration.

For present use at the Bussey Institution, from

Carroll Dunham	$100
James L. Little	23
	$123

Towards the erection and maintenance of the new Cancer Hospital, $40,000, from sundry subscriptions through J. Collins Warren.

From the Carnegie Foundation for the Advancement of Teaching, $37,971.69, to pay retiring allowances granted by the Executive Committee of this Foundation to persons connected with Harvard University.

Towards the support at Harvard University of Chinese students in addition to the sixteen students sent in 1906–07 by the Chinese Government, from

Henry L. Higginson	$1,500
Miss Ellen F. Mason	1,000
	$2,500

From Joseph H. Clark, $13.25, for binding books presented by him to the College Library.

From the Classical Association of New Engand, $25, towards the travelling expenses of a member of the Commission on Latin Entrance Requirements.

From the Department of the Classics, $200, in part payment of advances by the President and Fellows for the purchase of books for the Classical Library.

From the Department of the Classics, $150, for an additional University Scholarship for 1911–12.

To be added to the income available for the payment of salaries in the College, from

Mrs. Edward D. Brandegee	$500
D. Crawford Clark	250
Amos Tuck French	500
Alfred W. Hoyt	500
	$1,750

From Archibald Cary Coolidge, $1,000 additional, for the payment for services at the College Library.

From Archibald Cary Coolidge, $600, for the payment for additional services at the College Library.

From Archibald Cary Coolidge, $150, for an additional University Scholarship in History in the Graduate School of Arts and Sciences, for 1910–11.

From William T. Councilman, $1,775, to be used for the Pathological Laboratory.

For the use of the Division of Forestry, from

John S. Ames	$200	Amount brought forward	$2,335
Oakes Ames	200	David Pingree	1,000
Edward W. Atkinson	50	Mrs. Henry S. Russell	100
William Bacon	100	Miss Marian Russell	100
Blanchard Lumber Company	25	Sabin P. Sanger	250
Edward D. Brandegee	100	Charles O. Skinner	10
Peter C. Brooks	100	A. T. Stearns Lumber Company	100
I. Tucker Burr	500	E. Stetson Lumber Co.	250
Norman Cabot	20	Stone Lumber Company	10
Mrs. Edward M. Cary	100	Nathaniel H. Stone	100
Walstein R. Chester	25	John E. Thayer	200
J. Randolph Coolidge	50	Washington B. Thomas	100
George H. Davenport	100	Henry O. Underwood	500
Mrs. Robert D. Evans	200	Eliot Wadsworth	100
W. Cameron Forbes	200	John W. Weeks	100
Waldo E. Forbes	200	William P. Wharton	100
Charles C. Gardiner Lumber Company	50	Robert Winsor	50
Charles Holyoke	15	John M. Woods and Company	50
Amory A. Lawrence	100		$5,455
Amount carried forward	$2,335		

From John Craig, $500, $250 thereof for a prize in Dramatic Composition and $250 for the purchase of books on the History of the English Drama, for the College Library.

For the purchase of land, the erection of buildings, or the endowment of education and research, for the benefit of the Dental School, from

Amos I. Hadley	$200
Murdoch C. Smith	75
	$275

From Lawrence W. Baker, $100, to forward original research in the Dental School.

From Mrs. Henry Draper, $4,800 additional, to be spent by the Director of the Observatory in prosecuting the researches in the photography of stellar spectra with which the late Dr. Henry Draper's name is honorable associated.

From the estate of J. Rayner Edmands, $1,000, " for the Phillips Library or for such other application to the plant and operations of the astronomical observatory as the Director may determine."

For the use of the Department of English in publishing such contributions, either by students or instructors at Harvard, as may seem to merit preservation in permanent form, from

Laird Bell	$25	Amount brought forward	$700
William C. Boyden	25	Albert Matthews	50
Frederick I. Carpenter	50	John T. Morse, Jr.	150
George G. Crocker	50	Dudley L. Pickman	50
Edgar C. Felton	50	Mrs. Robert S. Russell	150
Frederick P. Fish	50	Lawrence E. Sexton	150
Samuel Hill	50	Moorfield Storey	50
Henry S. Howe	50	Francis J. Swayze	50
George G. Kennedy	50	Charles H. Tweed	50
George L. Kittredge	150	Kenneth G. T. Webster	50
Mrs. George L. Kittredge	50	George Wigglesworth	50
William Caleb Loring	50	Moses Williams	50
George D. Markham	50		$1,550
Amount carried forward	$700		

Towards the salary of an Instructor in the Department of Education, from

Mrs. Walter Channing	$200
Joseph Lee	2,300
	$2,500

Towards the purchase of a painting of The Holy Family attributed to Bonifasio, for The William Hayes Fogg Art Museum, from

Denman W. Ross	$100
Charles C. Walker	100
	$200

Towards the Degas exhibition at The William Hayes Fogg Art Museum, from

Francis Bullard	$10.00
Archibald Cary Coolidge	10.00
John T. Coolidge, Jr.	10.00
J. Randolph Coolidge, Jr.	25.00
Horatio G. Curtis	10.00
Francis G. Fitzpatrick	15.00
Edward W. Forbes	23.98
Denman W. Ross	25.00
	$128.98

Towards the fund for the erection of the Harvard Freshman dormitories, from

Frederick Ayer	$1,000
Francis B. Biddle	5
Charles C. Binney	100
William W. Bodine	25
Henry C. Brengle	100
John W. Brock, Jr.	25
John D. Brown	50
Henry D. Bushnell	5
Herbert L. Clark	1,000
Percy H. Clark	200
Sydney P. Clark	1,000
Charles A. Coffin	5,000
Edward K. Davis	5
Edgar C. Felton	500
Theodore Frothingham	1,000
Nathan Hayward	200
William H. R. Hilliard	10,000
Robert H. Hutchinson	25
Edward E. Jenkins	60
Amount carried forward	$20,300

Amount brought forward	$20,300
Charles H. Krumbhaar, Jr.	25
William F. Kurts	50
Percival Lowell	250
M. Phillips Mason	25
Charles E. Morgan, 3d	25
Kent Packard	2
Howard M. Paull	2
Richard A. F. Penrose, Jr.	100
Earl B. Putnam	100
Evan Randolph	10
Henry W. Schurr	5
Philip L. Spalding	100
Clarke Thomson	1,000
Charlemagne Tower	200
Mrs. Andrew C. Wheelwright	200
Clement B. Wood	40
Howard Wood, Jr.	20
William Woodward	10,000
	$32,454

From Franklin W. Moulton, $25, for loans to Freshmen.

From Otto H. Kahn, $1,000, for the purchase of reproductions of German art for the Germanic Museum, preferably toward the purchase of a bronze cast of the Schiller-Goethe monument at Weimar.

Towards a new chemical laboratory, in memory of Wolcott Gibbs, LL.D., Rumford Professor and Lecturer on the Application of Science to the Useful Arts, from 1863 to 1887, from

Walter C. Baylies	$1,000
Mrs. Edward M. Cary	2,000
John T. Davis	100
Mrs. J. Malcolm Forbes	500
Henry S. Howe	500
Amory A. Lawrence	1,000
Miss Fanny P. Mason	500
Robert Saltonstall	500
Stephen M. Weld	495
Robert Winsor	500
	$7,095

For two travelling scholarships to be awarded to students in Mining and Metallurgy doing the regular work of the first year in the Graduate School of Applied Science, from

Edgar C. Felton	$56.00
John Hays Hammond	55.56
Albert F. Holden	55.56
Hennen Jennings	55.56
Richard A. F. Penrose, Jr.	55.56
Charles P. Perin	55.56
Quincy A. Shaw	55.00
Frank H. Taylor	55.56
Benjamin B. Thayer	55.56
	$499.92

For the Gray Herbarium, from

Rodolphe L. Agassiz	$10	Amount brought forward	$220
Thomas Allen	10	Edward M. Brewer	10
Miss Mary S. Ames	10	William Brewster	10
Anonymous	50	Addison Brown	10
Anonymous	25	Mrs. William S. Bullard	10
Anonymous	25	Allston Burr	20
Edwin F. Atkins	10	" E. S. C."	25
Walter C. Baylies	10	" F. H. C."	10
Thomas P. Beal	10	Mrs. James B. Case	10
Arthur C. Bent	10	Horace D. Chapin	10
Mrs. Arthur W. Blake	10	Miss Cora H. Clarke	10
Francis Blake	10	Miss Louise H. Coburn	10
William P. Blake	10	Mr. and Mrs. James M. Codman	10
Mrs. John L. Bremer	10	Miss Helen Collamore	10
Miss Sarah F. Bremer	10	George G. Crocker	10
Amount carried forward	$220	Amount carried forward	$385

FOR THE GRAY HERBARIUM (continued)

Amount brought forward .	$385	Amount brought forward .	$1,050
Mrs. Charles P. Curtis . . .	10	Miss Katharine P. Loring . .	10
Henry P. Curtis	10	Miss Louisa P. Loring . .	10
Frank A. Day	25	Mrs. William Caleb Loring . .	20
Walter Deane	15	Mrs. Thornton K. Lothrop .	10
William Endicott	10	Mrs. George G. Lowell . . .	10
William Endicott, Jr. . . .	50	Arthur T. Lyman	10
Arthur F. Estabrook	100	Mrs. Gilbert N. MacMillan .	10
Charles F. Fairbanks	10	Miss Ellen F. Mason	10
Dudley B. Fay	10	Miss Fanny P. Mason . . .	10
Frederick P. Fish	10	Thomas Minns	10
Mrs. W. Scott Fitz	10	Mrs. Samuel T. Morse . . .	10
Francis A. Foster	10	Nathaniel C. Nash	10
Francis C. Foster	20	Grenville H. Norcross	10
Mrs. Francis C. Foster . . .	15	Mrs. Otis Norcross, Jr. . . .	10
Miss Harriet E. Freeman . .	10	Charles W. Parker	10
Miss Cornelia A. French . .	10	Miss Mary R. Peabody . . .	10
Robert H. Gardiner	10	Charles L. Peirson	25
George A. Goddard	10	Mrs. Anna T. Phillips . . .	10
Mrs. William H. Gorham . .	20	Mrs. Dudley L. Pickman . .	10
Miss Harriet Gray	10	David Pingree	20
Mrs. Henry S. Grew	10	Laban Pratt	5
Mrs. Augustus Hemenway .	10	Miss Elizabeth Putnam . . .	5
Miss Clara Hemenway . . .	10	Mr. and Mrs. George Putnam	25
Miss Annie P. Henchman . .	5	Miss Sarah E. Read	10
Joseph P. B. Henshaw . . .	10	Mrs. William Howell Reed .	10
Thomas Wentworth Higginson	5	George E. Richards	10
Miss Rose Hollingsworth . .	5	William L. Richardson . . .	25
Henry Hornblower	10	Denman W. Ross	10
Miss Katharine Horsford . .	25	Mrs. M. Denman Ross . . .	10
Clement S. Houghton	20	Mrs. Waldo O. Ross . . .	10
Miss Elizabeth G. Houghton .	10	Mrs. Robert S. Russell . . .	10
Henry S. Howe	10	Mrs. J. Montgomery Sears .	10
Charles W. Hubbard	10	Mrs. Knyvet W. Sears . . .	10
Mrs. John E. Hudson	5	Mrs. Phillip H. Sears . . .	10
Henry S. Hunnewell	25	Mrs. G. Howland Shaw . . .	10
Walter Hunnewell	10	David N. Skillings	10
Bernard Jenney	10	Francis Skinner	10
Edward C. Johnson	10	Francis P. Sprague	10
Frank L. Kennedy	5	Isaac Sprague	10
Charles A. Kidder	10	Mrs. Isaac Sprague	10
David P. Kimball	10	Nathaniel H. Stone	10
Mrs. David P. Kimball . . .	10	John E. Thayer	100
Miss Lulu S. Kimball	10	Miss Abby W. Turner . . .	10
Erasmus D. Leavitt	10	Charles H. Tweed	10
George V. Leverett	25	Charles C. Walker	10
Mrs. George Linder	10	Miss Caroline E. Ward . . .	10
Amount carried forward . .	$1,050	Amount carried forward . .	$1,655

For the Gray Herbarium (*continued*)

Amount brought forward	. $1,655	Amount brought forward	. $1,735
Miss Cornelia Warren	10	Mrs. Charles T. White	10
Benjamin L. Watson	10	George Wigglesworth	10
Frank G. Webster	25	Miss Adelia C. Williams	25
Mrs. Frank G. Webster	25	John D. Williams	20
Stephen M. Weld	10	Miss Mary Woodman	10
Amount carried forward . . $1,735			$1,810

From Jerome Davis Greene, $300, for a special scholarship to be called the "Mary Forbes Greene Scholarship for 1910–11."

From the Harvard Alumni Association, $50, towards certain travelling expenses incurred in connection with the College.

From the Committee on the Regulation of Athletic Sports, $5,000, to be added to its previous gifts for improvements upon, and additions to, The Soldier's Field, to be made by said Committee, with the approval of the Corporation.

From the Harvard Club of Boston, $1,000, for five scholarships of $200 each, to be given to successful candidates from the High Schools of Greater Boston, including the Roxbury Latin, for the year 1911–12.

From the Harvard Club of Chicago, $420, for the scholarship of the Club for 1909–10 and 1910–11.

From the Harvard Club of the Connecticut Valley, $200, for the scholarship of the Club for 1910–11.

From the Harvard Club of Fitchburg, $150, for the scholarship of the Club for 1910–11.

From the Harvard Club of Hawaii, $200, for the scholarship of the Club for 1910–11, "the award to be made with the understanding that it is a loan, repayable after a term of years."

From the Harvard Club of Hingham, $100, for the scholarship of the Club for 1910–11.

From the Harvard Club of Indiana, $200, for the scholarship of the Club for 1910–11.

From the Harvard Club of Lawrence, $100, the first payment for a scholarship for 1910–11.

From the Harvard Club of Lowell, $300, for two scholarships of $150 each, for the year 1910–11, the beneficiaries to be nominated by the Committee of the Club.

From the Harvard Club of Lynn, $100, for the scholarship of the Club for 1910–11.

From the Harvard Club of Milwaukee, $200, for the scholarship of the Club for 1910–11.

From the Harvard Club of Nebraska, $150, for the scholarship of the Club for 1910–11.

From the Harvard Club of New Jersey, $250, the third of three annual prizes of this amount to be awarded to that student from New Jersey who enters the Freshman Class in Harvard College with the highest credit in his examinations for admission.

From the Harvard Club of Western Pennsylvania, $300, for the scholarship of the Club for 1910–11.

From the Harvard Club of Rochester, New York, $200, for the scholarship of the Club for 1911–12.

From the Harvard Club of San Francisco, $500, for the scholarship of the Club for 1910–11.

From the Harvard Club of Washington, D. C., $101 additional, towards the maintenance of the scholarship of the Club for three years, beginning with 1909–10.

From the Harvard Club of Worcester, Mass., $200, for the scholarship of the Club for 1910–11.

From members of the Harvard Engineering Society of New York, $500, the second instalment of the "Student Fund of the Harvard Engineering Society of New York," to be loaned to students of engineering who are unable to meet the expenses of the summer courses in surveying, shopwork, and mining.

Towards refitting Holworthy Hall, from

Heman M. Burr	$50
I. Tucker Burr	100
T. Jefferson Coolidge, Jr.	60
William A. Gaston	100
Amount carried forward	$310

TOWARDS REFITTING HOLWORTHY HALL (*continued*)

Amount brought forward	$310
Edward W. Grew	25
Herbert C. Leeds	25
William Caleb Loring	200
George B. Ogden	100
Matthew V. Pierce	50
Ellery Sedgwick	100
Arthur M. Sherwood	100
Thomas C. Thacher	25
Robert D. Wrenn	50
	$985

From anonymous friends of the University, $200, for the Huide-koper Scholarship for 1910–11.

From James H. Hyde, $600, for the Fellowship of the Cercle Français de l'Université Harvard for 1910–11.

For the investigation of Infantile Paralysis, conducted by and under the direction of Dr. Theobald Smith, from

Francis R. Bangs	$50
Edward D. Brandegee	200
Frederick S. Converse	1,000
William H. Coolidge	100
Charles H. W. Foster	250
William H. Hill	100
Charles Jackson	1,000
Charles C. Jackson	1,000
Robert T. Paine, 2d	100
Frederick P. Royce	25
Frederic Schenck	50
Moses Williams	50
Moses Williams, Jr.	50
	$3,975

For the purchase of books for the College Library, from

Mrs. R. L. Adlercron, for books on Japan	$600.00
Anonymous, for books on Algiers	10.00
Anonymous, for books on Art	500.00
Anonymous, for books on English Literature	53.05
Anonymous, for books on Oceanic Linguistics	25.00
Robert Bacon	100.00
Thomas Barbour, for books on Oceanea	35.00
Harold W. Bell, for a set of the Numismatic Chronicle	137.00
Amount carried forward	$1,460.05

For the Purchase of Books for the College Library (*continued*)

Amount brought forward	$1,460.05
Alexander Cochrane	1,000.00
Archibald Cary Coolidge, for books on the History of France, and other subjects	2,137.48
Harold J. Coolidge, for books on China	50.00
Henry W. Cunningham	100.00
James F. Curtis, for books relating to the South . .	50.00
Estate of W. Bayard Cutting, Jr., for books on Florence	25.00
for books on Switzerland	25.00
for books relating to Napoleon or to the Napoleonic period	100.00
Dante Society	50.00
James Lloyd Derby, for books on the Philippine Islands	25.00
Ellis R. Dresel, for books on German Drama	50.00
William Endicott, Jr.	1,500.00
Department of English, for books in English literature	132.39
Jerome D. Greene, for a subscription to the "Japan Mail"	27.00
Editors of "The Harvard Crimson," in memory of their president, Fabian Fall, 1910, for extra books needed in large courses	250.00
William Thorn Kissel	5.00
George L. Kittredge, for books illustrating the history of Witchcraft	100.00
James Loeb, for "Labor Periodicals"	100.00
Edward P. Merritt	100.00
Godfrey Morse	50.00
Edwin Stanton Mullins, for books on Folk-lore . . .	50.00
Walter W. Naumburg, for books on Shakespere . .	200.00
William A. Neilson	6.31
Evan Randolph, for Encyclopaedia Britannica . . .	100.00
Saturday Club, of Boston, Mass.	600.00
Horace B. Stanton, for the Molière Collection . . .	25.00
Henry Stephens, 3d, for a set of the "Codex diplomaticus Hungariae ecclesiasticus ac civilis" . . .	550.00
James A. Stillman	100.00
Fund of the Twentieth Massachusetts Regiment . .	361.35
Horace E. Ware, for books on Comparative Philology	100.00
George Wigglesworth	100.00
Lucius Wilmerding, "to be used for the purchase of books at the sale of the library of Robert Hoe" .	150.00
	$9,679.58

From friends, in memory of Henry Weidemann Locke, S.B. 1902, $100 additional, for a scholarship for 1910–11 in Electrical Engineering in the Graduate School of Applied Science.

From Trustees under the will of Miss Harriet N. Lowell, of Boston, Mass., $4,000, the third and fourth payments under the following provision of her will:

" The remaining part of said net income shall during the life of the said . . . be paid in annual payments to the President and Fellows of Harvard College, in Cambridge, in said Commonwealth, to be used by the Medical Department of said College for scientific study and investigation in any department of surgery, and into the cause, treatment, prevention and cure of disease, including dental surgery and pathology, either in this country or in Europe or wherever such study and investigation may be most advantageously pursued."

To establish a Fellowship in Dramatic Composition to be called The MacDowell Fellowship, which may be held by a student of Harvard or Radcliffe, selected after open competition, by Professor George P. Baker of the English Department and accepted as holder of the Fellowship by the MacDowell Club of New York, from

George P. Baker	$50
The MacDowell Club of New York	550
	$600

From John Francis Manning, $50, to be added to the account " Lawrence Scientific School Loans Returned " to be loaned to a student in the Mining course who is recommended by some of the Instructors in that Department not merely for high marks but because he gives promise of making a practical, active Mining Engineer.

From Philippe Belknap Marcou, $50 additional, for a prize for French Composition, to be called the Jeremy Belknap Prize, as a memorial to Dr. Jeremy Belknap of the Class of 1762.

From the Massachusetts Society for Promoting Agriculture, $2,000 additional, " to be expended at the Arnold Arboretum by the Director, to increase the knowledge of trees."

From the Massachusetts Society for Promoting Agriculture, $1,200 additional, " to aid the College to enable Professor Theobald Smith to continue his experiments on bovine tuberculosis * * * ."

From J. Ewing Mears, $225, his second annual gift in accordance with the terms of his offer to establish a scholarship with an income of $225 a year, to be designated "The James Ewing Mears, M.D. Scholarship in Medicine," to be held by the beneficiary "for the full course of four years in the Medical School, subject to the standing he shall maintain in scholarship and to his good conduct as a student."

For three Zeiss microscopes, a paraboloid condenser, microtome and knife, and other apparatus, for the Medical School, $807.20 from

Richard Sisson Austin,
Alexander Maulins Burgess,
Oliver Street Hillman,
Archibald William Hunter,
Daniel Joseph Hurley,
Halsey Beach Loder,
Frank Burr Mallory.

From members of the Class of 1879 of the Harvard Medical School, $70 additional, to be added to "The Loan Fund of the Medical Class of 1879."

Towards the construction, at the Harvard Medical School, of tennis courts, squash courts, etc., for students' exercise, from

Through Henry S. Forbes	$800
Frederick C. Shattuck	100
George B. Shattuck	50
	$950

To be added to the income available for the payment of salaries in the Medical School, from

Henry L. Higginson	$5,000
William H. Walker	1,000
	$6,000

From Maurice H. Richardson, $800, towards defraying the expenses of the animal house erected for the Surgical Department of the Medical School.

From John F. Moors, $50, to be used for a certain scholarship for 1911–12.

For the use of the Division of Music, from

" An unknown donor "	$150
Percy L. Atherton	35
W. Kirkpatrick Brice	125
Frederick S. Converse	30
Carroll Dunham	25
Arthur Foote	30
Edward B. Hill	15
Philip L. Spalding	50
	$460

From James J. Putnam and Moorfield Storey, Trustees, $1,400 additional, towards the expenses of the Department of Neuropathology.

For the benefit and use of the Department of Neuropathology in the Medical School, from

Miss Katherine E. Bullard	$500
William N. Bullard	200
Mrs. William S. Bullard	500
	$1,200

For the Peabody Museum of American Archaeology and Ethnology, from

" A Friend "	$250.00
Anonymous	5,500.00
Mrs. E. N. Baylies	25.00
J. A. Lowell Blake	750.01
Clarence B. Moore	500.00
Miss Mary Lee Ware	480.00
	$7,505.01

From a friend, $75, for the Peabody Museum of American Archaeology and Ethnology, to be used towards the Explorations in the Delaware Valley.

From Henry W. Haynes, $55, his third annual gift of this amount to the Peabody Museum of American Archaeology and Ethnology, for the general purposes of the library, including binding current serials.

From John C. Phillips, $86, for the purchase of a new typewriter for the library of the Peabody Museum of American Archaeology and Ethnology.

From John B. Stetson, Jr., $150 additional, for books for the library of the Peabody Museum of American Archaeology and Ethnology.

From Mrs. William Hooper, $500, the first payment on account of her offer of $1,000 a year, in memory of her father, Charles Elliott Perkins, for the purchase of books and material bearing on the history and development of that part of America which lies beyond the Alleghanies.

From Edward Dyer Peters, $250, his fourth gift of like amount, for a scholarship in Mining and Metallurgy in the Graduate School of Applied Science for the year 1911–12.

From John C. Phillips, $3,000 additional, to be used under the direction of the Shattuck Professor of Pathological Anatomy, the Associate Professor of Pathological Anatomy and the donor, for work in the Department of Pathology.

From John C. Phillips, $200, for the payment for services at the University Museum.

From the Division of Philosophy, $50, for the Library of Philosophy in Emerson Hall.

From Reginald C. Robbins, $150, for the purchase of books for the Library of Philosophy in Emerson Hall.

From two anonymous givers, $300, towards a Scholarship in Philosophy for 1910–11.

From Theodore Lyman, $200, for the salary of an Assistant in Physics for 1910–11.

From Edward C. Pickering, $3,000 additional, for immediate use at the Observatory.

From John Winthrop Platner, $250, " for use in any department of the College work where it may be needed."

For the Department of Political Economy, from

Anonymous	$200
Arthur T. Lyman	500
Washington B. Thomas	100
Henry O. Underwood	500
	$1,300

From Murray Anthony Potter, $225, in memory of his mother, for two prizes in Comparative Literature, to be called the "Susan Anthony Potter Prizes," and a prize in Spanish Literature of the Golden Age.

From Andrew W. Preston, $3,333.33, to defray the cost of giving instruction in Central and South American Economics, Resources, and Commercial Organization, in the Graduate School of Business Administration and also in the High School of Commerce at Boston. This sum, together with $666.66, which has been given to the High School of Commerce, comprises the first two instalments of five yearly payments of two thousand dollars each.

The arrangement for the common utilization of this gift between the two institutions is as follows: during the year from September 1, 1909, to September 1, 1910, $666.66 goes to the High School of Commerce to assist in meeting the expenses of two travelling scholarships, and the balance, $1,333.33, is used at Harvard for the expenses of a course of lectures by experts in South American Trade conditions. After the year 1909–10, and beginning with September 1, 1910, the full sum of two thousand dollars goes to the Treasurer of Harvard University annually for four years, to pay the salary of a lecturer on South American Economics, Resources, and Commerce.

During the first of the four years the two thousand dollars will be used to pay the lecturer's expenses for an extended visit to various South American Countries. He will return to give instruction both at Harvard and in the Boston High School of Commerce. It is understood that he will give one-third of his time to the teaching of this subject in the High School of Commerce. The rest of his time will be devoted to the Graduate School of Business Administration at Harvard.

From Frederick Madison Allen, $787.50, for the Department of Preventive Medicine and Hygiene.

From Nelson Robinson, $15,000, for a certain salary in the Department of Architecture.

From Jacob H. Schiff, $2,000, one-half for buying and binding books for the Semitic Library, and one-half for the publication of a volume on the Babylonian tablets belonging to the Museum, any balance to be used for the Semitic Library.

From Horace S. Sears, $1,700, for the payment of certain lectures given in the Divinity School in 1910–11.

From Mrs. Joshua Montgomery Sears, $1,500 additional, for the Sears Prizes in the Law School.

From Henry L. Shattuck, $50 additional, toward the general expenses of undergraduate instruction in Harvard College.

From Francis Skinner, $3,000 additional, for the purchase of books for the Arnold Arboretum in memory of his father, Francis Skinner, of the Class of 1862.

From Jeremiah Smith, $250 additional, to be used for aid to students in the same manner as Scholarship Money Returned in the Law School is used.

From the Committee of Fifty, $300, for the purchase of books relating to the liquor question, for the Library of the Department of Social Ethics.

For the School for Social Workers, from

William S. Bigelow	$2,000
Joseph Lee	1,250
Mr. and Mrs. Frederick Nichols	500
	$3,750

From the Society for Promoting Theological Education, $714.27 additional, "for the purchase of books for the Library of the Divinity School and for the administration of said Library."

For the South End House Fellowship for 1910–11, from

Edward D. Brandegee	$100
Frederick P. Cabot	10
Archibald Cary Coolidge	10
Mrs. W. Scott Fits	100
Randolph C. Grew	100
Augustus Hemenway, Jr.	25
Robert Homans	3
Francis Welles Hunnewell, 2d	20
Frank Lowell Kennedy	5
Frederick Law Olmsted	5
Charles Weil	5
Alexander Whiteside	10
Robert A. Woods	7
	$400

For the South End House Fellowship in Social Education for the year 1910–11, from

Randolph C. Grew	$100
Through James Hardy Ropes	200
	$300

From Joseph E. Sterrett, $100, for the purchase of books or other material relating to accounting, for the Graduate School of Business Administration.

To forward original work in the Laboratory of Surgical Research, from

John S. Ames	$1,000.00
Anonymous	50.00
Through Robert B. Greenough	25.00
John Homans	5.20
John C. Phillips	25.00
	$1,105.20

From John E. Thayer, $500 additional, for the Bermuda Biological Station for Research.

From Frank Graham Thomson, $5,000 additional, for instruction in Municipal Government.

To pay the tuition of a certain student for 1911–12, from

William F. Bacon	$10
Edward E. Blodgett	10
Grosvenor Calkins	10
William H. Coolidge	10
Clift Rogers Clapp	10
William R. Dewey	10
Clinton L. Eddy	10
Robert S. Gorham	10
Percy S. Howe	10
James A. Lowell	10
George R. Pulsifer	10
Waldron H. Rand, Jr.	10
Frederick J. Ranlett	10
Alonzo R. Weed	10
Edward F. Woods	10
	$150

(These gifts have been returned to the givers.)

From Frederick Adams Woods, $400, for the " Adams Woods
Fellowship for the Study of Heredity in American History " for
1910–11.

For present use at the Museum of Comparative Zoölogy, from

Thomas Barbour	$50
Louis A. Shaw	250
	$300

*The total amount of these gifts for immediate use is $462,300.70
as shown in Exhibit B.*

SPECIAL INVESTMENTS
June 30, 1911

UNIVERSITY	Principal.	Net Income.
Walter F. Baker, Real Estate in Boston,	$46,000.00	......
John W. Carter, University Houses and Lands,	12,500.00	$554.39
George B. Dorr, University Houses and Lands,	115,966.56	5,143.85
George Draper, University Houses and Lands,	48,458.50	2,149.23
Robert H. Eddy, University Houses and Lands,	56,787.00	2,518.60
John Davis Williams French, University Houses and Lands,	5,322.09	236.04
John C. Gray, University Houses and Lands,	25,000.00	1,108.80
Walter Hastings, Real Estate, Sacramento St., Cambridge,	20,000.00	1,510.05
Henry L. Higginson, University Houses and Lands,	68,485.45	3,035.25
Insurance and Guaranty, Real Estate, Lucas St., Boston,	4,000.00	......
Joseph Lee, University Houses and Lands,	10,000.00	443.52
Henry S. Nourse (part), Mortgage on Real Estate in Chicago, Ill.	......	110.00
Francis E. Parker, University Houses and Lands,	113,817.44	5,048.08
Henry L. Pierce (Residuary) (part), Equipment at Memorial Hall	157,098.14	7,099.78
Riverside, 11 shares Harvard Riverside Associates,	11,000.00	......
Henry Villard, University Houses and Lands,	50,000.00	2,217.60
William F. Weld, University Houses and Lands,	100,000.00	4,435.20
Amounts carried forward,	$844,385.18	$35,609.84

45

	Principal.	Net Income.
Amounts brought forward, ...	$844,385.18	$35,609.84

COLLEGE

Daniel A. Buckley (part),

Real Estate in Cambridge, Mass., ...	66,345.59	7,302.44
" " Deer Isle, Me., ...	1.00	. . . . . .

George Newhall Clark,

100 shares St. Joseph R'y, Light, Heat & Power Co.,	10,000.00	500.00

Edward W. Codman (part),

$5,000 Kansas City, Fort Scott & Memphis R. R. Cons. M. 6's of 1928 (sold during the year), . .	. . . . . .	184.83
5,000 Northern Pacific–Great Northern Joint 4's (C. B. & Q. collateral) of 1921 (sold during the year), ...	. . . . . .	133.89
2 shares Pacific Mills, ...	4,600.00	240.00
15 " Barristers Hall Trust, ...	1,085.00	60.00
11 " Boston Real Estate Trust, ...	13,219.50	495.00
25 " Central Building Trust (sold during the year), ...	. . . . . .	136.67

Edward Erwin Coolidge,

200 shares U. S. Smelting, Ref. & Mining Co. pref'd,	9,000.00	700.00

T. Jefferson Coolidge, for Research in Physics,

625 shares Massachusetts Electric Cos., cum. pref'd,	57,500.00	2,500.00

Eliot Professorship (Jonathan Phillips's Gift),

$10,000 City of Boston 3½'s of 1920, ...	10,000.00	350.00

Professorship of Hygiene (part),

Policy of Mass. Hospital Life Insurance Co., . .	5,000.00	206.25
$16,000 Northern Pacific–Great Northern Joint 4's (C. B. & Q. collateral) of 1921 (sold during the year), ...	. . . . . .	428.44
6,000 New York Central & Hudson River R.R. (L. S. & M. S. Coll.) 3½'s of 1998 (sold during the year), ...	. . . . . .	180.54
35 shares American Smelting & Refining Co., . .	3,112.22	245.00
50 " American Tel. & Tel. Co., ...	5,350.00	400.00
25 " Canadian Pacific, ...	3,515.00	275.00
40 " Chicago, Milwaukee & St. Paul, ...	4,000.00	280.00

Charles Eliot Norton Fellowship,

$15,000 Northern Pacific–Great Northern Joint 4's (C. B. & Q. collateral) of 1921, ...	14,100.00	700.00
5,000 Louisville & Nashville Unified M. 4's of 1940,	5,000.00	200.00

George Foster Peabody Scholarship,

$6,000 Mexican Coal & Coke Co. 1st M., S. F. 5's of 1926, ...	4,800.00	150.00
Amounts carried forward, ...	$1,060,913.49	$51,277.90

	Principal	Net Income.
Amounts brought forward, ...	$1,060,913.49	$51,277.90
Sarah E. Potter Endowment (part),		
100 shares Boston & Albany, ...	18,500.00	625.00
100 " Massachusetts Electric Cos., cum. pref'd,	4,000.00	400.00
50 " Plymouth Cordage Co., ...	10,000.00	550.00
12 " Pureoxia Co., ...	60.00	4.80
William Reed Scholarship,		
$1,000 New York Central & H. R. Gold 3½'s of 1997,	1,000.00	35.00
1,000 Norfolk and Western Divisional 1st lien &		
gen. M. 4's of 1944, ...	1,000.00	40.00
2,000 Northern Pacific–Great Northern Joint 4's		
(C. B. & Q. collateral) of 1921, ...	2,000.00	100.00
Nelson Robinson Jr. Additional (part),		
1,750 shares Gauley Coal Land Co. preferred, . .	175,000.00	. . . . . .
Eliza O. and Mary P. Ropes (part),		
100 shares Chicago, Milwaukee & St. Paul, . . .	13,087.50	700.00
100 " Northern Pacific, ...	11,986.50	700.00
200 " Pennsylvania, ...	11,987.50	600.00
20 " " (50% paid), ...	500.00	. . . . . .
Dunlap Smith Scholarship,		
$5,000 Metropolitan West Side Elevated R. R. Extension M. 4's of 1938, ...	4,700.00	200.00
Stoughton Scholarship (part),		
Real Estate in Dorchester, ...	3,194.30	169.23
Teachers' Endowment (part),		
$5,000 Broadway Realty Co. Purchase Money, 2d M. 5's of 1916, ...	5,000.00	250.00
50,000 Wisconsin Central, Minneapolis Terminal Purchase Money M. 3½'s of 1950, ...	50,000.00	1,750.00
10 shares Harvard Riverside Associates, ...	10,000.00	. . . . . .
Wales Professorship of Sanskrit,		
Real Estate, Cornhill, Boston, ...	40,000.00	1,658.36
Samuel Ward's Gift (part),		
Ward's (Bumkin) Island, Boston Harbor, ...	1.00	. . . . . .
J. Palmer Welsh Memorial (part),		
$1,000 Ontario Power Co. 5's of 1948, ...	1,000.00	50.00

LIBRARY

William R. Castle,		
$1,000 Honolulu Gas Co., Limited, 6's of 1925, . .	1,000.00	60.00
Francis Parkman Memorial (part),		
$5,000 Louisville & Jeffersonville Bridge 1st M. Gold 4's of 1945, ...	4,500.00	200.00
Ichabod Tucker (part),		
Policy of Mass. Hospital Life Insurance Co., . . .	5,000.00	206.25
Amounts carried forward, ...	$1,434,480.29	$59,576.54

	Principal.	Net Inco
Amounts brought forward, ...	$1,434,430.29	$59,576

John Harvey Treat (part),

$2,000 Bethlehem Steel Corporation 1st M. 5's of 1926 (sold during the year), ...	. . . . . .	28
6,000 Interborough Rapid Transit conv. 6% Notes of 1911 (sold during the year), ...	. . . . . .	180
$3,000 Tri-City Railway & Light Co. 5's of 1923 (sold during the year), ...	. . . . . .	79
130 Shares Treat Hardware Supply Co., ...	6,500.00	390
70 " United Shoe Machinery Co., ...	4,050.00	. . .
Deposit in Andover Savings Bank (withdrawn), .	. . . . . .	34
" " Lawrence " "	1,644.76	. . .

MEDICAL SCHOOL

John C. Cutter Bequest,

6,250 Carthage Water Power Co., 1st M. 5% Notes,	1.00	
Deposit in Spencer Savings Bank, ...	500.00	. .
" " Leicester Savings Bank, ...	578.00	. . .

Calvin and Lucy Ellis (part),

$40,000 Northern Pacific–Great Northern Joint 4's (C. B. & Q. collateral) of 1921, ...	26,585.00	1,600
Real Estate in Boston (half interest in), ...	22,500.00	216
Real Estate in Eden, Bar Harbor, Maine, ...	10,000.00	. . .

Hamilton Kuhn Memorial (part),

14,000 Burl. & Mo. in Nebr. non-ex. 6's of 1918, .	14,570.00	930
20,000 Kansas C., Mem. & Birm. Inc. 5's of 1934, .	17,600.00	1,000
10,000 U. Elec. Sec. Coll. Tr. 5's of 1937, 26th ser.,	10,000.00	500
189 shares Edison Elec. Ill'm'ng Co. of Boston,	44,385.00	2,268

George C. Shattuck (part),

$25,000 Kansas City, Fort Scott & Memphis R. R. Cons. M. 6's of 1928 ($203.70 deducted from income for sinking premium), ...	28,463.00	1,296

Henry P. Walcott Fellowship in Clinical Medicine (part),

6,000 J. M. Guffey Petroleum Co. 1st M. 5's of 1912,	6,000.00	300
5,000 " " " 1913,	5,000.00	250
2,000 " " " 1914,	2,000.00	100

MUSEUM OF COMPARATIVE ZOÖLOGY

Maria Whitney,

$2,000 City of Providence 4's of 1911, ...	2,000.00	80
3,000 " " " 1921 (sold during the year), ...	. . . . . .	110

Alex. Agassiz Bequest, Clause XI,

Real Estate in Cambridge, ...	50,000.00	1,129
Amounts carried forward, ...	$1,686,807.05	$70,068

Principal. Net Income.

Amounts brought forward, ... $1,686,807.05 $70,068.60

OBSERVATORY

Advancement of Astronomical Science (1902),
15 shares Calumet & Hecla Mining Co., ... 9,000.00 390.00

Advancement of Astronomical Science (1901),
Real Estate in Cambridge, ... 2,476.81 . . . . . .

PEABODY MUSEUM OF AMERICAN ARCHAEOLOGY AND ETHNOLOGY

			Principal	Net Income
Peabody Building (part),	⎫	$54,000 Kansas & Mis- ⎧	11,512.72	622.32
Peabody Collection (part),	⎬	souri R. R. 1st M. 5's ⎨	19,218.64	1,088.84
Peabody Professor (part),	⎭	of 1922, ⎩	19,218.64	1,088.84

Thaw (part) ($8.47 deducted from income for sinking premium),
$20,000 Girard Point Storage Co. 1st M. 3½'s of 1940, 20,245.78 691.53

ARNOLD ARBORETUM

Robert Charles Billings,
$5,000 Butte Water Co. 1st M. 5's of 1921, ... 4,000.00 250.00

BUSSEY INSTITUTION
Woodland Hill,
Laboratory of Comparative Pathology building, . . 20,658.86 1,000.00

SPECIAL FUNDS

Francis H. Burr Memorial,
$19,000 Merrimack Valley Street Railway, 1st M.
5's of 1911 (paid during the year), ... 475.00
6,000 Cleveland, Cincinnati, Chicago & St. Louis
R.R. 5% Notes of 1911 (paid during the
year), ... 150.00

Bussey Trust (part),
Real Estate in Boston, ... 381,972.12 29,798.91

Fund of the Class of 1834,
Policy of Mass. Hospital Life Insurance Co., . . . 1,000.00 41.25

Fund of the Class of 1844,
Policy of Mass. Hospital Life Insurance Co., . . . 6,500.00 268.18

Fund of the Class of 1853,
Policy of Mass. Hospital Life Insurance Co., . . . 3,725.00 153.66

Calvin and Lucy Ellis Aid (part),
Real Estate in Boston (half interest in), ... 22,500.00 216.11

Charles L. Hancock Bequest (part),
Real Estate in Chelsea and Chicago, ... 65,001.00 4,252.00

Amounts carried forward, ... $2,273,836.62 $110,455.19

	Principal.	Net Income.
Amounts brought forward, ...	$2,273,836.62	$110,455.19

Anonymous,

	Principal.	Net Income.
20,000 Massachusetts 3's of 1930, ...	20,000.00	600.00
5,000 " " 1939, ...	5,000.00	150.00
19,000 " " 1941, ...	19,000.00	570.00
4,000 " 3½'s 1915, ...	4,000.00	70.00
6,000 " " 1916, ...	6,000.00	105.00
6,000 " " 1917, ...	6,000.00	105.00
2,000 Massachusetts 3's of 1918, ...	2,000.00	35.00
5,000 " " 1920, ...	5,000.00	87.50
10,000 " " 1923, ...	10,000.00	175.00
5,000 " " 1935, ...	5,000.00	87.50
12,000 " " 1940, ...	12,000.00	210.00
7,000 Boston Terminal Co. 3½'s of 1947 (sold during the year), ...	. . . .	23.82
17,000 City of Springfield 4's of 1914 (sold during the year), ...	. . . .	149.22

Robert Troup Paine (accumulating) ($187.38 deducted from income for sinking premiums),

	Principal.	Net Income.
$38,000 Massachusetts 3½'s of 1913, ...	38,361.88	1,185.25
5,000 " " 1916, ...	5,104.29	154.15
12,000 " " 1935, ...	12,247.22	409.08
4,000 " " 1938, ...	4,287.75	129.14

George Smith Bequest (part),

	Principal.	Net Income.
$10,000 Duquovn, Ill., Water Works Co. 6's of 1901, ...	1.00	. . . . . .
20,000 Laclede Gas Light Co. 5's of 1919, . . .	20,000.00	1,000.00
32,000 United States Steel Corporation 5's of 1963 (sold during the year), ...	. . . .	940.70
200 shares Laclede Gas Light Co., preferred, . . . } 20 " " " " " common. . . }	18,800.00	1,035.00

Frederick Sheldon (part),

	Principal.	Net Income.
$2,000 New York Gas & Electric Light, Heat & Power Co. 4's of 1949, ...	1,300.00	80.00
2,000 Twenty-eighth and Twenty-ninth Street Crosstown Ry. 1st M. 5's of 1996, . . .	500.00	. . . . . .
20 shares Astor Trust Co., ...	6,000.00	160.00
23 " Bank of America, ...	10,350.00	598.00
82 " Consolidated Gas Co. of New York,	6,734.25	451.00
11 " Corn Exchange Bank, ...	2,750.00	176.00
100 " Manhattan Trust Co., ...	12,900.00	360.00
23 " Mexican Telegraph Co., ...	4,370.00	230.00
50 " New York Loan & Improvement Co ,	6,500.00	325.00
7 " Newport Trust Co., ...	1,050.00	28.00
11 " Newport Water Works, ...	1,100.00	44.00
50 " Ontario Silver Mining Co., ...	200.00	. . . . . .
60 " U. S. Life Insurance Co., ...	1,815.00	126.00
100 15000th Trust Estate Hastings & Dak. Ry. Co.,	300 00	250.00

	Principal.	Net Income.
Amounts carried forward, ...	$2,522,508 01	$120,504.55

	Principal.	Net Income.
Amounts brought forward, ...	$2,522,508.01	$120,504.55

Gordon McKay Endowment (part),

	Principal.	Net Income.
$120,000 American Tel. & Tel. 4's of 1929, ...	114,000.00	4,800.00
18,000 Butte Electric & Power Co. 1st M. 5's of 1951,	16,650.00	900.00
20,000 Baltimore & Ohio R'y 3½'s of 1925 (sold during the year), ...	. . . .	237.23
6,000 Central Branch R'y 4's of 1919, ...	5,415.00	160.00
70,000 Florida East Coast R'y 1st M. 4½'s of 1959,	66,850.00	507.50
8,000 Freemont, Elkhorn & Mo. Valley R'y 6's of 1923 (sold during the year), ...	. . . .	345.33
8,000 General Electric Conv. 5's of 1917 (sold during the year), ...	. . . .	397.78
228,000 Interborough Rapid Transit 5's of 1952, .	227,166.75	6,006.11
221,000 Interborough R.T. Conv. 6% Notes of 1911 (sold during the year), ...	. . . .	6,555.00
35,000 Kansas City Railway & Light 6's of 1912, .	35,000.00	2,100.00
12,000 Madison River Power Co. 1st M. 5's of 1935,	11,975.00	. . . . . .
20,000 Main Central Improv. A, 4½'s of 1916 (sold during the year), ...	. . . .	1,270.00
45,000 Minneapolis General Electric 5's of 1934 (sold during the year), ...	. . . .	2,098.34
100,000 Kanawha & Michigan 5's of 1927, ...	95,500.00	5,000.00
80,000 New York, N. H. & H. Deb. 4's of 1955, .	78,800.00	3,200.00
61,000 N. Pacific–Great N. Joint 4's of 1921, . .	59,780.00	2,440.00
40,000 Puget Sound Electric 5's of 1910 (sold during the year), ...	. . . .	2,000.00
12,000 Puget Sound Electric 5's of 1932, ...	11,760.00	600.00
1,000 St. Joseph & Grand Island R'y 4's of 1947,	890.00	23.33
50,000 Seattle Electric Co. 5's of 1911 (sold during the year), ...	. . . .	1,666.67
50,000 Southern Railway Equip. 4½'s of 1912 (sold during the year), ...	. . . .	762.50
15,000 Wabash Equip. Serv. Co. 4½'s of 1910 (sold during the year), ...	. . . .	337.50
25,000 Wabash Equip. Serv. Co. 4½'s of 1915, .	23,800.00	1,125.00
300 shares Great Northern, ...	44,250.00	2,100.00
240 " Northern Pacific, ...	35,400.00	1,680.00
150 " Pennsylvania, ...	10,125.00	450.00
15 " " (50% paid), ...	875.00	. . . . . .
3,000 Washington Water Power Co. 5's of 1939 (sold during the year), ...	. . . .	67.08
14,000 West End Street R'y 4's of 1915 (sold during the year), ...	. . . .	233.33

Price Greenleaf. ($255.57 deducted from income for sinking premiums.) The total amount of this Fund is $794,898.98, which is invested as follows:

	Principal.	Net Income.
$70,000 Broadway Realty Co. Purchase money 1st M. 5's of 1926, ...	72,855.24	3,315.80
Amounts carried forward, ...	$3,433,100.00	$170,883.05

	Principal.	Net Income.
Amounts brought forward, . . .	$3,433,100.00	$170,883.05
$9,000 Burl. & Mo. River R. R. in Nebraska non-exempt 6's of 1918, ...	9,000.00	570.00
21,062.50 Central Crosstown Coll. Trust 5 % Notes of 1909, ...	20,239.58	. . . . . .
43,500 Central Vermont R'y 1st M. 4's of 1920, .	37,845.00	1,740.00
3,000 Chicago, Burl. & Quincy R. R. 4's of 1922,	2,880.00	120.00
50,000 Chicago Junction Railways & Union Stock Yards Coll. Trust 5's of 1915, ...	47,000.00	2,500.00
20,000 Cleveland R'y Ref. M. 5's of 1931, . . .	20,000.00	. . . . . .
30,000 Commonwealth Power Co. 1st M. 5's of 1924,	29,850.00	391.67
8,000 Kansas City, Fort Scott & Memphis cons. M. 6's of 1928, ...	9,213.35	408.63
50,000 Metropolitan Tel.&Tel.Co.1st M.5's of 1918,	49,750.00	2,500.00
34,000 New York Central & Hudson River R. R. (Michigan Central Collateral) 3½'s of 1998,	28,412.10	1,190.00
32,000 Northern Pacific–Great Northern Joint 4's (C. B. & Q. collateral) of 1921, ...	19,993.55	1,280.00
50,000 Seattle Electric Co. 5 % Notes of 1911 (sold during the year), ...	. . . .	2,500.00
50,000 Union Pacific R.R. 1st M.&L.G. 4's of 1947,	44,625.00	2,000.00
50,000 Note of Arlington Mills, ...	50,000.00	2,261.11
25,000 " " Hamilton Manufacturing Co., . .	25,000.00	1,218.75
50,000 " " Massachusetts Cotton Mills, . . .	50,000.00	2,250.00
360 shares Boston & Lowell R. R., ...	46,800.00	2,880.00
237 " Fitchburg R. R., preferred, ...	22,306.27	1,185.00
56 " Great Northern, preferred, ...	13,125.00	392.00
40 " " " Iron Ore Properties,	. . . .	60.00
355 " Old Colony R. R., ...	63,190.00	2,485.00
27 " N. Y. Central & Hudson River R. R., .	2,866.28	155.25
290 " Northern R. R. (N. H.), ...	29,290.00	1,740.00
52 " West End Street Railway, preferred, .	4,305.56	208.00
34 " Central Vermont R'y, ...	428.72	. . . . . .
707 " Pennsylvania R. R., ...	51,856.04	2,121.00
71 " " " (50 % paid), . .	1,775.00	. . . . . .
19 " Boston Real Estate Trust, ...	25,230.25	855.00
100 " Paddock Building Trust, ...	10,000.00	350.00
Cash in American Trust Co., ...	7,062.04	211.88
	$4,155,143.74	$204,456.34

SUMMARY :

Cash, Exhibit A, ...	$7,062.04
Securities, Exhibit A, ...	2,630,045.84
Land and Buildings, Exhibit A.	1,518,035.86
	$4,155,143.74
Interest and Dividends, Exhibit B, ...	$123,214.32
Rents, Land and Buildings, Exhibit B, ...	81,242.02
	$204,456.34

SECURITIES — GENERAL INVESTMENTS
June 30, 1911

Mortgages and Other Loans.	Principal.	Income.
Mortgages, ...	$867,000.00	
Advances to Bussey Trust, ...	312,499.08	
Abbeville Cotton Mills Note, ...	50,000.00	
American Woolen Co.'s Note, . . :	50,000.00	
Curtis and Sanger's Note, ...	50,000.00	
Darlington Manufacturing Co.'s Note, ...	50,000.00	
David Moffat Co. of Mass. Note, ...	100,000.00	
Indian Head Mills of Alabama Note, ...	50,000.00	
Merrimack Manufacturing Co.'s Note, ...	25,000.00	
Nashua Manufacturing Co.'s Note, ...	100,000.00	
Otis Elevator Co.'s Note, ...	100,000.00	
Pacific Mills Note, ...	50,000.00	
	$1,804,499.08	$76,958.44

Public Funds.

£3,500 Imperial Japanese Sterling 4½'s of 1925 (sold during the year), ...	. . . .	$607.23
$94,000 United States of Mexico 4's of 1954, . .	$87,250.00	3,760.00
	$87,250.00	$4,367.23

Railroad Bonds.

$100,000 Baltimore & Ohio 1st M. 4's of 1948, . .	$96,625.00	$4,000.00
100,000 B. & O. (S. W. Div.) 1st M. 3½'s of 1925,	89,750.00	3,500.00
100,000 Baltimore & Ohio (Pittsburg, Lake Erie & West Virginia) Ref. M. 4's of 1941,	99,250.00	4,000.00
125,000 Bangor & Aroostook Cons. Ref. M. 4's of 1951, ...	118,750.00	5,000.00
57,600 Burl. & Mo. in Nebr. non-ex. 6's of 1918,	57,600.00	4,116.00
444,000 Chicago, Burl. & Quincy 3½'s of 1949, . .	455,355.29	15,243.80
150,000 " " Gen. M. 4's of 1958,	145,250.00	6,000.00
200,000 C. B. & Q. (Illinois Div.) 4's of 1949, .	200,844.46	7,977.78
100,000 Chicago & No. Western Gen. M. 3½'s of 1987, ...	100,900.18	3,488.23
100,000 Chicago, Rock Island & Pacific Gen. M. 4's of 1988, ...	106,051.08	3,920.90
196,000 Duluth, Missabe & Northern General M. 5's of 1941, ...	209,847.62	9,423.81
100,000 Indiana, Ill. & Iowa 1st M. 4's of 1950,	96,500.00	4,000.00
200,000 Kansas City, Fort Scott & Memphis Cons. M. 6's of 1928, ...	232,827.61	10,068.97
114,000 Kansas City, Memphis & Birmingham (assented) Income 5's of 1934, . . .	103,500.00	5,700.00
Amounts carried forward, ...	$2,112,951.24	$66,439.49

	Principal.	Income.
Amounts brought forward, . . .	$2,112,951.24	$86,439.49

Railroad Bonds (*continued*).

	Principal.	Income.
$100,000 Lake Shore & Michigan Southern Deb. 4's of 1931, ...	98,250.00	2,133.33
100,000 Lake Shore & Michigan Southern Deb. 4's of 1928 (sold during the year), .	....	2,533.33
300,000 Long Island Unified M. 4's of 1949, . .	283,257.50	12,000.00
200,000 Louisville & Jeffersonville Bridge Co. 1st M. 4's of 1945, ...	191,000.00	8,000.00
100,000 Minneapolis Union 1st M. 5's of 1922, .	101,464.79	4,866.83
100,000 Montana Central 1st M. 6's of 1937, . .	129,656.22	4,859.37
300,000 New York Central & H. R. (L. S. & M. S. Coll.) 3½'s of 1998, ...	294,464.40	10,500.00
55,000 New York, New Haven & Hartford Convertible 3½'s of 1956 (sold during the year), ...	....	1,786.31
25,000 New York, New Haven & Hartford Convertible Deb. 6's of 1948, ...	25,000.00	1,500.00
100,000 New York, New Haven & Hartford Deb. 4's of 1955, ...	105,500.00	3,875.00
200,000 New York, Ontario & Western Ref. M. 4's of 1992, ...	209,385.23	7,884.13
343,000 Northern Pacific–Great Northern Joint 4's (C. B. & Q. Coll.) of 1921, . . .	164,325.92	13,720.00
100,000 Oregon Short Line Cons. 1st M. 5's of 1946,	114,593.77	4,583.03
100,000 Oregon Short Line Ref. M. 4's of 1929,	96,875.00	4,000.00
46,000 Pennsylvania Co. 3½'s of 1916, ...	48,875.00	1,715.00
250,000 Richmond–Washington Co. Coll. Trust 4's of 1943, Series C, ...	255,310.60	9,834.05
100,000 St. Louis & San Francisco Ref. M. 4's of 1951, ...	97,125.00	4,000.00
£40,000 St. Paul, Minneapolis & Manitoba (Pacific Extension) 4's of 1940, ...	200,367.07	7,535.52
$100,000 Southern Pacific 1st Ref. M. 4's of 1955,	97,062.50	4,000.00
100,000 Southern Pacific Conv. 4's of 1929 . .	99,625.00	4,000.00
200,000 Terminal R. R. Association of St. Louis Gen. M. Ref. 4's of 1953, ...	200,000.00	8,000.00
400,000 Union Pacific 1st M. & L. G. 4's of 1947,	353,114.75	16,000.00
100,000 " " Conv. 4's of 1927, ...	95,392.50	4,000.00
	$5,363,596.49	$227,765.39

Traction Bonds.

$150,000 Boston & Northern Street R'y 1st M. Ref. 4's of 1954, ...	$139,000.00	$6,000.00
84,250 Central Crosstown Coll. Trust 5% Notes of 1909, ...	88,625.00	......
200,000 Chicago Railways 1st M. 5's of 1927, .	198,388.90	4,944.45
100,000 Cleveland Railway Ref. M. 5's of 1931,	100,000.00	......
Amounts carried forward, ...	$521,013.90	$10,944.45

	Principal.	Income.
Amounts brought forward, ...	$521,018.90	$10,944.45

Traction Bonds (*continued*).

		Principal.	Income.
$300,000	Interborough-Metropolitan Coll. Trust 4¼'s of 1956, ...	254,782.50	13,500.00
300,000	Interborough Rapid Transit Co. Convertible 6% Gold Notes of 1911 (sold during the year), ...	. . . .	9,000.00
308,000	Interborough Rapid Transit Co. Gold M. 5's of 1952,	297,725.88	7,575.00
75,000	Kansas City Terminal R'y 1st M. Gold 4's	72,937.50	1,022.28
100,000	Metrop. Street R'y of Kansas City Consol. M. 5's of 1913, ...	99,000.00	888.89
100,000	Metrop. West Side Elevated 4's of 1938,	91,746.25	4,000.00
100,000	" " " Ext. M. 4's of 1938, ...	97,000.00	4,000.00
100,000	Northern Texas Traction Co. 1st M. 5's of 1933, ...	100,000.00	250.00
150,000	Old Colony Street R'y 1st M. Ref. 4's of 1954, ...	139,000.00	6,000.00
100,000	Second Ave. (N. Y.) Con. M. 5's of 1948,	115,789.60	. . . . . .
98,000	Third Avenue (N. Y.) 1st Consol. M. 4's of 2000, ...	94,052.86	. . . . . .
100,000	United Traction & Electric Co. 1st M. 5's of 1933, ...	109,599.97	4,563.68
		$1,992,647.46	$61,744.20

Sundry Bonds.

		Principal.	Income.
$100,000	American Agricultural Chemical Co. 5's of 1928, ...	$101,414.28	$719.84
800,000	American Tel. & Tel. Co. 4's of 1929, .	286,000.00	8,000.00
100,000	Boston Electric Light Co. 1st Cons. M. 5's of 1924, ...	109,173.06	4,820.51
145,000	Broadway Realty Co. Purchase money 1st M. 5's of 1926, ...	152,498.02	6,766.25
200,000	Calumet & Hecla Mining Co. 5% Coupon Notes of 1919, ...	201,600.00	9,800.00
140,000	Chicago Edison Co. 1st M. 5's of 1926 (sold during the year), ...	. . . .	6,709.60
250,000	Chicago Junction Railways and Union Stock Yards Coll. Trust 5's of 1915, .	250,080.55	12,479.85
100,000	Chicago Junction Railways and Union Stock Yards 4's of 1940, ...	98,500.00	4,000.00
150,000	Detroit Edison Co. 1st M. 5's of 1933, .	152,658.22	7,876.28
143,000	General Electric Co. Convertible Deb. 5's of 1917 (sold during the year), . .	. . . .	7,218.61
100,000	Madison River Power Co. 1st M. 5's of 1935, ...	85,000.00	5,000.00
	Amounts carried forward, . . .	$1,436,924.13	$72,385.94

	Principal.	Income.
Amounts brought forward, . .	$1,436,924.13	$72,385.94

Sundry Bonds (*continued*).

	Principal.	Income.
$50,000 Massachusetts Gas Co.'s S. F. 4½'s of 1929, ...	48,375.00	2,250.00
100,000 Metrop. Tel. & Tel. Co. 1st M. 5's of 1918 (sold during the year), ...	. . . .	4,180.67
100,000 Minneapolis General Electric Co. Gen. M. 5's of 1934, ...	101,991.56	4,915.26
100,000 Michigan State Telephone Co. 5's of 1924,	100,000.00	. . . . . .
100,000 Montreal Light, Heat and Power Co. 1st M. Coll. Trust 4½'s of 1932, ...	100,688.27	4,466.66
100,000 Municipal Gas & Electric Co. of Rochester, N. Y., 1st M. 4½'s of 1942, . . .	100,000.00	4,500.00
100,000 New England Tel. & Tel. Co. 5's of 1916,	104,705.84	4,058.82
75,000 New York Tel. Co. Gen. M. Gold S.F. 4½'s,	71,568.75	8,375.00
100,000 North American Co. Coll. Trust 5% Notes of 1912 (sold during the year), . . .	. . . .	972.22
100,000 Pacific Coast Power 5's of 1940, . . .	96,000,00	. . . . . .
100,000 Pejescot Paper Co. 1st M. 5's of 1917 and 1921, ...	99,000.00	5,000.00
200,000 Portland Gen'l Elec. 1st M. 5's of 1935,	202,953.86	9,876.93
100,000 Railway & Light Securities Co. Coll. Trust 5's of 1935, ...	100,818.20	4,965.90
100,000 Railway & Light Securities Co. Coll. Trust 5's of 1939, 2d series, ...	100,000.00	5,000.00
100,000 Railway & Light Securities Co. Coll. Trust 5's of 1939, 3rd series, ...	98,000.00	2,583.33
200,000 Southern Power Co. 1st M. Gold 5's, .	197,500.00	4,763.89
188,000 St. Louis National Stock Yards Co. 1st M. 4's of 1930, ...	181,945.00	6,443.33
100,000 Seattle Electric Co. 5% Notes of 1911, (sold during the year), ...	. . . .	5,000.00
100,000 Tacoma Railway & Power Co. 1st M. 5's of 1929, ...	100,960.00	4,980.00
50,000 United Electric Securities Co. Coll. Trust 5's of 1936, 24th series, . . .	50,000.00	2,500.00
75,000 United Electric Securities Co. Coll. Trust 5's of 1938, 27th series, . . .	75,000.00	3,750.00
50,000 United Electric Securities Co. Coll. Trust 5's of 1939, 29th series, . . .	50,997.80	4,203.76
100,000 United Fruit Co. 4½'s of 1925, ...	96,000.00	. . . . . .
100,000 Washington Water Power Co. 5's of 1939,	100,373.34	4,986.67
100,000 Western Elec. Co. Coll. Trust Gold 4½% Notes (sold during the year), . .	. . . .	4,250.00
200,000 Western Elec. Co. 1st M. 5's of 1922, .	199,000.00	. . . . . .
100,000 Westinghouse Electric Manufacturing Co. 5's Notes of 1917, ...	94,625.00	97.22
	$3,907,421.75	$169,505.60

Railroad Stocks.

			Principal.	Income.
700 shares		Baltimore & Ohio, ...	$70,362.50	$4,200.00
507	"	Chicago, Milwaukee & St. Paul, pfd.,	50,670.58	3,549.00
1268	"	Chicago, Milwaukee & St. Paul, . .	177,425.94	8,876.00
2282	"	Chicago & No. Western, ...	319,255.55	19,967.50
1337	"	Great Northern, preferred, ...	} 294,558.56	{ 9,359.00
955	"	Great Northern Iron Ore Properties,		{ 1,432.50
800	"	Louisville & Nashville, ...	98,924.00	5,600.00
8	"	Louisville Property	1.00	. . . . . .
700	"	Manhattan, ...	92,762.50	4,900.00
2088	"	New York Central & Hudson River, .	151,173.21	12,006.00
1367	"	New York, New Haven & Hartford, .	211,890.79	1,468.00
1000	"	Northern Pacific, ...	115,315.00	7,000.00
6229	"	Pennsylvania, ...	382,406.40	18,684.00
622	"	" (50% paid), ...	15,550.00	. . . . . .
500	"	Union Pacific, ...	91,437.50	5,000.00
			$2,066,733.53	$102,042.00

Manufacturing and Telephone Stocks.

2000 shares		American Smelters Securities Co. 5% cumulative preferred, series B, . .	$196,000.00	$10,000.00
1320	"	American Tel. & Tel. Co., ...	161,610.52	10,560.00
12	"	Amoskeag Manufacturing Co., . . .	3,654.00	1,440.00
2480	"	General Electric Co., ...	262,626.27	9,144.00
187	"	Merrimack Manufacturing Co., . . .	18,615.10	. . . . . .
24	"	Pacific Mills, ...	16,668.29	2,880.00
			$659,174.18	$34,024.00

Real Estate Trust Stocks.

1000 shares		Barristers Hall, ...	$92,766.00	$4,000.00
250	"	Business Real Estate, ...	23,750.00	. . . . . .
3500	"	Department Store, ...	220,291.88	11,250.00
1000	"	Essex Street, ...	100,000.00	4,000.00
750	"	Kimball Building, ...	75,000.00	2,250.00
1082	"	Paddock Building, ...	104,363.72	3,811.50
1000	"	Post Office Square Building, ...	103,000.00	4,000.00
1000	"	St. Paul Business Real Estate Assoc.	100,000.00	3,177.78
1000	"	Tremont Building, ...	100,000.00	2,187.50
1875	"	Western Real Estate Trust, ...	196,500.00	11,250.00
			$1,115,671.60	$45,926.78

Sundry Stocks.

611 shares		Edison Elec. Illum. Co., Boston, Mass., ...	$124,927.50	$7,332.00
1500	"	Massachusetts Gas Companies, pref'd,	132,107.00	6,000.00
1164	"	Trimountain Trust, ...	108,769.00	73.35
			$365,803.50	$13,405.35

SUMMARY :

	Principal.	Income.
Mortgages and Notes, ...	$1,804,499.08	$76,958.44
Public Funds, ...	87,250.00	4,367.23
Railroad Bonds, ...	5,363,596.49	237,765.39
Traction Bonds, ...	1,992,647.46	61,744.20
Sundry Bonds, ...	8,907,421.75	169,505.60
Railroad Stocks, ...	2,066,733.53	102,042.00
Manufacturing and Tel. Stocks, ...	659,174.18	34,024.00
Real Estate Trust Stocks, ...	1,115,671.60	45,926.78
Sundry Stocks, ...	365,803.50	13,405.35
Total, Exhibit A, ...	$17,362,797.59	
Total, Exhibit B, ...		$735,738.99

LAND AND BUILDINGS — GENERAL INVESTMENT
June 30, 1911

Real Estate in Boston.	Principal.	Net Income.
Adams Estate, Washington Street, ...	$250,000.00	$15,785.89
Amory Estate, Franklin Street, ...	165,615.81	9,075.66
Cowdin Estate, Haymarket Square, ...	36,000.00	2,065.21
Estate, 20 and 21 Haymarket Square, ...	58,913.52	1,338.89
Faneuil Hall Square Estate, ...	197,047.80	8,328.84
Gerrish Block, Blackstone and North Streets, . .	192,875.75	8,214.31
Gray Estate, Washington Street, ...	954,529.07	72,899.16
Lowell Estate, Washington Street, ...	464,368.91	26,421.29
Old Boston Music Hall Estate, ...	356,611.00	19,330.32
Townsend Estate, Hawkins Street, ...	44,419.49	1,787.27
Union and Friend Streets, ...	81,000.00	40.15
Webb Estate, Washington Street, ...	164,604.79	17,329.07
Total, Exhibit A, ...	$2,965,986.14	
Total, Exhibit B, ...		$182,616.06

FUNDS AND GIFTS

June 30, 1911

[The date following the title of a Fund shows the year of its establishment.]

Principal, July 1, 1910.	UNIVERSITY FUNDS	Principal, June 30, 1911.
$44,000.00	Anonymous (1910), ...	$136,568.75
. . . .	Walter F. Baker (1909), ...	46,877.95
2,000.00	William H. Baldwin, Jr. (1906),	2,000.00
1,143.00	Band Music (1903), ...	1,143.00
4,950.00	Andrew Bigelow (1898), ...	4,950.00
5,000.00	Stanton Blake (1889), ...	5,000.00
4,771.33	Charlotte F. Blanchard (1891), .	4,771.33
5,250.00	Samuel D. Bradford (1866), . .	5,250.00
50,000.00	Martin Brimmer (1907), ...	50,000.00
100,000.00	James C. Carter (1906), ...	100,000.00
12,500.00	John W. Carter (1898), ...	12,500.00
87,518.36	Class of 1883 (1908), ...	94,622.77
9,612.25	Edward Erwin Coolidge (1906),	9,777.10
153.67	Thomas Cotton (1727), ...	154.94
33,885.06	John Cowdin (1888), ...	33,885.06
115,966.56	George B. Dorr (1882), ...	115,966.56
48,458.50	George Draper (1892), ...	48,458.50
56,788.00	R. H. Eddy (1901), ...	56,788.00
101,225.49	Harvard Ellis (1895), ...	101,225.49
20,918.57	Richard W. Foster (1905), . . .	20,918.57
5,322.09	John Davis Williams French	
	(1901), ...	5,322.09
20,571.18	Gore (1834), ...	20,571.18
25,000.00	John C. Gray (1881), ...	25,000.00
20,000.00	Walter Hastings (1888), ...	20,000.00
100,000.00	Henry L. Higginson (1906), . .	100,000.00
5,000.00	George Baxter Hyde (1895), . .	5,000.00
4,000.00	Insurance and Guaranty (1860), . . .	4,000.00
16,871.63	Leonard Jarvis (1859), ...	16,871.63
10,000.00	Henry P. Kidder (1894), ...	10,000.00
10,000.00	Joseph Lee (1802), ...	10,000.00
10,000.00	Theodore Lyman (1898), ...	10,000.00
15,750.00	Israel Munson (1844), ...	15,750.00
50,000.00	Henry S. Nourse (1904), ...	49,980.00
113,817.44	Francis E. Parker (1886), . . .	113,817.44
4,005.59	George F. Parkman (1909), . . .	4,005.59
30,000.00	William Perkins (1888), ...	30,000.00
50,000.00	Henry L. Pierce (1898), ...	50,000.00
157,098.14	Henry L. Pierce(Residuary)(1898),	157,198.14
63,789.30	President's (1883), ...	64,334.47
370,081.87	Retiring Allowance (1879), ...	371,957.48
11,000.00	Riverside (1903), ...	11,000.00
$1,796,848.03	. . Amounts carried forward, . . .	$1,945,616.04

Principal, July 1, 1910.		Principal, June 30, 1911.	
$1,796,348.03	.. Amounts brought forward, . . .	$1,945,616.04	
23,370.03	John L. Russell (1889), ...	23,370.03	
2,116.62	Mary R. Searle (1903), ...	1,852.25	
46,918.13	Isaac Sweetser (1894), ...	46,918.13	
5,000.00	Seth Turner (1883), ...	5,000.00	
100,000.00	William F. Weld (1893), ...	100,000.00	$2,122,751.45

COLLEGE FUNDS

12,955.38	John W. P. Abbot (1874), . . .	$13,583.70	
27,748.64	Alford Professorship (1765), . . .	27,748.64	
7,806.86	Daniel Austin (1879), ...	7,806.86	
5,787.61	William H. Baldwin, Jr. 1885 (1906), ...	5,787.61	
....	Caroline M. Barnard Bequest (1911), ...	6,072.75	
666.67	John Barnard (1777), ...	666.67	
30,686.85	John B. Barringer (1873), . . .	30,686.85	
15,000.00	Robert Charles Billings, for Gray Herbarium (1903), ...	15,000.00	
1,050.00	John A. Blanchard (1873), . .	1,050.00	
39,780.00	Botanic Department (1880), ...	39,780.00	
28,337.40	Boylston Professorship (1772), . .	28,337.40	
11,224.65	Francis James Child Memorial (1897), ...	11,224.65	
7,105.12	Classical Publication Fund of the Class of 1856 (1888), ...	7,179.37	
103,669.41	Class of 1880 (1905).	103,669.41	
82,055.71	Fund of the Class of 1882 (1907),	91,924.30	
265.69	Class of 1883 Special Fund (1908),	278.59	
97,549.91	Class of 1884 (1909), ...	98,599.91	
105,097.01	Class of 1885 Gift (1910), ...	108,305.99	
....	Class of 1886 (1911), ...	100,000.00	
150,637.54	Class Subscription (1870), ...	150,637.54	
322,158.89	Edward W. Codman (1905), . .	321,399.84	
1,500.00	John Coggan (1652), ...	1,500.00	
58,018.63	T. Jefferson Coolidge, for Research in Physics, ...	57,521.55	
4,101.50	Paul Dudley (1751), ...	4,250.40	
111,434.26	Eaton Professorship (1903), . . .	111,838.81	
21,619.50	Eliot Professorship (1814), ...	21,619.50	
10,000.00	Eliot " (Jonathan Phillips's gift)(1854), ...	10,000.00	
3,500.01	Erving Professorship (1791), . . .	3,500.01	
35,990.99	Fisher " (1834), . . .	35,990.99	
431.07	Henry Flynt (1760), ...	434.57	
16,240.38	Fund for Permanent Tutors (1796), .	16,240.38	
1,033.57	Fund for Religious Services (1887), . .	1,033.57	
$3,287,201.06	.. Amounts carried forward, ...	$1,433,669.86	$2,122,751.45

Principal, July 1, 1910.		Principal, June 30, 1911.	
$3,287,201.06	. . Amounts brought forward, . . .	$1,433,669.86	$2,122,751.45
6,011.18	**George A. Gardner** (1892), . .	6,078.51	
15,013.68	**Godkin** Lectures (1903), ...	15,141.86	
7,837.79	**Gospel Church** (1868), ...	7,812.77	
32,711.00	**Asa Gray** Memorial (1898), . . .	32,711.00	
21,451.25	**Asa Gray** Professorship of Systematic Botany (1897), ...	21,451.25	
200,096.86	**Gurney** (1888), ...	200,096.86	
6,426.59	**George Silsbee** and **Ellen Sever Hale** (1904), ...	5,661.71	
15,289.80	**Harvard** Oriental Series (1899), . .	15,258.56	
20,655.91	**Herbarium** (1865), ...	20,655.91	
20,217.08	**Hersey** Professorship (1772), . . .	20,217.08	
21,744.18	**Hersey** Professorship (**Thomas Lee's** gift) (1856), ...	21,744.18	
520.00	**Thomas Hollis** (for Treasurer) (1721), ...	520.00	
34,517.60	**Hollis** Professorship of Divinity, .	34,517.60	
	Composed of these Funds : — **William Dummer** (1762), **Daniel Henchman** (1742), **Thomas Hollis** (1721), **Jonathan Mason** (1798), **James Townsend** (1738).		
3,747.33	**Hollis** Professorship of Mathematics,	3,747.33	
	Composed of these Funds : — **Thomas Brattle** (1713), **William Dummer** (1762), **Daniel Henchman** (1758), **Thomas Hollis** (1726).		
1,000.00	**Thomas Hubbard** (1774), . . .	1,000.00	
444.44	**Nathaniel Hulton** (1695), . . .	444.44	
233.33	**Thomas Hutchinson** (1739), . .	233.33	
6,159.78	**Ingersoll** Lecture (1894), ...	6,258.54	
61,536.43	**Abbott Lawrence** (1859), . . .	61,536.43	
50,375.00	**James Lawrence** (1865), ...	50,375.00	
11,537.00	Lectures on Political Economy (1889),	11,996.55	
15,796.97	**Lee** Fund for Reading (1863), . . .	15,796.97	
110,043.29	**Henry Lee** Professorship (1900), .	110,043.29	
. . . .	**Solomon Lincoln** Bequest (1911),	10,273.73	
7,720.00	**Joseph Lovering** for Physical Research (1891), ...	7,732.50	
68,257.31	**Lowell** Fund for a Botanic Garden (1882) (formerly Professorship of Natural History, 1805), ...	68,257.31	
20,040.72	**Woodbury Lowery** Memorial (1910), ...	20,212.81	
50,000.00	**Arthur T. Lyman** (1904), . . .	50,000.00	
$4,096,375.58	. . Amounts carried forward, . . .	$2,253,445.38	$2,122,751.45

Principal, July 1, 1910.		Principal, June 30, 1911.	
$4,096,375.58	. . Amounts brought forward, . . .	$2,253,445.38	$2,122,751.45
43,062.93	McLean Professorship (1834), . .	43,062.93	
1,302.26	Music Department (1903), ...	1,365.41	
333.33	John Newgate (1650), ...	333.33	
26,699.44	William Belden Noble Lectures		
	(1898), ...	26,788.83	
. . . .	Trenor L. Park Bequest (1911), .	21,914.79	
101,216.39	Francis Greenwood Peabody		
	Fund (1905), ...	100,396.53	
14,605.54	Daniel H. Peirce (1876), ...	14,676.38	
435.48	James Mills Peirce Bequest (bal.),	456.58	
21,000.00	Perkins Professorship (1841), . .	21,000.00	
31,500.00	Jonathan Phillips (1861), . . .	31,500.00	
75,000.00	Physical Laboratory Endowm't(1881),	75,000.00	
25,020.19	Plummer Foundation (1854), . .	25,020.19	
52,500.00	Pope Professorship (1868), ...	52,500.00	
189,655.98	Sarah E. Potter Endowment Fund,	189,655.98	
238,732.51	Professorship of Hygiene (1899), . .	238,871.83	
51,934.07	" " (1902), . .	52,340.17	
22,073.15	" " (1908), . .	32,555.25	
195,821.18	Nelson Robinson, Jr. Additional		
	(1906), ...	193,921.10	
3,535.00	Ezekiel Rogers (1701), ...	3,535.00	
117,134.99	Eliza O. and Mary P. Ropes, .	119,018.53	
56,368.73	Rumford Professorship (1819), . .	56,368.73	
1,514.00	Daniel Russell (1679), ...	1,514.00	
2,000.00	John L. Russell (1889), ...	2,000.00	
5,512.54	George William Sawin (1890),	5,779.92	
5,000.00	Robert W. Sayles (1906), . . .	5,000.00	
33,570.80	Shaler Memorial (1907), ...	33,498.99	
23,139.83	Smith Professorship (1816), . . .	23,139.83	
2,500.00	William M. Spackman (1905),	2,500.00	
2,042,744.93	Teachers' Endowment (1905), . . .	2,050,807.18	
16,303.16	John E. Thayer (1885), ...	15,988.30	
1,227.72	Elizabeth Torrey (1896), . . .	1,287.28	
13,552.42	Henry Warren Torrey (1890), .	13,807.26	
112,705.44	Twenty-fifth Anniversary Fund of the		
	Class of 1881 (1906), ...	113,975.44	
101,358.68	Unknown Memorial (1898), . . .	101,219.47	
50,000.00	Henry Villard (1902), ...	50,000.00	
40,000.00	Wales Professorship (1903), . . .	40,000.00	
17,638.95	Samuel Ward (1680), ...	18,494.39	
6,463.95	Cyrus M. Warren (1893), . . .	6,567.88	
119,213.37	Henry C. Warren (1899), . . .	119,528.34	
7,740.34	Sylvester Waterhouse (1896), .	8,115.73	
50,000.00	Increase Sumner Wheeler (1889),	50,000.00	
83.10	Jerome Wheelock (1903), . . .	97.42	
1,354.45	Chauncey Wright (1884), . . .	1,420.12	6,218,468.49
$8,017,930.43	. . Amounts carried forward, ...		$8,341,219.94

Principal, July 1, 1910.		Principal, June 30, 1911.
$8,017,930.48	. . Amounts brought forward, ...	$8,341,219.94

GIFTS FOR SPECIAL USE (BALANCES)

1,104.68	Anonymous Gift for Fellowship in Physical Research, ...	$648.84
. . . . . .	Anonymous Gift for Salary, 1911-12,	400.00
150.00	Anonymous Gift for Special Aid, . .	270.00
1,099.53	Bermuda Biological Station, ...	1,251.88
745.57	Cases, etc., at the Botanic Garden, .	760.48
30.27	**F. P. Bonney** Gift, ...	30.27
8.60	Common Room in Conant Hall, . . .	8.60
327.24	Harvard Economic Studies, ...	. . . . . .
. . . . . .	Department of English — Gift for Publications, ...	1,550.00
. . . . . .	Gift Department Economics, ...	578.71
78.08	Experimental Phonetics, ...	78.08
70.04	French Department Library, ...	70.04
14.50	Geographical Department, Lantern Slides, ...	14.50
84.00	Department of Geology, Exhibition Case for Photographs, ...	54.69
322.52	Collections for a Germanic Museum, .	322.52
. . . . . .	Department of Government — **F. G. Thomson** Gift.	476.80
36.15	**Augustus Hemenway** Gift, . .	36.15
1.339.87	Department of History, Books, . . .	1,029.91
94.50	Gift for Apparatus for Professor Jeffrey's Courses, ...	350.00
20.00	Gift for Land in New Hampshire, . .	20.00
10.23	**Lowell** Memorial Library, ...	10.23
24.18	**Arthur T. Lyman** Gift, ...	. . . . . .
122.62	**Edward Mallinckrodt** Gift, . .	47.62
30.00	Department of Mathematics, ...	30.00
200.00	International Committee on Teaching Mathematics, ...	100.00
. . . . . .	Mathematics Publication Fund, . .	490.47
9.60	Anonymous Gift (Mineralogy Exhibits).	. . . . . .
100.00	**Sir John Murray** Gift, ...	100.00
. . . . . .	Department Music. **John Knowles Paine** Memorial, ...	5.48
. . . . . .	Department Music, Gift, ...	74.16
61.18	Philosophical Library, ...	59.05
49.79	Physical Research, ...	. . . . . .
3,729.09	Plantation of Shrubs, etc., ...	3,803.67
76.88	Harvard Psychological Review, . . .	14.65
25.00	Political Economy Department, Library, ...	25.00
$8,027,894.55	. . Amounts carried forward, . . .	$12,711 80 $8,341,219.94

Principal, July 1, 1910.		Principal, June 30, 1911.	
$8,027,894.55	. . Amounts brought forward, . . .	$12,711.80	$8,841,219.94
6,594.22	Decorating the front of the Nelson Robinson Jr. Hall, ...	6,039.12	
2,118.90	Sanskrit Department, ...	2,366.93	
134.20	Semitic Library, ...	1,002.05	
1,862.47	Social Ethics, ...	4,813.38	
. . . .	Social Ethics Library, ...	300.00	
699.03	Furnishings for the Department of Social Ethics, ...	644.78	
785.72	Sugar-cane investigation, etc., . . .	801.43	28,679.49

FELLOWSHIP

. . . .	**Bayard Cutting** (1910), ...	$25,505.20	
. . . .	**W. Bayard Cutting, Jr.** Bequest (1910), ...	12,920.20	
5,604.94	**George W. Dillaway** (1903), . .	5,876.78	
26.17	Fellowship in Central American Archaeology (balance), ...	26.17	
11,846.54	**Ozias Goodwin** Memorial (1889),	11,896.12	
11,262.51	**Harris** (1868), ...	11,808.77	
26,322.36	**Edward William Hooper** (1905),	26,448.98	
11,410.32	**John Thornton Kirkland** (1871),	11,463.71	
12,271.61	**Henry Lee** Memorial (1889), . .	12,341.80	
19,066.40	**Charles Eliot Norton** (1901), .	19,166.40	
13,510.69	**Robert Treat Paine** (1887), . .	13,565.97	
62,129.51	**John Parker** (1873), ...	62,892.82	
10,449.37	**Francis Parkman** (1906), . . .	10,506.15	
10,200.00	**Princeton** (1910), ...	10,244.70	
33,454.38	**Rogers** (1869), ...	33,576.90	
12,607.03	**Henry Bromfield Rogers** Memorial (1889).	12,693.47	
500.00	Social Ethics, ...	524.25	
. . . .	South End House (balance), ...	100.00	
12,222.31	**John Tyndall** (1885).	12,815.08	
11,739.06	**James Walker** (1881), ...	11,808.26	
25,156.91	**Whiting** (1896), ...	25,477.03	331,658.76

SCHOLARSHIP

3,957.78	**Abbot** (1852), ...	$3,974.74	
2,737.27	**Alford** (1785), ...	2,870.01	
5,427.82	**Bartlett** (1881), ...	5,441.08	
5,712.75	**Bassett** (1876), ...	5,808.83	
13,855.86	**Bigelow** (1865), ...	13,927.88	
200.00	**Charles Sumner Bird**, ...	9.70	
3,418.86	**Samuel A. Borden** (1896), . . .	3,584.68	
116,405.05	**Bowditch** (1864), ...	116,759.02	
4,743.64	**Bright** (balance), ...	4,611.22	
$8,486,328.23	. . Amounts carried forward, ...	$156,987.16	$8,701,558.19

Principal, July 1, 1910.		Principal, June 30, 1911.	
$8,486,828.28	. . Amounts brought forward, . . .	$156,987.16	$8,701,558.19
4,044.28	Browne (1687), ...	4,065.41	
5,639.37	Morey Willard Buckminster (1898), ...	5,662.86	
35,678.57	Burr (1895), ...	35,889.00	
6,301.44	Ruluff Sterling Choate (1884),	6,332.04	
10,147.61	George Newhall Clark (1908),	10,154.79	
. . . .	Thomas William Clarke (1911),	5,066.45	
8,778.29	Class of 1802 (1870), ...	8,829.02	
3,377.24	" 1814 (1853), ...	3,391.02	
6,967.74	" 1815 (Kirkland) (1852),	7,005.69	
4,855.97	" 1817 (1852), ...	4,891.49	
3,574.52	" 1828 (1882), ...	3,547.91	
5,336.82	" 1835 (1853), ...	5,370.66	
5,430.66	" 1841 (1871), ...	5,469.06	
5,429.25	" 1852 (Dana) (1876), . .	5,467.56	
16,805.76	" 1856 (1885), ...	16,920.85	
5,061.61	" 1867 (1886), ...	7,311.63	
5,376.78	" 1877 (1902), ...	5,412.56	
6,357.72	" 1883 (1900), ...	6,391.08	
. . . .	Classical Department (Gift), ...	150.00	
12,838.55	Crowninshield (1877), ...	12,801.24	
. . . .	Warren H. Cudworth,	6,000.00	
6,575.47	Francis H. Cummings (1898), .	6,619.36	
5,655.79	George and Martha Derby (1881),	5,680.11	
6,469.74	Julius Dexter (1892), ...	6,558.53	
3,048.75	Orlando W. Doe (1893), ...	3,096.63	
. . . .	Edda Club (1911).	250.00	
5,577.68	William Samuel Eliot (1875), .	5,764.88	
31,731.40	George H. Emerson (1903), . .	32,920.85	
43,221.00	Joseph Eveleth (1896), ...	43,717.22	
2,566.26	Fall River (1893), ...	2,590.71	
6,622.53	Farrar (1873), ...	6,668.75	
4,998.77	George Fisher and Elizabeth Huntington Fisher (1908), . .	5,041.22	
12,050.10	Richard Augustine Gambrill (1890), ...	12,109.52	
8,074.13	Charles Haven Goodwin (1889),	8,115.72	
4,608.34	Greene (1863), ...	4,751.83	
100.00	Price Greenleaf (balance), . . .	100.00	
. . . .	Selwyn L. Harding Scholarship of the Class of 1886 (1911), . .	5,066.44	
1,000.00	Harvard Club of Boston, ...	1,048.50	
. . . .	" " Lawrence, ...	100.00	
. . . .	" " Rochester, N. Y., .	200.00	
50.00	" " San Francisco, . .	50.00	
456.12	" " Washington, D. C. (balance), ...	329.24	
$8,781,136.49	. . Amounts carried forward, . . .	$473,896.99	$8,701,558.19

Principal, July 1, 1910.		Principal, June 30, 1911.	
$8,781,136.49	. . Amounts brought forward, . . .	$473,896.99	$8,701,558.19
10,675.26	**John Appleton Haven** (1902), .	10,718.00	
25,459.97	**William Hilton** (1897), ...	25,794.78	
11,355.56	**Ebenezer Rockwood Hoar** (1895), ...	11,406.33	
6,645.75	**Levina Hoar,** for the town of Lincoln, Mass. (1876), ...	6,728.08	
13,850.46	**Hodges** (1878), ...	13,874.56	
6,636.59	**Hollis** (1722), ...	6,683.48	
11,276.59	**Henry B. Humphrey** (1890), . .	11,323.52	
32,409.36	**Charles L. Jones** (1901), ...	32,676.20	
11,035.43	**George Emerson Lowell** (1886),	11,120.63	
5,771.48	**Markoe** (1903), ...	5,801.37	
3,720.00	**Matthews** (balance), ...	3,355.26	
6,587.10	**Merrick** (1888), ...	6,631.57	
8,795.79	**Morey** (1868), ...	8,847.40	
6,151.18	**Lady Mowlson** (1643), ...	6,199.50	
2,942.86	Boston Newsboys' (1906), ...	3,085.60	
5,993.46	**Howard Gardner Nichols** (1897),	6,034.12	
6,330.13	**Lucy Osgood** (1873), ...	6,362.13	
. . . . . .	**George Herbert Palmer** (1911),	1,308.96	
5,524.90	**George Foster Peabody** (1902),	5,460.06	
4,396.15	**James Mills Peirce** Scholarship (1908), ...	4,609.36	
7,768.12	**Pennoyer** (1670), ...	8,144.87	
30,000.00	**Charles Elliott Perkins** Scholarships (1909), ...	30,000.00	
4,896.07	**Rebecca A. Perkins** (1869), . .	4,933.53	
11,286.36	Philadelphia (1904), ...	11,133.73	
1,798.58	**Wendell Phillips** Mem'l (1895),	1,810.83	
4,067.38	**William Reed** (1907), ...	4,070.63	
350.00	**Ricardo** Prize (balance), ...	350.00	
1,537.58	**Rodger** (1883), ...	1,612.17	
3,646.63	**Henry Bromfield Rogers** (1859),	3,673.51	
11,112.16	**Nathaniel Ropes, Jr.,** Scholarship (1909), ...	11,176.09	
15,496.81	**James Augustus Rumrill** (1909),	15,573.41	
6,059.94	**Edward Russell** (1877), ...	6,103.85	
6,005.97	**Sales** (1893), ...	6,047.26	
11,844.36	**Saltonstall** (1739), ...	11,893.79	
9,032.31	**Leverett Saltonstall** (1895), . .	9,070.36	
7,243.27	**Mary Saltonstall** (1730), ...	7,294.56	
3,282.13	**Sever** (1868), ...	3,291.31	
11,783.56	**Sewall** (1696), ...	11,855.08	
50,993.78	**Shattuck** (1854), ...	51,366.99	
6,311.23	**Slade** (1877), ...	6,342.31	
4,700.00	**Dunlap Smith** (1903), ...	4,700.00	
4,754.70	**Story** (1864), ...	4,785.32	
$9,180,665.45	. . Amounts carried forward, . . .	$877,147.50	$8,701,558.19

Principal, July 1, 1910.		Principal, June 30, 1911.	
$9,180,665.45	. . Amounts brought forward, . . .	$877,147.50	$8,701,558.19
3,552.12	**Stoughton** (1701), ...	3,593.56	
4,468.31	**Swift** (1899), ...	4,685.01	
84,150.32	**Thayer** (1857), ...	85,231.59	
4,560.39	**Gorham Thomas** (1865), ...	4,571.85	
8,104.50	**Toppan** (1868), ...	8,147.59	
27,090.08	**Townsend** (1861), ...	27,403.94	
. . . . . .	**Ira D. Van Duzee** (1911), . . .	4,919.10	
5,352.16	**Walcott** (1855), ...	5,411.73	
11,225.20	**Christopher M. Weld** (1899), .	11,269.61	
5,705.03	**Jacob Wendell** (1899), ...	5,732.55	
12,435.05	**Whiting** (1874), ...	12,488.15	
5,000.00	**Josiah Dwight Whitney** (1904),	5,000.00	
11,838.15	**Mary L. Whitney** (1903), . . .	11,912.29	
10,582.34	**Willard** (1907), ...	10,620.57	
2,076.40	**Augustus Woodbury** Scholarship (1909), ...	2,177.09	
10,500.91	**Charles Wyman** (1905), ...	10,560.21	1,090,872.34

BENEFICIARY AND LOAN

54,349.09	**Rebecca C. Ames** (1903), . . .	$54,515.02	
. . . . . .	Anonymous Gift for certain members of the Class of 1915, ...	650.00	
735.10	**Nathaniel Appleton** (1772), . .	770.75	
2,261.85	**Frank Bolles** Memorial (1894), .	2,271.56	
1,826.88	**William Brattle** (1717), ...	1,915.49	
90,098.19	**Daniel A. Buckley** (1905), . . .	95,274.52	
51,724.33	**Walter Channing Cabot** (1905),	51,732.94	
1,295.82	**Thomas Danforth** (1724), . . .	1,358.68	
5,473.64	**Moses Day** (1880), ...	5,473.64	
522.89	**John Ellery** (1738), ...	548.26	
1,353.69	**Exhibitions** (1796), ...	1,353.69	
1,920.00	Fines Loan (balance), ...	1,074.91	
951.73	**Thomas Fitch** (1737), ...	997.90	
565.26	**Ephraim Flynt** (1723), ...	592.66	
203.52	**Henry Flynt** (1760), ...	213.41	
4,741.27	Freshman Loan (balance), ...	3,166.15	
1,018.18	Freshman Loan, **Gove** Gift, ...	1,038.54	
588.40	**Henry Gibbs** (1722), ...	616.92	
4,030.27	**John Glover** (1653), ...	4,225.72	
14,324.65	**Price Greenleaf** Aid (balance), . .	16,635.29	
254.10	Student Fund of the **Harvard** Engineering Society of New York (1908) (balance), ...	751.90	
11,838.89	**Edwin A. W. Harlow** (1905), .	11,904.74	
5,615.26	**Robert Henry Harlow** (1908),	5,615.26	
438.70	**Edward Holyoke** (1743), . . .	459.99	
2,823.93	**Robert Keayne** (1659), ...	2,960.89	
$9,646,262.05	. . Amounts carried forward, . . .	$266,118.83	$9,792,430.53

Principal, July 1, 1910.		Principal, June 30, 1911.	
$9,646,262.05	. . Amounts brought forward, . . .	$266,118.83	$9,792,430.53
26,000.00	**Bertram Kimball** (1903), . . .	26,261.00	
2,272.42	**Harry Milton Levy** Loan (College) (balance), ...	1,877.61	
1,220.16	**Mary Lindall** (1812), ...	1,279.33	
5,988.87	**Susan B. Lyman** (1899), ...	5,988.87	
552.05	**Susan B. Lyman** Loans (College) (balance), ...	545.70	
285.00	**Anne Mills** (1725), ...	298.82	
. . . . . .	**John F. Moors'** Gift, Special aid for a member of the Class of 1915,	50.00	
10,962.91	**Munroe** (1880), ...	10,858.92	
2,236.43	**Palfrey** Exhibition (1821), ...	2,184.88	
5,467.96	**Dr. Andrew P. Peabody** Memorial (1896), ...	5,492.16	
5,192.29	Scholarship and Beneficiary Money Returned (balance), ...	1,844.89	
271.48	**Joseph Sewall** (1765), ...	284.62	
16,371.65	**Alexander Wheelock Thayer** (1899), ...	16,685.69	
11,171.94	**Quincy Tufts** (1877), ...	11,171.94	
366.50	**Benjamin Wadsworth** (1737), .	384.30	
7,160.00	**Stuart Wadsworth Wheeler** (1898),	7,739.69	359,067.25

PRIZE

50.00	**Jeremy Belknap**, ...	. . . .	
1,933.10	**James Gordon Bennett** (1893), .	$2,026.85	
417.15	**Philo Sherman Bennett** (1905),	437.37	
10,400.00	**Francis Boott** (1904), ...	10,500.00	
32,226.39	**Bowdoin** Prizes for Dissertations (1791), ...	32,298.55	
2,794.76	**Boylston** Prizes for Elocution (1817),	2,675.07	
5,840.49	**Coolidge** Debating (1899), ...	5,853.61	
50.00	**Dante** Prize (balance), ...	50.00	
2,714.02	**Lloyd McKim Garrison** Prize and Medal (1904), ...	2,736.93	
8.24	**Harvard** Club of New Jersey Prizes (balance), ...	8.24	
2,254.50	**Edward Hopkins** Gift for "Deturs" (1718) (balance), ...	2,308.65	
1,092.82	**George Arthur Knight** (1909),	1,145.83	
50.00	Patria Society Gift, ...	. . . .	
1,173.31	**Sales** (1892), ...	1,185.20	
2,821.91	**John O. Sargent** (1889), ...	2,758.78	
7,250.00	**George B. Sohier** (1890), ...	7,000.00	
4,253.06	**Charles Sumner** (1874), ...	4,359.33	
3,940.81	**Robert N. Toppan** (1894), . . .	4,131.95	
2,436.42	**Philip Washburn** (1899), . . .	2,404.57	
$9,823,488.69	. . Amounts carried forward, . . .	$81,880.93	$10,151,497.78

Principal, July 1, 1910.		Principal, June 30, 1911.	
$9,823,488.69	. . Amounts brought forward, . .	$81,880.93	$10,151,497.78
116,485.61	David A. Wells (1901), ...	116,332.76	
....	Elizabeth Wilder (1911), . . .	2,026.04	
....	Wister (1911), ...	816.59	201,056.82

SUMMER SCHOOL

10,531.80	Sayles, for Summer Course in Geology (1909), ...	$10,350.00	10,350.00

LIBRARY

57.71	Boott Income for Books (balance),	$56.35	
2,104.56	Bowditch (1861), ...	2,127.19	
58.67	Bright (balance), ...	313.08	
1,029.67	William R. Castle (1907), . . .	1,085.34	
847.01	Fund of the Class of 1851 (1899),	888.09	
834.10	" " " 1851 (C. F. Dunbar's Gift) (1899), ...	874.55	
3,598.18	Book Fund of the Class of 1881 (1906), ...	3,588.42	
27,896.40	Edwin Conant (1892), ...	27,901.38	
25,892.26	Constantius (1886), ...	25,892.26	
....	Archibald C. Coolidge and Clarence L. Hay (1910), . . .	4,708.89	
....	W. Bayard Cutting, Jr. Bequest (1910), ...	12,509.20	
....	Bayard Cutting Fellowship, Income for Books (balance), ...	17.70	
5,287.48	Denny (1875), ...	5,337.50	
5,593.63	Farrar (1871), ...	5,572.24	
....	Charles Gross Memorial (1910), .	1,590.07	
3,379.17	Haven (1844), ...	3,180.72	
10,009.26	Hayes (1885), ...	10,055.93	
5,375.93	Hayward (1864), ...	5,349.69	
1,259.35	R. M. Hodges (balance), ...	770.90	
2,348.45	Hollis (1774), ...	2,384.62	
2,172.65	Homer (1871), ...	2,140.84	
514.15	Jarvis (1885), ...	503.21	
5,261.88	Lane (1863), ...	5,329.17	
....	George C. Lodge and Joseph Trumbull Stickney Memorial Book Fund (1911), ...	3,125.55	
28,394.55	Lowell (1881), ...	28,750.98	
....	Francis Cabot Lowell (1911), .	10,000.00	
60,028.47	Minot (1870), ...	60,000.00	
8,954.92	Charles Eliot Norton (1905), .	9,065.91	
7,104.13	Lucy Osgood (1873), ...	7,213.67	
$10,158,458.68	. . Amounts carried forward, . . .	$240,333.45	$10,362,904.10

Principal, July 1, 1910.		Principal, June 30, 1911.
$10,158,458.68	. . Amounts brought forward, . . .	$240,333.45 $10,362,904.10
6,978.69	Mary Osgood (1860), ...	7,030.88
5,982.32	Francis Parkman Memorial (1908), ...	5,950.91
25,224.79	George F. Parkman (for books) (1909), ...	25,162.57
3,916.67	Sales (1892), ...	3,921.40
5,418.87	Salisbury (1858), ...	5,489.30
5,120.00	Stephen Salisbury (1907), . . .	5,120.00
20,534.96	Sever (1878), ...	20,382.61
3,949.87	Shapleigh (1801), ...	3,949.87
29.79	George B. Sohier Income for Books (balance), ...	126.08
2,512.71	Strobel Memorial, Class of 1877 (1909), ...	2,878.11
1,942.59	Strobel Memorial, Siam (1909), .	1,993.46
10,501.24	Subscription for Library (1859), . .	10,513.49
37,345.58	Sumner (1875), ...	37,488.88
5,159.35	Kenneth Matheson Taylor (1899), ...	5,075.64
11,925.34	Daniel Treadwell (1885), . . .	11,925.34
. . . .	John Harvey Treat Book Fund (1911), ...	41,521.99
5,176.47	Ichabod Tucker (1875), ...	5,208.34
. . . .	20th Mass. Regiment of Volunteer Infantry (1910), ...	615.08
245.68	Wales Income for Books (balance),	142.43
15,958.52	Walker (1875), ...	15,903.44
5,250.41	Ward (1858), ...	5,250.41
2,288.90	Julian Palmer Welsh Memorial (1910), ...	3,002.41
20,000.00	J. Huntington Wolcott (1891),	20,020.88
100,000.00	Eben Wright (1883), ...	100,000.00
7,297.17	Sundry Gifts for books (balances), .	4,141.37
.33	Sundry Gifts for services (balance), .	.33
. . . .	Gift for cases, ...	2,000.00
56.06	Duplicate Money, ...	58.68
887.78	Fines, ...	137.06
19.95	Gifts for Additional Service, ...	218.52 585,512.38

DIVINITY SCHOOL

71,427.02	New Endowment (1879), ...	$71,427.02
17,000.00	Oliver Ames (1880), ...	17,000.00
525.00	Hannah C. Andrews (1856), . .	525.00
1,115.26	Daniel Austin (1880), ...	1,115.26
1,000.00	Adams Ayer (1869), ...	1,000.00
15,275.00	Joseph Baker (1876), ...	15,275.00
$10,568,520.00	. . Amounts carried forward, . . .	$106,342.28 $10,948,416.48

Principal, July 1, 1910.		Principal, June 30, 1911.	
$10,568,520.00	. . Amounts brought forward, . . .	$106,342.28	$10,948,416.48
240.82	Beneficiary money returned (balance),	252.51	
4,296.17	Rushton Dashwood Burr (1894),	4,349.69	
37,583.74	Bussey Professorship (1862), . .	37,583.74	
2,177.95	Joshua Clapp (1836), ...	2,177.95	
5,000.00	Edwin Conant (1892), ...	8,794.32	
25,544.37	Dexter Lectureship (1810), . . .	25,544.37	
56,203.14	Frothingham Professorship(1892),	56,703.14	
1,050.00	Abraham W. Fuller (1847), . .	1,050.00	
911.34	Lewis Gould (1852), ...	911.34	
966.54	Louisa J.-Hall (1893), ...	979.15	
6,008.48	Hancock Professorship, ...	6,008.48	
	Composed of these Funds : —		
	Thomas Hancock (1765),		
	Stephen Sewall (1762).		
148,100.81	Charles L. Hancock (1891), . .	151,742.21	
5,000.00	Haven (1898), ...	5,000.00	
1,050.00	Samuel Hoar (1857), ...	1,050.00	
10,000.00	Henry P. Kidder (1881), . . .	10,000.00	
9,184.69	Henry Lienow (1841), ...	9,184.69	
1,050.00	Caroline Merriam (1867), . . .	1,050.00	
16,015.81	Parkman Professorship (1814), .	16,015.81	
682.94	John W. Quinby (1888), ...	716.07	
1,000.00	Abby Crocker Richmond (1881),	1,000.00	
1,000.00	John L. Russell (1890), ...	1,000.00	
. . . .	Horace S. Sears Gift Lectures, .	1,200.00	
10,000.00	William B. Spooner (1890), . .	10,000.00	
40,000.00	Thomas Tileston of New York		
	Endowment (1879), ...	40,000.00	
5,250.00	Mary P. Townsend (1861), . .	5,250.00	
2,100.00	Winthrop Ward (1862), ...	2,100.00	
58,345.73	Winn Professorship (1877), . . .	58,845.73	
1,038.20	Augustus Woodbury Bequest		
	(1909), ...	1,038.20	560,889.68

SCHOLARSHIP AND BENEFICIARY

2,651.04	Robert Charles Billings Prize		
	(1904), ...	$2,679.61	
13,597.50	Abner W. Buttrick (1880), . . .	13,682.00	
5,846.84	Thomas Cary (1820), ...	5,880.42	
2,934.95	George Chapman (1834), . . .	2,952.30	
4,696.18	Joshua Clapp (1839)	4,723.94	
15,469.81	Jackson Foundation (1835), . . .	15,580.11	
5,910.87	J. Henry Kendall (1863), . . .	5,947.55	
3,638.44	Nancy Kendall (1846), ...	3,662.88	
1,050.00	William Pomroy (1835), ...	1,058.92	56,167.73
$11,069,116.31	. . Amounts carried forward, ...		$11,565,473.84

$11,069,116.31 . . Amounts brought forward, ... $11,565,473.84

LAW SCHOOL

10,090.92	Ames (1910), ...	$10,580.33
657.70	James Barr Ames Loan (1904),	1,410.02
4,410.48	James Barr Ames Prize (1898),	4,224.37
93,979.27	Bemis Professorship (1879), . . .	98,537.25
2,173.00	Gift of James Munson Barnard and Augusta Barnard (balance),	2,216.46
23,979.82	Bussey Professorship (1862), . .	23,979.82
111,257.99	James C. Carter Professorship (1906), ...	110,654.00
13,052.95	James Coolidge Carter Loan (1906), ...	13,772.41
15,750.00	Dane Professorship (1829), ...	15,750.00
5,321.26	Samuel Phillips Prescott Fay, 1798, Fund and Scholarship (1907),	5,174.55
3,814.51	George Fisher Scholarship (1906),	3,849.54
.90	Hughes Loan (1903), ...	266.51
26,167.84	Langdell (1909), ...	26,286.99
47,021.25	Law School Book (1882), ...	47,021.25
100,000.00	Law School Library (1898), ...	100,000.00
2,604.58	Harry Milton Levy Loan (Law) (balance), ...	411.71
8,340.81	Royall Professorship (1781), . . .	8,340.81
1,641.61	Scholarship money returned (balance),	1,574.69
1,500.00	Joshua Montgomery Sears, Jr., Memorial Gift, ...	1,590.11
94,994.97	Weld Professorship (1882), . . .	94,994.97
. . . .	Gift for Research Scholarship, . . .	250.00

570,885.79

GRADUATE SCHOOL OF APPLIED SCIENCE

20,921.44	Julia Amory Appleton Fellowship (1906), ...	$20,936.11
1,253.24	Edward Austin Loans repaid (bal.),	1,193.24
4,197.49	Priscilla Clark Hodges Scholarship (1907), ...	4,226.04
11,819.79	Hennen Jennings Scholarship (1898), ...	11,868.06
4,591.74	Lawrence Scientific School Loans repaid (balance), ...	7,276.10
100.00	Henry Weidemann Locke Scholarship. Gift (balance), ...	200.00
615.00	Susan B. Lyman Loan (L.S.S.) (balance), ...	738.82
1,002,808.64	Gordon McKay Endowment (1909), ...	1,387,910.25

$12,682,683.51 . . Amounts carried forward, . . $1,434,348.62 $12,136,359.63

Principal, July 1, 1910.		Principal, June 30, 1911.
$12,682,683.51	. . Amounts brought forward, . .	$1,434,348.62$12,136,359.63
250.00	**Edward Dyer Peters** Scholarship (balance), ...	250.00
40,805.73	Professorship of Engineering (1847),	40,805.73
545,000.00	**Nelson Robinson, Jr.** (1899), .	550,000.00
25,000.00	Arthur Rotch (1895), ...	· 25,000.00
60,000.00	Gurdon Saltonstall (1901), . .	60,000.00
11,791.87	Josiah Stickney (1899), ...	11,791.87
. . . .	Ames-Butler Gift, ...	2,787.31
6,683.73	Gift for Equipment, Department of Architecture, ...	5,856.34
15.00	Gift Dept. of Forestry, Marsh house,	. . . .
.13	Gift for electrical apparatus, . . .	. . . .
18.97	Gift for Laboratory of Metallurgical Chemistry, ...	18.97
2,801.01	**Nelson Robinson, Jr.** Special Expense Gift, ...	2,276.07
. . . .	**Nelson Robinson, Jr.** Special Gift for Salaries, ...	13,112.69
1,230.57	Summer course Mining Camp Gift, .	809.61
. . . .	Mining and Metallurgy Scholarship (gift), ...	349.92 2,147,352.13

GRADUATE SCHOOL OF BUSINESS ADMINISTRATION

650.00	Gifts for Loans (balance), ...	$380.00
200.00	Gifts for Prizes (balances), ...	. . . .
. . . .	Gift of **Warren D. Robbins** — South American Course, ...	100.00
. . . .	Gift of **Joseph E. Sterrett,** Books on Accounting, ...	84.10 564.10

MUSEUM OF COMPARATIVE ZOÖLOGY

. . . .	**Alexander Agassiz** Bequest (1910),	$99,500.00
. . . .	**Alexander Agassiz** Bequest for Publications (1910), ...	94,794.56
297,933.10	**Agassiz** Memorial (1875), . . .	297,933.10
5,908.60	**Virginia Barret Gibbs** Scholarship (1892), ...	5,945.19
50,000.00	**Gray** Fund for Zoölogical Museum (1859), ...	50,000.00
106,511.23	**Sturgis Hooper** (1865), ...	107,391.03
7,740.66	**Humboldt** (1869), ...	7,740.66
5,000.00	**Willard Peele Hunnewell** (1901), , ...	5,000.00
117,469.34	Permanent (1859), ...	117,469.34
7,594.01	Teachers' and Pupils' (1875), . . .	7,594.01
5,526.10	**Maria Whitney** (1907), ...	5,830.57 799,198.46

$13,982,258.56	. . Amounts carried forward, ...	$15,083,474.32

Principal, July 1, 1910.		Principal, June 30, 1911.
$13,982,258.56	. . Amounts brought forward, ...	$15,083,474.32

GERMANIC MUSEUM

10,013.52	Germanic Museum (1909), ...	$10,013.52	
102,980.78	Germanic Museum Building (1908), .	209,268.49	
51,220.23	Germanic Museum Endowment(1909),	53,704.55	
26,335.00	Emperor William (1906), . . .	26,335.00	
. . . .	Gift for work of art, ...	1,000.00	300,321.56

PEABODY MUSEUM OF AMERICAN ARCHAEOLOGY AND ETHNOLOGY

12,642.79	Hemenway Fellowship (1891), .	$13,255.97	
. . . .	Mary Hemenway Fund for Archaeology (1910), ...	46,515.83	
28,355.56	Peabody Building (1866), . . .	28,355.56	
47,335.10	Peabody Collection (1866), . . .	47,335.10	
47,335.10	Peabody Professor (1866), . . .	47,335.10	
30,352.47	Thaw Fellowship (1890), ...	30,165.91	
10,000.00	Henry C. Warren Exploration (1899), ...	10,010.00	
5,000.00	Susan CorneliaWarren (1902),	5,000.00	
6,064.93	Robert C. Winthrop Scholarship (1895), ...	6,359.08	
20,000.00	Huntington FrothinghamWolcott (1891), ...	20,000.00	254,332.55

MEDICAL SCHOOL

5,650.16	Harvard Medical Alumni (1907),	$5,924.23	
1,250.00	Harvard Medical Alumni Gifts (balance), ...		
10,363.78	Anonymous Fund in the Department of Theory and Practice (1906), .	10,363.78	
11,303.10	Edward Austin (Bacteriological Laboratory) (1899), ...	11,699.40	
30,271.54	Edward M. Barringer (1881),	30,271.54	
100,000.00	Robert C. Billings (1900), . .	100,000.00	
6,593.70	J. Ingersoll Bowditch (1889),	6,044.84	
1,673.20	Boylston Fund for Medical Books (1800), ...	1,674.85	
24,826.83	John B. & Buckminster Brown Endowment (1896), ...	25,530.94	
76,115.99	Bullard Professorship of Neuropathology (1906), ...	76,251.06	
. . . .	Memorial Cancer Hospital Endowment (1910), ...	102,195.86	
. . . .	Memorial Cancer Hospital Maintenance (1910), ...	11,293 67	

$14,647,942.34	. . Amounts carried forward, . . .	$381,250.17	$15,638,128.43

Principal, July 1, 1910.		Principal, June 30, 1911.	
$14,647,942.34	. . Amounts brought forward, . .	$381,250.17	$15,688,128.43
95,788.65	Caroline Brewer Croft (1899),	92,846.07	
18,650.53	Dr. John C. Cutter Bequest (1910), ...	15,228.34	
386,265.36	Calvin and Lucy Ellis (1899),	387,141.80	
215,694.64	George Fabyan Foundation for Comparative Pathology (1906), .	207,940.88	
. . . .	George Fabyan Foundation Special (1910), ...	9,824.83	
52,552.79	Charles F. Farrington (1909),	52,601.61	
1,836.08	Samuel E. Fitz (1884), ...	1,836.08	
. . . .	Rebecca A. Greene (1911), . .	25,000.00	
4,915.66	F. B. Greenough (Surgical Research) (1901), ...	6,202.59	
105,368.85	George Higginson Professorship (1902), ...	106,479.25	
52,239.80	John Homans Memorial (1906),	52,239.80	
69,192.65	Jackson Professorship of Clinical Medicine (1859), ...	69,192.65	
102,997.46	Henry Jackson Endowment (1903), ...	102,738.57	
178,603.27	Hamilton Kuhn Memorial (1908),	179,060.17	
51,634.85	Walter Augustus Lecompte Professorship of Otology (1907),	52,120.38	
1,572.16	Harriet Newell Lowell (1907),	2,699.77	
2,324.28	Medical Library (1872), ...	2,326.60	
53,052.28	William O. Moseley (1897), . .	53,125.80	
38,850.00	New Subscription (1888), ...	38,850.00	
10,020.18	Lyman Nichols (1907), ...	10,020.18	
8,581.40	George F. Parkman (Medical) (1910), ...	8,581.40	
6,046.95	Gift for Pathological Laboratory, .	6,132.45	
500.00	Repayment Pathological Laboratory,	1,852.63	
38,779.88	Henry L. Pierce (Residuary) (1898), ...	39,216.62	
54,315.02	Proctor (1903), ...	52,895.72	
1,000,000.00	John D. Rockefeller Gift (1902),	1,000,000.00	
9,335.94	Dr. Ruppaner (1897), ...	9,335.94	
6,419.27	School of Comparative Medicine (1899), ...	6,730.59	
35,322.04	Henry Francis Sears Fund for Pathology (1907), ...	35,041.37	
77,000.00	George C. Shattuck (1853), . .	77,000.00	
10,857.39	James Skillen Memorial Fund (1907), ...	10,857.39	
117,180.93	James Stillman Professorship (1902), ...	117,564.21	
6,779.01	Surgical Laboratory (1897), ...	5,763.83	
$17,455,619.66	. . Amounts carried forward, . . .	$3,219,697.19	$15,638,128.43

Principal, July 1, 1910.		Principal, June 30, 1911.	
$17,455,619.66	. . Amounts brought forward, . .	$3,219,697.19	$15,638,128.43
15,765.11	Mary W. Swett (1884), ...	15,765.11	
20,000.00	Samuel W. Swett (1884), . . .	20,000.00	
2,000.00	Quincy Tufts (1879), ...	2,000.00	
10,734.13	Warren Fund for Anatomical Museum (1848), ...	11,254.73	
51,762.32	Edward Wigglesworth Professorship of Dermatology (1907),	52,292.78	
41,600.00	Charles Wilder (1900), ...	41,940.00	
47,054.42	Henry Willard Williams (1893),	48,836.54	
182.49	Gifts for Anatomical Research (bal.),	270.41	
2,580.01	Gift for Pathological Dep't. (bal.),	3,007.41	
121.20	Aesculapian Club Gift, ...	121.20	
3.21	Anonymous Gift for Theory and Practice, ...	3.21	
84.61	W. H. Walker Gift, ...	84.61	
133.61	Gift, Bacteriological Laboratory, .	46.86	
250.00	Mary R. Bremer Gift for Department of Anatomy, ...	4.87	
247.68	William N. and Katherine E. Bullard Gift, ...	322.90	
. . . .	Gift for a Salary, Cancer Commission, ...	200.00	
210.00	Gift for Diabetes Mellitus, ...	210.00	
. . . .	Sale of Duplicate Books, Library, .	2.90	
50.00	Experiments on Animals, ...	43.80	
. . . .	Gift, Investigation Infantile Paralysis,	3,730.96	
308.03	Loan Fund Medical Class of 1879, .	328.03	
727.91	Mass. Society for Promoting Agriculture, Department of Comparative Pathology, ...	1,688.43	
13.98	G. K. Sabine Gift, ...	13.98	
5.37	Sears Pathological Laboratory Publication Fund, ...	5.37	
132.53	Gifts for Department Neuropathology,	114.22	
16.05	Department of Physiology, ...	16.05	
. . . .	Gift for Recreation Grounds, . . .	950.00	
.24	Anonymous Gift for Investigation of Smallpox, ...	.24	
1,914.21	Gift for X-ray Apparatus, ...	1,058.48	3,424,010.28

FELLOWSHIP

8.32	Anonymous Gift for Teaching Fellowships in Histology and Embryology (balance), ...	$8.32	
13,259 82	Charles Follen Folsom Memorial (1908), ...	12,984.18	
$17,664,784.91	. . Amounts carried forward, ...	$12,992.50	$19,062,138.71

Principal, July 1, 1910.		Principal, June 30, 1911.	
$17,664,784.91	. . Amounts brought forward, . .	$12,992.50	$19,062,138.71
5,582.96	**George Cheyne Shattuck** Memorial (1891), ...	5,628.74	
5,998.88	**Charles Eliot Ware** Memorial (1891), ...	6,039.28	
5,523.51	**John Ware** Memorial (1891), . .	5,656.42	
17,000.00	**Henry P. Walcott** (1910), . .	25,310.99	55,627.98

SCHOLARSHIP

150.00	Aesculapian Club Scholarship, . . .	. . . .	
5,430.18	**Lucius F. Billings** (1900), . .	$5,468.53	
6,319.43	**James Jackson Cabot** (1906),	6,350.90	
5,950.03	**David Williams Cheever** (1889),	5,988.61	
3,331.19	**Cotting** Gift (1900), ...	3,367.74	
3,053.73	**Orlando W. Doe** (1893), . . .	3,101.85	
. . . .	**John Foster** income for Medical Students (balance), ...	3.60	
5,848.05	Lewis and Harriet Hayden (1894),	5,906.68	
. . . .	**William Otis Johnson** (1911),	2,026.29	
6,800.92	**Claudius M. Jones** (1893), . .	6,880.77	
. . . .	**John R. Kissinger** (1911), . .	3,018.33	
5,721.18	**Alfred Hosmer Linder** (1895),	5,748.65	
9,072.66	**Joseph Pearson Oliver** (1904),	9,112.70	
5,987.13	**Charles B. Porter** (1897), . . .	5,975.07	
5,366.54	**Francis Skinner** (1905), ...	5,476.84	
5,375.52	**Charles Pratt Strong** (1894), .	5,411.26	
6,838.39	**Isaac Sweetser** (1892), ...	6,920.03	
5,603.11	**John Thomson Taylor** (1899),	5,624.86	
5,747.49	**Edward Wigglesworth** (1897),	5,776.22	92,158.93

PRIZE

4,555.23	**Boylston** (1803), ...	$4,762.55	
9,425.65	**William H. Thorndike** (1895),	9,682.81	14,445.36

DENTAL SCHOOL

8,765.85	Dental School Endowment (1880), .	$12,000.85	
10.00	Dental School Endowment of the Class of 1909 (1910), ...	20.00	
25.00	Dental School Research Fund, . .	125.00	
5,713.33	**Harvard** Dental Alumni Endowment (1906), ...	6,195.33	
. . . .	**Harriet Newell Lowell** Gift,	1,000.00	
23,000.00	**Henry C. Warren** Endowment (1889), ...	23,000.00	
500.00	**Proctor** Bequest (1910), ...	500.00	
24.16	Gift for Surgical Instruments, . . .	15.16	
10,225.00	**Joseph Warren Smith, Jr.** Memorial (1909), ...	10,325.00	
40.27	Gifts for X-ray Apparatus, ...	40.27	53,221 61
$17,847,719.80	. . Amounts carried forward, ...		$19,277,592.54

Principal, July 1, 1910.		Principal, June 30, 1911.
$17,847,719.80	. . Amounts brought forward, ...	$19,277,592.54

OBSERVATORY

22,050.54	Advancement of Astronomical Science (1901), ...	$20,109.98	
20,000.00	Advancement of Astronomical Science (1902), ...	20,523.50	
5,000.00	**Thomas G. Appleton** (1884), .	5,000.00	
825.37	Bond Gifts (balance), ...	825.37	
2,500.00	**J. Ingersoll Bowditch** (1889), .	2,500.00	
200,000.00	**Uriah A. Boyden** (1887), . . .	200,000.00	
62.84	**Draper Memorial** (balance), . .	62.84	
2,000.00	**Charlotte Harris** (1877), . . .	2,000.00	
45,000.00	**Haven** (1898), ...	45,000.00	
21,000.00	**James Hayward** (1866), . . .	21,000.00	
50,000.00	**Observatory Endowment** (1882), .	50,000.00	
50,000.00	**Paine** Professorship (1886), . . .	50,000.00	
273,932.07	**Robert Treat Paine** (1886), . .	273,932.07	
110,293.88	**Edward B. Phillips** (1849), . .	110,293.88	
17,170.97	**Josiah Quincy** (1866), ...	12,995.12	
44,048.16	**David Sears** (1845), ...	45,116.33	
13,380.00	**Augustus Story** (1871), ...	13,380.00	
. . . .	**J. Rayner Edmands** Bequest (1911), ...	1,014.21	
42.35	Gift for publishing lunar photographs,	42.35	873,795.65

BUSSEY INSTITUTION

20,658.86	**Woodland Hill** (1895), ...	$20,658.86	20,658.86

ARNOLD ARBORETUM

129,230.00	**Arnold** Arboretum (1899), ...	$125,340.00	
162,885.42	**James Arnold** (1872), ...	162,779.20	
33,329.08	Arboretum Construction Gifts (balance),	42,309.99	
12,500.00	**Robert Charles Billings** (1904),	12,500.00	
20,000.00	**William L. Bradley** (1897), . .	20,000.00	
2,308.06	**Bussey** Fund for the **Arnold** Arboretum (1903), ...	2,308.06	
. . . .	Massachusetts Society for Promoting Agriculture (1911), ...	4,500.00	
20,000.00	**Francis Skinner** (1906), ...	20,000.00	
4,247.92	**Sears** Gift for Library, ...	3,132.12	
1,389.23	Gift for Expedition to China (balance),	2,250.68	395,120.05

PHILLIPS BROOKS HOUSE

10,506.66	**Phillips Brooks** House Endowment (1901), ...	$10,506.66	
11,343.64	**Ralph H. Shepard** (1900), . . .	11,343.64	
$19,152,924.85	. . . Amounts carried forward, . . .	$21,850.30	$20,567,167.10

Principal, July 1, 1910.		Principal, June 30, 1911.	
$19,152,924.85	. . Amounts brought forward, . . .	$21,850.30	$20,567,167.10
5,705.77	**Ralph Hamilton Shepard** Memorial (1898), ...	5,480.50	
6,758.78	**John W. and Belinda L. Randall** (1897), ...	7,086.59	34,417.39

WILLIAM HAYES FOGG ART MUSEUM

50,000.00	**William Hayes Fogg** (1892), .	$50,000.00	
16,087.93	**Gray** Fund for Engravings (1858),	16,000.28	
14,911.69	**William M. Prichard** (1898), .	15,016.47	
30,338.83	**John Witt Randall** (1892), . . .	80,000.00	111,016.75

STILLMAN INFIRMARY

7,727.78	**Stillman** Infirmary Gift (balance),	$8,102.58	
60,555.57	**Robert Charles Billings,** for Stillman Infirmary (1908), . .	60,555.57	
6,876.79	Free Bed Fund of the **Class of 1868** (1898), ...	6,876.79	
653.26	Free Bed Fund for **Stillman** Infirmary (1900), ...	653.26	
3,633.88	**Herbert Schurz** Memorial Free Bed (1908), ...	3,633.88	
3,204.16	**Henry P. Walcott** (1901), . . .	3,204.16	82,525.74

CLASS FUNDS

1,755.78	Fund of the **Class of 1834** (1887),	$1,833.70	
110.89	" " " **1842** (1908),	116.27	
10,184.51	" " " **1844** (1896),	10,888.70	
13,684.42	" " " **1846** (1905),	14,848.09	
3,720.35	" " " **1853** (1887),	3,725.00	
7,800.00	" " " **1856** (1904),	7,863.75	38,725.51

GIFTS FOR CONSTRUCTION

10,526.34	**Arnold** Arboretum Building Gifts,	$10,943.85	
421.74	Brighton Marsh Fence (balance), . .	421.74	
. . . .	**Francis H. Burr** Memorial, . . .	25,749.91	
. . . .	**Freshman** Dormitories, ...	32,587.89	
94,220.23	**Wolcott Gibbs** Memorial (1909),	105,852.40	
537.99	Gift for **Gray** Herbarium — Kidder Wing, ...	886.02	
. . . .	**Gray** Herbarium Library, ...	10,074.80	
. . . .	**Collis P. Huntington** Memorial Hospital, ...	7,975.85	
442.43	Semitic Building (balance), ...	442.43	
316,269.83	**Amey Richmond Sheldon** (1909),	331,608.98	
$19,818,553.30	. . Amounts carried forward, . . .	$526,043.32	$20,833,852.49

Principal, July 1, 1910.		Principal, June 30, 1911.	
$19,818,553.30	. . Amounts brought forward, . . .	$526,043.32	$20,833,852.49
37.97	John Simpkins Hall (balance), .	. . . .	
354,594.66	George Smith Bequest (1904), .	380,821.01	
11,977.89	Gift for a new University Library Building (balance), ...	12,558.27	919,422.60

SUNDRY

476,265.50	Edward Austin (1899), ...	$476,463.28	
50,000.00	Bright Legacy (1880), ...	50,000.00	
392,710.18	Bussey Trust (1861), ...	392,710.18	
165,859.27	Calvin and Lucy Ellis Aid (1899),	166,217.72	
3,171.50	John Foster (1840), ...	3,171.50	
794,942.67	Price Greenleaf (1887), ...	794,942.67	
29,939.33	Henry Harris (1883), ...	29,939.33	
1,745.88	Harvard Memorial Society (1898),	1,830.56	
62,434.95	Robert Troup Paine (1880), . .	64,421.50	
42,000.00	James Savage (1873), ...	42,000.00	
361,460.93	Frederick Sheldon (1909), . . .	366,425.97	
150,000.00	Edward Wigglesworth Memorial (1909), ...	150,000.00	
5,158.15	Gifts for Semitic Museum Collection (balance), ...	6,084.95	
24,815.09	Gifts for Excavations in Palestine (balance), ...	4,268.70	
. . . .	Gifts for Chinese Students (balance),	107.00	
33.96	Gifts for Cuban Teachers (balance),	33.96	2,548,617.32

FUNDS IN TRUST FOR PURPOSES NOT CONNECTED WITH THE COLLEGE

16,396.02	Daniel Williams (1716), ...	$16,506.47	
4,757.79	Sarah Winslow (1790), ...	4,795.66	21,302.18
$22,766,854.54			$24,833,194.54

GENERAL SUSPENSE

CREDIT BALANCES

June 30, 1911

July 1, 1910			June 30, 1911
$4,129.68	Cryptogamic Herbarium, ...		$4,777.20
550.66	Department of Forestry, ...		. . . .
6,779.81	Gray Herbarium, ...		5,778.41
3,135.47	Jefferson Physical Laboratory, ...		. . . .
751.37	School for Social Workers, ...		1,708.52
9,026.04	Graduate School of Business Administration, ...		12,337.44
. . . .	Graduate School of Applied Science.		
	Unexpended balances, ...	$8,854.52	
	Reserve, ...	2,045.60	10,900.12
16,094.50	Divinity School, ...		17,418.45
56,724.60	Law School, ...		66,151.52
18,488.52	Museum of Comparative Zoölogy, ...		18,826.43
. . . .	Peabody Museum of American Archaeology and		
	Ethnology, ...		2,457.56
564.64	Germanic Museum, ...		1,282.06
12,395.77	Bussey Institution, ...		5,838.46
16.18	Fogg Art Museum, ...		. . . .
65.92	Botanical Museum, ...		1,681.63
2,246.16	Botanic Garden, ...		3,366.96
. . . .	Laboratory Fees, Astronomy, ...		292.51
. . . .	" " Botany (Fernald), ...		110.00
. . . .	" " " (Thaxter), ...		105.08
. . . .	" " Chemistry, ...		251.23
. . . .	" " Geology, ...		157.70
. . . .	" " Hygiene, ...		319.96
. . . .	" " Mining and Metallurgy, ...		53.93
. . . .	Engineering Camp, Squam Lake, ...		571.61
. . . .	Baker Estate, ...		277.08
$130,969.32	Total — Exhibit A, ...		$154,158.81

GENERAL SUSPENSE

DEBIT BALANCES

June 30, 1911

July 1, 1910	Advances from General Investments to:	June 30, 1911
....	Adams Estate,	$8,345.02
$2,393.00	Aid to Chinese Students,	....
8,662.50	Aids, general,	4,787.50
1,823.95	Annals of Mathematics,	....
250.00	Anonymous Fund,	54.43
....	Anonymous Gift for Harvard Clinic,	746.02
....	Anonymous Gift for Research in Government,	325.00
....	Baker Estate,	8.82
14,625.90	Uriah A. Boyden Fund,	15,188.47
....	Business School, Gift for Prizes,	100.00
32,785.51	Bussey Trust (Real Estate),	39,238.23
.03	Carnegie Foundation Retiring Allowances,	....
108.94	Francis James Child Memorial Fund,	23.55
1,774.21	Classical Department,	1,574.21
374.25	Classical Library Fund,	486.65
384.59	Classical Publication Fund of the Class of 1856,	....
540.00	Warren H. Cudworth Scholarship,	889.55
225.00	Warren Delano Scholarship,	225.00
1,672.67	Dental School,	11,014.61
95,521.07	Dental School Building,	99,066.91
1,855.75	Dining Hall Committee,	1,855.75
150.00	Frank W. Draper Fund,	....
688.19	Estate No. 52 India St.,	813.67
829.31	" 21 Wharf St.,	829.68
....	Fogg Art Museum,	244.54
....	Department of Forestry,	1,584.66
2.00	Freight on Books,	....
.19	John Foster income for Medical Students,	....
....	Harvard Club of Buffalo Scholarship,	200.00
120.00	" " " Chicago Scholarship,	....
....	" " " Cleveland Scholarship,	400.00
....	" " " Fitchburg Scholarship,	8.50
....	Harvard Economic Studies,	980.02
830.56	Sturgis Hooper Fund,	....
....	Jefferson Physical Laboratory,	44.03
80.72	Joseph Lovering Fund for Physical Research,	....
18,588.30	Medical School,	27,742.09
....	Menorah Society Prize,	200.00
1,050.42	Mining and Metallurgy,	1,050.42
57.58	Division of Music Gifts,	....
$180,394.64	.. Amounts carried forward,	$217,977.33

July 1, 1910		June 30, 1911
$180,394.64	. . Amounts brought forward, ...	$217,977.33
350.00	New University Library Building, ...	350.00
4,500.00	Old Boston Music Hall Estate, ...	51,998.26
974.27	**Peabody** Museum of American Archaeology and Ethnology, ...	. . . .
272.76	**Charles Elliott Perkins** Scholarship Fund, . . .	17.76
95.94	Radcliffe College, ...	95.94
26,702.27	**Randall** Hall Association, ...	26,702.27
. . . .	**John Wirt Randall** Fund, ...	29.81
7.04	**Robert W. Sayles** Fund, ...	. . . .
. . . .	**Sayles,** for Summer Course in Geology, ...	1.25
. . . .	**Mary R. Searle** Fund, ...	49.16
. . . .	**Shaw** Fund, Business Research, ...	150.00
15,256.93	Improvements and Additions to The Soldier's Field, . .	10,875.94
94.74	**Dunlap Smith** Scholarship Fund, ...	94.74
380.91	**Stillman** Infirmary, ...	722.41
. . . .	**Townsend** Estate, ...	8,161.25
75.12	**Henry C. Warren** Exploration Fund, ...	. . . .
1,900.00	**Webb** Estate, ...	26,847.45
. . . .	**George Wigglesworth** Gift, ...	182.09
150.16	**Huntington Frothingham Wolcott** Fund, . .	310.16
5,518.84	**Woodland Hill** Fund, ...	5,902.90
. . . .	Laboratory Fees — Mineralogy, ...	10.61
	Library Funds :	
28.62	**Bowditch,**	. . . .
13.55	**Constantius,**	92.75
80.15	**Price Greenleaf,**	3.82
55.85	**Lane,**	. . . .
272.91	**Lowell,**	. . . .
389.78	**Minot,**	67.39
139.24	**Charles Eliot Norton,**	. . . .
329.11	**Henry L. Pierce,**	. . . .
40.50	**Sales,**	. . . .
20.78	**Shapleigh,**	8.62
24.26	**Strobel** Memorial (Siam), ...	. . . .
68.14	Subscription for Library, ...	. . . .
279.24	**Sumner,**	. . . .
43.46	**Daniel Treadwell,**	24.80
9.21	**Ward,**	69.84
115.30	**J. Huntington Wolcott,**	. . . .
$238,583.22	. . Total — Exhibit A, ...	$350,746.55

UNIVERSITY

INCOME AND EXPENDITURE

For the year ended June 30, 1911

INCOME

Income of the following Funds :

Walter F. Baker,	$996.38
Band Music,	55.44
John Barnard,	32.35
Andrew Bigelow,	240.08
Stanton Blake,	242.50
Charlotte F. Blanchard,	231.39
Samuel D. Bradford,	254.63
James C. Carter,	4,850.00
John W. Carter,	554.39
Class of 1883,	4,030.69
John Coggan,	72.75
Edward Erwin Coolidge (part),	164.85
Thomas Cotton,	7.47
John Cowdin,	1,641.00
George B. Dorr,	5,143.35
George Draper,	2,149.23
R. H. Eddy,	2,518.60
Harvard Ellis,	4,909.41
Richard W. Foster,	1,014.57
John Davis Williams French,	236.04
Gore,	997.69
John C. Gray,	1,108.80
Henry Harris (½ income),	726.02
Walter Hastings,	1,510.05
Henry L. Higginson,	4,566.15
Thomas Hollis,	25.22
Thomas Hubbard,	48.50
Nathaniel Hulton,	21.53
Thomas Hutchinson,	11.30
George Baxter Hyde,	242.50
Professorship of Hygiene (1899) (part),	1,000.00
Professorship of Hygiene (1902) (part),	200.00
Leonard Jarvis,	818.29
Henry P. Kidder,	485.00
Joseph Lee,	443.52
Theodore Lyman,	485.00
Israel Munson,	763.88
Henry S. Nourse (part),	1,528.66
Francis E. Parker,	5,048.03
George F. Parkman,	194.29
William Perkins,	1,455.00
Amount carried forward,	$51,024.55

UNIVERSITY (CONTINUED)

INCOME

Amount brought forward,	$51,024.55	
President's,	8,093.77	
Ezekiel Rogers,	171.45	
Daniel Russell,	78.48	
John L. Russell,	1,138.45	
Amey Richmond Sheldon,	15,839.10	
Isaac Sweetser,	2,275.28	
Seth Turner,	242.50	
William F. Weld,	4,435.20	$77,788.78
Care of the Sarah Winslow Fund,	$5.77	
Use of houses by College officers,	1,600.00	
Use of land by Harvard Union,	7,015.50	
Sale of University Directory,	9,866.58	
Sale of Annual Catalogue,	531.60	
Sale of Quinquennial Catalogue,	855.41	
Sale of Scrap Iron, etc.,	25.97	
Sale of wood,	52.50	
Share of the cost of Taxation Pamphlet received from other Colleges,	804.27	19,757.60
		$97,546.38

EXPENDITURE

Board of Overseers :		
Salaries and wages,	$220.00	
Printing Reports of President and Treasurer,	2,090.36	
Printing,	528.15	
Stationery, postage, telephone and telegraph,	39.33	
Auditing Treasurer's accounts,	150.00	
Advertising,	88.78	
Sundries,	.90	$3,112.52
Corporation's Office :		
Fuel, rent, etc.,	$2,603.08	
Less 80% transferred to the Treasurer's Office,	2,082.46	520.62
President's Office :		
Salaries :		
President,	$6,000.00	
Secretary to the President,	1,000.00	
Secretary to the Corporation,	1,000.00	
Keeper of the Corporation Records,	1,020.00	
Services and wages,	2,030.84	
Equipment and supplies,	89.65	
Stationery, postage, telephone and telegraph,	885.53	
Printing,	121.58	
Sundries,	34.17	
	$12,181.77	
Less 90% transferred to departments in proportion to the number of students,	10,963.60	
	$1,218.17	
Amounts carried forward,	$1,218.17	$3,633.14

UNIVERSITY (CONTINUED)

EXPENDITURE

Amounts brought forward, ...	$1,218.17	$3,633.14
Additional salary of President:		
From President's Fund, ...	2,548.60	
From Thomas Cotton Fund, ...	6.20	3,772.97
Treasurer's Office:		
Salaries:		
Treasurer, ...	$6,000.00	
Other salaries, ...	3,366.67	
Services and wages, ...	2,437.30	
Office supplies and expenses, ...	818.98	
Sundries, ...	897.07	
University charge:		
Corporation's Office, ...	2,082.46	
	$15,602.48	
Less transferred:		
To University General Expense for the keeping of the Corporation's Records, ... $750.00		
To Departments in proportion to the income of their Funds, ... 13,884.18	14,634.18	
The balance represents proportion on income of University Funds, ...		968.30
Bursar's Office:		
Salaries:		
Bursar, ...	$4,500.00	
Assistant Comptroller, ...	2,500.00	
Assistant Bursar, ...	2,083.36	
Services and wages, ...	9,792.59	
Office supplies and expenses, ...	2,847.85	
Sundries, ...	1,050.04	
	$22,773.84	
Less transferred:		
To the College for letting College rooms, ... $800.00		
To Departments in proportion to the Bursar's collections and payments, 21,420.47	22,220.47	
The balance represents proportion applicable to University collections and payments, ...		553.37
Publication Office:		
Salary:		
Publication Agent, ...	$2,500.00	
Services and wages, ...	1,686.36	
Office supplies and expenses, ...	6,978.94	
Sundries, ...	87.26	
	$11,252.56	
Less charged directly to Departments, ...	8,291.18	
Balance transferred to Departments in proportion to the free distribution of their publications,	$2,961.38	
Amount carried forward, ...		$3,927.78

UNIVERSITY (CONTINUED)

EXPENDITURE

Amount brought forward, ...		$8,927.78
Inspector of Grounds and Buildings:		
Salaries:		
Inspector of Grounds and Buildings, ...	$4,000.00	
Services and wages, ...	2,994.06	
Office supplies and expenses, ...	410.47	
Less transferred to Departments in proportion to the floor area of buildings in the Inspector's charge, ...	$7,404.58 7,404.58	
Janitor's Office:		
Services and wages, ...	$2,700.00	
Office supplies and expenses, ...	64.90	
	$2,764.90	
Less transferred to Departments in proportion to the floor area of buildings under Janitor's supervision,	2,764.90	
Quinquennial Catalogue:		
Services and wages, ...	$1,606.00	
Office expenses and printing, ...	4,520.20	
	$6,126.20	
Less sales, ...	855.41	
Amount to be apportioned to departments, ...	$5,270.79	
Less transferred to departments in proportion to space occupied, ...	3,057.05	
Amount paid by University:		
General Funds, 42%, ...	$2,213.74	
Amount paid by proceeds from sales, ...	855.41	3,069.15
Annual Catalogue:		
Printing and supplies, ...	$4,723.22	
Less sales, ...	531.60	
Amount to be apportioned to departments, ...	$4,191.62	
Less transferred to departments in proportion to space occupied, ...	3,520.96	
Amount paid by University:		
General Funds, 16%, ...	$670.66	
Amount paid by proceeds from sales, ...	531.60	1,202.26
General Expenses:		
University Gazette, ... $1,462.97		
Less sales, ... 212.53	$1,250.44	
Commencement Day, ...	1,804.20	
Professional services, ...	1,500.00	
Expenses of Professor at Berlin, ...	1,200.00	
Amounts carried forward, ...	$5,754.64	$13,199.19

UNIVERSITY (CONTINUED)

EXPENDITURE

Amounts brought forward, ...	$5,754.64	$13,199.19

General Expenses (*continued*):

Keeping of the Corporation's Records, Treasurer's Office, ...	750.00	
Expenses real estate in Lucas Street, ...	165.06	
Entertainment of National Education Association, .	705.06	
Descriptive pamphlet, ...	1,592.21	
University Guide Book, ... $181.98		
Less sales, ... 34.20	147.78	
Special guide book, Grounds and Buildings, ...	850.62	
Legal Services, ...	150.00	
Sundries, ...	395.96	10,511.33

Alumni List and Directory:

Services and wages, ...	$2,314.90	
Office supplies and expenses, ...	1,087.74	
Printing, ...	7,731.46	
	$11,134.10	
Less transferred to College, ...	1,767.52	
Amount paid from proceeds of sales, ...		9,366.58

Engineer, Services and Expenses, ...	$1,871.25	
Less transferred to Departments in proportion to the floor area of buildings under Engineer's Supervision, ...	1,871.25	

Labor in maintenance of grounds, ...	$10,282.51	
Less transferred to Cambridge Departments, . .	8,226.01	2,056.50

Watchmen:

In Yard, ...	$2,030.95	
Outside Yard, ...	1,156.62	
	$3,187.57	
Transferred to Departments in proportion to floor area of buildings, ...	3,187.57	

Medical Adviser's Office:

Salary Medical Adviser:

From Professorship of Hygiene (1899) Fund, ... $1,000.00		
From Professorship of Hygiene (1902) Fund, ... 200.00		
From General Funds, ... 2,800.00	$4,000.00	
Services and wages, ...	544.62	
Office supplies and expenses, ...	102.34	
Sundries, ...	373.25	
	$5,020.21	

Amounts carried forward, ...	$5,020.21	$35,133.60

UNIVERSITY (CONTINUED)

EXPENDITURE

Amounts brought forward, ...	$5,020.21	$35,133.60

General Expenses (*continued*):

Less amount paid from General Funds, transferred: $750 to the Stillman Infirmary and the remainder to Cambridge Departments in proportion to the number of students, ...	3,820.21	1,200.00

Memorial Hall and Sanders Theatre:

Repairs and equipment, ...	$1,265.71	
Caretaking, ...	669.36	
	$1,935.07	
Less 90% transferred to College, ...	1,741.57	193.50
Repairs and equipment, general, ...		934.36
Taxes, Harvard Union, ...		5,125.50

Secretary for Employment Office:

Salary of Secretary, ...	$1,200.00	
Services and wages, ...	2,983.27	
Office supplies and expenses, ...	1,080.11	
Transferred to College, ...	$5,263.38	

Payments made from University income for the following accounts:

Museum of Comparative Zoölogy	Sch. 23	$730.17	
Peabody Museum of American Archaeology and Ethnology	Sch. 24	2,064.82	
Semitic Museum	Sch. 25	966.91	
Germanic Museum	Sch. 26	142.89	
William Hayes Fogg Art Museum .	Sch. 27	292.24	
Appleton Chapel	Sch. 28	110.53	
Phillips Brooks House	Sch. 29	183.66	4,491.22
			$47,078.18

General Surplus, made up as follows:

Restricted Income unused, added to Funds and Gifts,	$16,050.39	
Surplus, carried to Schedule 10, ...	34,417.76	50,468.15
		$97,546.33

COLLEGE

(Including the Graduate School of Arts and Sciences)

INCOME AND EXPENDITURE

For the year ended June 30, 1911

INCOME

Income of Funds for Instruction and Gifts for Salaries.

Alford Professorship, ...	$1,345.83
Edward Austin (part).	
Austin Teaching Fellowships, ...	12,633.90
John B. Barringer, ...	1,488.32
Boylston Professorship, ...	1,374.34
Martin Brimmer, ...	2,425.00
Class of 1880, ...	5,027.95
Class Subscription, ...	7,305.94
Eaton Professorship, ...	5,404.55
Eliot Professorship, ...	1,048.52
Eliot " (Jon. Phillips' Gift), . .	350.00
Calvin and Lucy Ellis Aid (part), ...	4,794.02
Erving Professorship, ...	169.75
Fisher "	1,745.56
Henry Flynt (part), ...	16.55
Fund for Permanent Tutors, ...	787.64
Gospel Church (⅓ income used), ...	369.96
Gurney (part), ...	9,204.70
Charles L. Hancock, ...	4,400.00
Hersey Professorship (⅔ income), ...	588.31
Hersey Professorship (Thomas Lee's gift), . .	1,054.58
Hollis " (Mathematics), ...	181.73
Abbott Lawrence, ...	2,984.50
James Lawrence (part), ...	1,221.60
Henry Lee Professorship, ...	5,337.09
Thomas Lee, for Reading, ...	766.16
Arthur T. Lyman, ...	2,425.00
McLean Professorship, ...	2,088.56
Francis Greenwood Peabody (part), . .	3,000.00
Daniel H. Peirce, ...	708.39
Perkins Professorship, ...	1,018.50
Plummer Foundation, ...	1,213.47
Pope Professorship, ...	2,546.25
Nelson Robinson Jr. Additional (part), . .	1,000.00
Eliza O. and Mary P. Ropes, ...	5,883.54
Rumford Professorship, ...	2,733.90
Smith Professorship, ...	1,122.29
Teachers' Endowment :	
Interest, ... $98,070.83	
Gift, ... 400.00	98,470.83
Amount carried forward, ...	$194,237.23

COLLEGE (CONTINUED)
INCOME

Amount brought forward, ...	$194,287.23	

Income of Funds for Instruction and Gifts for Salaries (*continued*).

Unknown Memorial (part), ...	3,115.91	
Henry Villard, ...	2,217.60	
Henry W. Wales:		
Wales Professorship, ...	1,500.00	
Henry C. Warren (part), ...	4,000.00	
Sylvester Waterhouse, ...	375.39	
David A. Wells (part), ...	5,000.00	
Jerome Wheelock, ...	4.32	
Gifts for salaries, ...	6,300.00	$216,750.45

Income of Funds for General Purposes.

John W. P. Abbot (accumulating), ...	$628.32	
William H. Baldwin, Jr.	97.00	
John A. Blanchard, ...	50.93	
Twenty-fifth Anniversary Fund of the		
Class of 1881, ...	5,502.33	
Fund of the Class of 1882, ...	4,045.43	
Class of 1884, ...	4,731.18	
Class of 1885, ...	5,097.20	
Edward W. Codman, ...	15,616.58	
Charles L. Hancock, ...	3,017.03	
Trenor L. Park, ...	468.80	
Jonathan Phillips, ...	1,537.75	
William M. Spackman, ...	121.25	
Gifts for General Purposes, ...	2,650.01	43,563.81

Income of Fellowship Funds and Gifts for Fellowships.

Edward Austin (part):		
Edward Austin Fellowships, ...	$2,000.00	
Cercle Français de l'Université Harvard (gift),	600.00	
Bayard Cutting, ...	505.20	
Bayard Cutting (for Research in Physics), .	420.20	
George W. Dillaway, ...	271.84	
Ozias Goodwin Memorial, ...	574.58	
Harris, ...	546.26	
Edward William Hooper, ...	1,276.62	
John Thornton Kirkland, ...	553.89	
Henry Lee Memorial, ...	595.19	
Woodbury Lowery Memorial, ...	972.09	
MacDowell (gift), ...	600.00	
Charles Eliot Norton, ...	900.00	
Robert Treat Paine, ...	655.28	
John Parker, ...	3,018.31	
Francis Parkman, ...	506.78	
Amounts carried forward, ...	$13,990.74	$260,314.26

COLLEGE (CONTINUED)

INCOME

Amounts brought forward, ...	$13,990.74	$260,314.26

Income of Fellowship Funds and Gifts for Fellowships (*continued*).

Princeton Fellowship, ...	44.70	
Rogers, ...	1,622.52	
Henry Bromfield Rogers Memorial, . . .	611.44	
Frederick Sheldon (part), ...	15,221.56	
South End House (gift), ...	400.00	
South End House in Social Education (gift), . .	300.00	
Fellowship Department of Social Ethics, ...	24.25	
John Tyndall, ...	592.77	
James Walker, ...	569.20	
Whiting, ...	1,220.12	
Adams Woods (gift), ...	400.00	34,997.30

Income of Scholarship Funds and Gifts for Scholarships.

Abbot, ...		$191.96	
Alford (accumulating), ...		182.74	
Edward Austin (part):			
" " Scholarships for Teachers, .		3,465.00	
Bartlett, ...		263.26	
Bassett, ...		276.06	
Bigelow, ...		672.02	
Charles Sumner Bird, ...		9.70	
Borden (accumulating), ...		165.82	
Bowditch, ...		5,645.64	
W. G. Bowdoin (gift), ...		250.00	
Bright Scholarships (part):			
Interest on balance, ...	$230.08		
Bright Legacy (part income), . .	962.50	1,192.58	
Browne, ...		196.13	
Morey Willard Buckminster, ...		273.49	
Burr, ...		1,780.48	
Ruluff Sterling Choate, ...		305.60	
George Newhall Clark, ...		507.18	
Thomas William Clarke, ...		66.45	
Class of 1802, ...		425.73	
" 1814, ...		168.78	
" 1815 (Kirkland), ...		337.95	
" 1817, ...		285.52	
" 1828, ...		173.39	
" 1835, ...		258.84	
" 1841, ...		263.40	
" 1852 (Dana), ...		263.81	
" 1856, ...		815.09	
" 1867, ...		250.02	
Amounts carried forward, ...		$18,531.11	$295,311.56

COLLEGE (CONTINUED)

INCOME

Amounts brought forward, ...			$18,531.11	$295,311.56

Income of Scholarship Funds and Gifts for Scholarships (*continued*).

Class of 1877, ...		260.78
" 1883, ...		308.86
Classical Department (gift), ...		150.00
Crowninshield, ...		622.69
Warren H. Cudworth, ...		250.45
George and Martha Derby, ...		274.32
Julius Dexter, ...		313.79
Orlando W. Doe, ...		147.88
William Samuel Eliot, ...		270.58
George H. Emerson, ...		1,588.95
Joseph Eveleth (part), ...		896.22
Fall River, ...		124.45
Farrar, ...		321.22
George Fisher and Elizabeth Huntington Fisher, ...		242.45
Richard Augustine Gambrill, ...		584.42
Charles Haven Goodwin, ...		391.59
Benjamin D. Greene, ...		223.49
Mary Forbes Greene (gift), ...		300.00
Price Greenleaf (part) :		
Price Greenleaf Scholarships, ...		3,000.00
Selwyn L. Harding, ...		66.44
Harvard Club of Boston (gift), . .	$1,000.00	
Interest,	48.50	1,048.50
" " Chicago (gift), ...		420.00
" " Connecticut Valley (gift), .		200.00
" " Fitchburg (gift), ...		150.00
" " Hawaii (gift), ...		200.00
" " Hingham "		100.00
" " Indiana "		200.00
" " Lawrence "		100.00
" " Lowell "		300.00
" " Lynn "		100.00
" " Milwaukee "		200.00
" " Nebraska "		150.00
" " New Jersey "		250.00
" " Western Pennsylvania (gift),		300.00
" " Rochester, New York "		200.00
" " San Francisco (gift), ...		500.00
" " Washington (gift),	$101.00	
Interest,	22.12	123.12
Amounts carried forward, ...		$33,360.76 $295,311.56

COLLEGE (CONTINUED)

INCOME

Amounts brought forward, ... $33,360.76 $295,311.56

Income of Scholarship Funds and Gifts for Scholarships
   (*continued*).

Harvard Club of Worcester (gift), ...	200.00
John Appleton Haven, ...	517.74
William Hilton (part), ...	559.81
Ebenezer Rockwood Hoar, ...	550.77
Levina Hoar, for the town of Lincoln, ...	322.33
R. M. Hodges (part) :	
Hodges Scholarship, ...	299.10
Hollis, ...	321.89
Huidekoper (gift), ...	200.00
Henry B. Humphrey, ...	546.93
Charles L. Jones, ...	1,571.84
George Emerson Lowell, ...	535.20
Markoe, ...	279.89
Matthews Scholarships :	
Interest on balance, ... $180.42	
Matthews Hall, ½ net rents, . . . 3,954.84	4,135.26
William Merrick, ...	319.47
Morey, ...	426.61
Lady Mowlson, ...	298.32
Boston Newsboys', ...	142.74
Howard Gardner Nichols, ...	290.66
Lucy Osgood, ...	307.00
George Herbert Palmer, ...	7.52
George Foster Peabody, ...	185.16
James Mills Peirce, ...	213.21
Pennoyer, ...	376.75
Charles Eliot Perkins, ...	1,455.00
Rebecca A. Perkins, ...	237.46
Philadelphia	547.37
Wendell Phillips Memorial, ...	87.25
Philosophy (gift), ...	300.00
William Reed, ...	178.25
Ricardo Prize (gift), ...	350.00
Rodger, ...	74.59
Henry Bromfield Rogers, ...	176.88
Nathaniel Ropes Jr., ...	538.93
James A. Rumrill, ...	526.60
Edward Russell, ...	293.91
Sales, ...	291.29
Saltonstall, ...	574.43
Leverett Saltonstall, ...	438.05
Mary Saltonstall, ...	351.29

Amounts carried forward, ... $52,890.26 $295,311.56

COLLEGE (CONTINUED)

INCOME

Amounts brought forward, . . .	$52,390.26	$295,311.56

Income of Scholarship Funds and Gifts for Scholarships
(*continued*).

James Savage (part):

Savage Scholarship, ...		300.00
Sever, ...		159.18
Sewall, ...		571.52
Shattuck, ...		2,473.21
Slade, ...		306.08
Dunlap Smith, ...		200.00
Story, ...		230.62

Stoughton:

Interest, ...	$22.21	
Use of pasture, ...	169.23	191.44
Swift, ...		216.70
Thayer, ...		4,081.27
Gorham Thomas, ...		211.46
Toppan, ...		393.09
Townsend, ...		1,318.86
Ira D. Van Duzee		13.68
Walcott, ...		259.57
Christopher M. Weld, ...		544.41

Jacob Wendell:

Interest, ...	$277.52	
Gift, ...	50.00	327.52
Whiting, ...		603.10
Josiah Dwight Whitney, ...		242.50
Mary L. Whitney, ...		574.14
Willard, ...		513.23
Augustus Woodbury, ...		100.69
Charles Wyman, ...		509.30	66,726.83

Income of Beneficiary and Loan Funds and Repayments.

Rebecca C. Ames:

Interest, ...		$2,635.93

Anonymous gifts for benefit of certain members of the Class of 1915, ...		650.00
Anonymous gift for special aid for a member of the Graduate School of Arts and Sciences, . .		150.00
Nathaniel Appleton, ...		35.65

Edward Austin:

Interest, ...	$100.00	
Loans repaid by students, ...	63.88	163.88
Frank Bolles Memorial, ...		109.71
William Brattle, ...		88.61

Amounts carried forward, ...	$3,833.78	$362,038.39

COLLEGE (CONTINUED)

INCOME

Amounts brought forward, . . .		$8,833.78	$362,038.39

Income of Beneficiary and Loan Funds and Repayments (*continued*).

Daniel A. Buckley (part), ...		8,116.33
Walter Channing Cabot, ...		2,508.61
Chinese Students' Aid (gift), ...		2,500.00
Edward Erwin Coolidge (part), ...		564.83
Thomas Danforth, ...		62.86
Moses Day, ...		265.49
Calvin and Lucy Ellis Aid (part), ...		2,375.00
John Ellery, ...		25.87
Exhibitions, ...		65.67
Fines Loan Fund :		
For late registration, ...	$320.00	
For delayed payment of dues, . . .	486.25	
Loans returned, ...	20.25	
Interest, ...	93.12	919.62
Thomas Fitch, ...		46.17
Ephraim Flynt, ...		27.40
Henry Flynt, ...		9.89
Freshman Loan : Gift, ...	$25.00	
Interest, ...	80.03	
Loans repaid, ...	75.00	180.03
Freshman Loan (Gove Gift), ...		20.36
Henry Gibbs, ...		28.52
John Glover, ...		195.45
Price Greenleaf (part), ...	$16,944.55	
Price Greenleaf Aid :		
Interest, ...	694.76	
Price Greenleaf Aids returned,	50.67	17,689.98
Edwin A. W. Harlow :		
Interest, ...	$574.19	
Loans repaid, ...	50.00	624.19
Robert Henry Harlow, ...		272.38
Harvard Engineering Society Loan Fund :		
Gift, ...	$500.00	
Loans repaid, ...	72.80	572.80
Edward Holyoke, ...		21.29
Robert Keayne, ...		136.96
Bertram Kimball, ...		1,261.00
Harry Milton Levy Loan, ...		110.19
Mary Lindall, ...		59.17
The Loan, ...		6,125.00
Susan B. Lyman :		
Interest, ...		193.65

Amounts carried forward, ...		$48,811.94	$362,038.39

COLLEGE (CONTINUED)

INCOME

Amounts brought forward, ...	$48,811.94	$362,088.39

Income of Beneficiary and Loan Funds and Repayments (*continued*).

Anne Mills, ...		18.82	
John F. Moors Gift, special aid for a member of the Class of 1915, ...		50.00	
Munroe:			
Interest, ...	$531.71		
Loans repaid, ...	40.30	572.01	
Palfrey Exhibition, ...		108.45	
Dr. Andrew P. Peabody Memorial:			
Interest, ...	$265.20		
Loans repaid, ...	10.00	275.20	
Scholarship and Beneficiary Money Returned:			
Loans repaid, ...	$1,420.69		
Interest, ...	141.91	1,562.60	
Joseph Sewall, ...		13.14	
Alexander W. Thayer (part), ...		314.04	
Quincy Tufts, ...		541.84	
Benjamin Wadsworth, ...		17.80	
Stuart Wadsworth Wheeler:			
Interest, ...	$347.26		
Loans repaid, ...	232.43	579.69	52,860.53

Income of Prize Funds, and Gifts for Prizes:		
Jeremy Belknap (gift), ...	$50.00	
James Gordon Bennett, ...	93.75	
Philo Sherman Bennett, ...	20.22	
Francis Boott (part), ...	190.00	
Bowdoin Prizes for Dissertations, ...	1,562.96	
Boylston Prizes for Elocution, ...	185.56	
Coolidge Debating, ...	283.24	
John Craig (gift), ...	250.00	
Lloyd McKim Garrison, ...	131.63	
Edward Hopkins Gift for "Deturs":		
Interest on balance, ...	$109.32	
From Trustees, ...	230.79	340.11
George Arthur Knight, ...		53.01
Susan Anthony Potter Prizes (gift), . . .		225.00
Sales, ...		56.89
John O. Sargent, ...		186.87
George B. Sohier (part), ...		250.00
Charles Sumner, ...		206.27
Robert N. Toppan, ...		191.14
Philip Washburn, ...		118.15

Amounts carried forward, ...	$4,294.80	$414,898.92

COLLEGE (CONTINUED)

INCOME

Amounts brought forward, ...	$4,294.80	$414,898.92

Income of Prize Funds, and Gifts for Prizes (*continued*).

Elizabeth Wilder, ...	26.04	
Wister, ...	16.59	4,337.43

Income of Sundry Funds for Special Purposes:

Botanic Department (part):

½ for Cryptogamic Herbarium, . . $482.33		
½ for Laboratories of Botany, . . . 241.17	$723.50	
William H. Baldwin, Jr., 1885, ...	280.72	
Caroline M. Barnard Bequest, ...	72.75	
Francis Boott (part), ...	317.21	
Francis James Child Memorial, ...	544.41	

Classical Publication Fund of the Class of 1856:

Interest, ... $344.59		
Sales, ... 145.69	490.28	
Book Fund of the Class of 1881, ...	174.50	
Class of 1883 Special, ...	12.90	
Cryptogamic Herbarium, ...	165.19	
George A. Gardner, ...	291.53	
George Silsbee and Ellen Sever Hale, .	311.71	

Harvard Oriental Series:

Interest, ...	741.57	
Solomon Lincoln Bequest, ...	273.78	
Joseph Lovering for Physical Research, . .	374.42	
Music Department, ...	63.15	
Francis Greenwood Peabody (part), . .	1,857.18	
James Mills Peirce Bequest, ...	21.10	
Nelson Robinson, Jr. Additional (part), . .	9.82	
Robert W. Sayles, ...	242.50	
Sayles, for Summer Course in Geology, ...	510.80	
George William Sawin, ...	267.38	
Shaler Memorial, ...	1,628.19	
Elizabeth Torrey, ...	59.56	

Henry Warren Torrey:

Interest, ...	741.57	
Unknown Memorial (part), ...	1,800.00	
Samuel Ward, ...	855.44	
Cyrus M. Warren, ...	313.50	
Henry C. Warren (part), ...	1,781.83	
David A. Wells (part), ...	647.15	
Chauncey Wright, ...	65.67	
Amounts carried forward, ...	$15,754.57	$419,236.35

COLLEGE (CONTINUED)

INCOME

Amounts brought forward, ...	$15,754.57	$419,236.35

Income of Sundry Funds for Special Purposes (*continued*).

Jefferson Physical Laboratory:

Interest on balance, ...	152.05	
Physical Laboratory Endowment (interest), . . .	3,627.50	
T. Jefferson Coolidge for Research in Physics,	2,500.00	22,034.12

Sundry Gifts, Fees, etc., for Special Purposes.

For the Department of Botany:

Gift of **John S. Ames**, ...	$350.00	

For the Department of Classics:

Gift for Advances to Classical Department, .	200.00	
Sales of publications, ...	133.65	

For the Department of Economics:

Gift for Department, ... $1,300.00		
Interest, ... 6.75	1,306.75	

For the Department of English:

Gift for publications, ...	1,550.00	

For the Department of Government:

Gift of **Frank Graham Thomson,** . .	5,000.00	

For the Department of History (History 1):

Sales of publications, ... $240.28		
Interest, ... 26.80	267.08	

For the Department of Mathematics:

Sales of publications, ...	574.62	

For the Department of Music:

John K. Paine Memorial — Royalties on publications, ...	5.48	
Gift for Department, ...	560.00	

For the Department of Philosophy:

Gifts for Department Library, ...	200.00	
Sales of Psychological Review, ...	23.99	

For the Department of Physics:

Fellowship for Research in Physics — interest	44.16	

For the Department of Sanskrit:

Interest, ... $42.38		
Sales of publications, ... 205.65	248.03	

For the Department of Semitic:

Gift for Library, ...	1,000.00	

For the Department of Ethics of Social Questions:

Anonymous Gift for Department, $3,500.00		
Interest, ... 54.68		
Sales of publication, ... 495.03	4,049.71	
Special Gift for Department Library, . . .	300.00	
Gift for furnishing rooms — interest, ...	13.98	

Amounts carried forward, ...	$15,827.45	$441,681.77

COLLEGE (CONTINUED)

INCOME

Amounts brought forward, ...		$15,827.45	$441,681.77

Sundry Gifts, Fees, etc., for Special Purposes
(*continued*).

For the Department of Zoölogy:

Gift for Bermuda Biological Station,	$500.00		
Interest, ...	21.60	521.60	

For the School for Social Workers:

Gift, ...	$3,750.00		
Interest, ...	51.45		
Tuition fees, ...	100.00	3,901.45	
Gift Harvard Alumni Association —			
travelling expenses, ...		50.00	
Gift Plantation of Shrubs, interest, ...		74.58	20,375.08

Receipts from students.

Tuition Fees — Regular Programme:

College Regular, ...	$301,753.00		
" Special, ...	9,865.00		
Unclassified, ...	13,586.00	$325,204.00	

Tuition Fees — Additional Courses:

College Regular, ...	$31,173.34		
" Special, ...	1,033.74		
Unclassified, ...	710.00	32,917.08	

Tuition — Regular Programme:

Graduate School of Arts and Sciences, ...	$52,881.00		
Radcliffe students in University courses, ...	2,105.00		
For afternoon and Saturday courses for teachers, ...	15.00		
Summer Schools in Cambridge, .	21,277.67	76,278.67	

Registration Fees:

Summer Schools in Cambridge, ...		1,610.00	

Auditors' Fees:

Summer Schools in Cambridge, .	$850.00		
College, ...	50.00	900.00	

Examination fees:

Admission, ...	$10,345.00		
Condition, make-up and advanced standing, ...	2,742.00		
Doctor of Philosophy, ...	30.00	13,117.00	
Graduation fees, ...		8,120.00	

Laboratory fees:

Astronomy, ...	$895.00		
Botany, ...	1,277.50		
Amounts carried forward, .	$2,172.50	$458,146.75	$461,645.55

COLLEGE (CONTINUED)

INCOME

Amounts brought forward, .	$2,172.50	$458,146.75	$461,645.55

Receipts from Students (*continued*).

Chemistry, ...	14,649.37	
Geology, ...	1,460.00	
Mineralogy, ...	322.50	
Music, ...	70.00	
Hygiene, ...	1,845.00	
Physics, ...	3,265.00	
Psychology, ...	100.00	
Zoölogy, ...	1,205.00	25,089.37

College Dormitories: Hollis, Stoughton, Holworthy, Thayer, Weld, Wadsworth House, Walter Hastings, Perkins, and Conant, ...	$70,687.72	
Matthews Hall, ...	12,964.00	
	$83,651.72	
Less ½ net income from Matthews Hall, credited under income of Matthews Scholarship, ...	3,954.84	79,696.88
Summer School excursions, ...		87.71
Amount collected on account of unpaid term-bills previously charged off, ...		200.42	563,221.13

Sundries:

Sale of University Hymn Book, ...	$49.55	
" Address List, ...	2.25	
" Manual American History, ...	169.79	
" Annals of Mathematics, ...	854.80	
" old examination papers, ...	356.95	
" other publications, ...	525.20	
" Commencement Lunch tickets, ...	506.00	
Board from students at Mining Camp, ...	55.00	
Sale of Historical Monographs, ...	1.57	
Use of typewriters, ...	2.52	
Duplicate diplomas, ...	15.00	
Sale of photographs, ...	45.31	2,083.94
		$1,026,950.62

EXPENDITURE

From Fellowship Funds and Gifts.

Edward Austin, ...	$2,000.00
Cercle Français de l'Université **Harvard,** . . .	600.00
Ozias Goodwin Memorial, ...	525.00
Amount carried forward, ...	$3,125.00

COLLEGE (CONTINUED)

EXPENDITURE

Amount brought forward, ...	$3,125.00	
From Fellowship Funds and Gifts (*continued*).		
Edward William Hooper, ...	1,150.00	
John Thornton Kirkland, ...	500.00	
Henry Lee Memorial, ...	525.00	
Woodbury Lowery, ...	800.00	
MacDowell, ...	600.00	
Charles Eliot Norton, ...	800.00	
Robert Treat Paine, ...	600.00	
John Parker, ...	2,250.00	
Francis Parkman, ...	450.00	
Rogers, ...	1,500.00	
Henry Bromfield Rogers Memorial, . . .	525.00	
Frederick Sheldon (part), ...	14,596.85	
South End House, ...	300.00	
South End House Fellowship in Social Education,	300.00	
James Walker, ...	500.00	
Whiting, ...	900.00	
Adams Woods Fellowship, ...	400.00	29,821.35
From Scholarship Funds and Gifts.		
Abbot, ...	$175.00	
Edward Austin Scholarships for Teachers, .	3,465.00	
Bartlett, ...	250.00	
Bassett, ...	180.00	
Charles Sumner Bird, ...	200.00	
Bigelow, ...	600.00	
Bowditch, ...	5,291.67	
W. G. Bowdoin, Jr., Scholarship, ...	250.00	
Bright (part), ...	1,325.00	
Browne, ...	175.00	
Morey Willard Buckminster, ...	250.00	
Burr, ...	1,520.00	
Ruluff Sterling Choate, ...	275.00	
George Newhall Clark, ...	500.00	
Class of 1802, ...	375.00	
" 1814, ...	150.00	
" 1815 (Kirkland), ...	300.00	
" 1817, ...	200.00	
" 1828, ...	200.00	
" 1835, ...	225.00	
" 1841, ...	225.00	
" 1852 (Dana), ...	225.00	
" 1856, ...	700.00	
" 1877, ...	225.00	
" 1883, ...	275.00	
Amounts carried forward, ...	$17,556.67	$29,821.35

COLLEGE (CONTINUED)

EXPENDITURE

Amounts brought forward, . . . $17,556.67		$29,821.35

From Scholarship Funds and Gifts (*continued*).

Crowninshield, ...	660.00
Warren H. Cudworth, ...	600.00
George and Martha Derby, ...	250.00
Julius Dexter, ...	225.00
Orlando W. Doe, ...	100.00
William Samuel Eliot, ...	83.33
George H. Emerson, ...	349.50
Joseph Eveleth (part), ...	400.00
Fall River, ...	100.00
Farrar, ...	275.00
George Fisher and Elizabeth Huntington Fisher, ...	200.00
Richard Augustine Gambrill, ...	525.00
Charles Haven Goodwin, ...	350.00
Benjamin D. Greene, ...	80.00
Mary Forbes Greene, ...	300.00
Price Greenleaf (part), ...	3,000.00
Harvard Club of Boston, ...	1,000.00
" " Buffalo, ...	200.00
" " Chicago, ...	300.00
" " Cleveland, ...	400.00
" " Connecticut Valley, ...	200.00
" " Fitchburg, ...	158.50
" " Hawaii, ...	200.00
" " Hingham, ...	100.00
" " Indiana, ...	200.00
" " Lowell, ...	300.00
" " Lynn, ...	100.00
" " Milwaukee, ...	200.00
" " Nebraska, ...	150.00
" " New Jersey, ...	250.00
" " Western Pennsylvania, . . .	300.00
" " San Francisco, ...	500.00
" " Washington, ...	250.00
" " Worcester, ...	200.00
John Appleton Haven, ...	475.00
William Hilton (part), ...	225.00
Ebenezer Rockwood Hoar, ...	500.00
Levina Hoar, for the town of Lincoln, ...	240.00
R. M. Hodges (part), ...	275.00
Hollis, ...	275.00
Huidekoper Scholarship, ...	200.00
Henry B. Humphrey, ...	500.00

Amounts carried forward, ...	$32,753.00	$29,821.35

COLLEGE (CONTINUED)

EXPENDITURE

Amounts brought forward, ...	$32,753.00	$29,821.35

From Scholarship Funds and Gifts (*continued*).

Charles L. Jones, ...	1,305.00
George Emerson Lowell, ...	450.00
Markoe, ...	250.00
Matthews, ...	4,500.00
William Merrick, ...	275.00
Morey, ...	375.00
Lady Mowlson, ...	250.00
Howard Gardner Nichols, ...	250.00
Lucy Osgood, ...	275.00
George Foster Peabody, ...	250.00
C. E. Perkins Scholarship, ...	1,200.00
Rebecca A. Perkins, ...	200.00
Philadelphia, ...	700.00
Special Scholarship in Philosophy, ...	300.00
Wendell Phillips Memorial, ...	75.00
William Reed, ...	175.00
Ricardo Prize Gift, ...	350.00
Henry Bromfield Rogers, ...	150.00
Nathaniel Ropes, Jr., ...	475.00
James A. Rumrill, ...	450.00
Edward Russell, ...	250.00
Sales, ...	250.00
Saltonstall, ...	525.00
Leverett Saltonstall, ...	400.00
Mary Saltonstall, ...	300.00
James Savage (part), ...	300.00
Sever, ...	150.00
Sewall, ...	500.00
Shattuck, ...	2,100.00
Slade, ...	275.00
Dunlap Smith, ...	200.00
Story, ...	200.00
Stoughton, ...	150.00
Thayer, ...	3,000.00
Gorham Thomas, ...	200.00
Toppan, ...	350.00
Townsend, ...	1,000.00
Walcott, ...	200.00
Christopher M. Weld, ...	500.00
Jacob Wendell, ...	300.00
Whiting, ...	550.00
Josiah Dwight Whitney, ...	242.50
Mary L. Whitney, ...	500.00

Amounts carried forward, ...	$57,450.50	$29,821.35

COLLEGE (CONTINUED)

EXPENDITURE

Amounts brought forward, ...	$57,450.50	$29,821.35
From Scholarship Funds and Gifts (*continued*).		
Willard, ...	475.00	
Charles Wyman, ...	450.00	58,375.50
From Beneficiary and Loan Funds and Gifts.		
Rebecca C. Ames, ...	$2,470.00	
Anonymous Gift for Special Aid, ...	30.00	
Edward Austin Loan (Special Students), . .	100.00	
Frank Bolles Memorial, ...	100.00	
Daniel A. Buckley (part), ...	2,940.00	
Walter Channing Cabot, ...	2,500.00	
Edward Erwin Coolidge (part), ...	564.83	
Moses Day, ...	265.49	
Calvin and Lucy Ellis Aid (part), ...	2,875.00	
Exhibitions, ...	65.67	
Fines, Loan Fund, ...	1,764.71	
Freshman Loan, ...	1,755.15	
Price Greenleaf Aid, ...	15,879.84	
Edwin A. W. Harlow, ...	558.34	
Robert Henry Harlow, ...	272.83	
Student Fund of the **Harvard** Engineering		
Society of New York, ...	75.00	
Bertram Kimball, ...	1,000.00	
Harry Milton Levy Loan, ...	505.00	
The Loan, ...	6,125.00	
Susan B. Lyman, ...	200.00	
Munroe, ...	676.00	
Palfrey Exhibition, ...	160.00	
Dr. Andrew P. Peabody Memorial, ...	251.00	
Scholarship and Beneficiary Money Returned, . .	4,910.00	
Quincy Tufts, ...	541.84	45,584.70
From Prize Funds and Gifts for Prizes.		
Jeremy Belknap, ...	$100.00	
Francis Boott (part), ...	90.00	
Bowdoin Prizes for Dissertations, ...	1,490.80	
Boylston Prizes for Elocution, ...	255.25	
Coolidge Debating, ...	270.12	
John Craig, ...	250.00	
Lloyd McKim Garrison, ...	108.72	
Edward Hopkins Gift for "Deturs," . . .	285.96	
Menorah Society, ...	200.00	
Patria Society, ...	50.00	
Susan Anthony Potter Prizes, ...	225.00	
Sales, ...	45.00	
John O. Sargent, ...	200.00	
Amounts carried forward, ...	$3,570.85	$133,781.55

COLLEGE (CONTINUED)

EXPENDITURE

Amounts brought forward, ...	$3,570.85	$133,781.55

From Prize Funds and Gifts for Prizes (*continued*).

George B. Sohier, ...	500.00	
Charles Sumner, ...	100.00	
Philip Washburn, ...	150.00	4,320.85

For University Scholarships.
Undergraduate :

Normal, ...	$600.00	
Graduate School of Arts and Sciences, ...	6,120.00	6,720.00

From Sundry Funds and Balances for Special Purposes.

Francis Boott, books for the Department of Music, ...	$318.57	
Francis James Child Memorial, books, . .	459.02	
Classical Publication Fund of the Class of 1856 :		
Harvard Studies in Classical Philology, . .	31.44	
T. Jefferson Coolidge for Research in Physics,	2,997.08	
Book Fund of the Class of 1881, books for the Department of Chemistry, ...	184.26	
George A. Gardner, for photographs, etc., for the Department of Geology, ...	224.20	
Harvard Alumni Association, for travelling expenses, ...	50.00	
Harvard Oriental Series, publications, ...	772.81	
Harvard Economic Studies, ...	2,337.98	
Harvard Psychological Review, printing, . . .	86.22	
History Publication Fund (History 1), books, . .	577.04	
Joseph Lovering for Physical Research, . .	281.20	
Mathematics Publication Fund, books, ...	84.15	
Francis G. Peabody, ... $5,677.04		
Less amount paid for salaries, 3,000.00	2,677.04	
Nelson Robinson Jr. Additional (part).		
Psychological Laboratory, . . . $1,594.22		
Books, ... 280.89		
Expenses, ... 34.79		
Librarian Department Philosophy, 1,000.00		
$2,909.90		
Less paid for salaries, . . . 1,000.00	1,909.90	
Robert W. Sayles for Department of Geology,	235.46	
Shaler Memorial, ...	1,700.00	
Henry Warren Torrey, publications, . . .	602.04	
Unknown Memorial (part), services and expenses,	1,939.21	
Cyrus M. Warren, research in Chemistry, .	209.57	
Henry C. Warren, publications and books, .	1,466.86	
Summer Course in Geology, ...	1,043.85	
Amounts carried forward, ...	$20,187.90	$144,822.40

COLLEGE (CONTINUED)

EXPENDITURE

Amounts brought forward, ...	$20,187.90	$144,822.40

From Sundry Funds and Balances for Special
Purposes (*continued*).

Jefferson Physical Laboratory:

Services and wages, ...	$1,255.75		
Office supplies and expenses, . .	110.41		
Operating expense, . . . $5,904.23			
Less paid from General			
Income, ...	600.00	5,304.23	

University charge:

Treasurer's Office, care of invest-			
ments, ...	81.68		
Bursar's Office, collections and pay-			
ments, ...	128.32		
Watchmen, ...	78.66	6,959.05	27,146.95

From Gifts and Fees, etc., for Special Purposes.

For Department of Economics:		
Gift for Department, ...	$728.04	
Arthur T. Lyman, maps and charts, . .	24.18	
For Department of Mineralogy, Gift for exhibits,	9.60	
For Department of Mathematics:		
Gift for Expenses of Commission on teaching		
Mathematics, ...	100.00	
For Department of Chemistry:		
Edward Mallinckrodt gift, ...	75.00	
For Department of Philosophy:		
Philosophical Library Books, ...	202.13	
For Department of Ethics Social Questions, . .	1,098.80	
Furnishings for the Department of Social Ethics,	68.23	
For Division of Music, ...	485.84	
For Department of Physics, Physical Research, .	49.79	
Fellowship in Physical Research, . $500.00		
Less paid for salaries, ... 500.00		
Department of Botany, John S. Ames Gift, .	94.50	
" Zoölogy, Bermuda Biological Sta-		
tion, ...	369.25	
Department of Geology, Exhibition Case for		
Photographs, ...	29.31	
Semitic Library, books, ...	132.15	
Department of Classics, books, ...	196.05	
School for Social Workers, ... $2,944.80		
Less paid for salaries, ... 2,000.00	944.80	
Department of Government:		
Anonymous gift for Research, ...	325.00	
Amounts carried forward, ...	$4,932.17	$171,969.35

COLLEGE (CONTINUED)

EXPENDITURE

Amounts brought forward, ...	$4,932.17	$171,969.35

From Gifts and Fees, etc., for Special Purposes (*continued*).

Gift **F. G. Thomson**, ...	$4,523.20		
Less paid for salaries, ...	4,000.00	523.20	5,455.37

Administration Offices.

Dean of the Faculty of Arts and Sciences:

Salary, ...	$500.00	
Services and wages, ...	661.50	
Office supplies and expenses, ...	200.44	
Sundries, ...	1.36	1,363.30

Dean of Harvard College:

Salaries, ...	$11,020.84	
Services and wages, ...	7,680.42	
Office supplies and expenses, ...	2,558.19	
Sundries, ...	57.10	21,316.55

Dean and Secretary of the Graduate School of Arts and Sciences:

Salaries, ...	$2,500.00	
Services and wages, ...	688.15	
Office supplies and expenses, ...	769.12	3,957.27

Dean of the Graduate School of Business Administration:

Salary, ...	1,000.00

Secretary of the Faculty of Arts and Sciences:

Salaries, ...	$3,000.00	
Services and wages, ...	1,430.75	
Office supplies and expenses, ...	1,111.69	
Sundries, ...	3.06	5,545.50

From Appropriations.

Anthropology, ...	$50.00	
Astronomy, ...	30.67	
Botany, ...	7,305.74	
Classics, ...	800.00	
Comparative Literature, ...	42.80	
Economics, ...	$942.94	
Office expenses, ...	600.00	1,542.94
Education, ...	82.43	
English, ...	302.67	
Fine Arts, ...	588.12	
French and other Romance Languages, ...	1,397.25	
Geology, ...	150.00	
German, ...	543.84	
History, ...	1,063.00	
Mathematics, ...	462.10	

Amounts carried forward, ...	$14,361.06	$210,607.34

EXPENDITURE

Amounts brought forward, ...	$14,361.06	$210,607.84
From Appropriations (*continued*).		
Mineralogy and Petrography, ...	878.75	
Music, ...	150.00	
Physics, ...	711.61	
Psychology, ...	149.43	
Zoölogy, ...	1,792.21	17,543.06
From Laboratory Fees.		
Astronomy, ...	$602.49	
Botany, ...	1,062.47	
Chemistry, ...	14,398.14	
Geology, ...	1,302.30	
Hygiene, ...	1,525.04	
Mineralogy, ...	833.11	
Music, ...	70.00	
Physics, ...	3,265.00	
Psychology, ...	100.00	
Zoölogy, ...	1,205.00	23,863.55
For College Public Buildings, which are not valued in the Treasurer's books.		
Repairs and Equipment, ...	$8,319.09	
Caretaking and Operating Expenses, ...	21,546.99	29,866.08
For College Dormitories, Hollis, Stoughton, Holworthy, Thayer, Weld, Wadsworth House, Walter Hastings, Perkins, and Conant, which are not valued in the Treasurer's books; and for Matthews Hall.		
Repairs and Equipment, ...	$10,928.89	
Caretaking and Operating Expenses, ...	28,510.11	39,439.00
Summer School.		
Dean's Office:		

Salary of Dean, ...	$1,000.00		
Services and wages, ...	975.36		
Office supplies and expenses, . .	1,053.43		
Sundries, ...	38.40	$3,067.19	
Salaries, ...		17,318.00	
Services and wages, ...		228.50	
Office supplies and expenses, ...		721.57	
Receptions, ...		390.32	
Extra Janitor service, ...		54.10	
Remission of Tuition Fees, ...		140.00	
Sundries, ...		88.29	
School of Physical Education, ...		5,339.37	
Amounts carried forward, ...		$27,347.34	$321,319.03

COLLEGE (CONTINUED)

EXPENDITURE

Amounts brought forward, ...		$27,347.34	$321,319.03

Summer School (*continued*).

University charge:

Bursar's Office, collections and payments, ...	$454.40		
Publication Office, salaries and expenses, ...	236.91	691.31	28,038.65

General.

Salaries for Instruction:

Edward Austin (part):

Austin Teaching Fellowships, $12,500.00		
From Sundry Funds and Gifts, .	210,178.74	
From General Income, ...	260,186.89	$482,865.63

Services and wages, ...	5,365.49	
Proctors, ...	2,507.83	
Equipment and supplies, ...	1,047.02	
Blue-books, ...	522.50	
Printing, ...	6,472.25	
Pension for Bell-Ringer, ...	625.00	
Diplomas, ...	882.35	
Rooms for Visiting German Professor, ...	465.54	
Office Expenses, **Lawrence** Hall, ...	959.45	
Installation new boiler in **Peabody** Museum in 1909–10, ...	1,883.74	
Monitorships, ...	1,229.90	
Special lecturers, ...	600.00	
Subscription to American School of Classical Studies, ...	250.00	
Music Class Day, ...	125.00	
Fees for Summer Mining Camp received in 1909–10 and now paid to the Camp, ...	625.00	
Collection of term-bills, ...	95.79	
Refreshments at Faculty Meetings, ...	84.41	
Tuition fees of Students at Massachusetts Institute of Technology, ...	210.00	
College Entrance Examination Board, ...	100.00	
Graduate School Reception, ...	87.50	
Sundries, ...	929.10	507,933.50

Printing Office.

Services and wages, ...	$21,440.67	
Supplies and equipment, ...	18,289.91	
Printing, ...	7,159.78	
Repairs, ...	739.55	
Water, heat, light, and protection, ...	405.40	
Binding, ...	6,681.86	

Amounts carried forward, ...		$54,667.17	$857,291.18

EXPENDITURE

Amounts brought forward, ...	$54,667.17	$857,291.18
General (*continued*).		
New press and changes in office, ...	3,156.12	
Sundries, freight, etc., ...	115.97	
	$57,939.26	
Less sales to Departments, ...	56,677.59	1,261.67
Admission Examinations.		
Cambridge :		
Services and wages, ...	$3,059.72	
Reading books, ...	5,185.63	
Office supplies and expenses, ...	1,473.19	
Sundries, ...	588.77	10,307.31
Advertising, Graduate School of Arts and Sciences, ...		46.00
Annals of Mathematics, ...		2,789.96
Payments made from College Income for the following accounts :		
Jefferson Physical Laboratory, Schedule 8,	$600.00	
Graduate School of Applied Science, Schedule 11, ...	76,127.85	
Museum of Comparative Zoölogy, Schedule 23,	3,746.25	
Peabody Museum of American Archaeology and Ethnology, Schedule 24, ...	229.42	
William Hayes Fogg Art Museum, Schedule 27, ...	2,630.12	
Appleton Chapel, Schedule 28, ...	442.14	
Phillips Brooks House, Schedule 29, . .	1,191.12	
Hemenway Gymnasium, " 30, .	7,726.14	92,693.04
University charge.		
President's Office, salaries and expenses, ...	$7,138.40	
Treasurer's Office, care of investments, ...	5,976.21	
Bursar's Office :		
Collections and payments, ... $12,126.73		
Letting College rooms, ... 800.00	12,926.73	
Employment Office and Teachers' Agency, salaries and expenses, ...	5,096.72	
Medical Adviser, salary and expenses, ...	2,212.39	
Inspector of Grounds and Buildings, salary and expenses, ...	8,437.65	
Publication Office, salary and expenses, ...	2,221.04	
40 % Quinquennial Catalogue, ...	2,124.13	
57 % Annual Catalogue, ...	2,389.23	
90 % Memorial Hall and Sanders Theatre, expenses for the building, ...	1,741.57	
Watchmen, ...	1,995.44	
Amounts carried forward, ...	$47,259.51	$964,389.16

COLLEGE (continued)

EXPENDITURE

Amounts brought forward, ...		$47,259.51	$964,389.16
University charge (*continued*).			
Labor, etc., ...		7,458.95	
Alumni Office, ...		1,767.52	
Engineer, ...		1,143.51	
Janitor, ...		1,997.92	59,627.41
			$1,024,016.57

General surplus made up as follows:

Restricted Income unused carried to

Funds and Gifts, ...	$28,909.00	
General Suspense, ...	6,866.84	
	$35,275.84	

Less General Deficit made up as follows:

Advances to Funds and Gifts

carried to General Suspense,	$5,716.83		
Deficit carried to Schedule 10, .	26,624.96	32,341.79	2,934.05
			$1,026,950.62

SCHEDULE 9

LIBRARY

INCOME AND EXPENDITURE

For the year ended June 30, 1911

INCOME

Income of Book Funds and Gifts and Receipts for the
purchase of books.

Nathaniel I. Bowditch, ...		$102.09
Bright Legacy (½ income), ...	$1,212.50	
" Balance (interest), ...	2.86	1,215.36
William R. Castle, ...		61.46
Edwin Conant (¼ income), ...		338.24
Constantius (½ income), ...		627.88
Archibald C. Coolidge and Clarence L. Hay		208.89
W. Bayard Cutting Bequest, ...		420.20
Bayard Cutting Fellowship, ...		505.20
Denny, ...		256.42
Eliza Farrar, ...		271.31
Charles Gross Memorial, ...		44.87
Price Greenleaf (part), ...		1,000.00
Horace A. Haven, ...		163.86
Francis B. Hayes, ...		485.44
George Hayward, ...		260.74
Amount carried forward, ...		$5,961.96

LIBRARY (CONTINUED)

INCOME

Amount brought forward, ...	$5,961.96	
Income of Book Funds and Gifts and Receipts for the purchase of books (*continued*).		
Thomas Hollis, ...	113.88	
Sidney Homer, ...	105.39	
Jarvis, ...	24.98	
Frederick A. Lane, ...	255.21	
George C. Lodge and Joseph Trumbull Stickney Memorial, ...	23.15	
Lowell, ...	1,877.16	
Charles Minot, ...	2,911.36	
Charles Eliot Norton, ...	434.32	
Lucy Osgood, ...	344.55	
Mary Osgood, ...	338.24	
Francis Parkman Memorial, ...	271.88	
George F. Parkman, ...	1,223.41	
Francis Sales, ...	189.97	
Salisbury, ...	262.82	
Sever, ...	995.95	
Samuel Shapleigh, ...	191.58	
George B. Sohier (part), ...	103.08	
Strobel Memorial (Class of 1877), ...	126.00	
Strobel Memorial (Siam), ...	94.24	
Subscription, ...	509.30	
Charles Sumner, ...	1,811.38	
Kenneth Matheson Taylor, ...	250.21	
Daniel Treadwell (½ income), ...	289.18	
John Harvey Treat Book Fund, ...	899.85	
Ichabod Tucker, ...	214.79	
20th Mass. Regiment of Volunteer Infantry, . . .	15.08	
Wales Income for Books, ...	170.39	
James Walker, ...	774.01	
Thomas W. Ward, ...	254.63	
Julian Palmer Welsh Memorial, ...	138.51	
J. Huntington Wolcott, ...	970.00	
Gifts for books. Gifts, ... $10,429.58		
Interest, ... 172.17	10,601.75	
Sale of duplicate books, ...	285.04	
Received for books lost, ...	135.05	$32,618.05
Income of R. M. Hodges Fund (part).		
For publishing bibliographical contributions, ...		488.69
Income of Funds for general purposes.		
Daniel Austin, ...	$378.64	
Edwin Conant (¾ income), ...	1,014.72	
Constantius (½ income), ...	627.88	
Amounts carried forward, ...	$2,021.24	$33,051.74

LIBRARY (continued)

INCOME

Amounts brought forward, ...	$2,021.24	$33,051.74
Income of Funds for general purposes (continued).		
Fund of the **Class of 1851**, ...	41.08	
" " " " (**C. F. Dunbar's** Gift),	40.45	
Price Greenleaf (part), ...	15,944.54	
Henry L. Pierce, ...	2,425.00	
Henry L. Pierce, Residuary (part), ...	2,366.59	
Stephen Salisbury Bequest, ...	248.82	
James Savage (part), ...	1,802.75	
Daniel Treadwell (½ income), ...	289.18	
Eben Wright, ...	4,850.00	29,529.15
Fees for use of Library, ...	$105.00	
Fines, ...	549.85	
Gifts for additional service, ...	1,600.00	
Gift for cases, ...	2,000.00	
Gifts for general use, ...	13.25	
Sales of Bibliographical Contributions, ...	3.94	
Sales of Sundry publications, ...	2.48	4,273.97
		$66,854.86
General Deficit, made up as follows:		
Advances to Funds, carried to General Suspense, .	$207.22	
Deficit carried to Schedule 10, ...	36,325.64	
	$36,532.86	
Less Restricted Income unused, added to		
Funds and Gifts, ...	$3,954.22	
carried to General Suspense to repay		
former advances, ...	778.51	4,727.73	31,805.13
		$98,659.99

EXPENDITURE

For Books, from the following Funds, Gifts, etc.	
Bowditch, ...	$50.84
Bright, ...	960.95
Castle, ...	5.79
Edwin Conant, ...	333.26
Constantius, ...	707.08
W. Bayard Cutting Bequest, ...	411.00
Bayard Cutting Fellowship, ...	487.50
Denny, ...	206.40
Farrar, ...	292.70
Price Greenleaf (part), ...	928.67
Charles Gross Memorial, ...	30.86
Haven, ...	362.31
Hayes, ...	438.77
Amount carried forward, ...	$5,211.13

LIBRARY (CONTINUED)

EXPENDITURE

Amount brought forward, ...	$5,211.13	

For Books, from the following Funds, Gifts, etc. (continued).

Hayward, ...	286.98	
Hollis, ...	77.71	
Homer, ...	137.20	
Jarvis, ...	35.87	
Lane, ...	132.07	
Lowell, ...	826.28	
Minot, ...	3,007.22	
Charles Eliot Norton, ...	184.09	
Lucy Osgood, ...	285.01	
Mary Osgood, ...	281.05	
Francis Parkman Memorial, ...	303.29	
George F. Parkman, ...	1,285.68	
Sales, ...	144.74	
Salisbury, ...	192.39	
Sever, ...	1,148.30	
Shapleigh, ...	179.42	
George B. Sohier (part), ...	6.84	
Strobel Memorial (1877), ...	14.69	
" " (Siam), ...	19.11	
Subscription, ...	428.91	
Sumner, ...	1,717.98	
Kenneth Matheson Taylor, ...	333.92	
Daniel Treadwell, ...	270.52	
John Harvey Treat, ...	42.97	
Tucker, ...	182.92	
Wales, ...	273.54	
Walker, ...	829.09	
Ward, ...	315.26	
Julian Palmer Welsh Memorial, ...	75.00	
J. Huntington Wolcott, ...	834.32	
From Sundry gifts for books (balances), ...	9,757.55	
Duplicate money and receipts for lost books, . . .	367.47	
Fines, ...	1,300.07	$30,438.54
From R. M. Hodges Fund, publishing bibliographical contributions, ...		922.14

General.

Salaries, ...	$23,203.33	
Services and wages (part), ...	23,664.01	
Equipment and supplies, ...	2,684.13	
Stationery, postage, telephone and telegraph, . . .	793.92	
Binding, ...	4,521.99	
Freight, express, etc., ...	568.19	
Amounts carried forward, ...	$55,430.57	$31,360.68

LIBRARY (CONTINUED)

EXPENDITURE

Amounts brought forward, ...	$55,430.57	$31,360.68
General (*continued*).		
Moving and cleaning books, ...	359.50	
Laundry, ...	42.50	
Sundries, ...	395.92	
Special Reference Libraries, services, ...	1,451.90	
Repairs and equipment, land and building, ...	2,041.70	
Caretaking, land and building, ...	4,486.24	64,208.33
From Gifts.		
Additional service in main library, ...		1,401.43
University charge:		
Treasurer's Office, care of investments, ...	$747.08	
Bursar's Office, collections and payments, ...	439.90	
Inspector of Grounds and Buildings, salary and		
expenses, ...	220.66	
Annual Catalogue, ...	12.58	
Watchmen, ...	184.00	
Engineer, ...	85.33	1,689.55
		$98,659.99

SCHEDULE 10

UNIVERSITY, COLLEGE, AND LIBRARY COMBINED ACCOUNTS

For the year ended June 30, 1911

Deficit in College, Schedule 8, ...	$26,624.96	
Deficit in Library, Schedule 9, ...	36,325.64	$62,950.60
Surplus in University, Schedule 7, ...		34,417.76
Deficit met by the unrestricted principal of the **Walter F. Baker** Fund, ...		$28,532.84

GRADUATE SCHOOL OF APPLIED SCIENCE

INCOME AND EXPENDITURE

For the year ended June 30, 1911

INCOME

Income of Funds for Instruction or for General Purposes.

Edward Austin (part):

Austin Teaching Fellowships,	$1,500.00	
Henry Flynt (part),	4.35	
James Lawrence (part),	1,221.59	
Gordon McKay Endowment,	60,612.82	
Professorship of Engineering,	1,979.09	
Nelson Robinson, Jr. (part),	21,113.46	
Arthur Rotch,	1,212.50	
Gurdon Saltonstall,	2,910.00	
Josiah Stickney,	571.91	$91,125.72

Income of Fellowship Funds.

Julia Amory Appleton,	$1,014.67	
Nelson Robinson, Jr. (part),	983.32	
Frederick Sheldon (part),	1,200.00	3,197.99

Income of Scholarship Funds.

Edward Austin (part):

Austin Scholarships in Architecture,	$900.00	
Bright (part),	250.00	
Daniel A. Buckley (part),	150.00	
Francis H. Cummings,	318.89	
Joseph Eveleth (part),	600.00	
William Hilton (part),	225.00	
Priscilla Clark Hodges,	203.55	
Hennen Jennings,	573.27	
Henry Weidemann Locke (gift),	100.00	
Mining and Metallurgy Department (gift),	499.92	
Edward Dyer Peters (gift),	250.00	4,070.63

Income Loan Funds and Repayments.

Lawrence Scientific School Loans repaid:

Interest,	$222.71	
Loans repaid,	2,671.65	
Gift,	50.00	$2,944.36

Susan B. Lyman (L.S.S.):

Interest,	$96.82		
Loans repaid,	27.00	123.82	3,068.18

Income Sundry Funds and Gifts for Special Purposes.

Department of Architecture:

Nelson Robinson, Jr. Fund (part),	$4,335.72	
Gift for Equipment (interest),	251.00	

N. Robinson special gift for salary:

Gift,	$15,000.00	
Interest,	196.04	15,196.04

Amounts carried forward,	$19,782.76	$101,462.52

GRADUATE SCHOOL OF APPLIED SCIENCE (CONTINUED)

INCOME

Amounts brought forward, ...	$19,782.76	$101,462.52

Income Sundry Funds and Gifts for Special Purposes
(*continued*).

Department of Engineering:

Engineering Camp at Squam Lake, ...		18,916.81

Department of Forestry:

Gift for Division of Forestry, ...			5,455.00
Sales lumber, wood, etc., ...		$436.73	
Lodgings at Forestry House, . .		146.00	
Interest on balance, ...		26.72	609.45

Nelson Robinson, Jr., Special
Expense Gift:

Sale of Manual of Northern Woodsmen, ...		$748.25	
Interest on balance, ...		92.04	840.29

Department of Mining and Metallurgy:

Summer School Mining Camp — interest, . .		24.71	45,629.02

Receipts from Students.

Tuition fees, ...	$17,185.00	
Graduation fees, ...	800.00	

Laboratory fees:

Engineering, ...	$1,093.50	
Forestry, ...	95.00	
Mining and Metallurgy, ...	2,336.17	3,524.67
Shop-work fees, ...	1,059.00	22,568.67

Sundries.

Amount contributed from the General Funds of Harvard College for Salaries and Expenses, . .	$76,127.85	
Amount contributed by Bussey Institution to pay salary of instructor in Landscape Architecture,	1,800.00	77,927.85
		$247,588.06

EXPENDITURE

From Fellowship Funds.

Julia Amory Appleton, ...	$1,000.00	
Nelson Robinson, Jr., ...	983.32	
Frederick Sheldon (part), ...	1,200.00	$3,183.32

From Scholarship Funds and Gifts.

Edward Austin Scholarships in Architecture,	$900.00	
Bright, ...	250.00	
Daniel A. Buckley, ...	150.00	
Francis H. Cummings, ...	275.00	
Joseph Eveleth, ...	600.00	
William Hilton (part), ...	225.00	
Priscilla Clark Hodges, ...	175.00	
Hennen Jennings, ...	525.00	
Amounts carried forward, ...	$3,100.00	$3,183.32

GRADUATE SCHOOL OF APPLIED SCIENCE (CONTINUED)

EXPENDITURE

Amounts brought forward, ...	$3,100.00	$3,188.82

From Scholarship Funds and Gifts (*continued*).

Mining and Metallurgy Department Scholarship

(gift), ...	150.00	
Edward Dyer Peters, ...	250.00	3,500.00

From Loan Funds.

Edward Austin Loans repaid, ...	$60.00	
Lawrence Scientific School Loans repaid, . . .	260.00	320.00

For University Scholarships.

Architectural League, ...	$450.00	
General, ...	1,770.00	2,220.00

From Sundry Funds and Gifts for Special Purposes.

Department of Architecture :

Equipment, ...			$1,028.89

Nelson Robinson, Jr.:

Expense of Nelson Robinson, Jr.

Hall, ...		$3,925.17	

University charge :

Bursar, ...	$41.75		
Inspector of Grounds and			
Buildings, ...	125.86		
Janitor, ...	89.85		
Engineer, ...	48.50		
Watchman, ...	104.59	410.55	4,335.72

Department of Engineering :

Gift for Electrical Apparatus, ...	.18	
Engineering Camp at Squam Lake, ...	18,345.20	

Department of Forestry :

John S. Ames gift, ...	15.00	
Ames Butler gift, ... $2,717.69		
Less amount paid for salaries, 2,000.00	717.69	
Operations, ...	8,085.77	
House account, ...	186.07	
Nelson Robinson, Jr. special expense gift,	865.28	

Department of Mining and Metallurgy :

Summer Course Mining Camp gift, ...	95.67	28,674.87

Dean's Office :

Salary, ...	$2,500.00	
Services and wages, ...	907.75	
Equipment and supplies, ...	129.82	
Stationery, postage, telephone and telegraph, . .	160.24	
Printing, ...	37.40	
Sundries, ...	39.15	3,774.36

Amount carried forward, ...		$41,672.55

GRADUATE SCHOOL OF APPLIED SCIENCE (CONTINUED)
EXPENDITURE

Amount brought forward, ...		$41,672.55
From Appropriations:		
Architecture, ... :. .	$798.96	
Landscape Architecture, ...	1,950.86	
Engineering, ...	26,794.29	
Forestry, ...	270.77	
Mining and Metallurgy, ...	1,801.38	31,616.26
From Laboratory Fees:		
Engineering, ...	$1,093.50	
Forestry, ...	95.00	
Mining and Metallurgy, ...	2,282.24	3,470.74

General.

Salaries for Instruction:

Edward Austin (part):

Austin Teaching Fellowships,	$1,500.00	
From Sundry Funds and Gifts, .	27,688.38	
From General Income, ...	88,869.32	$118,057.70
Services and wages, ...		537.10
Equipment and supplies, ...		2.93
Stationery and postage, ...		42.48
Printing, ...		1,226.60
Travelling expenses, ...		500.00
Shop-work courses, ...		1,161.30
Taxes Harvard Forest, ...		2,955.29
Advertising, ...		50.00
Diplomas, ...		24.91
Sundries, ...		60.30
Repairs and Equipment, Pierce Hall and Rotch Building, ...		3,330.82
Caretaking, Pierce Hall and Rotch Building, . . .		6,602.01	134,551.44

University charge.

President's Office, salaries and expenses, ...	$322.33	
Treasurer's Office, care of investments, ...	1,194.04	
Bursar's Office, collections and payments, ...	1,204.83	
Publication Office, salary and expenses, ...	118.46	
Inspector of Grounds and Buildings, salary and expenses, ...	407.51	
Medical adviser, salary and expenses, ...	99.78	
Quinquennial Catalogue, ...	21.08	
Annual Catalogue, ...	146.71	
Watchmen, ...	167.97	
Engineer, ...	30.89	
Labor, etc., ...	3.34	3,716.94
Amount carried forward, ...		$215,027.93

GRADUATE SCHOOL OF APPLIED SCIENCE (continued)

EXPENDITURE

Amount brought forward, ...		$215,027.93
Phillips Brooks House, Schedule 29, ...	$53.72	
Hemenway Gymnasium, Schedule 30, ...	348.08	401.80
		$215,429.73

General Surplus, made up as follows:
Restricted Income unused, carried to
Funds and Gifts, ... $23,295.06
General Suspense, ... 625.54
Surplus carried to General Suspense.
Unexpended balances, $8,854.52
Reserve, ... 2,045.60 10,900.12 $34,820.72
Less advances carried to General Suspense, . . . 2,662.39 32,158.33

$247,588.06

GRADUATE SCHOOL OF BUSINESS ADMINISTRATION

INCOME AND EXPENDITURE

For the year ended June 30, 1911

INCOME

Graduate School of Business Administration Balance (interest), .		$361.04
Gifts for immediate use.		
Under the guarantee, ...	$26,750.00	
Other Gifts:		
For general use, ...	550.00	
For loans — interest, ...	20.00	
Gift of **Daniel W. Field**, Equipment of reading room, ...	500.00	
Gift of **Andrew W. Preston**, South American Course, ...	3,333.33	
Gift of **Warren D. Robbins**, South American Course, ...	100.00	
Gift of **Joseph E. Sterrett**, books on accounting, ...	100.00	31,353.33
Receipts from students.		
Tuition fees, ...	$8,625.00	
Graduation fees, ...	180.00	
Rental stop watches, ...	27.00	8,832.00
		$40,546.37

GRADUATE SCHOOL OF BUSINESS (CONTINUED)

EXPENDITURE

From Gifts for Loans,	$290.00	
From George O. May Gift for Prizes,	300.00	
From Joseph E. Sterrett Gift for Books,	15.90	
From Shaw Fund for Business Research,	150.00	$755.

Dean's Office.

Salary,	$500.00	
Services and wages,	923.62	
Expenses,	443.48	1,867.1

General.

Salaries,	$22,595.00	
Services and wages,	303.00	
Outside lecturers,	5,288.62	
Books,	1,499.60	
Expenses of course in Technique of Printing,	1,425.00	
Equipment and supplies,	286.29	
Stationery, postage, telephone and telegraph,	43.49	
Printing,	207.25	
Hospitality and travelling expenses,	472.44	
Scholarships from unrestricted income,	450.00	
Fitting up library in Lawrence Hall,	1,164.32	
Study Tours,	160.88	
Diplomas,	6.60	
Sundries,	96.26	33,998.7

University charge:

President's Office, salaries and expenses,	$192.98	
Bursar's Office, collections and payments,	342.38	
Medical Adviser, salary and expenses,	59.87	
Publication Office, salary and expenses,	236.91	
Annual Catalogue,	75.47	907.6

Phillips Brooks House, Schedule 29,	$32.23	
Hemenway Gymnasium, Schedule 30,	209.28	241.5
		$37,770.8

Reserve, carried to General Suspense, for use after the expiration of the guarantee,		$3,311.40	
Less principal of Sundry gifts used,	$285.90		
Advances to Sundry gifts carried to General Suspense,	250.00	535.90	2,775.

DIVINITY SCHOOL

INCOME AND EXPENDITURE

For the year ended June 30, 1911

INCOME

Income of Funds for Instruction or for General Purposes.

Divinity School balance (interest), ...	$780.56	
Endowment, ...	3,464.21	
Oliver Ames, ...	824.50	
Hannah C. Andrews, ...	25.46	
Daniel Austin, ...	54.08	
Adams Ayer, ...	48.50	
Joseph Baker, ...	740.84	
Beneficiary money returned (balance), ...	11.69	
Bussey Professorship, ...	1,822.82	
Bussey Trust (part), ...	5,246.34	
Joshua Clapp, ...	105.63	
Edwin Conant, ...	215.05	
Dexter Lectureship, ...	1,288.88	
Frothingham Professorship, ...	2,725.85	
Abraham W. Fuller, ...	50.92	
Lewis Gould, ...	44.18	
John Hancock Professorship, . . . $291.39		
Charles L. Hancock (part), . . 308.61	600.00	
Haven, ...	242.50	
Samuel Hoar, ...	50.93	
Hollis Professorship of Divinity, ...	1,674.12	
Henry P. Kidder, ...	485.00	
Henry Lienow, ...	445.47	
Caroline Merriam, ...	50.92	
John Newgate, ...	16.15	
Parkman Professorship, ...	776.78	
John W. Quinby, ...	88.13	
Abby Crocker Richmond, ...	48.50	
John L. Russell, ...	48.50	
William B. Spooner, ...	485.00	
Thomas Tileston of New York Endowment, .	1,940.00	
Mary P. Townsend, ...	254.63	
Winthrop Ward, ...	101.85	
Winn Professorship, ...	2,829.78	
Augustus Woodbury Bequest, ...	50.34	
Society for Promoting Theological Education Gift,		
Library, ...	714.27	$28,247.38

Income of Scholarship, Beneficiary and Prize Funds.

Robert Charles Billings (prizes), ...	$128.57	
Abner W. Buttrick, ...	659.50	
Thomas Cary, ...	283.58	
Amounts carried forward, ...	$1,071.65	$28,247.38

DIVINITY SCHOOL (CONTINUED)
INCOME

Amounts brought forward,.	$1,071.65	$38,247.38
Income of Scholarship, Beneficiary and Prize Funds (*continued*).		
George Chapman, ...	142.35	
Joshua Clapp, ...	227.76	
Jackson Foundation, ...	750.30	
J. Henry Kendall, ...	286.63	
Nancy Kendall, ...	174.44	
William Pomroy, ...	50.92	2,704.10
Income of Funds and Gifts.		
Rushton Dashwood Burr, ...	$208.36	
Louisa J. Hall, ...	46.90	
Horace S. Sears Gift, Lectures, ...	1,700.00	1,955.26
Receipts from Students.		
Tuition fees, regular courses, ...	$5,679.53	
Divinity Hall, rents, ...	3,010.00	
Library fines, ...	10.35	8,699.88
Summer School of Theology, Tuition fees, ...	$629.50	
Sale Dr. Everett's books, ...	8.00	
" General Catalogue, ...	85.00	
" Alumni Dinner Tickets, ...	102.00	824.50
		$42,431.12

EXPENDITURE

From Scholarship Funds.		
Thomas Cary, ...	$250.00	
George Chapman, ...	125.00	
Joshua Clapp, ...	200.00	
Jackson Foundation, ...	640.00	
J. Henry Kendall, ...	250.00	
Nancy Kendall, ...	150.00	$1,615.00
From Beneficiary Funds.		
Abner W. Buttrick, ...	$575.00	
William Pomroy, ...	42.00	617.00
From Robert Charles Billings Fund, prize, ...		100.00
From Funds and Gifts.		
Rushton Dashwood Burr, ...	$154.84	
Louisa J. Hall, ...	34.29	
Horace S. Sears Gift for Lectures, ...	500.00	689.13
Dean's Office.		
Stationery, postage, telephone and telegraph, . . .	$49.26	
Printing, ...	29.08	
Sundries, ...	2.25	80.59
Amount carried forward, ...		$3,101.72

DIVINITY SCHOOL (CONTINUED)

EXPENDITURE

Amount brought forward, ... $3,101.72

General.

Salaries, ...	$24,520.00	
Services and wages, ...	1,820.67	
Equipment and supplies, ...	67.84	
Stationery, postage, telephone and telegraph, . . .	97.59	
Books, ...	381.25	
Advertising, ...	427.06	
Care of grounds, ...	120.00	
Printing, ...	618.85	
Summer School of Theology, ...	1,076.07	
Alumni Dinner, ...	78.00	
Lectures, President Harada, ...	100.00	
Contribution American School of Archaeology, . .	100.00	
Binding, ...	48.20	
Sundries, ...	5.48	29,461.28

Divinity Library.

Repairs and equipment, land and building, ...	$57.11	
Caretaking, land and building, ...	1,084.70	1,141.81

Divinity Hall.

Repairs and equipment, land and building, ...	$378.21	
Caretaking, land and building, ...	1,960.98	2,339.19

University charge.

President's Office, salaries and expenses, ...	$99.77	
Treasurer's Office, care of investments, ...	519.85	
Bursar's Office, collections and payments, ...	264.03	
Medical Adviser, salary and expenses, ...	31.01	
Inspector of Grounds and Buildings, salary and expenses, ...	133.65	
Publication Office, salary and expenses, ...	14.81	
Quinquennial Catalogue, ...	73.79	
Annual Catalogue, ...	150.90	
Labor, etc., ...	360.93	
Watchmen, ...	54.92	
Engineer, ...	50.17	
Janitor, ...	92.91	1,846.74

Semitic Museum, Schedule 25, ...	$414.39	
Phillips Brooks House, Schedule 29, ...	16.69	
Hemenway Gymnasium, Schedule 30, ...	107.35	538.43
		$38,429.12

General Surplus, made up as follows:

Restricted Income unused, added to Funds and Gifts,	$2,683.05	
Surplus, carried to General Suspense, ...	1,318.95	4,002.00
		$42,431.12

LAW SCHOOL

INCOME AND EXPENDITURE

For the year ended June 30, 1911

INCOME

Income of Funds and Gifts.

Law School balance (interest),			$2,751.16
Ames Fund,			489.41
James Barr Ames Loan.			
Interest,		$31.91	
Repayments,		720.41	752.32
James Barr Ames Prize,			218.89
Gift of James Munson Barnard and Augusta Barnard (interest),			43.46
Bemis Professorship,			4,557.98
Bussey Professorship,			1,163.08
Bussey Trust (part),			5,246.32
James C. Carter Professorship,			5,396.01
James Coolidge Carter Loan:			
Interest,		$633.07	
Repayments,		86.39	719.46
Dane Professorship,			763.88
Samuel Phillips Prescott Fay 1798 Fund and Scholarship,			282.32
George Fisher Scholarship,			185.08
Hughes Loan.			
Repayments,			265.61
Langdell Scholarship,			1,269.15
Law School Book,			2,280.52
Law School Library,			4,850.00
Harry Milton Levy Loan:			
Interest,		$126.34	
Repayments,		396.04	522.38
Royall Professorship,			404.54
Weld "			4,607.26
Scholarship Money Returned:			
Gift,		$250.00	
Interest,		66.25	
Repayments,		1,226.83	1,543.08
Princeton Fellowship,			450.00
James A. Rumrill Scholarship,			225.00
Research Scholarship (gift),			250.00 $39,231.81

Gift for Prizes.

Joshua Montgomery Sears, Jr. Memorial:			
Gift,		$1,500.00	
Interest,		90.11	1,590.11
Tuition fees,			119,525.00
Sale of Quinquennial Catalogue,			11.50
Amount carried forward,			$160,358.42

LAW SCHOOL (CONTINUED)

INCOME

Amount brought forward,	$160,358.42
Sale of Library Catalogue,	55.00
Unclaimed locker deposits,	38.00
Fees for duplicate diplomas,	5.00
Amount collected on account of unpaid term-bills previously charged off,	59.52
	$160,515.94

EXPENDITURE

From Funds and Gifts.

James Barr Ames Prize,	$400.00	
Samuel Phillips Prescott Fay,	929.03	
George Fisher Scholarship,	150.00	
Langdell Scholarship,	1,150.00	
Harry Milton Levy Loan,	2,715.25	
Princeton Fellowship,	450.00	
James A. Rumrill Scholarship,	225.00	
Scholarship Money Returned Loan,	1,610.00	
Joshua M. Sears, Jr. Prize,	1,500.00	$9,129.28

Dean's and Secretary's Offices.

Salaries,	$2,500.00	
Services and wages,	828.58	
Stationery, postage, telephone and telegraph,	321.49	
Printing,	178.29	
Equipment and supplies,	162.51	
Sundries,	5.11	3,995.98
Scholarships from unrestricted income,		5,700.00

General.

Salaries,	$68,720.00	
Services and wages,	8,591.76	
Equipment and supplies,	674.47	
Stationery, postage, telephone and telegraph,	289.05	
Printing,	8,043.56	
Books,	21,189.51	
Binding,	2,192.46	
Advertising,	145.00	
Proctors,	728.00	
Freight,	851.16	
Travelling expenses,	194.30	
Diplomas,	257.99	
Diploma plate,	125.00	
Claim for injuries and legal expenses thereof,	1,090.85	
Sundries,	91.18	107,634.29
Repairs and equipment, land and buildings,		2,193.27
Caretaking, land and buildings,		8,033.81
Amount carried forward,		$136,686.63

LAW SCHOOL (CONTINUED)

EXPENDITURE

Amount brought forward, ... $136,686.63

University charge.

President's Office, salaries and expenses, ...	$2,152.15	
Treasurer's Office, care of investments, ...	555.00	
Bursar's Office, collections and payments, ...	2,580.24	
Medical Adviser, salary and expenses, ...	667.16	
Inspector of Grounds and Buildings, salary and expenses, ...	486.84	
Publication Office, salary and expenses, ...	7.40	
Quinquennial Catalogue, ...	426.94	
Annual Catalogue, ...	264.06	
Labor, etc., ...	289.69	
Watchmen, ...	200.28	
Janitor, ...	296.95	
Engineer, ...	160.25	8,086.96
Phillips Brooks House, Schedule 29, ...	$359.19	
Hemenway Gymnasium, Schedule 30, ...	2,330.31	2,689.50
		$147,463.09

General Surplus, made up as follows:

Restricted Income unused, added to Funds and Gifts,	$3,625.93	
Surplus, carried to General Suspense, ...	9,426.92	13,052.85
		$160,515.94

SCHEDULE 15

MEDICAL SCHOOL

INCOME AND EXPENDITURE

For the year ended June 30, 1911

INCOME

Income of Funds for Instruction and General Purposes.

Anonymous Fund in the Department of Theory and Practice, ...	$502.65
Edward M. Barringer (part), ...	968.19
Robert C. Billings, ...	4,850.00
John B. and **Buckminster Brown,**	1,204.11
Bullard Professorship of Neuropathology, . . .	3,691.63
John C. Cutter Bequest, ...	255.55
Calvin and **Lucy Ellis** (part), ...	17,528.80
Samuel E. Fitz, ...	89.05
Rebecca A. Greene Bequest, ...	15.96
Henry Harris (½ income), ...	726.02
Amount carried forward, ...	$29,831.96

MEDICAL SCHOOL (CONTINUED)

INCOME

Amount brought forward, ...		$29,831.96

Income of Funds for Instruction and General Purposes (*continued*).

Harvard Medical Alumni, ...	274.07	
Hersey Professorship (¾ income), ...	392.21	
George Higginson, ...	5,110.40	
John Homans Memorial, ...	2,533.64	
Jackson Professorship of Clinical Medicine, . .	3,355.86	
Hamilton Kuhn Memorial, ...	9,138.08	
William O. Moseley, ...	2,573.02	
New subscription, ...	1,884.23	
Lyman Nichols, ...	485.97	
George F. Parkman, Medical Fund, ...	416.18	

Henry L. Pierce (Residuary):

Sale of land, ...	$1,144.52		
Interest, ...	1,894.31	3,038.83	
John D. Rockefeller, ...		48,500.00	
Dr. Ruppaner, ...		452.80	
George C. Shattuck, ...		3,640.45	
James Stillman Professorship, ...		5,683.28	
Mary W. Swett, ...		764.60	
Samuel W. Swett, ...		970.00	
Quincy Tufts, ...		97.00	
Henry Willard Williams, ...		2,282.12	
Gifts for salaries, ...		6,300.00	
Gift toward cost new animal house, ...		800.00	$128,524.70

Income of Fellowship Funds.

Austin Teaching Fellowships, ...	$2,500.00	
Charles Follen Folsom Memorial, ...	643.11	
George Cheyne Shattuck Memorial, ...	270.78	
Frederick Sheldon, ...	1,335.13	
Charles Eliot Ware Memorial, ...	290.90	
John Ware "	267.91	
Henry P. Walcott, ...	1,060.99	6,368.82

Income of Funds and Gifts for Scholarships and Aids.

Anonymous Gift for Loans, ...	$150.00	
Edward M. Barringer (part), ...	500.00	
Lucius F. Billings, ...	263.35	
James Jackson Cabot, ...	306.47	
David Williams Cheever, ...	288.58	
Cotting Gift (interest), ...	161.55	
Orlando W. Doe, ...	148.12	
Joseph Eveleth (part), ...	600.00	
John Foster, ...	153.79	
Lewis and Harriet Hayden, ...	283.63	
Amounts carried forward, ...	$2,855.49	$134,893.52

MEDICAL SCHOOL (CONTINUED)
INCOME

Amounts brought forward, ...	$2,855.49	$134,893.52

Income of Funds and Gifts for Scholarships and Aids (*continued*).

William Hilton (part), ...	450.00	
William Otis Johnson, ...	26.29	
Claudius M. Jones, ...	329.85	
John R. Kissenger, ...	18.33	
Alfred Hosmer Linder, ...	277.47	
Loan Fund Medical School **Class of 1879** (Gift),	70.00	
James Ewing Mears (Gift), ...	225.00	
Joseph Pearson Oliver, ...	440.04	
Charles B. Porter, ...	287.94	
Francis Skinner, ...	260.30	
Charles Pratt Strong, ...	260.74	
Isaac Sweetser, ...	331.64	
John Thomson Taylor, ...	271.75	
Edward Wigglesworth, ...	278.78	6,383.57

Income of Prize Funds.

Ward Nicholas Boylston, ...	$220.92	
William H. Thorndike, ...	457.16	678.08

Income of Sundry Funds and Gifts for Special Purposes.

Frederick M. Allen Gift, Preventive Medicine,	$787.50	
Anatomical Research Gift, ...	500.00	
Edward Austin (Bacteriological Laboratory), .	548.20	
J. Ingersoll Bowditch, ...	319.81	
Boylston, for Medical Books, ...	81.14	
Katherine E. Bullard Gift, Neuropathology, .	1,200.00	
Gift for a salary, Cancer Commission, ...	450.00	
Memorial Cancer Hospital Endowment, ...	1,195.86	
Memorial Cancer Hospital Maintenance, ...	298.67	
Caroline Brewer Croft (part):		
Gifts, ...	$545.00	
Interest, ...	2,332.91	2,877.91
Sale Duplicate Books, Library, ...		191.46
George Fabyan Foundation for Comparative Pathology:		
Interest, ...	$10,006.71	
Sales, ...	161.65	10,168.36
George Fayban Foundation, Special, ...	454.44	
Charles F. Farrington, ...	2,548.82	
F. B. Greenough (for surgical research), . . .	286.98	
Henry Jackson Endowment, ...	4,995.85	
Walter Augustus Lecompte Professorship of Otology, ...	2,504.80	
Amounts carried forward, ...	$29,403.75	$141,955.17

MEDICAL SCHOOL (CONTINUED)

INCOME

Amounts brought forward, ... $29,408.75 $141,955.17

Income of Sundry Funds and Gifts for Special Purposes
  (*continued*).

Harriet Newell Lowell:

Gift, ...	$2,000.00	
Interest, ...	82.40	2,082.40

Massachusetts Society for Promoting Agriculture
  Gift, Comparative Pathology, ... 1,200.00
Medical Library, ... 112.71
Gift for Microscopes, etc., ... 807.20
Gift for Investigation of Infantile Paralysis:

Gift, ...	$3,975.00	
Interest, ...	111.98	4,086.98

Repayment Pathological Laboratory:

Gift, ...	$1,775.00	
Interest, ...	84.15	1,859.15

Gift for Pathological Laboratory (interest), ... 298 28

John C. Phillips Gift, Pathological
  Department. Gift, ... $8,000.00
  Interest, ... 79.44 8,079.44

Proctor, for the study of Chronic Diseases, . . . 2,634.28
Gift for Recreation Grounds, ... 950.00
Henry Francis Sears Fund for Pathology, . . 1,718.12
School of Comparative Medicine, ... 311.32
Storey Putnam Gift, Neuropathology, ... 1,400.00
Surgical Laboratory:

Gifts, ...	$1,105.20	
Interest, ...	263.11	1,368.31

X-ray Apparatus (interest), ... 88.28
Warren Fund for Anatomical Museum, ... 520.60
Edward Wigglesworth Professorship of Dermatology, ... 2,510.46 54,371.28

Sale of heat and power, ... $8,522.74
Clinic fees, ... 160.00 8,682.74

Receipts from students.
  Tuition Fees.

Regular courses, ...	$54,086.43	
Graduate courses, ...	4,045.88	
Dental students, ...	7,400.00	
Summer courses, ...	8,380.35	
Division of Medical Sciences, . . .	480.00	
Special students, ...	288.00	$74,680.66

Graduation fees, ... 60.00
Matriculation fees, ... 435.00

Amounts carried forward, ... $75,175.66 $200,009.19

MEDICAL SCHOOL (CONTINUED)

INCOME

Amounts brought forward, ...	$75,175.66	$200,009.19

Receipts from students (*continued*).

Examination fees, ...		117.00	

Laboratory fees and supplies.

Anatomy, ...	$935.00		
Comparative Anatomy, ...	53.75		
Chemistry, ...	1,094.58		
Clinical Laboratory, ...	99.18		
Histology, ...	357.25		
Physiology, ...	530.66		
Operative Surgery, ...	246.00		
Surgical Technique, ...	171.00	3,487.42	
Use of microscopes, ...		1,113.50	
Fines, ...		12.50	79,906.08
			$279,915.27

EXPENDITURE

From Fellowship Funds and Gifts.

Charles Follen Folsom Memorial, ...	$918.75	
George Cheyne Shattuck Memorial, ...	225.00	
Frederick Sheldon, ...	1,835.13	
Charles Eliot Ware Memorial, ...	250.00	
John Ware Memorial, ...	135.00	
Henry P. Walcott, ...	750.00	$3,613.88

From Scholarship and Aid Funds and Gifts.

Aesculapian Club, ...	$150.00	
Anonymous Gift for Loans, ...	150.00	
Edward M. Barringer (part), ...	500.00	
Lucius F. Billings, ...	225.00	
James Jackson Cabot, ...	275.00	
David Williams Cheever, ...	250.00	
Cotting Gift, ...	125.00	
Orlando W. Doe, ...	100.00	
Joseph Eveleth (part), ...	600.00	
John Foster, ...	150.00	
Lewis and Harriet Hayden, ...	225.00	
William Hilton (part), ...	450.00	
Claudius M. Jones, ...	250.00	
Alfred Hosmer Linder, ...	250.00	
Loan Fund Medical School Class of 1879, . . .	50.00	
James Ewing Mears, ...	225.00	
Joseph Pearson Oliver, ...	400.00	
Charles B. Porter, ...	250.00	
Francis Skinner, ...	150.00	
Charles Pratt Strong, ...	225.00	
Amounts carried forward, ...	$5,000.00	$3,613.88

MEDICAL SCHOOL (continued)

EXPENDITURE

Amounts brought forward	$5,000.00	$8,613.88

From Scholarship and Aid Funds and Gifts (*continued*).

Isaac Sweetser, ...	250.00	
John Thomson Taylor, ...	250.00	
Edward Wigglesworth, ...	250.00	5,750.00

From Prize Funds.

Boylston Prize expenses, ...	$13.60	
William H. Thorndike, ...	200.00	213.60

From Sundry Funds and Gifts for Special Purposes.

Frederick M. Allen Gift, Preventive Medicine,		$787.50	
Anatomical Research Gifts, ...		412.08	
Edward Austin (Bacteriological Laboratory), .		151.90	
Robert C. Billings, Journal of Medical Research,		300.00	
J. Ingersoll Bowditch, Physiology, ...		868.67	
Boylston, Medical Books, ...		79.49	
Mary L. Bremer Gift, Comparative Anatomy, .		245.13	
Katherine E. Bullard Gift, Neuropathology, .		1,124.78	
A. T. Cabot Gift, ...		6.20	
Gift for a salary, Cancer Commission, ...		250.00	
Caroline Brewer Croft (part):			
Cancer investigations, ...	$5,820.49		
Less paid for salaries, ...	3,500.00	2,320.49	
George Fabyan Foundation for Comparative			
Pathology, ...	$8,551.78		
Less paid for salaries, ...	5,000.00	3,551.78	
Gifts for the Investigation of Infantile Paralysis, .		356.02	
Henry Jackson Endowment:			
Warren Anatomical Museum, . .	$5,254.24		
Less paid for salaries, ...	2,500.00	2,754.24	
Walter Augustus Lecompte Pro-			
fessorship of Otology, ...	$2,018.77		
Less paid for salaries, ...	1,700.00	318.77	
Harriet Newell Lowell, ...		954.79	
Massachusetts Society for Promoting Agriculture			
Gift, Comparative Pathology, ...		239.48	
Medical Library, ...		110.89	
Gift for Microscopes, etc., ...		807.20	
Gift for Pathological Laboratory, ...		207.78	
Repayment Pathological Laboratory, ...		506.52	
John C. Phillips Gift, Pathological			
Department, ...	$2,652.04	.	
Less amount paid for salaries, . .	2,513.71	138.33	
Proctor, for the study of Chronic Diseases, . . .		3,053.58	
Henry Francis Sears Fund for Pathology, .		1,993.79	
Amounts carried forward, ...		$21,538.86	$9,577.48

MEDICAL SCHOOL (CONTINUED)
EXPENDITURE

Amounts brought forward,	$21,538.86	$9,577.48

From Sundry Funds and Gifts for Special Purposes (*continued*).

Storey Putnam Gifts, Neuropathology, $1,418.31		
Less amount paid for salaries, 300.00	1,118.31	
Surgical Laboratory,	1,883.49	
Edward Wigglesworth Professorship of Dermatology, $1,980.00		
Less paid for salaries, 1,500.00	480.00	
J. G. Wright Gift, Bacteriology,	86.75	
Gift for X-ray apparatus,	894.01	
Books, from proceeds of sale of duplicates,	188.56	25,689.98

Appropriations.

Advertising and catalogues,	$985.07	
Anatomy,	2,700.00	
Comparative Anatomy,	2,023.25	
Books and service for the library,	4,000.00	
Physiology,	1,928.10	
Comparative Physiology,	600.00	
Biological Chemistry,	2,503.69	
Bacteriology,	990.25	
Preventive Medicine and Hygiene,	2,061.09	
Materia Medica and Therapeutics,	998.78	
Theory and Practice of Physic,	1,884.72	
Clinical Medicine,	6.50	
Pediatrics,	149.58	
Surgery,	1,108.53	
Obstetrics,	50.00	
Neuropathology,	168.08	21,657.64

Dean's Office.

Salaries,	$1,500.00	
Services and wages,	2,100.00	
Equipment and supplies,	52.88	
Printing,	267.50	
Stationery, postage, telephone and telegraph,	501.55	4,421.93

General.

Salaries for instruction,	$126,961.93	
Summer courses. Fees repaid to instructors,	8,087.36	
Graduate courses. Fees repaid to instructors,	4,085.00	
Services and wages,	10,419.01	
Equipment and supplies,	1,115.97	
Stationery, postage, telephone and telegraph,	1,794.45	
Amounts carried forward,	$152,463.72	$61,347.03

MEDICAL SCHOOL (CONTINUED)

EXPENDITURE

Amounts brought forward, ...	$152,468.72	$61,347.03

General (*continued*).

Printing, ...	717.20	
Boston Medical Library, ...	300.00	
Diplomas, ...	97.34	
Travelling expense, ...	80.00	
Clinic, ...	1,949.18	
Proctors, ...	141.00	
Laying sidewalks, ...	217.00	
Printing and advertising for Summer courses, . . .	112.88	
Dues Association of Medical Colleges, ...	47.00	
Sundries, ...	42.48	
Repairs and equipment, land and buildings, ...	10,956.22	
Caretaking, land and buildings, ...	35,084.78	202,203.70
Retiring allowance, ...		1,000.00
Balance of payments on an annuity, Schedule 82, ...		273.44
Interest on advances, ...		929.41

University charge.

President's Office, salaries and expenses, ...	$746.60	
Treasurer's Office, care of investments, ...	2,330.17	
Bursar's Office, collections and payments, ...	1,960.06	
Inspector of Grounds and Buildings, salary and expenses, ...	1,480.17	
Publication Office, salary and expenses, ...	7.40	
Quinquennial Catalogue, ...	363.68	
Annual Catalogue, ...	402.86	7,290.44
		$273,049.02

General Surplus, made up as follows :

Restricted Income unused added to			
Funds and Gifts, ...		$16,765.87	
General Suspense, ...		.19	
		$16,766.06	
Less General Deficit carried to General Suspense :			
Advance to Gifts, ...	$746.02		
Deficit for year, ...	9,153.79	9,899.81	6,866.25
			$279,915.27

DENTAL SCHOOL

INCOME AND EXPENDITURE

For the year ended June 30, 1911

INCOME

Income of Funds and Gifts.

Dental School Endowment,	$470.94	
Harvard Dental Alumni Endowment,	278.58	
Joseph Warren Smith Jr.,	498.00	
Henry C. Warren Endowment,	1,115.50	
Proctor Bequest,	24.25	$2,387.27

Gifts for immediate use.

Dental School Research Fund,	$100.00	
Harriet Newell Lowell Gift for Research,	2,000.00	2,100.00

Receipts from students.

Tuition fees, regular courses, ... $19,188.57		
Less transferred to Medical School, 7,400.00	$11,788.57	
Tuition fees, evening courses,	500.00	
Chemistry, breakage and supplies,	664.89	
Amount collected on account of unpaid term-bills previously charged off,	.90	12,948.86
Fees from Infirmary,	. . . . .	8,944.63
Sale of gold,	$458.72	
" merchandise,	820.56	779.28

General Deficit made up as follows:

Deficit carried to General Suspense,	$9,841.94	
Less Restricted Income unused, added to Funds and Gifts,	1,091.00	8,350.94
		$35,410.98

EXPENDITURE

From Funds and Gifts.

Harriet Newell Lowell (salaries),	$1,000.00	
Gift for surgical instruments,	9.00	$1,009.00

Dean's Office.

Salaries,	$900.00	
Equipment and supplies,	69.60	
Stationery, postage, telephone and telegraph,	26.04	
Printing,	68.70	1,064.34

General.

Salaries for instruction,	$7,950.00	
Salaries, evening courses,	465.50	
Services and wages,	4,546.42	
Equipment and supplies,	7,194.66	
Stationery, postage, telephone and telegraph,	489.86	
Printing,	1,898.66	
Advertising,	725.08	
Amounts carried forward,	$22,770.13	$2,073.34

DENTAL SCHOOL (CONTINUED)

EXPENDITURE

Amounts brought forward,	$22,770.18	$2,073.84
General (*continued*).		
Binding Dental Journals,	11.25	
Mechanical Department sundries,	30.31	
Laundry,	581.29	
Quinquennial Catalogue,	5.50	
Diplomas,	26.88	
Rent of piano,	45.00	
Legal services,	30.00	
Laying sidewalk,	291.47	
Museum cases,	1,446.00	
Bronze tablet,	85.00	
Boston Medical Library,	50.00	
Dues to Dental Faculties Association of American Universities,	50.00	
Collation,	33.75	
Sundries,	88.50	25,495.08
Interest on advances,		88.68
Repairs and equipment, land and buildings,	$1,007.24	
Caretaking, land and buildings,	5,778.50	6,785.74
University charge.		
President's Office, salaries and expenses,	$311.37	
Treasurer's Office, care of investments,	35.64	
Bursar's Office, collections and payments,	350.28	
Inspector of Grounds and Buildings, salary and expenses,	104.40	
Publication Office, salary and expenses,	44.42	
Quinquennial Catalogue,	47.43	
Annual Catalogue,	79.65	973.19
		$35,410.98

SCHEDULE 17

BUSSEY INSTITUTION

INCOME AND EXPENDITURE

For the year ended June 30, 1911

INCOME

Income of Funds.		
Bussey Institution balance (interest),	$601.21	
Bussey Trust (part),	10,492.67	$11,093.88
Gifts for present use,		123.00
Sale of wood, hay, and sundries,	$20.68	
Board of animals,	83.35	
Amounts carried forward,	$104.03	$11,216.88

BUSSEY INSTITUTION (CONTINUED)
INCOME

Amounts brought forward, ...	$104.08	$11,216.88
Use of houses by College officers, ...	1,880.00	
Rent of Antitoxin stable, ...	1,008.82	
Sale of animals, ...	118.50	
Laboratory fees, ...	245.00	2,850.85
		$14,067.73
Deficit, met by accumulated income, carried to General Suspense, .		7,057.31
		$21,125.04

EXPENDITURE

Salaries, ...	$8,300.00	
Services and wages, ...	8,983.05	
Equipment and supplies, ...	4,891.15	
Stationery, postage, telephone and telegraph, ...	106.19	
Printing, ...	151.50	
Books, ...	502.41	
Legal services, ...	30.00	
Sundries, ...	111.15	
Repairs and equipment, land and buildings, ...	1,466.98	
Caretaking, land and buildings, ...	1,625.58	$20,668.01
University charge.		
Treasurer's Office, care of investments, ...	$187.13	
Bursar's Office, collections and payments, ...	175.11	
Inspector of Grounds and Buildings, salary and expenses, ...	94.79	457.03
		$21,125.04

ARNOLD ARBORETUM
INCOME AND EXPENDITURE
For the year ended June 30, 1911
INCOME

Income of Funds and Gifts.

Arnold Arboretum, ...		$6,285.80
James Arnold, ...		7,875.67
Arboretum Construction Gifts (interest), ...		1,780.09
Robert Charles Billings (part), ...		662.25
William L. Bradley Fund:		
Gift for present use, ...	$600.00	
Interest, ...	970.00	1,570.00
Amount carried forward, ...		$18,123.81

ARNOLD ARBORETUM (CONTINUED)
INCOME

Amount brought forward, ...		$18,123.81
Income of Funds and Gifts (*continued*).		
Francis Skinner, ...	970.00	
Bussey, for the **Arnold** Arboretum, ...	111.94	
Sears gift for Library, ...	206.08	$19,411.78
For botanical exploration in China.		
Interest, ...	$17.81	
Sale of photographs, ...	333.50	
Sale of botanical material, ...	3,342.85	
Gifts, ...	4,868.77	$8,562.93
Gifts for present uses, ...	22,625.00	
Gift for books :		
Gift, ...	$3,000.00	
Interest, ...	9.79	3,009.79
		34,197.72
Sale of publications, ...		75.00
		$53,684.50

EXPENDITURE

From **William L. Bradley** Fund, bibliography (part), ...		$1,570.00
From Chinese Exploration Gifts.		
Exploration in Northern China, ...	$2,920.00	
Third expedition, ...	4,766.71	
Carbon prints, ...	14.77	7,701.48
From gift for books, ...		3,009.79
From **Sears** Gift for Library, ...		1,321.88
General.		
Salaries, ...	$5,800.00	
Services and wages, ...	7,886.27	
Equipment and supplies, ...	3,883.30	
Stationery, postage, telephone and telegraph, . . .	273.03	
Printing, ...	499.27	
Labor, ...	9,923.92	
Water, heat, light, power and protection, ...	1,362.40	
Repairs and equipment, land and buildings, ...	1,818.66	
Rent of building, ...	150.00	
Bradley Bibliography of Trees, services, ...	2,655.42	
Expenses of expeditions for collecting, ...	961.53	
Freight, express, etc., ...	219.71	
Sundries, ...	84.00	35,517.51
University charge.		
Treasurer's Office, care of investments, ...	$261.39	
Bursar's Office, collections and payments, ...	182.16	443.55
		$49,564.16
Surplus made up as follows :		
Added to Sundry Funds and Gifts, ...	$139.43	
" " Arboretum Construction Gifts, ...	3,980.91	4,120.34
		$53,684.50

BOTANIC GARDEN

INCOME AND EXPENDITURE

For the year ended June 30, 1911

INCOME

Income of Funds.

Botanic Garden balance (interest), ...	$108.98	
Botanic Department (⅓ income), ...	1,205.83	
Lowell, for a Botanic Garden, ...	3,310.46	
John L. Russell (¼ income), ...	24.25	$4,649.47

Gifts.

For cases (interest), ...	$14.91	
For sugar-cane investigation (interest), ...	15.71	
For immediate use, ...	8,012.00	8,042.62
Laboratory fees in Botany, ...	$210.00	
Material supplied Radcliffe College, ...	100.00	
Sale of house and land, ...	3,000.00	3,310.00
		$16,002.09

EXPENDITURE

Services and wages, ...	$135.39	
Labor, ...	4,659.07	
Equipment and supplies, ...	785.11	
Stationery, postage, telephone and telegraph, ...	76.00	
Printing, ...	1.10	
Water, heat, light, power and protection, ...	1,019.48	
Repairs and equipment, land and buildings, ...	546.80	
Taxes, ...	157.30	
New greenhouses, ...	7,000.00	
Collecting plants and seeds, ...	250.00	
Books, ...	68.18	
Express and cartage, ...	44.96	
Sundries, ...	4.75	$14,748.14

University charge.

Treasurer's Office, care of investments, ...	$63.86	
Bursar's Office, collections and payments, ...	38.67	102.53
		$14,850.67

General surplus, made up as follows:

Restricted Income unused, added to Funds and Gifts,	$30.62	
Surplus, carried to General Suspense, ...	1,120.80	1,151.42
		$16,002.09

BOTANICAL MUSEUM

INCOME AND EXPENDITURE

For the year ended June 30, 1911

INCOME

Gift for present use.

Gift for Botanical Museum, ...		$3,050.00

EXPENDITURE

Services and wages, ...	$862.00	
Equipment and supplies, ...	311.06	
Telephone, ...	42.97	
Printing, ...	77.25	
Books, ...	76.41	
Repairs, ...	38.21	
Express, ...	2.00	$1,409.90
University charge.		
Bursar's Office, collections and payments, ...		24.39
		$1,434.29
Surplus carried to General Suspense, ...		1,615.71
		$3,050.00

GRAY HERBARIUM

INCOME AND EXPENDITURE

For the year ended June 30, 1911

INCOME

Income of Funds.

Gray Herbarium balance (interest), ...	$328.83	
Robert Charles Billings, ...	727.50	
Asa Gray Memorial, ...	1,586.48	
Asa Gray Professorship of Systematic Botany, . .	1,040.37	
Herbarium, ...	1,001.82	
Sarah E. Potter Endowment, ...	9,198.96	
John L. Russell (¼ income), ...	72.75	$13,956.71
Asa Gray's copyrights, ...		857.06
Gifts for immediate use, ...		1,810.00
Sale of card index, ...	$2,338.59	
" publications, ...	43.68	
" duplicate books and pamphlets, ...	25.00	2,407.27
		$19,031.04
Deficit, met by accumulated income, carried to General Suspense, .		1,001.40
		$20,032.44

GRAY HERBARIUM (CONTINUED)
EXPENDITURE

From **Asa Gray** Professorship of Systematic Botany Fund.

Salary of **Asa Gray** Professor (part), ...		$1,040.37
Salaries, ...	$5,730.45	
Services and wages, ...	2,869.70	
Equipment and supplies, ...	4,091.01	
Stationery, postage, telephone and telegraph, ...	70.09	
Printing, ...	975.11	
Books, ...	1,531.56	
Freight, express, and sundries, ...	52.15	
Expedition to Newfoundland, ...	426.62	
Commission and legal expenses on sale of Gray house, . .	166.27	
Amount paid Botanic Garden for removal of Gray house	2,000.00	
Repairs and equipment, land and buildings, ...	424.83	
Caretaking, land and buildings, ...	282.34	18,620.13

University charge.

Treasurer's Office, care of investments, ...	$200.48	
Bursar's Office, collections and payments, ...	132.26	
Inspector of Grounds and Buildings, salaries and expenses, ...	59.24	
Janitor, ...	42.58	
Engineer, ...	22.96	
	$457.52	
Less overcharge in University charge of 1908–09, .	85.58	371.94
		$20,032.44

OBSERVATORY
INCOME AND EXPENDITURE
For the year ended June 30, 1911
INCOME

Income of Funds and Gifts.

Advancement of Astronomical Science (1901), . .	$949.34
Advancement of Astronomical Science (1902), . .	923.50
Thomas G. Appleton, ...	242.50
J. Ingersoll Bowditch, ...	121.25
Uriah A. Boyden, ...	9,700.00
Charlotte Harris, ...	97.00
Haven, ...	2,182.50
James Hayward, ...	1,018.50
Observatory Endowment, ...	2,425.00
Paine Professorship, ...	2,425.00
Robert Treat Paine, ...	13,285.70
Amount carried forward, ...	$33,370.29

INCOME

Amount brought forward, ...	$33,370.29	
Income of Funds and Gifts (*continued*).		
Edward B. Phillips, ...	5,849.26	
Josiah Quincy, ...	882.79	
James Savage (¼ net income), ...	434.25	
David Sears, ...	2,136.33	
Augustus Story, ...	648.98	$42,771.85
Mrs. Henry Draper, gift for special research (additional), ...	$4,800.00	
J. Rayner Edmands Gift, Library.		
Gift, ... $1,000.00		
Interest, ... 14.21	1,014.21	
Gifts for present use, ...	3,000.00	8,814.21
Use of house by College officer, ...	$600.00	
Sale of Annals, ...	26.78	
" photographs, ...	15.00	641.78
		$52,227.84
General Deficit, made up as follows:		
Advance to Fund, carried to General Suspense, . .	$562.57	
Balances of sundry accounts used, ...	6,116.41	
	$6,678.98	
Less Restricted Income unused, added to Funds and Gifts, ...	2,605.88	4,073.10
		$56,300.94

EXPENDITURE

From Advancement of Astronomical Science Fund (1901), ...	$2,100.00	
From Advancement of Astronomical Science Fund (1902), ...	400.00	
From Uriah A. Boyden Fund.		
Salaries, ...	$5,151.50	
Services and wages, ...	1,554.29	
Equipment and supplies, ...	540.62	
Books, ...	53.47	
Expedition to Peru, ...	2,200.00	
Interest on advances, ...	721.89	
Sundries, ...	41.30	10,262.57
From Draper Memorial.		
Salaries, ...	$3,000.00	
Expedition to Peru, ...	1,800.00	4,800.00
From Josiah Quincy Fund, ...	. . . . . .	5,008.64
Salaries, ...	$14,282.66	
Services and wages, ...	11,852.75	
Equipment and supplies, ...	2,733.11	
Amounts carried forward, ...	$28,868.52	$22,571.21

OBSERVATORY (CONTINUED)
EXPENDITURE

Amounts brought forward,	$28,868.52	$22,571.21
Stationery, postage, telephone and telegraph,	324.72	
Printing,	356.75	
Binding,	832.81	
Books,	408.65	
Repairs and equipment, land and buildings,	599.49	
Caretaking, land and buildings,	2,905.45	
Taxes,	180.65	
Expedition to South Africa,	292.20	
Printing Annals,	3,402.13	
Use of house,	90.00	
Freight,	164.02	
Sundries,	26.56	
	$37,901.95	
Less cost printing certain Annals, transferred to the Josiah Quincy Fund,	5,008.64	32,893.31
University charge.		
Treasurer's Office, care of investments,	$613.40	
Bursar's Office, collections and payments,	223.02	836.42
		$56,300.94

SCHEDULE 23

MUSEUM OF COMPARATIVE ZOÖLOGY
INCOME AND EXPENDITURE
For the year ended June 30, 1911
INCOME

Income of Funds.		
Museum of Comparative Zoölogy balance (interest),	$896.72	
Agassiz Memorial,	14,449.75	
Virginia Barret Gibbs Scholarship,	286.59	
Gray Fund for Zoölogical Museum,	2,425.00	
Sturgis Hooper,	5,210.86	
Humboldt,	375.44	
Willard Peele Hunnewell,	242.50	
Permanent Fund for Museum of Zoölogy,	5,697.25	
Henry L. Pierce, Residuary (part),	4,733.19	
Teachers' and Pupils',	868.31	
Maria Whitney,	300.72	
Alexander Agassiz Bequest, General Purposes,	2,397.97	
" " " Publications,	2,908.40	$40,292.20
Amount carried forward,		$40,292.20

MUSEUM OF COMPARATIVE ZOÖLOGY (CONTINUED)

INCOME

Amount brought forward, ...		$40,292.20
Gift for present use, ...		500.00
Use of lecture rooms by Radcliffe College, ...	$700.00	
Sale of publications, ...	456.61	1,156.61
		$41,948.81

General Deficit, made up as follows :

Accumulated Income of **Sturgis Hooper** Fund,	$289.64		
Principal of **Alexander Agassiz** Bequest for			
Publications, ...	6,712.94		
	$7,002.58		
Less Restricted Income unused, added to			
Funds and Gifts, ...	$337.31		
Surplus carried to General Suspense, .	337.91	675.22	6,327.36
			$48,276.17

EXPENDITURE

From **Sturgis Hooper** Fund.

Salary of **Sturgis Hooper** Professor, ...	$5,500.00	
From **Alexander Agassiz** Bequest for Publications,	9,621.34	
From **Virginia Barret Gibbs** Scholarship Fund.		
Scholarship, ...	250.00	$15,371.34
Salaries, ...	$8,000.01	
Services and wages, ...	6,820.00	
Equipment and supplies, ...	4,026.73	
Stationery, postage, telephone and telegraph, ...	243.31	
Printing, ...	3,140.36	
Books, ...	2,056.04	
Water, heat, light, power and protection, ...	6,774.11	
Repairs and equipment, land and buildings, ...	2,762.61	
Binding, ...	1,087.90	
Collections, ...	1,034.97	
Freight and cartage, ...	332.94	
Boarding and lodging of students at Bermuda Biological		
Station, ...	363.60	
Sundries, ...	58.50	36,651.08
University charge.		
Treasurer's Office, care of investments, ...	$585.16	
Bursar's Office, collections and payments, ...	145.01	730.17
		$52,752.59

Less the following items transferred :

To the College, Schedule 8 :			
Heating and service, ...	$3,446.25		
Publishing contributions from the Laboratories			
of Geography and Zoölogy, ...	300.00		
	$3,746.25		
To the University, Schedule 7 :			
Total University charge, ...	730.17	4,476.42	
		$48,276.17	

PEABODY MUSEUM OF AMERICAN ARCHAEOLOGY AND ETHNOLOGY

INCOME AND EXPENDITURE

For the year ended June 80, 1911

INCOME

Income of Funds.

Hemenway Fellowship, ...	$618.18	
Mary Hemenway Fund for Archaeology, . . .	2,182.50	
Peabody Building, ...	1,439.20	
Peabody Collection, ...	2,402.47	
Peabody Professor, ...	2,402.47	
Thaw Fellowship, ...	1,167.61	
Henry C. Warren Exploration, ...	485.00	
Susan Cornelia Warren, ...	242.50	
Robert C. Winthrop Scholarship, ...	294.15	
Huntington Frothingham Wolcott, ...	970.00	
Anonymous Fellowship in Central American Archaeology, ...	600.00	$12,799.08
Gifts for present use, ...		7,121.00
Reimbursement by College for installation of boiler in 1909–10, . .		1,883.74
Returned by Dr. Farabee, South American Expedition account, .		56.54
		$21,860.86

EXPENDITURE

Anonymous Fellowship in Central American Archaeology,	$600.00	
Thaw Fellowship, ...	1,854.17	
Henry C. Warren Fund, explorations, ...	399.88	
Mary Hemenway Fund, ...	666.67	
Huntington Frothingham Wolcott Fund, specimens, ...	1,130.00	$4,150.72
Services and wages, ...	$4,054.94	
Equipment and supplies, ...	1,268.96	
Stationery, postage, telephone and telegraph, ...	253.08	
Printing, ...	28.95	
Books, ...	233.24	
Binding, ...	146.85	
Explorations, ...	363.15	
Collections, ...	5,500.00	
Professional services, ...	50.00	
Freight, ...	109.80	
Sundries, ...	58.96	
Repairs and equipment, land and buildings, ...	163.20	
Caretaking, land and buildings, ...	1,460.02	13,690.60
Interest on advances, ...		48.71
University charge.		
Treasurer's Office, care of investments, ...	$179.70	
Bursar's Office, collections and payments, ...	107.88	
Amounts carried forward, ...	$287.58	$17,890.03

PEABODY MUSEUM (CONTINUED)

EXPENDITURE

Amounts brought forward, ...	$287.58	$17,890.06
University charge (*continued*).		
Inspector of Grounds and Buildings, salary and expenses, ...	152.54	
Watchmen, ...	62.80	
Engineer, ...	58.89	
Janitor, ...	109.21	671.02
		$18,561.05
Less amounts transferred.		
Repairs, land and buildings, ...	$163.20	
Caretaking, land and buildings, ...	1,460.02	
University charge, ...	671.02	2,294.24
		$16,266.81
The above amounts are transferred as follows:		
90% to University, Schedule 7, ...	$2,064.82	
10% to College, Schedule 8, ...	229.42	
	$2,294.24	
General Surplus, made up as follows:		
Restricted Income unused, added to Funds and Gifts, ...	$2,346.60	
Amount carried to General Suspense to repay advance	75.12	
Surplus, carried to General Suspense, ...	3,431.83	
	$5,753.55	
Less advance to Fund, carried to General Suspense,	160.00	5,593.55
		$21,860.36

SEMITIC MUSEUM

INCOME AND EXPENDITURE

For the year ended June 30, 1911

INCOME

Gifts for Semitic Collection.		
Gift, ...	$1,000.00	
Interest, ...	203.88	$1,203.88
Gifts for excavations in Palestine.		
Interest, ...		182.50
Income from Charles L. Hancock Bequest, ...		500.00
		$1,886.38
General Deficit, made up as follows:		
Deficit, met by unrestricted principal of Gifts for excavations in Palestine, ...	$20,546.39	
Less Restricted Income unused, added to Funds and Gifts, ...	926.80	19,619.59
		$21,505.97

SEMITIC MUSEUM (CONTINUED)

EXPENDITURE

From gifts for Semitic Collection, ...	$277.08	
From gifts for excavations in Palestine, ...	20,728.89	$21,005.97
Curator, ...		500.00
Repairs and equipment, land and building, ...	$45.28	
Caretaking, land and building, ...	1,085.39	1,130.67
University charge.		
Treasurer's Office, care of investments, ...	$10.38	
Bursar's Office, collections and payments, ...	33.84	
Inspector of Grounds and Buildings, salary and		
expenses, ...	82.20	
Watchmen, ...	33.90	
Engineer, ...	31.70	
Janitor, ...	58.61	250.63
		$22,887.27
Less amounts transferred.		
General expenses, ...	$1,130.67	
University charge, ...	250.63	1,381.30
		$21,505.97
The above amounts are transferred as follows :		
70 % to University, Schedule 7, ...	$966.91	
30 % to Divinity School, Schedule 18, ...	414.39	
	$1,381.30	

GERMANIC MUSEUM

INCOME AND EXPENDITURE

For the year ended June 30, 1911

INCOME

Income of Funds and Gifts.		
Emperor William, ...	$1,277.25	
Germanic Museum balance (interest), ...	27.40	
Germanic Museum, ...	485.68	
Germanic Museum Endowment, ...	2,484.32	$4,274.65
Gift for special works of art, ...		1,000.00
Sale of Handbooks, ...		23.04
		$5,297.69

EXPENDITURE

General.		
Equipment and supplies, ...	$113.43	
Printing, ...	5.41	
Stationery and postage, ...	23.19	
Amount carried forward, ...	$142.03	

GERMANIC MUSEUM (CONTINUED)

EXPENDITURE

Amount brought forward, ...	$142.03	
General (*continued*).		
Sundries, ...	14.17	
Repairs and equipment, land and building, ...	24.40	
Caretaking, land and building, ...	915.35	$1,095.95
University charge.		
Treasurer's Office, care of investments, ...	$43.06	
Bursar's Office, collections and payments, ...	29.00	
Inspector of Grounds and Buildings, salary and		
expenses, ...	39.24	
Watchmen, ...	16.32	
Engineer, ...	15.27	142.89
		$1,238.84
Less University charge transferred to University, Schedule 7, . . .		142.89
		$1,095.95
General Surplus made up as follows:		
Restricted Income unexpended, added to Funds and		
Gifts, ...	$3,484.32	
Surplus carried to General Suspense, ...	717.42	4,201.74
		$5,297.69

SCHEDULE 27

WILLIAM HAYES FOGG ART MUSEUM

INCOME AND EXPENDITURE

For the year ended June 30, 1911

INCOME

Income of Funds.		
William Hayes Fogg, ...	$2,425.00	
Gray Fund for Engravings, ...	780.27	
William M. Prichard, ...	723.23	
John Witt Randall, ...	1,471.44	
Mary R. Searle, ...	102.67	$5,502.61
Sale of photographs and catalogues, ...	$46.01	
For work in connection with photographs sold, ...	43.75	
Gifts for special exhibit, ...	128.98	
Gift for paintings, ...	200.00	418.74
		$5,921.35
General Deficit, made up as follows:		
Accumulated income of Sundry Funds, ...	$586.07	
Advance to Fund carried to General Suspense, . .	78.97	
Deficit carried to General Suspense, ...	260.72	925.76
		$6,847.11

WILLIAM HAYES FOGG ART MUSEUM (CONTINUED)

EXPENDITURE

From the following Funds :

Gray Fund for Engravings.

Curator,	$250.00	
Services,	415.42	
Collections,	202.50	$867.92

William M. Prichard, collections, 618.45

John Witt Randall.

Curator,	$250.00	
Expenses,	1,590.08	1,840.08

Mary R. Searle, books, 416.20

From Gifts.

Paintings,	$200.00	
Special Exhibit,	128.98	328.98

General.

Director,	$500.00	
Services and wages,	1,509.80	
Equipment and supplies,	92.18	
Stationery, postage, telephone and telegraph,	20.12	
Printing,	8.80	
Professional services,	400.00	
Insurance,	131.75	
Repairs and equipment, building,	113.88	
Caretaking, building,	2,478.81	5,253.79

University charge

Treasurer's Office, care of investments,	$83.16	
Bursar's Office, collections and payments,	91.20	
Inspector of Grounds and Buildings, salary and expenses,	121.43	
Engineer,	46.91	
Watchmen,	101.85	444.05
		$9,769.47

Less amounts transferred.

Caretaking, building,	$2,478.81	
University charge,	444.05	2,922.86
		$6,847.11

The above amounts are transferred as follows :

10 % to University, Schedule 7,	$292.24	
90 % to College, Schedule 8,	2,630.12	
	$2,922.86	

APPLETON CHAPEL

INCOME AND EXPENDITURE

For the year ended June 30, 1911

INCOME

Income of Funds.

Fund for Religious Services, ...	$50.15	
Increase Sumner Wheeler, ...	2,425.00	
Edward Wigglesworth Memorial, ...	7,275.00	$9,750.15
Use of Organ, ...		33.19
		$9,783.34

General deficit made up as follows:

Advance to Gift, carried to General Suspense, . .	$182.09	
Deficit, transferred.		
20 % to University, Schedule 7, ...	110.53	
80 % to College, Schedule 8, ...	442.14	734.76
		$10,518.10

EXPENDITURE

From **George Wigglesworth** gift, ...		$182.09

General.

Preaching and morning services, ...	$3,975.00	
Administrator, ...	400.00	
Organist and Choir-master, ...	1,500.00	
Choir, ...	2,000.00	
Equipment and supplies, ...	101.42	
Stationery, postage, telephone and telegraph, . . .	1.07	
Printing, ...	71.15	
Repairs and equipment, land and buildings, ...	662.04	
Caretaking, land and buildings, ...	977.85	
Repairing and tuning organ, ...	91.21	
Music, ...	56.94	
Sundries, ...	115.65	9,952.33

University charge.

Treasurer's Office, care of investments, ...	$138.09	
Bursar's Office, collections and payments, ...	60.88	
Inspector of Grounds and Buildings, salary and		
expenses, ...	62.95	
Watchmen, ...	52.40	
Janitor, ...	45.07	
Engineer, ...	24.29	383.68
		$10,518.10

PHILLIPS BROOKS HOUSE

INCOME AND EXPENDITURE

For the year ended June 30, 1911

INCOME

Income of Funds.

Phillips Brooks House Endowment, ...	$509.59	
John W. and Belinda L. Randall, ...	327.81	
Ralph H. Shepard, ...	550.18	
Ralph Hamilton Shepard Memorial, ...	276.74	$1,664.32
		$1,664.32

EXPENDITURE

Secretaries of Phillips Brooks House Association, . . .	$1,000.00	
Equipment and supplies, ...	64.90	
Books, ...	2.90	
Receptions, ...	259.30	
Services of matron, ...	101.00	
Rent of piano, ...	45.00	
Sundries, ...	88.68	
Repairs and equipment, land and buildings, ...	84.99	
Caretaking, land and buildings, ...	1,541.44	$3,188.21
University charge.		
Treasurer's Office, care of investments, ...	$22.27	
Bursar's Office, collections and payments, ...	57.58	
Inspector of Grounds and Buildings, salary and		
expenses, ...	44.43	
Watchmen, ...	36.96	
Engineer, ...	17.14	
Janitor, ...	31.80	210.18
		$3,398.39
Less amounts transferred.		
Repairs and equipment, land and buildings, ...	$84.99	
Caretaking, land and buildings, ...	1,541.44	
University charge, ...	210.18	1,836.61
		$1,561.78
The above amounts are transferred as follows:		
10% to University, Schedule 7, ...	$183.66	
Remainder, divided in proportion to the number of		
students:		
College, Schedule 8, ...	1,191.12	
Graduate School of Applied Science, Sched-		
ule 11, ...	53.72	
Graduate School of Business Administration,		
Schedule 12, ...	32.23	
Amounts carried forward, ...	$1,460.78	$1,561.78

PHILLIPS BROOKS HOUSE (CONTINUED)

EXPENDITURE

Amounts brought forward, ...	$1,460.78	$1,561.78
Amounts transferred (*continued*).		
Divinity School, Schedule 13, ...	16.69	
Law School, Schedule 14, ...	359.19	
	$1,836.61	
General surplus made up as follows:		
Restricted Income unused, added to Funds and Gifts,	$327.81	
Less deficit met by the accrued income of the **Ralph**		
Hamilton Shepard Memorial Fund, ...	225.27	102.54
		$1,664.32

SCHEDULE 30

HEMENWAY GYMNASIUM

INCOME AND EXPENDITURE

For the year ended June 30, 1911

INCOME

Fees for the use of		
Lockers, by students, ...	$1,843.50	
Gymnasium, by graduates, ...	10.00	$1,853.50
Deficit transferred to the following departments in proportion to the number of students.		
College, Schedule 8, ...	$7,726.14	
Graduate School of Applied Science, Schedule 11, .	848.08	
Graduate School of Business Administration, Schedule 12, ...	209.28	
Divinity School, Schedule 13, ...	107.85	
Law School, Schedule 14, ...	2,830.31	
Episcopal Theological School, ...	122.54	10,843.70
		$12,697.20

EXPENDITURE

Salaries, ...	$5,500.00	
Services and wages, ...	1,147.19	
Apparatus, ...	548.38	
Equipment and supplies, ...	11.70	
Stationery, postage, telephone and telegraph, ...	91.16	
Printing, ...	73.70	
Rent of piano, ...	24.00	
Repairs and equipment, land and building, ...	511.95	
Caretaking, land and building, ...	4,271.07	$12,179.15
Amount carried forward, ...		$12,179.15

HEMENWAY GYMNASIUM (continued)
EXPENDITURE

Amount brought forward, ...		$12,179.15
University charge.		
Bursar's Office, collections and payments, ...	$90.54	
Inspector of Grounds and Buildings, salary and		
expenses, ...	237.69	
Watchmen, ...	97.98	
Engineer, ...	91.84	518.05
		$12,697.20

Schedule 31

STILLMAN INFIRMARY
INCOME AND EXPENDITURE
For the year ended June 30, 1911

INCOME

Income of Funds and Gifts.		
Robert Charles Billings, for **Stillman In-**		
firmary, ...	$2,986.97	
Free Bed Fund of the **Class of 1868,**	309.28	
" " for the **Stillman** Infirmary, . . .	31.67	
Herbert Schurz Memorial Free Bed Fund, . .	176.20	
Stillman Infirmary Gift, interest, ...	374.80	
Henry P. Walcott, ...	155.39	$3,984.31
Receipts from Students.		
Infirmary annual fees, ...	$14,604.00	
Receipts from patients, ...	4,496.78	19,100.78
		$23,085.09

EXPENDITURE

Services and wages, ...	$8,486.72	
Equipment and supplies, ...	7,241.27	
Stationery, postage, telephone and telegraph, ...	258.65	
Printing, ...	28.15	
Sundries, ...	20.80	
Repairs and equipment, land and buildings, ...	416.86	
Caretaking, land and buildings, ...	5,867.88	$21,820.33
Interest on advances, ...		19.04
University charge.		
Treasurer's Office, care of investments, ...	$56.43	
Bursar's Office, collections and payments, ...	136.01	
Medical Adviser, salary and expenses, ...	750.00	
Amounts carried forward, ...	$942.44	$21,839.37

STILLMAN INFIRMARY (CONTINUED)

EXPENDITURE

Amounts brought forward, ...	$942.44	$21,839.37
University charge (*continued*).		
Inspector of Grounds and Buildings, salary and		
expenses, ...	118.28	
Labor, etc., ...	118.10	
Engineer, ...	43.60	1,212.42
		$23,051.79
General Surplus, made up as follows :		
Restricted Income unused, added to Funds and Gifts,	$374.80	
Less Deficit carried to General Suspense, ...	341.50	33.30
		$23,085.09

SCHEDULE 32

FUNDS AND GIFTS FOR SPECIAL PURPOSES

INCOME AND EXPENDITURE

For the year ended June 80, 1911

INCOME

Anonymous Fund, ...		$3,545.57
Anonymous Gift for **Gray** Herbarium library building.		
Gift, ...	$10,000.00	
Interest, ...	74.80	10,074.80
Francis H. Burr Memorial Gift.		
Gift, ...	$25,000.00	
Interest, ...	827.16	25,827.16
Gifts for **Arnold** Arboretum Building.		
Interest, ...		510.51
Bussey Trust (part), ...		9,336.56
Gift from the **Carnegie** Foundation, ...		37,971.69
Class of 1834 Fund, ...		77.92
" 1842 "		5.38
" 1844 "		447.10
" 1846 "		663.67
" 1853 "		153.66
" 1856 "		363.75
Caroline Brewer Croft (part), ...		2,290.50
Dr. John C. Cutter Bequest (part), ...		409.72
Gifts for Dental School Building, ...		275.00
Paul Dudley Fund, ...		198.90
Calvin and Lucy Ellis Fund (part), ...		155.55
Amount carried forward, ...		$92,307.44

FUNDS AND GIFTS, ETC. (CONTINUED)

INCOME

Amount brought forward, ...		$92,307.44
Gift for Freshman Dormitories.		
Gifts, ...	$32,454.00	
Interest, ...	133.89	32,587.89
Germanic Museum Building.		
Gift, ...	$100,000.00	
Interest, ...	6,387.71	106,387.71
Wolcott Gibbs Memorial.		
Gifts, ...	$7,095.00	
Interest, ...	4,729.67	11,824.67
Godkin Lecture Fund, ...		728.18
Charles Gross Memorial Fund (part), ...		1.06
Gurney Fund (part), ...		500.00
Harvard Memorial Society (interest), ...		84.68
Charles L. Hancock Bequest, ...		15.68
Collis P. Huntington Memorial Hospital Building.		
Gift, ...	$40,000.00	
Interest, ...	164.62	40,164.62
Professorship of Hygiene, 1899 Fund (part), ...		10,572.89
" " 1902 "		2,271.51
" " 1908 "		1,617.75
Ingersoll Lecture Fund, ...		298.76
Gifts for a new University Library Building (interest), ...		580.88
G. C. Lodge and J. T. Stickney Memorial Fund (part), . . .		.61
William Belden Noble Lectures Fund.		
Interest, ...	$1,294.90	
Sales, ...	175.73	1,470.6
Henry S. Nourse Fund (part), ...		1,001.20
Robert Troup Paine, ...		1,986.55
Lectures on Political Economy Fund, ...		559.55
Retiring Allowance Fund, ...		17,946.55
Gift for Decorating Front of the Nelson Robinson, Jr. Hall		
(interest), ...		247.06
James Skillen Memorial Fund, ...		526.56
George Smith Bequest, ...		18,046.35
Gifts for Improvements and Additions to The Soldier's Field, . . .		5,000.00
Alexander W. Thayer Fund (part), ...		480.00
John E. Thayer Fund, Quarterly Journal of Economics.		
Interest, ...	$790.70	
Sales, ...	2,205.75	2,996.45
Charles Wilder Fund, ...		1,940.00
Daniel Williams Fund, ...		795.21
Sarah Winslow Fund, ...		230.76
Woodland Hill Fund, use of laboratory, ...		1,000.00
		$354,171.20

FUNDS AND GIFTS, ETC. (CONTINUED)

EXPENDITURE

Anonymous Fund (part) annuity,		$3,850.00
Francis H. Burr Memorial Gift,		77.25
Gifts for **Arnold** Arboretum Building Construction,		93.00
Bussey Trust (part).		
Annuities,	$4,000.00	
Taxes,	5,836.56	9,836.56
Gift from the **Carnegie** Foundation Retiring Allowances,		37,971.66
Class of 1853 Fund, Secretary of the Class,		149.01
" 1856 " " " "		300.00
Edwin Conant Fund (part) claim and legal expenses,		1,205.68
Caroline Brewer Croft Fund (part) annuity,		2,290.50
Dr. John C. Cutter Bequest, annuity,		409.72
Dental School Building.		
Interest on advances,		3,820.84
Paul Dudley Fund, legal services,		50.00
Calvin and **Lucy Ellis** Fund (part) taxes,		155.55
Germanic Museum Building.		
Collection charges on cheque in payment of gift,		100.00
Charles Gross Memorial Fund, exchange charges,		1.06
Wolcott Gibbs Memorial,		192.50
Godkin Lecture Fund, salary of lecturer,		600.00
Gurney Fund (part) annuities,		500.00
Gift for **Gray** Herbarium (**Kidder** Wing) construction,		151.97
Charles L. Hancock Bequest, taxes,		15.68
Collis P. Huntington Memorial Hospital Building,		32,189.27
Professorship of Hygiene, 1899 Fund (part) annuity,		10,013.78
" " 1902 " " "		1,865.41
" " 1908 " " "		1,158.15
Ingersoll Lecture Fund, salary lecturer,		200.00
G. C. Lodge and **J. F. Stickney** Memorial Fund, exchange charges on foreign subscriptions,		.61
William Belden Noble Lectures Fund,		1,381.24
Henry S. Nourse Fund.		
Annuity,	$1,000.00	
Insurance on house,	1.20	1,001.20
Lectures on Political Economy Fund,		100.00
Retiring Allowance Fund,		16,020.94
Henry L. Pierce Residuary (Medical) Fund, legal services,		707.78
Gift for Decorating Front of **Nelson Robinson, Jr.** Hall,		802.16
John Simpkins Hall,		37.97
James Skillen Memorial Fund, annuity,		800.00
George Smith Bequest, annuities,		900.00
Gifts for Improvements and Additions to The Soldier's Field.		
Interest on advances,		619.01
Alexander W. Thayer Fund, annuity,		480.00
Amount carried forward,		$129,048.45

FUNDS AND GIFTS, ETC. (CONTINUED)

EXPENDITURE

Amount brought forward, ...		$129,048.45
John E. Thayer Fund, Quarterly Journal of Economics, . . .		3,311.31
John H. Treat Fund, taxes, ...		33.75
Charles Wilder Fund, annuities, ...		1,600.00
Daniel Williams Fund.		
Treasurer of Herring Pond Indians, ...	$219.00	
Treasurer of Mashpee Indians, ...	465.76	684.76
Sarah Winslow.		
Teacher at Tyngsborough, ...	$93.56	
Minister " "	93.56	
Commission on income, credited to University, . .	5.77	192.89
Woodland Hill Fund.		
Taxes, ...	$1,108.64	
Interest on advances, ...	275.92	1,384.56
		$136,255.72
Less Balance of Annuity to Medical School, Schedule 15, ...		273.44
		$135,982.28
General Surplus, made up as follows:		
Unexpended balance of new gifts for buildings		
carried to Funds and Gifts, ...	$194,307.83	
Restricted Income unused carried to Funds and Gifts,	23,234.90	
Amount carried to General Suspense to repay former		
advances, ...	4,576.59	
	$222,119.32	
Less advances to Funds and Gifts carried to General		
Suspense, ...	3,930.40	218,188.92
		$354,171.20

Certificate of the Committee of the Overseers of Harvard College, for examining the Accounts of the Treasurer

The committee appointed by the Overseers of Harvard College to examine the accounts of the Treasurer for the year ending June 80, 1911, have, with the assistance of an expert chosen by them, examined and audited the Cash-book and Journal covering the period from July, 1910, to June 80, 1911, inclusive, and have seen that all the bonds, notes, mortgages, certificates of stock, and other evidences of property, which were on hand at the beginning of said year, or have been received by him during said year, are now in his possession, or are fully accounted for by entries made therein; they have also noticed all payments, both of principal and interest, indorsed on any of said bonds or notes, and have seen that the amounts so indorsed have been duly credited to the College.

They have in like manner satisfied themselves that all the entries for moneys expended by the Treasurer, or charged in his books to the College, are well vouched; such of them that are not supported by counter entries being proved by regular vouchers and receipts.

They have also, by the aid of said expert, satisfied themselves that all the entries for said year are duly transferred to the Ledger, and that the accounts there are rightly cast, and correctly balanced.

(Signed)

F. L. HIGGINSON, *Chairman,*
WILLIAM ENDICOTT, Jr.
WILLIAM A. GASTON,
ARTHUR LYMAN,
JOHN L. SALTONSTALL,
GRAFTON ST. L ABBOTT,
ALLAN FORBES,
RICHARD C. STOREY.

Of the Committee on behalf of the Board of Overseers.

BOSTON, January, 1912.

INDEX

OFFICIAL REGISTER OF
HARVARD UNIVERSITY

REPORTS OF THE
RESIDENT AND THE TREASURER
OF HARVARD COLLEGE

1911–12

PUBLISHED BY THE UNIVERSITY
CAMBRIDGE, MASS.

OFFICIAL REGISTER OF HARVARD UNIVERSITY

VOLUME X   FEBRUARY 20, 1913   NO. 2, PART I

REPORTS OF THE
PRESIDENT AND THE TREASURER
OF HARVARD COLLEGE

1911–12

PUBLISHED BY THE UNIVERSITY
CAMBRIDGE, MASS.

REPORTS OF THE
PRESIDENT AND THE TREASURER
OF HARVARD COLLEGE

1911–12

CAMBRIDGE
PUBLISHED BY THE UNIVERSITY
1913

CONTENTS

TREASURER'S STATEMENT

PRESIDENT'S REPORT FOR 1911–12

To the Board of Overseers: —

The President of the University has the honor to submit the following report for the academic year 1911–12: —

Since the last report was written the vacancy in the Corporation, caused by the death of Judge Francis Cabot Lowell on March 6, 1911, has been filled by the election of Robert Bacon, who relinquished his post as Ambassador to France to serve the University. He had hardly taken his place when another was left empty by the death on November 4, 1912, of Dr. Arthur Tracy Cabot, one of the most faithful and sagacious counsellors that we have ever had. Eminent as a surgeon, he had retired from his large practice a year before to give the rest of his life to public service; and we had looked forward to many years of coöperation and companionship with him.

The losses suffered in the instructing staff during the year covered by this report have been unusually heavy. Professor William Watson Goodwin died on June 15, 1912. Although on the retired list since 1901, and in declining health for the three last years, his name was an honor to the University, and the memory of his long service and great scholarship will not cease to be cherished. On July 30, Dr. Maurice Howe Richardson, Moseley Professor of Surgery, died suddenly in the full tide of his extraordinary activity. His devotion to the interests of the Medical School was constant, and he won the affection of vast numbers of patients in his private and hospital practice. Charles Robert Sanger, Professor of Chemistry and Director of the Chemical Laboratory, died after a prolonged illness on February 25th. His death thinned grievously the depleted ranks of the chemical staff. On April 7th died Abbott Lawrence Rotch, Professor of Meteorology, who founded and maintained at his own expense the Observatory at Blue Hill, which he devised to the University. A pioneer in a new field of science, his presence cannot soon be replaced.   At the close of the year Charles Loring Jackson, Erving Professor of Chemistry, retired, after a distinguished service of forty-four years as teacher and investigator; Arthur Searle, Phillips Professor of Astronomy, retired also, after devoting to the Observatory forty-three years; William Morris Davis, whose name is as well known abroad as in Cambridge, resigned the Sturgis-Hooper Professorship of Geology; and George Santayana, Professor of Philosophy, to our regret preferred in middle life to return to Europe.   The Medical School lost through resignation three of its most eminent clinical professors: Dr. Frederick Cheever Shattuck, Jackson Professor of Clinical Medicine; Dr. James Jackson Putnam, Professor of Diseases of the Nervous System; and Dr. Edward Hickling Bradford, Professor of Orthopedic Surgery.   The last of these was happily prevailed upon to accept the position of Dean of the School, in place of Dr. Henry Asbury Christian, who was obliged to resign because his professorship and his new duties as physician-in-chief of the Peter Bent Brigham Hospital will fill all his time.   Dr. Christian's work as Dean, in bringing about closer relations between the Medical School and the various hospitals, will mark an epoch in the progress of the School.

The new appointments made in the staff of the Medical School in consequence of these vacancies will be referred to in describing the condition of the School.   The appointments and promotions to professorships in the Faculty of Arts and Sciences have been as follows: —

Irving Babbitt,	Professor of French Literature.
Reginald Aldworth Daly,	Sturgis-Hooper Professor of Geology.
William Scott Ferguson,	Professor of Ancient History.
Elmer Peter Kohler.	Professor of Chemistry.
Arthur Michael.	Professor of Organic Chemistry.
William Bennett Munro,	Professor of Municipal Government.
Charles Palache,	Professor of Mineralogy.
Walter Raymond Spalding,	Associate Professor of Music.
Jay Backus Woodworth,	Associate Professor of Geology.
Charles Henry Conrad Wright,	Associate Professor of the French Language and Literature.

Although not strictly within the Faculty of Arts and Sciences, the promotion of Solon Irving Bailey to the Phillips Professorship of Astronomy may be mentioned here.

In the last annual report figures were presented concerning the number and geographical distribution of students admitted to Harvard College under the old and new methods of examination. In the second year of its trial the new method has been used more freely, and the proportion of candidates who failed, although larger than under the old method, was much less than at the first experiment, — perhaps because the nature of the test was better understood and fewer boys tried it merely on the chance that it would prove easy to pass. The number of candidates under the new plan and the percentage of failures for the two years have been as follows: —

	1911	1912
Applicants	185	259
Records not approved ...	46	46
Admitted	83 = 59.7%	154 = 72.3%
Rejected	56 = 40.3%	59 = 27.7%

Under the old plan in 1911 17.1 per cent of the candidates were rejected, and 8.1 per cent did not reappear to complete their examinations in September; in 1912, 19.1 per cent were rejected, and 6.1 per cent failed to reappear.

The distribution of the students admitted by the new method — geographically, and as between public and private schools,— does not differ much from last year, save that private preparatory schools in Massachusetts have begun to make some use of the new plan. Since it gives them greater freedom in their curricula, they are likely to resort to it more in the future. The following table shows the distribution for the two years by percentages: —

	1911		1912	
	Old Plan	New Plan	Old Plan	New Plan
From public schools	45.7	80.5	41.8	79
" private and endowed schools	54.2	19.4	58.1	20.9
" schools in Massachusetts	72	41	72.7	42.2
" schools in New England	85	47	87.1	51.2
" schools in other Atlantic States ..	8.5	31	8.1	28.5
" schools west of the Alleghanies ...	4.5	21	3.8	19.4

The results of the examinations will be found in greater detail in the report of the Chairman of the Committee on Admission.

That the new examinations are a good test of fitness for college work would seem clear from the records in their first year of the students recruited thereby, as shown in the report of the Dean of

Harvard College. The proportion of low grades among the seventy-nine Freshmen who entered in this way in 1911 is much less, and the proportion of high grades decidedly larger, than for the average of the class. These young men have proved that they are qualified to pursue college studies; and, whether they could have passed all the examinations required under the old plan or not, they are admitted without conditions. The result is that of the 598 men who were admitted by examination and actually entered the Freshman class in 1912, 402, or more than two thirds, entered clear. That is a great advantage both to them and to the College, for conditions are an additional burden upon students who ought to devote all their scholastic energy to college work. They are a heavy drag upon the Freshman year. Borne chiefly by the weakest, or least well equipped, they hold these men back and slow down the pace of the whole class.

The report for last year contained also a table showing the number of Freshmen who had chosen each of the fields of study for the concentration of their college work. The choices made by the Freshmen last May were not very different; but for that very reason, as showing a tendency rather than accident, a comparison of the two years is not without interest. The principal changes are increases in the actual numbers concentrating in Classics, English, Comparative Literature, Chemistry, Mathematics, and Philosophy; and a slight relative decrease in the number in the group of History, Economics, and Government.

CHOICES OF SUBJECTS OF CONCENTRATION

Subjects	Class of 1914	Class of 1915
The Classics	12	22
English	42	74
Romance Languages	45	39
Germanic Languages	9	14
Comparative Literature	3	12
History and Literature	9	4
Fine Arts	12	14
Music	9	6
Architecture	6	
Too vaguely expressed as Modern Languages	9	
Total, Group I	156	185

Subjects	Class of 1914	Class of 1915
Engineering	55	43
Chemistry	38	72
Biology	14	12
Geology	5	4
Physics	4	7
Anthropology	1	
Special Combinations		3
Too vaguely expressed as Natural Sciences	2	
Total, Group II	**119**	**141**
Economics	133	132
History	41	50
Government	25	33
Anthropology		2
Too vaguely expressed as History and Political Science	33	
Total, Group III	**232**	**217**
Mathematics	9	21
Philosophy	3	9
Total, Group IV	**12**	**30**

Percentages of Concentration

	Class of 1914	Class of 1915
Language, Literature, Fine Arts, and Music	30%	32%
Natural Sciences	23%	25%
Economics, History, Government	45%	38%
Mathematics and Philosophy	2%	5%

A few men have been allowed for good reasons to change their field of concentration, but they are not numerous enough to have a material effect upon the percentage. These tables indicate the main subjects of the students' work, but we must remember that they by no means express either the range of studies pursued by the individual student or the amount of instruction given by the several departments, for every undergraduate is obliged to distribute six of his courses among the groups in which his main work does not lie, and he may use his four free courses in the same way.

The oral examinations in French and German, which went into effect for the Class of 1914, required that no student should be registered as a Junior unless he could read one of those languages with fair ease and accuracy. The examinations were held three or four times a year; and the result, as stated in the last annual report, has been that each time about one half of the applicants failed. But the student may work on the language and try until he passes; and the upshot illustrates the general experience that students will rise to any reasonable standard which is seriously required; for by the end of October, 1912, only thirty-three members of the Class of 1914 had failed to pass the examination. Thus the object of the rule has been in large measure attained — that of ensuring among the upper classmen an ability to use books in at least one foreign language.

In the last annual report the adoption of general examinations in the Medical School, as a substitute for, or supplement to, the passing of a series of separate courses was described, and it was stated that the subject was under consideration in the Divinity School also. A general examination of this character has now been adopted for the degree of Bachelor of Divinity, and for that of Master of Divinity. The latter is a new degree conferred after a year of study, and designed to replace so far as possible the degree of Master of Arts hitherto conferred upon graduate students in the School by the Faculty of Arts and Sciences. The regulations for these general examinations in the Divinity School, and for the courses of study leading thereto, are printed in an appendix to this report.

The same principle has been discussed in Harvard College. After a year of careful study, the Division of History and Political Science,—comprising the Departments of History, Economics, and Government,—formulated a plan for a general examination before graduation of students concentrating in these subjects. The plan, which was brought before the Faculty this autumn, was adopted after debate in three meetings, and has since been approved by the governing boards. It lays down briefly the general principles, and, together with the outline of this plan prepared by the Division, will be found in a second appendix to this report.

In describing the general examinations for the Medical School something was said of the principle on which they are based; but the subject merits fuller treatment, because it involves a more radical change in American educational practice than anything the University has done for many years. It means a change not so much in machinery as in object; not of methods alone, but of the point of view. So far as I am aware, general examinations of some kind exist in all European universities, except for a degree with a mere pass in Scotland and the provincial universities of England. They have been used in the past in American colleges. In a very crude form they were at one time prescribed for graduation from Harvard; and in some other colleges they lasted until after the middle of the last century. Since the curriculum of those colleges comprised many subjects, the examination, which covered them all, was open to the criticism now heard of the general examination for graduation from the German gymnasium. It was almost of necessity a review of unconnected studies; an effort of memory, preceded by a strenuous cram. But whether in such a test the disadvantages outweigh the benefits or not, it was quite inapplicable after the elective system had been adopted in a thorough-going form at Harvard and more or less completely by other colleges. The student being allowed to select as he pleased among all the courses of instruction offered by the Faculty, a general examination would have covered a different ground for each student; would have been merely a repetition of the examinations in separate courses which the student had already passed; and could not have required reading outside of the courses, or demanded a correlation of information obtained in courses in diverse fields. But now that every student is obliged to take six courses in some one field, the situation has changed, and the way is open for this valuable instrument of education in that field. To the courses distributed among other subjects it is still inapplicable; but in the field of the student's concentration his attention can be directed, as it should be, to the subject pursued, rather than to the particular courses taken, which then become not ends in themselves but only efficient means to an end. By examinations well devised for the purpose the student can be made to reflect upon the subject as a whole, correlating the several parts; and the interest of an intelligent man follows his efforts. Moreover, he can be induced to read books outside the strict limits of his courses in order to fill in the gaps; for the habit of independent reading has fallen sadly out of use among undergraduates at the present day.

A general examination has drawbacks as well as merits. If it tends to fix attention on a subject wider than any single course, it tends also to make the passing of that examination the goal, and to lessen interest in matters unlikely to appear there; and hence, unskilfully used, it may lead to the cramming of information by expert tutors without serious effort to master the subject. But if skilfully used, it may be made a powerful instrument for promoting coördination of knowledge, a broad comprehension of the subject, a grasp of underlying principles instead of memory of detached facts, and in some subjects may provide an incentive to intellectual effort such as no other type of examination can offer.

The benefits to be gained from a general examination are not needed equally in all fields of learning. In some subjects, like Mathematics, Physics, and Chemistry, every advanced course must require familiarity with the principles taught in the more elementary ones, so that an examination in the higher branches measures fairly well the command of the whole subject. In other departments, notably History, there is little natural sequence, and a student may in his Senior year pass an excellent examination in a course on Europe in the nineteenth century although he has completely forgotten the American history he studied as a Sophomore,— and yet the events on the two sides of the Atlantic are intimately related parts of one movement in human progress. The general examination may well be applied, therefore, in one field while it is not in another; and the Faculty has been wise in allowing one division to adopt the plan without requiring uniformity in all.

If the general examination stood alone, the optimism of many undergraduates would lead them to postpone preparation until the time drew near, and then it would be too late. This could be justified only on the assumption that the function of the College was limited to providing earnest men with opportunities for education, probably with the result, witnessed in the German universities, that a large part of the students would make no attempt to obtain or earn a degree. No one would advocate such a plan for undergraduates here. American colleges must strive to form character, to induce habits of diligence; and they must do so all the more because, unlike the German universities, they are not groups of professional schools with the stimulus of direct preparation for one's career in life. It is not proposed, therefore, to abandon examinations in the several courses except so far as they occur at the same time as the general examination. Moreover, if the student is expected to study a subject, to regard his courses as means rather than ends, to do some outside reading, he must have special guidance beyond that which is provided in the courses he takes. There must be tutors, not unlike those at the English universities, who confer with the students frequently, not about their work in courses alone, but also about their outside reading and their preparation for the final test that lies before them. Tutors of this kind are an integral and necessary factor in the plan. To provide them will require money, part of which has been promised, while the rest must be sought from friends of the College; and the benefit to the students is well worth the expense involved. The great advantage for the average student of a general examination upon his principal field of study, lies in forcing him to correlate what he has studied, to keep it in mind as a body of connected learning, to fill in gaps by reading, to appreciate that all true education must be in great part self-education, a personal effort to advance on the difficult path of knowledge, not a half-reluctant transportation through college in perambulators pushed by instructors.

No one in close touch with American education has failed to deplore the lack among the mass of undergraduates of keen interest in their studies, the small regard for scholarly attainment; and a general examination upon a field of concentration seems to offer the most promising means of improvement. It was the method adopted in England a hundred years ago. The class tests at Oxford based on general public examinations began in 1802, and five years later they were divided into the Honour Schools of *Literae Humaniores* and Mathematics and Physics.* The effect in stimulating interest in scholarship and respect for high rank was rapid, profound, and permanent. Success in the examinations has been universally accepted as a test of ability and a gateway to the careers entered by Oxford and Cambridge men. The failure of American undergraduates, and, following their lead, of the American public at large, to value excellence in college scholarship is due in part, as the students themselves de-

---

* The Mathematical Tripos at Cambridge began in 1747, the Civil Law Classes in 1815, the Classical Tripos in 1824. The other triposes at Cambridge and Honour Schools at Oxford were established at various dates after the middle of the nineteenth century.

clare, to the fact that rank in courses depends upon the varying
standards maintained by different instructors.   It is due also to
a sincere doubt whether one who can accumulate the largest number of high marks in short stretches of work is really the ablest
man.   Much must be ascribed, moreover, to the absence of competition on a large scale.   So long as college men are all treading
separate paths, crossing at many points but never leading to a
common goal, there can be little of that conviction of superior
qualities which attaches to the man who succeeds in achieving
what many others are striving for.   A well-ordered general examination avoids all of these imperfections, for it provides a uniform
standard, a competitive test and a run long enough to call out the
whole power of the man.   The stimulus is not only good for those
who hope to win high distinction, but will tend also to leaven the
whole mass.

To turn from studies to athletics is to leave a region where competition has been neglected for one where it has been carried to an
extreme by the students themselves.   The prevailing interest in
athletic sports has done much for sobriety and cleanliness of life
in college, but the vast scale of the public games has brought its
problems.   They have long ceased to be an undergraduate diver-
sion, managed entirely by the students, and maintained by their
subscriptions.   They have become great spectacles supported by
the sale of tickets to thousands of people; while experience has
proved that skilful coaching will determine the victory between
teams of approximately equal strength.   The result has been an
enormous growth in expenditure until the authorities have felt
compelled to take part in supervising it.   The experiment of
control by an Athletic Committee composed of three members of
the Faculty and three graduates appointed by the Governing
Boards, and three undergraduates selected by the captains of the
teams, has brought improvement.   Extravagance has been cur-
tailed; but, with a revenue of about two hundred thousand dollars
a year, money comes easily and is easily spent under the spur of
intense public interest in the result of the major contests, and a
little laxity quickly leads to grave abuse.   Extravagance still
exists and vigilant supervision is required to reduce it.   Graduates,
who form public opinion on these matters, must realise that inter-

collegiate victories are not the most important objects of college education.   Nor must they forget the need of physical training for the mass of students by neglecting to encourage the efforts recently made to cultivate healthful sports among men who have no prospect of playing on the college teams.

The promotion of a better college life, physical, intellectual and moral, has received much attention of late among men engaged in education.   At Harvard we believe that a vital matter is to launch the student aright on the new freedom of college life by means of Freshman dormitories; and it is a pleasure to state that enough money has been subscribed to build three out of the four buildings projected.   These three will house over four hundred and fifty students, or by far the greater part of the present Freshman class that does not live at home.   One of them will be paid for by the bequest of the late George Smith, left to the College many years ago to accumulate until it reached the sum required to build a group of three dormitories of the collective size of one of the quadrangles designed.   Another has been generously given by Mrs. Russell Sage, and at her request will be named Standish Hall. The third is provided by a large number of subscriptions from alumni and others.   The project will not be complete until the fourth is given, but the erection of the first three will be begun early in the coming year, as soon as the working plans, now progressing rapidly, have been completed.   One of the quadrangles will be on Boylston Street, behind the Power House, while the others will be built farther to the east along the parkway as far as De Wolf Street.   Their buildings will stand on three sides of quadrangles, the fourth side facing the river being open to the south.   The architect, Mr. Charles A. Coolidge, has adapted to the purpose with great skill the colonial style of the older buildings in the College Yard.

People not very familiar with the progress of the plan have expressed a fear that the Freshmen would be treated like boys at boarding school; but that would defeat the very object in view, of teaching them to use sensibly the large liberty of college life. Liberty is taught to young men not by regulations, but by its exercise in a proper environment.   The vital matter is the atmosphere and the traditions in which the youth is placed on entering college. At present he is too much enchained in a narrow set of friends who copy one another, not always wisely, and come too little into contact with the broadening influences of the college community as a whole. Hence he fails to see how much he can get out of college life, or finds it out too late to reap the full benefit thereof. The Seniors show their appreciation of all this by rooming together in the Yard, but they end where they should have begun.

In the School of Applied Science important changes have taken place during the year. A number of technical courses have been removed from the list open to undergraduates, carrying forward the design of placing the School on a graduate basis. At the same time the plan of instruction has been modified and made more intensive in method, so that a college graduate without technical preparation can be taught his Engineering, Mining, or Architecture in the shortest possible period. No doubt it will take time for the community to learn that a man who hopes to rise high in his profession gains in the end by a college education preceding his technical studies. Engineering ought to stand among the liberal professions which are enriched by a general education, and in fact the number of college men who enter engineering schools, though still small, is increasing year by year.

The organization of the School has also been altered. At the suggestion of the instructors, the departments have been formed into Schools of Engineering, of Mining and Metallurgy, of Architecture and so forth, each under a Council of instructors, the whole being grouped under a new and distinct Faculty of Applied Science. This has the double advantage of giving the Schools a more strictly professional tone under the government of a body devoted wholly to their interests, and of relieving the Faculty of Arts and Sciences of questions hardly germane to its regular work. The new organization nominally went into effect in September, 1912, but in fact the Faculty of Applied Science began its services in the year covered by this report, and its members are glad to work out their common problems in a meeting of this kind.

The Graduate Schools of Applied Science possess an admirable staff of professors, and already in some directions excellent equipment, but as yet few students, for the reputation in the profession which fills the classes is naturally of slow growth. It cannot be stimulated rapidly, and depends upon the achievements of the men that the institution has produced. These are the principal means of recruiting fresh students for any school, and years must always pass before their influence in the community is strongly felt.

Since the last report was written the Massachusetts Institute of Technology has decided, at the request of great numbers of our fellow citizens, to erect its new buildings in Cambridge, and this brings home to us the question whether some coöperation between the two institutions is not possible in the training of students who are graduates of colleges or technical schools. That would not trench upon the principal field of the Institute of Technology, while it would add greatly to the efficiency of training college graduates, to whose needs the curriculum provided for boys coming from high schools is imperfectly adapted. The number of such college graduates is, and for an indefinite time to come will be, far too small to justify two separate schools; and that is even more true of the men who, after finishing the regular technical course, want to pursue advanced work. To maintain two distinct plants, fully staffed and equipped, for the teaching of an insufficient number of students in the most expensive of all kinds of education is not only a waste of educational resources, but entails an even more pitiful loss of efficiency. The momentum obtained by a combined effort would be far greater than that of two separate schools striving singly for the same object. No plan of coöperation has been devised, but the difficulties ought not to be insuperable if approached with mutual good will and a sense that an educational institution does not exist solely for its own glory, but as a means to a larger end.

Some comment was aroused by the decline in the number of students in the Law School at the opening of the term in October, 1912; but this is due, as the Dean explains in his report, not to the size of the entering class, which is substantially as large as ever, but to raising the standard for continuing in the School in the case of men whose work has been defective. Since the School has grown larger it has become both possible and necessary to insist on thoroughly satisfactory work by all students who attend the classes and who by their very presence affect the standard. The number of graduates of Harvard College who enter the School has, indeed, fallen off of late years; but this, as the elaborate report of the National Bureau of Education on the occupation of college graduates shows, is part of a general movement which is felt most promptly at Harvard. To inquire into its causes would not be possible here. It is enough to point out that the occupations in which college men engage have enlarged greatly, and the attractions of business life have grown stronger. The report of the Bureau, with its diagrams of historic changes in the proportion of graduates following different vocations, is highly interesting.

The year has been marked in the Medical School by the appointment of two new deans. That of Dr. Bradford as Dean of the School has already been mentioned. The other office is new. For many years courses of instruction, both clinical and in the laboratories, have been offered for the benefit of physicians and surgeons in active practice. A large part of these have been included in the Medical Summer School, while others have been given in term-time. The science and art of medicine are advancing so rapidly that many practitioners are glad of opportunities to gain a greater familiarity with recent methods than they can get from medical journals alone; and the Faculty felt that instruction of this character could profitably be made more systematic. A Graduate School of Medicine has, therefore, been created, with a separate dean and administrative board, and to some extent an additional staff of instructors, although not a distinct Faculty. Dr. Horace David Arnold has been appointed Dean; and the School opened its courses in October, 1912, with a very promising registration.

Reference has been made on a preceding page and in former reports to the closer relations between the Medical School and the different hospitals. The central factor in the movement is the alliance with the Peter Bent Brigham Hospital, situated opposite the main entrance to the School. The buildings are nearly completed, and will be ready for the first patients in a few weeks. In accordance with the arrangement for a joint selection of the staff of the Hospital and instructors in the School, Dr. Christian, our Hersey Professor of the Theory and Practice of Medicine, is the Physician-in-Chief of the Hospital, and Dr. Harvey Cushing, formerly of Johns Hopkins University, is Surgeon-in-Chief and has taken his chair as Moseley Professor of Surgery at the School. The other members of the staff have been selected by mutual understanding.

Notable also in the history of the School have been the opening of the Collis P. Huntington Memorial Hospital for cancer in close coöperation with the School, and the calling for the first time of a non-resident to a chair in the School and a leading position on the staff of the Massachusetts General Hospital. Dr. David Linn Edsall, formerly of the University of Pennsylvania and later of Washington University at St. Louis, was appointed chief of one of the two continuous medical services at the Hospital and Jackson Professor of Clinical Medicine in the School. The only other appointment to a full professorship has been the promotion of George Gray Sears to Clinical Professor of Medicine.

The year has been remarkable for a series of contributions to medical science made at the School. During the summer and autumn of 1912 Dr. Folin published his discoveries in metabolism, which made a profound impression, and his analysis of the blood in cases of rheumatism and gout; Dr. Mallory, his discovery of the germ of whooping cough; while Dr. Rosenau, with the coöperation of Dr. Richardson of the State Board of Health and Professor Wheeler of the Bussey Institution, ascertained that infantile paralysis was transmitted through a species of stable fly (*Stomoxys calcitrans*). Enlarging the bounds of knowledge is a function of a university no less essential than imparting it; and in no field are the two more closely connected today than in medicine. Three such discoveries in the course of a single year are, therefore, a deep source of gratification.

During the year we have been fortunate in our exchange professors, both in those we have received and those we have sent forth. From France came Dr. Charles Diehl, Professor of Byzantine History at the University of Paris; from Germany Dr. Willy Kükenthal, Professor of Zoölogy and Director of the

Zoölogical Institute at the University of Breslau.   To Berlin
we sent Professor Theobald Smith of the Medical School, and to
Paris Professor William Morris Davis of the Geological Department.   The alliance whereby we are to send annually a member
of our staff to lecture for a month at each of four Western colleges,
Knox, Beloit, Grinnell and Colorado, was inaugurated during the
second half of the year by Professor Albert Bushnell Hart.   Instructors were sent to Harvard by two only of these colleges.   They
were Walter Houghton Freeman, Instructor in Greek at Grinnell,
who acted as Assistant in Greek here; and Elijah Clarence Hill,
Head Professor of Romance Languages and Literature at Colorado,
who gave an independent course in Spanish-American poetry.

The University as a whole rejoices in the munificent offer of
a new library building by Mrs. George D. Widener.   Gore Hall
has long been lamentably insufficient to contain the books on
its catalogue.   Many thousands of them, in yearly increasing
numbers, have been stored in the basements of other buildings,
while Gore Hall itself has been far too crowded for a proper use
even of the volumes on its shelves.   Among the precious lives
lost on the " Titanic " was that of Harry Elkins Widener of the
Class of 1907, a rare collector of rare books.   His collection,
comprising many editions of great value and interest, he left
to his mother, with a request to give it to Harvard when there
was a building suitable for the purpose.   But Gore Hall was
not fireproof, and Mrs. Widener, in view of the conditions, generously determined to build a complete university library on the
general interior plan worked out by our committee of architects
a year ago, with additional rooms for her son's books in a part
of the open court in the centre of the building.   These rooms
and the volumes they contain are to be under the charge of a
special librarian selected by Mrs. Widener, who gives also a fund
of $150,000 to care for, and at her discretion to enlarge, the collec-
tion.   The other parts of the Harry Elkins Widener Memorial
Library will form the four sides of a quadrangle, whereof the
northern side, with the main entrance, will cover very nearly
the site of the present Gore Hall, and the south front will be about
one hundred feet from Massachusetts Avenue.   The building
will contain one large and several smaller reading-rooms on the

North, and rooms for seminars on the upper floor; while the greater part of the eastern, western and southern sections will be occupied by the stack, in which, however, there will be provided working rooms for professors and a large number of tables separated by glass screens for other readers. Such an arrangement is designed to make the stack as convenient of access as possible to the scholars who use it, so that they may work with all their tools at hand.

Housing our books where they would be safe and could be used during the construction of the new building was no easy problem. It has been solved partly by turning Upper and Lower Massachusetts into reading-rooms; partly by the hospitality of Andover Theological Seminary, which has kindly allowed us to use any vacant space on its shelves; partly by sending appropriate books to various departmental libraries; but chiefly by transferring the students' dining-tables from Randall Hall to Foxcroft, and building temporary stacks for four hundred thousand volumes in the Hall, one of the few fireproof buildings we possess. Although the transfer of the books was made in term-time, it was carried out by Professor Coolidge, the Director of the Library, with such skill that there has been almost no interruption in their use.

Another important gift of a building has been that of a chemical laboratory by the Hon. T. Jefferson Coolidge in memory of his son, Thomas Jefferson Coolidge, Jr., of the Class of 1884. This building will be nearly of the same size as the Wolcott Gibbs Laboratory, and will be used for quantitative analysis. It faces Divinity Avenue, and will form part of the proposed, and sorely needed, group of chemical laboratories between that Avenue and Oxford Street. Work upon it has been carried on as rapidly as possible, with the result that by the end of the year 1912 the outer walls were built and the timbers of the roof were laid, ensuring its readiness for use before the opening of the next college year.

Of the other gifts received the largest have been: that of Mrs. Sage for the Freshman Dormitory; $100,000 from the Class of 1887 on its twenty-fifth anniversary; $125,000 from Mr. Edmund Cogswell Converse to found a professorship of Banking in the School of Business Administration; $100,000 from Mrs. Collis P.

Huntington for the construction of the Cancer Hospital; $74,285.71 from the estate of Mrs. William O. Moseley for travelling fellowships in the Medical School; $50,000 from the estate of Miss Harriet E. Goodnow to keep poor students in Harvard College; $50,000 from Mr. George R. Agassiz for the use of the Museum of Comparative Zoölogy. These and many other benefactions are described more fully in the report of the Treasurer.

Recipients of such generosity seem churlish in asking for more, but our needs are ever outrunning our resources, and one of the objects of the annual report is to point them out. There is still a deficit in the University, College and Library account, although for the year 1911–12 it was reduced to $14,750.40. Until it disappears we cannot expect an expansion of those departments that are undermanned, and still less any increase in salaries. That the incomes of professors are inadequate in view of the grade of talent required is generally admitted, and the constant rise in prices has been reducing their purchasing power year by year. One of the most pressing special needs is more laboratories for instruction and research in Chemistry, perhaps the most promising field for scientific investigation and one in which our equipment is still singularly insufficient. Another is an endowment for the Dental School, the imperative need of which was urged in the last report with a reference to the great services rendered to the public by the operating rooms and the sacrifices of the clinical instructors. Still another is the endowment of professorships in the School of Business Administration. One such, in Banking, has been founded as already stated by the generosity of Mr. Converse, but three more are required, and efforts are being made to raise the funds by subscriptions. Every professional school has meant the substitution of thorough instruction in the principles of an art for the slower and less comprehensive process of learning them by apprenticeship; and this School is based on a belief that the principles governing business organization and methods, which have been wrought out in practice by the labor of a generation of expert administrators, can be taught in a way to save the time of the student and make him more efficient. No new professional school, moreover, demonstrates its full value swiftly, and we need not be surprised that most of the students in our

School still think a single year of its training sufficient. That the School, however, has already won recognition of its usefulness is proved by the rapid increase in the number of men entering it. During the first few years the progress was naturally slow, but the period of experiment appears to have passed; for the number of first-year students taking full work rose in the autumn of 1912 to 71 as against 45 the year before, and these 71 were graduates of 35 different colleges in all parts of the country.

Friends of the University are trying to raise money for a building for the Department of Music. The sum required to erect the building has been generously offered on condition that $50,000 is subscribed for its maintenance, and this is nearly accomplished. An effort is also being made to enlarge the Peabody Museum of Archaeology and Ethnology in accordance with the original plan, and the subscriptions for this purpose are well under way. The collections of American ethnology are large and constantly growing, too large already for the building now standing. When the addition is built the University Museum designed by Mr. Agassiz will be complete.

The University now possesses several special funds for the publication of books or periodicals on various subjects. These funds in the aggregate are considerable, but there is a growing conviction that a great institution of learning cannot attain its full usefulness without a university press which can publish the writings of its scholars. To that object the special funds now in hand would contribute greatly. Yet it is not enough that certain subjects are provided for. Nor do these funds enable the University to do its own printing. It would be an advantage, and in the long run an economy, if we could collect fonts of type in different languages which a commercial printer can ill afford to buy for the text or notes to an occasional book which may come into his hands. Many of the books issued by a university press would more than pay for themselves. Almost all of them would pay a part of their cost, but some works of great scholarly value yield little and can be published in no other way. If selected by a judicious committee, the publications of such a press would contribute much to the credit of the University, and, what is more important, would stimulate productive scholarship which still lags behind in America. Neither the initial cost of such a press nor the expense of maintenance is very large, but an endowment is absolutely essential if it is to be established. A committee has been appointed to consider the subject and ascertain whether the funds can be procured.

One word about the form of gifts that will ensure the greatest usefulness. Sometimes benefactors encumber their funds with provisions too inelastic in their application. The object may well be made precise, so that the intent shall be strictly observed; but the best means of attaining that object may vary in the course of time. Permanent funds endure into an indefinite future, and it is not wise to try to be wiser than all posterity. The details of application for the object named may often be left to the sagacity of those who will come hereafter.

In a brief annual report it is impossible even to touch upon all the manifold activities of the University. It is better to confine one's remarks to the matters of most common interest, without intending to imply that other things are of less importance. Nothing has, therefore, been said here of many of our great departments, such as the Observatory, the Arboretum, the Bussey Institution, the Museums, and the laboratories. For these, and for more detailed information about the different Faculties and Schools, the Overseers and friends of the University are respectfully referred to the reports of the Deans and Directors which are submitted and printed herewith.

A. LAWRENCE LOWELL, *President.*

APPENDIX TO PRESIDENT'S REPORT

I

NEW REQUIREMENTS FOR DEGREES IN THE DIVINITY SCHOOL

DEGREE OF BACHELOR OF DIVINITY

To be admitted as a candidate for the degree of Bachelor of Divinity a student must be a graduate of an approved college. He must present, with evidence of graduation, a certified record of his studies and testimonials of character.

The conditions on which the degree is conferred are: —

1. The completion of three years of theological study.*
2. The passing of satisfactory examinations in the following subjects: —
   (a) The Religion of Israel, with Judaism to the second century A.D.
   (b) Early Christianity, as it appears in the New Testament and the writings of the subapostolic age, with the environing religious conditions in the Greek and Roman world.
   (c) The History of Christianity, particularly the history of thought, and of the religious life, corporate and individual.
   (d) The History of Religions, especially the religions of civilized peoples.
   (e) Systematic Theology.
   (f) The Work of the Minister, including Social Ethics.

In these examinations the candidate will be expected to show that he possesses an adequate knowledge of the fundamental branches of theological study and the ability to apply his knowledge.

3. Satisfactory examinations in whatever other studies have been pursued as part of the candidate's professional education, whether more advanced studies in the fields specified above or studies in other subjects. To this end each student will present at the beginning of his last half-year a detailed account of his studies, including the courses he has taken and his reading in connection with them.

The examinations for the degree will be held at the end of the third year, and will be partly in writing, partly oral. To be admitted to them the candidate must have passed satisfactorily in the courses he has taken

---

* A student who enters the School at the beginning of the second half-year may, by special vote of the Faculty after two years of residence, be allowed to present himself for the Bachelor's examination at the end of two and one half years of residence.

in the School.   Candidates who pass the examinations with distinction
may be recommended for the degree *cum laude*.

Instructors may employ such means of satisfying themselves of the
progress of students in their courses as seem to them advisable, — by
examinations, theses, written reports, conferences, etc., — reporting the
results to the Dean in writing at the end of each half-year.

It is requested that, in the final report on the course, the instructor
expresses not merely his judgment of the student's performance, but his
impression of his quality.

ADVANCED STANDING

Students qualified for admission to candidacy for the degree in this
School, who have studied in an approved theological school, may be
admitted to advanced standing.   Applicants for advanced standing must
present a complete record of their previous studies.

Graduates of other theological schools having a three years' course of
study may be admitted to third-year standing, and may receive the degree
of Bachelor of Divinity on passing examinations in the prescribed fields
specified above and in the other professional studies they have pursued
here or elsewhere.

UNCLASSIFIED STUDENTS

Students admitted from other theological schools as candidates for the
degree of Bachelor of Divinity, when they cannot be assigned immediately
to a class, may be temporarily registered as unclassified students.   Qualified persons who are admitted to pursue special or partial studies in the
School will be designated in the same way.

STUDIES

On or before the second Monday of each academic year, every student
shall submit to the Committee on Studies for its approval a plan of studies
for the ensuing year.   At the beginning of the second year, along with the
plan for the year, shall be presented also a provisional plan for the rest of
the course.

It is advised that students take introductory courses in the subjects
designated by the letters (*a*), (*b*), (*c*), and (*d*), above (Religion of Israel,
Early Christianity, Church History, History of Religions), also in Homiletics, Social Ethics, and the Philosophical Basis of Theology (Theism),
as early as possible; they will thus pursue other studies with greater profit
and have more freedom of choice in subsequent years.   It is recommended,
further, that Systematic Theology be not begun before the second year,
and that it be preceded, if possible, by the History of Christian Thought.

The number and variety of the courses offered by the Faculty of Divinity
and in the Andover Theological Seminary give students large opportunity
to pursue more advanced studies, either concentrated in one or more
subjects or distributed over several fields according to individual preference or plans.   Many courses that may profitably be taken by theological
students are offered by the Faculty of Arts and Sciences.   The titles of
some such courses are included under the head of " Allied Courses " in
the list below.   Fuller information about them will be found in the announcements of that Faculty.

DEGREE OF MASTER OF DIVINITY

To be admitted as a candidate for the degree of Master of Divinity a student must present the same testimonials of character as are required for the degree of Bachelor of Divinity, must be a graduate of an approved college and of a theological school having a three years' course of study, or give evidence, by examination or otherwise, of equivalent attainment. Knowledge of Greek is required, except in the case of candidates in Practical Theology, of whom proficiency in modern languages may be accepted instead. The candidate's ability to make effective use of Latin and German for the purpose of his studies will be determined by examination within the first two weeks of the term.

The requirements for the degree can ordinarily be fulfilled by one year wholly devoted to advanced theological study; but candidates whose preparation for the studies they propose to undertake proves to be insufficient, or who for any reason are unable to give all their time to their studies, may need a proportionally longer period.

A candidate's studies must fall primarily in one of the main fields of theological study, but may include subsidiary studies in other fields. The plan of study must be coherent, and the studies comprised in it of advanced grade, ordinarily including one research, or seminary, course, and must be approved beforehand by the Faculty as affording proper preparation for the degree. Each candidate will be under the direction of a member of the Faculty in the department in which his work principally lies. In courses in which a mid-year examination is held, the candidate will be expected to pass this with high credit.

The examination for the degree will be in the subjects of the candidate's studies, rather than in the particular courses he has heard, and will include, besides such written tests as may be prescribed in each case, an oral examination before the Faculty or a committee appointed for the purpose.

DEGREES OF MASTER OF ARTS AND DOCTOR OF PHILOSOPHY

In special cases students in the Divinity School may, with the approval of the Faculty, be candidates for the degree of Master of Arts and of Doctor of Philosophy. These degrees are administered by the Faculty of Arts and Sciences, and the conditions will be found in the announcement of the Graduate School of Arts and Sciences. A candidate for the degree of Master of Arts cannot at the same time be registered as a candidate for a degree in Divinity.

II

NEW REQUIREMENT FOR THE BACHELOR'S DEGREE IN HISTORY, GOVERNMENT, AND ECONOMICS

1. That the Division of History, Government, and Economics be authorized to require of all students whose field of concentration lies in this Division, in addition to the present requirements stated in terms of courses for the Bachelor's degree, a special final examination upon each

student's field of concentration; and that the passing of this examination shall be necessary in order to fulfil the requirements for concentration in this Division.

2. That students who pass this special examination may be excused from the regular final examinations in such courses of their last year as fall within the Division of History, Government, and Economics in the same way that candidates for distinction who pass a public test may now be excused under the rules of the Faculty.

3. That this requirement go into effect with the class entering in 1913.

4. That the Division of History, Government, and Economics submit for the sanction of the Faculty the detailed rules for the final examinations and such a detailed scheme of tutorial assistance as may be adopted before these are put into effect by the Division.

OUTLINE OF THE PLAN FOR A GENERAL FINAL EXAMINATION IN THE DIVISION OF HISTORY, GOVERNMENT, AND ECONOMICS

I. GENERAL EXAMINATION. — In addition to the requirements now established in terms of courses for the degrees of Bachelor of Arts and Bachelor of Science, a general examination shall be taken as part of the requirement for the Bachelor's degree by all students concentrating within the Division of History, Government, and Economics. This examination will be held at or about the close of a student's final year of preparation, provision being made for those students who take their degree in the middle of the year.

(a) *Method of Examination.* — The examination will be both written and oral. The written examination will consist of not less than two three-hour papers. The first of these will be designed to test the general attainment of candidates in subjects within this Division; the second paper will be of a more special character. With the approval of the Examiners, however, candidates will be allowed to submit a suitable thesis in lieu of this special written examination or part thereof. The oral examination will be taken in the period intervening between the first written paper and the close of the college year.

(b) *Scope of the Examination.* — The examinations provided in the foregoing section will cover the entire work of each candidate in this Division and, specifically, a field of study (e. g., American history and government, or international law and diplomatic history, or accounting and corporations) represented approximately by three full courses, together with outside reading selected in connection with, or supplementary to, these courses. Suitable fields of study for purposes of this examination will be mapped out by the Division or by the Departments composing it; but provision will also be made for the approval of other suitable fields selected by candidates themselves.

(c) *Conduct of the Examination.* — The administration of the examinations will be placed in the hands of a Division committee of three, approved by the President. Members of this committee will be designated as Examiners and will be relieved from all their regular instruction for the second half-year or from its equivalent, except instruction in courses of research. The Division considers it a necessary part of the plan that the regular instruction from which the members of the committee are thus relieved be replaced both in quantity and quality. Examiners should be appointed for a three-year term, and the addition of an outside examiner will be arranged for, whenever practicable. The Examiners will prepare all questions for the written examinations, will read examination books, and will conduct the oral examination.

II. Preparation of Students for the General Examination. — Students concentrating in the Division will be encouraged to select their own fields of study, and, so far as possible, to carry forward their own preparation, including a mastery of the reading selected in courses or supplementary to them. But tutorial assistance also will be provided for each student who intends to take the general examination. This assistance will be given by Tutors under the direction of the Division. The work of these Tutors will be to guide students in their respective fields of study, to assist them in coördinating the knowledge which they have derived from different courses, and to stimulate in them the reading habit. Tutors will meet the students in small groups and at individual conferences. The Examiners will be authorized, however, to exempt from such conferences, upon the recommendation of a member of the Division, good students who are pursuing special work under his direction.

REPORTS OF DEPARTMENTS

THE FACULTY OF ARTS AND SCIENCES

To the President of the University: —

Sir, — I have the honor of presenting a report on the work of the Faculty of Arts and Sciences for the academic year 1911–12.

Besides the President, the Faculty contained eighty-nine Professors, sixty-one Assistant Professors, one Lecturer, twenty-five Instructors, the Acting Secretary, the Assistant Dean of Harvard College, and the Recorder, — in all, a hundred and eighty members.

Instruction in 1911–12

With the following list of courses of instruction that were actually given under the authority of the Faculty, I print a statement of the number and the classification of the students in each course. The figures are those officially returned to the Recorder by the several instructors at the close of the academic year, and take no account of persons who, regularly or irregularly, attended the exercises and did the work of a course without being officially recognized as members of it. The abbreviations are those ordinarily used in such lists: *Se.*, Senior; *Ju.*, Junior; *So.*, Sophomore; *Fr.*, Freshman; *Sp.*, Special Student; *uC.*, Unclassified; *Gr.*, Graduate School of Arts and Sciences; *G.S.*, Graduate School of Applied Science; *G.B.*, Graduate School of Business Administration; *R.*, Radcliffe; *Di.*, Divinity; *And.*, Andover; *Me.*, Medical School; *Ext.*, Department of University Extension; *Instr.*, Instructor. The number of " Freshmen " in courses for older students is misleading. Many " Freshmen " are Freshmen because of admission conditions, and are otherwise indistinguishable from Sophomores, Juniors, or Seniors.

COURSES OF INSTRUCTION GIVEN IN 1911–12

GROUP I

Semitic Languages and History

For Undergraduates and Graduates: —

1¹. Professor JEWETT. — Hebrew. Selections from the prose narratives of the Old Testament.   2 So., 1 Fr., 3 And.   Total 6.

2². Professor LYON. — Hebrew (second course).   Syntax.   Extensive reading in the Old Testament.   2 So., 2 Fr., 1 And.   Total 5.

4. Professor LYON. — The Old Testament, with special reference to the history and the literature of Israel.   9 Se., 17 Ju., 6 So., 5 F., 1 And.   Total 38.

A5. Professor ARNOLD. — Introduction to the Old Testament.   History of the text; the formation of the Canon; historico-critical study of the origin, form, and contents of the several books.   1 Se., 4 Di., 4 And.   Total 9.

12 *hf.* Professor LYON. — History of Babylonia and Assyria.
                    1 Gr., 4 Ju.   Total 5.

Primarily for Graduates: —

A4 ¹*hf.* Professor ARNOLD. — History of Israel.   1 Se., 1 Di., 7 And.   Total 9.

‡11. Professor LYON. — Assyrian (second course).   The Laws of Hammurabi; early historical records; mythological poems.   1 Gr.   Total 1.

‡14. Professor JEWETT. — Arabic (second course).   Selections from the Qorân, the Hadîth, and classical writers on geography and history.
                    1 Gr., 1 So.   Total 2.

18. Professor JEWETT. — Classical Aramaic (Syriac).   Selections from the Peshitto; Syriac prose of the classical period.   1 Di.   Total 1.

Course of Research

A20. Professor ARNOLD. — Old Testament Problems.   1 Gr.   Total 1.

Egyptology

For Undergraduates and Graduates: —

3 ¹*hf.* Asst. Professor REISNER. — History of Egypt.
                    24 Se., 24 Ju., 7 So., 2 Fr., 1 Sp.   Total 58.

Primarily for Graduates: —

6 ¹*hf.* Asst. Professor REISNER. — Archaeological Field Work.   Theory and practice of archaeological field work as a branch of historical research.
                    3 Gr., 1 Se.   Total 4.

Indic Philology

For Undergraduates and Graduates: —

1a ¹*hf.* Professor LANMAN. — Elementary Sanskrit.   4 Gr.   Total 4.

1b ²*hf.* Professor LANMAN. — Elementary Sanskrit (continued).   Bhagavad-Gîtâ.   Upanishads.   3 Gr.   Total 3.

Primarily for Graduates : —

2 ¹*hf.* Professor LANMAN. — Advanced Sanskrit. Mahā-Bhārata (rapid reading). Book 2 of the oldest Beast-fables of Kashmir, Tantra-ākhyāyika.
1 Gr. Total 1.

3 ²*hf.* Professor LANMAN. — Advanced Sanskrit (continued). Epigrams of Bhartri-hari with the native commentary. Selections from Vedas and Brāhmanas. 1 Gr. Total 1.

, The Classics

Primarily for Undergraduates : —

GREEK

G. Dr. K. K. SMITH. — Course for Beginners.
1 Gr., 3 So., 9 Fr., 1 Sp. Total 14.

A. Mr. MILLER. — Greek Literature. Homer, Odyssey; Euripides and Aristophanes. 3 Ju., 3 So., 16 Fr., 1 uC. Total 23.

B. Asst. Professor C. N. JACKSON, Dr. POST, and Dr. LITCHFIELD. — Greek Literature. Plato; Lysias; Elegiac, Iambic, and Lyric Poets; Euripides. Lectures on the History of Greek Literature.
4 Ju., 1 So., 26 Fr. Total 31.

E hf. Dr. WEBB. — Greek Prose Composition (first course).
1 Ju., 3 So., 2 Fr., 1 uC. Total 7.

1*a* ¹*hf.* Dr. LITCHFIELD. — Greek Literature. The Period of Athenian Supremacy. Herodotus; Aeschylus; Plutarch. 2 Fr., 1 uC. Total 3.

1*b* ²*hf.* Dr. POST. — Greek Literature. The Period of Athenian Supremacy. Thucydides; Aristophanes; Sophocles. 4 Fr., 1 uC. Total 5.

2. Professor C. P. PARKER and Asst. Professor C. N. JACKSON. — Greek Literature. Aristophanes; Thucydides; Aeschylus; Sophocles.
2 Se., 1 Ju., 5 So. Total 8.

3 *hf.* Asst. Professor CHASE. — Greek Prose Composition (second course).
4 Ju., 1 Fr., 1 uC. Total 6.

LATIN

A. Mr. MILLER. — Latin Literature. Cicero (selected speeches). Virgil.
1 Ju., 1 So., 5 Fr., 1 Sp., 1 uC. Total 9.

B. Professor E. K. RAND, Drs. WEBB, K. K. SMITH, LITCHFIELD, and Mr. MILLER. — Latin Literature. Livy; Terence; Horace.
1 Ju., 1 So., 99 Fr., 1 uC. Total 102.

E hf. Dr. LITCHFIELD. — Latin Composition (first course). Translation of English Narrative. 1 Se., 1 Ju., 4 So., 4 Fr. Total 10.

1. Professor CLIFFORD H. MOORE and Dr. WEBB. — Latin Literature. Tacitus; Catullus; Horace. 2 Se., 2 Ju., 15 So., 5 Fr. Total 24.

2*a* ¹*hf.* Dr. LITCHFIELD. — Latin Literature. General View of Latin Poetry.
4 So. Total 4.

2*b* ²*hf.* Dr. WEBB. — Latin Literature. Introduction to Latin Prose Literature. Tacitus. 1 Ju., 2 So., 1 Fr. Total 4.

3 *hf.* Dr. K. K. SMITH. — Latin Composition (second course). 4 Ju. Total 4.

For Undergraduates and Graduates : —

GREEK

6. Professor WEIR SMYTH and Dr. POST. — Greek Literature. Demosthenes; Aeschines; Aeschylus; Sophocles; Aristophanes.
1 Gr., 1 Se., 10 Ju., 1 So., 1 Fr., 1 uC. Total 15.

7 *hf.* Asst. Professor C. N. JACKSON. — Greek Prose Composition (third course).   4 Gr., 4 Se., 1 Ju. Total 9.

8. Professor C. P. PARKER. — Plato; Aristotle. Survey of Greek Philosophy from Thales to Aristotle.   1 Gr., 5 Se. Total 6.

15. Professor WEIR SMYTH and Dr. LITCHFIELD. — Greek Literature. The Homeric Poems, with studies of their literary influence. 2 Gr. Total 2.

LATIN

6. Professor A. A. HOWARD. — Latin Literature. Suetonius; Pliny; Juvenal; Martial.   4 Gr., 4 Se., 12 Ju., 1 uC. Total 21.

7 *hf.* Professor C. P. PARKER. — Latin Composition (third course).
4 Gr., 3 Se., 1 Ju. Total 8.

8. Professors CLIFFORD H. MOORE and E. K. RAND. — Latin Literature. Cicero; Lucretius; Plautus. 2 Gr., 6 Se., 2 Ju., 1 Fr., 1 uC. Total 12.

10. Professor CLIFFORD H. MOORE. — The Life and Thought of the Romans. Illustrated in the Monuments and in the Literature.
6 Se., 15 Ju., 1 Fr. Total 22.

12. Professor A. A. HOWARD. — History of Latin Literature to the middle of the Second Century.   3 Gr., 1 Se. Total 4.

Primarily for Graduates : —

CLASSICAL PHILOLOGY

25 ¹*hf.* Asst. Professor C. N. JACKSON. — Introduction to the Interpretation and Criticism of Classical Authors. History of Classical Studies.
3 Gr. Total 3.

‡37 ¹*hf.* Professor WEIR SMYTH. — Greek Lyric Poetry; The Elegy. With especial attention to the History of the Elegy.   4 Gr., 1 R. Total 5.

‡33 ²*hf.* Professor WEIR SMYTH. — Pindar.   8 Gr., 2 R., 1 Instr. Total 11.

43 ¹*hf.* Dr. POST. — Sophocles. Three Plays of Sophocles.
3 Gr., 2 Se., 1 Ju. Total 6.

‡40 ²*hf.* Professor WEIR SMYTH. — The Alexandrian Age. 2 Se., 1 R. Total 3.

‡59. Professor ROPES. — The Epistles of St. Paul. Selected portions.
3 Di. Total 3.

47 ¹*hf.* Professor A. A. HOWARD. — Terence. The Comedies of Terence.
6 Gr. Total 6.

58 ²*hf.* Asst. Professor C. N. JACKSON. — The later Roman Epic.
2 Gr., 1 Se. Total 3.

34 *hf*. Dr. K. K. SMITH. — Greek Grammar (Sounds and Inflections).   Study of Dialectic Inscriptions.   2 Gr.   Total 2.

28 *hf*. Professor A. A. HOWARD. — Latin Grammar (Syntax).   3 Gr.   Total 3.

50 *hf*. Professor CLIFFORD H. MOORE. — Introduction to Latin Epigraphy.
                                                6 Gr., 2 R., 1 Instr.   Total 9.

49 *hf*. Professor E. K. RAND. — Latin Palaeography.   Introduction to Latin Palaeography.   7 Gr.   Total 7.

29 *hf*. Professor CLIFFORD H. MOORE. — The Religion and Worship of the Greeks.   7 Gr., 1 Di., 1 Instr.   Total 9.

20.   *The Seminary of Classical Philology*

Professors C. P. PARKER and E. K. RAND, Directors for 1911–12. — Training in philological criticism and research.   Text-criticism and interpretation of Greek and Latin authors: for 1911–12, the Platonic Scholia and the Transmission of the text of Latin Authors in the Early Middle Ages.
                                                5 Gr.   Total 5.

CLASSICAL ARCHAEOLOGY

For Undergraduates and Graduates: —

1a *hf*. Asst. Professor CHASE. — Greek Archaeology.
                                5 Gr., 8 Se., 6 Ju., 1 So., 1 Fr.   Total 21.

1b *hf*. Asst. Professor CHASE. — Etruscan and Roman Archaeology.
                                3 Gr., 7 Se., 7 Ju., 2 So., 1 Sp.   Total 20.

Primarily for Graduates: —

6 *hf*. Asst. Professor CHASE. — Greek Vases.   3 Gr., 1 Ju.   Total 4.

English

ENGLISH COMPOSITION

Primarily for Undergraduates: —

A. Professors BRIGGS and HURLBUT, and Asst. Professor GREENOUGH, Drs. HANFORD, LEACH, LONG, WHITMORE, and Messrs. FRENCH, HERSEY, LEWIS, M. McLEOD, C. A. MOORE, SAVAGE, SHEAHAN, SHIPHERD, and WITHINGTON. — Rhetoric and English Composition.
                        1 G.B., 2 Ju., 10 So., 495 Fr., 12 Sp., 8 uC.   Total 528.
Of this number, 64 (1 Ju., 1 So., 61 Fr., 1 Sp.,) were relieved of the prescription of English at the end of the first half-year; 31 Fr., 1 uC., took the second half-year's work as an elective half-course.

D *hf*. Dr. WEBSTER, assisted by Messrs. O'CONOR and WITHINGTON. — English Composition.
                                1 Gr., 5 Se., 5 Ju., 34 So., 47 Fr., 2 uC.   Total 94.

31. Dr. BERNBAUM. — English Composition.
                                1 Se., 13 So., 4 Fr., 1 Sp., 5 uC.   Total 24.

22. Dr. MAYNADIER, assisted by Mr. COURS. — English Composition.
                        1 Gr., 13 Se., 30 Ju., 14 So., 8 Fr., 2 Sp., 8 uC.   Total 76.

18. Mr. STONE. — The Forms of Public Address.
                                15 Se., 30 Ju., 10 So., 1 Fr., 1 Sp., 2 uC.   Total 59.

30 *hf*. Mr. STONE. — Debating.   1 Gr., 5 Se., 5 Ju., 1 So., 1 Fr.,   Total 18.

For Undergraduates and Graduates : —

12. Asst. Professor COPELAND. — English Composition.

       7 Se., 15 Ju., 11 So., 1 Sp. Total 34.

57 *hf.* Professor BLISS PERRY. — English Composition.

       3 Gr., 1 Se., 2 Ju., 1 Sp., 1 Di. Total 8.

58 ¹*hf.* Professor WENDELL. — English Composition. 2 Se., 2 Ju., 1 So. Total 5.

Primarily for Graduates : —

5. Professor BRIGGS. — English Composition (advanced course).

      15 Gr., 6 Se., 7 Ju., 2 So., 1 Sp., 1 uC. Total 32.

47. Professor BAKER. — English Composition. The Technique of the Drama.

      11 Gr., 4 Ju., 1 So., 2 Sp., 1 uC., 2 Ext. Total 21.

ENGLISH LANGUAGE AND LITERATURE

Primarily for Undergraduates : —

28 *hf.* Professors BRIGGS, BLISS PERRY, KITTREDGE, BAKER, and NEILSON, and Dr. BERNBAUM. — History and Development of English Literature in outline.   58 Fr., 1 Sp., 1 uC. Total 60.

41. Professor WENDELL, assisted by Messrs. WITHINGTON and HUNT. — History of English Literature from the Elizabethan times to the present.

     1 Gr., 7 Se., 31 Ju., 48 So., 3 Fr., 2 Sp., 6 uC. Total 98.

37 ²*hf.* Dr. MAYNADIER. — The Story of King Arthur.

     13 Se., 19 Ju., 26 So., 9 Fr., 1 Sp., 4 uC. Total 72.

For Undergraduates and Graduates : —

8a ¹*hf.* Dr. WEBSTER. — Anglo-Saxon.

      17 Gr., 5 Se., 1 Ju., 2 So., 1 Fr. Total 26.

1. Professors NEILSON and F. N. ROBINSON. — Chaucer.

      21 Gr., 6 Se., 3 Ju., 1 So. Total 31.

2. Professor KITTREDGE. — Shakspere.

    16 Gr., 13 Se., 39 Ju., 17 So., 3 Fr., 1 Sp., 3 uC. Total 92.

11a ¹*hf.* Professor NEILSON. — Bacon.

     3 Gr., 7 Se., 15 Ju., 7 So., 5 Fr., 1 uC. Total 38.

11b ²*hf.* Professor NEILSON. — Milton.

     2 Gr., 5 Se., 12 Ju., 6 So., 4 Fr., 1 uC. Total 30.

61 ¹*hf.* Asst. Professor GREENOUGH. — Eighteenth Century Periodicals, particularly the Tatler, Spectator, Rambler, and Adventurer.

     6 Gr., 8 Se., 7 Ju., 3 So., 7 Fr., 2 uC. Total 33.

53 ²*hf.* Asst. Professor COPELAND, assisted by Mr. SHEAHAN. — Scott.

   3 Gr., 51 Se., 66 Ju., 40 So., 15 Fr., 2 Sp., 3 uC., 1 Law. Total 181.

16 ²*hf.* Professor BRIGGS. — History and Principles of English Versification.

     9 Gr., 3 Se., 8 Ju., 1 So., 3 Fr., 1 Sp., 1 uC. Total 26.

Primarily for Graduates : —

8b ²*hf.* Professors KITTREDGE and F. N. ROBINSON. — Anglo-Saxon. Béowulf.

      20 Gr., 4 Se. Total 24.

25 ²*hf*. Professor F. N. Robinson. — Anglo-Saxon Poetry. 6 Gr. Total 6.

Comparative Literature 25 *hf*. (See Comparative Literature, p. 48.)

44 ². Professor Kittredge. — Chaucer. Study of special topics.
10 Gr. Total 10.

14. Professor Baker. — The Drama in England from the Miracle Plays to the Closing of the Theatres.
32 Gr., 6 Se., 4 Ju., 1 So., 1 Sp., 2 uC. Total 46.

39. Professor Baker. — The Drama in England from 1642 to 1900.
16 Gr., 14 Se., 9 Ju., 3 So., 4 Sp., 2 uC., 1 Law. Total 49.

62 ¹*hf*. Asst. Professor Greenough. — The Character, with some Consideration of Related Forms. 8 Gr., 4 Se. Total 12.

56 ²*hf*. Dr. Bernbaum. — Eighteenth Century Sentimentalists and their Opponents. 10 Gr., 1 G.S., 1 Se., 1 Ju., 1 uC. Total 14.

59. Professor Bliss Perry. — The English Critical Essay.
15 Gr., 1 Fr., 1 Sp. Total 17.

24 ¹*hf*. Professor Neilson. — Studies in the Poets of the Romantic Period.
37 Gr., 4 Se., 3 Ju., 3 So., 2 Fr., 1 Sp. Total 50.

29 ¹*hf*. Dr. Maynadier. — The English Novel.
3 Gr., 2 Se., 4 Ju., 2 So., 1 Fr. Total 12.

33 ²*hf*. Professor Wendell. — The Literary History of America.
8 Gr., 4 Se. Total 12.

63 ²*hf*. Professor Bliss Perry. — Emerson
16 Gr., 31 Se., 26 Ju., 3 So., 1 Sp., 1 uC., 1 Di. Total 79.

Courses of Special Study

20. The instructors in English held themselves ready to assist and advise competent Graduate Students who might propose plans of special study in the language or literature of the periods or in the topics mentioned below. Such plans, however, must in each case have met the approval of the Department.

a. Professor F. N. Robinson. — Anglo-Saxon. 1 Gr. Total 1.

c. Professor Neilson. — Modern English Literature. 4 Gr. Total 4.

Professor Greenough. — Modern English Literature. 1 Gr. Total 1.

d. Professor Baker. — The English Drama: its history, and its relation to Continental Drama. 4 Gr. Total 4.

Public Speaking

Primarily for Undergraduates : —

A. Mr. Perret. — Voice Training, with Practice in Speaking and Reading.
4 Ju., 1 So., 16 Fr., 1 uC. Total 22.

2 *hf*. Asst. Professor Winter, and Mr. Bunker. — Masterpieces of Public Discourse. (*a*) Platform delivery — principles and practice. Selections from recent speeches. (*b*) Study of representative speeches, and practice in oral discussion. 8 Se., 8 Ju., 4 So., 5 Fr., 1 uC. Total 26.

3 *hf.* Asst. Professor WINTER, and Messrs. PERRET and PORTER. — Public Speaking. Practice in the delivery of original speeches, both prepared and extemporaneous. 23 Se., 40 Ju., 25 So., 3 Fr., 1 Sp. Total 92.

4 *hf.* Asst. Professor WINTER and Messrs. PERRET and BUNKER. — Vocal Interpretation of Dramatic Literature. Interpretative study, and training in speech and action. 1 Se., 3 Ju., 2 So., 2 Fr., 1 uC., 1 Ext. Total 10.

F². Asst. Professor WINTER. — Advanced Training in Platform Delivery.
2 Gr., 3 Se., 2 Law, 1 Me., 1 Instr. Total 9.

Germanic Languages and Literatures

GERMAN

Primarily for Undergraduates : —

A. Asst. Professor BIERWIRTH, Drs. EISERHARDT and PETTENGILL, and Messrs. IBERSHOFF, HERRICK, and A. E. RAND. — Elementary Course.
8 Gr., 5 Se., 7 Ju., 10 So., 186 Fr., 5 Sp., 8 uC., 4 Di. Total 233.

B. Mr. HERRICK. — Elementary Course (counting as two courses).
1 Se., 1 Jr., 1 So., 16 Fr., 2 Sp., 3 uC. Total 24.

C. Asst. Professor W. G. HOWARD, Drs. WEBER and EISERHARDT. — German Prose and Poetry. 1 Ju., 2 So., 39 Fr., 1 uC. Total 43.

1a. Drs. LIEDER and PETTENGILL. — German Prose and Poetry.
1 Se., 2 Ju., 37 So., 17 Fr., 3 uC. Total 60.

1b. Dr. WEBER. — German Prose. Subjects in History and Biography.
2 Gr., 1 Se., 11 Ju., 12 So., 16 Fr., 1 Sp., 1uC. Total 44.

1c. Dr. LIEDER. — German Scientific Prose. Subjects in Natural Science.
1 Gr., 2 Se., 14 Ju., 12 So., 14 Fr., 1 uC. Total 44.

F¹ *hf.* Mr. HERRICK. — Practice in speaking and writing German (first course).
6 Se., 9 Ju., 7 So., 15 Fr., 1 Sp., 1 uC. Total 39.

H² *hf.* Dr. EISERHARDT. — Practice in speaking and writing German (second course). 4 Se., 7 Ju., 7 So., 10 Fr., 2 uC. Total 30.

2a. Professor VON JAGEMANN and Dr. EISERHARDT. — Introduction to German Literature of the Eighteenth and Nineteenth Centuries. Lessing, Goethe, and Schiller. German Ballads and Lyrics.
10 Ju., 6 So., 26 Fr., 1 Sp., 2 uC. Total 45.

2b. Professor H. S. WHITE and Dr. LIEDER. — Introduction to German Literature of the Eighteenth and Nineteenth Centuries. Lessing, Goethe, and Schiller. German Ballads and Lyrics.
3 Se., 10 Ju., 16 So., 57 Fr., 1 uC. Total 87.

2c. Professor H. S. WHITE. — German Prose. Subjects in German History. Freytag; Below; Kugler; Biedermann; Tombo.
4 Ju., 9 So., 22 Fr., 1 uC. Total 36.

3. Asst. Professor BIERWIRTH. — Schiller and his Time. Der Dreissigjährige Krieg; Wallenstein; Maria Stuart; Die Jungfrau von Orleans; Die Braut von Messina; Gedichte.
1 Gr., 1 Se., 1 Ju., 13 So., 6 Fr., 2 uC. Total 24.

4. Professor WALZ and Dr. WEBER. — Goethe and his Time. Works of the Storm and Stress Period; Autobiographical Works; Poems; Egmont; Iphigenie; Tasso; Faust.

1 Gr., 6 Se., 13 Ju., 12 So., 4 Fr., 2 uC. Total 38.

25 ¹*hf.* Professor FRANCKE, assisted by Mr. GROSSMANN. — History of German Literature in outline.   29 Se., 27 Ju., 15 So., 10 Fr., 1 Sp. Total 82.

For Undergraduates and Graduates : —

18 *hf.* Dr. WEBER. — German Grammar and practice in writing German (advanced course).   2 Gr., 1 Ju., 2 So., 1 uC., 1 Law. Total 7.

8. Professor WALZ and Dr. WEBER. — German Literature in the Twelfth and Thirteenth Centuries. Nibelungenlied; Kudrun; Hartmann; Wolfram; Walther von der Vogelweide. Translation into modern German.

5 Gr., 1 Ju., 1 So. Total 7.

6 ¹*hf.* Professor FRANCKE. — History of German Culture from the End of the Thirty Years' War to the Death of Frederick the Great.

9 Gr., 2 Se., 6 Ju., 5 So., 2 Fr., 1 Sp. Total 25.

Comparative Literature 8²*hf.*   (See Comparative Literature, p. 43.)

26a ¹*hf.* Asst. Professor W. G. HOWARD. —German Literature in the first half of the Nineteenth Century. Kleist; Uhland; Heine.

4 Gr., 4 Se., 7 Ju., 2 uC. Total 17.

26b ²*hf.* Asst. Professor W. G. HOWARD. — German Literature in the second half of the Nineteenth Century. The Development of the Novel and the Drama.   5 Gr., 2 Se., 3 Ju., 2 So., 1 uC. Total 13.

29. Professor H. S. WHITE. — The Life and Writings of Richard Wagner. Selections from the texts of Richard Wagner's musical dramas, with some study of the legendary background, and with illustrations and elucidations from Wagner's other writings.

1 Gr., 7 Se., 8 Ju., 2 So., 3 Fr. Total 21.

33 ²*hf.* Dr. WEBER. — The German Novel in the Nineteenth Century.

3 Gr., 3 So., 1 uC. Total 7.

Primarily for Graduates : —

‡9 ¹*hf.* Professor FRANCKE. — German Religious Sculpture in the Middle Ages, with demonstrations in the Germanic Museum.

1 Gr., 1 Ju., 4 R. Total 6.

‡Comparative Literature 28 ¹*hf.*   (See Comparative Literature, p. 43.)

36 ²*hf.* Asst. Professor BIERWIRTH. — German Lyric Poetry since 1870.

5 Gr., 1 So., 3 R. Total 9.

‡12a ¹*hf.* Professor VON JAGEMANN. — Gothic. Introduction to the Study of Germanic Philology. General Introduction; phonology.

20 Gr., 7 R. Total 27.

‡12b ²*hf.* Professor VON JAGEMANN. — Introduction to the Study of Germanic Philology (continued). Morphology; etymology. 6 Gr., 3 R. Total 9.

‡15 ²*hf.* Professor WALZ. — Old High German.   6 Gr., 1 R. Total 7.

‡21. Professor VON JAGEMANN. — History of the German Language.

5 Gr., 1 R. Total 6.

Seminary Courses

‡20a ¹ʰf. Asst. Professor W. G. Howard. — Lessing's Laokoon. 5 Gr. Total 5.

‡20b ²ʰf. Professor Francke. — Schiller's Philosophical Poems.

2 Gr., 1 Sp. Total 3.

SCANDINAVIAN

For Undergraduates and Graduates:

1 ¹ʰf. Professor Schofield. — Dano-Norwegian. An introduction to the study of the Danish and Norwegian languages and literatures. Practice in the spoken language. Reading of selected texts.

4 Gr., 1 Se., 1 Ju., 2 So., 1 Sp. Total 9.

Primarily for Graduates:

5². Dr. Leach. — History of the Scandinavian Languages.

3 Gr., 1 Instr. Total 4.

Romance Languages and Literatures

FRENCH

Primarily for Undergraduates: —

A. Dr. Whittem, Drs. Hawkins and Wilkins, and Messrs. Lincoln, Weston, and Corley. — Elementary Course. French prose and composition.

17 Gr., 1 G.S., 3 Se., 10 Ju., 7 So., 85 Fr., 6 Sp., 10 uC., 2 And. Total 141.

1. Asst. Professor Babbitt, Drs. Hawkins and Wilkins, and Messrs. Raiche and Lincoln. — French Prose, historical and general. Translation from French into English. 9 Ju., 48 So., 49 Fr., 1 Sp., 11 uC. Total 118.

2c. Asst. Professor Potter, Drs. Hawkins and Whittem, and Messrs. Lincoln, Weston, and Corley. — French Prose and Poetry. Corneille; Racine; Molière; Victor Hugo; Alfred de Musset; Balzac; Mérimée; Flaubert; Daudet; Loti; Zola. Composition.

4 Se., 9 Ju., 84 So., 86 Fr., 2 Sp., 3 uC. Total 188.

2a. Asst. Professors Wright and Allard, and Messrs. Mercier, Raiche, Weston, and Atkin. — French Prose and Poetry. Corneille; Racine; Molière; Victor Hugo; Balzac; George Sand; Alfred de Musset; Rostand. Composition. 1 Gr., 4 Ju., 39 So., 118 Fr., 1 Sp., 1 uC. Total 164.

3. Mr. Raiche. — French Composition (elementary course).

2 Se., 8 Ju., 28 So., 11 Fr. Total 49.

4 ¹ʰf. Mr. Mercier. — French Composition (intermediate course).

1 Gr., 6 Se., 10 Ju., 16 So., 4 Fr., 1 Sp. Total 38.

5 ²ʰf. Mr. Mercier. — French Composition (advanced course).

1 Gr., 3 Se., 6 Ju., 12 So., 4 Fr., 1 uC. Total 27.

For Undergraduates and Graduates: —

6. Professors Grandgent and Ford, Asst. Professor Allard, and Mr. Mercier. — General View of French Literature.

2 Gr., 1 G.S., 5 Se., 18 Ju., 35 So., 5 Fr., 1 uC. Total 67.

8. Asst. Professor Allard. — French Literature in the Eighteenth Century.

2 Gr., 4 Se., 4 Ju., 4 So., 3 Fr. Total 17.

9. Asst. Professor WRIGHT. — French Literature in the Seventeenth Century.
5 Gr., 3 Se., 1 So.   Total 9.

17 *hf.* Asst. Professor BABBITT. — Literary Criticism in France, with special reference to the Nineteenth Century.   6 Gr., 2 Ju.   Total 8.

Comparative Literature 9.   (See Comparative Literature, p. 48.)

Primarily for Graduates : —

‡12. Professor SHELDON. — Old French Literature.   4 Gr., 1 R.   Total 5.

21 *hf.* Asst. Professor WRIGHT. — French Prose in the Sixteenth Century. Rabelais ; Montaigne.   9 Gr.   Total 9.

24 *hf.* Asst. Professor ALLARD. — Studies in the French Drama of the Nineteenth Century.   4 Gr.   Total 4.

ITALIAN

Primarily for Undergraduates : —

1. Dr. WILKINS and Mr. WESTON. — Italian Grammar.   Reading and Composition.   Modern Italian stories and plays.
1 Gr., 13 Ju., 6 So., 15 Fr., 2 uC.   Total 37.

For Undergraduates and Graduates : —

4 *hf.* Dr. WILKINS. — General View of Italian Literature.
5 Gr., 3 Se., 3 Ju., 1 So., 1 Fr.   Total 13.

2. Professor FORD and Mr. WESTON. — Italian Literature of the Fifteenth and Sixteenth Centuries.   Torquato Tasso ; Ariosto ; Machiavelli ; Benvenuto Cellini.   6 Gr., 3 Se., 2 Ju., 1 So.   Total 12.

10. Professor GRANDGENT. — The Works of Dante, particularly the Vita Nuova and the Divine Comedy.   7 Gr., 1 Se., 2 Ju.   Total 10.

Primarily for Graduates : —

3. Professor GRANDGENT and Dr. WILKINS. — Italian Literature of the Thirteenth and Fourteenth Centuries.   Selections from Boccaccio and Petrarch. Early Italian.   Monaci's Crestomazia italiana dei primi secoli.
9 Gr., 1 Ju.   Total 10.

Comparative Literature 17 *hf.*   (See Comparative Literature, p. 48.)

SPANISH

Primarily for Undergraduates : —

1. Asst. Professor POTTER, Dr. WHITTEM, and Messrs. LINCOLN, ATKIN, and RIVERA. — Spanish Grammar, reading, and composition.   Modern Spanish Novels and Plays.   1 Se., 37 Ju., 49 So., 35 Fr., 2 uC.   Total 124.

7 *hf.* Dr. WHITTEM. — Spanish Composition (elementary course).
1 G.B., 6 Ju., 2 So., 1 Fr.   Total 10.

For Undergraduates and Graduates : —

8 *hf.* Mr. RIVERA. — Spanish Composition and Conversation (advanced course).
2 Se., 2 Ju., 2 So.   Total 6.

5. Professor FORD and Dr. WHITTEM. — Spanish Prose and Poetry of the Eighteenth and Nineteenth Centuries.
7 Gr., 4 Se., 14 Ju., 12 So., 4 Fr.   Total 41.

6 ¹*hf.* Professor E. C. Hills (Colorado College). — Spanish American Poetry.
4 Gr., 1 Se., 7 Ju., 1 So.   Total 13.

Primarily for Graduates : —
Comparative Literature 17 *hf.*   (See Comparative Literature, p. 43.)

ROMANCE PHILOLOGY

Primarily for Graduates : —

3. Professor Sheldon. — Old French.   Phonology and inflections.   The oldest
texts.   La Chanson de Roland; Chrétien de Troyes; Aucassin et Nico-
lette.   21 Gr., 1 So.   Total 22.

5 *hf.* Professor Grandgent. — Low Latin.   14 Gr., 1 R.   Total 15.

6 ²*hf.* Professor Ford. — Portuguese.   Language and literature.   Old Portuguese lyric verse : Gil Vicente; Sá de Miranda; Camões.
5 Gr.   Total 5.

Course of Special Study

‡20. Professor Sheldon. — Investigation of Special Subjects in Romance Philology.   2 Gr.   Total 2.

Celtic

Primarily for Graduates : —

1 ¹*hf.* Professor F. N. Robinson. — Old Irish.   General Introduction to Celtic
Philology.   6 Gr.   Total 6.

2 ²*hf.* Professor F. N. Robinson. — Middle Irish.   Windisch's Irische Texte.
Lectures on the history of Irish Literature.   5 Gr.   Total 5.

Course of Special Study

20. Professor F. N. Robinson. — Investigation of Special Subjects in Celtic
Philology.   3 Gr.   Total 3.

The Celtic Conference

Fortnightly conferences were held in Celtic subjects for reading and for the
presentation of the results of investigation.   In 1911–12 the meetings were
chiefly devoted to the study of Ossianic texts in Irish and Scottish Gaelic.

Slavic Languages

For Undergraduates and Graduates : —

1a. Asst. Professor Wiener. — Russian.   1 Ju.   Total 1.

1b. Professor Wiener. — Literature of the Nineteenth Century.   Pushkin;
Gogol; Turgenev; Tolstoy.   Composition.   1 Se., 1 Ju.   Total 2.

4 ¹*hf.* Asst. Professor Wiener. — Introduction to the History of Russian Literature.   4 Se., 5 Ju., 2 So., 2 Fr.   Total 13.

5 ²*hf.* Asst. Professor Wiener. — Tolstoy and his time.
27 Se., 27 Ju., 10 So., 6 Fr., 1 uC.   Total 71.

Comparative Literature

Primarily for Undergraduates : —

1. Professor Wendell, assisted by Dr. Leach and Mr. Schenck. — European Literature.   General Survey.
27 Se., 37 Ju., 40 So., 19 Fr., 2 Sp., 2 uC.   Total 127.

For Undergraduates and Graduates: —

6a¹*hf.* Professor SCHOFIELD, assisted by Dr. WEBSTER. — The Literary History of England and its Relations to that of the Continent from the Beginning to Chaucer.   5 Gr., 27 Se., 22 Ju., 11 So., 10 Fr., 3 Sp.   Total 78.

6b²*hf.* Professor SCHOFIELD, assisted by Dr. WEBSTER. — The Literary History of England and its Relations to that of the Continent from Chaucer to Elizabeth.   5 Gr., 26 Se., 37 Ju., 23 So., 16 Fr., 2 Sp., 2 uC.   Total 111.

7. Asst. Professor POTTER. — Tendencies of European Literature in the Renaissance.   2 Gr., 2 Se., 3 Ju., 1 So.   Total 8.

30 ¹*hf.* Asst. Professor WRIGHT. — The Literary Relations of France and England in the Sixteenth and Seventeenth Centuries.
      3 Gr., 16 Se., 12 Ju., 3 So., 2 Fr.   Total 36.

9. Asst. Professor BABBITT. — Rousseau and his Influence.
      3 Gr., 1 Se., 2 Ju., 1 Fr.   Total 7.

12 ¹*hf.* Professor BLISS PERRY and Mr. SAVAGE. — Types of Fiction in the Eighteenth and Nineteenth Centuries.
      16 Gr., 48 Se., 61 Ju., 25 So., 6 Fr., 2 Sp., 3 uC., 1 Ext.   Total 162.

8²*hf.* Professor FRANCKE. — Goethe's Faust; with a study of kindred dramas in European Literature.
      3 Gr., 6 Se., 6 Ju., 8 So., 3 Fr., 1 uC.   Total 27.

13 ²*hf.* Professor SCHOFIELD. — Danish and Norwegian Dramatists. Holberg, Oehlenschläger, Björnson and Ibsen, and their relations to European literature.   4 Gr., 1 So.   Total 5.

Primarily for Graduates: —

‡14. Professor SHELDON. — Mediaeval Literature in the vulgar tongues, with especial reference to the Influence of France and Provence.
      2 Gr.   Total 2.

15 ²*hf.* Asst. Professor POTTER. — Epic Poetry. General characteristics. The heroic ballad, the national epic, the literary epic. Types of the popular epic.   1 Gr.   Total 1.

17 *hf.* Professor FORD. — The History of the Novel and the Tale in Italy and Spain from the Beginning of the Mediaeval Period to the Eighteenth Century.   5 Gr., 1 Se., 1 So.   Total 7.

18 ²*hf.* Professor NEILSON. — Studies in the Nature and History of Allegory. Lectures and theses.   14 Gr., 3 Ju.   Total 17.

25 ¹*hf.* Professor KITTREDGE. — The English and Scottish Popular Ballads.
      15 Gr.   Total 15.

27 ²*hf.* Professor SCHOFIELD. — English Literature of the Fourteenth and Fifteenth Centuries and its relations to Continental Literature.
      4 Gr.   Total 4.

‡28 ¹*hf.* Asst. Professor W. G. HOWARD. — German Literature in the Sixteenth Century and its relation to English Literature. Brant, Hutten, Luther, Hans Sachs, Fischart. Popular literature in prose and verse. The drama.
      7 Gr., 1 Se., 1 R.   Total 9.

35 ²*hf.* Dr. WEBSTER. — Life in the Middle Ages, as illustrated by Contemporary Literature.   1 Gr., 1 Se., 1 So.   Total 3.

Courses of Special Study

20*c*. Professor WEIR SMYTH. — The Relations of Greek Literature to European Literature in other Tongues. 1 Gr. Total 1.

20*h*. Professor FORD. — The Relations of Spanish Literature to European Literature in other Tongues. 2 Gr. Total 2.

20*j*. Professor WALZ. — The Relations of Middle High German Literature to European Literature in other Tongues. 2 Gr. Total 2.

20*k*. Professor WIENER. — The Relations of Slavic Literatures to European Literature in other Tongues. 1 Ju. Total 1.

The Fine Arts

Primarily for Undergraduates : —

1. Asst. Professor POPE and Mr. MOWER, assisted by Mr. R. E. JONES. — Principles of Drawing and Painting, with elementary practice.
2 G.S., 2 Se., 5 Ju., 5 So., 19 Fr., 3 uC. Total 36.

For Undergraduates and Graduates : —

2*a*. Asst. Professor POPE and Mr. MOWER. — Freehand Drawing (formerly Architecture 3*a*). 8 G.S., 8 Se., 8 Ju., 12 So., 3 Fr., 1 uC. Total 30.

2*b*. Mr. MOWER. — Freehand Drawing (advanced course).
2 G.S., 9 Se., 2 Ju., 4 So. Total 17.

3. Asst. Professor CHASE, assisted by Mr. FROST. — History of Ancient Art. Architecture, Sculpture, and Painting in Egypt, Assyria, and Greece, with some account of the lesser arts.
1 Gr., 1 G.S., 7 Se., 10 Ju., 17 So., 9 Fr. Total 45.

4*a*. Mr. FITZPATRICK, assisted by Mr. BORDEN. — The Fine Arts of the Middle Ages and the Renaissance. 11 Se., 18 Ju., 7 So., 3 Fr. Total 39.

4*b* ¹*hf*. Mr. FITZPATRICK. — History of Mediaeval Sculpture.
2 Se., 1 Ju., 1 So. Total 4.

4*c* ²*hf*. Asst. Professor POPE. — Painting of Venice and of Related Schools in the Sixteenth and Seventeenth Centuries. 8 Se., 3 Ju., 2 Fr. Total 13.

5 ¹*hf*. Mr. W. C. LANE. — The History of the Printed Book.
1 G.B., 1 Ju. Total 2.

8*a* ¹*hf*. (formerly Architecture 7*a*). Asst. Professor POPE and Mr. E. O. PARKER. — The Theory of Pure Design.
1 G.S., 2 Ju., 1 Fr., 1 uC. Total 5.

8*b* ²*hf*. (formerly Architecture 7*b*). Dr. ROSS and Mr. E. O. PARKER. — On Drawing and Painting: Theory and Practice.
1 G.S., 2 Se., 3 Ju., 2 So., 1 Fr., 1 uC. Total 10

9. Dr. POST. — The Art and Culture of Italy in the Middle Ages and the Renaissance. 10 Se., 17 Ju., 7 So., 2 Fr., 1 uC. Total 37.

Primarily for Graduates : —

Courses of Special Study

20*b*²*hf*. Mr. E. W. Forbes. — Florentine Painting in the Fifteenth Century.
1 G.B., 1 Se., 8 Ju.   Total 5.

20*c*²*hf*. (formerly Architecture 20*b*).   Dr. Ross. — Advanced Practice in Drawing and Painting.
2 Se., 2 Ju., 1 Fr.   Total 5.

20*f*. Dr. Post. — History of Italian Art.
1 Fr.   Total 1.

20*g*. Asst. Professor Pope. — History of Modern Painting.
1 Fr.   Total 1.

Architecture

For Undergraduates and Graduates : —

1*a*. Professor H. L. Warren and Mr. Frost. — Technical and Historical Development of the Ancient Styles, with especial reference to Classic Architecture.
1 G.S., 8 Se., 4 Ju., 9 So., 1 Fr., 2 uC.   Total 20.

1*c*. Professor H. L. Warren and Mr. Frost. — Technical and Historical Development of Renaissance and Modern Architecture.
7 G.S., 8 Se., 8 Ju., 1 Sp.   Total 24.

2*a*. Mr. Frost. — Elementary Architectural Drawing.   Elements of Architectural Form.   The Orders.
2 Se., 8 Ju., 1 So., 1 uC.   Total 12.

2*b*²*hf*. Mr. E. T. Putnam. — Stereotomy, Shades and Shadows, and Perspective.
1 G.S., 4 Se., 7 Ju., 5 So., 1 uC.   Total 18.

8*b*. Mr. H. B. Warren and Mr. Murphy. — Freehand Drawing.   Drawing from the Life.
8 G.S., 6 Se., 8 Ju., 1 So.   Total 18.

Primarily for Graduates : —

8*c*. Mr. H. B. Warren and Mr. Murphy. — Freehand Drawing.   Architectural Subjects and from the Life.
3 G.S., 1 Sp.   Total 4.

8*d*. Mr. H. B. Warren and Mr. Murphy. — Freehand Drawing.   Architectural Subjects and from the Life.
2 G.S.   Total 2.

4*a*. Mr. E. T. Putnam, with lectures by Professor H. L. Warren, and occasional criticism by Asst. Professor Humphreys. — Elementary Architectural Design.
2 G.S., 1 Ju.   Total 3.

4*b*. Asst. Professor Humphreys, with occasional criticism by Professor Duquesne. — Architectural Design (second course).
9 G.S., 2 Se.   Total 11.

4*c*. Professor Duquesne, assisted by Professor Humphreys. — Architectural Design (advanced course).
6 G.S.   Total 6.

5*a*. Asst. Professor Killam. — Materials and Methods of Building Construction.
1 G.S., 1 Se., 1 Ju.   Total 3.

5*b*. Asst. Professor Killam. — Theory of Building Construction; Statics; Resistance of Materials and Elementary Structural Design.
6 G.S., 1 Se.   Total 7.

6*hf*. Mr. Lawrie. — Modelling.   Practice in modelling architectural ornament in clay.
10 G.S.   Total 10.

7[1]. Professor SABINE. — Architectural Acoustics.   1 Gr., 10 G.S.   Total 11.

9[2]. Messrs. R. S. PEABODY, F. M. DAY, and GILBERT. — Professional Practice. Requirements of Special Classes of Buildings.   Nine lectures.
                        19 G.S., 2 Se., 3 Ju., 1 Sp.   Total 25.

Courses of Special Study

20a. Professor H. L. WARREN. — Study of Special Periods in the History of Architecture.   1 Gr., 2 G.S.   Total 3.

20d. Professor DUQUESNE. — Advanced Practice in Architectural Design.
                                        6 G.S.   Total 6.

Landscape Architecture

Primarily for Graduates : —

2. Asst. Professor H. V. HUBBARD. — Practice in Design (first course). Private estates and related problems. Study of local examples, with measured drawings, sketch plans, and reports; solution of original problems based on topographical surveys.   5 G.S.   Total 5.

3. Asst. Professor H. V. HUBBARD, with occasional instruction by Professor OLMSTED. — Practice in Design (second course).   Park and city planning.
                                        4 G.S.   Total 4.

4. Asst. Professor H. V. HUBBARD. — Principles of Construction (first course).
                                        5 G.S.   Total 5.

5. Asst. Professor H. V. HUBBARD, with occasional instruction by Professor OLMSTED. — Principles of Construction (second course).
                                        2 G.S.   Total 2.

6. Mr. WATSON. — Elements of Horticulture.   3 G.S.   Total 3.

7. Mr. WATSON. — Plants in Relation to Planting Design.   4 G.S.   Total 4.

8. Mr. WATSON. — Planting Design (first course).   3 G.S., 1 Se.   Total 4.

9. Mr. WATSON. — Planting Design (second course).   Advanced work following the methods of Course 8.   3 G.S., 1 Se.   Total 4.

11. Asst. Professor H. V. HUBBARD. — Elementary Drafting, with special reference to forms used in Landscape Design.   2 G.S., 2 Ju.   Total 4.

Music

For Undergraduates and Graduates : —

1. Asst. Professor HEILMAN, assisted by Dr. CLAPP. — Harmony, the Grammar of Music.
            2 Ju., 8 So., 22 Fr., 1 Sp., 2 uC., 1 And., 1 Ext.   Total 37.

1a hf. Asst. Professor SPALDING. — Advanced Harmony and Harmonic Analysis.
                        3 Gr., 3 Ju., 4 So., 1 Fr.   Total 11.

2. Asst. Professor SPALDING, assisted by Dr. DAVISON. — Counterpoint.
                        1 Gr., 1 Ju., 7 So., 3 Fr.   Total 12.

3. Asst. Professor SPALDING. — History of Music from the time of Palestrina to the present day.   2 Gr., 11 Se., 7 Ju., 8 So., 8 Fr.   Total 36.

4. Asst. Professors SPALDING and HEILMAN. — The Appreciation of Music; analytical study of masterpieces from the point of view of the listener.

1 Gr., 4 Se., 26 Ju., 20 So., 4 Fr., 1 Sp. Total 56.

4b hf. Mr. HILL. — D'Indy, Fauré, Debussy: a critical study of their respective contributions to modern music. 8 Gr., 2 Ju., 2 So. Total 7.

5 hf. Asst. Professor HEILMAN. — Canon and Fugue.

2 Gr., 4 Se., 1 Sp. Total 7.

Primarily for Graduates: —

‡6. Mr. HILL. — Instrumentation. 4 Gr., 1 Se., 5 Ju., 2 So., 1 Fr. Total 13.

7 hf. Mr. HILL. — A Preliminary Course in Composition, devoted chiefly to the smaller forms. 2 Gr., 4 Se., 3 Ju. Total 9.

GROUP II

History of Science

1 ¹hf. Asst. Professor HENDERSON. — History of the Physical and Biological Sciences (introductory course).

2 Gr., 11 Se., 19 Ju., 6 So., 4 Fr., 2 uC. Total 44.

Astronomy

Primarily for Undergraduates: —

1. Professor WILLSON and Dr. DUNCAN. — Descriptive Astronomy.

6 Se., 19 Ju., 35 So., 13 Fr., 4 uC. Total 77.

E ¹hf. Dr. DUNCAN. — Astronomy for Engineers. A modification of the first half-year of Astronomy 1, in which special attention was given to the methods of determining the meridian, finding the variation of the compass, time and latitude by theodolite, etc.

7 Se., 9 Ju., 4 So., 1 Fr., 1 Sp., 1 uC. Total 23.

2 ¹hf. Professor WILLSON. — Practical Astronomy. Application of Astronomy to Navigation and Exploration. 4 Se., 3 Ju. Total 7.

For Undergraduates and Graduates: —

8. Professor WILLSON. — Practical Astronomy. Portable and fixed instruments. Time and longitude by transit; latitude by zenith telescope; meridian circle. 1 uC. Total 1.

4a ¹hf. Dr. DUNCAN. — The Determination of Orbits. Olbers' method for the parabolic orbits; Gauss' method for elliptic orbits.

2 Ju., 1 Sp. Total 3.

4b ²hf. Dr. DUNCAN. — The Determination of Orbits. Leuschner's method for orbits of any eccentricity; orbits of visual and spectroscopic binary stars.

2 Ju. Total 2.

Primarily for Graduates: —

5. Professor WILLSON. — Practical Astronomy. Instruments of the fixed observatory. Meridian circle; almucantar; equatorial instrument; absolute determinations. 2 Se., 1 Ju. Total 3.

Physics

Primarily for Undergraduates : —

B. Professor HALL, Asst. Professor G. W. PIERCE, and Mr. EVANS. — Elementary Physics.   1 Ju., 9 So., 38 Fr., 2 Sp.   Total 50.

C. Professor SABINE, Asst. Professors H. W. MORSE and H. N. DAVIS, Dr. BRIDGMAN, and Messrs. HARRY CLARK, and D. L. WEBSTER. — Experimental Physics. Mechanics, Sound, Light, Magnetism, and Electricity.   5 Se., 15 Ju., 36 So., 70 Fr., 8 Sp., 4 uC. Total 138.

1. Professor HALL and Mr. EVANS. — General Descriptive Physics.   1 Gr., 5 Se., 7 Ju., 7 So., 15 Fr., 2 uC. Total 37.

11 ¹*hf.* Asst. Professor H. W. MORSE. — The Theory of Primary and Secondary Batteries.   2 Se., 4 Ju., 1 Fr., 1 Sp. Total 8.

14 ²*hf.* Asst. Professor H. W. MORSE. — The Theory of Photography.   3 Se., 3 Ju., 1 Fr., 2 Sp. Total 9.

For Undergraduates and Graduates : —

2 *hf.* Professor SABINE and Asst. Professor LYMAN. — Light.   3 Gr., 1 Sp.   Total 4.

8. Professor B. O. PEIRCE, assisted by Mr. KENT. — Electrostatics, Electrokinematics, and parts of Electromagnetism.   2 Gr., 4 G.S., 2 Se., 12 Ju., 2 So. Total 22.

12 ¹*hf.* Asst. Professor LYMAN.—Electric Conduction in Gases and Radioactivity, with special reference to Modern Theories of the Constitution of Matter.   2 Gr., 8 Ju., 1 So. Total 11.

17 ²*hf.* Asst. Professor G. W. PIERCE. — Electric Waves and their Application to Wireless Telegraphy.   1 Gr., 2 Se., 5 Ju., 1 Fr. Total 9.

4a ¹*hf.* Asst. Professor LYMAN and Dr. HAYES. — Magnetic Measurements and the Elementary Theory of Alternating Currents.   5 Gr., 4 G.S., 3 Se., 2 Ju. Total 14.

4b ²*hf.* Asst. Professor G. W. PIERCE. — Maxwell's Electromagnetic Theory. Electric Oscillations and Electric Waves.   3 Gr., 3 G.S. Total 6.

5. Professor SABINE. — Light.   4 Gr., 1 Sp. Total 5.

6a ¹*hf.* Professor HALL. — Elements of Thermodynamics.   4 Gr., 3 Ju., 1 So. Total 8.

6b ²*hf.* Professor HALL. — Modern Developments and Applications of Thermodynamics.   3 Gr., 1 G.S., 1 Se., 2 Ju. Total 7.

Primarily for Graduates : —

8 ²*hf.* Asst. Professor H. N. DAVIS. — Thermal Properties of Matter.   7 Gr.   Total 7.

‡10. Professor B. O. PEIRCE. — The Mathematical Theory of Electricity and Magnetism (second course).   5 Gr. Total 5.

Courses of Research

20*d*. Professor SABINE. — Light and Heat.   2 Gr.   Total 2.

20*e*. Asst. Professor G. W. PIERCE. — Radiation and Electromagnetic Waves.
    2 Gr.   Total 2.

20*g*. Asst. Professor LYMAN. — Light of Short Wave-Lengths.   1 Gr.   Total 1.

20*h*. Asst. Professor H. N. DAVIS. — Heat.   2 Gr.   Total 2.

Chemistry

Primarily for Undergraduates: —

1. Professor C. L. JACKSON and Mr. FISKE, assisted by Messrs. BARTLETT,
 DANIELS, JONES, and MELDRUM. — Descriptive Inorganic Chemistry.
    2 Gr., 7 Se., 20 Ju., 57 So., 238 Fr., 3 Sp., 6 uC.   Total 333.

2 ^1hf. Dr. KELLEY, assisted by Mr. EARLE. — Organic Chemistry (elementary
 course).
    2 Gr., 1 G.S., 17 Se., 30 Ju., 36 So., 8 Fr., 2 Sp., 4 uC., 1 Ext.   Total 101.

3. Professor SANGER and Dr. G. S. FORBES, assisted by Messrs. HUBBARD,
 WHITMORE, BRYAN, DAHL, and McLAUGHLIN. — Qualitative Analysis.
    9 Se., 31 Ju., 28 So., 8 Fr., 4 uC.   Total 80.

8 ^2hf. Professor RICHARDS and Dr. G. S. FORBES, assisted by Mr. BARRY. —
 Elementary Theoretical and Physical Chemistry, including the Historical
 Development of Chemical Theory.
    6 Gr., 9 Se., 27 Ju., 25 So., 2 Fr., 3 Sp., 3 uC.   Total 75.

For Undergraduates and Graduates: —

4. Asst. Professor BAXTER, assisted by Mr. VOTER. — Quantitative Analysis,
 gravimetric and volumetric.
    5 Gr., 7 Se., 14 Ju., 7 So., 1 Fr., 1 Sp., 3 uC.   Total 38.

9 ^1hf. Asst. Professor BAXTER, assisted by Dr. C. J. MOORE. — Advanced
 Quantitative Analysis.   7 Gr., 3 Se., 8 Ju.   Total 18.

10 ^2hf. Asst. Professor BAXTER, assisted by Dr. C. J. MOORE. — Gas Analysis.
    5 Gr., 3 Se., 7 Ju., 1 So.   Total 16.

5. Dr. KELLEY, assisted by Mr. PATCH. — The Carbon Compounds.
    9 Gr., 4 Se., 20 Ju., 3 So.   Total 36.

15 ^2hf. Asst. Professor HENDERSON. — General Biological Chemistry.
    3 Gr., 11 Se., 8 Ju., 1 So., 1 Sp., 1 uC., 1 Me.   Total 26.

11. Dr. LATHAM CLARKE. — Industrial Chemistry.
    7 Gr., 1 G.S., 7 Se., 18 Ju., 1 So.   Total 34.

18 ^1hf. Dr. LATHAM CLARKE. — Inorganic Preparations.   Chiefly laboratory
 work.   2 Gr., 4 Se.   Total 6.

19 ^2hf. Dr. LATHAM CLARKE. — Technical Analysis.   Chiefly laboratory work.
    3 Gr., 4 Se., 2 Ju.   Total 9.

Primarily for Graduates: —

6. Professor RICHARDS and Dr. G. S. FORBES, assisted by Mr. SHIPLEY. —
 Physical Chemistry.   12 Gr., 10 Se., 3 Ju.   Total 25.

12 ^1hf. Asst. Professor BAXTER, assisted by Mr. SHIPLEY. — Photochemistry, including the use of Optical Instruments in Chemistry.

                                          7 Gr., 1 Se. Total 8.

7 ^2hf. Dr. G. S. FORBES. — Electrochemistry.   6 Gr., 2 Se. Total 8.

13 ^2hf. Dr. G. S. FORBES, assisted by Mr. SHIPLEY. — Experimental Electrochemistry.

                                          4 Gr., 1 Se. Total 5.

16 ^1hf. Dr. KELLEY. — The General Reactions of Organic Chemistry.

                                          3 Gr., 6 Se., 2 Ju. Total 11.

17 ^2hf. Dr. KELLEY. — Special Topics in Advanced Organic Chemistry.

                          4 Gr., 6 Se., 3 Ju., 1 So., 1 Sp. Total 15.

Courses of Research

20*a*. Professor RICHARDS. — Inorganic Chemistry, including Determination of Atomic Weights.   3 Gr., 1 G.S. Total 4.

20*b*. Professor C. L. JACKSON. — Organic Chemistry.   4 Gr. Total 4.

20*c*. Dr. LATHAM CLARKE. — Organic Chemistry.   2 Gr. Total 2.

20*d*. Professor RICHARDS. — Physical Chemistry, including Electrochemistry.

                                          2 Gr. Total 2.

20*f*. Asst. Professor BAXTER. — Inorganic Chemistry, including Determination of Atomic Weights.   5 Gr., 1 Sp. Total 6.

20*g*. Asst. Professor BAXTER. — Physical Chemistry. Stoichiometry (determination of physicochemical constants).   1 Gr. Total 1.

20*h*. Dr. G. S. FORBES. — Physical Chemistry, including Electrochemistry.

                                          1 Gr. Total 1.

20*i*. Dr. LATHAM CLARKE. — Industrial Chemistry.   1 Se. Total 1.

20*k*. Asst. Professor HENDERSON. — Biological Chemistry.   1 Gr. Total 1.

Engineering

Primarily for Undergraduates : —

3*k*. Asst. Professors KENNEDY and A. E. NORTON, and Messrs. NINDE and THOROGOOD. — Mechanical Drawing. Use of instruments. Projections and descriptive geometry.

          1 Gr., 5 G.S., 7 Se., 17 Ju., 44 So., 19 Fr., 5 uC. Total 98.

3*l*. Asst. Professor A. E. NORTON, and Messrs. NINDE and THOROGOOD. — Elements of Engineering Design. Mechanism (gearing, linkages, etc.), machine drawing, and elementary design.

          1 G.S., 5 Se., 13 Ju., 6 So., 1 uC. Total 26.

10*a*. Mr. MARKHAM. — Chipping, Filing, and Fitting. Use of hand tools. Fitting by hand. Study of the metals in practical working.

          1 Se., 5 Ju., 6 So., 9 Fr., 1 Sp., 4 S.S. Total 26.

10*b*. Mr. MARKHAM. — Blacksmithing. Use of tools. Forging, welding, tool-dressing and tempering.

          1 Se., 5 Ju., 6 So., 9 Fr., 1 Sp., 7 S.S. Total 29.

10c. Mr. MARKHAM. — Pattern Making and Foundry Practice. Use of wood-working tools. Casting in iron and alloys.

6 Ju., 6 So., 9 Fr., 1 Sp., 4 S.S. Total 26.

10e. Mr. MARKHAM. — Machine Shop Practice.

1 Se., 6 Ju., 7 So., 6 Fr., 1 Sp., 7 S.S. Total 28.

☞ Engineering 10a, 10b, 10c, 10e count together as 1½ courses for the degree of S.B.

For Undergraduates and Graduates : —

3m. Asst. Professor KENNEDY and Mr. NINDE. — Engineering Design. Design of parts of machinery and other engineering structures. Proportioning the parts for strength and effect. 2 G.S., 8 Se., 6 Ju. Total 16.

4a hf. Asst. Professor HUGHES and assistants. — Surveying. Use of instruments; plane and topographical surveying; levelling; map drawing and field-practice.

8 Se., 15 Ju., 12 So., 20 Fr., 1 uC., 8 S. S., 8 from Associate Institutions.
Total 62.

4d. Asst. Professor HUGHES and assistants. — Railroad Engineering (first course). Railroad curves and location; field and office practice.

2 Se., 12 Ju., 11 So., 18 Fr., 1 uC., 4 S. S., 1 from an Associate Institution.
Total 44.

5a ¹hf. Professor L. J. JOHNSON, Asst. Professor H. N. DAVIS, and Mr. NICHOLS. — Kinetics (second course). 1 Gr., 2 G.S., 7 Se., 13 Ju. Total 28.

5b hf. Asst. Professor A. E. NORTON. — Elementary Statics. Graphic and Algebraic Methods. 1 Se., 3 Ju., 2 So. Total 6.

5c ²hf. Professor L. J. JOHNSON, Asst. Professor H. N. DAVIS, and Mr. NICHOLS. — Elementary Resistance of Materials.

3 G.S., 10 Se., 14 Ju., 1 So., 1 Fr., 1 Sp. Total 30.

5e hf. Asst. Professor A. E. NORTON. — Elementary Kinematics and Kinetics.

1 Se., 1 Ju., 1 So. Total 3.

6a ²hf. Asst. Professor HUGHES and Mr. PAIGE. — Elementary Hydraulics.

6 G.S., 1 G.B., 15 Se., 9 Ju., 1 So., 1 Sp. Total 33.

11a ²hf. Professor HOLLIS, and Messrs. MARKHAM, MERRIAM and SPOFFORD. — Steam Machinery (introductory course).

5 G.S., 19 Se.. 18 Ju., 23 So., 8 Fr., 1 uC. Total 74.

12b ¹hf. Professor MARKS and Mr. LOOMIS. — Elements of Thermodynamics. Theory of heat engines. 4 G.S., 13 Se., 23 Ju., 1 Sp. Total 41.

13a. Professor MARKS and Messrs. DODDS and MAKAREVICH. — Engineering Laboratory. A course in experimental methods.

7 G.S., 18 Se., 3 Ju., 1 So. Total 29.

16a. Professor KENNELLY, Messrs. CRANE, DOGGETT, and LIEBBRKNECHT. — Generation, Transmission, and Utilization of Electrical Energy (elementary course). 7 G.S., 19 Se., 14 Ju., 2 So., 1 Fr., 1 Sp. Total 44.

Primarily for Graduates : —

4e¹. Asst. Professor HUGHES and Mr. PAIGE. — Road Engineering.

4 G.S., 2 Se. Total 6.

4*f*². Asst. Professor HUGHES and Mr. PAIGE. — Railroad Engineering (second course). Problems in railroad construction and economics.
4 G.S., 1 G.B., 1 Se.   Total 6.

4*k*. Asst. Professor HUGHES and assistants. — Surveying: Use of Instruments; Plane and topographical surveying; levelling; map drawing and field practice.   1 G.S., 1 uC., 1 S.S.   Total 3.

5*f*. Professor L. J. JOHNSON and Mr. NICHOLS. — Mechanics of Structures.
9 G.S., 2 Se.   Total 11.

5*g*¹. Professor HOLLIS. — Mechanics of Machinery and Boilers.
2 G.S.   Total 2.

6*d*¹. Asst. Professor HUGHES, and Messrs. SAFFORD and PAIGE. — Hydraulics (second course).   Water measurements; water power; and miscellaneous problems in hydraulic engineering.   8 G.S., 2 Se.   Total 10.

7*b*. Professor SWAIN and Mr. NICHOLS. — Theory and Design of Structures of Wood, Stone, and Metal.   11 G.S.   Total 11.

8*a*¹. Asst. Professor KILLAM. — Foundations, Masonry, and Fireproofing.
9 G.S., 4 Se.   Total 13.

9*a*². Professor G. C. WHIPPLE, Messrs. J. W. M. BUNKER and M. C. WHIPPLE. — Sanitary Engineering (introductory course).
1 Gr., 11 G.S., 3 Se., 2 Me.   Total 17.

12*a*². Professor MARKS. — Efficiency and Economics of Heat Engines.
1 G.S., 1 Se.   Total 2.

13*b*². Professor MARKS, assisted by Messrs. DODDS and MAKAREVICH. — Mechanical Engineering Laboratory.   1 G.S.   Total 1.

14*b*¹. Professor HOLLIS, assisted by Mr. MERRIAM. — Machine Design.
2 G.S.   Total 2.

16*b*. Professor CLIFFORD and Mr. DOGGETT. — Generation, Transmission, and Distribution of Electrical Energy (second course).   6 Gr.   Total 6.

16*j*¹. Professor ADAMS and Messrs. CRANE and DOGGETT. — Direct Currents and Direct-Current Machinery.   2 G.S., 2 Se.   Total 4.

16*l*². Professor CLIFFORD, Messrs. CRANE and LIEBERKNECHT. — Alternating Currents.   3 G.S., 1 Se.   Total 4.

16*n*¹. Professor CLIFFORD, Messrs. CRANE and LIEBERKNECHT. — Alternating-Current Machinery.   6 G.S., 1 Sp.   Total 7.

16*p*². Professor KENNELLY and Mr. LIEBERKNECHT. — Electric Transmission and Distribution of Power.   4 G.S., 1 Sp.   Total 5.

17*b*¹. Professor KENNELLY and Mr. LIEBERKNECHT. — Telegraphy and Telephony.   3 G.S.   Total 3.

17*c*². Professor KENNELLY and Mr. LIEBERKNECHT. — Illumination and Photometry.   3 G.S., 1 Se., 1 Sp.   Total 5.

17*d*. Professor ADAMS and Mr. DOGGETT. — Dynamo Design. 3 G.S.   Total 3.

17*e*¹. Asst. Professor G. W. PIERCE and Dr. E. L. CHAFFEE. — Radiotelegraphic Engineering.   2 Gr., 5 G.S., 1 Se.   Total 8.

17*f.* Asst. Professor H. W. MORSE. — Storage Batteries and their Application in Electrical Engineering. 8 G.S. Total 8.

18*a*². Professor HOLLIS, assisted by Mr. MERRIAM. — Power Station Design. 8 G.S. Total 8.

21². Professors SWAIN, HOLLIS, KENNELLY, and CLIFFORD. — Conference on Engineering Subjects. 1 Gr., 10 G.S. Total 11.

22². Professor WYMAN. — Contracts and Specifications. General Principles of Common Law governing Construction Contracts. 12 G.S., 7 Se., 1 Ju. Total 20.

Courses in Special Fields

20*a*. Professor ADAMS. — Electrical Engineering Research. 2 G.S. Total 2.

20*b*. Professor CLIFFORD. — Electrical Engineering Research. 5 G.S. Total 5.

20*c*. Professor KENNELLY. — Electrical Engineering Research. 2 G.S. Total 2.

20*d*. Professor L. J. JOHNSON and Mr. NICHOLS. — Reinforced Concrete. 1 G.S. Total 1.

20*e*. Professor SWAIN. — Structures of Wood, Masonry, and Metal. 5 G.S. Total 5.

20*h*. Professor MARKS. — Internal Combustion Motors. 2 G.S. Total 2.

20*q*. Professor WHIPPLE. — Sanitary Engineering. 1 G.S., 1 Me. Total 2.

20*r*. Professor HOLLIS. — Steam Turbine. 2 G.S. Total 2.

20*s*. Asst. Professor G. W. PIERCE. — Wireless Telegraphy. 3 G.S. Total 3.

Botany

Primarily for Undergraduates: —

1 ¹*hf*. Asst. Professor OSTERHOUT, assisted by Messrs. BROOKS, HOAR, REED, and WHITE. — Botany (introductory course).
1 Gr., 9 Se., 13 Ju., 36 So., 65 Fr., 2 Sp., 7 uC. Total 133.

2 ¹*hf*. Professor THAXTER, assisted by Messrs. COLLEY and HOAR. — Morphology of Plants. 1 Gr., 4 Se., 3 Ju., 9 So., 2 Fr., 1 Sp. Total 20.

For Undergraduates and Graduates: —

3 ¹*hf*. Professor JEFFREY, assisted by Mr. EAMES. — General Morphology, Histology, and Cytology of Vascular Plants.
3 Gr., 1 G.S., 2 Ju., 1 So. Total 7.

4 ²*hf*. Professor THAXTER, assisted by Mr. COLLEY. — The Algae, Liverworts, and Mosses. 6 Gr., 2 Se., 2 Ju., 2 So., 1 Fr. Total 13.

7. Asst. Professor FERNALD, assisted by Messrs. BLAKE and HILL. — Classification and Distribution of Flowering Plants, with special reference to the Flora of New England and the Maritime Provinces.
2 Gr., 2 G.S. 1 Se., 1 Ju., 2 So. Total 8.

8 ¹*hf*. Professor JEFFREY and Mr. BAILEY, assisted by Mr. SINNOTT. — Structure of Woods: microscopic features. 2 Gr., 12 G.S. Total 14.

9 ^2hf. Professor JEFFREY, assisted by Mr. EAMES. — Special Morphology of the Lower Vascular Plants. The Lycopods, Equisetales, Ferns, Fossil and Lower Gymnosperms.   6 Gr., 1 G.S., 1 Ju., 1 So.   Total 9.

11 ^2hf. Professor W. E. CASTLE and Asst. Professor EAST.—Variation, Heredity, and the Principles of Animal and Plant Breeding. (See Zoölogy 11 ^2hf., below.)   4 Gr., 2 G.S., 4 Se., 2 Ju., 1 So., 1 Fr.   Total 14.

13. Asst. Professor OSTERHOUT. — Plant Physiology.
                                        7 Gr., 2 Se., 1 Ju.   Total 10.

Primarily for Graduates: —

Courses of Research

20a. Professor JEFFREY. — Structure and Development of Vascular Plants.
                                                       6 Gr.   Total 6.

20b. Professors FARLOW and THAXTER. — Structure and Development of Cryptogams.   4 Gr.   Total 4.

20d. Asst. Professor FERNALD. — Researches in Geographic Botany.
                                             2 Gr., 1 Se., 1 Ju.   Total 4.

20e. Asst. Professor OSTERHOUT. — Researches in Plant Physiology.
                                                       3 Gr.   Total 3.

20f. Asst. Professor EAST.— Variation, Heredity, and the Principles of Plant Breeding.   1 Gr., 1 G.S.   Total 2.

Zoölogy

Primarily for Undergraduates : —

1 ^1hf. Professors KÜKENTHAL and G. H. PARKER, Mr. SPAETH, and other assistants. — Zoölogy.
            3 Gr., 8 Se., 19 Ju., 36 So., 65 Fr., 3 Sp., 4 uC.   Total 138.

2 ^2hf. Professor W. E. CASTLE and Mr. DETLEFSEN. — Morphology of Animals.
                3 Gr., 5 Se., 6 Ju., 11 So., 3 Fr., 1 Sp.   Total 29.

For Undergraduates and Graduates : —

3. Asst. Professor H. W. RAND and Mr. GROSS. — Comparative Anatomy of Vertebrates.   1 Gr., 5 Se., 5 Ju., 1 So., 1 Fr., 1 Sp.   Total 14.

4 ^1hf. Asst. Professor H. W. RAND and Mr. D. W. DAVIS.—Microscopical Anatomy.   1 Gr., 3 Se., 3 Ju., 1 So., 1 Fr., 1 uC.   Total 10.

5b ^2hf. Professor MARK and Mr. KORNHAUSER. — Embryology of Vertebrates. Organogeny.   2 Gr., 1 G.S., 3 Se., 1 So., 1 uC.   Total 8.

11 ^2hf. Professor W. E. CASTLE and Asst. Professor EAST. — Variation, Heredity, and the Principles of Animal and Plant Breeding. (See Botany 11 ^2hf., above.)   4 Gr., 2 G.S., 4 Se., 2 Ju., 1 So., 1 Fr.   Total 14.

12 ^1hf. Professor MARK and Mr. KORNHAUSER. — Cytology, with special reference to Heredity.   3 Gr., 1 Ju.   Total 4.

Primarily for Graduates : —

7a ^2hf. Professor WHEELER and Mr. BRUES. — Morphology and Classification of Insects.   1 Gr., 1 G.S.   Total 2.

7b²*hf.* Professor WHEELER and Mr. BRUES. — Habits and Distribution of Insects.   1 Gr., 1 G.S.   Total 2.

7c²*hf.* Mr. BRUES. — Practical Entomology.   1 Se.   Total 1.

7d². Mr. BRUES. — Forest Entomology.   5 G.S.   Total 5.

‡14a¹*hf.* Professor G. H. PARKER. — The Structure and Functions of Sense Organs.   3 Gr., 1 G.S., 1 Se., 4 Ju., 1 Fr., 1 R.   Total 11.

17¹*hf.* Asst. Professor H. W. RAND. — Experimental Morphology. The Form-determining Factors in Development and Growth. 1 Gr., 1 G.S.   Total 2.

19¹*hf.* Professor KÜKENTHAL.—Certain Aspects of the Comparative Morphology of Vertebrates.   Lectures in German.   2 Gr., 1 Se.   Total 3.

Courses of Research

20a. Professor MARK. — Embryology.   1 Gr.   Total 1.

20b. Professor MARK. — Cytology, with special reference to Heredity.
                                                                 3 Gr.   Total 3.

20c. Professor G. H. PARKER. —The Structural and Functional Basis of Animal Reactions.   4 Gr.   Total 4.

20g. Asst. Professor H. W. RAND.—Experimental Morphology. 1 Gr.   Total 1.

APPLIED ZOÖLOGY

20d. Professor W. E. CASTLE. — Variation, Heredity, and the Principles of Animal Breeding.   4 G.S.   Total 4.

20f. Professor WHEELER. — Economic Entomology.   3 G.S.   Total 3.

Geology
GEOLOGY AND GEOGRAPHY
GENERAL GEOLOGY

Primarily for Undergraduates : —

4¹*hf.* Asst. Professor WOODWORTH, assisted by Messrs. HAYNES and WIGGLESWORTH. — Introduction to Geology. Dynamical and Structural Geology.   3 Gr., 14 Se., 22 Ju., 18 So., 12 Fr., 1 Sp., 1 uC.   Total 71.

5²*hf.* Asst. Professor WOODWORTH, assisted by Dr. LAHEE.— Introduction to Historical Geology. 1 Gr., 7 Se., 10 Ju., 7 So., 5 Fr., 1 Sp.   Total 31.

For Undergraduates and Graduates : —

8¹*hf.* Asst. Professor WOODWORTH. — Advanced General Geology.
                                         4 Gr., 1 G.S., 4 Se., 4 Ju., 1 Fr.   Total 14.

16²*hf.* Asst. Professor WOODWORTH. — Glacial Geology.
                                              3 Gr., 2 Se., 4 Ju., 1 So.   Total 10.

12. Dr. LAHEE. — Geological Field Work in the Vicinity of Boston.
                                                                 3 Gr.   Total 3.

Primarily for Graduates : —

20c. Professors DAVIS, WOLFF, and H. L. SMITH, and Asst. Professor WOODWORTH. — Geological Investigation in the Field and Laboratory.
                                                                 3 Gr.   Total 3.

PALÆONTOLOGY

20d². Professor RAYMOND. — Palæontology.   3 Gr., 1 G.S.   Total 4.

ECONOMIC GEOLOGY

For Undergraduates and Graduates : —

18 ²hf. Professor WOLFF and Asst. Professor PALACHE, and an assistant. —
Economic Geology of the Non-Metalliferous Substances.
                                              1 Se.   Total 1.

Primarily for Graduates : —

20b. Professor GRATON. — Economic Geology (research course).
                                              1 G.S.   Total 1.

GEOGRAPHY

Primarily for Undergraduates : —

A ¹hf. Asst. Professor D. W. JOHNSON and Mr. BROOKS. — Physical Geography
(introductory course).
              4 Se., 5 Ju., 12 So., 27 Fr., 1 Sp., 2 uC.   Total 51.

For Undergraduates and Graduates : —

10 ¹hf. Asst. Professor D. W. JOHNSON. — Geomorphology.
                                              1 Gr., 1 Ju.   Total 2.

2 ¹hf. Professor WARD. — Geography of South America.
                                3 Gr., 1 Se., 1 Ju., 1 So.   Total 6.

Primarily for Graduates : —

‡20a. Professor DAVIS and Asst. Professor D. W. JOHNSON. — Physiography
(research course).   1 Gr.   Total 1.

METEOROLOGY AND CLIMATOLOGY

Primarily for Undergraduates : —

B ²hf. Professor WARD, assisted by Mr. LINSLEY. — Meteorology (introductory
course).   4 Se., 5 Ju., 12 So., 31 Fr., 1 Sp., 1 uC.   Total 54.

For Undergraduates and Graduates : —

1 ¹hf. Professor WARD. — Climatology of North America.
                                1 Gr., 1 Se., 1 Ju., 1 So.   Total 4.

2 ¹hf. Professor WARD. — See Geography, above.

19 ¹hf. Professor WARD. — Climatology (general course).
                                     2 Se., 1 Ju., 2 So.   Total 5.

Primarily for Graduates : —

20e. Professor WARD. — Climatology (research course).   2 Gr.   Total 2.

20f. Professors ROTCH and WARD. — Meteorology (research course).
                                              2 Gr.   Total 2.

Mineralogy and Petrography

Primarily for Undergraduates : —

2. Asst. Professor PALACHE, assisted by Mr. R. E. SOMERS. — Mineralogy
(including Crystallography, Physical and Chemical Mineralogy, and
Descriptive Mineralogy).   1 Gr., 5 Se., 6 Ju., 1 So., 5 Fr.   Total 18.

For Undergraduates and Graduates : —

10 ²*hf.* Asst. Professor PALACHE. — Advanced Mineralogy. Lectures on selected topics. 3 Gr., 2 G.S., 1 Se.   Total 6.

12. Professor WOLFF, assisted by Mr. SOMERS. — Petrography.
4 Gr., 2 Se.   Total 6.

Primarily for Graduates : —

14 ¹*hf.* Professor WOLFF. — Advanced Petrography.   1 Gr., 7 G.S.   Total 8.

Mining and Metallurgy

Primarily for Undergraduates : —

B ²*hf.* Professors SAUVEUR and PETERS, assisted by Messrs. BOYLSTON and C. D. CRAWFORD. — General Metallurgy.
2 G.S., 10 Se., 21 Ju., 9 So., 9 Fr., 2 Sp.   Total 53.

1 ²*hf.* Professor H. L. SMYTH, Asst. Professor RAYMER, and Mr. WEEKS. — Elements of Mining. Prospecting and exploring; breaking ground; hydraulic and open-pit mining; stamp-milling and ore-concentration.
8 Se., 12 Ju., 3 Fr.   Total 23.

2. Professor H. L. SMYTH, Asst. Professor GRATON, and Mr. WEEKS. — Ore-deposits. Origin and occurrence.
1 Gr., 1 G.S., 3 Se., 4 Ju., 1 Fr.   Total 10.

3 ¹*hf.* Asst. Professor RAYMER, assisted by Mr. C. F. LEWIS. — Fire Assaying.
1 G.B., 1 G.S., 3 Se., 1 Ju., 1 Fr.   Total 7.

4 ²*hf.* Asst. Professor C. H. WHITE, assisted by Mr. C. F. LEWIS. — Metallurgical Chemistry. The Analysis of Ores.   1 Se., 2 Ju.   Total 3.

For Undergraduates and Graduates : —

7¹. Professor H. L. SMYTH and Mr. WEEKS. — Metal and Coal Mining; Exploitation.   4 G.S., 3 Se.   Total 7.

8 ²*hf.* Asst. Professor RAYMER. — Mining Plant.   2 G.S., 1 Se.   Total 3.

10. Mr. WEEKS. — Mining. The study of mining operations.
4 Ju., 3 So., 2 Fr., 2 S.S.   Total 11.

11 ¹*hf.* Professor SAUVEUR, assisted by Messrs. BOYLSTON and C. D. CRAWFORD. — Metallurgy of Iron and Steel.   8 G.S., 7 Se., 5 Ju., 2 Fr.   Total 22.

12 ²*hf.* Professor SAUVEUR, assisted by Mr. BOYLSTON. — Metallography.
6 G.S., 1 G.B., 2 Se., 1 Fr., 1 Sp.   Total 11.

14 ²*hf.* Professor PETERS and Mr. WEEKS. — Metallurgy of Copper, Lead, Zinc, and the Minor Metals, and of the Precious Metals in connection with Copper and Lead.   7 G.S., 1 Se., 1 Sp.   Total 9.

15 ²*hf.* Professor PETERS. — Metallurgy of Zinc, Nickel, Tin, Mercury, and the Minor Metals.   1 G.S., 1 Se., 1 Sp.   Total 3.

17 ². Asst. Professor RAYMER. — Ore-dressing, Concentration, and Milling.
4 G.S., 1 Sp.   Total 5.

19. Asst. Professor C. H. WHITE. — Metallurgical Chemistry (advanced course).
5 G.S., 1 Se.   Total 6.

Primarily for Graduates: —

21¹. Asst. Professor C. H. WHITE. — Leaching Processes for Gold and Silver Ores.   6 G.S.   Total 6.

22 ¹*hf.* Professor PETERS. — Advanced Course in the Metallurgy of Copper, Lead, and the Minor Metals.   2 G.S., 1 Se.   Total 3.

24². Professor H. L. SMYTH. — Mine Examination and Reports.
                                                     4 G.S.   Total 4.

25 ¹*hf.* Professor H. L. SMYTH. — Magnetic Methods of Prospecting. The dial-compass, dip-needle, and magnetometer.   1 G.S.   Total 1.

26¹. Asst. Professor RAYMER. — Mine Surveying.   4 G.S.   Total 4.

28 ¹*hf.* Dr. LAHEE. — Geological Surveying.   3 G.S.   Total 3.

29 ¹. Asst. Professor RAYMER. — Problems in the Treatment of Ores.
                                                     2 G.S.   Total 2.

30 ². Asst. Professor RAYMER. — Mining and Metallurgical Projects and Design.
                                                     5 G.S.   Total 5.

Courses of Research

20a. Professor SAUVEUR, assisted by Mr. BOYLSTON. — Metallurgy and the Physics of Metals.   5 G.S., 1 Fr.   Total 6.

20b. Asst. Professor GRATON. — Problems in ore-deposits.
                                                     3 G.S.   Total 3.

Physiology

1. Asst. Professor DARLING, and Drs. PROVANDIE, BACON, HAPGOOD, and GOODRIDGE. — Elementary Anatomy and Physiology. Personal Hygiene. Emergencies.
     1 Gr., 16 Se., 35 Ju., 47 So., 87 Fr., 3 Sp., 1 Ext.   Total 190.

GROUP III

History

INTRODUCTORY

Primarily for Undergraduates: —

History 1. Professor HASKINS and Dr. GRAY, assisted by Messrs. VARRELL, STEPHENSON, McDONALD, and F. E. CRAWFORD. — Mediaeval History (introductory course).   1 Se., 28 So., 211 Fr., 2 Sp., 8 uC.   Total 250.

History 2.   Modern European History.
   2a ¹*hf.* Asst. Professor MERRIMAN, assisted by Mr. KERNER. — History of Western Europe from the close of the Middle Ages to 1715.
            7 Se., 24 Ju., 58 So., 6 Fr., 3 Sp., 3 uC.   Total 101.

   2b ²*hf.* Professor COOLIDGE and Dr. LORD, assisted by Mr. KERNER. — History of Europe from 1715 to the present day.
            5 Se., 19 Ju., 51 So., 4 Fr., 3 Sp., 4 uC.   Total 86.

I. ANCIENT AND ORIENTAL HISTORY

For Undergraduates and Graduates : —

History 3. Asst. Professor FERGUSON. — History of Rome to the reign of Diocletian.   10 Gr., 4 Se., 2 Ju., 3 So., 1 Fr., 1 Sp. Total 21.

History 37 ²*hf*. Asst. Professor FERGUSON. — Character and Spread of Hellenistic Culture.   4 Gr., 7 Se., 9 Ju., 6 So., 3 Fr., 1 uC., 2 Di. Total 32.

Primarily for Graduates : —

History 51 ¹*hf*. Asst. Professor FERGUSON. — Studies in the Growth of the Roman Imperial System.   5 Gr. Total 5.

II. MEDIAEVAL HISTORY

For Undergraduates and Graduates : —

History 6. Professor EMERTON. — The First Eight Christian Centuries. The conflict of Christianity with Paganism. Origin and development of the Roman Papacy to its alliance with the Frankish state. The Germanic races as the basis of a new Christian civilization.
        1 Gr., 3 Se., 1 Ju., 1 So., 1 Fr., 1 uC., 4 Di., 6 And. Total 18.

History 8. Dr. GRAY. — History of France to the accession of Francis I.
                                1 Gr., 1 Ju., 1 So. Total 3.

History 9. Asst. Professor McILWAIN. — Constitutional History of England to the Sixteenth Century.   10 Gr., 1 Se., 5 Ju. Total 16.

History 38 ¹*hf*. Professor DIEHL (University of Paris). — Byzantine History.
                                4 Gr., 1 Ju., 1 So., 1 Di. Total 7.

History 52 ¹*hf*. Professor DIEHL (University of Paris). — France in the Orient in the Middle Ages. (Illustrated.)   1 Se., 1 So. Total 2.

Primarily for Graduates : —

History 25 *hf*. Professor HASKINS. — Historical Bibliography and Criticism.
                                8 Gr., 1 R., 1 Di. Total 10.

History 41 ²*hf*. Professor HASKINS. — Early Mediaeval Institutions.
                                                7 Gr. Total 7.

‡History 21 ¹*hf*. Professor HASKINS. — Introduction to the Sources of Mediaeval History.   4 Gr. Total 4.

Courses of Research

History 20a. Professor EMERTON. — Readings from Mediaeval Historical Literature.   2 Gr., 1 Di. Total 3.

History 20c. Professor HASKINS. — Mediaeval Institutions.   3 Gr. Total 3.

III. MODERN EUROPEAN HISTORY

For Undergraduates and Graduates : —

History 7. Professor EMERTON. — The Era of the Reformation in Europe from the rise of Italian Humanism to the close of the Council of Trent (1350–1563).   8 Gr., 3 Se., 7 Ju., 1 So., 2 Di., 1 And. Total 22.

History 11. Asst. Professor MERRIMAN. — History of England during the Tudor and Stuart Periods.   12 Gr., 4 Se., 9 Ju., 7 So., 1 Fr., 1 Sp Total 34.

History 12a *¹hf.* Mr. TEMPERLEY. — English History from the Revolution of
1688 to the Reform of Parliament.
2 Gr., 5 Se., 12 Ju., 10 So., 8 Fr., 2 uC.   Total 39.

History 40 *¹hf.* Dr. LORD. — History of France in the Seventeenth and Eighteenth
Centuries.   3 Gr., 6 Se., 7 Ju., 1 So., 1 Fr., 1 uC.   Total 19.

History 14 *²hf.* Asst. Professor JOHNSTON. — France under Napoleon I.
3 Gr., 25 Se., 20 Ju., 6 So., 1 Fr., 1 Sp., 2 uC.   Total 58.

History 28. Dr. LORD. — History of Modern Germany.
1 Gr., 1 Ju., 1 So., 1 Sp.   Total 4.

History 33 *²hf.* Asst. Professor JOHNSTON. — History of Italy from 1789–1870.
1 Gr., 6 Se., 5 Ju., 5 So.   Total 17.

History 19 *¹hf.* Professor COOLIDGE. — The Eastern Question.
1 Gr., 13 Se., 12 Ju., 5 So., 1 Sp., 1 uC.   Total 33.

History 30 *¹hf.* Mr. TEMPERLEY. — The Growth of the British Empire.
3 Gr., 7 Se., 8 Ju., 2 So., 1 Fr.   Total 21.

History 24a *¹hf.* Professor E. C. MOORE. — The History of the Christian Church
in Europe from the Reformation to the end of the Eighteenth Century.
1 G.B., 9 Se., 17 Ju., 9 So., 3 Fr., 2 Di., 1 And.   Total 42.

History 24b *²hf.* Professor E. C. MOORE. — The History of the Christian Church
in Europe and of the Expansion of Christendom in the East during the
Nineteenth Century. 11 Se., 18 Ju., 18 So., 8 Fr., 1 Sp., 5 Di.   Total 61.

Primarily for Graduates : —

History 29. Professor COOLIDGE. — Selected Topics in the History of the Nineteenth Century : European Expansion in North Africa.   3 Gr.   Total 3.

History 48. Dr LORD. — General History of Russia (advanced course).
1 Gr.   Total 1.

History 39 *²hf.* Asst. Professor MERRIMAN. — Comparative Studies in the Institutions of Western Europe, 1300–1600 (England, France, Spain).
2 Gr., 1 Se.   Total 3.

History 50 *²hf.* Asst. Professor JOHNSTON. — Studies in the Political Literature
of the Revolutionary Period in France and Italy.   1 Gr.   Total 1.

Courses of Research

History 20d. Professor COOLIDGE and Asst. Professor JOHNSTON. — History of
Continental Europe and of Asia in the Eighteenth and Nineteenth Centuries.   1 Gr., 1 Se.   Total 2.

History 20g. Asst. Professor MERRIMAN. — Topics in the History of Spain in
the Fifteenth and Sixteenth Centuries.   1 Gr.   Total 1.

IV. AMERICAN HISTORY

For Undergraduates and Graduates : —

History 10b *²hf.* Professor CHANNING. — American History : The Formation of the
Union (1760–1801).   3 Gr., 8 Se., 9 Ju., 17 So., 2 Sp., 4 uC.   Total 43.

History 48*b*²*hf.* Professor CHANNING. — Selected Readings in American History. The Administrations of Washington and Adams (1789–1801).

1 Se., 1 Ju. Total 2.

History 17. Professor TURNER, assisted by Mr. BROOKE. — The History of the West. 13 Gr., 21 Se., 31 Ju., 17 So., 4 Fr., 1 Sp., 5 uC. Total 92.

History 13. Professor A. B. HART and Dr. HOLCOMBE, assisted by Messrs. S. E. MORISON and RYAN. — Constitutional and Political History of the United States (1815–1911).

4 Gr., 12 Se., 47 Ju., 28 So., 7 Fr., 3 Sp., 2 uC. Total 103.

Primarily for Graduates: —

History 23*b*²*hf.* Professor CHANNING. — Selected Topics in the Historical Development of American Institutions. Constitutional History of the Administrations of Washington and John Adams (1789–1801).

4 Gr., 1 Ju. Total 5.

History 44. Professor TURNER. — Selected Topics in the History of the West (1840–1850). 8 Gr. Total 8.

‡History 46 *hf.* Mr. W. C. FORD. — Manuscript Materials of American History.

2 Gr., 1 R. Total 3.

Courses of Research

History 20*e.* Professor CHANNING. — American History. 1 Gr. Total 1.

History 20*k.* Professor TURNER. — American History. 3 Gr. Total 3.

V. ECONOMIC HISTORY

For Undergraduates and Graduates: —

Economics 6*a* ¹*hf.*, 6*b*²*hf.*, 11, 20*a.* Professor GAY. — (See Economics, pp. 64–65.)

VI. CHURCH HISTORY

History 5, 6, 7a, 24a, 24b, 26, and 20a are courses in Church History. In addition to these, the following courses in Andover Theological Seminary (offered Primarily for Graduates) were open to students in Harvard University: —

History A2. Professor PLATNER. — History of Christian Doctrine.

1 Ju., 1 Di., 4 And. Total 6.

History A6. Professor PLATNER. — History of Early Christian Literature.

1 Di., 1 And. Total 2.

VII. HISTORY OF RELIGIONS

Primarily for Undergraduates: —

History of Religions 10 ¹*hf.* Professor PLATNER. — The Elements of Christianity.

8 Se., 12 Ju., 5 So., 4 Fr. Total 29.

For Undergraduates and Graduates: —

History of Religions 1 ¹*hf.* Professor G. F. MOORE. — The Origin and Development of Religion. 1 Gr., 5 Se., 3 Ju., 1 So., 2 Di., 1 And. Total 13.

History of Religions 2. Professor G. F. Moore. — History of Religions in Out-line. — *First half-year:* The Religions of China and Japan, Egypt, Babylonia and Assyria, and the Western Semites (including Judaism and Mohammedanism). *Second half-year:* The Religions of India, Persia, the Greeks, Romans, Germans, and Celts; Christianity.

3 Se., 4 Ju., 1 Fr., 15 Di., 2 And.   Total 25.

Primarily for Graduates: —

History of Religion 3 ²*hf.* Professors Kittredge and F. N. Robinson. — Ger-manic and Celtic Religions. 3 Gr., 1 Se., 1 Di. Total 5.

Course of Research

History of Religions 20. Professor G. F. Moore. — Topics in Jewish Theology and Confucian Ethics. 1 Gr., 1 Di. Total 2.

Government

I. Introductory

Primarily for Undergraduates: —

Government 1. Asst. Professor Munro, assisted by Messrs. Cleary, Davis, S. C. McLeod, Cottrell, Kincaid, and R. H. Holt. — Constitutional Government.   1 Se., 2 Ju., 130 So., 328 Fr., 2 Sp., 16 uC. Total 479.

II. Modern Government

For Undergraduates and Graduates: —

Government 3a ¹. Dr. Holcombe. — Party Government.
1 Gr., 12 Se., 7 Ju., 9 So., 4 Fr., 1 uC. Total 34.

Government 17. Asst. Professor Munro, assisted by Mr. Hull. — Municipal Government.   4 Gr., 10 Se., 13 Ju., 22 So., 5 Fr., 1 Ext. Total 55.

Government 32a ¹*hf.* Dr. Holcombe. — Public Ownership and Control.
2 Gr., 1 G.S., 25 Se., 32 Ju., 22 So., 7 Fr., 2 uC. Total 91.

Government 32b ²*hf.* Dr. Holcombe. — Selected Problems in Public Owner-ship and Control.   4 Gr., 7 Se., 7 Ju., 1 So., 1 uC. Total 20.

Primarily for Graduates: —

Government 7. Mr. Matthews and Asst. Professor Munro. — Problems of Municipal Administration in Europe and America.

5 Gr., 2 Se., 4 Ju. Total 11.

Courses of Research

Government 20a. Asst. Professor Munro. — Selected Topics in Municipal Government. 1 Gr. Total 1.

Government 20c. Professor A. B. Hart. — American Institutions, National, State, Municipal and Insular. 5 Gr. Total 5.

III. Law and Political Theory

For Undergraduates and Graduates: —

Government 5. Asst. Professor McIlwain. — The Roman Law: its History, Principles, and Influence on European Institutions.

9 Gr., 8 Se., 9 Ju., 2 So., 1 uC. Total 24.

Government 6. Mr. YEOMANS. — Theories of the State and of Government.
9 Gr., 8 Se., 5 Ju., 1 uC., 1 Law. Total 19.

Government 25 ¹*hf.* Mr. JOSEPH WARREN. — History and System of the Common Law. 2 Gr., 24 Se., 6 Ju., 2 So., 2 And. Total 36.

Primarily for Graduates : —

Government 19. Messrs. YEOMANS and DALLINGER. — American Constitutional Law : A study of constitutional principles and limitations throughout the United States. 4 Gr., 1 Se., 1 Ju. Total 6.

IV. INTERNATIONAL LAW AND DIPLOMACY

For Undergraduates and Graduates : —

Government 4. Professor G. G. WILSON, assisted by Mr. PRIEST. — Elements of International Law. 8 Gr., 11 Se., 29 Ju., 1 So., 8 Sp., 1 uC. Total 58.

Primarily for Graduates : —

Government 14. Professors A. B. HART and G. G. WILSON. — American Diplomacy : Treaties ; Application of International Law ; Foreign Policy.
7 Gr., 5 Ju. Total 12.

Government 23. Professor G. G. WILSON. — Selected Cases in International Law. 7 Gr., 8 Se., 2 Ju., 2 Law. Total 14.

Course of Research

Government 20c. Professor G. G. WILSON. — International Law.
4 Gr., 8 Se. Total 7.

Economics

Primarily for Undergraduates : —

1. Professor TAUSSIG, assisted by Dr. E. E. DAY, and Messrs. JONES, BALCOM, J. S. DAVIS, BURBANK, and JAY MORRISON. — Principles of Economics.
1 Gr., 19 Se., 85 Ju., 252 So., 54 Fr., 4 Sp., 23 uC. Total 438.

I. ECONOMIC THEORY AND METHOD

For Undergraduates and Graduates : —

2. Professor TAUSSIG. — Economic Theory.
28 Gr., 11 Se., 16 Ju., 2 So., 1 Sp., 1 Di. Total 54.

4. Professor RIPLEY. — Statistics. Theory, method, and practice.
4 Gr., 1 G.B., 6 Se., 9 Ju. Total 20.

14a ¹*hf.* Professor CARVER, assisted by Mr. A. W. LAHEE. — The Distribution of Wealth. 6 Gr., 32 Se., 40 Ju., 11 So., 1 Fr., 2 Sp., 2 uC. Total 94.

14b ²*hf.* Professor CARVER. — Methods of Social Reform. Socialism, Communism, the Single Tax, etc.
5 Gr., 22 Se., 25 Ju., 9 So., 2 Sp., 2 uC. Total 65.

29 ¹*hf.* Dr. RAPPARD. — Socialism and the Social Movement in Europe.
3 Gr., 15 Se., 20 Ju., 3 So. Total 41.

Primarily for Graduates : —

13 ¹*hf.* Professor CARVER. — Methods of Economic Investigation.
2 Gr., 1 Ju., 1 So. Total 4.

‡15. Professor BULLOCK. — History and Literature of Economics to the year 1848. 6 Gr. Total 6.

22. Professor GAY. — French and German Economists of the Nineteenth Century. 5 Gr. Total 5.

II. ECONOMIC HISTORY

For Undergraduates and Graduates : —

6a ¹hf. Professor GAY, assisted by Mr. KLEIN. — European Industry and Commerce in the Nineteenth Century.
22 Gr., 5 Se., 28 Ju., 6 So., 2 Fr., 1 uC., 1 Ext. Total 65.

6b²hf. Professor GAY, assisted by Mr. KLEIN. — Economic and Financial History of the United States.
19 Gr., 11 Se., 48 Ju., 12 So., 3 Fr., 1 uC. Total 94.

11. Professor GAY. — Modern Economic History of Europe.
3 Gr., 1 Fr. Total 4.

III. APPLIED ECONOMICS

For Undergraduates and Graduates : —

5 ¹hf. Professor RIPLEY, assisted by Dr. DEWING. — Economics of Transportation. 4 Gr., 23 Se., 54 Ju., 14 So., 3 Fr., 1 Ext. Total 99.

7a ¹hf. Professor BULLOCK. — Introduction to Public Finance.
8 Gr., 5 Se., 11 Ju., 4 So., 1 uC. Total 24.

7b²hf. Professor BULLOCK. — The Theory and Methods of Taxation.
2 Gr., 10 Se., 16 Ju., 9 So. Total 37.

8. Dr. E. E. DAY, assisted by Mr. YORK. — Money, Banking, and Commercial Crises. 7 Gr., 16 Se., 70 Ju., 22 So., 4 Fr., 1 uC. Total 120.

9a ¹hf. Professor RIPLEY, assisted by Mr. HESS. — Problems of Labor.
3 Gr., 23 Se., 35 Ju., 8 So., 1 Di. Total 70.

9b²hf. Professor RIPLEY, assisted by Dr. DEWING. — Economics of Corporations. 9 Gr., 1 G.S., 41 Se., 72 Ju., 14 So., 2 Fr., 1 uC. Total 140.

23²hf. Professor CARVER. — Economics of Agriculture. With special reference to American conditions.
4 Gr., 36 Se., 44 Ju., 9 So., 1 Sp., 1 uC. Total 95.

30 ¹hf. Dr. DEWING. — The Financial Aspects of Industrial Combinations.
1 G.B., 8 Se., 9 Ju., 1 So. Total 19.

Primarily for Graduates : —

16. Professor BULLOCK. — Public Finance (advanced course).
11 Gr., 1 Se., 1 Ju. Total 13.

IV. COURSES PREPARING FOR A BUSINESS CAREER

For Undergraduates and Graduates : —

18. Asst. Professor COLE, assisted by Messrs. STONER and JOHNSON. — Principles of Accounting.
8 Gr., 7 G.S., 45 G.B., 129 Se., 68 Ju., 1 Sp., 3 Law. Total 261.

21 ¹hf. Professor WYMAN, assisted by Messrs. HUGHES and JOHNSON. — The Law of Competition and Combination.
2 Gr., 1 G.S., 107 Se., 44 Ju., 2 Sp. Total 156.

V. Sociology

For Undergraduates and Graduates: —

Economics 3. Professor CARVER, assisted by Mr. BRISTOL. — Principles of Sociology. Theories of Social Progress.

18 Gr., 24 Se., 35 Ju., 8 So., 2 Fr., 1 Sp., 5 uC., 2 Di.   Total 90.

Anthropology 12 ²*hf.*   (See Anthropology, p. 66.)

Social Ethics 1 ²*hf.*, 2 ²*hf.*, 4 ¹*hf.*, 6 ²*hf.*, 7 ¹*hf.*, ‡20*a*, ‡20*b*, 20*c*.   (See Social Ethics, p. 69.)

VI. Courses of Research in Economics

20*a*. Professor GAY. — The Economic History of England.   1 Gr.   Total 1.

‡20*b*. Professor CARVER. — Economic Theory.   1 Gr.   Total 1.

20*c*. Professor RIPLEY. — Principles of Corporation Finance.   8 Gr.   Total 8.

20*d*. Professor TAUSSIG. — The Economic History of the United States, with special reference to Tariff Legislation.   2 Gr.   Total 2.

20*e*. Professor BULLOCK. — American Taxation and Finance.   1 Gr.   Total 1.

20*g*. Asst. Professor SPRAGUE. — Banking.   1 Gr., 1 Ju.   Total 2.

The Seminary in Economics

Meetings were held by instructors and advanced students for the presentation of the results of investigation.

Education

For Undergraduates and Graduates: —

A ¹*hf.* (formerly 2*a*). Asst. Professor HOLMES. — Principles and Problems of Contemporary Education.

6 Gr., 1 G.B., 8 Se., 11 Ju., 2 So., 1 Fr., 1 And.   Total 30.

1. Asst. Professor A. O. NORTON. — History of Educational Practices and Theories.   7 Gr., 2 Se., 9 Ju., 1 Fr., 1 Sp.   Total 20.

5*a* ¹*hf.* Asst. Professor A. O. NORTON. — Modern Theories of Education. Critical study of recent views.

12 Gr., 1 Se., 2 Ju., 1 Fr., 2 Di.   Total 18.

5*b* ²*hf.* Asst. Professor A. O. NORTON. — The Education of the Individual. Study and treatment of both unusual and normal types.

11 Gr., 3 Se., 3 Ju., 2 Fr.   Total 19.

6*a* ¹*hf.* Asst. Professor HOLMES. — Educational Theory in the Early Nineteenth Century. Froebel. Constructive discussion of educational aims.

1 Gr., 2 Ju.   Total 8.

6*b* ²*hf.* Asst. Professor HOLMES. — Educational Theory in the Early Nineteenth Century. Pestalozzi and Herbart. Constructive discussion of educational methods.   2 Gr., 1 Ju.   Total 8.

Primarily for Graduates: —

8. Dr. F. E. SPAULDING (Superintendent of Schools, Newton). — Organization and Management of State and City Schools and School Systems. Duties and opportunities of superintendents and principals. Visits to schools, with special reference to the duties of supervising officers. Experimental study of problems in school administration.

8 Gr., 1 Se., 1 uC., 1 R.   Total 11.

8b *²hf.* Mr. WILLIAM ORR (Deputy Commissioner of Education, Commonwealth of Massachusetts) and Asst. Professor HOLMES. — Secondary Education : Public High Schools, Endowed and Private Schools. Visits to Schools. Practice teaching.   10 Gr., 8 Se., 1 So.   Total 19.

8c. Asst. Professor HOLMES. — Elementary Education. Programmes of study, administration, methods. Visits to schools. Practice teaching during the second half-year.   4 Gr., 2 Se. Total 6.

Seminary Course

‡20b. Asst. Professor A. O. NORTON. — Seminary in the History of Education.
4 Gr., 1 R.   Total 5.

Anthropology

Primarily for Undergraduates: —

1. Dr. TOZZER, assisted by Mr. KIDDER. — General Anthropology.
15 Se., 25 Ju., 46 So., 7 Fr., 1 Sp., 2 uC.   Total 96.

For Undergraduates and Graduates: —

5. Asst. Professor DIXON and Drs. FARABEE and TOZZER. — American Archaeology and Ethnography.   1 Gr., 3 Se., 1 So.   Total 5.

2. Dr. FARABEE. — Somatology.   2 Gr., 1 Se.   Total 3.

4 *²hf.* Dr. FARABEE. — Prehistoric European Archaeology and European Ethnography.   1 Gr., 2 Se., 2 Ju., 2 So.   Total 7.

7 *¹hf.* Asst. Professor DIXON. — Ethnography of Oceania.
1 Gr., 2 Se., 1 Sp.   Total 4.

11 *²hf.* Asst. Professor DIXON. — Ethnography of Asia.
2 Gr., 4 Se., 1 So., 1 Sp.   Total 8.

12 *²hf.* Dr. TOZZER. — Primitive Sociology, a History of Institutions.
6 Gr., 4 Se., 2 Ju., 1 Fr., 1 Sp.   Total 14.

Primarily for Graduates: —

‡8 *¹hf.* Asst. Professor DIXON. — American Indian Languages. Discussion and study of selected texts.   1 Gr.   Total 1.

9 *¹hf.* Dr. TOZZER. — Archaeology and Hieroglyphic Systems of Central America.   1 Sp.   Total 1.

Courses of Research

‡20a. Asst. Professor DIXON. — American Archaeology and Ethnology.
1 Gr., 1 Sp.   Total 2.

‡20b². Dr. FARABEE. — Advanced Somatology.   1 Gr.   Total 1.

‡20d. Asst. Professor DIXON. — General Ethnology.   1 Gr.   Total 1.

GROUP IV

Philosophy

Primarily for Undergraduates: —

A-E. INTRODUCTION TO PHILOSOPHY

A ¹*hf.* Professor PALMER. — History of Ancient Philosophy.
2 Se., 27 Ju., 111 So., 116 Fr., 1 Sp., 15 uC., 2 Ext. Total 274.

B ²*hf.* Professor CUSHMAN (Tufts College). — History of Modern Philosophy.
1 Se., 11 Ju., 48 So., 55 Fr., 10 uC., 2 Di., 1 Ext. Total 128.

C ¹*hf.* Professor ROYCE. — Logic.
1 Gr., 1 Se., 20 Ju., 28 So., 32 Fr., 3 Sp., 13 uC. Total 98.

D ¹*hf.* Asst. Professor R. B. PERRY. — General Problems of Philosophy.
1 Gr., 2 Se., 9 Ju., 24 So., 29 Fr., 2 Sp., 2 uC. Total 69.

E ²*hf.* Professor MÜNSTERBERG. — Psychology.
1 Gr., 1 G.S., 3 Se., 85 Ju., 121 So., 131 Fr., 1 Sp., 28 uC., 1 And., 1 Ext.
Total 373.

For Undergraduates and Graduates: —

3 ²*hf.* Asst. Professor G. P. ADAMS (University of California). — Philosophy of
Nature, with Especial Reference to Man's Place in Nature. Conceptions
of nature in the light of moral and religious interests.
10 Se., 9 Ju., 11 So., 2 Fr., 1 uC. Total 33.

4. Professor PALMER. — Ethics. The theory of morals, considered constructively.
15 Gr., 18 Se., 25 Ju., 7 So., 3 Fr., 1 uC., 4 Di., 6 And., 1 Ext. Total 75.

5a ¹*hf.* (formerly 22). Professor SANTAYANA. — Metaphysics. The order of
knowledge and the order of nature.
7 Gr., 9 Se., 10 Ju., 2 Sp., 1 uC., 1 Di. Total 30.

5b ²*hf.* Professor FITE (Indiana University). — Metaphysics. The fundamental
problems and conceptions of theoretical philosophy. — Idealism and realism, intellectualism and mysticism, in their relations.
5 Gr., 2 Se., 10 Ju., 1 So. Total 18.

6a ¹*hf.* (formerly 19). Professor E. C. MOORE. — Philosophy of Religion. —
The Nature of Religion. 3 Gr., 5 Se., 5 Ju., 4 Di., 1 Ext. Total 18.

6b ²*hf.* (formerly 19). Professor E. C. MOORE. — Philosophy of Religion. — The
Truths of Religion.
8 Se., 14 Ju., 8 So., 2 Fr., 3 Sp., 2 uC., 2 Di., 2 And., 1 Ext. Total 42.

7 ¹*hf.* (formerly 16). Professor FENN. — Theism. (Courses 6 and 7 are also
announced by the Faculty of Divinity.)
2 Gr., 1 Se., 7 Di., 2 And. Total 12.

8 (formerly 15). Professor ROYCE and Professor FITE (Indiana University). —
Advanced Logic. Modern doctrines regarding the thinking process and
regarding the principles of the exact sciences. — The relations of deduction
and induction. — Outlines of a theory of knowledge.
10 Gr., 2 Ju., 2 Di., 2 R. Total 16.

10 ¹*hf.* Professor SANTAYANA. — Philosophy of Art.
6 Gr., 13 Se., 17 Ju., 7 So., 3 Fr., 1 Sp., 2 uC. Total 49.

11 (formerly 18). Asst. Professor Woods. — Philosophical Systems of India, with special reference to Vedanta, Sankhya, and Yoga.

2 Gr., 1 Se., 1 Ju., 2 Di.   Total 6.

12. Asst. Professor Woods. — Greek Philosophy, with especial reference to Plato.   13 Gr., 3 Se., 5 Ju., 2 So., 1 Di., 1 And.   Total 25

14a²hf. (formerly 11a). Asst. Professor G. P. Adams (University of California) — Descartes, Spinoza, and Leibnitz.

7 Gr., 3 Ju., 1 uC., 1 And.   Total 12.

15 ¹hf. (formerly 8). Professor Royce. — The Kantian Philosophy.

11 Gr., 1 Se., 1 Ju., 1 So., 5 Di., 2 R.   Total 21.

16 ²hf. Professor Fite (Indiana University). — Representative Philosophical Thinkers of the Nineteenth Century.   Personal attitudes in philosophy and literature.   5 Gr., 6 Se., 10 Ju., 1 So., 1 Sp., 2 uC.   Total 25.

17 ¹hf. Professor E. C. Moore. — History of Christian Thought since Kant.

2 Se., 1 Sp., 7 Di., 3 And.   Total 13.

18 ¹hf. (formerly 24). Asst. Professor R. B. Perry. — Present Philosophical Tendencies.   A brief survey of contemporary Materialism, Idealism, Pragmatism, and Realism.   11 Gr., 8 Se., 11 Ju., 1 So., 3 Di.   Total 34.

19a ²hf. (formerly 7a). Asst. Professor G. P. Adams (University of California). — History of Ethics. — The Early English Moralists.   Hobbes, the Cambridge Platonists, Shaftesbury, Butler, and Adam Smith.

3 Gr., 2 Ju., 2 So.   Total 7.

21 ¹hf. (formerly 14). Dr. Langfeld. — Experimental Psychology (elementary laboratory course).   11 Gr., 4 Se., 7 Ju., 1 So.   Total 23.

22 ²hf. (formerly 2). Dr. Langfeld. — Advanced Psychology.

15 Gr., 4 Se., 7 Ju., 2 So., 2 Fr., 1 Di.   Total 31.

26a ¹hf. (formerly 13a). Asst. Professor Yerkes. — Comparative Psychology. — Mental Development in the Race.   13 Gr., 1 Se., 5 Ju., 2 So.   Total 21.

27 ²hf. (formerly 21a). Asst. Professor Yerkes. — Animal Psychology.   A study of forms of activity and consciousness in the animal kingdom.

2 Gr., 1 G.S., 1 Se.   Total 4.

28 ²hf. (formerly 6). Asst. Professor Yerkes. — Educational Psychology.   The psychological basis of educational practices.

11 Gr., 3 Se., 4 Ju., 1 So., 1 Fr., 1 Sp., 1 Di.   Total 22.

Primarily for Graduates: —

Courses of Special Study

‡20a. Professor Münsterberg, Asst. Professor Yerkes, and Dr. Langfeld. — Psychological Laboratory.   Experimental investigations in Human and Animal Psychology by advanced students.   12 Gr., 3 R.   Total 15.

20b. Professor Münsterberg. — Applied Psychology with special reference to Education, Jurisprudence and Medicine.

11 Gr., 2 Se., 2 Di., 1 And.   Total 16.

‡20c. Professors Royce and Southard. — Seminary in Logic.   A Comparative Study of Various Types of Scientific Method.   8 Gr., 4 R.   Total 12.

‡20*d*. Professor PALMER. — Seminary in Ethics. The Systematization of Ethics.
9 Gr., 2 Di., 1 R.   Total 12.

20*s* ¹*hf*. Asst. Professor R. B. PERRY. — Seminary in the Theory of Knowledge.
Ideas and their objects.   7 Gr., 1 Se., 2 Di., 1 R.   Total 11.

‡20*g*. Asst. Professor YERKES. — Seminary in Animal Psychology. The history
of the problems and methods of animal psychology.
1 Gr., 1 R.   Total 2.

The Classics

Primarily for Graduates

Greek 8 and Latin 8.   (See The Classics, p. 34.)

Social Ethics

For Undergraduates and Graduates : —

1 ¹*hf*. Professor PEABODY, Drs. FORD and FOERSTER. — Social Problems in
the light of Ethical Theory.
8 Gr., 11 Se., 12 Ju., 8 So., 2 Fr., 3 Di., 3 And., 1 Ext.   Total 48.

2 ¹*hf*. Dr. BRACKETT. — Practical Problems of Social Service : Public Aid,
Charity, and Neighborhood Work.
2 Gr., 4 Se., 5 Ju., 1 Sp., 1 uC., 1 Di.   Total 14.

4 ¹*hf*. Selected Topics in Social Ethics.
     Dr. BRACKETT. — The Ethics of Public Aid and Private Charity.
     Dr. FORD. — The Ethical Aspects of Industrial Coöperation.
     Dr. FOERSTER. — The Ethics of Immigration.
2 Gr., 2 Se., 5 Ju., 1 Di.   Total 10.

6 ²*hf*. Dr. FOERSTER. — Social Amelioration in Europe.
7 Gr., 5 Se., 7 Ju.   Total 19.
7 ¹*hf*. Dr. FORD. — Rural Social Development.
1 Gr., 8 Se., 7 Ju., 1 Fr.   Total 17.

Primarily for Graduates : —

Courses of Research

‡20*a*. Professor PEABODY. — Seminary of Social Ethics. The History of Social
Ethics from Fichte to Tolstoi.
5 Gr., 2 Se., 3 Di., 2 And., 1 R.   Total 13.

‡20*b*. Professor PEABODY. — Special Researches in Social Ethics.
1 Gr., 1 Di.   Total 2.
20*c*. Dr. BRACKETT. — The School for Social Workers.
4 Gr., 1 Se., 1 Ext.   Total 6.

Mathematics

Primarily for Undergraduates : —

A. Professor OSGOOD, assisted by Messrs. CUTTING, EDWARDS, and A. L. MILLER.
     — Trigonometry, Analytic Geometry, Introduction to the Calculus.
1 G.S., 3 Ju., 3 So., 77 Fr., 3 uC.   Total 87.

B. (formerly F). Asst. Professor BOUTON and Dr. DUNHAM JACKSON. — Trigonometry and Plane Analytic Geometry.
2 Se., 4 Ju., 10 So., 40 Fr., 1 Sp.   Total 57.

C. Asst. Professor COOLIDGE, assisted by Messrs. CATER and BEATLEY. — Plane and Solid Analytic Geometry.   2 Ju., 8 So., 69 Fr., 4 uC.   Total 83.

D $^2hf.$ Mr. DONAHUE. — Algebra. 3 Se., 10 Ju., 7 So., 39 Fr., 1 uC. Total 60.

E $^1hf.$ Mr. DONAHUE. — Solid Geometry.   4 Ju., 8 So., 27 Fr.   Total 39.

K $^2hf.$ (formerly *A*). Mr. DONAHUE. — Logarithms; Plane and Spherical Trigonometry.   9 Ju., 9 So., 24 Fr. Total 42.

L $^1hf.$ (formerly Engineering 1*d*). Mr. DONAHUE. — Plane Analytic Geometry.   1 Se., 7 So., 11 Fr., 1 Sp., 1 uC. Total 21.

G $^2hf.$ Asst. Professor BOUTON. — Descriptive Geometry.   1 G.S., 4 Se., 4 Ju., 5 So., 4 Fr.   Total 18.

2. Professors BYERLY and BÔCHER, and Messrs. GAYLORD, DONAHUE, and ETTLINGER. — Differential and Integral Calculus (first course).   1 Gr., 1 G.B., 2 G.S., 8 Se., 38 Ju., 62 So., 5 Fr., 7 uC. Total 124.

4. Asst. Professor H. N. DAVIS. — The Elements of Mechanics.   4 Gr., 2 G.S., 16 Se., 29 Ju., 8 So., 1 Sp. Total 60.

For Undergraduates and Graduates : —

8. Professor BYERLY. — Introduction to Modern Geometry and Modern Algebra.   4 Gr., 2 Ju., 2 So., 1 Sp. Total 9.

5. Professor OSGOOD. — Differential and Integral Calculus (second course).   6 Gr., 5 Se., 10 Ju., 2 So., 3 uC. Total 26.

9. Asst. Professor COOLIDGE. — Probability.   1 Gr., 1 Se., 4 Ju., 1 Sp. Total 7.

18 $^1hf.$ Asst. Professor BOUTON. — The Elementary Theory of Differential Equations.   5 Gr., 1 G.S., 2 Ju. Total 8.

6 $^1hf.$ Professor BÔCHER. — Vector Analysis.   5 Gr., 1 G.S., 3 Se., 1 Ju. Total 10.

8 $^2hf.$ Professor MAX MASON (University of Wisconsin). — Dynamics of Rigid and Elastic Bodies.   4 Gr., 1 G.S., 1 Se., 1 Ju. Total 7.

Primarily for Graduates : —

12 $^1hf.$ Dr. DUNHAM JACKSON. — Infinite Series and Products.   2 Gr., 2 Se., 2 Ju., 1 uC., 1 R. Total 8.

‡**13.** Professor OSGOOD. — The Theory of Functions (introductory course).   7 Gr., 1 Se., 1 uC., 1 R. Total 10.

‡**14a** $^2hf.$ Dr. DUNHAM JACKSON. — Algebra. The properties of polynomials; invariants.   5 Gr., 4 Se., 1 Ju., 1 uC., 1 R. Total 12.

‡**24.** Dr. DUNHAM JACKSON. — The Theory of Numbers, including the Theory of Ideals.   2 Gr., 3 Se., 1 R. Total 6.

22 $^1hf.$ Associate Professor G. A. BLISS (University of Chicago). — Differential Geometry of Curves and Surfaces.   4 Gr. Total 4.

‡**26.** Asst. Professor COOLIDGE. — Line Geometry. 3 Gr., 2 Se., 1 Ju. Total 6.

19. Professors BYERLY and B. O. PEIRCE. — Trigonometric Series. Introduction to Spherical Harmonics. The Potential Function.   9 Gr., 2 G.S., 1 Se., 1 Sp., 1 R. Total 14.

‡11 ¹*hf*. Professor B. O. Peirce. — Hydromechanics.   4 Gr., 1 G.S.   Total 5.

‡15. Asst. Professor Bouton. — Differential Equations.   With an introduction to Lie's theory of continuous groups.   7 Gr.   Total 7.

‡21 ²*hf*. Professor Bôcher. — Finite Differences and Difference Equations.
5 Gr., 1 Se., 1 uC.   Total 7.

30 ¹*hf*. Associate Professor G. A. Bliss (University of Chicago). — Partial Differential Equations.   8 Gr.   Total 8.

34 ²*hf*. Professor Max Mason (University of Wisconsin). — The Electron and the Electro-Magnetic Field.   1 G.S., 2 Gr.   Total 8.

Courses of Reading and Research

‡20c. Professor Osgood. — Topics in the Theory of Functions. 2 Gr.   Total 2.

‡20d. Professor Bôcher. — Topics in Analysis and Algebra.   1 Gr.   Total 1.

‡20e. Asst. Professor Bouton. — Topics in the Theory of Point-Transformations.
1 Gr.   Total 1.

‡20f. Asst. Professor Coolidge. — Topics in Higher Geometry. 3 Gr.   Total 3.

OUT OF GROUP
Business
I. Accounting

Economics 18. Asst. Professor Cole.   (See Economics, p. 64.)

Business 1. Asst. Professor Cole. — Accounting Practice.
4 Gr., 23 G.B.   Total 27.

2. Asst. Professor Cole. — Accounting Problems.   1 G.B.   Total 1.

II. Commercial Law

5. Asst. Professor Schaub. — Commercial Contracts.
2 Gr., 34 G.B.   Total 36.

6. Asst. Professor Schaub. — Law of Business Associations.
1 Gr., 6 G.B.   Total 7.

7 ¹*hf*. Asst. Professor Schaub. — Law of Banking Operations.
5 G.B.   Total 5.

III. Commercial Organization

10. Mr. Cherington. — Economic Resources and Commercial Organization of the United States.   1 Gr., 32 G.B., 1 Se., 1 Fr.   Total 35.

11. Mr. Cherington. — Problems of Commercial Organization.
22 G.B.   Total 22.

12 ²*hf*. Dr. Rappard. — Economic Resources and Commercial Policy of the Chief European States.   3 G.B., 1 G.S.   Total 4.

14 ¹*hf*. Mr. Martin. — Economic Resources and Commercial Organization of Central and South America.   7 G.B.   Total 7.

15 ²*hf*. Mr. Shaw, assisted by Mr. Martin. — Business Policy.
11 G.B.   Total 11.

16. Mr. Cherington. — Commercial Organization (advanced course).
2 G.B.   Total 2.

IV. Industrial Organization

17a ¹hf. Professor Gay and Mr. Gunn, and the following lecturers: Messrs. M. W. Alexander, C. G. L. Barth, C. C. Batchelder, M. L. Cooke, Charles Day, W. C. Fish, H. L. Gantt, C. B. Going, H. K. Hathaway᾽ W. J. Hoggson, J. T. Lincoln, W. C. Redfield, Russell Robb, J. E. Sterrett, and F. W. Taylor. — Industrial Organization.

1 Gr., 2 G.S., 39 G.B.   Total 42.

17b ²hf. Mr. Feiker and others. — Industrial Organization.   16 G.B.   Total 16.

19 ¹hf. Messrs. C. G. L. Barth, M. L. Cooke, H. K. Hathaway, and S. E· Thompson. — The Practice of Scientific Management.   5 G.B.   Total 5.

20c. Messrs. H. L. Baker, A. E. Barter, H. L. Bullen, J. C. Dana, C. W. Davis, A. W. Elson, A. W. Finlay, E. B. Hackett, H. B. Hatch, W. C. Huebner, F. T. Hull, H. L. Johnson, C. C. Lane, C. E. Mason, J. H. McFarland, H. M. Plimpton, C. Schweinler, W. S. Timmis, J. A. Ullman, D. B. Updike, and W. B. Wheelwright. — An Introduction to the Technique of Printing.   2 G.B.   Total 2.

20d. Messrs. C. C. Lane and Bruce Rogers. — Business Practice in Printing (advanced course).   1 G.B., 1 Sp.   Total 2.

V. Banking and Finance

21. Asst. Professor Sprague. — Banking.   1 Gr., 11 G.B.   Total 12.

22 ¹hf. Asst. Professor Sprague. — Banking (advanced course).
2 G.B.   Total 2.
24 ²hf. Mr. J. F. Moors. — Investments.
1 Gr., 39 G.B., 2 G.S., 1 Instr.   Total 43.

25. Asst. Professor Sprague. — Corporation Finance.   12 G.B.   Total 12.

VI. Transportation

27 ¹hf. Asst. Professor Cunningham. — Railroad Organization and Finance.
1 Gr., 1 G.S., 5 G.B., 1 Law.   Total 8.

28. Asst. Professor Cunningham. — Railroad Operation.   5 G.B.   Total 5.

29. Mr. Rich. — The Railroad and the Shipper: The Theory and Practice of Rate Making, with special reference to the Interstate Commerce Act.
2 G.B.   Total 2.

30 ²hf. Mr. Hobbs. — Railroad Accounting.   7 G.B.   Total 7.

31. Mr. Rich. — Railroad Rate Making (advanced course).   2 G.B.   Total 2.

VII. Insurance

35a ¹hf. Mr. Medlicott. — Fire Insurance.   1 Gr., 6 G.B.   Total 7.

35b ²hf. Mr. Dow. — Life Insurance.   5 G.B., 1 Sp.   Total 6.

Forestry

1a. Asst. Professor Fisher. — Silviculture. Silvical Studies. Forest description and treatment. Forest regions of the United States. Forest influences and the practice of forestry.   10 G.S.   Total 10.

1*b*. Asst. Professor JACK. — Forest Planting and Nursery Work.
11 G.S. Total 11.

2. Asst. Professor CARTER. — Forest Measurements. 12 G.S. Total 12.

3. Asst. Professor JACK. — Dendrology. Systematic study of American species of commercial trees. 11 G.S. Total 11.

4. Asst. Professor JACK. — Forest Protection. Diseases of trees, forest fires, etc.
6 G.S. Total 6.

5. Asst. Professor CARTER. — Forest Policy and Administration.
6 G.S. Total 6.

6. Mr. BAILEY. — Lumbering and Woods Practice. 5 G.S. Total 5.

7. Asst. Professor CARTER. — Forest Management. Theory of Forest Valuation and Regulation. Construction of a Complete Working Plan.
11 G.S. Total 11.

8 ^1hf. (See Botany, p. 53.)

9. Mr. BAILEY. — Forest Products. Gross features, properties, and utilization of woods. 14 G.S. Total 14.

10. Asst. Professor FISHER. — Forest Operation. 6 G.S. Total 6.

11. Asst. Professor CARTER. — Forest Investigations. Methods of Research in Problems of Technical Forestry. 6 G.S. Total 6.

12. Mr. BAILEY. — Forest Surveying and Timber Estimating. 5 G.S. Total 5.

13. Messrs. NICHOLS and MERRIAM. — Construction Engineering.
8 G.S. Total 8.

Engineering 4*a*. (See Engineering, p. 51.)

Zoölogy 7*d*^{2}. (See Zoölogy, p. 55.)

MEDICAL SCIENCES
Physiology

1. Professor CANNON, Asst. Professor MARTIN, and assistants. — Elementary Course. 4 Gr. Total 4.

20. Professor CANNON. — Research, Thesis, and Examination. 1 Gr. 1 Total.

Biochemistry

1. Professor FOLIN and Asst. Professor HENDERSON. — General Biological Chemistry. 2 Gr. Total 2.

5. Professor FOLIN and Asst. Professor HENDERSON. — Advanced Biological Chemistry. 2 Gr. Total 2.

20. Professor FOLIN and Asst. Professor HENDERSON. — Research and Biological Chemistry. 2 Gr. Total 2.

Pathology

1 *hf*. Professor COUNCILMAN and several assistants. — General Pathology.
2 Gr. Total 2.

2 *hf*. Professor COUNCILMAN and several assistants. — General and Special Pathology. 2 Gr. Total 2.

Neuropathology

1 *hf.* Professor Councilman. — Elementary Course.   2 Gr.   Total 2.

Bacteriology

1. Professor Ernst and several assistants. — Elementary Bacteriology.
                                                         1 Gr.   Total 1.
20. Professor Ernst. — Research.   1 Gr.   Total 1.

In accordance with the vote of the President and Fellows whereby the Faculty may under certain conditions authorize a Doctor of Philosophy or a Doctor of Science to give instruction gratuitously or for such fees as he may himself collect, Karl Schmidt, Ph.D., was authorized to give in the second half-year a course of lectures on " The Foundations of Mathematics."

On the recommendation of the Faculty Council of the Medical School, the President appointed a committee of the Faculty of Arts and Sciences to confer with a committee appointed by that Council and to "consider the correlation of courses in the Medical School with those of the University, especially as regards admission requirements to the Medical School." I give the exact words of the vote, though the use of the word " University " therein will not bear scrutiny.

The Faculty had a singularly uneventful year. Its most important act was the approval of a recommendation brought before it by the Dean of the Graduate School of Applied Science: —

That the Faculty recommend to the Corporation that certain Divisions and Departments in the Graduate School of Applied Science be organized as Schools: to wit: the School of Engineering, of Mining and Metallurgy, of Architecture and Landscape Architecture, of Forestry, of Applied Biology (Bussey Institution), — it being understood that additional schools of Applied Science may be hereafter organized.

That these Schools be grouped together as the Graduate Schools of Applied Science under a separate Faculty, to administer a self-contained graduate programme.

That this organization go into effect at the beginning of the next academic year.

The approval of the Faculty, though it may have been little more than formal, is regarded by some persons as a prophecy that the Faculty of Arts and Sciences will not long continue. This Faculty is a young body. It came into existence in 1890, when the growth of the Graduate Departments and the Lawrence Scientific School and their relation to Harvard College made a new organization of the government desirable and when the old

College Faculty had plainly become too large for the efficient handling of detailed College business. The College, the Scientific School, and the Graduate School were thenceforth to be governed by separate boards, each board with the appropriate Dean for its chairman. These boards, though appointed by the Corporation, were practically executive committees of the Faculty. Through their Deans they reported to the Faculty their most important doings and referred to the Faculty their most important questions, — in particular, questions which concerned more than one of the three schools. The Faculty thus comprising all the more stable teachers of candidates for degrees in arts or in sciences became known as the Faculty of Arts and Sciences.

This body has grown larger and larger, and has sent out as new offshoots the Graduate Schools of Applied Science and the Graduate School of Business Administration, each with its own Dean. The Committee on the Summer School also has been newly organized in connection with the work of University Extension and the degree of A.A. It now has its own Dean and is much like the other administrative boards. As the Faculty grows larger, and as more and more of its business passes into the hands of boards, it has fewer matters to discuss, and is more unwieldy in discussing them. It is obliged to rely on committees for nearly everything not managed by the administrative boards: but these committees, like the boards, are strictly accountable to the Faculty; their policy may at any time become a matter for Faculty discussion. The Faculty still serves as an admirable meeting-ground for the great body of University teachers not teaching exclusively in the professional schools. It holds its members together better than many members are aware and gives every man a glimpse of the character and the purposes of his fellow workers. Also, in a place as busy as Cambridge, the few minutes of social intercourse among men who ordinarily see little of their colleagues mean much. Best of all, the knowledge that a new and important measure must run the gauntlet of Faculty criticism and the risk of Faculty condemnation is a check to ill-considered and radical action. Responsibility to the Faculty, though often irksome, is a good thing for every member of it.

On the other hand, the Graduate Schools of Applied Science and the Graduate School of Business Administration, which is likely to ask for similar independence, are, to all intents and purposes, professional schools, eager to work in the same professional spirit that characterizes the schools of Law, Medicine,

and Divinity.   As professional schools they seek development
unhampered by the Faculty, and responsibility to the President
and Fellows only.   Many of the teachers still offering courses
under the Faculty of Arts and Sciences remain members of that
body.

Discussion of the new method of admission to Harvard College
I shall leave for the most part to Dean Hurlbut. A year's experience with this method strengthens my belief that the action of
the Faculty in establishing it was one of the most important and
most sensible acts ever committed by that body.   Thus far the
method has thoroughly justified itself.   Sure to be regarded by
the hostile or the sceptical as a lowering of the standard of admission, it has shown itself what it was meant to be, a peculiarly good
method for the better students.   These better students it relieves
of needless strain, while it applies a test so searching that anyone
who meets this test may confidently attack College work.   For
the boy who is coached into College rather than fitted for it, the
old method remains the only hope.

The new method depends wholly on the steady intelligence of
the committee which administers it.   Granted this steady intelligence, it is, in my opinion, the best scheme yet devised for admission to an American college.

L. B. R. BRIGGS, *Dean.*

THE COLLEGE

To the President of the University: —

Sir, — I have the honor of submitting to you a report on Harvard College for the academic year 1911–12.

The number of students in the College at the time the lists were compiled for the Catalogue of 1911–12 was two thousand two hundred and sixty-two, divided as follows: —

Seniors	372
Juniors	537
Sophomores	499
Freshmen	789
Total number of Undergraduates	2,147
Special Students	43
Unclassified Students	72
Total	2,262

Compared with the figures at the corresponding time of the preceding year these show a gain of forty-five: —

	Gain	Loss
Seniors		10
Juniors	55	
Sophomores		17
Freshmen	68	
Special Students		32
Unclassified Students		19
	123	78
Net gain	45	

As for a number of years past, therefore, I have again to report that in numbers the College remains practically stationary.

During the year the following students died: —

Edward Little Rogers, '13, ... November 23, 1911.
Joseph Brown Emerson, Unclassified, December 20, 1911.
Merle DeWitt Britten, '15, ... July 4, 1912.

Four hundred and nineteen candidates — nineteen in February and four hundred in June — received the degree of Bachelor of Arts in course. Of these two hundred and eighty-seven were registered as Seniors. The registration of the others is shown in the following table: —

On leave of absence all the year 22
On leave of absence first half-year 5
On leave of absence second half-year 20
Graduate Students in Arts and Sciences 9
Graduate Students in Applied Science 7
Registered in the Law School 15
Registered in the Medical School 4
Registered in the Business School 4
Registered in the Junior Class 14
Registered in the Freshman Class 1
Registered as a Special Student 1
                                                        ———
                                                        102
To be designated "as of 1912" in the *Quinquennial* . . . 30
                                                        ———
                                                        132

Fifty-two candidates received the degree of Bachelor of Science.
Their registration is indicated in the next table: —

Senior Class 42
Junior Class 1
                                                        ——
                                                        43
In Graduate School of Applied Science 2
In the Medical School 1
                                                        ——
                                                        46
On leave of absence first half-year 1
On leave of absence second half-year 4
                                                        ——
                                                        51
To be designated "as of 1913" in the *Quinquennial* . . . 1
                                                        ——
                                                        52

The last two tables show an increase, over the preceding year,
of five candidates for the degree of Bachelor of Arts and of eleven
for that of Bachelor of Science.

The next two tables show the losses and gains in the three lower
classes between November, 1911, and the latter part of October,
1912.

	November, 1911		Loss	Gain	November, 1912	
Class of 1913 . .	(Juniors)	587	211	71	(Seniors)	397
Class of 1914 . .	(Sophomores)	499	131	114	(Juniors)	482
Class of 1915 . .	(Freshmen)	789	173	93	(Sophomores)	659
			515	278		

Net loss in the three classes between Nov., 1911, and Nov., 1912, 237

	Class of 1913	Class of 1914	Class of 1915	Total for three classes
LOSSES				
Left College before the end of the year . .	14	16	40	70
Left College at the end of the year	148	24	23	195
Were "dropped" and left College	8	17	22	47
Entered a lower class	21	50	43	114
Entered a higher class	20	24	45	89
Total loss	211	131	173	515
GAINS				
From higher classes	4	21	50	75
From lower classes	34	36	..	70
Newly admitted	33	57	43	133
Total gain	71	114	93	278
Net loss	140	17	80	237
Net gain	..	..	..	..

The next table shows the losses and gains in the number of Special Students since December, 1911: —

*In attendance, December, 1911   43
Left College before the end of the year   4
Left College at the end of the year   21
Entered a College class   4
      Total loss   29
Reëntered College in 1912 as Special Students . . .   14
Newly admitted   14
      Total   28
      Net loss   15

The Freshman Class in 1912–13 numbers 661. The total for this year cannot justly be compared with the total, 740, of the preceding year, because of the adoption of the new rule whereby students with admission conditions are no longer held in the Freshman Class, but go on with their original class, being put on probation if before the beginning of their third year they have not removed their conditions. The number admitted by examination in 1911 was 593, 21 more than by examination in 1912. Twenty-five students admitted by examination before 1911 entered with the Class of 1915; 26 admitted by examination before 1912 entered with the Class of 1916.

* Catalogue figures, 1911–12.

Admitted by examination in 1912 572
Admitted by examination before 1912 26
Admitted from another college 12
*Admitted from a higher class 51
Admitted from the Special Students 00

Total 661

The members of the Administrative Board for 1911–12 were Professors Willson, Parker, Ward, Messrs. Wells, Hunt, the Assistant Dean (for the first half-year Mr. Castle, for the second Assistant Professor Yeomans), and the Dean. During the year one hundred and ten students were placed on probation for low records, of whom thirty-three were " dropped Freshmen "; eleven were put on probation for disciplinary reasons; the probation of ten students was closed (six of the ten were " dropped Freshmen ") ; six students were required to withdraw for various disciplinary reasons.

At the end of the year 1911–12 the Administrative Board, having three years before given notice to the Faculty and informally to the undergraduates that it should do so, abandoned the practice, which had existed for many years, of forgiving to a student who had been in residence for the full four undergraduate years two points of admission condition, provided that these were all that stood between him and his degree, and provided further that they were not in elementary German or elementary French. In practice these had as a general thing come to be in either elementary Algebra, Plane Geometry, or Science. That there was for this practice no excuse except the good nature of the Faculty was demonstrated by the fact that at Commencement, 1912, only three candidates lost their degrees on account of their failure to remove admission conditions. Either the mathematical lion that had stood in the way and paralysed travellers had lost his teeth, or the travellers had sharpened their swords. The forgiving of two points of condition, provided they are neither in French nor in German, is now accorded to a student only in case by high scholarship, the demonstration of real ability in college work, he wins a position in either the First or the Second Group of Scholars.

* Dropped from 1915 on account of low record 43
Readmitted as Freshmen, but were out of college last year, or withdrew during the
    college year : —
Formerly in 1914 3
Formerly in 1915 5

Total 51

An important change in the rules, logical and beneficial, will still further stimulate undergraduates early to remove their admission conditions. For many years there obtained a rule that a student might not register in a class higher than the Sophomore until he had removed his admission conditions. The Sophomore Class was, therefore, swollen, always the largest, for a student who had reduced his conditions to not more than two points, feeling sure that these would be forgiven at the time he came up for his degree, and for all purposes of undergraduate life being regarded by his fellows as a member of his original class, confidingly lay back and awaited the last meeting of the Faculty before Commencement. Only a prying few, to whom the matter could be easily explained, looked into the long list of names in the Catalogue, expressed surprise or asked embarrassing questions; and carrying about a study card of a color different from that of the cards of his original classmates brought a pang for but a single day at the opening of the year, the less sharp because the colors of the cards of the three upper classes might vary from year to year; and even if they did not they were not conspicuous, not the dearest color. Only a Freshman had always a crimson card.

In 1907 the Faculty amended this rule, and refused to allow a student to register in a class higher than the Freshman until his conditions were out of the way. This change reduced somewhat the number of conditioned men. A red card brought a keener pang, and there was likely to be more interest in the list of Freshmen as printed in the Catalogue than in the lists of the other classes. This change, however, produced an evil that far outweighed all the good it wrought. An erroneous impression concerning the number of the incoming Freshman Class, the only class in the numbers of which the public and the newspapers are interested, was spread broadcast through the country, involving each year elaborate explanations which, after all was said, never made the matter entirely clear.

By the plan now adopted a student will be given until the beginning of his third year in which to remove his admission conditions either by admission examinations or by "additional work" in College. (He can, also, by high standing win the forgiveness of two points.) If, however, by the beginning of his third year he has not cleared his record he is placed on probation, a logical and proper action for the Faculty to take, since it may well be debated whether a student who has not after two years

made up his admission deficiencies had not better be in some other
employment.   Certainly he ought to be required to give all of
his attention to his studies: he should not be allowed either to
represent the University publicly or to take part in public per-
formances.   Under the new rule, after a student has spent two
years in College, his privilege of removing an admission condition
by passing an admission examination is withdrawn;   he must
remove it by passing in a regular college course elected in addition
to the amount of work regularly prescribed for him.   The Faculty
may well consider whether the limitation of this privilege to two
years is wise: whether it would not be better to permit a student
to remove a condition by an admission examination at any
time when admission examinations are held.   Difficulties with
the new rule will surely arise when members of the classes to which
it applies, between whom and whose degrees after the classes
have graduated, stand only admission conditions, seek to complete the requirements for their degrees.   To require these men,
who have done in the College the work necessary for their degrees,
to return to College to take additional work simply to remove
admission conditions, will involve a hardship that may very well
be called unjust.   That the new rule is effective is shown by the
fact that of the students admitted in 1910, the first to whom the
new law has been applied, only twelve, present or past members
of the Class of 1914, have been placed on probation for failure
to remove their admission conditions.   This new rule is in line
with the tendency of the Board to use but two forms of censure, —
probation and some form of complete severance of a student's
connection with the College, either permanently or for a specific
time.   The practice is wise and salutary.   Probation means in
the language of the rule " serious danger of separation from College," doubt as to the wisdom of a student's remaining longer
a member thereof, unless he can prove by his conduct or his work
in College, or both, that he deserves to remain.   To have a youth
long on probation, unless a long time is specified when probation
is imposed, or repeatedly to incur the censure of probation, something that not infrequently occurs, is bad for him and for the College.   If he does not soon win restoration to good standing and
hold it, his connection with the College should be severed, either
finally or until such time as experience at work in the world with
men has shown him what a college can really give him, and he
stands ready to give his word that if he is allowed to resume his
studies he will work as a man should.

Forty-eight students won a place in the First Group of Scholars: of these thirteen, including the holder of the Jacob Wendell Scholarship (given to the student most distinguished in the work of the Freshman year, irrespective of his financial need) received honorary scholarships; thirty-five, scholarships with stipend. On the work of the year 1910–11, winning scholarships for the year 1911–12, fifty-three students won positions in the First Group: sixteen honorary scholarships, thirty-seven scholarships with stipend. One hundred and fifty-three won places in the Second Group of scholars: sixty-nine, honorary scholarships; eighty-four, scholarships with stipend. The preceding year one hundred and thirty-one won a position in this group: fifty-five holding honorary scholarships; seventy-six, scholarships with stipend. The First Group for the year 1912–13 is made up of twenty members of the Class of 1913, sixteen of the Class of 1914, twelve of the Class of 1915; the Second Group, of sixty-six members of 1913, thirty-four of 1914, and fifty-three of 1915. Compared by classes 1913 wins in the two groups eighty-six places; 1914, fifty; 1915, sixty-five. The total number of scholars in the two groups is two hundred and one, about ten per cent, roughly speaking, of the number of students in College eligible to compete for scholarships at the end of the year.

In his annual report on the work of the Faculty of Arts and Sciences for the year 1910–11 the Dean of the Faculty discussed " the most important act of the Faculty in the whole academic year — and its most important act in many years," the framing and the adoption of a "new plan" for admission to Harvard College. Men sceptical as to the wisdom of the plan could be found in our own Faculty; and in the faculties of other institutions were scornful sceptics who were sure that Harvard had " surrendered " to " the certificate system," — that under the new plan examinations were to be but formal, nominal. Those who used this argument showed merely that they knew little of the temper of the Harvard Faculty or of its committees. True, any system of examinations may become a mere form, and the new plan admits of this more easily than does the old; but to argue that at Harvard it is likely soon to become so is impossible for anyone who knows the Faculty as at present constituted. In accepting in place of the Harvard examinations the examinations of the College Entrance Examination Board, the Faculty did much to make Harvard more accessible to youths in remote parts of the country: first, because there is now practically no place in the United States or Western Europe which is not within fairly easy reach of some one of the Board's examination centres; and, second, because a candidate stands a better chance of passing the requisite examinations, since the adoption of the Board's definitions of subjects has done much to secure uniformity in teaching. Uniformity of requirements, even if only on paper, helps the work of the schools. Certainly conditions were greatly improved over those of thirty years ago, when to be able even to hope to secure admission a lad must have made his decision to enter years before he presented himself for examination. But with all the improvements a youth of promise might still find his " way to Harvard College blocked by an eccentricity of requirement "; there still existed " charactic differences " ; a certain number of points had to be secured. The difference between the emphasis of the old plan and that of the new is fundamental: it is no longer laid on points; it is on training, development, maturity of mind, — complete, not partial work. Has the candidate received a good secondary school education ? Has his preliminary training fitted him successfully to carry on College work ? If after the Committee on Admission is satisfied that a candidate has completed an approved school course, he can, by passing examinations in certain fundamental subjects and in a subject in which he has shown special aptitude, demonstrate this, he is admitted to College, unhampered by conditions, requirements that he must make up certain uncompleted tag ends of preliminary education. Theoretically the plan is ideal.

That the action of the Faculty was one of the most important in many years and also wise, the experience of a single year gives proof full of bright promise, almost convincing. That the change was welcome is shown by the fact that although the plan was not adopted until January 17, 1911, when, however, very wide notice of its adoption was given, no less than 185 candidates applied for permission to be examined under it. To 139 of these permission was given. Of the 139 examined 83 were admitted; 56 were rejected. Of the 83 admitted 79 entered College, 66 from public schools, 13 from private, representing, by residence of candidates, 20 states, the District of Columbia, and one foreign country; by schools, nineteen states and the District of Columbia. Among the schools three in New York State, one each in Maine, New Jersey, Pennsylvania, Alabama, Georgia, Illinois, Missouri and Nebraska had never before sent boys directly to Harvard College.

The distribution of the candidates by residence and by location of schools is shown in the following tables: —

MEN WHO ACTUALLY ENTERED HARVARD IN 1911 UNDER NEW PLAN

GEOGRAPHICALLY ARRANGED BY RESIDENCE		GEOGRAPHICALLY ARRANGED BY SCHOOLS	
Maine	2	Maine	2
Vermont	1	Vermont	1
Massachusetts	31	Massachusetts	33
New York	13	Connecticut	3
New Jersey	5	New York	12
Pennsylvania	4	New Jersey	5
	—	Pennsylvania	4
Total, North Atlantic Division	56		—
		Total, North Atlantic Division	60
District of Columbia	2		
Virginia	1	District of Columbia	3
Georgia	1	Georgia	1
	—		—
Total, South Atlantic Division	4	Total, South Atlantic Division	4
Colorado	2	Colorado	1
Washington	2	Washington	2
	—		—
Total, Western Division	4	Total, Western Division	3
Ohio	3	Ohio	3
Illinois	3	Illinois	2
Michigan	1	Michigan	1
Wisconsin	1	Wisconsin	1
Minnesota	1	Minnesota	0
Missouri	1	Missouri	2
Nebraska	1	Nebraska	1
Kansas	1		—
	—	Total, North Central Division	10
Total, North Central Division	12		
		Kentucky	1
Kentucky	1	Alabama	1
Alabama	1		—
	—	Total, South Central Division	2
Total, South Central Division	2		—
		Total	79
Mexico	1		
Total, Foreign	1		
	—		
Total	79		

Schools added to School and College List by men who actually entered Harvard in 1911 by the New Plan: —

MAINE	Skowhegan High.
NEW YORK	Fulton High.
NEW YORK	Hudson Falls High.
NEW YORK	Rochester, West High.
NEW JERSEY	Hammonton High.
PENNSYLVANIA	Bradford High.
ALABAMA	Marion Institute, Marion.
GEORGIA	Academy of Richmond County.
ILLINOIS	La Grange, Lyons Township High.
MISSOURI	Cape Girardeau Normal School.
NEBRASKA	Harvard High.

What has been the year's work of these men? The 79 elected, or rather carried until such time as some record could be secured in them, 408 courses. In these they secured the following grades: 61 A's; 147 B's; 155 C's; 34.5 D's; 6.5 E's; total, 404; from each of three courses a student was excluded; one student was absent from a final examination and therefore received no grade; total, 408. It will be seen that the number of grades of distinction, A and B, outnumbers all others. Of the 6.5 grades of failure, E, three were in the case of a single student, who was also excluded from a fourth course. The other 3.5 were divided among four students. Each of two other students was excluded from a single course, and one student of high record, mistaking the date of a final examination, was absent from the examination and thus lost credit for the course. All but thirteen had distinction in at least a half-course; and of these 64 all but two had distinction in more than this amount. The 34.5 grades of D were divided among 26 students. In the matter of freedom from official discipline the record is distinguished. One student was placed on probation during the course of the year, at the end of the year had his probation closed, and did not seek readmission. One other, failing at the end of the year to attain a grade above D, had his connection with the College severed, but on evidence of good work done during the summer was readmitted at the beginning of the present year to the Freshman Class. During the year a third student of this group was " admonished," — the mildest form of College censure, and in this case for a very minor offence in committing which he had much official sympathy. Four of the twelve members of the Class of 1915 winning positions in the First Group of Scholars in Harvard College, 33%, and eleven of the fifty-three winning positions in the Second Group, 20.7%, are numbered among these 79, fifteen out of the class total of sixty-five scholars. Of these sixty-five winners of scholarships five were admitted to College before 1911; sixty scholarships, therefore, were won by the 593 students admitted by examination in 1911, seventy-nine of whom entered by the new plan. In other words, 13.3% of the students admitted by examination in 1911 won 25% of the scholarships awarded to the class on the ground of academic distinction.

Brilliant as is this record, and surely it may be called brilliant, a prediction that the records of future years will be as brilliant cannot safely be made. Sixty-six of these boys came from public schools, picked youths; thirteen from private, — these also, for this year, picked. A just estimate can be made only when a larger number of private schools, the schools whose business it is to get into College not only every boy who wishes to go to College, but every boy whose parents wish him to go, and which " know how to prepare a boy to pass entrance examinations," make, if ever they do, liberal use of the new plan. That it can ever wholly supersede the old method appears, in view of its nature and the papers thus far set, extremely unlikely; it is not adapted to that type of boy (and a great many of them are well worth a college education) who, in the words of the headmaster of a once famous school, "whenever he gets a nugget should be allowed to run right up to the College and deposit it." But the hope of the Chairman of the Committee on Admission that by a modification of this new system for use in September, and the employment of the examinations of the College Board wholly in place of our own old system in June, we may be rid of the task of setting examination papers on the old system, seems very possible of realization.

The points on the other side, however, urged by Professor Edwin H. Hall, demand closest attention: the duty of watching with the utmost care the effect of the new plan upon secondary school education in general; the grave danger, when once candidates have the opportunity (which these had not) to shape their whole course for these examinations, that they will neglect so far as they dare those studies in which they know they shall not be examined; and the need of relief from the too great pressure of the colleges upon the schools, pressure of which the schools have long complained, and which any plan, no matter how good it be, framed only for the best students, does not afford.

Theoretically, as has already been said, the new plan is ideal, and the results of its first application are full of brilliant promise, amply justifying, so far as promise can, the labors and the hopes of the committee that drew it. The needs of the boys who are forced into college it does not, at least at present, appear to meet; but for that much more important class, those to whom college is a privilege, who love learning, in actual practice it far more nearly approaches the ideal than any other plan thus far devised. To schools that foster learning it should be an incentive and an inspiration.

B. S. HURLBUT, *Dean.*

ATHLETIC SPORTS

Sir, — As Chairman of the Committee on the Regulation of Athletic Sports, I have the honor of reporting on Harvard athletics in 1911–12.

Besides the Chairman, the Committee contained, as Faculty members, Dean Hurlbut and Acting Secretary Wells; as graduate members, Dr. E. H. Nichols, Mr. R. F. Herrick, and Mr. G. R. Fearing, Jr.; as undergraduate members, Mr. H. de Windt, Mr. A. M. Goodale, and Mr. H. L. Gaddis. In the latter part of the year Mr. de Windt was succeeded by Mr. R. S. Potter.

To facilitate business and to avoid unnecessary meetings, the Committee voted: —

That Mr. Edgar Wells be appointed Vice-Chairman of this Committee and that the Chairman and Vice-Chairman, or either of them, be vested with all the authority of the Committee over the control of athletics in the following matters: —

1. In all matters appertaining to qualification for participation in athletic sports.

2. In all matters affecting intercollegiate contests, expressly including the schedules for games and other contests, and the time and place for them, and including all matters relating to admissions to games and other contests and to distribution of tickets therefor.

3. The control and management of all receipts and expenditures on account of athletics.

Obviously this vote gave the Chairman and the Vice-Chairman large powers and might be so interpreted as to do away with all other members of the Committee. It was not so interpreted, however. All matters of importance were referred to the Committee except in such emergencies as compelled the officers to act quickly.

In 1911–12 the best spent money was used in reclaiming six more acres of the Soldiers' Field. In general, money is well spent when it increases opportunity for exercise among all students, or relieves all students of subscriptions; it is spent less well — some think it is spent ill — in the preparation of comparatively few men for single great contests, in costly journeys to the scenes of those contests, in prolonged use of the training table, and in some

other things which college athletics as now conducted demand.
On the other hand, without the great contests there would be less
money to spend; and there is, I suppose, some question whether
contests without elaborate preparation would be regarded as great.
In this question something may be learned from the game between
the Army and the Navy, which rivals in interest the game between
Yale and Harvard: —

"At West Point," says the *Yale News*, "where the daily practice lasts
about forty-five minutes, Yale Football Teams have twice in succession
been out-played, out-fought, and sent home — branded with defeat.   A
team of Army men, who find rest from strenuous labor in playing the
game — who do not pretend to supremacy in it — have thus, more than
Harvard and Princeton together, tarnished our football reputation."

Since the opportunity for students to use the Harvard swimming tank in the Y. M. C. A. Building revived and justified the
desire for a swimming team, the Committee voted to allow the
formation of a University Swimming Team for the year 1912–13
under certain conditions.

It is worth noting that the champion tennis player of the University is the first scholar of his class.

In the major sports the teams had only moderate success.   In
rowing Harvard failed, as usual, to win from Cornell, and again
won from Yale.   In track athletics Harvard won the dual meets
with Dartmouth and Yale, but made no remarkable score in the
intercollegiate games.   In football the speed and aggressiveness
of Princeton proved too much for a Harvard team with several
disabled players.   Yale and Harvard played once more a tie game
with no scoring.   In baseball Harvard succumbed to both Princeton and Yale.   When the size of Harvard University is considered
and her enormous outlay on athletic sports, it would seem that
she should win more of the great games; but since her University
teams contain neither Freshmen nor members of any graduate
or professional school, the number of men available for these teams
is smaller than the public supposes.   As to the enormous outlay
on teams, I am not sure that it has increased the chance of victory,
and I am sure that it has damaged some players.   In certain
things related to athletic games the College should spare no expense; for example, she should studiously and at any cost reduce
the danger to life and limb.   On the other hand, the College
should not watch her athletes with that kind of care which leads
them to think their nervous systems the most significant thing
in life and luxurious living a matter of course.   A boy poor when

he comes and poor when he goes gets a bad start in the struggle for a living if he has learned to regard limited trains, costly food, automobiles on the slightest provocation, and free entertainment in hours of leisure and refreshment as due from the world to him. In theory most persons favor economy; but in applying the theory to any one team, committees, coaches, managers, players, and captains have often been inclined — quite naturally — to consider everything before economy and to rely luxuriously on the great sums collected at games as more than covering the bills. What I have just said, though general, is by no means universal. Instances of courageous effort to keep expenses down are not infrequent among managers, and may at times be discerned even in captains and coaches. Moreover, there has been marked improvement in these matters within a very few years. The use of automobiles has been cut down; the waste in supplies has been diminished; and, in the present year, the cost per student at the football training table has been made altogether reasonable, with no signs of disaster to the team.

The dates of the boat-race and the baseball games have been disturbed by changes in the dates of Class Day and Commencement Day. In 1911, when Commencement was a week earlier at Yale than at Harvard, the Yale crew waited a week after everything at New Haven was over — a delay manifestly disadvantageous to Yale graduates, if not to the crew itself. In 1912, Commencement at Harvard was moved to the day following Commencement at Yale. Within a single week Class Day at Yale comes on Monday, Class Day at Harvard on Tuesday, Commencement at Yale on Wednesday, Commencement at Harvard on Thursday. The friends and graduates of Yale regarded a game of baseball at New Haven on Tuesday as almost essential to graduation week; the friends and graduates of Harvard regarded a game at Cambridge in close connection with Class Day, but not on that day, as almost essential to the festivities of the season. Neither college might fitly have the game in its own territory on its own Commencement Day. As a result the first game was played at New Haven on Tuesday, and the second at Cambridge on Wednesday, the Harvard Seniors in the team sacrificing their Class Day, the Yale Seniors their Commencement Day, and both teams undergoing two contests with no day between. This last consideration is not so important as members of a defeated team are disposed to think it. I question whether the strain of anticipation is not fully as great as the strain of reality, and whether it is not just as well to play these two games without a longer interval. The need of two pitchers in a team that may have one or none is a more serious drawback. Except for the players the dates were unquestionably the best; and, compared with the total number of interested persons, the players are few.

The boat-race was rowed on Friday, the first day after Commencement at Harvard and the second day after Commencement at Yale. This date leaves Thursday an off day in the Yale festivities. Thus the proposal of Friday, coming from Yale, was not merely fair but generous, a courtesy which Harvard men should appreciate. The dates were settled without a suspicion of friction between the Colleges, and settled by men who did not question, outwardly or inwardly, each other's sincerity. This would seem, and should be, a matter of course; my excuse for mentioning it is its inexcusable novelty.

Last year several of the larger colleges made a distinct effort to prevent "yapping" on the baseball field, and achieved considerable success: but umpires still fail to enforce the rules which limit the remarks of players; and student players, who get their training directly and indirectly from professional players, are constantly tempted to do what they know to be done — and done without censure — by the heroes of the American and National Leagues. We like to believe that recent Harvard teams, though by no means perfect, have honestly tried to resist such temptations and to play a clean game.

L. B. R. BRIGGS.

THE GRADUATE SCHOOL OF ARTS AND SCIENCES

To the President of the University: —

Sir, — As Dean of the Graduate School of Arts and Sciences, I have the honor to submit a report on the School for the academic year 1911–12.

The following tables present in summary form information concerning the number and distribution of the students, recommendations for degrees, and the assignment of fellowships and scholarships.

Table I shows that the number of students registered in the School was four hundred and seventy-five, a decrease of nine from the preceding year. Of this number four hundred and forty-seven were resident, and twenty-eight non-resident, all of whom were travelling fellows. Of the resident students three hundred and ninety-four were in attendance during the whole year, of whom three hundred and eight were doing full work. Of the remaining fifty-three resident students thirty-one entered the School after November 1 and twenty-two withdrew before the end of the year.

TABLE I. — NUMBER AND CLASSIFICATION OF STUDENTS

	1909–10	1910–11	1911–12
I. Resident Students doing full work in the School for the whole academic year	279	311	308
Resident students not doing full work or not working for the whole year as Resident Students	156	147	139
	—435	—458	—447
Non-Resident Students holding fellowships	15	26	28
Non-Resident Students not holding fellowships	2	0	0
	— 17	— 26	— 28
II. Students whose studies lay chiefly in			
Semitic Languages and History	0	2	1
Ancient Languages (Classics and Indic Philology)	26	22	17
Modern Languages (including Comparative Literature)	117	164	137
History and Political Science	77	93	108
Philosophy	59	52	62
Education	23	16	20
Fine Arts	2	5	2
Music	3	4	6
Mathematics	30	22	20
Physics	14	15	13
Chemistry	26	34	31
Biology	29	30	30
Geology	9	12	7
Anthropology	9	5	4
Medical Sciences	5	3	11
Unclassed Students	23	5	6
	—452	—484	—475
III. First-year Students	254	257	256
Second-year Students	110	136	109
Third-Year Students	53	53	65
Fourth-year Students	24	24	33
Students in fifth year or later	11	14	12
	—452	—484	—475
IV.*A.B.'s and S.B.'s of Harvard University and of no other institution	132	160	128
A.B.'s and S.B.'s (and holders of similar degrees) of other institutions and also of Harvard University	6	9	5
Students not holding the Harvard degree of A.B. or S.B.	314	315	342
	—452	—484	—475
V. Students holding the Harvard degree of A.M., S.M., Ph.D., or S.D.	106	120	133
*Students holding the Harvard degree of A.B. or S.B., but not of A.M., S.M., Ph.D., or S.D.	96	121	90
Students holding no Harvard degree in Arts, Philosophy, or Science	250	243	252
	—452	—484	—475

In Table II similar facts concerning residence and amount of work are set forth for a period of twenty years. Table III shows the percentage of students in their first and following years.

* Harvard College Seniors on leave of absence, with work for the bachelor's degree completed or nearly completed, are counted in this Table as holders of the degrees for which they are candidates in Harvard College.

TABLE II. — NUMBER OF STUDENTS: 1892–1912

	1892-93.	1893-94.	1894-95.	1895-96.	1896-97.	1897-98.	1898-99.	1899-1900.	1900-01.	1901-02.	1902-03.	1903-04.	1904-05.	1905-06.	1906-07.	1907-08.	1908-09.	1909-10.	1910-11.	1911-12.
Resident Students doing full work in the School for the whole academic year	127	162	161	175	194	171	218	227	226	218	216	289	278	260	281	287	290	279	311	308
Resident Students not doing full work or not working for the whole year as Resident Students	73	86	94	105	96	107	103	99	118	86	94	123	100	103	105	119	123	156	147	139
Whole number of Resident Students	200	248	255	280	290	278	321	326	339	304	310	412	378	363	386	406	413	435	458	447
Non-resident Fellows	9	10	12	13	14	15	12	13	14	11	15	14	15	16	21	17	15	15	26	28
Other Non-Resident Students	7	1	5	6	2	....	3	2	....	....	....	1	2	....	....	1	1	2	....	....
Whole number of Non-Resident Students	16	11	17	19	16	15	15	15	14	11	15	15	17	16	21	18	16	17	26	28
Whole number of students	216	259	272	299	306	293	336	341	353	315	325	427	395	409	407	424	429	452	484	475
Percentage of Resident Students doing full work for whole academic year	64	65	63	63	67	62	68	70	67	72	70	70	72	66	73	71	70	64	68	69

TABLE III. — PERCENTAGE OF STUDENTS IN THEIR FIRST
AND FOLLOWING YEARS: 1899–1912

	1899–1900.	1900–01.	1901–02.	1902–03.	1903–04.	1904–05.	1905–06.	1906–07.	1907–08.	1908–09.	1909–10.	1910–11.	1911–12.
	%	%	%	%	%	%	%	%	%	%	%	%	%
First-year Students	53	54	50	54	61	60	53	56	57	57	56	53	54
Second-year Students	25	23	26	26	21	24	26	21	23	24	25	28	23
Third-year Students	11	15	12	11	12	11	13	14	12	12	11	11	14
Fourth-year Students and Students of longer residence	11	8	12	9	6	5	8	9	8	7	8	8	9

Table IV shows a marked decline in the past year in the percentage of graduates of Harvard College studying in the Graduate School of Arts and Sciences. It is true that the proportion of Harvard men in 1910–11 was unusually large, but the percentage in 1911–12 is less than in any previous year, and may well indicate a tendency which should be watched in all departments of the University. Nevertheless, the quality of those who enter the Graduate School of Arts and Sciences shows no decline. It still remains true, as shown statistically in my report for 1909–10 and in the report prepared by Mr. Robinson in 1907–08, that the great majority of the honor men who continue their studies at Harvard enter the Graduate School of Arts and Sciences, and that this tendency increases with the grade of distinction achieved. Thus during the last five years, out of one hundred and seventeen who received the A.B. or S.B. *magna cum laude* fifty-three returned to the University the following year and thirty-five entered the Graduate School of Arts and Sciences; while of twenty-one graduating *summa cum laude* sixteen returned, all except three entering the Graduate School of Arts and Sciences. While it thus appears that in this respect the Graduate School of Arts and Sciences more than holds its own in comparison with the other graduate departments of the University, it is still true that the total number of Harvard men of promise who go on for advanced study in the humanities and pure science is less than it should be. Doubtless in America generally the career of a teacher and scholar does not offer the attractions it should offer to men of ability and ambition, but the colleges have also their responsibility, and we may well ask ourselves whether Harvard College is doing all that it might to develop the love of learning among its students.

TABLE IV. — PERCENTAGE OF GRADUATES OF HARVARD
COLLEGE: 1907–08 — 1911–12

	1907–08.	1908–09.	1909–10.	1910–11.	1911–12.
Total enrolment	424	429	452	484	475
*Number of graduates of Harvard College .	124	131	132	160	128
*Percentage of graduates of Harvard College	29%	30%	29%	37%	26%
Number of graduates of other colleges and universities	300	298	320	324	347
Percentage of graduates of other colleges and universities	71%	70%	71%	63%	74%

Tables V, VI, and VII indicate that the School continues to maintain its national character in the geographical distribution of its students and of the institutions from which they come to Harvard.

* Harvard College Seniors on leave of absence are reckoned as graduates of Harvard College.

TABLE V.—COLLEGES AND UNIVERSITIES REPRESENTED BY FOUR OR MORE GRADUATES IN THE SCHOOL: 1907–08, 1908–09, 1909–10, 1910–11, 1911–12

1907–08.		1908–09.		1909–10.		1910–11.		1911–12.	
Harvard	182	Harvard	182	Harvard	199	Harvard	218	Harvard	211
Amherst	10	Columbia	11	Amherst	14	Dartmouth	11	Yale	16
Michigan	9	Amherst	9	Dartmouth	10	Bowdoin	9	Dartmouth	13
Brown	8	Brown	9	Chicago	8	Amherst	8	Bowdoin	10
Dartmouth	8	Dartmouth	9	Haverford	8	Haverford	8	Boston Univ.	8
Rochester	8	Bowdoin	8	Princeton	8	Chicago	8	Haverford	8
Williams	7	Michigan	7	Williams	8	Northwestern (Ill.)	8	Indiana	8
Bowdoin	6	Princeton	7	Bowdoin	7	Boston Univ.	7	Kansas	7
Brown	6	Haverford	6	Kansas	7	Brown	7	Michigan	7
California	6	Mass. Inst. of Tech.	6	Missouri	7	Yale	7	Toronto	7
Texas	6	Northwestern	6	Syracuse	7	Indiana	6	Williams	7
Yale	6	Williams	6	Yale	7	Syracuse	6	California	6
Columbia	5	Boston University	6	Brown	6	North Carolina	6	McGill	6
Indiana	5	Chicago	5	Indiana	6	Toronto	6	Missouri	6
Ohio Wesleyan	5	Missouri	5	Mass. Inst. of Tech.	6	Missouri	6	North Carolina	6
Chicago	5	Mt. Allison	5	Michigan	6	Williams	6	Northwestern (Ill.)	6
Missouri	5	Texas	5	Northwestern	6	Central (Ky.)	5	Wisconsin	6
George Washington	4	Toronto	5	Texas	6	Columbia	5	Amherst	5
Leland Stanford Jr.	4	West Virginia	5	California	5	Cornell	5	Brown	5
Mass. Inst. of Tech.	4	Yale	5	Columbia	5	Monmouth	5	Chicago	5
Missouri	4	Acadia	4	Ohio State	5	Wisconsin	5	Ohio State	5
Mt. Allison	4	Allegheny	4	Tufts	5	Mt. Allison	5	Ohio Wesleyan	5
Princeton	4	California	4	Charleston	4	Mass. Inst. of Tech.	5	Colby	4
Toronto	4	Kansas	4	Georgia	4	Tufts	5	Columbia	4
Vanderbilt	4	Oberlin	4	Mt. Allison	4	Kansas	4	Dalhousie	4
Washington	4	Ohio Northern	4	Oberlin	4	Allegheny	4	DePauw	4
		Ohio State	4	Ohio Wesleyan	4	Dalhousie	4	Mass. Inst. of Tech.	4
		Southern California	4	Western Reserve	4	Leland Stanford Jr.	4	Monmouth	4
		Tufts	4			Ohio State	4	Syracuse	4
		Wesleyan (Conn.)	4			Ohio Wesleyan	4	Virginia	4
						Trinity (Conn.)	4	Wesleyan (Conn.)	4
						California	4		
						McGill	4		
Total Membership, 424		429		452		484		475	

TABLE VI. — HOLDERS OF DEGREES FROM HARVARD
AND TWENTY-FIVE OTHER COLLEGES AND UNIVERSITIES
1896–97 — 1911–12

	1896-97	1897-98	1898-99	1899-1900	1900-01	1901-02	1902-03	1903-04	1904-05	1905-06	1906-07	1907-08	1908-09	1909-10	1910-11	1911-12	Total
Harvard	174	178	196	191	197	189	174	232	192	197	185	182	182	199	218	211	3097
Amherst	7	5	5	7	10	8	10	14	8	8	7	10	9	14	8	5	135
Brown	5	7	8	5	11	8	11	12	7	12	4	8	9	6	7	5	125
Dartmouth	6	6	2	3	6	5	7	12	9	6	10	8	9	10	11	13	123
Bowdoin	4	3	6	4	9	8	7	7	5	3	5	6	8	7	9	10	111
Yale	2	4	10	4	7	4	6	9	7	8	7	6	5	7	7	16	109
Michigan	4	3	4	7	7	2	7	10	5	10	6	9	7	6	3	7	97
California	7	6	8	8	7	7	6	4	3	3	5	6	4	5	4	6	89
Haverford	2	3	5	5	4	4	5	7	5	5	5	3	6	8	8	8	83
Ohio Wesleyan	1	4	2	2	3	5	5	8	14	12	4	5	3	4	4	5	81
Williams	2	–	2	4	6	3	4	7	7	7	3	7	6	8	6	7	79
Toronto	1	5	6	5	6	6	3	4	5	3	8	4	5	2	6	7	76
Kansas	8	8	5	4	5	2	3	3	2	3	5	3	4	7	5	7	74
Boston Univ.	1	2	3	4	0	1	1	5	5	7	8	6	5	3	7	8	72
Indiana	6	4	5	4	2	3	3	2	3	4	5	5	3	6	6	8	69
Northwestern	2	5	6	6	5	1	6	2	2	1	1	2	6	6	8	6	65
Chicago	1	3	2	2	3	3	7	1	3	4	4	4	5	8	8	5	63
Tufts	5	2	6	5	5	4	6	6	3	1	2	–	4	5	5	2	61
Columbia	2	3	1	–	1	1	6	5	1	4	7	5	11	5	5	4	61
Leland Stanford Jr.	4	4	7	6	2	3	6	4	5	3	3	4	1	1	4	3	60
Oberlin	7	5	3	6	9	4	1	–	1	3	3	3	4	4	–	2	55
Princeton	3	5	1	2	3	4	3	2	–	3	4	4	7	8	3	3	55
Texas	2	2	1	3	3	3	5	5	3	1	2	6	5	6	3	2	53
Dalhousie	2	2	3	4	4	5	2	2	2	4	2	3	3	3	4	4	49
Mass. Inst. of Tech.	3	4	3	3	2	1	1	1	1	2	2	4	6	6	5	4	48
Total Membership	306	293	336	341	353	315	325	427	393	409	407	424	429	452	484	475	

TABLE VII. — BIRTHPLACES OF GRADUATE STUDENTS: 1909–12

	1909-10	1910-11	1911-12
Students born in the New England States	132	148	135
Students born in other Northern States east of the Mississippi River	160	158	164
Students born in Southern States east of the Mississippi River	37	42	43
Students born in States west of the Mississippi River	61	65	66
Students born in the Dominion of Canada	27	32	26
Students born in other foreign countries	35	39	41
Total number of students	452	484	475
Percentage of students born in New England	29	30	28
Percentage of students born elsewhere	71	70	72

Tables VIII and IX set forth the number of candidates recommended for higher degrees and their distribution throughout the various Divisions and Departments.

TABLE VIII. — RECOMMENDATIONS FOR DEGREES IN 1910–12

	1910	1911	1912
I. Graduate students recommended for A.M.	130	150	124
Graduate students recommended for S.M.	4	—	—
Graduate students recommended for Ph.D.	34	40	36
	—168	—190	—160
II. Professional students recommended for A.M. on special courses of study	13	14	5
Professional students recommended for Ph.D. on special courses of study	3 16	1 15	2 7
Total number recommended for A.M., S.M., and Ph.D.	184	205	167
III. Harvard Bachelors of Arts or Science, not previously graduated elsewhere	50	51	44
Harvard Bachelors of Arts or Science, previously graduated elsewhere	1	4	—
Students not Harvard Bachelors of Arts or Science	133	150	123
	—184	—205	—167

TABLE IX. — DIVISIONS AND DEPARTMENTS IN WHICH RECOMMENDATIONS FOR THE HIGHER DEGREES WERE MADE IN 1912

Division Department	Degrees	
	A.M.	Ph.D.
Semitic Languages and History	1	–
Ancient Languages	4	3
Modern Languages		
English	23	4
Germanic Languages and Literatures	2	2
French, and other Romance Languages	11	2
Comparative Literature	1	–
In more than one Department	1	–
Total in Modern Languages	— 38	— 8
History, Government, and Economics		
History	12	5
Government	6	1
Economics	11	1
Total in History, Government, and Economics	— 29	— 7
Philosophy	16	6
Education	6	1
Music	3	–
Mathematics	2	1
Physics	1	–
Chemistry	4	4
Biology		
Botany	6	1
Zoölogy	2	3
.Total in Biology	— 8	— 4
Geology	5	–
Anthropology	2	–
Medical Sciences	1	2
Undivisional	4	–
Professional Students:		
Divinity School	5	2
Total	129	38

The degree of Doctor of Philosophy was conferred upon the thirty-eight men named below.

GEORGE PLIMPTON ADAMS, A.B. 1904 (1903), A.M. 1907.
Subject, Philosophy. *Special Field*, Metaphysics. *Thesis*, "An Interpretation and Defence of the Principle of Idealism in Metaphysics." Assistant Professor of Philosophy, University of California.

ROGER ADAMS, A.B. 1909, A.M. 1910.
Subject, Chemistry. *Special Field*, Organic Chemistry. *Thesis*, I. "A Study of the Solubilities in Aqueous Alkalis of various Hydrazones of certain Aromatic Ortho-Hydroxyaldehydes and Ketones." II. "Nonanes." III. "A New Bottling Apparatus." Parker Fellow, at Bonn.

WALTER THEODORE BROWN, A.B. (*Univ. of Toronto*) 1907, A.M. (*ibid.*) 1908, A.M. (*Harvard Univ.*) 1911.
Subject, Philosophy. *Special Field*, Ethics. *Thesis*, "Studies in Individualism." Instructor in Philosophy, Bowdoin College.

ROBERT OSCAR BUSEY, A.B. (*Univ. of Illinois*) 1900, A.M. (*Harvard Univ.*) 1906.
Subject, Philology. *Special Field*, Germanic Philology. *Thesis*, "Observations on the Language of Georg Rudolf Weckherlin." Assistant Professor of German, Ohio State University.

EDMUND TROWBRIDGE DANA, A.B. 1909, A.M. 1910.
Subject, Philosophy. *Special Field*, Ethics. *Thesis*, "The True, the Right, and the Good." Cambridge.

TEIZABURO DEMURA, Gr., Theol. Course, *Tohoku Gakuin, Japan*, 1896, S.T.B. (*Pacific Theol. Seminary*) 1901, A.M. (*Yale Univ.*) 1902.
Subject, Philosophy. *Special Field*, Philosophy of Religion. *Thesis*, "The Nature of Religious Truth." Professor of Philosophy, Tohoku Gakuin, Sendai, Japan.

CARL SAWYER DOWNES, A.B. 1907, A.M. 1908.
Subject, Philology. *Special Field*, English Philology. *Thesis*, "Arnold's Poetry in its Relations to Romanticism." Instructor in English, University of Texas.

CURT JOHN DUCASSE, A.B. (*Univ. of Washington*) 1908, A.M. (*ibid.*) 1909.
Subject, Philosophy. *Special Field*, Metaphysics. *Thesis*, "The Fallacy of Counteraction, and its Metaphysical Significance." Instructor in Philosophy, University of Washington.

ARTHUR JOHNSON EAMES, A.B. 1908, A.M. 1910.
Subject, Biology. *Special Field*, Botany. *Thesis*, "The Morphology of Agathis australis (Lamb.) Steud." Instructor in Botany, Cornell University.

GUSTAVUS JOHN ESSELEN, Jr., A.B. 1909, A.M. 1911.
Subject, Chemistry. *Special Field*, Organic Chemistry. *Thesis*, "Studies on Benzhydrols. I. The Resolution of p-Aminobenzhydrol into its Optical Isomers. II. The Splitting of Benzhydrols by the Action of Bromine." Research Chemist, Research Laboratory, General Electric Company, West Lynn.

AUGUSTUS HENRY FISKE, A.B. 1901, A.M. 1902.
Subject, Chemistry. *Special Field*, Organic Chemistry. *Thesis*, I. "On certain Nitro Derivatives of Vicinal Tribrombenzol." II. "Decomposition of Tetrabromorthoquinone." III. "Hydrates of Sodium Carbonate and their Temperatures of Transition." Instructor in Chemistry, Harvard University.

FRED FORD FLANDERS, A.B. (*State Coll. of Washington*) 1902, A.M. (*ibid.*) 1905.
Subject, Chemistry. *Special Field*, Analytical Chemistry. *Thesis*, "The Determination and Metabolism of Benzoic Acid and Hippuric Acid." Chemist, Department of Standards, Massachusetts State Board of Insanity.

FRANCIS HOWARD FOBES, A.B. 1904, A.M. 1905.
Subject, Philology. *Special Field*, Classical Philology. *Thesis*, "De Libris aliquot Suetonianis. Instructor in Greek and Latin, Harvard University.

TOMLINSON FORT, A.B. (*Univ. of Georgia*) 1906, A.M. (*ibid.*) 1909, A.M. (*Harvard Univ.*) 1910.
Subject, Mathematics.   Special Field, Analysis.   Thesis, "Problems connected with Linear Difference Equations of the Second Order with special Reference to Equations with Periodic Coefficients."   John Thornton Kirkland Fellow, at Göttingen.

WALTER HOUGHTON FREEMAN, A.B. 1906 (1905), A.M. 1906.
Subject, Philology.   Special Field, Classical Philology.   Thesis, "De Textus Ovidi Carminum Amatoriorum Historia."   Instructor in Greek, Grinnell College.

ISAAC GOLDBERG, A.B. 1910, A.M. 1911.
Subject, Philology.   Special Field, Romance Philology.   Thesis, "Don José Echegaray: A Study in Modern Spanish Drama."   Editor, *Young Men's Hebrew Association Review*, Boston.

NORMAN SCOTT BRIEN GRAS, A.B. (*Western Univ.*) 1906, A.M. (*ibid.*) 1906, A.M. (*Harvard Univ.*) 1909.
Subject, History.   Special Field, Economic History.   Thesis, "The Evolution of the English Corn Market, 1100–1700."   Assistant Professor of History, Clark College.

ALFRED OTTO GROSS, A.B. (*Univ. of Illinois*) 1908.
Subject, Biology.   Special Field, Zoölogy.   Thesis, "The Reactions of Arthropods to Monochromatic Lights of Equal Intensities."   Instructor in Biology, Bowdoin College.

CARL HENRY IBERSHOFF, LITT.B. (*Univ. of Michigan*) 1899.
Subject, Philology.   Special Field, Germanic Philology.   Thesis, "The Sources of Bodmer's *Noah*."   Instructor in German, University of Wisconsin.

FRANKLIN PARADISE JOHNSON, A.B. (*Univ. of Missouri*) 1908, A.M. (*Harvard Univ.*) 1910.
Subject, Medical Sciences.   Special Field, Embryology.   Thesis, "The Development of the Mucosa of the Digestive Tube in the Human Embryo, with Notes on the Effects of Distention of the Intestine upon the Shape of Villi and Glands."   Assistant Professor of Anatomy, University of Missouri.

SIDNEY ISAAC KORNHAUSER, A.B. (*Univ. of Pittsburgh*) 1908, A.M. (*Harvard Univ.*) 1910.
Subject, Biology.   Special Field, Zoölogy.   Thesis, "A Comparative Study of the Chromosomes in the Spermatogenesis of Enchenopa binotata (Say) and Enchenopa (Campylenchia Stål) curvata (Fabr.)."   Edward William Hooper Fellow, at Halle.

WILLIAM SETCHEL LEARNED, A.B. (*Brown Univ.*) 1897, A.M. (*ibid.*) 1908.
Subject, Education.   Special Field, Educational Organisation.   Thesis, "The Development of the Professional and Social Organisation of Secondary Teachers in Germany."   Joseph Lee Fellow for Research in Education.

WILBERT LORNE MACDONALD, A.B. (*Univ. of Toronto*) 1908, A.M. (*Univ. of Wisconsin*) 1910.
Subject, Philology.   Special Field, English Philology.   Thesis, "The Beginnings of the English Essay."   Lecturer in English, University College, Toronto.

MALCOLM LEOD MACPHAIL, A.B. (*Franklin Coll., O.*) 1900, A.B. (*Boston Univ.*) 1901, Gr., *Auburn Theol. Seminary*, 1904, A.M. (*Harvard Univ.*) 1911.
Subject, Philosophy.   Special Field, Social Ethics.   Thesis, "Educated Men and the Church."   Pastor, First Presbyterian Church, North Side, Pittsburgh, Pa.

PERCY ALVIN MARTIN, A.B. (*Leland Stanford Jr. Univ.*) 1902, A.M. (*ibid.*) 1903, A.M. (*Harvard Univ.*) 1906.
Subject, History.   Special Field, Italian History.   Thesis, "The Biography of Matthew Schinner, Cardinal of Sion, with special reference to his Activity in Italy in the years 1510–1516."   Assistant Professor of European History, Leland Stanford Jr. University.

SELDEN OSGOOD MARTIN, A.B. (*Bowdoin Coll.*) 1903, A.M. (*Harvard Univ.*) 1904.
Subject, Economics.   Special Field, Economic History.   Thesis, "Recent Water Power Development in the United States."   Instructor in Commercial Organisation, Harvard University, on leave of absence.

SAMUEL ELIOT MORISON, A.B. 1908, A.M. 1909.
Subject, History. *Special Field*, American History. *Thesis*, "The Life and Correspondence of Harrison Gray Otis, 1765-1814." John Harvard Fellow.

SAMUEL COPELAND PALMER, A.B. (*Swarthmore Coll.*) 1895, A.M. (*ibid.*) 1907, A.M. (*Harvard Univ.*) 1909.
Subject, Biology. *Special Field*, Zoölogy. *Thesis*, "The Numerical Relations of the Histological Elements in the Vertebrate Retina." Assistant Professor of Biology and Geology, Swarthmore College.

WILLIS ALLEN PARKER, A.B. (*State Normal School, Emporia, Kan.*) 1909, A.M. (*Harvard Univ.*) 1911.
Subject, Philosophy. *Special Field*, Metaphysics. *Thesis*, "Pluralism and Irrationalism in the Philosophy of William James." Professor of Philosophy, Pomona College.

ROY MERLE PETERSON, A.B. (*Coe Coll.*) 1906, A.M. (*Harvard Univ.*) 1910.
Subject, Philology. *Special Field*, Classical Philology. *Thesis*, "De Vaticiniis apud Poetas Graecos." Professor of Latin, Missouri Valley College.

EUGENE LYMAN PORTER, A.B. 1904, A.M. (*Univ. of Michigan*) 1908.
Subject, Medical Sciences. *Special Field*, Physiology. *Thesis*, "Conditions affecting the Liminal Electrical Stimulus of a Spinal Reflex." Research Fellow in Physiology.

JOHN EDWARD ROUSE, A.B. (*Lincoln Coll.*) 1894, A.M. (*Univ. of Kansas*) 1896, A.M. (*Harvard Univ.*) 1901.
Subject, Philosophy. *Special Field*, Psychology. *Thesis*, "The Mental Life of Domestic Pigeons: An Experimental Study of certain Emotional and Associative Processes." Student, Harvard Graduate School of Medicine.

EDGAR FINLEY SHANNON, A.B. (*Central Univ. of Kentucky*) 1893, A.M. (*Harvard Univ.*) 1910.
Subject, Philology. *Special Field*, English Philology. *Thesis*, "The Influence of Ovid upon Chaucer." Professor of English, University of Arkansas.

MAHLON ELLWOOD SMITH, A.B. (*Syracuse Univ.*) 1906, A.M. (*Harvard Univ.*) 1909.
Subject, Philology. *Special Field*, English Philology. *Thesis*, "A History of the Fable in English to the Death of Pope." Assistant Professor of English, Syracuse University.

HARRY MAXWELL VARRELL, A.B. (*Bowdoin Coll.*) 1897, A.M. (*ibid.*) 1900, A.M. (*Harvard Univ.*) 1909.
Subject, History. *Special Field*, English History. *Thesis*, "The Early History of Ecclesiastical Jurisdiction in England." Instructor in History, Simmons College.

SAMUEL MONTEFIORE WAXMAN, A.B. 1907, A.M. 1910.
Subject, Philology. *Special Field*, Romance Philology. *Thesis*, "Chapters on Magic in Spanish Literature." Instructor in Romance Languages, Boston University.

FRANCIS HARDING WHITE, A.B. (*Princeton Univ.*) 1887, A.M. (*Harvard Univ.*) 1898.
Subject, Political Science. *Special Field*, American Government. *Thesis*, "The Administration of the General Land Office." Professor of History, Pomona College.

CARTER GODWIN WOODSON, LITT.B. (*Berea Coll.*) 1903, A.B. (*Univ. of Chicago*) 1907, A.M. (*ibid.*) 1908.
Subject, History. *Special Field*, American History. *Thesis*, "The Disruption of Virginia." Teacher of History and French, M Street High School, Washington, D. C.

TABLE X. — FELLOWSHIPS AND SCHOLARSHIPS (1910–13)

1. *Applications and Appointments*

	1910–11	1911–12	1912–13
Spring applicants for reappointment or promotion	59	73	78
Spring applicants for a first appointment	300	285	306
Later applicants	39	40	21
	—398	—398	—405
Appointed to fellowships	24	47	55
Appointed to scholarships	91	88	87
Appointed instructors, teaching fellows, or assistants	32	33	37
	—147	—168	—179
Deduct for repetitions	1	3	2
	—146	—165	—177
Entered or continued in the Graduate School of Arts and Sciences without receiving any of the above-named appointments	68	72	70
Entered undergraduate classes of Harvard College	2	0	0
Entered other Departments of the University	8	5	2
	— 78	— 77	— 72
Applicants who were at the University in the year following their applications..	224	242	249
Applicants not at the University in that year	174	156	156
	—398	—398	—405

2. *Classification of Applicants and Appointees*

	1910–11		1911–12		1912–13	
	Applicants	Appointees	Applicants	Appointees	Applicants	Appointees
Students of Philology	161	44	121	38	140	42
Students of History, Political Science, Philosophy, or Education	131	40	168	55	159	53
Students of Mathematics, Physics, or Chemistry	67	20	66	27	65	23
Students of Natural History	32	10	36	14	34	21
Students of other branches, or unclassified ..	7	1	7	1	7	3
	398	115	398	135	405	142
Students in Graduate School of Arts and Sciences	131	53	129	51	138	72
Students in Harvard College	22	4	18	5	18	11
Students in other Departments of the University	5	–	2	–	4	–
Former students in some Department of the University	33	8	37	9	36	9
Persons never previously members of the University	207	50	212	70	209	50
	398	115	398	135	405	142
Harvard Bachelors of Arts or Science, not previously graduated elsewhere	37	18	41	17	36	22
Harvard Bachelors of Arts or Science previously graduated elsewhere	6	3	3	1	3	3
Graduates of other institutions, not Harvard Bachelors of Arts or Science	298	70	303	93	282	83
Undergraduates of Harvard College or Lawrence Scientific School, not already graduated elsewhere	21	4	18	4	18	11
Undergraduates of other institutions and other non-graduates	36	20	33	20	66	23
	398	115	398	135	405	142

Forty-six fellowship were assigned for the year 1911–12, including three John Harvard Fellowships without stipend. There were nineteen resident and twenty-seven non-resident appointments. A list of the incumbents follows. After the name of each fellow is given the name of his fellowhip, the subject that he studied, and his present occupation. The place of study of the non-resident fellows is also indicated.

TRAVELLING FELLOWS

EDWARD SWITZER ALLEN, John Harvard Fellow. Mathematics. Rome.
Rogers Fellow, at Rome.

ROBERT PIERPONT BLAKE, John Harvard Fellow. Ancient History. St. Petersburg.
Instructor in History, University of Pennsylvania.

ALBERT RICHARD CHANDLER, Parker Fellow. Philosophy. Marburg.
Assistant in Philosophy. Third-year Graduate Student.

ALEXANDER FREDERICK BRUCE CLARK, Francis Parkman Fellow. Romance Languages. Paris and Madrid.
Thayer Fellow. Third-year Graduate Student.

CHARLES SAGER COLLIER, Frederick Sheldon Fellow. Economics and Government. Paris.
Student, Harvard Law School.

HARRY TODD COSTELLO, Frederick Sheldon Fellow. Philosophy. Paris.
Assistant in Philosophy.

HENRY WADSWORTH LONGFELLOW DANA, Frederick Sheldon Fellow. Comparative Literature. Paris.
Instructor in English and Comparative Literature, Columbia University.

EDWARD CARROLL DAY, Parker Fellow. Zoölogy. Bonn.
Frederick Sheldon Fellow, at Berlin.

GEORGE HAROLD EDGELL, John Harvard Fellow. Fine Arts. Rome.
Instructor in Fine Arts. Third-year Graduate Student.

FREDERICK MAY ELIOT, Frederick Sheldon Fellow. Municipal Government. London and other European cities.
Instructor in Municipal Government.

GRIFFITH CONRAD EVANS, Frederick Sheldon Fellow. Mathematics. Rome.
Assistant Professor of Mathematics, Rice Institute, Houston, Texas.

DONALD FISHER, James Walker Fellow. Philosophy. Berlin and Freiburg.
Assistant in Philosophy. Fifth-year Graduate Student.

NORMAN SCOTT BRIEN GRAS, Frederick Sheldon Fellow. Economic History. London.
Assistant Professor of History, Clark College.

WILLIAM CASPAR GRAUSTEIN, Rogers Fellow. Mathematics. Bonn.
Frederick Sheldon Fellow, at Bonn.

CLARENCE HENRY HARING, Bayard Cutting Fellow. History. Berlin and Seville.
Associate in History, Bryn Mawr College.

CLARENCE LEONARD HAY, Fellow in Central American Archaeology. Anthropology. Belize.
Continuing his studies at Washington, D. C.

HAROLD NEWCOMB HILLEBRAND, Frederick Sheldon Fellow. English. London.
Assistant in English. Fourth-year Graduate Student.

HENRY LAURENS, John Thornton Kirkland Fellow. Zoölogy. Bonn.
Instructor in Zoölogy, Yale University.

JOHN AVERY LOMAX, Frederick Sheldon Fellow. American Ballads. Austin, Texas.
Assistant Professor of English, University of Texas.

SERGIUS MORGULIS, Frederick Sheldon Fellow. Zoölogy. Charlottenburg.
Associate in Animal Metabolism, Nutrition Laboratory of the Carnegie Institution of Washington, Vila St., Boston.

LAURENCE BRADFORD PACKARD, Rogers Fellow. History. Paris.
Assistant in History. Fourth-year Graduate Student.

DEXTER PERKINS, James H. Hyde Fellow at the École Libre des Sciences
Politiques. History and Government. Paris.
Appointment continued.

CHAUNCEY J VALLETTE PETTIBONE, Frederick Sheldon Fellow. Biochemistry. Halle.
Instructor in Physiology and Biochemistry, Medical School, University of Minnesota.

JAMES HAMILTON PICKEN, Christopher M. Weld Scholar. Philosophy.
Berlin.
Fourth-year Graduate Student.

CYRUS ASHTON ROLLINS SANBORN, Frederick Sheldon Fellow. Classics.
Paris.
Continuing his studies in the American School, Athens.

THORBERGUR THORVALDSON, Edward William Hooper Fellow. Chemistry.
Dresden.
Frederick Sheldon Fellow, at Liverpool.

GEORGE ARTHUR UNDERWOOD, Parker Fellow. Romance Languages.
Paris.
Instructor in Romance Languages, University of Missouri.

RESIDENT FELLOWS

ROGER ADAMS, Edward Austin Fellow. Chemistry.
Parker Fellow, at Berlin.

WILLIAM T BOVIE, Edward Austin Fellow. Botany.
Reappointed.

THOMAS KITE BROWN, Jr., Thayer Fellow. German.
Instructor in German, Haverford College.

LLOYD MORGAN COSGRAVE, Henry Lee Memorial Fellow. Economics.
Instructor in Economics. Third-year Graduate Student.

EDWIN DEWITT DICKINSON, Ozias Goodwin Memorial Fellow. International Law.
Reappointed. Second-year Graduate Student.

WILFRED ELDRED, Harris Fellow. Economics.
Assistant in Economics. Third-year Graduate Student.

MENDAL GARBUTT FRAMPTON, Willard Scholar. English.
Professor of the English Language, Pomona College.

RALPH EMERSON HEILMAN, Robert Treat Paine Fellow. Social Science.
Instructor in Economics. Fourth-year Graduate Student.

YAMATO ICHIHASHI, Henry Bromfield Rogers Memorial Fellow. Ethics in
its relations to Sociology.
Continuing his studies towards the degree of Ph.D.

WILLIAM SETCHEL LEARNED, Edward Austin Fellow. Education.
Joseph Lee Fellow for Research in Education.

THOMAS COOKE McCRACKEN, South End House Fellow in Social Education.
Social Education.
Research Secretary of the Education Department, Women's Municipal League, Boston.
Fourth-year Graduate Student.

WILLIAM THOMAS MORGAN, Adams Woods Fellow. History and Government.
Third-Year Graduate Student.

DANA BRANNAN MURDOCK, South End House Fellow.   Social Problems.
Director, South Bay Union, Boston.

NILS ANDREAS OLSEN, Edward Austin Fellow.   History.
Herscher, Ill.

ROY MERLE PETERSON, Thayer Fellow.   Classics.
Professor of Latin, Missouri Valley College.

WILLIAM GORDON PETERSON, Thayer Fellow.   History.
Officer in the Canadian Permanent Force, at Halifax, N. S.

GARNETT GLADWIN SEDGEWICK, Thayer Fellow.   English.
Edward Austin Fellow.   Third-year Graduate Student.

MAHLON ELLWOOD SMITH, Harris Fellow.   English.
Assistant Professor of English, Syracuse University.

HOWARD MOFFITT TRUEBLOOD, John Tyndall Scholar.   Physics.
Bayard Cutting Fellow for Research in Physics.   Fourth-year Graduate Student.

The members of the Administrative Board for 1911–12 were
Professors Jackson, Mark, G. F. Moore, B. O. Peirce, H. W. Smyth,
Kittredge, Turner, Walz, Osterhout, R. B. Perry, and the Dean.
Seven meetings were held during the year.   The opening meeting
of the Graduate School of Arts and Sciences and of the Graduate
Schools of Applied Science and Business Administration was held
in the Faculty Room on the evening of Friday, October 6, 1911.
The chief address was by Professor Theodore W. Richards, who
discussed the general importance of chemical studies.   Professor
Willy Kükenthal of the University of Breslau, Exchange Professor of Zoölogy, also spoke briefly.

From every point of view the most important event in the
history of the Graduate School of Arts and Sciences during the
past year has been the gift of the Harry Elkins Widener Memorial
Library.   This munificent gift will not only house adequately
and safely the great collections upon which the advanced work
of the University chiefly rests, but will also enormously enlarge
the opportunities for their use on the part of professors and advanced students.   In spite of the limitations and inconveniences
of Gore Hall, the ready access to its shelves constituted one of
the most important privileges which the Graduate School of Arts
and Sciences has been able to offer, and the new seminary rooms
and the increased facilities for private study in the stack will be
of the greatest assistance in developing the higher work of the
School.   In its new home the Harvard Library will hold a unique
position, at least among university libraries, for, while there are
other libraries which are equally accessible and a few libraries
which are larger, there is probably none which combines in the
same degree one of the most valuable of existing collections of

books with great freedom of access on the part of professors and qualified students. Thus housed, the Harvard Library will be a resource of incalculable value to the University in attracting and holding the best men, both in its faculty and among its students.

As the resources of the library and the other opportunities for advanced work at Harvard become better known, we may expect an increasing resort to the University on the part of mature teachers and investigators who desire to spend a longer or shorter period of study and research in Cambridge. Such men will not be candidates for degrees or students in the ordinary sense, and it is worthy of serious consideration whether the University should not offer them its privileges without the payment of tuition fees. In individual cases this has sometimes been done, but never as a regular practice, nor in accordance with any fixed principle, and it would seem that the time has come for some general rule on the subject. I would suggest that the Faculty of Arts and Sciences be authorized to recommend to the Corporation for the privileges of the University, without the payment of tuition, men of established position as investigators or as college and university professors who do not desire to use their period of residence at the University in fulfilment of the conditions of candidacy for a degree. Nominations for this privilege could best be made by the Committee on Fellowships, after the consideration of each case by the department concerned. The number thus recommended would not be large in any one year, but such hospitality would be much appreciated and would tend to make the University more widely influential as a centre of learning.

From the point of view of both teaching and investigation, a most valuable feature of many American universities has been the sabbatical year, with its opportunities for travel, intellectual refreshment, and productive work. Its ultimate justification lies, of course, not in the convenience and pleasure of the professor, but in its contribution to his growth and efficiency, and it can accomplish its purpose only when advantage can be taken of it freely and frequently. Unfortunately the scale of university salaries taken in connection with the increased cost of living makes it in many cases impossible for professors to take their leave of absence as often as it is due, if indeed they can take it at all, and this is especially true in the earlier stages of a teacher's career, when a year of this sort is likely to yield the largest relative return. It might be seriously argued that the taking of sabbatical leave ought to be made compulsory; in any case it ought to be, under ordinary conditions, always possible, and this cannot be the case so long as a large sacrifice of salary is required. It would be of distinct help to the higher work of the university if Harvard should adopt the practice which exists in certain other universities of giving full salary during the sabbatical year or at least during half of it.

The productive work of professors, both in residence and on leave, would be greatly forwarded by the establishment of a fund for the assistance of research on the part of the Faculty. The Frederick Sheldon Fund, together with the various endowed fellowships, makes satisfactory provision for our advanced students, as far as their investigations take them away from Cambridge; and a similar fund, or series of funds, could be of even more value in the case of the more experienced investigators who are permanently connected with the University. In many instances professors have been compelled to postpone or abandon important researches for lack of such opportunities for work at a distance as many of our students already possess. The Woodbury Lowery Fellowship, founded by the Duchess of Arcos, and held for the past two years by Professor Channing for the study of the Spanish sources of American history, is an admirable example of what can be done by a special endowment of this sort, and so also, in a different way, is the Walter Channing Cabot Fellowship, now held by Professor Royce. It is also important to remember that leisure, or at least relief from benumbing and time-consuming routine, is even more important than special collections or apparatus, and that American universities have generally been more generous in providing the material facilities for advanced work than in giving their professors the time to avail themselves of these facilities.

CHARLES H. HASKINS, *Dean.*

THE GRADUATE SCHOOL OF APPLIED SCIENCE

To the President of the University: —

Sir, — As Dean of the Graduate School of Applied Science, I have the honor to present the following report for the year 1911-12.

The enrolment by subject in the Graduate School of Applied Science was as follows: —

	1906-07	1907-08	1908-09	1909-10	1910-11	1911-12
Civil Engineering	7	11	7	14	17	18
Mechanical Engineering .	0	4	4	7	3	6
Electrical Engineering . .	2	7	11	17	15	15
Mining and Metallurgy . .	3	12	14	18	26	14
Architecture	7	12	15	5	20	29
Landscape Architecture .	4	7	6	9	13	9
Forestry	5	7	10	12	19	19
Applied Physics	0	1	1	1	0	1
Applied Chemistry	1	1	1	0	1	2
Applied Zoölogy	0	0	1	0	0	0
Applied Geology	0	0	0	0	0	0
Applied Biology	0	1	0	4	9	7
	29	63	70	87	123	120

Subsequent to the issue of the Catalogue there were twenty-four additional enrolments distributed as follows: —

Civil Engineering	2
Mechanical Engineering	2
Electrical Engineering	2
Mining and Metallurgy	6
Architecture	7
Landscape Architecture	1
Forestry	1
Applied Physics	1
Applied Biology	2
	24

In several departments of the School the work is continuous throughout the calendar year. In Applied Biology, for reasons which are obvious and peculiar to that subject, special emphasis is laid on that period of the year which does not include the issue of the Catalogue,—from the first of February to the first of November. The enrolments not coincident with the issue of the Catalogue are therefore to be given a weight in considering the activity of the School to which they would not otherwise be entitled.

Of this total enrolment one hundred and thirteen were regular students, and thirty-one were special students not candidates for degrees. All regular students were graduates of some college or technical school. Of the special students four were graduates of colleges or technical schools, and all had professional attainments entitling them to special consideration. No one was admitted to the School as a special student who was not mature in years and who had not had at least three years of professional training or who did not satisfy the Division in which his work lay of his special preparation to profit by the instruction, and to contribute by his presence rather than detract from the efficiency of the course.

Fifty-one colleges and technical schools were represented as follows:—

Albany State Normal College	1	Middlebury College	1
Allegheny College	1	Norwich University	1
Amherst College	1	Ohio State University	1
Biltmore Forest School	1	Pennsylvania State College	1
Bowdoin College	1	Polytechnic Institute	1
Brown University	1	Princeton University	1
Carleton College	1	Randolph-Macon College	1
Case School of Applied Science	1	St. Lawrence University	1
College of the City of New York	1	St. Mary's College	1
Colorado College	1	St. Petersburg Institute of Technology	1
Columbia University	1		
Cornell University	3	South Dakota State College	1
Dartmouth College	4	South Eastern Agricultural College (England)	1
Denison University	1		
De Pauw University	1	Stevens Institute of Technology	1
Earlham College	2	Swarthmore College	1
Hamilton College	1	Trinity College (Conn.)	1
Harvard University	67	Tufts College	2
Heriot-Watt College (Edinburgh, Scotland)	1	United States Naval Academy	1
		University of Chicago	1
Iowa State College	1	University of Chile	1
Japanese Naval College	1	University of Michigan	1
Lafayette College	1	University of Minnesota	1
Lake Forest College	1	University of Wyoming	1
Leland Stanford Jr. University	2	Williams College	2
Massachusetts Agricultural College	2	Worcester Polytechnic Institute	1
		Yale University	4
Massachusetts Institute of Technology	1		

All the members of the staff of the School were in residence during the year. Professor Adams, who had received a sabbatical leave of absence, was unable to avail himself of the privilege. Indeed, it is a fact worthy of notice that in this, as in other laboratory subjects in the University, the instructors rarely avail themselves of the sabbatical privilege.   Throughout the University the sabbatical year is regarded as an opportunity for research and study. This can be best done in a laboratory, and in general nowhere so well as in one's own laboratory.   Of course exception is to be made to this in biological subjects calling for field work. The fact that there are so few sabbatical absences in scientific departments is therefore to be explained, neither by greater devotion to the University nor by less desire for research or special study, but rather by the nature of scientific investigations, and the fact that they are usually of long continuation and are essentially local in their pursuit.

During the academic year under review, a most important change in the organization of the School resulted from the following vote of the Corporation taken on the recommendation of the Administrative Board, after its approval by the Faculty of Arts and Sciences.

Voted under date of March 11, 1912: —

That certain Divisions and Departments in the Graduate School of Applied Science be organized as Schools: to wit: the School of Engineering, of Mining and Metallurgy, of Architecture and Landscape Architecture, of Forestry, of Applied Biology (Bussey Institution), — it being understood that additional schools of Applied Science may be hereafter organized.

That these Schools be grouped together as the Graduate Schools of Applied Science, under a separate Faculty, to administer a self-contained graduate programme.

That this organization go into effect at the beginning of the next academic year.

That the following disposition be made of the courses now open to undergraduates in Harvard College in the several Divisions concerned: —

ENGINEERING

That there be established in the Faculty of Arts and Sciences a Division of Engineering Sciences, and that the Degree with Distinction in Applied Mechanics be called the Degree with Distinction in Engineering Sciences.

That the following courses be withdrawn from the Faculty of Arts and Sciences:

Engineering 3*l*, 3*m*, 5*l*, 6*a*, 12*b*, 13*a*, 4*c* (courses now open to undergraduates) and all courses not open to undergraduates.

That the following courses be transferred to the Division of Engineering Sciences:

Engineering 3*k*, 5*k*, 4*a*, 4*d*, 11*a*, 16*a*, 10 (*a*, *b*, *c*, *e*).

MINING AND METALLURGY

That the following courses be withdrawn from the Faculty of Arts and Sciences:

Mining 1, 7, 8, 10; Metallurgy B, 11, 12, 14, 15, 17, 19 (courses now open to undergraduates) and all courses not open to undergraduates.

That Mining 2 be transferred to the Division of Geology, and that Mining 3 and Metallurgy 4 be transferred to the Division of Chemistry.

ARCHITECTURE AND LANDSCAPE ARCHITECTURE

That Architecture 1*a*, 1*b*, 1*c*, 2*a*, 2*b*, 3*b*, and Landscape Architecture 1 be transferred to the Department of Fine Arts and all other courses be withdrawn.

FORESTRY

That all courses be withdrawn from the Faculty of Arts and Sciences.

APPLIED BIOLOGY

That Zoölogy 20*d* and 20*f* and Botany 20*f* be withdrawn from the Faculty of Arts and Sciences.

That the courses in Engineering thus withdrawn be bracketed in the Elective Pamphlet of the Faculty of Arts and Sciences, with a note added that properly qualified Seniors may take the corresponding courses in the School of Engineering; this arrangement to be continued through the college year 1914–15.

This change of organization had its first consideration in the separate Divisions, the first to give its approval being the Division of Mining and Metallurgy. It was very shortly followed by the Division of Engineering and soon, although with some hesitation as to its effect, by the Division of Architecture and Landscape Architecture. Practically, Forestry has long been on such a basis. Complete separation of the work in Forestry has been necessitated by the fact that so large a part of its year is spent by the students away from Cambridge. To Applied Biology the change of organization was a matter of very minor moment.

By the initial organization of the Graduate School of Applied Science and by succeeding votes many courses had already been withdrawn from undergraduate election. By this vote four whole courses and three half-courses in Engineering, two whole courses and nine half-courses in Mining and Metallurgy, five whole courses and one half-course in Architecture were withdrawn, intensifying the graduate nature of the courses in the technical sciences.   The courses which remained as undergraduate courses were such as might reasonably compose a part of collegiate education for either a Bachelor of Arts or Bachelor of Science degree and are paralleled in other colleges not aiming toward technical training.   These courses are far less technical and professional than many collegiate courses in other departments.

The organization of a separate Faculty for the Schools of Applied Science provided a more attentive body for the consideration of such business as should properly receive Faculty consideration. The Faculty of Arts and Sciences had throughout the undergraduate as well as the graduate life of the Scientific School given but scant consideration to such business.   The real work of the School was therefore by necessity conducted in the Administrative Board, and thus lost the attention of all but the representatives of the several departments.   This situation was contrary to the spirit of the organization of the University and certainly contrary to efficient legislation.   It had the additional very great disadvantage of removing the thorough discussion of its problems from the immediate oversight of the President of the University.

The withdrawal of the courses from the Faculty of Arts and Sciences secured freedom from certain formal but trammelling conditions.   Under the Faculty of Arts and Sciences courses of instruction, presumably units of related work, must be of either of two magnitudes, a half course or a whole course.   In the several technical schools, where there are better opportunities for intimately following the programme of each student, such classification, devised for the sake of simplicity in numerical records, is not necessary.   The magnitude of any course may be adapted to the subject to which it is devoted.   The separate organization of the several schools further permitted the application, where such application was desirable, of the intensive method of instruction in which a part of the year should be wholly given to one subject. With this arrangement it became possible to secure a desirable sequence of courses.   Still a third advantage lay in the opportunity which it afforded of continuing the work throughout the calendar year and of reducing all vacation periods.

On the recommendation of the Administrative Board of the School, the Corporation passed the following votes: —

Under date of March 11th, 1912: —

Voted, That the School of Engineering be authorized to seek to establish the use of the Engineering Camp by other colleges similar to its use by Harvard College, offering to such institutions facilities for independent final examinations, the opportunity to read independently such examination books as are set by the instructors in the course, or such other arrangements as the colleges may find necessary in order to allow the work to count towards their own degrees.

That students from any college formally adopting such an arrangement and counting the work in Engineering towards its degree be admitted to the School on the same basis, as regards tuition fee, as students from Harvard College.

That special fees be charged only to such students in the Camp as are not registered in the School of Engineering or have not paid a full year's tuition fee in Harvard College or one of the associated institutions, and that this special fee be refunded, when charged, should the student subsequently enter any of the Graduate Schools of Applied Science.

Under date of April 8th, 1912: —

Voted, on recommendation of the Administrative Board of the Graduate School of Applied Science, that the courses in the Graduate Schools of Applied Science be opened, with the consent of the instructor, to properly qualified graduate students in other institutions on the same basis as to students in other Graduate Schools in the University, — on application from the other institutions and without registration in the University.

These votes of the Corporation formally opened the way for the widest possible coöperation between Harvard University and other neighboring educational institutions.

The invitation contained in the first vote to share in the use of the Engineering Camp has been accepted by several institutions, and the undergraduate courses there given have been included in the programme of courses counting toward the Bachelor's degree in Brown University and in Tufts College. In the future administration of the Summer Engineering Camp the assisting instructors will be, so far as possible, chosen from the institutions joining in this arrangement, in order that they may have as complete an understanding as possible of the nature of the work being done.

The second of the above votes, which was instigated mainly by the possibilities offered by the High Tension Laboratory, has been welcomed by the instructors in several neighboring institutions, but it has not as yet been a matter of formal action. It is our hope that this relationship may be a mutual one and that the Graduate Schools of Applied Science may receive as well as extend such special privileges.

The gift, for the time being anonymous, of $50,000, for a High Tension and High Frequency Electrical Laboratory, not merely gave promise of a unique equipment for the Department of Electrical Engineering but was peculiarly adapted to show the close relationship which should exist between the Applied and Pure Sciences in the University, that each had much to give to the other, and that their intimate physical relationship was of the utmost importance in the ultimate development of the scientific side of the University.   In considering the question of a site, it was evident that such a laboratory should not merely be near the main laboratory for Electrical Engineering but should also be near the laboratory of the Department of Physics.   The site chosen was at the south of Pierce Hall, and between it and the Physical Laboratory.   The gift of the building was followed by a gift from another donor of $12,000 for equipment.

Toward the end of the year it became evident to Professor Whipple that the work in Sanitary Engineering in the University could not be satisfactorily carried out on the basis of a half-time professorship, that it would need his full services, and that the department should be vigorously developed in respect to advanced instruction and research.   To make this possible, Mr. Ernest B. Dane contributed $5,000 for two years.   This generous gift assured the University a development in Sanitary Engineering which would make the work of preëminent quality.

The year was one of reasonable growth in the number of students and corresponding increment in staff.   There was also further relaxation in financial stringency under which some of the departments have been working.   The School can happily look forward to this in increasing measure through the steady enlargement of its endowment by the McKay bequest.

WALLACE C. SABINE, *Dean.*

THE GRADUATE SCHOOL OF BUSINESS ADMINISTRATION

To THE PRESIDENT OF THE UNIVERSITY: —

SIR, — I have the honor of presenting my report upon the Graduate School of Business Administration for the academic year 1911–12, the fourth year of the School's existence.

The number of students registered is shown in the following comparative table, counting as " regular " students college graduates taking full work in the School: —

	Number of Students			
	1908–09	1909–10	1910–11	1911–12
Regular students:				
First-year	33	42	43	55
Second-year	..	8	10	10
	—33	—50	—53	—65
Special students:				
(a) College graduates taking partial work	25	15	15	12
(b) Not holding college degrees	22	26	26	19
	—47	—41	—41	—31
Totals	80	91	94	96

GRADUATES OF COLLEGES

Albion College	1	Princeton University	2
Amherst College	2	University of Georgia	1
Case School of Applied Science ..	1	University of North Carolina ...	2
Clark College	1	Université de Rennes (France) ...	1
DePauw University	1	University of Rochester	1
Earlham College	2	University of Southern California	1
Grinnell College	1	University of Wisconsin	1
Harvard University	46	West Virginia University	1
Lewis Institute	1	West Virginia Wesleyan College .	1
McGill University	1	Williams College	2
Parsons College	3	Yale University	2
Pennsylvania State College	1		—
Peking University	1		77

(24 colleges represented, as compared with 14 in 1908–09, 19 in 1909–10, and 22 in 1910–11.)

Geographical distribution of students: —

STATES:

California	1
Connecticut	2
Georgia	1
Illinois	4
Indiana	4
Iowa	4
Maine	3
Maryland	1
Massachusetts	44
Michigan	2
Minnesota	1
Missouri	2
New York	10

STATES:

North Carolina	2
Ohio	3
Pennsylvania	2
Virginia	1
West Virginia	1
Wisconsin	1

FOREIGN COUNTRIES:

Canada	1
China	3
France	1
Germany	1
Hawaii	1

(19 states and 5 foreign countries, as compared with 12 states and 2 foreign countries in 1908–09, 16 states and 5 foreign countries in 1909–10, and 20 states and 2 foreign countries in 1910–11.)

Average ages of students (taking age in years and months on dates of registration in each academic year): —

	1908–09	1909–10	1910–11	1911–12
First-year men	23.22 years	22.95 years	23.26 years	22.62 years
Second-year men	—	24.75 "	24.67 "	25.69 "
Special students	31.65 years	32.06 "	31.68 "	28.34 "
With degree	30.11 "	27.89 "	27.63 "	27.43 "
Without "	32.66 "	34.47 "	34.01 "	28.91 "

The degree of Master in Business Administration was conferred in June, 1912, upon eight men, Bradshaw Langmaid receiving this degree " *with distinction.*" The names of the graduates and the subjects of the graduation theses are as follows: —

Sterling Ruffin Carrington, A.B. (*Univ. of North Carolina*) 1910.
    Thesis subject: "A Study of the Problems involved in a Specialty Store handling Women's Apparel doing its own Manufacturing."
Bradshaw Langmaid, A.B. 1911.
    Thesis subject: " The Principles underlying the Reasonableness in and of itself of any given Competitive Rate."
Charles LeDeuc, B.-ÈS-L.-PHIL. (*Univ. de Rennes*) 1899, D.ECON. (*ibid.*) 1905.
    Thesis subject: " The Relation of Cost of Service to Rate-Making."
William Wirt Leonard, A.B. (*Princeton Univ.*) 1896.
    Thesis subject: " Offset Printing."
Eliot Grinnell Mears, A.B. 1910.
    Thesis subject: " Stockholders' Privileged Subscriptions, 1906–11, inclusive: their effect on the Market Price of the Stocks."
Konrad Foeste Schreier, A.B. (*Univ. of Wisconsin*) 1910.
    Thesis subject: " State Banks and Trust Companies in Wisconsin."

Warren Bostwick Strong, A.B. 1910.
  Thesis subject: "The Northwestern Trust Company of Saint Paul
  and other Trust Companies in the State of Minnesota."
Carl Stewart Whittier, A.B. 1911.
  Thesis subject: "The Delivery System of the Mail Order Houses,
  with Special Reference to the Parcels Post."

The two prizes of one hundred dollars and fifty dollars, offered
annually by Mr. George Oliver May of New York, for the two
best graduation theses, were awarded to Mr. Carl Stewart Whittier and Mr. John Edward Hyde.

Mr. Hyde is the only person not holding a college degree who
has thus far been permitted to take the regular two-year course.
Experience has confirmed the wisdom of the School's regulation
that ordinarily special students not graduates of an approved
college will be permitted to take not more than a total of two
courses, whether in the same year or in successive years. Nevertheless, the provision admitting mature men not holding college degrees is avowedly based upon the assumption that in determining
upon the admission of students it is wise to give weight to various
factors in addition to the previous academic history of the appli-
cant. It is therefore reasonable that the extent of the privileges
of such special students be variable, depending upon all the facts
of each particular case, and that a man whose record in this School
has been exceptionally good should be permitted to take more
courses than the maximum number to which special students are
ordinarily limited. It is gratifying to be able to report that the
first man of this class to enjoy the full privileges of the School has
met the expectations of his instructors.

The five University Scholarships for the year 1911–12 were
awarded as follows: —

  Sterling Ruffin Carrington, A.B. (*Univ. of North Carolina*) 1910.
  George Ellsworth Thomas Cole, A.B. (*Clark Coll.*) 1911.
  Eli Mannus Libbman, A.B. 1912 (1911).
  Arthur Lister Rae, A.B. (*Williams Coll.*) 1911.
  Carl Stewart Whittier, A.B. 1911.

The following changes in courses were made from 1910–11:
Business 20c (An Introduction to the Technique of Printing) was
lengthened to a full course; Business 22 (Banking), advanced
course, was shortened to a half-course; Business 18 (Industrial
Organization), advanced course, was omitted. The following
courses which were omitted in 1910–11 were given during the
present year: Business 12^2 (Economic Resources and Commer-

cial Policy of the Chief European States); Business 27[1] (Railroad Organization and Finance).

The following courses were given for the first time: Business 15[2] (Business Policy), Mr. Shaw, assisted by Mr. Martin; Business 17b[2] (Industrial Organization), Mr. Feiker and others; Business 19[1] (The Practice of Scientific Management), Messrs. Barth, Cooke, Hathaway, and S. E. Thompson; Business 20d (Business Practice in Printing), advanced course, Mr. C. C. Lane.

The advisory committee of business men for the printing and publishing courses has been fortunate in securing the following additions to its committee: —

Mr. Theodore L. DeVinne of New York, honorary member.

Mr. J. Stearns Cushing of Norwood, Mass., President of United Typothetae of America.

Mr. Albert W. Finlay of Boston, Secretary and Manager, George H. Ellis Company.

Mr. William B. Howland of New York, Treasurer, *The Outlook*.

Mr. Edward L. Stone of Roanoke, Va., President of Stone Printing and Manufacturing Co.

The coöperative lecture courses in which business men assist as specialists have been conducted with increasing success. As was indicated in last year's report, changing conditions necessitate alterations from time to time in the amount of such outside assistance in any particular course. During the past year Business 14[2] (Economic Resources and Commercial Organization of Central and South America) and Business 25 (Corporation Finance) have had a much smaller number of outside lecturers than in previous years. The following lists, however, indicate the important part in the School's instruction during 1911–12 contributed by business men of large experience: —

BUSINESS 1: ACCOUNTING PRACTICE

Frank E. Webner of New York: " My Experience as a Cost Accountant."

BUSINESS 11: PROBLEMS OF COMMERCIAL ORGANIZATION

Harry Hodgson of Athens, Ga.: "The Manufacture and Sale of Commercial Fertilizers."

A. C. McGowin of Philadelphia: " A Discussion of Shoe Store Methods."

M. C. Rorty of New York: " Analytical Methods in Commercial Work."

J. R. Simpson of Boston: Five lectures on " Practical Problems of Department Store Organization and Management."

Thomas W. Slocum of New York: " Office Management."

BUSINESS 14 ²hf.: ECONOMIC RESOURCES AND COMMERCIAL ORGANIZATION OF CENTRAL AND SOUTH AMERICA

W. C. Downs of New York: " The Commission House in Latin American Trade "; " Latin American Trade Problems."

BUSINESS 15 ²hf.: BUSINESS POLICY

Walter H. Cottingham of Cleveland, O.: " Distribution of a Commodity (paint) direct from Producer to Dealer " (two lectures).
R. H. Grant of Dayton, O.: " Organisation and Handling of the Sales Force."
J. B. Hayward of New York: " The Policy of the Management toward the Competitor."
John S. Lawrence of Boston: " Distribution of a Commodity (textiles) by Middlemen, particularly the Selling Agent."

BUSINESS 17a ¹hf.: INDUSTRIAL ORGANIZATION

M. W. Alexander of Lynn: " Decentralised Management, as Exemplified by the General Electric Company."
Carl G. Barth of Philadelphia: " The Planning Department."
C. C. Batchelder of Boston: " Experience in Handling Two Strikes in the Lumber Business "; " Industrial Combinations in the Lumber Trade."
M. L. Cooke of Philadelphia: " The Essentials of Scientific Management."
Charles Day of Philadelphia: " Locating a Factory "; " Building a Plant."
W. C. Fish of Lynn: " Relations of Employer and Employee."
H. L. Gantt of New York: " The Task as a Basis of Proper Management "; " Preparing for Task Work."
C. B. Going of New York: " A Typical Factory Organisation "; " The Profession of the Industrial Engineer."
H. K. Hathaway of Philadelphia: " Scientific Management as Practised at the Tabor Manufacturing Company."
W. J. Hoggson of New York: " Office Organization."
J. T. Lincoln of Fall River: " The Relation of the Employer and Employee," with illustrations from the relations in the cotton industry in Fall River.
W. C. Redfield of New York: " Industrial Self-help."
Russell Robb of Boston: " Organization."
J. E. Sterrett of New York: " How a General Manager uses Accountants' Reports."
F. W. Taylor of Philadelphia: " Task Management "; " Task System and the Workmen "; " Factory Organization and Functional Foremanship."

BUSINESS 17b ²hf.: INDUSTRIAL ORGANIZATION

Frederick M. Feiker of Chicago: conduct of field work in course for six weeks, ending March 8, 1912.
Charles Day of Philadelphia: " Designing Industrial Plants."
H. K. Hathaway of Philadelphia: " Administration of the Tool Room."
Everett Morss of Boston: " Employers' Relations with Employees."
W. E. C. Nazro of Plymouth: " Relations of the Employer with the Employee."
C. K. Tripp of Lynn: " Apprenticeship System and Training School of the General Electric Company."

BUSINESS 19 ½hf.: THE PRACTICE OF SCIENTIFIC MANAGEMENT

Carl G. Barth of Philadelphia: " Classifying Stores "; " Stores Records "; " Laying out the Store Room "; " Installation of Stores Systems."

M. L. Cooke of Philadelphia: " Mechanical Handling of Stores "; " Standardisation."

H. K. Hathaway of Philadelphia: " Tool Room Administration "; " Classifying Tools."

Sanford E. Thompson of Newton Highlands: Special instruction in time-study in course for six weeks.

BUSINESS 20c: AN INTRODUCTION TO THE TECHNIQUE OF PRINTING

H. L. Baker of New York: " Cylinder Presses: Flat Bed and Rotary."

A. E. Barter of Norwood, Mass.: " Binding."

H. L. Bullen of Jersey City: " Job and Specialty Printing."

J. C. Dana of Newark, N. J.: " Introductory Lecture."

C. W. Davis of Harrisburg, Pa.: " Cost Accounting as Applied to the Printing Business."

A. W. Elson of Boston: " Reproducing Processes."

A. W. Finlay of Boston: " Printing Office Organisation."

E. B. Hackett of New Haven, Conn.: " Preparation of Manuscript "; " Proofs."

H. B. Hatch of Philadelphia: " Electrotyping."

W. C. Huebner of Buffalo: " Offset Printing."

Frank T. Hull of Cambridge: " The Comparative Cost of Hand and Machine Composition."

H. L. Johnson of Boston: " Principal Printing Offices of the World."

C. E. Mason of Boston: " Paper Making."

J. H. McFarland of Harrisburg, Pa.: " Printing Office Management."

H. M. Plimpton of Norwood, Mass.: " Book Binding."

Professor W. C. Sabine: " The Physics of the Three-color Process."

Charles Schweinler of New York: " Magasine Printing."

W. S. Timmis of New York: " Printing Office Construction."

J. A. Ullman of New York: " Printing Ink."

D. B. Updike of Boston: " Type and Composition."

W. B. Wheelwright of Boston: " Physical Qualities of Paper "; " Paper Making from Printer's Standpoint."

BUSINESS 20d: BUSINESS PRACTICE IN PRINTING (ADVANCED COURSE)

Bruce Rogers of Boston: "Conduct of Laboratory Work," in course from October to December, 1911, inclusive.

BUSINESS 21: BANKING

Roger W. Babson of Wellesley Hills: " Commercial Paper."

Ralph May of Boston: " Commercial Paper."

BUSINESS 25: CORPORATION FINANCE

Eliot Wadsworth of Boston: " Street Railway Financing."

BUSINESS 28: RAILROAD OPERATION

F. G. Athearn of San Francisco, Cal.: " The Work of the Bureau of Economics of the Southern Pacific Railroad Company."

W. G. Bealer of New York: "Some Phases of Emergency Railroad Work."

Major Charles Hine of Chicago: "The Unit System of Railroad Operating Organization."

George B. Leighton of Monadnock, N. H.: "Railway Track and Loading Gauges."

J. F. Moore of New York: "The Railroad Y. M. C. A. and its Relation to Operation."

L. G. Morphy of Boston: "Organization of Maintenance of Way Forces."

Edmund Rice of Boston: "Organization of the Purchasing and Equipment Departments."

BUSINESS 35b ²hf.: LIFE INSURANCE

James E. Rhodes, 2d, of Hartford, Conn.: "Liability Insurance."

The School was also able to secure a lecture of general business interest, open to the students of the University, by Mr. J. Horace McFarland, President of the Mount Pleasant Press, Harrisburg, Pa., on "Printing as a Profession."

The following should be added to the lists of firms in previous reports which have agreed to allow their plants to be inspected and studied by students of the School: —

> Aetna Mills, Watertown.
> American Tool and Machine Co., Hyde Park.
> American Type Founders' Co., Jersey City.
> Ayer and Co., Boston.
> Baldwin Locomotive Company, Philadelphia.
> Chadbourne and Moore, Chelsea.
> Champion International Paper Co., Lawrence.
> Chapple Publishing Co., Dorchester.
> Curtis Publishing Co., Philadelphia.
> Folsom and Sunergren Co., Boston.
> H. C. Hansen Type Foundry, Boston.
> A. H. Hews and Co., Inc., Cambridge.
> Hirsch and Guinsburg, Medway.
> Holtzer-Cabot Electric Co., Boston.
> Irving and Casson, East Cambridge.
> Lawrence Dye Works Co., Lawrence.
> Link-Belt Co., Philadelphia.
> A. D. Little Paper Testing Laboratory.
> Ludlow Manufacturing Associates, Boston.
> Magee Furnace Co., Chelsea.
> Manhattan Market, Cambridge.
> Merrymount Press, Boston.
> M. A. Packard Co., Brockton.
> Revere Sugar Refinery, East Cambridge.
> Charles Schweinler Press, New York.
> Simplex Electric Heating Co., Cambridge.
> D. and L. Slade Co., Revere.

Tabor Manufacturing Co., Philadelphia.
Union Carpet Lining Co., Watertown.
United States Worsted Co., Lawrence.
Wachusett Shirt Co., Leominster.
Walker Pratt Manufacturing Co., Watertown.
Walworth Manufacturing Co., South Boston.
Ward Corby Co., Cambridge.
Williams Printing Co., New York.

An encouraging beginning was made during the year in the undertaking to secure a permanent endowment fund for the School. A gift of one hundred and twenty-five thousand dollars ($125,000) was received from Mr. Edmund Cogswell Converse of New York to endow a professorship of banking. This generous and most opportune gift is the more welcome since it comes from a man of the highest character and standing, and expresses his confidence in the value of the training this School is attempting to provide as a preparation for a business career.

Attention was called in last year's report to the establishment in this School of the Shaw Fund for Business Research. This gift was made because of the donor's conviction that the individual business concern is not generally in a position to make a painstaking and systematic investigation of the conditions prevailing in his own line of business and that, with the exception of the national government which has thus far not undertaken work of this kind, no other institution is so well fitted to conduct such research as a high-grade school of business administration. Realizing that there is a special need for real facts about the different methods of market distribution, this field was selected as the first one to be investigated. For various reasons it was decided to begin with a study of retail conditions in the boot and shoe industry. On account of the variations in book-keeping on the part of shoe retailers it was absolutely essential in the first instance to devise a uniform system of accounts. This was done during the year 1910–11 through the coöperation of shoe retailers and accountants (among the ablest in the country) with members of the School's teaching staff who had already consulted with scores of shoe retailers in different parts of the country.

The past year has been devoted to introducing this system of accounts among such retailers as agree in return to furnish to this School their semi-annual figures made up on this basis. All individual data are and always will be held in strictest confidence by the School, but it is planned to prepare tables of averages and percentages which will be significant as to the prevailing and the possible costs of doing a retail shoe business. Such information will be issued in bulletin form to all coöperating retailers who will thus have the same kind of information about their business which railway managers of today have about their own and other roads through the medium of the published uniform railroad accounts.

A large number of shoe retailers in all parts of the country are coöperating with the School in this important undertaking and it is interesting to find that from returns already received from dealers tendencies toward certain standards can be noted.

This service to business men is, of course, but one function of the Bureau of Business Research. It has other functions of vital importance to the School. Obviously, it will furnish authoritative information on fundamental subjects taught in the School. But perhaps of still greater value is the spur it applies and the training it gives to members of the instructing staff in personally conducted investigations into modern business organization and methods, and its contribution toward an even more thoroughgoing application of the problem method of instruction to which the School is committed.

EDWIN F. GAY, *Dean.*

THE DIVINITY SCHOOL

To the President of the University: —

Sir, — As Dean of the Divinity School I have the honor to present the following report for the year 1911–12.

The most significant events of the year were the instituting of a new degree of S.T.M. to be administered by our Faculty, and a change in our requirements for the degree of S.T.B. For many years, an arrangement with the Graduate School has permitted students registered in the Divinity School to become candidates for the degrees of A.M. and Ph.D. under the conditions prescribed by the Graduate School for these degrees. It is manifest, however, that theological studies constitute an independent group not formally recognized in the regulations of the Graduate School, and therefore it has seemed desirable that there should be a higher degree in theology corresponding to the Master's degree in Arts which should be under the supervision of the Faculty of Divinity. In accordance with the rules of the Faculty, candidates for this degree must hold the degree of A.B. and be graduates of an approved theological school having a three years' course of study, and the degree is to be granted upon the basis of at least a full year of residence devoted to concentrated study in one of the recognized fields of theological learning in which the candidate's proficiency is to be tested by an examination, partly oral and partly written, at the end of the year.

The change in the requirements for the degree of S.T.B. does away with the old method by which the degree was granted upon the completion of fourteen courses approved by the Faculty to count towards the degree. By the new method, a student, already holding the degree of A.B., or admitted to equivalent standing, must devote three years to theological study and must pass at the end of the third year satisfactory examinations upon the entire field of theological learning and, in addition, upon such portions of it as he has selected for more detailed study. The purpose of the change is to ensure a more thorough and durable training for the work of the ministry and to enhance the value of the degree by increasing the difficulty of obtaining it.

Owing to political disturbances in the East, the Committee of the American Board of Commissioners for Foreign Missions, of which Professor E. C. Moore was a member, deemed it advisable to abandon its contemplated trip for which Professor Moore had been granted leave of absence during the second half-year, and therefore he was able to remain in residence throughout the year, giving courses as hereinafter reported.

The course in Religious Education provided by the generosity of Mr. Horace S. Sears was given during the second half-year by Professor George A. Coe of Union Theological Seminary. Although the course was formally taken by only a few students, since many of those most interested in the subject had attended the course conducted the year before by Professor Holmes, the lectures were well attended and students from other theological seminaries in the vicinity availed themselves of our invitation to visit the meetings of the course without charge. Special gratitude is due to Professor Coe for his kindness in coming to us, and to Union Seminary for its generosity in releasing him for this important service.

In a previous report I recommended the establishment of a three years' cycle of courses covering Church Music, Religious Education, and the Relation of the Minister to Social Problems, to the end that students taking the regular three years' course may receive instruction in all of these subjects during their term of residence. Through an arrangement with the Episcopal Theological School, which opens to our students a course given by Dean Hodges on Christian Liturgies, and the introduction of a Harvard-Andover course on Church Music by Dr. Davison, the first of the three topics mentioned is now satisfactorily covered except in the field of hymnody. It is to be hoped, also, that the course in Religious Education will be offered, at least in alternate years, by Professor Holmes of the Department of Education, who, in most trying circumstances, carried it through two years ago with remarkable success. But the deeply regretted resignation of Professor Peabody increases the need for a course on the Relation of the Minister to Social Problems. Furthermore, Professor Peabody's retirement will leave us with no member of the Faculty devoting himself primarily to the department of Homiletics and Pastoral Care, and the interests of the School imperatively demand that this highly important side of its work shall be materially strengthened. A school aiming to prepare men for the work of the ministry cannot honorably leave instruction bearing upon the technical and practical part of a minister's life to men whose primary interest necessarily lies in other departments to which they were specifically appointed. Moreover, the fact that many of our students are engaged for a part of their time in service to neighboring churches constitutes a problem which demands for its best solution the presence on the Faculty of a man who can organize these practical activities into a substantial part of the educational work of the School by helpful oversight and direction.

During the past year four students were in residence only during the first half-year, and five entered after the Mid-years. The distribution of the total enrolment was as follows: —

Resident Graduates	13
Senior Class	4
Middle Class	5
Junior Class	2
Special Students	7
Andover Students	22
Total	53

Thirty-five colleges were represented as follows: —

Alfred University	1	University of Minnesota	1
Amherst College	5	Nebraska Wesleyan University	1
Berea College	1	Northwestern University, Ill.	2
Brown University	3	Ohio Wesleyan University	1
Central Turkey College	1	Olivet College	1
Colgate University	1	Ripon College	1
Columbia University	2	University of Rochester	1
Cumberland University	1	Southwestern University	1
Dartmouth College	1	Syracuse University	1
University of Denver	1	University of Toronto	1
DePauw University	1	Transylvania University	1
Drake University	1	Wabash College	1
Drury College	1	Wesleyan University	1
Harvard University	12	Western Reserve University	2
Howard University	1	Yale University	1
State Normal School of Kansas	1		—
Lafayette College	1		57
McGill University	2	Counted more than once	9
Marietta College	2		—
University of Michigan	1		48

Fourteen theological seminaries were represented by graduates as follows: —

College of the Bible, Ky.	1
Boston University	4
Drake University	1
Episcopal Theological School, Cambridge	1
Garrett Biblical Institute	1
Harvard University	1
Harpoot Theological Seminary, Turkey	1
Lutheran Theological Seminary, Philadelphia	1
Meadville Theological School	1
Newton Theological Institution	1
Pacific Theological Seminary	1
Presbyterian College, Montreal	1
Rochester Theological Seminary	1
Tohoku Gakuin, Japan	1
	17
Counted more than once	1
	16

The interchange of instruction between the Faculty of the School and the Faculty of Arts and Sciences indicates the extent of the contribution made by the Divinity School to the general work of the University. This interchange between the two Faculties in 1911–12 was as follows: —
Divinity students electing courses offered primarily by the Faculty of Arts and Sciences: —

English	2 elections.
German	3 "
French	1 election.
History	4 elections.
Government	1 election.
Economics	4 elections.
Philosophy	29 "
Social Ethics	2 "
Education	3 "
Music	1 election.
	50

Non-Divinity students electing courses offered primarily by the Divinity School: —

Old Testament	47
Church History	125
History of Religions	18
Theology	56
Social Ethics	46
	292

The interchange of instruction between the Harvard Divinity School and Andover Theological Seminary was as follows: —

Harvard Divinity students electing courses offered primarily by Andover Theological Seminary: —

Old Testament	5
New Testament	7
Church History	3
Theology	7
Homiletics	10
	—
	32

Andover students electing courses offered primarily by the Divinity School: —

Old Testament	4
New Testament	6
Church History	7
History of Religions	2
Theology	8
Ethics	5
Homiletics	11
	—
	43

Three members of the School received the degree of S.T.B., four the degree of A.M., and three the degree of Ph.D.

The following is a list of the courses of instruction given in the School in the year 1911–12. With each course is a statement of the number of students electing it from the Divinity School, Andover Theological Seminary, the Graduate School of Arts and Sciences, and Harvard College. In such Andover courses as were taken only by Andover students, no record of attendance is given. A list of the lectures delivered in the Lowell Institute course in King's Chapel is appended to the list of regular courses.

COURSES OF INSTRUCTION

OLD TESTAMENT

1^1. Professor JEWETT. — Hebrew. — Morphology. Selections from the prose narratives of the Old Testament. *First half-year.* 3 And., 3 Col.

2^2. Professor LYON. — Hebrew (second course). — Syntax. Extensive reading in the Old Testament. *Second half-year.* 1 And., 4 Col.

18. Professor JEWETT. — Classical Aramaic (Syriac). — Brockelmann's Syrische Grammatik; selections from the Peshitto; Syriac prose of the classical period. 1 Div.

4. Professor LYON. — The Old Testament, with special reference to the History and the Literature of Israel. 37 Col.

A4 ¹hf. Professor ARNOLD. — History of Israel.   *Half-course (first half-year).*
                                             1 Div., 7 And., 1 Col.
A5. Professor ARNOLD. — Introduction to the Old Testament. — History of
    the text; the formation of the Canon; historico-critical study of the
    origin, form, and contents of the several books.   4 Div., 4 And., 1 Col.
11. Professor LYON. Assyrian (second course).   1 Gr.

NEW TESTAMENT

A1 hf. Professor RYDER. Introduction to the New Testament.   *Half-course.*
                                             4 Div., 4 And.
2 ¹hf. Professor ROPES. — Introduction to the Study of the New Testament.
    The Ideas of the New Testament.   *Half-course (second half-year).*
                                             3 Div., 4 And.
A3. Professor RYDER. — Interpretation of the Synoptic Gospels.
                                             1 Div., 6 And.
8. Professor ROPES. — The Epistles of Paul. — Selected portions.   3 Div.
15 ¹hf. Professor FENN. — The Theological Method of Jesus and Paul.   *Half-
    course (first half-year).*   2 Div., 2 And.
A17. Professor HINCKS. The Life of Christ.   2 Div., 5 And.

CHURCH HISTORY

1. Professor EMERTON. — The First Eight Christian Centuries. — The
    Conflict of Christianity with Paganism. Origin and Development of
    the Roman Papacy to its alliance with the Frankish State. The Ger-
    manic races as the basis of a new Christian civilization.
                                    4 Div., 6 And., 1 Gr., 7 Col.
A6. Professor PLATNER. — History of Early Christian Literature.
                                             1 Div., 1 And.
3. Professor EMERTON. — The Era of the Reformation in Europe, from the
    rise of Italian Humanism to the close of the Council of Trent (1350–
    1563).   2 Div., 1 And., 8 Gr., 11 Col.
4a ¹hf. Professor E. C. MOORE. — The History of the Christian Church in
    Europe from the Reformation to the End of the Eighteenth Century.
    Half-course (first half-year).   2 Div., 1 And., 1 Gr., 38 Col.
4b ²hf. Professor E. C. MOORE. — The History of the Christian Church in
    Europe and of the Expansion of Christendom in the East during the
    Nineteenth Century. *Half-course (second half-year).*   5 Div., 56 Col.
A8 ²hf. Professor PLATNER. History of Congregationalism.   *Half-course
    (second half-year).*   1 Div., 6 And.
A2. Professor PLATNER. History of Christian Doctrine.
                                             1 Div., 4 And., 1 Col.
6. Professor EMERTON. Practice in the Study and Use of Materials for
    Church History.   1 Div., 2 Gr.

HISTORY OF RELIGIONS

1 ¹hf. Professor G. F. MOORE. Origin and Development of Religion.   *Half-
    course (first half-year).*   2 Div., 1 And., 1 Gr., 9 Col.
2. Professor G. F. MOORE. — History of Religions in Outline.
                                             15 Div., 2 And., 8 Col.
20. Professor G. F. MOORE. Research Course.   1 Div., 1 Gr.

THEOLOGY

1 ¹*hf.* Professor FENN. — Theism. *Half-course (first half-year).*
6 Div., 2 And., 2 Gr., 1 Col.

A1 ¹*hf.* Professor EVANS. — The Philosophic Basis of the Christian Religion. *Half-course (first half-year).* 2 Div., 6 And.

2 ². Professor FENN. — Outlines of Systematic Theology. *Second half-year.*
1 Div.

5 ²*hf.* Professor FENN.— The History and Philosophy of Christian Mysticism. *Half-course (second half-year).* 11 Div., 3 And.

6 ¹*hf.* Professor E. C. MOORE. — History of Christian Thought since Kant. *Half-course (first half-year).* 7 Div., 3 And., 3 Col.

7a ¹*hf.* Professor E. C. MOORE. — Philosophy of Religion: The Nature of Religion. — Lectures, reading, and reports. *Half-course (first half-year).*
4 Div., 3 Gr., 10 Col.

7b ²*hf.* Professor E. C. MOORE. — Philosophy of Religion: The Truths of Religion. — Lectures, reading, and reports. *Half-course (second half-year).* 2 Div., 2 And., 37 Col.

ETHICS

1. Professor PEABODY, Dr. FORD, and Dr. FOERSTER. — Social Ethics. — The problems of Poor-Relief, the Family, Temperance, and various phases of the Labor Question, in the light of ethical theory. — Lectures, special researches, and prescribed reading.
3 Div., 3 And., 3 Gr., 33 Col., 1 Ext.

A3 ²*hf.* Professor EVANS. — Christian Ethics. *Half-course (second half-year).* 1 Div., 10 And.

20a. Professor PEABODY. — Seminary of Social Ethics. — *Subject for the year:* The History of Social Ethics from Fichte to Tolstoi.
3 Div., 2 And., 5 Gr., 2 Col., 1 R.

20b. Professor PEABODY will direct special researches of competent students in Social Ethics. 1 Div., 1 Gr.

HOMILETICS AND PASTORAL CARE

1 ¹*hf.* Professor PEABODY. — An Introduction to Preaching. *Half-course (first half-year).* 3 Div.

A1a ²*hf.* Professor FITCH. — The Office of the Ministry: The Historic Ideals and Present Possibilities of the Ministry. *Half-course (second half-year).* 3 Div., 10 And.

2. Professors PEABODY, E. C. MOORE, FENN, and FITCH. — Preaching.
8 Div., 4 And.

A3a ¹*hf.* Professor FITCH. — The Homiletical Use of the Old Testament. *Half-course (first half-year).* 1 Div., 5 And.

A3b ²*hf.* Professor FITCH. — The Homiletical Presentation of the Teaching of the New Testament. *Half-course (second half-year).* 6 Div., 7 And.

10 ¹*hf.* Professor COE and Asst. Professor H. W. HOLMES. — Principles and Methods of Religious Education. *Half-course (second half-year).*
3 Div.

11 ²*hf.* Dr. DAVISON. The History and Development of Church Music. *Half-course (second half-year).* 7 And.

PUBLIC SPEAKING

1. Asst. Professor WINTER and Mr. BUNKER. — Training in Voice and Speech. (Not counted for a degree.) 2 Div.

KING'S CHAPEL LECTURES

"THE THEOLOGY OF CONTEMPORARY RELIGION"

A. Professor E. C. MOORE. — Four lectures: "Within the Church."
B. Professor W. W. FENN. — Four lectures: "Without the Church."

In accordance with our agreement with Andover Theological Seminary, the libraries of the two institutions have been consolidated into the Andover-Harvard Theological Library, and the books in our stack have been transferred to the Andover building. The books on the reserved shelves in our Reading Room remain in place, and the room has been maintained as a working library for students. This arrangement entails considerable expense, both for attendance in the library during working hours, and also for the purchase of duplicates to books already in the Andover-Harvard collection,— an expense which can be justified only if our Reading Room is resorted to by a sufficient number of students. It must be said that during the past year this condition has not been fulfilled, but the experience of a single year does not furnish sufficient basis for judgment. In previous years the use of the Library by students has shown wide fluctuations and it may well be that the experience of last year gives no satisfactory evidence as to the value of the Reading Room to our students. Besides, in existing circumstances, it is exceedingly difficult to maintain the individuality of the School, and to give up our Library altogether would be perilous. During the past year, there were added to the Andover-Harvard Library 969 volumes and 608 pamphlets by purchase, and 1036 volumes and 932 pamphlets by gift, making the total of books in the combined libraries 102,521 and of pamphlets 48,303. Of these additions there are credited to the Harvard Divinity School, by purchase 386 volumes and 299 pamphlets, and by gift 577 volumes and 247 pamphlets, making the total of books owned by the Harvard Divinity School and contained in the Andover-Harvard Library, 39,757, and of pamphlets 11,175.

W. W. FENN, *Dean.*

THE LAW SCHOOL

To THE PRESIDENT OF THE UNIVERSITY: —

SIR, — I have the honor to present my report upon the Law School for the academic year 1911–12.

The first table below shows the growth of the School from year to year since 1870 in the number of students, the number and percentages of college graduates, and the number of colleges represented by their graduates.

The falling off in numbers with which the present year opens is not due to a reduction in the number of new students, as there has been no substantial change in the size of the entering class. The difference is in the second and third-year classes, and is largely due to greater stringency in excluding from the School students who have not reached the required standard. The large growth of the School is itself among the reasons which make it important to retain only such students as come up to a high standard of capacity and diligence; for the methods of instruction could not be effectively employed with the present large classes without an excellent quality and spirit among the students all through the class-room. Conditions in this particular are very fortunate.

The falling off in the number of Harvard graduates entering the School for some years past has been marked, although it has been rendered less conspicuous by the greater number of men from other colleges. Whether this decline in the number of graduates taking up law as a profession is merely a temporary and accidental fluctuation, or whether it is due to causes affecting also the other learned professions, has been somewhat discussed of late. But a matter of more concern is the decline which has also shown itself in the quality of the work of Harvard men in the School as compared with the work of men from other colleges. It is not to be supposed that this is due to any inferiority in the students themselves, or in their academic preparation; yet it has been too marked to be easily explained as accidental. I am inclined to think that one cause which has prevented Harvard men from distinguishing themselves when they otherwise would have done so is their attempt not infrequently to combine with

Year	Whole No. of Students	Total of College Graduates	Harvard Graduates	Graduates of other Colleges	Non-Graduates	Per cent of College Graduates	No. of Colleges represented
1870–71	165	77	27	50	88	47	27
1871–72	138	70	34	36	68	51	25
1872–73	117	66	34	32	51	56	25
1873–74	141	86	49	37	55	61	25
1874–75	144	82	63	19	62	57	18
1875–76	173	93	60	33	80	54	25
1876–77	199	116	74	42	88	58	30
1877–78	196	121	80	41	75	62	30
1878–79	169	109	71	38	60	64	24
1879–80	177	118	90	28	59	66	20
1880–81	161	112	82	30	49	70	19
1881–82	161	99	66	33	62	61	22
1882–83	138	93	58	35	45	67	32
1883–84	150	105	75	30	45	70	25
1884–85	156	122	85	37	34	78	31
1885–86	158	122	83	39	36	77	29
1886–87	188	143	88	55	45	76	34
1887–88	225	158	102	56	67	70	32
1888–89	225	158	105	53	67	70	32
1889–90	262	189	122	67	73	72	41
1890–91	285	200	135	65	85	70	33
1891–92	370	257	140	117	118	69	48
1892–93	405	266	132	134	139	66	54
1893–94	367	279	129	150	88	76	56
1894–95	413	310	139	171	103	75	74
1895–96	475	380	171	209	95	80	82
1896–97	490	408	186	222	82	83	82
1897–98	551	490	229	261	61	89	77
1898–99	564	503	212	291	61	89	78
1899–00	613	557	236	321	56	91	67
1900–01	655	605	252	353	50	92	83
1901–02	633	584	247	337	49	92	93
1902–03	644	600	241	359	44	93	94
1903–04	743	695	272	423	48	94	111
1904–05	766	711	286	425	55	93	114
1905–06	727	716	295	421	11	98	118
1906–07	705	696	260	436	9	99	126
1907–08	719	712	276	436	7	99	122
1908–09	690	680	256	424	10	99	121
1909–10	765	759	257	502	6	99	127
1910–11	790	778	240	538	12	98	135
1911–12	809	796	216	580	13	98	145
1912–13*	741	729	182†	547	12‡	98	133

their Law School course serious and exacting teaching work in the College.   I cannot but think it unfortunate that this situation should exist.   The School course is meant to occupy all the student's working time, and any considerable distraction of his activi-

* Up to October 30, 1912.

† 16 Harvard Seniors who have completed the full College course, but have not received their diplomas, are reckoned as graduates.   Prior to 1905–06 Harvard Seniors were not reckoned as graduates but as non-graduates.

‡ Seven of the twelve non-graduates are graduates of law schools.

ties is a misfortune. If necessity requires him to earn money during his course, the evil may be minimized by undertaking work which is not exacting either in the amount or distribution of the time for which it calls, or in the strain which it puts upon the student's mind or nerves. In all these respects some of the positions which are undertaken in the College seem among the worst. Not only do they make an undue demand upon the student's time, but the quality of the work is even more objectionable. The difficult task of effectively teaching mature pupils tends so to engage the thought of a conscientious man that his own study, carried on at the same time in another field, can hardly fail to become more or less perfunctory and superficial. At least it must lack something of the absorbed and excited interest which marks the work of the best students in the Law School. The fact that men of exceptional ability have been able to do the two things at once without actual failure, or even with apparent success, tempts others to undertake the combined work, and as a result the student loses, even under the most favorable conditions, the best features of his Law School course. He often fails to realize this until after graduation, when the harm has been done. If necessity requires a student to undertake such work he should realize that his true course is to postpone entering the Law School for another year.

The second table gives the courses of study and instruction during the year, the text-books used, the number of weekly exercises in each course, and the number of students who offered themselves for examination in each course at the end of the year. Few changes will be observed, the most important being those which resulted from the absence of Assistant Professor Scott during his service as Dean of the Law School of the University of Iowa. It is fortunate for the School that this absence has not continued beyond the year.

At Commencement the degree of Doctor of Law was conferred for the first time upon a graduate student. This marks the beginning of an interesting stage in the development of the School. It is not to be expected that the course for this degree will be pursued by a great number of students; but for men of exceptional quality who are proposing to devote themselves to scientific or scholarly work, either in teaching or in grappling with problems of legislation or administration, the opportunities which it offers are large. And this seems particularly true at a time when a new period of liberalization in our legal system brings the stu-

Instructors	Studies and Text-books	Exercises per week	Number of students examined
	First Year		
Prof. Wambaugh and Mr. Joseph Warren	Agency. Wambaugh's Cases on Agency	2	289
Mr. Seavey	Civil Procedure at Common Law. Ames's Cases on Pleading (2d ed.)	2	292
Prof. Williston Prof. Wyman	Contracts. Williston's Cases on Contracts	3	289
Prof. Beale	Criminal Law and Procedure. Beale's Cases on Criminal Law (2d ed.)	2	289
Prof. Warren	Property. Gray's Cases on Property, vols. 1, 2 (2d ed.)	2	315
Prof. Thayer	Torts. Cases on Torts: Ames, vol. 1 (3d ed.), Smith, vol. 2 (2d ed.)	2	298
	Second Year		
Prof. Brannan	Bills of Exchange and Promissory Notes. Ames's Cases on Bills and Notes and Brannan's Negotiable Instruments Law	2	194
Prof. Thayer	Evidence. Thayer's Cases on Evidence (2d ed.)	2	235
Prof. Pound	Jurisdiction and Procedure in Equity. Ames's Cases in Equity Jurisdiction, vol. 1	2	246
Prof. Gray and Mr. Gray	Property. Gray's Cases on Property, vols. 3, 4 (2d ed.)	2	234
Prof. Wyman	Public Service Companies. Beale's Cases on Carriers (2d ed.). Wyman's Cases on Public Service Companies (2d ed.)		
Prof. Williston	Sale of Personal Property. Williston's Cases on Sales	2	215
Prof. Wambaugh	Insurance. Wambaugh's Cases on Insurance	2	288
Prof. Brannan	Damages. Beale's Cases on Damages (2d ed.)	1	71
Mr. Joseph Warren	Persons. Smith's Cases on Persons	1	83

Third Year

Instructor	Course	Hrs.	No.
Prof. Beale	Conflict of Laws. Beale's Cases on the Conflict of Laws	2	214
Prof. Wambaugh	Constitutional Law. Thayer's Cases on Constitutional Law	2	160
Prof. Warren	Corporations. Warren's Cases on Private Corporations	2	286
Prof. Brannan	Partnership. Ames's Cases on Partnership	2	20
Prof. Gray	Property. Gray's Cases on Property, vols. 5, 6 (2d ed.)	2	75
Prof. Wyman	Suretyship and Mortgage. Ames's Cases on Suretyship. Wyman's Cases on Mortgage (revised ed.)	2	172
Prof. Pound	Trusts. Ames's Cases on Trusts (2d ed.)	2	203
Prof. Brannan	Bills of Exchange and Promissory Notes. Ames's Cases on Bills and Notes and Brannan's Negotiable Instruments Law	2	28
Prof. Thayer	Evidence. Thayer's Cases on Evidence	2	4
Prof. Pound	Jurisdiction and Procedure in Equity. Ames's Cases in Equity Jurisdiction, vol. 1	2	2
Prof. Gray and Mr. Gray	Property II. Gray's Cases on Property, vols. 3, 4 (2d ed.)	2	2
Prof. Williston	Sales of Personal Property. Williston's Cases on Sales	2	8
Prof. Williston	Bankruptcy. Williston's Cases on Bankruptcy	1	74
Prof. Brannan	Damages. Beale's Cases on Damages	1	14
Mr. Dutch	Equity III. Ames's Cases in Equity Jurisdiction, vol. 2	1	32
Prof. Wambaugh	Insurance. Wambaugh's Cases on Insurance	1	11
Prof. Beale	Municipal Corporations. Beale's Cases on Municipal Corporations	1	47
Prof. Wyman	Public Service Companies. Beale's Cases on Carriers (2d ed.). Wyman's Cases on Public Service Companies (2d ed.)	2	18
Mr. Joseph Warren	Persons. Smith's Cases on Persons	1	20
Mr. Schaub	Quasi-Contracts. Scott's Cases on Quasi-Contracts	1	14

Graduate Courses

Instructor	Course	Hrs.	No.
Mr. Dutch	Admiralty. Ames's Cases on Admiralty	1	1
Prof. Wambaugh	International Law. Scott's Cases on International Law	1	1
Prof. Beale	Jurisprudence. No text-book	1	2
Prof. Pound	Roman Law. No text-book	2	2
Prof. Pound	Theory of Law. No text-book	1	2
Prof. Wambaugh	Introduction to the Year Books. No text-book. (No examination)		

dent face to face with fundamental questions of the nature and possibilities of law.

The Research Scholarship referred to in the last report brought about work which it is believed will reflect credit upon the holder of the Scholarship and upon the School. The givers of the Scholarship have generously continued it for another year.

An event of signal importance has been the purchase of the library of the Marquis de Olivart. This great library contains nearly seven thousand titles (about twice as many volumes). Its completeness is indicated by the circumstance that the catalogue of this library is the standard bibliography of international law, referred to as such in recent treatises on the subject, for instance, Olivi, *Manuale di diritto internazionale* (1902), page 44; Bonfils, *Manuel de droit international public*, 4 ed. (1905), 147; the German edition of Bonfils, page 62; Hershey, *Essentials of International Public Law* (1912), 90. In the bibliography annexed to the article on the history of the law of nations in the *Cambridge Modern History*, volume 12, chapter 22, Sir Frederick Pollock says (page 954): " A list of such books would be out of place here but we may refer to the Marquis de Olivart's *Bibliographie du droit international*, Paris, 1905 and 1907 . . . this purports to note only works in the author's own library, but we know of nothing approaching it in completeness." The library is particularly rich in original documents, including some cases of importance of which it contains the single known copy, a full collection of documents and pamphlets relating to the international relations of Central and South American countries and the Spanish-American War of 1898, and also very full collections of documents and pamphlets relating to all recent international controversies. In addition there is a full collection of sixteenth, seventeenth, and eighteenth century writers on jurisprudence and public law, including some editions which are generally listed as unprocurable. Owing to a fortunate combination of circumstances, the School was able to obtain the library on very favorable terms, and the surplus accumulated in recent years justified the purchase.

More than 6,000 volumes were also added to the library as a result of our Assistant Librarian's trip abroad in the summer of 1911.

Largely as a result of these purchases 21,447 volumes and 3,594 pamphlets were added to the library during the period of eleven months from August 1, 1911, to June 30, 1912. On July 1, 1912, the library contained 148,337 volumes and about 17,570 pamphlets. From July 1, 1870, to July 1, 1912, the library has grown to be fifteen times as large as it was in the earlier year.

Among other important additions to the library during the year were a rare edition of Littleton's *Tenures*, published in 1540; early Upper Canada annual statutes and the earliest ordinances of the province of Quebec; a complete collection of the annual laws and decisions of Brazil; a volume of Choctaw Laws, the only known copy; the earliest laws of Kentucky and Mississippi; a very rare and valuable collection of Delaware laws, containing the revision of the laws from 1752 to 1762, and the annual session laws from 1763 to 1774; and several sessions of rare Oregon laws.

Thirty-three engraved portraits of judges and lawyers, three photographs, one lithograph and eleven prints of buildings, court-room interiors and trial scenes, have been added to the collection during the year.

The competition between second-year law clubs established from the income of Dean Ames's gift to the School took place for the first time during the year and was a great success. More than twenty clubs took part in the competition. It aroused keen interest among the students, and the quality of the work done, both in argument and preparation of briefs, was very good. The competition has also stimulated the work of the first-year courts, and the rule that clubs shall not be eligible for the competition in future years unless they have complied with the regulations prescribed by the Board of Advisers in their first-year work has had a good effect. In this and other respects the Advisers, with the experience of the past two years to guide them in developing and systematizing their action, have been able to give much help to the first-year men.

EZRA RIPLEY THAYER, *Dean.*

THE FACULTY OF MEDICINE

To the President of the University: —

Sir, — As Dean of the Faculty of Medicine I have the honor to present my report for the academic year 1911–12.

The current year has been one of much activity in both the Medical School and the Dental School. In the Dental School there has been a very gratifying increase in the number of students following the opening of the new buildings. An account of the activities of these two Schools will be found in the report of the Dean of the Medical School and that of the Dean of the Dental School.

The organization of a Graduate School of Medicine, referred to in the last report, was completed during the current year by the appointment of a Dean, Dr. Horace D. Arnold; a Secretary, and an Administrative Board.

The Collis P. Huntington Memorial Hospital under the direction of the Cancer Commission of Harvard University was completed and opened for patients during the year. Much construction work was done on the Peter Bent Brigham, the Infants' and the Children's Hospitals, on grounds adjacent to the Medical School.

The Faculty of Medicine lost during the year the services of an unusually large number of teachers. Professor F. C. Shattuck, Professor James J. Putnam, Professor Edward H. Bradford, and Professor John T. Bowen resigned from their Chairs, the first three under age retirement rules governing terms of service at hospitals. Professor Maurice H. Richardson died suddenly during the summer. These men had rendered conspicuous service to the cause of medical education during their connection with the Harvard Medical School.

The present Dean received leave of absence beginning May 1st, in order to visit and study hospitals and laboratories abroad in the interest of the Peter Bent Brigham Hospital, and tendered his resignation, to take effect at the end of the year, in order to undertake work in connection with that Hospital. As his successor was appointed Dr. Edward H. Bradford, Professor *Emeritus* of Orthopedic Surgery.

In February and June ninety-two men were recommended to the President and Fellows for degrees: —

Medical School
$\left\{\begin{array}{l}\end{array}\right.$
For the degree of M.D. (February) 8
" " " *cum laude* (February) 1
" " " (June) 32
" " " *cum laude* (June) . 20
" " Dr.P.H. (June) 3
                                    ――
                                    64

Dental School
$\left\{\begin{array}{l}\end{array}\right.$
For the degree of D.M.D. (February) . . . 4
" " " (June) 24
" " " *cum laude* (June) 0
                                    ――
                                    28

Total 92

HENRY A. CHRISTIAN, *Dean.*

THE MEDICAL SCHOOL

To THE PRESIDENT OF THE UNIVERSITY: —

SIR, — As Dean of the Medical School, I have the honor of presenting my report for the academic year 1911–12.

The Administrative Board was constituted as follows: Drs. H. A. Christian, C. M. Green, F. B. Harrington, G. G. Sears, F. B. Mallory, W. B. Cannon, John Warren, and E. E. Southard.

The Faculty Council was composed of the following: Drs. H. A. Christian, W. T. Councilman, G. G. Sears, John Warren, J. B. Blake, Abner Post, Otto Folin, and the President of the University.

During the year an important change was made in the method of instruction in the Harvard Medical School. For a long period of years it had been customary in the Medical School to hold an examination at the end of each individual course. As the result of the investigations of a Committee of the Faculty, and much discussion within the Faculty, it was decided to change from this plan to a plan which involved holding two general examinations, one after two years of medical study, and one after the close of a student's curriculum. These general examinations are to be conducted so as to measure the student's comprehension, judgment, and skill rather than to test chiefly his detailed information. They are to cover the subjects now taught in the first and second years of the medical curriculum in the case of the first general examination, and the subjects in the third and fourth years of the medical curriculum in the case of the second general examination. The examinations are to be held under the direction of a Committee and are to be in part oral, in part written. In addition there are to be practical tests held at the end of each course. The student's final mark will be based in part upon his practical tests, in part upon his general examinations. It is believed that this new plan of examinations will serve to stimulate the students to take a broader view of the subjects of medicine, to correlate more completely than was done in the past the component parts of their curriculum, and to serve as a far better test of the student's ability to meet the requirements of his profession after he leaves the Medical School. Information in regard to the details of this plan of general examinations will be found in the Annual Catalogue of the Medical School.

An examination of the Treasurer's Report for the current year will show that the many undertakings of the Medical School require the expenditure of a large sum of money. Though the School lived within its means during the year 1911–12, the present resources of the Medical School are completely used up in its various activities, and there is no money available for further development of these undertakings or for expansion, until additional funds are provided. Such funds are particularly needed for a more extended development of the clinical departments in order that the clinical departments may utilize in the very best way the clinical facilities made available by the construction of new hospitals and the reorganization of old hospitals. Other departments in the Medical School could be expanded very advantageously, were there money available. Money given now to the Harvard Medical School could be used almost entirely for the employment of teachers and investigators and for special apparatus for such investigations, inasmuch as an ample plant exists, and a large return could be expected from such new funds in the way of productive research. Particularly useful are funds for unrestricted use or whose use is restricted within broad limits, so that the ever changing problems of medical instruction and medical investigation may be met. Generous benefactors each year attest their faith in the work of the Medical School by gifts, and this year was no exception, as $301,619.30 was received, of which $119,988.35 was for immediate use, and $181,630.95 was for capital. Of this sum $149,891.24 was given for the work of the Cancer Commission of Harvard University; $151,728.06 for various uses in the Medical School, including an addition of $28,500 to the Rebecca A. Greene fund for unrestricted use mentioned in the last report, and the Julia A. Moseley bequest of $74,285.71 for two travelling fellowships to be awarded to students of the School. The Faculty of Medicine recognizes clearly its great responsibility in administering such large funds, but feels confident that the work being done in the various departments, much of which is referred to in this report, justifies the confidence shown in the past by benefactors. Large resources, with wise coöperation on the part of Boston hospitals, have made possible a plant capable of using intelligently and effectively yet larger resources.

A somewhat detailed report of Departments follows.

Buildings and Grounds. — Needed repair work has been done, and minor changes have been made in the various buildings.

Anatomy. — The Departments of Anatomy and Comparative Anatomy have been combined into a single Department, under which is conducted the instruction in gross anatomy, histology, embryology, and comparative anatomy. During this year for the first time Medical students were separated from Dental students in their instruction in gross anatomy. Inasmuch as the requirements of each are slightly different, the plan has been advantageous to both groups of students. For the benefit of Dental students, most of whom enter the School without previous training in biology, a special course in the anatomy of the cat was arranged under the direction of Dr. Williams, with the assistance of Dr. Johnson and Mr. Heuser, to serve as an introduction to the study of human anatomy and physiology. During the year the work for nine papers, on the anatomy of the guinea-pig, the development of mammalian blood and blood vessels, and the embryology of the digestive tract, was completed, and other studies are in progress. Professor Mangum of the University of North Carolina, Dr. Berstein of the Bender Laboratory of Albany, New York, and Professor Kingsbury of Cornell University visited the laboratory during the year and made use of its resources; Mr. Heuser received leave of absence during part of the year to serve as Assistant Professor of Zoölogy in the University of Kansas. Dr. Begg resigned as Teaching Fellow to serve as Professor of Histology in Drake University. Dr. Johnson resigned as Instructor to become Assistant Professor of Anatomy in the University of Missouri.

Physiology. — Professor Cannon has collated the results of his investigations on the movements of the alimentary canal, and they have been published in a series of International Medical Monographs. With Dr. Nice he has been studying the influence of emotional states on muscular efficiency. He has also served on a National Commission for Resuscitation from Electrical Shock. Assistant Professor Martin has completed his standardization of electrical stimulation and has collected in book form the various papers which he has published on the subject. His methods have been applied not only to the examination of the sensitiveness of isolated tissues, but of human beings. Mr. Grabfield has investigated the diurnal variations in the sensitiveness of men and women, and in both the Carnegie Nutrition Laboratory and the new Psychopathic Hospital the methods have been found useful in determining the status of the nervous system under abnormal conditions. Dr. Nice has made observations on the effects of various drugs on the spontaneous movement of mice, and Mr. Porter has continued his investigations on the effects of various agencies on the irritability of the nervous system. The effect of anaemia on the nerve plexus in the wall of the alimentary canal has been studied by Mr. Burket.

Biological Chemistry. — For the past three years the researches of this Department have been largely devoted to the discovery of more suitable analytical methods than have hitherto been available for the analysis of urine, blood, and tissues. These methods were published during the year just closed. By the help of these analytical methods, it became possible (for the first time) to follow experimentally the absorption and distribution through the blood and tissues of the digestion products of protein. Some noteworthy results were obtained in this field and have already been published. Dr. Kendall and Mr. Farmer have applied the methods to the study of bacterial metabolism. Taken altogether, the year was a most successful one from the standpoint of research.

Bacteriology. — Much of the material gathered by Assistant Professor Wolbach during the expedition to the Gambia, in association with Professor Todd of McGill University, Montreal, was worked up during the year, and a number of papers published under their joint authorship. Experimental work on trypanosomes was conducted by Assistant Professor Wolbach in conjunction with Messrs. Binger and Stevens, students in the Medical School. During the summer of 1912 Assistant Professor Wolbach began a study of the etiology of scarlet fever by means of experimental inoculations in monkeys. Dr. Floyd and Dr. Stanwood investigated the immunizing properties of certain acid-fast bacilli for the tubercle bacillus, and Dr. Floyd, in conjunction with Miss Dunbar, has been studying variations in virulence of tubercle bacilli isolated from the sputum. Dr. Langdon Frothingham has continued his studies of rabies, and in conjunction with Dr. O'Toole has been making a comparative study of anthrax bacilli. In addition they have conducted field work in the study of hog cholera and its management by the use of anti-hog-cholera serum. Dr. Page has completed work on the fermentative properties of bacteria for certain sugars, and other members of the Department have been active in investigation. Dr. Cobb and Dr. Nagel have completed several papers bearing upon the bacteriology of the nose and throat. In connection with the work of the Massachusetts State Board of Health, Dr. Spooner has been given a place in the laboratory for the preparation of anti-typhoid vaccine.   The teaching work of the Department has been slightly changed by the introduction into the course for second-year students of a series of demonstrations illustrating some of the immunity reactions of animals to bacteria.

Pathology. — The method of instruction of the undergraduate in the course of pathology has been expanded in the past year. In the place of a general didactic course, there was substituted a study of individual cases of disease, and this was facilitated by the preparation by Professor Councilman of a teaching manual of pathology for the students' use.   In addition there was added a course in experimental pathology under the direction of Assistant Professor Karsner.   The expense of this course was met by a generous gift from Dr. J. C. Phillips.   This course has proven a valuable addition to the general course in that it shows the effect produced by the lesions of disease and serves as a stimulus to the students.   A beautiful memorial tablet was placed in the Laboratory by the family of Dr. W. R. Brinckerhoff, and the sum of $5000 was given by them to the Department for the investigation of disease.   Dr. Barkan resigned as Instructor to enter upon the study of ophthalmology.   Dr. Boretti resigned as Assistant to accept a position as Assistant Professor of Pathology in Northwestern University.   During the year 322 post-mortem examinations were made, and 1,025 specimens reported upon by the Pathological Department.

Comparative Pathology. — During the year the activities of the Department were somewhat reduced owing to the absence of Professor Smith, who left early in December to serve as Harvard Exchange Professor at the University of Berlin, where he was associated in teaching and research with Professor Flügge, Director of the Hygienic Institute.   Dr. Fabyan concluded important work on infectious abortion in cattle, and the work of tracing possible sources of infection of poliomyelitis among the lower domestic animals was continued by Mr. Ten Broeck.

Preventive Medicine and Hygiene. — Nine students entered for the work leading to the degree of Doctor of Public Health.   The degree was awarded at the end of the year to Dr. H. L. Amoss, who presented a thesis on "A Chemical Study upon Organic Matters in the Expired Breath"; Dr. W. G. Anderson, with a thesis on "Heat, Moisture and Carbon Dioxid considered as Fatigue Factors in their Relation to Health"; Dr. E. H. Schorer, with a thesis on " Experimental Studies of Milk, with Special Reference to the Uniformity of Different Grades of Milk and the Effects of Storage upon Certified, Inspected, and Pasteurized Milk." Dr. Allen continued his study of diabetes and glycosuria; Dr. Kendall, with Mr. Farmer, their studies on bacterial metabolism; Dr. Sheppard, his investigations of infantile paralysis, carried on under the auspices of the Massachusetts State Board of Health. Professor Rosenau is engaged on investigations of the mode of transmission of infantile paralysis, the presence of the virus of this disease in the secretion from the nose and throat, pasteurization of milk, and a study of organic matter in the expired air. One of the rooms in the Department is being utilized by officers of the United States Navy in studies of the purity of the air in sub-marine boats. Members of the Department have taken an active part in the work of various agencies not directly connected with the Medical School which have a philanthropic and public motive.

Theory and Practice of Physic. — Studies of experimental nephritis have been conducted by Professor Christian and Dr. O'Hare; experimental pancreatic lesions in relation to metabolic changes, by Drs. Pratt and Spooner, and experimental arteriosclerosis by Dr. C. Frothingham, Jr. During the latter part of the year Professor Christian and Dr. Frothingham were abroad studying foreign medical clinics in the interests of the Peter Bent Brigham Hospital.

Clinical Medicine. — The most important changes in this Department concern themselves with the reorganization of the medical service at the Massachusetts General Hospital, under which it was possible to call Dr. David L. Edsall to Boston as the successor of Professor Shattuck. Under the new organization, Dr. Edsall becomes Chief of Service in one medical service at the Massachusetts General Hospital, with Dr. Cabot as colleague and Chief of Service in the other medical service. Dr. Henry Jackson, after many years of faithful and conspicuous service in the instruction of the Department, resigned. The value to the Department of the Henry P. Walcott Fellowship is great. The work of Dr. Lawrence, its first incumbent, has been published, and the present incumbent, Dr. Palmer, is carrying out investigations upon nephritis.

Pediatrics. — The extended facilities for clinical teaching in pediatrics referred to in the last Annual Report have been taken advantage of effectively, and the interest in pediatrics among the students has been much enhanced by these added facilities. The Department has been enlarged by the addition of three assistants.

Surgery. — An important and material change in the work of the Department was the division of fourth-year elective work into separate elective courses. This was done in order to give greater latitude to the student in selecting the particular kinds of surgical work which would be most helpful to him in later years. The laboratory of surgical research was under the immediate charge of Dr. John Homans. Dr. Homans completed his metabolic investigations on the hypophysectomized dog in collaboration with Dr. Benedict of the Carnegie Nutrition Laboratory. Drs. Osgood, Lucas, and Low continued their study of anterior poliomyelitis, and Drs. Risley and Irving studied experimentally produced jaundice in dogs, and the therapeutic relation of transfusion to this condition.

Obstetrics and Gynaecology. — In the last Annual Report the very large amount of clinical material available to the Medical School for the teaching of obstetrics was referred to. In the class receiving the M.D. degree in 1912, only one man was satisfied to have a minimum requirement of six obstetric cases, while one student attended 53 cases. The average number of cases personally attended by the class was 25; this in addition to the cases observed under the care of other students and members of the hospital staff. Under the plan referred to last year, through the generosity of the Harvard Medical Alumni Association, an Alumni Assistant was provided for the Department, and Dr. Toppan, who held this position, conducted instruction in addition to that previously furnished by the regular teaching staff. In Gynaecology the School is likewise richly provided with clinical material. The courses in both subjects have remained essentially unchanged from that of the preceding year. Dr. Leo V. Friedman resigned as Assistant in Obstetrics at the close of the year, after eleven years of faithful and efficient service.

Warren Anatomical Museum. — Many valuable specimens were added to the Museum during the year. Particularly should be mentioned those prepared by Dr. Leonard W. Williams, whose recent sudden death was such a sad shock to the School. Dr. Williams was an excellent preparer, and his assistance will be greatly missed in the Museum. Two additional marble busts, those of Professor John Ware and Professor Henry P. Bowditch, were placed in the Museum during the year.

The Proctor Fund for the Study of Chronic Disease. — This fund, which has served so important a purpose in the past in the investigation of disease, shows an increasing usefulness. Each year the requests for assistance from the fund increase, as does also the value of the work done under its assistance. In the year 1911–12, grants were made to Dr. Pratt, for studies of the pathology of the pancreas; to Drs. Lucas and Osgood, for investigations on the occurrence of the virus of poliomyelitis in the tissues of the tonsils and pharynx; to Dr. O'Hare, for studies of experimental nephritis; to Dr. Ghoreyeb, for the hydro-dynamic study of organs under pathological conditions; and to Dr. Allen, for studies on diabetes.

Cancer Commission of Harvard University. — On March 26th of this year the Collis P. Huntington Memorial Hospital was formally opened. Since that time somewhat over 100 patients have been cared for, and investigations for which the Hospital was planned are now in progress. The organization of the Hospital in its dual relation to the treatment of patients and the investigation of cancer has been perfected, and its activities have been coördinated with those of the laboratory in which, up to this time, the work of the Cancer Commission has been conducted. New fields of investigation have been opened to the workers of this Commission by means of the Hospital, and former lines of investigation have been continued.

Scholarships and Student Aid. — In connection with the award of scholarships and in aiding deserving students, Dr. Dexter, Director of Scholarships, interviewed 99 Medical students, many of them a number of times. In addition to scholarship awards twenty students were aided by loans or gifts amounting to $1,296.75. This work, to which Dr. Dexter gives much time, is of great helpfulness to our students and deserves the encouragement of gifts for its enlargement.

FINAL EXAMINATIONS

	1908				1909				1910				1911				1912			
	Passed	Failed	Total	% Failed	Passed	Failed	Total	% Failed	Passed	Failed	Total	% Failed	Passed	Failed	Total	% Failed	Passed	Failed	Total	% Failed
FIRST CLASS:—																				
Comparative Anatomy	79	7	86	8	51	3	54	5	54	3	57	6	59	8	67	12	73	3	76	4
Biological Chemistry	64	15	79	19	47	17	64	26	58	5	63	9	48	11	59	18	76	3	79	4
Anatomy	65	16	81	20	54	9	63	14	62	2	64	3	61	6	67	10	70	7	77	9
Physiology	77	16	93	17	56	13	69	18	54	12	66	22	66	6	72	8	74	5	79	6
SECOND CLASS:—																				
Pathological Anatomy	66	13	79	16	84	12	96	12	50	3	53	6	56	3	59	5	64	4	68	6
Bacteriology	62	22	84	26	81	12	93	12	53	2	55	4	59	4	63	6	61	5	66	8
Hygiene	73	5	78	6	87	3	90	3	48	3	51	6	58	0	58	0	64	0	64	0
THIRD CLASS:—																				
Theory and Practice	60	6	66	9	60	7	67	10	95	3	98	3	53	2	55	4	60	6	66	9
Surgery	62	3	65	5	68	1	69	1	90	0	90	0	50	0	50	0	43	1	44	2
Obstetrics	58	9	67	13	69	16	85	19	84	9	93	10	51	2	53	4	64	1	65	2
Pediatrics	67	0	67	0	75	0	75	0	89	3	92	3	51	2	53	4	64	1	65	2
Dermatology	61	8	69	12	70	7	77	9	93	2	95	3	53	2	55	4	62	1	63	2
Gynaecology	57	10	67	15	72	5	77	6	75	19	94	25	54	2	56	4	65	1	66	2
Neurology	66	4	70	6	74	2	76	2	87	6	93	7	55	2	57	4	64	8	67	4
Therapeutics	59	13	72	18	68	14	82	17	84	10	94	12	51	4	55	7	63	5	68	7
Clinical Medicine	63	7	70	10	75	5	80	6	89	3	92	3	56	0	56	0	64	6	64	8
Clinical Surgery	61	0	61	0	73	0	73	0	90	0	90	0	54	0	54	0	65	3	64	3
Syphilis	64	4	68	6	78	0	78	0	87	4	91	5	52	2	54	4	65	1	65	0
Ophthalmology	59	7	66	10	69	11	80	14	91	2	93	2	49	2	51	4	61	1	62	2
Otology	67	3	67	5	74	0	74	0	92	1	93	1	58	0	53	0	64	0	65	0
Laryngology	64	2	68	3	72	1	73	1	90	2	92	2	58	0	58	0	66	0	66	0
Psychiatry	65	3	68	4	73	2	75	2	91	0	91	0	53	0	53	0	65	0	65	0

Fourth Class. — Electives:*—

Anatomy	33	33	38	38	31	30	34	33	49	49
Comparative Anatomy	0	0	3	3	4	4	3	3	.	.
Embryology	0	0	0	0	0	0	.	.	3	3
Physiology	2	2	3	3	3	3	2	2	10	10
Comparative Physiology	0	0	1	1	0	0	0	0	2	2
Biochemistry	3	3	2	2	2	2	1	1	5	5
Bacteriology	6	6	4	4	1	1	0	0	.	.
Pathology	19	19	42	42	32	32	30	30	14	14
Comparative P.logy	9	9	5	5	1	1	3	3	2	2
Protozoölogy	0	0	0	0	2	2	.	.	.	.
Neuropathology	2	2	3	3	4	4	1	1	.	.
Preventive e and Hygiene	6	6	19	19	3	3	0	0	1	1
Pharmacol	1	1	5	5	9	9	.	.	.	.
Medicine	71	71	110	110	111	111	50	49	84	83
Theory an e	16	16	63	63	59	59	46	46	45	45
Pediatrics	59	59	93	93	72	72	47	47	70	70
Clinical S Pathology	0	0	3	3	1	1	0	0	2	2
Roentgen	5	5	4	4	1	1	.	.	.	.
urgery	141	141	95	95	94	94	59	58	102	102
Surgical Patho gy	0	0	0	0	1	1	3	3	6	6
Obstetrics	28	28	23	23	17	17	21	21	19	19
Gynaecology	0	0	0	0	1	1	0	0	2	2
Dermatology d Syphilis	40	40	72	72	58	58	50	50	58	58
Neurology Psychiatry	17	17	40	40	24	24	24	24	25	25
Ophthalmo	16	16	17	17	1	1	8	8	3	3
Otology	16	16	14	14	22	22	11	11	28	28
Laryngolo	4	4	5	5	3	3	1	1	9	9
	6	6	7	7	2	2	2	2	7	7
	28	28	21	21	13	13	11	11	16	16

* In the table of electives, not the total number of students taking electives are enumerated, but the number of courses elected. Each course represents the work of one student for a period of one month. Eight electives constitute the work of the fourth year, but a student may take more than one month's work in a single subject. This system of fourth-year work went into effect in 1906.

FINAL EXAMINATIONS

	1908 Passed	1908 Failed	1908 Total	1908 %Failed	1909 Passed	1909 Failed	1909 Total	1909 %Failed	1910 Passed	1910 Failed	1910 Total	1910 %Failed	1911 Passed	1911 Failed	1911 Total	1911 %Failed	1912 Passed	1912 Failed	1912 Total	1912 %Failed
First Class:—																				
Comparative Anatomy	79	7	86	8	51	3	54	5	54	3	57	6	59	8	67	12	73	3	76	4
Biological Chemistry	64	15	79	19	47	17	64	26	58	5	63	9	48	11	59	18	76	3	79	4
Anatomy	65	16	81	20	54	9	63	14	62	2	64	3	61	6	67	10	70	7	77	9
Physiology	77	16	93	17	56	13	69	18	54	12	66	22	66	6	72	8	74	5	79	6
Second Class:—																				
Pathological Anatomy	66	13	79	16	84	12	96	12	50	3	53	6	56	3	59	5	64	4	68	6
Bacteriology	62	22	84	26	81	12	93	12	53	2	55	4	59	4	63	6	61	5	66	8
Hygiene	73	5	78	6	87	3	90	3	48	3	51	6	58	0	58	0	64	0	64	0
Third Class:—																				
Theory and Practice	60	6	66	9	60	7	67	10	95	3	98	3	53	2	55	4	60	6	66	9
Surgery	62	3	65	5	68	1	69	1	90	0	90	0	50	0	50	0	43	1	44	2
Obstetrics	58	9	67	13	69	16	85	19	84	9	93	10	51	2	53	4	64	1	65	2
Pediatrics	67	0	67	0	75	0	75	0	89	3	92	3	51	2	53	4	64	1	65	2
Dermatology	61	8	69	12	70	7	77	9	93	2	95	2	53	2	55	4	62	1	63	2
Gynaecology	57	10	67	15	72	5	77	6	75	19	94	25	54	2	56	4	65	1	66	2
Neurology	66	4	70	6	74	2	76	2	87	6	93	7	55	2	57	4	64	8	67	12
Therapeutics	59	13	72	18	68	14	82	17	84	10	94	10	51	4	55	7	63	5	68	7
Clinical Medicine	63	7	70	10	75	5	80	6	89	3	92	3	56	0	56	0	62	2	64	3
Clinical Surgery	61	0	61	0	73	0	73	0	90	0	90	0	54	0	54	0	64	1	65	2
Syphilis	64	4	68	6	78	0	78	0	87	4	91	5	52	2	54	4	65	0	65	0
Ophthalmology	59	7	66	10	69	11	80	14	91	2	93	2	49	2	51	4	61	1	62	2
Otology	64	3	67	5	74	0	74	0	92	1	93	1	53	0	53	0	64	1	65	2
Laryngology	66	2	68	3	72	1	73	1	90	2	92	2	53	0	53	0	66	0	66	0
Psychiatry	65	3	68	4	73	2	75	2	91	0	91	0	53	0	58	0	65	0	65	0

FOURTH CLASS. — ELECTIVES :* —

Subject					
Anatomy	49	33	31	38	33
Comparative Anatomy	.	3	4	3	0
Embryology	3	.	0	0	0
Physiology	10	2	3	3	2
Comparative Physiology	2	0	0	1	0
Biochemistry	5	1	2	2	3
Bacteriology	.	1	1	4	6
Pathology	14	30	32	42	19
Comparative Pathology	2	3	1	5	9
Protozoology	.	.	2	0	0
Neuropathology	.	1	4	3	2
Preventive Medicine and Hygiene	1	0	3	19	6
Pharmacology	.	.	9	5	1
Medicin[e], Theory [an]d Practice	83	49	111	110	71
Pediatri[cs]	45	46	59	63	16
Clinical [and S]urgical Pathology	70	47	72	93	59
Roentge[n] Ray	2	0	1	3	0
Surgery	.	.	1	4	5
Surgery	102	58	94	95	141
Surgical Pathology	6	3	1	0	0
[Obstetri]cs	19	21	17	23	28
Gynaecology	2	0	1	0	0
Dermatology and Syphilis	58	50	58	72	40
Neurology and Psychiatry	25	24	24	40	17
Ophthalmology	3	8	1	17	16
Otology	28	11	22	14	16
Laryngology	9	1	3	5	4
	7	2	2	7	6
	16	11	13	21	28

* In the table of electives, the figures are not the total number of students taking electives are enumerated, but the number of courses elected. Each course represents the work of one student for a period of one month. Eight electives constitute the work of the fourth year, but a student may take more than one month's work in a single subject. This system of fourth-year work went into effect in 1905.

GENERAL STATISTICS OF THE SCHOOL

Candidates for the Degree of Doctor of Medicine

New matriculants   90

The number of students in attendance : —

Fourth Class   50
Third Class   56
Second Class   57
First Class   95
Special Students   12

Total   270

Applicants for Degree of M.D. (February)   9
Applicants for Degree of M.D. (June)   54

68

Rejected   2
Graduated   61

Of the 61 students who received the degree of Doctor of Medicine, 21 received the degree *sum laude*.

Candidates for the Degree of Doctor of Public Health

The number of students in attendance   5
Applicants for Degree of Dr.P.H. (June)   4
Rejected   1
Graduated   3

	SUMMER COURSES					GRADUATE COURSES				
	1908	1909	1910	1911	1912	1907–08	1908–09	1909–10	1910–11	1911–12
Courses taken	178	291	299	510	485	125	128	151	184	222
Students . .	186	210	197	267	219	81	111	111	153	155
Receipts . .	$4886.50	$8729.50	$8622	$13370	$11684.50	$2982.50	$3187	$3605.77	$4085	$5077

Students in courses of the regular medical curriculum . . .   270
Students in Graduate Medical courses   219
Students in Summer Medical courses   155
Students in Doctor of Public Health courses   5
Total students, October 1, 1911, to October 1, 1912, . .   649

HENRY A. CHRISTIAN, *Dean.*

THE DENTAL SCHOOL

To the President of the University: —

Sir, — I have the honor to submit my report on the Dental School for the academic year 1911-12.

The total number of students registered was 154, an increase of 38 over the registration of last year.

The registration by classes was as follows: —

Third-year students	42
Second-year students	55
First-year students	57
	154

Instruction was given as follows: —

Anatomy.—Asst. Professor Warren, Demonstrator Cheever, Instructors Mosher, R. M. Green, and Shepard, Assistants Hartwell, Boothby, Ehrenfried, Whittemore, and Young, Fellow Adams. 424 hours.

Comparative Anatomy. — Professor Minot, Asst. Professor Lewis, Demonstrator Bremer, Instructors Williams, Shepard, Johnson, Teaching Fellow Begg, Austin Teaching Fellow Heuser. 252 hours.

Physiology. — Professor Cannon, Asst. Professor Martin, Instructor Nice, Teaching Fellows Burket, Myers, Austin Teaching Fellow Porter. 348 hours.

Physiological and Dental Chemistry. — Lecturer H. Carlton Smith, Assistant Fred M. Rice. 302 hours.

Bacteriology.—Professor H. C. Ernst, Asst. Professor Wolbach, Instructors Frothingham, Page, Assistants Perry, Worthington, Everett, Dane, Stanwood, Austin Teaching Fellow Floyd. 160 hours.

Materia Medica and Therapeutics.—Professor E. C. Briggs, Assistant O'Connell. 42 hours.

Dental Pathology.— Professor C. A. Brackett. 32 hours.

Neurology. —Instructor E. W. Taylor. 4 hours.

Crown and Bridge Work.— Professor Cooke, Instructors Eldred, Belliveau, Hovestadt, Beckford, and Peters. 128 hours.

Orthodontia. — Professor E. H. Smith, Asst. Professor Baker, Instructors Howe, Gilpatric, and Assistant Pierce. 180 hours.

Orthodontia, Second Year. — Asst. Professor Baker. 10 hours.

Prosthetic Dentistry, Second Year. — Asst. Professor Cross. 32 hours.

Prosthetic Dentistry, Laboratory, Third Year. — Asst. Professor Cross, Instructors Hayden, Haley, L. A. Rogers, Langley, Weston, Clark, Demonstrator Kazanjian, Assistants McCullagh, Sykora, Provan, Lane, Ruelberg, Shannon. 496 hours.

Prosthetic Dentistry, Laboratory, Second Year. — Asst. Professor Cross, Instructors Dort, Eames, Demonstrator Kazanjian, Assistants Fernald, Parker, Mackintosh, Shinn, Travis, Morgan, Loomer, Weinz, Flagg, Jenkins, Malmstrom, Stoddard. 544 hours.

Prosthetic Dentistry, Laboratory, First Year.— Asst. Professor CROSS, Demonstrator KAZANJIAN, Assistant F. W. HOVESTADT. 44 hours.

Anatomical Articulation, Mechanical Treatment of Fractured Jaws, Cleft Palates, and other Deformities. — Asst. Professor CROSS. 21 hours.

Extracting and Anaesthesia. — Professor POTTER, Instructors FARRINGTON, MIDGLEY, NORWOOD, Assistants WOLFE, ANDREWS, and RING. 477 hours.

Porcelain Inlays and Carving Teeth.— Instructors OLDHAM, HADLEY, and MOFFATT, Assistant NESBETT. 142 hours.

Roentgenology. — Instructor CUMMINGS, 8 lectures and 350 radiographs.

Surgery, Surgical Pathology, and Oral Surgery.— Professor MONKS, 23 lectures and demonstrations; Professor MONKS, Instructor MINER, Assistant TAFT, clinics, 160 hours; Instructor BLAKE, 9 clinics at City Hospital.

Syphilis. — Instructor C. MORTON SMITH. 6 lectures and clinics.

Operative Dentistry, Seniors. — Professor POTTER. 32 hours.

Operative Dentistry, Juniors. — Lecturer DILL. 32 hours.

Operative Dentistry, Infirmary, Seniors. — Professor SMITH, Instructors LOVELAND, JEWELL, EDDY, BLAISDELL, STANLEY, PAUL, FURFEY, CHUTE, ELLIOTT, PIKE, WHITEHILL, STONE, FURBISH, WHITCHURCH, Assistants VAUGHAN, HURLEY, W. A. DAVIS, CASWELL, CATHERON, DREA, MacDONALD, EMERSON. 624 hours.

Operative Dentistry, Infirmary, Juniors. — Lecturer DILL, Instructors SPINNEY, McPHERSON, F. T. TAYLOR, TISHLER, WYMAN, LEAVITT, STEVENS, Assistants HALLET, FREEMAN, SPEERS, PETERSON, ESTES, O'CONNELL, O. S. SMITH, ANDREWS, SAFFORD, EMERSON. 535 hours.

The work of the year is outlined in the following table: —

OPERATIVE DENTISTRY

No. of treatments of teeth and gums	2,958
" " " pyorrhoea alveolaris	212
" sets of teeth cleaned	2,024
" fillings — gold	1,776
" " gutta percha	298
" " cement	2,126
" " amalgam	2,438
" " amalgam and cement	2,280
" " silicate	266
" patients	4,126
" operations	14,887

PROSTHETIC DENTISTRY

SERVICE TO PATIENTS

No. of sets of artificial teeth	224
" " " " repaired	99
" partial sets of artificial teeth	195
" patients	716

PRACTICE WORK

No. of specimen plates	365

CROWN AND BRIDGE WORK
Service to Patients

No. of crowns and caps 207
" crowns repaired 41
" pieces of bridge work 109
' " " repaired 17

Practice Work

No. of crowns and caps 268
" bridges 158
" carved teeth models 28

ORTHODONTIA
Service to Patients

No. of patients treated for irregularities of the teeth 87
" appliances 254
" models of regulating cases 172

Practice Work

No. of appliances for irregularities of the teeth 104
" models for regulating cases 52

INLAY WORK
Service to Patients

No. of porcelain inlays and tips 9
" gold inlays 53

Practice Work

No. of porcelain inlays 48
" gold inlays 43

FRACTURED JAWS
Service to Patients

No. of cases 28
" appliances 28

Practice Work

No. of appliances 104

SURGICAL DEPARTMENT

No. of cases of alveolar abscess, from infected teeth . . . 22
" " " " " imbedded roots . . . 2
" " " " following fracture 4
" " absorption following abscess 3
" " antrum empyema 10
" " arsenic poisoning 1
" " ankylosis 2
" " adenoids 1

SURGICAL DEPARTMENT. — Continued

No. of cases of amputation of root		1
"	" Bell's palsy	1
"	" carcinoma	1
"	" cleft palates	8
"	" curettement of socket	2
"	" dentigerous cysts	8
"	" epulis	8
"	" excision of frenum	2
"	" fracture of alveolar process	2
"	" " " jaw	4
"	" " " tooth	2
"	" gangrene	2
"	" hypertrophied tissue	2
"	" hemorrhage	1
"	" imbedded and impacted third molars	11
"	" imbedded cuspid	1
"	" inflammation of tonsils	1
'	" " maxillary joint	1
"	" lead poisoning	1
"	" leucoplakia	1
"	" necrosis of jaw	6
"	" neuritis	8
"	" osteomyelitis	1
"	" pyorrhoea	8
"	" ranula	1
"	" syphilis	1
"	" stomatitis	1
"	" sinus of cheek	1
"	" " " alveolar process	1
"	" supernumerary teeth	1
"	" submaxillary abscess	1
"	" tri-facial neuralgia	4
"	" tubercular glands	1
"	" imflammation of the gustatory nerve	1

SUMMARY

No. of operations in Prosthetic Department		1,553
"	" Operative Department	14,387
"	" Surgical Department	5,679
		21,619

The library now contains 1,961 bound volumes, 241 volumes having been added during the past year. The cataloguing of the books is now practically completed and the usefulness of the library very much increased. It is open to students and to teachers until ten o'clock each week-day evening.

The specimens in the Museum have been carefully examined and many that were comparatively worthless as specimens have been cast aside. A number of them consisted of gold dentures, which have been broken up and sold, netting the sum of $672, which has been placed to the account of the Endowment Fund.

Professor William H. Potter has delivered public lectures as follows: —

Jan. 9, 1912. Haverhill Dental Society, Haverhill, Mass., "Local Anaesthesia, Nitrous Oxide and Oxygen Anaesthesia."

Jan. 22, 1912. Cambridge Young Men's Christian Association, "Oral Hygiene."

Feb. 29, 1912. Brockton, Mass., "Oral Hygiene."

Mar. 22, 1912. "Oral Hygiene for Teachers," given in Professor A. O. Norton's course at Harvard University.

Mar. 29, 1912. "The Care of the Teeth of School Children," before American School Hygiene Association, Harvard Medical School.

Professor William P. Cooke read a paper before the Massachusetts Dental Society on "The Prevention and Control of Dental Caries." He has also been active in societies and with legislative committees in the interest of a bill which shall legalize the dental nurse.

Professor Harold DeW. Cross read a paper on "Anatomical Occlusion," before the Lynn Dental Society. Dr. Cross has also experimented in casting processes and made investigations in the several processes of administering nitrous oxide and oxygen for complete and partial anaesthesia.

Dr. LeR. M. S. Miner has continued his studies on new growths of the alveolar process and presented his findings in a paper read before the Massachusetts Dental Society. The work included the production of experimental lesions in guinea-pigs which microscopically resemble the human lesions. He has now under way studies of the so-called abscess sacs found on the apices of roots of teeth.

Dr. George H. Wright read a paper on "The Teeth and their Relations to the Body," before the Massachusetts Medical Society (published in the *Boston Medical and Surgical Journal*). He has also been experimenting to obtain an artificial means of replacing a jaw lost through surgical extirpation; also, a method of using naso-pharyngeal plate to prevent adhesion of the soft palate to the pharyngeal wall after operations on adenoids and tonsils.

The Research Committee completed their work in the establishment of the Harriet N. Lowell Society for Dental Research. The Society has been doing excellent work during the year. The student body has become much interested in research work and several papers of interest have been read before the society. The income of the Harriet N. Lowell Fund for Dental Research has been used by Dr. Miner in furtherance of his investigations.

Mr. H. Carlton Smith has continued his studies on oxydizing enzymes and has been fairly successful in the isolation and preservation of enzymes, particularly of oxideses, by separating the enzymes in an atmosphere free from oxygen, and preserving it in capsules covered with a very thin coating of stearic acids. In the investigation of the character of salivary acidity he has found that in a great majority of cases the acidity is wholly due to carbon dioxide. He has devised special apparatus for this experiment and is now at work on the relation of the viscosity of the saliva to the mucin content.

At the urgent request of members of the Boston Social Union the Infirmary was opened one evening a week during March and April, to provide an opportunity for the low-wage earners to obtain dental treatment without loss of income. Some 350 letters were sent to our Alumni and members of the Metropolitan District Hospital Association, outlining our plans and asking for volunteer workers. The Infirmary was opened on the evening of March 7, with nine practicing dentists in attendance and pledges on hand to insure that number one evening each week.

During the following eight weeks 284 patients were treated. Though the demand for the work increased rapidly, we were obliged to close the clinic on account of the expense. There is dire need for this kind of a clinic which cannot be met without an endowment.

In making the report of the men who during the past year have by research work and public lectures added to the knowledge of the profession, I wish to call your attention to our large staff of faithful teachers who continue to give their time at a great financial sacrifice. Were it not for their unselfish devotion we should be obliged to close the School. This condition is to be deplored and a substantial endowment is the only remedy.

EUGENE H. SMITH, *Dean.*

REPORT OF THE DIRECTOR OF SCHOLARSHIPS IN THE MEDICAL AND DENTAL SCHOOLS

To THE PRESIDENT OF THE UNIVERSITY: —

SIR, — I respectfully beg leave to submit the account of my work as Director of Scholarships for the past year: —

	Medical.	Dental.	Total.
Number of applicants for first-year scholarships . .	16		16
Number of applicants for other scholarships . . .	42		42
Number of students interviewed	99	20	119
Total number of interviews	336	46	382
Number of letters received and answered	347	56	403
Total number of students aided (exclusive of scholarships).	20	10	30
Number to whom money was loaned	18	10	28
Number to whom money was given	4		4
Amount of money loaned	$988.00	$525	$1,513.00
Amount of money given	308.75		308.75
Sources from which money was obtained			
Private Fund	1038.00	525	1,563.00
Francis Skinner Fund	18.75		18.75
Anonymous Gifts	200.00		200.00
Loan Fund of Class of 1879	40.00		40.00
Amount of money refunded	463.00	415	878.00

FRANKLIN DEXTER,
Director of Scholarships.

THE LIBRARY

To the President of the University: —

Sir, — As Director of the University Library and Chairman of the Council of the College Library, I beg to submit my report covering the year July 1, 1911, to June 30, 1912.

Except perhaps for the years 1638, when the Harvard Library was founded, and 1764, when it was burned down, the past year has been the most notable in its history. Never has there been greater activity in its different branches, never have the accessions, immediate or prospective, been so numerous and of such value, and, above all, never has it received a gift comparable to the Harry Elkins Widener Memorial Library, to which it now looks forward. Thanks to the princely generosity of Mrs. George D. Widener, the Harvard College Library is at last assured of a home that will house its treasures in an adequate manner and provide for their best administration and use. In the centre of the building will be Harry Widener's own priceless collection of books and manuscripts, — a lasting memorial to his character and to his tastes and even more to his affection for Harvard. The prospect is indeed splendid, but further comment on it may be reserved for future reports, when our dream of so many years past will have become a wonderful reality.

The growth of the College Library in 1911–12 has been satisfactory. The amount expended for books by it alone has been greater by fifty per cent than in any previous twelve months, though the total of volumes acquired has been exceeded twice before, when there have been gifts of large collections. The quality of the purchases has been unusually high, for besides those made from our ordinary income, perforce reserved for commonplace necessities, they have included many rare volumes and costly sets, which we owe to the use of certain restricted funds, and still more to the generosity of various donors. But this last source, however gratifying, is precarious. An important part of our accessions came from two trips in Europe made by Dr. Walter Lichtenstein (Librarian of Northwestern University, but also buying for Harvard and other institutions), who picked up books for us with admirable skill and judgment. It is true, we were at our wits' ends as to where to house our acquisitions, but this apparently insoluble problem, which tormented us for so long, is at last almost pleasing as a reminiscence. For the next year or two the Library will cheerfully store its new books in any sort of safe temporary quarters, and with the glorious opportunity for usefulness now ahead, it must not relax for an instant its efforts to keep adding to the value of its collections.

The chief events in the administration of the College Library have been the substitution wherever possible of the printed standard size cards of the Congressional Library for our small written ones, and the beginning to print new standard cards of our own. Both of these operations have necessitated an amount of labor that would surprise any one not familiar with the complexities of such an enterprise. The quantity of comparison, correction, and revision it has meant has been rather appalling. Towards the end of August, 1911, after the necessary new catalogue cases had been put in, the work of the insertion of Library of Congress and other standard cards was taken up and was not completed until about November 1, 1912. During that time 323,000 new cards were prepared and inserted in the trays and about an equal number of old ones taken out. In spite of the difficulty and cost of the operation and the inconvenience to which it temporarily put many people, experience has only further convinced us of its necessity. Our own printing of cards started on November 1st, and has proceeded slowly and cautiously. The subscription of several other libraries to our cards helps to lighten a cost which otherwise might be heavy.

The pressing task of classification and reclassification has proceeded as fast as our straitened conditions have permitted. In 1911–12 18,038 volumes were arranged into new groups. Amidst the press of other business but little could be done for the subject catalogues except the carrying out of reforms previously decided upon.

The last year has been a notable one in the history of the Law School Library. Its growth has been unprecedented, — 21,447 volumes and 3,594 pamphlets. This will of course remain exceptional and the library may never again make a single splendid acquisition equal to the Olivart Collection,* yet there is reason to believe that its rapid increase in recent years will continue, the

* For details, see the Report of the Dean of the Law School.

more so as it is paying attention to fields it has hitherto rather neglected.

Between October 31st and November 8th, 1911, the library of the Divinity School was brought over into the new building of the Andover Theological Seminary. The two collections are now being merged into one, but the process must be slow.

The new wing of the Gray Herbarium has been completed, thus providing excellent and much needed accommodation for several thousand volumes.

As the various branches of the University Library increase, the tendency will be for them to spread out and to enrich their collections without asking whether the books they desire are already to be found in some other part of Cambridge. Considerable duplication is doubtless inevitable, for many works are useful to scholars in several subjects and should be represented at Harvard by several copies conveniently located. The professors in charge of the Departmental and of the special libraries are naturally quick to resent any suggestion that they are not the best judges of their own needs and of those of their pupils, and that they should be limited in their disposition of funds, which in many cases are due to their personal efforts. And yet from the point of view of the proper use of the University's resources, it is not satisfactory to have several departments buy copies of expensive books but rarely used in any of them. Harvard has some four or five separate and one might almost say rival botanical libraries, differing from each other in scope, yet tending to overlap in their purchases. In the case of the Law School, the Olivart Collection just acquired contains thousands of volumes duplicating ones already in the possession of the College. This is not of much consequence, even if we may question whether it would not be well to part with a few, rather than go to the expense of cataloguing them. It would be more serious if the Law School were to interpret the meaning of International Law as broadly as did Marquis Olivart, and embark on a policy of buying numerous works on international affairs, of the kind that are acquired by the College Library for historical and general purposes. For instance, today both have collections (between which there is little to choose) on such subjects as Morocco, Cuba, Latin American boundary disputes, etc. The need of an adjustment at least for the future is plain. As between the College and the Andover-Harvard Divinity libraries, the division is simpler, but even here such an important topic as Church History lies obviously in the field of both, as does

Canon Law which is also of interest to the Law School. Every one of our libraries thinks first of its own readers and wishes to possess whatever may be useful to them, regardless of conditions elsewhere. It is not always an easy matter to reconcile this natural and legitimate feeling with the broader policy of the University.

ARCHIBALD CARY COOLIDGE.

APPENDIX TO THE LIBRARY REPORT

I

ACCESSIONS

The accessions to the University Library for the year and the present extent of each of its parts are shown in the following table: —

ACCESSIONS	Volumes added	Present extent in	
		Volumes	Pamphlets
College Library : —			
Gore Hall Collections	26,125	586,872	400,350
Thirty-six Special Reference Libraries	5,290	66,284	. .
Law School	21,477	148,387	17,570
Divinity School	963	39,757	11,175
Medical School	957	18,637	39,994
Dental School	229	1,806	13,000
Bussey Institution	292	3,062	12,051
Museum of Zoölogy	1,136	49,155	45,535
Peabody Museum	1,369	4,800	4,497
Astronomical Observatory	250	13,762	31,165
Gray Herbarium	610	13,396	10,457
Arnold Arboretum	1,958	26,706	6,640
Total	60,656		
Deduct, transfers between Gore Hall and Department Libraries	283		
Totals	60,373	972,574	592,434
Andover Theological Seminary	. .	62,764	37,128
Total number of volumes and pamphlets		1,664,900	. .

The additions to the College Library collection alone, excluding the special reference libraries, for the last five years have been as follows: —

ADDITIONS TO GORE HALL	1907-08	1908-09	1909-10 11 mos.	1910-11	1911-12
Volumes by purchase or exchange .	8,765	9,759	8,577	9,939	14,817
Do. by binding serials	1,699	1,841	1,924	2,882	2,308
Do. by binding pamphlets . . .	1,099	1,122	974	1,815	1,594
Do. by gift	7,153	17,939	9,141	9,547	7,358
Do. of pamphlets bound together				48	53
Total volumes added	18,716	30,661	20,616	23,231	26,125
Maps in sheets	699	1,131	525	555	498
Pamphlets and serials * by purchase or exchange	2,010	1,820	3,051	2,044	6,184
Pamphlets by gift	14,872	19,611	17,848	21,848	17,120
Total gifts (vols., pams. and serials).	22,025	37,450	26,489	31,395	24,478

INCOME AND EXPENDITURE FOR BOOKS

The following table shows the income of the book-funds, receipts from other sources for the purchase of books, and expenditures for books during the last six years: —

INCOME AND EXPENDITURE	1906-07	1907-08	1908-09	1909-10 11 mos.	1910-11	1911-12
From book funds, —						
Balance from previous year .	$5,140	$5,726	$5,723	$5,029	$2,163	$4,257
Income of the year	20,259	19,773	20,917	19,111	21,426	23,788
Total available	25,399	25,499	26,640	24,140	23,589	28,045
Spent for books	19,673	19,776	21,611	21,977	19,332	24,594
Balance to next year	5,726	5,723	5,029	2,163	4,257	3,451
Special gifts, sales, etc. —						
Balance from previous year .	4,279	8,802	3,321	4,860	†4,241	4,337
Received during the year . .	10,115	5,351	7,246	11,948	11,521	19,164
Total available	14,394	9,153	10,567	16,808	15,762	23,501
Spent for books	10,592	5,832	5,707	8,567	11,425	22,463
Balance to next year	3,802	3,321	4,860	8,241	4,337	1,038
Total spent for books, —						
College Library	$30,265	$25,608	$27,318	$30,544	$30,757	$47,057
Dep't and Spec. Ref. Librarie (orders through Coll. Lib.)	7,642	5,914	7,436	8,339	9,239	‡7,058
Total	$37,907	$31,522	$34,754	$38,883	$39,996	$54,115

* Not including current periodicals recorded on the periodical cards.
† The balance of the previous year was diminished by the transfer of $4,000 to the Coolidge-Hay Fund.   ‡ 1911-12 figures are for Special Reference Libraries only.

SPECIAL REFERENCE LIBRARIES

The present extent of these libraries is as follows: —

SPECIAL REFERENCE LIBRARIES	Permanent	On Deposit	Totals
1. Chemical Lab. *Boylston Hall*	3,260	1,255	4,515
2. Physical Lab. *Jefferson Phys. Lab.*	690	19	709
3. Botanical Lab. *University Museum*	1,279	120	1,399
4. Geological Lab. *Do.*	241	. .	241
5. Mineralogical Lab. *Do.*	894	212	1,106
6. Phys. Geography Lab. *Do.*	259	184	448
7. Zoölogical Lab. *Do.*	422	. .	422
8. Plant Physiology Laboratory. *Botanic Garden* .	153	. .	153
9. Astronomical Lab.	82	. .	82
10. Statistical Lab. *Dane Hall*	247	. .	247
11. Graduate Economics. *Dane Hall*	76	. .	76
12. Physiological Lab. *Lawrence Hall*	65	. .	65
13. Classics. *Harvard Hall 3*	4,951	148	5,099
14. History. *Harvard Hall R. R.*	5,961	39	6,000
15. Economics. *Do.*	1,766	84	1,800
16. Social Ethics. *Emerson Hall.*	3,397	. .	3,397
17. Philosophy (Robbins Library and Psychol. Lab.). *Emerson Hall*	4,403	44	4,447
18. Child Memorial (English). *Warren House* . . .	5,301	90	5,391
19. Lowell Memorial (Romance). *Do.* . . .	1,644	6	1,650
20. German. *Do.* . . .	1,579	. .	1,579
21. French. *Do.* . . .	2,634	. .	2,634
22. Sanskrit. *Do.* . . .	1,036	31	1,067
23. Semitic. *Semitic Museum*	1,887	24	1,911
24. Mathematics. *Sever 22*	997	94	1,091
25. Mining and Metallurgy. *Rotch Laboratory* . . .	409	71	480
26. Engineering. *Pierce Hall*	8,112	200	8,312
27. Forestry. *Do.*	17	39	56
28. Music. *Holden Chapel*	1,168	. .	1,168
29. Education. *Lawrence Hall*	6,772	. .	6,772
30. Business. *Do.*	793	1,075	1,868
31. Fine Arts (incl. Gray and Randall Coll.). *Fogg Museum*	1,257	13	1,270
32. Architecture. *Robinson Hall*	1,530	45	1,575
33. Landscape Architecture. *Robinson Hall*	1,000	10	1,010
34. Bureau for Municipal Research. *Wadsworth House*	1,316	499	1,815
35. Preachers' Library. *Wadsworth House*	186	. .	186
36. Phillips Brooks House Library	500	. .	500
Totals	66,284	4,252	70,536

SHELF DEPARTMENT

During the year the following groups were permanently classified:

Ancient History	5,100
Egyptology	296
Modern Latin Literature	1,014
United States History (in part)	11,628
Total	18,038

II

FROM THE REPORT OF THE LIBRARIAN

The gifts of the year include no collections of great size, as has often been the case previously, but four at least deserve to be separately mentioned and described.

On March 19th, Professor Palmer celebrated his seventieth birthday by presenting to the Library his George Herbert collection, to which he has devoted years of loving care. This collection, which numbers 158 volumes, includes, besides the complete series of editions of Herbert's Works and copies of all the important manuscripts of his poems, the chief biographies from Walton down, the works of his six brothers, with autographs of each of them, works relating to Nicholas Ferrar, the head of Little Gidding, and whatever else "might incidentally throw light on the scenery and events of Herbert's life, his scholarly and political associates, and the sources from which he derived literary material." All of these books are described in "A Herbert Bibliography," compiled by Professor Palmer and published as number 59 of the Library's "Bibliographical Contributions." On the occasion of the presentation of the books, a company of Professor Palmer's friends and associates were invited to meet him in the Treasure Room of the College Library, when he described felicitously the pleasure he had had in bringing the collection together, its character, and his purpose in presenting it to the Library.

Mr. Thomas Hall, Jr., '93, who had been an Instructor in English in the University for fifteen years, died in August, 1911. From his library we received an unusually well selected collection of about 600 volumes of English literature, including many plays and some out-of-the-way and rare works.

From the late W. Bayard Cutting, Jr., who died on March 10, 1910, and who had for many years shown his keen interest in the growth of the Library, we received a bequest of about one thousand volumes from his own library, mainly of standard works on French and English history.

On the death of Rev. Edward H. Hall, '51, of Cambridge, a number of rare and early editions and other books, amounting in all to 120 volumes, were sent to the Library by his executors.

From many friends we have received gifts of money for the purchase of books, amounting altogether to $16,951. A full list of the names of donors will be found in the Treasurer's report. The principal gifts have been: —

From Mrs. Louis Bettmann, of Cincinnati, in memory of her son, Milton Bettmann, '97, and of the quindecennial celebration of his class, and supplementing a former gift made some years ago, $100.

From Mrs. E. D. Brandegee, of Brookline, for incunabula to be added to the Weld Memorial Collection, $1,250.

From the Committee to visit the Department of Economics, for books on economics, $745.12.

From Professor A. C. Coolidge, '87, for books on French and German history and for other purchases, $5,500.

From Lady Sybil Cutting, for books on the history and art of Florence and other cities of Northern Italy, in memory of her husband, W. Bayard Cutting, Jr., '00, $100.

From James L. Derby, '08, of New York, for books on the Philippines, $50.

From William Endicott, Jr., '87, of Boston, $1,500.

From Evan Randolph, '03, of Philadelphia, $100.

For books in English literature and English history, from Alexander Cochrane, of Boston, $1,000; from Ernest B. Dane, '92, of Boston, $1,000; from the English Department, $339.95; from Edward N. Fenno, Jr., '97, of Boston, $100; from Charles Jackson, '98, of Boston, $2,000; from Francis Skinner, '92, of Dedham, $200; from Frank G. Thomson, '97, of Philadelphia, $100; from Lucius Wilmerding, '01, of New York, $50.

For additions to the Lefferts Pope collection, from William R. Castle, Jr., '00, of Boston, $90; from John L. Saltonstall, '00, of Boston, $50; and from Mr. Lefferts, the original owner of the collection, an early edition of Pope's Letters, acquired from a bookseller.

For early editions of Defoe, gifts amounting to $220 from Ezra H. Baker, '81, of Boston; Tracy Dows, '94, of New York; Ogden L. Mills, '05, of New York; and Grenville H. Norcross, '75, of Boston.

For two years we have been indebted to Professor Roger B. Merriman, '96, for a gift of $100 each year, for the purchase of books on Spanish history. A portion of the Cutting income has been devoted to the same purpose.

Annual gifts or gifts made in continuation of earlier ones have been received from Lawrence S. Butler, '98, of New York, $50 for books on Paris; from Harold J. Coolidge, '92, of Boston, $50 for books on China; from John Craig, of Boston, $250 for books on the Theatre in connection with his Prize for Dramatic Composition; from the Dante Society, $50 for books on Dante; from Ellis L. Dresel, '87, of Boston, $50 for German drama; from J. Hays Gardiner, '85, $10 for books on Burmah; from George L. Kittredge, '82, $60 for books illustrating the history of witchcraft; from John S. Lawrence, '01, $10 for biographies of successful men; from James Loeb, '88, of New York, now of Munich, $100 for labor periodicals; from Edwin S. Mullins, '93, of Hyannisport, $50 for Folklore; from Walter W. Naumburg, '89, of New York, $100 for the Shakespeare collection; from an anonymous giver, for books on Western History as a memorial to Charles Elliott Perkins, $1,000; from William Phillips, '00, Secretary of the American Embassy in London, $100 for books on London; from the Saturday Club, of Boston, $300; from Horace B. Stanton, '00, of Boston, $25 for books on Molière. These numerous gifts for special purposes add greatly to the strength and reputation of the Library by building up special collections in ways quite beyond what our ordinary income would provide for.

APPLETON CHAPEL
AND PHILLIPS BROOKS HOUSE

To the President of the University: —

Sir, — No significant changes have taken place in the administration of the University Chapel during the past year. Experience has abundantly justified the change of the Sunday service to the morning hour. The attendance of the Cambridge public at that service has diminished; that of the University constituency, apart from the students, has increased. The average attendance of students remains about as last year. In the uniformity of this attendance there has been great gain. The report of the Chapel Committee, appointed by the Phillips Brooks House Association, contains the following paragraph: " The student attendance is now almost as large as is possible under the present arrangements, as two hundred and fifty men more than fill the south side of the Chapel. For this reason, many students who come late are now unable to find seats, there being no seats in the gallery owing to the large numbers of the Cambridge public attending every Sunday. The average total attendance for the last six months has been exactly four hundred. As more than half of these are students, and only two hundred seats are reserved for them, under the present system it seems that the day is not far distant when the number of seats reserved for outsiders will have to be materially decreased." On an October Sunday, 1912, in accordance with this suggestion, the south gallery was reserved for students and practically filled by them.

A special service for Freshmen was held on a week day evening last year, at which the President, Professor Bliss Perry and the Chairman of the Board of Preachers spoke. The Committee above mentioned has made it its business to bring the work of the Chapel to the attention of every member of the Freshman class. At eleven o'clock on the morning of Good Friday, without suspension of the regular university exercises, at the written request of nearly two hundred students, the Communion of the Lord's Supper was observed in the Chapel. This service was attended by two hundred and fifty-nine persons, two hundred and twenty-eight of whom were students. Owing no doubt to the greater place held in the university life by the Sunday service, and to the closer relation which now obtains with the Phillips Brooks House, the attendance at the daily service of morning prayers shows an increase in the average of about ten per cent as compared with the previous year.

In my last report I stated that the greatest need of the Chapel was that of a new organ.   This need has now been met through the generosity of two friends of the University especially interested in the Chapel work.   The organ has been built by the E. M. Skinner Co., of Dorchester, and is of the highest order.   It should have been in place on the 20th of September; it is hoped that it may be in use before Thanksgiving Day.   Too much cannot be said of the work of Dr. Davison, the organist and choirmaster, and of the student choir under his direction.   They have been able to avail themselves of music, both mediaeval and modern, which is little used in ordinary choirs, but most appropriate for a university chapel.   The Christmas Choral Service has taken its place in the university life.

It has always been the ideal that the Chapel and the Phillips Brooks House should work in close coöperation, the House being the parish house of the Chapel and furnishing the organization and apparatus for the charitable, philanthropic and social activities of the men, one centre at least of whose devotional life is in the Sunday and daily services of worship.   This ideal has never so nearly approached fulfilment as at present.   The House has never stood better in the mind of the University as a whole, the interests of the Chapel have never been more truly considered or more earnestly furthered by the organizations at the House. Both House and Chapel owe much to the aid which *The Crimson* and other student periodicals generously afford.   Chapel and Brooks House topics have place in student discussion in a manner which is gratifying.   In the manner here indicated, suggestion has made been that the revision of the University Hymn Book be not too long postponed.

Mr. Arthur Beane, who served as Graduate Secretary last year, has been re-elected for a period of three years.   The administration of the House is thus given a permanence which it has greatly lacked.   The necessary expenses of the Phillips Brooks House Association, the central organization at the House, have increased of late years, although it is believed that this increase is only in proportion to the efficiency of the work.   The margin of these costs, over and above the income of a small endowment fund which the University holds in the name of the House, has always been sought in the way of private subscription from interested friends.   It is the opinion of the Advisory Committee that material addition should be made to the endowment.   For the first time, this year we have a regularly appointed Assistant Secretary for the Law and Graduate Schools, and the great increase in the membership and activity of these branch associations is one of the things which we have to record.   The University Bureau of Information for new students has been placed entirely in the hands of the Brooks House Association, and is conducted at the House. This Bureau was opened two weeks before the opening of the term and with the annual Harvard Handbook, also published by the Association, rendered great service to new men.

The individual societies which together constitute the Brooks House Association have membership as follows: —

Phillips Brooks House Association (direct)	184
Harvard University Christian Association	305
St. Paul's Society	300
St. Paul's Catholic Club	250
Graduate School Christian Association	60
Harvard-Andover Divinity Club	55
Total	1,154

The above-named total number is one-third larger than the corresponding figure for last year.   Making all deduction for graduate student membership, it appears that nearly half of the undergraduate body is connected with one or another of the societies having their centre at the Brooks House.

The work of the Social Service Committee has been in charge of Mr. D. P. Ranney, who has had the assistance of Mr. Elliott Dunlap Smith, the former Social Service Secretary.   Three hundred and forty-eight men have been engaged in the work, eighty per cent of these being undergraduates.   The attitude of the Settlements and of the other organizations in Boston and vicinity toward the men sent out by the University is one of uniform appreciation.   The spring conference at the Brooks House between settlement leaders and student workers, and the system of inspection of student work by a representative of the House, is largely responsible for the gain in this regard.   The Harvard Medical School in China, which has begun its active work in Shanghai this year, has been granted the use of an office in the Phillips Brooks House.

EDWARD CALDWELL MOORE.

THE GRAY HERBARIUM

To THE PRESIDENT OF THE UNIVERSITY:—

SIR, — During the past academic year the regularly employed staff of the Herbarium has consisted of a Curator (Asa Gray Professor of Systematic Botany), an Assistant Professor of Botany, a Librarian, an assistant in the library, an assistant engaged chiefly in the sorting and distribution of specimens, and an assistant occupied chiefly with the mounting of specimens. As supplementary aids the following persons have been employed for portions of the year: Mr. C. A. Weatherby, from July 1 to September 30, in determinative work and in the distribution of specimens; Miss H. E. Day, in bibliographical indexing; Mr. A. F. Hill, as an assistant in instruction, and Mr. H. T. Darlington, in field work.

The more noteworthy collections of plants received have been as follows: I. *By gift or in exchange:* from the United States National Museum, 1,015 miscellaneous duplicates, including 188 plants of Maryland collected by Mr. G. H. Shull, and 121 specimens in continuation of Mr. C. L. Pollard's series illustrating the North American forms of the genus *Viola;* from the United States Bureau of Plant Industry, 162 specimens of *Gramineae,* largely of the genus *Bouteloua;* from Dr. A. S. Pease, 6,589 specimens, being all of his personal herbarium except the New England plants and comprising a carefully mounted collection of well selected specimens, including a considerable number from Switzerland, Italy, and Greece; from Professor J. F. Collins, 1,021 specimens of vascular plants from his private herbarium; from the New York Botanical Garden, 587 plants of Cuba; from the University of California, 433 plants, chiefly of California and including many of exceptional rarity and interest; from the Geological Survey of Canada, 148 plants, mostly from the shores of Hudson Bay; from Mr. F. S. Collins, 128 plants of the Bermuda Islands; from Mr. John Davis, 194 plants of Missouri; from Mr. F. F. Forbes, 100 specimens to be used in the continuation of the *Exsiccatae Grayanae;* from Mr. Earl E. Sherff, 103 plants of Illinois; from Professor L. H. Pammel, 119 plants of western Canada. II. *Acquired by purchase:* from Mr. T. S. Brandegee, 464 plants of Mexico, collected by Dr. C. A. Purpus; from Mr. C. M. Weber, 267 plants of the Philippine Islands; from Professor I. Urban, 192 plants of San Domingo, collected by H. von Türckheim; from Mr. R. M. Holman, 100 plants of the Philippine Islands; from Dr. H. A. Gleason, his personal herbarium, including 5,116 specimens, in large part representative of the prairies of the Mississippi Valley; from Professor Aven Nelson, 1,724 plants of Idaho; from Professor A. A. Heller, 202 plants of Nevada, Utah, and Montana; from Mr. B. F. Bush, 326 plants of Missouri; from Mr. Earl E. Sherff, 551 plants of Illinois, Missouri, and Arizona; *from dealers*: Kneucker's *Glumaceae Exsiccatae*, fascicles 47–49; Fiori's *Flora Italica Exsiccata*, centuries 15 and 16; Petrak's *Flora Bohemiae et Moraviae Exsiccata*, distributions 1–8, including 843 specimens; Buchtien's *Herbarium Bolivianum*, century 1; and Ross's *Herbarium Siculum*, century 8. III. *Collected by members of the staff:* by Professor Fernald and assistants, 10,554 specimens from Newfoundland; by the Curator, 196 plants of the Bermuda Islands and 603 plants from the coastal portions of South Carolina and Virginia.

The entire number of specimens received from all sources has been 27,059. The number of sheets of mounted specimens added to the organized portion of the Gray Herbarium has been 16,960, being the largest annual addition recorded, and bringing the whole number of sheets in the collection to 484,541.

To the library of the Herbarium there have been added 610 volumes and 442 pamphlets. The library contained, June 30th, 13,396 volumes and 10,457 pamphlets. There have been published four issues of the Card-index of New Genera and Species of American Plants, together amounting to 8,074 cards. This exceedingly useful bibliographical index, edited by Miss Mary A. Day and published by the Gray Herbarium, now contains 100,781 cards and has become by far the most extensive botanical undertaking of its kind.

Again notable progress has been made toward the safe housing and far more perfect equipment of the Herbarium. With generous gifts mentioned in the last report, it has been possible during the year to rebuild in a thoroughly safe manner and on a considerably enlarged scale two more sections of the building. One of these, forming a wing toward Garden Street and being the gift of an anonymous donor, provides ample and highly perfected accommodation for the library of the Herbarium, also two private offices, a room for convenient disposition of stored publications, maps, files of correspondence, labels, etc.; also, in the basement, a pressing room, conveniently arranged for the preparation of specimens and systematic storage of presses, driers, vascula, and the various implements used in equipping collectors, two store-rooms, and a well-ventilated photographic dark-room.

In the opposite direction, toward the conservatories, a two-storied fireproof wing, to be known as the George Robert White Laboratories of Systematic Botany, has been built with Mr. White's gift for the purpose, recorded in the last report. This wing, replacing a smaller one built in 1871, by Mr. H. H. Hunne-well, contains two excellent laboratories, fully appointed as to plumbing, electricity, microscope-lockers, projecting lantern, etc., an instrument room, a room for stored collections, a private office, and a room which is being put at the disposition of the New England Botanical Club for its large and valuable local herbarium; also, in the basement, the engine room, work-shop, etc.

Work upon these important additions was somewhat delayed by a variety of difficulties, such as exceptionally unfavorable weather conditions, the enforced absence of the Curator during a portion of the year from considerations of health, and the tem-porary leave of absence accorded to the Inspector of Buildings. However, it is a pleasure to report that the structures have at length been completed in a very satisfactory manner and at a cost well within the anticipated expense.

At the end of the academic year the only portion of the building still to be reconstructed was the central section, about fifty-five feet deep and thirty-five in frontage. A generous gift of $10,000, from a donor who wishes to be anonymous, has recently been received to permit the rebuilding of the front portion of this central section, that is to say, the part in front of a transverse wall and to be in its reconstructed form a three-storied structure containing a vestibule and five rooms for special purposes, which can be described in greater detail in the next report. The gift is very highly valued as it will permit the completion without great delay of the main façade of the building, so that final grading and appropriate planting of the surrounding grounds may be undertaken in a manner to give the building a proper setting in the Garden. The plans for this part of the building being already carefully prepared, it has been possible to let the contract at once and the work is already started.

The subsequent rebuilding of the large central room, about thirty-five feet by thirty, will still be necessary to complete the

whole programme. It is an undertaking of little structural difficulty, but will entail considerable expense from the large amount
of steel furnishings, chiefly herbarium cases, needful to complete
it in accord with the high standard carefully preserved in all other
portions of the building.

The reconstruction, a portion at a time, of a large building, filled
with extensive, delicate, and valuable collections, is naturally
an undertaking involving due caution, careful planning, and time-
consuming re-arrangements of collections, re-numbering, re-
indexing, etc., all of which must of necessity temporarily hamper
more scientific work. Nevertheless, the Herbarium has been
kept continuously open to visitors, both the plants and the library
having been almost continuously accessible for consultation.
Furthermore, determinative work, investigation, correspondence,
publication, field-work, bibliographical indexing, and the mounting
and distribution of specimens have all proceeded without serious
interruption, the additions to the organized collection actually
being more numerous than in any previous year. During the
rebuilding of the laboratories, it was necessary to conduct the
elementary course in systematic botany at the Botanical Museum,
a room being kindly supplied for the purpose by the Honorary
Curator of the Museum.

The newly built portions of the Herbarium already furnish
convenient work rooms and shelving for the whole library and
more than half of the plant collections, so that the completion
of the rebuilding can be effected with even less interruption to the
scientific activities of the staff or accessibility of the collections.

During the summer of 1911 Professor Fernald, in company with
Professor Karl M. Wiegand of Wellesley College and Mr. Edwin
B. Bartram, and assisted by Mr. H. T. Darlington, made another
highly successful collecting expedition to Newfoundland, exploring
chiefly the eastern-central and southeastern portions and acquiring
not merely a large amount of interesting material for study and
exchange, but also exceptionally telling data regarding plant-
distribution in general and the origin of the Newfoundland flora
in particular, — data which strongly corroborate Professor Fernald's convincing hypothesis of a former land bridge between
Newfoundland and the eastern coast of Nova Scotia and coastal
plain of New England.

The Curator in two southern journeys, from January to May,
made as extensive collections as time and season permitted in the
Bermuda Islands, coastal South Carolina, and " tide-water Vir-

ginia," thereby considerably amplifying the representation of the spring flora of these regions in the Gray Herbarium.

As for many years past the Visiting Committee has shown loyal and helpful interest in the work of the Herbarium, issuing again their annual circular to which 110 contributors gave cordial response in gifts ranging from three to one hundred dollars, donations recorded in the report of the Treasurer.

During the year twenty-nine scientific papers have been published by the Gray Herbarium. As their titles have been fully recorded in the *University Gazette*, they need not be repeated here.

B. L. ROBINSON, *Curator*.

THE BOTANIC GARDEN

To the President of the University: —

Sir, — As Director I have the honor to present my third annual report on the progress and condition of the Botanic Garden.

As a matter of record the report of Mr. Robert Cameron, Head Gardener, is here included: —

The early part of the year was dry and unfavorable for the growth and welfare of the plants in the Garden. Fortunately, copious rains in the fall completely revived them. The fall was exceptionally mild and much work was done in replanting and renovating the order beds.

The winter was very cold, but few losses were sustained.

The spring flowers, such as tulips, hyacinths, and irises, bloomed unusually well and attracted much attention.

June was the driest month we have experienced in many years, and vegetation suffered severely.

The population in the part of Cambridge where the Garden is located has increased in the last decade and consequently the Garden is visited by larger numbers of people, especially in the spring and fall.

School teachers with their classes visit us more frequently than in former years.

Students of the University take much more interest in the plants. This is especially true of those who are studying landscape architecture.

The plants in the greenhouses are all in good, healthy condition.

From J. M. Bailey, Director of the Botanic Garden at Brisbane, Australia, a series of Australian orchids and ferns was received early in the year which added many desirable species of botanical interest to the collections.

As in former years, Messrs. R. & J. Farquhar & Co. presented bulbs and seeds, which have been useful for supplying material for study and decoration.

In addition to supplying specimens for laboratory studies and for the lecture room the collections are beginning to mean more to the students in Botany 1 than heretofore through the influence of supervised excursions. In small sections the students are conducted to the Garden, several times through the spring, and as a result of these excursions it has been found that some of the students return for voluntary study. Professor Osterhout continued to use the laboratory, and the space assigned to him in the greenhouses, for work in Botany 13 and for research.

Mr. B. M. Watson's class in Landscape Architecture 6 met regularly at the Garden on Saturdays from November to April, studying practical horticulture. Aside from the instruction given relative to grafting, propagation by cuttings and the care of seedlings, the students were able by independent observations to become familiar with the more useful and ornamental garden plants.

In connection with the State Forester's Office, the propagation and distribution of the fungus disease, *Entomophthora Aulicae*, of the brown-tail moth larvae was continued. From April 1 to June 30, under the direction of Mr. R. H. Colley, Austin Teaching Fellow in Cryptogamic Botany, the work was carried on in House 14. By the use of improved methods in handling and infecting the caterpillars the distribution of a larger number of diseased larvae was made possible than in any previous season. With the coöperation of the State Forester's Office diseased caterpillars were planted in badly infested areas all over eastern Massachusetts. Besides this distribution approximately one hundred tubes of infected larvae were mailed to private individuals. Under the very favorable weather conditions of May and June the fungus spread rapidly and caused a mortality which in some localities ran as high as 98–100%. This wholesale destruction was also in evidence in areas planted in the fall of 1911, where a marked decrease was found in the number of larvae which survived the fall epidemic and the winter. By June 10th these areas appeared to be practically free from infestation. There is every reason to believe that the propagation and distribution of this fungus disease is materially reducing the number of brown-tail caterpillars in Massachusetts.

In the disease of the chestnut, caused by a fungus parasite which is at present incompletely understood, we have a very serious danger to guard against. Where this disease has appeared the chestnut has been practically exterminated in spite of every remedy applied. In June, in connection with the work being done at the Garden to control the brown-tail and gypsy moths, experiments were started, under the supervision of Dr. Farlow, for the purpose of obtaining a clearer knowledge than we now have of the chestnut blight, with a view to the discovery of some means to hold it in check. In 1906 the fungus which causes the disease was described as a new species under the name *Diaporthe parasitica*. Whether or not this fungus is a new species, its systematic position is at this time of interest and importance, in revealing its origin, whether endemic or exotic.

At the Harvard Experiment Station near Cienfuegos, Cuba, the production of seedling sugar cane was continued and studies of introduced economic plants carried on by Mr. Robert M. Grey. Mr. Grey's monthly reports indicate that the work at the station is progressing satisfactorily. In August, the seedling canes raised in 1912 numbered 2,200. Among this number are several canes which give promise of excellent qualities advantageously combined.

Throughout the year, in connection with the Bureau of Science at Manila, the Director has carried on his studies of the orchid flora of the Philippines. The results of these studies are published from time to time in the *Philippine Journal of Science.*

To maintain the Garden in its present state of efficiency expenditures greatly exceed the income. A substantial increase in invested funds is not only necessary to remove the need for annual subscriptions but to enable the Director to increase the collections and to keep the greenhouses and grounds in first-class condition.

OAKES AMES, *Director.*

THE BOTANICAL MUSEUM

To the President of the University: —

Sir, — I have the honor of presenting the following report on the condition of the Botanical Museum.

Considerable accessions to the stock of illustrative material in Economic Botany have been received during the past year, and a large part of this has already been safely stored in the new form of containers, where it can be conveniently examined as occasion requires. These occasions for consulting our specimens are becoming more frequent, since year by year it is more widely known that our collections are available for comparison and identification of " raw materials."

The space which we can devote to the installation of type-specimens in exhibition-cases is very limited, and therefore it has been found necessary to withdraw from our shelves certain groups of manufactured products, which, although extremely interesting in connection with the plants from which they are derived, belong more strictly in a technological cabinet. For instance, some exceedingly fine illustrations of manila rope have been taken out of the exhibition-case of fibres, to give room to the specimens of untwisted strands. Unquestionably a technological exhibit would prove highly useful in connection with certain of our college courses, but we cannot longer develop this side of our Botanical Museum without throwing the rest out of proportion. For the present, we shall retain in our reserve a great part of these manufactured products, and we shall stand ready to transfer them to an industrial collection at the proper time.

But, wherever it is possible to do so, we shall keep in our cases some of the more striking products, which do not encroach too much on our space, as illustrations of the drift of modern industry. Thus among the newer developments in the cellulose industry, we have installed interesting specimens of artificial silk, produced from wood-pulp or its equivalent, by the three most successful processes.

We are retaining among our forest-products on the exhibition-shelves, certain barks and leaves formerly much used in tanning, but now falling into disuse, on account of their being displaced by the newer chrome methods.   And we shall exhibit for some time longer, illustrative specimens of the madders and indigo which are being crowded out of cultivation by the anilin and alizarin dyes. It must be understood that type-specimens of most of these plant-products are accessible in our store-rooms, in sufficient quantities for physical and chemical investigation.

Very few changes have been made in the collection of fossil-plants, but the specimens selected by Dr. Robert T. Jackson for exhibition on the third floor have been provided with more distinctive labels.

Mr. Rudolph Blaschka states that the next invoice of glass models of flowers will be ready for shipment the coming winter. He had expected to finish this series, consisting of illustrations of insect visits to flowers, some months ago, but the extreme difficulty of constructing the models of insects has delayed him. We have made some changes in the arrangement of a few of the specimens illustrating the economic plants, but without disturbing the general plan.

It is pleasant to note the greatly increased use of this popular display of glass-models by the teachers of our public schools. It is becoming almost impossible to furnish pupils in our cities with good specimens of our common wild flowers: in the Ware collection of Blaschka models the wild flowers are faithfully shown and the principal parts exhibited on an enlarged scale.   The importance of the collection as a synoptic view of our flowering plants will be best realized when it is known that 147 natural families, 520 genera, and 694 species are now fully illustrated. Moreover, practically every important term employed in the description of all Phaenogamia is clearly illustrated in this collection by the roots, stems, and leaves, and by over 2,900 magnified details.   It is gratifying to report that as a rule the school teachers make use of the exhibition-rooms without causing inconvenience to the increasing number of our visitors.   The pamphlet issued for general distribution last year has proved useful, and an enlarged edition is in contemplation.

The most interesting acquisition during the year was a volume of exquisite paintings of all the plants described in Rev. Henry N. Ellacombe's "Plant-lore and Garden-craft of Shakespeare." These water-colors are full of artistic merit.   It has not yet been finally determined how the plates can be most advantageously displayed.   The collection consists of 182 paintings by the late

Miss Rosa M. Towne of Philadelphia, and is the gift to the University from the Estate of William E. Towne of the same city. It gives me pleasure to report that the expenses of the Museum have been met by the gifts of a few friends of the University. No attempt has yet been made towards securing a permanent fund for the maintenance of the Botanical Museum, but it will be absolutely necessary in the near future to provide for the care of the Museum, when its present Curator retires.

GEORGE LINCOLN GOODALE,
Honorary Curator.

THE ARNOLD ARBORETUM

To the President of the University: —

Sir, — I have the honor to submit the following report on the progress and condition of the Arnold Arboretum during the year ending June 30, 1912.

Little new construction has been undertaken during the year, and work in the Arboretum has been largely confined to the care and extension of existing plantations, and to the protection of these and the natural woods from the attacks of destructive insects which in many species abound in the Arboretum. To keep these in check now means much hard work and a large expenditure of money, and greatly increases the difficulty of properly maintaining a garden like the Arboretum.

Mr. William Purdom has completed his three years' contract to explore northern and western China for the Arboretum, and returned to Europe in May. He left Peking late in the winter of 1911 and was able to reach Min-Chau on the T'asho River in southern Kansu in the spring of that year. He was prevented, however, owing to the disturbed condition of the country, from extending his journey to the high mountains surrounding the Monastery of Chusan, near the Tibetan border of Kansu, which it was hoped he would be able to explore. Political disturbances, too, delayed his return journey to Peking and caused the loss of a part of his collections. His three years' explorations, while they did not result in the introduction of a large number of new species of plants, were on the whole successful, and he was able to make valuable contributions to the knowledge of the Chinese flora. His most interesting discovery is, perhaps, the wild form of the Moutan or Tree Peony, which he found growing on a mountain in southern Shensi, in the region believed to be the cradle of the Chinese race. Forms of this Peony have been cultivated for centuries in eastern Asia, where they are among the most beloved of all plants, but the wild origin of the cultivated plant has remained unknown to Americans and Europeans until Purdom found it in 1910 and sent seeds and a few roots to the Arboretum.

The library now contains 26,706 bound volumes and 6,640 unbound pamphlets, 1,959 volumes and 102 pamphlets having been added during the year.

During the year 6,300 sheets have been inserted in the herbarium; and 2,895 sheets of duplicates have been distributed in exchange. In addition to these, sets of duplicates of the dried plants collected by Wilson in China, as far as these have been named, have been acquired by the Smithsonian Institution, the British Museum, the Royal Gardens at Kew and at Edinburgh, the Imperial Botanic Garden at St. Petersburg, the Hamburgische Botanische Staatsinstitute and the Naturhistorisches Hofmuseum at Vienna.

The interchange of plants and seeds with other horticultural and botanical establishments has been continued during the year. 8,052 plants, including grafts and cuttings, and 484 packets of seeds have been distributed as follows: To the United States, 7,244 plants and 153 packets of seeds; to Great Britain, 515 plants and 189 packets of seeds; to the continent of Europe, 293 plants and 116 packets of seeds; to Japan, 26 packets of seeds. There have been received 844 plants and 452 packets of seeds; of these, 767 plants and 161 packets of seeds came from the United States; from the continent of Europe, 77 plants and 111 packets of seeds; from Japan, 32 packets of seeds; from China, 147 packets of seeds; and from New Zealand, 1 packet of seeds.

During the year instruction in dendrology has been given at the Arboretum by Assistant Professor Jack to students in forestry and to a class of twenty-three special students, principally teachers.

Two parts of the *Plantae Wilsonianae*, or about one-third of the work, have been published during the year. This is an enumeration of the woody plants collected by Wilson in China for the Arboretum, with descriptions of the new species and the elaboration of some of the important genera as represented in the whole of China. In this work the staff of the Arboretum has received valuable assistance from several European specialists. Dr. E. Koehne of Berlin has elaborated Philadelphus and Prunus; Dr. E. Janczewski of Krakow, Ribes; Dr. W. O. Focke of Bremen, Rubus; Dr. Th. Loesener of Berlin, Ilex; Dr. F. Gagnepain of Paris, the Vitaceae; and Dr. Camillo Schneider of Vienna, Syringa.

During the year the first volume of the *Bradley Bibliography* has appeared and the printing of the second volume has been completed. This work, which will be finished in five volumes, contains an account of all printed books and of all articles in any way relating to woody plants in periodicals and other serial publications in all languages published before the end of the last century. Volume I includes all botanical publications containing references to these plants, except those which are restricted to a particular family, genus, or species which are found in the second volume. The third volume will contain the titles of publications dealing with the economic products and uses of woody plants, and with arboriculture, including the ornamental value and uses of trees and shrubs. The fourth volume will be devoted to publications on forestry, and the fifth volume will contain an index to all titles enumerated in the work arranged alphabetically according to authors and titles. This work, which has involved a large amount of labor, has been in charge of Mr. Alfred Rehder of the Arboretum staff, who has devoted most of his time to it during the last twelve years and who has examined for it all the principal botanical, horticultural, and forestry libraries in the United States and Europe and obtained the assistance of many European specialists.

Twenty numbers of the *Bulletin of Popular Information* have been issued during the year. The object of this Bulletin is to give at irregular intervals information about plants in the Arboretum of special interest. The Bulletins are issued gratuitously to any one on application and now go to many parts of the United States and to several European countries. The fact that these Bulletins are often reproduced in horticultural journals and in daily papers seems to show an increasing interest in the cultivation of the plants which they describe.

It has only been possible to administer the Arboretum, to increase its activities and to meet the demands which are made on it from all parts of the world by the interest and generosity of many persons living in the neighborhood of Boston and in other parts of the country. Four years ago, following the example of the Massachusetts General Hospital and the Museum of Fine Arts, an effort was made to increase the income of the Arboretum by application to its friends for annual subscriptions. During the year 1908–09 this subscription produced $15,810; in 1909–10 it amounted to $19,110; in 1910–11, to $20,625; and in 1911–12, to $26,755. Annual subscriptions have been usually in sums of $100; a few only have been for smaller amounts, and some have been larger. The success of these subscriptions is largely due to the assistance which I have received in this undertaking from the Committee appointed by the Overseers to visit the Arboretum.

Without the industry, enthusiasm, and influence of the members of this Committee it would have been impossible to continue the development of the Arboretum, and I take this opportunity to express my obligation to them for the help they have given me in carrying out the provisions of the Trust established by the executors of James Arnold.

C. S. SARGENT, Director.

THE CHEMICAL LABORATORY

To the President of the University: —

Sir, — Owing to the death of Professor Sanger, Director of the Chemical Laboratory, in February, Assistant Professor Baxter served as Acting Director for the remainder of the year.

A well-marked and very encouraging increase of about twenty per cent in the total number of students taking courses in chemistry over the number in 1910–11 brought the registration well above the previous maximum of 1904–05. The increase occurred chiefly in the elementary courses, although the advanced courses were almost universally larger than the year before.

The number of research students also was slightly larger. The following subjects were investigated by students under the direction of members of the Division: —

Professor Jackson: Sulphoorthoquinones; iodanil; the action of sodium hydroxide on tetrabromorthoquinone; some reactions of iodtribromnitrobenzol; the replacement of halogen by hydrogen in derivatives of benzol containing the nitro groups and halogens.

Professor Richards: Revisions of the atomic weights of uranium through uranium tetrabromide, of aluminum through aluminum bromide, of carbon through the ratio of sodium carbonate to sodium sulphate, and of silver through the analysis of lithium perchlorate; the compressibility of homologous hydrocarbons; the heats of combustion of homologous hydrocarbons; the heats of neutralization of typical alkalies and acids as determined by adiabatic calorimetry; the electro-motive force of thallium amalgams.

Assistant Professor Baxter: Revisions of the atomic weights of phosphorus by the analysis of phosphorus tribromide, of iron by the reduction of ferric oxide, of arsenic by the titration of arsenious acid against iodic acid, of neodymium by the analysis of neodymium chloride; the preparation of pure praeseodymium salts; the determination of potassium as chloroplatinate; the changes in volume during the solution of certain salts in water.

Assistant Professor Henderson: The racemization of glucose.

Dr. Forbes: The constancy of transference numbers as determined with the use of a partially rectified current; a new apparatus to measure the pressure of corrosive gases at constant volume;

concentration cells involving complex argentichloride ions; the relation between heats of fusion of eutectic mixtures and the heats of fusion of their components; the reduction of chromic acid at a platinum cathode.

Dr. Clarke: Preparation of certain paraffine hydrocarbons in homologous series of hexanes, heptanes, octanes, and nonanes; the splitting of aminobenzhydrols and aminoaryl benzhydrols by halogens; the action of fuming nitric acid on iodanil; the reduction of zinc ores.

Dr. Kelley: Cyclic ketones.

Twenty-one papers were published, chiefly on investigations conducted during 1910–11. The titles of these papers may be found in the *University Gazette*.

The laboratory continued to benefit by the generosity of the Carnegie Institution of Washington from grants in aid of research, of $3,000 to Professor Richards and of $1,000 to Assistant Professor Baxter.

Mrs. Charles R. Sanger has very generously given to the Chemical library a large number of valuable text-books and sets of periodicals which belonged to Professor Sanger.

Work upon the Wolcott Gibbs Memorial Laboratory which was interrupted by the winter was recommenced early in the spring, and the building is rapidly nearing completion, so that it will be ready for occupancy by January 1.

The plans of the Division of Chemistry for a group of new buildings devoted to chemistry were furthered by the gift of $50,000, later increased to not exceeding $60,000, by T. Jefferson Coolidge, '50, to build a laboratory in memory of his son, T. Jefferson Coolidge, Jr., '84. The building will be called the T. Jefferson Coolidge, Jr., Memorial Laboratory. It will be located on Divinity Avenue, near the Wolcott Gibbs Memorial Laboratory, and will resemble the latter building closely in exterior appearance. The new laboratory will be devoted to quantitative analysis, and will contain, besides a lecture room, three class laboratories and six small private laboratories with balance rooms. The foundations have been laid and it is hoped that the walls and roof will be completed before winter, so that the building may be ready for use in September, 1913.

ARTHUR B. LAMB, *Director*.

JEFFERSON PHYSICAL LABORATORY

To the President of the University: —

Sir, — The members of the teaching staff have all been actively engaged in research during the last year. The results of their labors will be found in the appropriate volume of the Contributions from this Laboratory.

Among the graduate students, Mr. Sawtelle has brought a long and difficult piece of work to a successful conclusion. Mr. Royster and Mr. Trueblood have continued their researches in Heat. Mr. Swan has concluded his research in Sound. Mr. Webster has continued his study of the Absorption of Light. Mr. Clark has begun a research in Magnetism, and Mr. Chamberlin has done work on Vacuum Tube Rectifiers for Alternating Currents. Mr. Yabu and Mr. Maddox, students in the Graduate School of Applied Science, have carried on work in Wireless Telegraphy under Professor G. W. Pierce.

This year, the Cutting Fellowship was awarded to Mr. H. M. Trueblood.

Following the policy of Professor Trowbridge, graduate students engaged in research have been allowed free access to the building during the evening and on holidays. At such times, the janitors are not on duty. The risk from fire is increased by the policy. It is hoped that the sprinkler system which has recently been installed will tend to minimize this risk.

The overcrowding from which the elementary laboratories and the class-rooms continue to suffer is chiefly felt because of the lack of ventilation. Owing to the very substantial construction of the building, which makes all changes difficult, the evil cannot be easily remedied.

In conclusion, the Director must repeat his statement of last year: the endowment fund is inadequate for the present needs of the Laboratory.

THEODORE LYMAN, *Director.*

PSYCHOLOGICAL LABORATORY

To the President of the University: —

Sir, — The year in the Psychological Laboratory was characterized by very eager research work carried on by advanced graduates who were all on the road to the Doctor's degree. A list of the investigations which absorbed the chief energy of the Laboratory may indicate the manifoldness of directions in which the psychological experiment is proceeding. Of problems which have essentially theoretical bearing, I may mention the following. Mr. I. L. Williamson studied the fluctuations of memory. The ability to reproduce material which has been learned appears to increase at first after the completion of the learning process by a non-conscious slow organization of the memory dispositions. This change after the learning was studied by a new method, through which the firmness of the memory connections can be established for any given time period. Mr. E. C. Tolman investigated the relations between memory and the feeling tones as they are produced by pleasant and unpleasant sounds, smells, and so on. Mr. P. Rowland tried to develop methods by which the intensity of the will impulse toward particular actions could be measured through the amount of mental resistance which it overcomes. This resistance was set by the known suggestive power of certain objects which demanded opposite actions. Mr. J. W. Bridges approached the field of the psychology of decision. The decisions of individuals vary as to their rapidity, their firmness, their constancy and so on, and the aim was to determine how far these characteristics in the act of decision are correlated to a large number of other mental functions of the personality. Mr. E. R. Riesen was engaged with the question which nowadays is much discussed in experimental psychology, the influence of similarity on the learning process. From studies with similar ideas, he was led to an inquiry into the mutual relations of similar motor processes. A painstaking research in the borderland of psychology and aesthetics was that of Mr. R. C. Givler, who investigated the psychophysical effects of the predominant speech elements of various poets. After an exact statistical analysis of the various consonants and vowels in a large number of English poets, artificially constructed combinations of sounds in rhythm were studied, with subtlest methods in their effect on the system of psychophysical reactions, in order to determine how far the speech elements contribute to the characteristic impressions of the various authors.

Among problems which besides their theoretical interest have a more or less direct relation to the field of applied psychology may be mentioned an investigation by Mr. H. S. Townsend on the psychophysical effect of conscious misstatements with special reference to the time relations of untrue answers by a witness. Another research which may be of consequence for questions of law was that of Mr. G. A. Feingold, who aimed toward the development of methods by which the degree of mental similarity in the impressions from imitations might be measured. In view of the legal uncertainty in determining the justified similarity of goods in the market it seems important to gain objective standards for the appearance of likeness. Mr. J. Elliott, after finishing a shorter investigation concerning reversals in localization of sound, turned to a broad research into the psychophysical conditions of handwriting. In contrast to the popular graphology, he began with exact experimental methods to trace the variations of characteristic elements of writing under a great variety of mental conditions. Miss A. B. Copeland studied under the point of view of vocational guidance the psychophysical tests with which individual differences may be quickly determined.

Besides these investigations in the field of human psychology which were carried on under my own guidance and that of Dr. Langfeld, research work of students in the field of animal psychology conducted by Professor Yerkes included the following. Mr. H. C. Bingham continued his experimental study of size and form perception in chickens. Mr. C. A. Coburn began a study of the transmission of certain mental traits in mice; attention was given especially to wildness, savageness, and certain peculiar vocal expressions.

Of investigations which instructors of the laboratory carried on themselves, Professor Yerkes, in coöperation with Professor J. B. Watson of Johns Hopkins University, completed his study on methods of studying vision in animals. In coöperation with certain other comparative psychologists he undertook a critical study of the maze method in order to effect standardization. He also conducted an experimental investigation concerning acquisition of habits by earth-worms and their relations to the nervous system.   Dr. Langfeld made investigations upon the process of suppression both of movements and ideas under both positive and negative instructions.   My own experimental work, besides the above mentioned investigations carried on with students, was concerned with a development of experimental methods for the determination of the fitness of industrial workers.   I tried to develop experimental methods by which, for instance, motormen of electric railways, employees in the telephone service, employees in the ship service, and so on, may be examined as to their mental suitability.

All the various introductory and training courses of the laboratory and the lecture courses, which also make use of the means of the Laboratory, were well attended.   The elementary psychology course reached such a size that the largest hall in Emerson Hall proved insufficient.   While the courses related to the Laboratory moved along the lines of work in previous years, as far as human psychology was concerned, some changes were introduced in the field of animal psychology.   During the first half-year an introduction to comparative psychology was given as a lecture and demonstration course, and this was followed in the second half-year by a laboratory training course in animal psychology.   It is planned that the lecture course prepare students for the laboratory training course and that it in turn fit them for advanced work in comparative psychology, either in thesis courses or in laboratory courses.   When the plan which is now being developed is perfected, three full courses in comparative psychology will be offered, each year an introductory lecture course, one term, combined with a laboratory training course, one term; secondly, advanced comparative psychology, a thesis course, and thirdly, a research course in the psychological laboratory.

The equipment of the Laboratory has been supplemented in many respects, especially by a large number of devices which the able mechanic of the Laboratory, Mr. Thain, has worked out. The only difficulty with which the Laboratory has still to contend is the continuing lack of an ample fund for the independent publication of the students' work.

HUGO MÜNSTERBERG.

THE OBSERVATORY

To THE PRESIDENT OF THE UNIVERSITY: —

SIR, — The plan of work advocated in recent reports has been greatly improved and extended during the past year. When a method, which commends itself to other astronomers, has been developed, if it can be applied to a large number of objects, results of great value will be achieved. It is of the first importance that the accuracy of the measures shall not be diminished, but with this condition the value is often proportional to the number of objects observed. Examples of such researches are the Revised Draper Catalogue and the Durchmusterung of Selected Areas, described more in detail below. As increased efficiency is of great importance, many of the methods of " Scientific Management " can be applied to advantage. The continual requests for facts which can only be obtained from the Harvard photographs is evidence that these lines of work are approved by astronomers and no other observatory is prepared or inclined to supply this demand. A large number of investigations, some of them requiring several years for their completion, are now in progress here. Another important feature of our present work is the extensive coöperation with other observatories and astronomical associations, both in America and Europe.

The retirement of Professor Arthur Searle, at the age of seventy-five years, deprives the Observatory of an active and efficient officer after a service of forty-three years. His devotion of a quarter of a century of his life to the discussion and reduction of the zone $-10°$ to $-14°$ provides one of the largest contributions of America, to Astronomy. Fortunately, he has been enabled to see this great work practically completed.

The Observatory has suffered a serious loss by the death of Professor A. Lawrence Rotch, Director of the Blue Hill Meteorological Observatory. His friendly coöperation with this Observatory has prevented needless duplication of work and has filled seven volumes of our Annals. These investigations have done much to change Meteorology from the mere work of collecting routine observations to a living science giving us the laws of the atmosphere. His study of the upper air by means of kites and balloons placed him in the front rank in these investigations. It is hoped that his wish, expressed in the Preface to Volume 20 of our Annals, for " the ultimate consolidation of the two institutions," may be fulfilled.

Observatory Instruments

East Equatorial. — The observations with the 15-inch East Equatorial have been made by Professor O. C. Wendell, and have been of the same general character as in previous years. More than nine thousand photometric comparisons have been made, mainly with the polarizing photometer with achromatic prisms. A part of the measurements relate to stars of the Algol type, others to stars whose variability is small, or doubtful, this instrument permitting slight changes to be detected, with certainty. 1,380 settings have been made on Nova Geminorum No. 2, and its comparison stars. A series of measurements, comprising 752 settings, has also been made on S Ursae Majoris while its light was diminishing. The observations of a selected list of Fourth Type stars have been continued, 368 settings having been made. The brightness of the nucleus of Brooks' Comet 1911c was observed on two nights. With a second photometer, adapted to the measure of adjacent objects, four eclipses of Jupiter's satellites have been observed, making 914 in all, and 224 settings have been made on δ Orionis, suspected of variability. Other observations of a miscellaneous character have also been obtained.

Meridian Circle. — The work of this instrument may now be regarded as completed, except that the study of the proper motion of the stars in the zone −10° to −14° is still in progress. Two great investigations have been completed with it, the zone +50° to +55° containing 8,627 stars, and the zone −10° to −14° containing 8,337 stars. Each of these investigations occupied the time of an observer and corps of computers for more than twenty years. The results fill eleven of the quarto volumes of the Annals, and the expense in salaries alone was about a hundred thousand dollars in each case. The instrument is still in use for time observations. It is believed that its work could now be advantageously replaced by photography, and experiments are in progress here with that end in view. It certainly would not be wise to undertake any large investigation with it, in its present condition. Great improvement might be expected by the application to it of methods recently devised.

HENRY DRAPER MEMORIAL

The number of photographs taken with the 11-inch Draper Telescope is 28, making 18,358 in all; with the 8-inch Draper Telescope, 713, making the total number 38,015.   The total number of stellar photographs taken here during the year is 4,155. The first of these instruments has been mounted at Mandeville, Jamaica, where it has been in regular use by Professor W. H. Pickering, mainly in a study of the changes in the surface of the Moon, and in the ellipticity of Jupiter's Satellites.   The atmospheric conditions there appear to be exceptionally good both as regards clearness and steadiness of the air.

Miss Cannon has been appointed Curator of Astronomical Photographs in the place of the late Mrs. Fleming.   From an examination of the spectra she has found four faint stars in which the line $H\beta$ is bright, and twelve stars whose spectra are composite.   The most important work she has undertaken, and one of the largest attempted by this Observatory, is the formation of a Revised Draper Catalogue.   This work will include the class of spectrum, the photometric magnitude and the photographic magnitude of more than a hundred thousand stars distributed over the entire sky.   As a basis for this catalogue Miss Cannon is classifying five thousand stars a month and has now classified 50,024.

The new star in Gemini afforded an excellent example of the value of our collection of photographs.   Two plates taken of the region on March 10, 1912, showed no sign of the star, which appeared at nearly full brightness on two plates taken March 11; on March 12 it was discovered in Norway, and a photograph of its spectrum on March 13 showed that it closely resembled an ordinary star; on March 14 bright lines appeared in its spectrum, and on March 17 the spectrum had entirely changed, and become like those of other Novae.

BOYDEN DEPARTMENT

The Arequipa Station has continued under the charge of Mr. Leon Campbell.   The cloudy weather has seriously interfered with the work, although the conditions have greatly improved, and it seems probable that we shall again have the clear weather of former years.   The number of photographs taken with the 13-inch Boyden Telescope is 29, making 12,988 in all; 792 photographs have been taken with the 8-inch Bache Telescope, making 43,528 in all.   The total number of stellar photographs taken at the station during the year was 2,141.   In coöperation with the Smithsonian Institution, a pyrheliometer was mounted at Arequipa, on August 13, 1912, and during 49 days preceding October 1, 1,584 readings were obtained, on 38 days.

Bruce Photographic Telescope

The number of photographs taken with the 24-inch Bruce Telescope was 105, making a total of 10,614, in all.   Photographs have been obtained of several of the Selected Areas of Kapteyn. Of the 24 equatorial and 118 southern regions, all have now been taken but 30, of which 10 are equatorial, and 20 are southern.

Blue Hill Meteorological Observatory

Professor A. Lawrence Rotch, the Founder and Director of the Observatory, died on April 7, 1912.   Beginning in 1885, by the most assiduous effort, he built up and brought the Observatory to its present important position in the field of meteorology.   Until its formal transfer to the University of Harvard is effected, the Observatory is being maintained and supported by Mrs. Rotch.

The regular observations and records were continued at the Observatory and at its lower station, and the weather forecasts were displayed at the gate daily.   The upper air research was continued and kite-flights were made on twelve days named by the International Commission for Scientific Aeronautics, to a mean maximum altitude of 5,990 feet.   The maximum altitude attained by the meteorograph in any flight was 10,615 feet.   In July and August, Mr. E. G. Linsley, a student in Geology 20f, secured, during fogs, eighteen aerological records by means of kites flown from a motor-boat at Seal Harbor, Maine, as a part of a research on fog commenced during the winter.   Mr. L. A. Wells continued as observer-in-charge.   Mr. A. H. Palmer was succeeded by Mr. C. F. Brooks as research assistant.

Miscellaneous

Needs of the Observatory. — The needs of the Observatory remain the same as in former years.   The greatest need is provision for a number of computers to utilize the vast amount of material contained in the Harvard collection of photographs.   It may be compared to a library of two hundred thousand volumes with only a dozen readers.   Five thousand dollars a year, or any portion of this sum, could be expended to great advantage in this way, and would yield results wholly out of proportion to its amount. This is well illustrated by the acceptable gift of Mr. George R. Agassiz, who supplied the means for employing two additional assistants. Fireproof buildings are also greatly needed to contain the Library and additional photographs. The sum of thirty thousand dollars would be sufficient for this purpose.

Variable Stars. — The organization for the observation of variable stars has greatly increased during the past year. Photographic maps have now been prepared of 582 variable stars, and the magnitudes of a sequence of comparison stars for each have been determined on a uniform scale. It thus becomes easy to estimate directly the brightness of these variables. As a result, 8,443 observations have been received as follows: Amherst College Observatory, 1,276; Mr. M. W. Jacobs, Jr., Harrisburg, Pa., 1,163; Dr. E. Gray, Eldridge, Cal., 998; Mr. W. T. Olcott, Norwich, Conn., 995; Mount Holyoke College Observatory, 787; Mr. J. B. Lacchini, Firenze, Italy, 610; Vassar College Observatory, 468; Mr. E. L. Forsyth, Needles, Cal., 342; Mr. H. W. Vrooman, Kokomo, Indiana, 318; Rev. T. C. H. Bouton, Hudson, N. H., 256; Mr. A. P. C. Craig, Corona, Cal., 229; Miss H. M. Swartz, South Norwalk, Conn., 188; Mr. F. E. Hathorn, Des Moines, Iowa, 182; Mr. S. C. Hunter, New Rochelle, N. Y., 159; Mr. H. C. Bancroft, West Collingswood, N. J., 130; Mr. C. Y. McAteer, Pittsburgh, Pa., 129; Dr. E. Padova, Catania, Italy, 104; Mr. W. P. Hoge, Pasadena, Cal., 56; Mr. W. N. Bixby, Cambridge, Mass., 22; Mr. E. A. Perkins, Lynn, Mass., 21; and Mr. T. Dunham, Jr., Northeast Harbor, Maine, 10.

All those sending their observations here early in each month are mentioned in a series of articles sent to *Popular Astronomy* showing the brightness of each variable. The observations will also be published in the Annals of the Observatory, if they have not been printed elsewhere. In addition to the observations mentioned above, 1,332 were made here, comprising 1,082 by Mr. P. G. O'Reilly, 210 by Miss I. E. Woods, and 40 by Miss M. Harwood. 342 observations were made at Arequipa, by Mr. L. Campbell. The total number is, therefore, 10,117. The important aims are to secure observations, at short intervals, of the principal variables of long period, and to obtain useful results from large numbers of owners of small telescopes whose work, otherwise, might be but of little value. Both of these conditions seem now to be fulfilled in a highly satisfactory manner.

Observatory of the Rev. J. H. Metcalf. — 209 photographs have been taken by Mr. Metcalf and his assistant, with the 12-inch and 6-inch Telescopes, with an average exposure of 70 minutes. The total number of photographs to October 1, 1912, is 1,362. More than a hundred observations of asteroids have been made. Several new ones were found, three of which had their orbits computed by the Rechen Institute of Berlin. One of these proved to be an old asteroid, which had been lost. The other two were new. A zone for following asteroids has been assigned to Mr. Metcalf by the Rechen Institute. Observations in it are now in progress.

The 16-inch Metcalf Telescope has continued in regular use in Cambridge. 720 photographs have been taken, making the total number 2,017. All of the 110 Selected Areas of Kapteyn, north of the Equator, have been photographed except nine, seven systematic, and two special, regions. The determination of the position of the Moon by photography has now become a part of the regular routine work of this instrument. 183 photographs have been taken, making 289 in all. Plans have been completed for the regular measurement and discussion of these plates under the direction of Professor Russell of Princeton.

Additional Investigations. — The total number of unpublished investigations now in progress exceeds forty. Perhaps the most important of these is the determination of the photographic magnitude of the stars on a uniform scale. Miss Leavitt is still continuing the study of a sequence of stars near the North Pole. By the courtesy of the Director of the Mount Wilson Observatory, photographs taken with the 60-inch Telescope have enabled us to extend this work to stars fainter than the twentieth magnitude. This scale is also being transferred to the forty-nine other regions distributed over the sky and including one near the South Pole. The possibility of determining the photographic magnitudes and colors of stars on a uniform scale with an accuracy equal to that of photometric magnitudes, now seems within our reach.

Another research of the greatest importance is the measurement by Professor Kapteyn of all the stars in his Selected Areas. Photographs of the southern regions were taken with the 24-inch Bruce Telescope in Arequipa, those of the northern regions, with the 16-inch Metcalf Telescope in Cambridge. Measures have been made in Groningen of the diameters and positions of 181,497 stars on these photographs. Plans have been completed for the publication of these measurements in our Annals as soon as a satisfactory method has been found for reducing the diameters to photographic magnitudes. It is expected that the total number of stars will be about 300,000, and that they will fill five volumes of our Annals.

Library. — The Library of the Observatory has been increased by 294 volumes and 1,462 pamphlets, making the total number, 13,824 volumes and 32,734 pamphlets. It is scattered through the various rooms of the Observatory, and continues in constant danger of destruction by fire.

Telegraphic Announcements. — Thirty-two telegraphic announcements have been made, mainly relating to the discovery and observation of comets. They are sent to all who wish for them, free of expense beyond that charged in each case by the telegraph company. The messages are generally sent by "Night Letter," and can thus be transmitted in ordinary language, instead of in cipher, without increased expense, and generally without serious delay.

Cablegrams intended for this Observatory should be addressed "Observatory, Boston," and all telegrams "Harvard College Observatory, Cambridge, Mass." All correspondence should be addressed to the Director.

Thirty-five bulletins have been issued, making the total number 501. The bulletins, beginning with No. 501, are now printed, instead of neostyled, with a great improvement in their appearance and legibility, and but little, if any, loss of time. Many interesting facts are communicated to us and are thus distributed without additional charge to those receiving the telegrams. An example of the promptness with which facts of astronomical importance are now made known throughout the world is afforded by the New Star in Gemini which appeared last spring. Although it was first seen in Norway, observations were obtained of it here and at other American observatories the following evening.

Publications. — A large part of the work of this Observatory is devoted to the publication of results in its Annals. During the last year Volumes 47, Part 2; 56, Nos. 6 and 7; 59, Nos. 9 and 10; 61, Part 3; 63, Part 1; 71, No. 2; 72, Nos. 1, 2, and 3, have been distributed; 56, No. 8, Comparison of Objective Prism and Slit Spectrograms, is nearly ready for the printer; 63, Part 2, Sequences of Comparison Stars for 285 Variables, is in preparation; 64, No. 8, Basis of Meridian Photometric Magnitudes, is ready for printing; 67, Catalogue of 8,337 Stars in the Zone $-9°\ 50'$ to $-14°\ 10'$, is completed, and will be distributed as soon as it reaches the Observatory; 71, No. 3, Standard North Polar Sequence, is nearly ready for the printer; **72**, No. **4**, Observations with the Rumford Photometer, is partly printed; **72**, No. **5**, Light Curves of Eros and other Asteroids, has been sent to the printer; **73**, Part **1**, Blue Hill Meteorological Observatory, 1909, is in process of publication and 35 pages are in type; **74**, General Catalogue of Faint Stars, is about one third in type; **75**, Bond Zones of Faint Equatorial Stars, is nearly all in type. A quarto pamphlet of thirty-six pages, giving the contents of the Annals, **1** to **73**, has been distributed, together with a plan for the sale of these volumes at cost. The set of Annals, from **1** to **70**, is therefore completed and distributed with the exception of **56**, No. **8**; **63**, Part **2**; **64**, No. **8**, and **69**, Part **2**. Portions of **71** and **72** have also been distributed.

From a comparison with previous reports it will be seen that good progress has been made in filling the gaps in the series of Annals, and it is expected that further progress will be made during the coming year.

Ten Circulars have been issued whose numbers, titles, and dates are as follows: —

167. Stars having Peculiar Spectra. 31 New Variable Stars. September 20, 1911.
168. The Variable Star, 232848, Z Andromedae. November 10, 1911.
169. Photometric Observations of Asteroids. December 14, 1911.
170. Adopted Photographic Magnitudes of 96 Polar Stars. February 21, 1912.
171. Five Variable Stars having Secondary Minima. February 21, 1912.
172. Photographic Magnitudes of Asteroids. February 22, 1912.
173. Periods of 25 Variable Stars in the Small Magellanic Cloud. March 3, 1912.
174. Variability of the Pole Star. April 8, 1912.
175. Photometric Measurements of Nova Geminorum, No. 2. July 16, 1912.
176. Nova Geminorum, No. 2. July 29, 1912.

Various other publications by officers of the Observatory are described in the *Harvard University Gazette*, each month.

EDWARD C. PICKERING, *Director.*

MUSEUM OF COMPARATIVE ZOÖLOGY

To THE PRESIDENT OF THE UNIVERSITY: —

SIR, — During the academic year 1911–12 nineteen courses were given to two hundred and sixty-three students in Harvard University.

Two of these courses were given by the German Exchange Professor, Dr. Willy Kükenthal of Breslau, and were taken by one hundred and forty-one students.

The instruction in the other courses was given by Professors Mark, Parker, Wheeler, Castle, Rand, East, and Mr. Brues.

The Assistants in these courses were Messrs. C. T. Brues, D. W. Davis, T. R. Goethals, A. O. Gross, S. I. Kornhauser, Jonathan Risser, R. A. Spaeth, and P. W. Whiting.

The Virginia Barret Gibbs Scholarship was held by Mr. James W. Mavor. The income of the Humboldt Fund aided five students, three at the Bermuda Station for Research, and two at the Laboratory of the U. S. Bureau of Fisheries at Woods Hole.

The instruction in Radcliffe was given by Professors Mark and Rand, and Mr. D. W. Davis.

Five courses were given to thirty-four students.

The number of courses and of students in 1910–11 was: — *Harvard*, twenty courses, two hundred and fifty-four students; *Radcliffe*, five courses, thirty-five students.

The instruction in the Department of Geology and Geography was given by Professors Rotch, Ward, Woodworth, Johnson, and Raymond and Dr. Lahee, assisted by Messrs. D. C. Barton, W. P. Haynes, E. G. Linsley, and Edward Wigglesworth. Dr. Lahee also served as Assistant to Professor Woodworth in one course.

Seventeen courses were taken by two hundred and sixty-eight students in Harvard University and three courses were taken by twenty-three students of Radcliffe College.

The income of the Josiah Dwight Whitney Scholarship Fund was used to aid two students in their geological and geographical work in the Rocky Mountain region.

In 1910–11 the number of courses and of students was: — *Harvard*, seventeen courses, three hundred and fifteen students; *Radcliffe*, six courses, twenty-one students.

The resignation of Professor William M. Davis as Sturgis Hooper Professor of Geology will not, it is hoped, deprive his Museum associates of his wise and critical counsel, while Professor Reginald A. Daly's appointment as Professor Davis's successor is an assurance that the high ideals of the Sturgis Hooper professorship will be maintained.

The title of the officers in charge of the collections was changed, by vote of the Museum Faculty, from Assistant to Curator; following this change the Corporation appointed the former Curator of the Museum, Director.

Two additions have been made to the working staff of the Museum, namely, Dr. Percy E. Raymond as Curator of Invertebrate Palaeontology, and Dr. Thomas Barbour as Associate Curator of Reptiles and Amphibians. Dr. Raymond has also been appointed Assistant Professor of Palaeontology in the University. It is anticipated that Professor Raymond's appointments will be of mutual advantage. His previous service with the Carnegie Museum, Pittsburgh, and more recently with the Geological Survey of Canada, together with the resources of the collection and library of this Museum, should attract students. Recent reports of the Museum give ample evidence of Dr. Barbour's interest in the work of the Museum.

On the 28th of May, 1912, Dr. William McM. Woodworth of the Museum staff died in Cambridge. Dr. Woodworth graduated from Harvard in 1888. Appointed in 1889 Assistant in Microscopical Anatomy in the University, he held various offices in the University and the Museum and served continuously from the date of his first appointment until his death. As a privileged Assistant, Dr. Woodworth accompanied Mr. Agassiz on most of his expeditions to the tropics, and thus enjoyed advantages unusual for a zoölogist. A skilled technician and an intelligent collector of books, Dr. Woodworth, by his will, bequeathed to the Museum a number of zoölogical books and pamphlets, a collection of specimens, an especially valuable series of works relating to the South Seas, and also many desirable instruments.

Through the generosity of Mr. George R. Agassiz, fifty thousand dollars ($50,000) has been added to the permanent funds, the income available for the general use of the Museum.

For monetary gifts applicable for the acquisition of desirable material or for the expenses attendant on collecting the same, acknowledgment is due Miss A. A. Sprague, Mrs. Mary L. Russell, Mrs. Louis A. Shaw, and Messrs. Thomas Barbour, C. L. Hay, E. C. Lee, J. C. Phillips, and J. E. Thayer.

As in previous years, valuable specimens of mammals and birds have been added this year to the collections of the Museum through the generosity of Mr. John E. Thayer.   A number of Birds-of-Paradise, some of marked beauty, are among Mr. Thayer's gifts.

To Dr. J. C. Phillips the Museum is indebted for a large series of skulls, horns, and antlers of mammals, mostly game ungulates. Many of these were new to the Museum collections.   Dr. Phillips has also presented very many skins of pheasants and ducks, both terms used in their widest significance, and many of the species of these two important groups of birds included in Dr. Phillips's gift were also not well represented in the collection.   It is to Dr. Phillips's liberality that the Museum owes the services of its second Preparator.   In addition to the above gifts Dr. Phillips was instrumental in securing for the Museum the Bryant-Palmer collection of Javan birds and mammals.   This collection contains nearly one thousand skins of birds, more than one hundred of which were not represented previously in the collection of the Museum.   The Bryant-Palmer accession contains also a few nests and eggs of birds and several hundred mammals, skins and skulls.

Mr. L. J. de G. de Milhau has been good enough to continue his gift of Icelandic birds, and to Dr. S. B. Wolbach the Museum owes several mammals, birds, reptiles, and arachnids obtained while he was attached to the expedition of the Liverpool School of Tropical Medicine to the Gambia in 1911.

Col. John Caswell has sent to the Museum a few mounted birds and a number of mounted heads of African ungulates.   Some of the latter, the Giraffe, Rhinoceros, and Hippopotamus, make a notable addition to the series of heads and horns on exhibition in the Divinity Avenue entrance hall.

There are many specimens of scientific interest among the skeletons, skulls, and casts of bones of vertebrates contained in the kind gift of Dr. R. T. Jackson.

The Museum is indebted to Messrs. J. H. Emerton and R. V. Chamberlin for the type specimens of new species of Araneida and of Myriopoda described by them.

From Dr. P. P. Calvert and Mr. E. B. Williamson the Museum has received a large number of Odonata; many of these are new to the collection and all are most desirable as representing especially rare forms or such as extend the distribution of the species as shown by the Museum collection.

To the U. S. Bureau of Fisheries the Museum is under obligations for two large series of marine invertebrates, both collected during cruises of the "Albatross." One of these collections, the schizopods, obtained during the 1899–1900 and the 1904–05 expeditions, has been in the hands of Dr. H. J. Hansen of Copenhagen. His report forms number 4 of Volume 35 of the Memoirs of the Museum. This collection was received in Cambridge in perfect condition and its value is very much enhanced by Dr. Hansen's careful and exact labelling. The labelling of similar collections is too frequently done in a purely mechanical way by inexperienced hands and is consequently without the authority that original material should have. The second accession, the gift of the Bureau, is the series of Hydromedusae, Scyphomedusae, siphonophores and ctenophores collected by the "Albatross" during 1904–05 and 1906; the reports on the scientific results obtained from these collections have been prepared by Dr. Bigelow.

The Museum is also indebted to Miss H. E. Hooker and to Messrs. W. L. Allen, Henry Hales, A. H. Higginson, and Harry W. Smith for additions to the collection of domestic animals; to Yale University, through Professor Charles Schuchert, for a set of casts of a Pteranodon, and to Mrs. Walter Channing, for some interesting birds.

The thanks of the Museum are due Messrs. Faxon, Brewster, Bangs, Bigelow, and Sayles for their interest in the collections entrusted to their care, and also to Dr. Thomas Barbour, who makes his first report as Associate Curator of Reptiles and Amphibians.

The Museum collections benefit each year from the visits of specialists. Two noteworthy instances during the year may be mentioned. Dr. Kükenthal studied critically a large part of the alcyonarian corals, and received as a loan for a detailed examination at his convenience a small series of foetal whales and sirenians. Dr. Carlos de la Torre has added very many rare and desirable Cuban species of vertebrates and invertebrates to the collection, and the Museum is especially indebted to him for a thorough and critical revision of a very large part of its Cuban land shells. Dr. de la Torre's exact knowledge of the Cuban Pulmonifera and his personal relations with earlier students of West Indian Mollusca enabled him to disentangle many doubtful points of identification and of nomenclature.

The collection of Araneida has been increased in size and improved scientifically by the voluntary work of Miss E. B. Bryant

Field work carried on during the year has contributed a large amount of valuable material. This work may be briefly summarized: —

Mr. W. P. Haynes spent a week searching for fossil insects in the Carboniferous area in the vicinity of Pawtucket, R. I. A cursory examination of the material secured shows that plants, crustaceans, and some tracks, possibly amphibian, were collected; also a few fragmentary specimens that more careful study may prove to be the wings of insects. While in the Rocky Mountain region of Montana, Mr. Haynes also collected a large series of Cambrian, Devonian, and Carboniferous invertebrates. This collection was made mainly in the vicinity of Three Forks; it is as yet unstudied.

By the courtesy of the Hon. G. M. Bowers, U. S. Commissioner of Fisheries, the U. S. F. C. Schooner "Grampus" was placed at Dr. H. B. Bigelow's disposal during July and August. Accompanied by Messrs. W. W. Welsh and H. E. Metcalf as Assistants, Dr. Bigelow undertook a partial survey of the Gulf of Maine. Forty-six off-shore stations were occupied and a large number of interesting observations relative to temperatures, salinities, currents, and plankton were made; these will form the basis for a detailed report. With the coöperation of Professor J. S. Kingsley, a week was devoted to trawling in Casco Bay and vicinity, but with this exception little attention was given to work with the trawl or dredge. The collections obtained by the "Grampus," though rich in a few groups, were not large.

In two short trips, one to George's Bank and a second to eastern and northern Maine, Mr. W. F. Clapp secured enormous series of shells. The series from George's is estimated at 20,000 specimens and that from Maine at 50,000. Some of the species collected by Mr. Clapp are most desirable additions to the collection, and very many of the others provide specimens for advantageous exchanges. Mr. Clapp's trip to George's was made on the trawler "Crest," Captain Green, through the courtesy of the Bay State Fish Company.

Dr. Thomas Barbour worked in western and central Cuba for about two months, January–March, 1912; he secured a large number of new and little-known reptiles and amphibians as well as other interesting vertebrates and invertebrates. He received much kind assistance from Dr. Carlos de la Torre and Messrs. R. M. Grey, Victor Rodiguez, and Jesus Valdivia.

Dr. H. L. Clark, at the kind invitation of Dr. A. G. Mayer of the Marine Biological Department of the Carnegie Institution, Washington, spent six weeks, February and March, 1912, at Montego Bay, Jamaica. While there he collected fifty-seven species of echinoderms, many of them in considerable series; he also preserved a large amount of material that will aid in tracing the history of the postlarval development of the brittle-stars.

With the kind assent of Mr. Clarence L. Hay, Mr. J. L. Peters accompanied the 1910–11 Central American expedition of the Peabody Museum. Working in extreme southern Mexico along the border of British Honduras, Mr. Peters collected many desirable reptiles, birds, and mammals.

During the year Mr. George Nelson of the Museum staff made two trips to the Swan Islands, Caribbean Sea, spending about eight weeks collecting on the two islands. Mr. Nelson secured what is probably a complete series of reptiles, resident birds, and mammals, together with some of the more conspicuous terrestrial invertebrates.

Professor Theodore Lyman left Cambridge late in May for a short trip to the Altai Mountains. He was accompanied by Mr. N. Hollister of the U. S. National Museum. Professor Lyman arranged that the scientific results of his trip should be shared by the U. S. National Museum and the Museum of Comparative Zoölogy. This Museum will receive the birds collected, the U. S. National Museum the mammals. After the publication of the reports, the material will be divided between the two Museums.

The reports of the Curators give the details of the work and of the additions received in the several departments during the year.

Mr. George Nelson's collecting trips to the Swan Islands have been mentioned already. His work at the Museum has been directed chiefly toward the improvement of the exhibition collections of vertebrates. He has mounted a number of recent reptiles, birds, and mammals, among the last a specimen of Père David's Milou Deer, *Elaphurus davidianus;* he has completed the remounting of the mammalian skeletons, with the exception of the largest specimens, and has also remounted many skeletons of birds. His time is not infrequently given up to photographic work, either for the illustration of Museum publications or in answer to the requests of scientific institutions and investigators.

Mr. W. R. Zappey has mounted a number of birds and mammals for exhibition; the more noteworthy of the latter are: — a male

Impala, *Aepyceros melampus suava*, from Guaso Nyiro, British East Africa, a gift of Dr. William Lord Smith, and an East Tibetan Serow, *Capricornis sumatrensis milne edwardsi*, shot by Mr. Zappey at Tachienlu, and a gift to the Museum from Mr. J. E. Thayer. Mr. Zappey has also accomplished in a most satisfactory way a large amount of taxidermic drudgery.

Since April, 1912, Mr. J. D. Sornborger has worked conscientiously upon the osteological specimens received in recent years.

As for several years assistance in addition to the Museum staff has been employed, from time to time, for the care and development of the research collections. Dr. G. M. Allen, as in recent years, has worked for three days of each week upon the collection of mammals. He has completed a revision of the collection of skins; with the exception of a few recent accessions, the entire series is arranged and card catalogued. Dr. Allen has also begun the incorporation of the fossil Mammalia with the osteological specimens of recent forms.

Mr. W. F. Clapp's work upon the Mollusca has been confined in large part to the North American Pulmonifera, and to such aid as he could give Dr. de la Torre in the revision of the Cuban land shells. Mr. Clapp's great success in collecting has been referred to.

Since October, 1911, Miss Elvira Wood has worked upon the collection of fossil crinoids. This collection, with the exception of the Camerata, has been rearranged according to the 1900 English translation of Zittel; the classification of Wachsmuth and Springer has been used for the Camerata. With the rearrangement, the work of identification, verification of previous identifications, and the relabelling of the specimens has been effected. Many specimens have been developed, and others repaired. All the types and figured specimens have been compared with the original descriptions and figures, and catalogued.

Three new cases have been built in the exhibition halls and the many new accessions to the research collections have necessitated additional cases for the collections of echinoderms, insects, and birds. In two of the new cases in the gallery devoted to the North American fauna, the invertebrates and lower vertebrates have been rearranged. The improved methods of mounting fishes for exhibition have been very marked during recent years. With due care these methods prove satisfactory for large and medium sized specimens, but have failed hitherto for small fishes. Recently, however, Mr. Nelson has mounted specimens of the Redside

Darter, *Boleichthys fusiformis*, less than two inches in length, which are in all respects masterly pieces of taxidermy, by far the finest mounted fishes in the Museum.

By purchase the Museum has acquired the W. G. Dietz collection of Microlepidoptera. This collection is rich in types, in series of specimens, and in specimens of recently described species new to the Museum. With the Chambers and Zeller material, the Dietz collection makes the Museum series of Palaearctic and Nearctic forms a large and important one.

The Library consists of 49,155 volumes and 45,535 pamphlets; 1,136 volumes and 1,093 pamphlets have been added during the year.

The publications for the year include seven numbers of the Memoirs, thirteen numbers of the Bulletin, and the Annual Report, a total of 1,229 (907 quarto, 322 octavo) pages, and 156 (133 quarto, 23 octavo) plates. One number of the Bulletin contains the third annual report of the Harvard Seismographic Station, and four numbers contain Contributions from the Zoölogical Laboratory. Three numbers of the Bulletin and six numbers of the Memoirs contain Reports on the scientific results of the expeditions carried on under Mr. Agassiz's direction, and five numbers of the Bulletin and one number of the Memoirs represent work based upon Museum collections.

The Corporation has granted, as in recent years, the sum of $350, to assist in the publication of contributions from the Zoölogical and Geological Laboratories.

By vote of the Corporation (13 November, 1911), "the buildings of the Museum of Comparative Zoölogy" will be known hereafter as Agassiz Hall.

SAMUEL HENSHAW, *Director*.

THE ZOÖLOGICAL LABORATORY

To the President of the University: —

Sir, — The Department of Zoölogy was favored during the past year by the presence of the German Exchange Professor selected for 1911–12, — Doctor Willy Kükenthal, Professor of Zoölogy and Director of the Zoölogical Museum at the University of Breslau. His term of service at Harvard fell in the first half-year, during which time he conducted, in German, one course for advanced students, and gave in English the lectures in the elementary course on general zoölogy. With this exception, and the changes due to alternation of certain courses in successive years, the courses in zoölogy were substantially the same as in 1910–11.

The tables which follow show the number of students in each of the several classes who were enrolled in the zoölogical courses during the year 1911–12, — the first for students in Harvard University, the second for students in Radcliffe College.

TABLE I

Courses 1911-12	Graduate A. & S.	Graduate Ap. Sci.	Senior	Junior	Soph.	Fresh.	Special	Uncl.	Total
Zoölogy 1	3	. . .	8	19	36	65	3	4	138
" 2	3	. . .	5	6	11	3	1	. . .	29
" 3	1	. . .	5	5	1	1	. . .	1	14
" 4	1	. . .	3	3	1	1	. . .	1	10
" 5b	2	1	3	. . .	1	. . .	. . .	1	8
" 7a	1	1	. . .	. . .	. . .	. . .	. . .	. . .	2
" 7b	1	1	. . .	. . .	. . .	. . .	. . .	. . .	2
" 7c	. . .	. . .	2	. . .	. . .	. . .	. . .	. . .	2*
" 7d	. . .	5	. . .	. . .	. . .	. . .	1	. . .	6*
" 11	4	2	4	2	1	1	. . .	. . .	14
" 12	2	1	. . .	1	. . .	. . .	. . .	. . .	4
" 14a	3	1	2	2	1	. . .	. . .	1	10
" 17	2	. . .	. . .	. . .	. . .	. . .	. . .	. . .	2
" 19	2	. . .	1	. . .	. . .	. . .	. . .	. . .	3
" 20a, b	4	. . .	. . .	. . .	. . .	. . .	. . .	. . .	4
" 20c	4	. . .	. . .	. . .	. . .	. . .	. . .	. . .	4
" 20d	. . .	5	. . .	. . .	. . .	. . .	. . .	. . .	5
" 20f	. . .	5	. . .	. . .	. . .	. . .	. . .	. . .	5*
" 20g	1	. . .	. . .	. . .	. . .	. . .	. . .	. . .	1
Sums ..	34	22	33	38	52	71	5	8	263

* These numbers include students enrolled in the summer courses.

TABLE II

Courses 1911–12	Gr.	Senior	Junior	Soph.	Fresh.	Special	Total
Zoölogy 1	. . .	1	6	2	12	2	23
" 2	1	. . .	. . .	2	2	. . .	5
" 4	. . .	. . .	1	. . .	. . .	1	2
5b	2	. . .	. . .	. . .	. . .	1	3
" 14a	. . .	. . .	. . .	. . .	. . .	1	1
Sums	3	1	7	4	14	5	34

Nineteen students (nine registered in the Graduate School of Arts and Sciences and ten in the Graduate School of Applied Science) were enrolled in courses of research, four each under supervision of Professors Mark and Parker, five each under Professors Wheeler and Castle, and one under Assistant Professor Rand.

Two of these, named below, completed the requirements for the degree of Doctor of Philosophy, which was conferred on them in June. The thesis of Alfred O. Gross was entitled "The Reactions of Arthropods to Monochromatic Lights of Equal Intensities," and that of Sidney I. Kornhauser, "A Comparative Study of the Chromosomes in the Spermatogenesis of Enchenopa binotata (Say) and Enchenopa (Campylenchia Stål) curvata (Fabr.)." The thesis of Donald W. Davis, entitled "Asexual Multiplication and Regeneration in Sagartia luciae Verrill," was approved, and Mr. Davis will come up later for his final examination. Mr. Samuel C. Palmer, whose thesis was mentioned in the last report, received the degree of Ph.D. at mid-year.

Three students were granted aid from the income of the Humboldt Fund to the amount of $205.71 while carrying on work at the Bermuda Biological Station, and two to the amount of $61.71 while working at Woods Hole.

The Bermuda Biological Station was open from June 24 till August 10. Of the four persons enrolled, three were connected with Harvard University. Two numbers of the Contributions from the Station were published during the year.

In November Professor Kükenthal presented before the National Academy of Science, as guest at its meeting in New York City, a paper subsequently published as one (No. 230) of the Contributions from the Zoölogical Laboratory.

In March Professor Parker read by invitation a paper entitled " Sensory Appropriation, as Illustrated by the Organs of Taste in Vertebrates " at the centennial celebration of the founding of the Philadelphia Academy of Natural Sciences, and in May he gave an address before the Biological Club of Trinity College, Hartford, on " The Nature of the Primitive Nervous System."

The Zoölogical Club held twenty-four meetings, at which twenty-two original papers and fourteen reviews were presented.

During the year forty-six zoölogical papers, including those in applied zoölogy, have been published.   Their titles have been recorded in the *University Gazette* and in part in the Report of the Director of the Museum of Comparative Zoölogy.

EDWARD L. MARK, *Director.*

MINERALOGICAL MUSEUM AND LABORATORIES OF MINERALOGY AND PETROGRAPHY

To the President of the University: —

Sir, — Besides the addition of individual specimens from various sources the Museum has been enabled to do its own collecting on a large scale through the generosity of Mr. Albert F. Holden, Class of '88, who provided a considerable sum of money for that purpose. · Accordingly Professor Palache visited last summer the localities of New Hampshire and Maine famous for their beryls, tourmalines, and a number of rarer minerals, and obtained a large amount of material for exhibition and research. Mr. Holden also gave a large New Hampshire beryl of great beauty and a huge celestite group from Ohio. Alfred Mosely, Esq., of London, obtained from the De Beers Mining Co. of Kimberley a valuable series illustrating the occurrence of the diamond. The Curator purchased a local mineral collection of some 600 specimens. Four new meteorites were given to that collection at a cost to the donor of $1,000; two being representatives of recent daylight falls in the United States. The Curator visited the Corundum mines of Southern Ontario and the gold districts in the north of that province, obtaining some good material. He has described under the name, "Sheridanite," a new variety of the mineral chlorite, from Wyoming.

JOHN E. WOLFF, *Curator.*

THE PEABODY MUSEUM OF AMERICAN ARCHAE-
OLOGY AND ETHNOLOGY

To the President of the University: —

Sir, — The matter of greatest importance to the Museum at the present time is the success of the Committee appointed by the Corporation to secure the means for the completion of the University Museum building. When the money is obtained and the building is completed, the original plan of the Museum, made by Louis Agassiz fifty-three years ago, will have been carried out. The additional space to be provided is allotted to the Anthropological Section of the University Museum, and will give the long desired room for its further development. The plans provide for the addition to the Peabody Museum of five exhibition halls, each 100 by 60 feet, a stack room for the library, several much needed work rooms and offices, a photographic room, an elevator, and other conveniences.

During the past year the Museum has continued its explorations in several fields. Acting under the Committee for Central American Research, from January to June Mr. R. E. Merwin, Field Director of the Central American Expedition, Mr. C. L. Hay, Chief Assistant, and Mr. J. L. Peters, Zoölogist, were exploring the region north of the Hondo River, the boundary line between Yucatan and British Honduras. Several prehistoric Maya cities were discovered and many photographs were taken of ruins heretofore unknown. A thorough search was made for stelae and hieroglyphic inscriptions which seem to be very rare in the region explored. Mr. Merwin is now preparing a report on the expedition which will be published as a Museum Memoir.

Mr. A. V. Kidder, Austin Teaching Fellow, in continuation of his studies of the several culture groups of the ancient peoples of the pueblos and cliff dwellings of New Mexico, Colorado, Nevada, and Utah, visited about 100 ancient sites and secured much material for study, particularly in relation to the designs on the pottery. He also obtained a good collection of old pottery from the existing pueblos in New Mexico, and an important lot of objects from the cliff houses in the Navajo mountains.

Mr. F. H. Sterns, Hemenway Fellow, has been engaged in a study of the prehistoric sites in Douglas County, Nebraska.

These consist of more or less extended groups of earth circles and depressions covering an area of about seven square miles in Douglas County. There are other similar groups in Washington County and on the other side of the Missouri River in Iowa. The thorough exploration of three of these sites showed them to be ruins of rectangular habitations. Many objects of pottery, stone and bone were found and brought to the Museum for study. Mr. Sterns is preparing a map showing the distribution of these habitation sites which extend over this large area. In connection with Mr. R. F. Gilder of Omaha, Mr. Sterns explored one house site in Sarpy County where human bones were found. Mr. Gilder kindly added to the collection obtained for the Museum the collection of human bones and other objects he had previously found at this site.

Mr. S. J. Guernsey in continuation of his archaeological researches in the valley of Charles River has discovered several rock shelters, and three pits containing caches of stone implements. An interesting site on the grounds of the U. S. Arsenal was explored by the kind permission of the Commandant. The Metropolitan Park Commissioners also have shown their interest in these researches by granting permission to explore an Indian rock shelter on the park near Newton Lower Falls. There are many old Indian sites in the valley and the Museum solicits information of any that may be known or hereafter discovered, that the Indian occupation of the valley may be studied and the sites mapped. Information is also desired of the location of Indian village sites, shell heaps, or burial places in other parts of the state. Stone implements picked up on the surface will be welcome, as they are of interest in many ways and often indicate an ancient village site. Mr. Guernsey also found and examined three Indian burial places, two village sites, and several shell heaps at Martha's Vineyard.

Mr. Ernest Volk has continued the explorations in the Delaware Valley. Taking advantage of numerous excavations in the glacial gravels that have been made for foundations of buildings and by the Pennsylvania Railroad, as well as excavations in the bottom of the Delaware River itself, he has obtained interesting results both geological and archaeological. The Museum is indebted to the Duke of Loubat and Dr. Peabody for the means of carrying on this research.

Dr. Charles Peabody has been in Europe during a portion of the year, and he has made trips to certain archaeological sites in

England and on the Continent.   He has secured by his own
collecting, by gifts of friends, and by purchase, several collections
for the division of European Archaeology of which he is in charge.
One large and valuable collection, which he secured by purchase
and presented to the Museum, is from the Cavern of Espélugues,
Lourdes, France.   This collection of stone and bone implements
of various kinds includes many carved bones, and is a very important addition to our palaeolithic collection from Europe.   Dr.
Peabody represented the Museum and presented papers at the
Anthropological Congresses held at London, Angoulême, Geneva,
and Rome during the past summer.   He was also an official
delegate from the United States to the International Congress of
Prehistoric Anthropology and Archaeology at Geneva.

Professor Henry Williamson Haynes, who died on February
16, 1912, was an early friend of the Museum.   He was sincerely
interested in its work and development and served on the Museum
Visiting Committee from the time that committee was appointed
by the Board of Overseers in 1890.   By his will he bequeathed to
the Museum his private collections of prehistoric archaeology and
his books and pamphlets relating to archaeology and ethnology.
Professor Haynes' collections were made by himself during his
travels in Egypt, France, Switzerland, Italy, Greece, Austria,
Hungary, Denmark, Sweden, England, and Ireland, as well as in
various parts of our own country.   It was Professor Haynes who
first brought to this country a series of implements of palaeolithic
forms from Egypt.   These he secured in 1877 and described and
illustrated in the Memoirs of the American Academy of Arts and
Sciences in 1881.   The only specimens in this country of the
much discussed flints or "pseudo-eoliths" from Theney are
also in the collection.   His archaeological collecting trips in Europe
began in 1873 and continued nearly to the time of his death.   In
August, 1911, he brought home the last specimens to be added
to his already large museum which overflowed one good-sized
room in his home.   For several years Professor Haynes had given
to the Museum fifty dollars annually for binding serials in the
library.   By his will he left $1,000 as a fund, the income of which,
by vote of the Museum Faculty, will be devoted to the same
purpose.

From Mrs. N. E. Baylies the Museum has received one thousand
dollars to be kept as a fund in memory of the late Francis C.
Lowell, who was a Trustee of the Peabody Funds and later a
member of the Faculty of the Museum.

The Museum has also received its portion of the income for the year of the bequest of Eliza O. and Mary P. Ropes to Harvard University.

For current expenses, for the purchase of books, repairs of the halls, and for special explorations, independent of the Central American Expeditions, there have been gifts amounting to $2,435.63, which are recorded in the report of the Treasurer of the University.

The income of the Huntington Frothingham Wolcott Fund was applied to the purchase of several small lots of Indian objects and ethnological collections from British Guiana, Africa, and the Pacific Islands.

The income of the Henry C. Warren Fund for Explorations was used for several limited explorations in this country.

The income of the Susan C. Warren Fund was in part used for the construction of cases and in part for current expenses.

A portion of the income of the Mary Hemenway Fund for Archaeology was devoted to the salary of the Hemenway Assistant in Archaeology and for Mr. Kidder's researches in the pueblo region of the Southwest.

In addition to the collection received by the bequest of Professor Haynes, many important and, in several instances, unique specimens of great value have been received as gifts. These gifts can only be briefly mentioned here.

From Mr. Lewis H. Farlow, a collection illustrating the customs of the Moki Indians of Arizona and the Pueblo Indians of the Rio Grande region of New Mexico, and many old and rare objects from the Apache, Navajo, Ute, Cocopa, Mono, Shasta, and Paiute tribes; from Dr. Charles Peabody, about 2,000 specimens, principally of bone and stone, from various places in France, the greater part being from the Cavern of Espélugues, Lourdes; from Mr. Charles P. Bowditch, Japanese prayers and charms; from General George M. Sternberg, U. S. A., through Dr. H. P. Walcott, three medicine masks and a medicine man in miniature, carved in wood, from the Northwest Coast Indians; from Dr. Thomas Barbour, a decorated skull from Vella Lavella Island, Solomon Group, a decorated skull from the Namau District, Papuan Gulf, New Guinea, and three shrunken human heads from the Jivaro Indians of Peru and Ecuador; from Mr. Clarence L. Hay, a shrunken head of a Rio Santiago Indian obtained from the Aguaruna Indians of northern Peru; from Mr. Oric Bates, weapons and a fringed leather apron from the Egyptian Sudan, and a throwing stick from near Bor, White Nile; from Captain W. I.

Moore, six pieces of Peruvian pottery, a number of ethnological specimens from Samoa and the Solomon Islands, and 50 photographs of ethnological types from various countries; from Dr. H. F. Lawrence, U. S. N., through Dr. L. C. Jones, tapa cloth, a kava strainer, kava root and native tobacco from Samoa, a mat from Wallis Island and tapa cloth from the Horne Islands; from Mr. Alanson Skinner, a boy's beaded belt and a birchbark box from the Menominee Indians, a pair of Cayuga moccasins, and 22 photographs of the Menominee Indians; from Mr. Wheeler Sammons, a slate box, six pottery dishes, and explosive arrows from Korea; from Mr. Clarence B. Moore, a representative lot of pottery from the burial mounds of Arkansas; from Dr. Langdon Warner, a bone necklace and a bow from Luzon; from Dr. F. G. Speck, a bone snowshoe needle and a bone die for plate and dice game of the Penobscot Indians; from Miss Ellen M. Cram, a Zulu snuff box; from Mr. Griscom Bettle, 40 chipped implements and a collection of potsherds from Florida; from Mrs. Frances W. Boyden, 17 native weapons from the southern Philippine Islands; from Mr. Frank Wachter, beads, bracelet, pipe and shell ornaments from Indian grave at Trenton, N. J.; from Professor J. B. Woodworth, pottery cup from Teotihuacan, Mexico, chipped implements from old French and Indian fort at Schuylerville, N. Y., stone adze from Lexington, Mass.; from the Misses Norton, 52 pottery heads from Teotihuacan, Mexico, collected by A. F. Bandelier about 1875; from Miss Grace Norton, a cooking basket of the Pomo Indians; from Miss Edith Morrill Hooper, a stone adze from Sebasticook River; from Mr. Philip Hinkle, a cast of the "Cincinnati Tablet"; from Dr. R. B. Dixon, tapa cloth from the Fiji Islands; from Rev. Perley C. Grant, stone adze from Enfield, N. H.; from Mr. H. T. Deane, bones from an Indian grave, Prouts Neck, Maine; from Dr. Carlos de la Torre, a stone adze, three human crania and other bones from caves in Cuba; from Señor Ivan Ciseo Moreno, a stone axe and a shell spoon from Cuba; from Señor Tomas Mora, five stone axe blades from Fajado, Porto Rico; from Mrs. H. W. Price, two stone blades from North Island, New Zealand; from Professor Harrison W. Smith, a cliff-dweller's skull, Colorado, basketry, clothing, weapons, models of a boat and dwelling, and other objects illustrating the life of the natives of Borneo; from Mrs. Herbert Clarke Emery, a stone metate, pottery, shell objects and two ceremonial axes from Nicaragua and Costa Rica, pottery and three gold ornaments from Colombia, also modern pottery and carved calabash cups from

Nicaragua and Colombia; from Dr. C. C. Abbott, several stone implements and bones from the yellow soil at Trenton, N. J.; from Miss Grace Nicholson, 25 photographs taken among the Paiute, Maidu and Pomo Indians of California; from Dr. Thomas Barbour, a book of photographs of Pacific Island natives from negatives by A. E. Pratt and enlargements from copies of other photographs from negatives purchased by the late Dr. C. G. Weld during his visits to Samoa, New Zealand, and Australia; from Mr. S. V. Kidder, 73 photographs of pueblo pottery mostly from New Mexico; from Mr. George W. Nash, 13 photographs of Indians taken in the early days of the wet plate process; from Mr. Charles P. Bowditch, photographs of pictographs from Arizona and California, 211 lantern slides, mostly Maya subjects; from the Buffalo Society of Natural Sciences, four lantern slides of bone-pits in Orangeport, N. Y.; from Mr. George D. Markham, a fine miniature portrait of George Peabody, the founder of the Museum.

On request of the Trustees of the Museum of Fine Arts and by vote of the Faculty of the Museum, an exhibit illustrating the artistic work of the prehistoric peoples of Central America was made in a special room at the Art Museum, from April 16 to May 16. The objects were selected from our Central American collection by Dr. Denman W. Ross. The exhibit comprised many carvings in stone and ornaments made of stone, particularly of jadeite; ornaments in bone, shell, wood, copper, and gold; and pottery of various shapes and ornamentation in color. This exhibit, which attracted much attention and was visited by 5,400 persons, proved a surprise to most of the visitors and acted as an incentive to visit the Peabody Museum for further examination of the prehistoric art of America. On the opening day of the exhibit, Dr. Tozzer, Assistant in Central American Archaeology, gave a lecture, illustrated by lantern slides, on the ruined Maya cities. This was followed by remarks by Dr. Ross, who pointed out many artistic features of special interest in the objects exhibited.

Much work has been accomplished by the assistants in the Museum in cataloguing and caring for the numerous collections received during the year. Mr. Willoughby, Assistant Curator, assisted by Mr. Guernsey, has reinstalled the collections from Central America and Mexico. This hall, thanks to Mr. Hemenway, has been renovated and repainted. The rearrangement has enabled us to make a much larger exhibit of the collections obtained by the Museum Expeditions of recent years. Several new exhibits have been placed in the South American and African rooms, and numerous specimens have been added to the North American gallery. Many printed labels have been added to the exhibits during the year. Mr. Willoughby has also superintended the construction of a miniature house group of the Seminole Indians of the Florida Everglades from data and photographs furnished by Mr. Alanson Skinner who had recently returned from an exploration of that region for the American Museum of Natural History.

For several months preceding the death of Professor Haynes, Dr. Charles Peabody spent much time with him in the preparation of notes on the specimens in the Haynes collection which were to come to the Museum.

Assistant Professor Dixon, Assistant in Ethnology and Librarian of the Museum, has leave of absence from the University for 1912–13 to travel in the East in connection with his new course on the Ethnography of Asia. In his absence Mr. Carroll, Library Assistant, has prepared the report on the Library for Librarian Lane. The Library now contains 4,800 volumes and 4,497 pamphlets. In addition to the Haynes bequest, the Library has received many gifts of importance, including 73 volumes and 169 pamphlets from Mr. Charles P. Bowditch, and gifts of money from Mr. John B. Stetson, Jr., and Mr. Clarence L. Hay for the purchase of two important Russian anthropological journals. Two new stacks have been added to the Library and there is now no further possibility of extension of the Library except by the completion of the University Museum building.

F. W. PUTNAM,
Honorary Curator of the Museum.

THE SEMITIC MUSEUM

To the President of the University: —

Sir, — The death of Dr. John Orne, Curator of Arabic Manuscripts in the Semitic Museum, occurred on November 11, 1911. Dr. Orne was for many years a teacher of Chemistry and Physics in the Cambridge High School, but his favorite study was Arabic. His office of curator was honorary, and was created by the Corporation in recognition of his voluntary work on the manuscripts. But while honorary, the office was no sinecure. Dr. Orne gave much time to the study of the manuscripts, and prepared several volumes filled with careful descriptions of their condition and contents.

A year ago the Department was much in need of an additional instructor. Through the generosity of a friend, this need has been met by the appointment of Mr. Martin Sprengling, who is now with us conducting courses in Hebrew and Aramaic.

It may not be inappropriate to mention a new honor which has come to Professor Crawford H. Toy, *Emeritus*, long a member of the Department. A volume of Studies in the History of Religions, presented to him by pupils, colleagues, and friends, was published early in November by the Macmillan Company of New York. Of the sixteen essays in the volume six are contributed by colleagues in Harvard University. The volume is intended to be an expression of affection for the man and of admiration for his work.

The growth of the Semitic Museum for the past year has been mainly in additions to its collections of inscriptions from Babylonia and of specimens of wood from Palestine. The Museum fulfils a useful function in furnishing material for illustrating the Semitic instruction. It is also much visited by classes in schools and colleges and by the public.

In the year 1911–12 William E. M. Aitken, who took his Ph.D. degree with us in June, 1911, held the Joseph Henry Thayer Scholarship in the American Archaeological School at Jerusalem. For the current year Harry Wolfson, '11, is holder of a Sheldon Fellowship, and is spending the year abroad studying Mediaeval Jewish Philosophy.

The report of a year ago mentioned the desirability of the publication of a series of Semitic studies in connection with the Department. Since then the Corporation has voted its approval, and has appointed a committee to have charge of the new series, which will consist of occasional volumes in the field of Semitic exploration, philology, literature, history, and religion.

Volume III has recently appeared, and bears the imprint of the University and of the J. C. Hinrichs'sche Buchhandlung, of Leipzig. The title is "Sumerian Tablets in the Harvard Semitic Museum, Part 1, Chiefly from the Reigns of Lugalanda and Urukagina of Lagash. Copied, with Introduction and Index of Names of Persons, by Mary Inda Hussey, Ph.D." There are thirty-six pages of Introduction and Index, seventy-five lithographed plates of the cuneiform texts, and six photographic plates. The Hon. Jacob H. Schiff, who has done so much to foster Semitic research at Harvard, has generously borne the cost of the publication.

Volumes I and II in the series are to give the account of the Harvard expedition to Samaria in the years 1908–10. The appearance of these volumes has been delayed by conditions beyond the control of the editorial committee. I am glad to report that the manuscript has now (December, 1912,) been received. The committee will use all possible despatch in getting the work through the press.

There has been no exploration at Samaria since 1910. It is most desirable that the work should be resumed, either by the University or by other responsible parties. And when the importance of the site is more widely recognized there ought to be no difficulty in finding the means.

DAVID G. LYON, *Curator.*

THE FOGG ART MUSEUM

To the President of the University: —

Sir, — I have the honor to present the following report on the Fogg Art Museum for the year 1911–12.

This year the following works of art have been received as gifts: from Alfred Atmore Pope, Esq., of Farmington, Conn., a Tondo of the late Italian school, representing the Adoration of the Shepherds; from Paul J. Sachs, of the Class of 1900, 12 etchings by Herman A. Webster, which complete the collection of Webster's work to date, 11 lithographs by Joseph Pennell, 6 lithographs by Alexandre Calame, and one etching by Jules Ferdinand Jacquemart; from the Misses Norton, 38 objects, including Greek vases, terra-cottas, etc.; from the estate of the Rev. Edward H. Hall, of the Class of 1851, four small drawings and two portions of pages of a Choral; and from R. Ederbeimer, the Holy Family, an engraving by Albrecht Altdörfer.

Five prints have been added to the Gray Collection by purchase: The Adoration of the Magi and S. Thomas, engravings by Martin Schongauer; Dumbarton Rock, Leader Sea-Piece, and Morpeth, etchings from the series of Turner's Liber Studiorum. Three prints have been purchased for the Randall Collection, namely: The Climbers, engraving by Marcantonio after Michelangelo (this reproduces a portion of the famous cartoon of the "Battle with the Pisans," which was executed by Michelangelo in preparation for his proposed fresco in the Council Hall of the Palazzo Vecchio; the fresco was never painted, the cartoon disappeared, and the print by Marcantonio is one of the few remaining traces of this work of genius); a fine impression of the Judgment of Paris, also by Marcantonio, after Raphael; and Holy Island Cathedral, etching by Turner for the Liber Studiorum.

The Museum has received the following objects as loans: a Tondo, representing the Mystic Marriage of S. Catherine, which was formerly attributed to Filippino Lippi, but now is thought to be by Raffaelino di Carli, lent by Mrs. Francis P. Nash; a Madonna and Child with Angels, by Sano di Pietro, a water-color painting by Dante Gabriel Rossetti, called "Before the Battle," a Venetian Scene by Francesco Guardi, and a Risen Christ by William Blake, all lent by the Misses Norton; a Madonna and Child of the Florentine school, a Madonna and Child of the Venetian school, and an Annunciation attributed to Lazzaro Bastiani, lent by Hervey E. Wetzel, of the Class of 1911; a German painting of the sixteenth century, representing the weighing of a human soul by three saints, and an early Flemish copy of Michelangelo's Holy Family, lent by the Museum of Fine Arts, Boston; an oil marine by Daubigny, lent by Mrs. Warren K. Blodgett; and 13 Dürer prints, lent by Francis Bullard, of the Class of 1886, for the exhibition of early German engraving.

In March, 1912, the exhibition of nineteenth century etchings in the Print Room was replaced by an exhibition of the works of the fifteenth century German engravers and Dürer.

The photograph department has received as gifts 85 photographs from Mr. Bernhard Berenson, 263 from the Haynes bequest to the Classical Department, and 6 from other sources, making a total of 354. 121 photographs were purchased, so that the photograph collection at present numbers 43,783. 313 photographs have been catalogued during the year, and in the department of Italian painting approximately 1,540 photographs have been revised.

The slide collection has received as gifts 20 slides from Miss Louise Nichols, 21 slides from Professor C. H. Moore, and 57 slides from Mr. E. W. Forbes. 229 slides were purchased for the collection, most of which were of Spanish architecture. The slide collection now numbers 5,110. During the year 327 slides have been catalogued.

The library of the Museum has received 11 volumes as gifts, and 66 volumes were purchased. Of the whole number, four were gallery catalogues, and 16 were for students' use.

During the year photographs have been lent 141 times to various members of the University, and occasionally to outside individuals. In the same manner, slides were lent 276 times. The sum of $31.34 has been received from the sale of catalogues, photographs, and post-cards during the year, and $11.56 for outside work.

The total number of prints catalogued was 915, of which five belong to the Gray Collection, 880 to the Randall Collection, and 30 to the Museum Collection. The number of visits to the print department made by outsiders was 69.

At the suggestion of Professor James H. Ropes, Dean in charge of University Extension, the Fogg Museum bought a set of thirty

Greek slides and a set of thirty-three Roman slides. Notices were sent to all the high schools and some of the private schools in Massachusetts, asking if they would like to have these slides as loans, for use in the schoolroom. A number of schools were interested, and, although the plan was not started until March, the slides were actually sent to twenty schools. Several of the principals expressed enthusiasm in the plan, and were much pleased to receive the slides. The success of the start which was made last year makes it probable that in the future this work can be done on a larger scale.

The need of improvement in the Fogg Museum building has been apparent for many years, and has been referred to more than once in the Director's reports. The Committee on the Fogg Museum and members of the Fine Arts Department have been studying this problem for some time. At last a solution has been discovered which seems to offer hopes of great improvement in the building. The generous gift of $9,000 from Mr. Alfred Atmore Pope, of Farmington, Connecticut, has made it possible to effect the desired changes on the ground floor. About one-half of the money needed for alterations on the second story has been raised, but about $10,000 is still needed to complete the proposed improvements in the building. It is hoped that this money may be raised in time to do the rest of the work next summer; that is, to increase the number of skylights, to raise the ones already in existence, to get more windows, and make some changes in the interior walls which will give more light and air in the whole upper floor, including the main galleries, administration and photograph rooms, and the print room.

The work which Mr. Pope's generosity has enabled us to carry on was started during the summer months, and will be completed on or about the first of November. The most important change is in the large lecture hall. A semi-circular wall has been built, dividing this room into two parts, — a lecture hall, capable of holding about 205 people, with a raised platform at the back suitable for the exhibition of large casts; and a semi-circular corridor outside the lecture room, for the exhibition of other casts. This will add materially to the exhibition space in the Museum, and will make it possible to separate the casts and the original works of art. The lecture hall will be smaller and more useful than before for classes of the size of the courses in fine arts. Certain changes also have been made in the small rooms on either side of the main entrance hall. Plaster belts and cornices have been removed, one door and one recess have been filled in with plaster, and one other door reduced in size, thus increasing the wall space available for exhibition. Two of these rooms cannot be used for Museum purposes for a year or two, because the fine arts books belonging to the College Library are at present housed in them. Radical changes have been made in the system of keeping the semi-circular part of the building water tight. The gutters have been altered, and in one part the porous stone has been painted in such a way that the painting is scarcely noticeable, and it is hoped that it will leak no more. We trust that next year the rest of the building may be made waterproof. Thus the Fogg Museum has been much improved, and its usefulness should increase.

EDWARD W. FORBES, *Director*.

THE GERMANIC MUSEUM

Sir, — The academic year 1911–12 was marked by one striking advance in the Museum cause: the formal laying of the corner-stone of the new Museum building, which took place on June 8, 1912. Unfortunately, the donor of the building, Mr. Adolphus Busch, was prevented by illness from attending. He was, however, represented by Mrs. Busch, and by Mr. and Mrs. Hugo Reisinger, his son-in-law and daughter. The German Ambassador, Count von Bernstorff, who performed the ceremony, brought greetings from His Majesty, the German Emperor, and from the Imperial Chancellor. After the ceremony, the Germanic Museum Association gave a luncheon at the Harvard Union, at which President Lowell, Count von Bernstorff, and Professor Francke made addresses. In addition, President Lowell read a communication from ex-President Andrew D. White of Cornell University, who as Ambassador to Germany had taken a part in the beginnings of our undertaking; and Mr. Reisinger read a message from Mr. Busch, from which the following passages may here be inserted: —

We German-Americans have every reason to do what we can to bring to its consummation an undertaking which appeals both to our allegiance to the country of our choice and to our love for the land of our birth. We have found in this country the realization of hopes and aspirations which, to many of us, at least, would have been denied in our old home. We have found here greater opportunity for work on a large scale, we have found here a better chance for the average man to rise above the restrictions of class and tradition; we have found here a public life based upon the ideals of political freedom and civic independence. We are grateful for all this and we shall do our part in maintaining lawful liberty in this country. But we cannot forget that Germany is above all countries the home of free inquiry and of individual conviction, that it is the land of earnest and manly devotion to the public weal, the land of rational social reform, the land of serious thought and of harmless enjoyment of life, the land of sentiment and song. And we should be faithless to our obligations to our adopted country if we did not try to implant upon American life something of this German honesty and independence of moral conviction, of this German genuineness and wealth of feeling, of this German power for simple and healthy enjoyment.

We German-Americans, therefore, are bound to see in this Germanic Museum connected with an American university a symbol of our twofold relation to American life and a visible and solemn appeal to do justice to both.   Lastly, we Americans of German descent are particularly glad that it is Harvard University, the oldest and most venerable American institution of learning, which has opened its hospitable doors to these treasures of German art.   Harvard has always in a conspicuous manner stood for the German ideals of free scientific inquiry and of individual moral responsibility, and it is largely due to her leadership that these ideals are now dominant in all the universities throughout our land.

I doubt not that in this museum matter also Harvard's leadership will serve as an example to other educational institutions and I look forward to a time when we shall have Germanic museums at Columbia and Wisconsin universities, in Chicago, St. Louis, and San Francisco.   Meanwhile it is for us to see to it that this first Germanic Museum in America grows up to the full measure of the auspicious foundations which have been laid today; and I repeat, every German-American should consider it his patriotic obligation to help in its upbuilding.   As for myself, I am proud of my connections with it, and shall be as long as I live.

It is unfortunate that, owing to certain contract obligations, the Corporation is at present unable to get possession of the land assigned to us, so that the further work of construction must be delayed, possibly for two years more.   The time will be utilized by the architect, Professor Bestelmeyer, in working out every detail of his plan, so that we may ultimately look forward to a building unusually well appointed and in every way adapted to our needs.

The plan includes a number of rooms for a Seminary and a special Library on the History of German Culture.   I am now ordering books to make a beginning of such a Library, using the income of the $10,000 given by Mr. Frohman, which is to be spent at the discretion of the Curator for defraying current expenses.

The Museum has suffered a great loss in the death last spring of Mr. Henry W. Putnam.   Ever since the plan of a Germanic Museum was first suggested, Mr. Putnam was one of its most earnest and effective supporters.   He himself gave liberally to its collections, he helped to raise the Emperor William Fund, for more than ten years he was Chairman of the Board of Directors of the Germanic Museum Association, and he was at all times willing and eager to give work and counsel.   It was a grief to his associates that this trusted and faithful friend should not have been with them at the laying of the corner-stone of the new museum building, in which he himself had taken such keen and generous interest.

KUNO FRANCKE, *Curator*.

PUBLICATION OFFICE

To the President of the University: —

Sir, — I have the honor to submit my report for the academic year 1911–12.

During this period the work of the Publication Office has increased materially. In the course of the year the University took over the publication of the Harvard Economic Studies (7 volumes), the Harvard Historical Studies (16 volumes), the Harvard Law Review, and twenty case-books written by professors in the Law School. A new periodical, The Architectural Quarterly of Harvard University, has also been added to the list of publications with the Harvard imprint. Altogether more than eighty books and periodicals are now distributed from the Publication Office. These publications are sold in the principal bookstores throughout the country, and the Oxford University Press keeps a stock of them in London and supplies dealers in Great Britain and on the continent.

Leaving out of consideration the books acquired during the year, the receipts from the sale of publications amounted to more than $14,000, an increase of $3,000 over the corresponding figures for the preceding year. The printing done in the small plant operated by the University represented a business of approximately $42,000.

The University has not only a much longer list of publications than ever before but it also has a greater number of new books in preparation. Among the latter volumes the following may be mentioned as noteworthy: —

Lectures on Legal History. By James Barr Ames.
The Granger Movement in the United States. By S. J. Buck.
The Barrington-Bernard Correspondence. Edited by Edward Channing.
The Cotton Manufacturing Industry in the United States. By M. T. Copeland.
The Year Books of Richard II. By G. F. Deiser.
Complete sets of the Harvard Law Review. (Reprints of the 25 volumes already issued.)
The Ottoman Empire in the Time of Suleiman the Magnificent. By A. H. Lybyer.
Chivalry in English Literature. By W. H. Schofield.
The History of the Grain Trade in France. By A. P. Usher.
Cases on Constitutional Law. By Eugene Wambaugh.

The increased activity of the Publication Office has served to emphasize more than ever the need for a real University Press. The reasons for the establishment of such an institution may be briefly summarized as follows: —

1. The University has several funds for the publication of special series and an adequately endowed University Press could far more efficiently and economically secure the proper distribution of these works than is at present possible with the University's meagre publication facilities.

2. There are several learned publications edited by committees of the Faculty which must now be issued elsewhere; their publication by a Harvard Press would more closely connect these valuable researches with the name of the University.

3. The University spends more than $100,000 for printing each year, and owing to lack of space only a fraction of this work can be handled in the existing plant. Even the work which is now undertaken is done under great difficulties. More accurate and satisfactory work at a lower cost could be secured if the University maintained an adequate Press.

4. A Harvard Press could do much to add to the prestige of the University by connecting its name more closely with works of scholarly distinction. At present many important contributions to learning by members of the Faculty are issued under the imprints of commercial publishers, sometimes even of other universities, and are not connected in the public mind with the institution at which they were produced.

5. A Harvard University Press could also contribute materially to the advancement of knowledge. At present a number of works of high scholarship are being produced by members of the University and because of our lack of publication funds and our inadequate equipment many of these books are never issued.

6. With the establishment of a University Press it will be possible to increase the effectiveness of the instruction in printing now offered in the Graduate School of Business Administration. This course has met with hearty approval from members of the Typothetae and from other employing printers. To reach its greatest usefulness, however, such a well equipped laboratory as a University Press would provide is needed.

7. This institution would also make possible the establishment of a national testing laboratory for printers. Several master printers have suggested the need for such an institution for research and investigation, and the financial support of such experimentation seems assured. As a workroom for these investigations, however, a well equipped University Press is needed.

That the need for such an institution is becoming generally recognized is shown by the recent establishment of presses at several universities in this country. No one of these universities, however, maintains a publishing plant comparable with the Presses at Oxford and Cambridge, and in that fact seems to lie the opportunity for Harvard University. "There is a very definite need in this country," to quote from my last year's report,

" for a learned press where large fonts of type of Arabic, Hebrew, Sanskrit, Russian, and other tongues might be found, where compositors skilled in setting foreign languages and mathematical formulae might be gathered, and where work of scholarly accuracy might be executed.   The first press of adequate scope to be established in the United States will draw to it, from all parts of the country, learned work which is now sent abroad, and Harvard University has still the chance to establish such an institution. The opportunity is not one that can be postponed, however, for the need is so well recognized and the advantages to be derived are so considerable that within the next few years some university is sure to take advantage of the situation."

C. CHESTER LANE, *Publication Agent.*

UNIVERSITY EXTENSION

To the President of the University: —

Sir, — The following report covers the work of University Extension for the academic year 1911–12, including the Summer School of Arts and Sciences for 1912.

I. The Summer School of Arts and Sciences

The general courses of the Summer School were given by thirty-two officers of the Faculty of Arts and Sciences, including three professors, two lecturers, eight assistant professors, fourteen instructors, one fellow for research, four assistants; together with five professors, one assistant professor, and one instructor from other institutions; and two gentlemen not holding academic positions. In addition, one Harvard instructor offered a course for which a sufficient number of persons did not apply to justify giving the course. Eight persons were employed as assistants in the summer courses. The usual courses at the Hemenway Gymnasium and the Engineering Camp engaged the services of a large number of other instructors, lecturers, and assistants.

The list of courses, as formerly given in the Report of the Dean of the Faculty, follows. In order to make the record complete, the lists also for 1910 and 1911, which were not given in previous reports, are here included.

SUMMER COURSES OF INSTRUCTION

All courses met five times a week, for six weeks.

The degrees (A.B., S.B., A.A.) for which a course was accepted are indicated after the name of the course. The courses accepted for a degree are valued as half-courses, unless otherwise stated.

For summer courses in Engineering and Shopwork, see pp. 50–51.

Harvard students are designated by their status in the academic year preceding the Summer School.

1910

Architecture

84a. Mr. E. T. Putnam. — Elementary Design. (A.B., S.B., A.A.)
2 So., 1 Ju., 2 Sp., 1 Gr., 1 Law, 2 S.S. Total 9.

ASTRONOMY

S1. Dr. J. C. DUNCAN. — Elementary Astronomy. (A.B., S.B., A.A.)
5 S.S. Total 5.

Dr. J. C. DUNCAN. — Special Course. (A.B., S.B., A.A.)
1 So. Total 1.

BOTANY

S1. Asst. Professor W. J. V. OSTERHOUT. — Elementary Botany. (A.B., S.B., A.A.) 1 Fr., 1 Ju., 4 S.S. Total 6.

S2. Asst. Professor W. J. V. OSTERHOUT. — Plant Physiology. (A.B., S.B., A.A.) 1 Ju., 3 S.S. Total 4.

S20. Asst. Professor W. J. V. OSTERHOUT. — Research in Plant Physiology. (A.B., S.B., A.A.) 1 S.S. Total 1.

CHEMISTRY

S1. Asst. Professor G. P. Baxter. — Elementary Chemistry. (A.B., S.B., A.A.) 2 Fr., 1 So., 1 Ju., 17 S.S. Total 21.

S2. Professor W. L. JENNINGS (Worcester Polytechnic Institute). —Organic Chemistry. (A.B., S.B., A.A.) 1 So., 1 Ju., 10 S.S. Total 12.

S3. Professor W. L. JENNINGS (Worcester Polytechnic Institute). — Qualitative Analysis. (A.B., S.B., A.A.)
1 Fr., 2 Se., 1 Sp., 7 S.S. Total 11.

S4. Asst. Professor G. P. BAXTER. — Quantitative Analysis. (A.B., S.B., A.A.) 1 So., 2 Ju., 2 S.S. Total 5.

S6. Dr. G. S. FORBES. — Physical Chemistry. (A.B., S.B., A.A.)
1 So., 2 Se., 1 S.M., 5 S.S. Total 9.

S20c. Professor W. L. JENNINGS (Worcester Polytechnic Institute). — Research in Organic Chemistry. (A.B., S.B., A.A.) 1 S.S. Total 1.

S20f. Asst. Professor G. P. BAXTER. — Research in Inorganic Chemistry. (A.B., S.B., A.A.) 1 Gr., 2 S.S. Total 3.

ECONOMICS

S1. Professor A. B. WOLFE (Oberlin College). — Principles of Economics.
10 S.S. Total 10.

EDUCATION

S2a. Asst. Professor A. O. NORTON.— General Principles. (A.B., S.B., A.A.)
1 Gr., 3 So., 1 Ju., 1 Se., 1 Sp., 13 S.S. Total 20.

S3a. Professor P. H. HANUS. — Organization and Administration of Schools. (A.B., S.B., A.A.) 1 So., 1 Gr., 33 S.S. Total 35.

S5b. Asst. Professor A. O. NORTON.— Education of the Individual. (A.B., S.B., A.A.) 1 Sp., 13 S.S. Total 14.

S20. Professor P. H. HANUS. — Seminary in Education. (A.B., S.B., A.A.)
6 S.S. Total 6.

ENGLISH *

SA. Mr. H. R. SHIPHERD. — Composition, first course. (A.B., S.B., A.A.)
1 Fr., 36 S.S. Total 37.

* The courses in English Composition were accepted for A.B. and S.B., and the courses in Fine Arts for any degree, only under special conditions.

SB. Professor E. A. Greenlaw (Adelphi College). — Composition, second course. (A.B., S.B., A.A.)   20 S.S.   Total 20.

SC. Associate Professor R. P. Utter (Amherst College). — Composition, third course. (A.B., S.B., A.A.)   1 Se., 1 Sp., 18 S.S.   Total 20.

S3. Professor J. W. Rankin (University of Vermont). — Anglo-Saxon. (A.B., S.B., A.A.)   2 Gr., 8 S.S.   Total 10.

S28. Professor E. A. Greenlaw (Adelphi College). — Development of English Literature in Outline. (A.B., S.B., A.A.)   16 S.S.   Total 16.

S45. Mr. C. T. Copeland. — English Literature in the Nineteenth Century. (A.A.)   1 Fr., 23 S.S.   Total 24.

S60. Associate Professor R. P. Utter (Amherst College). — College Admission Requirements in English.   19 S.S.   Total 19.

Fine Arts

S1. Asst. Professor Arthur Pope. — Theory of Pure Design. (A.B., S.B., A.A.)   8 S.S.   Total 8.

S2. Mr. Martin Mower. — Drawing and Painting in Representation. (A.B., S.B., A.A.)   1 Fr., 1 S.M., 9 S.S.   Total 11.

S3. Professor H. N. Fowler (Western Reserve University). — History of Ancient Art. (A.B., S.B., A.A.)   2 So., 3 Ju., 1 Se., 3 S.S.   Total 9.

French

S1. Dr. A. F. Whittem.— Intermediate Course for Teachers. (A.B., S.B., A.A.)   1 Gr., 16 S.S.   Total 17.

S2. Mr. Alphonse Brun. — French Conversation.
          1 So., 1 Gr., 15 S.S.   Total 17.

Geology

S5. Asst. Professor J. B. Woodworth. — Field Work in Montana. (A.B., S.B., A.A.)   1 Fr., 2 So., 4 Ju., 4 Se., 1 Sc., 1 Gr., 3 S.S.   Total 16.

S20a. Professor W. M. Davis. — Physiographic Field Investigation. (A.B., S.B., A.A.)   1 Ju.   Total 1.

S20c. Professor J. E. Wolff.— Structural or Glacial Field Work. (A.B., S.B., A.A.)   1 S.S.   Total 1.

German

S1. Dr. A. W. Boesche.— Intermediate German for Teachers. (A.B., S.B., A.A.)   15 S.S.   Total 15.

S2. Dr. A. W. Boesche. — German Conversation.   13 S.S.   Total 13.

S3. Dr. H. J. Weber. — German Dramatists of the Nineteenth Century. (A.B., S.B., A.A.)   1 Fr., 1 So., 1 Ju., 7 S.S.   Total 10.

Government

S1. Dr. A. N. Holcombe. — Civil Government. (A.B., S.B., A.A.)
          1 Gr., 3 S.S.   Total 4.

Greek

SG. Dr. D. P. Lockwood. — Greek for Beginners.   2 Sp., 3 S.S.   Total 5.

HISTORY

S2. Asst. Professor W. S. FERGUSON. — Ancient History for Teachers. (A.B., S.B., A.A.) 14 S.S. Total 14.

S4. Professor WILLIAM MACDONALD (Brown University). — History of England from 1689. (A.B., S.B., A.A.) 1 Ju., 1 Gr., 13 S.S. Total 15.

S5. Professor WILLIAM MACDONALD (Brown University). — American History to 1783. (A.B., S.B., A.A.) 13 S.S. Total 13.

S20d. Professor A. C. COOLIDGE. — Research in Modern European History. (A.B., S.B., A.A.) 1 S.S. Total 1.

S20e. Professor WILLIAM MACDONALD (Brown University). — Research in American History. (A.B., S.B., A.A.) 1 Gr. Total 1.

S20i. Asst. Professor W. S. FERGUSON. — Research in Greek and Roman History. (A.B., S.B., A.A.) 2 S.S. Total 2.

LATIN

S1. Professor C. H. MOORE. — Latin for Teachers. 17 S.S. Total 17.

S2. Professor C. H. MOORE.— Life and Works of Virgil. (A.B., S.B., A.A.) 2 So., 5 S.S. Total 7.

MATHEMATICS

SAB. Asst. Professor E. V. HUNTINGTON. — Trigonometry and Analytical Geometry. (A.B., S.B., A.A.) 5 Fr., 1 So., 12 S.S. Total 18.

SD. Asst. Professor C. L. BOUTON.— Advanced Algebra. (A.B., S.B., A.A.) 5 S.S. Total 5.

S2. Professor W. F. OSGOOD. — Calculus. 1 Ju., 1 Se., 9 S.S. Total 11.

S3. Asst. Professor C. L. BOUTON. — Introduction to Modern Geometry. (A.B., S.B., A.A.) 3 S.S. Total 3.

S20d. Professor W. F. OSGOOD.— Topics in the Theory of Functions. (A.B., S.B., A.A.) 2 S.S. Total 2.

S20e. Asst. Professor C. L. BOUTON. — Subject Matter of Elementary Mathematics. (A.B., S.B., A.A.) 1 S.S. Total 1.

METALLURGY

S12. Mr. H. M. BOYLSTON. — Metallography. (S.B., A.A.) 3 S.S. Total 3.

MUSIC

S1. Asst. Professor J. P. MARSHALL (Boston University). — Appreciation of Music. (A.B., S.B., A.A.) 13 Fr., 5 So., 5 Ju., 1 Sp., 1 Me., 9 S.S. Total 34.

S2. Asst. Professor J. P. MARSHALL (Boston University). — Elementary Harmony. (A.B., S.B., A.A.) 1 Fr., 1 Ju., 1 Gr., 2 S.S. Total 5.

S3. Asst. Professor J. P. MARSHALL (Boston University). — Advanced Harmony. (A.B., S.B., A.A.) 9 S.S. Total 9.

S4. Professor C. H. FARNSWORTH (Columbia University). — School Music, Practice. 4 S.S. Total 4.

S5. Professor C. H. FARNSWORTH (Columbia University). — School Music, Theory of Teaching. 8 S.S. Total 8.

PHILOSOPHY

S1. Asst. Professor R. B. PERRY. — General Introduction to Philosophy. (A.B., S.B., A.A.)   6 Fr., 1 So., 1 Ju., 1 Sp., 6 S.S.   Total 15.

S2. Asst. Professor R. B. PERRY. — Introduction to Ethics. (A.B., S.B., A.A.)   1 Fr., 1 So., 1 Ju., 1 uC., 1 Sp., 6 S.S.   Total 11.

S20. Asst. Professor R. B. PERRY. — Seminary in Philosophy. (A.B., S.B., A.A.)   1 Ju., 1 S.S.   Total 2.

PHYSICS

SB. Mr. H. C. HAYES and Mr. E. L. CHAFFEE. — Elementary Experimental Physics. (A.B., S.B., A.A.)
     1 Fr., 1 Sp., 1 Dn., 15 S.S.   Total 18.

SC. Dr. P. W. BRIDGMAN. — Experimental Physics. (A.B., S.B., A.A.)
     1 Gr., 6 S.S.   Total 7.

PSYCHOLOGY

S1. Asst. Professor R. M. YERKES. — Descriptive Psychology. (A.B., S.B., A.A.)   1 So., 1 Se., 1 Gr., 14 S.S.   Total 17.

S2. Asst. Professor R. M. YERKES. — Applications of Psychology. (A.B., S.B., A.A.)   9 S.S.   Total 9.

S20. Asst. Professor R. M. YERKES. — Advanced Experimental Work. (A.B., S.B., A.A.)   1 S.S.   Total 1.

PUBLIC SPEAKING *

S1. Mr. B. G. WILLARD. — Vocal Technique. (A.B., S.B., A.A.)
     1 Gr., 8 S.S.   Total 9.

S3. Asst. Professor I. L. WINTER and Associate Professor THOMAS CROSBY (Brown University). — Delivery of Speeches. (A.B., S.B., A.A.)
     1 So., 12 S.S.   Total 13.

S4. Asst. Professor I. L. WINTER and Associate Professor THOMAS CROSBY (Brown University). — Vocal Interpretation for Teachers of English. (A.B., S.B., A.A.)   1 So., 1 Se., 7 S.S.   Total 9.

S7. Asst. Professor I. L. WINTER. — Advanced Course. (A.B., S.B., A.A.)
     1 Se., 5 S.S.   Total 6.

S12. Asst. Professor I. L. WINTER. — Course of Readings.
     1 Se., 1 Gr., 20 S.S.   Total 22.

SOCIOLOGY

S1. Professor A. B. WOLFE (Oberlin College). — General Principles of Sociology. (A.B., S.B., A.A.)   7 S.S.   Total 7.

1911

ASTRONOMY

S1. Dr. J. C. DUNCAN. — Elementary Astronomy. (A.B., S.B., A.A.)
     4 uC., 2 S.S.   Total 6.

---

* Any two courses in Public Speaking (not including S12) taken in the same year were accepted as one half-course toward the degree of A.B., S.B., or A.A.

CHEMISTRY

81. Asst. Professor G. P. BAXTER. — Elementary Theoretical and Descriptive Chemistry. (A.B., S.B., A.A.) 1 Fr., 2 Ju., 11 S.S. Total 14.

82. Dr. G. L. KELLEY. — Organic Chemistry. (A.B., S.B., A.A.)
2 Fr., 1 Me., 12 S.S. Total 15.

83. Dr. G. S. FORBES. — Qualitative Analysis. (A.B., S.B., A.A.)
1 So., 6 S.S. Total 7.

84. Asst. Professor G. P. BAXTER. — Quantitative Analysis. (A.B., S.B., A.A.) 1 Ju., 1 S.S. Total 2.

86. Dr. G. S. FORBES. — Physical Chemistry. (A.B., S.B., A.A.)
2 Se., 1 Gr., 4 S.S. Total 7.

823f. Asst. Professor G. P. BAXTER. — Research in Inorganic and Physical Chemistry. (A.B., S.B., A.A.) 1 Gr., 2 S.S. Total 3.

ECONOMICS

81. Professor A. B. WOLFE (Oberlin College). — Principles of Economics. (A.A.) 6 S.S. Total 6.

EDUCATION

82a. Asst. Professor F. W. BALLOU (University of Cincinnati). — Organization and Administration of Schools and School Systems. (A.B., S.B., A.A.) 1 Sp., 29 S.S. Total 30.

87. Mr. MEYER BLOOMFIELD (Vocation Bureau, Boston). — Vocational Guidance. 41 S.S. Total 41.

ENGLISH *

8A. Mr. H. R. SHIPHERD. — English Composition and Methods of Teaching. (A.B., S.B., A.A.) 49 S.S. Total 49.

8B. Professor E. A. GREENLAW (Adelphi College). — English Composition, second course. (A.B., S.B., A.A.) 1 Ju., 20 S.S. Total 21.

8C. Mr. H. M. RIDEOUT.— English Composition, third course. (A.B., S.B., A.A.) 1 uC., 18 S.S. Total 19.

83. Dr. T. P. CROSS.— Anglo-Saxon. (A.B., S.B., A.A.) 9 S.S. Total 9.

828. Professor E. A. GREENLAW (Adelphi College). — History and Development of English Literature in Outline. (A.B., S.B., A.A.)
8 S.S. Total 8.

845. Mr. H. M. RIDEOUT. — History of English Literature in the Nineteenth Century. (A.A.) 13 S.S. Total 13.

FINE ARTS *

81. Dr. D. W. ROSS. — Drawing and Painting. (A.B., S.B., A.A.)
2 uC., 1 Gr., 23 S.S. Total 26.

82. Dr. D. W. ROSS. — Practice in Pure Design. (A.B., S.B., A.A.)
14 S.S. Total 14.

83. Mr. MARTIN MOWER. — Drawing and Painting in Representation. (A.B., S.B., A.A.) 2 uC., 1 Se., 9 S.S. Total 12.

* The courses in English Composition were accepted for A.B. and S.B., and courses in Fine Arts for any degree, only under special conditions.

S5. Asst. Professor A. Pope. — Turner and the Landscape Painting of His Time. (A.B., S.B., A.A.)   2 S.S.   Total 2.

S9. Dr. C. R. Post. — Sculpture and Painting of the Italian Renaissance. (A.B., S.B., A.A.)   1 Fr., 1 So., 2 Ju., 8 S.S.   Total 12.

FRENCH

S1. Mr. G. L. Lincoln. — French for Teachers. (A.B., S.B., A.A.)
                                                              8 S.S.   Total 8.

S2. Mr. R. E. Pellissier. — French Conversation.   10 S.S.   Total 10.

S4. Dr. E. H. Wilkins. — Second-year College French. (A.B., S.B., A.A.)
                                          5 Fr., 2 So., 1 Se., 6 S.S.   Total 14.

GEOLOGY

S5. Asst. Professor J. B. Woodworth. — Field Geology. (A.B., S.B., A.A.)
                                  3 So., 2 Ju., 1 Se., 1 Gr., 1 S.S.   Total 8.

S20c. Professor J. E. Wolff. — Structural or Glacial Field Work. (A.B., S.B., A.A.)   1 Gr.   Total 1.

GERMAN

S1. Dr. H. J. Weber. — German for Teachers. (A.B., S.B., A.A.)
                                                        1 Gr., 5 S.S.   Total 6.

S2. Dr. Ewald Eiserhardt. — German Conversation.   4 S.S.   Total 4.

S3. Dr. H. J. Weber. — German Literature. (A.B., S.B., A.A.)
                                                        1 Ju., 8 S.S.   Total 9.

S4. Mr. A. H. Herrick. — Second-year College German. (A.B., S.B., A.A.)
                                                        6 Fr., 4 S.S.   Total 10.

      Dr. H. J. Weber. Special Course.   1 S.S.   Total 1.

GOVERNMENT

S1. Dr. A. N. Holcombe. — Civil Government. (A.B., S.B., A.A.)
                                                              6 S.S.   Total 6.

HISTORY

S2. Asst. Professor W. S. Ferguson. — Ancient History for Teachers. (A.B., S.B., A.A.)   1 Fr., 13 S.S.   Total 14.

S5. Professor William MacDonald (Brown University). — American History from 1783 to 1829. (A.B., S.B., A.A.) 2 Ju., 18 S.S. Total 20.

S20e. Professor William MacDonald (Brown University). — Research in American History. (A.B., S.B., A.A.)   3 S.S.   Total 3.

ITALIAN

S1. Dr. E. H. Wilkins. — Elementary Italian. (A.B., S.B., A.A.)
                                              1 So., 1 Ju., 5 S.S.   Total 7.

LATIN

S1. Professor J. C. Rolfe (University of Pennsylvania). — Latin for Teachers. (A.A.)   17 S.S.   Total 17.

S2. Professor J. C. Rolfe (University of Pennsylvania). — Life and Works of Virgil. (A.B., S.B., A.A.)   8 S.S.   Total 8.

MATHEMATICS

S*A*. Mr. H. D. GAYLORD. — Trigonometry. (A.B., S.B., A.A.)
10 Fr., 1 So., 2 Ju., 1 Se., 4 S.S. Total 18.

S*B*. Asst. Professor E. V. HUNTINGTON.— Analytic Geometry. (A.B., S.B., A.A.)
2 Fr., 2 S.S. Total 4.

S2. Asst. Professor E. V. HUNTINGTON. — Calculus. (A.A.)
1 Ju., 4 S.S. Total 5.

METALLURGY

S12. Mr. H. M. BOYLSTON. — Metallography. (S.B., A.A.)
1 So., 1 S.S. Total 2.

MUSIC

S1. Asst. Professor J. P. MARSHALL (Boston University). — Appreciation of Music. (A.B., S.B., A.A.) 1 So., 1 Ju., 1 uC., 13 S.S. Total 16.

S2. Asst. Professor J. P. MARSHALL (Boston University). — Elementary Harmony. (A.B., S.B., A.A.) 1 So., 6 S.S. Total 7.

S3. Asst. Professor J. P. MARSHALL (Boston University). — Advanced Harmony. (A.B., S.B., A.A.) 5 S.S. Total 5.

S4. Mr. G. H. GARTLAN (Assistant Supervisor of Music, New York City).—School Music for Grade Teachers. (A.A.) 6 S.S. Total 6.

PHILOSOPHY

S1. Asst. Professor R. B. PERRY. — General Introduction to Philosophy. (A.B., S.B., A.A.) 1 So., 1 uC., 1 Me., 7 S.S. Total 13.

S2. Asst. Professor R. B. PERRY. — Introduction to Ethics. (A.B., S.B., A.A.) 1 So., 5 S.S. Total 6.

S20. Asst. Professor R. B. PERRY. — Seminary in Philosophy. (A.B., S.B., A.A.) 2 S.S. Total 2.

PHYSICS

S*B*. Mr. H. C. HAYES. — Elementary Experimental Physics for Teachers. (A.A., S.B., A.A.) 17 S.S. Total 17.

PSYCHOLOGY

S1. Asst. Professor R. M. YERKES.— Descriptive Psychology (A.B., S.B, A.A.) 12 S.S. Total 12.

S2. Asst. Professor R. M. YERKES.— Educational Psychology. (A.B., S.B., A.A.) 1 uC., 17 S.S. Total 18.

S20. Asst. Professor R. M. YERKES.— Advanced Experimental Work. (A.B., S.B., A.A.) 2 S.S. Total 2.

PUBLIC SPEAKING *

S1. Mr. B. G. WILLARD. — Vocal Technique in Speaking and Reading. (A.B., S.B., A.A.) 11 S.S. Total 11.

S3. Asst. Professor I. L. WINTER. — Training in the Delivery of Speeches. (A.B., S.B., A.A.) 13 S.S. Total 13.

S4. Asst. Professor I. L. WINTER. — Vocal Interpretation of English Prose and Poetry. (A.B., S.B., A.A.) 15 S.S. Total 15.

* Two courses in Public Speaking taken in the same year were accepted as one half-course toward the degree of A.B., S.B., or A.A.

S7.   Asst. Professor I. L. WINTER. — Advanced Course for Teachers.
      (A.B., S.B., A.A.)   10 S.S.   Total 10.

SOCIOLOGY

S1.   Professor A. B. WOLFE (Oberlin College). — Social Problems.   (A.B.,
      S.B., A.A.)   12 S.S.   Total 12.

SPANISH

S1.   Mr. G. L. LINCOLN. — Elementary Spanish.   (A.B., S.B., A.A.)
                                           1 Se., 8 S.S.   Total 9.

1912

CHEMISTRY

S1.   Asst. Professor G. P. BAXTER. — Elementary Theoretical and Descrip-
      tive Chemistry. (A.B., S.B., A.A.) 1 Fr., 2 Se., 14 S.S. Total 17.

S2.   Dr. G. L. KELLEY. — Organic Chemistry.   (A.B., S.B., A.A.)
                                      1 Fr., 1 Se., 10 S.S.   Total 12.

S3.   Asst. Professor G. P. BAXTER. — Qualitative Analysis.   (A.B., S.B.,
      A.A.)   1 Fr., 1 Me., 4 S.S.   Total 6.

S6.   Dr. G. S. FORBES. — Physical Chemistry.   (A.B., S.B., A.A.)
                                1 uC., 3 Ju., 1 Se., 3 S.S.   Total 8.

S13. Dr. G. S. FORBES.—Experimental Electrochemistry. (A.B., S.B., A.A.)
                                                   2 Gr.   Total 2.

S20f. Asst. Professor G. P. BAXTER. — Research in Inorganic Chemistry.
      (A.B., S.B., A.A.)   3 Gr., 2 S.S.   Total 5.

S20h. Dr. G. S. FORBES. — Research in Physical Chemistry.   (A.B., S.B.,
      A.A.)   1 Me., 1 S.S.   Total 2.

ECONOMICS

S1.   Professor GARRETT DROPPERS (Williams College). — Principles of Eco-
      nomics. (A.A.)   1 Sc., 12 S.S.   Total 13.

EDUCATION

S2a. Professor ERNEST C. MOORE (Yale University). — General Principles
      of Education. (A.B., S.B., A.A.)   1 Ju., 20 S.S.   Total 21.

S3a. Professor ERNEST C. MOORE (Yale University). — Organization and
      Administration of Schools. (A.B., S.B., A.A.)   22 S.S.   Total 22.

S7.   Mr. MEYER BLOOMFIELD (Vocation Bureau, Boston). — Vocational
      Guidance. (A.A.)   26 S.S.   Total 26.

ENGLISH *

SA.   Mr. H. R. SHIPHERD.—English Composition and Methods of Teaching.
      (A.B., S.B., A.A.)   31 S.S.   Total 31.

SB.   Mr. H. J. SAVAGE. — English Composition, second course.   (A.B.,
      S.B., A.A.)   12 S.S.   Total 12.

* The courses in English Composition are accepted for A.B. and S.B., and courses in Fine
Arts for any degree, only under special conditions.

8C. Professor R. M. ALDEN (University of Illinois). — English Composition, third course. (A.B., S.B., A.A.)   1 Gr., 15 S.S. Total 16.

S3. Dr. K. G. T. WEBSTER.— Anglo-Saxon. (A.B., S.B., A.A.)
                                                      3 S.S. Total 3.

S16. Professor R. M. ALDEN (University of Illinois). — Poetics. (A.A.)
                                                      1 Ju., 7 S.S. Total 8.

S45. Asst. Professor C. T. COPELAND. — Nineteenth Century English Literature. (A.A.)   20 S.S. Total 20.

S70. Professor W. A. NEILSON. — Shakespeare. (A.B., S.B., A.A.)
                                        2 Fr., 1 So., 2 Ju., 31 S.S. Total 36.

FINE ARTS *

S1. Dr. D. W. ROSS. — Lectures on the Principles of Pure Design and of Representation. (A.B., S.B., A.A.)   1 So., 1 Se., 31 S.S. Total 33.

S2. Dr. D. W. ROSS. — Practice in Pure Design. (A.B., S.B., A.A.)
                                                      13 S.S. Total 13.

S3. Mr. MARTIN MOWER. — Drawing and Painting in Representation. (A.B., S.B., A.A.)   1 So., 1 Se., 5 S.S. Total 7.

S4. Asst. Professor G. H. CHASE. — Greek Art. (A.B., S.B., A.A.)
                                                      2 Ju., 5 S.S. Total 7.

FRENCH

S1. Mr. G. L. LINCOLN. — French for Teachers. (A.B., S.B., A.A.)
                                                      1 Ju., 15 S.S. Total 16.

S2. Mr. R. E. PELLISSIER (Leland Stanford Jr. University). — French Conversation.   1 Ju., 1 Gr., 9 S.S. Total 11.

S3. Mr. L. J. A. MERCIER. — General View of the History of French Literature. (A.B., S.B., A.A.)   1 Se., 3 S.S. Total 4.

S4. Dr. E. H. WILKINS. — Second-year College French. (A.B., S.B., A.A.)
                                        6 Fr., 1 So., 2 uC., 4 S.S. Total 13.

S5. Mr. L. J. A. MERCIER. — French for Oral Examination.
                                                      1 Fr., 2 So. Total 3.

GEOLOGY

S5. Asst. Professor J. B. WOODWORTH. — Field Geology. (A.B., S.B., A.A.)
                                              3 So., 1 Gr., 2 S.S. Total 6.

S20c. Professor J. E. WOLFF. — Geological and Petrographical Studies. (A.B., S.B., A.A.)   4 Gr. Total 4.

GERMAN

S3. Dr. H. J. WEBER. — German Literature. (A.B., S.B., A.A.)
                                                      1 Ju., 14 S.S. Total 15.

S4. Mr. A. H. HERRICK. — Second-year College German. (A.B., S.B., A.A.)
                                              5 Fr., 2 So., 4 S.S. Total 11.

S5. Dr. F. W. C. LIEDER. — German for Oral Examinations.
                                                      1 So., 1 S.S. Total 2.

GOVERNMENT

S1. Mr. E. A. COTTRELL. — Civil Government. (A.B., S.B., A.A.)
                                                      1 Ju., 1 S.S. Total 2.

---

* The courses in English Composition are accepted for A.B. and S.B., and courses in Fine Arts for any degree, only under special conditions.

S2.   Mr. E. A. COTTRELL. — Municipal Government.   (A.B., S.B., A.A.)
                                              1 uC., 2 S.S.   Total 3.

HISTORY

S2.   Asst. Professor W. S. FERGUSON. — Ancient History for Teachers.
      (A.B., S.B., A.A.)   16 S.S.   Total 16.

S4.   Professor E. D. ADAMS (Leland Stanford Jr. University). — English
      Governmental and Parliamentary Attitude toward the American
      Civil War.   (A.B., S.B., A.A.)   1 uC.   Total 1.

S5.   Professor E. D. ADAMS (Leland Stanford Jr. University). — History
      of the United States since 1830.   (A.B., S.B., A.A.)
                                      1 Sc., 2 Ju., 17 S.S.   Total 20.

S20s. Professor E. D. ADAMS (Leland Stanford Jr. University). — Research
      in American History.   (A.B., S.B., A.A.)   4 S.S.   Total 4.

ITALIAN

S1.   Dr. E. H. WILKINS. — Elementary Italian.   (A.B., S.B., A.A.)
                                              1 Gr., 5 S.S.   Total 6.

LATIN

S1.   Asst. Professor A. S. PEASE (University of Illinois). — Latin for
      Teachers.   (A.A.)   12 S.S.   Total 12.

S2.   Asst. Professor A. S. PEASE (University of Illinois). — Life and Works
      of Virgil.   (A.B., S.B., A.A.)   3 S.S.   Total 3.

MATHEMATICS

SK.   Mr. H. D. GAYLORD. — Logarithms and Trigonometry.   (A.B., S.B.,
      A.A.)   13 Fr., 4 So., 3 S.S.   Total 20.

SM.   Mr. H. D. GAYLORD. — Logarithms and Trigonometry for Teachers.
      (A.A.)   7 S.S.   Total 7.

S2.   Professor W. F. OSGOOD. — Calculus.   (A.A.)   6 S.S.   Total 6.

METALLURGY

S12. Mr. H. M. BOYLSTON. — Metallography.   (S.B., Met. E., A.A.)
                                              1 Se., 3 S.S.   Total 4.

MUSIC

S1.   Asst. Professor W. R. SPALDING. — Appreciation of Music.   (A.B.,
      S.B., A.A.)   1 Fr., 2 Ju., 1 Se., 4 S.S.   Total 8.

S2.   Dr. A. T. DAVISON, Jr. — Elementary Harmony.   (A.B., S.B., A.A.)
                                                 5 S.S.   Total 5.

S3.   Asst. Professor W. R. SPALDING. — Advanced Harmony.   (A.B., S.B.,
      A.A.)   6 S.S.   Total 6.

PHILOSOPHY

S1.   Asst. Professor G. P. ADAMS (University of California). — General
      Introduction to Philosophy.   (A.B., S.B., A.A.)   5 S.S.   Total 5.

PHYSICS

SB.   Dr. H. C. HAYES. — Elementary Experimental Physics for Teachers.
      (A.B., S.B., A.A.)   1 Se., 14 S.S.   Total 15.

PSYCHOLOGY

S1. Asst. Professor R. M. YERKES. — Descriptive Psychology. (A.B., S.B., A.A.)   2 Fr., 4 S.S. Total 6.

S2. Asst. Professor R. M. YERKES. — Educational Psychology. (A.B., S.B., A.A.)   7 S.S. Total 7.

S3. Dr. WILLIAM HEALY (Juvenile Psychopathic Institute, Chicago). — Psychology and Training of the Mentally and Morally Abnormal. (A.A.)   24 S.S. Total 24.

S20. Asst. Professor R. M. YERKES. — Advanced Work in Psychology. (A.B., S.B., A.A.)   1 S.S. Total 1.

PUBLIC SPEAKING *

S1. Mr. G. R. BUNKER. — Vocal Technique in Speaking and Reading. (A.B., S.B., A.A.)   11 S.S. Total 11.

S3. Asst. Professor I. L. WINTER. — Training in the Delivery of both Selected and Original Speeches. (A.B., S.B., A.A.) 13 S.S. Total 13.

S4. Asst. Professor I. L. WINTER. — Vocal Interpretation of English Prose and Poetry. (A.B., S.B., A.A.)   7 S.S. Total 7.

S7. Asst. Professor I. L. WINTER. — Vocal Interpretation and Public Speaking. (A.B., S.B., A.A.)   12 S.S. Total 12.

SOCIOLOGY

S1. Professor GARRETT DROPPERS (Williams College). — Principles of Sociology and Social Problems. (A.B., S.B., A.A.)
                                                        1 Ju., 23 S.S. Total 24.

SPANISH

S1. Mr. G. L. LINCOLN. — Elementary Spanish. (A.B., S.B., A.A.).
                                                        2 So., 9 S.S. Total 11.

In numbers of students enrolled, the general courses of the Summer School of 1912 substantially held their own, while there was a marked increase in the normal courses in Physical Education, given at the Hemenway Gymnasium under Dr. Sargent.

The total number in attendance was as follows: —

	1909	1910	1911	1912
Total number of students	933	873	787	823
" " " men	438	476	400	423
" " " women	495	397	387	405
Percentage of men	47%	54.5%	51%	51%

* Any two courses in Public Speaking taken together in the same year count as one half-course.

This body of students was made up as follows: —

	1909	1910	1911	1912
Students at Engineering Camp *	12	31	19	10
Harvard students of preceding academic year: †..				
Members of graduate and professional schools	17	19	10	16
Undergraduates in good standing	46	61	43	48
Undergraduates with deficient record	42	57	35	35
Radcliffe students of preceding academic year ...	7	11	6	12
Students in Physical Education courses	160	170	186	222
Students from outside in general courses	653	528	492	485
	937	877	791	828
Names counted twice	4	4	4	5
	933	873	787	823

The composition of the group entitled " Students from outside in general courses," was as follows: —

	1909	1910	1911	1912
Teachers and school officers:				
Professors and college instructors	52	40	40	29
Normal school teachers	16	14	5	7
High school teachers	121	98	94	88
Grade school teachers	63	100	75	72
Endowed and private school teachers	64	54	52	43
Other teachers	86	34	38	29
Superintendents, supervisors, and principals .	59	55	50	52
Total, teachers and school officers	461	395	354	320
Men	163	162	135	135
Women	298	233	219	185
Percentage of men	35%	40%	38%	42%
Students from other colleges	48	39	27	30
Students from preparatory schools	2	7	5	7
Other students	47	21	11	9
Other occupation than teaching	33	34	45	82
Occupation not given	62	32	50	37
	192	133	138	165
	461	395	354	320
Total, students from outside taking general courses	653	528	492	485
Men	261	243	209	224
Women	392	285	283	261
Percentage of men	40%	46%	42.5%	46%

* Not including Engineering Camp students who were at the time members of Harvard University.

† Not including Harvard students in Shopwork courses.

In this body of " students from outside " there were: —

	1909	1910	1911	1912
Holders of A.B., S.B., or some equivalent degree	173	148	170	151
Holders of a higher degree	71	57	48	47
Members of the Summer School in one of preceding five years	146	99	136	154

The geographical distribution of this same group was as follows:

	1909	1910	1911	1912
New England States	327	257	261	275
Middle States	157	124	94	76
South Atlantic States	57	26	36	33
South Central States	19	26	26	15
North Central States	66	72	52	73
Western States	6	5	5	9
Foreign Countries	21	18	18	4
	653	528	492	485

The general courses of the Summer School cost in 1912 over $1,000 more than they earned. This deficit is, however, more than balanced by the surplus in the courses in Physical Education.

II. Commission on Extension Courses

The Commission on Extension Courses, representing the following institutions: —

Harvard University	Boston University
Tufts College	Museum of Fine Arts
Mass. Institute of Technology	Wellesley College
Boston College	Simmons College

offered in 1911–12 the following courses, all of which, by vote of the Faculty of Arts and Sciences, were accepted for the Harvard degree of A.A. The table shows for each course the number of students in the course, and the number of certificates granted.

	Students	Certificates
Shakespeare (Professor Neilson, Harvard University)......	45	18
English Composition (Mr. Hersey, Harvard University) ..	74	29
Music (Professor Marshall, Boston University)	112	47
Elementary Economics (Professor Baldwin, Boston Univ.) .	65	27
Industrial Organization (Professor Metcalf, Tufts College) .	47	36
Psychology (Professor Yerkes, Harvard University)	69	22
Accounting (Professor Cole, Harvard University)	132	22
Commercial Organization (Mr. Cherington, Harvard University)	61	4
Advanced Composition (Professor Sharp, Boston University)	116	35
English Literature (Professor Black, Boston University) ..	83	48
Elementary German (Professor Perrin, Boston University)	78	41
Moslem Art (Mr. Borden, Harvard University)	82	12
Greek Mythology (Dr. Fairbanks, Museum of Fine Arts) .	36	12
Historical Geology (Professor Barton)	31	12
Petrology (Professor Barton)	32	11
Geography (Professor Johnson, Harvard University)	56	40
Botany (Professor Osterhout, Harvard University)	31	17
	1,150	433

As the figures show, the proportion of certificates to the total enrolment was just under 38 per cent.

All the courses were accepted for the degree of A.A. by Radcliffe College and Tufts College, as well as by Harvard University; Wellesley College accepted all except those in Accounting and in Commercial Organization.

The financial statement of the Commission's courses is as follows: —

Expenses

Salaries...		$16,857.40
Lecture-room expenses		1,012.40
Advertising		234.96
Printing and stationery		339.12
Postage		224.95
Office and clerical expense		148.98
Teachers' School of Science general expenses (not including salaries):		
Equipment and administration	$258.04	
Less sale of microscopes	10.00	248.04
		$19,065.85

Income

Fees	$7,320.00
Lowell Institute	11,217.08
Mrs. Shepherd Brooks's gift for Teachers' School of Science	147.15
Chamber of Commerce subscription	381.62
	$19,065.85

III.

In 1911–12, eleven persons were registered as "Extension Students," admitted to regular courses under the Faculty of Arts and Sciences. These were in nearly all cases either members of other neighboring institutions or persons engaged in some regular calling (such as playing in the Boston Symphony Orchestra), but able to give a part of their time to study. Under former conditions some of them would have been admitted as Special Students in Harvard College. As "Extension Students" they are not members of Harvard College, but are affiliated students of the University. The Committee on Admission of the Faculty of Arts and Sciences has now consented to take charge of the admission of students to this status.

The Dean was able in the course of the year to coöperate with the Fogg Art Museum in an interesting undertaking whereby sets of slides illustrating Greek and Roman civilization and art are lent to Massachusetts high schools. This piece of extension work is more fully described in the report of the Director of the Museum.

JAMES HARDY ROPES, *Dean.*

To the President of the University: —

Sir, — I have the honor to submit the report of Radcliffe College for the academic year 1911–12.

The number of students in actual attendance during the year was 566, as against 500 during the preceding year.

Graduate Students	85
Seniors	78
Juniors	66
Sophomores	67
Freshmen	117
Special Students	142
Unclassified Students	11
Total	566

At Commencement in June, 1912, eighty-one students, four of whom had completed their residence in an earlier year, received the degree of Bachelor of Arts. Two students who had not been registered as Seniors received the degree, and three students who had been so registered failed to receive it. One of the eighty-one received the degree *summa cum laude;* six received it *magna cum laude;* twenty-six, *cum laude.*

Thirty-four candidates received the degree of Master of Arts. Twelve of the thirty-four had taken their first degree at Radcliffe; the others represented the following colleges: Boston University, Colby College, Colorado College. Dalhousie University, Irving College, Mount Holyoke College, Pomona College, Smith College, Swarthmore College, Teachers' College, Tufts College, Vassar College, Wellesley College, and the Universities of Alabama, Cincinnati, Idaho, Illinois, New Brunswick, Rochester, and Wisconsin. Eighteen received the degree in English, five in French and Other Romance Languages and Literatures, two each in the Classics, in History and Political Science, in Philosophy, and in Botany, and one each in German, in Education, and in Social Ethics.

The degree of Doctor of Philosophy was conferred upon two candidates, both in the special field of English Philology: Charlotte Farrington Babcock, A.B. (Radcliffe) 1906, A.M. (*ibid.*) 1909, and Bertha Marion Pillsbury, A.B. (University of Illinois) 1895, A.M. (Radcliffe) 1898.

One hundred and twenty-nine candidates took the preliminary examinations, and one hundred and thirty the final examinations. Three of the four candidates who took wholly or in part the examinations of the College Entrance Examination Board were admitted to the Freshman Class. The new plan of admission was tried by thirty-eight candidates in June and in September, thirty-four of whom passed. Of the six candidates who were rejected under this plan in June three tried the new plan again in September and passed; and one completed her examinations in September under the old plan. Fifteen schools, chiefly in distant places, which have not regularly prepared pupils for Radcliffe, sent candidates for the examinations under the new plan. The results of the final examinations are given in the following table: —

	Admitted	Admitted "clear"	Rejected
June	79	51	10
September	30	15	5
	109	66	15
Total rejected	15		
Candidates in June who did not reappear in September	6		
	130		

The entering class of 1912–13 numbers ninety-seven, who were admitted, ninety-one in 1912, four in 1911, one in 1910, and one in 1909.

Eighty-five graduate students registered during the year 1911–12, fifty-five of whom were from colleges other than Radcliffe. Fourteen students were admitted to ten whole courses, and thirty-six students to twenty half-courses of the "Courses Primarily for Graduates in Harvard University open to competent students of Radcliffe College."

The Caroline I. Wilby Prize was awarded to Charlotte Farrington Babcock for her Doctor's dissertation. The Captain Jonathan Fay Diploma and Scholarship were awarded to Bessie London, 1912. The Sylvia Platt Prize of fifty dollars, offered for the first time in 1912 by Mary Caroline Hardy, 1901, for the best poem by a Radcliffe student, was awarded to Abbie Huston Evans, a special student. The Alice Freeman Palmer Fellowship in

the award of Wellesley College was awarded for 1912–13 to Bessie
Marion Coats, A.B. (Vassar) 1907, A.M. (Radcliffe) 1912. The
European · Fellowship of the Association of Collegiate Alumnae
and the Fellowship of the Archaeological Institute of America
were awarded for 1912–13 to Margaret Coleman Waites, A.B.
(Radcliffe) 1905, Ph.D. (*ibid.*) 1910. The Astronomical Fellowship of the Nantucket Maria Mitchell Association, offered for the
first time in 1912, was awarded for 1912–13 to Margaret Harwood,
A.B. (Radcliffe) 1907.

Two prizes open to competition by the students of Harvard
University and of Radcliffe College were awarded in 1912 as
follows: the Old Testament Prize to Grace Martha Harriman,
1912, and the Craig Prize in Dramatic Composition to Elizabeth
Apthorp McFadden, B.L. (Smith) 1898, Radcliffe graduate
student, 1908–09, 1910–11. The Charles Eliot Norton Fellowship in Greek Studies in Harvard University was awarded for
1911–12 to Hetty Goldman, A.B. (Bryn Mawr) 1903, A.M.
(Radcliffe) 1910, who held the same fellowship in 1910–11.

The members of the Academic Board for 1911–12 were Professor
Byerly (Chairman), and Professors E. L. Mark, H. S. White,
E. H. Hall, H. W. Smyth, A. A. Howard, G. L. Kittredge, C. H.
Grandgent, E. F. Gay.

The close of the college year was saddened by the death of
Professor William Watson Goodwin. Radcliffe College, together
with Harvard College, bears witness to her indebtedness to Professor Goodwin. He was one of the signers of the Articles of
Association of the Society for the Collegiate Instruction of Women,
together with Mrs. Agassiz, Professor and Mrs. Gurney, Professors Child, Greenough, Norton, and Peirce, and others now living,
whose approval gave adequate assurance in the eyes of many that
the experiment they had undertaken would be carried out according to the highest ideals of scholarship. He remained an Associate until his death.

At the meeting of the Associates on October 18, 1911, the
resignation of Mr. John Forbes Perkins from the Associates was
accepted with regret. There were five elections of members of
the Associates during the year 1911–12: Mrs. Mabel Harris Lyon,
of the Class of 1897, an Associate since 1909, nominated by the
Alumnae, was reëlected for a term of three years from 1911; Mrs.
Mary Lowell Barton, an Associate since 1906, was reëlected for
a term of three years from 1912; Professor James Hardy Ropes,
an Associate since 1906, whose term of office expired in February,

1912, was reëlected in June for a term of one year from 1912; Professor Gregory Paul Baxter was elected for a term of two years; and Professor George Howard Parker was elected for a term of three years. Radcliffe College has had the good fortune in the past to have in its Board of Associates several members of the Harvard Faculty. It is suggested that for these Associates there be rotation of office, as in the case of the Harvard Overseers. Professor Fred Norris Robinson was reëlected member of the Council for a term of seven years from 1912. Miss Margaret Gilman, a special student in Radcliffe in 1885–86, a daughter of Mr. Arthur Gilman, who was the first Secretary of the College, was appointed Mistress of Sarah Whitman Hall for the year 1912–13.

The College is still young and still poor, but much the richer for receiving last year $170,290. This sum came through divers channels. Little came by begging. The largest gift came from a patron of education who knew where and how to give. The gifts, bequests, and legacies include the following: —

From the Division of Modern Languages, and the Departments of English and History, $315, for the purchase of books for the Radcliffe Library. From the Class of 1902, as its decennial gift, $1,200, toward the fund for instruction. From the estate of Elnathan Pratt, of Worcester, $4,775, in payment of a legacy to establish a scholarship to be known as the Elnathan Pratt Scholarship, the income to be given by preference to a student coming from Worcester, Massachusetts. From the estate of Mrs. Josiah Parsons Cooke, $5,000. Mrs. Cooke left this sum to found a scholarship to be called the Josiah Parsons Cooke Scholarship, the income to be given by preference to a student wishing to pursue scientific study. From the executors of the estate of Andrew C. Slater, $5,000, for a scholarship, the income to be given to needy and deserving students. From the estate of Mrs. Rebecca A. Greene, $39,000, in addition to the $175,000 received in 1910–11. From the estate of Mrs. Lydia Augusta Barnard, $115,000: $75,000 is for a hall of residence to be known as James and Augusta Barnard Hall; $30,000 is to found the Anna Parsons Scholarships; $10,000, which is subject to the payment of certain annuities, is to found the James and Augusta Barnard Scholarships.

These gifts show that Radcliffe has kept old friends, and has found new friends who believe in her possibilities. From the income of the several sums here enumerated for the purpose, ten new scholarships have become available for 1912–13. There is no better service to be rendered than to open the way into college to those able and deserving young women who cannot work their way as easily as men do, and who run the risk of working it at too great a cost.

Bertram Hall and Grace Hopkinson Eliot Hall, given by Mrs. D. P. Kimball in 1901 and 1906, not only have served the purpose for which they were given, but have done more than anyone expected. The ladies in charge have succeeded in establishing something like family life, free from artificial restraints, among the young women who live in the buildings, and in averting the disadvantages that were looked for by some persons in dormitories for girls.

The complete success of these halls has led to the erection of another of the same type, — Sarah Whitman Hall, built in memory of Mrs. Sarah Wyman Whitman. It was ready for occupation on the first day of the college year, 1912. It stands in Walker Street, near the corner of Shepard Street, facing the Radcliffe field. In the material of which it is built, namely, brick with stone trimmings, it resembles its neighbors, but in the plan of the interior is somewhat different from the other two. It accommodates fifty students, and contains, in addition to bedrooms, rooms for the mistress, parlors, a dining-room, kitchen, and laundry. The portrait of Mrs. Whitman, painted by her friend, Mrs. Daniel Merriman, hangs in the living room. A considerable sum of money toward the building of this hall was given by friends of Mrs. Whitman, with very little solicitation. Radcliffe can never thank adequately those friends for their generosity and devotion to Mrs. Whitman in thus caring for the best interests of the College. The money needed in excess of subscriptions was supplied by the College, and is to be repaid by a sinking fund. It is hoped, however, that further contributions toward this hall will be made later.

James and Augusta Barnard Hall is to be built on the Radcliffe field, at right angles to Bertram Hall, facing Sarah Whitman Hall. This fourth hall will be most acceptable, because the College has land to put it on, and students to put into it. Radcliffe has needed more halls in order to make the resort to the College broad and national. With registered students to the number of 563 in 1912–13, it should certainly have halls for the accommodation of at least 250 students.

A readjustment has been made in the prices of the rooms for 1912–13. In the three halls there are eighteen rooms at $72 a year, sixty-two at $108, and nineteen at $144. There are a few special combinations of bedrooms and studies in Bertram Hall which are at higher rates. Table board remains as before, $216 for the thirty-six weeks in the college year. This makes the minimum expense for tuition and for board and lodging in the halls about $500. It costs more to send a girl to Radcliffe than to send a boy to Harvard.

The interest in the health record of college women students is so general that it may be of interest to state that there have been no deaths in the College this year, and three only among the alumnae.

The Radcliffe alumnae number 1,237, and of these a fourth are married, a large proportion in view of the fact that the early classes were very small, and that the members of the recent large classes are young. More than half of the remainder are employed in a wage-earning occupation.

In 1897–98 the number of students was 424. It remained, with slight variations from year to year, between 400 and 500 until 1910–11, when it reached exactly 500. In 1911–12 it rose suddenly to 566. It is as hard to explain this quick gain in numbers as to account for temporary losses in the past. The increase in 1911–12 was in the Freshman Class, the graduate students, and the special students. There were more Freshmen from outside Massachusetts than before. Perhaps Radcliffe is beginning to illustrate the truth of the statement that women will go on with advanced work if they can go on at the college where they have taken their undergraduate work. This may also be a reason for the increase of the Freshmen. One hundred and one, or one out of twelve, of the holders of the Radcliffe A.B. hold the A.M. or the Ph.D. degree from Radcliffe, whereas only one out of forty hold these degrees from other institutions.

Radcliffe is not trying to do too many things at once, but it has been able, as a rule, to attract students who come well prepared to do their own work, and expect to do it well, eager for the high rewards of scholarship. These women are trying to show that they realize that they are living in a century which "is generous to women in granting them new opportunities, a large share in the learning and intellectual property of the world." Indeed the positions that the Radcliffe graduates are asked to fill call for all the capacities and virtues which they can acquire, from the intellectual to the domestic. Five of them are deans of women in coeducational colleges; sixteen hold appointments as professors or instructors in colleges, several hold important positions as heads of private schools for girls, in public schools, as social workers, and as mistresses of halls of residence.   They are doing distinguished service in various communities, and they are able to do this because they have enjoyed the incomparable opportunities to come in touch with the highest scholarship and to attain modern ideals of equipment through the gifts made to Radcliffe from year to year and through the generosity of Harvard College.

MARY COES, *Dean.*

APPENDIX

REPORT OF THE CHAIRMAN OF THE COMMITTEE ON ADMISSION

To THE PRESIDENT OF THE UNIVERSITY: —

SIR, — I have the honor to submit to you my report as Chairman of the Committee on Admission. During the past year, the Committee have received and acted upon 1,066 applications for admission to Harvard College. The action of the Committee upon these applications is indicated in the tables that immediately follow. With them, I have given, for purposes of comparison, the similar tables for 1910–11.

Applications for Admission to the Freshman Class by Examination

	1911	1912
Admitted without conditions (Old Plan)	309	272
Admitted without conditions (New Plan)	83	154
Total admitted without conditions	392	426
Admitted with conditions (Old Plan)	248	219
Total admitted by examination	640	645
Refused admission (Old Plan)	128	125
Refused admission (New Plan)	56	59
Total refused admission	184	184
Candidates in June who did not reappear in September	61	40
Total number of candidates	885	869

The percentage of men admitted from Public Schools is a little short of that for last year, but not enough to cause any anxiety. As the following figures will show, we have been steadily increasing our representation from the Public High Schools: —

	1906	1907	1908	1909	1910	1911	1912
Percentage of men admitted from Public Schools	40.4	42.4	45.3	45.5	43.0	50.9	48.2
Percentage of men admitted from Private and Endowed Schools..	59.4	57.4	54.5	54.4	56.9	49.0	51.7

The effect of the New Plan on our representation from Public High Schools is very noticeable.

I regret that I am obliged to report that our representation from different parts of the country does not increase except in the North Atlantic Division, and possibly in the North Central Division. The following figures represent the numbers of men who have actually entered Harvard College after examination according to the geographical situation of their schools: —

	1906	1907	1908	1909	1910	1911	1912
New England	424	416	357	400	410	473	451
North Atlantic (including New England)	496	485	415	460	464	542	521
South Atlantic	9	3	3	7	5	4	6
Western	6	13	5	4	3	3	5
North Central	26	22	33	35	24	31	43
South Central	0	2	2	0	1	3	2
Foreign	2	1	3	1	8	4	2
Insular Territories and Dependencies	0	3	2	2	2	1	0
	539	529	463	509	507	588	579

It is to be hoped that our New Plan of Admission will enable us to increase our representation from outside New England and the North Atlantic Division of states. There is some ground for this hope in the increase in the number of new schools with which we have become connected during the past two years. The following figures represent the numbers of new schools each year which have not appeared before in our School and College List, i. e., the list of schools and colleges from which men have actually entered Harvard: —

1906	1907	1908	1909	1910	1911	1912
32	31	26	28	27	36	35

Of the thirty-six new schools in 1911 and the thirty-five in 1912, the two years during which we have had the New Plan, thirteen in 1911 and twenty-five in 1912 were added by the New Plan, and of these all but one in 1911 and all but seven in 1912 were outside New England.

The New Plan was devised with special reference to high schools, and has already more than justified itself by proving its adaptability to cases of boys who have made their decision to come to Harvard late in their last school year after a course not planned according to examinations under the Old Plan. The proportions of New Plan men according to the kinds of schools they attended are as follows: —

	1911	1912
Percentage of Candidates from Public Schools	80.5	79.0
Percentage of Candidates from Private and Endowed Schools	19.4	20.9

Similar figures for candidates for admission by the Old Plan are as follows: —

	1911	1912
Percentage of Candidates from Public Schools	45.7	41.8
Percentage of Candidates from Private and Endowed Schools	54.2	58.1

The attitude of preparatory schools towards the New Plan seems to be, for the most part, one of indifference or of distrust. Such schools are, in a measure, under contract to put their boys into college, and cannot afford to risk what they conceive to be the "chances" of the New Plan, especially before they have had a good opportunity to observe how it works — on others. They conceive that the method of scoring used in the Old Plan is safer, and that the greater number of examinations and the possibility of dividing them provide more incentives to work than are provided for under the New Plan.

From this kind of school have come already two objections to certain provisions of the New Plan, both relating to the prescription of certain examinations. The first objection comes from teachers of Mathematics who fear that the prescription of an examination in either Mathematics or Science will work to the disadvantage of Mathematics by leading to the discontinuance of Mathematics as a fourth-year subject in school. The other objection is that the prescription of an examination in Latin for candidates for the degree of A.B. practically extends the definition of the requirement in Latin by a whole year's work, and by compelling a boy to take Latin in his fourth school year restricts unduly his freedom in planning his course. The objections are such as would be felt chiefly in schools of the "preparatory" type; and as yet such schools have not to any great extent used the New Plan. The Committee have both these objections under careful consideration.

The statistics concerning the admission of students from other colleges present no unusual features. Under the new rules for the choice of electives, the work of administering this class of students has greatly increased in amount and difficulty; and undoubtedly these rules will tend to restrict the numbers of men admitted to a class higher than the Sophomore Class. This, however, is a matter which need give us no concern. The statistics for 1910–11 and 1911–12 are as follows: —

	1910–11	1911–12
Admitted as Unclassified Students	92	99
" " Freshmen	12	3
" " Sophomores	14	19
" " Juniors	16	12
" " Seniors	2	1
Refused admission	25	34
Total number of applicants	161	168

The number of applicants for admission as Special Students continues to decline. The figures for 1910–11 and 1911–12 are as follows: —

	1910–11	1911–12
Admitted	28	21
Refused admission	23	8
Total number of applicants	51	29

This falling off in the number of Special Students is partly or wholly accounted for by the fact that the Department of University Extension now affords a much better way of meeting all legitimate desires for instruction in one or two subjects on the part of men who do not fit into the definition of a regular member of the College.   It has seemed to the Committee that it may be well to abolish the category of Special Students, and provide for all who can properly be admitted to our instruction outside of those who are candidates for degrees by means of the provisions for University Extension.   The Committee is coöperating with the Dean of the Department of University Extension in an investigation of the subject, and may report to the Faculty later this year.

During the past year, the Old Plan of admission has been simplified by the dropping of examinations in some subjects which have not proved to be useful, and by a revision of our examinations in History to make them uniform with similar examinations of the College Entrance Examination Board.   The unsolved problems now before the Committee are the difficulties created under the Old Plan by the present ratings of the modern languages and the difficulties which arise from having two different plans of admission side by side.   At present, the outlook is not hopeful for a discontinuance of the Old Plan of admission.   If we could find some way of administering that plan wholly by means of the College Entrance Examination Board, we should greatly simplify our administration of admission, and expedite the successful working out of all problems connected with the New Plan.   It seems very doubtful to me if we shall ever succeed in establishing the examinations we hope for under the New Plan until we are disembarrassed of the Old Plan examinations.

JOHN GODDARD HART,
Chairman of the Committee on Admission.

REPORT OF THE MEDICAL ADVISER

To THE PRESIDENT OF THE UNIVERSITY: —

SIR, — I have the honor to present the report of illness among Harvard students for the academic year 1911–12.

The 499 patients cared for at the Stillman Infirmary and listed in Table III are included in Tables I and II. Among these 499 patients Table III mentions two deaths. They were: —

Joseph B. Emerson, December 20, acute pulmonary tuberculosis.
Garrick M. Borden, May 24, septicaemia.

Other deaths among students were: —

Edward L. Rogers, November 23, of injuries received in an automobile accident.
Merle D. Britten, July 4, head crushed by two electric cars.

In addition to the usual Tables I, II and III, Table IV is a report of the more common serious illnesses treated at the Stillman Infirmary since it was opened in 1902. It may be seen that among 157 cases of appendicitis, with 94 operations, since 1905–06, there has not been a death.

Of the sixty-three cases of diphtheria in the ten years there has been no death.

The provision by the University of a Medical Adviser with an office in the College Yard, where he may be easily and freely consulted, is largely responsible for these good results, in that it facilitates early diagnosis, with immediate operation when called for in the case of appendicitis, and the early administration of antitoxin in the case of diphtheria.

The large proportion of the diagnoses of diphtheria are established by culture before it is possible to determine them clinically. The students ill with diphtheria receive their antitoxin so early that it is the exception to be very ill, and difficult for the majority of them to appreciate that their illness should be considered serious.

Much credit for these and other good results must be given to our Stillman Infirmary, which has every modern equipment, including the best of trained nurses, for the care of the sick. The Stillman Infirmary differs from most other hospitals in one particular, in that it maintains no training school for nurses, but employs only those who have graduated from a thorough course of training in some hospital of established reputation. Nineteen cases of typhoid fever without a death, fifty-five cases of scarlet fever with one death, and thirty-four cases of pneumonia with only four deaths, reflect great credit on the skill and faithfulness of our nurses. Further, I think it is the aim of every one connected with the Infirmary to make it as attractive as possible for the boy who is ill away from home. The sunny atmosphere at the Infirmary and the harmony among its employees are largely due to those qualities in the matron in charge, plus her unusual tact and executive ability. The student at the Infirmary is made to feel much more at home by the kindly interest shown by visits from his college adviser, professor, and Dean. The frequent visits of Mrs. Lowell have added a great deal of sunshine to many a sick student.

TABLE I.—Illness Report, 1911-12

Diseases	Sept.	Oct.	Nov.	Dec.	Jan.	Feb.	Mar.	Apr.	May	June	Total
Abscesses	..	1	1	..	3	2	5	1	2	2	17
Appendicitis	1	7	4	2	5	2	8	5	3	2	39
Asthma	..	..	..	4	1	..	1	1	..	..	7
Bronchitis	..	5	6	4	10	3	5	4	2	..	39
Catarrh	..	..	1	..	1	1	1	..	2	..	6
Chicken-pox	..	..	..	1	2	1	5	2	1	..	12
Colds — unclassified	1	8	25	34	53	40	52	23	30	..	266
Coryza	..	1	5	2	3	7	7	6	5	..	36
Dementia Praecox	..	..	..	..	..	1	..	..	..	..	1
Diarrhoea	..	..	..	1	1	2	4	2	1	1	12
Diphtheria	..	..	2	..	..	1	9	..	..	..	12
Ear, of the	..	..	1	3	4	2	2	1	1	1	15
Eye, of the	..	7	15	16	15	13	25	19	11	4	125
General Debility	..	3	10	13	11	17	23	19	18	9	118
German Measles	..	..	..	..	..	..	2	23	19	..	44
Grippe	..	10	23	20	18	27	26	18	5	1	148
Heart, of the	..	..	1	3	3	1	..	..	..	..	8
Indigestion	1	6	6	11	12	12	7	15	7	5	82
Infections localized	1	12	10	12	6	21	15	14	7	1	99
Insomnia	..	1	1	2	1	4	3	..	5	1	18
Jaundice	..	1	1	1	3	..	1	2	2	..	11
Laryngitis	..	3	..	1	2	1	3	1	..	..	11
Lumbago	..	..	1	..	..	..	1	..	..	..	2
Malaria	..	..	..	..	..	..	..	1	..	..	1
Measles	1	..	..	..	..	..	..	3	..	..	4
Miscellaneous Med.	..	13	14	20	23	21	39	25	31	9	195
Miscellaneous Surg.	4	20	33	19	27	22	27	34	33	15	234
Mumps	..	..	..	..	2	..	1	..	1	1	5
Nephritis	..	..	..	..	..	..	..	2	..	..	2
Neuralgia	..	1	..	1	..	2	1	1	2	..	8
Neuritis	..	2	..	..	..	..	..	..	..	..	2
Pharyngitis	..	..	2	1	5	10	9	7	1	..	35
Pleuritis	..	..	..	..	1	2	..	..	..	..	3
Pneumonia	..	..	1	..	..	1	4	1	..	1	8
Rheumatism	..	..	1	2	6	1	5	2	2	..	19
Skin, of the	..	5	1	2	2	3	3	3	2	1	22
Teeth, of the	..	1	2	6	..	2	2	4	1	2	20
Tonsillitis	1	5	11	19	13	38	42	33	22	3	187
Tuberculosis	..	..	..	1	..	..	1	..	..	..	2
Typhoid	..	2	..	..	..	..	..	..	..	2	4
Whooping Cough	..	..	..	..	..	1	..	..	..	..	1
No diagnosis	..	5	11	5	4	4	4	3	3	..	39
Totals	10	119	189	206	237	265	343	275	214	61	1919
Visits	6	89	154	123	163	155	209	130	90	69	1188
Office consultations, med.	9	169	200	200	253	271	352	297	268	91	2110
Office consultations, surg.	5	115	97	106	157	173	131	136	87	31	1038
Total No. consultations	20	373	451	429	573	599	692	563	445	191	4336

Cases not seen by the Medical Adviser 1176

TABLE II.—ILLNESS REPORT AS RELATED TO THE DIFFERENT SCHOOLS

Diseases	College						Law	Graduate	G. B.	G. S.	Div.	Med.	Instructors	Totals
	1	2	3	4	Sp.	Un.								
Abscesses	4	2	2	3	..	..	3	3	..	..	..	..	..	17
Appendicitis	4	6	7	8	1	..	3	6	1	..	..	3	..	39
Asthma	3	1	3	..	..	..	..	..	..	..	..	..	..	7
Bronchitis	16	9	6	4	..	..	2	2	..	..	..	..	..	39
Catarrh	2	3	..	1	..	..	..	..	..	..	..	..	..	6
Chicken-pox	2	5	1	..	..	..	3	1	..	..	..	..	..	12
Colds, unclassified	115	67	43	29	..	3	7	1	..	..	1	..	..	266
Coryza	8	15	5	3	..	1	2	1	1	..	..	..	..	36
Dementia Praecox	..	..	1	..	..	..	..	..	..	..	..	..	..	1
Diarrhoea	4	3	5	..	..	..	..	..	..	..	..	..	..	12
Diphtheria	1	1	1	1	..	..	5	2	..	..	..	..	1	12
Ear, of the	3	2	2	5	..	..	3	..	..	..	..	..	..	15
Eye, of the	48	23	33	15	..	4	1	1	..	..	..	..	..	125
General Debility	31	23	30	14	2	4	6	5	..	..	2	..	1	118
German Measles	28	4	5	1	..	..	1	3	1	1	..	..	..	44
Grippe	50	32	29	18	..	1	11	3	2	..	1	..	1	148
Heart, of the	4	4	..	..	..	..	..	..	..	..	..	..	..	8
Indigestion	27	24	14	6	1	1	4	4	..	..	1	..	..	82
Infections localized	31	24	17	10	1	1	5	4	3	2	1	..	..	99
Insomnia	2	4	4	1	..	2	3	2	..	..	..	..	..	18
Jaundice	4	3	1	3	..	..	..	..	..	..	..	..	..	11
Laryngitis	2	3	2	4	..	..	..	..	..	..	..	..	..	11
Lumbago	1	..	..	..	1	..	..	..	..	..	..	..	..	2
Malaria	..	..	..	..	..	..	..	1	..	..	..	..	..	1
Measles	1	2	..	..	..	1	..	..	..	..	..	..	..	4
Miscellaneous Med.	75	38	20	23	..	5	13	14	2	1	2	..	2	195
Miscellaneous Surg.	71	46	45	28	3	3	21	11	3	2	2	1	3	234
Mumps	3	1	1	..	..	..	..	..	..	..	..	..	..	5
Nephritis	..	1	1	..	..	..	..	..	..	..	..	..	..	2
Neuralgia	2	2	..	3	..	..	1	..	..	..	..	..	..	8
Neuritis	..	..	..	..	..	..	..	1	..	..	1	..	..	2
Pharyngitis	7	10	4	5	..	..	4	5	..	..	..	..	..	35
Pleuritis	1	..	..	..	1	1	..	..	..	..	..	..	..	3
Pneumonia	4	2	..	1	..	..	1	..	..	..	..	..	..	8
Rheumatism	7	2	4	2	..	..	2	1	..	..	1	..	..	19
Skin, of the	6	3	1	1	..	1	6	3	..	..	..	..	1	22
Teeth, of the	5	6	5	2	..	..	1	..	..	..	..	..	1	20
Tonsillitis	62	48	29	25	..	1	11	7	1	1	..	2	..	187
Tuberculosis	..	1	..	..	..	1	..	..	..	..	..	..	..	2
Typhoid	1	..	..	..	..	..	1	..	..	..	..	..	..	4
Whooping Cough	..	..	1	..	..	..	..	..	..	..	..	..	..	1
No diagnosis	12	7	15	4	..	..	1	..	..	..	..	..	..	39
Totals	647	427	337	217	10	30	121	81	14	7	12	6	10	1919
No. of Students	739	499	537	372	43	72	808	454	79	123	48	275	..	
% of "Sign-offs"	88	86	68	58	23	42	15	18	18	6	25	2	..	
No. of Students at Infirmary	98	74	74	58	8	13	94	36	14	8	6	6	10	
% of "Sign-offs"	13	15	14	16	19	18	12	8	18	7	13	2	..	

TABLE III

STILLMAN INFIRMARY

List of Cases, 1911–12

Abscess — miscellaneous	13	Laryngitis	4
" peritonsillar	6	Lumbago	1
Appendicitis	25	Malaria	1
Bronchitis	11	Measles	2
Chicken-pox	10	Miscellaneous Medical	24
Colds — unclassified	20	Miscellaneous Surgical	88
Coryza	5	Mumps	3
Dementia Praecox	1	Neuralgia	1
Diarrhoea	2	Pharyngitis	5
Diphtheria	12	Pleuritis	2
Ear, of the	6	Pneumonia	1
Eye, of the	2	Rheumatism	9
Fractures	6	Skin, of the	4
General Debility	17	Teeth, of the	3
German Measles	31	Tonsillitis	64
Grippe	47	Tuberculosis	1
Heart, of the	1	Typhoid	1
Indigestion	23	No diagnosis	9
Infections — localized	31		
Insomnia	8	Total	499
Jaundice	4		

Room patients	85
Ward patients	414
Total	499

Discharged — well	310
" relieved	181
" not relieved	3
Died	2
Transferred to other hospitals	3
Total	499

Total number of hospital days	3,074
Daily average	11.42
Total number of operations	52
Operations for Appendicitis	17

TABLE IV

STILLMAN INFIRMARY

ABBREVIATED SUMMARY FOR THE TEN YEARS SINCE THE INFIRMARY
WAS OPENED

Academic Year	Total number Patients	Appendicitis	Operations for Appendicitis	Deaths from Appendicitis	Diphtheria	Deaths from Diphtheria	Pneumonia	Deaths from Pneumonia	Scarlet Fever	Deaths from Scarlet Fever	Typhoid Fever	Deaths from Typhoid Fever
1902–03	223	17	9	0	2	0	7	0	0	0	5	0
1903–04	290	19	10	2	0	0	5	2	0	0	2	0
1904–05	377	22	9	0	5	0	3	1	0	0	5	0
1905–06	432	27	21	1	29	0	0	0	6	0	1	0
1906–07	467	22	15	0	2	0	2	0	5	0	2	0
1907–08	541	27	16	0	5	0	4	0	33	1	2	0
1908–09	459	29	17	0	2	0	0	0	3	0	1	0
1909–10	575	36	19	0	3	0	5	1	3	0	0	0
1910–11	581	18	10	0	3	0	7	0	5	0	0	0
1911–12	499	25	17	0	12	0	1	0	0	0	1	0
Total	4444	242	143	3	63	0	34	4	55	1	19	0

Deaths from other causes were as follows : —

1904–05, 3; 1906–07, 1; 1909–10, 2; 1911–12, 2; making the total number of deaths, sixteen for the ten years.

The causes of the above-mentioned deaths were as follows : —

Auto accident, 1; cancer, 1; carbuncle, 1; cerebro-spinal meningitis, 1; endo- and pericarditis and meningitis, 1; septicaemia, 1; tuberculosis, 2.

Table V is a Summary of the more common contagious diseases for the last eighteen years.

TABLE V

PROPORTION OF FOUR CONTAGIOUS DISEASES FOR THE PAST EIGHTEEN YEARS

	Diphtheria	Measles	Mumps	Scarlet Fever	Total
1894–95	3	21	65	12	101
1895–96	3	21	20	2	46
1896–97	2	47	11	4	64
1897–98	5	19	95	2	121
1898–99	0	48	2	0	50
1899–1900 . . .	5	106	44	3	158
1900–01	12	1	66	4	83
1901–02	4	42	3	2	51
1902–03	7	7	12	7	33
1903–04	13	75	28	7	123
1904–05	11	20	24	0	55
1905–06	35	28	19	8	90
1906–07	4	18	29	9	60
1907–08	5	36	9	46	96
1908–09	2	16	36	5	59
1909–10	3	20	31	9	68
1910–11	4	26	3	7	40
1911–12	12	4	5	0	21

Table VI is given for comparison between the University and the City of Cambridge, but such comparison is made difficult because while the

TABLE VI

PROPORTION OF DIPHTHERIA, MEASLES, AND SCARLET FEVER
FOR THE CITY OF CAMBRIDGE FOR THE PAST
EIGHTEEN YEARS

	Diphtheria	Measles	Scarlet Fever	Total
1894	176		901	1077
1895	573	249	293	1115
1896	455	288	198	941
1897	321	410	231	962
1898	152	53	122	327
1899	502	473	158	1133
1900	925	138	176	1239
1901	615	562	101	1278
1902	460	407	199	1066
1903	322	80	188	590
1904	330	481	135	946
1905	350	112	150	612
1906	517	631	166	1314
1907	323	60	414	797
1908	422	1197	495	2114
1909	278	542	365	1185
1910	310	287	349	946
1911	397	605	213	1215

University statistics in Table V are for the academic year, the statistics for the City of Cambridge are for the calendar year.

Mumps is not mentioned in Table VI, because the Cambridge Board of Health keeps no record of that disease.

MARSHALL H. BAILEY, *Medical Adviser.*

REPORT OF THE APPOINTMENT OFFICE

To the President of the University: —

Sir, — The following Report, rendered by the Appointment Office, describes the work of that Office in 1911–12. The work consists of the recommendation of Harvard men (A) to fill *academic* positions in universities, colleges, schools, or institutions of research; (B) to fill positions *not academic*, including institutional, technical, or business positions. These recommendations may be made by the Chairmen or other representatives of the Divisions and Departments of the Faculty of Arts and Sciences, by the Deans of the Professional Schools,* by the representatives of the Faculty in coöperation with the Office of the General Secretary of The Harvard Alumni Association, or by that Office independently.

In reading the following statement it must be remembered that there are doubtless many positions that have been filled through the influence of individual members of the Faculty which have never come to the attention of this Office.

The statistical tables indicate some interesting facts. The classification according to subject shows that by recommendation of the Faculty, 30 appointments as teacher of English were made. The Reports of the Appointment Office for the last six years show that the Department of English fills each year not less than 10 more positions than any other Department. In the year 1909–10, 27 teachers of English were placed, the next in number being History, 14. In 1910–11, an exceptional year both for demands and for candidates, appointments in English rose to 50; in History, to 15. In 1911–12 the numbers are: English, 30; History, 13; Biology, 12†; Greek and Latin, 9; German, 8; Chemistry, 8; Mathematics, 8; Philosophy and Psychology, 8.

In the table of the general summary, showing comparative figures, it appears that in 1911–12, 194 academic (teaching and research) appointments have been made as against 200 in 1910–11. The loss of 6 occurs in the university and college appointments, which in 1911–12 number 94 as against 122 in 1910–11. This difference in figures of 28 is due not to any noticeable shortage in the demands on the Faculty for such teachers, but to the fact that in 1910–11, when 122 college and university positions were filled by the Office, there was an unusually large registration of men ready to accept elementary instructorships. A large proportion of the calls from colleges and universities is for teachers of elementary classes at a salary of about $1,000. The men registered for such positions are naturally candidates for the degree of Master of Arts, with an occasional unusually well-trained Senior. The disproportion between the men registered in any one year and the men placed is, therefore, readily explained by the fact that only a small number of the men registered can afford to be candidates for such modest college positions as are commonly offered. The majority of men registered in any year have positions already but hope for better ones. It is evident that there must be a variation from year to year in the number of college or university positions which the Appointment Office can fill, dependent on the number and type of grad-

---

* No official report has been received from the Schools of Divinity, Law, Medicine, or Mining.

† In 1910–11 the Division of Biology filled 7 positions.

uate students, candidates for the higher degrees, or on the opportunities presented for transferring Harvard teachers already holding college or university appointments to higher posts. To some extent this condition of affairs affects the placing of men in technical positions through the various Scientific Departments. Even in this year, when statistics show a loss of 6, almost every Department placed all its newly registered men.

A cause for encouragement in the statistics of the present year is in the fact that the number of appointments in the public schools has risen from 13 in 1911 to 22 in 1912. The private school record is even more encouraging: 53 positions filled in 1912 as compared with 40 in 1911.

It is further noticeable in 1912 that 113 out of 194 academic appointments, or about 58%, are in the North Atlantic Section of the United States. Out of the 95 appointments not academic, 80, or about 85%, are in that same section. In 1911, out of 200 academic appointments, 97, or about 48%, were in the North Atlantic States, and out of 112 appointments not academic, 89, or about 79%, were in the same section.

The statistics concerning business positions reported by the Faculty and by The Harvard Alumni Association show 95 in 1912 as against 112 in 1911. Of these 95, 63 are reported by the Office of the Alumni Association and 32 by the Faculty, compared with 66 reported by the Alumni Association in 1911, and 46 by the Faculty in the same year. This variation in figures may be accounted for by the fact that 1911 was an unusually full year in all Departments, both for opportunities and for candidates, and also by the fact that the record of appointments submitted by the Chairmen may not cover all the positions filled. The decrease in the percentage of positions filled by The Harvard Alumni Association is due perhaps to several causes. There has been an increasing number of candidates for positions in manufacturing, mercantile, and publishing houses, and an insufficient number of such positions. The calls from the bond and brokerage concerns, however, have increased, while the number of applicants has steadily fallen off. At the same time it is interesting to note that there is a gain in 1912 of 5 insurance and 4 mercantile positions, 6 of the mercantile positions being in department stores, — a growing field for college men.

In 1912 the average salary reported for academic positions is $1,382; in 1911 it was $1,310; the average salary reported for a position not academic in 1912 is $977; in 1911 it was $888.

APPOINTMENTS

(A) ACADEMIC

(a) Teaching and Administrative

	Number of Positions	Number of Salaries Reported	Aggregate Salaries Reported
1. Universities or Colleges	94	83	$114,425
2. Technical Schools	9	8	11,116
3. Normal Schools	4	3	2,150
4. Vocational School	1	1	5,000
5. Public Schools	22	20	27,550
6. Private or Endowed Schools	53	52	67,205
Total	183	167	$227,446

Classification according to Subject and Department: —

1. Subject

	Number of Positions Filled	
Group I		
Greek and Latin	2	
Latin	4	
with Ancient History	1	
with Ancient History and Mathematics	1	
with English	1	
with other subjects	1	
Roman Archaeology	1	
Greek	2	
with Latin and Ancient History	1	
with Ancient History	1	15
English	30	
with Latin	2	
with Public Speaking	1	
with History	1	
with other subjects	2	36
German	8	
with Latin	2	10
French and German	5	5
Romance Languages	4	
French	4	
with German and Latin	2	
with German, Latin, and English	1	
with German and Chemistry........................	1	
with English and History	1	
with Spanish	2	
with other subjects (baseball)	1	
Italian	1	17
Fine Arts		
Architecture	1	
Landscape Gardening	1	2
Music	2	2
Carried forward		87

Number of
Positions
Filled

Brought forward		87
GROUP II		
Physics and Chemistry	6	
Physics	1	
Chemistry	8	15
Engineering	2	2
Biology	8	
Botany	4	
Zoölogy	8	
with Embryology	1	
Genetics	1	12
Geology	2	
Economic Geology	1	8
Natural History	▲	▲
GROUP III		
History	18	
with Government	1	14
Economics	6	
with Sociology	8	9
Education and Psychology	▲	▲
GROUP IV		
Philosophy and Psychology	1	
Philosophy	4	
Psychology	8	8
Mathematics	8	
with Science, Mechanical Drawing, and English	1	
with Athletics	1	10
Carried forward...................		162

	Number of Positions Filled	
Brought forward...................	162	

OUT OF GROUP

Business	1	ı
Commercial Subjects	1	ı
Manual Training	ı	ı
General Combined Subjects	2	2
Physical Training	1	
with other subjects	3	ı

2. DEPARTMENT (ADMINISTRATIVE)

Principal	7	7
Superintendent	2	2
Assistant Superintendent	ı	ı
Registrar...	ı	ı
Head of Junior Department of Boys' School	1	1
Total	183	

(b) Research

	Number of Positions		Number of Salaries Reported	Aggregate Salaries Reported
1. Economic	1	1		
2. Educational	5	5		
3. Sociological	2	2		
4. Scientific				
Biology:				
Botany	1			
Zoölogy	1	2		
5. Chemistry	1	1		
Total	11		10	$15,641

(B) Not Academic

	Number of Positions secured through		Number of Salaries Reported	Aggregate Salaries Reported
	Faculty	Harvard Alumni Association		
(a) Business				
1. Accounting and auditing		2	2	2	$1,500
		—			
2. Banking and Brokerage				
Office	2	2		
Advertising	..	1	5	3	. 2,300
		—			
3. Engineering (Construction and Consulting)	5	3	8	6	4,864
	—	—			
4. Forestry				
Consulting Foresters	ʒ			
United States Forest Service	2			
State Association	1			
	—			
5. Insurance		6	6	6	5,460
6. Journalism				
Editing		3		
Advertising		2	5	5	5,828
		—			
7. Architecture	ʌ			
	—			
8. Landscape Architecture	2		2	1	1,300
	—			
9. Manufacturing:				
Office and Manufacturing proper	1	17		
Efficiency	1	2		
Chemistry	1	2	24	22	17,696
	—	—			
10. Mercantile:				
Wholesale		5		
Retail (including Department Stores)	3	3	11	11	6,136
	—	—			
11. Public Service Corporation				
Railroad (Engineering) .	4	3		
Telephone (Office)	1	3		
Municipal Engineering	1			
Sewerage	1		13	8	6,254
	—			
	—	—	—	—	
Carried forward........	30	54	84	64	$51,338

	Faculty	Number of Positions secured through Harvard Alumni Association	Number of Salaries Reported	Aggregate Salaries Reported
Brought forward	30	54	84	64	$51,338
12. Publishing		2			
Translating	1		3	3	4,340
		—			
13. Real Estate		2	2	2	1,420
		—			
14. Secretaryships					
Executive					
Learned Foundation ...	1				
Public Library					
Private					
Diplomatic		2			
Museum		1			
State Reservation Commission		1	6	4	8,900
	—	—	—	—	
	32	63	95	73	$65,998

(C) GEOGRAPHICAL DISTRIBUTION

	Universities Colleges	Technical Schools	Normal Schools	Vocational Schools	Public Schools	Private Schools	Research	Not Academic	Totals for States	Totals for Divisions
NORTH ATLANTIC DIVISION:										193
Maine	3	..	..	..	..	..	..	1	4	..
New Hampshire	2	..	..	..	..	6	..	..	8	..
Vermont	2	..	..	..	..	1	..	..	3	..
Massachusetts	11	5	..	..	12	13	6	62	109	..
Rhode Island	1	..	..	..	..	1	..	..	2	..
Connecticut	4	..	..	1	1	2	..	..	8	..
New York	11	..	..	..	..	7	3	13	34	..
New Jersey	1	..	..	..	2	3	..	1	7	..
Pennsylvania	9	1	..	..	..	5	..	3	18	..
SOUTH ATLANTIC DIVISION:	..	..	..	..	..	..	..	..	..	18
Maryland	..	..	..	..	..	1	..	1	2	..
District of Columbia	..	..	..	..	..	..	2	2	4	..
Virginia	3	..	..	..	..	..	..	..	3	..
West Virginia	..	..	1	..	..	..	..	..	1	..
North Carolina	3	..	..	..	..	1	..	2	6	..
South Carolina	..	..	..	..	..	1	..	..	1	..
Georgia	..	..	..	..	..	..	..	1	1	..
SOUTH CENTRAL DIVISION:										6
Tennessee	..	..	..	..	1	..	..	..	1	..
Texas	2	1	..	..	..	..	..	..	3	..
Arkansas	2	..	..	..	..	..	..	..	2	..
NORTH CENTRAL DIVISION:										42
Ohio	..	..	..	..	..	..	..	2	2	..
Indiana	2	..	1	..	2	..	..	..	5	..
Illinois	8	..	..	..	..	2	..	1	11	..
Michigan	..	..	..	..	..	..	..	2	2	..
Wisconsin	2	..	..	..	1	1	..	1	5	..
Minnesota	1	..	..	..	..	..	..	..	1	..
Iowa	2	..	..	..	1	..	..	..	3	..
Missouri	6	..	..	..	..	..	..	..	6	..
North Dakota	..	..	1	..	..	..	..	..	1	..
South Dakota	2	1	..	..	..	..	..	..	3	..
Kansas	2	..	..	..	1	..	..	..	3	..
WESTERN DIVISION:										23
Colorado	1	..	..	..	1	2	..	..	4	..
Arizona	..	..	..	..	..	1	..	..	1	..
Utah	1	1	..	..	..	..	..	..	2	..
Washington	3	..	..	..	..	..	..	..	3	..
Oregon	1	..	..	..	..	..	..	..	1	..
California	7	..	..	..	..	4	..	..	11	..
CUBA	..	..	..	..	..	..	..	1	1	1
CANADA	2	..	1	..	..	..	..	..	3	3
ENGLAND	..	..	..	..	..	..	..	1	1	1
GERMANY	..	..	..	..	..	2	..	..	2	2
AUSTRIA	..	..	..	..	..	..	..	1	1	1
Total Positions	94	9	4	1	22	53	11	95	289	289

(D) SUMMARY OF APPOINTMENTS

Geographical Distribution	Academic 1912	Not Academic 1912	Academic 1911	Not Academic 1911
North Atlantic	113	80	97	89
South Atlantic	12	6	17	7
South Central	6	0	23	0
North Central	36	6	31	11
Western	22	0	20	1
Dependencies	0	1	3	1
Foreign Countries	5	2	9	3
	194	95	200	112
Total		289		312
Aggregate Salaries	$243,087	$65,598	$229,821	$76,992

L. B. R. BRIGGS, *Dean,*
Faculty of Arts and Sciences.

E. H. WELLS, *General Secretary,*
The Harvard Alumni Association.

REPORT OF THE SECRETARY FOR STUDENT EMPLOYMENT

The following report, submitted by the Secretary of the Students' Employment Office, describes the work of that Office in 1911–12.

The office undertakes to recommend Harvard students and graduates as tutors, or for such part time work as is available in and about Cambridge. It also endeavors, as far as possible, to increase the demand for this work. It is essential that students who secure employment render punctual and efficient service, and it is the policy of the Office to recommend for positions men who by their knowledge, experience, and personality are best qualified to fill them, regardless of the fact that there may be other men of less ability more in need. Experience shows that many positions are lost either through inefficient work or through the unbusiness-like attitude of students toward their employers and the Office.

In comparison with 1910–11, the following figures show an increase of 41 men employed and a decrease of about $6,000 in the amount earned.

	1910–11	1911–12
Men registered for term-time work	599	559
Men who secured term-time work	272	306
Men registered for summer work	638	611
Men who secured summer work	138	145
Total registration for term-time and summer work, allowing for men registered for both	1021 *	1015 *

A decrease of 6 men registered and an increase of 41 employed.

The division of registration among the different Departments of the University is as follows: —

College	687	Dental	14
Medical	42	Scientific	32
Law	92	Special	9
Graduate	113	Unclassified	8
Business	6	Assistants	6
Divinity	6		
		Total	1015

* 1910–11........216 duplicate registrations
1911–12........155 duplicate registrations

Men employed and amount earned through the aid of the Students' Employment Office, the Departments of the University, and The Harvard Alumni Association: —

	Men employed	Amount earned 1910–11	1911–12
Term-time	278	63,263.29	......
Term-time	312 *	......	56,773.01
Summer, 1911	157	23,568.64	......
Summer, 1912	157 †	......	23,769.66
		86,831.93	80,542.67
Amount reported independently earned during year		31,823.55	27,169.29
		118,655.48	107,711.96

* 306 men employed through the aid of the Office.
  6 men employed through the aid of the Departments of the University and The Harvard Alumni Association.

† 145 men employed through the aid of the Office.
  12 men employed through the aid of Departments of the University and The Harvard Alumni Association.

The following table shows the number of temporary positions filled — 2,455 in all — through the aid of the Office, the Departments of the University, and The Harvard Alumni Association: —

Agent	8	Library Messenger	1
Assistant	2	Literary Work	2
Attendant	6	Model	4
Bath-house Employee	1	Monitor	479
Boatman	3	Musician	8
Book-keeper	1	Newspaper Correspondent	1
Boy Scout Leader	1	Night School Teacher	4
Camp Councillor	10	Office Boy	1
Canvasser, Solicitor	4	Organiser	1
Caretaker	1	Playground Director	3
Cataloguer	3	Proctor	92
Chauffeur	4	Proof-reader	2
Chemist	1	Pylon Man	1
Choreman	54	Reader	5
Clerk	115	Room for Services	6
Club Employee	1	Salesman	5
Coach	8	Scene Shifter, Chair Mover	5
Companion	21	Secretary	7
Computer	4	Settlement Worker	4
Conductor	1	Stenographer	26
Draftsman	12	Substitute for Schools	5
Electrician	2	Supernumerary	2
Engineer	2	Supervisor of Study	20
Entertainer	1	Supervisor and Tutor	1
Errandman	50	Surveyor	2
Expressman	1	Teacher in Chemistry	1
Farm Hand	2	Ticket Taker	589
Gardener	3	Telegraph Operator	1
Gate Keeper, Guard, Usher	3	Translator	9
General Man on Estate	9	Tutor and Companion	31
Guide	447	Tutor	95
Hotel Employee	8	Typewriter	132
Ice Man	1	Waiter	109
Illustrator	1	Watchman	2
Inspector	2		
Janitor	2	Total	2,455
Library Work	4		

TERM-TIME EMPLOYMENT
October 2, 1911 — June 29, 1912

Positions	No. of positions	Amount	No. of men employed	Avg. amt. earned per man
Agent	3	$44.00	4	$11.00
Attendant	3	377.00	4	94.25
Canvasser, Solicitor	4	90.83	22	4.13
Cataloguer	3	91.50	2	45.75
Chauffeur	1	240.00	1	240.00
Choreman	46	561.49	28	20.05
Civil Engineer	1	210.00	1	210.00
*Clerk [1]	103	1,120.01	87	12.87
Coach	7	1,052.00	7	150.28
Companion	6	1,218.00	6	203.00
Computer	4	70.55	4	17.54
*Draftsman	10	196.50	7	28.07
Electrician	1	2.00	1	2.00
Entertainer	1	10.00	2	5.00
Errandman	47	46.13	33	1.40
Expressman	1	19.00	2	9.50
Gate Keeper	3	269.60	13	20.74
*General Man	4	951.00	4	237.75
Guide	133	145.15	25	5.80
Hotel Employee	1	712.50	1	712.50
Inspector	2	95.00	3	31.67
Janitor	2	343.00	2	171.50
Library Messenger	1	135.00	1	135.00
*Library Work	3	335.00	3	111.67
Literary Work	2	70.00	2	35.00
Model	4	62.50	4	15.62
Monitor	479	1,338.60	13	102.97
Musician [1]	7	107.00	7	15.29
Night School Teacher	4	478.00	6	79.66
Organiser	1	15.00	1	15.00
Proctor	92	2,775.77	102	27.21
Proof-reader	1	140.00	3	46.67
Reader	4	11.70	3	3.90
Room for Services	6	873.00	6	145.50
Salesman	5	128.50	12	10.71
Scene Shifter and Chair Mover	5	31.33	10	3.13
Secretary	6	1,776.62	8	222.08
Settlement Worker	4	2,442.00	4	610.50
Stenographer	20	730.50	8	90.06
*Substitute for School	5	443.00	5	88.60
Supernumerary	2	5.60	10	.56
Supervisor	20	1,130.00	16	70.63
Supervisor and Tutor	1	1,800.00	1	1,800.00
Surveyor	2	508.60	3	169.53
Teacher in Chemistry	1	310.00	1	310.00
Ticket Taker	550	896.75	8	112.09
Translator	6	323.00	6	53.83
Tutor [1]	59	6,892.99	49	140.67
Tutor and Companion	16	14,291.20	16	893.20
Typewriter	126	1,174.80	24	48.95
Waiter	108	9,691.29	108	89.73
	1,926	$56,773.01		

[1] Statistics compiled on number who reported only. Seven men have not reported.
* Six positions filled by the Departments of the University or The Harvard Alumni Association.

Positions	No. of positions	Amount	No. of men employed	Avg. amt. earned per man
Agent	5	$317.20	9	$35.24
*Assistant	2	450.00	2	225.00
Attendant	3	312.00	3	104.00
Bath House Employee	1	115.00	1	115.00
Boatman	3	381.17	3	127.06
*Boy Scout Leader	1	100.00	1	100.00
Book-keeper	1	73.32	1	73.32
Camp Councillor	10	2,014.00	10	201.40
Caretaker	1	126.50	1	126.50
*Chauffeur	3	315.00	3	105.00
*Chemist	1	76.00	1	76.00
Choreman [1]	8	97.33	11	8.85
*Clerk [1]	12	608.60	12	50.72
Club Employee	1	336.00	2	168.00
Coach	1	255.00	1	255.00
Companion [1]	15	4,078.50	16	254.90
Conductor [1]	1	110.25	1	110.25
*Draftsman [1]	2	325.00	2	162.50
Electrician	1	108.00	1	108.00
*Engineer	1	24.00	1	24.00
Farm Hand	2	135.00	2	67.50
Gardener	3	200.65	3	66.88
General Man on Estate	5	483.13	4	120.78
Guides	314	861.56	6	143.59
Hotel Employee	7	878.00	9	97.55
Ice Man	1	80.00	1	80.00
Illustrator	1	60.00	1	60.00
Library Work	1	121.50	1	121.50
Messenger	3	106.75	7	15.25
Musician	1	5.00	1	5.00
*Newspaper Work	1	2.00	1	2.00
Office Boy	1	10.75	1	10.75
Playground Director	3	310.00	4	77.50
Proof-reader	1	7.13	1	7.13
Pylon Men	1	105.00	10	10.50
Reader	1	34.00	1	34.00
*Secretary	1	418.50	1	418.50
*Stenographer	6	296.15	4	74.04
*Telegraph Operator	1	467.00	1	467.00
Ticket Taker	39	200.00	48	4.17
Translator	3	128.50	3	42.83
Tutor [1]	36	2,993.25	28	106.90
Tutor and Companion	15	5,494.92	15	366.33
Typewriter	6	145.50	4	36.37
Waiter	1	2.50	1	2.50
Watchman [1]	2	..	..	..
	529	$23,769.66		

[1] Statistics compiled upon number of men who reported only. Seven men have not reported.

* Twelve positions filled by the Departments of the University or The Harvard Alumni Association.

MORRIS GRAY, JR.,
Secretary for Student Employment.

ORDINARY DEGREES CONFERRED, 1908–12

	1908	1909	1910	1911	1912
Bachelors of Arts	379	421	452	414	419
Bachelors of Arts out of course	60	73	52	62	57
Bachelors of Science	50	60	57	44	52
Bachelors of Science out of course	10	18	12	25	8
Bachelors of Divinity	12	12	6	6	3
Bachelors of Laws	159	163	182	168	186
Bachelors of Laws out of course	13	14	11	13	13
Doctor of Law	0	0	0	0	1
Bachelors of Agricultural Science	7	5	1	0	0
Bachelors of Agricultural Science out of course	0	0	1	0	0
Doctors of Public Health	0	0	0	2	3
Doctors of Medicine	69	55	73	85	60
Doctors of Medicine out of course	2	3	0	2	1
Doctors of Dental Medicine	18	10	24	12	28
Doctors of Dental Medicine out of course . . .	0	5	0	0	0
Doctor of Veterinary Medicine out of course . .	0	0	0	0	1
Masters of Arts	116	112	142	163	131
Masters of Arts out of course	8	7	0	0	0
Masters of Science	4	3	4	0	0
Doctors of Philosophy	43	38	37	41	38
Doctors of Science	0	0	0	1	3
Metallurgical Engineers	0	0	0	1	0
Mining Engineers	3	5	3	8	4
Masters in Civil Engineering	1	2	1	5	5
Masters in Mechanical Engineering	3	0	4	1	1
Masters in Electrical Engineering	1	3	4	8	8
Masters in Electrical Engineering out of course	0	0	1	0	0
Masters in Architecture	1	2	2	0	2
Masters in Landscape Architecture	1	0	1	4	4
Masters in Forestry	4	5	3	5	5
Masters in Forestry out of course	0	0	0	1	0
Masters of Science in Botany	0	0	0	3	1
Masters of Science in Chemistry	0	0	0	1	1
Master of Science in Geology	0	0	0	0	1
Masters of Science in Zoology	0	0	0	1	3
Masters in Business Administration	0	0	8	8	8
Master in Business Administration out of course	0	0	0	0	1
Totals	964	1011	1081	1084	1048

Commencement Certificates	1	1	1	1	0

INDEX

TREASURER'S STATEMENT

TREASURER'S STATEMENT FOR 1911–12

To THE BOARD OF OVERSEERS OF HARVARD COLLEGE: —

The Treasurer submits the annual statement of the financial affairs of the University, for the year ending June 30, 1912.

The net income of the general investments for this period was divided at the rate of 4.95 per cent among the Funds to which these investments belong.

From the income of all bonds bought at a premium for general investments $7,766.36 was credited to the various accounts concerned, and for special investments $594.81, as the fair yearly repayment to make good the premiums at the maturity of the bonds.

CHARLES F. ADAMS, 2D, *Treasurer.*

BOSTON, November, 1912.

BALANCE SHEET

June 30, 1912

ASSETS

CASH IN BANKS:

Bursar, ...	$46,517.33	
Treasurer — General, ...	176,338.07	
Treasurer — Special — Schedule 1, ...	433.30	$223,288.70

ACCOUNTS RECEIVABLE:

Term Bills of January, 1912, ...	$841.22	
Term Bills of June, 1912, ...	105,963.19	
Sundry accounts of Bursar's office, ...	9,083.51	
Interest accrued, ...	4,638.31	120,526.23

INVENTORY — Stores, ... 10,483.72

INSURANCE UNEXPIRED, ... 26,784.18

INVESTMENTS:

Securities — Special — Schedule 1, ...	$2,469,684.73	
Securities — General — Schedule 2, ...	18,631,588.70	
Land and Buildings — Special — Schedule 1,	1,465,926.72	
Land and Buildings — General — Schedule 3,	3,301,666.87	25,868,867.02

$26,249,949.85

BALANCE SHEET

June 30, 1912

LIABILITIES

ACCOUNTS PAYABLE:

Salaries, ...	$165,112.08	
Deposits and Advance Payments, ...	14,400.96	$179,513.04

CAPITAL:

Gains and Losses for General Investments, ...			555,647.48
Income on General Investments Unapportioned, ...			4,381.67
Funds and Gifts, July 1, 1911, ...	$24,338,194.54		
General Suspense, July 1, 1911, ...	196,587.74		
		$24,126,606.80	
Gifts for Capital — Exhibit D, $932,409.21			
Gains and losses in valuation			
of Special Investments, . . 41,726.09			
Unexpended balances of new			
gifts for buildings, ... 443,282.78			
Other capital receipts, ... 886.08			
$1,418,304.16			
Less expenditures charged to			
capital account, ... 8,584.59			
$1,409,719.57			
Expenditures charged to General Suspense, ... 9,730.79		1,399,988.78	
		$25,526,595.58	
General Deficit — Exhibit B, ...		16,187.92	
Funds and Gifts — June 30, 1912,			
Schedule 4, ... $25,752,720.39			
General Suspense, Credit			
Balances, June 30, 1912,			
Schedule 5, ... 133,435.06			
$25,886,155.45			
Less General Suspense, Debit			
Balances, June 30, 1912,			
Schedule 6, ... 375,747.79 $25,510,407.66		25,510,407.66	
			$26,249,949.85

CONSOLIDATED STATEMENT OF INCOME AND EXPENDITURE

For the year ended June 30, 1912

INCOME

RESTRICTED INCOME:

FROM SPECIAL INVESTMENTS,

Interest and Dividends — Schedule 1, ...		$108,038.01	
Rents of Land and Buildings, . .	$153,390.54		
Less Operating Expenses, . . .	89,549.09	63,841.45	
Net income — Schedule 1, ...			$171,879.46

FROM GENERAL INVESTMENTS,

Interest and Dividends on

Securities — Schedule 2, . . .	$797,636.22		
Bank Balances, ...	3,512.26		
Advances to Departments and			
Miscellaneous, ...	15,688.04	$816,836.52	
Rents of Land and Buildings, . .	$306,726.12		
Less Operating Expenses, . . .	97,752.46		
Net Income — Schedule 3, ...		208,973.66	
Total Income General Investments, . . .		$1,025,810.18	
Amount of Income unapportioned during previous years, now used, ...		1,255.98	
Amount from General Investments apportioned, ...			1,027,066.16
Gifts for Immediate Use — Exhibit E, ...		$771,772.20	
Less Unexpended balances of new gifts for buildings, added to Funds and Gifts — Exhibit A, ...		443,282.78	328,489.42
Miscellaneous income, ...			53,656.07

GENERAL INCOME:

Tuition Fees, ...	$670,890.88	
Laboratory Fees, ...	36,789.31	
Other Fees, ...	66,502.31	
Gross Rents of College Dormitories, etc.	88,915.16	
Miscellaneous income, ...	*114,976.92	978,074.58
		$2,559,165.69
General Deficit to Exhibit A, ...		16,187.92
		$2,575,353.61

* Included in this amount is $71,695.58 received by the Graduate School of Applied Science from Harvard College — see contra.

CONSOLIDATED STATEMENT OF INCOME AND EXPENDITURE

For the year ended June 30, 1912

EXPENDITURE

From RESTRICTED INCOME for:

Administrative Purposes,	$5,501.24	
Educational Purposes,	453,940.44	
Other Activities,	604,496.73	
Aids,	177,426.81	$1,241,365.22

From GENERAL INCOME for:

Administrative Purposes,	$92,526.01	
Educational Purposes,	*985,517.02	
Other Activities,	94,897.02	
Aids,	14,575.00	1,187,515.05
Repairs and equipment of College dormitories,	$16,345.90	
Caretaking and operating expenses of College dormitories,	31,187.09	47,532.99
Repairs and equipment of land and buildings for general purposes,	$25,034.81	
Caretaking and operating expenses of land and buildings for general purposes,	73,905.54	98,940.35

$2,575,353.61

* Included in this amount is $71,695.58 paid by Harvard College to the Graduate School of Applied Science — see contra.

INCOME AND EXPENDITURE

For the year ended

	INCOME		
	Restricted	General	Total
University (Sch. 7), ...	$65,996.83	$10,662.07	$76,658.90
College, including Graduate School of Arts and Sciences (Sch. 8), . .	480,215.25	559,227.62	1,089,442.87
Library (Sch. 9), ...	73,947.12	1,481.26	75,428.38
Summer Schools (Sch. 11), ...	882.33	23,868.47	24,750.80
Graduate School of Applied Science (Sch. 12), ...	133,726.61	96,761.98	230,488.59
Graduate School of Business Administration (Sch. 13), ...	30,122.23	10,641.40	40,763.63
Divinity School (Sch. 14), ...	36,658.22	8,558.83	45,217.05
Law School (Sch. 15), ...	36,154.69	119,360.25	155,514.94
Medical School (Sch. 16), ...	197,693.73	93,943.07	291,636.80
Graduate School of Medicine (Sch. 17),	. . . . . .	. . . . . .	. . . . . .
Dental School (Sch. 18), ...	3,277.40	32,938.82	36,216.22
Bussey Institution (Sch. 19), ...	13,504.92	107.50	13,612.42
Arnold Arboretum (Sch. 20), ...	55,284.38	. . . . . .	55,284.38
Botanic Garden (Sch. 21), ...	8,112.05	. . . . . .	8,112.05
Botanical Museum (Sch. 22), ...	2,583.26	. . . . . .	2,583.26
Gray Herbarium (Sch. 23), ...	18,662.50	. . . . . .	18,662.50
Observatory (Sch. 24), ...	53,217.70	. . . . . .	53,217.70
Museum of Comp. Zoölogy (Sch. 25),	46,859.33	. . . . . .	46,859.33
Peabody Museum of American Archaeology and Ethnology (Sch. 26), . .	16,410.22	. . . . . .	16,410.22
Semitic Museum (Sch. 27), ...	769.99	. . . . . .	769.99
Germanic Museum (Sch. 28), ...	4,543.91	. . . . . .	4,543.91
William Hayes Fogg Art Museum (Sch. 29), ...	18,742.90	. . . . . .	18,742.90
Appleton Chapel (Sch. 30), ...	10,320.62	. . . . . .	10,320.62
Phillips Brooks House (Sch. 31), . .	1,703.74	. . . . . .	1,703.74
Hemenway Gymnasium (Sch. 32), . .	. . . . . .	2,118.50	2,118.50
Stillman Infirmary (Sch. 33), ...	4,085.02	18,404.81	22,489.83
Funds and Gifts for Special Purposes (Sch. 34), . . $710,898.94			
Less Unexpended balances of new gifts for buildings, 443,282.78	267,616.16	. . . . . .	267,616.16
Less Deficit of Hemenway Gymnasium included in the above expenditure of other departments and deducted to show the total net expenditure :			
	$1,581,091.11	$978,074.58	$2,559,165.69

BY DEPARTMENTS

June 30, 1912

EXPENDITURE	GENERAL		Disposition of General Deficit or Surplus			
			FUNDS AND GIFTS		GENERAL SUSPENSE	
	Deficit	Surplus	Debit	Credit	Debit	Credit
$41,137.52	......	$35,521.38	......	$35,521.38	......	......
1,008,238.77	......	31,204.10	$18,084.57	50,125.64	$4,618.63	$3,781.66
130,542.38	$55,114.00	......	55,707.06	1,963.40	1,628.94	258.60
23,597.20	......	1,153.60	......	61.08	......	1,092.52
231,544.96	1,056.87	......	7,402.11	6,378.23	409.26	376.77
37,995.94	......	2,767.69	145.00	1,983.67	46.63	975.65
51,972.39	6,755.34	......	1,200.00	1,422.21	6,977.55	......
172,141.91	16,626.97	......	5,565.56	2,360.20	18,421.61	......
281,469.81	......	10,166.99	10,800.05	23,436.49	3,715.47	746.02
1,129.89	1,129.89	......	......	......	1,129.89	......
40,514.06	4,297.84	......	1,046.29	580.50	3,832.05	......
18,759.54	5,147.12	......	......	......	5,147.12	......
54,397.74	......	886.64	2,435.07	3,321.71	......	......
7,009.22	......	1,102.83	......	31.23	......	1,071.60
3,574.55	991.29	......	......	......	991.29	......
16,582.11	......	2,080.89	......	......	......	2,080.89
57,028.71	3,811.01	......	4,910.32	1,800.47	701.16	......
56,724.54	9,865.21	......	8,892.45	580.76	1,553.52	......
13,552.14	......	2,858.08	......	833.57	185.23	2,209.74
3,437.17	2,667.18	......	2,667.18	......	......	......
1,402.91	......	3,141.00	......	2,658.40	......	482.60
4,947.21	......	13,795.69	213.48	13,714.31	......	294.81
9,950.09	......	370.53	......	188.44	......	182.09
1,562.33	......	141.41	209.40	350.81	......	......
12,058.00	......	......	......	......	......	......
21,803.55	......	686.28	......	401.09	......	285.19
282,218.47	14,602.31	......	49,059.67	40,216.08	5,758.72	......
$2,585,293.11						

9,989.50

$2,575,353.61	$122,064.58	$105,876.61	$167,838.16	$187,929.67	$50,117.07	$18,837.64
	105,876.61			167,838.16	13,837.64	
	$16,187.92			$20,091.51	$36,279.43	

GIFTS FOR CAPITAL

June 30, 1912

ESTABLISHING NEW FUNDS OR INCREASING OLD ONES

From George R. Agassiz, $50,000, for the general use of the Museum of Comparative Zoölogy.

From an anonymous giver, $30,000, for the Harvard Foundation for exchanges with Sorbonne and Universities of France.

From an anonymous giver, $5,000, " In Memory of Lawrence Carteret Fenno," to establish a fund for the treatment of cancer by " Light " rays, at the Collis P. Huntington Memorial Hospital.

From an anonymous giver, $5,000, to establish the " Lawrence Carteret Fenno Memorial Free Bed Fund " in the Collis P. Huntington Memorial Hospital.

For addition to the principal of the Fund for the Professorship of Hygiene, $10,000, from the anonymous founder of this Fund.

From the Trustees of the estate of Edward Whitney, $1,000, to be used in protecting and providing suitable housing for birds in the Arnold Arboretum.

From Benjamin F. Keith, $120, for the Arnold Arboretum Fund.

From the estate of Walter Farnsworth Baker, of the Class of 1893, of Boston, Mass., $2,506.33 in cash, and securities valued at $2,644, on account of his unrestricted bequest " to the corporation of Harvard University to be used for any purpose to help my beloved Alma Mater," . . .

From the estate of Caroline M. Barnard (Mrs. Robert M. Barnard), of Everett, Mass., $24,000 additional, on account of her bequest as follows: " The balance, if any, remaining after these payments, I give and devise to the several Benevolent, Religious, Charitable and Educational Institutions, Corporations and Societies named as Beneficiaries in this my said Will . . . to be shared by them pro rata; that is to say, in the proportion which the respective bequests, hereinbefore given to each, bear to the total amount of all the bequests to said several Societies, Institutions, and Corporations . . ."

From the estate of Lydia Augusta Barnard (Mrs. James Munson Barnard) of Milton, Mass., $25,000, on account of her bequest to the President and Fellows of Harvard College, " to be kept as a separate and distinct fund to be known as the ' James and Augusta Barnard Law Fund,' the net income of the fund to be expended by them for the advancement, improvement and study of jurisprudence, legislation, administration and allied subjects in the United States of America when and where and in the manner they shall think best and, if they deem advisable, for the purchase of law books for the law library of said College; . . ."

From the estate of Henry Pickering Bowditch, of the Class of 1861, of Jamaica Plain, Mass., $4,000, to be added to the J. Ingersoll Bowditch Fund, " the income of which shall be expended under the direction of the Professor of Physiology for the promotion of original investigation in the Physiological laboratory of the Harvard Medical School, with special power to use the income . . . for the purchase of books."

To be added to the endowment fund of the Collis P. Huntington Memorial Hospital, from

Additional subscriptions received through	
Dr. J. Collins Warren	$6,953.27
Anonymous	2,816.97
	$9,770.24

From Thomas W. Lamont, $250, to be added to the maintenance fund of the Collis P. Huntington Memorial Hospital.

From George P. Castle and family, $5,000, in memory of Walter Remsen Brinckerhoff, to establish a fund in the Harvard Medical School to be known as the " Brinckerhoff Fund," the income to be used under the direction of the Shattuck Professor of Pathological Anatomy for the promotion of medical knowledge.

From members of the Class of 1881, $60, to be added to the " Twenty-fifth Anniversary Fund of the Class of 1881."

From members of the Class of 1882, $3,045.88, to be added to the Fund of the Class of 1882, established on the twenty-fifth anniversary of their graduation.

From members of the Class of 1883, $100, to be added to the "Class of 1883 Fund," established on the twenty-fifth anniversary of their graduation.

From members of the Class of 1884, $1,500, the final payment on account of their gift of $100,000, to be added to the "Class of 1884 Fund," established on the twenty-fifth anniversary of their graduation.

From members of the Class of 1887, to commemorate the twenty-fifth anniversary of their graduation, $100,000, to establish the "Class of 1887 Fund, the income only to be used and that only for the general purposes of the College as distinguished from the graduate schools and special departments of the University."

From William J. Riley, in memory of his nephew Clement Harlow Condell, of the Class of 1907, and later a student in the Law School, $25,000, " to be perpetually held in trust, the income to be applied to such scholarship or scholarships as may from time to time be approved by you (the President and Fellows), such scholarship or scholarships to be known and designated as the ' Clement Harlow Condell Scholarship.' "

From Edmund Cogswell Converse, $125,000, to establish "The Edmund Cogswell Converse Professorship of Banking" in the Graduate School of Business Administration. "The income only of this fund shall be used to maintain a Professorship in the Graduate School of Business Administration so long as that School endures, and thereafter in the College for similar purposes. It is my desire that this Professor shall give instruction and conduct or promote investigations in the subject of banking and finance. While it is my desire that this income shall ordinarily secure the services of an eminent instructor, it is also my desire to promote teaching and research, and if for any reason the Professorship should be temporarily vacant, or in the discretion of the President and Fellows it should be unnecessary to apply the entire income of this fund to maintain the Professorship, the

President and Fellows are authorized to use the income in securing instruction and research in the subjects named in such way as they see fit."

From Archibald Cary Coolidge and Clarence Leonard Hay, $500, to be added to " The Archibald Cary Coolidge and Clarence Leonard Hay Fund," the income to be used for the purchase of books relating to South America, for the College Library, with the right to withdraw the whole or such part of the principal as may be necessary for the purchase of any library or collection of books on South America.

To establish the Thomas Dwight Memorial Fund, " the income only to be used for anatomical research under the direction of the Department of Anatomy at the Harvard Medical School and with the express stipulation that no part of this income shall be applied directly or indirectly to diminish the amount which would otherwise and without this fund be appropriated for the maintenance of the Department of Anatomy aforesaid," from

George R. Agassiz	$1,000
Walter C. Baylies	200
Alexander Cochrane	500
Charles C. Jackson	100
Augustus Hemenway	250
Horatio A. Lamb	100
George Wigglesworth	100
Moses Williams	75
	$2,325

From five anonymous givers, $115 additional, to be added to the Harvard Dental Alumni Endowment Fund.

From W. Vernon Ryder, $20, to be added to the endowment fund for the benefit of the Harvard Dental School, to be used for education, research, or the general expenses of the Infirmary.

From Waldo E. Boardman, $50, to be applied to the Dental School Endowment Fund of the Class of 1886.

From William F. Drea, $10 additional, towards the Class of 1909 Dental Endowment Fund.

From the estate of Calvin and Lucy Ellis, additional securities valued at $1, to be added to the Calvin and Lucy Ellis Aid Fund.

From the estate of Miss Harriet E. Goodnow, of Sterling, Mass.,
$50,000, on account of her bequest "in memory of Reverend
Josiah Kendall Waite, Esther Kendall Waite, Catherine A. Goodnow and Lucy Ann Waite . . . to be held in trust and known as
the 'Waite Memorial Fund,' the income to be added to and
become a part of the principal until the principal amounts to one
hundred and fifty thousand dollars, and thereafter the income
only to be used in assisting worthy, poor young men of any denom-
ination, desiring a college education at Harvard College ; . . ."

From the estate of Rebecca A. Greene (Mrs. Francis B. Greene),
of Dartmouth, Mass., $28,500 additional, for the use of the
Medical School.

To be added to the fund established by friends and former
pupils, in memory of Professor Charles Gross, $10.05, the income
of the fund to be used for the purchase of books on English History,
especially in those branches of the subject in which Professor
Gross's studies lay.

From the estate of Charles L. Hancock, $28.55 additional,
to be added to the Charles L. Hancock Fund.

To be added to the Harvard Edda Club Scholarship Fund for
Scandinavian students, from

The Harvard Edda Club	$170.00
Swedish Society Vega, of Boston	50.00
Vasa Orden af Amerika, Logen Sofia No. 94	17.52
	$237.52

Through the Harvard Medical Alumni Association, $500, to
be added to the principal of the Harvard Medical Alumni Fund,
established in 1907 by the Association. The income of the Fund
is to added to the principal, or applied to increase the salary of
one or more of the younger instructors in the Medical School,
or to be applied otherwise in accordance with the wishes of the
Association.

To "commemorate the life and work of Richard Hodgson,
M.A., LL.D. (Melbourne), A.B., A.M. (Cambridge), who was
born in Melbourne, Australia, in 1855, and who served as secretary
of the American Society for Psychical Research and of the Ameri-

can Branch of the English Society for Psychical Research successively from 1887 until his death in Boston in 1905, devoting throughout those years a generous character and rare abilities to the investigation and study of phenomena which purported to furnish evidence of human immortality," the contributors "realize that enquiries of the kind with which Richard Hodgson's work in psychical research especially identified him may from time to time be most profitably pursued in ways not now predictable, and they desire to establish a fund for the encouragement of such work that may be broadly administered and that shall thus become a fitting and permanent tribute to his memory.

Accordingly the contributors direct that the fund shall be known as the Richard Hodgson Memorial Fund and that, subject only to the provisions for permitting accumulations hereinafter named, the income shall be expended in the sole discretion of the President and Fellows in any manner designed to encourage the investigation and study of mental or physical phenomena the origin or expression of which appears to be independent of the ordinary sensory channels.

The contributors further direct that one third, but not more, of the annual income of the fund and of all additions thereto, may from time to time be added to the principal in the discretion of the President and Fellows. Nothing herein shall be construed to require the expenditure of income annually.

It is the hope of the contributors, this statement of which shall not limit or restrict the discretion of the President and Fellows, that a preference will be given in the expenditure of income to the endowment of investigation and research as distinguished from lectureships and that, unless and until the fund reaches such proportions that its income is sufficient to justify the permanent appointment of an instructor or investigator the income will be accumulated for such reasonable periods as shall be necessary to make possible its expenditure in amounts adequate for important uses," from

Henry James, Jr.	$20.00
Mrs. David P. Kimball	3,380.50
Mrs. Richard FitzHugh Ledyard	1,100.00
Miss Edith Perry	10.00
Amount carried forward, ...	$4,510.50

Amount brought forward,	. . . .	$4,510.50
Miss Margaret Perry	. . . .	10.00
Mr. and Mrs. Thomas Sergeant Perry	. . . . . .	200.00
Miss Theodate Pope	. . . .	100.00
Mrs. William G. Webb	. . . .	5,000.00
Interest	. . . .	179.50

$10,000.00

From the estate of Mary Upham Johnson (Mrs. William Otis Johnson), $2,000 additional, to be added to the principal of the "William Otis Johnson Scholarship" in the Medical School.

From the estate of John C. Kimball, of Greenfield, Mass., $500, "to the Harvard Divinity School . . . the income from which is to go to any worthy poor student or students who are preparing for the Unitarian Ministry."

To be added to the George Cabot Lodge and Joseph Trumbull Stickney Memorial Book Fund, $220, from

Louis Aubert
F. R. Shipman
Mrs. Austin Stickney.

From the estate of Gordon McKay, $100,265.83 in cash, and securities valued at $64,611.67, to be added to the Gordon McKay Endowment Fund.

From the Massachusetts Society for Promoting Agriculture, $500 additional, to be added to the Massachusetts Society for Promoting Agriculture Fund, established in 1911 with previous gifts amounting to $4,500, "the principal to be maintained as a part of the permanent fund of the Arnold Arboretum, the income to be applied yearly for the maintenance of said Arboretum."

From the estate of Julia M. Moseley (Mrs. William O. Moseley), of Newburyport, Mass., $74,285.71, being her bequest of $60,000, plus the pro rata distribution of $50,000, to establish the "William O. Moseley Jr. Fund," "for the following purposes and upon conditions as follows viz.: — Two young men who shall have attended the Harvard Medical School connected with said College for three or four years or for the Medical course and who have given evidence of their diligence in the study of medicine and of their ability and likelihood of success shall be selected from time to time by the President and proper officers connected with the said Medical School and to each of said two young men shall be given annually one half the income of this fund for the purpose of going to Europe and whilst there they shall continue the study of medicine in such manner and for such time and under such rules and restrictions as said President and officers shall determine wise and best."

Towards the maintenance fund for the new building for the use of the Department of Music, from

J. Arthur Beebe	$1,000
Blair Fairchild	110
Frank E. Peabody	5,000
George Foster Peabody	100
Norton Perkins	500
	$6,710

From Elkan Naumburg, $10,000, to found "The Elkan Naumburg Fellowship in Music for the use of graduates who have shown a marked ability in musical composition during their college course.

I . . . desire that the income of the fund be used to aid in the support of such graduate for a term not exceeding two years, so far as possible immediately following his graduation, while further pursuing his musical studies in this country or abroad. I wish the award to be made by a committee appointed by the Department of Music of Harvard College, who shall also fix the length of the term and direct the place where the studies are to be pursued, — the award to be made regardless of the financial ability of the candidate.

I desire that if any year there should be no candidate worthy in the judgment of the committee to receive the fellowship, the income from the sum should be added to the principal, until the fund becomes sufficient to produce an annual income of $500 after which, in any such case, the income for that year shall be used for the library of the University, for the purchase of works, pertaining preferably to music."

From Mrs. John Knowles Paine, securities valued at $28,000, for the establishment, after a certain specified time, of "two fellowships, of equal value, in Music, said fellowships to be called the ' John Knowles Paine Fellowships in Music,' and to be open to undergraduates, except freshmen, and resident students of the Graduate School of Harvard University; the full annual income of which shall be paid to the holder of said Fellowships. The said student must have shown distinguished talent and originality in musical composition and high musical scholarship. The terms of said Fellowships may be for one, two, or three years, according to the recommendation of the Division of Music and the judgment of the Administrative Board of said Graduate School. . . ."

To be added to the George Herbert Palmer Fund, $214, from

> Miss Margaret V. Cobb
> James E. Gregg
> Miss Laura A. Knott
> Walter L. Leighton
> Osgood Putnam.

From the estate of Elnathan Pratt, of Worcester, Mass., $4,775, " To the President and Fellows of Harvard College, . . . to establish a scholarship, to be known as the Elnathan Pratt Scholarship, the income of which shall be devoted annually to the support of one deserving and needy student in the undergraduate department of said college, the preference to be given to a student coming from Worcester, Massachusetts."

From Mrs. Redfield Proctor, $25,000, " in trust, to be used towards the maintenance of the new Cancer Hospital, which the Cancer Commission of Harvard University has recently built on the grounds of the Harvard Medical School, and for the care of patients therein to its normal capacity. The principal of said sum or any part of it may be used for said purpose, or said Trustee may in its discretion keep said fund or any part of it invested and apply the income only therefrom for said purpose; provided, however, that if there should at any time be a shortage of income for the maintenance of said Hospital and the proper care of patients to its normal capacity, then and in that event such part of the principal as may be necessary therefor shall be used to supply such deficiency rather than leave empty beds or patients not properly cared for."

From the estate of Miss Mary P. Ropes, of Salem, Mass., $2,845.71, " for the support of or to assist in endowing a Professorship to be known as the Nathaniel Ropes Chair of Political Economy. If the income . . . is more than sufficient for the support of the professorship, the Peabody Museum of Archaeology and Ethnology of which Professor F. W. Putnam is at the present time Curator, to annually receive the surplus."

From Mrs. Joshua Montgomery Sears, securities valued at $34,000, the income to be used towards the maintenance of the Joshua Montgomery Sears, Jr. Prizes in the Law School.

From the estate of Grace R. Shaw (Mrs. Henry R. Shaw), $35,000, in trust, to be separately invested and to be known as the " Henry Russell Shaw Fund," " the income thereof to be applied at the discretion of the President to enable one or more graduates of Harvard College upon the completion of their undergraduate studies, to pass a few months in European travel. The purpose of this gift is to make it possible for young men of promise to supplement their formal education by the broadening and cultivating influence which comes from acquaintance with other countries. While I recognize that great good is done by travelling fellowships intended to provide the means of study and research for young men who are preparing themselves for a scholar's career, I have in mind a different object, which is that of benefiting young men of worth, who without necessarily having attained to the highest scholarship in college, have made good use of their opportunities and give promise of success in professional or business careers. I therefore do not prescribe any formal tests, such as relative rank in scholarship, as the basis of awarding the income of this fund, nor do I consider it necessary that the award should be made in formal competition; for I believe that the qualities which should determine the award can be better judged through the personal acquaintance of the President and his advisers with the candidates."

For the Teachers' Endowment Fund, $1,843.40 additional, from previous contributors.

From the estate of John Harvey Treat, of Lawrence, Mass., $276 additional, on account of his residuary bequest, " to be called the Treat Fund, the income whereof to be used for the benefit of the Library for the purchase of books relating to the Church of England and Churches in Communion with her, the Roman and Greek Churches, and the Episcopal Church in the United States of America, especially as regards ritual matters, . . . my desire is to make this Department of the Library as full as possible for the benefit of scholars. If the funds are more than sufficient for the purpose designated, they may be used for other departments at the direction of the Librarian. . . ."

From Mrs. Walter M. Underhill, $10,000, to establish a fund, the income of which shall be used "for the purpose of original investigation into diseases and disturbances of function of the nervous system, especially into those nervous or mental disorders caused or affected by disorders of the body at large, or by shock, strain, physical injury, glandular disease, and the like. If at any time these investigations have become unnecessary or are sufficiently provided for, the income of the fund may be used for other objects as nearly akin thereto as possible . . ."

From the estate of Jerome Wheelock of Worcester, Mass., $10, the ninth payment of that amount for establishing the Jerome Wheelock Fund of $100,000.

From the estate of James Lyman Whitney, of Cambridge, Mass., $58.32, "to form a Maria Whitney and James Lyman Whitney Fund, the income only to be expended for the benefit of the Whitney Library, established by my brother, Professor Josiah D. Whitney at the Museum of Comparative Zoölogy in Cambridge, Massachusetts."

From Charles H. Wilder, $10,000, "to the President and Fellows of Harvard College, . . . to be added to the 'Charles Wilder Fund' to establish a chair in the Medical department of said College which is to bear the family name of 'Wilder,' . . ."

The total amount of these gifts for capital account is $932,409.81, as shown in Exhibit A.

GIFTS FOR IMMEDIATE USE
June 30, 1912

From Edwin H. Abbot, $400, in accordance with the terms of his letter of gift, to be added to the income of the Teachers' Endowment Fund.

From the Aesculapian Club, $150, for a scholarship in the Medical School, to be awarded during the year 1911–12.

From George R. Agassiz, $1,000, for assistance in completing a revised Draper Catalogue for the Observatory.

From an anonymous friend, securities valued at $5,000, for an anonymous purpose.

From an anonymous giver, $250, for the salary of a secretary for The Cancer Commission of Harvard University.

From an anonymous giver, $200, to secure a certain salary under The Cancer Commission of Harvard University.

From an anonymous giver, $500, for the payment of an additional salary in the Medical School.

From an anonymous giver, $500, to increase the Bayard Cutting Fellowship for Research in Physics for 1912–13.

From an anonymous friend, $200, towards the cost of a book upon the history of the English Customs for the use of the Department of Economics.

From an anonymous giver, $11,750, " For the new high-voltage electrical laboratory."

From an anonymous giver, $1,000, the first payment on account of the offer of $1,000 a year for five years, for the collection of material on American Government.

From anonymous donors, $200, for a special scholarship in the Graduate School of Applied Science for 1911–12.

From an anonymous giver, $300, for a special scholarship in the Graduate School of Arts and Sciences for 1911–12.

From an anonymous giver, $15,000 additional, for the rebuilding and extension, as well as the furnishing, of the Library of the Gray Herbarium.

From an anonymous giver, $250, for a special scholarship in the Medical School for 1912–13.

From an anonymous giver, $300, " towards a salary in the Medical School."

From an anonymous giver, $746.02 additional, towards the support of the Clinic at the Harvard Medical School.

From an anonymous donor, $100, to be awarded in equal prizes in 1911–12 and 1912–13, to that undergraduate of Harvard or Radcliffe College who shall show, by competitive examination, the best acquaintance with the contents of the Old Testament.

To be added to the Anonymous Gift for Physical Research, from

Anonymous $500
Anonymous   15
                                                       $515

From an anonymous giver, $1,000, for the salary of an Assistant in Physics for 1912–13.

From an anonymous giver, $25, for a second prize for the encouragement of the study of the Old Testament among undergraduates in Harvard and Radcliffe Colleges.

From an anonymous friend, $1,200, for the expenses of the exchange professor to France for the year 1911–12.

From an anonymous giver, $350, for the Ricardo Prize Scholarship for 1912–13.

From anonymous donors, $525, for a special scholarship for 1911–12.

From an anonymous giver, $50, to be used as the income of Scholarship Funds is used.

From an anonymous giver, $50, for lectures in the Summer School.

From an anonymous giver, $600, for a scholarship in the International School of American Archaeology and Ethnology at Mexico City.

To increase the income of the Arnold Arboretum for the year 1911–12, from

Gordon Abbott	$50	Amount brought forward .	$6,885
Mrs. George R. Agassiz	1,000	W. Murray Crane	100
Thomas Allen	100	Zenas Crane	100
Frederick L. Ames	1,000	Mrs. Charles P. Curtis	100
John S. Ames	200	Mrs. Charles H. Dalton	100
Miss Mary S. Ames	1,000	Mr. and Mrs. Ernest B. Dane	500
Oliver Ames	100	Mrs. Arthur E. Davis	100
Lars Anderson	100	Frank A. Day	100
Mrs. Lars Anderson	100	Philip Dexter	100
Anonymous	300	George B. Dorr	100
Anonymous	200	Mr. and Mrs. Eben S. Draper	100
Anonymous	200	Mrs. George A. Draper	100
Anonymous	100	Miss Hannah M. Edwards	100
Mrs. S. Reed Anthony	100	Mrs. George R. Emmerton	100
Charles F. Ayer	100	William Endicott, Jr.	100
Miss Ellen S. Bacon	100	Mr. and Mrs. William C.	
Walter C. Baylies	100	Endicott	100
Boylston A. Beal	10	Arthur F. Estabrook	100
E. Pierson Beebe	100	Mrs. Robert D. Evans	200
William S. Bigelow	100	Mr. and Mrs. Francis W.	
Charles S. Bird	150	Fabyan	100
George Nixon Black	100	Charles S. Fairchild	100
Mrs. Wilmon W. Blackmar	25	Mr. and Mrs. J. Brooks Fenno	25
Mrs. Arthur W. Blake	100	Mrs. L. Carteret Fenno	100
Francis Blake	100	Sewall H. Fessenden	100
Mr. and Mrs. Edward D.		Mrs. W. Scott Fitz	100
Brandegee	100	Mrs. J. Malcolm Forbes	50
Mrs. John L. Bremer	100	Mrs. William H. Forbes	50
Miss Helen O. Brice	100	Miss Cornelia A. French	100
Peter C. Brooks	100	Mrs. Frederick Frelinghuysen	100
Shepherd Brooks	100	Henry C. Frick	1,000
" E. S. C."	.100	Mrs. Henry C. Frick	1,000
Arthur E. Childs	50	A Friend	200
Mrs. Arthur E. Childs	50	Robert H. Gardiner	50
Mrs. J. Dudley Clark	100	George A. Gardner	100
Alexander Cochrane	100	Miss Sarah H. Gaston	100
Mr. and Mrs. James M. Cod-		William A. Gaston	250
man	100	Mrs. William A. Gaston	100
Miss Alice S. Coffin	100	J. E. Gay	50
Charles A. Coffin	150	R. H. I. Goddard	100
Frederick G. Crane	100	Mrs. Marie T. Green	10
Amount carried forward .	$6,885	Amount carried forward .	$12,870

Amount brought forward	$12,870	Amount brought forward	$17,645
Mrs. Henry S. Grew	100	Thomas E. Proctor	100
Charles Hayden	100	William A. Read	100
Augustus Hemenway	200	Arthur W. Rice	10
Mrs. Augustus Hemenway	100	William K. Richardson	50
Henry Hornblower	100	William L. Richardson	100
Mr. and Mrs. Clement S.		Mrs. Jacob C. Rogers	100
Houghton	100	Mr. and Mrs. John L. Salton-	
Henry S. Howe	100	stall	500
Mrs. John E. Hudson	100	Richard M. Saltonstall	100
Henry S. Hunnewell	100	Charles S. Sargent	100
Mrs. Henry S. Hunnewell	100	Mr. and Mrs. Charles S. Sar-	
Walter Hunnewell	100	gent	250
Mrs. Oscar Iasigi	100	Charles S. Sargent, Jr.	100
George G. Kennedy	100	Winthrop Sargent	100
Nathaniel T. Kidder	100	Mrs. Winthrop Sargent	100
Mrs. David P. Kimball	100	Henry F. Sears	100
Mr. and Mrs. Horatio A.		Mrs. J. Montgomery Sears	200
Lamb	100	Mrs. Knyvet W. Sears	100
Gardiner M. Lane	200	Mrs. G. Howland Shaw	100
John M. Longyear	100	Mrs. Robert G. Shaw	100
Arthur T. Lyman	100	Abraham Shuman	100
Mrs. George S. Mandell	100	Charles D. Sias	100
Thomas L. Manson	100	C. R. Simpkins	100
Miss Ellen F. Mason	100	Frank E. Simpson	100
Miss Fanny P. Mason	100	Frederic E. Snow	100
George von L. Meyer	100	Charles A. Stone	100
George H. Mifflin	100	Mrs. Charles A. Stone	100
Thomas Minns	100	Galen L. Stone	250
J. Pierpont Morgan	100	Nathaniel H. Stone	100
Mr. and Mrs. J. Pierpont		Charles E. Stratton	100
Morgan, Jr.	100	Charles H. Taylor	100
John T. Morris	·100	Mr. and Mrs. Bayard Thayer	500
Mrs. John T. Morse	100	Eugene V. R. Thayer	100
Frederick S. Moseley	100	Mr. and Mrs. John E. Thayer	500
A. R. Nicol	25	Washington B. Thomas	100
Robert Osgood	100	Samuel Thorne	50
John Parkinson	100	Robert E. Townsend	100
Frank E. Peabody	100	Theodore N. Vail	1,000
George A. Peabody	100	William A. Wadsworth	100
Charles L. Peirson	100	Charles C. Walker	100
Mrs. John C. Phillips	100	Mr. and Mrs. William B.	
Dudley L. Pickman	100	Walker	100
Mrs. Dudley L. Pickman	100	Edwin S. Webster	100
Wallace L. Pierce	100	Mrs. Edwin S. Webster	100
David Pingree	500	Frank G. Webster	100
Mrs. Benjamin F. Pitman	50	Mrs. Frank G. Webster	100
Amount carried forward	$17,645	Amount carried forward	$24,255

For the Arnold Arboretum (*continued*)

Amount brought forward	$24,255	Amount brought forward.	$25,155
Laurence J. Webster	100	J. Reed Whipple Company .	100
Mrs. Laurence J. Webster .	100	George R. White	1,000
Mrs. Charles G. Weld . . .	100	William Whitman	100
C. Minot Weld	100	Trustees of the Estate of	
Stephen M. Weld	200	Edward Whitney	100
Mrs. William G. Weld . . .	100	Charles W. Whittier	100
Mrs. Henry C. Weston . . .	100	John D. Williams	100
William P. Wharton	100	Robert Winsor	100
Amount carried forward .	$25,155		$26,755

From James H. Veitch and Sons, $1,453.62 additional, for the botanical exploration of Western China, begun in 1906 by Ernest Henry Wilson, on behalf of the Arnold Arboretum.

For present use at the Botanic Garden, from

Oliver Ames	$100
Edwin F. Atkins	200
Ernest B. Dane	250
Miss Caroline L. W. French	100
	$650

For present use at the Botanical Museum, from

" A friend "	$800
Anonymous	1,500
Anonymous	200
	$2,500

From W. Graham Bowdoin, Jr., $250, for the " W. Graham Bowdoin Jr. Scholarship " for 1911–12.

From Miss Abby A. Bradley, $600 additional, to be added to the income of the William L. Bradley Fund for the Arnold Arboretum.

Towards meeting the fourth year's expenses of the Graduate School of Business Administration, in accordance with the pledges which made the undertaking possible, from

Oliver Ames	$500	Amount brought forward .	$1,700
George F. Baker, Jr.	100	Allston Burr	100
Walter C. Baylies	500	Benjamin P. Cheney	1,000
Charles S. Bird	500	Charles A. Coffin	200
Edward D. Brandegee . . .	100	" E "	1,200
Amount carried forward . .	$1,700	Amount carried forward . .	$4,200

FOR GRADUATE SCHOOL OF BUSINESS ADMINISTRATION (*continued*)

Amount brought forward	. $4,200	Amount brought forward	$19,100
Estate of Robert D. Evans	. 1,000	Nathaniel C. Nash	100
Charles S. Fairchild	500	Bradley W. Palmer	100
William A. Gaston	100	Estate of George L. Peabody	400
General Education Board . .	9,700	James H. Proctor	100
Robert Goelet	250	Estate of William B. Rice .	500
Robert Walton Goelet . . .	250	Horace S. Sears	200
Henry S. Howe	100	Herbert N. Straus ⎫	
A. Lawrence Lowell	1,000	Jesse I. Straus ⎬	500
Arthur T. Lyman	500	Percy S. Straus ⎭	
George S. Mandell	500	Members of the Class of 1879	1,200
J. Pierpont Morgan, Jr. . .	1,000		
	———		———
			$22,200
Amount carried forward .	$19,100		

For the general purposes of the Graduate School of Business Administration, from

Everett Morss	$25
Frederick W. Taylor	150
	———
	$175

From John R. Simpson, $125, to be added to the Loan Fund in the Graduate School of Business Administration.

Towards the support of the Course in Printing, in the Graduate School of Business Administration, from

Thomas E. Donnelley	$25.00
Albert W. Finlay, for books and materials	25.00
Charles E. Mason	100.00
Charles Schweinler, for illustrative materials and apparatus	50.00
The Society of Printers	507.88
	———
	$707.88

From members of " The Club of Odd Volumes," $600, towards defraying the expenses of a course of practical instruction in Printing and Fine Book Making, given in the Graduate School of Business Administration during the year 1911–12.

From William Endicott, Jr., $100, for the purchase of books on Transportation for the Graduate School of Business Administration.

Towards the support of the Course in Printing in the Graduate School of Business Administration during the year 1912–13, $1,000, from

Thurber C. Adams	Benjamin Kimball
Samuel P. Avery	Gardiner M. Lane
Francis Bartlett	Joseph J. Little
The Blade Printing and Paper Company	The Meyer-Rotier Printing Company
Francis Bullard	The C. H. Morgan Company
Ogden Codman	J. Pierpont Morgan
Theodore L. De Vinne	Henry P. Porter
The Dover Press	Abraham Rothschild
William Green	Toby Rubovits
J. Eveleth Griffith	Paul J. Sachs
H. C. Hansen	Grenville Winthrop.
William B. Howland	

To be added to the "Shaw Fund for Business Research," in the Graduate School of Business Administration, from

Walter H. Cottingham	$100
Jonathan B. Hayward	50
	$150

From Harry Hodgson, $75, for a prize or prizes to be awarded in the Graduate School of Business Administration during the year 1912–13.

From George O. May, $300 additional, for prizes awarded in the Graduate School of Business Administration in 1910–11 and 1911–12.

From Carroll Dunham, $100 additional, for present use at the Bussey Institution.

For the purchase of books for the Bussey Institution, from

Walter C. Baylies	$50
Carroll Dunham	50
	$100

Towards the work of The Cancer Commission of Harvard University, from

Anonymous	$20
Anonymous	20
Anonymous	5
In memory of Mrs. Curtis S. Bushnell, from Curtis C. Bushnell	16
	$61

Towards the current expenses of the Collis P. Huntington Memorial Hospital, from

George R. Agassiz	$500
Mrs. Arthur W. Blake	20
Miss Georgina S. Cary	25
Charles A. Dean	25
Charles A. King	50
Mrs. Alexander S. Porter, Jr.	15
William L. Richardson	100
Wallace F. Robinson	25
Francis Skinner	100
Galen L. Stone	100
John E. Thayer	250
Henry O. Underwood	100
Daniel G. Wing	50
	$1,360

From Mrs. Collis P. Huntington, $100,000, for the construction of the Cancer Hospital to be known as the " Collis P. Huntington Memorial Hospital."

From George R. White, $2,500, towards furnishing the Collis P. Huntington Memorial Hospital.

From the Carnegie Foundation for the Advancement of Teaching, $39,539.16, to pay retiring allowances granted by the Executive Committee of this Foundation to persons connected with Harvard University.

From members of the Class of 1901, $300, for a scholarship, to be known as " The 1901 Decennial Scholarship," to be given to a first-year student during the year 1911–12.

From Gardiner M. Lane, $1,000, for lectures in the Department of the Classics during the year 1911–12.

To be added to the income available for the payment of salaries in the College, from

Charles P. Bowditch	$1,000
W. Kirkpatrick Brice	100
D. Crawford Clark	250
Amos Tuck French	500
Alfred W. Hoyt	500
Gardiner M. Lane	100
	$2,450

For additions to the permanent equipment of the Laboratory of Comparative Anatomy, $304.76, representing the balance of the following subscriptions after the payment of bills amounting to $195.24:

Charles P. Bowditch	$50
" A friend "	100
Francis L. Higginson	100
Harris Kennedy	50
Amory A. Lawrence	100
Laurence Minot	100
	$500

From T. Jefferson Coolidge, $50,000, for use in the construction of a chemical laboratory building, to be erected " In memory of T. Jefferson Coolidge of the Class of 1884."

From Archibald Cary Coolidge, $10 additional, the proceeds from the sale of copies of the Hohenzollern book-plate.

From Mrs. J. Randolph Coolidge, $36, for the purchase of a globe and a map of Boston, for the College Library.

From the Dante Society, $100 additional, to maintain the annual prize of this amount, first offered in 1885, for the best essay on a subject drawn from the Life or Works of Dante.

From Lawrence W. Baker, $100 additional, to forward original research in the Dental School.

From Mrs. Henry Draper, $4,800 additional, to be spent by the Director of the Observatory in prosecuting the researches in the photography of stellar spectra with which the late Dr. Henry Draper's name is honorably associated.

From David A. Ellis, $25, for the purchase of books on School Administration for the use of the Department of Municipal Government.

From Francis J. Swayze, $50, for the use of the Department of Economics.

For the use of the Department of English in publishing such

contributions, either by students or instructors at Harvard, as may seem to merit preservation in permanent form, from

Laird Bell	$25	Amount brought forward .	$500
William C. Boyden	25	George D. Markham	50
Frederic I. Carpenter	50	Albert Matthews	50
George G. Crocker	50	Dudley L. Pickman	50
Frederick P. Fish	50	Charles A. Snow	50
Robert Grant	50	Francis J. Swayze	50
Henry S. Howe	50	Charles H. Tweed	50
George G. Kennedy	50	Kenneth G. T. Webster	50
Mrs. George L. Kittredge	100	Moses Williams	50
William Caleb Loring	50		
Amount carried forward . .	$500		$900

Towards improvements in The William Hayes Fogg Art Museum, from

Anonymous	$2,000
George Nixon Black	1,000
Mrs. Edward M. Cary	2,000
Mrs. William H. Forbes	3,000
Alfred Atmore Pope	5,000
	$13,000

Towards the expenses of work at The William Hayes Fogg Art Museum in connection with loaning slides of Greek and Roman subjects to various high schools in Massachusetts, from

Frederick P. Fish	$25
Robert S. Morison	10
James Hardy Ropes	5
	$40

From Francis Bullard, $30, towards the purchase of a print, by Marcantonio, for The William Hayes Fogg Art Museum.

For the Division of Forestry, from

John S. Ames	$200	Amount brought forward .	$1,110
Oakes Ames	200	David N. Skillings	100
George J. Barker	20	Charles O. Skinner	10
The Blanchard Lumber Company	25	Nathaniel H. Stone	100
		The Stone Lumber Company .	10
Warner R. Butler	200	John E. Thayer	200
J. Randolph Coolidge	50	Washington B. Thomas	100
George B. Dorr	100	Eliot Wadsworth	100
Charles Holyoke	15	John W. Weeks	100
Amory A. Lawrence	100	William P. Wharton	100
Mrs. Henry S. Russell	100	The John M. Woods Company	50
Miss Marian S. Russell	100		
Amount carried forward . .	$1,110		$1,980

Towards the fund for the erection of the Harvard Freshman Dormitories, from

Horace F. Baker	$10.00	Amount brought forward	$91,649.10
Samuel B. Booth	5.00	Arthur T. Lyman	5,000.00
Henry S. Bowers	100.00	James E. MacCloskey, Jr.	10.00
Daniel H. Burnham	1,000.00	Sidney R. Miner	15.00
Henry D. Bushnell	10.00	Kent Packard	2.00
Harrison K. Caner	1,600.00	George L. Paine	300.00
Frederic I. Carpenter	100.00	Potter Palmer, Jr.	1,000.00
Herbert L. Clark	2,000.00	Harry D. Parkin	10.00
Percy H. Clark	400.00	A. J. Drexel Paul	5,000.00
Sydney P. Clark	2,000.00	Howard M. Paull	2.00
Frederic A. Delano	2,500.00	George A. Peabody	5,000.00
Edgar C. Felton	1,000.00	Charles Elliott Perkins	250.00
Mrs. J. Malcolm Forbes	1,000.00	David Pingree	1,500.00
Mrs. William H. Forbes	5,000.00	Evan Randolph	20.00
Harry R. Fulton	7.50	Norman C. Riggs	5.00
Richard Haughton	6.50	Mrs. Russell Sage	225,000.00
Stevens Heckscher	100.00	Henry W. Schurr	20.00
Augustus Hemenway	25,000.00	Mrs. Robert G. Shaw	500.00
Francis L. Higginson	20,000.00	Albert L. Smith	10.00
M. Dennison Hull	2,500.00	Philip L. Spalding	100.00
George S. Jackson	100.00	Redmond D. Stephens	200.00
Edward E. Jenkins	120.10	Nathaniel H. Stone	5,000.00
Charles F. Judson	5.00	James E. Switzer	50.00
Kidder, Peabody and		Nathaniel N. Thayer	200.00
Company	25,000.00	Charlemagne Tower	400.00
George C. Kimball	10.00	Henry O. Underwood	500.00
Charles H. Krumbhaar, Jr.	50.00	Sidney J. Watts	1.00
Arthur H. Lea	1,000.00	Donald R. Wegg	50.00
Walter F. Lewis	5.00	Alvin W. Wise	25.00
Lawrence Litchfield	20.00	Clement B. Wood	40.00
Arthur Lyman	1,000.00	Howard Wood, Jr.	20.00

Amount carried forward . $91,649.10 $341,879.10

From The General Theological Seminary, $50, to defray, in part, the expenses of Volume XXIII of " The Harvard Studies in Classical Philology."

From Archer O'Reilly, $25, towards a new chemical laboratory, in memory of Wolcott Gibbs, LL.D., Rumford Professor and Lecturer on the Application of Science to the Useful Arts from 1863 to 1887, at this University.

From William Bennett Munro, $108.30, towards defraying certain expenses connected with his courses in Government.

For the Gray Herbarium, from

Rodolphe L. Agassiz	$10	Amount brought forward.	
Miss Mary S. Ames	10	Clement S. Houghton	
Anonymous	25	Charles W. Hubbard	
Anonymous	25	Mrs. John E. Hudson	
Edwin F. Atkins	10	Henry S. Hunnewell	
Walter C. Baylies	10	Walter Hunnewell	1
Thomas P. Beal	10	Edward C. Johnson	1
Arthur C. Bent	10	Frank L. Kennedy	
Mrs. Arthur W. Blake	10	Charles A. Kidder	1
Mrs. John L. Bremer	10	David P. Kimball	1
Miss Sarah F. Bremer	10	Mrs. David P. Kimball	1
Edward M. Brewer	10	Miss Harriet M. Laughlin	1
William Brewster	10	Erasmus D. Leavitt	1
Addison Brown	10	George V. Leverett	
Mrs. William S. Bullard	10	Mrs. George Linder	1
Allston Burr	10	Miss Louisa P. Loring	1
Mrs. James B. Case	10	Mrs. Thornton K. Lothrop	1
Horace D. Chapin	10	Mrs. George G. Lowell	1
Estate of Charles F. Choate	10	Arthur T. Lyman	1
Miss Cora H. Clarke	10	Mrs. Gilbert N. MacMillan	1
Mrs. James M. Codman	10	Miss Ellen F. Mason	1
Miss Helen Collamore	10	Miss Susan Minns	
George G. Crocker	10	Thomas Minns	1
Mrs. Charles A. Cummings	10	Nathaniel C. Nash	1
Mrs. Charles P. Curtis	10	Grenville H. Norcross	1
Mrs. Abram E. Cutter	10	Mrs. Otis Norcross, Jr.	1
N. H. Daniels	5	James L. Paine	1
Frank A. Day	25	Charles W. Parker	1
Walter Deane	15	Miss Mary R. Peabody	1
Mrs. John W. Elliott	10	Mrs. John C. Phillips	1
William Endicott	10	Mrs. Dudley L. Pickman	1
William Endicott, Jr.	10	David Pingree	
" D. B. F."	10	Laban Pratt	
Charles F. Fairbanks	10	Miss Elizabeth C. Putnam	
Mrs. W. Scott Fits	10	Mrs. George Putnam	1
Francis A. Foster	10	George E. Richards	1
Francis C. Foster	20	William L. Richardson	
Mrs. Francis C. Foster	15	Denman W. Ross	1
Miss Cornelia A. French	10	Mrs. M. Denman Ross	1
George A. Goddard	10	Mrs. Waldo O. Ross	1
Miss Harriet Gray	10	Mrs. Robert S. Russell	1
Mrs. Henry S. Grew	10	Robert Saltonstall	1
Mrs. Augustus Hemenway	10	Mrs. J. Montgomery Sears	1
Miss Clara Hemenway	10	Mrs. Knyvet W. Sears	1
Joseph P. B. Henshaw	10	Mrs. G. Howland Shaw	1
Henry Hornblower	10	David N. Skillings	1
Miss Katharine Horsford	25	Francis Skinner	1
Amount carried forward	$545	Amount carried forward	$1,

For the Gray Herbarium (*continued*)

Amount brought forward . $1,088		Amount brought forward . $1,278	
Francis P. Sprague	10	Miss Cornelia Warren . . .	10
Isaac Sprague	10	Benjamin M. Watson	10
Mrs. Isaac Sprague	20	Frank G. Webster	20
Robert H. Stevenson	10	Mrs. Frank G. Webster . . .	20
Nathaniel H. Stone	10	Mrs. Charles T. White . . .	10
John E. Thayer	100	George Wigglesworth	10
Charles H. Tweed	10	Miss Adelia C. Williams . .	25
Charles C. Walker	10	John D. Williams	20
Miss Caroline E. Ward . . .	10	Miss Mary Woodman	10

Amount carried forward . . $1,278			$1,413

From George R. White, $31,500, to be expended in the erection of a building at the Gray Herbarium, to be known as the " George Robert White Laboratories of Systematic Botany."

From Mrs. Edwin Farnham Greene, $100, "to be awarded during the year 1912–13 as a prize or as prizes for essays upon the subject of international arbitration in accordance with regulations to be prescribed by the Department of Government and to be known as the Lake Mohonk Prize and to be open for competition to undergraduates of Harvard University."

From the Harvard Club of Boston, $1,000, for five scholarships of $200 each, to be awarded during the year 1912–13, " to properly qualified graduates of public High and Latin Schools (including the Roxbury Latin School), within a radius of twenty miles from the State House in Boston, during their first year in Harvard College as candidates for the degree of A.B. or S.B."

From the Harvard Club of Buffalo, $400, for the scholarship of the Club for 1910–11 and 1911–12.

From the Harvard Club of Cleveland, $650, for the scholarship of the Club for 1910–11 and 1911–12.

From the Harvard Club of the Connecticut Valley, $200, for the scholarship of the Club for 1911–12.

From the Harvard Club of Fitchburg, $150, for the scholarship of the Club for 1911–12.

From the Harvard Club of Hawaii, $200, for the scholarship of the Club for 1911–12.

From the Harvard Club of Hingham, $100, for the scholarship of the Club for 1911–12.

From the Harvard Club of Kansas City, Missouri, $150, for the scholarship of the Club for 1912–13, to "be awarded to an applicant who is a resident of Jackson County, Mo. or Wyandotte County, Ks., if such a person applies; otherwise . . . to an applicant who is a resident of the state of Missouri or of the state of Kansas; and that it be awarded to an applicant as above for use while he is a member of the Freshman Class in Harvard College."

From the Harvard Club of Louisiana, $257.14, for the scholarship of the Club for 1911–12.

From the Harvard Club of Lowell, $350, for two scholarships for the year 1911–12, the beneficiaries to be nominated by a committee of the Club.

From the Harvard Club of Lynn, $100, for the scholarship of the Club for 1911–12.

From the Harvard Club of Maine, $150, for the scholarship of the Club for 1911–12.

From the Harvard Club of Nebraska, $150, for the scholarship of the Club for 1911–12.

From the Harvard Club of New Jersey, $250, the fourth annual prize of this amount to be awarded to that student from New Jersey who enters the Freshman Class in Harvard College with the highest credit in his examinations for admission.

From the Harvard Club of Western Pennsylvania, $600, to maintain three scholarships during the year 1911–12.

From the Harvard Club of Rhode Island, $150, for the scholarship of the Club for 1911–12.

From the Harvard Club of Rochester, N. Y., $200, for the scholarship of the Club for 1912–13.

From the Harvard Club of San Francisco, $500, for the scholarship of the Club for 1911–12.

From the Harvard Club of Seattle, $200, for the scholarship of the Club for 1911–12.

From the Harvard Club of St. Louis, $300, for the scholarship of the Club for 1911–12.

From the Harvard Club of St. Louis, $140.10, for a special scholarship of the Club for 1911–12.

From the Harvard Club of Syracuse, $200, for the scholarship of the Club for 1911–12.

From the Harvard Club of Worcester, Mass., $100, for the scholarship of the Club for 1911–12.

From the Harvard Medical Alumni Association, $2,000 additional, to be used to increase the salaries of some of the younger Instructors and Assistants in the Medical School.

Towards refitting Holworthy Hall, from

Richard H. Dana	$100
William Farnsworth	50
	$150

From anonymous friends of the University, $200, the third annual scholarship of this amount, to maintain the Huidekoper Scholarship, established in 1909–10, in memory of Edgar Huidekoper and Frances Shippen Huidekoper of Meadville, Pa., " to be enjoyed by a properly qualified graduate of Allegheny College, Meadville, Pennsylvania, who may desire to pursue his studies in one of the graduate departments of the University. The incumbent of the scholarship is to be chosen in the usual manner after conference with the proper authorities at Allegheny College. This scholarship may be held in two or three successive years by the same student if there be no other candidates."

From James H. Hyde, $600, for the Fellowship at the Ecole des Sciences Politiques, for the year 1911–12.

Towards the investigation of Infantile Paralysis, conducted by and under the direction of Dr. Theobald Smith, from

Thomas F. Baxter	$100
William A. L. Baseley	100
Edmund D. Codman	100
Amount carried forward	$300

TOWARDS INVESTIGATION OF INFANTILE PARALYSIS (*continued*)

Amount brought forward	$300
Edmund W. Converse	200
Stephen V. R. Crosby	100
Frederick L. Dabney	100
Sewall H. Fessenden	100
Eben D. Jordan	200
David P. Kimball	100
Neal Rantoul	100
George T. Rice	200
Richard C. Storey	100
Edwin S. Webster	250
George Wigglesworth	100
	$1,850

From Gardiner M. Lane, $150, for an additional University Scholarship for 1912–13 in the Graduate School of Arts and Sciences.

From Deen Lombard Robinson, $450, repayment of scholarships received by him while in the Law School.

From Joseph Lee, $250, towards the support of the course in School Music at the Summer School of 1911.

From Joseph Lee, $5,000, for the salary of an instructor in the Department of Education for 1910–11 and 1911–12.

For the purchase of books for the College Library, from

Anonymous	$10.95
Ezra H. Baker, } for a collection of the writings of Daniel Defoe {	20.00
Grenville H. Norcross, }	25.00
Thomas Barbour, for books on Oceania	5.00
Mrs. Louis Bettman, for books, as a permanent memorial of the quindecennial celebration of the Class of 1897, of which her son, Dr. Milton Bettman, was a member	100.00
Lawrence S. Butler, for books on Paris	50.00
William R. Castle, Jr., } for additions to the collection of the works {	90.00
John L. Saltonstall, } of Alexander Pope {	50.00
Alexander Cochrane	1,000.00
Archibald Cary Coolidge, for books on French History, German History, and other subjects	5,500.00
Harold J. Coolidge, for books on China	50.00
J. Randolph Coolidge, for a set of the Bradley Bibliography, published by the Arnold Arboretum	100.00
John Craig, for books on the history of the English Drama	250.00
Amount carried forward	**$7,250.95**

For the Purchase of Books for the College Library (*continued*)

Amount brought forward	$7,250.95
The Lady Sybil Cutting, for books on the history of Florence and other cities of Northern Italy, to be added to the William Bayard Cutting, Jr. Collection	100.00

Ernest B. Dane,	1,000.00
John H. Sedgwick, for books on English Literature	10.00
Francis Skinner,	200.00
Lucius Wilmerding,	50.00

Dante Society	50.00
James Lloyd Derby, for books on the Philippine Islands	50.00
Ellis L. Dresel, for books on German Drama	50.00
Tracy Dows	100.00
William Endicott, Jr., for works in history	1,500.00
Department of English, for English Poetry	359.95
Edward N. Fenno, Jr.	100.00
Robert F. Foerster	6.85
John Hays Gardiner, for books on Burmah	10.00
Ernest L. Gay, for ballad-operas . . . .'. . .	8.00
Franklin Mott Gunther, for books on Central America	10.00
Charles Jackson, for books on English History and English Literature	2,000.00
George L. Kittredge, for books illustrating the history of Witchcraft	60.00
John S. Lawrence, for books on the lives of successful men . . .	10.00
Marshall C. Lefferts, for an edition of the letters of Alexander Pope	9.20
James Loeb, for " Labor Periodicals "	100.00
Percival Hall Lombard	25.00
Ogden L. Mills	75.00
Edwin Stanton Mullins, for books on Folk-lore	50.00
Walter W. Naumburg, for books on Shakespere	100.00
William Phillips, for books on London	100.00
Saturday Club of Boston, Mass.	300.00
Horace B. Stanton, for the Molière Collection	25.00
Frank Graham Thomson	100.00
	$13,809.95

Towards defraying the expenses of architectural studies in connection with enlarging Gore Hall, from

Francis R. Appleton	$200
Edward D. Brandegee	200
William A. Gaston	200
Henry S. Howe	200
Gardiner M. Lane	200
Francis Shaw	200
Interest	50
	$1,250

From J. Pierpont Morgan, Jr., $1,000, towards providing additional service at the College Library.

From friends, in memory of Henry Weidemann Locke, S.B. 1902, $100 additional, for a scholarship for 1911–12 in Electrical Engineering in the Graduate School of Applied Science.

To maintain The MacDowell Fellowship in Dramatic Composition, established in 1910–11, which may be held by a student of Harvard or Radcliffe College selected, after open competition, by Professor George P. Baker of the Department of English and accepted as holder of the Fellowship by The MacDowell Club of New York, from

George P. Baker	$25
The MacDowell Club of New York	550
	$575

From Philippe Belknap Marcou, $50 additional, for a prize for French Composition, to be called the Jeremy Belknap Prize, as a memorial to Dr. Jeremy Belknap of the Class of 1762.

From the Massachusetts Society for Promoting Agriculture, $2,000 additional, "to be expended at the Arnold Arboretum by the Director, to increase the knowledge of trees."

From the Massachusetts Society for Promoting Agriculture, $1,200 additional, "to aid the College to enable Professor Theobald Smith to continue his experiments on bovine tuberculosis . . . ."

From J. Ewing Mears, $225, his third annual gift in accordance with the terms of his offer to establish a scholarship with an income of $225 a year, to be designated "The James Ewing Mears, M.D. Scholarship in Medicine," to be held by the beneficiary "for the full course of four years in the Medical School, subject to the standing he shall maintain in scholarship and to his good conduct as a student."

For a Zeiss microscope, Minot rotary microtome, and other laboratory supplies for the Medical School, $267.42 additional from

Richard Sisson Austin	Oliver Street Hillman
Alexander Manlius Burgess	Frank Burr Mallory
Russell Richardson.	

From Walter P. Bowers, $50, to be added to " The Loan Fund of the Medical Class of 1879."

From George G. Sears, $20, towards the construction, at the Medical School, of tennis courts, squash courts, etc. for students' exercise.

To be added to the income available for the payment of salaries in the Medical School, from

Charles S. Minot	$200
William H. Walker	1,000
	$1,200

For the use of the Division of Music, from

Frederick S. Converse	$30
Arthur W. Foote	30
James Loeb	100
Dave H. Morris	100
Horace E. Smith	75
Philip L. Spalding	50
	$385

From Miss Katherine E. Bullard, $500 additional, for the benefit and use of the Department of Neuropathology in the Medical School.

From James J. Putnam and Moorfield Storey, Trustees of the fund created by Arthur W. Blake, $600 additional, for the Department of Neuropathology, for researches bearing on the knowledge and treatment of diseases of the nervous system.

From Grafton D. Cushing, $25, to be added to the income of the Boston Newsboys' Scholarship Fund, for 1911–12.

For the purchase of a freezing microtome, travelling microscope, slide boxes, typewriter, and other apparatus, for the Department of Pathology in the Medical School, $290.40, from

Richard Sisson Austin
Alexander Manlius Burgess
Frank Burr Mallory.

From the Patria Society of Harvard University, $50, to be awarded by the Corporation of Harvard College, during the year

1911–12, to the winner of a prize essay contest, open only to undergraduates, upon the subject, "Harvard Men in the Revolution."

For the Peabody Museum of American Archaeology and Ethnology, from

Mrs. N. E. Baylies	$25.00
J. A. Lowell Blake	249.99
Clarence B. Moore	500.00
	$774.99

For the Peabody Museum of American Archaeology and Ethnology, towards explorations in the Delaware Valley, from

"A Friend"	$75
Le Duc de Loubat	400
Charles Peabody	450
	$925

From Henry W. Haynes, $50, his fourth annual gift to the Peabody Museum of American Archaeology and Ethnology, for the general purposes of the Library, including binding current serials.

From Charles Peabody, $25, for the payment of transportation charges on European Collections for the Peabody Museum of American Archaeology and Ethnology.

From Miss Mary L. Ware, $540, towards the salary of an Assistant in the Peabody Museum of American Archaeology and Ethnology.

From Mrs. William Hooper, $1,000 additional, on account of her offer of one thousand dollars a year, in memory of her father, Charles Elliott Perkins, for the purchase of books and material bearing on the history and development of that part of America which lies beyond the Alleghanies.

From Edward Dyer Peters, $250, his fifth gift of like amount, for a scholarship in Mining and Metallurgy in the Graduate School of Applied Science for the year 1912–13.

From John C. Phillips, $3,000 additional, to be used under the direction of the Shattuck Professor of Pathological Anatomy, the Associate Professor of Pathological Anatomy, and the donor, for work in the Department of Pathology.

From John C. Phillips, $700, towards the salary of an Assistant at the Bussey Institution for 1911–12.

From Reginald C. Robbins, $60, towards meeting the deficit in the Library of Philosophy in Emerson Hall incurred during the year 1910–11.

From Reginald C. Robbins, $200, for the use of the Library of Philosophy in Emerson Hall during the year 1911–12.

From Theodore Lyman, $200, for the salary of an Assistant in Physics for 1911–12.

From Edward C. Pickering, $3,000 additional, for immediate use at the Observatory.

For the Department of Political Economy, from

"A Friend"	$200
Gordon Abbott	100
Thomas P. Beal	200
Benjamin P. Cheney	200
T. Jefferson Coolidge, Jr.	100
William Endicott, Jr.	200
Thomas W. Lamont	100
George B. Leighton	100
Robert Treat Paine	100
Arthur Perry	100
Eliot Wadsworth	100
George Wigglesworth	200
	$1,700

From Murray Anthony Potter, $125, towards the support of a course in Spanish Composition during the year 1911–12.

From Murray Anthony Potter, $225, in memory of his mother, for two prizes in Comparative Literature, to be called the "Susan Anthony Potter Prizes," and for a prize in Spanish Literature of the Golden Age.

From Andrew W. Preston, $2,000 additional, for the salary of a lecturer on South American Economics, Resources and Commerce.

From Frederick Madison Allen, $393.75 additional, for the Department of Preventive Medicine and Hygiene.

From Evan Randolph, $100, to Harvard University, without restriction.

From Francis Bullard, $20, to be added to the Mary R. Searle Fund.

From Mrs. Joshua Montgomery Sears, $650 additional, to be added to the income of the Joshua Montgomery Sears, Jr. Prize Fund, to be distributed, during the year 1911–12 in not exceeding four prizes, to students in one or more or all of the classes in the Harvard Law School.

From Clift Rogers Clapp, $10, to be added to Scholarship and Beneficiary Money Returned.

From Henry L. Shattuck, $50 additional, towards the general expenses of undergraduate instruction in Harvard College.

From Arch Wilkinson Shaw, $1,200, to be used for research work in connection with the Graduate School of Business Administration, the gift to be known as the "Shaw Fund for Business Research."

From Francis Skinner, $2,000 additional, for the purchase of books for the Arnold Arboretum in memory of his father, Francis Skinner, of the Class of 1862.

From Mr. and Mrs. Frederick Nichols, $500 additional, for the School for Social Workers.

From the Society for Promoting Theological Education, $1,091.11, "for the purchase of books for the library of the Harvard Divinity School and for the administration of said Library."

For the South End House Fellowship for 1911–12, from

Archibald Cary Coolidge	$10
Randolph C. Grew	200
Augustus Hemenway, Jr.	25
Robert Homans	3
Francis Welles Hunnewell, 2d	15
F. Lowell Kennedy	5
Frederick Law Olmsted	5
Charles Weil	5
Alexander Whiteside	10
	$278

For the South End House Fellowship in Social Education for the year 1911–12, from

South End House Association	$150
Trustees of the estate of Caroline A. R. Whitney	200
	$350

From Joseph E. Sterrett, $100 additional, for the purchase of books relating to accounting, for the Graduate School of Business Administration.

From John B. Stetson, Jr., $100 additional, for books and periodicals for the Library of the Peabody Museum of American Archaeology and Ethnology.

To forward original work in the Laboratory of Surgical Research, from

Anonymous	$20
John S. Ames	1,000
	$1,020

For the purchase of books for the Surgical Library, from

William Sturgis Bigelow	$100
Mrs. F. Gordon Dexter	50
Augustus Hemenway	100
	$250

From Francis J. Swayze, $75, "for such purpose as Professor Taussig approves."

From John E. Thayer, $500 additional, for the Bermuda Biological Station for Research.

From Frank Graham Thomson, $5,000 additional, for additional instruction in Municipal Government.

Towards the support of the Bureau of Municipal Research in connection with the course in Municipal Government, from

Clarke Thomson	$1,250
Frank Graham Thomson	1,250
	$2,500

From Mrs. Walter M. Underhill, $500, for researches in Neurology under the direction of Professor E. E. Southard.

For the purchase of incunabula to be added to the Weld Memorial Library, from

Edward D. Brandegee	$750
Mrs. Edward D. Brandegee	500
	$1,250

From Alfred T. White, $2,500 additional, for immediate use, " to be expended under the direction of the Department of Social Ethics."

From George Wigglesworth, $295, towards defraying the expenses of the Choir in Appleton Chapel during the year 1910–11.

From George Wigglesworth, $70, to defray the expenses of the Choir in Appleton Chapel during the session of the Summer School of 1911.

From Mrs. William Barbour, $1,785.50, to be used for the illustrations of a forthcoming Memoir of the Museum of Comparative Zoölogy.

The total amount of these gifts for immediate use is $771,772.20, as shown in Exhibit B.

SPECIAL INVESTMENTS

June 30, 1912

UNIVERSITY	Principal.	Net Income.
Walter F. Baker,		
Real Estate in Boston (sold during the year), . .	......	......
4 shares New York, New Haven & Hartford R.R.,	$560.00	$24.00
5 " Boston & Maine R.R., ...	500.00	15.00
6 " West End Street R.R., ...	522.00	10.50
2 " " " " " preferred, ...	206.00	4.00
4 " Am. Tel. & Tel. Co., ...	552.00	16.00
2 " Municipal Real Estate Trust, ...	204.00	4.00
1 " Belvidere Woolen Manufacturing Co., .	100.00	......
John W. Carter,		
University Houses and Lands, ...	12,500.00	223.31
George B. Dorr,		
University Houses and Lands, ...	115,966.56	2,071.70
George Draper,		
University Houses and Lands, ...	48,458.50	865.69
Robert H. Eddy,		
University Houses and Lands, ...	56,787.00	1,014.51
John Davis Williams French,		
University Houses and Lands, ...	5,322.09	95.27
John C. Gray,		
University Houses and Lands, ...	25,000.00	446.63
Walter Hastings,		
Real Estate, Sacramento St., Cambridge, ...	20,000.00	1,197.72
Henry L. Higginson,		
University Houses and Lands, ...	81,435.45	1,454.80
Insurance and Guaranty,		
Real Estate, Lucas St., Boston, ...	4,000.00	......
Joseph Lee,		
University Houses and Lands, ...	10,000.00	178.65
Henry S. Nourse (part),		
Mortgage on Real Estate in Chicago, Ill.	......	110.00
Francis E. Parker,		
University Houses and Lands, ...	113,817.44	2,033.33
Henry L. Pierce (Residuary) (part),		
Equipment at Memorial Hall, ...	157,098.14	7,069.42
Amounts carried forward, ...	$653,029.18	$16,834.53

	Principal.	Net Income.
Amounts brought forward, ...	$653,029.18	$16,834.53
Riverside,		
11 shares Harvard Riverside Associates, ...	11,000.00	. . . . . .
Henry Villard,		
University Houses and Lands, ...	50,000.00	893.24
William F. Weld,		
University Houses and Lands, ...	100,000.00	1,786.47

COLLEGE

	Principal.	Net Income.
Daniel A. Buckley (part),		
Real Estate in Cambridge, Mass., ...	66,345.59	7,045.08
" " Deer Isle, Me., ...	1.00	. . . . . .
George Newhall Clark,		
100 shares St. Joseph R'y, Light, Heat & Power Co. pref'd, ...	10,000.00	500.00
Edward W. Codman (part),		
2 shares Pacific Mills, ...	4,600.00	160.00
15 " Barristers Hall Trust, ...	1,085.00	60.00
12 " Boston Real Estate Trust, ...	14,341.50	517.50
Edward Erwin Coolidge,		
200 shares U. S. Smelting, Ref. & Mining Co. pref'd,	9,000.00	700.00
T. Jefferson Coolidge, for Research in Physics,		
648 shares Massachusetts Electric Cos., cum. pref'd,	59,805.25	2,500.00
Eliot Professorship (Jonathan Phillips's Gift),		
$10,000 City of Boston 3½'s of 1920, ...	10,000.00	350.00
Professorship of Hygiene (part),		
Policy of Mass. Hospital Life Insurance Co., . .	5,000.00	206.25
35 shares American Smelting & Refining Co., . .	3,112.22	285.83
60 " American Tel. & Tel. Co., ...	6,250.00	420.00
40 " Chicago, Milwaukee & St. Paul, ...	4,000.00	240.00
Charles Eliot Norton Fellowship,		
$15,000 Northern Pacific–Great Northern Joint 4's (C. B. & Q. collateral) of 1921, ...	14,100.00	600.00
5,000 Louisville & Nashville Unified M. 4's of 1940,	5,000.00	200.00
George Foster Peabody Scholarship,		
$6,000 Mexican Coal & Coke Co. 1st M., S. F. 5's of 1926, ...	4,800.00	. . . . . .
John K. Paine Music Fellowship,		
Mortgage Notes, ...	28,000.00	371.25
Sarah E. Potter Endowment (part),		
100 shares Boston & Albany (sold during the year),	. . . . . .	250.00
100 " Massachusetts Electric Cos., cum. pref'd (sold during the year),	. . . . . .	200.00
60 " Plymouth Cordage Co., ...	11,000.00	420.00
12 " Pureoxia Co., ...	60.00	5.40
Amounts carried forward, ...	$1,070,529.74	$34,545.55

	Principal.	Net Income.
Amounts brought forward, ...	$1,070,529.74	$34,545.55

William Reed Scholarship,

$1,000 New York Central & H. R. Gold 3½'s of 1997,	1,000.00	35.00
1,000 Norfolk and Western Divisional 1st lien & gen. M. 4's of 1944, ...	1,000.00	40.00
2,000 Northern Pacific–Great Northern Joint 4's (C. B. & Q. collateral) of 1921, ...	2,000.00	80.00

Nelson Robinson Jr. Additional (part),

1,750 shares Gauley Coal Land Co. preferred, . .	175,000.00	. . . . . .

Eliza O. and **Mary P. Ropes** (part),

100 shares Chicago, Milwaukee & St. Paul, . . .	18,087.50	600.00
100 " Northern Pacific, ...	11,986.50	700.00
220 " Pennsylvania, ...	12,987.50	645.00

Dunlap Smith Scholarship,

$5,000 Metropolitan West Side Elevated R. R. Extension M. 4's of 1938, ...	4,700.00	200.00

Stoughton Scholarship (part),

Real Estate in Dorchester, ...	3,294.30	70.48

Teachers' Endowment (part),

$5,000 Broadway Realty Co. Purchase Money, 2d M. 5's of 1916, ...	5,000.00	250.00
50,000 Wisconsin Central, Minneapolis Terminal Purchase Money M. 3½'s of 1950, ...	50,000.00	1,750.00
10 shares Harvard Riverside Associates, ...	10,000.00	. . . . . .

Wales Professorship of Sanskrit,

Real Estate, Cornhill, Boston (sold during the year),	. . . . . .	1,290.71

Samuel Ward's Gift (part),

Ward's (Bumkin) Island, Boston Harbor, ...	1.00	. . . . . .

J. Palmer Welsh Memorial (part),

$1,000 Ontario Power Co. 5's of 1943, ...	1,000.00	50.00

LIBRARY

William R. Castle,

$1,000 Honolulu Gas Co., Limited, 6's of 1925, . .	1,000.00	60.00

Francis Parkman Memorial (part),

$5,000 Louisville & Jeffersonville Bridge 1st M. Gold 4's of 1945, ...	4,500.00	200.00

Ichabod Tucker (part),

Policy of Mass. Hospital Life Insurance Co., . . .	5,000.00	206.25

John Harvey Treat (part),

130 Shares Treat Hardware Supply Co., ...	6,500.00	390.00
75 " United Shoe Machinery Co., ...	4,050.00	150.00
Deposit in Lawrence Savings Bank (withdrawn), .	. . . . . .	32.88
Amounts carried forward, ...	$1,382,636.54	$41,295.87

	Principal.	Net Income.
Amounts brought forward, ...	$1,382,636.54	$41,295.87

LAW SCHOOL

Joshua M. Sears Memorial,

$14,000 Illinois Steel Co. Deb. 5's of 1913, . . .	14,000.00	350.00
10,000 Minneapolis General Electric, Gold M. 5's of 1934, ...	10,000.00	. . . . . .
10,000 New England R.R. Consol. M. 5's of 1945,	10,000.00	. . . . . .

MEDICAL SCHOOL

John C. Cutter Bequest,

$6,000 Carthage Water Power Co., 1st M. 5% Notes,	1.00	. . . . . .
Deposit in Leicester Savings Bank (withdrawn during the year), ...	. . . . . .	10.00

Calvin and Lucy Ellis (part),

$40,000 Northern Pacific–Great Northern Joint 4's (C. B. & Q. collateral) of 1921, ...	26,585.00	1,600.00
Real Estate in Boston (half interest in), (sold during the year), ...	. . . . . .	102.67
Real Estate in Eden, Bar Harbor, Maine, ...	10,000.00	. . . . . .

Hamilton Kuhn Memorial (part),

$14,000 Burl. & Mo. in Nebr. non-ex. 6's of 1918, .	14,570.00	840.00
20,000 Kansas C., Mem. & Birm. Inc. 5's of 1934, .	17,600.00	1,000.00
10,000 U. Elec. Sec. Coll. Tr. 5's of 1937, 26th ser.,	10,000.00	500.00
189 shares Edison Elec. Ill'm'ng Co. of Boston (sold during the year), ...	. . . . . .	1,184.00

Robert Charles Billings (part),

Real Estate, Wigglesworth St. & Power House, Vila St., Boston, ...	68,267.67	. . . . . .

George C. Shattuck (part),

$25,000 Kansas City, Fort Scott & Memphis R. R. Cons. M. 6's of 1928 ($203.70 deducted from income for sinking premium), ...	28,259.30	1,296.30

Henry P. Walcott Fellowship in Clinical Medicine (part),

$6,000 J. M. Guffey Petroleum Co. 1st M. 5's of 1912 (paid during the year), ...	. . . . . .	300.00
5,000 J. M. Guffey Petroleum Co. 1st M. 5's of 1913,	5,000.00	250.00
2,000 " " " 1914,	2,000.00	100.00

MUSEUM OF COMPARATIVE ZOÖLOGY

Maria Whitney,

$2,000 City of Providence 4's of 1911 (paid during the year), ...	. . . . . .	40.00

Alex. Agassiz Bequest, Clause XI,

Real Estate in Cambridge, ...	50,000.00	. . . . . .
Amounts carried forward, ...	$1,648,919.51	$48,818.84

Principal.   Net Income.

Amounts brought forward, ... $1,648,919.51 $48,818.84

OBSERVATORY

Advancement of Astronomical Science (1902),
15 shares Calumet & Hecla Mining Co., ...   9,000.00   450.00

PEABODY MUSEUM OF AMERICAN ARCHAEOLOGY AND ETHNOLOGY

Peabody Building (part), } $54,000 Kansas & Mis- { 11,512.72		622.32
Peabody Collection (part), } souri R. R. 1st M. 5's { 19,218.64		1,038.84
Peabody Professor (part), } of 1922, { 19,218.64		1,038.84

Thaw (part) ($8.47 deducted from income for sinking premium),
$20,000 Girard Point Storage Co. 1st M. 3½'s of 1940,   20,237.31   691.58

ARNOLD ARBORETUM

Robert Charles Billings,
$5,000 Butte Water Co. 1st M. 5's of 1921, ...   4,000.00   250.00

BUSSEY INSTITUTION
Woodland Hill,
Laboratory of Comparative Pathology building, . .   20,658.86   1,000.00

SPECIAL FUNDS

Anonymous (1912),
$5,000 Newton Street Railway 1st M. 5's of 1912, .   5,000.00   . . . . . .

Bussey Trust (part),
Real Estate in Boston, ...   381,972.12   30,133.14

Fund of the Class of 1834,
Policy of Mass. Hospital Life Insurance Co., . . .   1,000.00   41.25

Fund of the Class of 1844,
Policy of Mass. Hospital Life Insurance Co., . . .   6,500.00   268.13

Fund of the Class of 1853,
Policy of Mass. Hospital Life Insurance Co., . . .   3,725.00   153.66

Calvin and Lucy Ellis Aid (part),
Real Estate in Boston (half interest in), (sold during
the year), ...   102.68
11 shares Massachusetts Cremation Society, . . .   1.00   5.50

Charles L. Hancock Bequest (part),
Real Estate in Chelsea and Chicago, ...   65,001.00   4,765.95

Freshman Dormitories,
$20,000 Mahoning & Shenango R'y & Light, 1st
Consol. Ref. M. 5's of 1916, ...   20,000.00   . . . . . .

Amounts carried forward, ... $2,235,964.80 $89,380.68

	Principal.	Net Income.
Amounts brought forward, ...	$2,235,964.80	$89,880.68

Anonymous,

	Principal.	Net Income.
$20,000 Massachusetts 3's of 1930, ...	20,000.00	600.00
5,000 " " 1939, ...	5,000.00	150.00
19,000 " " 1941, ...	19,000.00	570.00
4,000 " 3½'s 1915 (sold during year),	. . . .	95.28
6,000 " " 1916, " " "	. . . .	142.92
6,000 " " 1917, " " "	. . . .	142.92
2,000 " 3's 1918, " " "	. . . .	47.64
5,000 " " 1920, " " "	. . . .	104.52
10,000 " " 1923. " " "	. . . .	175.00
5,000 " " 1935, " " "	. . . .	148.26
12,000 " " 1940, " " "	. . . .	280.00
189 shares Edison Electric Ill'm'ng Co. of Boston,	55,188.00	1,134.00

Robert Troup Paine (accumulating) ($127.07 deducted from income for sinking premiums),

	Principal.	Net Income.
$38,000 Massachusetts 3½'s of 1913 (sold during year),	. . . .	1,275.11
5,000 " " 1916, ...	5,083.44	154.15
29,000 " " 1935, ...	28,258.80	343.85
31,000 " .. 1938, ...	29,623.14	25.98
2,000 " " 1936, ...	1,885.00	. . . . . .

George Smith Bequest (part),

	Principal.	Net Income.
$10,000 Duquoin, Ill., Water Works Co. 6's of 1901, ...	1.00	. . . . . .
20,000 Laclede Gas Light Co. 5's of 1919, . . .	20,000.00	1,000.00
200 shares Laclede Gas Light Co., preferred, . . }	18,800.00	1,140.00
20 " " " " " common, . . }		

Frederick Sheldon (part),

	Principal.	Net Income.
$2,000 New York Gas & Electric Light, Heat & Power Co. 4's of 1949 (sold during year),	. . . .	98.67
2,000 Twenty-eighth and Twenty-ninth Street Crosstown Ry. 1st M. 5's of 1996, . . .	500.00	. . . . . .
20 shares Astor Trust Co. (sold during year),	. . . .	120.00
23 " Bank of America, " " "	. . . .	621.00
82 " Consolidated Gas Co. of New York (sold during the year), ...	. . . .	369.00
11 " Corn Exchange Bank (sold during the year), ...	. . . .	132.00
100 " Manhattan Trust Co. (sold during the year), ...	. . . .	540.00
23 " Mexican Telegraph Co., ...	4,370.00	230.00
50 " New York Loan & Improvement Co., (sold during the year), ...	. . . .	175.00
7 " Newport Trust Co. (sold during the year), ...	. . . .	35.00
11 " Newport Water Works (sold during the year), ...	. . . .	44.00
Amounts carried forward, ...	$2,443,674.18	$99,274.98

	Principal.	Net Income.
Amounts brought forward, ...	$2,443,674.18	$99,274.98

Frederick Sheldon (part) (*continued*).
60 shares U. S. Life Insurance Co. (sold during the year), ...	. . . .	126.00
100/15000th Trust Estate Hastings & Dak. Ry. Co.,	300.00	137.50

Gordon McKay Endowment (part),
21,000 American Agricultural & Chemical Co. 4½'s of 1928, ...	21,367.50	. . . . . .
$120,000 American Tel. & Tel. 4's of 1929, ...	114,000.00	4,800.00
18,000 Butte Electric & Power Co. 1st M. 5's of 1951 (sold during the year), ...	. . . .	430.00
6,000 Central Branch R'y 4's of 1919 (sold during the year), ...	. . . .	195.33
70,000 Florida East Coast R'y 1st M. 4½'s of 1959 (sold during the year), ...	. . . .	3,184.25
200,000 Interborough Rapid Transit 5's of 1952, .	203,505.50	10,645.28
35,000 Kansas City Railway & Light 6's of 1912, .	35,000.00	1,050.00
12,000 Madison River Power Co. 1st M. 5's of 1935,	11,975.00	300.00
16,000 Minneapolis General Electric 5's of 1934,	16,120.00	. . . . . .
100,000 Kanawha & Michigan 5's of 1927, ...	95,500.00	5,000.00
25,000 National Railways of Mexico 4½'s of 1957,	22,343.75	. . . . . .
80,000 New York, N. H. & H. Deb. 4's of 1955, .	78,800.00	3,200.00
61,000 N. Pacific–Great N. Joint 4's of 1921 (sold during the year), ...	. . . .	1,572.44
12,000 Puget Sound Electric 5's of 1932, ...	11,760.00	300.00
1,000 St. Joseph & Grand Island R'y 4's of 1947 (sold during the year), ...	. . . .	35.78
14,000 Seattle Electric R'y 5's of 1952, ...	4,160.00	. . . . . .
25,000 Wabash Equip. Serv. Co. 4½'s of 1915 (sold during the year), ...	. . . .	1,006.25
300 shares Great Northern, ...	44,250.00	2,100.00
240 " Northern Pacific, ...	35,400.00	1,680.00
165 " Pennsylvania, ...	10,875.00	483.75

Price Greenleaf. ($255.57 deducted from income for sinking premiums.) The total amount of this Fund is $787,013.82, which is invested as follows :
$70,000 Broadway Realty Co. Purchase money 1st M. 5's of 1926, ...	72,671.04	3,315.80
4,000 Burl. & Mo. River R. R. in Nebraska non-exempt 6's of 1918.	4,000.00	510.00
43,500 Central Vermont R'y 1st M. 4's of 1920, .	37,845.00	1,740.00
3,000 Chicago, Burl. & Quincy R. R. 4's of 1922,	2,880.00	120.00
50,000 Chicago Junction Railways & Union Stock Yards Coll. Trust 5's of 1915, ...	47,000.00	2,500.00
20,000 Cleveland R'y Ref. M. 5's of 1931, . . .	20,000.00	975.00
30,000 Commonwealth Power Co. 1st M. 5's of 1924,	29,850.00	1,500.00
35,000 Galveston Electric Co. 1st M. 5's of 1940,	32,900.00	481.25
Amounts carried forward, ...	$3,396,176.97	$146,663.61

	Principal.	Net Income.
Amounts brought forward, . . .	$3,896,176.97	$146,663.61

Price Greenleaf (*continued*).

	Principal.	Net Income.
$8,000 Kansas City, Fort Scott & Memphis cons. M. 6's of 1928, ...	9,141.98	408.63
50,000 Metropolitan Tel. & Tel. Co. 1st M. 5's of 1918,	49,750.00	2,500.00
34,000 New York Central & Hudson River R. R. (Michigan Central Collateral) 3½'s of 1998,	28,412.10	1,190.00
3,644.25 New York Railways Co. 1st R. E. & Ref. M. 4's of 1942, ...	2,860.73	. . . . . .
18,000 New York Railways Co. Adj. M. 5's of 1942,	9,450.00	. . . . . .
32,000 Northern Pacific–Great Northern Joint 4's (C. B. & Q. collateral) of 1921, ...	19,993.55	1,280.00
50,000 Union Pacific R. R. 1st M. & L. G. 4's of 1947,	44,625.00	2,000.00
50,000 Note of Arlington Mills, ...	50,000.00	2,281.25
25,000 " " Hamilton Manufacturing Co (paid during the year), ...	. . . .	593.75
50,000 " " Massachusetts Cotton Mills, . . .	50,000.00	2,312.50
360 shares Boston & Lowell R. R., ...	46,800.00	2,880.00
237 " Fitchburg R. R., preferred, ...	22,306.27	1,185.00
56 " Great Northern, preferred, ...	13,125.00	392.00
40 " " " Iron Ore Properties,	. . . .	. . . . . .
355 " Old Colony R. R., ...	68,190.00	2,485.00
27 " N. Y. Central & Hudson River R. R., .	2,866.28	135.00
290 " Northern R. R. (N. H.), ...	29,290.00	1,740.00
52 " West End Street Railway, preferred, .	4,805.56	208.00
34 " Central Vermont R'y, ...	428.72	. . . . . .
778 " Pennsylvania R. R., ...	55,406.04	2,280.75
21 " Boston Real Estate Trust, ...	27,483.25	900.00
100 " Paddock Building Trust, ...	10,000.00	350.00
Cash in American Trust Co., ...	433.30	93.97
	$3,936,044.75	$171,879.46

SUMMARY:

Cash, Exhibit A, ...	$433.30	
Securities, Exhibit A, ...	2,469,684.73	
Land and Buildings, Exhibit A.	1,465,926.72	
	$3,936,044.75	
Interest and Dividends, Exhibit B, ...		$108,038.01
Rents, Land and Buildings, Exhibit B, ...		63,841.45
		$171,879.46

SECURITIES—GENERAL INVESTMENTS
June 30, 1912

Mortgages and Other Loans.	Principal.	Income.
Mortgages, ...	$906,000.00	
Advances to Bussey Trust, ... : . .	312,499.08	
Abbeville Cotton Mills Note, ...	50,000.00	
American Woolen Co.'s Note, ...	50,000.00	
Boott Mills Notes, ...	50,000.00	
Curtis and Sanger's Note, ...	50,000.00	
Everett Mills Note, ...	50,000.00	
Hamilton Manufacturing Co.'s Note, ...	50,000.00	
Harmony Mills Notes, ...	50,000.00	
Indian Head Mills of Alabama Note, ...	50,000.00	
Merchant & Miners Transportation Co.'s Notes, .	50,000.00	
Merrimack Manufacturing Co.'s Note, ...	25,000.00	
Nashua Manufacturing Co.'s Note, ...	100,000.00	
New England Cotton Yarn Co.'s Note, ...	50,000.00	
Pacific Mills Note, ...	100,000.00	
Waltham Watch Co.'s Note, ...	50,000.00	
York Manufacturing Co.'s Note, ...	50,000.00	
	$2,043,499.08	$87,272.68

Public Funds.		
$94,000 United States of Mexico 4's of 1954, . .	$87,250.00	$3,760.00

Railroad Bonds.		
$100,000 Baltimore & Ohio 1st M. 4's of 1948, . .	$96,625.00	$4,000.00
100,000 B. & O. (S. W. Div.) 1st M. 3½'s of 1925,	89,750.00	3,500.00
100,000 Baltimore & Ohio (Pittsburg, Lake Erie & West Virginia) Ref. M. 4's of 1941,	99,250.00	4,000.00
125,000 Bangor & Aroostook Cons. Ref. M. 4's of 1951,	118,750.00	5,000.00
51,000 Burl. & Mo. in Nebr. non-ex. 6's of 1918,	51,000.00	3,866.00
50,000 Canadian Northern R'y Equipment 4½'s of 1913, ...	50,000.00	. . . .
444,000 Chicago, Burl. & Quincy 3½'s of 1949, . .	454,959.09	15,243.80
150,000 " " Gen. M. 4's of 1958,	145,250.00	6,000.00
200,000 C. B. & Q. (Illinois Div.) 4's of 1949, .	200,822.24	7,977.78
28,700 Chicago, Milwaukee, & St. Paul Conv. 4½'s of 1932, ...	28,700.00	. . . .
100,000 Chicago & No. Western Gen. M. 3½'s of 1987, ...	100,888.41	3,488.23
100,000 Chicago, Rock Island & Pacific Gen. M. 4's of 1988, ...	105,971.98	3,920.90
192,000 Duluth, Missabe & Northern General M. 5's of 1941, ...	205,171.43	9,223.81
Amounts carried forward, ...	$1,747,138.15	$65,720.52

	Principal.	Income.
Amounts brought forward, . . .	$1,747,138.15	$65,720.52

Railroad Bonds (*continued*).

	Principal.	Income.
$100,000 Indiana, Ill. & Iowa 1st M. 4's of 1950,	96,500.00	4,000.00
200,000 Kansas City, Fort Scott & Memphis Cons. M. 6's of 1928, ...	230,896.58	10,068.97
114,000 Kansas City, Memphis & Birmingham (assented) Income 5's of 1934, . . .	103,500.00	5,700.00
100,000 Lake Shore & Michigan Southern Deb. 4's of 1931, ...	93,250.00	4,000.00
300,000 Long Island Unified M. 4's of 1949, . .	283,257.50	12,000.00
200,000 Louisville & Jeffersonville Bridge Co. 1st M. 4's of 1945, ...	191,000.00	8,000.00
100,000 Minneapolis Union 1st M. 5's of 1922, .	101,331.62	4,866.83
100,000 Montana Central 1st M. 6's of 1937, . .	128,515.59	4,859.37
300,000 New York Central & H. R. (L. S. & M. S. Coll.) 3½'s of 1998, ...	294,464.40	10,500.00
25,000 New York, New Haven & Hartford Convertible Deb. 6's of 1948, ...	25,000.00	1,500.00
100,000 New York, New Haven & Hartford Deb. 4's of 1955, ...	105,375.00	3,875.00
200,000 New York, Ontario & Western Ref. M. 4's of 1992, ...	209,269.36	7,884.13
343,000 Northern Pacific–Great Northern Joint 4's (C. B. & Q. Coll.) of 1921, . . .	164,325.92	13,720.00
100,000 Oregon Short Line Cons.1st M.5's of 1946,	114,176.80	4,583.03
100,000 Oregon Short Line Ref. M. 4's of 1929,	96,875.00	4,000.00
40,000 Pennsylvania Co. 3½'s of 1916, ...	37,875.00	1,505.00
250,000 Richmond-Washington Co. Coll. Trust 4's of 1943, Series C, ...	255,144.65	9,834.05
100,000 St. Louis & San Francisco Ref. M. 4's of 1951, ...	97,125.00	4,000.00
£40,000 St. Paul, Minneapolis & Manitoba (Pacific Extension) 4's of 1940, ...	200,145.42	7,535.55
$100,000 Southern Pacific 1st Ref. M. 4's of 1955,	97,062.50	4,000.00
100,000 Southern Pacific Conv. 4's of 1929 . .	99,625.00	4,000.00
200,000 Terminal R. R. Association of St. Louis Gen. M. Ref 4's of 1953.	200,000.00	8,000.00
400,000 Union Pacific 1st M. & L. G. 4's of 1947,	353,114.75	16,000.00
100,000 " " Conv. 4's of 1927, ...	95,392.50	4,000.00
	$5,420,360.74	$224,152.45

Traction Bonds

	Principal.	Income.
$150,000 Boston & Northern Street R'y 1st M. Ref. 4's of 1954 (sold during the year),	. . . .	$6,577.78
200,000 Chicago Railways 1st M 5's of 1927, .	198,333.35	9,930.56
100,000 Cleveland Railway Ref. M 5's of 1931,	100,000.00	4,875.00
300,000 Interborough–Metropolitan Coll. Trust 4½'s of 1956, ...	254,782.50	13,500.00
Amounts carried forward, ...	$553,115.85	$34,883.34

	Principal.	Income.
Amounts brought forward, ...	$553,115.85	$34,883.34

Traction Bonds (*continued*).

	Principal.	Income.
$303,000 Interborough Rapid Transit Co. Gold M. 5's of 1952, ...	297,725.38	15,150.0
75,000 Kansas City Terminal R'y 1st M. Gold 4's (sold during the year), ...	. . . .	1,608.33
100,000 Metrop. Street R'y of Kansas City Consol. M. 5's of 1913, ...	99,000.00	5,000.00
100,000 Metrop. West Side Elevated 4's of 1938,	91,746.25	4,000.00
100,000 " " " Ext. M. 4's of 1938, ...	97,000.00	4,000.00
150,000 Montreal Tramways Co. 1st M. Ref. 5's of 1941, ...	149,625.00	770.84
70,632.50 New York Railways Co. Adj. M. 5's of 1942, ...	37,082.06	. . . . . .
15,222 New York Railways Co. 1st R. E & Ref. M. 4's of 1942, ...	11,949.27	. . . . . .
100,000 New York, Westchester & Boston R'y 1st M. 4½'s of 1946, ...	96,250.00	1,837.50
100,000 Northern Texas Traction Co. 1st M. 5's of 1933, ...	100,000.00	2,500.00
300,000 Old Colony Street R'y 1st M. Ref. 4's of 1954, ...	270,500.00	5,844.44
200,000 Puget Sound Traction, Light & Power Co. 5% M. Gold Notes of 1914, . . .	201,000.00	. . . . . .
100,000 Portland R'y Light & Power Co., 1st M. 5's of 1942, ...	95,500.00	. . . . . .
100,000 Second Ave. (N. Y.) Con. M. 5's of 1948,	115,789.60	. . . . . .
93,000 Third Avenue (N. Y.) 1st Consol. M. 4's of 2000, ...	94,052.36	. . . . . .
100,000 United Traction & Electric Co. 1st M. 5's of 1933, ...	109,163.60	4,563.63
	$2,419,499.87	$80,158.08

Sundry Bonds.

	Principal.	Income.
$100,000 American Agricultural Chemical Co. 5's of 1928, ...	$101,328.56	$4,914.28
300,000 American Tel. & Tel. Co. 4's of 1929, .	286,000.00	11,800.00
100,000 Boston Electric Light Co. 1st Cons. M. 5's of 1924 (sold during the year), . .	. . . .	2,111.12
145,000 Broadway Realty Co. Purchase money 1st M. 5's of 1926, ...	152,014.27	6,766.25
100,000 Calumet & Hecla Mining Co. 5% Coupon Notes of 1919, ...	101,400.00	7,397.22
250,000 Chicago Junction Railways and Union Stock Yards Coll. Trust 5's of 1915, .	250,060.40	12,479.85
100,000 Chicago Junction Railways and Union Stock Yards 4's of 1940, ...	98,500.00	4,000.00
Amounts carried forward, . . .	$989,303,23	$49,468.72

	Principal.	Income.
Amounts brought forward, . .	$989,808.23	$49,468.72

Sundry Bonds (*continued*).

	Principal.	Income.
$100,000 Chicago Telephone Co. 5's of 1923, . .	102,250.00	291.67
150,000 Detroit Edison Co. 1st M. 5's of 1933, .	152,534.50	7,376.28
50,000 Electric Securities Corp. 5's of 1940, 9th series, ...	50,000.00	1,430.56
300,000 Illinois Steel Co. Deb. 4½'s of 1940, . . .	284,250.00	8,537.50
100,000 Madison River Power Co. 1st M. 5's of 1935, ...	85,000.00	5,000.00
50,000 Massachusetts Gas Co.'s S. F. 4½'s of 1929, ...	48,375.00	2,250.00
100,000 Minneapolis General Electric Co. Gen. M. 5's of 1934, ...	101,906.82	4,915.26
100,000 Michigan State Telephone Co. 5's of 1924,	100,000.00	4,583.33
100,000 Montreal Light, Heat and Power Co. 1st M. Coll. Trust 4½'s of 1932 (sold during the year), ...	. . . .	4,837.50
100,000 Municipal Gas & Electric Co. of Rochester, N. Y., 1st M. 4½'s of 1942, . . .	100,000.00	4,500.00
100,000 New England Tel. & Tel. Co. 5's of 1916,	103,764.66	4,058.82
75,000 New York Tel. Co. Gen. M. Gold S.F. 4½'s (sold during the year), ...	. . . .	1,128.40
100,000 Pacific Coast Power 5's of 1940, . . .	96,000.00	4,069.40
55,000 Pejescot Paper Co. 1st M. 5's of 1917	54,450.00	2,750.00
45,000 " " " " " of 1921	44,550.00	2,250.00
200,000 Portland Gen'l Elec. 1st M. 5's of 1935,	202,830.79	9,876.93
100,000 Railway & Light Securities Co. Coll. Trust 5's of 1935, 1st series	100,784.10	4,965.90
100,000 Railway & Light Securities Co. Coll. Trust 5's of 1939, 2d series, ...	100,000.00	5,000.00
100,000 Railway & Light Securities Co. Coll. Trust 5's of 1939, 3rd series, ...	98,000.00	5,000.00
200,000 San Francisco Gas & Electric Co. 4½'s of 1933, ...	187,000.00	4,312.50
200,000 Southern Power Co. 1st M. 5's, of 1930,	197,500.00	8,805.55
191,000 St. Louis National Stock Yards Co. 1st M. 4's of 1930, ...	184,465.00	7,353.11
100,000 Tacoma Railway & Power Co. 1st M. 5's of 1929, ...	100,940.00	4,980.00
50,000 United Electric Securities Co. Coll. Trust 5's of 1936, 24th series, . . .	50,000.00	2,500.00
50,000 United Electric Securities Co. Coll. Trust 5's of 1938, 27th series, ...	49,250.00	3,034.72
50,000 United Electric Securities Co. Coll. Trust 5's of 1939, 29th series (sold during the year), ...	. . . .	1,076.39
25,000 United Electric Securities Co. Coll. Trust 5's of 1940, 32nd series, . . .	25,241.07	699.40
Amounts carried forward, . . .	$3,608,895.17	$164,551.94

	Principal.	Income.
Amount brought forward, ...	$3,608,895.17	$164,551.64

Sundry Bonds (*continued*).

		Principal.	Income.
$100,000	United Electric Securities Co., Coll. Trust 5's of 1942, 36th series, . . .	100,000.00	. . . . . .
150,000	United Fruit Co. 4½'s of 1925, ...	143,750.00	6,206.25
100,000	United States Smelting, Refining & Mining Co. 5's of 1914, ...	98,000.00	1,986.11
100,000	Washington Water Power Co. 5's of 1939,	100,360.01	4,986.67
200,000	Western Elec. Co. 1st M. 5's of 1922, .	199,000.00	9,944.44
100,000	Westinghouse Electric Manufacturing Co. 5% Notes of 1917, ...	94,625.00	5,000.00
		$4,344,130.18	$192,675.41

Railroad Stocks.

		Principal.	Income.
700 shares	Baltimore & Ohio, ...	$70,362.50	$4,200.00
507 "	Chicago, Milwaukee & St. Paul, pfd.,	50,670.58	3,549.00
1268 "	Chicago, Milwaukee & St. Paul, . .	177,425.94	7,608.00
2282 "	Chicago & No. Western, ...	319,255.55	15,974.00
1337 "	Great Northern, preferred, ...	} 294,558.56	{ 9,359.00
955 "	Great Northern Iron Ore Properties,		. . . . . .
800 "	Louisville & Nashville, ...	93,924.00	5,600.00
8 "	Louisville Property	1.00	. . . . . .
700 "	Manhattan, ...	92,762.50	4,900.00
2088 "	New York Central & Hudson River, .	151,173.21	10,440.00
867 "	New York, New Haven & Hartford, .	141,729.80	6,936.00
1000 "	Northern Pacific, ...	115,315.00	7,000.00
6851 "	Pennsylvania, ...	413,506.40	20,086.50
500 "	Union Pacific, ...	91,437.50	5,000.00
		$2,012,122.54	$100,652.50

Manufacturing and Telephone Stocks.

		Principal.	Income.
2000 shares	American Smelters Securities Co. 5% cumulative preferred, series B, . .	$196,000.00	$8,333.33
2584 "	American Tel. & Tel. Co., ...	320,447.53	12,448.00
240 "	Amoskeag Manufacturing Co., pref.,	} 8,654.00	1,800.00
360 "	" " " " . .		
2430 "	General Electric Co., ...	262,626.27	16,580.00
187 "	Merrimack Manufacturing Co., . . .	18,615.10	. . . . . .
24 "	Pacific Mills, ...	16,668.29	1,920.00
		$818,011.19	$41,081.33

Real Estate Trust Stocks.

		Principal.	Income.
1000 shares	Barristers Hall, ...	$92,766.00	$4,000.00
250 "	Business Real Estate, ...	23,750.00	1,125.00
2500 "	Department Store, ...	220,291.88	11,250.00
1000 "	Essex Street, ...	100,000.00	4,000.00
750 "	Kimball Building, ...	75,000.00	2,250.00
1069 "	Paddock Building, ...	104,363.72	3,811.50
1000 "	Post Office Square Building, ...	108,000.00	4,000.00
1000 "	St. Paul Business Real Estate Assoc.	100,000.00	4,000.00
	Amounts carried forward, . . .	$819,171.60	$34,436.50

			Principal.	Income.
	Amounts brought forward.		$819,171.60	$34,436.50
Real Estate Trust Stocks (*continued*).				
1000	"	Tremont Building.	100,000.00	4,500.00
1875	"	Western Real Estate Trust, ...	196,500.00	11,718.75
			$1,115,671.60	$50,655.25
Sundry Stocks.				
611 shares		Edison Elec. Illum. Co., Boston, Mass., ...	$124,927.50	$7,332.00
1500	"	Massachusetts Gas Companies, pref'd,	132,107.00	6,000.00
1222	"	Trimountain Trust.	114,009.50	3,896.57
			$371,044.00	$17,228.57

SUMMARY :

	Principal	Income
Mortgages and Notes.	$2,043,499.06	$87,272.63
Public Funds, ...	87,250.00	3,760.00
Railroad Bonds, ...	5,420,360.74	224,152.45
Traction Bonds, ...	2,419,499.37	80,158.08
Sundry Bonds, ...	4,344,130.18	192,675.41
Railroad Stocks, ...	2,012,122.54	100,652.50
Manufacturing and Tel. Stocks, ...	818,011.19	41,081.33
Real Estate Trust Stocks, ...	1,115,671.60	50,655.25
Sundry Stocks, ...	371,044.00	17,228.57
Total, Exhibit A, ...	$18,631,588.70	
Total. Exhibit B, ...		$797,636.22

Schedule 3

LAND AND BUILDINGS — GENERAL INVESTMENT
June 30, 1912

Real Estate in Boston.	Principal.	Net Income.
Adams Estate, Washington Street, ...	$250,000.00	$15,641.73
Amory Estate, Franklin Street, ...	165,615.81	11,507.34
Cowdin Estate, Haymarket Square, ...	36,000.00	1,877.13
Estate, 17 and 19 Haymarket Square, ...	13,500.00	1,246.06
Estate, 20 and 21 Haymarket Square, ...	58,913.52	2,942.05
Estate, 364 and 366 Washington St., ...	110,000.00	5,509.84
Estate, 31 and 33 Otis and 112 Arch Streets, . .	55,000.00	733.34
Estate, 16 to 18 Union and 3 to 11 Friend Streets,	81,000.00	2,739.84
Faneuil Hall Square Estate, ...	197,047.80	8,328.84
Gerrish Block, Blackstone and North Streets, . .	192,875.75	7,928.25
Gray Estate, Washington Street, ...	949,709.80	72,585.76
Jaynes Estate, Washington and Hanover Streets,	162,000.00	6,658.57
Lowell Estate, Washington Street, ...	464,368.91	28,888.19
Old Boston Music Hall Estate, ...	356,611.00	22,422.38
Townsend Estate, Hawkins Street, ...	44,419.49	716.72
Webb Estate, Washington Street, ...	164,604.79	19,256.92
Total, Exhibit A, ...	$3,301,666.87	
Total, Exhibit B, ...		$208,973.66

FUNDS AND GIFTS

June 30, 1912

[The date following the title of a Fund shows the year of its establishment.]

Principal, July 1, 1911.	UNIVERSITY FUNDS	Principal, June 30, 1912.
$136,568.75	Anonymous (1910), ...	$134,766.25
46,877.95	**Walter F. Baker** (1909), ...	24,602.11
2,000.00	**William H. Baldwin, Jr.** (1906),	2,000.00
1,148.00	Band Music (1903), ...	1,148.00
4,950.00	**Andrew Bigelow** (1898), ...	4,950.00
5,000.00	**Stanton Blake** (1889), ...	5,000.00
4,771.38	**Charlotte F. Blanchard** (1891), .	4,771.38
5,250.00	**Samuel D. Bradford** (1866), . .	5,250.00
50,000.00	**Martin Brimmer** (1907), ...	50,000.00
100,000.00	**James C. Carter** (1906), ...	100,000.00
12,500.00	**John W. Carter** (1898), ...	12,500.00
94,622.77	**Class of 1883** (1908), ...	94,722.77
9,777.10	**Edward Erwin Coolidge** (1906),	9,815.55
154.94	Thomas Cotton (1727), ...	155.09
38,885.06	John Cowdin (1888), ...	38,885.06
115,966.56	**George B. Dorr** (1882), ...	115,966.56
48,458.50	**George Draper** (1892), ...	48,458.50
56,788.00	**R. H. Eddy** (1901), ...	56,788.00
101,225.49	Harvard Ellis (1895), ...	101,225.49
20,918.57	**Richard W. Foster** (1905), . . .	20,918.57
5,322.09	**John Davis Williams French** (1901), ...	5,322.09
20,571.18	**Gore** (1834), ...	20,571.18
25,000.00	**John C. Gray** (1881), ...	25,000.00
20,000.00	**Walter Hastings** (1888), ...	20,000.00
100,000.00	**Henry L. Higginson** (1906), . .	100,000.00
5,000.00	**George Baxter Hyde** (1895), . .	5,000.00
4,000.00	Insurance and Guaranty (1860), . . .	4,000.00
16,871.63	Leonard Jarvis (1859), ...	16,871.63
10,000.00	**Henry P. Kidder** (1894), ...	10,000.00
10,000.00	**Joseph Lee** (1802), ...	10,000.00
10,000.00	**Theodore Lyman** (1898), ...	10,000.00
15,750.00	Israel Munson (1844), ...	15,750.00
49,980.00	**Henry S. Nourse** (1904), ...	50,000.00
113,817.44	**Francis E. Parker** (1886), . . .	113,817.44
4,005.59	**George F. Parkman** (1909), . . .	4,005.59
30,000.00	**William Perkins** (1888), ...	30,000.00
50,000.00	**Henry L. Pierce** (1898), ...	50,000.00
157,198.14	Henry L. Pierce(Residuary)(1898),	157,198.14
64,334.47	President's (1883), ...	64,425.24
371,957.48	Retiring Allowance (1879), ...	378,159.96
11,000.00	Riverside (1903), ...	11,000.00
$1,945,616.04	. . Amounts carried forward, . . .	$1,927,989.55

Principal, July 1, 1911.		Principal, June 30, 1912.	
$1,945,616.04	. . Amounts brought forward, . .	$1,927,989.55	
23,370.03	John L. Russell (1889), ...	23,370.03	
1,852.25	Mary R. Searle (1903), ...	1,852.25	
46,913.13	Isaac Sweetser (1894), ...	46,913.13	
5,000.00	Seth Turner (1883), ...	5,000.00	
100,000.00	William F. Weld (1893), ...	100,000.00	$2,105,124.96

COLLEGE FUNDS

13,583.70	John W. P. Abbot (1874), . . .	$14,256.10	
27,748.64	Alford Professorship (1765), . . .	27,748.64	
7,806.86	Daniel Austin (1879), ...	7,806.86	
5,787.61	William H. Baldwin, Jr. 1885 (1906), ...	5,588.96	
666.67	John Barnard (1777), ...	666.67	
30,686.85	John B. Barringer (1873), . . .	30,686.85	
15,000.00	Robert Charles Billings, for Gray Herbarium (1908), ...	15,000.00	
1,050.00	John A. Blanchard (1873), . .	1,050.00	
39,780.00	Botanic Department (1880), ...	39,780.00	
28,837.40	Boylston Professorship (1772), . .	28,837.40	
11,224.65	Francis James Child Memorial (1897), ...	11,224.65	
7,179.37	Classical Publication Fund of the Class of 1856 (1888), ...	7,179.37	
108,669.41	Class of 1880 (1905), ...	108,669.41	
91,924.30	Fund of the Class of 1882 (1907),	94,970.18	
278.59	Class of 1883 Special Fund (1908),	292.40	
98,599.91	Class of 1884 (1909), ...	100,099.91	
108,305.99	Class of 1885 Gift (1910), ...	108,305.99	
100,000.00	Class of 1886 (1911), ...	100,000.00	
. . . .	Class of 1887 (1912), ...	100,000.00	
150,637.54	Class Subscription (1870), ...	150,637.54	
321,399.84	Edward W. Codman (1905), . .	321,399.84	
1,500.00	John Coggan (1652), ...	1,500.00	
57,521.55	T. Jefferson Coolidge, for Research in Physics, ...	59,860.06	
4,250.40	Paul Dudley (1751), ...	4,260.78	
111,838.81	Eaton Professorship (1903), . . .	112,374.84	
21,619.50	Eliot Professorship (1814), ...	21,619.50	
10,000.00	Eliot " (Jonathan Phillips's gift) (1854), ...	10,000.00	
3,500.01	Erving Professorship (1791), . . .	3,500.01	
35,990.99	Fisher " (1834), . . .	35,990.99	
484.57	Henry Flynt (1760), ...	435.21	
16,240.38	Fund for Permanent Tutors (1796), .	16,240.38	
1,033.57	Fund for Religious Services (1887), .	1,033.57	
6,078.51	George A. Gardner (1892), . .	6,130.66	
$3,556,427.07	. . Amounts carried forward, . . .	$1,541,646.77	$2,105,124.96

Principal, July 1, 1911.		Principal, June 30, 1912.	
$3,556,427.07	.. Amounts brought forward, ...	$1,541,646.77	$2,105,124.96
15,141.86	**Godkin** Lectures (1903), ...	15,891.89	
7,812.77	**Gospel** Church (1868), ...	8,006.14	
32,711.00	**Asa Gray** Memorial (1898), . . .	32,711.00	
21,451.25	**Asa Gray** Professorship of Systematic Botany (1897), ...	21,451.25	
200,096.86	**Gurney** (1888), ...	200,096.86	
5,661.71	**George Silsbee** and **Ellen Sever Hale** (1904), ...	5,941.98	
. . . .	**Harvard** Foundation for Exchanges with French Universities (1912), .	30,352.98	
15,258.56	**Harvard** Oriental Series (1899), . .	15,486.64	
20,655.91	**Herbarium** (1865), ...	20,655.91	
20,217.08	**Hersey** Professorship (1772), . . .	20,217.08	
21,744.18	**Hersey** Professorship (**Thomas Lee's** gift) (1856), ...	21,744.18	
. . . .	**Richard Hodgson** Memorial (1912), ...	10,012.18	
520.00	**Thomas Hollis** (for Treasurer) (1721), ...	520.00	
3,747.33	**Hollis** Professorship of Mathematics, Composed of these Funds : — **Thomas Brattle** (1713), **William Dummer** (1762), **Daniel Henchman** (1758), **Thomas Hollis** (1726).	3,747.33	
1,000.00	**Thomas Hubbard** (1774), . . .	1,000.00	
444.44	**Nathaniel Hulton** (1695), . . .	444.44	
233.33	**Thomas Hutchinson** (1739), . .	233.33	
6,258.54	**Ingersoll** Lecture (1894), ...	6,522.62	
61,536.43	**Abbott Lawrence** (1859), . . .	61,536.43	
50,375.00	**James Lawrence** (1865), ...	50,375.00	
11,996.55	**Lectures** on Political Economy (1889),	12,315.40	
15,796.97	**Lee** Fund for Reading (1863), . . .	15,796.97	
110,043.29	**Henry Lee** Professorship (1900), .	110,043.29	
10,273.73	**Solomon Lincoln** Bequest (1911),	10,782.29	
7,732.50	**Joseph Lovering** for Physical Research (1891), ...	7,747.94	
68,257.31	**Lowell** Fund for a Botanic Garden (1882) (formerly Professorship of Natural History, 1805), ...	68,257.31	
20,212.81	**Woodbury Lowery** Memorial (1910), ...	20,232.75	
50,000.00	**Arthur T. Lyman** (1904), . . .	50,000.00	
43,062.93	**McLean** Professorship (1834), . .	43,062.93	
. . . .	**Music** Building Maintenance Fund (1911), ...	6,852.51	
1,365.41	**Music** Department (1903), ...	1,432.97	
$4,380,034.82	.. Amounts carried forward, . . .	$2,415,117.87	$2,105,124.96

Principal, July 1, 1911.		Principal, June 30, 1912.	
$4,380,084.82	. . Amounts brought forward, . . . $2,415,117.87	$2,105,124.96	
333.33	John Newgate (1650), ...	333.33	
26,788.88	William Belden Noble Lectures (1898), ...	26,929.98	
21,914.79	Trenor L. Park Bequest (1911), .	21,914.79	
100,396.58	Francis Greenwood Peabody Fund (1905), ...	101,866.18	
14,676.38	Daniel H. Peirce (1876), ...	14,749.08	
456.58	James Mills Peirce Bequest (bal.),	479.20	
21,000.00	Perkins Professorship (1841), . .	21,000.00	
31,500.00	Jonathan Phillips (1861), . . .	31,500.00	
75,000.00	Physical Laboratory Endowm't(1881),	75,000.00	
25,020.19	Plummer Foundation (1854), . .	25,020.19	
52,500.00	Pope Professorship (1868), ...	52,500.00	
189,655.98	Sarah E. Potter Endowment Fund,	198,620.97	
238,871.83	Professorship of Hygiene (1899), . .	239,008.97	
52,340.17	" " (1902), . .	52,391.63	
32,555.25	" " (1908), . .	45,593.71	
. . . .	General Publication Fund (1912), .	2,782.39	
193,921.10	Nelson Robinson, Jr. Additional (1906), ...	192,266.01	
8,535.00	Ezekiel Rogers (1701), ...	8,535.00	
119,018.53	Eliza O. and Mary P. Ropes, .	121,864.24	
56,368.73	Rumford Professorship (1819), . .	56,368.73	
1,514.00	Daniel Russell (1679), ...	1,514.00	
2,000.00	John L. Russell (1889), ...	2,000.00	
5,779.92	George William Sawin (1890),	6,066.03	
5,000.00	Robert W. Sayles (1906), . . .	5,238.87	
33,498.99	Shaler Memorial (1907), ...	35,128.19	
23,139.83	Smith Professorship (1816), . . .	23,139.83	
2,500.00	William M. Spackman (1905),	2,500.00	
2,050,807.18	Teachers' Endowment (1905), . . .	2,052,650.58	
15,988.30	John E. Thayer (1885), ...	16,414.91	
1,287.28	Elizabeth Torrey (1896), . . .	1,155.59	
13,807.26	Henry Warren Torrey (1890), .	14,156.47	
113,975.44	Twenty-fifth Anniversary Fund of the Class of 1881 (1906), ...	114,035.44	
101,219.47	Unknown Memorial (1898), . . .	100,189 99	
50,000.00	Henry Villard (1902), ...	50,000.00	
40,000.00	Wales Professorship (1903), . . .	39,540.20	
18,494.39	Samuel Ward (1680), ...	19,409.79	
6,567.88	Cyrus M. Warren (1893), . . .	6,335.28	
119,528.34	Henry C. Warren (1899), . . .	119,531.46	
8,115.73	Sylvester Waterhouse (1896), .	8,517.48	
50,000.00	Increase Sumner Wheeler (1889),	50,000.00	
97.42	Jerome Wheelock (1903), . . .	112.52	
1,420.12	Chauncey Wright (1884), . . .	1,490.41	6,367,964.21
$8,300,629.59	. . Amounts carried forward, ...	$8,473,089.17	

Principal, July 1, 1911.		Principal, June 30, 1912.
$8,300,629.59	. . Amounts brought forward, ...	$8,473,089.17

GIFTS FOR SPECIAL USE (BALANCES)

648.84	Anonymous Gift for Fellowship in Physical Research, ...	$148.84
. . . . . .	Anonymous Gift to be added to the 1912–13 income of the **W. Bayard Cutting** Fellowship in Physics, . .	500.00
400.00	Anonymous Gift for Salary, 1911–12,	. . . . . .
270.00	Anonymous Gift for Special Aid, . .	270.00
1,251.88	Bermuda Biological Station, ...	1,340.30
760.48	Cases, etc., at the Botanic Garden, .	775.69
30.27	**F. P. Bonney** Gift, ...	30.27
8.60	Common Room in Conant Hall, . . .	8.60
. . . . . .	Harvard Economic Studies, ...	2,576.52
1,550.00	Department of English — Gift for Publications, ...	2,498.00
578.71	Gift Department Economics, ...	. . . . . .
. . . . . .	Department Economics, Special Use,	75.00
78.08	Experimental Phonetics, ...	78.08
. . . . . .	Gift Department of Fine Arts, . . .	15.00
70.04	French Department Library, ...	70.04
14.50	Geographical Department, Lantern Slides, ...	14.50
54.69	Department of Geology, Exhibition Case for Photographs, ...	. . . . . .
322.52	Collections for a Germanic Museum, .	322.52
476.80	Department of Government—**F. G. Thomson** Gift, ...	1,568.69
. . . . . .	Department of Government — Gift **David A. Ellis**, Books, ...	9.14
. . . . . .	Department of Government — Gift for special expenses in Municipal Government, ...	108.80
36.15	**Augustus Hemenway** Gift, . .	36.15
1,029.91	History Book Fund, ...	1,346.62
350.00	Gift for Apparatus for Professor Jeffrey's Courses, ...	. . . . . .
20.00	Gift for Land in New Hampshire, . .	20.00
10.23	**Lowell** Memorial Library, ...	10.23
47.62	**Edward Mallinckrodt** Gift, . .	33.21
30.00	Department of Mathematics, ...	30.00
100.00	International Committee on Teaching Mathematics, ...	. . . . . .
490.47	Mathematics Book Fund, ...	516.61
100.00	**Sir John Murray** Gift, ...	100.00
74.16	Department Music, Gift, ...	50.87

Principal, July 1, 1911.			Principal, June 30, 1912.
$8,309,433.54	. . Amounts carried forward, . . .	$12,548.18	$8,473,089.17

Principal, July 1, 1911.		Principal, June 30, 1911	
$8,309,433.54	. . Amounts brought forward, . . .	$12,548.18	$8,473,089.17
59.05	Philosophical Library, ...	180.67	
3,803.67	Plantation of Shrubs, etc., ...	. . . . . .	
14.65	Harvard Psychological Review, . . .	21.61	
25.00	Political Economy Department, Library, ...	25.00	
6,089.12	Decorating the front of the Nelson Robinson Jr. Hall, ...	6,280.68	
. . . .	Gift for salaries, 1912–13, ...	2,000.00	
2,366.93	Sanskrit Department, ...	2,473.54	
1,002.05	Semitic Library, ...	879.82	
4,813.38	Social Ethics, ...	4,645.82	
300.00	Social Ethics Library, ...	293.10	
644.78	Furnishings for the Department of Social Ethics, ...	450.27	
801.43	Sugar-cane investigation, etc., . . .	817.45	30,616.14

FELLOWSHIP

25,505.20	Bayard Cutting (1910), ...	$25,642.69	
12,920.20	W. Bayard Cutting, Jr. Bequest (1910), ...	12,984.74	
5,876.78	George W. Dillaway (1903), . .	5,942.69	
26.17	Fellowship in Central American Archaeology (balance), ...	26.17	
11,896.12	Ozias Goodwin Memorial (1889),	11,959.97	
11,808.77	Harris (1868), ...	11,393.31	
26,448.98	Edward William Hooper(1905),	26,608.21	
11,463.71	John Thornton Kirkland(1871),	11,531.17	
12,341.80	Henry Lee Memorial (1889), . .	12,427.73	
. . . .	Elkan Naumburg (1911), . . .	10,281.31	
19,166.40	Charles Eliot Norton (1901), .	19,169.67	
5.48	John Knowles Paine (1912), .	28,384.07	
13,565.97	Robert Treat Paine (1887), . .	13,637.48	
62,892.82	John Parker (1873), ...	63,381.03	
10,506.15	Francis Parkman (1906), . . .	10,426.20	
10,244.70	Princeton (1910), ...	10,301.82	
33,576.90	Rogers (1869), ...	33,738.96	
12,693.47	Henry Bromfield Rogers Memorial (1889), ...	12,796.77	
. . . .	Henry Russell Shaw (1912), .	35,264.83	
524.25	Social Ethics, ...	100.18	
100.00	South End House (balance), ...	. . . .	
12,815.08	John Tyndall (1885), ...	12,899.43	
11,808.26	James Walker (1881), ...	11,867.76	
25,477.03	Whiting (1896), ...	25,838.13	406,604.21
$8,660,967.84	. . Amounts carried forward, ...		$8,910,309.63

Principal, July 1, 1911.		Principal, June 30, 1912.
$8,660,967.84	. . Amounts brought forward, ...	$8,910,809.63

SCHOLARSHIP

3,974.74	Abbot (1852), ...	$3,996.51
2,870.01	Alford (1785), ...	3,012.08
. . . .	Scholarship at International School of American Archaeology and Ethnology at Mexico City (gift), . .	600.00
6,072.75	Caroline M. Barnard Bequest (1911), ...	29,972.75
5,441.08	Bartlett (1831), ...	5,460.41
5,808.83	Bassett (1876), ...	5,826.88
13,927.88	Bigelow (1865), ...	14,017.82
9.70	Charles Sumner Bird, ...	. . . .
3,584.68	Samuel A. Borden (1896), . . .	3,762.14
116,759.02	Bowditch (1864), ...	117,288.59
4,611.22	Bright (balance), ...	4,826.96
4,065.41	Browne (1687), ...	4,091.62
5,662.86	Morey Willard Buckminster (1898), ...	5,693.18
35,889.00	Burr (1895), ...	36,065.51
6,332.04	Ruluff Sterling Choate (1884),	6,370.47
10,154.79	George Newhall Clark (1908),	10,162.47
5,066.45	Thomas William Clarke (1911),	5,092.22
8,829.02	Class of 1802 (1870), ...	8,891.06
3,391.02	" 1814 (1853), ...	3,408.87
7,005.69	" 1815(Kirkland)(1852),	7,052.49
4,891.49	" 1817 (1852), ...	4,933.59
3,547.91	" 1828 (1882), ...	3,528.54
5,370.66	" 1835 (1858), ...	5,411.52
5,469.06	" 1841 (1871), ...	5,514.78
5,467.56	" 1852 (Dana) (1876), . .	5,513.23
16,920.85	" 1856 (1885), ...	17,008.43
7,311.63	" 1867 (1886), ...	7,348.57
5,412.56	" 1877 (1902), ...	5,455.50
6,391.08	" 1883 (1900), ...	6,432.43
150.00	Classical Department (Gift), ...	157.42
. . . .	Clement Harlow Condell (1911),	25,000.00
12,801.24	Crowninshield (1877), ...	12,884.88
6,000.00	Warren H. Cudworth, ...	6,000.00
6,619.36	Francis H. Cummings (1898), .	6,672.00
5,680.11	George and Martha Derby (1881),	5,711.27
6,558.53	Julius Dexter (1892), ...	6,658.20
3,096.68	Orlando W. Doe (1898), ...	3,149.93
250.00	Edda Club (1911), ...	508.21
5,764.88	William Samuel Eliot (1875), .	5,800.24
32,920.85	George H. Emerson (1908), . . .	33,875.44

| $9,051,048.43 | . . Amounts carried forward, . . . | $443,150.21 $8,910,809.63 |

Principal, July 1, 1911.		Principal, June 30, 1912.	
$9,051,048.43	. . Amounts brought forward, . . .	$443,150.21	$8,910,309.63
43,717.22	Joseph Eveleth (1896), ...	44,481.23	
2,590.71	Fall River (1898), ...	2,618.96	
6,668.75	Farrar (1873), ...	6,723.87	
5,041.22	George Fisher and Elizabeth Huntington Fisher (1908), . .	5,090.75	
12,109.52	Richard Augustine Gambrill (1890), ...	12,183.97	
8,115.72	Charles Haven Goodwin(1889),	8,167.47	
4,751.83	Greene (1863), ...	4,787.05	
100.00	Price Greenleaf (balance), . . .	220.00	
5,066.44	Selwyn L. Harding Scholarship of the Class of 1886 (1911), . .	5,092.21	
1,048.50	Harvard Club of Boston, ...	1,048.50	
. . . .	" " Kansas City, . . .	150.00	
100.00	" " Lawrence, ...	. . . .	
200.00	" " Rochester, N. Y., .	200.00	
50.00	" " San Francisco, . .	50.00	
329.24	" " Washington, D. C. (balance), ...	79.24	
10,718.00	John Appleton Haven (1902), .	10,773.54	
25,794.78	William Hilton (1897), ...	26,171.64	
11,406.33	Ebenezer Rockwood Hoar (1895), ...	11,470.93	
6,728.08	Levina Hoar, for the town of Lincoln, Mass. (1876), ...	6,761.12	
13,874.56	Hodges (1878), ...	13,906.07	
6,683.48	Hollis (1722), ...	6,739.29	
11,323.52	Henry B. Humphrey (1890), . .	11,384.05	
32,676.20	Charles L. Jones (1901), ...	32,943.66	
11,120 63	George Emerson Lowell (1886),	11,221.12	
5,801.37	Markoe (1903), ...	5,838.52	
3,355.26	Matthews (balance), ...	1,663.31	
6,631.57	Merrick (1888), ...	6,684.85	
8,847.40	Morey (1868), ...	8,910.33	
6,199.50	Lady Mowlson (1643), ...	6,256.40	
3,085.60	Boston Newsboys' (1906), ...	3,113.36	
6,034.12	Howard Gardner Nichols (1897),	6,082.80	
6,362.13	Lucy Osgood (1873), ...	6,402.05	
1,308.96	George Herbert Palmer (1911),	1,593.79	
5,460.06	George Foster Peabody (1902),	5,242.73	
4,609.36	James Mills Peirce Scholarship (1908), ...	4,837.50	
8,144.87	Pennoyer (1670).	8,468.05	
30,000.00	Charles Elliott Perkins Scholarships (1909), ...	30,267.24	
4,933.53	Rebecca A. Perkins (1869), . .	4,977.76	
11,133.73	Philadelphia (1904), ...	11,184.86	
$9,383,170.62	. . Amounts carried forward, . . .	$776,938.43	$8,910,309.63

Principal, July 1, 1911.		Principal, June 30, 1912.	
$9,383,170.62	. . Amounts brought forward, . . .	$776,938.43	$8,910,309.63
1,810.83	**Wendell Phillips** Mem'l (1895),	1,825.47	
. . . .	**Elnathan Pratt** (1912), ...	4,847.96	
4,070.63	**William Reed** (1907), ...	4,054.14	
350.00	**Ricardo** Prize (balance), ...	350.00	
1,612.17	**Rodger** (1883), ...	1,691.96	
3,673.51	**Henry Bromfield Rogers** (1859),	3,705.37	
11,176.09	**Nathaniel Ropes, Jr.,** Scholarship		
	(1909), ...	11,254.31	
15,573.41	**James Augustus Rumrill** (1909),	15,669.27	
6,103.85	**Edward Russell** (1877), ...	6,155.99	
6,047.26	**Sales** (1893), ...	6,096.59	
11,893.79	**Saltonstall** (1739), ...	11,957.54	
9,070.36	**Leverett Saltonstall** (1895), . .	9,119.33	
7,294.56	**Mary Saltonstall** (1730), ...	7,355.66	
3,291.31	**Sever** (1868), ...	3,304.22	
11,855.08	**Sewall** (1696), ...	11,941.91	
51,366.99	**Shattuck** (1854), ...	51,809.65	
6,342.31	**Slade** (1877), ...	6,381.24	
4,700.00	**Dunlap Smith** (1903), ...	4,700.00	
4,785.32	**Story** (1864), ...	4,822.18	
3,593.56	**Stoughton** (1701), ...	3,533.79	
4,685.01	**Swift** (1899), ...	4,716.92	
85,231.59	**Thayer** (1857), ...	85,950.57	
4,571.85	**Gorham Thomas** (1865), ...	4,598.16	
8,147.59	**Toppan** (1868), ...	7,850.92	
27,403.94	**Townsend** (1861), ...	27,760.43	
. . . .	University (gift), ...	150.00	
4,919.10	**Ira D. Van Duzee** (1911), . . .	4,917.41	
5,411.73	**Walcott** (1855), ...	5,479.62	
11,269.61	**Christopher M. Weld** (1899), .	11,327.48	
5,732.55	**Jacob Wendell** (1899), ...	5,766.33	
12,488.15	**Whiting** (1874), ...	12,556.31	
5,000.00	**Josiah Dwight Whitney** (1904),	5,005.00	
11,912.29	**Mary L. Whitney** (1903), . . .	12,001.93	
10,620.57	**Willard** (1907), ...	10,671.31	
2,177.09	**Augustus Woodbury** Scholar-		
	ship '(1909), ...	2,284.85	
10,560.21	**Charles Wyman** (1905), ...	10,632.93	1,159,185.18

BENEFICIARY AND LOAN

54,515.02	**Rebecca C. Ames** (1903), . . .	$54,878.52	
650.00	Anonymous Gift for certain members		
	of the Class of 1915, ...	32.18	
770.75	**Nathaniel Appleton** (1772), . .	770.75	
2,271.56	**Frank Bolles** Memorial (1894), .	2,294.02	
1,915.49	**William Brattle** (1717), ...	1,915.49	
95,274.52	**Daniel A. Buckley** (1905), . . .	97,100.04	
$9,913,310.27	. . Amounts carried forward, . . .	$156,991.00	$10,069,494.81

Principal, July 1, 1911.		Principal, June 30, 1912.	
$9,913,310.27	. . Amounts brought forward, . .	$156,991.00	$10,069,494.81
51,782.94	Walter Channing Cabot (1905),	52,293.72	
1,858.68	Thomas Danforth (1724), . . .	1,858.68	
5,473.64	Moses Day (1880), ...	5,473.64	
. . . .	Dean's Loan, Harvard College, . . .	500.00	
548.26	John Ellery (1788), ...	548.26	
1,853.69	Exhibitions (1796), ...	1,853.69	
1,074.91	Fines Loan (balance), ...	2,875.67	
997.90	Thomas Fitch (1737), ...	1,047.80	
592.66	Ephraim Flynt (1723), ...	592.66	
213.41	Henry Flynt (1760), ...	213.41	
3,166.15	Freshman Loan (balance), ...	2,707.87	
1,088.54	Freshman Loan, Gove Gift, ...	1,059.80	
616.92	Henry Gibbs (1722), ...	616.92	
4,225.72	John Glover (1653), ...	4,268.83	
16,635.29	Price Greenleaf Aid (balance), .	19,818.68	
751.90	Student Fund of the Harvard Engineering Society of New York (1908) (balance), ...	789.12	
11,904.74	Edwin A. W. Harlow (1905), .	12,239.04	
5,615.26	Robert Henry Harlow (1908),	5,677.86	
459.99	Edward Holyoke (1743), . . .	460.91	
2,960.89	Robert Keayne (1659), ...	2,960.89	
26,261.00	Bertram Kimball (1903), . . .	26,299.92	
1,877.61	Harry Milton Levy Loan (College) (balance), ...	1,530.56	
1,279.83	Mary Lindall (1812), ...	1,279.83	
5,988.87	Susan B. Lyman (1899), ...	5,988.87	
545.70	Susan B. Lyman Loans (College) (balance), ...	504.09	
298.82	Anne Mills (1725), ...	298.82	
50.00	John F. Moors' Gift, Special aid for a member of the Class of 1915,	. . . . . .	
10,858.92	Munroe (1880), ...	11,081.98	
2,184.88	Palfrey Exhibition (1821), ...	2,298.04	
5,492.16	Dr. Andrew P. Peabody Memorial (1896), ...	5,591.26	
1,844.89	Scholarship and Beneficiary Money Returned (balance), ...	1,123.68	
284.62	Joseph Sewall (1765), ...	298.72	
16,685.69	Alexander Wheelock Thayer (1899), ...	16,685.69	
11,171.94	Quincy Tufts (1877), ...	11,171.94	
384.80	Benjamin Wadsworth (1737),	384.80	
. . . .	Waite Memorial (1912), ...	50,696.52	
7,789.69	Stuart Wadsworth Wheeler (1898), ...	8,259.82	416,730.49
$10,116,980.18	. . Amounts carried forward, ...		$10,486,225.30

Principal, July 1, 1911.		Principal, June 30, 1912.
$10,116,980.18	. . Amounts brought forward, ...	$10,486,225.80

PRIZE

2,026.85	James Gordon Bennett (1893), .	$2,087.19
487.87	Philo Sherman Bennett (1905),	459.01
10,500.00	Francis Boott (1904), ...	10,600.00
32,298.55	Bowdoin Prizes for Dissertations (1791), ...	32,612.82
2,675.07	Boylston Prizes for Elocution (1817),	2,597.49
5,853.61	Coolidge Debating (1899), ...	5,924.35
50.00	Dante Prize (balance), ...	50.00
2,736.93	Lloyd McKim Garrison Prize and Medal (1904), ...	2,760.66
8.24	Harvard Club of New Jersey Prizes (balance), ...	8.24
2,808.65	Edward Hopkins Gift for "Deturs" (1718) (balance), ...	2,527.46
1,145.83	George Arthur Knight (1909),	1,202.56
. . . .	Lake Mohonk (1912), ...	100.00
. . . .	Old Testament Study (1912), . . .	50.00
. . . .	Patria Society Gift, ...	50.00
1,185.20	Sales (1892), ...	1,198.86
2,758.78	John O. Sargent (1889), ...	2,795.35
7,000.00	George B. Sohier (1890), ...	7,000.00
4,859.83	Charles Sumner (1874), ...	4,575.10
4,131.95	Robert N. Toppan (1894), . . .	4,186.48
2,404.57	Philip Washburn (1899), . . .	2,448.62
116,382.76	David A. Wells (1901), ...	113,795.69
2,026.04	Elizabeth Wilder (1911), . . .	2,126.33
816.59	Wister (1911), ...	857.04 200,013.25

SUMMER SCHOOL

10,350.00	Sayles, for Summer Course in Geology (1909), ...	$10,361.08
. . . .	Gift for lectures, School of 1912, . .	50.00 10,411.08

LIBRARY

56.35	Boott Income for Books (balance),	$156.29
2,127.19	Bowditch (1861), ...	2,124.63
313.08	Bright (balance), ...	68.30
1,085.34	William R. Castle (1907), . . .	1,020.02
888.09	Fund of the Class of 1851 (1899),	888.09
874.55	" " " 1851 (C. F. Dunbar's Gift) (1899), ...	874.55
3,588.42	Book Fund of the Class of 1881 (1906), ...	3,500.00
$10,837,319.52	. . Amounts carried forward, . . .	$8,631.88 $10,696,649.63

Principal, July 1, 1911.		Principal, June 30, 1912.
$10,837,319.52	. . Amounts brought forward, . . .	$8,631.88 $10,696,649.63
27,901.38	Edwin Conant (1892), ...	27,768.38
25,892.26	Constantius (1886), ...	26,096.12
4,708.89	Archibald C. Coolidge and Clarence L. Hay (1910), . . .	5,420.23
12,509.20	W. Bayard Cutting, Jr. Bequest (1910), ...	12,547.14
17.70	Bayard Cutting Fellowship, Income for Books (balance), ...	. . . .
5,337.50	Denny (1875), ...	5,255.02
5,572.24	Farrar (1871), ...	5,253.74
. . . .	Price Greenleaf (balance), . . .	.23
1,590.07	Charles Gross Memorial (1910), .	1,614.58
3,180.72	Haven (1844), ...	3,121.90
10,055.93	Hayes (1885), ...	10,000.00
5,349.69	Hayward (1864), ...	5,254.96
770.90	R. M. Hodges (balance), ...	809.53
2,384.62	Hollis (1774), ...	2,375.10
2,140.84	Homer (1871), ...	2,150.08
503.21	Jarvis (1885), ...	500.62
5,329.17	Lane (1863), ...	5,273.82
3,125.55	George C. Lodge and Joseph Trumbull Stickney Memorial Book Fund (1911), ...	3,325.48
28,750.98	Lowell (1881), ...	29,541.81
10,000.00	Francis Cabot Lowell (1911), .	10,068.83
60,000.00	Minot (1870), ...	60,106.83
9,065.91	Charles Eliot Norton (1905), .	8,995.48
7,213.67	Lucy Osgood (1873), ...	7,188.32
7,030.88	Mary Osgood (1860), ...	6,991.07
5,950.91	Francis Parkman Memorial (1908), ...	5,986.06
25,162.57	George F. Parkman (for books) (1909), ...	25,007.31
. . . .	Charles Elliott Perkins Memorial (1911), ...	289.32
3,921.40	Sales (1892), ...	3,916.67
5,489.30	Salisbury (1858), ...	5,534.99
5,120.00	Stephen Salisbury (1907), . . .	5,120.00
20,382.61	Sever (1878), ...	20,054.13
3,949.87	Shapleigh (1801), ...	3,949.87
126.08	George B. Sohier Income for Books (balance), ...	47.79
2,878.11	Strobel Memorial, Class of 1877 (1909), ...	2,987.02
1,998.46	Strobel Memorial, Siam (1909), .	2,047.83
10,513.49	Subscription for Library (1859), . .	10,525.01
37,438.88	Sumner (1875), ...	37,372.67
$10,698,677.46	. . Amounts carried forward, . . .	$371,029.32 $10,696,649.63

Principal, July 1, 1911.		Principal, June 30, 1912.	
$10,698,677.46	. . Amounts brought forward, . . .	$371,029.32	$10,696,649.63
5,075.64	Kenneth Matheson Taylor (1899), ...	5,013.32	
11,925.84	Daniel Treadwell (1885), . . .	11,929.54	
41,521.99	John Harvey Treat Book Fund (1911), ...	41,436.06	
5,208.34	Ichabod Tucker (1875), ...	5,115.36	
615.08	20th Mass. Regiment of Volunteer Infantry (1910), ...	645.52	
142.43	Wales Income for Books (balance),	327.10	
15,903.44	Walker (1875), ...	15,802.60	
5,250.41	Ward (1858), ...	5,280.06	
3,002.41	Julian Palmer Welsh Memorial (1910), ...	3,008.89	
20,020.38	J. Huntington Wolcott (1891),	20,033.71	
100,000.00	Eben Wright (1883), ...	100,000.00	
4,141.37	Sundry Gifts for books (balances), .	679.61	
.33	Sundry Gifts for services (balance), .	. . . .	
2,000.00	Gift for cases, ...	. . . .	
58.68	Duplicate Money, ...	65.98	
137.06	Fines, ...	3.22	
218.52	Gifts for Additional Service, ...	. . . .	580,370.29

DIVINITY SCHOOL

71,427.02	New Endowment (1879), ...	$71,427.02	
17,000.00	Oliver Ames (1880), ...	17,000.00	
525.00	Hannah C. Andrews (1836), . .	525.00	
1,115.26	Daniel Austin (1880), ...	1,115.26	
1,000.00	Adams Ayer (1869), ...	1,000.00	
15,275.00	Joseph Baker (1876), ...	15,275.00	
252.51	Beneficiary money returned (balance),	265.08	
4,349.69	Rushton Dashwood Burr (1894),	4,380.23	
37,583.74	Bussey Professorship (1862), . .	37,583.74	
2,177.95	Joshua Clapp (1836), ...	2,177.95	
3,794.32	Edwin Conant (1892), ...	3,794.32	
25,544.37	Dexter Lectureship (1810), . . .	25,544.37	
56,703.14	Frothingham Professorship(1892),	57,203.14	
1,050.00	Abraham W. Fuller (1847), . .	1,050.00	
911.84	Lewis Gould (1852), ...	911.84	
979.15	Louisa J. Hall (1893), ...	985.11	
6,008.43	Hancock Professorship, ...	6,008.43	
	Composed of these Funds : — Thomas Hancock (1765), Stephen Sewall (1762).		
151,742.21	Charles L. Hancock (1891), . .	151,770.76	
5,000.00	Haven (1898), ...	5,000.00	
1,050.00	Samuel Hoar (1857), ...	1,050.00	
$11,317,388.01	. . Amounts carried forward, . . .	$404,066.70	$11,277,019.92

Principal, July 1, 1911.		Principal, June 30, 1912.	
$11,817,888.01	. . Amounts brought forward, . .	$404,066.70	$11,277,019.92
34,517.60	Hollis Professorship of Divinity, .	34,517.60	
	Composed of these Funds :—		
	William Dummer (1762),		
	Daniel Henchman (1742),		
	Thomas Hollis (1721),		
	Jonathan Mason (1798),		
	James Townsend (1738).		
10,000.00	Henry P. Kidder (1881), . . .	10,000.00	
9,184.69	Henry Lienow (1841), ...	9,184.69	
1,050.00	Caroline Merriam (1867), . . .	1,050.00	
16,015.81	Parkman Professorship (1814), .	16,015.81	
716.07	John W. Quinby (1888), ...	726.52	
1,000.00	Abby Crocker Richmond (1881),	1,000.00	
1,000.00	John L. Russell (1890), ...	1,000.00	
1,200.00	Horace S. Sears Gift Lectures, .	. . . .	
10,000.00	William B. Spooner (1890), . . .	10,000.00	
40,000.00	Thomas Tileston of New York		
	Endowment (1879), ...	40,000.00	
5,250.00	Mary P. Townsend (1861), . .	5,250.00	
2,100.00	Winthrop Ward (1862), ...	2,100.00	
58,845.73	Winn Professorship (1877), . . .	59,345.73	
1,038.20	Augustus Woodbury Bequest		
	(1909), ...	1,038.20	595,295.25

SCHOLARSHIP AND BENEFICIARY

2,679.61	Robert Charles Billings Prize		
	(1904), ...	$2,712.27	
18,682.00	Abner W. Buttrick (1880), . . .	18,722.26	
5,880.42	Thomas Cary (1820), ...	5,921.48	
2,952.30	George Chapman (1834), . . .	2,969.34	
4,723.94	Joshua Clapp (1889)	4,757.77	
15,580.11	Jackson Foundation (1835), . . .	15,718.32	
5,947.55	J. Henry Kendall (1863), . . .	5,991.98	
3,662.88	Nancy Kendall (1846), ...	3,674.20	
. . . .	John C. Kimball (1912), . . .	507.43	
1,058.92	William Pomroy (1835), ...	1,060.42	57,080.47

LAW SCHOOL

10,580.33	Ames (1910), ...	$10,679.04	
1,410.02	James Barr Ames Loan (1904),	450.28	
4,224.37	James Barr Ames Prize (1898),	4,438.61	
98,537.25	Bemis Professorship (1879), . .	98,914.83	
. . . .	James and Augusta Barnard		
	Law (1912), ...	25,206.27	
2,216.46	Gift of James Munson Barnard		
	and Augusta Barnard (balance),	2,305.10	
$11,682,442.27	. . Amounts carried forward, . .	$141,989.12	$11,929,345.64

Principal, July 1, 1911.		Principal, June 30, 1912.	
$11,682,442.27	. . Amounts brought forward, . .	$141,989.13	$11,929,845.64
28,979.82	**Bussey** Professorship (1862), . .	28,979.82	
110,654.00	**James C. Carter** Professorship (1906), ...	109,181.37	
13,772.41	**James Coolidge Carter** Loan (1906), ...	13,929.57	
15,750.00	**Dane** Professorship (1829), ...	15,750.00	
5,174.55	**Samuel Phillips Prescott Fay,** 1798, Fund and Scholarship (1907),	5,205.37	
3,849.54	**George Fisher** Scholarship (1906),	3,890.11	
266.51	**Hughes** Loan (1903), ...	77.00	
26,286.99	**Langdell** (1909), ...	26,438.20	
47,021.25	Law School Book (1882), ...	47,021.25	
100,000.00	Law School Library (1898), ...	100,000.00	
411.71	**Harry Milton Levy** Loan (Law) (balance), ...	267.69	
8,340.81	**Royall** Professorship (1781), . . .	8,340.81	
1,574.69	Scholarship money returned (balance),	591.52	
1,590.11	**Joshua Montgomery Sears, Jr.,** Memorial Fund for Prizes (1912),	35,090.11	
94,994.97	**Weld** Professorship (1882), . . .	94,994.97	
250.00	Gift for Research Scholarship, . . .	. . . .	626,696.92

GRADUATE SCHOOL OF APPLIED SCIENCE

20,936.11	**Julia Amory Appleton** Fellowship (1906), ...	$20,972.45	
1,193.24	**Edward Austin** Loans repaid (bal.),	922.29	
4,226.04	**Priscilla Clark Hodges** Scholarship (1907), ...	4,260.23	
11,868.06	**Hennen Jennings** Scholarship (1898), ...	11,930.53	
7,276.10	**Lawrence** Scientific School Loans repaid (balance), ...	7,935.64	
200.00	**Henry Weidemann Locke** Scholarship. Gift (balance), ...	200.00	
738.82	**Susan B. Lyman** Loan (L. S. S.) (balance), ...	887.64	
1,387,910.25	**Gordon McKay** Endowment (1909), ...	1,554,532.75	
250.00	**Edward Dyer Peters** Scholarship (balance), ...	250.00	
40,805.73	Professorship of Engineering (1847),	40,805.73	
550,000.00	**Nelson Robinson, Jr.** (1899), .	555,000.00	
25,000.00	**Arthur Rotch** (1895), ...	25,000.00	
60,000.00	**Gurdon Saltonstall** (1901), . .	60,000.00	
11,791.87	**Josiah Stickney** (1899), ...	11,791.87	
2,737.31	**Ames-Butler** Gifts, ...	3,155.85	
$14,261,293.16	. . Amounts carried forward, . .	$2,297,594.48	$12,556,042.56

Principal, July 1, 1911.		Principal, June 30, 1912.	
$14,261,293.16	Amounts brought forward,	$2,297,594.48	$12,556,042.56
5,856.84	Gift for Equipment, Department of Architecture,	3,450.69	
13.97	Gift for Laboratory of Metallurgical Chemistry,	13.97	
2,276.07	**Nelson Robinson, Jr.** Special Expense Gift,	....	
13,112.69	**Nelson Robinson, Jr.** Special Gift for Salaries,	8,537.18	
809.61	Summer course Mining Camp Gift,	825.80	
349.92	Mining and Metallurgy Scholarship (gift),	199.92	2,310,632.04

GRADUATE SCHOOL OF BUSINESS ADMINISTRATION

....	**Edmund Cogswell Converse** Professorship of Banking (1912),	$125,745.87	
380.00	Gifts for Loans (balance),	335.00	
....	Gift of **William Endicott, Jr.,** Books on Transportation,	100.00	
....	Gift for Hodgson Prize,	75.00	
....	" " **George O. May** Prizes,	50.00	
....	" " Courses in Printing,	1,000.00	
100.00	" of **Warren D. Robbins** — South American Course,	100.00	
84.10	Gift of **Joseph E. Sterrett,** Books on Accounting,	96.90	127,502.77

MUSEUM OF COMPARATIVE ZOÖLOGY

99,500.00	**Alexander Agassiz** Bequest (1910),	$99,500.00	
94,794.56	**Alexander Agassiz** Bequest for Publications (1910),	86,086.26	
297,933.10	**Agassiz** Memorial (1875),	297,933.10	
....	**George R. Agassiz** (1911),	50,000.00	
5,945.19	**Virginia Barret Gibbs** Scholarship (1892),	5,989.47	
50,000.00	**Gray** Fund for Zoölogical Museum (1859),	50,000.00	
107,391.08	**Sturgis Hooper** (1865),	107,206.88	
7,740.66	**Humboldt** (1869),	7,927.27	
5,000.00	**Willard Peele Hunnewell** (1901),	5,105.49	
117,469.84	Permanent (1859),	117,469.84	
7,594.01	Teachers' and Pupils' (1875),	7,594.01	
5,880.57	**Maria Whitney** (1907),	6,073.66	
....	**Maria Whitney** and **James Lyman Whitney** (1912),	59.61	840,945.09
$15,083,474.32	Amounts carried forward,		$15,835,112.46

Principal, July 1, 1911.		Principal, June 30, 1912.
$15,063,474.82	. . Amounts brought forward, ...	$15,835,112.46

GERMANIC MUSEUM

10,013.52	Germanic Museum (1909), ...	$10,013.52	
209,268.49	Germanic Museum Building (1908), .	217,589.07	
53,704.55	Germanic Museum Endowment(1909),	56,362.95	
26,385.00	**Emperor William** (1906), . . .	26,385.00	
1,000.00	Gift for work of art, ...	1,000.00	311,300.54

PEABODY MUSEUM OF AMERICAN ARCHAEOLOGY AND ETHNOLOGY

13,255.97	**Hemenway** Fellowship (1891), .	$13,912.14	
46,515.88	**Mary Hemenway** Fund for Archaeology (1910), ...	46,618.37	
28,355.56	**Peabody** Building (1866), . . .	28,355.56	
47,335.10	**Peabody** Collection (1866), . . .	47,335.10	
47,335.10	**Peabody** Professor (1866), . . .	47,335.10	
30,165.91	**Thaw** Fellowship (1890), ...	30,180.87	
10,010.00	**Henry C. Warren** Exploration (1899), ...	10,030.50	
5,000.00	**Susan Cornelia Warren** (1902),	5,000.00	
6,359.08	**Robert C. Winthrop** Scholarship (1895), ...	6,173.85	
20,000.00	**Huntington Frothingham Wolcott** (1891), ...	20,039.40	254,980.89

MEDICAL SCHOOL

5,924.23	**Harvard** Medical Alumni (1907),	$6,729.84	
10,363.78	Anonymous Fund in the Department of Theory and Practice (1906), .	10,363.78	
11,699.40	**Edward Austin** (Bacteriological Laboratory) (1899), ...	11,103.13	
30,271.54	**Edward M. Barringer** (1881),	30,271.54	
100,000.00	**Robert C. Billings** (1900), . .	100,000.00	
6,044.84	**J. Ingersoll Bowditch** (1889),	10,092.68	
1,674.85	**Boylston** Fund for Medical Books (1800), ...	1,678.21	
. . . .	**Brinckerhoff** Fund (1911), . . .	5,145.38	
25,530.94	**John B. & Buckminster Brown** Endowment (1896), ...	26,294.72	
76,251.06	**Bullard** Professorship of Neuropathology (1906), ...	76,333.85	
102,195.86	Memorial Cancer Hospital Endowment (1910), ...	100,876.27	
11,293.67	Memorial Cancer Hospital Maintenance (1910), ...	6,287.72	

$16,019,878.60	. . Amounts carried forward, . . .	$385,177.12	$16,401,393.89

Principal, July 1, 1911.		Principal, June 30, 1912.
$16,019,378.60	. . Amounts brought forward, . .	$385,177.12 $16,401,393.89
. . . .	Memorial Cancer Hospital Proctor Maintenance (1912), ...	25,000.00
92,846.07	**Caroline Brewer Croft** (1899),	98,868.52
15,228.34	**Dr. John C. Cutter** Bequest (1910), ...	15,348.56
. . . .	**Thomas Dwight** Memorial (1912),	2,328.07
387,141.80	**Calvin and Lucy Ellis** (1899),	393,515.72
207,940.88	**George Fabyan** Foundation for Comparative Pathology (1906), .	210,798.75
9,824.83	**George Fabyan** Foundation Special (1910), ...	10,639.82
52,601.61	**Charles F. Farrington** (1909),	52,431.81
. . . .	**Lawrence Carteret Fenno** (1911),	5,135.90
. . . .	**Lawrence Carteret Fenno** Memorial Free Bed Fund (1912), . .	5,063.55
1,836.08	**Samuel E. Fitz** (1884), ...	1,836.08
25,000.00	**Rebecca A. Greene** (1911), . .	53,500.00
6,202.59	**F. B. Greenough** (Surgical Research) (1901), ...	6,509.64
106,479.25	**George Higginson** Professorship (1902), ...	107,249.96
52,239.80	**John Homans** Memorial (1906),	52,239.80
. . . .	**Franklin H. Hooper** Memorial Free Bed Fund (1911), ...	5,247.50
69,192.65	**Jackson** Professorship of Clinical Medicine (1859), ...	69,192.65
102,738.57	**Henry Jackson** Endowment (1903), ...	103,111.28
179,060.17	**Hamilton Kuhn** Memorial (1908),	190,356.88
52,120.38	**Walter Augustus Lecompte** Professorship of Otology (1907),	52,229.44
2,699.77	**Harriet Newell Lowell** (1907),	1,901.58
2,326.60	Medical Library (1872), ...	2,331.28
53,125.80	**William O. Moseley** (1897), . .	53,254.99
88,850.00	New Subscription (1888), ...	88,850.00
10,020.18	**Lyman Nichols** (1907), ...	10,020.18
8,581.40	**George F. Parkman** (Medical) (1910), ...	8,581.40
6,132.45	Gift for Pathological Laboratory, .	6,285.85
1,852.63	Repayment Pathological Laboratory,	1,406.81
. . . .	**Clara Endicott Payson** Memorial Free Bed Fund (1911), .	5,247.50
39,216.62	**Henry L. Pierce** (Residuary) (1898), ...	39,216.62
52,895.72	**Proctor** (1903), ...	52,410.96
1,000,000.00	**John D. Rockefeller** Gift (1902),	1,000,000.00
9,335.94	**Dr. Ruppaner** (1897), ...	9,335.94
$18,604,868.23	. . Amounts carried forward, . . .	$3,069,123.61 $16,401,393.89

Principal, July 1, 1911.		Principal, June 30, 1912.
$18,604,868.23	. . Amounts brought forward, . .	$3,069,123.61$16,401,898.89
6,780.59	School of Comparative Medicine (1899), ...	7,063.77
85,041.37	**Henry Francis Sears** Fund for Pathology (1907), ...	85,084.99
77,000.00	**George C. Shattuck** (1853), . . .	77,000.00
10,857.39	**James Skillen** Memorial Fund (1907), ...	10,857.39
117,564.21	**James Stillman** Professorship (1902), ...	118,083.62
5,763.88	Surgical Laboratory (1897), ...	5,942.95
15,765.11	**Mary W. Swett** (1884), ...	15,765.11
20,000.00	**Samuel W. Swett** (1884), . . .	20,000.00
2,000.00	**Quincy Tufts** (1879), ...	2,000.00
11,254.78	**Warren** Fund for Anatomical Museum (1848), ...	11,811.86
52,292.78	**Edward Wigglesworth** Professorship of Dermatology (1907),	54,374.88
41,940.00	**Charles Wilder** (1900), ...	52,200.47
48,886.54	**Henry Willard Williams** (1893),	50,353.97
. . . .	**Zoe D. Underhill** (1912), . . .	10,109.54
270.41	Gifts for Anatomical Research (bal.),	8.83
3,007.41	Gift for Pathological Dep't. (bal.),	2,784.21
121.20	Aesculapian Club Gift, ...	121.20
3.21	Anonymous Gift for Theory and Practice, ...	3.21
84.61	**W. H. Walker** Gift, ...	80.11
46.86	Gift, Bacteriological Laboratory, .	43.46
4.87	**Mary R. Bremer** Gift for Department of Anatomy, ...	4.87
322.90	**William N.** and **Katherine E. Bullard** Gift, ...	272.88
200.00	Gift for a Salary, Cancer Commission, ...	200.00
. . . .	Gift Equipment Laboratory Comparative Anatomy, ...	196.76
210.00	Gift for Diabetes Mellitus, ...	142.73
2.90	Sale of Duplicate Books, Library, .	467.57
43.80	Experiments on Animals, ...	24.98
3,730.96	Gift, Investigation Infantile Paralysis,	4,666.46
328.08	Loan Fund Medical Class of 1879, .	388.08
1,688.43	Mass. Society for Promoting Agriculture, Department of Comparative Pathology, ...	2,879.61
18.98	**G. K. Sabine** Gift, ...	18.98
5.37	**Sears** Pathological Laboratory Publication Fund, ...	5.37
114.22	Gifts for Department Neuropathology,	168.90
$19,060,113.94	. . Amounts carried forward, . . .	$3,552,140.27$16,401,898.89

Principal, July 1, 1911.		Principal, June 30, 1912.	
$19,060,118.94	.. Amounts brought forward, ..	$3,552,140.27	$16,401,593.89
16.05	Department of Physiology, ...	16.05	
950.00	Gift for Recreation Grounds, ...	646.53	
.24	Anonymous Gift for Investigation of Smallpox,............	.24	
....	Gift for Surgical Library, ...	250.00	
1,058.48	Gift for X-ray Apparatus, ...	1,079.64	3,554,132.73

FELLOWSHIP

8.32	Anonymous Gift for Teaching Fellowships in Histology and Embryology (balance),........	$8.32	
12,984.18	**Charles Follen Folsom** Memorial (1908), ...	13,101.88	
....	**William O. Moseley, Jr.** (1912),	75,943.47	
5,628.74	**George Cheyne Shattuck** Memorial (1891), ...	5,682.38	
6,089.28	**Charles Eliot Ware** Memorial (1891),............	6,088.21	
5,656.42	**John Ware** Memorial (1891),..	5,711.40	
25,310.99	**Henry P. Walcott** (1910), ..	26,011.79	132,547.45

SCHOLARSHIP

5,468.53	**Lucius F. Billings** (1900), ..	$5,514.24	
6,350.90	**James Jackson Cabot** (1906),	6,390.27	
5,988.61	**David Williams Cheever** (1889),	6,085.07	
3,367.74	**Cotting** Gift (1900), ...	3,409.45	
3,101.85	**Orlando W. Doe** (1893), ...	3,155.40	
3.60	**John Foster** income for Medical Students (balance), ...	3.60	
5,906.68	**Lewis** and **Harriet Hayden**(1894),	5,949.08	
2,026.29	**William Otis Johnson** (1911),	4,071.16	
6,880.77	**Claudius M. Jones** (1893), ..	6,971.38	
3,018.33	**John R. Kissinger** (1911), ..	3,167.72	
5,748.65	**Alfred Hosmer Linder** (1895),	5,783.23	
9,112.70	**Joseph Pearson Oliver** (1904),	9,163.79	
5,975.07	**Charles B. Porter** (1897), ...	6,020.83	
5,476.84	**Francis Skinner** (1905), ...	5,729.21	
....	Special Scholarship 1912–13, ...	250.00	
5,411.26	**Charles Pratt Strong** (1894), .	5,454.11	
6,920.03	**Isaac Sweetser** (1892), ...	7,012.57	
5,624.86	**John Thomson Taylor** (1899),	5,653.31	
5,776.22	**Edward Wigglesworth** (1897),	5,812.13	95,546.55

PRIZE

4,762.55	**Boylston** (1803), ...	$4,985.82	
9,682.81	**William H. Thorndike** (1895),	10,162.07	15,147.89
$19,224,370.93	.. Amounts carried forward, ...		$20,198,768.51

Principal, July 1, 1911.		Principal, June 30, 1912.	
$19,224,870.93	. . Amounts brought forward, ...	$20,198,768.51	

DENTAL SCHOOL

12,000.85	Dental School Endowment (1880), .	$12,601.35	
. . . .	Dental School Endowment of the Class of 1886 (1911), ...	50.00	
20.00	Dental School Endowment of the Class of 1909 (1910), ...	30.00	
125.00	Dental School Research Fund, . .	113.71	
6,195.33	Harvard Dental Alumni Endowment (1906), ...	6,310.33	
1,000.00	Harriet Newell Lowell Gift,	. . . .	
23,000.00	Henry C. Warren Endowment (1889), ...	23,000.00	
500.00	Proctor Bequest (1910), ...	500.00	
15.16	Gift for Surgical Instruments, . . .	15.16	
10,325.00	Joseph Warren Smith, Jr. Memorial (1909), ...	10,325.00	
40.27	Gifts for X-ray Apparatus, ...	5.27	52,950.82

OBSERVATORY

20,109.98	Advancement of Astronomical Science (1901), ...	$19,262.31	
20,523.50	Advancement of Astronomical Science (1902), ...	20,000.00	
. . . .	George R. Agassiz Gift, Revising Draper Catalogue, ...	583.34	
5,000.00	Thomas G. Appleton (1884), .	5,000.00	
825.37	Bond Gifts (balance), ...	. . . .	
2,500.00	J. Ingersoll Bowditch (1889), .	2,500.00	
200,000.00	Uriah A. Boyden (1887), . . .	200,000.00	
62.84	Draper Memorial (balance), . .	. . . .	
1,014.21	J. Rayner Edmands Bequest (1911), ...	1,014.21	
2,000.00	Charlotte Harris (1877), . . .	2,000.00	
45,000.00	Haven (1898), ...	45,000.00	
21,000.00	James Hayward (1866), . . .	21,000.00	
50,000.00	Observatory Endowment (1882), .	50,000.00	
50,000.00	Paine Professorship (1886), . . .	50,000.00	
273,932.07	Robert Treat Paine (1886), . .	273,932.07	
110,293.88	Edward B. Phillips (1849), . .	110,293.88	
12,995.12	Josiah Quincy (1866), ...	13,095.62	
45,116.83	David Sears (1845), ...	46,282.96	
18,380.00	Augustus Story (1871), ...	18,380.00	
42.35	Gift for publishing lunar photographs,	42.35	873,336.74

$20,151,888.19	. . Amounts carried forward, ...	$21,125,056.07	

Principal,
July 1, 1911.   Principal, June 30, 1912.

$20,151,388.19 . . Amounts brought forward, ... $21,125,056.07

BUSSEY INSTITUTION

20,658.86 Woodland Hill (1895), ... 20,658.86   20,658.86

ARNOLD ARBORETUM

125,340.00	Arnold Arboretum (1899), . . . -.	$125,460.00
162,779.20	James Arnold (1872), ...	163,182.08
42,309.99	Arboretum Construction Gifts (balance),	40,228.82
12,500.00	Robert Charles Billings (1904),	12,500.00
20,000.00	William L. Bradley (1897), . .	20,000.00
2,308.06	Bussey Fund for the Arnold Arboretum (1903), ...	2,308.06
4,500.00	Massachusetts Society for Promoting Agriculture (1911), ...	5,000.00
20,000.00	Francis Skinner (1906), ...	20,000.00
8,132.12	Sears Gift for Library, ...	2,182.51
. . . .	Bayard and Ruth S. Thayer (1911), ...	15,000.00
. . . .	Edward Whitney (1912), . . .	1,000.00
2,250.68	Gift for Expedition to China (balance),	765.22	407,626.69

PHILLIPS BROOKS HOUSE

10,506.66	Phillips Brooks House Endowment (1901), ...	$10,506.66
11,343.64	Ralph H. Shepard (1900), . . .	11,343.64
5,480.50	Ralph Hamilton Shepard Memorial (1898), ...	5,271.10
7,086.59	John W. and Belinda L. Randall (1897), ...	7,437.40	34,558.80

WILLIAM HAYES FOGG ART MUSEUM

50,000.00	William Hayes Fogg (1892), .	$50,029.27
16,000.28	Gray Fund for Engravings (1858),	15,786.85
15,016.47	William M. Prichard (1898), .	15,595.04
30,000.00	John Witt Randall (1892), . . .	30,074.99
. . . .	Gift for Improvements, ...	13,031.48	124,517.63

STILLMAN INFIRMARY

8,102.58	Stillman Infirmary Gift (balance),	$8,503.67
60,555.57	Robert Charles Billings, for Stillman Infirmary (1903), . .	60,555.57
6,376.79	Free Bed Fund of the Class of 1868 (1898), ...	6,376.79
653.26	Free Bed Fund for Stillman Infirmary (1900), ...	653.26

$20,788,289.44 . . Amounts carried forward, . . . $76,089.29 $21,712,418.05

Principal, July 1, 1911.		Principal, June 30, 1912.	
$20,788,289.44	.. Amounts brought forward, ...	$76,089.29	$21,712,418.05
3,633.88	Herbert Schurz Memorial Free Bed (1908), ...	3,633.88	
3,204.16	Henry P. Walcott (1901), ...	3,204.16	82,926.83

CLASS FUNDS

1,888.70	Fund of the Class of 1834 (1887),	$1,916.23	
116.27	" " " 1842 (1908),	122.02	
10,888.70	" " " 1844 (1896),	11,821.12	
14,848.09	" " " 1846 (1905),	15,058.82	
8,725.00	" " " 1853 (1887),	8,725.00	
7,868.75	" " " 1856 (1904),	7,871.25	40,013.94

GIFTS FOR CONSTRUCTION

10,948.85	Arnold Arboretum Building Gifts,	$990.57	
421.74	Brighton Marsh Fence (balance), ..	....	
25,749.91	Francis H. Burr Memorial, ...	....	
....	T. Jefferson Coolidge Gift for a Chemical Laboratory, ...	50,049.20	
82,587.89	Freshman Dormitories, ...	385,196.00	
....	High Voltage Electrical Laboratory Building, ...	11,828.38	
105,852.40	Wolcott Gibbs Memorial (1909),	82,785.51	
886.02	Gift for Gray Herbarium — Kidder Wing, ...	228.61	
10,074.80	Gray Herbarium Library, ...	18,333.73	
....	Gray Herbarium, gift for George R. White Laboratories, ...	16,119.00	
7,975.85	Collis P. Huntington Memorial Hospital, ...	17,394.56	
442.43	Semitic Building (balance), ...	442.43	
331,608.93	Amey Richmond Sheldon (1909),	348,023.58	
380,821.01	George Smith Bequest (1904), .	398,991.00	
12,558.27	Gift for a new University Library Building (balance), ...	1,956.35	
....	Gift for Architectural Studies, New Library Building, ...	484.00	1,827,767.87

SUNDRY

476,463.28	Edward Austin (1899), ...	$476,463.28	
50,000.00	Bright Legacy (1880), ...	50,000.00	
392,710.18	Bussey Trust (1861), ...	392,710.18	
....	Carnegie Foundation Retiring Allowance, ...	.33	
166,217.72	Calvin and Lucy Ellis Aid (1899),	172,056.69	
3,171.50	John Foster (1840), ...	3,328.46	
$22,841,887.77	.. Amounts carried forward, ..	$1,094,558.94	$23,168,126.69

Principal, July 1, 1911.		Principal, June 30, 1912.	
$22,841,887.77	. . Amounts brought forward, . .	$1,094,558.94	$23,163,126.63
794,942.67	Price Greenleaf (1887), ...	787,018.82	
29,939.33	Henry Harris (1883), ...	29,939.33	
1,880.56	Harvard Memorial Society (1898),	1,750.10	
64,421.50	Robert Troup Paine (1880), . .	65,976.16	
42,000.00	James Savage (1873), ...	42,000.00	
366,425.97	Frederick Sheldon (1909), . . .	388,873.50	
150,000.00	Edward Wigglesworth Memorial (1909), ...	150,188.44	
6,084.95	Gifts for Semitic Museum Collection (balance), ...	3,927.88	
4,268.70	Gifts for Excavations in Palestine (balance), ...	3,758.59	
107.00	Gifts for Chinese Students (balance),	107.00	
33.96	Gifts for Cuban Teachers (balance),	33.96	2,568,127.72

FUNDS IN TRUST FOR PURPOSES NOT CONNECTED WITH THE COLLEGE

16,506.47	Daniel Williams (1716), ...	$16,551.34	
4,795.66	Sarah Winslow (1790), ...	4,914.64	21,465.98
$24,823,194.54			$25,752,720.39

GENERAL SUSPENSE

CREDIT BALANCES

June 80, 1912

July 1, 1911		June 30, 1912
$4,777.20	Cryptogamic Herbarium, ...	$5,459.56
5,778.41	**Gray** Herbarium, ...	7,858.80
1,708.52	School for Social Workers, ...	593.52
12,337.44	Graduate School of Business Administration, ...	13,213.09
10,900.12	Graduate School of Applied Science.	
	Unexpended balances, ... $5,554.79	
	Reserve, ... 4,936.07	10,490.86
. . . .	Summer Schools, ...	1,091.27
17,413.45	Divinity School, ...	10,435.90
66,151.52	Law School, ...	52,729.91
18,826.43	Museum of Comparative Zoölogy, ...	17,272.91
2,457.56	**Peabody** Museum of American Archaeology and Ethnology, ...	4,357.14
1,282.06	Germanic Museum, ...	1,764.66
5,338.46	**Bussey** Institution, ...	191.34
1,681.63	Botanical Museum, ...	690.34
3,366.96	Botanic Garden, ...	4,438.56
292.51	Laboratory Fees, Astronomy, ...	. . . .
110.00	" " Botany (Fernald), ...	. . . .
105.03	" " " (Thaxter), ...	193.06
251.23	" " Chemistry, ...	206.28
. . . .	" " Forestry, ...	24.40
157.70	" " Geology, ...	324.34
319.96	" " Hygiene, ...	542.87
53.93	" " Mining and Metallurgy, ...	268.82
. . . .	" " Physics, ...	403.94
. . . .	" " Zoölogy, ...	53.48
571.61	Engineering Camp, Squam Lake, ...	577.47
277.08	**Baker Estate,**	. . . .
. . . .	**Robert C. Billings** (Medical) Fund, Advance interest, ...	252.54
$154,158.81	Total — Exhibit A, ...	$133,435.06

GENERAL SUSPENSE

DEBIT BALANCES

June 30, 1912

July 1, 1911	Advances from General Investments to :	June 30, 1912
$8,845.02	**Adams** Estate,	$5,007.02
4,787.50	Aids, general,	4,356.25
54.43	Anonymous Fund,	72.06
746.02	Anonymous Gift for **Harvard** Clinic,	....
325.00	Anonymous Gift for Research in Government,	278.86
8.82	**Baker** Estate,	....
15,188.47	**Uriah A. Boyden** Fund,	15,882.28
100.00	Business School, Gift for Prizes,	....
....	Business School, Study tours,	250.00
39,238.23	**Bussey** Trust (Real Estate),	37,438.23
28.55	**Francis James Child** Memorial Fund,	2.55
1,574.21	Classical Department,	....
436.65	Classical Library Fund,	453.70
....	Classical Publication Fund of the **Class of 1856,**	771.30
....	**C. H. Condell** Scholarship,	63.41
....	Book Fund of the Class of 1881,	14.58
....	**Draper** Memorial Fund,	7.35
889.55	**Warren H. Cudworth** Scholarship,	294.83
225.00	**Warren Delano** Scholarship,	17.50
11,014.61	Dental School,	14,846.66
99,066.91	Dental School Building,	104,020.26
1,855.75	Dining Hall Committee,	....
....	Gift Department of Economics,	703.02
813.67	Estate No. 52 India St.,	....
829.68	" 21 Wharf St.,	....
244.54	**Fogg** Art Museum,	....
1,584.66	Department of Forestry,	1,453.04
....	**Gerrish** Block,	2,500.00
200.00	**Harvard** Club of Buffalo Scholarship,	....
400.00	" " " Cleveland "	150.00
8.50	" " " Fitchburg "	8.50
....	" " " Lawrence "	100.00
....	" " " Seattle "	100.00
....	" " " Worcester "	100.00
980.02	**Harvard** Economic Studies,	....
....	Gift for changes, Holworthy Hall,	6,957.04
44.08	**Jefferson** Physical Laboratory,	....
....	Gifts for University Library expenses,	1,500.00
....	**MacDowell** Fellowship,	25.00
....	**Matchett** Bequest,	50.00
$188,984.82	.. Amounts carried forward,	$197,423.42

July 1, 1911		June 30, 1912
$188,984.82	. . Amounts brought forward, ...	$197,428.42
27,742.09	Medical School, ...	81,457.56
. . . .	Graduate School of Medicine, ...	1,129.89
200.00	Menorah Society Prize, ...	800.00
1,050.42	Mining and Metallurgy, ...	1,050.42
350.00	New University Library Building, ...	. . . .
51,998.26	Old Boston Music Hall Estate, ...	46,798.46
17.76	**Charles Elliott Perkins** ScholarshipFund, . . .	. . . .
95.94	Radcliffe College, ...	. . . .
26,702.27	**Randall** Hall Association, ...	26,702.27
29.81	**John Wirt Randall** Fund, ...	. . . .
1.25	**Sayles,** for Summer Course in Geology, ...	. . . .
49.16	**Mary R. Searle** Fund, ...	28.70
150.00	**Shaw** Fund, Business Research, ...	196.63
10,875.94	Improvements and Additions to The Soldier's Field, . .	11,269.74
94.74	**Dunlap Smith** Scholarship Fund, ...	94.74
. . . .	South End House Fellowship, ...	95.05
722.41	**Stillman** Infirmary, ...	437.22
. . . .	**Charles Sumner** Scholarship, ...	189.80
. . . .	Gift for changes in Thayer Hall, ...	3,252.14
8,161.25	**Townsend** Estate, ...	22,976.94
26,847.45	**Webb** Estate, ...	25,433.45
182.09	**George Wigglesworth** Gift, ...	. . . .
810.16	**Huntington Frothingham Wolcott** Fund, . .	. . . .
5,902.90	Woodland Hill Fund, ...	6,296.84
. . . .	**Adams Woods** Fellowship, ...	400.00
. . . .	Laboratory Fees — Astronomy, ...	61.17
. . . .	" " — Botany (**Osterhout**), ...	15.79
10.61	" " — Mineralogy, ...	. . . .
	Library Funds :	
92.75	**Constantius,**	. . . .
. . . .	**Denny,**	14.86
. . . .	**Elisa Farrar,**	22.46
3.82	**Price Greenleaf,**	. . . .
. . . .	**Horace A. Haven,**	8.44
. . . .	**Francis B. Hayes,**	84.63
67.89	**Minot,**	.
. . . .	**Sales,**	23.02
8.62	**Shapleigh,**	13.92
24.80	**Daniel Treadwell,**	. . . .
. . . .	**James Walker,**	20.23
69.84	**Ward,**	. . . .
$850,746.55	. . Total — Exhibit A, ...	$375,747.79

UNIVERSITY

INCOME AND EXPENDITURE

For the year ended June 30, 1912

INCOME

Income of the following Funds:

Walter F. Baker,	$1,134.84
Band Music,	56.58
John Barnard,	33.02
Andrew Bigelow,	245.08
Stanton Blake,	247.50
Charlotte F. Blanchard,	236.16
Samuel D. Bradford,	259.88
James C. Carter,	4,950.00
John W. Carter,	223.31
Class of 1883,	4,686.71
John Coggan,	74.25
Edward Erwin Coolidge (part),	38.45
Thomas Cotton,	7.62
John Cowdin,	1,674.84
George B. Dorr,	2,071.70
George Draper,	865.69
R. H. Eddy,	1,014.51
Harvard Ellis,	5,010.63
Richard W. Foster,	1,035.49
John Davis Williams French,	95.27
Gore,	1,018.26
John C. Gray,	446.63
Henry Harris (½ income),	741.02
Walter Hastings,	1,197.72
Henry L. Higginson,	2,469.25
Thomas Hollis,	25.74
Thomas Hubbard,	49.50
Nathaniel Hulton,	21.98
Thomas Hutchinson,	11.53
George Baxter Hyde,	247.50
Professorship of Hygiene (1899) (part),	1,000.00
Professorship of Hygiene (1902) (part),	200.00
Leonard Jarvis,	835.16
Henry P. Kidder,	495.00
Joseph Lee,	178.65
Theodore Lyman,	495.00
Israel Munson,	779.63
Henry S. Nourse (part),	1,544.11
Francis E. Parker,	2,083.83
George F. Parkman,	198.25
William Perkins,	1,485.00
President's,	3,184.54
Ezekiel Rogers,	174.98
Amount carried forward,	$42,794.26

UNIVERSITY (CONTINUED)

INCOME

Amount brought forward, ...	$42,794.26	
Daniel Russell, ...	74.94	
John L. Russell, ...	1,156.82	
Amey Richmond Sheldon, ...	16,414.65	
Isaac Sweetser, ...	2,322.19	
Seth Turner, ...	247.50	
William F. Weld, ...	1,786.47	$64,796.83
Gift for expenses Professor at France, ...		1,200.00
Care of the Sarah Winslow Fund, ...	$5.94	
Use of houses by College officers, ...	1,600.00	
Use of land by Harvard Union, ...	5,730.62	
Sale of University Directory, ...	2,398.02	
Sale of Annual Catalogue, ...	443.57	
Sale of Quinquennial Catalogue, ...	119.28	
Sale of Scrap Iron, etc., ...	75.00	
Sale of wood, ...	15.00	
Sale of Guide Book, ...	34.96	
Checks drawn by Bursar July 1, 1872 to October 15, 1909, and not presented at Bank for payment, now credited, ...	289.68	10,662.07
		$76,658.90

EXPENDITURE

Board of Overseers :		
Salaries and wages, ...	$200.00	
Printing Reports of President and Treasurer, . . .	2,172.85	
Printing, ...	285.90	
Stationery, postage, telephone and telegraph, . . .	63.18	
Auditing Treasurer's accounts, ...	150.00	
Advertising, ...	80.00	$2,951.93
Corporation's Office :		
Fuel, rent, etc., ...	$2,556.19	
Less 80% transferred to the Treasurer's Office,	2,044.95	511.24
President's Office :		
Salaries :		
President, ...	$6,000.00	
Comptroller, ...	263.43	
Secretary to the Corporation, ...	1,041.67	
Keeper of the Corporation Records, ...	1,020.00	
Services and wages, ...	2,856.50	
Equipment and supplies, ...	507.17	
Stationery, postage, telephone and telegraph, . .	824.91	
Printing, ...	186.68	
Sundries, ...	26.92	
	$12,227.28	
Less 90% transferred to departments in proportion to the number of students, ...	11,003.20	
Amounts carried forward, ...	$1,224.08	$3,463.17

UNIVERSITY (CONTINUED)

EXPENDITURE

Amounts brought forward, ...	$1,224.08	$3,463.17
Additional salary of President:		
From President's Fund, ...	3,093.77	
From **Thomas Cotton** Fund, ...	7.47	4,325.32
Treasurer's Office:		
Salaries:		
Treasurer, ...	$6,000.00	
Other salaries, ...	3,400.00	
Services and wages, ...	2,367.44	
Office supplies and expenses, ...	781.42	
Rent of Safes, ...	750.00	
University charge:		
Corporation's Office, ...	2,044.95	
Less transferred:	$15,343.81	
To Departments in proportion to the		
income of their Funds, ...	13,655.99	
The balance represents proportion on income of		
University Funds, ...		1,687.82
Bursar's Office:		
Salaries:		
Bursar, ...	$4,500.00	
Assistant Comptroller, ...	2,500.00	
Services and wages, ...	11,079.95	
Office supplies and expenses, ...	2,236.55	
Mercantile Agency, ...	825.00	
Less transferred:	$21,141.50	
To the College for letting College		
rooms, ... $800.00		
To Departments in proportion to the		
Bursar's collections and payments, 19,842.13	20,642.13	
The balance represents proportion applicable to		
University collections and payments, ...		499.37
Publication Office:		
Salary:		
Publication Agent, ...	$2,500.00	
Services and wages, ...	1,600.23	
Office supplies and expenses, ...	5,342.61	
Sundries, ...	100.39	
	$9,543.23	
Less charged directly to Departments, ...	5,958.30	
Balance transferred to Departments in proportion		
to the free distribution of their publications,	$3,584.93	
Amount carried forward, ...		$9,975.68

UNIVERSITY (CONTINUED)
EXPENDITURE

Amount brought forward, ...		$9,975.68
Inspector of Grounds and Buildings:		
Salary:		
Inspector of Grounds and Buildings, ...	$3,305.75	
Services and wages, ...	3,452.58	
Office supplies and expenses, ...	752.38	
Less transferred to Departments in proportion to	$7,510.71	
the floor area of buildings in the Inspector's		
charge, ...	7,510.71	
Janitor's Office:		
Services and wages, ...	$2,700.00	
Office supplies and expenses, ...	57.73	
	$2,757.73	
Less transferred to Departments in proportion to the		
floor area of buildings under Janitor's supervision,	2,757.73	
Quinquennial Catalogue:		
Salaries, ...	$500.00	
Services and wages, ...	1,415.25	
Office expenses and printing, ...	310.26	
	$2,225.51	
Less sales, ...	119.28	
Amount to be apportioned to departments, ...	$2,106.23	
Less transferred to departments in proportion to		
space occupied, ...	1,221.61	
Amount paid by University:		
General Funds, ...	$884.62	
Amount paid by proceeds from sales, ...	119.28	1,003.90
Annual Catalogue:		
Printing and supplies, ...	$4,330.69	
Less sales, ...	443.57	
Amount to be apportioned to departments, ...	$3,887.12	
Less transferred to departments in proportion to		
space occupied, ...	3,181.22	
Amount paid by University:		
General Funds, ...	$705.90	
Amount paid by proceeds from sales, ...	443.57	1,149.47
General Expenses:		
Salary Secretary Commission on Finance, ...	$2,333.32	
Auto truck account, ...	2,070.53	
Expenses Real Estate in Lucas St., Boston, ...	128.77	
Tablet Agassiz Hall, ...	209.35	
Planting in rear Anti-Toxin stable Bussey Inst., . .	522.00	
University Gazette, ... $1,717.88		
Less sales, ... 200.70	1,517.18	
Amounts carried forward, ...	$6,781.15	$12,129.05

UNIVERSITY (CONTINUED)

EXPENDITURE

Amounts brought forward, ...	$6,781.15	$12,129.05
General Expenses (*continued*):		
Commencement Day, ...	2,731.84	
Expenses of Professor at Berlin, ...	1,200.00	
" " France, ...	1,200.00	
" " Colorado College, . . .	200.00	
Expenses Exhibit Cambridge Industrial Carnival, .	101.56	
Work on pictures, ...	97.76	
Dues to American Association of Universities, . .	80.00	
Expenses of Delegates, ...	159.95	
Sundries, ...	60.38	12,612.64
Alumni List and Directory:		
Services and wages, ...	$1,774.30	
Office supplies and expenses, ...	765.13	
	$2,539.43	
Less transferred to College, ...	141.41	
Amount paid from proceeds of sales, ...		2,398.02
Engineer, Services and Expenses, ...	$1,888.92	
Less transferred to Departments in proportion to the floor area of buildings under Engineer's supervision, ...	1,888.92	
Labor in maintenance of grounds, ...	$13,038.07	
Less transferred to Cambridge Departments, . .	10,430.45	2,607.62
Watchmen:		
In Yard, ...	$1,773.24	
Outside Yard, ...	1,145.33	
	$2,918.57	
Transferred to Departments in proportion to floor area of buildings, ...	2,918.57	
Medical Adviser's Office:		
Salary Medical Adviser:		
From Professorship of Hygiene (1899) Fund, ... $1,000.00		
From Professorship of Hygiene (1902) Fund, ... 200.00		
From General Funds, ... 2,800.00	$4,000.00	
Services and wages, ...	360.00	
Office supplies and expenses, ...	207.99	
Sundries, ...	345.00	
	$4,912.99	
Amounts carried forward, ...	$4,912.99	$39,747.33

UNIVERSITY (CONTINUED)

EXPENDITURE

Amounts brought forward, ...	$4,912.99	$29,747.33
Medical Adviser's Office (*continued*):		
Less amount paid from General Funds, transferred: $750 to the Stillman Infirmary and the remainder to Cambridge Departments in proportion to the number of students, ...	3,712.99	1,200.00
Purchasing Agent:		
Salary and expenses, ...	$366.26	
Transferred to Departments, ...	366.26	
Memorial Hall and Sanders Theatre:		
Repairs and equipment, ...	$570.32	
Caretaking, ...	752.44	
	$1,322.76	
Less 90% transferred to College, ...	1,190.48	132.28
Repairs and equipment, general, ...		289.00
Taxes, Harvard Union, ...		5,074.50
Students Employment Office and Appointment Office:		
Salary of Secretary, ...	$1,200.00	
Services and wages, ...	3,132.70	
Office supplies and expenses, ...	1,122.42	
	$5,455.12	
Transferred to College, ...	5,455.12	
Payments made from University income for the following accounts:		
Museum of Comparative Zoölogy . . . . Sch. 25	$714.15	
Peabody Museum of American Archaeology and Ethnology . . . . Sch. 26	2,040.44	
Semitic Museum . . . . Sch. 27	1,163.11	
Germanic Museum . . . . Sch. 28	315.26	
William Hayes Fogg Art Museum . Sch. 29	285.56	
Phillips Brooks House . . . . . . Sch. 31	175.89	4,694.41
		$41,137.52
General Surplus, made up as follows:		
Restricted Income unused, added to Funds and Gifts,	$16,564.02	
Surplus, carried to Schedule 10, ...	18,957.36	35,521.38
		$76,658.90

COLLEGE

(Including the Graduate School of Arts and Sciences)

INCOME AND EXPENDITURE

For the year ended June 30, 1912

INCOME

Income of Funds for Instruction and Gifts for Salaries.

Alford Professorship,	$1,873.57
Edward Austin (part).	
Austin Teaching Fellowships,	12,052.61
John B. Barringer,	1,519.01
Bemis Professorship,	4,500.00
Boylston Professorship,	1,402.67
Martin Brimmer,	2,475.00
Class of 1880,	5,131.62
Class Subscription,	7,456.58
Eaton Professorship,	5,536.03
Eliot Professorship,	1,070.14
Eliot " (Jon. Phillips' Gift),	350.00
Calvin and Lucy Ellis Aid (part),	4,714.71
Erving Professorship,	173.25
Fisher "	1,781.55
Henry Flynt,	21.54
Fund for Permanent Tutors,	803.88
Gospel Church (⅔ income used),	386.74
Gurney (part),	9,404.80
Hersey Professorship (⅞ income),	600.45
Hersey Professorship (Thomas Lee's gift),	1,076.32
Hollis " (Mathematics),	185.48
Abbott Lawrence,	3,046.04
James Lawrence (part),	1,246.79
Henry Lee Professorship,	5,447.13
Thomas Lee, for Reading,	781.96
Arthur T. Lyman,	2,475.00
McLean Professorship,	2,131.62
Francis Greenwood Peabody,	4,969.65
Daniel H. Peirce,	726.47
Perkins Professorship,	1,039.50
Plummer Foundation,	1,238.49
Pope Professorship,	2,598.75
Nelson Robinson Jr. Additional (part),	936.59
Eliza O. and Mary P. Ropes (part),	4,500.00
Rumford Professorship,	2,790.27
Smith Professorship,	1,145.43

Teachers' Endowment:

Interest,	$100,325.12	
Gift,	400.00	100,725.12
Amount carried forward,		$197,814.76

94

COLLEGE (CONTINUED)

INCOME

Amount brought forward, ... $197,814.76

Income of Funds for Instruction and Gifts for Salaries
  (continued).

Unknown Memorial (part), ...	3,210.84	
Henry Villard, ...	893.24	
Henry W. Wales:		
Wales Professorship, ...	1,500.00	
Henry C. Warren (part), ...	4,000.00	
Sylvester Waterhouse, ...	401.75	
David A. Wells (part), ...	5,000.00	
Jerome Wheelock, ...	5.10	
Gifts for salaries, ...	9,875.00	$222,200.19

Income of Funds for General Purposes.

John W. P. Abbot (accumulating), ...	$672.40	
William H. Baldwin, Jr.	99.00	
John A. Blanchard, ...	51.98	
Twenty-fifth Anniversary Fund of the		
Class of 1881, ...	5,644.00	
Fund of the Class of 1882, ...	4,601.12	
Class of 1884, ...	4,880.70	
Class of 1885, ...	5,361.15	
Class of 1886, ...	4,950.00	
Class of 1887, ...	202.85	
Edward W. Codman, ...	15,678.53	
Charles L. Hancock (part), ...	3,842.26	
Trenor L. Park, ...	1,084.79	
Jonathan Phillips, ...	1,569.25	
William M. Spackman, ...	123.75	
Gifts for General Purposes, ...	449.99	49,211.77

Income of Fellowship Funds and Gifts for Fellowships.

Edward Austin (part):			
Edward Austin Fellowships, ...		$2,000.00	
Bayard Cutting, ...		1,262.49	
W. Bayard Cutting, Jr., Bequest (for			
Research in Physics) Interest, . . .	$639.54		
Gift, ...	500.00	1,139.54	
George W. Dillaway, ...		290.91	
Fellowship at Ecole Libre des Sciences Politiques			
(gift), ...		600.00	
Osias Goodwin Memorial, ...		588.85	
Harris, ...		584.54	
Edward William Hooper, ...		1,309.28	
John Thornton Kirkland, ...		567.46	
Henry Lee Memorial, ...		610.93	

Amounts carried forward, ... $8,953.95 $271,411.96

COLLEGE (continued)

INCOME

Amounts brought forward, ...	$8,953.95	$271,411.96

Income of Fellowship Funds and Gifts for Fellowships (*continued*).

Woodbury Lowery Memorial, ...	992.03
MacDowell (gift), ...	575.00
Elkan Naumburg, ...	281.31
Charles Eliot Norton, ...	803.27

John K. Paine, Interest, ... $371.25		
Royalties, . . .	7.34	378.59

Robert Treat Paine, ...	671.51
John Parker, ...	3,113.21
Francis Parkman, ...	520.05
Princeton Fellowship (part), ...	57.12
Rogers, ...	1,662.06
Henry Bromfield Rogers Memorial, . . .	628.30
Henry Russell Shaw, ...	264.88
Frederick Sheldon (part), ...	17,372.85

South End House, Gift, ... $278.00		
Interest, ...	4.95	282.95

South End House in Social Education (gift), . .	350.00	
Fellowship Department of Social Ethics, ...	25.93	
John Tyndall, ...	634.85	
James Walker, ...	584.50	
Whiting, ...	1,261.10	39,413.91

Income of Scholarship Funds and Gifts for Scholarships.

Abbot, ...	$196.77
Alford (accumulating), ...	142.07
Scholarship at International School of American Archaeology and Ethnology at Mexico City (gift),	600.00
Edward Austin (part):	
" " Scholarships for Teachers, .	4,000.00
Caroline M. Barnard Bequest, ...	597.72
Bartlett, ...	269.33
Bassett, ...	287.55
Bigelow, ...	689.44
Charles Sumner Bird, ...	.50
Borden (accumulating), ...	177.46
Bowditch, ...	5,779.57
Bright Scholarships (part):	

Interest on balance, ... $228.24		
Bright Legacy (part income), . . 1,237.50	1,465.74	

Browne, ...	201.21
Morey Willard Buckminster, ...	280.32
Burr, ...	1,776.51

Amounts carried forward, ...	$16,464.19	$310,824.87

COLLEGE (CONTINUED)

INCOME

Income of Scholarship Funds and Gifts for Scholarships
(*continued*).

Ruluff Sterling Choate, ...	313.43
George Newhall Clark, ...	507.68
Thomas William Clarke, ...	250.77
Class of 1802, ...	437.04
" 1814, ...	167.85
" 1815 (Kirkland), ...	346.80
·· 1817, ...	242.10
·· 1828, ...	175.63
·· 1835, ...	265.86
·· 1841, ...	270.72
" 1852 (Dana), ...	270.67
·· 1856, ...	837.58
·· 1867, ...	361.94
·· 1877, ...	267.94
·· 1883, ...	316.85
" 1901 (gift), ...	300.00
Classical Department, ...	7.42
Clement Harlow Condell, ...	936.59
Crowninshield, ...	633.64
Warren H. Cudworth, ...	297.00
George and Martha Derby, ...	281.16
Julius Dexter, ...	324.67
Orlando W. Doe, ...	153.30
Edda Club, ...	20.69
William Samuel Eliot, ...	285.36
George H. Emerson, ...	1,179.59
Joseph Eveleth (part), ...	1,164.01
Fall River, ...	128.25
Farrar, ...	830.12
George Fisher and Elizabeth Huntington Fisher, ...	249.53
Richard Augustine Gambrill, ...	599.45
Charles Haven Goodwin, ...	401.75
Benjamin D. Greene, ...	235.22
Price Greenleaf (part):	
Price Greenleaf Scholarships, ...	8,000.00
Selwyn L. Harding, ...	250.77
Harvard Club of Boston (gift), ...	1,000.00
" " Buffalo "	400.00
" " Cleveland (gift), ...	650.00
" " Connecticut Valley (gift), .	200.00
" " Fitchburg (gift), ...	150.00

COLLEGE (CONTINUED)

INCOME

Amounts brought forward, ... $84,675.07 $310,824.87

Income of Scholarship Funds and Gifts for Scholarships
(*continued*).

Harvard Club of Hawaii (gift), ...		200.00	
"	"	Hingham "	100.00
"	"	Kansas City (gift), ...	150.00
"	"	Louisiana (gift), ...	257.14
"	"	Lowell (gift), ...	350.00
"	"	Lynn "	100.00
"	"	Maine "	150.00
"	"	Nebraska "	150.00
"	"	New Jersey "	250.00
"	"	Western Pennsylvania (gift),	600.00
"	"	Rhode Island (gift), ...	150.00
"	"	Rochester, New York (gift),	200.00
"	"	St. Louis (gift), ...	440.10
"	"	San Francisco (gift), ...	500.00
"	"	Seattle (gift), ...	200.00
"	"	Syracuse (gift), ...	200.00
"	"	Worcester "	100.00

John Appleton Haven, ...   530.54
William Hilton (part), ...   601.86
Scholarship in American History (gift), ...   300.00
Ebenezer Rockwood Hoar, ...   564.60
Levina Hoar, for the town of Lincoln, ...   333.04
R. M. Hodges (part) :
    Hodges Scholarship, ...   306.51
Hollis, ...   330.81
Henry B. Humphrey, ...   560.53
Charles L. Jones, ...   1,617.46
George Emerson Lowell, ...   550.49
Markoe, ...   287.15
Matthews Scholarships :
    Interest on balance, ... $166.08
    Matthews Hall, ½ net rents, . . . 2,841.97   3,008.05
William Merrick, ...   328.28
Morey, ...   437.93
Lady Mowlson, ...   306.90
Boston Newsboys', Interest, ... $152.76
    Gift, ... 25.00   177.76
Howard Gardner Nichols, ...   298.68
Lucy Osgood, ...   314.92
George Herbert Palmer, ...   70.83
George Foster Peabody, ...   32.67
James Mills Peirce, ...   228.14

Amounts carried forward, ... $49,959.46 $310,824.87

COLLEGE (CONTINUED)

INCOME

| | Amounts brought forward, . . . | $49,959.46 | $310,824.87 |

Income of Scholarship Funds and Gifts for Scholarships
(*continued*).

Pennoyer, ...	328.18
Charles Eliot Perkins, ...	1,185.00
Rebecca A. Perkins, ...	244.23
Philadelphia, ...	551.18
Wendell Phillips Memorial, ...	89.64
Elnathan Pratt, ...	72.96
Ricardo Prize (gift), ...	850.00
Rodger, ...	79.79
Henry Bromfield Rogers, ...	181.86
Nathaniel Ropes Jr., ...	553.22
James A. Rumrill, ...	770.86
Edward Russell, ...	302.14
Sales, ...	299.83
Saltonstall, ...	588.75
Leverett Saltonstall, ...	448.97
Mary Saltonstall, ...	861.10

James Savage (part):

Savage Scholarship, ...	300.00
Sever, ...	162.91
Sewall, ...	586.88
Shattuck, ...	2,542.66
Slade, ...	313.93
Dunlap Smith, ...	200.00
Story, ...	236.86

Stoughton:

Interest, ...	$19.75	
Use of pasture, ...	70.48	90.23
Swift, ...		231.91
Thayer, ...		4,218.98
Gorham Thomas, ...		226.81
Toppan, ...		408.83
Townsend, ...		1,856.49
University (gift) 1912–18, ...		150.00
Ira D. Van Duzee (part), ...		8.31
Walcott, ...		267.89
Christopher M. Weld, ...		557.67

Jacob Wendell:

Interest, ...	$283.78	
Gift, ...	50.00	333.78
Whiting, ...		618.16
Josiah Dwight Whitney, ...		247.50
Mary L. Whitney, ...		589.64

| | Amounts carried forward, ... | $70,005.21 | $310,824.87 |

COLLEGE (CONTINUED)

INCOME

Amounts brought forward, . . .	$70,005.21	$310,824.8

Income of Scholarship Funds and Gifts for Scholarships
(*continued*).

Willard, ...	525.74	
Augustus Woodbury, ...	107.76	
Charles Wyman, ...	522.72	71,161.43

Income of Beneficiary and Loan Funds and Repayments.

Rebecca C. Ames:		
Interest, ...	$2,698.50	
Loans repaid by Students, . . .	100.00	$2,798.50
Anonymous gifts for benefit of certain members		
of the **Class of 1915,** Gifts, . .	$525.00	
Interest, .	32.18	557.18
Nathaniel Appleton, ...		38.16
Edward Austin:		
Interest, ...	$257.30	
Loans repaid by students, ...	106.70	364.00
Frank Bolles Memorial, ...		112.46
William Brattle, ...		94.80
Daniel A. Buckley (part), ...		8,025.52
Walter Channing Cabot, ...		2,560.78
Edward Erwin Coolidge (part), ...		700.00
Thomas Danforth, ...		67.27
Moses Day, ...		270.96
Calvin and **Lucy Ellis** Aid (part), ...		2,880.00
John Ellery, ...		27.13
Exhibitions, ...		67.02
Fines Loan Fund:		
For late registration, ...	$435.00	
For delayed payment of dues, . . .	553.75	
Loans returned, ...	563.54	
Interest, ...	53.22	1,605.51
Thomas Fitch, ...		49.40
Ephraim Flynt, ...		29.35
Henry Flynt, ...		10.54
Freshman Loan:		
Interest, ...	$156.72	
Loans repaid, ...	270.00	426.72
Freshman Loan (**Gove** Gift), ...		20.76
Henry Gibbs, ...		30.55
John Glover, ...		209.19
Price Greenleaf (part), ...	$16,678.95	
Price Greenleaf Aid:		
Interest, ...	823.44	
Price Greenleaf Aids returned,	145.00	17,647.39
Amounts carried forward, ...	$38,593.19	$381,986.30

COLLEGE (CONTINUED)

INCOME

Amounts brought forward, ...	$38,593.19	$381,986.30

Income of Beneficiary and Loan Funds and Repayments (*continued*).

Edwin A. W. Harlow:

Interest, ...		589.30

Robert Henry Harlow:

Interest, ... ∴ .	$277.95	
Loans repaid, ...	25.65	303.60

Harvard Engineering Society Loan Fund:

Interest, ...		37.22

Edward Holyoke, ...		22.77
Robert Keayne, ...		146.57
Bertram Kimball, ...		1,299.92

Harry Milton Levy Loan:

Interest, ...	$92.95	
Loans repaid, ...	85.00	127.95

Mary Lindall, ...		68.31
The Loan, ...		7,944.00

Susan B. Lyman:

Interest, ...		197.64

Anne Mills, ...		14.80

Munroe:

Interest, ...	$537.52	
Loans repaid, ...	105.54	648.06

Palfrey Exhibition:

Interest, ...	$108.16	
Award of 1910–11 returned, . . .	80.00	188.16

Dr. Andrew P. Peabody Memorial:

Interest, ...		271.85

Scholarship and Beneficiary Money Returned:

Gift, ...	$10.00	
Loans repaid, ...	1,515.78	
Interest, ...	78.01	1,603.79

Joseph Sewall, ...		14.10
Alexander W. Thayer (part), ...		345.95
Quincy Tufts, ...		553.01
Benjamin Wadsworth, ...		19.00

Stuart Wadsworth Wheeler:

Interest, ...	$333.13	
Loans repaid, ...	187.00	520.13

Waite Memorial, ...	696.52	54,195.84

Income of Prize Funds, and Gifts for Prizes:

Jeremy Belknap (gift), ...	$50.00	
James Gordon Bennett, ...	100.34	
Amounts carried forward, ...	$150.34	$436,182 14

COLLEGE (CONTINUED)

INCOME

Amounts brought forward, ...	$150.34	$436,182.14

Income of Prize Funds, and Gifts for Prizes
(*continued*).

Philo Sherman Bennett, ...	21.64	
Francis Boott (part), ...	190.00	
Bowdoin Prizes for Dissertations, ...	1,598.65	
Boylston Prizes for Elocution, ...	132.42	
Coolidge Debating, ...	289.77	
Dante Prize (gift), ...	100.00	
Lloyd McKim Garrison, ...	135.48	
Edward Hopkins Gift for "Deturs":		
Interest on balance, ... $114.30		
From Trustees, ... 233.25	347.55	
George Arthur Knight, ...	56.73	
Lake Mohonk (gift), ...	100.00	
Old Testament Study (gifts), ...	125.00	
Patria Society (gift), ...	50.00	
Susan Anthony Potter Prizes (gift), . . .	225.00	
Sales, ...	58.66	
John O. Sargent, ...	136.57	
George B. Sohier (part), ...	250.00	
Charles Sumner, ...	215.77	
Robert N. Toppan, ...	204.53	
Philip Washburn, ...	119.05	
Elizabeth Wilder, ...	100.29	
Wister, ...	40.45	4,647.90

Income of Sundry Funds for Special Purposes:

Botanic Department (part):		
¼ for Cryptogamic Herbarium, . . $492.28		
¼ for Laboratories of Botany, . . . 246.14	$738.42	
William H. Baldwin, Jr., 1885, ...	286.51	
Francis Boott (part), ...	329.75	
Francis James Child Memorial, ...	555.64	
Classical Publication Fund of the Class of 1856:		
Interest, ... $355.36		
Sales, ... 104.26	459.62	
Book Fund of the Class of 1881, ...	177.61	
Class of 1883 Special, ...	13.81	
Cryptogamic Herbarium, ...	190.08	
George A. Gardner, ...	300.91	
George Silsbee and Ellen Sever Hale, .	280.27	
Harvard Economic Studies:		
Sales of publications, ... $487.67		
Grant from accumulated income of		
David A. Wells Fund, . . 2,637.52	3,125.19	
Amounts carried forward, ...	$6,457.81	$440,830.04

COLLEGE (CONTINUED)

INCOME

Amounts brought forward, ...	$6,457.81	$440,830.04

Income of Sundry Funds for Special Purposes
(continued).

Harvard Foundation for exchanges with French Universities, ...		352.98
Harvard Oriental Series:		
Interest, ...		755.32
History Book Fund (History 1):		
Sales of publications, ...	$402.56	
Interest, ...	20.53	423.09
Richard Hodgson Memorial, ...		12.18
Solomon Lincoln Bequest, ...		508.56
Joseph Lovering for Physical Research, . .		882.78
Mathematics Book Fund: Sales of publications,		91.89
Music Building Maintenance Fund, ...		142.51
Music Department, ...		67.56
James Mills Peirce Bequest, ...		22.62
General Publication Fund:		
Sales of publications, ...	$419.95	
Interest, ...	86.37	506.32
Nelson Robinson, Jr. Additional (part) gift,		60.00
Robert W. Sayles, ...		247.50
George William Sawin, ...		286.11
Shaler Memorial, ...		1,658.20
Elizabeth Torrey, ...		63.71
Henry Warren Torrey:		
Interest, ...	$683.45	
Sales, ...	265.51	948.96
Unknown Memorial (part), ...		1,800.00
Samuel Ward, ...		915.40
Cyrus M. Warren, ...		325.12
Henry C. Warren (part), ...		1,916.64
David A. Wells (part), ...		758.48
Chauncey Wright, ...		70.29
Physical Laboratory Endowment (interest), . . .		3,702.50
T. Jefferson Coolidge for Research in Physics,	2,501.09	24,977.57

Sundry Gifts, Fees, etc., for Special Purposes.

For the Department of Classics:		
Gift for Lecturers, ...	$1,000.00	
" " Harvard Studies in Classical Philology,	50.00	
Sales of publications, ...	31.42	
For the Department of Economics:		
Gifts for Department, ...	1,004.88	
" " " Special use, ...	75.00	
" " Publishing History English Customs,	200.00	
Amounts carried forward, ...	$2,361.30	$465,807.61

COLLEGE (CONTINUED)

INCOME

Amounts brought forward, ...	$2,361.30	$465,807.61

Sundry Gifts, Fees, etc., for Special Purposes
(*continued*).

For the Department of English:
Gifts for publications, ...	$900.00	
Interest, ...	43.00	943.00

For the Department of Fine Arts:
Gift for Expenses, ...	40.00

For the Department of Government:
Gift for Research in Government, ...	1,000.00
" of David A. Ellis, books, ...	25.00
" for Special Expenses in Munic. Govt.,	108.30
" of Frank Graham Thomson, . .	5,000.00
" " Frank Graham Thomson and Clarke Thomson, ...	2,500.00

For the Department of Music:
Gifts for Department, ...	385.00
" " Special Salary, ...	100.00

For the Department of Philosophy:
Gifts for Department Library, ...	200.00
Sales of Psychological Review, ...	6.96

For the Department of Physics:
Gifts for Physical Research, ...	515.00

For the Department of Sanskrit:
Interest, ...	$47.34	
Sales of publications, ...	59.27	106.61

For the Department of Semitic:
Gift for Library — Interest, ...	19.20

For the Department of Ethics of Social Questions:
Anonymous Gift for Department,	$2,500.00	
Interest, ...	92.14	
Sales of publication, ...	200.04	2,792.18
Gift for furnishing rooms — interest, ...		11.59

For the School for Social Workers:
Gift, ...	$500.00	
Interest, ...	34.16	
Tuition fees, ...	210.00	744.16

For the Department of Zoölogy:
Gift for Bermuda Biological Station,	$500.00	
Interest, ...	25.25	525.25
Gift Plantation of Shrubs — interest, ...	76.06	17,459.61
Amount carried forward, ...		$483,367.22

COLLEGE (CONTINUED)

INCOME

Amount brought forward, ...		$483,267.22

Receipts from students.

Tuition Fees — Regular Programme:

College Regular, ...	$315,470.00	
" Special, ...	5,635.00	
Unclassified, ...	11,020.00	$382,125.00

Tuition Fees — Additional Courses:

College Regular, ...	$31,402.02	
" Special, ...	380.00	
Unclassified, ...	202.66	31,984.68

Tuition — Regular Programme:

Graduate School of Arts and Sciences, ...	$52,645.00	
Radcliffe students in University courses, ...	1,755.00	54,400.00

Auditors' Fees:

College, ...		35.00

Examination fees:

Admission, ...	$9,920.00	
Condition, make-up and advanced standing, ...	2,064.00	
Doctor of Philosophy, ...	30.00	12,014.00

Graduation fees, ...		8,680.00

Laboratory fees:

Astronomy, ...	$1,045.00	
Botany, ...	1,272.50	
Chemistry, ...	15,486.41	
Geology, ...	1,240.00	
Mineralogy, ...	315.00	
Music, ...	150.00	
Hygiene, ...	2,070.00	
Physics, ...	3,568.00	
Psychology, ...	235.00	
Zoölogy, ...	1,333.87	26,715.78

College Dormitories: Hollis, Stoughton, Holworthy, Thayer, Weld, Wadsworth House, Walter Hastings, Perkins, and Conant, ...	$74,017.66	
Matthews Hall, ...	12,057.50	
	$86,075.16	
Less ½ net income from Matthews Hall, credited under income of Matthews Scholarship, ...	2,841.97	83,233.19
Amount collected on account of unpaid term-bills previously charged off, ...	100.00	549,287.65

Amount carried forward, ...		$1,032,554.87

COLLEGE (CONTINUED)
EXPENDITURE

Amount brought forward, ... $1,032,554.87

Sundries:
Sale of University Hymn Book, ... 156.62
"   Manual American History, ... 170.27
"   Annals of Mathematics, ... 63.21
"   old examination papers, ... 372.06
"   other publications, ... 412.32
"   Commencement Lunch tickets, ... 682.50
"   Historical Monographs, ... 2.12
Duplicate diplomas, ... 25.00
Sale of photographs, ... 29.38
Gift for Brighton Marsh Fence credited to College
Account, ... 421.74
Conscience money, ... 1.00
Royalty on Sales Agamemnon of Aeschylus, . . 3.40
Receipts at College Printing Office, . $41,930.33
Less Expenses contra, ... 37,381.95   4,548.38   6,888.00

$1,039,442.87

EXPENDITURE

From Fellowship Funds and Gifts.
Edward Austin:
From Income, ... $2,000.00
From Gift, ... 400.00 $2,400.00

Bayard Cutting Fellowship, ... 1,125.00
W. Bayard Cutting, Jr., Bequest, ... 575.00
George W. Dillaway, ... 225.00
Fellowship at École Libre des Sciences Politiques, 600.00
Ozias Goodwin Memorial, ... 525.00
Harris, ... 1,000.00
Edward William Hooper, ... 1,150.00
John Thornton Kirkland, ... 500.00
Henry Lee Memorial, ... 525.00
Woodbury Lowery, ... 972.09
MacDowell, ... 600.00
Charles Eliot Norton, ... 800.00
Robert Treat Paine, ... 600.00
John Parker, ... 2,625.00
Francis Parkman, ... 600.00
Rogers, ... 1,500.00
Henry Bromfield Rogers Memorial, . . . 525.00
Frederick Sheldon (part), ... 12,150.00
Social Ethics, ... 450.00
South End House, ... 478.00

Amount carried forward, ... $29,925.09

COLLEGE (CONTINUED)

EXPENDITURE

Amount brought forward, ... $29,925.09

From Fellowship Funds and Gifts (*continued*).

South End House Fellowship in Social Education,	350.00	
John Tyndall, ...	550.00	
James Walker, ...	525.00	
Whiting, ...	900.00	
Adams Woods Fellowship, ...	400.00	32,650 09

From Scholarship Funds and Gifts.

Abbot, ...	$175.00	
Edward Austin Scholarships for Teachers, .	4,000.00	
Bartlett, ...	250.00	
Bassett, ...	270.00	
Bigelow, ...	600.00	
Bowditch, ...	5,250.00	
Bright (part), ...	1,250.00	
Browne, ...	175.00	
Morey Willard Buckminster, ...	250.00	
Burr, ...	1,600.00	
Ruluff Sterling Choate, ...	275.00	
George Newhall Clark, ...	500.00	
Thomas William Clarke, ...	225.00	
Class of 1802, ...	375.00	
" 1814, ...	150.00	
" 1815 (Kirkland), ...	300.00	
" 1817, ...	200.00	
" 1828, ...	200.00	
" 1835, ...	225.00	
" 1841, ...	225.00	
" 1852 (Dana), ...	225.00	
" 1856, ...	750.00	
" 1867, ...	325.00	
" 1877, ...	225.00	
" 1883, ...	275.00	
" 1901, ...	300.00	
Clement Harlow Condell, ...	1,000.00	
Crowninshield, ...	550.00	
Warren H. Cudworth, ...	300.00	
George and Martha Derby, ...	250.00	
Julius Dexter, ...	225.00	
Orlando W. Doe, ...	100.00	
William Samuel Eliot, ...	250.00	
George H. Emerson, ...	225.00	
Joseph Eveleth (part), ...	400.00	
Fall River, ...	100.00	
Farrar, ...	275.00	
Amounts carried forward, ...	$22,270.00	$32,650.09

COLLEGE (CONTINUED)

EXPENDITURE

Amounts brought forward, ... $22,270.00 $32,650.09

From Scholarship Funds and Gifts (*continued*).

George Fisher and Elizabeth Huntington Fisher, ...	200.00	
Richard Augustine Gambrill, ...	525.00	
Charles Haven Goodwin, ...	350.00	
Benjamin D. Greene, ...	200.00	
Price Greenleaf (part), ...	2,880.00	
Selwyn L. Harding, ...	225.00	
Harvard Club of Boston, ...	1,000.00	
" " Buffalo, ...	200.00	
" " Cleveland, ...	400.00	
" " Connecticut Valley, . . .	200.00	
" " Fitchburg, ...	150.00	
" " Hawaii, ...	200.00	
" " Hingham, ...	100.00	
" " Lawrence, ...	200.00	
" " Louisiana, ...	257.14	
" " Lowell, ...	350.00	
" " Lynn, ...	100.00	
" " Maine, ...	150.00	
" " Nebraska, ...	150.00	
" " New Jersey, ...	250.00	
" " Western Pennsylvania, . . .	600.00	
" " Rhode Island, ...	150.00	
" " Rochester, N.Y., ...	200.00	
" " St. Louis, ...	440.10	
" " San Francisco, ...	500.00	
" " Seattle, ...	300.00	
" " Syracuse, ...	200.00	
" " Washington, ...	250.00	
" " Worcester, ...	200.00	
John Appleton Haven, ...	475.00	
William Hilton (part), ...	225.00	
Scholarship in American History, ...	300.00	
Ebenezer Rockwood Hoar, ...	500.00	
Levina Hoar, for the town of Lincoln, . . .	300.00	
R. M. Hodges (part), ...	275.00	
Hollis, ...	275.00	
Henry B. Humphrey, ...	500.00	
Charles L. Jones, ...	1,350.00	
George Emerson Lowell, ...	450.00	
Markoe, ...	250.00	
Matthews, ...	4,700.00	
William Merrick, ...	275.00	

Amounts carried forward, ... $43,072.24 $32,650.09

COLLEGE (CONTINUED)

EXPENDITURE

Amounts brought forward, ...	$43,072.24	$32,650.09

From Scholarship Funds and Gifts (*continued*).

Morey, ...	375.00
Lady Mowlson, ...	250.00
Boston Newsboys', ...	150.00
Howard Gardner Nichols, ...	250.00
Lucy Osgood, ...	275.00
George Foster Peabody, ...	250.00
C. E. Perkins Scholarship,	900.00
Rebecca A. Perkins, ...	200.00
Philadelphia, ...	500.00
Wendell Phillips Memorial, ...	75.00
Ricardo Prize Gift, ...	350.00
Henry Bromfield Rogers, ...	150.00
Nathaniel Ropes, Jr., ...	475.00
James A. Rumrill, ...	675.00
Edward Russell, ...	250.00
Sales, ...	250.00
Saltonstall, ...	525.00
Leverett Saltonstall, ...	400.00
Mary Saltonstall, ...	300.00
James Savage (part), ...	300.00
Sever, ...	150.00
Sewall, ...	500.00
Shattuck, ...	2,100.00
Slade, ...	275.00
Dunlap Smith, ...	200.00
Story, ...	200.00
Stoughton, ...	150.00
Charles Sumner, ...	200.00
Swift, ...	200.00
Thayer, ...	8,500.00
Gorham Thomas, ...	200.00
Toppan, ...	700.00
Townsend, ...	1,000.00
Walcott, ...	200.00
Christopher M. Weld, ...	500.00
Jacob Wendell, ...	300.00
Whiting, ...	550.00
Josiah Dwight Whitney, ...	242.50
Mary L. Whitney, ...	500.00
Willard, ...	475.00
Charles Wyman, ...	450.00

		62,564.74
Amount carried forward, ...		$95,214.83

COLLEGE (CONTINUED)

EXPENDITURE

Amount brought forward, ...		$95,214.83
From Beneficiary and Loan Funds and Gifts.		
Rebecca C. Ames, ...	$2,435.00	
Anonymous Gifts for Special Aid, ...	1,175.00	
Nathaniel Appleton, ...	38.16	
Edward Austin Loan (Special Students), . .	364.00	
Frank Bolles Memorial, ...	90.00	
William Brattle, ...	94.80	
Daniel A. Buckley (part), ...	6,200.00	
Walter Channing Cabot, ...	2,000.00	
Edward Erwin Coolidge (part), ...	700.00	
Thomas Danforth, ...	67.27	
Moses Day, ...	270.96	
John Ellery, ...	27.13	
Calvin and Lucy Ellis Aid (part), ...	2,880.00	
Exhibitions, ...	67.02	
Fines, Loan Fund, ...	304.75	
Ephraim Flynt, ...	29.85	
Henry Flynt, ...	10.54	
Freshman Loan, ...	885.00	
Henry Gibbs, ...	30.55	
John Glover, ...	166.58	
Price Greenleaf Aid, ...	14,469.00	
Edwin A. W. Harlow, ...	255.00	
Robert Henry Harlow, ...	241.00	
Student Fund of the Harvard Engineering Society of New York, ...	50.00	
Edward Holyoke, ...	21.85	
Robert Keayne, ...	146.57	
Bertram Kimball, ...	1,261.00	
Harry Milton Levy Loan, ...	475.00	
Mary Lindall, ...	63.31	
The Loan, ...	7,944.00	
Susan B. Lyman, ...	239.25	
Anne Mills, ...	14.80	
John F. Moors' Gift, ...	50.00	
Munroe, ...	470.00	
Palfrey Exhibition, ...	80.00	
Dr. Andrew P. Peabody Memorial, ...	172.75	
Scholarship and Beneficiary Money Returned, . .	2,325.00	
Alexander Wheelock Thayer, ...	345.95	
Quincy Tufts, ...	553.01	
Benjamin Wadsworth, ...	19.00	47,082.60
From Prize Funds and Gifts for Prizes.		
Jeremy Belknap, ...	$50.00	
James Gordon Bennett, ...	40.00	
Francis Boott (part), ...	90.00	
Amounts carried forward, ...	$180.00	$142,247.43

COLLEGE (CONTINUED)

EXPENDITURE

Amounts brought forward, ...	$180.00	$142,247.43

From Prize Funds and Gifts for Prizes (*continued*).

Bowdoin Prizes for Dissertations, ...	1,284.38	
Boylston Prizes for Elocution, ...	210.00	
Coolidge Debating, ...	219.03	
Dante, ...	100.00	
Lloyd McKim Garrison, ...	111.75	
Edward Hopkins Gift for "Deturs," . . .	128.74	
Menorah Society, ...	100.00	
Susan Anthony Potter Prizes, ...	225.00	
Sales, ...	45.00	
John O. Sargent, ...	100.00	
George B. Sohier, ...	250.00	
Old Testament Study, ...	75.00	
Robert N. Toppan, ...	150.00	
Philip Washburn, ...	75.00	
David A. Wells, ... :	658.03	3,911.93

For University Scholarships.

Undergraduate:

Normal, ...	$600.00	
Graduate School of Arts and Sciences, ...	4,940.00	5,540.00

From Sundry Funds and Balances for Special Purposes.

Francis Boott, books for the Department of Music, ...	$229.81	
Francis James Child Memorial, books, . .	534.62	
Classical Publication Fund of the Class of 1856:		
Harvard Studies in Classical Philology, . .	1,280.92	
T. Jefferson Coolidge for Research in Physics,	2,462.58	
Book Fund of the Class of 1881, books for the Department of Chemistry, ...	280.61	
George A. Gardner, for photographs, etc., for the Department of Geology, ...	248.76	
Harvard Oriental Series, publications, ...	527.24	
Harvard Economic Studies, ...	53.81	
History Book Fund (History 1), ...	106.88	
Joseph Lovering for Physical Research, . .	367.29	
Mathematics Book Fund, ...	65.75	

Francis G. Peabody, ...	$3,500.00		
Less amount paid for salaries,	3,500.00		

Nelson Robinson Jr. Additional (part).

Psychological Laboratory, . . .	$1,301.62		
Books, ...	311.29		
Expenses, ...	38.77		
Librarian Department Philosophy,	1,000.00		
	$2,651.68		
Less paid for salaries, . . .	1,000.00	1,651.68	

Amounts carried forward, ...	$7,809.45	$151,699.36

COLLEGE (CONTINUED)

EXPENDITURE

Amounts brought forward, ...	$7,809.45	$151,699.36
From Sundry Funds and Balances for Special		
Purposes (*continued*).		
Robert W. Sayles for Department of Geology,	8.63	
Shaler Memorial, ...	29.00	
Elizabeth Torrey Bequest, ...	195.40	
Henry Warren Torrey, publications, . . .	599.75	
Unknown Memorial (part), services and expenses,	2,829.48	
Cyrus M. Warren, research in Chemistry, .	557.72	
Henry C. Warren, publications and books, .	1,913.52	
David A. Wells, Harvard Economic Studies,	2,637.52	
Jefferson Physical Laboratory :		
Services and wages, ... $2,042.75		
Operating expense, . . . $1,906.31		
Less paid from General		
Income, ... 600.00 1,306.31		
University charge :		
Treasurer's Office, care of invest-		
ments, ... 82.85		
Bursar's Office, collections and pay-		
ments, ... 148.68		
Watchmen, ... 77.88	8,658.47	20,238.94
From Gifts and Fees, etc., for Special Purposes.		
For Department of Economics :		
Gift for Department, ... $2,286.61		
Less paid for Salaries, ... 1,550.00	736.61	
Gift for Publishing History of English Customs,	200.00	
For Department of Fine Arts, ...	25.00	
For Department of Mathematics :		
Gift for Expenses of Commission on teaching		
Mathematics, ...	100.00	
For Department of Chemistry :		
Edward Mallinckrodt gift, ...	14.41	
For Department of Philosophy :		
Philosophical Library Books, ...	78.38	
For Department of Ethics Social Questions, general,	2,959.74	
" " " " " Gift for		
books, ...	6.90	
Furnishings for the Department of Social Ethics,	206.10	
For Division of Music, ...	408.29	
" " " Gift for services, ...	100.00	
For Department of Physics, Physical Research, .	515.00	
Fellowship in Physical Research, . $500.00		
Less paid for salaries, ... 500.00		
Amounts carried forward, ...	$5,350.48	$171,938.30

COLLEGE (CONTINUED)

EXPENDITURE

Amounts brought forward, ...	$5,350.48	$171,988.30

From Gifts and Fees, etc., for Special Purposes (*continued*).

Department of Botany, **John S. Ames** Gift, .	350.00	
" Zoölogy, Bermuda Biological Station, ...	436.83	
Department of Geology, Exhibition Case for Photographs, ...	54.69	
Semitic Library, books, ...	141.43	
Department of Classics, books, ...	248.47	
" " " Lecturers, ...	1,000.00	
School for Social Workers, ... $1,859.16		
Less paid for salaries, ... 1,000.00	859.16	
Department of Government :		
Anonymous gift for Research, ...	953.86	
Gift **David A. Ellis**, books, ...	15.86	
Gift **F. G. Thomson**, ... $3,908.11		
Less paid for salaries, ... 2,750.00	1,158.11	
Gifts **F. G. Thomson** and **Clarke Thomson**, for Bureau of Municipal Research, ...	2,500.00	
Gift for Plantation of Shrubs, etc., ...	3,879.73	16,948.57

Administration Offices.

Dean of the Faculty of Arts and Sciences :		
Salary, ...	$500.00	
Services and wages, ...	874.66	
Office supplies and expenses, ...	167.97	1,542.63
Dean of **Harvard** College :		
Salaries, ...	$10,300.00	
Services and wages, ...	7,435.62	
Office supplies and expenses, ...	2,399.27	20,134.89
Dean and Secretary of the Graduate School of Arts and Sciences :		
Salaries, ...	$3,500.00	
Services and wages, ...	834.00	
Office supplies and expenses, ...	592.93	3,926.93
Dean of the Graduate School of Business Administration :		
Salary, ...		1,000.00
Secretary of the Faculty of Arts and Sciences :		
Salaries, ...	$2,750.00	
Services and wages, ...	2,326.75	
Office supplies and expenses, ...	991.31	6,068.06
Amount carried forward, ...		$221,559.38

COLLEGE (CONTINUED)

EXPENDITURE

Amount brought forward, ...		$221,559.38
From Appropriations.		
Anthropology, ...	$41.76	
Botany, ...	3,349.00	
Classics, ...	200.00	
Economics, ... $199.70		
Office expenses, ... 600.00	799.70	
Education, ...	118.95	
English, ...	280.10	
Fine Arts, ...	554.31	
French and other Romance Languages, ...	1,400.00	
Geology, ...	50.00	
German, ...	741.59	
Government, ...	97.81	
History, ...	812.50	
Mathematics, ...	225.00	
Mineralogy and Petrography, ...	330.24	
Music, ...	250.00	
Philosophy, ...	100.00	
Physics, ...	1,000.00	
Psychology, ...	141.18	
Zoölogy, ...	65.93	10,558.07
From Laboratory Fees.		
Astronomy, ...	$1,398.68	
Botany, ...	1,310.26	
Chemistry, ...	15,531.36	
Geology, ...	1,073.36	
Hygiene, ...	1,847.09	
Mineralogy, ...	304.39	
Music, ...	150.00	
Physics, ...	3,164.06	
Psychology, ...	235.00	
Zoölogy, ...	1,280.39	26,294.59
For College Public Buildings, which are not valued in the Treasurer's books.		
Repairs and Equipment, ...	$9,939.14	
Caretaking and Operating Expenses, ...	23,104.58	33,043.72
For College Dormitories: Hollis, Stoughton, Holworthy, Thayer, Weld, Wadsworth House, Walter Hastings, Perkins, and Conant, which are not valued in the Treasurer's books; and for Matthews Hall.		
Repairs and Equipment, ...	$10,759.19	
Caretaking and Operating Expenses, ...	29,155.30	39,914.49
Amount carried forward, ...		$331,370.25

COLLEGE (CONTINUED)

EXPENDITURE

Amount brought forward, ...		$331,370.25
General.		
Salaries for Instruction:		
Edward Austin (part):		
Austin Teaching Fellowships, $12,052.61		
From Sundry Funds and Gifts, . 220,797.18		
From General Income, ... 265,232.20 $498,081.99		
Services and wages, ...	5,882.55	
Proctors, ...	2,606.64	
Equipment and supplies, ...	1,108.79	
Blue-books, ...	438.08	
Printing, ...	8,563.36	
Pension for Bell-Ringer, ...	625.00	
Diplomas, ...	588.71	
Stationery, postage, telephone, etc., ...	562.88	
Monitorships, ...	1,267.95	
Special lecturers, ...	125.00	
Subscription to American School of Classical Studies, ...	250.00	
Music Class Day, ...	125.00	
Collection of term-bills, ...	88.09	
Refreshments at Faculty Meetings, ...	67.78	
College Entrance Examination Board, ...	100.00	
Graduate School Reception, ...	84.66	
Sundries, ...	763.90	521,225.28
Printing Office.		
Services and wages, ...	$19,477.29	
Supplies and equipment, ...	13,737.07	
Printing, ...	268.80	
Repairs, ...	117.88	
Binding, ...	3,627.76	
Sundries, ...	153.15	
	$37,381.95	
Expenses carried contra and deducted from sales to Departments, ...	37,381.95	
Admission Examinations.		
Cambridge:		
Services and wages, ...	$1,823.95	
Reading books, ...	4,114.20	
Office supplies and expenses, ...	1,144.60	7,082.75
Outside Cambridge:		
Service, ...	$2,371.00	
Expenses, ...	1,084.72	3,455.72
Annals of Mathematics, ...		251.01
Amount carried forward, ...		$868,385.01

COLLEGE (CONTINUED)

EXPENDITURE

Amount brought forward, ...		$863,385.01

General (*continued*).

Payments made from College Income for the following accounts:

Jefferson Physical Laboratory, Schedule 8,	$600.00	
Graduate School of Applied Science, Schedule 12, ...	71,695.58	
Museum of Comparative Zoölogy, Schedule 25,	3,977.50	
Peabody Museum of American Archaeology and Ethnology, Schedule 26, ...	226.71	
William Hayes Fogg Art Museum, Schedule 29, ...	2,570.10	
Phillips Brooks House, Schedule 31, .	1,146.57	
Hemenway Gymnasium, " 32, .	7,141.53	87,357.99

University charge.

President's Office, salaries and expenses, ...	$7,154.28	
Treasurer's Office, care of investments, ...	5,506.90	
Bursar's Office:		
Collections and payments, ... $11,571.99		
Letting College rooms, ... 800.00	12,371.99	
Students Employment Office and Appointment Office, salaries and expenses, ...	5,455.12	
Medical Adviser, salary and expenses, ...	2,146.09	
Inspector of Grounds and Buildings, salary and expenses, ...	3,481.66	
Publication Office, salary and expenses, ...	2,688.83	
Quinquennial Catalogue, ...	848.82	
Annual Catalogue, ...	2,032.57	
90% Memorial Hall and Sanders Theatre, expenses for the building, ...	1,190.48	
Watchmen, ...	1,792.09	
Labor, etc., ...	9,455.76	
Alumni Office, ...	141.41	
Engineer, ...	1,154.30	
Janitor, ...	1,992.73	
Purchasing Agent, ...	82.74	57,495.77
		$1,008,238.77

General surplus made up as follows:

Restricted Income unused carried to Funds and Gifts, ...	$47,472.90	
General Suspense, ...	3,781.66	
Surplus for year carried to Schedule 10, ...	2,652.74	
	$53,907.30	

Less General Deficit made up as follows:

Advances to Funds and Gifts carried to General Suspense,	$4,618.63		
Accumulated income of Funds and Gifts used, ...	18,084.57	22,703.20	31,204.10
			$1,039,442.87

LIBRARY

INCOME AND EXPENDITURE

For the year ended June 30, 1912

INCOME

Income of Book Funds and Gifts and Receipts for the
purchase of books.

Nathaniel I. Bowditch,		$105.29
Bright Legacy (½ income),	$1,237.50	
" Balance (interest),	15.49	1,252.99
William R. Castle,		64.20
Edwin Conant (¼ income),		845.27
Constantius (½ income),		640.82
Archibald C. Coolidge and Clarence L. Hay		243.84
W. Bayard Cutting Bequest,		619.20
Denny,		264.19
Eliza Farrar,		275.81
Price Greenleaf (part),		1,000.00
Charles Gross Memorial,		78.90
Horace A. Haven,		157.46
Francis B. Hayes,		497.77
George Hayward,		264.84
Thomas Hollis,		118.06
Sidney Homer,		105.98
Jarvis,		24.90
Frederick A. Lane,		263.79
George C. Lodge and Joseph Trumbull Stickney Memorial,		164.98
Lowell,		1,423.17
Francis Cabot Lowell,		495.00
Charles Minot,		2,970.00
Charles Eliot Norton,		448.77
Lucy Osgood,		857.09
Mary Osgood,		848.08
Francis Parkman Memorial,		271.82
George F. Parkman,		1,246.05
Francis Sales,		194.09
Salisbury,		271.71
Sever,		1,008.95
Samuel Shapleigh,		195.53
George B. Sohier (part),		96.50
Strobel Memorial (Class of 1877),		142.46
Strobel Memorial (Siam),		98.65
Subscription,		520.89
Charles Sumner,		1,853.23
Kenneth Matheson Taylor,		251.26
Daniel Treadwell (½ income),		295.14
John Harvey Treat Book Fund,		2,117.00
Amount carried forward,		$21,093.08

LIBRARY (CONTINUED)

INCOME

Amount brought forward, ...			$31,093.08

Income of Book Funds and Gifts and Receipts for the purchase of books (*continued*).

Ichabod Tucker, ...		216.55	
20th Mass. Regiment of Volunteer Infantry, . . .		30.44	
Wales Income for Books, ...		285.71	
James Walker, ...		787.19	
Thomas W. Ward, ...		259.88	
Julian Palmer Welsh Memorial, ...		149.10	
J. Huntington Wolcott, ...		990.99	
Gifts for books. Gifts, ... $16,951.07			
Interest, ... 282.32		17,233.39	
Sale of duplicate books, ...		1,282.80	
Received for books lost, ...		77.35	$42,406.43

Income of R. M. Hodges Fund (part).

For publishing bibliographical contributions, ...			418.46

Income of Funds for general purposes.

Daniel Austin, ...		$386.44	
Edwin Conant (¼ income), ...		1,085.83	
Constantius (½ income), ...		640.83	
Fund of the Class of 1851, ...		43.96	
" " " " (C. F. Dunbar's Gift),		43.31	
Price Greenleaf (part), ...		15,678.95	
Henry L. Pierce, ...		2,475.00	
Henry L. Pierce, Residuary (part), ...		2,358.12	
Stephen Salisbury Bequest, ...		253.44	
James Savage (part), ...		1,834.25	
Daniel Treadwell (¼ income), ...		295.14	
Eben Wright, ...		4,950.00	29,495.37
Fees for use of Library, ...		$95.00	
Fines, ...		570.23	
Gifts for additional service, return of part payment made in 1910–11, ...		56.68	
Gifts for general use, ...		1,000.00	
Sales of Bibliographical Contributions, ...		3.20	
Sales of Sundry publications, ...		14.35	
Sales printed cards, ...		1,368.71	3,108.17
			$75,428.58

General Deficit, made up as follows :

Funds and Gifts, accumulated income, ...		$19,346.56	
Advances to Funds, carried to General Suspense, .		1,628.94	
Deficit carried to Schedule 10, ...		86,360.50	
		$57,336.00	
Less Restricted Income unused, added to Funds and Gifts, ...	$1,963.40		
Restricted Income carried to General Suspense to repay former advances,	258.60	2,222.00	55,114.00
			$130,542.58

LIBRARY (CONTINUED)

EXPENDITURE

For Books, from the following Funds, Gifts, etc.

Bowditch,	$107.85
Bright,	1,497.77
Castle,	129.52
Edwin Conant,	478.27
Constantius,	344.21
A. C. Coolidge and C. L. Hay,	82.50
W. Bayard Cutting Bequest,	581.26
Bayard Cutting Fellowship,	17.70
Denny,	361.53
Farrar,	616.77
Price Greenleaf (part),	995.95
Charles Gross Memorial,	64.44
Haven,	224.72
Hayes,	588.33
Hayward,	359.57
Hollis,	127.58
Homer,	96.74
Jarvis,	27.49
Lane,	319.14
G. C. Lodge and J. T. Stickney Memorial,	185.00
Lowell,	632.34
Francis Cabot Lowell,	426.17
Minot,	2,796.28
Charles Eliot Norton,	519.20
Lucy Osgood,	432.44
Mary Osgood,	387.84
Francis Parkman Memorial,	236.67
George F. Parkman,	1,401.31
Sales,	221.84
Salisbury,	226.02
Sever,	1,337.43
Shapleigh,	200.83
George B. Sohier (part),	174.74
Strobel Memorial (1877),	83.55
" " (Siam),	44.28
Subscription,	508.87
Sumner,	1,919.44
Kenneth Matheson Taylor,	313.58
Daniel Treadwell,	266.14
John Harvey Treat,	2,478.93
Tucker,	309.53
Wales,	101.04
Walker,	908.26
Ward,	160.39
Amount carried forward,	$23,243.46

LIBRARY (CONTINUED)

EXPENDITURE

Amount brought forward, ...	$23,248.46	
For Books, from the following Funds, Gifts, etc. (*continued*).		
Julian Palmer Welsh Memorial, ...	142.62	
J. Huntington Wolcott, ...	977.66	
From Sundry gifts for books (balances), ...	20,405.83	
Duplicate money and receipts for lost books, . . .	1,352.85	
Fines, ...	704.07	$46,836.49
From **R. M. Hodges** Fund, publishing bibliographical contributions, ...		379.83
General.		
Salaries, ...	$23,696.68	
Services and wages (part), ...	34,489.81	
Equipment and supplies, ...	5,791.27	
Stationery, postage, telephone and telegraph, . . .	836.03	
Binding, ...	4,378.64	
General printing, ...	529.25	
Printed cards, ...	4,596.64	
Moving and cleaning books, ...	550.81	
Laundry, ...	66.00	
Sundries, ...	91.19	
Special Reference Libraries, services, ...	1,278.00	
Repairs and equipment, land and building, ...	1,293.07	
Caretaking, land and building, ...	4,127.08	81,724.42
University charge:		
Treasurer's Office, care of investments, ...	$722.68	
Bursar's Office, collections and payments, ...	380.84	
Inspector of Grounds and Buildings, salary and expenses, ...	223.82	
Annual Catalogue, ...	16.32	
Watchmen, ...	160.65	
Engineer, ...	86.14	
Purchasing Agent, ...	21.19	1,611.64
		$130,542.38

UNIVERSITY, COLLEGE, AND LIBRARY
COMBINED ACCOUNTS

For the year ended June 30, 1912

Deficit in Library, Schedule 9, ...		$36,360.50
Surplus in University, Schedule 7, ...	$18,957.36	
Surplus in College, Schedule 8, ...	2,652.74	21,610.10

Deficit met by the unrestricted principal of the **Walter F. Baker** Fund, ... $14,750.40

SUMMER SCHOOLS
FACULTY OF ARTS AND SCIENCES

INCOME AND EXPENDITURE

For the year ended June 30, 1912

INCOME

School of 1911.

Gift for expenses at Appleton Chapel,	$70.00		
" course in Music, ...	250.00	$320.00	
Receipts from students :			
Tuition fees, ...	$20,469.00		
Registration fees, ...	2,229.00		
Auditors fees, ...	910.00		
Historical Excursions, ...	145.14	23,753.14	
Sundries, ...		108.33	24,181.47

School of 1912.

Income of **Sayles** Fund, Summer Course in Geology,	$512.33		
Gift for lectures, ...	50.00		
Sundries, ...	7.00	569.33	
			$24,750.80

EXPENDITURE

School of 1911.

Dean's Office :			
Salary of Dean, ...	$1,000.00		
Services and wages, ...	148.33		
Office supplies, ...	48.87		
Printing, ...	136.40	$1,333.60	
Salaries for Instruction, ...		12,080.00	
General Expenses, ...		301.47	
Public Exercises and Historical Excursions, ...		551.77	
Hospitality, ...		351.31	
Amount carried forward, ...		$14,618.15	

SUMMER SCHOOLS (CONTINUED)

EXPENDITURE

Amount brought forward, ... $14,618.15

School of 1911 (*continued*).

Postage, ...		8.62	
Shop-work courses, ...		528.00	
Catalogue of students, ...		111.45	
Scholarships, ...		95.00	

University charge :

Bursar's Office, collections and payments, ...	$359.77		
Publication Office, Expenses, . . .	215.06		
	$574.83		
Less amount transferred to Schedule 8,	279.77	295.06	$15,656.28
School of Physical Education, ...			4,852.25

School of 1912.

From Sayles Fund, ...		$500.00	

Dean's Office :

Services and wages, ...	$838.12		
Office supplies, ...	148.43		
Printing, ...	47.20		
Sundries, ...	2.00	1,035.75	
General Expenses, ...		239.95	
Advertising, ...		1,060.88	
Postage, ...		168.76	3,004.79
School of Physical Education, ...			83.88
			$23,597.20

General Surplus made up as follows :

Restricted Income carried to General Suspense to repay former advance, ...		$1.25	
Restricted Income unused, added to Funds and Gifts,		61.08	
Surplus, carried to General Suspense, ...		1,091.27	1,153.60
			$24,750.80

GRADUATE SCHOOL OF APPLIED SCIENCE

INCOME AND EXPENDITURE

For the year ended June 30, 1912

INCOME

Income of Funds for Instruction or for General Purposes.

Graduate School of Applied Science Balance, interest, ...	$539.55	
Edward Austin (part):		
Austin Teaching Fellowships, ...	1,500.00	
James Lawrence (part), ...	1,246.78	
Gordon McKay Endowment, ...	69,255.80	
Professorship of Engineering, ...	2,019.90	
Nelson Robinson, Jr. (part), ...	20,926.54	
Arthur Rotch, ...	1,237.50	
Gurdon Saltonstall, ...	2,970.00	
Josiah Stickney, ...	583.70	$100,279.77

Income of Fellowship Funds.

Julia Amory Appleton, ...	$1,036.34	
Nelson Robinson, Jr. (part), ...	1,016.68	
Frederick Sheldon (part), ...	1,000.00	3,053.02

Income of Scholarship Funds.

Edward Austin (part):		
Austin Scholarships in Architecture, . . .	$900.00	
Daniel A. Buckley (part), ...	300.00	
Francis H. Cummings, ...	327.64	
George H. Emerson (part), ...	450.00	
Joseph Eveleth (part), ...	400.00	
William Hilton (part), ...	225.00	
Priscilla Clark Hodges, ...	209.19	
Hennen Jennings, ...	587.47	
Henry Weidemann Locke (gift), ...	100.00	
Edward Dyer Peters (gift), ...	250.00	
Special Scholarship (gift), ...	200.00	3,949.30

Income Loan Funds and Repayments.

Edward Austin Loans repaid, interest, ...		$59.05	
Lawrence Scientific School Loans repaid:			
Interest, ...	$360.17		
Loans repaid, ...	299.37	659.54	
Susan B. Lyman (L.S.S.), interest, ...		98.82	817.41

Income Sundry Funds and Gifts for Special Purposes.

Department of Architecture:		
Nelson Robinson, Jr. Fund (part), . .	$5,281.78	
Gift for Equipment (interest), ...	179.70	
N. Robinson special gift for salary:		
Interest, ...	424.49	
Amounts carried forward, ...	$5,885.97	$108,099.50

GRADUATE SCHOOL OF APPLIED SCIENCE (CONTINUED)

INCOME

Amounts brought forward, ...	$5,885.97	$108,099.50

Income Sundry Funds and Gifts for Special Purposes (*continued*).

Department of Engineering:

Engineering Camp at Squam Lake, ...		12,519.99

Department of Forestry:

Gift for Division of Forestry:

Gift, ...	$1,980.00	
Interest, ...	108.47	2,088.47
Sales lumber, wood, etc., ...	$4,919.99	
Lodgings at Forestry House, . .	196.50	5,116.49

Department of Mining and Metallurgy:

Summer School Mining Camp — interest, . .		16.19	25,627.11

Receipts from Students.

Tuition fees, ...	$16,985.00	
Graduation fees, ...	720.00	

Laboratory fees:

Engineering, ...	$1,083.25	
Forestry, ...	98.45	
Mining and Metallurgy, ...	2,548.74	3,730.44
Shop-work fees, ...		1,677.00
Registration fees in Architecture, ...	15.00	23,127.44

Sundries.

Amount contributed from the General Funds of Harvard College for Salaries and Expenses, . .	$71,695.58	
Amount contributed by Bussey Institution to pay salary of instructor in Landscape Architecture,	1,800.00	
Sales of Architectural Quarterly, ...	138.96	73,634.54
		$230,488.59

General Deficit made up as follows:

Accumulated Income and Gifts used, ...	$7,402.11	
Deficit for 1911–12, carried to General Suspense, .	409.26	
	$7,811.37	

Less Restricted Income unused, carried to

Funds and Gifts, ...	$6,378.23		
General Suspense, ...	376.77	6,755.00	1,056.37
			$231,544.96

EXPENDITURE

From Fellowship Funds.

Julia Amory Appleton, ...	$1,000.00	
Nelson Robinson, Jr., ...	1,016.68	
Frederick Sheldon (part), ...	1,000.00	$3,016.68
Amount carried forward, ...		$3,016.68

GRADUATE SCHOOL OF APPLIED SCIENCE (CONTINUED)
EXPENDITURE

Amount brought forward, ...		$3,016.68

From Scholarship Funds and Gifts.

Edward Austin Scholarships in Architecture,	$900.00	
Daniel A. Buckley, ...	300.00	
Francis H. Cummings, ...	275.00	
George H. Emerson (part), ...	450.00	
Joseph Eveleth, ...	400.00	
William Hilton (part), ...	225.00	
Priscilla Clark Hodges, ...	175.00	
Hennen Jennings, ...	525.00	
Henry Weidemann Locke (gift), ...	100.00	
Mining and Metallurgy Department Scholarship (gift), ...	150.00	
Edward Dyer Peters, ...	250.00	
Special Scholarship (gift), ...	200.00	3,950.00

From Loan Funds.

Edward Austin Loans repaid, ...		330.00

For University Scholarships.

Architectural League, ...	$540.00	
General, ...	1,950.00	2,490.00

From Sundry Funds and Gifts for Special Purposes.

Department of Architecture:

Equipment, ...		$2,585.35	
Nelson Robinson, special gift for salaries, ...	$5,000.00		
Less amount charged for salaries,	5,000.00		

Nelson Robinson, Jr.:

Expense of Nelson Robinson, Jr. Hall, ...		$4,863.76	
University charge:			
Bursar, ...	$60.42		
Inspector of Grounds and Buildings, ...	127.68		
Janitor, ...	89.63		
Engineer, ...	48.96		
Watchman, ...	91.33	418.02	5,281.78

Department of Engineering:

Engineering Camp at Squam Lake, ...	12,514.13	

Department of Forestry:

Ames Butler gift, ...	$1,670.43		
Less amount paid for salaries,	1,300.00	370.43	
Operations, ...		4,749.13	
House account, ...		235.74	25,736.56

Amount carried forward, ...		$35,523.24

GRADUATE SCHOOL OF APPLIED SCIENCE (CONTINUED)

EXPENDITURE

Amount brought forward, ...		$35,523.24
Dean's Office:		
Salary, ...	$2,500.00	
Services and wages, ...	934.11	
Equipment and supplies, ...	52.60	
Stationery, postage, telephone and telegraph, . .	310.41	
Printing, ...	22.70	
Sundries, ...	5.80	3,825.62
From Appropriations:		
Architecture, ...	$951.66	
Landscape Architecture, ...	1,630.42	
Engineering, ...	37,708.28	
Forestry, ...	229.23	
Mining and Metallurgy, ...	1,135.76	
Quarterly Journal of Architecture, ...	2,006.68	43,662.03
From Laboratory Fees:		
Engineering, ...	$1,083.25	
Forestry, ...	74.05	
Mining and Metallurgy, ...	2,333.85	3,491.15
General.		
Salaries for Instruction:		
Edward Austin (part):		
Austin Teaching Fellowships, $1,500.00		
From Sundry Funds and Gifts, . 30,284.42		
From General Income, ... 94,283.35	$126,067.77	
Services and wages, ...	1,044.24	
Equipment and supplies, ...	92.43	
Printing, ...	1,198.21	
Travelling expenses, ...	155.96	
Shop-work courses, ...	1,097.61	
Taxes Harvard Forest, ...	964.77	
Advertising, ...	91.63	
Diplomas, ...	34.68	
Legal services, ...	40.00	
Expenses of lecture, ...	36.83	130,834.13
Repairs and Equipment, Pierce Hall and Rotch Building, ...	$2,128.07	
Caretaking, Pierce Hall and Rotch Building, . . .	7,592.65	9,720.72
University charge.		
President's Office, salaries and expenses, ...	$322.39	
Treasurer's Office, care of investments, ...	1,445.38	
Bursar's Office, collections and payments, ...	1,067.82	
Publication Office, salary and expenses, ...	358.45	
Inspector of Grounds and Buildings, salary and expenses, ...	413.48	
Amounts carried forward, ...	$3,607.52	$227,046.89

GRADUATE SCHOOL OF APPLIED SCIENCE (CONTINUED)
EXPENDITURE

Amounts brought forward, ...	$3,607.52	$227,046.89
University charge (*continued*).		
Medical adviser, salary and expenses, ...	96.90	
Quinquennial Catalogue, ...	8.42	
Annual Catalogue, ...	176.47	
Watchmen, ...	166.83	
Engineer, ...	81.18	
Labor, etc., ...	4.26	
Purchasing Agent, ...	88.19	4,124.27
Phillips Brooks House, Schedule 31, ...	$51.76	
Hemenway Gymnasium, Schedule 32, ...	822.04	873.80
		$231,544.96

SCHEDULE 13

GRADUATE SCHOOL OF BUSINESS ADMINISTRATION
INCOME AND EXPENDITURE
For the year ended June 30, 1912
INCOME

Graduate School of Business Administration Balance (interest), .		$493.48
Edward Cogswell Converse Professorship in Banking, interest, ...		745.87
Daniel A. Buckley Scholarship, interest (part), ...		150.00
Gifts for immediate use:		
Under the guarantee, ...	$22,200.00	
Other Gifts:		
For general use, ...	175.00	
For loans, ...	125.00	
For courses in printing, ...	2,307.88	
For **Shaw** Fund, Business Research, ...	1,350.00	
William Endicott, Jr., Books on Transportation, ...	100.00	
Harry Hodgson, prizes, ...	75.00	
George O. May, prizes, ...	800.00	
Andrew W. Preston, South American Course, ...	2,000.00	
Joseph E. Sterrett, books on accounting, .	100.00	28,732.88
Receipts from students.		
Tuition fees, ...	$10,460.00	
Graduation fees, ...	160.00	
Laboratory fees, ...	9.00	
Sale Business 10 pamphlet, ...	12.40	10,641.40
		$40,768.63

GRADUATE SCHOOL OF BUSINESS (CONTINUED)

EXPENDITURE

From Gifts for Loans,		$270.00	
George O. May Gift for Prizes,		150.00	
Joseph E. Sterrett Gift for Books,		87.20	
Shaw Fund for Business Research,		1,896.63	
D. A. Buckley Scholarship,		150.00	
A. W. Preston Gift,	$2,000.00		
Less amount paid for salaries,	2,000.00		
Gifts in support of Printing Courses,	$1,307.88		
Less amount paid for salaries,	500.00	807.88	$3,861.71

Dean's Office.

Salary,	$500.00	
Services and wages,	897.00	
Expenses,	325.90	1,722.90

General.

Salaries,	$23,500.00	
Services and wages,	20.00	
Outside lecturers,	4,672.73	
Books,	1,144.94	
Equipment and supplies,	188.72	
Printing,	407.96	
Hospitality and travelling expenses,	376.22	
Scholarships from unrestricted income,	750.00	
Study Tours,	498.07	
Reading room,	466.51	
Adjustment, amount credited to general account in 1910–11, and belonging to Loan Fund account,	100.00	
Sundry expenses in courses,	102.66	
Legal services,	75.00	
Sundries,	45.43	32,298.24

University charge :

President's Office, salaries and expenses,	$206.86	
Bursar's Office, collections and payments,	332.66	
Medical Adviser, salary and expenses,	61.98	
Publication Office, salary and expenses,	179.23	
Annual Catalogue,	80.09	
Inspector of Grounds and Buildings, salary and expenses,	6.97	
Watchmen,	2.80	
Labor,	2.72	873.26

Phillips Brooks House, Schedule 31,	$33.09	
Hemenway Gymnasium, Schedule 32,	206.74	239.83
Amount carried forward,		$37,995.94

GRADUATE SCHOOL OF BUSINESS (CONTINUED)

EXPENDITURE

Amount brought forward, ...		$37,995.94
General Surplus made up as follows :		
Restricted Income unused carried to Funds and Gifts,	$1,983.67	
Amount carried to General Suspense to repay former advance, ...	100.00	
Reserve, carried to General Suspense, for use after the expiration of the guarantee, ...	875.65	
	$2,959.32	

Less amount of accumulated income of Funds and Gifts used, ...	$145.00		
Amount of advance to Fund carried to General Suspense, ...	46.68	191.68	2,767.69
			$40,763.63

SCHEDULE 14

DIVINITY SCHOOL

INCOME AND EXPENDITURE

For the year ended June 30, 1912

INCOME

Income of Funds for Instruction or for General Purposes.

Divinity School balance (interest), ...		$861.94
Endowment, ...		3,535.64
Oliver Ames, ...		841.50
Hannah C. Andrews, ...		25.98
Daniel Austin, ...		55.24
Adams Ayer, ...		49.50
Joseph Baker, ...		756.11
Beneficiary money returned (balance), ...		12.52
Bussey Professorship, ...		1,860.40
Bussey Trust (part), ...		5,296.29
Joshua Clapp, ...		107.81
Edwin Conant, ...		187.80
Dexter Lectureship, ...		1,264.42
Frothingham Professorship, ...		2,806.80
Abraham W. Fuller, ...		51.97
Lewis Gould, ...		45.09
John Hancock Professorship, . . .	$297.40	
Charles L. Hancock (part), . .	4,702.60	5,000.00
Haven, ...		247.50
Samuel Hoar, ...		51.98
Hollis Professorship of Divinity, ...		1,708.64
Henry P. Kidder, ...		495.00
Amount carried forward, ...		$25,262.13

DIVINITY SCHOOL (CONTINUED)
INCOME

Amount brought forward, ... $25,262.13

Income of Funds for Instruction or for General Purposes
(*continued*).

Henry Lienow, ...	454.66	
Caroline Merriam, ...	51.97	
John Newgate, ...	16.48	
Parkman Professorship, ...	792.80	
John W. Quinby, ...	35.45	
Abby Crocker Richmond, ...	49.50	
John L. Russell, ...	49.50	
William B. Spooner, ...	495.00	
Thomas Tileston of New York Endowment, .	1,980.00	
Mary P. Townsend, ...	259.88	
Winthrop Ward, ...	103.95	
Winn Professorship, ...	2,912.88	
Augustus Woodbury Bequest, ...	51.38	
Society for Promoting Theological Education Gift, Library, ...	1,091.11	$33,606.69

Income of Scholarship, Beneficiary and Prize Funds.

Robert Charles Billings (prizes), ...	$132.66	
Abner W. Buttrick, ...	677.26	
Thomas Cary, ...	291.06	
George Chapman, ...	146.12	
Joshua Clapp, ...	233.83	
Jackson Foundation, ...	771.21	
J. Henry Kendall, ...	294.43	
Nancy Kendall, ...	181.32	
John C. Kimball, ...	7.43	
William Pomroy, ...	52.42	2,787.74

Income of Funds and Gifts.

Rushton Dashwood Burr, ...	$215.33	
Louisa J. Hall, ...	48.46	263.79

Receipts from Students.

Tuition fees, regular courses, ...	$3,925.00	
" " Andover students, ...	1,756.33	
Divinity Hall, rents, ...	2,840.00	8,521.33

Sale Dr. Everett's books, ...	4.50	
" Alumni Dinner Tickets, ...	33.00	37.50
		$45,217.05

General Deficit made up as follows:

Principal of gift used, ...	$1,200.00	
Deficit, met by accumulated income, carried to General Suspense, ...	6,977.55	
	$8,177.55	
Less Income unused carried to Funds and Gifts, .	1,422.21	6,755.34
		$51,972.39

DIVINITY SCHOOL (CONTINUED)

EXPENDITURE

From Scholarship Funds.

Thomas Cary,	$250.00	
George Chapman,	129.08	
Joshua Clapp,	200.00	
Jackson Foundation,	638.00	
J. Henry Kendall,	250.00	
Nancy Kendall,	170.00	$1,637.08

From Beneficiary Funds.

Abner W. Buttrick,	$637.00	
William Pomroy,	50.92	687.92
From Robert Charles Billings Fund, prize,		100.00

From Funds and Gifts.

Rushton Dashwood Burr,	$184.79	
Louisa J. Hall,	42.50	
John W. Quinby,	25.00	
Horace S. Sears Gift for Lectures,	1,200.00	1,452.29

Dean's Office.

Stationery, postage, telephone and telegraph,	$44.66	
Printing,	21.30	65.96

General.

Salaries,	$30,600.00	
Services and wages,	2,131.35	
Equipment and supplies,	205.03	
Stationery, postage, telephone and telegraph,	101.19	
Books,	575.65	
Advertising,	41.96	
Care of grounds,	120.00	
Printing,	153.65	
Alumni Dinner,	98.00	
Lectures,	150.00	
Contribution American School of Oriental Study and Research,	100.00	
Binding,	48.20	
Share heat and light, Andover Theological Library,	711.65	
" salaries, Andover Theological Library,	1,145.83	
Instruction at Andover Theological School,	687.10	
Moving books,	90.25	
Board walks,	89.01.	
Sundries,	65.78	37,109.65

Divinity Library.

Repairs and equipment, land and building,	$36.11	
Caretaking, land and building,	941.19	977.30

Divinity Hall.

Repairs and equipment, land and building,	$5,586.71	
Caretaking, land and building,	2,031.79	7,618.50
Amount carried forward,		$49,648.70

DIVINITY SCHOOL (CONTINUED)
EXPENDITURE

Amount brought forward, ...		$49,648.70
University charge.		
President's Office, salaries and expenses, ...	$73.72	
Treasurer's Office, care of investments, ...	443.37	
Bursar's Office, collections and payments, ...	224.35	
Medical Adviser, salary and expenses, ...	22.22	
Inspector of Grounds and Buildings, salary and		
expenses, ...	134.68	
Publication Office, salary and expenses, ...	35.84	
Quinquennial Catalogue, ...	29.50	
Annual Catalogue, ...	122.44	
Labor, etc., ...	457.32	
Watchmen, ...	54.04	
Engineer, ...	50.64	
Janitor, ...	92.66	1,740.78
Semitic Museum, Schedule 27, ...	$498.48	
Phillips Brooks House, Schedule 31, ...	11.87	
Hemenway Gymnasium, Schedule 32, ...	72.56	582.91
		$51,972.39

SCHEDULE 15

LAW SCHOOL

INCOME AND EXPENDITURE

For the year ended June 30, 1912

INCOME

Income of Funds and Gifts.		
Law School balance (interest), ...		$3,274.52
Ames Fund, ...		523.71
James Barr Ames Loan:		
Interest, ...	$69.79	
Repayments, ...	410.05	479.84
James Barr Ames Prize, ...		209.24
James and Augusta Barnard, Law, ...		206.27
Gift of James Munson Barnard and Augusta		
Barnard (interest), ...		88.64
Bemis Professorship (part), ...		377.58
W. G. Bowdoin, Jr. Scholarship (gift), . . .		250.00
Bussey Professorship, ...		1,187.01
Bussey Trust (part), ...		5,296.29
James C. Carter Professorship, ...		5,477.37
Amount carried forward, ...		$17,370.47

LAW SCHOOL (CONTINUED)
INCOME

Amount brought forward,			$17,370.47

Income of Funds and Gifts (*continued*).

James Coolidge Carter Loan:

Interest,		$681.66	
Repayments,		85.50	767.16
Dane Professorship,			779.62
Samuel Phillips Prescott Fay 1798 Fund and Scholarship,			256.17
George Fisher Scholarship,			190.57
Hughes Loan, Interest,		$18.22	
Repayments,		12.27	25.49
Huidekoper Scholarship (gift),			200.00
Langdell Scholarship,			1,801.21
Law School Book,			2,327.54
Law School Library,			4,950.00
Harry Milton Levy Loan:			
Repayments,			275.98
Pennoyer Scholarship (part),			80.00
Charles Elliott Perkins Scholarship (part),			300.00
Princeton Fellowship,			450.00
William Reed Scholarship,			158.51
Royall Professorship,			412.88
Joshua Montgomery Sears, Jr. Memorial:			
Interest,		$350.00	
Gift,		650.00	1,000.00
Weld Professorship,			4,702.26
Scholarship Money Returned:			
Gift,		$450.00	
Interest,		23.52	
Repayments,		133.31	606.83
			$36,154.69
Tuition fees,			119,280.00
Sale of Quinquennial Catalogue,			6.25
Sale of Library Catalogue,			5.00
Unclaimed locker deposits,			69.00
			$155,514.94

General Deficit, made up as follows:

Accumulated Income and Gifts used,		$5,565.56	
Deficit, met by accumulated income, carried to General Suspense,		13,421.61	
		$18,987.17	
Less Restricted Income unused, carried to Funds and Gifts,		2,360.20	16,626.97
			$172,141.91

LAW SCHOOL (CONTINUED)

EXPENDITURE

From Funds and Gifts.

Ames Fund,	$425.00	
James Barr Ames Loan,	1,439.58	
W. G. Bowdoin, Jr. Scholarship,	250.00	
James Coolidge Carter Loan,	610.00	
Samuel Phillips Prescott Fay,	225.35	
George Fisher Scholarship,	150.00	
Hughes Loan,	215.00	
Huidekoper Scholarship,	200.00	
Langdell Scholarship,	1,150.00	
Harry Milton Levy Loan,	420.00	
Pennoyer Scholarship,	80.00	
Charles Elliott Perkins Scholarship,	300.00	
Princeton Fellowship,	450.00	
William Reed Scholarship,	175.00	
Research Scholarship,	250.00	
Scholarship Money Returned Loan,	1,590.00	
Joshua M. Sears, Jr. Prize,	1,500.00	$9,429.93

Dean's and Secretary's Offices.

Salaries,	$2,500.00	
Services and wages,	851.50	
Stationery, postage, telephone and telegraph,	486.21	
Printing,	162.03	
Equipment and supplies,	77.34	4,077.08

Scholarships from unrestricted income,		5,700.00

General.

Salaries,	$76,425.00	
Services and wages,	10,350.30	
Equipment and supplies,	1,152.76	
Stationery, postage, telephone and telegraph,	307.19	
Printing,	620.64	
Books,	20,908.87	
Binding,	3,168.65	
Advertising,	180.50	
Proctors,	453.50	
Freight,	73.15	
Travelling expenses of assistant librarian,	1,817.99	
Diplomas,	108.40	
Collation, American Bar Association,	311.15	
Services messenger Supreme Judicial Court,	50.00	
Reading examination books,	80.00	
Moving books,	35.50	
Olivart Library and expenses of purchase,	14,928.84	
Sundries,	45.78	130,918.22

Repairs and equipment, land and buildings,	$4,294.81	
Caretaking, land and buildings,	7,595.49	11,890.30
Amount carried forward,		$162,015.53

LAW SCHOOL (CONTINUED)

EXPENDITURE

Amount brought forward, ...		$162,015.58
University charge.		
President's Office, salaries and expenses, ...	$2,119.22	
Treasurer's Office, care of investments, ... ·.	527.84	
Bursar's Office, collections and payments, ...	2,380.18	
Medical Adviser, salary and expenses, ...	635.85	
Inspector of Grounds and Buildings, salary and expenses, ...	492.93	
Publication Office, salary and expenses, ...	11.94	
Quinquennial Catalogue, ...	170.59	
Annual Catalogue, ...	802.04	
Labor, etc., ...	366.97	
Watchmen, ...	198.03	
Janitor, ...	296.20	
Engineer, ...	161.75	
Purchasing agent, ...	5.02	7,668.56
Phillips Brooks House, Schedule 31, ...	$339.71	
Hemenway Gymnasium, Schedule 32, ...	2,118.11	2,457.82
		$172,141.91

SCHEDULE 16

MEDICAL SCHOOL

INCOME AND EXPENDITURE

For the year ended June 30, 1912

INCOME

Income of Funds for Instruction and General Purposes.		
Anonymous Fund in the Department of Theory and Practice, ...		$513.01
Edward M. Barringer (part), ...		998.46
Robert C. Billings, ...		3,573.36
John B. and Buckminster Brown, ...		1,263.78
Bullard Professorship of Neuropathology, . . .		3,774.42
John C. Cutter Bequest:		
Interest, ...	$296.59	
Royalties on publications, ...	118.63	
Miscellaneous sales, ...	5.00	420.22
Calvin and Lucy Ellis (part), ...		18,148.59
Samuel E. Fitz, ...		90.89
Rebecca A. Greene Bequest, ...		2,836.05
Henry Harris (½ income), ...		741.01
Amount carried forward, ...		$31,859.79

MEDICAL SCHOOL (CONTINUED)
INCOME

Amount brought forward, ... $31,859.79

Income of Funds for Instruction and General Purposes
(*continued*).

Harvard Medical Alumni, ...	305.61	
Harvard Medical Alumni (gifts), ...	2,000.00	
Hersey Professorship (¾ income), ...	400.29	
George Higginson, ...	5,270.71	
John Homans Memorial, ...	2,585.88	
Jackson Professorship of Clinical Medicine, . .	3,425.05	
Hamilton Kuhn Memorial, ...	9,874.21	
William O. Moseley, ...	2,629.69	
New subscription, ...	1,923.08	
Lyman Nichols, ...	496.00	
George F. Parkman, Medical Fund, ...	424.76	
Henry L. Pierce (Residuary), ...	1,941.25	
John D. Rockefeller, ...	49,500.00	
Dr. Ruppaner, ...	462.14	
George C. Shattuck, ...	3,698.89	
James Stillman Professorship, ...	5,819.41	
Mary W. Swett, ...	780.37	
Samuel W. Swett, ...	990.00	
Quincy Tufts, ...	99.00	
Henry Willard Williams, ...	2,417.43	
Gifts for salaries, ...	1,500.00	$128,403.56

Income of Fellowship Funds.

Austin Teaching Fellowships, ...	$2,875.00	
Charles Follen Folsom Memorial, ...	642.70	
William O. Moseley, Jr., ...	1,657.76	
George Cheyne Shattuck Memorial, ...	278.64	
Frederick Sheldon (part), ...	164.87	
Charles Eliot Ware Memorial, ...	298.93	
John Ware "	279.98	
Henry P. Walcott, ...	1,284.14	7,482.02

Income of Funds and Gifts for Scholarships and Aids.

Aesculapian Club (gift), ...	$150.00	
Edward M. Barringer (part), ...	500.00	
Lucius F. Billings, ...	270.71	
James Jackson Cabot, ...	314.37	
David Williams Cheever, ...	296.46	
Cotting Gift (interest), ...	166.71	
Orlando W. Doe, ...	153.55	
Joseph Eveleth (part), ...	600.00	
John Foster, ...	156.96	
Lewis and Harriet Hayden, ...	292.40	

Amounts carried forward, ... $2,901.16 $135,885.58

MEDICAL SCHOOL (CONTINUED)

INCOME

Amounts brought forward, ...	$2,901.16	$135,885.58

Income of Funds and Gifts for Scholarships and Aids *(continued)*.

William Hilton (part), ...	450.00	
William Otis Johnson, ...	141.12	
Claudius M. Jones, ...	340.61	
John R. Kissenger, ...	149.89	
Alfred Hosmer Linder, ...	284.58	
Loan Fund Medical School Class of 1879 (gift),	50.00	
James Ewing Mears (gift), ...	225.00	
Joseph Pearson Oliver, ...	451.09	
Charles B. Porter, ...	295.76	
Francis Skinner, ...	271.12	
Charles Pratt Strong, ...	267.85	
Isaac Sweetser, ...	342.54	
John Thomson Taylor, ...	278.45	
Edward Wigglesworth, ...	285.91	
Special Scholarship for 1912–13 (gift), ...	250.00	6,984.58

Income of Prize Funds.

Ward Nicholas Boylston, ...	$235.77	
William H. Thorndike, ...	479.26	715.03

Income of Sundry Funds and Gifts for Special Purposes.

Frederick M. Allen Gift, Preventive Medicine,	$393.75	
Laboratory of Comparative Anatomy (gift), . . .	304.76	
Edward Austin (Bacteriological Laboratory), .	579.10	
J. Ingersoll Bowditch, ...	349.52	
Boylston, for Medical Books, ...	82.92	
Brinckerhoff Fund, ...	145.88	
Katherine E. Bullard Gift, Neuropathology, .	500.00	
Gift for a salary, Cancer Commission, ...	250.00	
Memorial Cancer Hospital Endowment :		
Interest, ... $4,720.17		
Gift, ... 500.00	5,220.17	
Memorial Cancer Hospital Maintenance, ...	406.80	
Memorial Cancer Hospital Proctor Maintenance, .	238.29	
Lawrence Carteret Fenno Memorial, . . .	185.90	
Lawrence Carteret Fenno Free Bed Fund, .	63.55	
Franklin H. Hooper Memorial Free Bed Fund,	247.50	
Clara Endicott Payson Memorial Free Bed Fund, ...	247.50	
Memorial Cancer Hospital Subscription (gifts), . .	1,860.00	
Caroline Brewer Croft (part) :		
Gifts, ... $261.00		
Interest, ... 2,344.98		
Fees and sales, ... 63.10	2,669.08	
Amounts carried forward, ...	$13,188.67	$143,585.19

MEDICAL SCHOOL (continued)

INCOME

Amounts brought forward, ...	$13,188.67	$143,585.19

Income of Sundry Funds and Gifts for Special Purposes
(continued).

Sale Duplicate Books, Library, ...	586.10	
Thomas Dwight Memorial, ...	3.07	
George Fabyan Foundation for Comparative Pathology, ...	10,293.09	
George Fabyan Foundation, Special:		
Interest, ... $486.34		
Sales, ... 167.00	653.34	
Charles F. Farrington, ...	2,603.80	
F. B. Greenough (for surgical research), . . .	307.05	
Harvard Clinic (gift), ...	746.02	
Henry Jackson Endowment, ...	5,085.58	
Walter Augustus Lecompte Professorship of Otology, ...	2,579.94	
Harriet Newell Lowell, ...	133.65	
Massachusetts Society for Promoting Agriculture Gift, Comparative Pathology:		
Gift, ... $1,200.00		
Interest, ... 48.42	1,248.42	
Medical Library, ...	115.19	
Gift for Microscopes, etc., ...	557.82	
Gift for Investigation of Infantile Paralysis:		
Gift, ... $1,850.00		
Interest, ... 80.42	1,930.42	
Gift Research in Neurology, ...	500.00	
Repayment Pathological Laboratory (interest), . .	63.23	
Gift for Pathological Laboratory (interest), ...	303.53	
John C. Phillips Gift, Pathological Department. Gift, ... $3,000.00		
Interest, ... 76.74	3,076.74	
Proctor, for the study of Chronic Diseases, . . .	2,618.36	
Gift for Recreation Grounds, ...	20.00	
School of Comparative Medicine, ...	333.18	
Henry Francis Sears Fund for Pathology, . .	1,734.49	
Storey Putnam Gift, Neuropathology, ...	600.00	
Surgical Laboratory:		
Gifts, ... $1,020.00		
Interest, ... 280.52	1,300.52	
Gift for Surgical Library, ...	250.00	
Zoe D. Underhill Research, ...	109.54	
X-ray Apparatus (interest), ...	21.16	
Warren Fund for Anatomical Museum, ...	557.13	
Amounts carried forward, ...	$51,520.04	$143,585.19

MEDICAL SCHOOL (CONTINUED)

INCOME

Amounts brought forward, ...	$51,520.04	$143,585.19

Income of Sundry Funds and Gifts for Special Purposes (*continued*).

Edward Wigglesworth Professorship of Dermatology, ...	2,588.50	54,108.54
Sale of heat and power, ...	$7,003.39	
Clinic fees, ...	84.63	
Repayment of appropriation for lenses, ...	188.00	
Rent of sign, ...	65.00	7,341.02

Receipts from students.

Tuition Fees.

Regular courses, ...	$53,132.50		
Graduate courses, ...	5,116.12		
Dental students, ...	8,550.00		
Summer courses, ...	13,870.00		
Division of Medical Sciences, . . .	940.00		
Special students, ...	190.00		
Candidates for degree D.P.H., . .	566.25	$81,864.87	
Graduation fees, ...		60.00	
Matriculation fees, ...		490.00	
Examination fees, ...		96.00	

Laboratory fees and supplies.

Anatomy, ...	$996.00		
Comparative Anatomy, ...	208.00		
Chemistry, ...	1,441.13		
Clinical Laboratory, ...	48.61		
Histology, ...	411.00		
Physiology, ...	567.44		
Operative Surgery, ...	227.00		
Surgical Technique, ...	192.00	4,091.18	86,602.05
			$291,636.80

EXPENDITURE

From Fellowship Funds and Gifts.

Charles Follen Folsom Memorial, ...	$525.00	
George Cheyne Shattuck Memorial, ...	225.00	
Frederick Sheldon, ...	164.87	
Charles Eliot Ware Memorial, ...	250.00	
John Ware Memorial, ...	225.00	
Henry P. Walcott, ...	583.34	$1,973.21

From Scholarship and Aid Funds and Gifts.

Aesculapian Club, ...	$150.00	
Edward M. Barringer (part), ...	500.00	
Lucius F. Billings, ...	225.00	
Amounts carried forward, ...	$875.00	$1,973.21

MEDICAL SCHOOL (continued)

EXPENDITURE

Amounts brought forward, ...	$875.00	$1,973.31

From Scholarship and Aid Funds and Gifts (*continued*).

James Jackson Cabot, ...	275.00
David Williams Cheever, ...	250.00
Cotting Gift, ...	125.00
Orlando W. Doe, ...	100.00
Joseph Eveleth (part), ...	600.00
Lewis and Harriet Hayden, ...	250.00
William Hilton (part), ...	450.00
William Otis Johnson, ...	96.25
Claudius M. Jones, ...	250.00
Alfred Hosmer Linder, ...	250.00
Loan Fund Medical School Class of 1879, . . .	40.00
James Ewing Mears, ...	225.00
Joseph Pearson Oliver, ...	400.00
Charles B. Porter, ...	250.00
Francis Skinner, ...	18.75
Charles Pratt Strong, ...	225.00
Isaac Sweetser, ...	250.00
John Thomson Taylor, ...	250.00
Edward Wigglesworth, ...	250.00

5,430.00

From Prize Funds.

Boylston Prize expenses, ...	12.50

From Sundry Funds and Gifts for Special Purposes.

Frederick M. Allen Gift, Preventive Medicine,	$393.75
Anatomical Research Gifts, ...	266.58
Gift for Equipment Comparative Anatomy Laboratory,	108.00
Edward Austin (Bacteriological Laboratory), . .	1,175.37
Robert C. Billings, Journal of Medical Research,	600.00
J. Ingersoll Bowditch, Physiology, ...	301.68
Boylston, Medical Books, ...	79.56
Katherine E. Bullard Gift, Neuropathology, .	550.02
A. T. Cabot Gift, ...	18.87
Dr. John C. Cutter Bequest, ...	300.00
Gift for Study Diabetes Mellitus, ...	67.27

George Fabyan Foundation for Comparative

Pathology, ...	$7,273.57	
Less paid for salaries, ...	5,000.00	2,273.57

Charles F. Farrington, ...	$2,774.10	
Less paid for salaries, ...	1,500.00	1,274.10

Gifts for the Investigation of Infantile Paralysis, .	994.92

Henry Jackson Endowment:

Warren Anatomical Museum, . .	$4,712.92	
Less paid for salaries, ...	2,800.00	1,912.92

Amounts carried forward, ...	$10,316.61	$7,415.71

MEDICAL SCHOOL (continued)

EXPENDITURE

Amounts brought forward, ...		$10,816.61	$7,415.71

From Sundry Funds and Gifts for Special Purposes (*continued*).

Walter Augustus Lecompte Professorship of Otology, ...	$2,470.88		
Less paid for salaries, ...	1,800.00	670.88	
Harriet Newell Lowell, ...		931.84	
Massachusetts' Society for Promoting Agriculture Gift, Comparative Pathology, ...		57.24	
Medical Library, ...		110.51	
Gift for Microscopes, etc., ...		557.82	
Gift for Pathological Laboratory, ...		150.18	
Repayment Pathological Laboratory, ...		509.05	
John C. Phillips Gift, Pathological Department, ...	$3,299.94		
Less amount paid for salaries, . .	2,000.00	1,299.94	
Proctor, for the study of Chronic Diseases, . . .		2,108.12	
Henry Francis Sears Fund for Pathology, .		1,740.87	
Storey Putnam Gifts, Neuropathology,	$545.82		
Less amount paid for salaries, . . .	300.00	245.82	
Surgical Laboratory, ...		1,121.40	
Gift, Research in Neurology, ...		500.00	
W. H. Walker Gift, ...		4.50	
Edward Wigglesworth Professorship of Dermatology, ...		506.40	
J. G. Wright Gift, Bacteriology, ...		3.40	
Books, from proceeds of sale of duplicates, ...		121.48	
Gift for Recreation Grounds, ...		823.47	
Cancer Hospital:			
Memorial Cancer Hospital Endowment Fund, ...	$6,000.00		
Less paid for salaries, . . .	3,500.00	2,500.00	
Gift for current expenses, ...		1,860.00	
Memorial Cancer Hospital Maintenance Fund,		6,972.25	
Caroline Brewer Croft Fund (part), . .		2,146.58	
Gift salary Secretary Cancer Commission, . .		250.00	
Memorial Cancer Hospital **Proctor** Maintenance Fund, ...		288.29	34,736.05

Appropriations.

Advertising and catalogues, ...	$1,098.87	
Anatomy, ...	2,250.00	
Comparative Anatomy, ...	1,869.00	
Books and service for the library, ...	4,000.00	
Physiology, ...	2,084.57	
Comparative Physiology, ...	419.51	
Amounts carried forward, ...	$11,721.95	$42,151.76

MEDICAL SCHOOL (continued)

EXPENDITURE

Amounts brought forward, ...	$11,721.95	$42,151.76

Appropriations (*continued*).

Biological Chemistry, ...	2,727.40	
Bacteriology, ...	900.00	
Preventive Medicine and Hygiene, ...	2,066.21	
Materia Medica and Therapeutics, ...	870.98	
Theory and Practice of Physic, ...	1,152.73	
Clinical Medicine, ...	7.50	
Pediatrics, ...	109.71	
Surgery, ...	1,048.49	
Obstetrics, ...	75.00	
Neuropathology, ...	835.00	21,014.97

Dean's Office.

Salaries, ...	$1,166.68	
Services and wages, ...	2,032.22	
Equipment and supplies, ...	40.95	
Printing, ...	166.32	
Stationery, postage, telephone and telegraph, . . .	468.55	3,874.72

General.

Salaries for instruction, ...	$126,090.65	

Summer courses.

Fees repaid to instructors, ...	$12,033.00	
Salary of director, ...	500.00	
Stationery, postage, printing, etc., .	863.91	13,396.91

Graduate courses.

Fees repaid to instructors, ...	5,077.10	
Services and wages, ...	11,564.11	
Equipment and supplies, ...	705.72	
Stationery, postage, telephone and telegraph, . . .	1,751.70	
Printing, ...	110.65	
Boston Medical Library, ...	150.00	
Diplomas, ...	53.06	
Travelling expense, ...	92.00	
Clinic, ...	1,704.85	
Proctors, ...	24.00	
Dues Association of Medical Colleges, ...	25.00	
Legal services, ...	50.00	
Sundries, ...	48.08	
Repairs and equipment, land and buildings, ...	5,001.25	
Caretaking, land and buildings, ...	18,652.69	
Heat and Power, ...	25,247.59	204,745.36
Retiring allowance, ...		1,000.00
Balance of payments on an annuity, Schedule 34, ...		262.58
Interest on advances, ...		1,387.10
Amount carried forward, ...		$374,436.49

MEDICAL SCHOOL (CONTINUED)
EXPENDITURE

Amount brought forward, ... $274,436.49

University charge.

President's Office, salaries and expenses, ...	$721.81	
Treasurer's Office, care of investments, ...	2,432.00	
Bursar's Office, collections and payments, ...	1,844.56	
Inspector of Grounds and Buildings, salary and expenses, ...	1,501.89	
Publication Office, salary and expenses, ...	11.95	
Quinquennial Catalogue, ...	145.32	
Annual Catalogue, ...	873.53	
Purchasing Agent, ...	2.76	7,033.32

$281,469.81

General Surplus, made up as follows:

Restricted Income unused added to

Funds and Gifts, ...	$23,436.49		
General Suspense, ...	746.02		
	$24,182.51		
Less Amount of accumulated income of			
Funds and Gifts used, ... $10,300.05			
*Deficit for the year carried to			
General Suspense, ... 8,715.47	14,015.52	10,166.99	

$291,636.80

* A promised gift of $5,000.00 for certain expenses of 1911-12 was not received until after the close of the fiscal year; otherwise there would have been a surplus for the year of $1,284.53.

SCHEDULE 17

GRADUATE SCHOOL OF MEDICINE
EXPENDITURE

For the year ended June 30, 1912

Dean's Office.

Salaries, ...	$661.47	
Services and wages, ...	94.67	
Stationery and postage, ...	100.80	
Printing, ...	61.95	$918.89
General.		
Printing, ...		211.00
Deficit for year carried to General Suspense, ...		$1,129.89

DENTAL SCHOOL

INCOME AND EXPENDITURE

For the year ended June 30, 1912

INCOME

Income of Funds and Gifts.

Dental School Endowment, Interest, . .	$607.55		
" " " Sale specimens from Museum, ...	580.50	$1,188.05	
Dental School Endowment of the Class of 1886,		2.48	
" " " " " 1909,		.99	
Harvard Dental Alumni Endowment, ...		811.55	
Proctor Bequest, ...		24.75	
Joseph Warren Smith Jr., ...		511.08	
Henry C. Warren Endowment, ...		1,138.50	$3,177.40

Gifts for immediate use.

Dental School Research Fund, ...			100.00

Receipts from students.

Tuition fees, regular courses, ...	$26,420.00		
Less transferred to Medical School,	8,550.00	$17,870.00	
Chemistry, breakage and supplies, ...		755.41	
Examination fees, ...		86.00	18,661.41
Fees from Infirmary, ...			18,238.65
Sale of gold, ...	$615.62		
" merchandise, ...		423.14	1,038.76
			$36,216.22

General Deficit made up as follows:

Deficit carried to General Suspense, ...	$3,832.05		
Accumulated Income used, ...	1,046.29		
	$4,878.34		
Less Restricted Income unused, added to Funds and Gifts, ...		580.50	4,297.84
			$40,514.06

EXPENDITURE

From Funds and Gifts.

Harriet Newell Lowell (salaries), ...	$1,000.00		
Gift for X-ray apparatus, ...	35.00		
Dental School Research Fund, ...	111.29	$1,146.29	

Dean's Office.

Salaries, ...	$900.00		
Services and wages, ...	2.88		
Stationery, postage, telephone and telegraph, . . .	171.43		
Printing, ...	14.55	1,088.86	
Amount carried forward, ...			$2,235.15

DENTAL SCHOOL (CONTINUED)

EXPENDITURE

Amount brought forward, ...		$2,285.15

General.

Salaries for instruction, ...	$8,085.00	
Services and wages, ...	5,687.70	
Equipment and supplies, ...	12,678.58	
Stationery, postage, telephone and telegraph, . . .	509.10	
Printing, ...	893.38	
Advertising, ...	702.68	
Books, ...	108.40	
Mechanical Department sundries, ...	58.25	
Laundry, ...	798.49	
Diplomas, ...	15.82	
Rent of piano, ...	45.00	
Legal services, ...	125.00	
Boston Medical Library, ...	50.00	
Dues to Dental Faculties Association of American Universities, ...	50.00	
Dues to Institute of Dental Pedagogics, ...	20.00	
Collation, ...	56.00	
Expenses Delegate to Iowa City, ...	125.00	
Hospital service, ...	25.00	
Sundries, ...	78.16	29,561.06
Interest on advances, ...		550.73
Repairs and equipment, land and buildings, ...	$1,054.20	
Caretaking, land and buildings, ...	6,103.49	7,157.69

University charge.

President's Office, salaries and expenses, ...	$404.92	
Treasurer's Office, care of investments, ...	33.76	
Bursar's Office, collections and payments, ...	356.18	
Inspector of Grounds and Buildings, salary and expenses, ...	105.90	
Publication Office, salary and expenses, ...	11.95	
Quinquennial Catalogue, ...	18.96	
Annual Catalogue, ...	77.76	1,009.43
		$40,514.06

BUSSEY INSTITUTION

INCOME AND EXPENDITURE

For the year ended June 30, 1912

INCOME

Income of Funds.

Bussey Institution balance (interest), ...	$264.22	
Bussey Trust (part), ...	10,592.57	$10,856.79
Gifts for present use, ...		200.00
Board of animals, ...	$52.21	
Use of houses by College officers, ...	1,380.00	
Rent of Antitoxin stable, ...	1,008.32	
Sale of animals, ...	7.60	
Laboratory fees, ...	107.50	2,555.63
		$13,612.42
Deficit, met by accumulated income, carried to General Suspense, .		5,147.12
		$18,759.54

EXPENDITURE

Salaries, ...	$8,300.00	
Services and wages, ...	3,992.92	
Equipment and supplies, ...	2,681.14	
Stationery, postage, telephone and telegraph, ...	134.53	
Printing, ...	211.83	
Books, ...	490.93	
Labor, ...	278.00	
Binding books, ...	81.60	
Sundries, ...	22.68	
Repairs and equipment, land and buildings, ...	265.64	
Caretaking, land and buildings, ...	1,868.26	$18,327.53
University charge.		
Treasurer's Office, care of investments, ...	$217.89	
Bursar's Office, collections and payments, ...	117.97	
Inspector of Grounds and Buildings, salary and expenses, ...	96.15	432.01
		$18,759.54

ARNOLD ARBORETUM

INCOME AND EXPENDITURE

For the year ended June 30, 1912

INCOME

Income of Funds and Gifts.

Arnold Arboretum,		$6,207.49	
James Arnold,		8,057.56	
Arboretum Construction Gifts (interest),		2,094.35	
Robert Charles Billings (part),		670.75	
William L. Bradley Fund:			
Gift for present use,	$990.00		
Interest,	600.00		
Sales,	640.00	2,230.00	
Francis Skinner,		990.00	
Bussey, for the Arnold Arboretum,		114.25	
Sears gift for Library,		155.03	
Massachusetts Society for Promoting Agriculture,		238.24	
Bayard and Ruth S. Thayer,		742.50	$21,500.17

For botanical exploration in China.

Interest,	$22.53		
Sale of photographs and pamphlet,	488.75		
Sale of botanical material,	701.75		
Gifts,	1,453.62	$2,666.65	
Gifts for present use,		28,755.00	
Gift for books,		2,000.00	33,421.65
Sale of publications,			184.56
Sale of surplus material,			178.00
			$55,284.38

EXPENDITURE

From William L. Bradley Fund, bibliography (part),	$2,230.00	
From Chinese Exploration Gifts,	4,152.11	
From gift for books,	2,000.00	
From Sears Gift for Library,	1,104.64	$9,486.75

General.

Salaries,	$5,800.00	
Services and wages,	9,737.08	
Equipment and supplies,	8,090.78	
Stationery, postage, telephone and telegraph,	210.94	
Printing,	539.54	
Labor,	13,483.39	
Water, heat, light, power and protection,	839.88	
Repairs and equipment, land and buildings,	708.44	
Rent of building,	150.00	
Bradley Bibliography of Trees,	7,906.47	
Expenses of expeditions for collecting,	1,159.47	
Freight, express, etc.,	393.12	
Amounts carried forward,	$44,018.61	$9,486.75

ARNOLD ARBORETUM (CONTINUED)

EXPENDITURE

Amounts brought forward, ...	$44,018.61	$9,486.75
General (*continued*).		
Taxes on house, ...	321.44	
Liability Insurance, ...	73.00	
Sundries, ...	59.31	44,472.36
University charge.		
Treasurer's Office, care of investments, ...	$260.85	
Bursar's Office, collections and payments, ...	177.78	438.63
		$54,397.74
General Surplus made up as follows :		
Added to Sundry Funds and Gifts, ...	$402.88	
" " Arboretum Construction Gifts, ...	2,918.83	
	$3,321.71	
Less Accumulated Income Funds and Gifts used, .	2,435.07	886.64
		$55,284.38

BOTANIC GARDEN

INCOME AND EXPENDITURE

For the year ended June 30, 1912

INCOME

Income of Funds.		
Botanic Garden balance (interest), ...	$166.66	
Botanic Department (⅓ income), ...	1,230.69	
Lowell, for a Botanic Garden, ...	3,378.72	
John L. Russell (¼ income), ...	24.75	$4,800.82
Gifts.		
For cases (interest), ...	$15.21	
For sugar-cane investigation (interest), ...	16.02	
For immediate use, ...	650.00	681.23
Botanical Museum, in adjustment of prior joint budget,	$2,000.00	
Laboratory fees in Botany, ...	210.00	
Material supplied Radcliffe College, ...	150.00	
Interest on mortgage, ...	250.00	
Sale of junk, ...	20.00	2,630.00
		$8,112.05

EXPENDITURE

Labor, ...	$4,536.31
Equipment and supplies, ...	554.71
Stationery, postage, telephone and telegraph, ...	39.49
Printing, ...	4.25
Amount carried forward, ...	$5,134.76

BOTANIC GARDEN (CONTINUED)

EXPENDITURE

Amount brought forward, ...	$5,184.76	
Water, heat, light, power and protection, ...	1,051.04	
Repairs and equipment, land and buildings, ...	605.17	
Taxes, ...	59.70	
Express and cartage, ...	55.77	
Sundries, ...	14.65	$6,921.09
University charge.		
Treasurer's Office, care of investments, ...	$62.91	
Bursar's Office, collections and payments, ...	25.22	88.13
		$7,009.22
General surplus, made up as follows :		
Restricted Income unused, added to Funds and Gifts,	$31.23	
Surplus, carried to General Suspense, ...	1,071.60	1,102.83
		$8,112.05

SCHEDULE 22

BOTANICAL MUSEUM

INCOME AND EXPENDITURE

For the year ended June 30, 1912

INCOME

Botanical Museum balance, interest, ...		$83.26
Gift for present use.		
Gift for Botanical Museum, ...		2,500.00
		$2,583.26
Deficit, met by accumulated gifts, carried to General Suspense, . .		991.29
		$3,574.55

EXPENDITURE

Services and wages, ...	$1,064.15	
Equipment and supplies, ...	103.62	
Stationery, postage, telephone, etc., ...	55.45	
Printing, ...	65.58	
Books, ...	17.45	
Botanic Garden, in adjustment of prior joint budget, . .	2,000.00	
Expenses collection of plant specimens, ...	250.00	$3,556.25
University charge.		
Bursar's Office, collections and payments, ...		18.30
		$3,574.55

GRAY HERBARIUM

INCOME AND EXPENDITURE

For the year ended June 30, 1912

INCOME

Income of Funds.

Gray Herbarium balance (interest), ...	$286.01	
Robert Charles Billings, ...	742.50	
Asa Gray Memorial, ...	1,619.19	
Asa Gray Professorship of Systematic Botany, . .	1,061.82	
Herbarium, ...	1,022.48	
Sarah E. Potter Endowment, ...	10,048.44	
John L. Russell (¼ income), ...	74.25	$14,854.69
Asa Gray's copyrights, ...		713.71
Gifts for immediate use, ...		1,413.00
Sale of card index, ...	$1,619.69	
" publications, ...	50.81	
" duplicate plants, ...	10.60	1,681.10
		$18,662.50

EXPENDITURE

From **Asa Gray** Professorship of Systematic Botany Fund.

Salary of **Asa Gray** Professor (part), ...		$1,061.82
Salaries, ...	$5,588.18	
Services and wages, ...	3,636.59	
Equipment and supplies, ...	1,126.53	
Stationery, postage, telephone and telegraph, ...	106.63	
Printing, ...	1,210.32	
Books, ...	2,401.49	
Binding, ...	105.90	
Freight, express, and sundries, ...	56.74	
Expedition to Magdalena Islands, ...	500.00	
Repairs and equipment, land and buildings, ...	45.57	
Caretaking, land and buildings, ...	286.60	15,064.55

University charge.

Treasurer's Office, care of investments, ...	$193.83	
Bursar's Office, collections and payments, ...	136.69	
Inspector of Grounds and Buildings, salaries and expenses, ...	60.08	
Janitor, ...	42.47	
Engineer, ...	23.17	455.74
		$16,582.11
Surplus for the year carried to General Suspense, ...		2,080.39
		$18,662.50

OBSERVATORY

INCOME AND EXPENDITURE

For the year ended June 30, 1912

INCOME

Income of Funds and Gifts.

Advancement of Astronomical Science (1901), . .	$936.20	
Advancement of Astronomical Science (1902), . .	1,020.44	
Thomas G. Appleton, ...	247.50	
J. Ingersoll Bowditch, ...	123.75	
Uriah A. Boyden, ...	9,900.00	
J. Rayner Edmands, ...	50.19	
Charlotte Harris, ...	99.00	
Haven, ...	2,227.50	
James Hayward, ...	1,089.50	
Observatory Endowment, ...	2,475.00	
Paine Professorship, ...	2,475.00	
Robert Treat Paine, ...	18,559.63	
Edward B. Phillips, ...	5,459.55	
Josiah Quincy, ...	643.25	
James Savage (¼ net income), ...	444.75	
David Sears, ...	2,283.25	
Augustus Story, ...	662.31	$43,596.82
George R. Agassiz Gift, Catalogue, ...	$1,000.00	
Mrs. Henry Draper, gift for special research (additional), ...	4,800.00	
Gifts for present use, ...	3,000.00	8,800.00
Use of house by College officer, ...	$600.00	
Sale of Annals, ...	125.33	
" photographs, ...	89.55	
Subscriptions to Bulletins, ...	6.00	820.88
		$53,217.70
General Deficit, made up as follows:		
Advances to Funds, carried to General Suspense, .	$701.16	
Balances of sundry accounts used, ...	4,910.32	
	$5,611.48	
Less Restricted Income unused, added to Funds and Gifts, ...	1,800.47	3,811.01
		$57,028.71

EXPENDITURE

From Advancement of Astronomical Science Fund (1901), ...	$1,175.00
From Advancement of Astronomical Science Fund (1902), ...	1,050.00
From George R. Agassiz Gift, ...	416.66
From Uriah A. Boyden Fund.		
Salaries, ...	$4,048.50	
Services and wages, ...	1,436.13	
Amounts carried forward, ...	$5,484.63	$2,641.66

151

OBSERVATORY (CONTINUED)

EXPENDITURE

Amounts brought forward, ...	$5,484.68	$2,641.66
From Uriah A. Boyden Fund (*continued*).		
Equipment and supplies, ...	422.64	
Expedition to Jamaica, ...	3,000.00	
Expedition to Peru, ...	795.94	
Interest on advances, ...	759.44	
Sundries, ...	131.16	10,593.81
From Draper Memorial.		
Expedition to Peru, ...	$2,400.00	
Other payments, ...	2,470.19	4,870.19
From Josiah Quincy Fund, ...	. . . . .	542.75
Salaries, ...	$15,500.00	
Services and wages, ...	10,458.46	
Equipment and supplies, ...	3,798.59	
Stationery, postage, telephone and telegraph, ...	645.16	
Printing, ...	687.72	
Binding, ...	538.69	
Books, ...	232.47	
Repairs and equipment, land and buildings, ...	407.91	
Caretaking, land and buildings, ...	2,924.01	
Taxes, ...	129.35	
Printing Annals, ...	4,303.69	
Use of house, ...	90.00	
Freight and teaming, ...	344.74	
Sundries, ...	24.44	
	$40,085.23	
Less cost printing certain Annals, paid by other Funds,	2,446.23	37,639.00
University charge.		
Treasurer's Office, care of investments, ...	$487.95	
Bursar's Office, collections and payments, ...	211.59	
Purchasing Agent, ...	41.76	741.30
		$57,028.71

MUSEUM OF COMPARATIVE ZOÖLOGY

INCOME AND EXPENDITURE

For the year ended June 30, 1912

INCOME

Income of Funds.

Museum of Comparative Zoölogy balance (interest),	$931.88	
Agassiz Memorial, ...	14,747.69	
Alexander Agassiz Bequest, General Purposes, (part), ...	2,311.90	
Alexander Agassiz Bequest for Publications, .	4,692.36	
George R. Agassiz, ...	1,507.96	
Virginia Barret Gibbs Scholarship, ...	294.28	
Gray Fund for Zoölogical Museum, ...	2,475.00	
Sturgis Hooper, ...	5,815.85	
Humboldt, ...	883.18	
Willard Peele Hunnewell, ...	247.50	
Permanent Fund for Museum of Zoölogy, ...	5,814.72	
Henry L. Pierce, Residuary (part), ...	4,716.25	
Teachers' and Pupils', ...	375.90	
Maria Whitney, ...	323.63	
Maria Whitney and James Lyman Whitney,	1.29	$44,144.39
Gift Mrs. William Barbour, for illustrations, ...		1,785.50
Use of lecture rooms by Radcliffe College, ...	$700.00	
Sale of publications, ...	226.44	
Lost books, ...	3.00	929.44
		$46,859.33
General Deficit, made up as follows:		
Accumulated Income of Sturgis Hooper Fund,	$184.15	
Principal of Alexander Agassiz Bequest for Publications, ...	8,708.30	
Deficit met by accumulated Income, carried to General Suspense, ...	1,553.52	
	$10,445.97	
Less Restricted Income unused, added to Funds and Gifts, ...	580.76	9,865.21
		$56,724.54

EXPENDITURE

From Sturgis Hooper Fund.

Salary of Sturgis Hooper Professor, ...	$5,500.00	
Alexander Agassiz Bequest for Publications, . . .	13,400.66	
Humboldt Fund, ...	196.57	
Willard Peele Hunnewell Fund, ...	142.01	
Maria Whitney Fund, ...	85.54	
Virginia Barret Gibbs Scholarship Fund. Scholarship, ...	250.00	
Gift Mrs. William Barbour, for illustrations, . . .	1,785.50	$21,360.28
Amount carried forward, ...		$21,360.28

MUSEUM OF COMPARATIVE ZOÖLOGY (continued)

EXPENDITURE

Amount brought forward, ...		$21,360.28
Salaries, ...	$10,183.31	
Services and wages, ...	8,193.89	
Equipment and supplies, ...	4,024.96	
Stationery, postage, telephone and telegraph, ...	188.57	
Printing, ...	3,097.96	
Books, ...	2,114.48	
Water, heat, light, power and protection, ...	6,616.10	
Repairs and equipment, land and buildings, ...	1,679.26	
Binding, ...	692.88	
Collections, ...	2,016.98	
Freight and cartage, ...	348.51	
Travelling expenses, ...	91.60	
Laundry work, ...	58.25	
Sundries, ...	35.01	39,341.76
University charge.		
Treasurer's Office, care of investments, ...	$575.44	
Bursar's Office, collections and payments, ...	138.71	714.15
		$61,416.19
Less the following items transferred :		
To the College, Schedule 8 :		
Heating and service, ...	$3,427.50	
Publishing contributions from the Laboratories		
of Geography and Zoölogy, ...	300.00	
Services of librarian, ...	250.00	
	$3,977.50	
To the University, Schedule 7 :		
Total University charge, ...	714.15	4,691.65
		$56,724.54

PEABODY MUSEUM OF AMERICAN ARCHAEOLOGY AND ETHNOLOGY

INCOME AND EXPENDITURE

For the year ended June 30, 1912

INCOME

Income of Funds.

Peabody Museum balance (interest), ...	$121.70
Hemenway Fellowship, ...	656.17
Mary Hemenway Fund for Archaeology, . . .	2,302.54
Peabody Building, ...	1,456.04
Peabody Collection, ...	2,430.59
Amount carried forward, ...	$6,967.04

PEABODY MUSEUM (CONTINUED)
INCOME

Amount brought forward, ...	$6,967.04	
Income of Funds (*continued*).		
Peabody Professor, ...	2,430.59	
Eliza O. and Mary P. Ropes (part), ...	1,568.54	
Thaw Fellowship, ...	1,182.57	
Henry C. Warren Exploration, ...	495.50	
Susan Cornelia Warren, ...	247.50	
Robert C. Winthrop Scholarship, ...	814.77	
Huntington Frothingham Wolcott, ...	990.00	$14,196.51
Gifts for present use, ...		2,165.00
Overcharge for interest in 1910–11, ...		48.71
		$16,410.22

EXPENDITURE

Thaw Fellowship, ...	$1,167.61	
Henry C. Warren Fund, explorations, ...	475.00	
Mary Hemenway Fund, ...	2,200.00	
Huntington Frothingham Wolcott Fund, specimens, ...	640.44	
Robert C. Winthrop Scholarship, ...	500.00	$4,983.05
Services and wages, ...	$4,448.25	
Equipment and supplies, ...	825.36	
Stationery, postage, telephone and telegraph, ...	239.76	
Printing, ...	104.00	
Books, ...	221.48	
Binding, ...	147.55	
Explorations, ...	1,799.20	
Collections, ...	234.60	
Freight, ...	238.80	
Travelling expenses, ...	227.61	
Rent space in deposit vaults, ...	33.00	
Sundries, ...	55.08	
Repairs and equipment, land and buildings, ...	177.11	
Caretaking, land and buildings, ...	1,415.77	10,161.97
University charge.		
Treasurer's Office, care of investments, ...	$162.65	
Bursar's Office, collections and payments, ...	125.90	
Inspector of Grounds and Buildings, salary and expenses, ...	154.71	
Watchmen, ...	62.19	
Engineer, ...	59.44	
Janitor, ...	108.92	
Purchasing Agent, ...	.46	674.27
Amount carried forward, ...		$15,819.29

PEABODY MUSEUM (CONTINUED)

EXPENDITURE

Amount brought forward, ...		$15,819.29
Less amounts transferred.		
Repairs, land and buildings, ...	$177.11	
Caretaking, land and buildings, ...	1,415.77	
University charge, ...	674.27	2,267.15
		$18,552.14
The above amounts are transferred as follows:		
90% to University, Schedule 7, ...	$2,040.44	
10% to College, Schedule 8, ...	226.71	
	$2,267.15	
General Surplus, made up as follows:		
Restricted Income unused, added to Funds and Gifts, ...	$833.57	
Amount carried to General Suspense to repay advance	310.16	
Surplus, carried to General Suspense, ...	1,899.58	
	$3,043.31	
Less advance to Fund, carried to General Suspense,	185.23	2,858.08
		$16,410.22

SCHEDULE 27

SEMITIC MUSEUM

INCOME AND EXPENDITURE

For the year ended June 30, 1912

INCOME

Gifts for Semitic Collection.		
Interest, ...		$192.41
Gifts for excavations in Palestine.		
Interest, ...		77.58
Income from **Charles L. Hancock** Bequest, ...		500.00
		$769.99
Deficit, met by unrestricted principal of Gifts, ...		2,667.18
		$3,437.17

EXPENDITURE

From gifts for Semitic Collection, ...	$2,349.48	
From gifts for excavations in Palestine, ...	587.69	$2,937.17
Curator, ...		500.00
Repairs and equipment, land and building, ...	$123.21	
Caretaking, land and building, ...	1,285.94	1,409.15
University charge.		
Treasurer's Office, care of investments, ...	$12.28	
Bursar's Office, collections and payments, ...	32.75	
Amounts carried forward, ...	$45.03	$4,846.32

SEMITIC MUSEUM (continued)

EXPENDITURE

Amounts brought forward, ...	$45.08	$4,846.32
University charge (*continued*).		
Inspector of Grounds and Buildings, salary and expenses, ...	88.38	
Watchmen, ...	38.56	
Engineer, ...	82.01	
Janitor, ...	58.46	252.44
		$5,098.76
Less amounts transferred.		
General expenses, ...	$1,409.15	
University charge, ...	252.44	1,661.59
		$3,437.17
The above amounts are transferred as follows:		
70 % to University, Schedule 7, ...	$1,163.11	
30 % to Divinity School, Schedule 14, ...	498.48	
	$1,661.59	

GERMANIC MUSEUM

INCOME AND EXPENDITURE

For the year ended June 30, 1912

INCOME

Income of Funds and Gifts.		
Germanic Museum balance (interest), ...	$63.46	
Emperor William, ...	1,303.59	
Germanic Museum, ...	495.69	
Germanic Museum Endowment, ...	2,658.40	$4,521.14
Sale of Handbooks, ...		22.77
		$4,543.91

EXPENDITURE

General.		
Services and wages, ...	$4.75	
Equipment and supplies, ...	77.55	
Printing, ...	33.35	
Stationery and postage, ...	28.57	
Freight, ...	82.83	
Expenses of reception, ...	41.16	
Dues to Museum associations, ...	20.00	
Sundries, ...	39.75	
Repairs and equipment, land and building, ...	83.47	
Caretaking, land and building, ...	991.48	$1,402.91
Amount carried forward, ...		$1,402.91

GERMANIC MUSEUM (CONTINUED)

EXPENDITURE

Amount brought forward, ... $1,402.91

University charge.

Treasurer's Office, care of investments, ...	$211.75	
Bursar's Office, collections and payments, ...	32.14	
Inspector of Grounds and Buildings, salary and expenses, ...	39.81	
Watchmen, ...	16.15	
Engineer, ...	15.41	315.26

$1,718.17

Less University charge transferred to University, Schedule 7, . . .   315.26

$1,402.91

General Surplus made up as follows:

Restricted Income unexpended, added to Funds and Gifts, ...	$2,658.40	
Surplus carried to General Suspense, ...	482.60	3,141.00

$4,543.91

SCHEDULE 29

WILLIAM HAYES FOGG ART MUSEUM

INCOME AND EXPENDITURE

For the year ended June 30, 1912

INCOME

Income of Funds.

William Hayes Fogg, ...		$2,475.00	
Gray Fund for Engravings, ...		792.00	
William M. Prichard, ...		748.30	
John Witt Randall, Interest, . . .	$1,485.00		
Gift, ...	30.00	1,515.00	
Mary R. Searle, Interest, ...	91.67		
Gift, ...	20.00	111.67	
Gift for Improvements, Gift, ...	$13,000.00		
Interest, . . .	31.48	13,031.48	$18,668.45

Sale of photographs and catalogues.	$36.96	
For work in connection with photographs sold, ...	13.86	
Balance subscriptions for purchase of drawings, ...	23.63	74.45

$18,742.90

WILLIAM HAYES FOGG ART MUSEUM (CONTINUED)

EXPENDITURE

From the following Funds:

Gray Fund for Engravings.

Curator,	$250.00	
Services,	146.00	
Collections,	609.43	$1,005.43
William M. Prichard, collections,		164.73

John Witt Randall.

Curator,	$250.00	
Expenses,	1,160.20	1,410.20
Mary R. Searle, books,		91.21

General.

Director,	$500.00	
Services and wages,	1,246.24	
Equipment and supplies,	83.48	
Stationery, postage, telephone and telegraph,	64.57	
Printing,	2.65	
Legal services,	75.00	
Insurance,	200.73	
Sundries,	8.97	
Interest on advances,	12.23	
Repairs and equipment, building,	81.77	
Caretaking, building,	2,459.22	4,784.86

University charge.

Treasurer's Office, care of investments,	$72.12	
Bursar's Office, collections and payments,	65.30	
Inspector of Grounds and Buildings, salary and expenses,	123.17	
Engineer,	47.36	
Watchmen,	88.49	396.44
		$7,802.87

Less amounts transferred.

Caretaking, building,	$2,459.22	
University charge,	396.44	2,855.66
		$4,947.21

The above amounts are transferred as follows:

10 % to University, Schedule 7,	$285.56
90 % to College, Schedule 8,	2,570.10
	$2,855.66

General Surplus, made up as follows:

Income of Restricted Funds and Gifts not used,	$13,714.31	
Income Restricted Funds carried to General Suspense to repay former advances,	294.81	
	$14,009.12	
Less Accumulated Income of Funds and Gifts used,	213.43	13,795.69
		$18,742.90

APPLETON CHAPEL

INCOME AND EXPENDITURE

For the year ended June 30, 1912

INCOME

Income of Funds.

Fund for Religious Services, ...	$51.18	
Increase Sumner Wheeler, ...	2,475.00	
Edward Wigglesworth Memorial, ...	7,425.00	$9,951.18
Gift for choir expenses, ...		295.00
Use of Organ, ...		74.44
		$10,320.62

EXPENDITURE

From George Wigglesworth gift, ...		$135.91

General.

Preaching and morning services, ...	$3,945.00	
Administrator, ...	400.00	
Organist and Choir-master, ...	1,500.00	
Choir, ...	1,989.00	
Equipment and supplies, ...	186.71	
Stationery, postage, telephone and telegraph, . . .	.57	
Printing, ...	71.10	
Repairs and equipment, land and buildings, ...	104.84	
Caretaking, land and buildings, ...	1,042.44	
Repairing and tuning organ, ...	50.59	
Music, ...	117.25	
Sundries, ...	44.12	9,451.12

University charge.

Treasurer's Office, care of investments, ...	$128.87	
Bursar's Office, collections and payments, . . .· . . .	55.13	
Inspector of Grounds and Buildings, salary and expenses, ...	63.84	
Watchmen, ...	45.75	
Janitor, ...	44.95	
Engineer, ...	24.52	363.06
		$9,950.09

General surplus made up as follows:

Restricted Income unexpended, added to Funds and Gifts, ...	$188.44	
Carried to General Suspense to repay former advances, ...	182.09	370.53
		$10,320.62

PHILLIPS BROOKS HOUSE

INCOME AND EXPENDITURE

For the year ended June 30, 1912

INCOME

Income of Funds.

Phillips Brooks House Endowment,	$520.10	
John W. and Belinda L. Randall,	350.81	
Ralph H. Shepard,	561.52	
Ralph Hamilton Shepard Memorial,	271.31	$1,703.74
		$1,703.74

EXPENDITURE

Secretaries of Phillips Brooks House Association,	$1,000.00	
Equipment and supplies,	72.08	
Books,	3.45	
Receptions,	300.00	
Services of matron,	100.00	
Rent of piano,	45.00	
Sundries,	41.80	
Repairs and equipment, land and buildings,	76.69	
Caretaking, land and buildings,	1,489.03	$3,128.05

University charge.

Treasurer's Office, care of investments,	$21.47	
Bursar's Office, collections and payments,	45.36	
Inspector of Grounds and Buildings, salary and expenses,	45.06	
Watchmen,	32.27	
Engineer,	17.30	
Janitor,	31.71	193.17
		$3,321.22

Less amounts transferred.

Repairs and equipment, land and buildings,	$76.69	
Caretaking, land and buildings,	1,489.03	
University charge,	193.17	1,758.89
		$1,562.33

The above amounts are transferred as follows:

10% to University, Schedule 7,	$175.89	
Remainder, divided in proportion to the number of students:		
College, Schedule 8,	1,146.57	
Graduate School of Applied Science, Schedule 12,	51.76	
Graduate School of Business Administration, Schedule 13,	33.09	
Amounts carried forward,	$1,407.31	$1,562.33

PHILLIPS BROOKS HOUSE (CONTINUED)

EXPENDITURE

Amounts brought forward, ...	$1,407.31	$1,562.33
Amounts transferred (*continued*).		
Divinity School, Schedule 14, ...	11.87	
Law School, Schedule 15, ...	339.71	
	$1,758.89	
General surplus made up as follows:		
Restricted Income unused, added to Funds and Gifts,	$350.81	
Less deficit met by the accrued income of the **Ralph**		
Hamilton Shepard Memorial Fund, ...	209.40	141.41
		$1,703.74

SCHEDULE 32

HEMENWAY GYMNASIUM

INCOME AND EXPENDITURE

For the year ended June 30, 1912

INCOME

Fees for the use of		
Lockers, by students, ...	$2,108.50	
Gymnasium, by graduates, ...	10.00	$2,118.50
Deficit transferred to the following departments in proportion to the number of students.		
College, Schedule 8, ...	$7,141.53	
Graduate School of Applied Science, Schedule 12, .	322.04	
Graduate School of Business Administration, Schedule 13, ...	206.74	
Divinity School, Schedule 14, ...	72.56	
Law School, Schedule 15, ...	2,118.11	
Episcopal Theological School, ...	78.52	9,939.50
		$12,058.00

EXPENDITURE

Salaries, ...	$5,500.00	
Services and wages, ...	1,241.89	
Apparatus, ...	266.38	
Equipment and supplies, ...	10.49	
Stationery, postage, telephone and telegraph, ...	91.92	
Printing, ...	80.85	
Rent of piano, ...	54.00	
Sundries, ...	1.75	
Repairs and equipment, land and building, ...	271.48	
Caretaking, land and building, ...	4,085.28	$11,553.54
Amount carried forward, ...		$11,553.54

EXPENDITURE

Amount brought forward, ...		$11,558.54
University charge.		
Bursar's Office, collections and payments, ...	$78.64	
Inspector of Grounds and Buildings, salary and expenses, ...	241.09	
Watchmen, ...	97.01	
Engineer, ...	92.72	504.46
		$12,058.00

STILLMAN INFIRMARY

INCOME AND EXPENDITURE

For the year ended June 30, 1912

INCOME

Income of Funds and Gifts.		
Robert Charles Billings, for Stillman Infirmary, ...	$2,997.53	
Free Bed Fund of the Class of 1868, ...	315.66	
" " for the Stillman Infirmary, . . .	32.32	
Herbert Schurz Memorial Free Bed Fund, . .	179.83	
Stillman Infirmary Gift, interest, ...	401.09	
Henry P. Walcott, ...	158.59	$4,085.02
Receipts from Students.		
Infirmary annual fees, ...	$14,788.00	
Receipts from patients, ...	3,616.81	18,404.81
		$22,489.83

EXPENDITURE

Services and wages, ...	$6,951.29	
Equipment and supplies, ...	6,889.59	
Stationery, postage, telephone and telegraph, ...	217.35	
Printing, ...	17.85	
Sundries, ...	9.40	
Repairs and equipment, land and buildings, ...	765.96	
Caretaking, land and buildings, ...	5,691.97	$20,543.41
Interest on advances, ...		36.12
University charge.		
Treasurer's Office, care of investments, ...	$53.70	
Bursar's Office, collections and payments, ...	117.97	
Medical Adviser, salary and expenses, ...	750.00	
Amounts carried forward, ...	$921.67	$20,579.53

STILLMAN INFIRMARY (CONTINUED)
EXPENDITURE

Amounts brought forward, ...	$921.67	$20,579.53
University charge (*continued*).		
Inspector of Grounds and Buildings, salary and expenses, ...	114.91	
Labor, etc., ...	143.42	
Engineer, ...	44.02	1,224.02
		$21,803.55
General Surplus, made up as follows :		
Restricted Income unused, added to Funds and Gifts,	$401.09	
Surplus carried to General Suspense, ...	285.19	686.28
		$22,489.83

SCHEDULE 34

FUNDS AND GIFTS FOR SPECIAL PURPOSES
INCOME AND EXPENDITURE
For the year ended June 30, 1912
INCOME

Alexander Agassiz Bequest (part), ...		$138.35
Anonymous Fund, ...		5,582.37
Anonymous Gift for Anonymous Purpose, ...		5,000.00
Anonymous Gift for Gray Herbarium library building.		
Gift, ...	$15,000.00	
Interest, ...	374.99	15,374.99
Walter F. Baker (part), ...		143.64
Daniel A. Buckley Fund (part), ...		1.50
Gifts for Arnold Arboretum Building (interest), ...		46.72
Bussey Trust (part), ...		9,479.52
Gift from the Carnegie Foundation, ...		39,539.16
Class of 1834 Fund, ...		82.53
" 1842 "		5.75
" 1844 "		482.42
" 1846 "		710.23
" 1853 "		153.66
" 1856 "		371.25
T. Jefferson Coolidge Gift, construction chemical laboratory.		
Gift, ...	$50,000.00	
Interest, ...	49.20	50,049.20
Caroline Brewer Croft (part), ...		2,231.60
Dr. John C. Cutter Bequest (part), ...		467.15
Paul Dudley Fund, ...		210.88
Amount carried forward, ...		$130,070.42

FUNDS AND GIFTS, ETC. (CONTINUED)
INCOME

Amount brought forward, ...		$130,070.42
High Voltage Electrical Laboratory Building.		
Gift, ...	$11,750.00	
Interest, ...	78.33	11,828.33
Calvin and Lucy Ellis Fund (part), ...		165.39
Gift for Freshman Dormitories.		
Gifts, ...	$341,879.10	
Interest, ...	11,009.57	352,888.67
Germanic Museum Building (interest), ...		8,370.72
Wolcott Gibbs Memorial.		
Gift, ...	$25.00	
Interest, ...	2,014.24	2,089.24
Godkin Lecture Fund, ...		749.53
Gurney Fund (part), ...		500.00
Harvard Memorial Society (interest), ...		90.63
Charles L. Hancock Bequest (part), ...		15.26
Collis P. Huntington Memorial Hospital Building.		
Gift, ...	$102,500.00	
Interest, ...	827.39	103,327.39
Professorship of Hygiene, 1899 Fund (part), ...		10,705.03
" " 1902 "		2,322.97
" " 1908 "		2,043.59
Ingersoll Lecture Fund, ...		809.82
Gifts for a new University Library Building (interest), ...		621.58
Gift for Architectural Studies, New Library Building, ...		1,250.00
William Belden Noble Lectures Fund.		
Interest, ...	$1,326.06	
Sales, ...	89.82	1,415.88
Henry S. Nourse Fund (part), ...		1,089.90
Robert Troup Paine, ...		1,946.10
Lectures on Political Economy Fund, ...		593.85
Quarterly Journal of Economics.		
Income of **John E. Thayer** Fund, ...	$791.41	
Sales, ...	2,604.61	3,396.02
Retiring Allowance Fund, ...		18,411.92
Gift for Decorating Front of the **Nelson Robinson, Jr.** Hall		
(interest), ...		241.56
Frederick Sheldon Fund (part), ...		20.00
James Skillen Memorial Fund, ...		537.42
George Smith Bequest, ...		19,069.99
Alexander W. Thayer Fund (part), ...		480.00
John Harvey Treat Fund (part), ...		3.00
George Robert White Laboratories of Systematic Botany.		
Gift, ...	$31,500.00	
Interest, ...	454.62	31,954.62
Amount carried forward, ...		$706,408.83

FUNDS AND GIFTS, ETC. (CONTINUED)

INCOME

Amount brought forward, ...	$706,408.83
Ira D. Van Dusee Scholarship Fund (part), ...	235.18
Charles Wilder Fund, ...	2,200.47
Daniel Williams Fund, ...	817.05
Sarah Winslow Fund, ...	237.41
Woodland Hill Fund, use of laboratory, ...	1,000.00
	$710,898.94

EXPENDITURE

Agassiz Estate, expenses, ...		$138.35
Anonymous Fund (part) annuity, ...		5,600.00
Anonymous Gift for Anonymous Purpose, ...		5,000.00
Walter F. Baker Fund, expenses, ...		143.64
Daniel A. Buckley Fund, taxes, ...		1.50
Francis H. Burr Memorial Gift, ...		25,749.91
Bussey Trust (part).		
Annuities, ...	$4,000.00	
Taxes and legal expenses, ...	5,479.52	9,479.52
Gift from the Carnegie Foundation Retiring Allowances, ...		39,538.83
Class of 1853 Fund, Secretary of the Class, ...		153.66
" 1856 " " " "		363.75
Caroline Brewer Croft Fund (part) annuity, ...		2,231.60
Dr. John O. Cutter Bequest, annuity, ...		467.15
Dental School Building.		
Interest on advances, ...		4,953.35
Paul Dudley Fund, lectures, ...		200.00
Calvin and Lucy Ellis Fund (part) taxes, ...		165.39
Freshman Dormitories gifts, ...		280.56
Germanic Museum Building, ...		50.14
Wolcott Gibbs Memorial, ...		25,106.13
Gurney Fund (part) annuities, ...		500.00
Gift for Gray Herbarium (Kidder Wing) construction, ...		162.41
Gray Herbarium, gift for Library wing, ...		12,116.06
" " gift for George Robert White laboratories,		15,835.62
Charles L. Hancock Bequest, taxes, ...		15.26
Harvard Memorial Society Fund, ...		171.09
Collis P. Huntington Memorial Hospital Building, ...		93,908.18
Professorship of Hygiene, 1899 Fund (part) annuity, ...		10,572.89
" " 1902 " " "		2,271.51
" " 1908 " " "		1,617.75
Ingersoll Lecture Fund, printing, ...		45.74
Library Building Architectural Studies gift, ...		816.00
William Belden Noble Lectures Fund, ...		1,274.78
Amount carried forward, ...		$258,930.77

FUNDS AND GIFTS, ETC. (CONTINUED)

EXPENDITURE

Amount brought forward, ... $258,980.77

Henry S. Nourse Fund.

Annuity, ... $1,000.00

Insurance and repairs on house, ... 89.90   1,089.90

Lectures on Political Economy Fund, ... 275.00

Quarterly Journal of Economics, ... 2,969.41

Retiring Allowance Fund, ... 12,209.44

Frederick Sheldon Fund, care of securities, ... 20.00

James Skillen Memorial Fund, annuity, ... 800.00

George Smith Bequest, annuities, ... 900.00

Gifts for Improvements and Additions to The Soldier's Field.

Interest on advances, ... 898.80

Alexander W. Thayer Fund, annuity, ... 480.00

John H. Treat Fund, legal services, ... 8.00

Ira D. Van Duzee Scholarship Fund, expenses, ... 235.18

Charles Wilder Fund, annuities, ... 1,940.00

Daniel Williams Fund.

Treasurer of Herring Pond Indians, ... $265.07

Treasurer of Mashpee Indians, ... 507.11   772.18

Sarah Winslow.

Minister at Tyngsborough, ... $112.49

Commission on income, credited to University, . . 5.94   118.43

Woodland Hill Fund.

Taxes, ... $1,098.80

Interest on advances, ... 295.14   1,893.94

           $282,481.05

Less Balance of Annuity to Medical School, Schedule 16, ... 262.58

           $282,218.47

General Surplus, made up as follows:

Unexpended balance of new gifts for buildings

carried to Funds and Gifts, ... $443,282.78

Restricted Income unused carried to Funds and Gifts, 40,216.08

           $483,498.86

Less advances to Funds and Gifts carried

to General Suspense, ... $5,758.72

Accumulated Income and Gifts used, . 49,059.67   54,818.39   428,680.47

           $710,898.94

Certificate of the Committee of the Overseers of Harvard College, for examining the Accounts of the Treasurer

The committee appointed by the Overseers of Harvard College to examine the accounts of the Treasurer for the year ending June 30, 1912, have, with the assistance of an expert chosen by them, examined and audited the Cash-book and Journal covering the period from July 1, 1911, to June 30, 1912, inclusive, and have seen that all the bonds, mortgages, notes, certificates of stock, and other evidences of property, which were on hand at the beginning of said year, or have been received by him during said year, are now in his possession, or are fully accounted for by entries made therein; they have also noticed all payments, both of principal and interest, indorsed on any of said bonds or notes, and have seen that the amounts so indorsed have been duly credited to the College.

They have in like manner satisfied themselves that all the entries for moneys expended by the Treasurer, or charged in his books to the College, are well vouched; such of them that are not supported by counter entries being proved by regular vouchers and receipts.

They have also, by the aid of said expert, satisfied themselves that all the entries for said year are duly transferred to the Ledger, and that the accounts there are rightly cast, and correctly balanced.

(Signed)

F. L. HIGGINSON, *Chairman,*
GRAFTON ST. L. ABBOTT,
WILLIAM A. GASTON,
WILLIAM ENDICOTT, Jr.
WILLIAM C. ENDICOTT.

Of the Committee on behalf of the Board of Overseers.

Boston, January, 1913.

INDEX

172

Lightning Source UK Ltd.
Milton Keynes UK
UKHW022018151118
332420UK00017B/1384/P

9 781528 456081